Principles of Distributed Database Systems

M. Tamer Özsu • Patrick Valduriez

Principles of Distributed Database Systems

Third Edition

 Springer

M. Tamer Özsu
David R. Cheriton School of
Computer Science
University of Waterloo
Waterloo Ontario
Canada N2L 3G1
Tamer.Ozsu@uwaterloo.ca

Patrick Valduriez
INRIA
LIRMM
161 rue Ada
34392 Montpellier Cedex
France
Patrick.Valduriez@inria.fr

This book was previously published by: Pearson Education, Inc.

Additional material to this book can be downloaded from http://extras.springer.com.

ISBN 978-1-4939-4174-2   ISBN 978-1-4419-8834-8 (eBook)
DOI 10.1007/978-1-4419-8834-8
Springer New York Dordrecht Heidelberg London

Printed on acid-free paper

Springer is part of Springer Science+Business Media (www.springer.com)

To my family
 and my parents
 M.T.Ö.

 To Esther, my daughters Anna, Juliette and
Sarah, and my parents
 P.V.

Preface

It has been almost twenty years since the first edition of this book appeared, and ten years since we released the second edition. As one can imagine, in a fast changing area such as this, there have been significant changes in the intervening period. Distributed data management went from a potentially significant technology to one that is common place. The advent of the Internet and the World Wide Web have certainly changed the way we typically look at distribution. The emergence in recent years of different forms of distributed computing, exemplified by data streams and cloud computing, has regenerated interest in distributed data management. Thus, it was time for a major revision of the material.

We started to work on this edition five years ago, and it has taken quite a while to complete the work. The end result, however, is a book that has been heavily revised – while we maintained and updated the core chapters, we have also added new ones. The major changes are the following:

1. Database integration and querying is now treated in much more detail, reflecting the attention these topics have received in the community in the past decade. Chapter 4 focuses on the integration process, while Chapter 9 discusses querying over multidatabase systems.

2. The previous editions had only brief discussion of data replication protocols. This topic is now covered in a separate chapter (Chapter 13) where we provide an in-depth discussion of the protocols and how they can be integrated with transaction management.

3. Peer-to-peer data management is discussed in depth in Chapter 16. These systems have become an important and interesting architectural alternative to classical distributed database systems. Although the early distributed database systems architectures followed the peer-to-peer paradigm, the modern incarnation of these systems have fundamentally different characteristics, so they deserve in-depth discussion in a chapter of their own.

4. Web data management is discussed in Chapter 17. This is a difficult topic to cover since there is no unifying framework. We discuss various aspects

of the topic ranging from web models to search engines to distributed XML processing.

5. Earlier editions contained a chapter where we discussed "recent issues" at the time. In this edition, we again have a similar chapter (Chapter 18) where we cover stream data management and cloud computing. These topics are still in a flux and are subjects of considerable ongoing research. We highlight the issues and the potential research directions.

The resulting manuscript strikes a balance between our two objectives, namely to address new and emerging issues, and maintain the main characteristics of the book in addressing the principles of distributed data management.

The organization of the book can be divided into two major parts. The first part covers the fundamental principles of distributed data management and consist of Chapters 1 to 14. Chapter 2 in this part covers the background and can be skipped if the students already have sufficient knowledge of the relational database concepts and the computer network technology. The only part of this chapter that is essential is Example 2.3, which introduces the running example that we use throughout much of the book. The second part covers more advanced topics and includes Chapters 15 – 18. What one covers in a course depends very much on the duration and the course objectives. If the course aims to discuss the fundamental techniques, then it might cover Chapters 1, 3, 5, 6–8, 10–12. An extended coverage would include, in addition to the above, Chapters 4, 9, and 13. Courses that have time to cover more material can selectively pick one or more of Chapters 15 – 18 from the second part.

Many colleagues have assisted with this edition of the book. S. Keshav (University of Waterloo) has read and provided many suggestions to update the sections on computer networks. Renée Miller (University of Toronto) and Erhard Rahm (University of Leipzig) read an early draft of Chapter 4 and provided many comments, Alon Halevy (Google) answered a number of questions about this chapter and provided a draft copy of his upcoming book on this topic as well as reading and providing feedback on Chapter 9, Avigdor Gal (Technion) also reviewed and critiqued this chapter very thoroughly. Matthias Jarke and Xiang Li (University of Aachen), Gottfried Vossen (University of Muenster), Erhard Rahm and Andreas Thor (University of Leipzig) contributed exercises to this chapter. Hubert Naacke (University of Paris 6) contributed to the section on heterogeneous cost modeling and Fabio Porto (LNCC, Petropolis) to the section on adaptive query processing of Chapter 9. Data replication (Chapter 13) could not have been written without the assistance of Gustavo Alonso (ETH Zürich) and Bettina Kemme (McGill University). Tamer spent four months in Spring 2006 visiting Gustavo where work on this chapter began and involved many long discussions. Bettina read multiple iterations of this chapter over the next one year criticizing everything and pointing out better ways of explaining the material. Esther Pacitti (University of Montpellier) also contributed to this chapter, both by reviewing it and by providing background material; she also contributed to the section on replication in database clusters in Chapter 14. Ricardo Jimenez-Peris also contributed to that chapter in the section on fault-tolerance in database clusters. Khuzaima Daudjee (University of Waterloo) read and provided comments on this chapter as well. Chapter 15 on Distributed Object Database Management was reviewed by Serge Abiteboul (INRIA), who provided important critique of the material and suggestions for its improvement. Peer-to-peer data management (Chapter 16) owes a lot to discussions with Beng Chin Ooi (National University of Singapore) during the four months Tamer was visiting NUS in the fall of 2006. The section of Chapter 16 on query processing in P2P systems uses material from the PhD work of Reza Akbarinia (INRIA) and Wenceslao Palma (PUC-Valparaiso, Chile) while the section on replication uses material from the PhD work of Vidal Martins (PUCPR, Curitiba). The distributed XML processing section of Chapter 17 uses material from the PhD work of Ning Zhang (Facebook) and Patrick Kling at the University of Waterloo, and Ying Zhang at CWI. All three of them also read the material and provided significant feedback. Victor Muntés i Mulero (Universitat Politècnica de Catalunya) contributed to the exercises in that chapter. Özgür Ulusoy (Bilkent University) provided comments and corrections on Chapters 16 and 17. Data stream management section of Chapter 18 draws from the PhD work of Lukasz Golab (AT&T Labs-Research), and Yingying Tao at the University of Waterloo. Walid Aref (Purdue University) and Avigdor Gal (Technion) used the draft of the book in their courses, which was very helpful in debugging certain parts. We thank them, as well as many colleagues who had helped out with the first two editions, for all their assistance. We have not always followed their advice, and, needless to say, the resulting problems and errors are ours. Students in two courses at the University of Waterloo (Web Data Management in Winter 2005, and Internet-Scale Data Distribution in Fall 2005) wrote surveys as part of their coursework that were very helpful in structuring some chapters. Tamer taught courses at ETH Zürich (PDDBS – Parallel and Distributed Databases in Spring 2006) and at NUS (CS5225 – Parallel and Distributed Database Systems in Fall 2010) using parts of this edition. We thank students in all these courses for their contributions and their patience as they had to deal with chapters that were works-in-progress – the material got cleaned considerably as a result of these teaching experiences.

You will note that the publisher of the third edition of the book is different than the first two editions. Pearson, our previous publisher, decided not to be involved with the third edition. Springer subsequently showed considerable interest in the book. We would like to thank Susan Lagerstrom-Fife and Jennifer Evans of Springer for their lightning-fast decision to publish the book, and Jennifer Mauer for a ton of hand-holding during the conversion process. We would also like to thank Tracy Dunkelberger of Pearson who shepherded the reversal of the copyright to us without delay.

As in earlier editions, we will have presentation slides that can be used to teach from the book as well as solutions to most of the exercises. These will be available from Springer to instructors who adopt the book and there will be a link to them from the book's site at springer.com.

Finally, we would be very interested to hear your comments and suggestions regarding the material. We welcome any feedback, but we would particularly like to receive feedback on the following aspects:

1. any errors that may have remained despite our best efforts (although we hope there are not many);

2. any topics that should no longer be included and any topics that should be added or expanded; and

3. any exercises that you may have designed that you would like to be included in the book.

M. Tamer Özsu (Tamer.Ozsu@uwaterloo.ca)
Patrick Valduriez (Patrick.Valduriez@inria.fr)
November 2010

Contents

Chapter 1
Introduction

Distributed database system (DDBS) technology is the union of what appear to be two diametrically opposed approaches to data processing: *database system* and *computer network* technologies. Database systems have taken us from a paradigm of data processing in which each application defined and maintained its own data (Figure 1.1) to one in which the data are defined and administered centrally (Figure 1.2). This new orientation results in *data independence*, whereby the application programs are immune to changes in the logical or physical organization of the data, and vice versa.

One of the major motivations behind the use of database systems is the desire to integrate the operational data of an enterprise and to provide centralized, thus controlled access to that data. The technology of computer networks, on the other hand, promotes a mode of work that goes against all centralization efforts. At first glance it might be difficult to understand how these two contrasting approaches can possibly be synthesized to produce a technology that is more powerful and more promising than either one alone. The key to this understanding is the realization

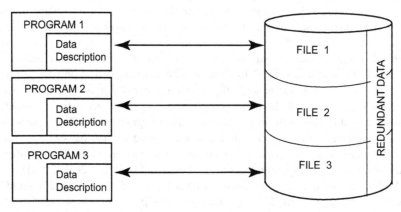

Fig. 1.1 Traditional File Processing

M.T. Özsu and P. Valduriez, *Principles of Distributed Database Systems: Third Edition*,
DOI 10.1007/978-1-4419-8834-8_1, © Springer Science+Business Media, LLC 2011

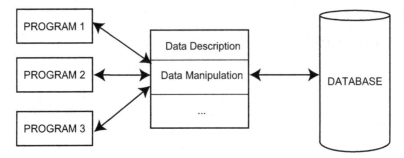

Fig. 1.2 Database Processing

that the most important objective of the database technology is *integration*, not *centralization*. It is important to realize that either one of these terms does not necessarily imply the other. It is possible to achieve integration without centralization, and that is exactly what the distributed database technology attempts to achieve.

In this chapter we define the fundamental concepts and set the framework for discussing distributed databases. We start by examining distributed systems in general in order to clarify the role of database technology within distributed data processing, and then move on to topics that are more directly related to DDBS.

1.1 Distributed Data Processing

The term *distributed processing* (or *distributed computing*) is hard to define precisely. Obviously, some degree of distributed processing goes on in any computer system, even on single-processor computers where the central processing unit (CPU) and in-put/output (I/O) functions are separated and overlapped. This separation and overlap can be considered as one form of distributed processing. The widespread emergence of parallel computers has further complicated the picture, since the distinction be-tween distributed computing systems and some forms of parallel computers is rather vague.

In this book we define distributed processing in such a way that it leads to a definition of a distributed database system. The working definition we use for a *distributed computing system* states that it is a number of autonomous processing elements (not necessarily homogeneous) that are interconnected by a computer network and that cooperate in performing their assigned tasks. The "processing element" referred to in this definition is a computing device that can execute a program on its own. This definition is similar to those given in distributed systems textbooks (e.g., [Tanenbaum and van Steen, 2002] and [Colouris et al., 2001]).

A fundamental question that needs to be asked is: What is being distributed? One of the things that might be distributed is the *processing logic*. In fact, the definition of a distributed computing system given above implicitly assumes that the processing logic or processing elements are distributed. Another possible distribution is according to *function*. Various functions of a computer system could be delegated to various pieces of hardware or software. A third possible mode of distribution is according to *data*. Data used by a number of applications may be distributed to a number of processing sites. Finally, *control* can be distributed. The control of the execution of various tasks might be distributed instead of being performed by one computer system. From the viewpoint of distributed database systems, these modes of distribution are all necessary and important. In the following sections we talk about these in more detail.

Another reasonable question to ask at this point is: Why do we distribute at all? The classical answers to this question indicate that distributed processing better corresponds to the organizational structure of today's widely distributed enterprises, and that such a system is more reliable and more responsive. More importantly, many of the current applications of computer technology are inherently distributed. Web-based applications, electronic commerce business over the Internet, multimedia applications such as news-on-demand or medical imaging, manufacturing control systems are all examples of such applications.

From a more global perspective, however, it can be stated that the fundamental reason behind distributed processing is to be better able to cope with the large-scale data management problems that we face today, by using a variation of the well-known divide-and-conquer rule. If the necessary software support for distributed processing can be developed, it might be possible to solve these complicated problems simply by dividing them into smaller pieces and assigning them to different software groups, which work on different computers and produce a system that runs on multiple processing elements but can work efficiently toward the execution of a common task.

Distributed database systems should also be viewed within this framework and treated as tools that could make distributed processing easier and more efficient. It is reasonable to draw an analogy between what distributed databases might offer to the data processing world and what the database technology has already provided. There is no doubt that the development of general-purpose, adaptable, efficient distributed database systems has aided greatly in the task of developing distributed software.

1.2 What is a Distributed Database System?

We define a *distributed database* as *a collection of multiple, logically interrelated databases distributed over a computer network*. A *distributed database management system* (distributed DBMS) is then defined as *the software system that permits the management of the distributed database and makes the distribution transparent to the users*. Sometimes "distributed database system" (DDBS) is used to refer jointly to the distributed database and the distributed DBMS. The two important terms in these definitions are "*logically interrelated*" and "*distributed over a computer network*." They help eliminate certain cases that have sometimes been accepted to represent a DDBS.

A DDBS is not a "collection of files" that can be individually stored at each node of a computer network. To form a DDBS, files should not only be logically related, but there should be structured among the files, and access should be via a common interface. We should note that there has been much recent activity in providing DBMS functionality over semi-structured data that are stored in files on the Internet (such as Web pages). In light of this activity, the above requirement may seem unnecessarily strict. Nevertheless, it is important to make a distinction between a DDBS where this requirement is met, and more general distributed data management systems that provide a "DBMS-like" access to data. In various chapters of this book, we will expand our discussion to cover these more general systems.

It has sometimes been assumed that the physical distribution of data is not the most significant issue. The proponents of this view would therefore feel comfortable in labeling as a distributed database a number of (related) databases that reside in the same computer system. However, the physical distribution of data is important. It creates problems that are not encountered when the databases reside in the same computer. These difficulties are discussed in Section 1.5. Note that physical distribution does not necessarily imply that the computer systems be geographically far apart; they could actually be in the same room. It simply implies that the communication between them is done over a network instead of through shared memory or shared disk (as would be the case with *multiprocessor systems*), with the network as the only shared resource.

This suggests that multiprocessor systems should not be considered as DDBSs. Although shared-nothing multiprocessors, where each processor node has its own primary and secondary memory, and may also have its own peripherals, are quite similar to the distributed environment that we focus on, there are differences. The fundamental difference is the mode of operation. A multiprocessor system design is rather symmetrical, consisting of a number of identical processor and memory components, and controlled by one or more copies of the same operating system that is responsible for a strict control of the task assignment to each processor. This is not true in distributed computing systems, where heterogeneity of the operating system as well as the hardware is quite common. Database systems that run over multiprocessor systems are called *parallel database systems* and are discussed in Chapter 14.

A DDBS is also not a system where, despite the existence of a network, the database resides at only one node of the network (Figure 1.3). In this case, the problems of database management are no different than the problems encountered in a centralized database environment (shortly, we will discuss client/server DBMSs which relax this requirement to a certain extent). The database is centrally managed by one computer system (site 2 in Figure 1.3) and all the requests are routed to that site. The only additional consideration has to do with transmission delays. It is obvious that the existence of a computer network or a collection of "files" is not sufficient to form a distributed database system. What we are interested in is an environment where data are distributed among a number of sites (Figure 1.4).

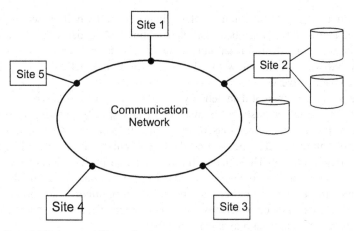

Fig. 1.3 Central Database on a Network

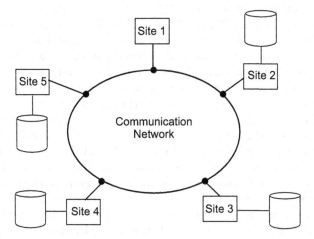

Fig. 1.4 DDBS Environment

1.3 Data Delivery Alternatives

In distributed databases, data are "delivered" from the sites where they are stored to where the query is posed. We characterize the data delivery alternatives along three orthogonal dimensions: *delivery modes*, *frequency* and *communication methods*. The combinations of alternatives along each of these dimensions (that we discuss next) provide a rich design space.

The alternative delivery modes are pull-only, push-only and hybrid. In the *pull-only* mode of data delivery, the transfer of data from servers to clients is initiated by a client pull. When a client request is received at a server, the server responds by locating the requested information. The main characteristic of pull-based delivery is that the arrival of new data items or updates to existing data items are carried out at a server without notification to clients unless clients explicitly poll the server. Also, in pull-based mode, servers must be interrupted continuously to deal with requests from clients. Furthermore, the information that clients can obtain from a server is limited to when and what clients know to ask for. Conventional DBMSs offer primarily pull-based data delivery.

In the *push-only* mode of data delivery, the transfer of data from servers to clients is initiated by a server push in the absence of any specific request from clients. The main difficulty of the push-based approach is in deciding which data would be of common interest, and when to send them to clients – alternatives are periodic, irregular, or conditional. Thus, the usefulness of server push depends heavily upon the accuracy of a server to predict the needs of clients. In push-based mode, servers disseminate information to either an unbounded set of clients (random broadcast) who can listen to a medium or selective set of clients (multicast), who belong to some categories of recipients that may receive the data.

The hybrid mode of data delivery combines the client-pull and server-push mechanisms. The continuous (or continual) query approach (e.g., [Liu et al., 1996],[Terry et al., 1992],[Chen et al., 2000],[Pandey et al., 2003]) presents one possible way of combining the pull and push modes: namely, the transfer of information from servers to clients is first initiated by a client pull (by posing the query), and the subsequent transfer of updated information to clients is initiated by a server push.

There are three typical frequency measurements that can be used to classify the regularity of data delivery. They are *periodic*, *conditional*, and *ad-hoc* or *irregular*.

In periodic delivery, data are sent from the server to clients at regular intervals. The intervals can be defined by system default or by clients using their profiles. Both pull and push can be performed in periodic fashion. Periodic delivery is carried out on a regular and pre-specified repeating schedule. A client request for IBM's stock price every week is an example of a periodic pull. An example of periodic push is when an application can send out stock price listing on a regular basis, say every morning. Periodic push is particularly useful for situations in which clients might not be available at all times, or might be unable to react to what has been sent, such as in the mobile setting where clients can become disconnected.

In conditional delivery, data are sent from servers whenever certain conditions installed by clients in their profiles are satisfied. Such conditions can be as simple as a given time span or as complicated as event-condition-action rules. Conditional delivery is mostly used in the hybrid or push-only delivery systems. Using conditional push, data are sent out according to a pre-specified condition, rather than any particular repeating schedule. An application that sends out stock prices only when they change is an example of conditional push. An application that sends out a balance statement only when the total balance is 5% below the pre-defined balance threshold is an example of hybrid conditional push. Conditional push assumes that changes are critical to the clients, and that clients are always listening and need to respond to what is being sent. Hybrid conditional push further assumes that missing some update information is not crucial to the clients.

Ad-hoc delivery is irregular and is performed mostly in a pure pull-based system. Data are pulled from servers to clients in an ad-hoc fashion whenever clients request it. In contrast, periodic pull arises when a client uses polling to obtain data from servers based on a regular period (schedule).

The third component of the design space of information delivery alternatives is the communication method. These methods determine the various ways in which servers and clients communicate for delivering information to clients. The alternatives are *unicast* and *one-to-many*. In unicast, the communication from a server to a client is one-to-one: the server sends data to one client using a particular delivery mode with some frequency. In one-to-many, as the name implies, the server sends data to a number of clients. Note that we are not referring here to a specific protocol; one-to-many communication may use a multicast or broadcast protocol.

We should note that this characterization is subject to considerable debate. It is not clear that every point in the design space is meaningful. Furthermore, specification of alternatives such as conditional **and** periodic (which may make sense) is difficult. However, it serves as a first-order characterization of the complexity of emerging distributed data management systems. For the most part, in this book, we are concerned with pull-only, ad hoc data delivery systems, although examples of other approaches are discussed in some chapters.

1.4 Promises of DDBSs

Many advantages of DDBSs have been cited in literature, ranging from sociological reasons for decentralization [D'Oliviera, 1977] to better economics. All of these can be distilled to four fundamentals which may also be viewed as promises of DDBS technology: transparent management of distributed and replicated data, reliable access to data through distributed transactions, improved performance, and easier system expansion. In this section we discuss these promises and, in the process, introduce many of the concepts that we will study in subsequent chapters.

1.4.1 Transparent Management of Distributed and Replicated Data

Transparency refers to separation of the higher-level semantics of a system from lower-level implementation issues. In other words, a transparent system "hides" the implementation details from users. The advantage of a fully transparent DBMS is the high level of support that it provides for the development of complex applications. It is obvious that we would like to make all DBMSs (centralized or distributed) fully transparent.

Let us start our discussion with an example. Consider an engineering firm that has offices in Boston, Waterloo, Paris and San Francisco. They run projects at each of these sites and would like to maintain a database of their employees, the projects and other related data. Assuming that the database is relational, we can store this information in two relations: EMP(<u>ENO</u>, ENAME, TITLE)[1] and PROJ(<u>PNO</u>, PNAME, BUDGET). We also introduce a third relation to store salary information: SAL(<u>TITLE</u>, AMT) and a fourth relation ASG which indicates which employees have been assigned to which projects for what duration with what responsibility: ASG(<u>ENO, PNO</u>, RESP, DUR). If all of this data were stored in a centralized DBMS, and we wanted to find out the names and employees who worked on a project for more than 12 months, we would specify this using the following SQL query:

```
SELECT  ENAME, AMT
FROM    EMP, ASG, SAL
WHERE   ASG.DUR > 12
AND     EMP.ENO = ASG.ENO
AND     SAL.TITLE = EMP.TITLE
```

However, given the distributed nature of this firm's business, it is preferable, under these circumstances, to localize data such that data about the employees in Waterloo office are stored in Waterloo, those in the Boston office are stored in Boston, and so forth. The same applies to the project and salary information. Thus, what we are engaged in is a process where we partition each of the relations and store each partition at a different site. This is known as *fragmentation* and we discuss it further below and in detail in Chapter 3.

Furthermore, it may be preferable to duplicate some of this data at other sites for performance and reliability reasons. The result is a distributed database which is fragmented and replicated (Figure 1.5). Fully transparent access means that the users can still pose the query as specified above, without paying any attention to the fragmentation, location, or replication of data, and let the system worry about resolving these issues.

For a system to adequately deal with this type of query over a distributed, fragmented and replicated database, it needs to be able to deal with a number of different types of transparencies. We discuss these in this section.

1.4.1.1 Data Independence

Data independence is a fundamental form of transparency that we look for within a DBMS. It is also the only type that is important within the context of a centralized DBMS. It refers to the immunity of user applications to changes in the definition and organization of data, and vice versa.

As is well-known, data definition occurs at two levels. At one level the logical structure of the data are specified, and at the other level its physical structure. The former is commonly known as the *schema definition*, whereas the latter is referred to as the *physical data description*. We can therefore talk about two types of data

---

[1] We discuss relational systems in Chapter 2 (Section 2.1) where we develop this example further. For the time being, it is sufficient to note that this nomenclature indicates that we have just defined a relation with three attributes: ENO (which is the key, identified by underlining), ENAME and TITLE.

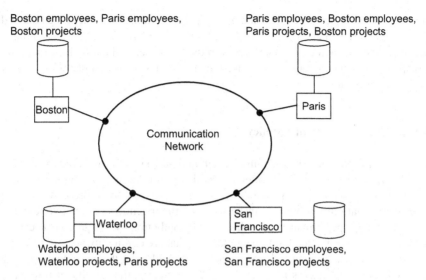

Fig. 1.5 A Distributed Application

independence: logical data independence and physical data independence. *Logical data independence* refers to the immunity of user applications to changes in the logical structure (i.e., schema) of the database. *Physical data independence*, on the other hand, deals with hiding the details of the storage structure from user applications. When a user application is written, it should not be concerned with the details of physical data organization. Therefore, the user application should not need to be modified when data organization changes occur due to performance considerations.

1.4.1.2 Network Transparency

In centralized database systems, the only available resource that needs to be shielded from the user is the data (i.e., the storage system). In a distributed database environment, however, there is a second resource that needs to be managed in much the same manner: the network. Preferably, the user should be protected from the operational details of the network; possibly even hiding the existence of the network. Then there would be no difference between database applications that would run on a centralized database and those that would run on a distributed database. This type of transparency is referred to as *network transparency* or *distribution transparency*.

One can consider network transparency from the viewpoint of either the services provided or the data. From the former perspective, it is desirable to have a uniform means by which services are accessed. From a DBMS perspective, distribution transparency requires that users do not have to specify where data are located.

Sometimes two types of distribution transparency are identified: location transparency and naming transparency. *Location transparency* refers to the fact that the command used to perform a task is independent of both the location of the data and the system on which an operation is carried out. *Naming transparency* means that a unique name is provided for each object in the database. In the absence of naming transparency, users are required to embed the location name (or an identifier) as part of the object name.

1.4.1.3 Replication Transparency

The issue of replicating data within a distributed database is introduced in Chapter 3 and discussed in detail in Chapter 13. At this point, let us just mention that for performance, reliability, and availability reasons, it is usually desirable to be able to distribute data in a replicated fashion across the machines on a network. Such replication helps performance since diverse and conflicting user requirements can be more easily accommodated. For example, data that are commonly accessed by one user can be placed on that user's local machine as well as on the machine of another user with the same access requirements. This increases the locality of reference. Furthermore, if one of the machines fails, a copy of the data are still available on another machine on the network. Of course, this is a very simple-minded description of the situation. In fact, the decision as to whether to replicate or not, and how many copies of any database object to have, depends to a considerable degree on user applications. We will discuss these in later chapters.

Assuming that data are replicated, the transparency issue is whether the users should be aware of the existence of copies or whether the system should handle the management of copies and the user should act as if there is a single copy of the data (note that we are not referring to the placement of copies, only their existence). From a user's perspective the answer is obvious. It is preferable not to be involved with handling copies and having to specify the fact that a certain action can and/or should be taken on multiple copies. From a systems point of view, however, the answer is not that simple. As we will see in Chapter 11, when the responsibility of specifying that an action needs to be executed on multiple copies is delegated to the user, it makes transaction management simpler for distributed DBMSs. On the other hand, doing so inevitably results in the loss of some flexibility. It is not the system that decides whether or not to have copies and how many copies to have, but the user application. Any change in these decisions because of various considerations definitely affects the user application and, therefore, reduces data independence considerably. Given these considerations, it is desirable that replication transparency be provided as a standard feature of DBMSs. Remember that replication transparency refers only to the existence of replicas, not to their actual location. Note also that distributing these replicas across the network in a transparent manner is the domain of network transparency.

1.4.1.4 Fragmentation Transparency

The final form of transparency that needs to be addressed within the context of a distributed database system is that of fragmentation transparency. In Chapter 3 we discuss and justify the fact that it is commonly desirable to divide each database relation into smaller fragments and treat each fragment as a separate database object (i.e., another relation). This is commonly done for reasons of performance, availability, and reliability. Furthermore, fragmentation can reduce the negative effects of replication. Each replica is not the full relation but only a subset of it; thus less space is required and fewer data items need be managed.

There are two general types of fragmentation alternatives. In one case, called *horizontal fragmentation*, a relation is partitioned into a set of sub-relations each of which have a subset of the tuples (rows) of the original relation. The second alternative is *vertical fragmentation* where each sub-relation is defined on a subset of the attributes (columns) of the original relation.

When database objects are fragmented, we have to deal with the problem of handling user queries that are specified on entire relations but have to be executed on subrelations. In other words, the issue is one of finding a query processing strategy based on the fragments rather than the relations, even though the queries are specified on the latter. Typically, this requires a translation from what is called a *global query* to several *fragment queries*. Since the fundamental issue of dealing with fragmentation transparency is one of query processing, we defer the discussion of techniques by which this translation can be performed until Chapter 7.

1.4.1.5 Who Should Provide Transparency?

In previous sections we discussed various possible forms of transparency within a distributed computing environment. Obviously, to provide easy and efficient access by novice users to the services of the DBMS, one would want to have full transparency, involving all the various types that we discussed. Nevertheless, the level of transparency is inevitably a compromise between ease of use and the difficulty and overhead cost of providing high levels of transparency. For example, Gray argues that full transparency makes the management of distributed data very difficult and claims that "applications coded with transparent access to geographically distributed databases have: poor manageability, poor modularity, and poor message performance" [Gray, 1989]. He proposes a remote procedure call mechanism between the requestor users and the server DBMSs whereby the users would direct their queries to a specific DBMS. This is indeed the approach commonly taken by client/server systems that we discuss shortly.

What has not yet been discussed is who is responsible for providing these services. It is possible to identify three distinct layers at which the transparency services can be provided. It is quite common to treat these as mutually exclusive means of providing the service, although it is more appropriate to view them as complementary.

We could leave the responsibility of providing transparent access to data resources to the access layer. The transparency features can be built into the user language, which then translates the requested services into required operations. In other words, the compiler or the interpreter takes over the task and no transparent service is provided to the implementer of the compiler or the interpreter.

The second layer at which transparency can be provided is the operating system level. State-of-the-art operating systems provide some level of transparency to system users. For example, the device drivers within the operating system handle the details of getting each piece of peripheral equipment to do what is requested. The typical computer user, or even an application programmer, does not normally write device drivers to interact with individual peripheral equipment; that operation is transparent to the user.

Providing transparent access to resources at the operating system level can obviously be extended to the distributed environment, where the management of the network resource is taken over by the distributed operating system or the middleware if the distributed DBMS is implemented over one. There are two potential problems with this approach. The first is that not all commercially available distributed operating systems provide a reasonable level of transparency in network management. The second problem is that some applications do not wish to be shielded from the details of distribution and need to access them for specific performance tuning.

The third layer at which transparency can be supported is within the DBMS. The transparency and support for database functions provided to the DBMS designers by an underlying operating system is generally minimal and typically limited to very fundamental operations for performing certain tasks. It is the responsibility of the DBMS to make all the necessary translations from the operating system to the higher-level user interface. This mode of operation is the most common method today. There are, however, various problems associated with leaving the task of providing full transparency to the DBMS. These have to do with the interaction of the operating system with the distributed DBMS and are discussed throughout this book.

A hierarchy of these transparencies is shown in Figure 1.6. It is not always easy to delineate clearly the levels of transparency, but such a figure serves an important instructional purpose even if it is not fully correct. To complete the picture we have added a "language transparency" layer, although it is not discussed in this chapter. With this generic layer, users have high-level access to the data (e.g., fourth-generation languages, graphical user interfaces, natural language access).

1.4.2 Reliability Through Distributed Transactions

Distributed DBMSs are intended to improve reliability since they have replicated components and, thereby eliminate single points of failure. The failure of a single site, or the failure of a communication link which makes one or more sites unreachable, is not sufficient to bring down the entire system. In the case of a distributed database, this means that some of the data may be unreachable, but with proper care, users

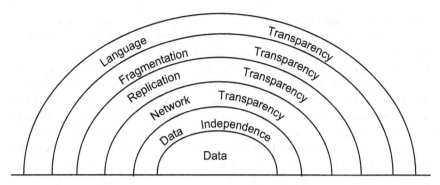

Fig. 1.6 Layers of Transparency

may be permitted to access other parts of the distributed database. The "proper care" comes in the form of support for distributed transactions and application protocols.

We discuss transactions and transaction processing in detail in Chapters 10–12. A *transaction* is a basic unit of consistent and reliable computing, consisting of a sequence of database operations executed as an atomic action. It transforms a consistent database state to another consistent database state even when a number of such transactions are executed concurrently (sometimes called *concurrency transparency*), and even when failures occur (also called *failure atomicity*). Therefore, a DBMS that provides full transaction support guarantees that concurrent execution of user transactions will not violate database consistency in the face of system failures as long as each transaction is correct, i.e., obeys the integrity rules specified on the database.

Let us give an example of a transaction based on the engineering firm example that we introduced earlier. Assume that there is an application that updates the salaries of all the employees by 10%. It is desirable to encapsulate the query (or the program code) that accomplishes this task within transaction boundaries. For example, if a system failure occurs half-way through the execution of this program, we would like the DBMS to be able to determine, upon recovery, where it left off and continue with its operation (or start all over again). This is the topic of failure atomicity. Alternatively, if some other user runs a query calculating the average salaries of the employees in this firm while the original update action is going on, the calculated result will be in error. Therefore we would like the system to be able to synchronize the *concurrent* execution of these two programs. To encapsulate a query (or a program code) within transactional boundaries, it is sufficient to declare the begin of the transaction and its end:

Begin_transaction SALARY_UPDATE
begin
```
   EXEC SQL UPDATE    PAY
               SET       SAL = SAL*1.1
```
end.

Distributed transactions execute at a number of sites at which they access the local database. The above transaction, for example, will execute in Boston, Waterloo, Paris and San Francisco since the data are distributed at these sites. With full support for distributed transactions, user applications can access a single logical image of the database and rely on the distributed DBMS to ensure that their requests will be executed correctly no matter what happens in the system. "Correctly" means that user applications do not need to be concerned with coordinating their accesses to individual local databases nor do they need to worry about the possibility of site or communication link failures during the execution of their transactions. This illustrates the link between distributed transactions and transparency, since both involve issues related to distributed naming and directory management, among other things.

Providing transaction support requires the implementation of distributed concurrency control (Chapter 11) and distributed reliability (Chapter 12) protocols — in particular, two-phase commit (2PC) and distributed recovery protocols — which are significantly more complicated than their centralized counterparts. Supporting replicas requires the implementation of replica control protocols that enforce a specified semantics of accessing them (Chapter 13).

1.4.3 Improved Performance

The case for the improved performance of distributed DBMSs is typically made based on two points. First, a distributed DBMS fragments the conceptual database, enabling data to be stored in close proximity to its points of use (also called *data localization*). This has two potential advantages:

1. Since each site handles only a portion of the database, contention for CPU and I/O services is not as severe as for centralized databases.

2. Localization reduces remote access delays that are usually involved in wide area networks (for example, the minimum round-trip message propagation delay in satellite-based systems is about 1 second).

Most distributed DBMSs are structured to gain maximum benefit from data localization. Full benefits of reduced contention and reduced communication overhead can be obtained only by a proper fragmentation and distribution of the database.

This point relates to the overhead of distributed computing if the data have to reside at remote sites and one has to access it by remote communication. The argument is that it is better, in these circumstances, to distribute the data management functionality to where the data are located rather than moving large amounts of data. This has lately become a topic of contention. Some argue that with the widespread use of high-speed, high-capacity networks, distributing data and data management functions no longer makes sense and that it may be much simpler to store data at a central site and access it (by downloading) over high-speed networks. This argument, while appealing, misses the point of distributed databases. First of all, in most of today's applications, data are distributed; what may be open for debate is how and where we process it. Second, and more important, point is that this argument does not distinguish between bandwidth (the capacity of the computer links) and latency (how long it takes for data to be transmitted). Latency is inherent in the distributed environments and there are physical limits to how fast we can send data over computer networks. As indicated above, for example, satellite links take about half-a-second to transmit data between two ground stations. This is a function of the distance of the satellites from the earth and there is nothing that we can do to improve that performance. For some applications, this might constitute an unacceptable delay.

The second case point is that the inherent parallelism of distributed systems may be exploited for inter-query and intra-query parallelism. Inter-query parallelism results from the ability to execute multiple queries at the same time while intra-query parallelism is achieved by breaking up a single query into a number of subqueries each of which is executed at a different site, accessing a different part of the distributed database.

If the user access to the distributed database consisted only of querying (i.e., read-only access), then provision of inter-query and intra-query parallelism would imply that as much of the database as possible should be replicated. However, since most database accesses are not read-only, the mixing of read and update operations requires the implementation of elaborate concurrency control and commit protocols.

1.4.4 Easier System Expansion

In a distributed environment, it is much easier to accommodate increasing database sizes. Major system overhauls are seldom necessary; expansion can usually be handled by adding processing and storage power to the network. Obviously, it may not be possible to obtain a linear increase in "power," since this also depends on the overhead of distribution. However, significant improvements are still possible.

One aspect of easier system expansion is economics. It normally costs much less to put together a system of "smaller" computers with the equivalent power of a single big machine. In earlier times, it was commonly believed that it would be possible to purchase a fourfold powerful computer if one spent twice as much. This was known as Grosh's law. With the advent of microcomputers and workstations, and their price/performance characteristics, this law is considered invalid.

This should not be interpreted to mean that mainframes are dead; this is not the point that we are making here. Indeed, in recent years, we have observed a resurgence in the world-wide sale of mainframes. The point is that for many applications, it is more economical to put together a distributed computer system (whether composed of mainframes or workstations) with sufficient power than it is to establish a single, centralized system to run these tasks. In fact, the latter may not even be feasible these days.

1.5 Complications Introduced by Distribution

The problems encountered in database systems take on additional complexity in a distributed environment, even though the basic underlying principles are the same. Furthermore, this additional complexity gives rise to new problems influenced mainly by three factors.

First, data may be replicated in a distributed environment. A distributed database can be designed so that the entire database, or portions of it, reside at different sites of a computer network. It is not essential that every site on the network contain the database; it is only essential that there be more than one site where the database resides. The possible duplication of data items is mainly due to reliability and efficiency considerations. Consequently, the distributed database system is responsible for (1) choosing one of the stored copies of the requested data for access in case of retrievals, and (2) making sure that the effect of an update is reflected on each and every copy of that data item.

Second, if some sites fail (e.g., by either hardware or software malfunction), or if some communication links fail (making some of the sites unreachable) while an update is being executed, the system must make sure that the effects will be reflected on the data residing at the failing or unreachable sites as soon as the system can recover from the failure.

The third point is that since each site cannot have instantaneous information on the actions currently being carried out at the other sites, the synchronization of transactions on multiple sites is considerably harder than for a centralized system.

These difficulties point to a number of potential problems with distributed DBMSs. These are the inherent complexity of building distributed applications, increased cost of replicating resources, and, more importantly, managing distribution, the devolution of control to many centers and the difficulty of reaching agreements, and the exacerbated security concerns (the secure communication channel problem). These are well-known problems in distributed systems in general, and, in this book, we discuss their manifestations within the context of distributed DBMS and how they can be addressed.

1.6 Design Issues

In Section 1.4, we discussed the promises of distributed DBMS technology, highlighting the challenges that need to be overcome in order to realize them. In this section we build on this discussion by presenting the design issues that arise in building a distributed DBMS. These issues will occupy much of the remainder of this book.

1.6.1 Distributed Database Design

The question that is being addressed is how the database and the applications that run against it should be placed across the sites. There are two basic alternatives to placing data: *partitioned* (or *non-replicated*) and *replicated*. In the partitioned scheme the database is divided into a number of disjoint partitions each of which is placed at a different site. Replicated designs can be either *fully replicated* (also called *fully duplicated*) where the entire database is stored at each site, or *partially replicated* (or *partially duplicated*) where each partition of the database is stored at more than one site, but not at all the sites. The two fundamental design issues are *fragmentation*, the separation of the database into partitions called *fragments*, and *distribution*, the optimum distribution of fragments.

The research in this area mostly involves mathematical programming in order to minimize the combined cost of storing the database, processing transactions against it, and message communication among sites. The general problem is NP-hard. Therefore, the proposed solutions are based on heuristics. Distributed database design is the topic of Chapter 3.

1.6.2 Distributed Directory Management

A directory contains information (such as descriptions and locations) about data items in the database. Problems related to directory management are similar in nature to the database placement problem discussed in the preceding section. A directory may be global to the entire DDBS or local to each site; it can be centralized at one site or distributed over several sites; there can be a single copy or multiple copies. We briefly discuss these issues in Chapter 3.

1.6.3 Distributed Query Processing

Query processing deals with designing algorithms that analyze queries and convert them into a series of data manipulation operations. The problem is how to decide on a strategy for executing each query over the network in the most cost-effective way, however cost is defined. The factors to be considered are the distribution of data, communication costs, and lack of sufficient locally-available information. The objective is to optimize where the inherent parallelism is used to improve the performance of executing the transaction, subject to the above-mentioned constraints. The problem is NP-hard in nature, and the approaches are usually heuristic. Distributed query processing is discussed in detail in Chapter 6 - 8.

1.6.4 Distributed Concurrency Control

Concurrency control involves the synchronization of accesses to the distributed database, such that the integrity of the database is maintained. It is, without any doubt, one of the most extensively studied problems in the DDBS field. The concurrency control problem in a distributed context is somewhat different than in a centralized framework. One not only has to worry about the integrity of a single database, but also about the consistency of multiple copies of the database. The condition that requires all the values of multiple copies of every data item to converge to the same value is called *mutual consistency*.

The alternative solutions are too numerous to discuss here, so we examine them in detail in Chapter 11. Let us only mention that the two general classes are *pessimistic*, synchronizing the execution of user requests before the execution starts, and *optimistic*, executing the requests and then checking if the execution has compromised the consistency of the database. Two fundamental primitives that can be used with both approaches are *locking*, which is based on the mutual exclusion of accesses to data items, and *timestamping*, where the transaction executions are ordered based on timestamps. There are variations of these schemes as well as hybrid algorithms that attempt to combine the two basic mechanisms.

1.6.5 Distributed Deadlock Management

The deadlock problem in DDBSs is similar in nature to that encountered in operating systems. The competition among users for access to a set of resources (data, in this case) can result in a deadlock if the synchronization mechanism is based on locking. The well-known alternatives of prevention, avoidance, and detection/recovery also apply to DDBSs. Deadlock management is covered in Chapter 11.

1.6.6 Reliability of Distributed DBMS

We mentioned earlier that one of the potential advantages of distributed systems is improved reliability and availability. This, however, is not a feature that comes automatically. It is important that mechanisms be provided to ensure the consistency of the database as well as to detect failures and recover from them. The implication for DDBSs is that when a failure occurs and various sites become either inoperable or inaccessible, the databases at the operational sites remain consistent and up to date. Furthermore, when the computer system or network recovers from the failure, the DDBSs should be able to recover and bring the databases at the failed sites up-to-date. This may be especially difficult in the case of network partitioning, where the sites are divided into two or more groups with no communication among them. Distributed reliability protocols are the topic of Chapter 12.

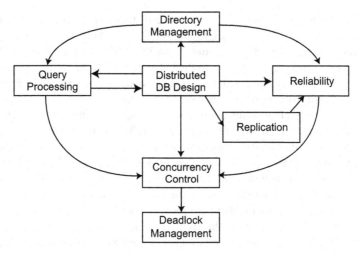

Fig. 1.7 Relationship Among Research Issues

1.6.7 Replication

If the distributed database is (partially or fully) replicated, it is necessary to implement protocols that ensure the consistency of the replicas,i.e., copies of the same data item have the same value. These protocols can be *eager* in that they force the updates to be applied to all the replicas before the transaction completes, or they may be *lazy* so that the transaction updates one copy (called the *master*) from which updates are propagated to the others after the transaction completes. We discuss replication protocols in Chapter 13.

1.6.8 Relationship among Problems

Naturally, these problems are not isolated from one another. Each problem is affected by the solutions found for the others, and in turn affects the set of feasible solutions for them. In this section we discuss how they are related.

The relationship among the components is shown in Figure 1.7. The design of distributed databases affects many areas. It affects directory management, because the definition of fragments and their placement determine the contents of the directory (or directories) as well as the strategies that may be employed to manage them. The same information (i.e., fragment structure and placement) is used by the query processor to determine the query evaluation strategy. On the other hand, the access and usage patterns that are determined by the query processor are used as inputs to the data distribution and fragmentation algorithms. Similarly, directory placement and contents influence the processing of queries.

The replication of fragments when they are distributed affects the concurrency control strategies that might be employed. As we will study in Chapter 11, some concurrency control algorithms cannot be easily used with replicated databases. Similarly, usage and access patterns to the database will influence the concurrency control algorithms. If the environment is update intensive, the necessary precautions are quite different from those in a query-only environment.

There is a strong relationship among the concurrency control problem, the deadlock management problem, and reliability issues. This is to be expected, since together they are usually called the *transaction management* problem. The concurrency control algorithm that is employed will determine whether or not a separate deadlock management facility is required. If a locking-based algorithm is used, deadlocks will occur, whereas they will not if timestamping is the chosen alternative.

Reliability mechanisms involve both local recovery techniques and distributed reliability protocols. In that sense, they both influence the choice of the concurrency control techniques and are built on top of them. Techniques to provide reliability also make use of data placement information since the existence of duplicate copies of the data serve as a safeguard to maintain reliable operation.

Finally, the need for replication protocols arise if data distribution involves replicas. As indicated above, there is a strong relationship between replication protocols and concurrency control techniques, since both deal with the consistency of data, but from different perspectives. Furthermore, the replication protocols influence distributed reliability techniques such as commit protocols. In fact, it is sometimes suggested (wrongly, in our view) that replication protocols can be used instead of implementing distributed commit protocols.

1.6.9 Additional Issues

The above design issues cover what may be called "traditional" distributed database systems. The environment has changed significantly since these topics started to be investigated, posing additional challenges and opportunities.

One of the important developments has been the move towards "looser" federation among data sources, which may also be heterogeneous. As we discuss in the next section, this has given rise to the development of multidatabase systems (also called *federated databases* and *data integration systems*) that require re-investigation of some of the fundamental database techniques. These systems constitute an important part of today's distributed environment. We discuss database design issues in multidatabase systems (i.e., *database integration*) in Chapter 4 and the query processing challenges in Chapter 9.

The growth of the Internet as a fundamental networking platform has raised important questions about the assumptions underlying distributed database systems. Two issues are of particular concern to us. One is the re-emergence of peer-to-peer computing, and the other is the development and growth of the World Wide Web (web for short). Both of these aim at improving data sharing, but take different approaches and pose different data management challenges. We discuss peer-to-peer data management in Chapter 16 and web data management in Chapter 17.

We should note that peer-to-peer is not a new concept in distributed databases, as we discuss in the next section. However, their new re-incarnation has significant differences from the earlier versions. In Chapter 16, it is these new versions that we focus on.

Finally, as earlier noted, there is a strong relationship between distributed databases and parallel databases. Although the former assumes each site to be a single logical computer, most of these installations are, in fact, parallel clusters. Thus, while most of the book focuses on issues that arise in managing data distributed across these sites, interesting data management issues exist within a single logical site that may be a parallel system. We discuss these issues in Chapter 14.

1.7 Distributed DBMS Architecture

The architecture of a system defines its structure. This means that the components of the system are identified, the function of each component is specified, and the interrelationships and interactions among these components are defined. The specification of the architecture of a system requires identification of the various modules, with their interfaces and interrelationships, in terms of the data and control flow through the system.

In this section we develop three "reference" architectures[2] for a distributed DBMS: client/server systems, peer-to-peer distributed DBMS, and multidatabase systems. These are "idealized" views of a DBMS in that many of the commercially available systems may deviate from them; however, the architectures will serve as a reasonable framework within which the issues related to distributed DBMS can be discussed.

We first start with a brief presentation of the "ANSI/SPARC architecture", which is a *datalogical* approach to defining a DBMS architecture – it focuses on the different user classes and roles and their varying views on data. This architecture is helpful in putting certain concepts we have discussed so far in their proper perspective. We then have a short discussion of a generic architecture of a centralized DBMSs, that we subsequently extend to identify the set of alternative architectures for a distributed DBMS. Whithin this characterization, we focus on the three alternatives that we identified above.

1.7.1 ANSI/SPARC Architecture

In late 1972, the Computer and Information Processing Committee (X3) of the American National Standards Institute (ANSI) established a Study Group on Database

---

[2] A reference architecture is commonly created by standards developers to clearly define the interfaces that need to be standardized.

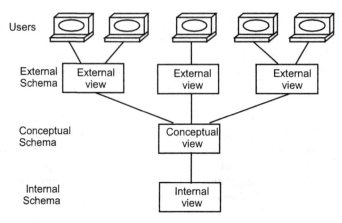

Fig. 1.8 The ANSI/SPARC Architecture

Management Systems under the auspices of its Standards Planning and Requirements Committee (SPARC). The mission of the study group was to study the *feasibility* of setting up standards in this area, as well as determining which aspects should be standardized if it was feasible. The study group issued its interim report in 1975 [ANSI/SPARC, 1975], and its final report in 1977 [Tsichritzis and Klug, 1978]. The architectural framework proposed in these reports came to be known as the "ANSI/SPARC architecture," its full title being "ANSI/X3/SPARC DBMS Framework." The study group proposed that the interfaces be standardized, and defined an architectural framework that contained 43 interfaces, 14 of which would deal with the physical storage subsystem of the computer and therefore not be considered essential parts of the DBMS architecture.

A simplified version of the ANSI/SPARC architecture is depicted in Figure 1.8. There are three views of data: the *external view*, which is that of the end user, who might be a programmer; the *internal view*, that of the system or machine; and the *conceptual view*, that of the enterprise. For each of these views, an appropriate schema definition is required.

At the lowest level of the architecture is the internal view, which deals with the physical definition and organization of data. The location of data on different storage devices and the access mechanisms used to reach and manipulate data are the issues dealt with at this level. At the other extreme is the external view, which is concerned with how users view the database. An individual user's view represents the portion of the database that will be accessed by that user as well as the relationships that the user would like to see among the data. A view can be shared among a number of users, with the collection of user views making up the external schema. In between these two ends is the conceptual schema, which is an abstract definition of the database. It is the "real world" view of the enterprise being modeled in the database [Yormark, 1977]. As such, it is supposed to represent the data and the relationships among data without considering the requirements of individual applications or the restrictions of the physical storage media. In reality, however, it is not possible to ignore these requirements completely, due to performance reasons. The transformation between these three levels is accomplished by mappings that specify how a definition at one level can be obtained from a definition at another level.

This perspective is important, because it provides the basis for data independence that we discussed earlier. The separation of the external schemas from the conceptual schema enables *logical data independence*, while the separation of the conceptual schema from the internal schema allows *physical data independence*.

1.7.2 A Generic Centralized DBMS Architecture

A DBMS is a reentrant program shared by multiple processes (*transactions*), that run database programs. When running on a general purpose computer, a DBMS is interfaced with two other components: the communication subsystem and the operating system. The communication subsystem permits interfacing the DBMS with other subsystems in order to communicate with applications. For example, the terminal monitor needs to communicate with the DBMS to run interactive transactions. The operating system provides the interface between the DBMS and computer resources (processor, memory, disk drives, etc.).

The functions performed by a DBMS can be layered as in Figure 1.9, where the arrows indicate the direction of the data and the control flow. Taking a top-down approach, the layers are the interface, control, compilation, execution, data access, and consistency management.

The *interface layer* manages the interface to the applications. There can be several interfaces such as, in the case of relational DBMSs discussed in Chapter 2, SQL embedded in a host language, such as C and QBE (Query-by-Example). Database application programs are executed against external *views* of the database. For an application, a view is useful in representing its particular perception of the database (shared by many applications). A view in relational DBMSs is a virtual relation derived from base relations by applying relational algebra operations.[3] These concepts are defined more precisely in Chapter 2, but they are usually covered in undergraduate database courses, so we expect many readers to be familiar with them. View management consists of translating the user query from external data to conceptual data.

The *control layer* controls the query by adding semantic integrity predicates and authorization predicates. Semantic integrity constraints and authorizations are usually specified in a declarative language, as discussed in Chapter 5. The output of this layer is an enriched query in the high-level language accepted by the interface.

The *query processing* (or *compilation*) layer maps the query into an optimized sequence of lower-level operations. This layer is concerned with performance. It

---

[3] Note that this does not mean that the real-world views are, or should be, specified in relational algebra. On the contrary, they are specified by some high-level data language such as SQL. The translation from one of these languages to relational algebra is now well understood, and the effects of the view definition can be specified in terms of relational algebra operations.

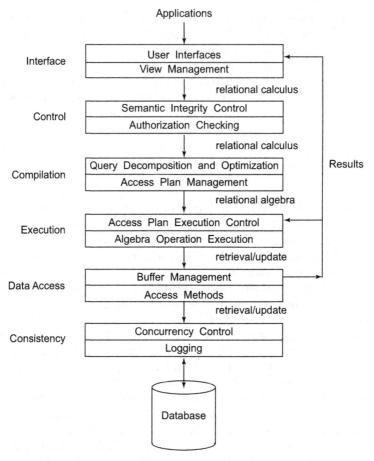

Fig. 1.9 Functional Layers of a Centralized DBMS

decomposes the query into a tree of algebra operations and tries to find the "optimal" ordering of the operations. The result is stored in an access plan. The output of this layer is a query expressed in lower-level code (algebra operations).

The *execution layer* directs the execution of the access plans, including transaction management (commit, restart) and synchronization of algebra operations. It interprets the relational operations by calling the data access layer through the retrieval and update requests.

The *data access layer* manages the data structures that implement the files, indices, etc. It also manages the buffers by caching the most frequently accessed data. Careful use of this layer minimizes the access to disks to get or write data.

Finally, the *consistency layer* manages concurrency control and logging for update requests. This layer allows transaction, system, and media recovery after failure.

1.7.3 Architectural Models for Distributed DBMSs

We now consider the possible ways in which a distributed DBMS may be architected. We use a classification (Figure 1.10) that organizes the systems as characterized with respect to (1) the autonomy of local systems, (2) their distribution, and (3) their heterogeneity.

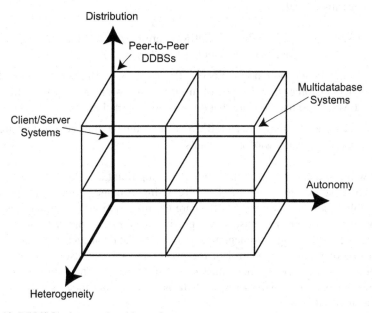

Fig. 1.10 DBMS Implementation Alternatives

1.7.4 Autonomy

Autonomy, in this context, refers to the distribution of control, not of data. It indicates the degree to which individual DBMSs can operate independently. Autonomy is a function of a number of factors such as whether the component systems (i.e., individual DBMSs) exchange information, whether they can independently execute transactions, and whether one is allowed to modify them. Requirements of an autonomous system have been specified as follows [Gligor and Popescu-Zeletin, 1986]:

1. The local operations of the individual DBMSs are not affected by their participation in the distributed system.

2. The manner in which the individual DBMSs process queries and optimize them should not be affected by the execution of global queries that access multiple databases.

3. System consistency or operation should not be compromised when individual DBMSs join or leave the distributed system.

On the other hand, the dimensions of autonomy can be specified as follows [Du and Elmagarmid, 1989]:

1. Design autonomy: Individual DBMSs are free to use the data models and transaction management techniques that they prefer.

2. Communication autonomy: Each of the individual DBMSs is free to make its own decision as to what type of information it wants to provide to the other DBMSs or to the software that controls their global execution.

3. Execution autonomy: Each DBMS can execute the transactions that are submitted to it in any way that it wants to.

We will use a classification that covers the important aspects of these features. One alternative is *tight integration*, where a single-image of the entire database is available to any user who wants to share the information, which may reside in multiple databases. From the users' perspective, the data are logically integrated in one database. In these tightly-integrated systems, the data managers are implemented so that one of them is in control of the processing of each user request even if that request is serviced by more than one data manager. The data managers do not typically operate as independent DBMSs even though they usually have the functionality to do so.

Next we identify *semiautonomous* systems that consist of DBMSs that can (and usually do) operate independently, but have decided to participate in a federation to make their local data sharable. Each of these DBMSs determine what parts of their own database they will make accessible to users of other DBMSs. They are not fully autonomous systems because they need to be modified to enable them to exchange information with one another.

The last alternative that we consider is *total isolation*, where the individual systems are stand-alone DBMSs that know neither of the existence of other DBMSs nor how to communicate with them. In such systems, the processing of user transactions that access multiple databases is especially difficult since there is no global control over the execution of individual DBMSs.

It is important to note at this point that the three alternatives that we consider for autonomous systems are not the only possibilities. We simply highlight the three most popular ones.

1.7.5 Distribution

Whereas autonomy refers to the distribution (or decentralization) of control, the distribution dimension of the taxonomy deals with data. Of course, we are considering the physical distribution of data over multiple sites; as we discussed earlier, the user sees the data as one logical pool. There are a number of ways DBMSs have been distributed. We abstract these alternatives into two classes: *client/server* distribution and *peer-to-peer* distribution (or *full* distribution). Together with the non-distributed option, the taxonomy identifies three alternative architectures.

The client/server distribution concentrates data management duties at servers while the clients focus on providing the application environment including the user interface. The communication duties are shared between the client machines and servers. Client/server DBMSs represent a practical compromise to distributing functionality. There are a variety of ways of structuring them, each providing a different level of distribution. With respect to the framework, we abstract these differences and leave that discussion to Section 1.7.8, which we devote to client/server DBMS architectures. What is important at this point is that the sites on a network are distinguished as "clients" and "servers" and their functionality is different.

In *peer-to-peer systems*, there is no distinction of client machines versus servers. Each machine has full DBMS functionality and can communicate with other machines to execute queries and transactions. Most of the very early work on distributed database systems have assumed peer-to-peer architecture. Therefore, our main focus in this book are on peer-to-peer systems (also called *fully distributed*), even though many of the techniques carry over to client/server systems as well.

1.7.6 Heterogeneity

Heterogeneity may occur in various forms in distributed systems, ranging from hardware heterogeneity and differences in networking protocols to variations in data managers. The important ones from the perspective of this book relate to data models, query languages, and transaction management protocols. Representing data with different modeling tools creates heterogeneity because of the inherent expressive powers and limitations of individual data models. Heterogeneity in query languages not only involves the use of completely different data access paradigms in different data models (set-at-a-time access in relational systems versus record-at-a-time access in some object-oriented systems), but also covers differences in languages even when the individual systems use the same data model. Although SQL is now the standard relational query language, there are many different implementations and every vendor's language has a slightly different flavor (sometimes even different semantics, producing different results).

1.7.7 Architectural Alternatives

The distribution of databases, their possible heterogeneity, and their autonomy are orthogonal issues. Consequently, following the above characterization, there are 18 different possible architectures. Not all of these architectural alternatives that form the design space are meaningful. Furthermore, not all are relevant from the perspective of this book.

In Figure 1.10, we have identified three alternative architectures that are the focus of this book and that we discuss in more detail in the next three subsections: (A0, D1, H0) that corresponds to client/server distributed DBMSs, (A0, D2, H0) that is a peer-to-peer distributed DBMS and (A2, D2, H1) which represents a (peer-to-peer) distributed, heterogeneous multidatabase system. Note that we discuss the heterogeneity issues within the context of one system architecture, although the issue arises in other models as well.

1.7.8 Client/Server Systems

Client/server DBMSs entered the computing scene at the beginning of 1990's and have made a significant impact on both the DBMS technology and the way we do computing. The general idea is very simple and elegant: distinguish the functionality that needs to be provided and divide these functions into two classes: server functions and client functions. This provides a *two-level architecture* which makes it easier to manage the complexity of modern DBMSs and the complexity of distribution.

As with any highly popular term, client/server has been much abused and has come to mean different things. If one takes a process-centric view, then any process that requests the services of another process is its client and vice versa. However, it is important to note that "client/server computing" and "client/server DBMS," as it is used in our context, do not refer to processes, but to actual machines. Thus, we focus on what software should run on the client machines and what software should run on the server machine.

Put this way, the issue is clearer and we can begin to study the differences in client and server functionality. The functionality allocation between clients and serves differ in different types of distributed DBMSs (e.g., relational versus object-oriented). In relational systems, the server does most of the data management work. This means that all of query processing and optimization, transaction management and storage management is done at the server. The client, in addition to the application and the user interface, has a *DBMS client* module that is responsible for managing the data that is cached to the client and (sometimes) managing the transaction locks that may have been cached as well. It is also possible to place consistency checking of user queries at the client side, but this is not common since it requires the replication of the system catalog at the client machines. Of course, there is operating system and communication software that runs on both the client and the server, but we only focus on the DBMS related functionality. This architecture, depicted in Figure 1.11,

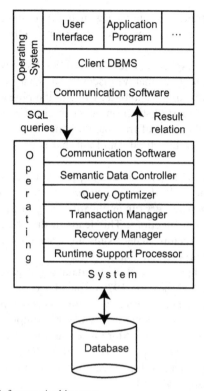

Fig. 1.11 Client/Server Reference Architecture

is quite common in relational systems where the communication between the clients and the server(s) is at the level of SQL statements. In other words, the client passes SQL queries to the server without trying to understand or optimize them. The server does most of the work and returns the result relation to the client.

There are a number of different types of client/server architecture. The simplest is the case where there is only one server which is accessed by multiple clients. We call this *multiple client/single server*. From a data management perspective, this is not much different from centralized databases since the database is stored on only one machine (the server) that also hosts the software to manage it. However, there are some (important) differences from centralized systems in the way transactions are executed and caches are managed. We do not consider such issues at this point. A more sophisticated client/server architecture is one where there are multiple servers in the system (the so-called *multiple client/multiple server* approach). In this case, two alternative management strategies are possible: either each client manages its own connection to the appropriate server or each client knows of only its "home server" which then communicates with other servers as required. The former approach simplifies server code, but loads the client machines with additional responsibilities. This leads to what has been called "heavy client" systems. The latter approach, on the other hand, concentrates the data management functionality at the servers. Thus, the transparency of data access is provided at the server interface, leading to "light clients."

From a datalogical perspective, client/server DBMSs provide the same view of data as do peer-to-peer systems that we discuss next. That is, they give the user the appearance of a logically single database, while at the physical level data **may** be distributed. Thus the primary distinction between client/server systems and peer-to-peer ones is not in the level of transparency that is provided to the users and applications, but in the architectural paradigm that is used to realize this level of transparency.

Client/server can be naturally extended to provide for a more efficient function distribution on different kinds of servers: *client servers* run the user interface (e.g., web servers), *application servers* run application programs, and *database servers* run database management functions. This leads to the present trend in three-tier distributed system architecture, where sites are organized as specialized servers rather than as general-purpose computers.

The original idea, which is to offload the database management functions to a special server, dates back to the early 1970s [Canaday et al., 1974]. At the time, the computer on which the database system was run was called the *database machine*, *database computer*, or *backend computer*, while the computer that ran the applications was called the *host computer*. More recent terms for these are the *database server* and *application server*, respectively. Figure 1.12 illustrates a simple view of the database server approach, with application servers connected to one database server via a communication network.

The database server approach, as an extension of the classical client/server architecture, has several potential advantages. First, the single focus on data management makes possible the development of specific techniques for increasing data reliability and availability, e.g. using parallelism. Second, the overall performance of database management can be significantly enhanced by the tight integration of the database system and a dedicated database operating system. Finally, a database server can also exploit recent hardware architectures, such as multiprocessors or clusters of PC servers to enhance both performance and data availability.

Although these advantages are significant, they can be offset by the overhead introduced by the additional communication between the application and the data servers. This is an issue, of course, in classical client/server systems as well, but in this case there is an additional layer of communication to worry about. The communication cost can be amortized only if the server interface is sufficiently high level to allow the expression of complex queries involving intensive data processing.

The application server approach (indeed, a n-tier distributed approach) can be extended by the introduction of multiple database servers and multiple application servers (Figure 1.13), as can be done in classical client/server architectures. In this case, it is typically the case that each application server is dedicated to one or a few applications, while database servers operate in the multiple server fashion discussed above.

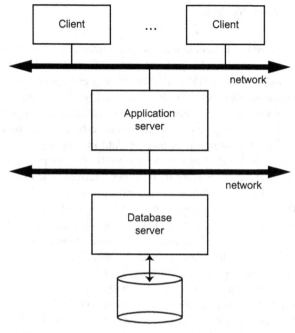

Fig. 1.12 Database Server Approach

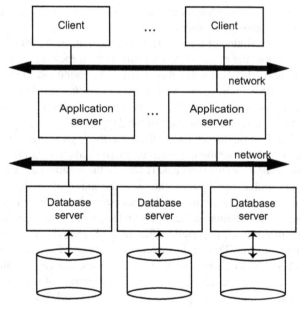

Fig. 1.13 Distributed Database Servers

1.7.9 Peer-to-Peer Systems

If the term "client/server" is loaded with different interpretations, "peer-to-peer" is even worse as its meaning has changed and evolved over the years. As noted earlier, the early works on distributed DBMSs all focused on peer-to-peer architectures where there was no differentiation between the functionality of each site in the system[4]. After a decade of popularity of client/server computing, peer-to-peer have made a comeback in the last few years (primarily spurred by file sharing applications) and some have even positioned peer-to-peer data management as an alternative to distributed DBMSs. While this may be a stretch, modern peer-to-peer systems have two important differences from their earlier relatives. The first is the massive distribution in current systems. While in the early days we focused on a few (perhaps at most tens of) sites, current systems consider thousands of sites. The second is the inherent heterogeneity of every aspect of the sites and their autonomy. While this has always been a concern of distributed databases, as discussed earlier, coupled with massive distribution, site heterogeneity and autonomy take on an added significance, disallowing some of the approaches from consideration.

Discussing peer-to-peer database systems within this backdrop poses real challenges; the unique issues of database management over the "modern" peer-to-peer architectures are still being investigated. What we choose to do, in this book, is to initially focus on the classical meaning of peer-to-peer (the same functionality of each site), since the principles and fundamental techniques of these systems are very similar to those of client/server systems, and discuss the modern peer-to-peer database issues in a separate chapter (Chapter 16).

Let us start the description of the architecture by looking at the data organizational view. We first note that the physical data organization on each machine may be, and probably is, different. This means that there needs to be an individual internal schema definition at each site, which we call the *local internal schema* (LIS). The enterprise view of the data is described by the *global conceptual schema* (GCS), which is global because it describes the logical structure of the data at all the sites.

To handle data fragmentation and replication, the logical organization of data at each site needs to be described. Therefore, there needs to be a third layer in the architecture, the *local conceptual schema* (LCS). In the architectural model we have chosen, then, the global conceptual schema is the union of the local conceptual schemas. Finally, user applications and user access to the database is supported by *external schemas* (ESs), defined as being above the global conceptual schema.

This architecture model, depicted in Figure 1.14, provides the levels of transparency discussed earlier. Data independence is supported since the model is an extension of ANSI/SPARC, which provides such independence naturally. Location and replication transparencies are supported by the definition of the local and global conceptual schemas and the mapping in between. Network transparency, on the other hand, is supported by the definition of the global conceptual schema. The user

---

[4] In fact, in the first edition of this book which appeared in early 1990 and whose writing was completed in 1989, there wasn't a single mention of the term "client/server".

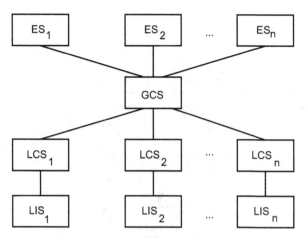

Fig. 1.14 Distributed Database Reference Architecture

queries data irrespective of its location or of which local component of the distributed database system will service it. As mentioned before, the distributed DBMS translates global queries into a group of local queries, which are executed by distributed DBMS components at different sites that communicate with one another.

The detailed components of a distributed DBMS are shown in Figure 1.15. One component handles the interaction with users, and another deals with the storage. The first major component, which we call the *user processor*, consists of four elements:

1. The *user interface handler* is responsible for interpreting user commands as they come in, and formatting the result data as it is sent to the user.

2. The *semantic data controller* uses the integrity constraints and authorizations that are defined as part of the global conceptual schema to check if the user query can be processed. This component, which is studied in detail in Chapter 5, is also responsible for authorization and other functions.

3. The *global query optimizer and decomposer* determines an execution strategy to minimize a cost function, and translates the global queries into local ones using the global and local conceptual schemas as well as the global directory. The global query optimizer is responsible, among other things, for generating the best strategy to execute distributed join operations. These issues are discussed in Chapters 6 through 8.

4. The *distributed execution monitor* coordinates the distributed execution of the user request. The execution monitor is also called the *distributed transaction manager*. In executing queries in a distributed fashion, the execution monitors at various sites may, and usually do, communicate with one another.

The second major component of a distributed DBMS is the *data processor* and consists of three elements:

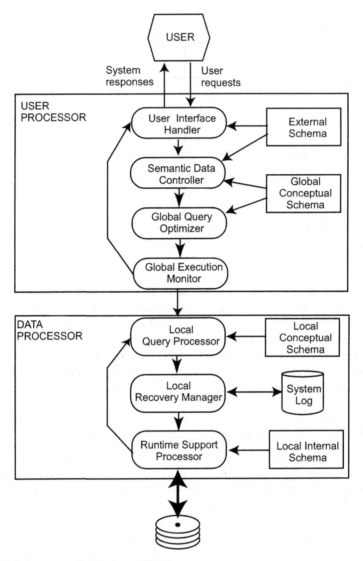

Fig. 1.15 Components of a Distributed DBMS

1. The *local query optimizer*, which actually acts as the *access path selector*, is responsible for choosing the best access path[5] to access any data item (touched upon briefly in Chapter 8).

2. The *local recovery manager* is responsible for making sure that the local database remains consistent even when failures occur (Chapter 12).

3. The *run-time support processor* physically accesses the database according to the physical commands in the schedule generated by the query optimizer. The run-time support processor is the interface to the operating system and contains the *database buffer* (or *cache*) *manager*, which is responsible for maintaining the main memory buffers and managing the data accesses.

It is important to note, at this point, that our use of the terms "user processor" and "data processor" does not imply a functional division similar to client/server systems. These divisions are merely organizational and there is no suggestion that they should be placed on different machines. In peer-to-peer systems, one expects to find both the user processor modules and the data processor modules on each machine. However, there have been suggestions to separate "query-only sites" in a system from full-functionality ones. In this case, the former sites would only need to have the user processor.

In client/server systems where there is a single server, the client has the user interface manager while the server has all of the data processor functionality as well as semantic data controller; there is no need for the global query optimizer or the global execution monitor. If there are multiple servers and the home server approach described in the previous section is employed, then each server hosts all of the modules except the user interface manager that resides on the client. If, however, each client is expected to contact individual servers on its own, then, most likely, the clients will host the full user processor functionality while the data processor functionality resides in the servers.

1.7.10 Multidatabase System Architecture

Multidatabase systems (MDBS) represent the case where individual DBMSs (whether distributed or not) are fully autonomous and have no concept of cooperation; they may not even "know" of each other's existence or how to talk to each other. Our focus is, naturally, on distributed MDBSs, which is what the term will refer to in the remainder. In most current literature, one finds the term *data integration system* used instead. We avoid using that term since data integration systems consider non-database data sources as well. Our focus is strictly on databases. We discuss these systems and their relationship to database integration in Chapter 4. We note, however, that there is considerable variability of the use of the term "multidatabase" in literature. In this

---

[5] The term *access path* refers to the data structures and the algorithms that are used to access the data. A typical access path, for example, is an index on one or more attributes of a relation.

book, we use it consistently as defined above, which may devitate from its use in some of the existing literature.

The differences in the level of autonomy between the distributed multi-DBMSs and distributed DBMSs are also reflected in their architectural models. The fundamental difference relates to the definition of the global conceptual schema. In the case of logically integrated distributed DBMSs, the global conceptual schema defines the conceptual view of the *entire* database, while in the case of distributed multi-DBMSs, it represents only the collection of *some* of the local databases that each local DBMS wants to share. The individual DBMSs may choose to make some of their data available for access by others (i.e., federated database architectures) by defining an *export schema* [Heimbigner and McLeod, 1985]. Thus the definition of a *global database* is different in MDBSs than in distributed DBMSs. In the latter, the global database is equal to the union of local databases, whereas in the former it is only a (possibly proper) subset of the same union. In a MDBS, the GCS (which is also called a mediated *schema*) is defined by integrating either the external schemas of local autonomous databases or (possibly parts of their) local conceptual schemas.

Furthermore, users of a local DBMS define their own views on the local database and do not need to change their applications if they do not want to access data from another database. This is again an issue of autonomy.

Designing the global conceptual schema in multidatabase systems involves the integration of either the local conceptual schemas or the local external schemas (Figure 1.16). A major difference between the design of the GCS in multi-DBMSs and in logically integrated distributed DBMSs is that in the former the mapping is from local conceptual schemas to a global schema. In the latter, however, mapping is in the reverse direction. As we discuss in Chapters 3 and 4, this is because the design in the former is usually a bottom-up process, whereas in the latter it is usually a top-down procedure. Furthermore, if heterogeneity exists in the multidatabase system, a canonical data model has to be found to define the GCS.

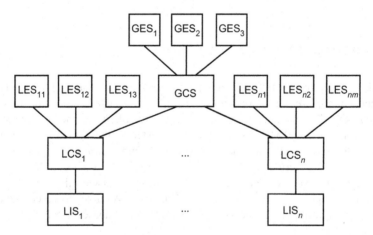

Fig. 1.16 MDBS Architecture with a GCS

Once the GCS has been designed, views over the global schema can be defined for users who require global access. It is not necessary for the GES and GCS to be defined using the same data model and language; whether they do or not determines whether the system is homogeneous or heterogeneous.

If heterogeneity exists in the system, then two implementation alternatives exist: unilingual and multilingual. A *unilingual* multi-DBMS requires the users to utilize possibly different data models and languages when both a local database and the global database are accessed. The identifying characteristic of unilingual systems is that any application that accesses data from multiple databases must do so by means of an external view that is defined on the global conceptual schema. This means that the user of the global database is effectively a different user than those who access only a local database, utilizing a different data model and a different data language.

An alternative is *multilingual* architecture, where the basic philosophy is to permit each user to access the global database (i.e., data from other databases) by means of an external schema, defined using the language of the user's local DBMS. The GCS definition is quite similar in the multilingual architecture and the unilingual approach, the major difference being the definition of the external schemas, which are described in the language of the external schemas of the local database. Assuming that the definition is purely local, a query issued according to a particular schema is handled exactly as any query in the centralized DBMSs. Queries against the global database are made using the language of the local DBMS, but they generally require some processing to be mapped to the global conceptual schema.

The component-based architectural model of a multi-DBMS is significantly different from a distributed DBMS. The fundamental difference is the existence of full-fledged DBMSs, each of which manages a different database. The MDBS provides a layer of software that runs on top of these individual DBMSs and provides users with the facilities of accessing various databases (Figure 1.17). Note that in a distributed MDBS, the multi-DBMS layer may run on multiple sites or there may be central site where those services are offered. Also note that as far as the individual DBMSs are concerned, the MDBS layer is simply another application that submits requests and receives answers.

A popular implementation architecture for MDBSs is the mediator/wrapper approach (Figure 1.18) [Wiederhold, 1992]. A *mediator* "is a software module that exploits encoded knowledge about certain sets or subsets of data to create information for a higher layer of applications." Thus, each mediator performs a particular function with clearly defined interfaces. Using this architecture to implement a MDBS, each module in the multi-DBMS layer of Figure 1.17 is realized as a mediator. Since mediators can be built on top of other mediators, it is possible to construct a layered implementation. In mapping this architecture to the datalogical view of Figure 1.16, the mediator level implements the GCS. It is this level that handles user queries over the GCS and performs the MDBS functionality.

The mediators typically operate using a common data model and interface language. To deal with potential heterogeneities of the source DBMSs, *wrappers* are implemented whose task is to provide a mapping between a source DBMSs view and the mediators' view. For example, if the source DBMS is a relational one, but the

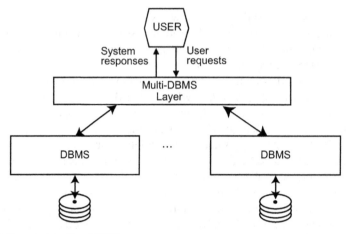

Fig. 1.17 Components of an MDBS

mediator implementations are object-oriented, the required mappings are established by the wrappers. The exact role and function of mediators differ from one implementation to another. In some cases, thin mediators have been implemented who do nothing more than translation. In other cases, wrappers take over the execution of some of the query functionality.

One can view the collection of mediators as a middleware layer that provides services above the source systems. Middleware is a topic that has been the subject of significant study in the past decade and very sophisticated middleware systems have been developed that provide advanced services for development of distributed applications. The mediators that we discuss only represent a subset of the functionality provided by these systems.

1.8 Bibliographic Notes

There are not many books on distributed DBMSs. Ceri and Pelagatti's book [Ceri and Pelagatti, 1983] was the first on this topic though it is now dated. The book by Bell and Grimson [Bell and Grimson, 1992] also provides an overview of the topics addressed here. In addition, almost every database book now has a chapter on distributed DBMSs. A brief overview of the technology is provided in [Özsu and Valduriez, 1997]. Our papers [Özsu and Valduriez, 1994, 1991] provide discussions of the state-of-the-art at the time they were written.

Database design is discussed in an introductory manner in [Levin and Morgan, 1975] and more comprehensively in [Ceri et al., 1987]. A survey of the file distribution algorithms is given in [Dowdy and Foster, 1982]. Directory management has not been considered in detail in the research community, but general techniques can be found in Chu and Nahouraii [1975] and [Chu, 1976]. A survey of query processing

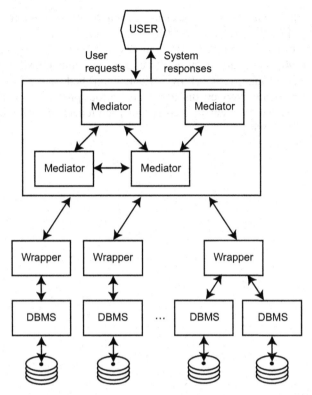

Fig. 1.18 Mediator/Wrapper Architecture

techniques can be found in [Sacco and Yao, 1982]. Concurrency control algorithms are reviewed in [Bernstein and Goodman, 1981] and [Bernstein et al., 1987]. Deadlock management has also been the subject of extensive research; an introductory paper is [Isloor and Marsland, 1980] and a widely quoted paper is [Obermarck, 1982]. For deadlock detection, good surveys are [Knapp, 1987] and [Elmagarmid, 1986]. Reliability is one of the issues discussed in [Gray, 1979], which is one of the landmark papers in the field. Other important papers on this topic are [Verhofstadt, 1978] and [Härder and Reuter, 1983]. [Gray, 1979] is also the first paper discussing the issues of operating system support for distributed databases; the same topic is addressed in [Stonebraker, 1981]. Unfortunately, both papers emphasize centralized database systems.

There have been a number of architectural framework proposals. Some of the interesting ones include Schreiber's quite detailed extension of the ANSI/SPARC framework which attempts to accommodate heterogeneity of the data models [Schreiber, 1977], and the proposal by Mohan and Yeh [Mohan and Yeh, 1978]. As expected, these date back to the early days of the introduction of distributed DBMS technology. The detailed component-wise system architecture given in Figure 1.15 derives from

[Rahimi, 1987]. An alternative to the classification that we provide in Figure 1.10 can be found in [Sheth and Larson, 1990].

Most of the discussion on architectural models for multi-DBMSs is from [Özsu and Barker, 1990]. Other architectural discussions on multi-DBMSs are given in [Gligor and Luckenbaugh, 1984], [Litwin, 1988], and [Sheth and Larson, 1990]. All of these papers provide overview discussions of various prototype and commercial systems. An excellent overview of heterogeneous and federated database systems is [Sheth and Larson, 1990].

Chapter 2
Background

As indicated in the previous chapter, there are two technological bases for distributed database technology: database management and computer networks. In this chapter, we provide an overview of the concepts in these two fields that are more important from the perspective of distributed database technology.

2.1 Overview of Relational DBMS

The aim of this section is to define the terminology and framework used in subsequent chapters, since most of the distributed database technology has been developed using the relational model. In later chapters, when appropriate, we introduce other models. Our focus here is on the language and operators.

2.1.1 Relational Database Concepts

A *database* is a structured collection of data related to some real-life phenomena that we are trying to model. A *relational database* is one where the database structure is in the form of tables. Formally, a relation R defined over n sets $D_1, D_2, \ldots, D_n$ (not necessarily distinct) is a set of *n-tuples* (or simply *tuples*) $\langle d_1, d_2, \ldots, d_n \rangle$ such that $d_1 \in D_1, d_2 \in D_2, \ldots, d_n \in D_n$.

Example 2.1. As an example we use a database that models an engineering company. The entities to be modeled are the *employees* (EMP) and *project*s (PROJ). For each employee, we would like to keep track of the employee number (ENO), name (ENAME), title in the company (TITLE), salary (SAL), identification number of the project(s) the employee is working on (PNO), responsibility within the project (RESP), and duration of the assignment to the project (DUR) in months. Similarly, for each project we would like to store the project number (PNO), the project name (PNAME), and the project budget (BUDGET).

M.T. Özsu and P. Valduriez, *Principles of Distributed Database Systems: Third Edition*, 41
DOI 10.1007/978-1-4419-8834-8_2, © Springer Science+Business Media, LLC 2011

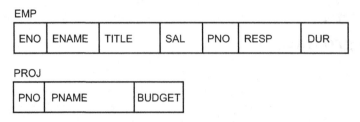

Fig. 2.1 Sample Database Scheme

The *relation schemas* for this database can be defined as follows:

EMP(<u>ENO</u>, ENAME, TITLE, SAL, <u>PNO</u>, RESP, DUR)

PROJ(<u>PNO</u>,PNAME, BUDGET)

In relation scheme EMP, there are seven *attributes*: ENO, ENAME, TITLE, SAL, PNO, RESP, DUR. The values of ENO come from the *domain* of all valid employee numbers, say D_1, the values of ENAME come from the domain of all valid names, say D_2, and so on. Note that each attribute of each relation does not have to come from a distinct domain. Various attributes within a relation or from a number of relations may be defined over the same domain.   ♦

The *key* of a relation scheme is the minimum non-empty subset of its attributes such that the values of the attributes comprising the key uniquely identify each tuple of the relation. The attributes that make up key are called *prime* attributes. The superset of a key is usually called a *superkey*. Thus in our example the key of **PROJ** is PNO, and that of **EMP** is the set (ENO, PNO). Each relation has at least one key. Sometimes, there may be more than one possibility for the key. In such cases, each alternative is considered a *candidate key*, and one of the candidate keys is chosen as the *primary key*, which we denote by underlining. The number of attributes of a relation defines its *degree*, whereas the number of tuples of the relation defines its *cardinality*.

In tabular form, the example database consists of two tables, as shown in Figure 2.1. The columns of the tables correspond to the attributes of the relations; if there were any information entered as the rows, they would correspond to the tuples. The empty table, showing the structure of the table, corresponds to the *relation schema*; when the table is filled with rows, it corresponds to a *relation instance*. Since the information within a table varies over time, many instances can be generated from one relation scheme. Note that from now on, the term *relation* refers to a relation instance. In Figure 2.2 we depict instances of the two relations that are defined in Figure 2.1.

An attribute value may be undefined. This lack of definition may have various interpretations, the most common being "unknown" or "not applicable". This special value of the attribute is generally referred to as the *null value*. The representation of a null value must be different from any other domain value, and special care should be given to differentiate it from zero. For example, value "0" for attribute DUR is

EMP

ENO	ENAME	TITLE	SAL	PNO	RESP	DUR
E1	J. Doe	Elect. Eng.	40000	P1	Manager	12
E2	M. Smith	Analyst	34000	P1	Analyst	24
E2	M. Smith	Analyst	34000	P2	Analyst	6
E3	A. Lee	Mech. Eng.	27000	P3	Consultant	10
E3	A. Lee	Mech. Eng.	27000	P4	Engineer	48
E4	J. Miller	Programmer	24000	P2	Programmer	18
E5	B. Casey	Syst. Anal.	34000	P2	Manager	24
E6	L. Chu	Elect. Eng.	40000	P4	Manager	48
E7	R. Davis	Mech. Eng.	27000	P3	Engineer	36
E8	J. Jones	Syst. Anal.	34000	P3	Manager	40

PROJ

PNO	PNAME	BUDGET
P1	Instrumentation	150000
P2	Database Develop.	135000
P3	CAD/CAM	250000
P4	Maintenance	310000

Fig. 2.2 Sample Database Instance

known information (e.g., in the case of a newly hired employee), while value "null" for DUR means unknown. Supporting null values is an important feature necessary to deal with *maybe* queries [Codd, 1979].

2.1.2 Normalization

The aim of normalization is to eliminate various anomalies (or undesirable aspects) of a relation in order to obtain "better" relations. The following four problems might exist in a relation scheme:

1. *Repetition anomaly.* Certain information may be repeated unnecessarily. Consider, for example, the EMP relation in Figure 2.2. The name, title, and salary of an employee are repeated for each project on which this person serves. This is obviously a waste of storage and is contrary to the spirit of databases.

2. *Update anomaly*. As a consequence of the repetition of data, performing updates may be troublesome. For example, if the salary of an employee changes, multiple tuples have to be updated to reflect this change.

3. *Insertion anomaly*. It may not be possible to add new information to the database. For example, when a new employee joins the company, we cannot add personal information (name, title, salary) to the EMP relation unless an appointment to a project is made. This is because the key of EMP includes the attribute PNO, and null values cannot be part of the key.

4. *Deletion anomaly*. This is the converse of the insertion anomaly. If an employee works on only one project, and that project is terminated, it is not possible to delete the project information from the EMP relation. To do so would result in deleting the only tuple about the employee, thereby resulting in the loss of personal information we might want to retain.

Normalization transforms arbitrary relation schemes into ones without these problems. A relation with one or more of the above mentioned anomalies is split into two or more relations of a higher *normal form*. A relation is said to be in a normal form if it satisfies the conditions associated with that normal form. Codd initially defined the *first*, *second*, and *third* normal forms (1NF, 2NF, and 3NF, respectively). Boyce and Codd [Codd, 1974] later defined a modified version of the third normal form, commonly known as the *Boyce-Codd normal form* (BCNF). This was followed by the definition of the *fourth* (4NF) [Fagin, 1977] and *fifth* normal forms (5NF) [Fagin, 1979].

The normal forms are based on certain dependency structures. BCNF and lower normal forms are based on *functional dependencies* (FDs), 4NF is based on *multi-valued dependencies*, and 5NF is based on *projection-join dependencies*. We only introduce functional dependency, since that is the only relevant one for the example we are considering.

Let R be a relation defined over the set of attributes $A = \{A_1, A_2, \ldots, A_n\}$ and let $X \subset A$, $Y \subset A$. If for each value of X in R, there is only one associated Y value, we say that "X *functionally determines* Y" or that "Y is *functionally dependent* on X." Notationally, this is shown as $X \rightarrow Y$. The key of a relation functionally determines the non-key attributes of the same relation.

Example 2.2. For example, in the PROJ relation of Example 2.1 (one can observe these in Figure 2.2 as well), the valid FD is

PNO → (PNAME, BUDGET)

In the EMP relation we have

(ENO, PNO) → (ENAME,TITLE,SAL,RESP,DUR)

This last FD is not the only FD in EMP, however. If each employee is given unique employee numbers, we can write

ENO → (ENAME, TITLE, SAL)

(ENO, PNO) → (RESP, DUR)

It may also happen that the salary for a given position is fixed, which gives rise to the FD

TITLE → SAL

◆

We do not discuss the normal forms or the normalization algorithms in detail; these can be found in database textbooks. The following example shows the result of normalization on the sample database that we introduced in Example 2.1.

Example 2.3. The following set of relation schemes are normalized into BCNF with respect to the functional dependencies defined over the relations.

EMP(<u>ENO</u>, ENAME, TITLE)

PAY(<u>TITLE</u>, SAL)

PROJ(<u>PNO</u>, PNAME, BUDGET)

ASG(<u>ENO, PNO</u>, RESP, DUR)

The normalized instances of these relations are shown in Figure 2.3.   ◆

2.1.3 *Relational Data Languages*

Data manipulation languages developed for the relational model (commonly called *query languages*) fall into two fundamental groups: *relational algebra* languages and *relational calculus* languages. The difference between them is based on how the user query is formulated. The relational algebra is procedural in that the user is expected to specify, using certain high-level operators, how the result is to be obtained. The relational calculus, on the other hand, is non-procedural; the user only specifies the relationships that should hold in the result. Both of these languages were originally proposed by Codd [1970], who also proved that they were equivalent in terms of expressive power [Codd, 1972].

2.1.3.1 Relational Algebra

Relational algebra consists of a set of operators that operate on relations. Each operator takes one or two relations as operands and produces a result relation, which, in turn, may be an operand to another operator. These operations permit the querying and updating of a relational database.

EMP

ENO	ENAME	TITLE
E1	J. Doe	Elect. Eng
E2	M. Smith	Syst. Anal.
E3	A. Lee	Mech. Eng.
E4	J. Miller	Programmer
E5	B. Casey	Syst. Anal.
E6	L. Chu	Elect. Eng.
E7	R. Davis	Mech. Eng.
E8	J. Jones	Syst. Anal.

ASG

ENO	PNO	RESP	DUR
E1	P1	Manager	12
E2	P1	Analyst	24
E2	P2	Analyst	6
E3	P3	Consultant	10
E3	P4	Engineer	48
E4	P2	Programmer	18
E5	P2	Manager	24
E6	P4	Manager	48
E7	P3	Engineer	36
E8	P3	Manager	40

PROJ

PNO	PNAME	BUDGET
P1	Instrumentation	150000
P2	Database Develop.	135000
P3	CAD/CAM	250000
P4	Maintenance	310000

PAY

TITLE	SAL
Elect. Eng.	40000
Syst. Anal.	34000
Mech. Eng.	27000
Programmer	24000

Fig. 2.3 Normalized Relations

There are five fundamental relational algebra operators and five others that can be defined in terms of these. The fundamental operators are *selection*, *projection*, *union*, *set difference*, and *Cartesian product*. The first two of these operators are unary operators, and the last three are binary operators. The additional operators that can be defined in terms of these fundamental operators are *intersection*, $\theta - join$, *natural join*, *semijoin* and *division*. In practice, relational algebra is extended with operators for grouping or sorting the results, and for performing arithmetic and aggregate functions. Other operators, such as *outer join* and *transitive closure*, are sometimes used as well to provide additional functionality. We only discuss the more common operators.

The operands of some of the binary relations should be *union compatible*. Two relations R and S are union compatible if and only if they are of the same degree and the i-th attribute of each is defined over the same domain. The second part of the definition holds, obviously, only when the attributes of a relation are identified by their relative positions within the relation and not by their names. If relative ordering of attributes is not important, it is necessary to replace the second part of the definition by the phrase "the corresponding attributes of the two relations should be defined over the same domain." The correspondence is defined rather loosely here.

Many operator definitions refer to "formula", which also appears in relational calculus expressions we discuss later. Thus, let us define precisely, at this point, what we mean by a formula. We define a formula within the context of first-order predicate calculus (since we use that formalism later), and follow the notation of Gallaire et al. [1984]. First-order predicate calculus is based on a *symbol alphabet* that consists of (1) variables, constants, functions, and predicate symbols; (2) parentheses; (3) the logical connectors $\wedge$ (and), $\vee$ (or), $\neg$ (not), $\rightarrow$ (implication), and $\leftrightarrow$ (equivalence); and (4) quantifiers $\forall$ (for all) and $\exists$ (there exists). A *term* is either a constant or a variable. Recursively, if f is an n-ary function and $t_1, \ldots, t_n$ are terms, $f(t_1, \ldots, t_n)$ is also a term. An *atomic formula* is of the form $P(t_1, \ldots, t_n)$, where P is an n-ary predicate symbol and the t_i's are terms. A *well-formed formula* (*wff*) can be defined recursively as follows: If w_i and w_j are wffs, then (w_i), $\neg(w_i)$, $(w_i) \wedge (w_j)$, $(w_i) \vee (w_j)$, $(w_i) \rightarrow (w_j)$, and $(w_i) \leftrightarrow (w_j)$ are all wffs. Variables in a wff may be *free* or they may be *bound* by one of the two quantifiers.

Selection.

Selection produces a horizontal subset of a given relation. The subset consists of all the tuples that satisfy a formula (condition). The selection from a relation R is

$$\sigma_F(R)$$

where R is the relation and F is a formula.

The formula in the selection operation is called a *selection predicate* and is an atomic formula whose terms are of the form $A\theta c$, where A is an attribute of R and θ is one of the arithmetic comparison operators $<, >, =, \neq, \leq,$ and $\geq$. The terms can be connected by the logical connectors $\wedge, \vee,$ and $\neg$. Furthermore, the selection predicate does not contain any quantifiers.

Example 2.4. Consider the relation EMP shown in Figure 2.3. The result of selecting those tuples for electrical engineers is shown in Figure 2.4. $\blacklozenge$

$$\sigma_{\text{TITLE="Elect. Eng."}}(\text{EMP})$$

ENO	ENAME	TITLE
E1	J. Doe	Elect. Eng
E6	L. Chu	Elect. Eng.

Fig. 2.4 Result of Selection

Projection.

Projection produces a vertical subset of a relation. The result relation contains only those attributes of the original relation over which projection is performed. Thus the degree of the result is less than or equal to the degree of the original relation.

The projection of relation R over attributes A and B is denoted as

$$\Pi_{A,B}(R)$$

Note that the result of a projection might contain tuples that are identical. In that case the duplicate tuples may be deleted from the result relation. It is possible to specify projection with or without duplicate elimination.

Example 2.5. The projection of relation PROJ shown in Figure 2.3 over attributes PNO and BUDGET is depicted in Figure 2.5.   ♦

$$\Pi_{PNO,BUDGET}(PROJ)$$

PNO	BUDGET
P1	150000
P2	135000
P3	250000
P4	310000

Fig. 2.5 Result of Projection

Union.

The union of two relations R and S (denoted as $R \cup S$) is the set of all tuples that are in R, or in S, or in both. We should note that R and S should be union compatible. As in the case of projection, the duplicate tuples are normally eliminated. Union may be used to insert new tuples into an existing relation, where these tuples form one of the operand relations.

Set Difference.

The set difference of two relations R and S ($R - S$) is the set of all tuples that are in R but not in S. In this case, not only should R and S be union compatible, but the operation is also asymmetric (i.e., $R - S \neq S - R$). This operation allows the

EMP x PAY

ENO	ENAME	EMP.TITLE	PAY.TITLE	SAL
E1	J. Doe	Elect. Eng.	Elect. Eng.	40000
E1	J. Doe	Elect. Eng.	Syst. Anal.	34000
E1	J. Doe	Elect. Eng.	Mech. Eng.	27000
E1	J. Doe	Elect. Eng.	Programmer	24000
E2	M. Smith	Syst. Anal.	Elect. Eng.	40000
E2	M. Smith	Syst. Anal.	Syst. Anal.	34000
E2	M. Smith	Syst. Anal.	Mech. Eng.	27000
E2	M. Smith	Syst. Anal.	Programmer	24000
E3	A. Lee	Mech. Eng.	Elect. Eng.	40000
E3	A. Lee	Mech. Eng.	Syst. Anal.	34000
E3	A. Lee	Mech. Eng.	Mech. Eng.	27000
E3	A. Lee	Mech. Eng.	Programmer	24000
≈	≈	≈	≈	≈
E8	J. Jones	Syst. Anal.	Elect. Eng.	40000
E8	J. Jones	Syst. Anal.	Syst. Anal.	34000
E8	J. Jones	Syst. Anal.	Mech. Eng.	27000
E8	J. Jones	Syst. Anal.	Programmer	24000

Fig. 2.6 Partial Result of Cartesian Product

deletion of tuples from a relation. Together with the union operation, we can perform modification of tuples by deletion followed by insertion.

Cartesian Product.

The Cartesian product of two relations R of degree k_1 and S of degree k_2 is the set of $(k_1 + k_2)$-tuples, where each result tuple is a concatenation of one tuple of R with one tuple of S, for all tuples of R and S. The Cartesian product of R and S is denoted as $R \times S$.

It is possible that the two relations might have attributes with the same name. In this case the attribute names are prefixed with the relation name so as to maintain the uniqueness of the attribute names within a relation.

Example 2.6. Consider relations EMP and PAY in Figure 2.3. EMP $\times$ PAY is shown in Figure 2.6. Note that the attribute TITLE, which is common to both relations, appears twice, prefixed with the relation name. ♦

Intersection.

Intersection of two relations R and S ($R \cap S$) consists of the set of all tuples that are in both R and S. In terms of the basic operators, it can be specified as follows:

$$R \cap S = R - (R - S)$$

θ-Join.

Join is a derivative of Cartesian product. There are various forms of join; the primary classification is between *inner join* and *outer join*. We first discuss inner join and its variants and then describe outer join.

The most general type of inner join is the θ-join. The θ-join of two relations R and S is denoted as

$$R \bowtie_F S$$

where F is a formula specifying the *join predicate*. A join predicate is specified similar to a selection predicate, except that the terms are of the form $R.A\theta S.B$, where A and B are attributes of R and S, respectively.

The join of two relations is equivalent to performing a selection, using the join predicate as the selection formula, over the Cartesian product of the two operand relations. Thus

$$R \bowtie_F S = \sigma_F (R \times S)$$

In the equivalence above, we should note that if F involves attributes of the two relations that are common to both of them, a projection is necessary to make sure that those attributes do not appear twice in the result.

Example 2.7. Let us consider that the EMP relation in Figure 2.3 and add two more tuples as depicted in Figure 2.7(a). Then Figure 2.7(b) shows the θ-join of relations EMP and ASG over the join predicate EMP.ENO=ASG.ENO.

The same result could have been obtained as

$$\text{EMP} \bowtie_{\text{EMP.ENO=ASG.ENO}} \text{ASG} =$$
$$\Pi_{\text{ENO, ENAME, TITLE, SAL}} (\sigma_{\text{EMP.ENO =PAY.ENO}} (\text{EMP} \times \text{ASG}))$$

Notice that the result does not have tuples E9 and E10 since these employees have not yet been assigned to a project. Furthermore, the information about some employees (e.g., E2 and E3) who have been assigned to multiple projects appear more than once in the result.   ♦

This example demonstrates a special case of θ-join which is called the *equi-join*. This is a case where the formula F only contains equality (=) as the arithmetic operator. It should be noted, however, that an equi-join does not have to be specified over a common attribute as the example above might suggest.

EMP   EMP ⋈ EMP.ENO=ASG.ENO ASG

ENO	ENAME	TITLE
E1	J. Doe	Elect. Eng
E2	M. Smith	Syst. Anal.
E3	A. Lee	Mech. Eng.
E4	J. Miller	Programmer
E5	B. Casey	Syst. Anal.
E6	L. Chu	Elect. Eng.
E7	R. Davis	Mech. Eng.
E8	J. Jones	Syst. Anal.
E9	A. Hsu	Programmer
E10	T. Wong	Syst. Anal.

ENO	ENAME	TITLE	PNO	RESP	DUR
E1	J. Doe	Elect. Eng.	P1	Manager	12
E2	M. Smith	Syst. Anal.	P1	Analyst	12
E2	M. Smith	Syst. Anal.	P2	Analyst	12
E3	A. Lee	Mech. Eng.	P3	Consultant	12
E3	A. Lee	Mech. Eng.	P4	Engineer	12
E4	J. Miller	Programmer	P2	Programmer	12
E5	J. Miller	Syst. Anal.	P2	Manager	12
E6	L. Chu	Elect. Eng.	P4	Manager	12
E7	R. Davis	Mech. Eng.	P3	Engineer	12
E8	J. Jones	Syst. Anal.	P3	Manager	12

                    (a)   (b)

Fig. 2.7 The Result of Join

A natural join is an equi-join of two relations over a specified attribute, more specifically, over attributes with the same domain. There is a difference, however, in that usually the attributes over which the natural join is performed appear only once in the result. A natural join is denoted as the join without the formula

$$R \bowtie_A S$$

where A is the attribute common to both R and S. We should note here that the natural join attribute may have different names in the two relations; what is required is that they come from the same domain. In this case the join is denoted as

$$R_A \bowtie_B S$$

where B is the corresponding join attribute of S.

Example 2.8. The join of EMP and ASG in Example 2.7 is actually a natural join. Here is another example – Figure 2.8 shows the natural join of relations EMP and PAY in Figure 2.3 over the attribute TITLE.

◆

Inner join requires the joined tuples from the two operand relations to satisfy the join predicate. In contrast, outer join does not have this requirement – tuples exist in the result relation regardless. Outer join can be of three types: left outer join (⋈̄), right outer join (⋈̄) and full outer join (⋈̄). In the left outer join, the tuples from the left operand relation are always in the result, in the case of right outer join, the tuples from the right operand are always in the result, and in the case of full outer relation, tuples from both relations are always in the result. Outer join is useful in those cases where we wish to include information from one or both relations even if the do not satisfy the join predicate.

EMP ⋈ TITLE PAY

ENO	ENAME	TITLE	SAL
E1	J. Doe	Elect. Eng.	40000
E2	M. Smith	Analyst	34000
E3	A. Lee	Mech. Eng.	27000
E4	J. Miller	Programmer	24000
E5	B. Casey	Syst. Anal.	34000
E6	L. Chu	Elect. Eng.	40000
E7	R. Davis	Mech. Eng.	27000
E8	J. Jones	Syst. Anal.	34000

Fig. 2.8 The Result of Natural Join

Example 2.9. Consider the left outer join of EMP (as revised in Example 2.7) and ASG over attribute ENO (i.e., EMP ⋉$_{ENO}$ ASG). The result is given in Figure 2.9. Notice that the information about two employees, E9 and E10 are included in the result even thought they have not yet been assigned to a project with "Null" values for the attributes from the ASG relation.   ♦

EMP ⋉ $_{ENO}$ ASG

ENO	ENAME	TITLE	PNO	RESP	DUR
E1	J. Doe	Elect. Eng.	P1	Manager	12
E2	M. Smith	Syst. Anal.	P1	Analyst	12
E2	M. Smith	Syst. Anal.	P2	Analyst	12
E3	A. Lee	Mech. Eng.	P3	Consultant	12
E3	A. Lee	Mech. Eng.	P4	Engineer	12
E4	J. Miller	Programmer	P2	Programmer	12
E5	J. Miller	Syst. Anal.	P2	Manager	12
E6	L. Chu	Elect. Eng.	P4	Manager	12
E7	R. Davis	Mech. Eng.	P3	Engineer	12
E8	J. Jones	Syst. Anal.	P3	Manager	12
E9	A. Hsu	Programmer	Null	Null	Null
E10	T. Wong	Syst. Anal.	Null	Null	Null

Fig. 2.9 The Result of Left Outer Join

Semijoin.

The semijoin of relation R, defined over the set of attributes A, by relation S, defined over the set of attributes B, is the subset of the tuples of R that participate in the join of R with S. It is denoted as $R \ltimes_F S$ (where F is a predicate as defined before) and can be obtained as follows:

$$R \ltimes_F S = \Pi_A(R \bowtie_F S) = \Pi_A(R) \bowtie_F \Pi_{A \cap B}(S)$$
$$= R \bowtie_F \Pi_{A \cap B}(S)$$

The advantage of semijoin is that it decreases the number of tuples that need to be handled to form the join. In centralized database systems, this is important because it usually results in a decreased number of secondary storage accesses by making better use of the memory. It is even more important in distributed databases since it usually reduces the amount of data that needs to be transmitted between sites in order to evaluate a query. We talk about this in more detail in Chapters 3 and 8. At this point note that the operation is asymmetric (i.e., $R \ltimes_F S \neq S \ltimes_F R$).

Example 2.10. To demonstrate the difference between join and semijoin, let us consider the semijoin of EMP with PAY over the predicate EMP.TITLE = PAY.TITLE, that is,

EMP $\ltimes_{\text{EMP.TITLE = PAY.TITLE}}$ PAY

The result of the operation is shown in Figure 2.10. We encourage readers to compare Figures 2.7 and 2.10 to see the difference between the join and the semijoin operations. Note that the resultant relation does not have the PAY attribute and is therefore smaller.   ◆

EMP $\bowtie_{\text{EMP.TITLE=PAY.TITLE}}$ PAY

ENO	ENAME	TITLE
E1	J. Doe	Elect. Eng.
E2	M. Smith	Analyst
E3	A. Lee	Mech. Eng.
E4	J. Miller	Programmer
E5	B. Casey	Syst. Anal.
E6	L. Chu	Elect. Eng.
E7	R. Davis	Mech. Eng.
E8	J. Jones	Syst. Anal.

Fig. 2.10 The Result of Semijoin

Division.

The division of relation R of degree r with relation S of degree s (where $r > s$ and $s \neq 0$) is the set of $(r - s)$-tuples t such that for all s-tuples u in S, the tuple tu is in R. The division operation is denoted as $R \div S$ and can be specified in terms of the fundamental operators as follows:

$$R \div S = \Pi_{\bar{A}}(R) - \Pi_{\bar{A}}((\Pi_{\bar{A}}(R) \times S) - R)$$

where $\bar{A}$ is the set of attributes of R that are not in S [i.e., the $(r - s)$-tuples].

Example 2.11. Assume that we have a modified version of the ASG relation (call it ASG$'$) depicted in Figure 2.11a and defined as follows:

ASG$'$ = $\Pi_{\text{ENO,PNO}}$ (ASG) $\bowtie_{\text{PNO}}$ PROJ

If one wants to find the employee numbers of those employees who are assigned to all the projects that have a budget greater than \$200,000, it is necessary to divide ASG$'$ with a restricted version of PROJ, called PROJ$'$ (see Figure 2.11b). The result of division (ASG$' \div$ PROJ$'$) is shown in Figure 2.11c.

The keyword in the query above is "*all*." This rules out the possibility of doing a selection on ASG$'$ to find the necessary tuples, since that would only give those which correspond to employees working on *some* project with a budget greater than \$200,000, not those who work on all projects. Note that the result contains only the tuple $\langle$E3$\rangle$ since the tuples $\langle$E3, P3, CAD/CAM, 250000$\rangle$ and $\langle$E3, P4, Maintenance, 310000$\rangle$ both exist in ASG$'$. On the other hand, for example, $\langle$E7$\rangle$ is not in the result, since even though the tuple $\langle$E7, P3, CAD/CAM, 250000$\rangle$ is in ASG$'$, the tuple $\langle$E7, P4, Maintenance, 310000$\rangle$ is not.   ♦

Since all operations take relations as input and produce relations as outputs, we can nest operations using a parenthesized notation and represent relational algebra programs. The parentheses indicate the order of execution. The following are a few examples that demonstrate the issue.

Example 2.12. Consider the relations of Figure 2.3. The retrieval query

"Find the names of employees working on the CAD/CAM project"

can be answered by the relational algebra program

$\Pi_{\text{ENAME}}(((\sigma_{\text{PNAME = "CAD/CAM"}} \text{ PROJ}) \bowtie_{\text{PNO}} \text{ASG}) \bowtie_{\text{ENO}} \text{EMP})$

The order of execution is: the selection on PROJ, followed by the join with ASG, followed by the join with EMP, and finally the project on ENAME.

An equivalent program where the size of the intermediate relations is smaller is

$\Pi_{\text{ENAME}} (\text{EMP} \ltimes_{\text{ENO}} (\Pi_{\text{ENO}}(\text{ASG} \ltimes_{\text{PNO}} (\sigma_{\text{PNAME= "CAD/CAM"}} \text{PROJ}))))$ ♦

ASG'

ENO	PNO	PNAME	BUDGET
E1	P1	Instrumentation	150000
E2	P1	Instrumentation	150000
E2	P2	Database Develop.	135000
E3	P3	CAD/CAM	250000
E3	P4	Maintenance	310000
E4	P2	Database Develop.	135000
E5	P2	Database Develop.	135000
E6	P4	Maintenance	310000
E7	P3	CAD/CAM	250000
E8	P3	CAD/CAM	250000

(a)

PROJ'

PNO	PNAME	BUDGET
P3	CAD/CAM	250000
P4	Maintenance	310000

(b)

(ASG' ÷ PROJ')

ENO
E3

(c)

Fig. 2.11 The Result of Division

Example 2.13. The update query

"Replace the salary of programmers by \$25,000"

can be computed by

$$(\text{PAY} - (\sigma_{\text{TITLE} = \text{"Programmer"}} \text{PAY})) \cup (\langle \text{Programmer}, 25000 \rangle)$$

◆

2.1.3.2 Relational Calculus

In relational calculus-based languages, instead of specifying *how* to obtain the result, one specifies *what* the result is by stating the relationship that is supposed to hold for the result. Relational calculus languages fall into two groups: *tuple relational calculus* and *domain relational calculus*. The difference between the two is in terms of the primitive variable used in specifying the queries. We briefly review these two types of languages.

Relational calculus languages have a solid theoretical foundation since they are based on first-order predicate logic as we discussed before. Semantics is given to formulas by interpreting them as assertions on the database. A relational database can be viewed as a collection of tuples or a collection of domains. Tuple relational calculus interprets a variable in a formula as a tuple of a relation, whereas domain relational calculus interprets a variable as the value of a domain.

Tuple relational calculus.

The primitive variable used in tuple relational calculus is a *tuple variable* which specifies a tuple of a relation. In other words, it ranges over the tuples of a relation. Tuple calculus is the original relational calculus developed by Codd [1970].

In tuple relational calculus queries are specified as $\{t|F(t)\}$, where t is a tuple variable and F is a well-formed formula. The atomic formulas are of two forms:

1. *Tuple-variable membership expressions.* If t is a tuple variable ranging over the tuples of relation R (predicate symbol), the expression "tuple t belongs to relation R" is an atomic formula, which is usually specified as $R.t$ or $R(t)$.

2. *Conditions.* These can be defined as follows:

    (a) $s[A]\theta t[B]$, where s and t are tuple variables and A and B are components of s and t, respectively. θ is one of the arithmetic comparison operators $<$, $>$, $=$, $\neq$, $\leq$, and $\geq$. This condition specifies that component A of s stands in relation θ to the B component of t: for example, $s[SAL] > t[SAL]$.

    (b) $s[A]\theta c$, where s, A, and θ are as defined above and c is a constant. For example, $s[ENAME] =$ "Smith".

Note that A is defined as a component of the tuple variable s. Since the range of s is a relation instance, say S, it is obvious that component A of s corresponds to attribute A of relation S. The same thing is obviously true for B.

There are many languages that are based on relational tuple calculus, the most popular ones being SQL[1] [Date, 1987] and QUEL [Stonebraker et al., 1976]. SQL is now an international standard (actually, the only one) with various versions released: SQL1 was released in 1986, modifications to SQL1 were included in the 1989 version, SQL2 was issued in 1992, and SQL3, with object-oriented language extensions, was released in 1999.

---

[1] Sometimes SQL is cited as lying somewhere between relational algebra and relational calculus. Its originators called it a "mapping language." However, it follows the tuple calculus definition quite closely; hence we classify it as such.

SQL provides a uniform approach to data manipulation (retrieval, update), data definition (schema manipulation), and control (authorization, integrity, etc.). We limit ourselves to the expression, in SQL, of the queries in Examples 2.14 and 2.15.

Example 2.14. The query from Example 2.12,

"Find the names of employees working on the CAD/CAM project"

can be expressed as follows:

```
SELECT  EMP.ENAME
FROM    EMP,ASG,PROJ
WHERE   EMP.ENO = ASG.ENO
AND     ASG.PNO = PROJ.PNO
AND     PROJ.PNAME = "CAD/CAM"
```
◆

Note that a retrieval query generates a new relation similar to the relational algebra operations.

Example 2.15. The update query of Example 2.13,

"Replace the salary of programmers by $25,000"

is expressed as

```
UPDATE  PAY
SET     SAL = 25000
WHERE   PAY.TITLE = "Programmer"
```
◆

Domain relational calculus.

The domain relational calculus was first proposed by Lacroix and Pirotte [1977]. The fundamental difference between a tuple relational language and a domain relational language is the use of a *domain variable* in the latter. A domain variable ranges over the values in a domain and specifies a component of a tuple. In other words, the range of a domain variable consists of the domains over which the relation is defined. The wffs are formulated accordingly. The queries are specified in the following form:

$$x_1, x_2, ..., x_n | F(x_1, x_2, ..., x_n)$$

where F is a wff in which $x_1, ..., x_n$ are the free variables.

The success of domain relational calculus languages is due mainly to QBE [Zloof, 1977], which is a visual application of domain calculus. QBE, designed only for interactive use from a visual terminal, is user friendly. The basic concept is an *example*: the user formulates queries by providing a possible example of the answer. Typing relation names triggers the printing, on screen, of their schemes. Then, by supplying keywords into the columns (domains), the user specifies the query. For instance, the attributes of the project relation are given by P, which stands for "Print."

EMP	ENO	ENAME	TITLE
	E2	P.	

ASG	ENO	PNO	RESP	DUR
	E2	P3		

PROJ	PNO	PNAME	BUDGET
	P3	CAD/CAM	

Fig. 2.12 Retrieval Query in QBE

By default, all queries are retrieval. An update query requires the specification of U under the name of the updated relation or in the updated column. The retrieval query corresponding to Example 2.12 is given in Figure 2.12 and the update query of Example 2.13 is given in Figure 2.13. To distinguish examples from constants, examples are underlined.

PAY	TITLE	SAL
	Programmer	U.25000

Fig. 2.13 Update Query in QBE

2.2 Review of Computer Networks

In this section we discuss computer networking concepts relevant to distributed database systems. We omit most of the details of the technological and technical issues in favor of discussing the main concepts.

We define a *computer network* as an *interconnected collection of autonomous computers that are capable of exchanging information among themselves* (Figure 2.14). The keywords in this definition are *interconnected* and *autonomous*. We want the computers to be autonomous so that each computer can execute programs on its own. We also want the computers to be interconnected so that they are capable of exchanging information. Computers on a network are referred to as *nodes, hosts, end systems*, or *sites*. Note that sometimes the terms *host* and *end system* are used to refer

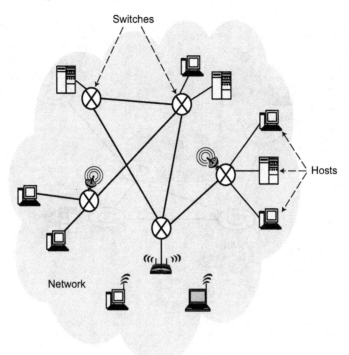

Fig. 2.14 A Computer Network

simply to the equipment, whereas *site* is reserved for the equipment as well as the software that runs on it. Similarly, *node* is generally used as a generic reference to the computers or to the switches in a network. They form one of the fundamental hardware components of a network. The other fundamental component is special purpose devices and links that form the communication path that interconnects the nodes. As depicted in Figure 2.14, the hosts are connected to the network through switches (represented as circles with an X in them)[2], which are special-purpose equipment that *route* messages through the network. Some of the hosts may be connected to the switches directly (using fiber optic, coaxial cable or copper wire) and some via wireless base stations. The switches are connected to each other by communication links that may be fiber optics, coaxial cable, satellite links, microwave connections, etc.

The most widely used computer network these days is the Internet. It is hard to define the Internet since the term is used to mean different things, but perhaps the best definition is that it is a network of networks (Figure 2.15). Each of these

---

[2] Note that the terms "switch" and "router" are sometimes used interchangeably (even within the same text). However, other times they are used to mean slightly different things: switch refers to the devices inside a network whereas router refers to one that is at the edge of a network connecting it to the backbone. We use them interchangeably as in Figures 2.14 and 2.15.

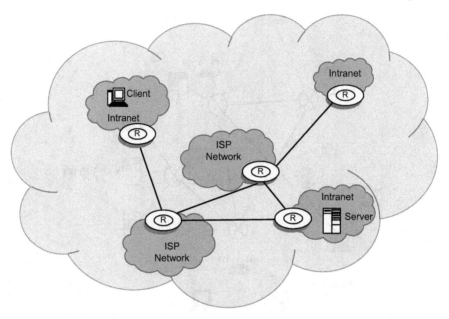

Fig. 2.15 Internet

networks is referred to as an *intranet* to highlight the fact that they are "internal" to an organization. An intranet, then, consists of a set of links and routers (shown as "R" in Figure 2.15) administered by a single administrative entity or by its delegates. For instance, the routers and links at a university constitute a single administrative domain. Such domains may be located within a single geographical area (such as the university network mentioned above), or, as in the case of large enterprises or Internet Service Provider (ISP) networks, span multiple geographical areas. Each intranet is connected to some others by means of links provisioned from ISPs. These links are typically high-speed, long-distance duplex data transmission media (we will define these terms shortly), such as a fiber-optic cable, or a satellite link. These links make up what is called the Internet backbone. Each intranet has a router interface that connects it to the backbone, as shown in Figure 2.15. Thus, each link connects an intranet router to an ISP's router. ISP's routers are connected by similar links to routers of other ISPs. This allows servers and clients within an intranet to communicate with servers and clients in other intranets.

2.2.1 Types of Networks

There are various criteria by which computer networks can be classified. One criterion is the geographic distribution (also called *scale* [Tanenbaum, 2003]), a second criterion is the *interconnection structure* of nodes (also called *topology*), and the third is the mode of transmission.

2.2.1.1 Scale

In terms of geographic distribution, networks are classified as wide area networks, metropolitan area networks and local area networks. The distinctions among these are somewhat blurred, but in the following, we give some general guidelines that identify each of these networks. The primary distinction among them are probably in terms of propagation delay, administrative control, and the protocols that are used in managing them.

A wide area network (WAN) is one where the link distance between any two nodes is greater than approximately 20 kilometers (km) and can go as large as thousands of kilometers. Use of switches allow the aggregation of communication over wider areas such as this. Owing to the distances that need to be traveled, long delays are involved in wide area data transmission. For example, via satellite, there is a minimum delay of half a second for data to be transmitted from the source to the destination and acknowledged. This is because the speed with which signals can be transmitted is limited to the speed of light, and the distances that need to be spanned are great (about 31,000 km from an earth station to a satellite).

WANs are typically characterized by the heterogeneity of the transmission media, the computers, and the user community involved. Early WANs had a limited capacity of less than a few megabits-per-second (Mbps). However, most of the current ones are broadband WANs that provide capacities of 150 Mbps and above. These individual channels are aggregated into the backbone links; the current backbone links are commonly OC48 at 2.4 Gbps or OC192 at 10Gbps. These networks can carry multiple data streams with varying characteristics (e.g., data as well as audio/video streams), the possibility of negotiating for a level of quality of service (QoS) and reserving network resources sufficient to fulfill this level of QoS.

Local area networks (LANs) are typically limited in geographic scope (usually less than 2 km). They provide higher capacity communication over inexpensive transmission media. The capacities are typically in the range of 10-1000 Mbps per connection. Higher capacity and shorter distances between hosts result in very short delays. Furthermore, the better controlled environments in which the communication links are laid out (within buildings, for example) reduce the noise and interference, and the heterogeneity among the computers that are connected is easier to manage, and a common transmission medium is used.

Metropolitan area networks (MANs) are in between LANs and WANs in scale and cover a city or a portion of it. The distances between nodes is typically on the order of 10 km.

2.2.1.2 Topology

As the name indicates, interconnection structure or topology refers to the way nodes
on a network are interconnected. The network in Figure 2.14 is what is called an
irregular network, where the interconnections between nodes do not follow any
pattern. It is possible to find a node that is connected to only one other node, as well
as nodes that have connections to a number of nodes. Internet is a typical irregular
network.

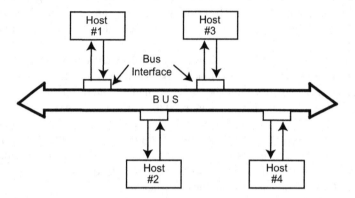

Fig. 2.16 Bus Network

Another popular topology is the bus, where all the computers are connected to a
common channel (Figure 2.16). This type of network is primarily used in LANs. The
link control is typically performed using *carrier sense medium access with collision
detection* (CSMA/CD) protocol. The CSMA/CD bus control mechanism can best be
described as a "listen before and while you transmit" scheme. The fundamental point
is that each host listens continuously to what occurs on the bus. When a message
transmission is detected, the host checks if the message is addressed to it, and takes
the appropriate action. If it wants to transmit, it waits until it detects no more activity
on the bus and then places its message on the network and continues to listen to bus
activity. If it detects another transmission while it is transmitting a message itself,
then there has been a "collision." In such a case, and when the collision is detected,
the transmitting hosts abort the transmission, each waits a random amount of time,
and then each retransmits the message. The basic CSMA/CD scheme is used in the
Ethernet local area network[3].

Other common alternatives are star, ring, bus, and mesh networks.

---

[3] In most current implementations of Ethernet, multiple busses are linked via one or more switches
(called *switched hubs*) for expanded coverage and to better control the load on each bus segment.
In these systems, individual computers can directly be connected to the switch as well. These are
known as switched Ethernet.

- *Star* networks connect all the hosts to a central node that coordinates the transmission on the network. Thus if two hosts want to communicate, they have to go through the central node. Since there is a separate link between the central node and each of the others, there is a negotiation between the hosts and the central node when they wish to communicate.

- *Ring* networks interconnect the hosts in the form of a loop. This type of network was originally proposed for LANs, but their use in these networks has nearly stopped. They are now primarily used in MANs (e.g., SONET rings). In their current incarnation, data transmission around the ring is usually bidirectional (original rings were unidirectional), with each station (actually the interface to which each station is connected) serving as an active repeater that receives a message, checks the address, copies the message if it is addressed to that station, and retransmits it.

  Control of communication in ring type networks is generally controlled by means of a *control token*. In the simplest type of token ring networks, a token, which has one bit pattern to indicate that the network is free and a different bit pattern to indicate that it is in use, is circulated around the network. Any site wanting to transmit a message waits for the token. When it arrives, the site checks the token's bit pattern to see if the network is free or in use. If it is free, the site changes the bit pattern to indicate that the network is in use and then places the messages on the ring. The message circulates around the ring and returns to the sender which changes the bit pattern to free and sends the token to the next computer down the line.

- *Complete* (or *mesh*) interconnection is one where each node is interconnected to every other node. Such an interconnection structure obviously provides more reliability and the possibility of better performance than that of the structures noted previously. However, it is also the costliest. For example, a complete connection of 10,000 computers would require approximately $(10,000)^2$ links.[4]

2.2.2 Communication Schemes

In terms of the physical communication schemes employed, networks can be either *point-to-point* (also called *unicast*) networks, or *broadcast* (sometimes also called *multi-point*) networks.

In point-to-point networks, there are one or more (direct or indirect) links between each pair of nodes. The communication is always between two nodes and the receiver and sender are identified by their addresses that are included in the message header. Data transmission from the sender to the receiver follows one of the possibly many links between them, some of which may involve visiting other intermediate nodes. An intermediate node checks the destination address in the message header and if it is not addressed to it, passes it along to the next intermediate node. This is the

---

[4] The general form of the equation is $n(n-1)/2$, where n is the number of nodes on the network.

process of *switching* or *routing*. The selection of the links via which messages are sent is determined by usually elaborate routing algorithms that are beyond our scope. We discuss the details of switching in Section 2.2.3.

The fundamental transmission media for point-to-point networks are twisted pair, coaxial or fiber optic cables. Each of these media have different capacities: twisted pair 300 bps to 10 Mbps, coaxial up to 200 Mbps, and fiber optic 10 Gbps and even higher.

In broadcast networks, there is a common communication channel that is utilized by all the nodes in the network. Messages are transmitted over this common channel and received by all the nodes. Each node checks the receiver address and if the message is not addressed to it, ignores it.

A special case of broadcasting is *multicasting* where the message is sent to a subset of the nodes in the network. The receiver address is somehow encoded to indicate which nodes are the recipients.

Broadcast networks are generally radio or satellite-based. In case of satellite transmission, each site beams its transmission to a satellite which then beams it back at a different frequency. Every site on the network listens to the receiving frequency and has to disregard the message if it is not addressed to that site. A network that uses this technique is HughesNet™.

Microwave transmission is another mode of data communication and it can be over satellite or terrestrial. Terrestrial microwave links used to form a major portion of most countries' telephone networks although many of these have since been converted to fiber optic. In addition to the public carriers, some companies make use of private terrestrial microwave links. In fact, major metropolitan cities face the problem of microwave interference among privately owned and public carrier links. A very early example that is usually identified as having pioneered the use of satellite microwave transmission is ALOHA [Abramson, 1973].

Satellite and microwave networks are examples of wireless networks. These types of wireless networks are commonly referred to as *wireless broadband* networks. Another type of wireless network is one that is based on *cellular* networks. A cellular network control station is responsible for a geographic area called a *cell* and coordinates the communication from mobile hosts in their cell. These control stations may be linked to a "wireline" backbone network and thereby provide access from/to mobile hosts to other mobile hosts or stationary hosts on the wireline network.

A third type of wireless network with which most of us may be more familiar are *wireless LANs* (commonly referred to as Wi-LAN or WiLan). In this case a number of "base stations" are connected to a wireline network and serve as connection points for mobile hosts (similar to control stations in cellular networks). These networks can provide bandwidth of up to 54 Mbps.

A final word on broadcasting topologies is that they have the advantage that it is easier to check for errors and to send messages to more than one site than to do so in point-to-point topologies. On the other hand, since everybody listens in, broadcast networks are not as secure as point-to-point networks.

2.2.3 Data Communication Concepts

What we refer to as data communication is the set of technologies that enable two hosts to communicate. We are not going to be too detailed in this discussion, since, at the distributed DBMS level, we can assume that the technology exists to move bits between hosts. We, instead, focus on a few important issues that are relevant to understanding delay and routing concepts.

As indicated earlier hosts are connected by *links*, each of which can carry one or more *channels*. Link is a physical entity whereas channel is a logical one. Communication links can carry signals either in digital form or in analog form. Telephone lines, for example, can carry data in analog form between the home and the central office – the rest of the telephone network is now digital and even the home-to-central office link is becoming digital with voice-over-IP (VoIP) technology. Each communication channel has a *capacity*, which can be defined as the amount of information that can be transmitted over the channel in a given time unit. This capacity is commonly referred to as the *bandwidth* of the channel. In analog transmission channels, the bandwidth is defined as the difference (in hertz) between the lowest and highest frequencies that can be transmitted over the channel per second. In digital links, *bandwidth* refers (less formally and with abuse of terminology) to the number of bits that can be transmitted per second (bps).

With respect to delays in getting the user's work done, the bandwidth of a transmission channel is a significant factor, but it is not necessarily the only ones. The other factor in the transmission time is the software employed. There are usually overhead costs involved in data transmission due to the redundancies within the message itself, necessary for error detection and correction. Furthermore, the network software adds headers and trailers to any message, for example, to specify the destination or to check for errors in the entire message. All of these activities contribute to delays in transmitting data. The actual rate at which data are transmitted across the network is known as the *data transfer rate* and this rate is usually less than the actual bandwidth of the transmission channel. The software issues, that generally are referred as *network protocols*, are discussed in the next section.

In computer-to-computer communication, data are usually transmitted in *packets*, as we mentioned earlier. Usually, upper limits on frame sizes are established for each network and each contains data as well as some control information, such as the destination and source addresses, block error check codes, and so on (Figure 2.17). If a message that is to be sent from a source node to a destination node cannot fit one frame, it is split over a number of frames. This is be discussed further in Section 2.2.4.

There are various possible forms of switching/routing that can occur in point-to-point networks. It is possible to establish a connection such that a dedicated channel exists between the sender and the receiver. This is called *circuit switching* and is commonly used in traditional telephone connections. When a subscriber dials the number of another subscriber, a circuit is established between the two phones by means of various switches. The circuit is maintained during the period of conversation and is broken when one side hangs up. Similar setup is possible in computer networks.

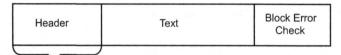

- Source address
- Destination address
- Message number
- Packet number
- Acknowledgment
- Control information

Fig. 2.17 Typical Frame Format

Another form of switching used in computer communication is *packet switching*, where a message is broken up into packets and each packet transmitted individually. In our discussion of the TCP/IP protocol earlier, we referred to messages being transmitted; in fact the TCP protocol (or any other transport layer protocol) takes each application package and breaks it up into fixed sized packets. Therefore, each application message may be sent to the destination as multiple packets.

Packets for the same message may travel independently of each other and may, in fact, take different routes. The result of routing packets along possibly different links in the network is that they may arrive at the destination out-of-order. Thus the transport layer software at the destination site should be able to sort them into their original order to reconstruct the message. Consequently, it is the individual packages that are routed through the network, which may result in packets reaching the destination at different times and even out of order. The transport layer protocol at the destination is responsible for collating and ordering the packets and generating the application message properly.

The advantages of packet switching are many. First, packet-switching networks provide higher link utilization since each link is not dedicated to a pair of communicating equipment and can be shared by many. This is especially useful in computer communication due to its bursty nature – there is a burst of transmission and then some break before another burst of transmission starts. The link can be used for other transmission when it is idle. Another reason is that packetizing may permit the parallel transmission of data. There is usually no requirement that various packets belonging to the same message travel the same route through the network. In such a case, they may be sent in parallel via different routes to improve the total data transmission time. As mentioned above, the result of routing frames this way is that their in-order delivery cannot be guaranteed.

On the other hand, circuit switching provides a dedicated channel between the receiver and the sender. If there is a sizable amount of data to be transmitted between the two or if the channel sharing in packet switched networks introduces too much delay or delay variance, or packet loss (which are important in multimedia applications), then the dedicated channel facilitates this significantly. Therefore, schemes similar to circuit switching (i.e., reservation-based schemes) have gained favor in the broadband networks that support applications such as multimedia with very high data transmission loads.

2.2.4 Communication Protocols

Establishing a physical connection between two hosts is not sufficient for them to communicate. Error-free, reliable and efficient communication between hosts requires the implementation of elaborate software systems that are generally called *protocols*. Network protocols are "layered" in that network functionality is divided into layers, each layer performing a well-defined function relying on the services provided by the layer below it and providing a service to the layer above. A protocol defines the services that are performed at one layer. The resulting layered protocol set is referred to as a *protocol stack* or *protocol suite*.

There are different protocol stacks for different types of networks; however, for communication over the Internet, the standard one is what is referred to as TCP/IP that stands for "Transport Control Protocol/Internet Protocol". We focus primarily on TCP/IP in this section as well as some of the common LAN protocols.

Before we get into the specifics of the TCP/IP protocol stack, let us first discuss how a message from a process on host C in Figure 2.15 is transmitted to a process on server S, assuming both hosts implement the TCP/IP protocol. The process is depicted in Figure 2.18.

The appropriate application layer protocol takes the message from the process on host C and creates an application layer message by adding some application layer header information (oblique hatched part in Figure 2.18) details of which are not important for us. The application message is handed over to the TCP protocol, which repeats the process by adding its own header information. TCP header includes the necessary information to facilitate the provision of TCP services we discuss shortly. The Internet layer takes the TCP message that is generated and forms an Internet message as we also discuss below. This message is now physically transmitted from host C to its router using the protocol of its own network, then through a series of routers to the router of the network that contains server S, where the process is reversed until the original message is recovered and handed over to the appropriate process on S. The TCP protocols at hosts C and S communicate to ensure the end-to-end guarantees that we discussed.

2.2.4.1 TCP/IP Protocol Stack

What is referred to as TCP/IP is in fact a family of protocols, commonly referred to as the *protocol stack*. It consists of two sets of protocols, one set at the *transport layer* and the other at the *network (Internet) layer* (Figure 2.19).

The transport layer defines the types of services that the network provides to applications. The protocols at this layer address issues such as data loss (can the

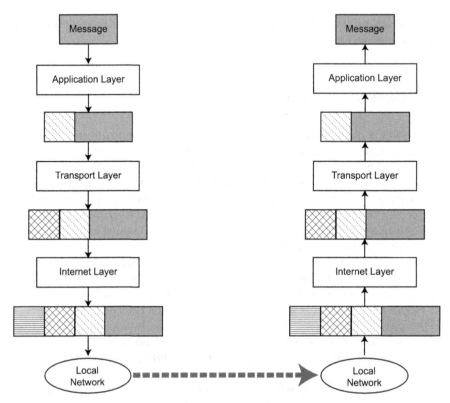

Fig. 2.18 Message Transmission using TCP/IP

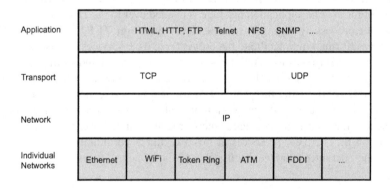

Fig. 2.19 TCP/IP Protocol

application tolerate losing some of the data during transmission?), bandwidth (some applications have minimum bandwidth requirements while others can be more elastic in their requirements), and timing (what type of delay can the applications tolerate?). For example, a file transfer application can not tolerate any data loss, can be flexible in its bandwidth use (it will work whether the connection is high capacity or low capacity, although the performance may differ), and it does not have strict timing requirements (although we may not like a file transfer to take a few days, it would still work). In contrast, a real-time audio/video transmission application can tolerate a limited amount of data loss (this may cause some jitter and other problems, but the communication will still be "understandable"), has minimum bandwidth requirement (5-128 Kbps for audio and 5 Kbps-20 Mbps for video), and is time sensitive (audio and video data need to be synchronized).

To deal with these varying requirements (at least with some of them), at the transport layer, two protocols are provided: TCP and UDP. TCP is connection-oriented, meaning that prior setup is required between the sender and the receiver before actual message transmission can start; it provides reliable transmission between the sender and the receiver by ensuring that the messages are received correctly at the receiver (referred to as "end-to-end reliability"); ensures flow control so that the sender does not overwhelm the receiver if the receiver process is not able to keep up with the incoming messages, and ensures congestion control so that the sender is throttled when network is overloaded. Note that TCP does not address the timing and minimum bandwidth guarantees, leaving these to the application layer.

UDP, on the other hand, is a connectionless service that does not provide the reliability, flow control and congestion control guarantees that TCP provides. Nor does it establish a connection between the sender and receiver beforehand. Thus, each message is transmitted hoping that it will get to the destination, but no end-to-end guarantees are provided. Thus, UDP has significantly lower overhead than TCP, and is preferred by applications that would prefer to deal with these requirements themselves, rather than having the network protocol handle them.

The network layer implements the Internet Protocol (IP) that provides the facility to "package" a message in a standard Internet message format for transmission across the network. Each Internet message can be up to 64KB long and consists of a header that contains, among other things, the IP addresses of the sender and the receiver machines (the numbers such as 129.97.79.58 that you may have seen attached to your own machines), and the message body itself. The message format of each network that makes up the Internet can be different, but each of these messages are encoded into an Internet message by the Internet Protocol before they are transmitted[5].

The importance of TCP/IP is the following. Each of the intranets that are part of the Internet can use its own preferred protocol, so the computers on that network implement that particular protocol (e.g., the token ring mechanism and the CSMA/CS technique described above are examples of these types of protocols). However, if they are to connect to the Internet, they need to be able to communicate using TCP/IP, which are implemented on top of these specific network protocols (Figure 2.19).

---

[5] Today, many of the Intranets also use TCP/IP, in which case IP encapsulation may not be necessary.

2.2.4.2 Other Protocol Layers

Let us now briefly consider the other two layers depicted in Figure 2.19. Although these are not part of the TCP/IP protocol stack, they are necessary to be able to build distributed applications. These make up the top and the bottom layers of the protocol stack.

The Application Protocol layer provides the specifications that distributed applications have to follow. For example, if one is building a Web application, then the documents that will be posted on the Web have to be written according to the HTML protocol (note that HTML is not a networking protocol, but a document encoding protocol) and the communication between the client browser and the Web server has to follow the HTTP protocol. Similar protocols are defined at this layer for other applications as indicated in the figure.

The bottom layer represents the specific network that may be used. Each of those networks have their own message formats and protocols and they provide the mechanisms for data transmission within those networks.

The standardization for LANs is spearheaded by the Institute of Electrical and Electronics Engineers (IEEE), specifically their Committee No. 802; hence the standard that has been developed is known as the IEEE 802 Standard. The three layers of the IEEE 802 local area network standard are the physical layer, the medium access control layer, and the logical link control layer.

The physical layer deals with physical data transmission issues such as signaling. Medium access control layer defines protocols that control who can have access to the transmission medium and when. Logical link control layer implements protocols that ensure reliable packet transmission between two adjacent computers (not end-to-end). In most LANs, the TCP and IP layer protocols are implemented on top of these three layers, enabling each computer to be able to directly communicate on the Internet.

To enable it to cover a variety of LAN architectures, the 802 local area network standard is actually a number of standards rather than a single one. Originally, it was specified to support three mechanisms at the medium access control level: the CSMA/CD mechanism, token ring, and token access mechanism for bus networks.

2.3 Bibliographic Notes

This chapter covered the basic issues related to relational database systems and computer networks. These concepts are discussed in much greater detail in a number of excellent textbooks. Related to database technology, we can name [Ramakrishnan and Gehrke, 2003; Elmasri and Navathe, 2011; Silberschatz et al., 2002; Garcia-Molina et al., 2002; Kifer et al., 2006], and [Date, 2004]. For computer networks one can refer to [Tanenbaum, 2003; Kurose and Ross, 2010; Leon-Garcia and Widjaja, 2004; Comer, 2009]. More focused discussion of data communication issues can be found in [Stallings, 2011].

Chapter 3
Distributed Database Design

The design of a distributed computer system involves making decisions on the placement of *data* and *programs* across the sites of a computer network, as well as possibly designing the network itself. In the case of distributed DBMSs, the distribution of applications involves two things: the distribution of the distributed DBMS software and the distribution of the application programs that run on it. Different architectural models discussed in Chapter 1 address the issue of application distribution. In this chapter we concentrate on distribution of data.

It has been suggested that the organization of distributed systems can be investigated along three orthogonal dimensions [Levin and Morgan, 1975] (Figure 3.1):

1. Level of sharing
2. Behavior of access patterns
3. Level of knowledge on access pattern behavior

In terms of the level of sharing, there are three possibilities. First, there is *no sharing*: each application and its data execute at one site, and there is no communication with any other program or access to any data file at other sites. This characterizes the very early days of networking and is probably not very common today. We then find the level of *data sharing*; all the programs are replicated at all the sites, but data files are not. Accordingly, user requests are handled at the site where they originate and the necessary data files are moved around the network. Finally, in *data-plus-program sharing*, both data and programs may be shared, meaning that a program at a given site can request a service from another program at a second site, which, in turn, may have to access a data file located at a third site.

Levin and Morgan draw a distinction between data sharing and data-plus-program sharing to illustrate the differences between homogeneous and heterogeneous distributed computer systems. They indicate, correctly, that in a heterogeneous environment it is usually very difficult, and sometimes impossible, to execute a given program on different hardware under a different operating system. It might, however, be possible to move data around relatively easily.

M.T. Özsu and P. Valduriez, *Principles of Distributed Database Systems: Third Edition*,
DOI 10.1007/978-1-4419-8834-8_3, © Springer Science+Business Media, LLC 2011

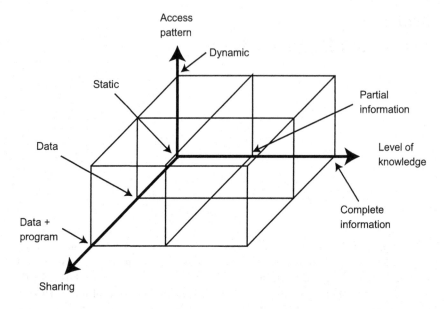

Fig. 3.1 Framework of Distribution

Along the second dimension of access pattern behavior, it is possible to identify two alternatives. The access patterns of user requests may be *static*, so that they do not change over time, or *dynamic*. It is obviously considerably easier to plan for and manage the static environments than would be the case for dynamic distributed systems. Unfortunately, it is difficult to find many real-life distributed applications that would be classified as static. The significant question, then, is not whether a system is static or dynamic, but how dynamic it is. Incidentally, it is along this dimension that the relationship between the distributed database design and query processing is established (refer to Figure 1.7).

The third dimension of classification is the level of knowledge about the access pattern behavior. One possibility, of course, is that the designers do not have any information about how users will access the database. This is a theoretical possibility, but it is very difficult, if not impossible, to design a distributed DBMS that can effectively cope with this situation. The more practical alternatives are that the designers have *complete information*, where the access patterns can reasonably be predicted and do not deviate significantly from these predictions, or *partial information*, where there are deviations from the predictions.

The distributed database design problem should be considered within this general framework. In all the cases discussed, except in the no-sharing alternative, new problems are introduced in the distributed environment which are not relevant in a centralized setting. In this chapter it is our objective to focus on these unique problems.

Two major strategies that have been identified for designing distributed databases are the *top-down approach* and the *bottom-up approach* [Ceri et al., 1987]. As the names indicate, they constitute very different approaches to the design process. Top-down approach is more suitable for tightly integrated, homogeneous distributed DBMSs, while bottom-up design is more suited to multidatabases (see the classification in Chapter 1). In this chapter, we focus on top-down design and defer bottom-up to the next chapter.

3.1 Top-Down Design Process

A framework for top-down design process is shown in Figure 3.2. The activity begins with a requirements analysis that defines the environment of the system and "elicits both the data and processing needs of all potential database users" [Yao et al., 1982a]. The requirements study also specifies where the final system is expected to stand with respect to the objectives of a distributed DBMS as identified in Section 1.4. These objectives are defined with respect to performance, reliability and availability, economics, and expandability (flexibility).

The requirements document is input to two parallel activities: view design and conceptual design. The *view design* activity deals with defining the interfaces for end users. The *conceptual design*, on the other hand, is the process by which the enterprise is examined to determine entity types and relationships among these entities. One can possibly divide this process into two related activity groups [Davenport, 1981]: entity analysis and functional analysis. *Entity analysis* is concerned with determining the entities, their attributes, and the relationships among them. *Functional analysis*, on the other hand, is concerned with determining the fundamental functions with which the modeled enterprise is involved. The results of these two steps need to be cross-referenced to get a better understanding of which functions deal with which entities.

There is a relationship between the conceptual design and the view design. In one sense, the conceptual design can be interpreted as being an integration of user views. Even though this *view integration* activity is very important, the conceptual model should support not only the existing applications, but also future applications. View integration should be used to ensure that entity and relationship requirements for all the views are covered in the conceptual schema.

In conceptual design and view design activities the user needs to specify the data entities and must determine the applications that will run on the database as well as statistical information about these applications. Statistical information includes the specification of the frequency of user applications, the volume of various information, and the like. Note that from the conceptual design step comes the definition of global conceptual schema discussed in Section 1.7. We have not yet considered the implications of the distributed environment; in fact, up to this point, the process is identical to that in a centralized database design.

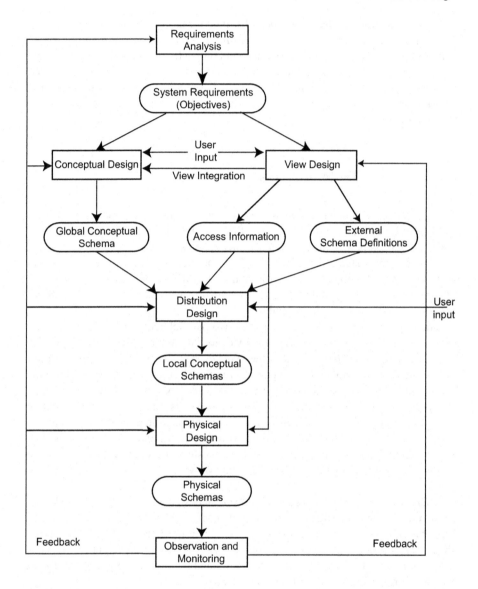

Fig. 3.2 Top-Down Design Process

The global conceptual schema (GCS) and access pattern information collected as a result of view design are inputs to the *distribution design* step. The objective at this stage, which is the focus of this chapter, is to design the local conceptual schemas (LCSs) by distributing the entities over the sites of the distributed system. It is possible, of course, to treat each entity as a unit of distribution. Given that we use the relational model as the basis of discussion in this book, the entities correspond to relations.

Rather than distributing relations, it is quite common to divide them into subrelations, called *fragments*, which are then distributed. Thus, the distribution design activity consists of two steps: *fragmentation* and *allocation*. The reason for separating the distribution design into two steps is to better deal with the complexity of the problem. However, this raises other concerns as we discuss at the end of the chapter.

The last step in the design process is the physical design, which maps the local conceptual schemas to the physical storage devices available at the corresponding sites. The inputs to this process are the local conceptual schema and the access pattern information about the fragments in them.

It is well known that design and development activity of any kind is an ongoing process requiring constant monitoring and periodic adjustment and tuning. We have therefore included observation and monitoring as a major activity in this process. Note that one does not monitor only the behavior of the database implementation but also the suitability of user views. The result is some form of feedback, which may result in backing up to one of the earlier steps in the design.

3.2 Distribution Design Issues

In the preceding section we indicated that the relations in a database schema are usually decomposed into smaller fragments, but we did not offer any justification or details for this process. The objective of this section is to fill in these details.

The following set of interrelated questions covers the entire issue. We will therefore seek to answer them in the remainder of this section.

1. Why fragment at all?
2. How should we fragment?
3. How much should we fragment?
4. Is there any way to test the correctness of decomposition?
5. How should we allocate?
6. What is the necessary information for fragmentation and allocation?

3.2.1 Reasons for Fragmentation

From a data distribution viewpoint, there is really no reason to fragment data. After all, in distributed file systems, the distribution is performed on the basis of entire files. In fact, the very early work dealt specifically with the allocation of files to nodes on a computer network. We consider earlier models in Section 3.4.

With respect to fragmentation, the important issue is the appropriate unit of distribution. A relation is not a suitable unit, for a number of reasons. First, application views are usually subsets of relations. Therefore, the locality of accesses of applications is defined not on entire relations but on their subsets. Hence it is only natural to consider subsets of relations as distribution units.

Second, if the applications that have views defined on a given relation reside at different sites, two alternatives can be followed, with the entire relation being the unit of distribution. Either the relation is not replicated and is stored at only one site, or it is replicated at all or some of the sites where the applications reside. The former results in an unnecessarily high volume of remote data accesses. The latter, on the other hand, has unnecessary replication, which causes problems in executing updates (to be discussed later) and may not be desirable if storage is limited.

Finally, the decomposition of a relation into fragments, each being treated as a unit, permits a number of transactions to execute concurrently. In addition, the fragmentation of relations typically results in the parallel execution of a single query by dividing it into a set of subqueries that operate on fragments. Thus fragmentation typically increases the level of concurrency and therefore the system throughput. This form of concurrency, which we refer to as *intraquery concurrency*, is dealt with mainly in Chapters 7 and 8, under query processing.

Fragmentation raises difficulties as well. If the applications have conflicting requirements that prevent decomposition of the relation into mutually exclusive fragments, those applications whose views are defined on more than one fragment may suffer performance degradation. It might, for example, be necessary to retrieve data from two fragments and then take their join, which is costly. Minimizing distributed joins is a fundamental fragmentation issue.

The second problem is related to semantic data control, specifically to integrity checking. As a result of fragmentation, attributes participating in a dependency may be decomposed into different fragments that might be allocated to different sites. In this case, even the simpler task of checking for dependencies would result in chasing after data in a number of sites. In Chapter 5 we return to the issue of semantic data control.

3.2.2 Fragmentation Alternatives

Relation instances are essentially tables, so the issue is one of finding alternative ways of dividing a table into smaller ones. There are clearly two alternatives for this: dividing it *horizontally* or dividing it *vertically*.

Example 3.1. In this chapter we use a modified version of the relational database scheme developed in Section 2.1. We have added to the PROJ relation a new attribute (LOC) that indicates the place of each project. Figure 3.3 depicts the database instance we will use. Figure 3.4 shows the PROJ relation of Figure 3.3 divided horizontally into two relations. Subrelation PROJ$_1$ contains information about projects whose

EMP

ENO	ENAME	TITLE
E1	J. Doe	Elect. Eng
E2	M. Smith	Syst. Anal.
E3	A. Lee	Mech. Eng.
E4	J. Miller	Programmer
E5	B. Casey	Syst. Anal.
E6	L. Chu	Elect. Eng.
E7	R. Davis	Mech. Eng.
E8	J. Jones	Syst. Anal.

ASG

ENO	PNO	RESP	DUR
E1	P1	Manager	12
E2	P1	Analyst	24
E2	P2	Analyst	6
E3	P3	Consultant	10
E3	P4	Engineer	48
E4	P2	Programmer	18
E5	P2	Manager	24
E6	P4	Manager	48
E7	P3	Engineer	36
E8	P3	Manager	40

PROJ

PNO	PNAME	BUDGET	LOC
P1	Instrumentation	150000	Montreal
P2	Database Develop.	135000	New York
P3	CAD/CAM	250000	New York
P4	Maintenance	310000	Paris

PAY

TITLE	SAL
Elect. Eng.	40000
Syst. Anal.	34000
Mech. Eng.	27000
Programmer	24000

Fig. 3.3 Modified Example Database

budgets are less than \$200,000, whereas $PROJ_2$ stores information about projects with larger budgets. ◆

Example 3.2. Figure 3.5 shows the PROJ relation of Figure 3.3 partitioned vertically into two subrelations, $PROJ_1$ and $PROJ_2$. $PROJ_1$ contains only the information about project budgets, whereas $PROJ_2$ contains project names and locations. It is important to notice that the primary key to the relation (PNO) is included in both fragments. ◆

The fragmentation may, of course, be nested. If the nestings are of different types, one gets *hybrid fragmentation*. Even though we do not treat hybrid fragmentation as a primitive fragmentation strategy, many real-life partitionings may be hybrid.

3.2.3 Degree of Fragmentation

The extent to which the database should be fragmented is an important decision that affects the performance of query execution. In fact, the issues in Section 3.2.1 concerning the reasons for fragmentation constitute a subset of the answers to the question we are addressing here. The degree of fragmentation goes from one extreme, that is, not to fragment at all, to the other extreme, to fragment to the level of

PROJ$_1$

PNO	PNAME	BUDGET	LOC
P1	Instrumentation	150000	Montreal
P2	Database Develop.	135000	New York

PROJ$_2$

PNO	PNAME	BUDGET	LOC
P3	CAD/CAM	255000	New York
P4	Maintenance	310000	Paris

Fig. 3.4 Example of Horizontal Partitioning

PROJ$_1$

PNO	BUDGET
P1	150000
P2	135000
P3	250000
P4	310000

PROJ$_2$

PNO	PNAME	LOC
P1	Instrumentation	Montreal
P2	Database Develop.	New York
P3	CAD/CAM	New York
P4	Maintenance	Paris

Fig. 3.5 Example of Vertical Partitioning

individual tuples (in the case of horizontal fragmentation) or to the level of individual attributes (in the case of vertical fragmentation).

We have already addressed the adverse effects of very large and very small units of fragmentation. What we need, then, is to find a suitable level of fragmentation that is a compromise between the two extremes. Such a level can only be defined with respect to the applications that will run on the database. The issue is, how? In general, the applications need to be characterized with respect to a number of parameters. According to the values of these parameters, individual fragments can be identified. In Section 3.3 we describe how this characterization can be carried out for alternative fragmentations.

3.2.4 Correctness Rules of Fragmentation

We will enforce the following three rules during fragmentation, which, together, ensure that the database does not undergo semantic change during fragmentation.

1. *Completeness.* If a relation instance R is decomposed into fragments $F_R = \{R_1, R_2, \ldots, R_n\}$, each data item that can be found in R can also be found in one or more of R_i's. This property, which is identical to the *lossless decomposition* property of normalization (Section 2.1), is also important in fragmentation since it ensures that the data in a global relation are mapped into fragments without any loss [Grant, 1984]. Note that in the case of horizontal fragmentation, the "item" typically refers to a tuple, while in the case of vertical fragmentation, it refers to an attribute.

2. *Reconstruction.* If a relation R is decomposed into fragments $F_R = \{R_1, R_2, \ldots, R_n\}$, it should be possible to define a relational operator $\triangledown$ such that

    $$R = \triangledown R_i, \quad \forall R_i \in F_R$$

    The operator $\triangledown$ will be different for different forms of fragmentation; it is important, however, that it can be identified. The reconstructability of the relation from its fragments ensures that constraints defined on the data in the form of dependencies are preserved.

3. *Disjointness.* If a relation R is horizontally decomposed into fragments $F_R = \{R_1, R_2, \ldots, R_n\}$ and data item d_i is in R_j, it is not in any other fragment R_k $(k \neq j)$. This criterion ensures that the horizontal fragments are disjoint. If relation R is vertically decomposed, its primary key attributes are typically repeated in all its fragments (for reconstruction). Therefore, in case of vertical partitioning, disjointness is defined only on the non-primary key attributes of a relation.

3.2.5 Allocation Alternatives

Assuming that the database is fragmented properly, one has to decide on the allocation of the fragments to various sites on the network. When data are allocated, it may either be replicated or maintained as a single copy. The reasons for replication are reliability and efficiency of read-only queries. If there are multiple copies of a data item, there is a good chance that some copy of the data will be accessible somewhere even when system failures occur. Furthermore, read-only queries that access the same data items can be executed in parallel since copies exist on multiple sites. On the other hand, the execution of update queries cause trouble since the system has to ensure that all the copies of the data are updated properly. Hence the decision regarding replication is a trade-off that depends on the ratio of the read-only queries to the update queries. This decision affects almost all of the distributed DBMS algorithms and control functions.

A non-replicated database (commonly called a *partitioned* database) contains fragments that are allocated to sites, and there is only one copy of any fragment on the network. In case of replication, either the database exists in its entirety at each site (*fully replicated* database), or fragments are distributed to the sites in such a way that copies of a fragment may reside in multiple sites (*partially replicated* database). In the latter the number of copies of a fragment may be an input to the allocation algorithm or a decision variable whose value is determined by the algorithm. Figure 3.6 compares these three replication alternatives with respect to various distributed DBMS functions. We will discuss replication at length in Chapter 13.

	Full replication	Partial replication	Partitioning
QUERY PROCESSING	Easy	← Same difficulty →	
DIRECTORY MANAGEMENT	Easy or nonexistent	← Same difficulty →	
CONCURRENCY CONTROL	Moderate	Difficult	Easy
RELIABILITY	Very high	High	Low
REALITY	Possible application	Realistic	Possible application

Fig. 3.6 Comparison of Replication Alternatives

3.2.6 Information Requirements

One aspect of distribution design is that too many factors contribute to an optimal design. The logical organization of the database, the location of the applications, the access characteristics of the applications to the database, and the properties of the computer systems at each site all have an influence on distribution decisions. This makes it very complicated to formulate the distribution problem.

The information needed for distribution design can be divided into four categories: database information, application information, communication network information, and computer system information. The latter two categories are completely quantitative in nature and are used in allocation models rather than in fragmentation algorithms. We do not consider them in detail here. Instead, the detailed information requirements of the fragmentation and allocation algorithms are discussed in their respective sections.

3.3 Fragmentation

In this section we present the various fragmentation strategies and algorithms. As mentioned previously, there are two fundamental fragmentation strategies: horizontal and vertical. Furthermore, there is a possibility of nesting fragments in a hybrid fashion.

3.3.1 Horizontal Fragmentation

As we explained earlier, horizontal fragmentation partitions a relation along its tuples. Thus each fragment has a subset of the tuples of the relation. There are two versions of horizontal partitioning: primary and derived. *Primary horizontal fragmentation* of a relation is performed using predicates that are defined on that relation. *Derived horizontal fragmentation*, on the other hand, is the partitioning of a relation that results from predicates being defined on another relation.

Later in this section we consider an algorithm for performing both of these fragmentations. However, first we investigate the information needed to carry out horizontal fragmentation activity.

3.3.1.1 Information Requirements of Horizontal Fragmentation

Database Information.

The database information concerns the global conceptual schema. In this context it is important to note how the database relations are connected to one another, especially with joins. In the relational model, these relationships are also depicted as relations. However, in other data models, such as the entity-relationship (E–R) model [Chen, 1976], these relationships between database objects are depicted explicitly. Ceri et al. [1983] also model the relationship explicitly, within the relational framework, for purposes of the distribution design. In the latter notation, directed *links* are drawn between relations that are related to each other by an equijoin operation.

Example 3.3. Figure 3.7 shows the expression of links among the database relations given in Figure 2.3. Note that the direction of the link shows a one-to-many relationship. For example, for each title there are multiple employees with that title; thus there is a link between the PAY and EMP relations. Along the same lines, the many-to-many relationship between the EMP and PROJ relations is expressed with two links to the ASG relation.   ◆

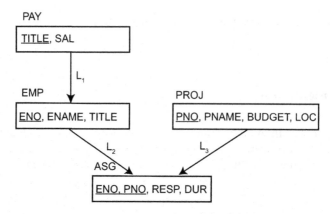

Fig. 3.7 Expression of Relationships Among Relations Using Links

The links between database objects (i.e., relations in our case) should be quite familiar to those who have dealt with network models of data. In the relational model, they are introduced as join graphs, which we discuss in detail in subsequent chapters on query processing. We introduce them here because they help to simplify the presentation of the distribution models we discuss later.

The relation at the tail of a link is called the *owner* of the link and the relation at the head is called the *member* [Ceri et al., 1983]. More commonly used terms, within the relational framework, are *source* relation for owner and *target* relation for member. Let us define two functions: *owner* and *member*, both of which provide mappings from the set of links to the set of relations. Therefore, given a link, they return the member or owner relations of the link, respectively.

Example 3.4. Given link L_1 of Figure 3.7, the *owner and member* functions have the following values:

$$owner(L_1) = \text{PAY}$$
$$member(L_1) = \text{EMP}$$

$\blacklozenge$

The quantitative information required about the database is the cardinality of each relation R, denoted $card(R)$.

Application Information.

As indicated previously in relation to Figure 3.2, both qualitative and quantitative information is required about applications. The qualitative information guides the fragmentation activity, whereas the quantitative information is incorporated primarily into the allocation models.

The fundamental qualitative information consists of the predicates used in user queries. If it is not possible to analyze all of the user applications to determine these predicates, one should at least investigate the most "important" ones. It has been suggested that as a rule of thumb, the most active 20% of user queries account for 80% of the total data accesses [Wiederhold, 1982]. This "80/20 rule" may be used as a guideline in carrying out this analysis.

At this point we are interested in determining *simple predicates*. Given a relation $R(A_1, A_2, \ldots, A_n)$, where A_i is an attribute defined over domain D_i, a simple predicate p_j defined on R has the form

$p_j : A_i \; \theta \; Value$

where $\theta \in \{=, <, \neq, \leq, >, \geq\}$ and *Value* is chosen from the domain of A_i (*Value* $\in D_i$). We use Pr_i to denote the set of all simple predicates defined on a relation R_i. The members of Pr_i are denoted by p_{ij}.

Example 3.5. Given the relation instance PROJ of Figure 3.3,

PNAME = "Maintenance"

is a simple predicate, as well as

BUDGET $\leq$ 200000

♦

Even though simple predicates are quite elegant to deal with, user queries quite often include more complicated predicates, which are Boolean combinations of simple predicates. One combination that we are particularly interested in, called a *minterm predicate*, is the conjunction of simple predicates. Since it is always possible to transform a Boolean expression into conjunctive normal form, the use of minterm predicates in the design algorithms does not cause any loss of generality.

Given a set $Pr_i = \{p_{i1}, p_{i2}, \ldots, p_{im}\}$ of simple predicates for relation R_i, the set of minterm predicates $M_i = \{m_{i1}, m_{i2}, \ldots, m_{iz}\}$ is defined as

$$M_i = \{m_{ij} | m_{ij} = \bigwedge_{p_{ik} \in Pr_i} p_{ik}^*\}, \; 1 \leq k \leq m, \; 1 \leq j \leq z$$

where $p_{ik}^* = p_{ik}$ or $p_{ik}^* = \neg p_{ik}$. So each simple predicate can occur in a minterm predicate either in its natural form or its negated form.

It is important to note that the negation of a predicate is meaningful for equality predicates of the form *Attribute = Value*. For inequality predicates, the negation should be treated as the complement. For example, the negation of the simple predicate *Attribute $\leq$ Value* is *Attribute > Value*. Besides theoretical problems of complementation in infinite sets, there is also the practical problem that the complement may be difficult to define. For example, if two simple predicates are defined of the form *Lower_bound $\leq$ Attribute_1*, and *Attribute_1 $\leq$ Upper_bound*, their complements are $\neg(Lower\_bound \leq Attribute\_1)$ and $\neg(Attribute\_1 \leq Upper\_bound)$. However, the original two simple predicates can be written as *Lower_bound $\leq$ Attribute_1 $\leq$ Upper_bound* with a complement $\neg(Lower\_bound \leq Attribute\_1 \leq Upper\_bound)$

that may not be easy to define. Therefore, the research in this area typically considers only simple equality predicates [Ceri et al., 1982b; Ceri and Pelagatti, 1984].

Example 3.6. Consider relation PAY of Figure 3.3. The following are some of the possible simple predicates that can be defined on PAY.

p_1: TITLE = "Elect. Eng."
p_2: TITLE = "Syst. Anal."
p_3: TITLE = "Mech. Eng."
p_4: TITLE = "Programmer"
p_5: SAL $\leq$ 30000

The following are *some* of the minterm predicates that can be defined based on these simple predicates.

m_1: TITLE = "Elect. Eng." $\wedge$ SAL $\leq$ 30000
m_2: TITLE = "Elect. Eng." $\wedge$ SAL $>$ 30000
m_3: $\neg$(TITLE = "Elect. Eng.") $\wedge$ SAL $\leq$ 30000
m_4: $\neg$(TITLE = "Elect. Eng.") $\wedge$ SAL $>$ 30000
m_5: TITLE = "Programmer" $\wedge$ SAL $\leq$ 30000
m_6: TITLE = "Programmer" $\wedge$ SAL $>$ 30000

$\blacklozenge$

There are a few points to mention here. First, these are not all the minterm predicates that can be defined; we are presenting only a representative sample. Second, some of these may be meaningless given the semantics of relation PAY; we are not addressing that issue here. Third, these are simplified versions of the minterms. The minterm definition requires each predicate to be in a minterm in either its natural or its negated form. Thus, m_1, for example, should be written as

m_1: TITLE = "Elect. Eng." $\wedge$ TITLE $\neq$ "Syst. Anal." $\wedge$ TITLE $\neq$ "Mech. Eng." $\wedge$ TITLE $\neq$ "Programmer" $\wedge$ SAL $\leq$ 30000

However, clearly this is not necessary, and we use the simplified form. Finally, note that there are logically equivalent expressions to these minterms; for example, m_3 can also be rewritten as

m_3: TITLE $\neq$ "Elect. Eng." $\wedge$ SAL $\leq$ 30000

In terms of quantitative information about user applications, we need to have two sets of data.

1. *Minterm selectivity*: number of tuples of the relation that would be accessed by a user query specified according to a given minterm predicate. For example, the selectivity of m_1 of Example 3.6 is 0 since there are no tuples in PAY that satisfy the minterm predicate. The selectivity of m_2, on the other hand, is 0.25

since one of the four tuples in PAY satisfy m_2. We denote the selectivity of a minterm m_i as $sel(m_i)$.

2. *Access frequency*: frequency with which user applications access data. If $Q = \{q_1, q_2, \ldots, q_q\}$ is a set of user queries, $acc(q_i)$ indicates the access frequency of query q_i in a given period.

Note that minterm access frequencies can be determined from the query frequencies. We refer to the access frequency of a minterm m_i as $acc(m_i)$.

3.3.1.2 Primary Horizontal Fragmentation

Before we present a formal algorithm for horizontal fragmentation, we intuitively discuss the process for primary (and derived) horizontal fragmentation. A *primary horizontal fragmentation* is defined by a selection operation on the owner relations of a database schema. Therefore, given relation R, its horizontal fragments are given by

$$R_i = \sigma_{F_i}(R), \ 1 \leq i \leq w$$

where F_i is the selection formula used to obtain fragment R_i (also called the *fragmentation predicate*). Note that if F_i is in conjunctive normal form, it is a minterm predicate (m_i). The algorithm we discuss will, in fact, insist that F_i be a minterm predicate.

Example 3.7. The decomposition of relation PROJ into horizontal fragments $PROJ_1$ and $PROJ_2$ in Example 3.1 is defined as follows[1]:

$$PROJ_1 = \sigma_{BUDGET \leq 200000} (PROJ)$$
$$PROJ_2 = \sigma_{BUDGET > 200000} (PROJ)$$

◆

Example 3.7 demonstrates one of the problems of horizontal partitioning. If the domain of the attributes participating in the selection formulas are continuous and infinite, as in Example 3.7, it is quite difficult to define the set of formulas $F = \{F_1, F_2, \ldots, F_n\}$ that would fragment the relation properly. One possible course of action is to define ranges as we have done in Example 3.7. However, there is always the problem of handling the two endpoints. For example, if a new tuple with a BUDGET value of, say, \$600,000 were to be inserted into PROJ, one would have had to review the fragmentation to decide if the new tuple is to go into $PROJ_2$ or if the fragments need to be revised and a new fragment needs to be defined as

---

[1] We assume that the non-negativity of the BUDGET values is a feature of the relation that is enforced by an integrity constraint. Otherwise, a simple predicate of the form $0 \leq BUDGET$ also needs to be included in *Pr*. We assume this to be true in all our examples and discussions in this chapter.

$$\text{PROJ}_2 = \sigma_{200000 < \text{BUDGET} \leq 400000} (\text{PROJ})$$
$$\text{PROJ}_3 \quad = \sigma_{\text{BUDGET} > 400000} (\text{PROJ})$$

Example 3.8. Consider relation PROJ of Figure 3.3. We can define the following horizontal fragments based on the project location. The resulting fragments are shown in Figure 3.8.

$$\text{PROJ}_1 = \sigma_{\text{LOC}=\text{"Montreal"}} (\text{PROJ})$$
$$\text{PROJ}_2 = \sigma_{\text{LOC}=\text{"New York"}} (\text{PROJ})$$
$$\text{PROJ}_3 \quad = \sigma_{\text{LOC}=\text{"Paris"}} (\text{PROJ})$$

◆

PROJ$_1$

PNO	PNAME	BUDGET	LOC
P1	Instrumentation	150000	Montreal

PROJ$_2$

PNO	PNAME	BUDGET	LOC
P2	Database Develop.	135000	New York
P3	CAD/CAM	250000	New York

PROJ$_3$

PNO	PNAME	BUDGET	LOC
P4	Maintenance	310000	Paris

Fig. 3.8 Primary Horizontal Fragmentation of Relation PROJ

Now we can define a horizontal fragment more carefully. A horizontal fragment R_i of relation R consists of all the tuples of R that satisfy a minterm predicate m_i. Hence, given a set of minterm predicates M, there are as many horizontal fragments of relation R as there are minterm predicates. This set of horizontal fragments is also commonly referred to as the set of *minterm fragments*.

From the foregoing discussion it is obvious that the definition of the horizontal fragments depends on minterm predicates. Therefore, the first step of any fragmentation algorithm is to determine a set of simple predicates that will form the minterm predicates.

An important aspect of simple predicates is their *completeness*; another is their *minimality*. A set of simple predicates Pr is said to be *complete* if and only if there is an equal probability of access by every application to any tuple belonging to any minterm fragment that is defined according to Pr^2.

Example 3.9. Consider the fragmentation of relation PROJ given in Example 3.8. If the only application that accesses PROJ wants to access the tuples according to the location, the set is complete since each tuple of each fragment PROJ$_i$ (Example 3.8) has the same probability of being accessed. If, however, there is a second application which accesses only those project tuples where the budget is less than or equal to \$200,000, then Pr is not complete. Some of the tuples within each PROJ$_i$ have a higher probability of being accessed due to this second application. To make the set of predicates complete, we need to add (BUDGET $\leq$ 200000, BUDGET $>$ 200000) to Pr:

$$Pr = \{\text{LOC="Montreal", LOC="New York", LOC="Paris",}$$
$$\text{BUDGET} \leq 200000, \text{BUDGET} > 200000\}$$

♦

The reason completeness is a desirable property is because fragments obtained according to a complete set of predicates are logically uniform since they all satisfy the minterm predicate. They are also statistically homogeneous in the way applications access them. These characteristics ensure that the resulting fragmentation results in a balanced load (with respect to the given workload) across all the fragments. Therefore, we will use a complete set of predicates as the basis of primary horizontal fragmentation.

It is possible to define completeness more formally so that a complete set of predicates can be obtained automatically. However, this would require the designer to specify the access probabilities for *each* tuple of a relation for *each* application under consideration. This is considerably more work than appealing to the common sense and experience of the designer to come up with a complete set. Shortly, we will present an algorithmic way of obtaining this set.

The second desirable property of the set of predicates, according to which minterm predicates and, in turn, fragments are to be defined, is minimality, which is very intuitive. It simply states that if a predicate influences how fragmentation is performed (i.e., causes a fragment f to be further fragmented into, say, f_i and f_j), there should be at least one application that accesses f_i and f_j differently. In other words, the simple predicate should be *relevant* in determining a fragmentation. If all the predicates of a set Pr are relevant, Pr is *minimal*.

A formal definition of relevance can be given as follows [Ceri et al., 1982b]. Let m_i and m_j be two minterm predicates that are identical in their definition, except that m_i contains the simple predicate p_i in its natural form while m_j contains $\neg p_i$. Also, let f_i and f_j be two fragments defined according to m_i and m_j, respectively. Then p_i is *relevant* if and only if

---

[2] It is clear that the definition of completeness of a set of simple predicates is different from the completeness rule of fragmentation given in Section 3.2.4.

$$\frac{acc(m_i)}{card(f_i)} \neq \frac{acc(m_j)}{card(f_j)}$$

Example 3.10. The set *Pr* defined in Example 3.9 is complete and minimal. If, however, we were to add the predicate

PNAME = "Instrumentation"

to *Pr*, the resulting set would not be minimal since the new predicate is not relevant with respect to *Pr* – there is no application that would access the resulting fragments any differently.   ◆

We can now present an iterative algorithm that would generate a complete and minimal set of predicates *Pr'* given a set of simple predicates *Pr*. This algorithm, called COM_MIN, is given in Algorithm 3.1. To avoid lengthy wording, we have adopted the following notation:

Rule 1: each fragment is accessed differently by at least one application.'

f_i *of Pr'*: fragment f_i defined according to a minterm predicate defined over the predicates of *Pr'*.

Algorithm 3.1: COM_MIN Algorithm

Input: *R*: relation; *Pr*: set of simple predicates
Output: *Pr'*: set of simple predicates
Declare: *F*: set of minterm fragments
begin
    find $p_i \in Pr$ such that p_i partitions *R* according to *Rule 1* ;
    $Pr' \leftarrow p_i$;
    $Pr \leftarrow Pr - p_i$;
    $F \leftarrow f_i$ {f_i is the minterm fragment according to p_i} ;
    repeat
        find a $p_j \in Pr$ such that p_j partitions some f_k of *Pr'* according to *Rule 1* ;
        $Pr' \leftarrow Pr' \cup p_j$;
        $Pr \leftarrow Pr - p_j$;
        $F \leftarrow F \cup f_j$;
        if $\exists p_k \in Pr'$ *which is not relevant* **then**
            $Pr' \leftarrow Pr' - p_k$;
            $F \leftarrow F - f_k$;
    until *Pr'* *is complete* ;
end

The algorithm begins by finding a predicate that is relevant and that partitions the input relation. The **repeat-until** loop iteratively adds predicates to this set, ensuring minimality at each step. Therefore, at the end the set Pr' is both minimal and complete.

The second step in the primary horizontal design process is to derive the set of minterm predicates that can be defined on the predicates in set Pr'. These minterm predicates determine the fragments that are used as candidates in the allocation step. Determination of individual minterm predicates is trivial; the difficulty is that the set of minterm predicates may be quite large (in fact, exponential on the number of simple predicates). We look at ways of reducing the number of minterm predicates that need to be considered in fragmentation.

This reduction can be achieved by eliminating some of the minterm fragments that may be meaningless. This elimination is performed by identifying those minterms that might be contradictory to a set of implications I. For example, if $Pr' = \{p_1, p_2\}$, where

$p_1 : att = value\_1$
$p_2 : att = value\_2$

and the domain of att is $\{value\_1, value\_2\}$, it is obvious that I contains two implications:

$i_1 : (att = value\_1) \Rightarrow \neg(att = value\_2)$
$i_2 : \neg(att = value_1) \Rightarrow (att = value\_2)$

The following four minterm predicates are defined according to Pr':

$m_1 : (att = value\_1) \wedge (att = value\_2)$
$m_2 : (att = value\_1) \wedge \neg(att = value\_2)$
$m_3 : \neg(att = value\_1) \wedge (att = value\_2)$
$m_4 : \neg(att = value\_1) \wedge \neg(att = value\_2)$

In this case the minterm predicates m_1 and m_4 are contradictory to the implications I and can therefore be eliminated from M.

The algorithm for primary horizontal fragmentation is given in Algorithm 3.2. The input to the algorithm PHORIZONTAL is a relation R that is subject to primary horizontal fragmentation, and Pr, which is the set of simple predicates that have been determined according to applications defined on relation R.

Example 3.11. We now consider the design of the database scheme given in Figure 3.7. The first thing to note is that there are two relations that are the subject of primary horizontal fragmentation: PAY and PROJ.

Suppose that there is only one application that accesses PAY, which checks the salary information and determines a raise accordingly. Assume that employee records are managed in two places, one handling the records of those with salaries less than

---

Algorithm 3.2: PHORIZONTAL Algorithm

Input: R: relation; Pr: set of simple predicates
Output: M: set of minterm fragments
begin

    $Pr' \leftarrow$ COM_MIN(R, Pr) ;
    determine the set M of minterm predicates ;
    determine the set I of implications among $p_i \in Pr'$;
    foreach $m_i \in M$ **do**
        if m_i *is contradictory according to* I **then**
            $M \leftarrow M - m_i$

end

---

or equal to \$30,000, and the other handling the records of those who earn more than \$30,000. Therefore, the query is issued at two sites.

The simple predicates that would be used to partition relation PAY are

p_1: SAL $\leq$ 30000
p_2: SAL $>$ 30000

thus giving the initial set of simple predicates $Pr = \{p_1, p_2\}$. Applying the COM_MIN algorithm with $i = 1$ as initial value results in $Pr' = \{p_1\}$. This is complete and minimal since p_2 would not partition f_1 (which is the minterm fragment formed with respect to p_1) according to Rule 1. We can form the following minterm predicates as members of M:

m_1: (SAL $<$ 30000)
m_2: $\neg$(SAL $\leq$ 30000) = SAL $>$ 30000

Therefore, we define two fragments $F_s = \{S_1, S_2\}$ according to M (Figure 3.9).

PAY $_1$

TITLE	SAL
Mech. Eng.	27000
Programmer	24000

PAY $_2$

TITLE	SAL
Elect. Eng.	40000
Syst. Anal.	34000

Fig. 3.9 Horizontal Fragmentation of Relation PAY

Let us next consider relation PROJ. Assume that there are two applications. The first is issued at three sites and finds the names and budgets of projects given their location. In SQL notation, the query is

```
SELECT PNAME, BUDGET
FROM   PROJ
WHERE  LOC=Value
```

For this application, the simple predicates that would be used are the following:

p_1: LOC = "Montreal"
p_2: LOC = "New York"
p_3: LOC = "Paris"

The second application is issued at two sites and has to do with the management of the projects. Those projects that have a budget of less than or equal to \$200,000 are managed at one site, whereas those with larger budgets are managed at a second site. Thus, the simple predicates that should be used to fragment according to the second application are

p_4: BUDGET $\leq$ 200000
p_5: BUDGET $>$ 200000

If the COM_MIN algorithm is followed, the set $Pr' = \{p_1, p_2, p_4\}$ is obviously complete and minimal. Actually COM_MIN would add any two of p_1, p_2, p_3 to Pr'; in this example we have selected to include p_1, p_2.

Based on Pr', the following six minterm predicates that form M can be defined:

m_1: (LOC = "Montreal") $\wedge$ (BUDGET $\leq$ 200000)
m_2: (LOC = "Montreal") $\wedge$ (BUDGET $>$ 200000)
m_3: (LOC = "New York") $\wedge$ (BUDGET $\leq$ 200000)
m_4: (LOC = "New York") $\wedge$ (BUDGET $>$ 200000)
m_5: (LOC = "Paris") $\wedge$ (BUDGET $\leq$ 200000)
m_6: (LOC = "Paris") $\wedge$ (BUDGET $>$ 200000)

As noted in Example 3.6, these are not the only minterm predicates that can be generated. It is, for example, possible to specify predicates of the form

$$p_1 \wedge p_2 \wedge p_3 \wedge p_4 \wedge p_5$$

However, the obvious implications

$i_1 : p_1 \Rightarrow \neg p_2 \wedge \neg p_3$
$i_2 : p_2 \Rightarrow \neg p_1 \wedge \neg p_3$
$i_3 : p_3 \Rightarrow \neg p_1 \wedge \neg p_2$
$i_4 : p_4 \Rightarrow \neg p_5$
$i_5 : p_5 \Rightarrow \neg p_4$
$i_6 : \neg p_4 \Rightarrow p_5$
$i_7 : \neg p_5 \Rightarrow p_4$

eliminate these minterm predicates and we are left with m_1 to m_6.

Looking at the database instance in Figure 3.3, one may be tempted to claim that the following implications hold:

i_8: LOC = "Montreal" $\Rightarrow \neg$ (BUDGET > 200000)
i_9: LOC = "Paris" $\Rightarrow \neg$ (BUDGET ≤ 200000)
i_{10}: $\neg$ (LOC = "Montreal") $\Rightarrow$ BUDGET ≤ 200000
i_{11}: $\neg$ (LOC = "Paris") $\Rightarrow$ BUDGET > 200000

However, remember that implications should be defined according to the semantics of the database, not according to the current values. There is nothing in the database semantics that suggest that the implications i_8 through i_{11} hold. Some of the fragments defined according to $M = \{m_1, \ldots, m_6\}$ may be empty, but they are, nevertheless, fragments.

The result of the primary horizontal fragmentation of PROJ is to form six fragments $F_{PROJ} = \{PROJ_1, PROJ_2, PROJ_3, PROJ_4, PROJ_5, PROJ_6\}$ of relation PROJ according to the minterm predicates M (Figure 3.10). Since fragments $PROJ_2$, and $PROJ_5$ are empty, they are not depicted in Figure 3.10.   ◆

PROJ$_1$

PNO	PNAME	BUDGET	LOC
P1	Instrumentation	150000	Montreal

PROJ$_3$

PNO	PNAME	BUDGET	LOC
P2	Database Develop.	135000	New York

PROJ$_4$

PNO	PNAME	BUDGET	LOC
P3	CAD/CAM	250000	New York

PROJ$_6$

PNO	PNAME	BUDGET	LOC
P4	Maintenance	310000	Paris

Fig. 3.10 Horizontal Partitioning of Relation PROJ

3.3.1.3 Derived Horizontal Fragmentation

A derived horizontal fragmentation is defined on a member relation of a link according to a selection operation specified on its owner. It is important to remember two points. First, the link between the owner and the member relations is defined as an equi-join. Second, an equi-join can be implemented by means of semijoins. This second point is especially important for our purposes, since we want to partition a member relation according to the fragmentation of its owner, but we also want the resulting fragment to be defined *only* on the attributes of the member relation.

Accordingly, given a link L where $owner(L) = S$ and $member(L) = R$, the derived horizontal fragments of R are defined as

$$R_i = R \ltimes S_i, 1 \leq i \leq w$$

where w is the maximum number of fragments that will be defined on R, and $S_i = \sigma_{F_i}(S)$, where F_i is the formula according to which the primary horizontal fragment S_i is defined.

Example 3.12. Consider link L_1 in Figure 3.7, where $owner(L_1) = $ PAY and $member(L_1) = $ EMP. Then we can group engineers into two groups according to their salary: those making less than or equal to \$30,000, and those making more than \$30,000. The two fragments EMP_1 and EMP_2 are defined as follows:

$$EMP_1 = EMP \ltimes PAY_1$$
$$EMP_2 = EMP \ltimes PAY_2$$

where

$$PAY_1 = \sigma_{SAL \leq 30000}(PAY)$$
$$PAY_2 = \sigma_{SAL > 30000}(PAY)$$

The result of this fragmentation is depicted in Figure 3.11.   ◆

EMP$_1$

ENO	ENAME	TITLE
E3	A. Lee	Mech. Eng.
E4	J. Miller	Programmer
E7	R. Davis	Mech. Eng.

EMP$_2$

ENO	ENAME	TITLE
E1	J. Doe	Elect. Eng.
E2	M. Smith	Syst. Anal.
E5	B. Casey	Syst. Anal.
E6	L. Chu	Elect. Eng.
E8	J. Jones	Syst. Anal.

Fig. 3.11 Derived Horizontal Fragmentation of Relation EMP

To carry out a derived horizontal fragmentation, three inputs are needed: the set of partitions of the owner relation (e.g., PAY_1 and PAY_2 in Example 3.12), the member relation, and the set of semijoin predicates between the owner and the member (e.g., EMP.TITLE = PAY.TITLE in Example 3.12). The fragmentation algorithm, then, is quite trivial, so we will not present it in any detail.

There is one potential complication that deserves some attention. In a database schema, it is common that there are more than two links into a relation R (e.g., in Figure 3.7, ASG has two incoming links). In this case there is more than one possible derived horizontal fragmentation of *R*. The choice of candidate fragmentation is based on two criteria:

1. The fragmentation with better join characteristics

2. The fragmentation used in more applications

Let us discuss the second criterion first. This is quite straightforward if we take into consideration the frequency with which applications access some data. If possible, one should try to facilitate the accesses of the "heavy" users so that their total impact on system performance is minimized.

Applying the first criterion, however, is not that straightforward. Consider, for example, the fragmentation we discussed in Example 3.1. The effect (and the objective) of this fragmentation is that the join of the EMP and PAY relations to answer the query is assisted (1) by performing it on smaller relations (i.e., fragments), and (2) by potentially performing joins in parallel.

The first point is obvious. The fragments of EMP are smaller than EMP itself. Therefore, it will be faster to join any fragment of PAY with any fragment of EMP than to work with the relations themselves. The second point, however, is more important and is at the heart of distributed databases. If, besides executing a number of queries at different sites, we can parallelize execution of one join query, the response time or throughput of the system can be expected to improve. In the case of joins, this is possible under certain circumstances. Consider, for example, the join graph (i.e., the links) between the fragments of EMP and PAY derived in Example 3.10 (Figure 3.12). There is only one link coming in or going out of a fragment. Such a join graph is called a *simple* graph. The advantage of a design where the join relationship between fragments is simple is that the member and owner of a link can be allocated to one site and the joins between different pairs of fragments can proceed independently and in parallel.

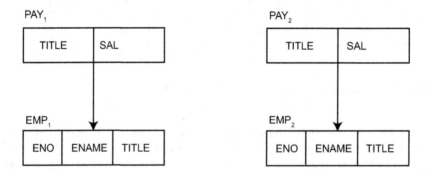

Fig. 3.12 Join Graph Between Fragments

Unfortunately, obtaining simple join graphs may not always be possible. In that case, the next desirable alternative is to have a design that results in a *partitioned* join graph. A partitioned graph consists of two or more subgraphs with no links between them. Fragments so obtained may not be distributed for parallel execution as easily as those obtained via simple join graphs, but the allocation is still possible.

Example 3.13. Let us continue with the distribution design of the database we started in Example 3.11. We already decided on the fragmentation of relation EMP according to the fragmentation of PAY (Example 3.12). Let us now consider ASG. Assume that there are the following two applications:

1. The first application finds the names of engineers who work at certain places. It runs on all three sites and accesses the information about the engineers who work on local projects with higher probability than those of projects at other locations.

2. At each administrative site where employee records are managed, users would like to access the responsibilities on the projects that these employees work on and learn how long they will work on those projects.

The first application results in a fragmentation of ASG according to the (non-empty) fragments $PROJ_1$, $PROJ_3$, $PROJ_4$ and $PROJ_6$ of PROJ obtained in Example 3.11. Remember that

$PROJ_1$: $\sigma_{LOC=\text{"Montreal"} \wedge BUDGET \leq 200000}$ (PROJ)
$PROJ_3$: $\sigma_{LOC=\text{"New York"} \wedge BUDGET \leq 200000}$ (PROJ)
$PROJ_4$: $\sigma_{LOC=\text{"New York"} \wedge BUDGET > 200000}$ (PROJ)
$PROJ_6$: $\sigma_{LOC=\text{"Paris"} \wedge BUDGET > 200000}$ (PROJ)

Therefore, the derived fragmentation of ASG according to $\{PROJ_1, PROJ_2, PROJ_3\}$ is defined as follows:

$ASG_1 = ASG \ltimes PROJ_1$
$ASG_2 = ASG \ltimes PROJ_3$
$ASG_3 = ASG \ltimes PROJ_4$
$ASG_4 = ASG \ltimes PROJ_6$

These fragment instances are shown in Figure 3.13.

The second query can be specified in SQL as

```
SELECT RESP, DUR
FROM    ASG, EMPᵢ
WHERE   ASG.ENO = EMPᵢ.ENO
```

where $i = 1$ or $i = 2$, depending on the site where the query is issued. The derived fragmentation of ASG according to the fragmentation of EMP is defined below and depicted in Figure 3.14.

$ASG_1 = ASG \ltimes EMP_1$
$ASG_2 = ASG \ltimes EMP_2$

◆

ASG$_1$

ENO	PNO	RESP	DUR
E1	P1	Manager	12
E2	P1	Analyst	24

ASG$_2$

ENO	PNO	RESP	DUR
E2	P2	Analyst	6
E4	P2	Programmer	18
E5	P2	Manager	24

ASG$_3$

ENO	PNO	RESP	DUR
E3	P3	Consultant	10
E7	P3	Engineer	36
E8	P3	Manager	40

ASG$_4$

ENO	PNO	RESP	DUR
E3	P4	Engineer	48
E6	P4	Manager	48

Fig. 3.13 Derived Fragmentation of ASG with respect to PROJ

ASG$_1$

ENO	PNO	RESP	DUR
E3	P3	Consultant	10
E3	P4	Engineer	48
E4	P2	Programmer	18
E7	P3	Engineer	36

ASG$_2$

ENO	PNO	RESP	DUR
E1	P1	Manager	12
E2	P1	Analyst	24
E2	P2	Analyst	6
E5	P2	Manager	24
E6	P4	Manager	48
E8	P3	Manager	40

Fig. 3.14 Derived Fragmentation of ASG with respect to EMP

This example demonstrates two things:

1. Derived fragmentation may follow a chain where one relation is fragmented
   as a result of another one's design and it, in turn, causes the fragmentation of
   another relation (e.g., the chain PAY→EMP→ASG).

2. Typically, there will be more than one candidate fragmentation for a relation
   (e.g., relation ASG). The final choice of the fragmentation scheme may be a
   decision problem addressed during allocation.

3.3.1.4 Checking for Correctness

We should now check the fragmentation algorithms discussed so far with respect to the three correctness criteria presented in Section 3.2.4.

Completeness.

The completeness of a primary horizontal fragmentation is based on the selection predicates used. As long as the selection predicates are complete, the resulting fragmentation is guaranteed to be complete as well. Since the basis of the fragmentation algorithm is a set of *complete* and *minimal* predicates, Pr', completeness is guaranteed as long as no mistakes are made in defining Pr'.

The completeness of a derived horizontal fragmentation is somewhat more difficult to define. The difficulty is due to the fact that the predicate determining the fragmentation involves two relations. Let us first define the completeness rule formally and then look at an example.

Let R be the member relation of a link whose owner is relation S, where R and S are fragmented as $F_R = \{R_1, R_2, \ldots, R_w\}$ and $F_S = \{S_1, S_2, \ldots, S_w\}$, respectively. Furthermore, let A be the join attribute between R and S. Then for each tuple t of R_i, there should be a tuple t' of S_i such that $t[A] = t'[A]$.

For example, there should be no ASG tuple which has a project number that is not also contained in PROJ. Similarly, there should be no EMP tuples with TITLE values where the same TITLE value does not appear in PAY as well. This rule is known as *referential integrity* and ensures that the tuples of any fragment of the member relation are also in the owner relation.

Reconstruction.

Reconstruction of a global relation from its fragments is performed by the union operator in both the primary and the derived horizontal fragmentation. Thus, for a relation R with fragmentation $F_R = \{R_1, R_2, \ldots, R_w\}$,

$$R = \bigcup R_i, \quad \forall R_i \in F_R$$

Disjointness.

It is easier to establish disjointness of fragmentation for primary than for derived horizontal fragmentation. In the former case, disjointness is guaranteed as long as the minterm predicates determining the fragmentation are mutually exclusive.

In derived fragmentation, however, there is a semijoin involved that adds considerable complexity. Disjointness can be guaranteed if the join graph is simple. Otherwise, it is necessary to investigate actual tuple values. In general, we do not want a tuple of a member relation to join with two or more tuples of the owner relation when these tuples are in different fragments of the owner. This may not be very easy to establish, and illustrates why derived fragmentation schemes that generate a simple join graph are always desirable.

Example 3.14. In fragmenting relation PAY (Example 3.11), the minterm predicates $M = \{m_1, m_2\}$ were

   m_1: SAL $\leq$ 30000
   m_2: SAL $>$ 30000

Since m_1 and m_2 are mutually exclusive, the fragmentation of PAY is disjoint. For relation EMP, however, we require that

1. Each engineer has a single title.

2. Each title have a single salary value associated with it.

Since these two rules follow from the semantics of the database, the fragmentation of EMP with respect to PAY is also disjoint.   ♦

3.3.2 Vertical Fragmentation

Remember that a vertical fragmentation of a relation R produces fragments $R_1, R_2,$ $\ldots, R_r$, each of which contains a subset of R's attributes as well as the primary key of R. The objective of vertical fragmentation is to partition a relation into a set of smaller relations so that many of the user applications will run on only one fragment. In this context, an "optimal" fragmentation is one that produces a fragmentation scheme which minimizes the execution time of user applications that run on these fragments.

Vertical fragmentation has been investigated within the context of centralized database systems as well as distributed ones. Its motivation within the centralized context is as a design tool, which allows the user queries to deal with smaller relations, thus causing a smaller number of page accesses [Navathe et al., 1984]. It has also been suggested that the most "active" subrelations can be identified and placed in a faster memory subsystem in those cases where memory hierarchies are supported [Eisner and Severance, 1976].

Vertical partitioning is inherently more complicated than horizontal partitioning. This is due to the total number of alternatives that are available. For example, in horizontal partitioning, if the total number of simple predicates in Pr is n, there are 2^n possible minterm predicates that can be defined on it. In addition, we know that some of these will contradict the existing implications, further reducing the candidate fragments that need to be considered. In the case of vertical partitioning, however, if a relation has m non-primary key attributes, the number of possible fragments is equal to $B(m)$, which is the mth Bell number [Niamir, 1978]. For large values of

$m, B(m) \approx m^m$; for example, for $m=10$, $B(m) \approx 115,000$, for $m=15$, $B(m) \approx 10^9$, for $m=30$, $B(m) = 10^{23}$ [Hammer and Niamir, 1979; Navathe et al., 1984].

These values indicate that it is futile to attempt to obtain optimal solutions to the vertical partitioning problem; one has to resort to heuristics. Two types of heuristic approaches exist for the vertical fragmentation of global relations:

1. *Grouping:* starts by assigning each attribute to one fragment, and at each step, joins some of the fragments until some criteria is satisfied. Grouping was first suggested for centralized databases [Hammer and Niamir, 1979], and was used later for distributed databases [Sacca and Wiederhold, 1985].

2. *Splitting:* starts with a relation and decides on beneficial partitionings based on the access behavior of applications to the attributes. The technique was also first discussed for centralized database design [Hoffer and Severance, 1975]. It was then extended to the distributed environment [Navathe et al., 1984].

In what follows we discuss only the splitting technique, since it fits more naturally within the top-down design methodology, since the "optimal" solution is probably closer to the full relation than to a set of fragments each of which consists of a single attribute [Navathe et al., 1984]. Furthermore, splitting generates non-overlapping fragments whereas grouping typically results in overlapping fragments. We prefer non-overlapping fragments for disjointness. Of course, non-overlapping refers only to non-primary key attributes.

Before we proceed, let us clarify an issue that we only mentioned in Example 3.2, namely, the replication of the global relation's key in the fragments. This is a characteristic of vertical fragmentation that allows the reconstruction of the global relation. Therefore, splitting is considered only for those attributes that do not participate in the primary key.

There is a strong advantage to replicating the key attributes despite the obvious problems it causes. This advantage has to do with semantic integrity enforcement, to be discussed in Chapter 5. Note that the dependencies briefly discussed in Section 2.1 is, in fact, a constraint that has to hold among the attribute values of the respective relations at all times. Remember also that most of these dependencies involve the key attributes of a relation. If we now design the database so that the key attributes are part of one fragment that is allocated to one site, and the implied attributes are part of another fragment that is allocated to a second site, every update request that causes an integrity check will necessitate communication among sites. Replication of the key attributes at each fragment reduces the chances of this occurring but does not eliminate it completely, since such communication may be necessary due to integrity constraints that do not involve the primary key, as well as due to concurrency control.

One alternative to the replication of the key attributes is the use of *tuple identifiers* (TIDs), which are system-assigned unique values to the tuples of a relation. Since TIDs are maintained by the system, the fragments are disjoint at a logical level.

3.3.2.1 Information Requirements of Vertical Fragmentation

The major information required for vertical fragmentation is related to applications. The following discussion, therefore, is exclusively focused on what needs to be determined about applications that will run against the distributed database. Since vertical partitioning places in one fragment those attributes usually accessed together, there is a need for some measure that would define more precisely the notion of "togetherness." This measure is the *affinity* of attributes, which indicates how closely related the attributes are. Unfortunately, it is not realistic to expect the designer or the users to be able to easily specify these values. We now present one way by which they can be obtained from more primitive data.

The major information requirement related to applications is their access frequencies. Let $Q = \{q_1, q_2, \dots, q_q\}$ be the set of user queries (applications) that access relation $R(A_1, A_2, \dots, A_n)$. Then, for each query q_i and each attribute A_j, we associate an *attribute usage value*, denoted as $use(q_i, A_j)$, and defined as follows:

$$use(q_i, A_j) = \begin{cases} 1 \text{ if attribute } A_j \text{ is referenced by query } q_i \\ 0 \text{ otherwise} \end{cases}$$

The $use(q_i, \bullet)$ vectors for each application are easy to define if the designer knows the applications that will run on the database. Again, remember that the 80-20 rule discussed earlier should be helpful in this task.

Example 3.15. Consider relation PROJ of Figure 3.3. Assume that the following applications are defined to run on this relation. In each case we also give the SQL specification.

q_1: Find the budget of a project, given its identification number.

```
SELECT BUDGET
FROM   PROJ
WHERE  PNO=Value
```

q_2: Find the names and budgets of all projects.

```
SELECT  PNAME, BUDGET
FROM    PROJ
```

q_3: Find the names of projects located at a given city.

```
SELECT PNAME
FROM   PROJ
WHERE  LOC=Value
```

q_4: Find the total project budgets for each city.

```
SELECT SUM(BUDGET)
FROM   PROJ
WHERE  LOC=Value
```

According to these four applications, the attribute usage values can be defined. As a notational convenience, we let A_1 = PNO, A_2 = PNAME, A_3 = BUDGET, and A_4 = LOC. The usage values are defined in matrix form (Figure 3.15), where entry (i, j) denotes $use(q_i, A_j)$. ♦

$$\begin{array}{c@{\quad}c@{\quad}c@{\quad}c@{\quad}c}
 & A_1 & A_2 & A_3 & A_4 \\
q_1 & 1 & 0 & 1 & 0 \\
q_2 & 0 & 1 & 1 & 0 \\
q_3 & 0 & 1 & 0 & 1 \\
q_4 & 0 & 0 & 1 & 1
\end{array}$$

Fig. 3.15 Example Attribute Usage Matrix

Attribute usage values are not sufficiently general to form the basis of attribute splitting and fragmentation. This is because these values do not represent the weight of application frequencies. The frequency measure can be included in the definition of the attribute affinity measure $aff(A_i, A_j)$, which measures the bond between two attributes of a relation according to how they are accessed by applications.

The attribute affinity measure between two attributes A_i and A_j of a relation $R(A_1, A_2, \ldots, A_n)$ with respect to the set of applications $Q = \{q_1, q_2, \ldots, q_q\}$ is defined as

$$aff(A_i, A_j) = \sum_{k|use(q_k,A_i)=1 \wedge use(q_k,A_j)=1} \sum_{\forall S_l} ref_l(q_k)acc_l(q_k)$$

where $ref_l(q_k)$ is the number of accesses to attributes (A_i, A_j) for each execution of application q_k at site S_l and $acc_l(q_k)$ is the application access frequency measure previously defined and modified to include frequencies at different sites.

The result of this computation is an $n \times n$ matrix, each element of which is one of the measures defined above. We call this matrix the *attribute affinity matrix (AA)*.

Example 3.16. Let us continue with the case that we examined in Example 3.15. For simplicity, let us assume that $ref_l(q_k)$ = 1 for all q_k and S_l. If the application frequencies are

$$acc_1(q_1) = 15 \; acc_2(q_1) = 20 \; acc_3(q_1) = 10$$
$$acc_1(q_2) = 5 \;\;\; acc_2(q_2) = 0 \;\;\;\; acc_3(q_2) = 0$$
$$acc_1(q_3) = 25 \; acc_2(q_3) = 25 \; acc_3(q_3) = 25$$
$$acc_1(q_4) = 3 \;\;\; acc_2(q_4) = 0 \;\;\;\; acc_3(q_4) = 0$$

then the affinity measure between attributes A_1 and A_3 can be measured as

$$aff(A_1, A_3) = \sum_{k=1}^{1} \sum_{l=1}^{3} acc_l(q_k) = acc_1(q_1) + acc_2(q_1) + acc_3(q_1) = 45$$

since the only application that accesses both of the attributes is q_1. The complete attribute affinity matrix is shown in Figure 3.16. Note that the diagonal values are not computed since they are meaningless.   ♦

$$\begin{array}{c c} & \begin{array}{c c c c} A_1 & A_2 & A_3 & A_4 \end{array} \\ \begin{array}{c} A_1 \\ A_2 \\ A_3 \\ A_4 \end{array} & \left[\begin{array}{c c c c} - & 0 & 45 & 0 \\ 0 & - & 5 & 75 \\ 45 & 5 & - & 3 \\ 0 & 75 & 3 & - \end{array} \right] \end{array}$$

Fig. 3.16 Attribute Affinity Matrix

The attribute affinity matrix will be used in the rest of this chapter to guide the fragmentation effort. The process involves first clustering together the attributes with high affinity for each other, and then splitting the relation accordingly.

3.3.2.2 Clustering Algorithm

The fundamental task in designing a vertical fragmentation algorithm is to find some means of grouping the attributes of a relation based on the attribute affinity values in *AA*. It has been suggested that the bond energy algorithm (BEA) [McCormick et al., 1972] should be used for this purpose ([Hoffer and Severance, 1975] and [Navathe et al., 1984]). It is considered appropriate for the following reasons [Hoffer and Severance, 1975]:

1. It is designed specifically to determine groups of similar items as opposed to, say, a linear ordering of the items (i.e., it clusters the attributes with larger affinity values together, and the ones with smaller values together).

2. The final groupings are insensitive to the order in which items are presented to the algorithm.

3. The computation time of the algorithm is reasonable: $O(n^2)$, where n is the number of attributes.

4. Secondary interrelationships between clustered attribute groups are identifiable.

The bond energy algorithm takes as input the attribute affinity matrix, permutes its rows and columns, and generates a *clustered affinity matrix (CA)*. The permutation is done in such a way as to *maximize* the following *global affinity measure (AM)*:

$$AM = \sum_{i=1}^{n} \sum_{j=1}^{n} aff(A_i, A_j)[aff(A_i, A_{j-1}) + aff(A_i, A_{j+1})$$
$$+ aff(A_{i-1}, A_j) + aff(A_{i+1}, A_j)]$$

where

$$aff(A_0, A_j) = aff(A_i, A_0) = aff(A_{n+1}, A_j) = aff(A_i, A_{n+1}) = 0$$

The last set of conditions takes care of the cases where an attribute is being placed in *CA* to the left of the leftmost attribute or to the right of the rightmost attribute during column permutations, and prior to the topmost row and following the last row during row permutations. In these cases, we take 0 to be the *aff* values between the attribute being considered for placement and its left or right (top or bottom) neighbors, which do not exist in *CA*.

The maximization function considers the nearest neighbors only, thereby resulting in the grouping of large values with large ones, and small values with small ones. Also, the attribute affinity matrix (*AA*) is symmetric, which reduces the objective function of the formulation above to

$$AM = \sum_{i=1}^{n} \sum_{j=1}^{n} aff(A_i, A_j)[aff(A_i, A_{j-1}) + aff(A_i, A_{j+1})]$$

The details of the bond energy algorithm are given in Algorithm 3.3. Generation of the clustered affinity matrix (*CA*) is done in three steps:

1. *Initialization.* Place and fix one of the columns of *AA* arbitrarily into *CA*. Column 1 was chosen in the algorithm.

2. *Iteration.* Pick each of the remaining $n - i$ columns (where i is the number of columns already placed in *CA*) and try to place them in the remaining $i + 1$ positions in the *CA* matrix. Choose the placement that makes the greatest contribution to the global affinity measure described above. Continue this step until no more columns remain to be placed.

3. *Row ordering.* Once the column ordering is determined, the placement of the rows should also be changed so that their relative positions match the relative positions of the columns.[3]

---

[3] From now on, we may refer to elements of the *AA* and *CA* matrices as $AA(i, j)$ and $CA(i, j)$, respectively. This is done for notational convenience only. The mapping to the affinity measures is $AA(i, j) = aff(A_i, A_j)$ and $CA(i, j) = aff($attribute placed at column i in *CA*, attribute placed at column j in *CA*). Even though *AA* and *CA* matrices are identical except for the ordering of attributes, since the algorithm orders all the *CA* columns before it orders the rows, the affinity measure of *CA* is specified with respect to columns. Note that the endpoint condition for the calculation of the affinity measure (*AM*) can be specified, using this notation, as $CA(0, j) = CA(i, 0) = CA(n+1, j) = CA(i, n+1) = 0$.

Algorithm 3.3: BEA Algorithm

Input: *AA*: attribute affinity matrix
Output: *CA*: clustered affinity matrix
begin
    {initialize; remember that *AA* is an $n \times n$ matrix}
    $CA(\bullet, 1) \leftarrow AA(\bullet, 1)$;
    $CA(\bullet, 2) \leftarrow AA(\bullet, 2)$;
    $index \leftarrow 3$;
    while *index* $\leq n$ **do**   {choose the "best" location for attribute AA_{index}}
        for *i from 1 to index* -1 *by 1* **do** calculate $cont(A_{i-1}, A_{index}, A_i)$;
        calculate $cont(A_{index-1}, A_{index}, A_{index+1})$;   {boundary condition}
        loc $\leftarrow$ placement given by maximum *cont* value ;
        for *j from index to loc by* -1 **do**
            $CA(\bullet, j) \leftarrow CA(\bullet, j-1)$ {shuffle the two matrices}
        $CA(\bullet, loc) \leftarrow AA(\bullet, index)$;
        $index \leftarrow index + 1$
    order the rows according to the relative ordering of columns
end

For the second step of the algorithm to work, we need to define what is meant by the contribution of an attribute to the affinity measure. This contribution can be derived as follows. Recall that the global affinity measure *AM* was previously defined as

$$AM = \sum_{i=1}^{n} \sum_{j=1}^{n} aff(A_i, A_j)[aff(A_i, A_{j-1}) + aff(A_i, A_{j+1})]$$

which can be rewritten as

$$AM = \sum_{i=1}^{n} \sum_{j=1}^{n} [aff(A_i, A_j)aff(A_i, A_{j-1}) + aff(A_i, A_j)aff(A_i, A_{j+1})]$$

$$= \sum_{j=1}^{n} \left[\sum_{i=1}^{n} aff(A_i, A_j)aff(A_i, A_{j-1}) + \sum_{i=1}^{n} aff(A_i, A_j)aff(A_i, A_{j+1}) \right]$$

Let us define the *bond* between two attributes A_x and A_y as

$$bond(A_x, A_y) = \sum_{z=1}^{n} aff(A_z, A_x)aff(A_z, A_y)$$

Then *AM* can be written as

$$AM = \sum_{j=1}^{n} [bond(A_j, A_{j-1}) + bond(A_j, A_{j+1})]$$

Now consider the following n attributes

$$\underbrace{A_1 \, A_2 \, \ldots \, A_{i-1}}_{AM'} \, A_i \, A_j \, \underbrace{A_{j+1} \, \ldots \, A_n}_{AM''}$$

The global affinity measure for these attributes can be written as

$$
\begin{aligned}
AM_{old} &= AM' + AM'' \\
&\quad + bond(A_{i-1}, A_i) + bond(A_i, A_j) + bond(A_j, A_i) + bond(A_j, A_{j+1}) \\
&= \sum_{l=1}^{i} [bond(A_l, A_{l-1}) + bond(A_l, A_{l+1})] \\
&\quad + \sum_{l=i+2}^{n} [bond(A_l, A_{l-1}) + bond(A_l, A_{l+1})] \\
&\quad + 2bond(A_i, A_j)
\end{aligned}
$$

Now consider placing a new attribute A_k between attributes A_i and A_j in the clustered affinity matrix. The new global affinity measure can be similarly written as

$$
\begin{aligned}
AM_{new} &= AM' + AM'' + bond(A_i, A_k) + bond(A_k, A_i) \\
&\quad + bond(A_k, A_j) + bond(A_j, A_k) \\
&= AM' + AM'' + 2bond(A_i, A_k) + 2bond(A_k, A_j)
\end{aligned}
$$

Thus, the net *contribution*[4] to the global affinity measure of placing attribute A_k between A_i and A_j is

$$
\begin{aligned}
cont(A_i, A_k, A_j) &= AM_{new} - AM_{old} \\
&= 2bond(A_i, A_k) + 2bond(A_k, A_j) - 2bond(A_i, A_j)
\end{aligned}
$$

Example 3.17. Let us consider the *AA* matrix given in Figure 3.16 and study the contribution of moving attribute A_4 between attributes A_1 and A_2, given by the formula

$$cont(A_1, A_4, A_2) = 2bond(A_1, A_4) + 2bond(A_4, A_2) - 2bond(A_1, A_2)$$

Computing each term, we get

$$
\begin{aligned}
bond(A_1, A_4) &= 45*0 + 0*75 + 45*3 + 0*78 = 135 \\
bond(A_4, A_2) &= 11865 \\
bond(A_1, A_2) &= 225
\end{aligned}
$$

Therefore,

---

[4] In literature [Hoffer and Severance, 1975] this measure is specified as $bond(A_i, A_k) + bond(A_k, A_j) - 2bond(A_i, A_j)$. However, this is a pessimistic measure which does not follow from the definition of *AM*.

$$cont(A_1,A_4,A_2) = 2*135+2*11865-2*225 = 23550$$

♦

Note that the calculation of the bond between two attributes requires the multiplication of the respective elements of the two columns representing these attributes and taking the row-wise sum.

The algorithm and our discussion so far have both concentrated on the columns of the attribute affinity matrix. We can also make the same arguments and redesign the algorithm to operate on the rows. Since the AA matrix is symmetric, both of these approaches will generate the same result.

Another point about Algorithm 3.3 is that to improve its efficiency, the second column is also fixed and placed next to the first one during the initialization step. This is acceptable since, according to the algorithm, A_2 can be placed either to the left of A_1 or to its right. The bond between the two, however, is independent of their positions relative to one another.

Finally, we should indicate the problem of computing *cont* at the endpoints. If an attribute A_i is being considered for placement to the left of the leftmost attribute, one of the bond equations to be calculated is between a non-existent left element and A_k [i.e., $bond(A_0,A_k)$]. Thus we need to refer to the conditions imposed on the definition of the global affinity measure AM, where $CA(0,k) = 0$. The other extreme is if A_j is the rightmost attribute that is already placed in the CA matrix and we are checking for the contribution of placing attribute A_k to the right of A_j. In this case the $bond(k,k+1)$ needs to be calculated. However, since no attribute is yet placed in column $k+1$ of CA, the affinity measure is not defined. Therefore, according to the endpoint conditions, this *bond* value is also 0.

Example 3.18. We consider the clustering of the PROJ relation attributes and use the attribute affinity matrix AA of Figure 3.16.

According to the initialization step, we copy columns 1 and 2 of the AA matrix to the CA matrix (Figure 3.17a) and start with column 3 (i.e., attribute A_3). There are three alternative places where column 3 can be placed: to the left of column 1, resulting in the ordering (3-1-2), in between columns 1 and 2, giving (1-3-2), and to the right of 2, resulting in (1-2-3). Note that to compute the contribution of the last ordering we have to compute $cont(A_2,A_3,A_4)$ rather than $cont(A_1,A_2,A_3)$. Furthermore, in this context A_4 refers to the fourth index position in the CA matrix, which is empty (Figure 3.17b), not to the attribute column A_4 of the AA matrix. Let us calculate the contribution to the global affinity measure of each alternative.

Ordering (0-3-1):

$$cont(A_0,A_3,A_1) = 2bond(A_0,A_3)+2bond(A_3,A_1)-2bond(A_0,A_1)$$

We know that

$$bond(A_0,A_1) = bond(A_0,A_3) = 0$$
$$bond(A_3,A_1) = 45*45+5*0+53*45+3*0 = 4410$$

$$
\begin{array}{c}
\begin{array}{cc} A_1 & A_2 \end{array} \\
\begin{array}{c} A_1 \\ A_2 \\ A_3 \\ A_4 \end{array}
\left[\begin{array}{cc}
45 & 0 \\
0 & 80 \\
45 & 5 \\
0 & 75
\end{array} \right]
\end{array}
\qquad
\begin{array}{c}
\begin{array}{ccc} A_1 & A_3 & A_2 \end{array} \\
\begin{array}{c} A_1 \\ A_2 \\ A_3 \\ A_4 \end{array}
\left[\begin{array}{ccc}
45 & 45 & 0 \\
0 & 5 & 80 \\
45 & 53 & 5 \\
0 & 3 & 75
\end{array} \right]
\end{array}
$$

(a)   (b)

$$
\begin{array}{c}
\begin{array}{cccc} A_1 & A_3 & A_2 & A_4 \end{array} \\
\begin{array}{c} A_1 \\ A_2 \\ A_3 \\ A_4 \end{array}
\left[\begin{array}{cccc}
45 & 45 & 0 & 0 \\
0 & 5 & 80 & 75 \\
45 & 53 & 5 & 3 \\
0 & 3 & 75 & 78
\end{array} \right]
\end{array}
\qquad
\begin{array}{c}
\begin{array}{cccc} A_1 & A_3 & A_2 & A_4 \end{array} \\
\begin{array}{c} A_1 \\ A_3 \\ A_2 \\ A_4 \end{array}
\left[\begin{array}{cccc}
45 & 45 & 0 & 0 \\
45 & 53 & 5 & 3 \\
0 & 5 & 80 & 75 \\
0 & 3 & 75 & 78
\end{array} \right]
\end{array}
$$

(c)   (d)

Fig. 3.17 Calculation of the Clustered Affinity (CA) Matrix

Thus

$$cont(A_0, A_3, A_1) = 8820$$

Ordering (1-3-2):

$$cont(A_1, A_3, A_2) = 2bond(A_1, A_3) + 2bond(A_3, A_2) - 2bond(A_1, A_2)$$
$$bond(A_1, A_3) \quad = bond(A_3, A_1) = 4410$$
$$bond(A_3, A_2) \quad = 890$$
$$bond(A_1, A_2) \quad = 225$$

Thus

$$cont(A_1, A_3, A_2) = 10150$$

Ordering (2-3-4):

$$cont(A_2, A_3, A_4) = 2bond(A_2, A_3) + 2bond(A_3, A_4) - 2bond(A_2, A_4)$$
$$bond(A_2, A_3) \quad = 890$$
$$bond(A_3, A_4) \quad = 0$$
$$bond(A_2, A_4) \quad = 0$$

Thus

$$cont(A_2,A_3,A_4) = 1780$$

Since the contribution of the ordering (1-3-2) is the largest, we select to place A_3 to the right of A_1 (Figure 3.17b). Similar calculations for A_4 indicate that it should be placed to the right of A_2 (Figure 3.17c).

Finally, the rows are organized in the same order as the columns and the result is shown in Figure 3.17d.   ◆

In Figure 3.17d we see the creation of two clusters: one is in the upper left corner and contains the smaller affinity values and the other is in the lower right corner and contains the larger affinity values. This clustering indicates how the attributes of relation PROJ should be split. However, in general the border for this split may not be this clear-cut. When the *CA* matrix is big, usually more than two clusters are formed and there are more than one candidate partitionings. Thus, there is a need to approach this problem more systematically.

3.3.2.3 Partitioning Algorithm

The objective of the splitting activity is to find sets of attributes that are accessed solely, or for the most part, by distinct sets of applications. For example, if it is possible to identify two attributes, A_1 and A_2, which are accessed only by application q_1, and attributes A_3 and A_4, which are accessed by, say, two applications q_2 and q_3, it would be quite straightforward to decide on the fragments. The task lies in finding an algorithmic method of identifying these groups.

Consider the clustered attribute matrix of Figure 3.18. If a point along the diagonal is fixed, two sets of attributes are identified. One set $\{A_1,A_2,\ldots,A_i\}$ is at the upper left-hand corner and the second set $\{A_{i+1},\ldots,A_n\}$ is to the right and to the bottom of this point. We call the former set *top* and the latter set *bottom* and denote the attribute sets as *TA* and *BA*, respectively.

We now turn to the set of applications $Q = \{q_1,q_2,\ldots,q_q\}$ and define the set of applications that access only *TA*, only *BA*, or both. These sets are defined as follows:

$$AQ(q_i) = \{A_j | use(q_i,A_j) = 1\}$$
$$TQ = \{q_i | AQ(q_i) \subseteq TA\}$$
$$BQ = \{q_i | AQ(q_i) \subseteq BA\}$$
$$OQ = Q - \{TQ \cup BQ\}$$

The first of these equations defines the set of attributes accessed by application q_i; *TQ* and *BQ* are the sets of applications that only access *TA* or *BA*, respectively, and *OQ* is the set of applications that access both.

There is an optimization problem here. If there are n attributes of a relation, there are $n-1$ possible positions where the dividing point can be placed along the diagonal

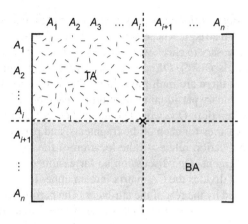

Fig. 3.18 Locating a Splitting Point

of the clustered attribute matrix for that relation. The best position for division is one which produces the sets TQ and BQ such that the total accesses to *only one* fragment are maximized while the total accesses to *both* fragments are minimized. We therefore define the following cost equations:

$$CQ = \sum_{q_i \in Q} \sum_{\forall S_j} ref_j(q_i) acc_j(q_i)$$

$$CTQ = \sum_{q_i \in TQ} \sum_{\forall S_j} ref_j(q_i) acc_j(q_i)$$

$$CBQ = \sum_{q_i \in BQ} \sum_{\forall S_j} ref_j(q_i) acc_j(q_i)$$

$$COQ = \sum_{q_i \in OQ} \sum_{\forall S_j} ref_j(q_i) acc_j(q_i)$$

Each of the equations above counts the total number of accesses to attributes by applications in their respective classes. Based on these measures, the optimization problem is defined as finding the point x $(1 \le x \le n)$ such that the expression

$$z = CTQ * CBQ - COQ^2$$

is maximized [Navathe et al., 1984]. The important feature of this expression is that it defines two fragments such that the values of CTQ and CBQ are as nearly equal as possible. This enables the balancing of processing loads when the fragments are distributed to various sites. It is clear that the partitioning algorithm has linear complexity in terms of the number of attributes of the relation, that is, $O(n)$.

There are two complications that need to be addressed. The first is with respect to the splitting. The procedure splits the set of attributes two-way. For larger sets of attributes, it is quite likely that m-way partitioning may be necessary.

Designing an m-way partitioning is possible but computationally expensive. Along the diagonal of the CA matrix, it is necessary to try $1, 2, \ldots, m-1$ split points, and for each of these, it is necessary to check which place maximizes z. Thus, the complexity of such an algorithm is $O(2^m)$. Of course, the definition of z has to be modified for those cases where there are multiple split points. The alternative solution is to recursively apply the binary partitioning algorithm to each of the fragments obtained during the previous iteration. One would compute TQ, BQ, and OQ, as well as the associated access measures for each of the fragments, and partition them further.

The second complication relates to the location of the block of attributes that should form one fragment. Our discussion so far assumed that the split point is unique and single and divides the CA matrix into an upper left-hand partition and a second partition formed by the rest of the attributes. The partition, however, may also be formed in the middle of the matrix. In this case, we need to modify the algorithm slightly. The leftmost column of the CA matrix is shifted to become the rightmost column and the topmost row is shifted to the bottom. The shift operation is followed by checking the $n-1$ diagonal positions to find the maximum z. The idea behind shifting is to move the block of attributes that should form a cluster to the topmost left corner of the matrix, where it can easily be identified. With the addition of the shift operation, the complexity of the partitioning algorithm increases by a factor of n and becomes $O(n^2)$.

Assuming that a shift procedure, called SHIFT, has already been implemented, the partitioning algorithm is given in Algorithm 3.4. The input of the PARTITION is the clustered affinity matrix CA, the relation R to be fragmented, and the attribute usage and access frequency matrices. The output is a set of fragments $F_R = \{R_1, R_2\}$, where $R_i \subseteq \{A_1, A_2 \ldots, A_n\}$ and $R_1 \cap R_2 =$ the key attributes of relation R. Note that for n-way partitioning, this routine should either be invoked iteratively, or implemented as a recursive procedure.

Example 3.19. When the PARTITION algorithm is applied to the CA matrix obtained for relation PROJ (Example 3.18), the result is the definition of fragments $F_{PROJ} = \{PROJ_1, PROJ_2\}$, where $PROJ_1 = \{A_1, A_3\}$ and $PROJ_2 = \{A_1, A_2, A_4\}$. Thus

$$PROJ_1 \quad = \{PNO, BUDGET\}$$
$$PROJ_2 = \{PNO, PNAME, LOC\}$$

Note that in this exercise we performed the fragmentation over the entire set of attributes rather than only on the non-key ones. The reason for this is the simplicity of the example. For that reason, we included PNO, which is the key of PROJ in $PROJ_2$ as well as in $PROJ_1$.   ◆

3.3.2.4 Checking for Correctness

We follow arguments similar to those of horizontal partitioning to prove that the PARTITION algorithm yields a correct vertical fragmentation.

Algorithm 3.4: PARTITION Algorithm

Input: CA: clustered affinity matrix; R: relation; ref: attribute usage matrix;
  acc: access frequency matrix
Output: F: set of fragments
begin
  {determine the z value for the first column}
  {the subscripts in the cost equations indicate the split point}
  calculate CTQ_{n-1} ;
  calculate CBQ_{n-1} ;
  calculate COQ_{n-1} ;
  $best \leftarrow CTQ_{n-1} * CBQ_{n-1} - (COQ_{n-1})^2$;
  repeat
    {determine the best partitioning}
    for i *from* $n-2$ *to* 1 *by* -1 **do**
      calculate CTQ_i ;
      calculate CBQ_i ;
      calculate COQ_i ;
      $z \leftarrow CTQ * CBQ_i - COQ_i^2$;
      if $z > best$ **then** $best \leftarrow z$ {record the split point within shift}
    call SHIFT(CA)
  until *no more SHIFT is possible* ;
  reconstruct the matrix according to the shift position ;
  $R_1 \leftarrow \Pi_{TA}(R) \cup K$;   {K is the set of primary key attributes of R}
  $R_2 \leftarrow \Pi_{BA}(R) \cup K$;
  $F \leftarrow \{R_1, R_2\}$
end

Completeness.

Completeness is guaranteed by the PARTITION algorithm since each attribute of the global relation is assigned to one of the fragments. As long as the set of attributes A over which the relation R is defined consists of

$$A = \bigcup R_i$$

completeness of vertical fragmentation is ensured.

Reconstruction.

We have already mentioned that the reconstruction of the original global relation is made possible by the join operation. Thus, for a relation R with vertical fragmentation $F_R = \{R_1, R_2, \ldots, R_r\}$ and key attribute(s) K,

$$R = \bowtie_K R_i, \forall R_i \in F_R$$

Therefore, as long as each R_i is complete, the join operation will properly reconstruct R. Another important point is that either each R_i should contain the key attribute(s) of R, or it should contain the system assigned tuple IDs (TIDs).

Disjointness.

As we indicated before, the disjointness of fragments is not as important in vertical fragmentation as it is in horizontal fragmentation. There are two cases here:

1. TIDs are used, in which case the fragments are disjoint since the TIDs that are replicated in each fragment are system assigned and managed entities, totally invisible to the users.

2. The key attributes are replicated in each fragment, in which case one cannot claim that they are disjoint in the strict sense of the term. However, it is important to realize that this duplication of the key attributes is known and managed by the system and does not have the same implications as tuple duplication in horizontally partitioned fragments. In other words, as long as the fragments are disjoint except for the key attributes, we can be satisfied and call them disjoint.

3.3.3 Hybrid Fragmentation

In most cases a simple horizontal or vertical fragmentation of a database schema will not be sufficient to satisfy the requirements of user applications. In this case a vertical fragmentation may be followed by a horizontal one, or vice versa, producing a tree-structured partitioning (Figure 3.19). Since the two types of partitioning strategies are applied one after the other, this alternative is called *hybrid* fragmentation. It has also been named *mixed* fragmentation or *nested* fragmentation.

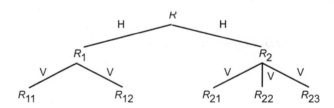

Fig. 3.19 Hybrid Fragmentation

A good example for the necessity of hybrid fragmentation is relation PROJ, which we have been working with. In Example 3.11 we partitioned it into six horizontal fragments based on two applications. In Example 3.19 we partitioned the same relation vertically into two. What we have, therefore, is a set of horizontal fragments, each of which is further partitioned into two vertical fragments.

The number of levels of nesting can be large, but it is certainly finite. In the case of horizontal fragmentation, one has to stop when each fragment consists of only one tuple, whereas the termination point for vertical fragmentation is one attribute per fragment. These limits are quite academic, however, since the levels of nesting in most practical applications do not exceed 2. This is due to the fact that normalized global relations already have small degrees and one cannot perform too many vertical fragmentations before the cost of joins becomes very high.

We will not discuss in detail the correctness rules and conditions for hybrid fragmentation, since they follow naturally from those for vertical and horizontal fragmentations. For example, to reconstruct the original global relation in case of hybrid fragmentation, one starts at the leaves of the partitioning tree and moves upward by performing joins and unions (Figure 3.20). The fragmentation is complete if the intermediate and leaf fragments are complete. Similarly, disjointness is guaranteed if intermediate and leaf fragments are disjoint.

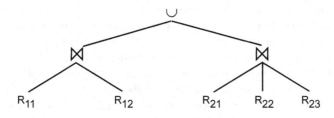

Fig. 3.20 Reconstruction of Hybrid Fragmentation

3.4 Allocation

The allocation of resources across the nodes of a computer network is an old problem that has been studied extensively. Most of this work, however, does not address the problem of distributed database design, but rather that of placing individual files on a computer network. We will examine the differences between the two shortly. We first need to define the allocation problem more precisely.

3.4.1 Allocation Problem

Assume that there are a set of fragments $F = \{F_1, F_2, \ldots, F_n\}$ and a distributed system consisting of sites $S = \{S_1, S_2, \ldots, S_m\}$ on which a set of applications $Q = \{q_1, q_2, \ldots, q_q\}$ is running. The allocation problem involves finding the "optimal" distribution of F to S.

The optimality can be defined with respect to two measures [Dowdy and Foster, 1982]:

1. *Minimal cost.* The cost function consists of the cost of storing each F_i at a site S_j, the cost of querying F_i at site S_j, the cost of updating F_i at all sites where it is stored, and the cost of data communication. The allocation problem, then, attempts to find an allocation scheme that minimizes a combined cost function.

2. *Performance.* The allocation strategy is designed to maintain a performance metric. Two well-known ones are to minimize the response time and to maximize the system throughput at each site.

Most of the models that have been proposed to date make this distinction of optimality. However, if one really examines the problem in depth, it is apparent that the "optimality" measure should include both the performance and the cost factors. In other words, one should be looking for an allocation scheme that, for example, answers user queries in minimal time while keeping the cost of processing minimal. A similar statement can be made for throughput maximization. One can then ask why such models have not been developed. The answer is quite simple: complexity.

Let us consider a *very* simple formulation of the problem. Let F and S be defined as before. For the time being, we consider only a single fragment, F_k. We make a number of assumptions and definitions that will enable us to model the allocation problem.

1. Assume that Q can be modified so that it is possible to identify the update and the retrieval-only queries, and to define the following for a *single* fragment F_k:

$$T = \{t_1, t_2, \ldots, t_m\}$$

where t_i is the read-only traffic generated at site S_i for F_k, and

$$U = \{u_1, u_2, \ldots, u_m\}$$

where u_i is the update traffic generated at site S_i for F_k.

2. Assume that the communication cost between any two pair of sites S_i and S_j is fixed for a unit of transmission. Furthermore, assume that it is different for updates and retrievals in order that the following can be defined:

$$C(T) = \{c_{12}, c_{13}, \ldots, c_{1m}, \ldots, c_{m-1,m}\}$$
$$C'(U) = \{c'_{12}, c'_{13}, \ldots, c'_{1m}, \ldots, c'_{m-1,m}\}$$

where c_{ij} is the unit communication cost for retrieval requests between sites S_i and S_j, and c'_{ij} is the unit communication cost for update requests between sites S_i and S_j.

3. Let the cost of storing the fragment at site S_i be d_i. Thus we can define $D = \{d_1, d_2, \ldots, d_m\}$ for the storage cost of fragment F_k at all the sites.

4. Assume that there are no capacity constraints for either the sites or the communication links.

Then the allocation problem can be specified as a cost-minimization problem where we are trying to find the set $I \subseteq S$ that specifies where the copies of the fragment will be stored. In the following, x_j denotes the decision variable for the placement such that

$$x_j = \begin{cases} 1 & \text{if fragment } F_k \text{ is assigned to site } S_j \\ 0 & \text{otherwise} \end{cases}$$

The precise specification is as follows:

$$\min \left[\sum_{i=1}^{m} \left(\sum_{j|S_j \in I} x_j u_j c'_{ij} + t_j \min_{j|S_j \in I} c_{ij} \right) + \sum_{j|S_j \in I} x_j d_j \right]$$

subject to

$$x_j = 0 \; or \; 1$$

The second term of the objective function calculates the total cost of storing all the duplicate copies of the fragment. The first term, on the other hand, corresponds to the cost of transmitting the updates to all the sites that hold the replicas of the fragment, and to the cost of executing the retrieval-only requests at the site, which will result in minimal data transmission cost.

This is a very simplistic formulation that is not suitable for distributed database design. But even if it were, there is another problem. This formulation, which comes from Casey [1972], has been proven to be NP-complete [Eswaran, 1974]. Various different formulations of the problem have been proven to be just as hard over the years (e.g., [Sacca and Wiederhold, 1985] and [Lam and Yu, 1980]). The implication is, of course, that for large problems (i.e., large number of fragments and sites), obtaining optimal solutions is probably not computationally feasible. Considerable research has therefore been devoted to finding good heuristics that may provide suboptimal solutions.

There are a number of reasons why simplistic formulations such as the one we have discussed are not suitable for distributed database design. These are inherent in all the early file allocation models for computer networks.

1. One cannot treat fragments as individual files that can be allocated one at a time, in isolation. The placement of one fragment usually has an impact on the placement decisions about the other fragments which are accessed together since the access costs to the remaining fragments may change (e.g., due to distributed join). Therefore, the relationship between fragments should be taken into account.

2. The access to data by applications is modeled very simply. A user request is issued at one site and all the data to answer it is transferred to that site. In distributed database systems, access to data is more complicated than this simple "remote file access" model suggests. Therefore, the relationship between the allocation and query processing should be properly modeled.

3. These models do not take into consideration the cost of integrity enforcement, yet locating two fragments involved in the same integrity constraint at two different sites can be costly.

4. Similarly, the cost of enforcing concurrency control mechanisms should be considered [Rothnie and Goodman, 1977].

In summary, let us remember the interrelationship between the distributed database problems as depicted in Figure 1.7. Since the allocation is so central, its relationship with algorithms that are implemented for other problem areas needs to be represented in the allocation model. However, this is exactly what makes it quite difficult to solve these models. To separate the traditional problem of file allocation from the fragment allocation in distributed database design, we refer to the former as the *file allocation problem* (FAP) and to the latter as the *database allocation problem* (DAP).

There are no general heuristic models that take as input a set of fragments and produce a near-optimal allocation subject to the types of constraints discussed here. The models developed to date make a number of simplifying assumptions and are applicable to certain specific formulations. Therefore, instead of presenting one or more of these allocation algorithms, we present a relatively general model and then discuss a number of possible heuristics that might be employed to solve it.

3.4.2 Information Requirements

It is at the allocation stage that we need the quantitative data about the database, the applications that run on it, the communication network, the processing capabilities, and storage limitations of each site on the network. We will discuss each of these in detail.

3.4.2.1 Database Information

To perform horizontal fragmentation, we defined the selectivity of minterms. We now need to extend that definition to fragments, and define the selectivity of a fragment F_j with respect to query q_i. This is the number of tuples of F_j that need to be accessed in order to process q_i. This value will be denoted as $sel_i(F_j)$.

Another piece of necessary information on the database fragments is their size. The size of a fragment F_j is given by

$$size(F_j) = card(F_j) * length(F_j)$$

where $length(F_j)$ is the length (in bytes) of a tuple of fragment F_j.

3.4.2.2 Application Information

Most of the application-related information is already compiled during the fragmentation activity, but a few more are required by the allocation model. The two important measures are the number of read accesses that a query q_i makes to a fragment F_j during its execution (denoted as RR_{ij}), and its counterpart for the update accesses (UR_{ij}). These may, for example, count the number of block accesses required by the query.

We also need to define two matrices UM and RM, with elements u_{ij} and r_{ij}, respectively, which are specified as follows:

$$u_{ij} = \begin{cases} 1 & \text{if query } q_i \text{ updates fragment } F_j \\ 0 & \text{otherwise} \end{cases}$$

$$r_{ij} = \begin{cases} 1 & \text{if query } q_i \text{ retrieves from fragment } F_j \\ 0 & \text{otherwise} \end{cases}$$

A vector O of values $o(i)$ is also defined, where $o(i)$ specifies the originating site of query q_i. Finally, to define the response-time constraint, the maximum allowable response time of each application should be specified.

3.4.2.3 Site Information

For each computer site, we need to know its storage and processing capacity. Obviously, these values can be computed by means of elaborate functions or by simple estimates. The unit cost of storing data at site S_k will be denoted as USC_k. There is also a need to specify a cost measure LPC_k as the cost of processing one unit of work at site S_k. The work unit should be identical to that of the RR and UR measures.

3.4.2.4 Network Information

In our model we assume the existence of a simple network where the cost of communication is defined in terms of one frame of data. Thus g_{ij} denotes the communication cost per frame between sites S_i and S_j. To enable the calculation of the number of messages, we use $fsize$ as the size (in bytes) of one frame. There is no question that there are more elaborate network models which take into consideration the channel capacities, distances between sites, protocol overhead, and so on. However, the derivation of those equations is beyond the scope of this chapter.

3.4.3 Allocation Model

We discuss an allocation model that attempts to minimize the total cost of processing and storage while trying to meet certain response time restrictions. The model we use has the following form:

min(Total Cost)

subject to

    response-time constraint
    storage constraint
    processing constraint

In the remainder of this section we expand the components of this model based on the information requirements discussed in Section 3.4.2. The decision variable is x_{ij}, which is defined as

$$x_{ij} = \begin{cases} 1 \text{ if the fragment } F_i \text{ is stored at site } S_j \\ 0 \text{ otherwise} \end{cases}$$

3.4.3.1 Total Cost

The total cost function has two components: query processing and storage. Thus it can be expressed as

$$TOC = \sum_{\forall q_i \in Q} QPC_i + \sum_{\forall S_k \in S} \sum_{\forall F_j \in F} STC_{jk}$$

where QPC_i is the query processing cost of application q_i, and STC_{jk} is the cost of storing fragment F_j at site S_k.

Let us consider the storage cost first. It is simply given by

$$STC_{jk} = USC_k * size(F_j) * x_{jk}$$

and the two summations find the total storage costs at all the sites for all the fragments.

The query processing cost is more difficult to specify. Most models of the file allocation problem (FAP) separate it into two components: the retrieval-only processing cost, and the update processing cost. We choose a different approach in our model of the database allocation problem (DAP) and specify it as consisting of the processing cost (PC) and the transmission cost (TC). Thus the query processing cost (QPC) for application q_i is

$$QPC_i = PC_i + TC_i$$

According to the guidelines presented in Section 3.4.1, the processing component, PC, consists of three cost factors, the access cost (AC), the integrity enforcement cost (IE), and the concurrency control cost (CC):

$$PC_i = AC_i + IE_i + CC_i$$

The detailed specification of each of these cost factors depends on the algorithms used to accomplish these tasks. However, to demonstrate the point, we specify AC in some detail:

$$AC_i = \sum_{\forall S_k \in S} \sum_{\forall F_j \in F} (u_{ij} * UR_{ij} + r_{ij} * RR_{ij}) * x_{jk} * LPC_k$$

The first two terms in the above formula calculate the number of accesses of user query q_i to fragment F_j. Note that $(UR_{ij} + RR_{ij})$ gives the total number of update and retrieval accesses. We assume that the local costs of processing them are identical. The summation gives the total number of accesses for all the fragments referenced by q_i. Multiplication by LPC_k gives the cost of this access at site S_k. We again use x_{jk} to select only those cost values for the sites where fragments are stored.

A very important issue needs to be pointed out here. The access cost function assumes that processing a query involves decomposing it into a set of subqueries, each of which works on a fragment stored at the site, followed by transmitting the results back to the site where the query has originated. As we discussed earlier, this is a very simplistic view which does not take into consideration the complexities of database processing. For example, the cost function does not take into account the cost of performing joins (if necessary), which may be executed in a number of ways, studied in Chapter 8. In a model that is more realistic than the generic model we are considering, these issues should not be omitted.

The integrity enforcement cost factor can be specified much like the processing component, except that the unit local processing cost would probably change to reflect the true cost of integrity enforcement. Since the integrity checking and concurrency control methods are discussed later in the book, we do not need to study these cost components further here. The reader should refer back to this section after reading Chapters 5 and 11 to be convinced that the cost functions can indeed be derived.

The transmission cost function can be formulated along the lines of the access cost function. However, the data transmission overhead for update and that for retrieval requests are quite different. In update queries it is necessary to inform all the sites where replicas exist, while in retrieval queries, it is sufficient to access only one of the copies. In addition, at the end of an update request, there is no data transmission back to the originating site other than a confirmation message, whereas the retrieval-only queries may result in significant data transmission.

The update component of the transmission function is

$$TCU_i = \sum_{\forall S_k \in S} \sum_{\forall F_j \in F} u_{ij} * x_{jk} * g_{o(i),k} + \sum_{\forall S_k \in S} \sum_{\forall F_j \in F} u_{ij} * x_{jk} * g_{k,o(i)}$$

The first term is for sending the update message from the originating site $o(i)$ of q_i to all the fragment replicas that need to be updated. The second term is for the confirmation.

The retrieval cost can be specified as

$$TCR_i = \sum_{\forall F_j \in F} \min_{S_k \in S}(r_{ij} * x_{jk} * g_{o(i),k} + r_{ij} * x_{jk} * \frac{sel_i(F_j) * length(F_j)}{fsize} * g_{k,o(i)})$$

The first term in TCR represents the cost of transmitting the retrieval request to those sites which have copies of fragments that need to be accessed. The second term accounts for the transmission of the results from these sites to the originating site. The equation states that among all the sites with copies of the same fragment, only the site that yields the minimum total transmission cost should be selected for the execution of the operation.

Now the transmission cost function for query q_i can be specified as

$$TC_i = TCU_i + TCR_i$$

which fully specifies the total cost function.

3.4.3.2 Constraints

The constraint functions can be specified in similar detail. However, instead of describing these functions in depth, we will simply indicate what they should look like. The response-time constraint should be specified as

execution time of $q_i \leq$ maximum response time of $q_i, \forall q_i \in Q$

Preferably, the cost measure in the objective function should be specified in terms of time, as it makes the specification of the execution-time constraint relatively straightforward.

The storage constraint is

$$\sum_{\forall F_j \in F} STC_{jk} \leq \text{storage capacity at site } S_k, \forall S_k \in S$$

whereas the processing constraint is

$$\sum_{\forall q_i \in Q} \text{processing load of } q_i \text{ at site } S_k \leq \text{processing capacity of } S_k, \forall S_k \in S$$

This completes our development of the allocation model. Even though we have not developed it entirely, the precision in some of the terms indicates how one goes about formulating such a problem. In addition to this aspect, we have indicated the important issues that need to be addressed in allocation models.

3.4.4 Solution Methods

In the preceding section we developed a generic allocation model which is considerably more complex than the FAP model presented in Section 3.4.1. Since the FAP model is NP-complete, one would expect the solution of this formulation of the database allocation problem (DAP) to be NP-complete as well. Even though we will not prove this conjecture, it is indeed true. Thus one has to look for heuristic methods that yield suboptimal solutions. The test of "goodness" in this case is, obviously, how close the results of the heuristic algorithm are to the optimal allocation.

A number of different heuristics have been applied to the solution of FAP and DAP models. It was observed early on that there is a correspondence between FAP and the plant location problem that has been studied in operations research. In fact, the isomorphism of the simple FAP and the single commodity warehouse location problem has been shown [Ramamoorthy and Wah, 1983]. Thus heuristics developed by operations researchers have commonly been adopted to solve the FAP and DAP problems. Examples are the knapsack problem solution [Ceri et al., 1982a], branch-and-bound techniques [Fisher and Hochbaum, 1980], and network flow algorithms [Chang and Liu, 1982].

There have been other attempts to reduce the complexity of the problem. One strategy has been to assume that all the candidate partitionings have been determined together with their associated costs and benefits in terms of query processing. The problem, then, is modeled so as to choose the optimal partitioning and placement for each relation [Ceri et al., 1983]. Another simplification frequently employed is to ignore replication at first and find an optimal non-replicated solution. Replication is handled at the second step by applying a greedy algorithm which starts with the non-replicated solution as the initial feasible solution, and tries to improve upon it ([Ceri et al., 1983] and [Ceri and Pernici, 1985]). For these heuristics, however, there is not enough data to determine how close the results are to the optimal.

3.5 Data Directory

The distributed database schema needs to be stored and maintained by the system. This information is necessary during distributed query optimization, as we will discuss later. The schema information is stored in a *data dictionary/directory*, also called a *catalog* or simply a directory. A directory is a meta-database that stores a number of information.

Within the context of the centralized ANSI/SPARC architecture discussed in Section 1.7.1, directory is the system component that permits mapping between different data organizational views. It should at least contain schema and mapping definitions. It may also contain usage statistics, access control information, and the like. It is clearly seen that the data dictionary/directory serves as the central component in both processing different schemas and in providing mappings among them.

In the case of a distributed database, as depicted in Figure 1.14 and discussed earlier in this chapter, schema definition is done at the global level (i.e., the global conceptual schema – GCS) as well as at the local sites (i.e., local conceptual schemas – LCSs). Consequently, there are two types of directories: a *global directory/dictionary* (GD/D)[5] that describes the database schema as the end users see it, and that permits the required global mappings between external schemas and the GCS, and the *local directory/dictionary* (LD/D), that describes the local mappings and describes the schema at each site. Thus, the local database management components are integrated by means of global DBMS functions.

As stated above, the directory is itself a database that contains *metadata* about the actual data stored in the database. Therefore, the techniques we discussed in this chapter with respect to distributed database design also apply to directory management. Briefly, a directory may be either *global* to the entire database or *local* to each site. In other words, there might be a single directory containing information about all the data in the database, or a number of directories, each containing the information stored at one site. In the latter case, we might either build hierarchies of directories to facilitate searches, or implement a distributed search strategy that involves considerable communication among the sites holding the directories.

The second issue has to do with location. In the case of a global directory, it may be maintained *centrally* at one site, or in a *distributed* fashion by distributing it over a number of sites. Keeping the directory at one site might increase the load at that site, thereby causing a bottleneck as well as increasing message traffic around that site. Distributing it over a number of sites, on the other hand, increases the complexity of managing directories. In the case of multi-DBMSs, the choice is dependent on whether or not the system is distributed. If it is, the directory is always distributed; otherwise of course, it is maintained centrally.

The final issue is replication. There may be a *single* copy of the directory or *multiple* copies. Multiple copies would provide more reliability, since the probability of reaching one copy of the directory would be higher. Furthermore, the delays

---

[5] In the remainder, we will simply refer to this as the *global directory*.

in accessing the directory would be lower, due to less contention and the relative proximity of the directory copies. On the other hand, keeping the directory up to date would be considerably more difficult, since multiple copies would need to be updated. Therefore, the choice should depend on the environment in which the system operates and should be made by balancing such factors as the response-time requirements, the size of the directory, the machine capacities at the sites, the reliability requirements, and the volatility of the directory (i.e., the amount of change experienced by the database, which would cause a change to the directory).

3.6 Conclusion

In this chapter, we presented the techniques that can be used for distributed database design with special emphasis on the fragmentation and allocation issues. There are a number of lines of research that have been followed in distributed database design. For example, Chang has independently developed a theory of fragmentation [Chang and Cheng, 1980], and allocation [Chang and Liu, 1982]. However, for its maturity of development, we have chosen to develop this chapter along the track developed by Ceri, Pelagatti, Navathe, and Wiederhold. Our references to the literature by these authors reflect this quite clearly.

There is a considerable body of literature on the allocation problem, focusing mostly on the simpler file allocation issue. We still do not have sufficiently general models that take into consideration all the aspects of data distribution. The model presented in Section 3.4 highlights the types of issues that need to be taken into account. Within this context, it might be worthwhile to take a somewhat different approach to the solution of the distributed allocation problem. One might develop a set of heuristic rules that might accompany the mathematical formulation and reduce the solution space, thus making the solution feasible.

We have discussed, in detail, the algorithms that one can use to fragment a relational schema in various ways. These algorithms have been developed quite independently and there is no underlying design methodology that combines the horizontal and vertical partitioning techniques. If one starts with a global relation, there are algorithms to decompose it horizontally as well as algorithms to decompose it vertically into a set of fragment relations. However, there are no algorithms that fragment a global relation into a set of fragment relations some of which are decomposed horizontally and others vertically. It is commonly pointed out that most real-life fragmentations would be mixed, i.e., would involve both horizontal and vertical partitioning of a relation, but the methodology research to accomplish this is lacking. What is needed is a distribution design methodology which encompasses the horizontal and vertical fragmentation algorithms and uses them as part of a more general strategy. Such a methodology should take a global relation together with a set of design criteria and come up with a set of fragments some of which are obtained via horizontal and others obtained via vertical fragmentation.

The second part of distribution design, namely allocation, is typically treated independently of fragmentation. The process is, therefore, linear when the output of fragmentation is input to allocation. At first sight, the isolation of the fragmentation and the allocation steps appears to simplify the formulation of the problem by reducing the decision space. However, closer examination reveals that isolating the two steps actually contributes to the complexity of the allocation models. Both steps have similar inputs, differing only in that fragmentation works on global relations whereas allocation considers fragment relations. They both require information about the user applications (e.g., how often they access data, what the relationships of individual data objects to one another are, etc.), but ignore how each other makes use of these inputs. The end result is that the fragmentation algorithms decide how to partition a relation based partially on how applications access it, but the allocation models ignore the part that this input plays in fragmentation. Therefore, the allocation models have to include all over again detailed specification of the relationship among the fragment relations and how user applications access them. What would be more promising is to formulate a methodology that more properly reflects the interdependence of the fragmentation and the allocation decisions. This requires extensions to existing distribution design strategies. We recognize that integrated methodologies such as the one we propose here may be considerably complex. However, there may be synergistic effects of combining these two steps enabling the development of quite acceptable heuristic solution methods. There are a few studies that follow such an integrated methodology (e.g., [Muro et al., 1983, 1985; Yoshida et al., 1985]). These methodologies build a simulation model of the distributed DBMS, taking as input a specific database design, and measure its effectiveness. Development of tools based on such methodologies, which aid the human designer rather than attempt to replace him, is probably the more appropriate approach to the design problem.

Another aspect of the work described in this chapter is that it assumes a static environment where design is conducted only once and this design can persist. Reality, of course, is quite different. Both physical (e.g., network characteristics, available storage at various sites) and logical (e.g., migration of applications from one site to another, access pattern modifications) changes occur necessitating redesign of the database. This problem has been studied to some extent. In a dynamic environment, the process becomes one of design-redesign-materialization of the redesign. The design step follows techniques that have been described in this chapter. Redesign can either be limited in that only parts of the database are affected, or total, requiring a complete redistribution [Wilson and Navathe, 1986]. Materialization refers to the reorganization of the distributed database to reflect the changes required by the redesign step. Limited redesign, in particular, the materialization issue is studied in [Rivera-Vega et al., 1990; Varadarajan et al., 1989]. Complete redesign and materialization issues have been studied in [Karlapalem et al., 1996b; Karlapalem and Navathe, 1994; Kazerouni and Karlapalem, 1997]. In particular, Kazerouni and Karlapalem [1997] describes a stepwise redesign methodology which involves a split phase where fragments are further subdivided based on the changed application requirements until no further subdivision is profitable based on a cost function. At this point, the merging phase starts where fragments that are accessed together by a set of applications are merged into one fragment.

3.7 Bibliographic Notes

Most of the known results about fragmentation have been covered in this chapter. Work on fragmentation in distributed databases initially concentrated on horizontal fragmentation. Most of the literature on this has been cited in the appropriate section. The topic of vertical fragmentation for distribution design has been addressed in several papers ([Navathe et al., 1984] and [Sacca and Wiederhold, 1985]. The original work on vertical fragmentation goes back to Hoffer's dissertation [Hoffer, 1975; Hoffer and Severance, 1975] and to Hammer and Niamir's work ([Niamir, 1978] and [Hammer and Niamir, 1979]).

It is not possible to be as exhaustive when discussing allocation as we have been for fragmentation, given there is no limit to the literature on the subject. The investigation of FAP on wide area networks goes back to Chu's work [Chu, 1969, 1973]. Most of the early work on FAP has been covered in the excellent survey by Dowdy and Foster [1982]. Some theoretical results about FAP are reported by Grapa and Belford [1977] and Kollias and Hatzopoulos [1981].

The DAP work dates back to the mid-1970s to the works of Eswaran [1974] and others. In their earlier work, Levin and Morgan [1975] concentrated on data allocation, but later they considered program and data allocation together [Morgan and Levin, 1977]. The DAP has been studied in many specialized settings as well. Work has been done to determine the placement of computers and data in a wide area network design [Gavish and Pirkul, 1986]. Channel capacities have been examined along with data placement [Mahmoud and Riordon, 1976] and data allocation on supercomputer systems [Irani and Khabbaz, 1982] as well as on a cluster of processors [Sacca and Wiederhold, 1985]. An interesting work is the one by Apers, where the relations are optimally placed on the nodes of a virtual network, and then the best matching between the virtual network nodes and the physical network are found [Apers, 1981].

Some of the allocation work has also touched upon physical design. The assignment of files to various levels of a memory hierarchy has been studied by Foster and Browne [1976] and by Navathe et al. [1984]. These are outside the scope of this chapter, as are those that deal with general resource and task allocation in distributed systems (e.g., [Bucci and Golinelli, 1977], [Ceri and Pelagatti, 1982], and [Haessig and Jenny, 1980]).

We should finally point out that some effort was spent to develop a general methodology for distributed database design along the lines that we presented (Figure 3.2). Ours is similar to the DATAID-D methodology [Ceri and Navathe, 1983; Ceri et al., 1987]. Other attempts to develop a methodology are due to Fisher et al. [1980], Dawson [1980]; Hevner and Schneider [1980] and Mohan [1979].

Exercises

Problem 3.1 (*). Given relation EMP as in Figure 3.3, let p_1: TITLE < "Programmer" and p_2: TITLE > "Programmer" be two simple predicates. Assume that character strings have an order among them, based on the alphabetical order.

(a) Perform a horizontal fragmentation of relation EMP with respect to $\{p_1, p_2\}$.
(b) Explain why the resulting fragmentation (EMP$_1$, EMP$_2$) does not fulfill the correctness rules of fragmentation.
(c) Modify the predicates p_1 and p_2 so that they partition EMP obeying the correctness rules of fragmentaion. To do this, modify the predicates, compose all minterm predicates and deduce the corresponding implications, and then perform a horizontal fragmentation of EMP based on these minterm predicates. Finally, show that the result has completeness, reconstruction and disjointness properties.

Problem 3.2 (*). Consider relation ASG in Figure 3.3. Suppose there are two applications that access ASG. The first is issued at five sites and attempts to find the duration of assignment of employees given their numbers. Assume that managers, consultants, engineers, and programmers are located at four different sites. The second application is issued at two sites where the employees with an assignment duration of less than 20 months are managed at one site, whereas those with longer duration are managed at a second site. Derive the primary horizontal fragmentation of ASG using the foregoing information.

Problem 3.3. Consider relations EMP and PAY in Figure 3.3. EMP and PAY are horizontally fragmented as follows:

$$EMP_1 = \sigma_{\text{TITLE="Elect.Eng."}}(EMP)$$
$$EMP_2 = \sigma_{\text{TITLE="Syst.Anal."}}(EMP)$$
$$EMP_3 = \sigma_{\text{TITLE="Mech.Eng."}}(EMP)$$
$$EMP_4 = \sigma_{\text{TITLE="Programmer"}}(EMP)$$

$$PAY_1 = \sigma_{\text{SAL} \geq 30000}(PAY)$$
$$PAY_2 = \sigma_{\text{SAL} < 30000}(PAY)$$

Draw the join graph of EMP $\ltimes_{\text{TITLE}}$ PAY. Is the graph simple or partitioned? If it is partitioned, modify the fragmentation of either EMP or PAY so that the join graph of EMP $\ltimes_{\text{TITLE}}$ PAY is simple.

Problem 3.4. Give an example of a *CA* matrix where the split point is not unique and the partition is in the middle of the matrix. Show the number of shift operations required to obtain a single, unique split point.

Problem 3.5 (**). Given relation PAY as in Figure 3.3, let p_1: SAL < 30000 and p_2: SAL $\geq$ 30000 be two simple predicates. Perform a horizontal fragmentation of PAY with respect to these predicates to obtain PAY$_1$, and PAY$_2$. Using the fragmentation of PAY, perform further derived horizontal fragmentation for EMP. Show completeness, reconstruction, and disjointness of the fragmentation of EMP.

Problem 3.6 (**). Let $Q = \{q_1, \ldots, q_5\}$ be a set of queries, $A = \{A_1, \ldots, A_5\}$ be a set of attributes, and $S = \{S_1, S_2, S_3\}$ be a set of sites. The matrix of Figure 3.21a describes the attribute usage values and the matrix of Figure 3.21b gives the application access frequencies. Assume that $ref_i(q_k) = 1$ for all q_k and S_i and that A_1 is the key attribute. Use the bond energy and vertical partitioning algorithms to obtain a vertical fragmentation of the set of attributes in A.

	A_1	A_2	A_3	A_4	A_5
q_1	0	1	1	0	1
q_2	1	1	1	0	1
q_3	1	0	0	1	1
q_4	0	0	1	0	0
q_5	1	1	1	0	0

	S_1	S_2	S_3
q_1	10	20	0
q_2	5	0	10
q_3	0	35	5
q_4	0	10	0
q_5	0	15	0

(a)   (b)

Fig. 3.21 Attribute Usage Values and Application Access Frequencies in Exercise 3.6

Problem 3.7 (**). Write an algorithm for derived horizontal fragmentation.

Problem 3.8 (**). Assume the following view definition

```
CREATE VIEW    EMPVIEW(ENO, ENAME, PNO, RESP)
AS         SELECT EMP.ENO, EMP.ENAME, ASG.PNO,
               ASG.RESP
           FROM    EMP, ASG
           WHERE   EMP.ENO=ASG.ENO
           AND     DUR=24
```

is accessed by application q_1, located at sites 1 and 2, with frequencies 10 and 20, respectively. Let us further assume that there is another query q_2 defined as

```
SELECT ENO, DUR
FROM    ASG
```

which is run at sites 2 and 3 with frequencies 20 and 10, respectively. Based on the above information, construct the $use(q_i, A_j)$ matrix for the attributes of both relations EMP and ASG. Also construct the affinity matrix containing all attributes of EMP and ASG. Finally, transform the affinity matrix so that it could be used to split the relation into two vertical fragments using heuristics or BEA.

Problem 3.9 (**). Formally define the three correctness criteria for derived horizontal fragmentation.

Problem 3.10 (*). Given a relation $R(K,A,B,C)$ (where K is the key) and the following query

```
SELECT *
FROM    R
WHERE   R.A = 10 AND R.B=15
```

(a) What will be the outcome of running PHF on this query?
(b) Does the COM_MIN algorithm produce in this case a complete and minimal predicate set? Justify your answer.

Problem 3.11 (*). Show that the bond energy algorithm generates the same results using either row or column operation.

Problem 3.12 (**). Modify algorithm PARTITION to allow n-way partitioning, and compute the complexity of the resulting algorithm.

Problem 3.13 (**). Formally define the three correctness criteria for hybrid fragmentation.

Problem 3.14. Discuss how the order in which the two basic fragmentation schemas are applied in hybrid fragmentation affects the final fragmentation.

Problem 3.15 (**). Describe how the following can be properly modeled in the database allocation problem.

(a) Relationships among fragments
(b) Query processing
(c) Integrity enforcement
(d) Concurrency control mechanisms

Problem 3.16 (**). Consider the various heuristic algorithms for the database allocation problem.

(a) What are some of the reasonable criteria for comparing these heuristics? Discuss.
(b) Compare the heuristic algorithms with respect to these criteria.

Problem 3.17 (*). Pick one of the heuristic algorithms used to solve the DAP, and write a program for it.

Problem 3.18 (**). Assume the environment of Exercise 3.8. Also assume that 60% of the accesses of query q_1 are updates to PNO and RESP of view EMPVIEW and that ASG.DUR is not updated through EMPVIEW. In addition, assume that the data transfer rate between site 1 and site 2 is half of that between site 2 and site 3. Based on the above information, find a reasonable fragmentation of ASG and EMP and an optimal replication and placement for the fragments, assuming that storage costs do not matter here, but copies are kept consistent.

Hint: Consider horizontal fragmentation for ASG based on DUR=24 predicate and the corresponding derived horizontal fragmentation for EMP. Also look at the affinity matrix obtained in Example 3.8 for EMP and ASG together, and consider whether it would make sense to perform a vertical fragmentation for ASG.

Chapter 4
Database Integration

In the previous chapter, we discussed top-down distributed database design, which is suitable for tightly integrated, homogeneous distributed DBMSs. In this chapter, we focus on bottom-up design that is appropriate in multidatabase systems. In this case, a number of databases already exist, and the design task involves integrating them into one database. The starting point of bottom-up design is the individual local conceptual schemas. The process consists of integrating local databases with their (local) schemas into a global database with its global conceptual schema (GCS) (also called the *mediated schema*).

Database integration, and the related problem of querying multidatabases (see Chapter 9), is only one part of the more general *interoperability* problem. In recent years, new distributed applications have started to pose new requirements regarding the data source(s) they access. In parallel, the management of "legacy systems" and reuse of the data they generate have gained importance. The result has been a renewed consideration of the broader question of information system interoperability, including non-database sources and interoperability at the application level in addition to the database level.

Database integration can be either physical or logical [Jhingran et al., 2002]. In the former, the source databases are integrated and the integrated database is *materialized*. These are known as *data warehouses*. The integration is aided by *extract-transform-load* (ETL) tools that enable extraction of data from sources, their transformation to match the GCS, and their loading (i.e., materialization). *Enterprise Application Integration* (EAI), which allows data exchange between applications, perform similar transformation functions, although data are not entirely materialized. This process is depicted in Figure 4.1. In logical integration, the global conceptual (or mediated) schema is entirely *virtual* and not materialized. This is also known as *Enterprise Information Integration* (EII)[1].

These two approaches are complementary and address differing needs. Data warehousing [Inmon, 1992; Jarke et al., 2003] supports decision support applications,

---

[1] It has been (rightly) argued that the second "I" should stand for Interoperability rather than Integration (see J. Pollock's contribution in [Halevy et al., 2005]).

M.T. Özsu and P. Valduriez, *Principles of Distributed Database Systems: Third Edition*,   131
DOI 10.1007/978-1-4419-8834-8_4, © Springer Science+Business Media, LLC 2011

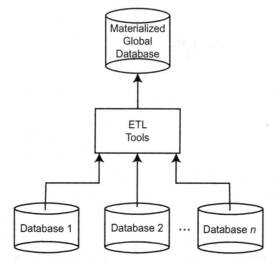

Fig. 4.1 Data Warehouse Approach

which are commonly termed *On-line Analytical Processing* (OLAP) [Codd, 1995] to better reflect their different requirements relative to the On-Line Transaction Processing (OLTP) applications. OLTP applications, such as airline reservation or banking systems, are high-throughput transaction-oriented. They need extensive data control and availability, high multiuser throughput and predictable, fast response times. In contrast, OLAP applications, such as trend analysis or forecasting, need to analyze historical, summarized data coming from a number of operational databases. They use complex queries over potentially very large tables. Because of their strategic nature, response time is important. The users are managers or analysts. Performing OLAP queries directly over distributed operational databases raises two problems. First, it hurts the OLTP applications' performance by competing for local resources. Second, the overall response time of the OLAP queries can be very poor because large quantities of data must be transferred over the network. Furthermore, most OLAP applications do not need the most current versions of the data, and thus do not need direct access to most up-to-date operational data. Consequently, data warehouses gather data from a number of operational databases and materialize them. As updates happen on the operational databases, they are propagated to the data warehouse (also referred to as *materialized view maintenance* [Gupta and Mumick, 1999b]).

By contrast, in logical data integration, the integration is only virtual and there is no materialized global database (see Figure 1.18). The data resides in the operational databases and the GCS provides a virtual integration for querying over them similar to the case described in the previous chapter. The difference is that the GCS may not be the union of the local conceptual schamas (LCSs). It is possible for the GCS not to capture all of the information in each of the LCSs. Furthermore, in some cases, the GCS may be defined bottom-up, by "integrating" parts of the LCSs of the local operational databases rather than being defined up-front (more on this shortly). User queries are posed over this global schema, which are then decomposed and shipped to the local operational databases for processing as is done in tightly-integrated systems. The main differences are the autonomy and potential heterogeneity of the local systems. These have important effects on query processing that we discuss in Chapter 9. Although there is ample work on transaction management in these systems, supporting global updates is quite difficult given the autonomy of the underlying operational DBMSs. Therefore, they are primarily read-only.

Logical data integration, and the resulting systems, are known by a variety of names; *data integration* and *information integration* are perhaps the most common terms used in literature. The generality of these terms point to the fact that the underlying data sources do not have to be databases. In this chapter we focus our attention on the integration of autonomous and (possibly) heterogeneous databases; thus we will use the term *database integration* (which also helps to distinguish these systems from data warehouses).

4.1 Bottom-Up Design Methodology

Bottom-up design involves the process by which information from participating databases can be (physically or logically) integrated to form a single cohesive multi-database. There are two alternative approaches. In some cases, the global conceptual (or mediated) schema is defined first, in which case the bottom-up design involves mapping LCSs to this schema. This is the case in data warehouses, but the practice is not restricted to these and other data integration methodologies may follow the same strategy. In other cases, the GCS is defined as an integration of parts of LCSs. In this case, the bottom-up design involves both the generation of the GCS and the mapping of individual LCSs to this GCS.

If the GCS is defined up-front, the relationship between the GCS and the local conceptual schemas (LCS) can be of two fundamental types [Lenzerini, 2002]: local-as-view, and global-as-view. In local-as-view (LAV) systems, the GCS definition exists, and each LCS is treated as a view definition over it. In global-as-view systems (GAV), on the other hand, the GCS is defined as a set of views over the LCSs. These views indicate how the elements of the GCS can be derived, when needed, from the elements of LCSs. One way to think of the difference between the two is in terms of the results that can be obtained from each system [Koch, 2001]. In GAV, the query results are constrained to the set of objects that are defined in the GCS, although the local DBMSs may be considerably richer (Figure 4.2a). In LAV, on the other hand, the results are constrained by the objects in the local DBMSs, while the GCS definition may be richer (Figure 4.2b). Thus, in LAV systems, it may be necessary to deal with incomplete answers. A combination of these two approaches has also been proposed as global-local-as-view (GLAV) [Friedman et al., 1999] where the relationship between GCS and LCSs is specified using both LAV and GAV.

Bottom-up design occurs in two general steps (Figure 4.3): *schema translation* (or simply *translation*) and *schema generation*. In the first step, the component

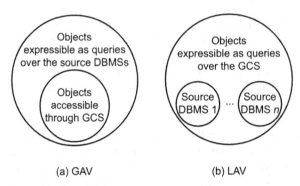

Fig. 4.2 GAV and LAV Mappings (Based on [Koch, 2001])

database schemas are translated to a common intermediate canonical representation $(InS_1, InS_2, \ldots, InS_n)$. The use of a canonical representation facilitates the translation process by reducing the number of translators that need to be written. The choice of the canonical model is important. As a principle, it should be one that is sufficiently expressive to incorporate the concepts available in all the databases that will later be integrated. Alternatives that have been used include the entity-relationship model [Palopoli et al., 1998, 2003b; He and Ling, 2006], object-oriented model [Castano and Antonellis, 1999; Bergamaschi et al., 2001], or a graph [Palopoli et al., 1999; Milo and Zohar, 1998; Melnik et al., 2002; Do and Rahm, 2002] that may be simplified to a tree [Madhavan et al., 2001]. The graph (tree) models have become more popular as XML data sources have proliferated, since it is fairly straightforward to map XML to graphs, although there are efforts to target XML directly [Yang et al., 2003]. In this chapter, we will simply use the relational model as our canonical data model, because we have been using it throughout the book, and the graph models used in literature are quite diverse with no common graph representation. The choice of the relational model as the canonical data representation does not affect in any fundamental way the discussion of the major issues of data integration. In any case, we will not discuss the specifics of translating various data models to relational; this can be found in many database textbooks.

Clearly, the translation step is necessary only if the component databases are heterogeneous and local schemas are defined using different data models. There has been some work on the development of system federation, in which systems with similar data models are integrated together (e.g., relational systems are integrated into one conceptual schema and, perhaps, object databases are integrated to another schema) and these integrated schemas are "combined" at a later stage (e.g., AURORA project [Yan, 1997; Yan et al., 1997]). In this case, the translation step is delayed, providing increased flexibility for applications to access underlying data sources in a manner that is suitable for their needs.

In the second step of bottom-up design, the intermediate schemas are used to generate a GCS. In some methodologies, *local external* (or *export*) *schemas* are considered for integration rather than full database schemas, to reflect the fact that

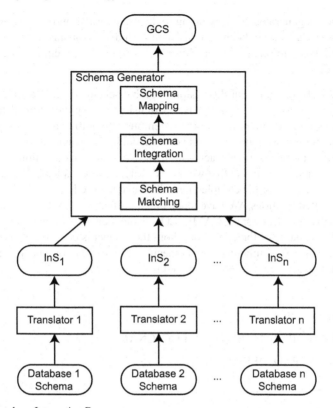

Fig. 4.3 Database Integration Process

local systems may only be willing to contribute some of their data to the multidatabase [Sheth and Larson, 1990].

The schema generation process consists of the following steps:

1. Schema matching to determine the syntactic and semantic correspondences among the translated LCS elements or between individual LCS elements and the pre-defined GCS elements (Section 4.2).

2. Integration of the common schema elements into a global conceptual (mediated) schema if one has not yet been defined (Section 4.3).

3. Schema mapping that determines how to map the elements of each LCS to the other elements of the GCS (Section 4.4).

It is also possible that the schema mapping step may be divided into two phases [Bernstein and Melnik, 2007]: mapping constraint generation and transformation generation. In the first phase, given correspondences between two schemas, a transformation function such as a query or view definition over the source schema is generated that would "populate" the target schema. In the second phase, an executable code is generated corresponding to this transformation function that would actually generate a target database consistent with these constraints. In some cases, the constraints are implicitly included in the correspondences, eliminating the need for the first phase.

Example 4.1. To facilitate our discussion of global schema design in multidatabase systems, we will use an example that is an extension of the engineering database we have been using throughout the book. To demonstrate both phases of the database integration process, we introduce some data model heterogeneity into our example.

Consider two organizations, each with their own database definitions. One is the (relational) database example that we have developed in Chapter 2. We repeat that definition in Figure 4.4 for completeness. The underscored attributes are the keys of the associated relations. We have made one modification in the PROJ relation by including attributes LOC and CNAME. LOC is the location of the project, whereas CNAME is the name of the client for whom the project is carried out. The second database also defined similar data, but is specified according to the entity-relationship (E-R) data model [Chen, 1976] as depicted in Figure 4.5.

EMP(ENO, ENAME, TITLE)

PROJ(PNO, PNAME, BUDGET, LOC, CNAME)

ASG(ENO, PNO, RESP, DUR)

PAY(TITLE, SAL)

Fig. 4.4 Relational Engineering Database Representation

We assume that the reader is familiar with the entity-relationship data model. Therefore, we will not describe the formalism, except to make the following points regarding the semantics of Figure 4.5. This database is similar to the relational engineering database definition of Figure 4.4, with one significant difference: it also maintains data about the clients for whom the projects are conducted. The rectangular boxes in Figure 4.5 represent the entities modeled in the database, and the diamonds indicate a relationship between the entities to which they are connected. The type of relationship is indicated around the diamonds. For example, the CONTRACTED-BY relation is a many-to-one from the PROJECT entity to the CLIENT entity (e.g., each project has a single client, but each client can have many projects). Similarly, the WORKS-IN relationship indicates a many-to-many relationship between the two connected relations. The attributes of entities and the relationships are shown as elliptical circles.   ♦

Example 4.2. The mapping of the E-R model to the relational model is given in Figure 4.6. Note that we have renamed some of the attributes in order to ensure name uniqueness.   ♦

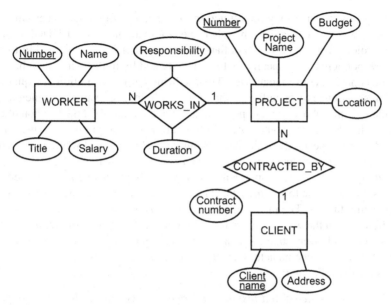

Fig. 4.5 Entity-Relationship Database

WORKER(<u>WNUMBER</u>, NAME, TITLE, SALARY)

PROJECT(<u>PNUMBER</u>, PNAME, BUDGET)

CLIENT(<u>CNAME</u>, ADDRESS)

WORKS_IN(<u>WNUMBER, PNUMBER</u>, RESPONSIBILITY, DURATION)

CONTRACTED_BY(<u>PNUMBER, CNAME</u>, CONTRACTNO)

Fig. 4.6 Relational Mapping of E-R Schema

4.2 Schema Matching

Schema matching determines which concepts of one schema match those of another. As discussed earlier, if the GCS has already been defined, then one of these schemas is typically the GCS, and the task is to match each LCS to the GCS. Otherwise, matching is done on two LCSs. The matches that are determined in this phase are then used in schema mapping to produce a set of directed mappings, which, when applied to the source schema, would map its concepts to the target schema.

The matches that are defined or discovered during schema matching are specified as a set of rules where each rule (r) identifies a *correspondence* (c) between two elements, a *predicate* (p) that indicates when the correspondence may hold, and a *similarity value* (s) between the two elements identified in the correspondence. A correspondence (c) may simply identify that two concepts are similar (which we will denote by $\approx$) or it may be a function that specifies that one concept may be derived by a computation over the other one (for example, if the BUDGET value of one project is specified in US dollars while the other one is specified in Euros, the correspondence may specify that one is obtained by multiplying the other one with the appropriate exchange rate). The predicate (p) is a condition that qualifies the correspondence by specifying when it might hold. For example, in the budget example specified above, p may specify that the rule holds only if the location of one project is in US while the other one is in the Euro zone. The similarity value (s) for each rule can be specified or calculated. Similarity values are real values in the range [0,1]. Thus, a set of matches can be defined as $\mathcal{M} = \{r\}$ where $r = \langle c, p, s \rangle$.

As indicated above, correspondences may either be discovered or specified. As much as it is desirable to automate this process, as we discuss below, there are many complicating factors. The most important is schema heterogeneity, which refers to the differences in the way real-world phenomena are captured in different schemas. This is a critically important issue, and we devote a separate section to it (Section 4.2.1). Aside from schema heterogeneity, other issues that complicate the matching process are the following:

- *Insufficient schema and instance information:* Matching algorithms depend on the information that can be extracted from the schema and the existing data instances. In some cases there is some ambiguity of the terms due to the insufficient information provided about these items. For example, using short names or ambiguous abbreviations for concepts, as we have done in our examples, can lead to incorrect matching.

- *Unavailability of schema documentation:* In most cases, the database schemas are not well documented or not documented at all. Quite often, the schema designer is no longer available to guide the process. The lack of these vital information sources adds to the difficulty of matching.

- *Subjectivity of matching:* Finally, we need to note (and admit) that matching schema elements can be highly subjective; two designers may not agree on a single "correct" mapping. This makes the evaluation of a given algorithm's accuracy significantly difficult.

Despite these difficulties, serious progress has been made in recent years in developing algorithmic approaches to the matching problem. In this section, we discuss a number of these algorithms and the various approaches.

A number of issues affect the particular matching algorithm [Rahm and Bernstein, 2001]. The more important ones are the following:

- *Schema versus instance matching.* So far in this chapter, we have been focusing on schema integration; thus, our attention has naturally been on matching concepts of one schema to those of another. A large number of algorithms have been developed that work on "schema objects." There are others, however, that have focused instead on the data instances or a combination of schema information and data instances. The argument is that considering data instances can help alleviate some of the semantic issues discussed above. For example, if an attribute name is ambiguous, as in "contact-info", then fetching its data may help identify its meaning; if its data instances have the phone number format, then obviously it is the phone number of the contact agent, while long strings may indicate that it is the contact agent name. Furthermore, there are a large number of attributes, such as postal codes, country names, email addresses, that can be defined easily through their data instances.

Matching that relies solely on schema data may be more efficient, because it does not require a search over data instances to match the attributes. Furthermore, this approach is the only feasible one when few data instances are available in the matched databases, in which case learning may not be reliable. However, in peer-to-peer systems (see Chapter 16), there may not be a schema, in which case instance-based matching is the only appropriate approach.

- *Element-level vs. structure-level.* Some matching algorithms operate on individual schema elements while others also consider the structural relationships between these elements. The basic concept of the element-level approach is that most of the schema semantics are captured by the elements' names. However, this may fail to find complex mappings that span multiple attributes. Match algorithms that also consider structure are based on the belief that, normally, the structures of matchable schemas tend to be similar.

- *Matching cardinality.* Matching algorithms exhibit various capabilities in terms of cardinality of mappings. The simplest approaches use 1:1 mapping, which means that each element in one schema is matched with exactly one element in the other schema. The majority of proposed algorithms belong to this category, because problems are greatly simplified in this case. Of course there are many cases where this assumption is not valid. For example, an attribute named "Total price" could be mapped to the sum of two attributes in another schema named "Subtotal" and "Taxes". Such mappings require more complex matching algorithms that consider 1:M and N:M mappings.

These criteria, and others, can be used to come up with a taxonomy of matching approaches [Rahm and Bernstein, 2001]. According to this taxonomy (which we will follow in this chapter with some modifications), the first level of separation is between schema-based matchers versus instance-based matchers (Figure 4.7). Schema-based matchers can be further classified as element-level and structure-level, while for instance-based approaches, only element-level techniques are meaningful. At the lowest level, the techniques are characterized as either linguistic or constraint-based. It is at this level that fundamental differences between matching algorithms are exhibited and we focus on these algorithms in the remainder, discussing linguistic approaches in Section 4.2.2, constraint-based approaches in Section 4.2.3, and learning-based techniques in Section 4.2.4. Rahm and Bernstein [2001] refer to all of these as *individual matcher* approaches, and their combinations are possible by developing either *hybrid matchers* or *composite matchers* (Section 4.2.5).

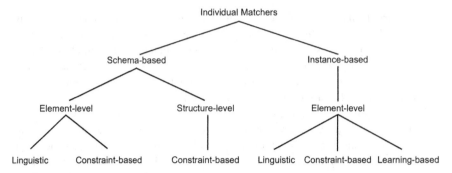

Fig. 4.7 Taxonomy of Schema Matching Techniques

4.2.1 Schema Heterogeneity

Schema matching algorithms deal with both structural heterogeneity and semantic heterogeneity among the matched schemas. We discuss these in this section before presenting the different match algorithms.

Structural conflicts occur in four possible ways: as *type conflicts*, *dependency conflicts*, *key conflicts*,, or *behavioral conflicts* [Batini et al., 1986]. Type conflicts occur when the same object is represented by an attribute in one schema and by an entity (relation) in another. Dependency conflicts occur when different relationship modes (e.g., one-to-one versus many-to-many) are used to represent the same thing in different schemas. Key conflicts occur when different candidate keys are available and different primary keys are selected in different schemas. Behavioral conflicts are implied by the modeling mechanism. For example, deleting the last item from one database may cause the deletion of the containing entity (i.e., deletion of the last employee causes the dissolution of the department).

Example 4.3. We have two structural conflicts in the example we are considering. The first is a type conflict involving clients of projects. In the schema of Figure 4.5, the client of a project is modeled as an entity. In the schema of Figure 4.4, however, the client is included as an attribute of the PROJ entity.

The second structural conflict is a dependency conflict involving the WORKS_IN relationship in Figure 4.5 and the ASG relation in Figure 4.4. In the former, the relationship is many-to-one from the WORKER to the PROJECT, whereas in the latter, the relationship is many-to-many. ◆

Structural differences among schemas are important, but their identification and resolution is not sufficient. Schema matching has to take into account the (possibly different) semantics of the schema concepts. This is referred to as *semantic hetero-geneity*, which is a fairly loaded term without a clear definition. It basically refers to the differences among the databases that relate to the meaning, interpretation, and intended use of data [Vermeer, 1997]. There are attempts to formalize semantic heterogeneity and to establish its link to structural heterogeneity [Kashyap and Sheth,

1996; Sheth and Kashyap, 1992]; we will take a more informal approach and discuss some of the semantic heterogeneity issues intuitively. The following are some of these problems that the match algorithms need to deal with.

- *Synonyms, homonyms, hypernyms.* Synonyms are multiple terms that all refer to the same concept. In our database example, PROJ and PROJECT refer to the same concept. Homonyms, on the other hand, occur when the same term is used to mean different things in different contexts. Again, in our example, BUDGET may refer to the gross budget in one database and it may refer to the net budget (after some overhead deduction) in another, making their simple comparison difficult. Hypernym is a term that is more generic than a similar word. Although there is no direct example of it in the databases we are considering, the concept of a Vehicle in one database is a hypernym for the concept of a Car in another (incidentally, in this case, Car is a *hyponym* of Vehicle). These problems can be addressed by the use of *domain ontologies* that define the organization of concepts and terms in a particular domain.

- *Different ontology:* Even if domain ontologies are used to deal with issues in one domain, it is quite often the case that schemas from different domains may need to be matched. In this case, one has to be careful of the meaning of terms across ontologies, as they can be highly dependent on the domain they are used in. For example, an attribute called "load" may imply a measure of resistance in an electrical ontology, but in a mechanical ontology, it may represent a measure of weight.

- *Imprecise wording:* Schemas may contain ambiguous names. For example the LOCATION and LOC attributes in our example database may refer to the full address or just the city name. Similarly, an attribute named "contact-info" may imply that the attribute contains the name of the contact agent or his/her telephone number. These types of ambiguities are common.

4.2.2 Linguistic Matching Approaches

Linguistic matching approaches, as the name implies, use element names and other textual information (such as textual descriptions/annotations in schema definitions) to perform matches among elements. In many cases, they may use external sources, such as thesauri, to assist in the process.

Linguistic techniques can be applied in both schema-based approaches and instance-based ones. In the former case, similarities are established among schema elements whereas in the latter, they are specified among elements of individual data instances. To focus our discussion, we will mostly consider schema-based linguistic matching approaches, briefly mentioning instance-based techniques. Consequently, we will use the notation $\langle$ SC1.element-1 $\approx$ SC2.element-2, $p, s \rangle$ to represent that element-1 in schema SC1 corresponds to element-2 in schema SC2 if predicate p

holds, with a similarity value of s. Matchers use these rules and similarity values to determine the similarity value of schema elements.

Linguistic matchers that operate at the schema element-level typically deal with the names of the schema elements and handle cases such as synonyms, homonyms, and hypernyms. In some cases, the schema definitions can have annotations (natural language comments) that may be exploited by the linguistic matchers. In the case of instance-based approaches, linguistic matchers focus on information retrieval techniques such as word frequencies, key terms, etc. In these cases, the matchers "deduce" similarities based on these information retrieval measures.

Schema linguistic matchers use a set of linguistic (also called terminological) rules that can be hand-crafted or may be "discovered" using auxiliary data sources such as thesauri, e.g., WordNet [Miller, 1995] (http://wordnet.princeton.edu/). In the case of hand-crafted rules, the designer needs to specify the predicate p and the similarity value s as well. For discovered rules, these may either be specified by an expert following the discovery, or they may be computed using one of the techniques we will discuss shortly.

The hand-crafted linguistic rules may deal with capitalization, abbreviations, concept relationships, etc. In some systems, the hand-crafted rules are specified for each schema individually (*intraschema rules*) by the designer, and *interschema rules* are then "discovered" by the matching algorithm [Palopoli et al., 1999]. However, in most cases, the rule base contains both intra and interschema rules.

Example 4.4. In the relational database of Example 4.2, the set of rules may have been defined (quite intuitively) as follows where RelDB refers to the relational schema and ERDB refers to the translated E-R schema:

⟨uppercase names $\approx$ lower case names, $true$, 1.0⟩
⟨uppercase names $\approx$ capitalized names, $true$, 1.0⟩
⟨capitalized names $\approx$ lower case names, $true$, 1.0⟩
⟨RelDB.ASG $\approx$ ERDB.WORKS_IN, $true$, 0.8⟩
  ...

The first three rules are generic ones specifying how to deal with capitalizations, while the fourth one specifies a similarity between the ASG element of RelDB and the WORKS_IN element of ERDB. Since these correspondences always hold, $p = true$.
◆

As indicated above, there are ways of determining the element name similarities automatically. For example, COMA [Do and Rahm, 2002] uses the following techniques to determine similarity of two element names:

- The *affixes*, which are the common prefixes and suffixes between the two element name strings are determined.

- The *n-grams* of the two element name strings are compared. An n-gram is a substring of length n and the similarity is higher if the two strings have more n-grams in common.

- The *edit distance* between two element name strings is computed. The edit distance (also called the Lewenstein metric) determines the number of character modifications (additions, deletions, insertions) that one has to perform on one string to convert it to the second string.

- The *soundex code* of the element names is computed. This gives the phonetic similarity between names based on their soundex codes. Soundex code of English words are obtained by hashing the word to a letter and three numbers. This hash value (roughly) corresponds to how the word would sound. The important aspect of this code in our context is that two words that sound similar will have close soundex codes.

Example 4.5. Consider matching the RESP and the RESPONSIBILITY attributes in the two example schemas we are considering. The rules defined in Example 4.4 take care of the capitalization differences, so we are left with matching RESP with RESPONSIBILITY. Let us consider how the similarity between these two strings can be computed using the edit distance and the n-gram approaches.

The number of editing changes that one needs to do to convert one of these strings to the other is 10 (either we add the characters 'O', 'N', 'S', 'I', 'B', 'I', 'L', 'I', 'T', 'Y', to RESP or delete the same characters from RESPONSIBILITY). Thus the ratio of the required changes is $10/14$, which defines the edit distance between these two strings; $1 - (10/14) = 4/14 = 0.29$ is then their similarity.

For n-gram computation, we need to first fix the value of n. For this example, let $n = 3$, so we are looking for 3-grams. The 3-grams of RESP are 'RES' and 'ESP'. Similarly, there are twelve 3-grams of RESPONSIBILITY: 'RES', 'ESP', 'SPO', 'PON', 'ONS', 'NSI', 'SIB', 'IBI', 'BIP', 'ILI', 'LIT', and 'ITY'. There are two matching 3-grams out of twelve, giving a 3-gram similarity of $2/12 = 0.17$.   ◆

The examples we have covered in this section all fall into the category of 1:1 matches – we matched one element of a particular schema to an element of another schema. As discussed earlier, it is possible to have 1:N (e.g., Street address, City, and Country element values in one database can be extracted from a single Address element in another), N:1 (e.g., Total_price can be calculated from Subtotal and Taxes elements), or N:M (e.g., Book_title, Rating information can be extracted via a join of two tables one of which holds book information and the other maintains reader reviews and ratings). Rahm and Bernstein [2001] suggest that 1:1, 1:N, and N:1 matchers are typically used in element-level matching while schema-level matching can also use N:M matching, since, in the latter case the necessary schema information is available.

4.2.3 Constraint-based Matching Approaches

Schema definitions almost always contain semantic information that constrain the values in the database. These are typically data type information, allowable ranges for data values, key constraints, etc. In the case of instance-based techniques, the existing ranges of the values can be extracted as well as some patterns that exist in the instance data. These can be used by matchers.

Consider data types that capture a large amount of semantic information. This information can be used to disambiguate concepts and also focus the match. For example, RESP and RESPONSIBILITY have relatively low similarity values according to computations in Example 4.5. However, if they have the same data type definition, this may be used to increase their similarity value. Similarly, the data type comparison may differentiate between elements that have high lexical similarity. For example, ENO in Figure 4.4 has the same edit distance and n-gram similarity values to the two NUMBER attributes in Figure 4.5 (of course, we are referring to the *names* of these attributes). In this case, the data types may be of assistance – if the data type of both ENO and worker number (WORKER.NUMBER) are integer while the data type of project number (PROJECT.NUMBER) is a string, the likelihood of ENO matching WORKER.NUMBER is significantly higher.

In structure-based approaches, the structural similarities in the two schemas can be exploited in determining the similarity of the schema elements. If two schema elements are structurally similar, this enhances our confidence that they indeed represent the same concept. For example, if two elements have very different names and we have not been able to establish their similarity through element matchers, but they have the same properties (e.g., same attributes) that have the same data types, then we can be more confident that these two elements may be representing the same concept.

The determination of structural similarity involves checking the similarity of the "neighborhoods" of the two concepts under consideration. Definition of the neighborhood is typically done using a graph representation of the schemas [Madhavan et al., 2001; Do and Rahm, 2002] where each concept (relation, entity, attribute) is a node and there is a directed edge between two nodes if and only if the two concepts are related (e.g., there is an edge from a relation node to each of its attributes, or there is an edge from a foreign key attribute node to the primary key attribute node it is referencing). In this case, the neighborhood can be defined in terms of the nodes that can be reached within a certain path length of each concept, and the problem reduces to checking the similarity of the subgraphs in this neighborhood.

The traversing of the graph can be done in a number of ways; for example CUPID [Madhavan et al., 2001] converts the graphs to trees and then looks at similarities of subtrees rooted at the two nodes in consideration, while COMA [Do and Rahm, 2002] considers the paths from the root to these element nodes. The fundamental point of these algorithms is that if the subgraphs are similar, this increases the similarity of the roots of these subtrees. The similarity of the subgraphs are determined in a bottom-up process, starting at the leaves whose similarity are determined using element matching (e.g., name similarity to the level of synonyms, or data type compatibility). The similarity of the two subtrees is recursively determined based on the similarity of the nodes in the subtree. A number of formulae may be used to for this recursive computation. CUPID, for example, looks at the similarity of two leaf nodes and if it is higher than a threshold value, then those two leaf nodes are said to be *strongly linked*. The similarity of two subgraphs is then defined as the fraction of leaves in the two subtrees that are strongly linked. This is based on the assumption that leafs carry more information and that the structural similarity of two non-leaf schema elements is determined by the similarity of the leaf nodes in their respective subtrees, even if their immediate children are not similar. These are heuristic rules and it is possible to define others.

Another interesting approach to considering neighborhood in directed graphs while computing similarity of nodes is *similarity flooding* [Melnik et al., 2002]. It starts from an initial graph where the node similarities are already determined by means of an element matcher, and propagates, iteratively, to determine the similarity of each node to its neighbors. Hence, whenever any two elements in two schemas are found to be similar, the similarity of their adjacent nodes increases. The iterative process stops when the node similarities stabilize. At each iteration, to reduce the amount of work, a subset of the nodes are selected as the "most plausible" matches, which are then considered in the subsequent iteration.

Both of these approaches are agnostic to the edge semantics. In some graph representations, there is additional semantics attached to these edges. For example, *containment edges* from a relation or entity node to its attributes may be distinguished from *referential edges* from a foreign key attribute node to the corresponding primary key attribute node. Some systems exploit these edge semantics (e.g., DIKE [Palopoli et al., 1998, 2003a]).

4.2.4 Learning-based Matching

A third alternative approach that has been proposed is to use machine learning techniques to determine schema matches. Learning-based approaches formulate the problem as one of classification where concepts from various schemas are classified into classes according to their similarity. The similarity is determined by checking the features of the data instances of the databases that correspond to these schemas. How to classify concepts according to their features is learned by studying the data instances in a training data set.

The process is as follows (Figure 4.8). A training set (τ) is prepared that consists of instances of example correspondences between the concepts of two databases D_i and D_j. This training set can be generated after manual identification of the schema correspondences between two databases followed by extraction of example training data instances [Doan et al., 2003a], or by the specification of a query expression that converts data from one database to another [Berlin and Motro, 2001]. The learner uses this training data to acquire probabilistic information about the features of the data sets. The classifier, when given two other database instances (D_k and D_l), then uses this knowledge to go through the data instances in D_k and D_l and make predictions about classifying the elements of D_k and D_l.

This general approach applies to all of the proposed learning-based schema matching approaches. Where they differ is the type of learner that they use and how they adjust this learner's behavior for schema matching. Some have used neural networks (e.g., SEMINT [Li and Clifton, 2000; Li et al., 2000]), others have used Naïve Bayesian learner/classifier (Autoplex [Berlin and Motro, 2001], LSD [Doan

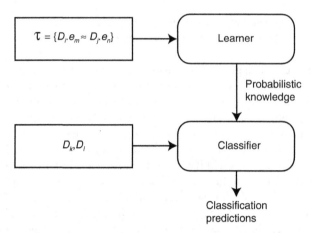

Fig. 4.8 Learning-based Matching Approach

et al., 2001, 2003a] and [Naumann et al., 2002]), and decision trees [Embley et al., 2001, 2002]. Discussing the details of these learning techniques are beyond our scope.

4.2.5 Combined Matching Approaches

The individual matching techniques that we have considered so far have their strong points and their weaknesses. Each may be more suitable for matching certain cases. Therefore, a "complete" matching algorithm or methodology usually needs to make use of more than one individual matcher.

There are two possible ways in which matchers can be combined [Rahm and Bernstein, 2001]: hybrid and composite. *Hybrid* algorithms combine multiple matchers within one algorithm. In other words, elements from two schemas can be compared using a number of element matchers (e.g., string matching as well as data type matching) and/or structural matchers within one algorithm to determine their overall similarity. Careful readers will have noted that in discussing the constraint-based matching algorithms that focused on structural matching, we followed a hybrid approach since they were based on an initial similarity determination of, for example, the leaf nodes using an element matcher, and these similarity values were then used in structural matching. *Composite* algorithms, on the other hand, apply each matcher to the elements of the two schemas (or two instances) individually, obtaining individual similarity scores, and then they apply a method for combining these similarity scores. More precisely, if $s_i(C_j^k, C_l^m)$ is the similarity score using matcher i ($i = 1, ..., q$) over two concepts C_j from schema k and C_l from schema m, then the composite similarity of the two concepts is given by $s(C_j^k, C_l^m) = f(s_1, ..., s_q)$ where f is the function that is used to combine the similarity scores. This function can be as simple as average, max, or min, or it can be an adaptation of more complicated ranking aggregation functions [Fagin, 2002] that we will discuss further in Chapter 9. Composite approach has been proposed in the LSD [Doan et al., 2001, 2003a] and iMAP [Dhamankar et al., 2004] systems for handling 1:1 and N:M matches, respectively.

4.3 Schema Integration

Once schema matching is done, the correspondences between the various LCSs have been identified. The next step is to create the GCS, and this is referred to as *schema integration*. As indicated earlier, this step is only necessary if a GCS has not already been defined and matching was performed on individual LCSs. If the GSC was defined up-front, then the matching step would determine correspondences between it and each of the LCSs and there would be no need for the integration step. If the GCS is created as a result of the integration of LCSs based on correspondences identified during schema matching, then, as part of integration, it is important to identify the correspondences between the GCS and the LCSs. Although tools (e.g., [Sheth et al., 1988a]) have been developed to aid in the integration process, human involvement is clearly essential.

Example 4.6. There are a number of possible integrations of the two example LCSs we have been discussing. Figure 4.9 shows one possible GCS that can be generated as a result of schema integration.   ◆

Employee(<u>ENUMBER</u>, ENAME, TITLE)

Pay(<u>TITLE</u>, SALARY)

Project(<u>PNUMBER</u>, PNAME, BIDGET, LOCATION)

Client(<u>CNAME</u>, ADDRESS, CONTRACTNO, PNUMBER)

Works(<u>ENUMBER, PNUMBER</u>, RESP, DURATION)

Fig. 4.9 Example Integrated GCS

Integration methodologies can be classified as binary or *n*ary mechanisms [Batini et al., 1986] based on the manner in which the local schemas are handled in the first phase (Figure 4.10). Binary integration methodologies involve the manipulation of two schemas at a time. These can occur in a stepwise (ladder) fashion (Figure 4.11a) where intermediate schemas are created for integration with subsequent schemas [Pu, 1988], or in a purely binary fashion (Figure 4.11b), where each schema is integrated with one other, creating an intermediate schema for integration with other intermediate schemas ([Batini and Lenzirini, 1984] and [Dayal and Hwang, 1984]).

Other binary integration approaches do not make this distinction [Melnik et al., 2002].

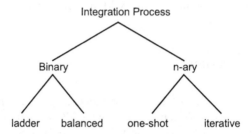

Fig. 4.10 Taxonomy of Integration Methodologies

*N*ary integration mechanisms integrate more than two schemas at each iteration. One-pass integration (Figure 4.12a) occurs when all schemas are integrated at once, producing the global conceptual schema after one iteration. Benefits of this approach include the availability of complete information about all databases at integration time. There is no implied priority for the integration order of schemas, and the trade-offs, such as the best representation for data items or the most understandable structure, can be made between all schemas rather than between a few. Difficulties with this approach include increased complexity and difficulty of automation.

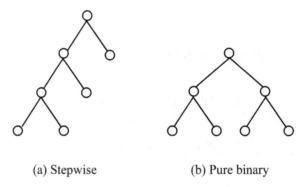

(a) Stepwise   (b) Pure binary

Fig. 4.11 Binary Integration Methods

Iterative *n*ary integration (Figure 4.12b) offers more flexibility (typically, more information is available) and is more general (the number of schemas can be varied depending on the integrator's preferences). Binary approaches are a special case of iterative *n*ary. They decrease the potential integration complexity and lead toward automation techniques, since the number of schemas to be considered at each step is more manageable. Integration by an *n*ary process enables the integrator to perform the operations on more than two schemas. For practical reasons, the majority of

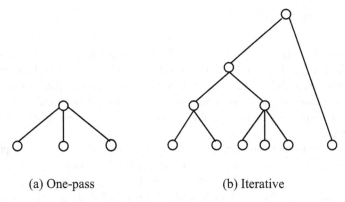

(a) One-pass   (b) Iterative

Fig. 4.12 *N*ary Integration Methods

systems utilize binary methodology, but a number of researchers prefer the *n*ary approach because complete information is available ([Elmasri et al., 1987; Yao et al., 1982b; He et al., 2004]).

4.4 Schema Mapping

Once a GCS (or mediated schema) is defined, it is necessary to identify how the data from each of the local databases (source) can be mapped to GCS (target) while preserving semantic consistency (as defined by both the source and the target). Although schema matching has identified the correspondences between the LCSs and the GCS, it may not have identified explicitly how to obtain the global database from the local ones. This is what schema mapping is about.

In the case of data warehouses, schema mappings are used to explicitly extract data from the sources, and translate them to the data warehouse schema for populating it. In the case of data integration systems, these mappings are used in query processing phase by both the query processor and the wrappers (see Chapter 9).

There are two issues related to schema mapping that we will be studying: *mapping creation*, and *mapping maintenance*. Mapping creation is the process of creating explicit queries that map data from a local database to the global data. Mapping maintenance is the detection and correction of mapping inconsistencies resulting from schema evolution. Source schemas may undergo structural or semantic changes that invalidate mappings. Mapping maintenance is concerned with the detection of broken mappings and the (automatic) rewriting of mappings such that semantic consistency with the new schema and semantic equivalence with the current mapping are achieved.

4.4.1 *Mapping Creation*

Mapping creation starts with a source LCS, the target GCS, and a set of schema matches $\mathcal{M}$ and produces a set of queries that, when executed, will create GCS data instances from the source data. In data warehouses, these queries are actually executed to create the data warehouse (global database) while in data integration systems, these queries are used in the reverse direction during query processing (Chapter 9).

Let us make this more concrete by referring to the canonical relational representation that we have adopted. The source LCS under consideration consists of a set of relations $\mathcal{S} = \{S_1, \ldots, S_m\}$, the GCS consists of a set of global (or target) relations $\mathcal{T} = \{T_1, \ldots, T_n\}$, and $\mathcal{M}$ consists of a set of schema match rules as defined in Section 4.2. We are looking for a way to generate, for each T_k, a query Q_k that is defined on a (possibly proper) subset of the relations in $\mathcal{S}$ such that, when executed, will generate data for T_k from the source relations.

An algorithm due to Miller et al. [2000] accomplishes this iteratively by considering each T_k in turn. It starts with $M_k \subseteq \mathcal{M}$ (M_k is the set of rules that only apply to the attributes of T_k) and divides it into subsets $\{M_k^1, \ldots, M_k^s\}$ such that each M_k^j specifies one possible way that values of T_k can be computed. Each M_k^j can be mapped to a query q_k^j that, when executed, would generate *some* of T_k's data. The union of all of these queries gives $Q_k(= \cup_j q_k^j)$ that we are looking for.

The algorithm proceeds in four steps that we discuss below. It does not consider the similarity values in the rules. It can be argued that the similarity values would be used in the final stages of the matching process to finalize correspondences, so that their use during mapping is unnecessary. Furthermore, by the time this phase of the integration process is reached, the concern is how to map source relation (LCS) data to target relation (GCS) data. Consequently, correspondences are not symmetric equivalences ($\approx$), but mappings ($\mapsto$): attribute(s) from (possibly multiple) source relations are mapped to an attribute of a target relation (i.e., $(S_i.attribute_k, S_j.attribute_l) \mapsto T_w.attribute_z)$).

Example 4.7. To demonstrate the algorithm, we will use a different example database than what we have been working with, because it does not incorporate all the complexities that we wish to demonstrate. Instead, we will use the following abstract example.

Source relations (LCS):

$S_1(A_1, A_2)$
$S_2(B_1, B_2, B_3)$
$S_3(C_1, C_2, C_3)$
$S_4(D_1, D_2)$

Target relation (GCS)

$T(W_1, W_2, W_3, W_4)$

We consider only one relation in GCS, since the algorithm iterates over target relations one-at-a-time, so this is sufficient to demonstrate the operation of the algorithm.

The foreign key relationships between the attributes are as follows:

Foreign key	Refers to
A_1	B_1
A_2	B_1
C_1	B_1

The following matches have been discovered for attributes of relation T (these make up M_T). In the subsequent examples, we will not be concerned with the predicates, so they are not explicitly specified.

$$r_1 = \langle A_1 \mapsto W_1, p \rangle$$
$$r_2 = \langle A_2 \mapsto W_2, p \rangle$$
$$r_3 = \langle B_2 \mapsto W_4, p \rangle$$
$$r_4 = \langle B_3 \mapsto W_3, p \rangle$$
$$r_5 = \langle C_1 \mapsto W_1, p \rangle$$
$$r_6 = \langle C_2 \mapsto W_2, p \rangle$$
$$r_7 = \langle D_1 \mapsto W_4, p \rangle$$

◆

In the first step, M_k (corresponding to T_k) is partitioned into its subsets $\{M_k^1, \ldots, M_k^n\}$ such that each M_k^j contains at most one match for each attribute of T_k. These are called *potential candidate sets*, some of which may be *complete* in that they include a match for every attribute of T_k, but others may not be. The reasons for considering incomplete sets are twofold. First, it may be the case that no match is found for one or more attributes of the target relation (i.e., none of the match sets are complete). Second, for large and complex database schemas, it may make sense to build the mapping iteratively so that the designer specifies the mappings incrementally.

Example 4.8. M_T is partitioned into the following fifty-three subsets (i.e., potential candidate sets). The first eight of these are complete, while the rest are not. To make it easier to read, the complete rules are listed in the order of the target attributes to which they map (e.g., the third rule in M_T^1 is r_4, because this rule maps to attribute W_3):

$$M_T^1 = \{r_1, r_2, r_4, r_3\} \quad M_T^2 = \{r_1, r_2, r_4, r_7\}$$
$$M_T^3 = \{r_1, r_6, r_4, r_3\} \quad M_T^4 = \{r_1, r_6, r_4, r_7\}$$
$$M_T^5 = \{r_5, r_2, r_4, r_3\} \quad M_T^6 = \{r_5, r_2, r_4, r_7\}$$
$$M_T^7 = \{r_5, r_6, r_4, r_3\} \quad M_T^8 = \{r_5, r_6, r_4, r_7\}$$
$$M_T^9 = \{r_1, r_2, r_3\} \quad M_T^{10} = \{r_1, r_2, r_4\}$$
$$M_T^{11} = \{r_1, r_3, r_4\} \quad M_T^{12} = \{r_2, r_3, r_4\}$$

$$M_T^{13} = \{r_1, r_3, r_6\} \qquad M_T^{14} = \{r_3, r_4, r_6\}$$

$$\cdots \qquad\qquad\qquad \cdots$$

$$M_T^{47} = \{r_1\} \qquad\qquad M_T^{48} = \{r_2\}$$
$$M_T^{49} = \{r_3\} \qquad\qquad M_T^{50} = \{r_4\}$$
$$M_T^{51} = \{r_5\} \qquad\qquad M_T^{52} = \{r_6\}$$
$$M_T^{53} = \{r_7\}$$

$\blacklozenge$

In the second step, the algorithm analyzes each potential candidate set M_k^j to see if a "good" query can be produced for it. If all the matches in M_k^j map values from a single source relation to T_k, then it is easy to generate a query corresponding to M_k^j. Of particular concern are matches that require access to multiple source relations. In this case the algorithm checks to see if there is a referential connection between these relations through foreign keys (i.e., whether there is a join path through the source relations). If there isn't, then the potential candidate set is eliminated from further consideration. In case there are multiple join paths through foreign key relationships, the algorithm looks for those paths that will produce the most number of tuples (i.e., the estimated difference in size of the outer and inner joins is the smallest). If there are multiple such paths, then the database designer needs to be involved in selecting one (tools such as Clio [Miller et al., 2001], OntoBuilder [Roitman and Gal, 2006] and others facilitate this process and provide mechanisms for designers to view and specify correspondences [Yan et al., 2001]). The result of this step is a set $\overline{M_k} \subseteq M_k$ of *candidate sets*.

Example 4.9. In this example, there is no M_k^j where the values of all of T's attributes are mapped from a single source relation. Among those that involve multiple source relations, rules that involve S_1, S_2 and S_3 can be mapped to "good" queries since there are foreign key relationships between them. However, the rules that involve S_4 (i.e., those that include rule r_7) cannot be mapped to a "good" query since there is no join path from S_4 to the other relations (i.e., any query would involve a cross product, which is expensive). Thus, these rules are eliminated from the potential candidate set. Considering only the complete sets, M_k^2, M_k^4, M_k^6, and M_k^8 are pruned from the set. In the end, the candidate set $(\overline{M_k})$ contains thirty-five rules (the readers are encouraged to verify this to better understand the algorithm). $\blacklozenge$

In the third step, the algorithm looks for a cover of the candidate sets $\overline{M_k}$. The cover $\mathcal{C}_k \subseteq \overline{M_k}$ is a set of candidate sets such that each match in $\overline{M_k}$ appears in $\mathcal{C}_k$ at least once. The point of determining a cover is that it accounts for all of the matches and is, therefore, sufficient to generate the target relation T_k. If there are multiple covers (a match can participate in multiple covers), then they are ranked in increasing number of the candidate sets in the cover. The fewer the number of candidate sets in the cover, the fewer are the number of queries that will be generated in the next step; this improves the efficiency of the mappings that are generated. If there are multiple covers with the same ranking, then they are further ranked in decreasing order of the total number of unique target attributes that are used in the candidate sets constituting the cover. The point of this ranking is that covers with higher number of attributes generate fewer null values in the result. At this stage, the designer may need to be consulted to choose from among the ranked covers.

Example 4.10. First note that we have six rules that define matches in $\overline{M_k}$ that we need to consider, since M_k^j that include rule r_7 have been eliminated. There are a large number of possible covers; let us start with those that involve M_k^1 to demonstrate the algorithm:

$$\mathcal{C}_T^1 = \{\underbrace{\{r_1, r_2, r_4, r_3\}}_{M_T^1}, \underbrace{\{r_1, r_6, r_4, r_3\}}_{M_T^3}, \underbrace{\{r_2\}}_{M_T^{48}}\}$$

$$\mathcal{C}_T^2 = \{\underbrace{\{r_1, r_2, r_4, r_3\}}_{M_T^1}, \underbrace{\{r_5, r_2, r_4, r_3\}}_{M_T^5}, \underbrace{\{r_6\}}_{M_T^{50}}\}$$

$$\mathcal{C}_T^3 = \{\underbrace{\{r_1, r_2, r_4, r_3\}}_{M_T^1}, \underbrace{\{r_5, r_6, r_4, r_3\}}_{M_T^7}\}$$

$$\mathcal{C}_T^4 = \{\underbrace{\{r_1, r_2, r_4, r_3\}}_{M_T^1}, \underbrace{\{r_5, r_6, r_4\}}_{M_T^{12}}\}$$

$$\mathcal{C}_T^5 = \{\underbrace{\{r_1, r_2, r_4, r_3\}}_{M_T^1}, \underbrace{\{r_5, r_6, r_3\}}_{M_T^{19}}\}$$

$$\mathcal{C}_T^6 = \{\underbrace{\{r_1, r_2, r_4, r_3\}}_{M_T^1}, \underbrace{\{r_5, r_6\}}_{M_T^{32}}\}$$

At this point we observe that the covers consist of either two or three candidate sets. Since the algorithm prefers those with fewer candidate sets, we only need to focus on those involving two sets. Furthermore, among these covers, we note that the number of target attributes in the candidate sets differ. Since the algorithm prefers covers with the largest number of target attributes in each candidate set, $\mathcal{C}_T^3$ is the preferred cover in this case.

Note that due to the two heuristics employed by the algorithm, the only covers we need to consider are those that involve M_T^1, M_T^3, M_T^5, and M_T^7. Similar covers can be defined involving M_T^3, M_T^5, and M_T^7; we leave that as an exercise. In the remainder, we will assume that the designer has chosen to use $\mathcal{C}_T^3$ as the preferred cover. ◆

The final step of the algorithm builds a query q_k^j for each of the candidate sets in the cover selected in the previous step. The union of all of these queries (UNION ALL) results in the final mapping for relation T_k in the GCS.

Query q_k^j is built as follows:

- SELECT clause includes all correspondences (c) in each of the rules (r_k^i) in M_k^j.

- FROM clause includes all source relations mentioned in r_k^i and in the join paths determined in Step 2 of the algorithm.
- WHERE clause includes conjunct of all predicates (p) in r_k^i and all join predicates determined in Step 2 of the algorithm.
- If r_k^i contains an aggregate function either in c or in p
    - GROUP BY is used over attributes (or functions on attributes) in the SELECT clause that are not within the aggregate;
    - If aggregate is in the correspondence c, it is added to SELECT, else (i.e., aggregate is in the predicate p) a HAVING clause is created with the aggregate.

Example 4.11. Since in Example 4.10 we have decided to use cover $\mathcal{C}_T^3$ for the final mapping, we need to generate two queries: q_T^1 and q_T^7 corresponding to M_T^1 and M_T^7, respectively. For ease of presentation, we list the rules here again:

$$r_1 = \langle A_1 \mapsto W_1, p \rangle$$
$$r_2 = \langle A_2 \mapsto W_2, p \rangle$$
$$r_3 = \langle B_2 \mapsto W_4, p \rangle$$
$$r_4 = \langle B_3 \mapsto W_3, p \rangle$$
$$r_5 = \langle C_1 \mapsto W_1, p \rangle$$
$$r_6 = \langle C_2 \mapsto W_2, p \rangle$$

The two queries are as follows:

q_k^1 : SELECT A_1, A_2, B_2, B_3
    FROM S_1, S_2
    WHERE p_1 AND p_2 AND p_3 AND p_4
             AND $S_1.A_1 = S_2.B_1$ AND $S_1.A_2 = S_2.B_1$

q_k^7 : SELECT B_2, B_3, C_1, C_2
    FROM S_2, S_3
    WHERE p_3 AND p_4 AND p_5 AND p_6
             AND $S_3.c_1 = S_2.B_1$

Thus, the final query Q_k for target relation T becomes q_k^1 UNION ALL q_k^7.   ♦

The output of this algorithm, after it is iteratively applied to each target relation T_k is a set of queries $\mathcal{Q} = \{Q_k\}$ that, when executed, produce data for the GCS relations. Thus, the algorithm produces GAV mappings between relational schemas – recall that GAV defines a GCS as a view over the LCSs and that is exactly what the set of mapping queries do. The algorithm takes into account the semantics of the source schema since it considers foreign key relationships in determining which queries to generate. However, it does not consider the semantics of the target, so that the tuples that are generated by the execution of the mapping queries are not guaranteed to satisfy target semantics. This is not a major issue in the case when the GCS is integrated from the LCSs; however, if the GCS is defined independent of the LCSs, then this is problematic.

It is possible to extend the algorithm to deal with target semantics as well as source semantics. This requires that inter-schema tuple-generating dependencies be considered. In other words, it is necessary to produce GLAV mappings. A GLAV mapping, by definition, is not simply a query over the source relations; it is a relationship between a query over the source (i.e., LCS) relations and a query over the target (i.e., GCS) relations. Let us be more precise. Consider a schema match v that specifies a correspondence between attribute A of a source LCS relation S and attribute B of a target GCS relation T (in the notation we used in this section we have $v = \langle S.A \approx T.B, p, s \rangle$). Then the source query specifies how to retrieve $S.A$ and the target query specifies how to obtain $T.B$. The GLAV mapping, then, is a relationship between these two queries.

An algorithm to accomplish this [Popa et al., 2002] also starts, as above, with a source schema, a target schema, and $\mathcal{M}$, and "discovers" mappings that satisfy both the source and the target schema semantics. The algorithm is also more powerful than the one we discussed in this section in that it can handle nested structures that are common in XML, object databases, and nested relational systems.

The first step in discovering all of the mappings based on schema match correspondences is *semantic translation*, which seeks to interpret schema matches in $\mathcal{M}$ in a way that is consistent with the semantics of both the source and target schemas as captured by the schema structure and the referential (foreign key) constraints. The result is a set of *logical mappings* each of which captures the design choices (semantics) made in both source and target schemas. Each logical mapping corresponds to one target schema relation. The second step is *data translation* that implements each logical mapping as a rule that can be translated into a query that would create an instance of the target element when executed.

Semantic translation takes as inputs the source $\mathcal{S}$ and target schemas $\mathcal{T}$, and $\mathcal{M}$ and performs the following two steps:

- It examines intra-schema semantics within the $\mathcal{S}$ and $\mathcal{T}$ separately and produces for each a set of *logical relations* that are semantically consistent.

- It then interprets inter-schema correspondences $\mathcal{M}$ in the context of logical relations generated in Step 1 and produces a set of queries into $\mathcal{Q}$ that are semantically consistent with $\mathcal{T}$.

4.4.2 Mapping Maintenance

In dynamic environments where schemas evolve over time, schema mappings can be made invalid as the result of structural or constraint changes made to the schemas.

Thus, the detection of invalid/inconsistent schema mappings and the adaptation of such schema mappings to new schema structures/constraints becomes important.

In general, automatic detection of invalid/inconsistent schema mappings is desirable as the complexity of the schemas, and the number of schema mappings used in database applications, increases. Likewise, (semi-)automatic adaptation of mappings to schema changes is also a goal. It should be noted that automatic adaptation of schema mappings is not the same as automatic schema matching. Schema adaptation aims to resolve semantic correspondences using known changes in intra-schema semantics, semantics in existing mappings, and detected semantic inconsistencies (resulting from schema changes). Schema matching must take a much more "from scratch" approach at generating schema mappings and does not have the ability (or luxury) of incorporating such contextual knowledge.

4.4.2.1 Detecting invalid mappings

In general, detection of invalid mappings resulting from schema change can either happen proactively, or reactively. In proactive detection environments, schema mappings are tested for inconsistencies as soon as schema changes are made by a user. The assumption (or requirement) is that the mapping maintenance system is completely aware of any and all schema changes, as soon as they are made. The ToMAS system [Velegrakis et al., 2004], for example, expects users to make schema changes through its own schema editors, making the system immediately aware of any schema changes. Once schema changes have been detected, invalid mappings can be detected by doing a semantic translation of the existing mappings using the logical relations of the updated schema.

In reactive detection environments, the mapping maintenance system is unaware of when and what schema changes are made. To detect invalid schema mappings in this setting, mappings are tested at regular intervals by performing queries against the data sources and translating the resulting data using the existing mappings. Invalid mappings are then determined based on the results of these mapping tests.

An alternative method that has been proposed is to use machine learning techniques to detect invalid mappings (as in the Maveric system [McCann et al., 2005]). What has been proposed is to build an ensemble of trained *sensors* (similar to multiple learners in schema matching) to detect invalid mappings. Examples of such sensors include value sensors for monitoring distribution characteristics of target instance values, trend sensors for monitoring the average rate of data modification, and layout and constraint sensors that monitor translated data against expected target schema syntax and semantics. A weighted combination of the findings of the individual sensors is then calculated where the weights are also learned. If the combined result indicates changes and follow-up tests suggest that this may indeed be the case, an alert is generated.

4.4.2.2 Adapting invalid mappings

Once invalid schema mappings are detected, they must be adapted to schema changes and made valid once again. Various high-level mapping adaptation approaches have been proposed [Velegrakis et al., 2004]. These can be broadly described as *fixed rule approaches* that define a re-mapping rule for every type of expected schema change, *map bridging approaches* that compare original schema S and the updated schema S', and generate new mapping from S to S' in addition to existing mappings, and *semantic rewriting approaches*, which exploit semantic information encoded in existing mappings, schemas, and semantic changes made to schemas to propose map rewritings that produce semantically consistent target data. In most cases, multiple such rewritings are possible, requiring a ranking of the candidates for presentation to users who make the final decision (based on scenario- or business-level semantics not encoded in schemas or mappings).

Arguably, a complete remapping of schemas (i.e. from scratch, using schema matching techniques) is another alternative to mapping adaption. However, in most cases, map rewriting is cheaper than map regeneration as rewriting can exploit knowledge encoded in existing mappings to avoid computation of mappings that would be rejected by the user anyway (and to avoid redundant mappings).

4.5 Data Cleaning

Errors in source databases can always occur, requiring cleaning in order to correctly answer user queries. Data cleaning is a problem that arises in both data warehouses and data integration systems, but in different contexts. In data warehouses where data are actually extracted from local operational databases and materialized as a global database, cleaning is performed as the global database is created. In the case of data integration systems, data cleaning is a process that needs to be performed during query processing when data are returned from the source databases.

The errors that are subject to data cleaning can generally be broken down into either schema-level or instance-level concerns [Rahm and Do, 2000]. Schema-level problems can arise in each individual LCS due to violations of explicit and implicit constraints. For example, values of attributes may be outside the range of their domains (e.g. 14th month or negative salary value), attribute values may violate implicit dependencies (e.g., the age attribute value may not correspond to the value that is computed as the difference between the current date and the birth date), uniqueness of attribute values may not hold, and referential integrity constraints may be violated. Furthermore, in the environment that we are considering in this chapter, the schema-level heterogeneities (both structural and semantic) among the LCSs that we discussed earlier can all be considered problems that need to be resolved. At the schema level, it is clear that the problems need to be identified at the schema match stage and fixed during schema integration.

Instance level errors are those that exist at the data level. For example, the values of some attributes may be missing although they were required, there could be misspellings and word transpositions (e.g., "M.D. Mary Smith" versus "Mary Smith, M.D.") or differences in abbreviations (e.g., "J. Doe" in one source database while "J.N. Doe" in another), embedded values (e.g., an aggregate address attribute that includes street name, value, province name, and postal code), values that were erroneously placed in other fields, duplicate values, and contradicting values (the salary value appearing as one value in one database and another value in another database). For instance-level cleaning, the issue is clearly one of generating the mappings such that the data are cleaned through the execution of the mapping functions (queries).

The popular approach to data cleaning has been to define a number of operators that operate either on schemas or on individual data. The operators can be composed into a data cleaning plan. Example schema operators add or drop columns from table, restructure a table by combining columns or splitting a column into two [Raman and Hellerstein, 2001], or define more complicated schema transformation through a generic "map" operator [Galhardas et al., 2001] that takes a single relation and produces one ore more relations. Example data level operators include those that apply a function to every value of one attribute, merging values of two attributes into the value of a single attribute and its converse split operator [Raman and Hellerstein, 2001], a matching operator that computes an approximate join between tuples of two relations, clustering operator that groups tuples of a relation into clusters, and a tuple merge operator that partitions the tuples of a relation into groups and collapses the tuples in each group into a single tuple through some aggregation over them [Galhardas et al., 2001], as well as basic operators to find duplicates and eliminate them (this has long been known as the purge/merge problem [Hernández and Stolfo, 1998]). Many of the data level operators compare individual tuples of two relations (from the same or different schemas) and decide whether or not they represent the same fact. This is similar to what is done in schema matching, except that it is done at the individual data level and what is considered are not individual attribute values, but entire tuples. However, the same techniques we studied under schema matching (e.g., use of edit distance or soundex value) can be used in this context. There have been proposals for special techniques for handling this efficiently within the context of data cleaning (e.g., [Chaudhuri et al., 2003]).

Given the large amount of data that needs to be handled, data level cleaning is expensive and efficiency is a significant issue. The physical implementation of each of the operators we discussed above is a considerable concern. Although cleaning can be done off-line as a batch process in the case of data warehouses, for data integration systems, cleaning needs to be done online as data are retrieved from the sources. The performance of data cleaning is, of course, more critical in the latter case. In fact, the performance and scalability concerns in the latter systems have resulted in proposals where data cleaning is forfeited in favor of querying that is tolerant to conflicts [Yan and Özsu, 1999].

4.6 Conclusion

In this chapter we discussed the bottom-up database design process, which we called database integration. This is the process of creating a GCS (or a mediated schema) and determining how each LCS maps to it. A fundamental separation is between data warehouses where the GCS is instantiated and materialized, and data integration systems where the GCS is merely a virtual view.

Although the topic of database integration has been studied extensively for a long time, almost all of the work has been fragmented. Individual projects focus on schema matching, or data cleaning, or schema mapping. There is a serious lack of research that considers end-to-end methodology for database integration. The lack of a methodology is made more serious by the fact that each of these research activities work on different assumptions related to data models, types of heterogeneities and so on. A notable exception is the work of Bernstein and Melnik [2007], which provides the beginnings of a comprehensive "end-to-end" methodology. This is probably the most important topic that requires attention.

A related concept that has received considerable discussion in literature is *data exchange*. This is defined as "the problem of taking data structured under a source schema and creating an instance of a target schema that reflects the source data as accurately as possible." [Fagin et al., 2005]. This is very similar to the physical integration (i.e., materialized) data integration, such as data warehouses, that we discussed in this chapter. A difference between data warehouses and the materialization approaches as addressed in data exchange environments is that data warehouse data typically belongs to one organization and can be structured according to a well-defined schema while in data exchange environments data may come from different sources and contain heterogeneity [Doan et al., 2010]. However, for most of the discussions of this chapter, this is not a major concern.

Our focus in this chapter has been on integrating *databases*. Increasingly, however, the data that are used in distributed applications involve those that are not in a database. An interesting new topic of discussion among researchers is the integration of *structured* data that is stored in databases and *unstructured* data that is maintained in other systems (Web servers, multimedia systems, digital libraries, etc) [Halevy et al., 2003; Somani et al., 2002]. In next generation systems, ability to handle both types of data will be increasingly important.

Another issue that we ignored in this chapter is interoperability when a GCS does not exist or cannot be specified. As we discussed in Chapter 1, there have been early objections to interoperable access to multiple data sources through a GCS, arguing instead that the languages should provide facilities to access multiple heterogeneous sources without requiring a GCS. The issue becomes critical in the modern peer-to-peer systems where the scale and the variety of data sources make it quite difficult (if not impossible) to design a GCS. We will discuss data integration in peer-to-peer systems in Chapter 16.

4.7 Bibliographic Notes

A large volume of literature exists on the topic of this chapter. The work goes back to early 1980's and which is nicely surveyed by Batini et al. [1986]. Subsequent work is nicely covered by Elmagarmid et al. [1999] and Sheth and Larson [1990].

There is an upcoming book on this topic that provides the broadest coverage of the subject [Doan et al., 2010]. There are a number of recent overview papers on the topic. Bernstein and Melnik [2007] provides a very nice discussion of the integration methodology. It goes further by comparing the model management work with some of the data integration research. Halevy et al. [2006] reviews the data integration work in the 1990's, focusing on the Information Manifold system [Levy et al., 1996c], that uses a LAV approach. The paper provides a large bibliography and discusses the research areas that have been opened in the intervening years. Haas [2007] takes a comprehensive approach to the entire integration process and divides it into four phases: understanding that involves discovering relevant information (keys, constraints, data types, etc), analyzing it to assess quality, an to determine statistical properties; standardization whereby the best way to represent the integrated information is determined; specification, that involves the configuration of the integration process; and execution, which is the actual integration. The specification phase includes the techniques defined in this paper. Doan and Halevy [2005] is another very good overview of the various schema matching techniques. They propose a different, and simpler, classification of the techniques as rule-based, learning-based, and combined.

A large number of systems have been developed that have tested the LAV versus GAV approaches. Many of these focus on querying over integrated systems, so we will discuss them in Chapter 9. Examples of LAV approaches are described in the papers [Duschka and Genesereth, 1997; Levy et al., 1996a; Manolescu et al., 2001] while examples of GAV are presented in papers [Adali et al., 1996a; Garcia-Molina et al., 1997; Haas et al., 1997b].

Topics of structural and semantic heterogeneity have occupied researchers for quite some time. While the literature on this topic is quite extensive, some of the interesting publications that discuss structural heterogeneity are and those that focus on semantic heterogeneity are [Dayal and Hwang, 1984; Kim and Seo, 1991; Breitbart et al., 1986; Krishnamurthy et al., 1991] [Hull, 1997; Ouksel and Sheth, 1999; Kashyap and Sheth, 1996; Bright et al., 1994; Ceri and Widom, 1993]. We should note that this list is seriously incomplete.

More recent works in schema matching are surveyed by Rahm and Bernstein [2001] and Doan and Halevy [2005]. In particular, Rahm and Bernstein [2001] gives a very nice comparison of various proposals.

A number of systems have been developed demonstrating the feasibility of various schema matching approaches. Among rule-based techniques, one can cite DIKE [Palopoli et al., 1998, 2003b,a], DIPE, which is an earlier version of this system [Palopoli et al., 1999], TranSCM [Milo and Zohar, 1998], ARTEMIS [Bergamaschi et al., 2001], similarity flooding [Melnik et al., 2002], CUPID [Madhavan et al., 2001], and COMA [Do and Rahm, 2002].

Exercises

Problem 4.1. Distributed database systems and distributed multidatabase systems represent two different approaches to systems design. Find three real-life applications for which each of these approaches would be more appropriate. Discuss the features of these applications that make them more favorable for one approach or the other.

Problem 4.2. Some architectural models favor the definition of a global conceptual schema, whereas others do not. What do you think? Justify your selection with detailed technical arguments.

Problem 4.3 (*). Give an algorithm to convert a relational schema to an entity-relationship one.

Problem 4.4 (**). Consider the two databases given in Figures 4.13 and 4.14 and described below. Design a global conceptual schema as a union of the two databases by first translating them into the E-R model.

DIRECTOR(<u>NAME</u>, PHONE_NO, ADDRESS)
LICENSES(<u>LIC_NO</u>, CITY, DATE, ISSUES, COST, DEPT, CONTACT)
RACER(<u>NAME, ADDRESS</u>, MEM_NUM)
SPONSOR(<u>SP_NAME</u>, CONTACT)
RACE(<u>R_NO</u>, LIC_NO, DIR, MAL_WIN, FRM_WIN, SP_NAME)

Fig. 4.13 Road Race Database

Figure 4.13 describes a relational race database used by organizers of road races and Figure 4.14 describes an entity-relationship database used by a shoe manufacturer. The semantics of each of these database schemas is discussed below. Figure 4.13 describes a relational road race database with the following semantics:

DIRECTOR is a relation that defines race directors who organize races; we assume that each race director has a unique name (to be used as the key), a phone number, and an address.

LICENSES is required because all races require a governmental license, which is issued by a CONTACT in a department who is the ISSUER, possibly contained within another government department DEPT; each license has a unique LIC_NO (the key), which is issued for use in a specific CITY on a specific DATE with a certain COST.

RACER is a relation that describes people who participate in a race. Each person is identified by NAME, which is not sufficient to identify them uniquely, so a compound key formed with the ADDRESS is required. Finally, each racer may have a MEM_NUM to identify him or her as a member of the racing fraternity, but not all competitors have membership numbers.

SPONSOR indicates which sponsor is funding a given race. Typically, one sponsor funds a number of races through a specific person (CONTACT), and a number of races may have different sponsors.

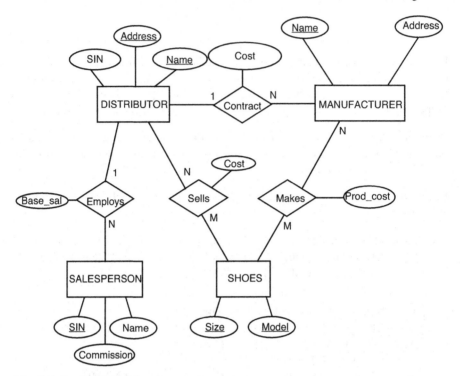

Fig. 4.14 Sponsor Database

RACE uniquely identifies a single race which has a license number (LIC_NO) and
race number (R_NO) (to be used as a key, since a race may be planned without
acquiring a license yet); each race has a winner in the male and female groups
(MAL_WIN and FEM_WIN) and a race director (DIR).

Figure 4.14 illustrates an entity-relationship schema used by the sponsor's database
system with the following semantics:

SHOES are produced by sponsors of a certain MODEL and SIZE, which forms the
key to the entity.

MANUFACTURER is identified uniquely by NAME and resides at a certain AD-
DRESS.

DISTRIBUTOR is a person that has a NAME and ADDRESS (which are necessary
to form the key) and a SIN number for tax purposes.

SALESPERSON is a person (entity) who has a NAME, earns a COMMISSION,
and is uniquely identified by his or her SIN number (the key).

Makes is a relationship that has a certain fixed production cost (PROD_COST). It
indicates that a number of different shoes are made by a manufacturer, and that
different manufacturers produce the same shoe.

Sells is a relationship that indicates the wholesale COST to a distributor of shoes. It
indicates that each distributor sells more than one type of shoe, and that each type
of shoe is sold by more than one distributor.

Contract is a relationship whereby a distributor purchases, for a COST, exclusive rights to represent a manufacturer. Note that this does not preclude the distributor from selling different manufacturers' shoes.

Employs indicates that each distributor hires a number of salespeople to sell the shoes; each earns a BASE_SALARY.

Problem 4.5 (*). Consider three sources:

- Database 1 has one relation Area(Id, Field) providing areas of specialization of employees; the Id field identifies an employee.

- Database 2 has two relations, Teach(Professor, Course) and In(Course, Field); Teach indicates the courses that each professor teaches and In that specifies possible fields that a course can blong to.

- Database 3 has two relations, Grant(Researcher, GrantNo) for grants given to researchers, and For(GrantNo, Field) indicating which fields the grants are for.

The objective is to build a GCS with two relations: Works(Id, Project) stating that an employee works for a particular project, and Area(Project, Field) associating projects with one or more fields.

(a) Provide a LAV mapping between Database 1 and the GCS.
(b) Provide a GLAV mapping between the GCS and the local schemas.
(c) Suppose one extra relation, Funds(GrantNo, Project), is added to Database 3. Provide a GAV mapping in this case.

Problem 4.6. Consider a GCS with the following relation: Person(Name, Age, Gender). This relation is defined as a view over three LCSs as follows:

```
CREATE VIEW Person AS
SELECT Name, Age, "male" AS Gender
FROM   SoccerPlayer
UNION
SELECT Name, NULL AS Age, Gender
FROM   Actor
UNION
SELECT Name, Age, Gender
FROM   Politician
WHERE  Age > 30
```

For each of the following queries, discuss which of the three local schemas (SoccerPlayer, Actor, and Politician) contribute to the global query result.

(a) `SELECT Name FROM person`
(b) `SELECT Name FROM Person`
     `WHERE Gender = "female"`
(c) `SELECT Name FROM Person WHERE Age > 25`
(d) `SELECT Name FROM Person WHERE Age < 25`
(e) `SELECT Name FROM Person`
     `WHERE Gender = "male" AND Age = 40`

Problem 4.7. A GCS with the relation Country(Name, Continent, Population, Has-Coast) describes countries of the world. The attribute HasCoast indicates if the country has direct access to the sea. Three LCSs are connected to the global schema using the LAV approach as follows:

```
CREATE VIEW EuropeanCountry AS
SELECT Name, Continent, Population, HasCoast
FROM   Country
WHERE  Continent = "Europe"

CREATE VIEW BigCountry AS
SELECT Name, Continent, Population, HasCoast
FROM   Country
WHERE  Population >= 30000000

CREATE VIEW MidsizeOceanCountry AS
SELECT Name, Continent, Population, HasCoast
FROM   Country
WHERE  HasCoast = true AND Population > 10000000
```

(a) For each of the following queries, discuss the results with respect to their completeness, i.e., verify if the (combination of the) local sources cover all relevant results.

1. ```
   SELECT Name FROM Country
   ```

2. ```
   SELECT Name FROM Country
   WHERE Population > 40
   ```

3. ```
   SELECT Name FROM Country
   WHERE Population > 20
   ```

(b) For each of the following queries, discuss which of the three LCSs are necessary for the global query result.

1. ```
   SELECT Name FROM Country
   ```

2. ```
   SELECT Name FROM Country
   WHERE Population > 30
   AND Continent = "Europe"
   ```

3. ```
   SELECT Name FROM Country
   WHERE Population < 30
   ```

4. ```
   SELECT Name FROM Country
   WHERE Population > 30
   AND HasCoast = true
   ```

Problem 4.8. Consider the following two relations PRODUCT and ARTICLE that are specified in a simplified SQL notation. The perfect schema matching correspondences are denoted by arrows.
   ```

PRODUCT $\longrightarrow$ ARTICLE
  Id: int PRIMARY KEY $\longrightarrow$ Key: varchar(255) PRIMARY KEY
  Name: varchar(255) $\longrightarrow$ Title: varchar(255)
  DeliveryPrice: float $\longrightarrow$ Price: real
  Description: varchar(8000) $\longrightarrow$ Information: varchar(5000)

(a) For each of the five correspondences, indicate which of the following match approaches will probably identify the correspondence:

    1. Syntactic comparison of element names, e.g., using edit distance string similarity

    2. Comparison of element names using a synonym lookup table

    3. Comparison of data types

    4. Analysis of instance data values

(b) Is it possible for the listed matching approaches to determine false correspondences for these match tasks? If so, give an example.

Problem 4.9. Consider two relations $S(a,b,c)$ and $T(d,e,f)$. A match approach determines the following similarities between the elements of S and T:

	$T.d$	$T.e$	$T.f$
$S.a$	0.8	0.3	0.1
$S.b$	0.5	0.2	0.9
$S.c$	0.4	0.7	0.8

Based on the given matcher's result, derive an overall schema match result with the following characteristics:

- Each element participates in exactly one correspondence.
- There is no correspondence where both elements match an element of the opposite schema with a higher similarity than its corresponding counterpart.

Problem 4.10 (*). Figure 4.15 illustrates the schema of three different data sources:

- MyGroup contains publications authored by members of a working group;
- MyConference contains publications of a conference series and associated workshops;
- MyPublisher contains articles that are published in journals.

The arrows show the foreign key-to-primary key relationships.
The sources are defined as follows:
MyGroup

- Publication

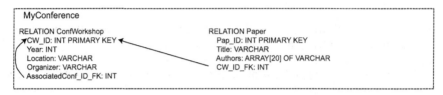

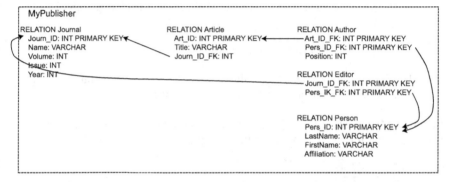

Fig. 4.15 Figure for Exercise 10

- Pub_ID: unique publication ID
- VenueName: name of the journal, conference or workshop
- VenueType: "journal", "conference", or "workshop"
- Year: year of publication
- Title: publication's title

- AuthorOf

  - many-to-many relationship representing "group member is author of publication"

- GroupMember

  - Member_ID: unique member ID
  - Name: name of the group member
  - Email: email address of the group member

MyConference

- ConfWorkshop
  - CW_ID: unique ID for the conference/workshop
  - Name: name of the conference or workshop
  - Year: year when the event takes place
  - Location: event's location
  - Organizer: name of the organizing person
  - AssociatedConf_ID_FK: value is NULL if it is a conference, ID of the associated conference if the event is a workshop (this is assuming that workshops are organized in conjunction with a conference)
- Paper
  - Pap_ID: unique paper ID
  - Title: paper's title
  - Author: array of author names
  - CW_ID_FK: conference/workshop where the paper is published

MyPublisher

- Journal
  - Journ_ID: unique journal ID
  - Name: journal's name
  - Year: year when the event takes place
  - Volume: journal volume
  - Issue: journal issue
- Article
  - Art_ID: unique article ID
  - Title: title of the article
  - Journ_ID_FK: journal where the article is published
- Person
  - Pers_ID: unique person ID
  - LastName: last name of the person
  - FirstName: first name of the person
  - Affiliation: person's affiliation (e.g., the name of a university)
- Author
  - represents the many-to-many relationship for "person is author of article"

- Position: author's position in the author list (e.g., first author has Position 1)

- Editor

  - represents the many-to-many relationship for "person is editor of journal issue"

(a) Identify all schema matching correspondences between the schema elements of the sources. Use the names and data types of the schema elements as well as the given description.

(b) Classify your correspondences along the following dimensions:

   1. Type of schema elements (e.g., attribute-attribute or attribute-relation)

   2. Cardinality (e.g., 1:1 or 1:N)

(c) Give a consolidated global schema that covers all information of the source schemas.

Problem 4.11 (*). Figure 4.16 illustrates (using a simplified SQL syntax) two sources S_1 and S_2. S_1 has two relations, Course and Tutor, and S_2 has only one relation, Lecture. The solid arrows denote schema matching correspondences. The dashed arrow represents a foreign key relationship between the two relations in S_1.

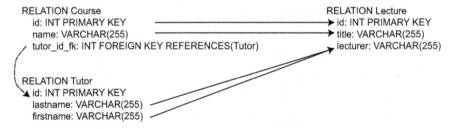

Fig. 4.16 Figure for Exercise 11

The following are four schema mappings (represented as SQL queries) to transform S_1's data into S_2.

```
1. SELECT C.id, C.name as Title, CONCAT(T.lastname,
            T.firstname) AS Lecturer)
   FROM   Course AS C
   JOIN   Tutor AS T ON (C.tutor_id_fk = T.id)

2. SELECT C.id, C.name AS Title, NULL AS Lecturer)
   FROM   Course AS C
   UNION
   SELECT T.id AS ID, NULL AS Title, T,
            lastname AS Lecturer)
```

```
FROM    Course AS C
FULL OUTER JOIN Tutor AS T ON(C.tutor_id_fk=T.id)
```

3. `SELECT C.id, C.name as Title, CONCAT(T.lastname,`
`        T.firstname) AS Lecturer)`
`FROM    Course AS C`
`FULL OUTER JOIN Tutor AS T ON(C.tutor_id_fk=T.id)`

Discuss each of these schema mappings with respect to the following questions:

(a) Is the mapping meaningful?
(b) Is the mapping complete (i.e., are all data instances of S_1 transformed)?
(c) Does the mapping potentially violate key constraints?

Problem 4.12 (*). Consider three data sources:

- Database 1 has one relation AREA(ID, FIELD) providing areas of specialization of employees where ID identifies an employee.

- Database 2 has two relations: TEACH(PROFESSOR, COURSE) and IN(COURSE, FIELD) specifying possible fields a course can belong to.

- Database 3 has two relations: GRANT(RESEARCHER, GRANT#) for grants given to researchers, and FOR(GRANT#, FIELD) indicating the fields that the grants are in.

Design a global schema with two relations: WORKS(ID, PROJECT) that records which projects employees work in, and AREA(PROJECT, FIELD) that associates projects with one or more fields for the following cases:

(a) There should be a LAV mapping between Database 1 and the global schema.
(b) There should be a GLAV mapping between the global schema and the local schemas.
(c) There should be a GAV mapping when one extra relation FUNDS(GRANT#, PROJECT) is added to Database 3.

Problem 4.13 (**). Logic (first-order logic, to be precise) has been suggested as a uniform formalism for schema translation and integration. Discuss how logic can be useful for this purpose.

Chapter 5
Data and Access Control

An important requirement of a centralized or a distributed DBMS is the ability to support semantic data control, i.e., data and access control using high-level semantics. Semantic data control typically includes view management, security control, and semantic integrity control. Informally, these functions must ensure that *authorized* users perform *correct* operations on the database, contributing to the maintenance of database integrity. The functions necessary for maintaining the physical integrity of the database in the presence of concurrent accesses and failures are studied separately in Chapters 10 through 12 in the context of transaction management. In the relational framework, semantic data control can be achieved in a uniform fashion. Views, security constraints, and semantic integrity constraints can be defined as rules that the system automatically enforces. The violation of some rules by a user program (a set of database operations) generally implies the rejection of the effects of that program (e.g., undoing its updates) or propagating some effects (e.g., updating related data) to preserve the database integrity.

The definition of the rules for controlling data manipulation is part of the administration of the database, a function generally performed by a database administrator (DBA). This person is also in charge of applying the organizational policies. Well-known solutions for semantic data control have been proposed for centralized DBMSs. In this chapter we briefly review the centralized solution to semantic data control, and present the special problems encountered in a distributed environment and solutions to these problems. The cost of enforcing semantic data control, which is high in terms of resource utilization in a centralized DBMS, can be prohibitive in a distributed environment.

Since the rules for semantic data control must be stored in a catalog, the management of a distributed directory (also called a catalog) is also relevant in this chapter. We discussed directories in Section 3.5. Remember that the directory of a distributed DBMS is itself a distributed database. There are several ways to store semantic data control definitions, according to the way the directory is managed. Directory information can be stored differently according to its type; in other words, some information might be fully replicated whereas other information might be distributed. For example, information that is useful at compile time, such as security control

M.T. Özsu and P. Valduriez, *Principles of Distributed Database Systems: Third Edition*,
DOI 10.1007/978-1-4419-8834-8_5, © Springer Science+Business Media, LLC 2011

information, could be replicated. In this chapter we emphasize the impact of directory management on the performance of semantic data control mechanisms.

This chapter is organized as follows. View management is the subject of Section 5.1. Security control is presented in Section 5.2. Finally, semantic integrity control is treated in Section 5.3. For each section we first outline the solution in a centralized DBMS and then give the distributed solution, which is often an extension of the centralized one, although more difficult.

5.1 View Management

One of the main advantages of the relational model is that it provides full logical data independence. As introduced in Chapter 1, external schemas enable user groups to have their particular *view* of the database. In a relational system, a view is a *virtual relation*, defined as the result of a query on *base relations* (or real relations), but not materialized like a base relation, which is stored in the database. A view is a dynamic window in the sense that it reflects all updates to the database. An external schema can be defined as a set of views and/or base relations. Besides their use in external schemas, views are useful for ensuring data security in a simple way. By selecting a subset of the database, views *hide* some data. If users may only access the database through views, they cannot see or manipulate the hidden data, which are therefore secure.

In the remainder of this section we look at view management in centralized and distributed systems as well as the problems of updating views. Note that in a distributed DBMS, a view can be derived from distributed relations, and the access to a view requires the execution of the distributed query corresponding to the view definition. An important issue in a distributed DBMS is to make view materialization efficient. We will see how the concept of materialized views helps in solving this problem, among others, but requires efficient techniques for materialized view maintenance.

5.1.1 Views in Centralized DBMSs

Most relational DBMSs use a view mechanism where a view is a relation derived from base relations as the result of a relational query (this was first proposed within the INGRES [Stonebraker, 1975] and System R [Chamberlin et al., 1975] projects). It is defined by associating the name of the view with the retrieval query that specifies it.

Example 5.1. The view of system analysts (SYSAN) derived from relation EMP (ENO,ENAME,TITLE), can be defined by the following SQL query:

SYSAN

ENO	ENAME
E2	M.Smith
E5	B.Casey
E8	J.Jones

Fig. 5.1 Relation Corresponding to the View SYSAN

```
CREATE VIEW    SYSAN(ENO, ENAME)
AS       SELECT ENO, ENAME
         FROM    EMP
         WHERE   TITLE = "Syst. Anal."
```
◆

The single effect of this statement is the storage of the view definition in the catalog. No other information needs to be recorded. Therefore, the result of the query defining the view (i.e., a relation having the attributes ENO and ENAME for the system analysts as shown in Figure 5.1) is *not* produced. However, the view SYSAN can be manipulated as a base relation.

Example 5.2. The query

"Find the names of all the system analysts with their project number and responsibility(ies)"

involving the view SYSAN and relation ASG(ENO,PNO,RESP,DUR) can be expressed as

```
SELECT ENAME, PNO, RESP
FROM    SYSAN, ASG
WHERE   SYSAN.ENO = ASG.ENO
```
◆

Mapping a query expressed on views into a query expressed on base relations can be done by *query modification* [Stonebraker, 1975]. With this technique the variables are changed to range on base relations and the query qualification is merged (ANDed) with the view qualification.

Example 5.3. The preceding query can be modified to

```
SELECT ENAME, PNO, RESP
FROM    EMP, ASG
WHERE   EMP.ENO = ASG.ENO
AND     TITLE = "Syst. Anal."
```

The result of this query is illustrated in Figure 5.2.   ◆

The modified query is expressed on base relations and can therefore be processed by the query processor. It is important to note that view processing can be done at compile time. The view mechanism can also be used for refining the access controls to include subsets of objects. To specify any user from whom one wants to hide data, the keyword USER generally refers to the logged-on user identifier.

ENAME	PNO	RESP
M.Smith	P1	Analyst
M.Smith	P2	Analyst
B.Casey	P3	Manager
J.Jones	P4	Manager

Fig. 5.2 Result of Query involving View SYSAN

Example 5.4. The view ESAME restricts the access by any user to those employees having the same title:

```
CREATE VIEW   ESAME
AS      SELECT *
        FROM    EMP E1, EMP E2
        WHERE   E1.TITLE = E2.TITLE
        AND     E1.ENO = USER
```

In the view definition above, * stands for "all attributes" and the two tuple variables (E1 and E2) ranging over relation EMP are required to express the join of one tuple of EMP (the one corresponding to the logged-on user) with all tuples of EMP based on the same title. For example, the following query issued by the user J. Doe,

```
SELECT *
FROM    ESAME
```

returns the relation of Figure 5.3. Note that the user J. Doe also appears in the result. If the user who creates ESAME is an electrical engineer, as in this case, the view represents the set of all electrical engineers.   ◆

ENO	ENAME	TITLE
E1	J. Doe	Elect. Eng
E2	L. Chu	Elect. Eng

Fig. 5.3 Result of Query on View ESAME

Views can be defined using arbitrarily complex relational queries involving selection, projection, join, aggregate functions, and so on. All views can be interrogated as base relations, but not all views can be manipulated as such. Updates through views can be handled automatically only if they can be propagated correctly to the base relations. We can classify views as being updatable and not updatable. A view is updatable only if the updates to the view can be propagated to the base relations without ambiguity. The view SYSAN above is updatable; the insertion, for example, of a new system analyst ⟨201, Smith⟩ will be mapped into the insertion of a new employee ⟨201, Smith, Syst. Anal.⟩. If attributes other than TITLE were hidden by the view, they would be assigned *null values*.

Example 5.5. The following view, however, is not updatable:

```
CREATE VIEW   EG(ENAME, RESP)
AS      SELECT DISTINCT ENAME, RESP
        FROM   EMP, ASG
        WHERE  EMP.ENO = ASG.ENO
```

The deletion, for example, of the tuple ⟨Smith, Analyst⟩ cannot be propagated, since it is ambiguous. Deletions of Smith in relation EMP or analyst in relation ASG are both meaningful, but the system does not know which is correct.   ♦

Current systems are very restrictive about supporting updates through views. Views can be updated only if they are derived from a single relation by selection and projection. This precludes views defined by joins, aggregates, and so on. However, it is theoretically possible to automatically support updates of a larger class of views [Bancilhon and Spyratos, 1981; Dayal and Bernstein, 1978; Keller, 1982]. It is interesting to note that views derived by join are updatable if they include the keys of the base relations.

5.1.2 Views in Distributed DBMSs

The definition of a view is similar in a distributed DBMS and in centralized systems. However, a view in a distributed system may be derived from fragmented relations stored at different sites. When a view is defined, its name and its retrieval query are stored in the catalog.

Since views may be used as base relations by application programs, their definition should be stored in the directory in the same way as the base relation descriptions. Depending on the degree of site autonomy offered by the system [Williams et al., 1982], view definitions can be centralized at one site, partially duplicated, or fully duplicated. In any case, the information associating a view name to its definition site should be duplicated. If the view definition is not present at the site where the query is issued, remote access to the view definition site is necessary.

The mapping of a query expressed on views into a query expressed on base relations (which can potentially be fragmented) can also be done in the same way as in centralized systems, that is, through query modification. With this technique, the qualification defining the view is found in the distributed database catalog and then merged with the query to provide a query on base relations. Such a modified query is a *distributed query*, which can be processed by the distributed query processor (see Chapter 6). The query processor maps the distributed query into a query on physical fragments.

In Chapter 3 we presented alternative ways of fragmenting base relations. The definition of fragmentation is, in fact, very similar to the definition of particular views. It is possible to manage views and fragments using a unified mechanism [Adiba, 1981]. This is based on the observation that views in a distributed DBMS can be defined with rules similar to fragment definition rules. Furthermore, replicated data can be handled in the same way. The value of such a unified mechanism is to facilitate distributed database administration. The objects manipulated by the database administrator can be seen as a hierarchy where the leaves are the fragments from which relations and views can be derived. Therefore, the DBA may increase locality of reference by making views in one-to-one correspondence with fragments. For example, it is possible to implement the view SYSAN illustrated in Example 5.1 by a fragment at a given site, provided that most users accessing the view SYSAN are at the same site.

Evaluating views derived from distributed relations may be costly. In a given organization it is likely that many users access the same view which must be recomputed for each user. We saw in Section 5.1.1 that view derivation is done by merging the view qualification with the query qualification. An alternative solution is to avoid view derivation by maintaining actual versions of the views, called *materialized views*. A *materialized view* stores the tuples of a view in a database relation, like the other database tuples, possibly with indices. Thus, access to a materialized view is much faster than deriving the view, in particular, in a distributed DBMS where base relations can be remote. Introduced in the early 1980s [Adiba and Lindsay, 1980], materialized views have since gained much interest in the context of data warehousing to speed up On Line Analytical Processing (OLAP) applications [Gupta and Mumick, 1999c]. Materialized views in data warehouses typically involve aggregate (such as SUM and COUNT) and grouping (GROUP BY) operators because they provide compact database summaries. Today, all major database products support materialized views.

Example 5.6. The following view over relation PROJ(PNO,PNAME,BUDGET,LOC) gives, for each location, the number of projects and the total budget.

```
CREATE VIEW     PL(LOC, NBPROJ, TBUDGET)
AS      SELECT  LOC, COUNT(*),SUM(BUDGET)
        FROM    PROJ
        GROUP BY LOC
```

♦

5.1.3 Maintenance of Materialized Views

A materialized view is a copy of some base data and thus must be kept consistent with that base data which may be updated. *View maintenance* is the process of updating (or refreshing) a materialized view to reflect the changes made to the base data. The issues related to view materialization are somewhat similar to those of database replication which we will address in Chapter 13. However, a major difference is that materialized view expressions, in particular, for data warehousing, are typically more complex than replica definitions and may include join, group by and aggregate operators. Another major difference is that database replication is concerned with more general replication configurations, e.g., with multiple copies of the same base data at multiple sites.

A view maintenance policy allows a DBA to specify *when* and *how* a view should be refreshed. The first question (when to refresh) is related to consistency (between the view and the base data) and efficiency. A view can be refreshed in two modes: *immediate* or *deferred*. With the immediate mode, a view is refreshed immediately as part as the transaction that updates base data used by the view. If the view and the base data are managed by different DBMSs, possibly at different sites, this requires the use of a distributed transaction, for instance, using the two-phase commit (2PC) protocol (see Chapter 12). The main advantages of immediate refreshment are that the view is always consistent with the base data and that read-only queries can be fast. However, this is at the expense of increased transaction time to update both the base data and the views within the same transactions. Furthermore, using distributed transactions may be difficult.

In practice, the deferred mode is preferred because the view is refreshed in separate (refresh) transactions, thus without performance penalty on the transactions that update the base data. The refresh transactions can be triggered at different times: *lazily*, just before a query is evaluated on the view; *periodically*, at predefined times, e.g., every day; or *forcedly*, after a predefined number of updates to the base data. Lazy refreshment enables queries to see the latest consistent state of the base data but at the expense of increased query time to include the refreshment of the view. Periodic and forced refreshment allow queries to see views whose state is not consistent with the latest state of the base data. The views managed with these strategies are also called *snapshots* [Adiba, 1981; Blakeley et al., 1986].

The second question (how to refresh a view) is an important efficiency issue. The simplest way to refresh a view is to recompute it from scratch using the base data. In some cases, this may be the most efficient strategy, e.g., if a large subset of the base data has been changed. However, there are many cases where only a small subset of view needs to be changed. In these cases, a better strategy is to compute the view *incrementally*, by computing only the changes to the view. Incremental view maintenance relies on the concept of differential relation. Let u be an update of relation R. R^+ and R^- are *differential relations* of R by u, where R^+ contains the tuples inserted by u into R, and R^- contains the tuples of R deleted by u. If u is an insertion, R^- is empty. If u is a deletion, R^+ is empty. Finally, if u is a modification, relation R can be obtained by computing $(R - R^-) \cup R^+$. Similarly, a materialized view V can be refreshed by computing $(V - V^-) \cup V^+$. Computing the changes to the view, i.e., V^+ and V^-, may require using the base relations in addition to differential relations.

Example 5.7. Consider the view EG of Example 5.5 which uses relations EMP and ASG as base data and assume its state is derived from that of Example 3.1, so that EG has 9 tuples (see Figure 5.4). Let EMP$^+$ consist of one tuple ⟨E9, B. Martin, Programmer⟩ to be inserted in EMP, and ASG$^+$ consist of two tuples ⟨E4, P3, Programmer, 12⟩ and ⟨E9, P3, Programmer, 12⟩ to be inserted in ASG. The changes to the view EG can be computed as:

```
EG+ =    (SELECT   ENAME, RESP
          FROM      EMP, ASG+
          WHERE     EMP.ENO = ASG+.ENO)
                    UNION
          (SELECT   ENAME, RESP
          FROM      EMP+, ASG
          WHERE     EMP+.ENO = ASG.ENO)
                    UNION
          (SELECT   ENAME, RESP
          FROM      EMP+, ASG+
          WHERE     EMP+.ENO = ASG+.ENO)
```

which yields tuples ⟨B. Martin, Programmer⟩ and ⟨J. Miller, Programmer⟩. Note that integrity constraints would be useful here to avoid useless work (see Section 5.3.2). Assuming that relations EMP and ASG are related by a referential constraint that says that ENO in ASG must exist in EMP, the second SELECT statement is useless as it produces an empty relation.   ◆

EG

ENAME	RESP
J. Doe	Manager
M. Smith	Analyst
A. Lee	Consultant
A. Lee	Engineer
J. Miller	Programmer
B. Casey	Manager
L. Chu	Manager
R. Davis	Engineer
J.Jones	Manager

Fig. 5.4 State of View EG

Efficient techniques have been devised to perform incremental view maintenance using both the materialized views and the base relations. The techniques essentially differ in their views' expressiveness, their use of integrity constraints, and the way they handle insertion and deletion. Gupta and Mumick [1999a] classify these techniques along the view expressiveness dimension as non-recursive views, views involving outerjoins, and recursive views. For non-recursive views, i.e., select-project-join (SPJ) views that may have duplicate elimination, union and aggregation, an elegant solution is the counting algorithm [Gupta et al., 1993]. One problem stems from the fact that individual tuples in the view may be derived from several tuples in the base relations, thus making deletion in the view difficult. The basic idea of the counting algorithm is to maintain a count of the number of derivations for each tuple in the view, and to increment (resp. decrement) tuple counts based on insertions (resp. deletions); a tuple in the view of which count is zero can then be deleted.

Example 5.8. Consider the view EG in Figure 5.4. Each tuple in EG has one derivation (i.e., a count of 1) except tuple ⟨M. Smith, Analyst⟩ which has two (i.e., a count of 2). Assume now that tuples ⟨E2, P1, Analyst, 24⟩ and ⟨E3, P3, Consultant, 10⟩ are deleted from ASG. Then only tuple ⟨A. Lee, Consultant⟩ needs to be deleted from EG. ♦

We now present the basic counting algorithm for refreshing a view V defined over two relations R and S as a query $q(R, S)$. Assuming that each tuple in V has an associated derivation count, the algorithm has three main steps (see Algorithm 5.1). First, it applies the view differentiation technique to formulate the differential views V^+ and V^- as queries over the view, the base relations, and the differential relations. Second, it computes V^+ and V^- and their tuple counts. Third, it applies the changes V^+ and V^- in V by adding positive counts and subtracting negative counts, and deleting tuples with a count of zero.

Algorithm 5.1: COUNTING Algorithm

Input: V: view defined as $q(R, S)$; R, S: relations; R^+, R^-: changes to R
begin
    $V^+ = q^+(V, R^+, R, S)$;
    $V^- = q^-(V, R^-, R, S)$;
    compute V^+ with positive counts for inserted tuples;
    compute V^- with negative counts for deleted tuples;
    compute $(V - V^-) \cup V^+$ by adding positive counts and substracting
    negative counts deleting each tuple in V with count $= 0$;
end

The counting algorithm is optimal since it computes exactly the view tuples that are inserted or deleted. However, it requires access to the base relations. This implies that the base relations be maintained (possibly as replicas) at the sites of the materialized view. To avoid accessing the base relations so the view can be stored at a different site, the view should be maintainable using only the view and the differential relations. Such views are called *self-maintainable* [Gupta et al., 1996].

Example 5.9. Consider the view SYSAN in Example 5.1. Let us write the view definition as SYSAN=q(EMP) meaning that the view is defined by a query q on EMP. We can compute the differential views using only the differential relations, i.e., SYSAN$^+ = q$(EMP$^+$) and SYSAN$^- = q$(EMP$^-$). Thus, the view SYSAN is self-maintainable.   ◆

Self-maintainability depends on the views' expressiveness and can be defined with respect to the kind of updates (insertion, deletion or modification) [Gupta et al., 1996]. Most SPJ views are not self-maintainable with respect to insertion but are often self-maintainable with respect to deletion and modification. For instance, an SPJ view is self-maintainable with respect to deletion of relation R if the key attributes of R are included in the view.

Example 5.10. Consider the view EG of Example 5.5. Let us add attribute ENO (which is key of EMP) in the view definition. This view is not self-maintainable with respect to insertion. For instance, after an insertion of an ASG tuple, we need to perform the join with EMP to get the corresponding ENAME to insert in the view. However, this view is self-maintainable with respect to deletion on EMP. For instance, if one EMP tuple is deleted, the view tuples having same ENO can be deleted.   ◆

5.2 Data Security

Data security is an important function of a database system that protects data against unauthorized access. Data security includes two aspects: *data protection* and *access control*.

Data protection is required to prevent unauthorized users from understanding the physical content of data. This function is typically provided by file systems in the context of centralized and distributed operating systems. The main data protection approach is data encryption [Fernandez et al., 1981], which is useful both for information stored on disk and for information exchanged on a network. Encrypted (encoded) data can be decrypted (decoded) only by authorized users who "know" the code. The two main schemes are the Data Encryption Standard [NBS, 1977] and the public-key encryption schemes ([Diffie and Hellman, 1976] and [Rivest et al., 1978]). In this section we concentrate on the second aspect of data security, which is more specific to database systems. A complete presentation of database security techniques can be found in [Castano et al., 1995].

Access control must guarantee that only authorized users perform operations they are allowed to perform on the database. Many different users may have access to a large collection of data under the control of a single centralized or distributed system. The centralized or distributed DBMS must thus be able to restrict the access of a subset of the database to a subset of the users. Access control has long been provided by operating systems, and more recently, by distributed operating systems [Tanenbaum, 1995] as services of the file system. In this context, a centralized control is offered. Indeed, the central controller creates objects, and this person may allow particular users to perform particular operations (read, write, execute) on these objects. Also, objects are identified by their external names.

Access control in database systems differs in several aspects from that in traditional file systems. Authorizations must be refined so that different users have different rights on the same database objects. This requirement implies the ability to specify subsets of objects more precisely than by name and to distinguish between groups of users. In addition, the decentralized control of authorizations is of particular importance in a distributed context. In relational systems, authorizations can be uniformly controlled by database administrators using high-level constructs. For example, controlled objects can be specified by predicates in the same way as is a query qualification.

There are two main approaches to database access control [Lunt and Fernández, 1990]. The first approach is called *discretionary* and has long been provided by DBMS. Discretionary access control (or *authorization control*) defines access rights based on the users, the type of access (e.g., SELECT, UPDATE) and the objects to be accessed. The second approach, called *mandatory* or *multilevel* [Lunt and Fernández, 1990; Jajodia and Sandhu, 1991] further increases security by restricting access to classified data to cleared users. Support of multilevel access control by major DBMSs is more recent and stems from increased security threats coming from the Internet.

From solutions to access control in centralized systems, we derive those for distributed DBMSs. However, there is the additional complexity which stems from the fact that objects and users can be distributed. In what follows we first present discretionary and multilevel access control in centralized systems and then the additional problems and their solutions in distributed systems.

5.2.1 Discretionary Access Control

Three main actors are involved in discretionary access control control: the *subject* (e.g., users, groups of users) who trigger the execution of application programs; the *operations*, which are embedded in application programs; and the *database objects*, on which the operations are performed [Hoffman, 1977]. Authorization control consists of checking whether a given triple (subject, operation, object) can be allowed to proceed (i.e., the user can execute the operation on the object). An authorization can be viewed as a triple (subject, operation type, object definition) which specifies that the subjects has the right to perform an operation of operation type on an object. To control authorizations properly, the DBMS requires the definition of subjects, objects, and access rights.

The introduction of a subject in the system is typically done by a pair (user name, password). The user name uniquely *identifies* the users of that name in the system, while the password, known only to the users of that name, *authenticates* the users. Both user name and password must be supplied in order to log in the system. This prevents people who do not know the password from entering the system with only the user name.

The objects to protect are subsets of the database. Relational systems provide finer and more general protection granularity than do earlier systems. In a file system, the protection granule is the file, while in an object-oriented DBMS, it is the object type. In a relational system, objects can be defined by their type (view, relation, tuple, attribute) as well as by their content using selection predicates. Furthermore, the view mechanism as introduced in Section 5.1 permits the protection of objects simply by hiding subsets of relations (attributes or tuples) from unauthorized users.

A right expresses a relationship between a subject and an object for a particular set of operations. In an SQL-based relational DBMS, an operation is a high-level statement such as SELECT, INSERT, UPDATE, or DELETE, and rights are defined (granted or revoked) using the following statements:

GRANT ⟨operation type(s)⟩ ON ⟨object⟩ TO ⟨subject(s)⟩
REVOKE ⟨operation type(s)⟩ FROM ⟨object⟩ TO ⟨subject(s)⟩

The keyword *public* can be used to mean all users. Authorization control can be characterized based on who (the grantors) can grant the rights. In its simplest form, the control is centralized: a single user or user class, the database administrators, has all privileges on the database objects and is the only one allowed to use the GRANT and REVOKE statements.

A more flexible but complex form of control is decentralized [Griffiths and Wade, 1976]: the creator of an object becomes its owner and is granted all privileges on it. In particular, there is the additional operation type GRANT, which transfers all the rights of the grantor performing the statement to the specified subjects. Therefore, the person receiving the right (the grantee) may subsequently grant privileges on that object. The main difficulty with this approach is that the revoking process must be recursive. For example, if A, who granted B who granted C the GRANT privilege on object O, wants to revoke all the privileges of B on O, all the privileges of C on O must also be revoked. To perform revocation, the system must maintain a hierarchy of grants per object where the creator of the object is the root.

The privileges of the subjects over objects are recorded in the catalog (directory) as authorization rules. There are several ways to store the authorizations. The most convenient approach is to consider all the privileges as an *authorization matrix*, in which a row defines a subject, a column an object, and a matrix entry (for a pair ⟨subject, object⟩), the authorized operations. The authorized operations are specified by their operation type (e.g., SELECT, UPDATE). It is also customary to associate with the operation type a predicate that further restricts the access to the object. The latter option is provided when the objects must be base relations and cannot be views. For example, one authorized operation for the pair ⟨Jones, relation EMP⟩ could be

```
SELECT WHERE TITLE = "Syst.Anal."
```

which authorizes Jones to access only the employee tuples for system analysts. Figure 5.5 gives an example of an authorization matrix where objects are either relations (EMP and ASG) or attributes (ENAME).

	EMP	ENAME	ASG
Casey	UPDATE	UPDATE	UPDATE
Jones	SELECT	SELECT	SELECT WHERE RESP ≠ "Manager"
Smith	NONE	SELECT	NONE

Fig. 5.5 Example of Authorization Matrix

The authorization matrix can be stored in three ways: by row, by column, or by element. When the matrix is stored by *row*, each subject is associated with the list of objects that may be accessed together with the related access rights. This approach makes the enforcement of authorizations efficient, since all the rights of the logged-on user are together (in the user profile). However, the manipulation of access rights per object (e.g., making an object public) is not efficient since all subject profiles must be accessed. When the matrix is stored by *column*, each object is associated with the list of subjects who may access it with the corresponding access rights. The advantages and disadvantages of this approach are the reverse of the previous approach.

The respective advantages of the two approaches can be combined in the third approach, in which the matrix is stored by *element*, that is, by relation (subject, object, right). This relation can have indices on both subject and object, thereby providing fast-access right manipulation per subject and per object.

5.2.2 Multilevel Access Control

Discretionary access control has some limitations. One problem is that a malicious user can access unauthorized data through an authorized user. For instance, consider user A who has authorized access to relations R and S and user B who has authorized access to relation S only. If B somehow manages to modify an application program used by A so it writes R data into S, then B can read unauthorized data without violating authorization rules.

Multilevel access control answers this problem and further improves security by defining different security levels for both subjects and data objects. Multilevel access control in databases is based on the well-known Bell and Lapaduda model designed for operating system security [Bell and Lapuda, 1976]. In this model, subjects are processes acting on a user's behalf; a process has a security level also called *clearance* derived from that of the user. In its simplest form, the security levels are Top Secret (TS), Secret (S), Confidential (C) and Unclassified (U), and ordered as $TS > S > C > U$, where ">" means "more secure". Access in read and write modes by subjects is restricted by two simple rules:

1. A subject S is allowed to read an object of security level l only if $level(S) \geq l$.

2. A subject S is allowed to write an object of security level l only if $class(S) \leq l$.

Rule 1 (called "no read up") protects data from unauthorized disclosure, i.e., a subject at a given security level can only read objects at the same or lower security levels. For instance, a subject with secret clearance cannot read top-secret data. Rule 2 (called "no write down") protects data from unauthorized change, i.e., a subject at a given security level can only write objects at the same or higher security levels. For instance, a subject with top-secret clearance can only write top-secret data but cannot write secret data (which could then contain top-secret data).

In the relational model, data objects can be relations, tuples or attributes. Thus, a relation can be classified at different levels: relation (i.e., all tuples in the relation have the same security level), tuple (i.e., every tuple has a security level), or attribute (i.e., every distinct attribute value has a security level). A classified relation is thus called *multilevel relation* to reflect that it will appear differently (with different data) to subjects with different clearances. For instance, a multilevel relation classified at the tuple level can be represented by adding a security level attribute to each tuple. Similarly, a multilevel relation classified at attribute level can be represented by adding a corresponding security level to each attribute. Figure 5.6 illustrates a multilevel relation PROJ* based on relation PROJ which is classified at the attribute level. Note that the additional security level attributes may increase significantly the size of the relation.

PROJ*

PNO	SL1	PNAME	SL2	BUDGET	SL3	LOC	SL4
P1	C	Instrumentation	C	150000	C	Montreal	C
P2	C	Database Develop.	C	135000	S	New York	S
P3	S	CAD/CAM	S	250000	S	New York	S

Fig. 5.6 Multilevel relation PROJ* classified at the attribute level

The entire relation also has a security level which is the lowest security level of any data it contains. For instance, relation PROJ* has security level C. A relation can then be accessed by any subject having a security level which is the same or higher. However, a subject can only access data for which it has clearance. Thus, attributes for which a subject has no clearance will appear to the subject as null values with an associated security level which is the same as the subject. Figure 5.7 shows an instance of relation PROJ* as accessed by a subject at a confidential security level.

Multilevel access control has strong impact on the data model because users do not see the same data and have to deal with unexpected side-effects. One major side-effect is called *polyinstantiation* [Lunt et al., 1990] which allows the same object to have different attribute values depending on the users' security level. Figure 5.8 illustrates a multirelation with polyinstantiated tuples. Tuple of primary key P3 has two instantiations, each one with a different security level. This may result from a subject S with security level C inserting a tuple with key="P3" in relation PROJ* in

PROJ*C

PNO	SL1	PNAME	SL2	BUDGET	SL3	LOC	SL4
P1	C	Instrumentation	C	150000	C	Montreal	C
P2	C	Database Develop.	C	Null	C	Null	C

Fig. 5.7 Confidential relation PROJ*C

Figure 5.6. Because *S* (with confidential clearance level) should ignore the existence of tuple with key="P3" (classified as secret), the only practical solution is to add a second tuple with same key and different classification. However, a user with secret clearance would see both tuples with key="E3" and should interpret this unexpected effect.

PROJ**

PNO	SL1	PNAME	SL2	BUDGET	SL3	LOC	SL4
P1	C	Instrumentation	C	150000	C	Montreal	C
P2	C	Database Develop.	C	135000	S	New York	S
P3	S	CAD/CAM	S	250000	S	New York	S
P3	C	Web Develop.	C	200000	C	Paris	C

Fig. 5.8 Multilevel relation with polyinstantiation

5.2.3 Distributed Access Control

The additional problems of access control in a distributed environment stem from the fact that objects and subjects are distributed and that messages with sensitive data can be read by unauthorized users. These problems are: remote user authentication, management of discretionary access rules, handling of views and of user groups, and enforcing multilevel access control.

Remote user authentication is necessary since any site of a distributed DBMS may accept programs initiated, and authorized, at remote sites. To prevent remote access by unauthorized users or applications (e.g., from a site that is not part of the distributed DBMS), users must also be identified and authenticated at the accessed site. Furthermore, instead of using passwords that could be obtained from sniffing messages, encrypted certificates could be used.

Three solutions are possible for managing authentication:

1. Authentication information is maintained at a central site for *global users* which can then be authenticated only once and then accessed from multiple sites.

2. The information for authenticating users (user name and password) is replicated at all sites in the catalog. Local programs, initiated at a remote site, must also indicate the user name and password.

3. All sites of the distributed DBMS identify and authenticate themselves similar to the way users do. Intersite communication is thus protected by the use of the site password. Once the initiating site has been authenticated, there is no need for authenticating their remote users.

The first solution simplifies password administration significantly and enables single authentication (also called single sign on). However, the central authentication site can be a single point of failure and a bottleneck. The second solution is more costly in terms of directory management given that the introduction of a new user is a distributed operation. However, users can access the distributed database from any site. The third solution is necessary if user information is not replicated. Nevertheless, it can also be used if there is replication of the user information. In this case it makes remote authentication more efficient. If user names and passwords are not replicated, they should be stored at the sites where the users access the system (i.e., the home site). The latter solution is based on the realistic assumption that users are more static, or at least they always access the distributed database from the same site.

Distributed authorization rules are expressed in the same way as centralized ones. Like view definitions, they must be stored in the catalog. They can be either fully replicated at each site or stored at the sites of the referenced objects. In the latter case the rules are duplicated only at the sites where the referenced objects are distributed. The main advantage of the fully replicated approach is that authorization can be processed by query modification [Stonebraker, 1975] at compile time. However, directory management is more costly because of data duplication. The second solution is better if locality of reference is very high. However, distributed authorization cannot be controlled at compile time.

Views may be considered to be objects by the authorization mechanism. Views are composite objects, that is, composed of other underlying objects. Therefore, granting access to a view translates into granting access to underlying objects. If view definition and authorization rules for all objects are fully replicated (as in many systems), this translation is rather simple and can be done locally. The translation is harder when the view definition and its underlying objects are all stored separately [Wilms and Lindsay, 1981], as is the case with site autonomy assumption. In this situation, the translation is a totally distributed operation. The authorizations granted on views depend on the access rights of the view creator on the underlying objects. A solution is to record the association information at the site of each underlying object.

Handling user groups for the purpose of authorization simplifies distributed database administration. In a centralized DBMS, "all users" can be referred to as *public*. In a distributed DBMS, the same notion is useful, the public denoting all the users of the system. However an intermediate level is often introduced to specify the public at a particular site, denoted by public@site_s [Wilms and Lindsay, 1981]. The public is a particular user group. More precise groups can be defined by the command

```
DEFINE GROUP ⟨group_id⟩ AS ⟨list of subject ids⟩
```

The management of groups in a distributed environment poses some problems since the subjects of a group can be located at various sites and access to an object may be granted to several groups, which are themselves distributed. If group information as well as access rules are fully replicated at all sites, the enforcement of access rights is similar to that of a centralized system. However, maintaining this replication may be expensive. The problem is more difficult if site autonomy (with decentralized control) must be maintained. Several solutions to this problem have been identified [Wilms and Lindsay, 1981]. One solution enforces access rights by performing a remote query to the nodes holding the group definition. Another solution replicates a group definition at each node containing an object that may be accessed by subjects of that group. These solutions tend to decrease the degree of site autonomy.

Enforcing multilevel access control in a distributed environment is made difficult by the possibility of indirect means, called *covert channels*, to access unauthorized data [Rjaibi, 2004]. For instance, consider a simple distributed DBMS architecture with two sites, each managing its database at a single security level, e.g., one site is confidential while the other is secret. According to the "no write down" rule, an update operation from a subject with secret clearance could only be sent to the secret site. However, according to the "no read up" rule, a read query from the same secret subject could be sent to both the secret and the confidential sites. Since the query sent to the confidential site may contain secret information (e.g., in a select predicate), it is potentially a covert channel. To avoid such covert channels, a solution is to replicate part of the database [Thuraisingham, 2001] so that a site at security level l contains all data that a subject at level l can access. For instance, the secret site would replicate confidential data so that it can entirely process secret queries. One problem with this architecture is the overhead of maintaining the consistency of replicas (see Chapter 13 on replication). Furthermore, although there are no covert channels for queries, there may still be covert channels for update operations because the delays involved in synchronizing transactions may be exploited [Jajodia et al., 2001]. The complete support for multilevel access control in distributed database systems, therefore, requires significant extensions to transaction management techniques [Ray et al., 2000] and to distributed query processing techniques [Agrawal et al., 2003].

5.3 Semantic Integrity Control

Another important and difficult problem for a database system is how to guarantee *database consistency*. A database state is said to be consistent if the database satisfies a set of constraints, called *semantic integrity constraints*. Maintaining a consistent database requires various mechanisms such as concurrency control, reliability, protection, and semantic integrity control, which are provided as part of transaction management. Semantic integrity control ensures database consistency by rejecting update transactions that lead to inconsistent database states, or by activating specific actions on the database state, which compensate for the effects of the update transactions. Note that the updated database must satisfy the set of integrity constraints.

In general, semantic integrity constraints are rules that represent the *knowledge* about the properties of an application. They define static or dynamic application properties that cannot be directly captured by the object and operation concepts of a data model. Thus the concept of an integrity rule is strongly connected with that of a data model in the sense that more semantic information about the application can be captured by means of these rules.

Two main types of integrity constraints can be distinguished: structural constraints and behavioral constraints. *Structural constraints* express basic semantic properties inherent to a model. Examples of such constraints are unique key constraints in the relational model, or one-to-many associations between objects in the object-oriented model. *Behavioral constraints*, on the other hand, regulate the application behavior. Thus they are essential in the database design process. They can express associations between objects, such as inclusion dependency in the relational model, or describe object properties and structures. The increasing variety of database applications and the development of database design aid tools call for powerful integrity constraints that can enrich the data model.

Integrity control appeared with data processing and evolved from procedural methods (in which the controls were embedded in application programs) to declarative methods. Declarative methods have emerged with the relational model to alleviate the problems of program/data dependency, code redundancy, and poor performance of the procedural methods. The idea is to express integrity constraints using assertions of predicate calculus [Florentin, 1974]. Thus a set of semantic integrity assertions defines database consistency. This approach allows one to easily declare and modify complex integrity constraints.

The main problem in supporting automatic semantic integrity control is that the cost of checking for constraint violation can be prohibitive. Enforcing integrity constraints is costly because it generally requires access to a large amount of data that are not directly involved in the database updates. The problem is more difficult when constraints are defined over a distributed database.

Various solutions have been investigated to design an integrity manager by combining optimization strategies. Their purpose is to (1) limit the number of constraints that need to be enforced, (2) decrease the number of data accesses to enforce a given constraint in the presence of an update transaction, (3) define a preventive strategy that detects inconsistencies in a way that avoids undoing updates, (4) perform as much integrity control as possible at compile time. A few of these solutions have been implemented, but they suffer from a lack of generality. Either they are restricted to a small set of assertions (more general constraints would have a prohibitive checking cost) or they only support restricted programs (e.g., single-tuple updates).

In this section we present the solutions for semantic integrity control first in centralized systems and then in distributed systems. Since our context is the relational model, we consider only declarative methods.

5.3.1 Centralized Semantic Integrity Control

A semantic integrity manager has two main components: a language for expressing and manipulating integrity assertions, and an enforcement mechanism that performs specific actions to enforce database integrity upon update transactions.

5.3.1.1 Specification of Integrity Constraints

Integrity constraints should be manipulated by the database administrator using a high-level language. In this section we illustrate a declarative language for specifying integrity constraints [Simon and Valduriez, 1987]. This language is much in the spirit of the standard SQL language, but with more generality. It allows one to specify, read, or drop integrity constraints. These constraints can be defined either at relation creation time, or at any time, even if the relation already contains tuples. In both cases, however, the syntax is almost the same. For simplicity and without lack of generality, we assume that the effect of integrity constraint violation is to abort the violating transactions. However, the SQL standard provides means to express the propagation of update actions to correct inconsistencies, with the CASCADING clause within the constraint declaration. More generally, *triggers* (event-condition-action rules) [Ramakrishnan and Gehrke, 2003] can be used to automatically propagate updates, and thus to maintain semantic integrity. However, triggers are quite powerful and thus more difficult to support efficiently than specific integrity constraints.

In relational database systems, integrity constraints are defined as assertions. An assertion is a particular expression of tuple relational calculus (see Chapter 2), in which each variable is either universally ($\forall$) or existentially ($\exists$) quantified. Thus an assertion can be seen as a query qualification that is either true or false for each tuple in the Cartesian product of the relations determined by the tuple variables. We can distinguish between three types of integrity constraints: predefined, precondition, or general constraints.

Examples of integrity constraints will be given on the following database:

EMP(ENO, ENAME, TITLE)

PROJ(PNO, PNAME, BUDGET)

ASG(ENO, PNO, RESP, DUR)

Predefined constraints are based on simple keywords. Through them, it is possible to express concisely the more common constraints of the relational model, such as non-null attribute, unique key, foreign key, or functional dependency [Fagin and Vardi, 1984]. Examples 5.11 through 5.14 demonstrate predefined constraints.

Example 5.11. Employee number in relation EMP cannot be null.

```
ENO NOT NULL IN EMP
```

♦

Example 5.12. The pair (ENO, PNO) is the unique key in relation ASG.

```
(ENO, PNO) UNIQUE IN ASG
```
                                                                              ◆

Example 5.13. The project number PNO in relation ASG is a foreign key matching
the primary key PNO of relation PROJ. In other words, a project referred to in
relation ASG must exist in relation PROJ.

```
PNO IN ASG REFERENCES PNO IN PROJ
```
                                                                              ◆

Example 5.14. The employee number functionally determines the employee name.

```
ENO IN EMP DETERMINES ENAME
```
                                                                              ◆

Precondition constraints express conditions that must be satisfied by all tuples in a
relation for a given update type. The update type, which might be INSERT, DELETE,
or MODIFY, permits restricting the integrity control. To identify in the constraint
definition the tuples that are subject to update, two variables, NEW and OLD, are
implicitly defined. They range over new tuples (to be inserted) and old tuples (to
be deleted), respectively [Astrahan et al., 1976]. Precondition constraints can be
expressed with the SQL CHECK statement enriched with the ability to specify the
update type. The syntax of the CHECK statement is

```
CHECK ON ⟨relation name⟩ WHEN⟨update type⟩
         (⟨qualification over relation name⟩)
```

Examples of precondition constraints are the following:

Example 5.15. The budget of a project is between 500K and 1000K.

```
CHECK ON PROJ (BUDGET+ >= 500000 AND  BUDGET <= 1000000)
```
                                                                              ◆

Example 5.16. Only the tuples whose budget is 0 may be deleted.

```
CHECK ON PROJ WHEN DELETE (BUDGET = 0)
```
                                                                              ◆

Example 5.17. The budget of a project can only increase.

```
CHECK ON PROJ (NEW.BUDGET > OLD.BUDGET
AND NEW.PNO = OLD.PNO)
```
                                                                              ◆

General constraints are formulas of tuple relational calculus where all variables
are quantified. The database system must ensure that those formulas are always
true. General constraints are more concise than precompiled constraints since the
former may involve more than one relation. For instance, at least three precompiled
constraints are necessary to express a general constraint on three relations. A general
constraint may be expressed with the following syntax:

```
CHECK ON list of <variable name>:<relation name>,
(<qualification>)
```

Examples of general constraints are given below.

Example 5.18. The constraint of Example 5.8 may also be expressed as

```
CHECK ON e1:EMP, e2:EMP
    (e1.ENAME = e2.ENAME IF e1.ENO = e2.ENO)
```

◆

Example 5.19. The total duration for all employees in the CAD project is less than 100.

```
CHECK ON g:ASG, j:PROJ (SUM(g.DUR WHERE
    g.PNO=j.PNO)<100 IF j.PNAME="CAD/CAM")
```

◆

5.3.1.2 Integrity Enforcement

We now focus on enforcing semantic integrity that consists of rejecting update transactions that violate some integrity constraints. A constraint is violated when it becomes false in the new database state produced by the update transaction. A major difficulty in designing an integrity manager is finding efficient enforcement algorithms. Two basic methods permit the rejection of inconsistent update transactions. The first one is based on the *detection* of inconsistencies. The update transaction u is executed, causing a change of the database state D to D_u. The enforcement algorithm verifies, by applying tests derived from these constraints, that all relevant constraints hold in state D_u. If state D_u is inconsistent, the DBMS can try either to reach another consistent state, D'_u, by modifying D_u with compensation actions, or to restore state D by undoing u. Since these tests are applied *after* having changed the database state, they are generally called *posttests*. This approach may be inefficient if a large amount of work (the update of D) must be undone in the case of an integrity failure.

The second method is based on the *prevention* of inconsistencies. An update is executed only if it changes the database state to a consistent state. The tuples subject to the update transaction are either directly available (in the case of insert) or must be retrieved from the database (in the case of deletion or modification). The enforcement algorithm verifies that all relevant constraints will hold after updating those tuples. This is generally done by applying to those tuples tests that are derived from the integrity constraints. Given that these tests are applied *before* the database state is changed, they are generally called *pretests*. The preventive approach is more efficient than the detection approach since updates never need to be undone because of integrity violation.

The query modification algorithm [Stonebraker, 1975] is an example of a preventive method that is particularly efficient at enforcing domain constraints. It adds the assertion qualification to the query qualification by an AND operator so that the modified query can enforce integrity.

Example 5.20. The query for increasing the budget of the CAD/CAM project by 10%, which would be specified as

```
UPDATE PROJ
SET     BUDGET = BUDGET*1.1
WHERE   PNAME= "CAD/CAM"
```

will be transformed into the following query in order to enforce the domain constraint discussed in Example 5.9.

```
UPDATE PROJ
SET     BUDGET = BUDGET * 1.1
WHERE   PNAME= "CAD/CAM"
AND     NEW.BUDGET ≥ 500000
AND     NEW.BUDGET ≤ 1000000
```
◆

The query modification algorithm, which is well known for its elegance, produces pretests at run time by ANDing the assertion predicates with the update predicates of each instruction of the transaction. However, the algorithm only applies to tuple calculus formulas and can be specified as follows. Consider the assertion $(\forall x \in R)F(x)$, where F is a tuple calculus expression in which x is the only free variable. An update of R can be written as $(\forall x \in R)(Q(x) \Rightarrow update(x))$, where Q is a tuple calculus expression whose only free variable is x. Roughly speaking, the query modification consists in generating the update $(\forall x \in R)((Q(x) \text{ and } F(x)) \Rightarrow update(x))$. Thus x needs to be universally quantified.

Example 5.21. The foreign key constraint of Example 5.13 that can be rewritten as

$$\forall g \in \text{ASG}, \exists j \in \text{PROJ} : g.\text{PNO} = j.\text{PNO}$$

could not be processed by query modification because the variable j is not universally quantified.   ◆

To handle more general constraints, pretests can be generated at constraint definition time, and enforced at run time when updates occur [Bernstein et al., 1980a; Bernstein and Blaustein, 1982; Blaustein, 1981; Nicolas, 1982]. The method described by Nicolas [1982] is restricted to updates that insert or delete a *single* tuple of a single relation. The algorithm proposed by Bernstein et al. [1980a] and Blaustein [1981] is an improvement, although updates are single single tuple. The algorithm builds a pretest at constraint definition time for each constraint and each update type (insert, delete). These pretests are enforced at run time. This method accepts multirelation, monovariable assertions, possibly with aggregates. The principle is the substitution of the tuple variables in the assertion by constants from an updated tuple. Despite its important contribution to research, the method is hardly usable in a real environment because of the restriction on updates.

In the rest of this section, we present the method proposed by Simon and Valduriez [1986, 1987], which combines the generality of updates supported by Stonebraker [1975] with at least the generality of assertions for which pretests can be produced by Blaustein [1981]. This method is based on the production, at assertion definition time, of pretests that are used subsequently to prevent the introduction of inconsistencies in the database. This is a general preventive method that handles the entire set of constraints introduced in the preceding section. It significantly reduces the proportion of the database that must be checked when enforcing assertions in the presence of updates. This is a major advantage when applied to a distributed environment.

The definition of pretest uses differential relations, as defined in Section 5.1.3. A *pretest* is a triple (R, U, C) in which R is a relation, U is an update type, and C is an assertion ranging over the differential relation(s) involved in an update of type U. When an integrity constraint I is defined, a set of pretests may be produced for the relations used by I. Whenever a relation involved in I is updated by a transaction u, the pretests that must be checked to enforce I are only those defined on I for the update type of u. The performance advantage of this approach is twofold. First, the number of assertions to enforce is minimized since only the pretests of type u need be checked. Second, the cost of enforcing a pretest is less than that of enforcing I since differential relations are, in general, much smaller than the base relations.

Pretests may be obtained by applying transformation rules to the original assertion. These rules are based on a syntactic analysis of the assertion and quantifier permutations. They permit the substitution of differential relations for base relations. Since the pretests are simpler than the original ones, the process that generates them is called *simplification*.

Example 5.22. Consider the modified expression of the foreign key constraint in Example 5.15. The pretests associated with this constraint are

(ASG, **INSERT**, C_1), (PROJ, **DELETE**, C_2) and (PROJ, **MODIFY**, C_3)

where C_1 is

$$\forall \text{ NEW} \in \text{ASG}^+, \exists j \in \text{PROJ: NEW.PNO} = j.\text{PNO}$$

C_2 is

$$\forall g \in \text{ASG}, \forall \text{ OLD} \in \text{PROJ}^- : g.\text{PNO} \neq \text{OLD.PNO}$$

and C_3 is

$$\forall g \in \text{ASG}, \forall \text{OLD} \in \text{PROJ}^-, \exists \text{ NEW} \in \text{PROJ}^+ : g.\text{PNO} \neq \text{OLD.PNO OR}$$
$$\text{OLD.PNO} = \text{NEW.PNO}$$

◆

The advantage provided by such pretests is obvious. For instance, a deletion on relation ASG does not incur any assertion checking.

The enforcement algorithm [Simon and Valduriez, 1984] makes use of pretests and is specialized according to the class of the assertions. Three classes of constraints are distinguished: single-relation constraints, multirelation constrainss, and constraints involving aggregate functions.

Let us now summarize the enforcement algorithm. Recall that an update transaction updates all tuples of relation R that satisfy some qualification. The algorithm acts in two steps. The first step generates the differential relations R^+ and R^- from R. The second step simply consists of retrieving the tuples of R^+ and R^-, which do not satisfy the pretests. If no tuples are retrieved, the constraint is valid. Otherwise, it is violated.

Example 5.23. Suppose there is a deletion on PROJ. Enforcing (PROJ, **DELETE**, C_2) consists in generating the following statement:

> *result* ← retrieve all tuples of PROJ⁻ where ¬(C_2)

Then, if the result is empty, the assertion is verified by the update and consistency is preserved.   ◆

5.3.2 Distributed Semantic Integrity Control

In this section we present algorithms for ensuring the semantic integrity of distributed databases. They are extensions of the simplification method discussed previously. In what follows, we assume global transaction management capabilities, as provided for homogeneous systems or multidatabase systems. Thus, the two main problems of designing an integrity manager for such a distributed DBMS are the definition and storage of assertions, and the enforcement of these constraints. We will also discuss the issues involved in integrity constraint checking when there is no global transaction support.

5.3.2.1 Definition of Distributed Integrity Constraints

An integrity constraint is supposed to be expressed in tuple relational calculus. Each assertion is seen as a query qualification that is either true or false for each tuple in the Cartesian product of the relations determined by the tuple variables. Since assertions can involve data stored at different sites, the storage of the constraints must be decided so as to minimize the cost of integrity checking. There is a strategy based on a taxonomy of integrity constraints that distinguishes three classes:

1. *Individual constraints*: single-relation single-variable constraints. They refer only to tuples to be updated independently of the rest of the database. For instance, the domain constraint of Example 5.15 is an individual assertion.

2. *Set-oriented constraints*: include single-relation multivariable constraints such as functional dependency (Example 5.14) and multirelation multivariable constraints such as foreign key constraints (Example 5.13).

3. *Constraints involving aggregates*: require special processing because of the cost of evaluating the aggregates. The assertion in Example 5.19 is representative of a constraint of this class.

The definition of a new integrity constraint can be started at one of the sites that store the relations involved in the assertion. Remember that the relations can be fragmented. A fragmentation predicate is a particular case of assertion of class 1. Different fragments of the same relation can be located at different sites. Thus, defining an integrity assertion becomes a distributed operation, which is done in two steps. The first step is to transform the high-level assertions into pretests, using the techniques discussed in the preceding section. The next step is to store pretests according to the class of constraints. Constraints of class 3 are treated like those of class 1 or 2, depending on whether they are individual or set-oriented.

Individual constraints.

The constraint definition is sent to all other sites that contain fragments of the relation involved in the constraint. The constraint must be compatible with the relation data at each site. Compatibility can be checked at two levels: predicate and data. First, predicate compatibility is verified by comparing the constraint predicate with the fragment predicate. A constraint C is not compatible with a fragment predicate p if "C is true" implies that "p is false," and is compatible with p otherwise. If non-compatibility is found at one of the sites, the constraint definition is globally rejected because tuples of that fragment do not satisfy the integrity constraints. Second, if predicate compatibility has been found, the constraint is tested against the instance of the fragment. If it is not satisfied by that instance, the constraint is also globally rejected. If compatibility is found, the constraint is stored at each site. Note that the compatibility checks are performed only for pretests whose update type is "insert" (the tuples in the fragments are considered "inserted").

Example 5.24. Consider relation EMP, horizontally fragmented across three sites using the predicates

$$p_1 : 0 \leq \text{ENO} < \text{"E3"}$$
$$p_2 : \text{"E3"} \leq \text{ENO} \leq \text{"E6"}$$
$$p_3 : \text{ENO} > \text{"E6"}$$

and the domain constraint C: ENO < "E4". Constraint C is compatible with p_1 (if C is true, p_1 is true) and p_2 (if C is true, p_2 is not necessarily false), but not with p_3 (if C is true, then p_3 is false). Therefore, constraint C should be globally rejected because the tuples at site 3 cannot satisfy C, and thus relation EMP does not satisfy C.   ◆

Set-oriented constraints.

Set-oriented constraint are multivariable; that is, they involve join predicates. Although the assertion predicate may be multirelation, a pretest is associated with a single relation. Therefore, the constraint definition can be sent to all the sites that store a fragment referenced by these variables. Compatibility checking also involves fragments of the relation used in the join predicate. Predicate compatibility is useless here, because it is impossible to infer that a fragment predicate p is false if the constraint C (based on a join predicate) is true. Therefore C must be checked for compatibility against the data. This compatibility check basically requires joining each fragment of the relation, say R, with all fragments of the other relation, say S, involved in the constraint predicate. This operation may be expensive and, as any join, should be optimized by the distributed query processor. Three cases, given in increasing cost of checking, can occur:

1. The fragmentation of R is derived (see Chapter 3) from that of S based on a semijoin on the attribute used in the assertion join predicate.

2. S is fragmented on join attribute.

3. S is not fragmented on join attribute.

In the first case, compatibility checking is cheap since the tuple of S matching a tuple of R is at the same site. In the second case, each tuple of R must be compared with at most one fragment of S, because the join attribute value of the tuple of R can be used to find the site of the corresponding fragment of S. In the third case, each tuple of R must be compared with all fragments of S. If compatibility is found for all tuples of R, the constraint can be stored at each site.

Example 5.25. Consider the set-oriented pretest (ASG, **INSERT**, C_1) defined in Example 5.16, where C_1 is

$$\forall \, \textbf{NEW} \in ASG^+, \exists j \in PROJ : \textbf{NEW}.PNO = j.PNO$$

Let us consider the following three cases:

1. ASG is fragmented using the predicate

   $$ASG \ltimes_{PNO} PROJ_i$$

   where $PROJ_i$ is a fragment of relation PROJ. In this case each tuple **NEW** of ASG has been placed at the same site as tuple j such that **NEW**.PNO $= j$.PNO. Since the fragmentation predicate is identical to that of C_1, compatibility checking does not incur communication.

2. PROJ is horizontally fragmented based on the two predicates

   $$p_1 : PNO < \text{“P3”}$$
   $$p_2 : PNO \geq \text{“P3”}$$

In this case each tuple **NEW** of ASG is compared with either fragment PROJ$_1$, if **NEW**.PNO < "P3", or fragment PROJ$_2$ if **NEW**.PNO $\geq$ "P3".

3. PROJ is horizontally fragmented based on the two predicates

p_1 : PNAME = "CAD/CAM"

p_2 : PNAME $\neq$ "CAD/CAM"

In this case each tuple of ASG must be compared with both fragments PROJ$_1$ and PROJ$_2$.

◆

5.3.2.2 Enforcement of Distributed Integrity Assertions

Enforcing distributed integrity assertions is more complex than needed in centralized DBMSs, even with global transaction management support. The main problem is to decide where (at which site) to enforce the integrity constraints. The choice depends on the class of the constraint, the type of update, and the nature of the site where the update is issued (called the *query master site*). This site may, or may not, store the updated relation or some of the relations involved in the integrity constraints. The critical parameter we consider is the cost of transferring data, including messages, from one site to another. We now discuss the different types of strategies according to these criteria.

Individual constraints.

Two cases are considered. If the update transaction is an insert statement, all the tuples to be inserted are explicitly provided by the user. In this case, all individual constraints can be enforced at the site where the update is submitted. If the update is a qualified update (delete or modify statements), it is sent to the sites storing the relation that will be updated. The query processor executes the update qualification for each fragment. The resulting tuples at each site are combined into one temporary relation in the case of a delete statement, or two, in the case of a modify statement (i.e., R^+ and R^-). Each site involved in the distributed update enforces the assertions relevant at that site (e.g., domain constraints when it is a delete).

Set-oriented constraints.

We first study single-relation constraints by means of an example. Consider the functional dependency of Example 5.14. The pretest associated with update type INSERT is

(EMP, **INSERT**, C)

where C is

$$(\forall e \in \text{EMP})(\forall \textbf{NEW1} \in \text{EMP})(\forall \textbf{NEW2} \in \text{EMP}) \tag{1}$$

$$(\textbf{NEW1}.\text{ENO} = e.\text{ENO} \Rightarrow \textbf{NEW1}.\text{ENAME} = e.\text{ENAME}) \wedge \tag{2}$$

$$(\textbf{NEW1}.\text{ENO} = \textbf{NEW2}.\text{ENO} \Rightarrow \textbf{NEW1}.\text{ENAME} = \textbf{NEW2}.\text{ENAME}) \tag{3}$$

The second line in the definition of C checks the constraint between the inserted tuples (NEW1) and the existing ones (e), while the third checks it between the inserted tuples themselves. That is why two variables (NEW1 and NEW2) are declared in the first line.

Consider now an update of EMP. First, the update qualification is executed by the query processor and returns one or two temporary relations, as in the case of individual constraints. These temporary relations are then sent to all sites storing EMP. Assume that the update is an INSERT statement. Then each site storing a fragment of EMP will enforce constraint C described above. Because e in C is universally quantified, C must be satisfied by the local data of each site. This is due to the fact that $\forall x \in \{a_1, \ldots, a_n\} f(x)$ is equivalent to $[f(a_1) \wedge f(a_2) \wedge \cdots \wedge f(a_n)]$. Thus the site where the update is submitted must receive for each site a message indicating that this constraint is satisfied and that it is a condition for all sites. If the constraint is not true for one site, this site sends an error message indicating that the constraint has been violated. The update is then invalid, and it is the responsibility of the integrity manager to decide if the entire transaction must be rejected using the global transaction manager.

Let us now consider multirelation constraints. For the sake of clarity, we assume that the integrity constraints do not have more than one tuple variable ranging over the same relation. Note that this is likely to be the most frequent case. As with single-relation constraints, the update is computed at the site where it was submitted. The enforcement is done at the query master site, using the ENFORCE algorithm given in Algorithm 5.2.

Example 5.26. We illustrate this algorithm through an example based on the foreign key constraint of Example 5.13. Let u be an insertion of a new tuple into ASG. The previous algorithm uses the pretest (ASG, **INSERT**, C), where C is

$$\forall \textbf{NEW} \in \text{ASG}^+, \exists j \in \text{PROJ} : \textbf{NEW}.\text{PNO} = j.\text{PNO}$$

For this constraint, the retrieval statement is to retrieve all new tuples in ASG$^+$ where C is not true. This statement can be expressed in SQL as

```
SELECT NEW.*
FROM   ASG+ NEW, PROJ
WHERE  COUNT(PROJ.PNO WHERE NEW.PNO = PROJ.PNO)=0
```

Note that **NEW**.* denotes all the attributes of ASG$^+$.   ◆

Thus the strategy is to send new tuples to sites storing relation PROJ in order to perform the joins, and then to centralize all results at the query master site. For each

---

Algorithm 5.2: ENFORCE Algorithm

Input: U: update type; R: relation
begin
    retrieve all compiled assertions (R, U, C_i) ;
    inconsistent ← **false** ;
    for *each compiled assertion* **do**
        ⌊ *result* ← all new (respectively old), tuples of R where $\neg(C_i)$
    if *card(result)* $\neq$ 0 **then**
        ⌊ *inconsistent* ← **true**
    if $\neg$*inconsistent* **then**
        | send the tuples to update to all the sites storing fragments of R
    else
        ⌊ reject the update
end

---

site storing a fragment of PROJ, the site joins the fragment with ASG$^+$ and sends the result to the query master site, which performs the union of all results. If the union is empty, the database is consistent. Otherwise, the update leads to an inconsistent state and should be rejected, using the global transaction manager. More sophisticated strategies that notify or compensate inconsistencies can also be devised.

Constraints involving aggregates.

These constraints are among the most costly to test because they require the calculation of the aggregate functions. The aggregate functions generally manipulated are MIN, MAX, SUM, and COUNT. Each aggregate function contains a projection part and a selection part. To enforce these constraints efficiently, it is possible to produce pretest that isolate redundant data which can be stored at each site storing the associated relation [Bernstein and Blaustein, 1982]. This data is what we called *materialized views* in Section 5.1.2.

5.3.2.3 Summary of Distributed Integrity Control

The main problem of distributed integrity control is that the communication and processing costs of enforcing distributed constraints can be prohibitive. The two main issues in designing a distributed integrity manager are the definition of the distributed assertions and of the enforcement algorithms, which minimize the cost of distributed integrity checking. We have shown in this chapter that distributed integrity control can be completely achieved, by extending a preventive method based on the compilation of semantic integrity constraints into pretests. The method is general since all types of constraints expressed in first-order predicate logic can be handled.

It is compatible with fragment definition and minimizes intersite communication. A better performance of distributed integrity enforcement can be obtained if fragments are defined carefully. Therefore, the specification of distributed integrity constraints is an important aspect of the distributed database design process.

The method described above assumes global transaction support. Without global transaction support as in some loosely-coupled multidatabase systems, the problem is more difficult [Grefen and Widom, 1997]. First, the interface between the constraint manager and the component DBMS is different since constraint checking can no longer be part of the global transaction validation. Instead, the component DBMSs should notify the integrity manager to perform constraint checking after some events, e.g., as a result of local transactions's commitments. This can be done using triggers whose events are updates to relations involved in global constraints. Second, if a global constraint violation is detected, since there is no way to specify global aborts, specific correcting transactions should be provided to produce global database states that are consistent. A family of protocols for global integrity checking has been proposed [Grefen and Widom, 1997]. The root of the family is a simple strategy, based on the computation of differential relations (as in the previous method), which is shown to be safe (correctly identifies constraint violations) but inaccurate (may raise an error event though there is no constraint violation). Inaccuracy is due to the fact that producing differential relations at different times at different sites may yield *phantom* states for the global database, i.e., states that never existed. Extensions of the basic protocol with either timestamping or using local transaction commands are proposed to solve that problem.

5.4 Conclusion

Semantic data and access control includes view management, security control, and semantic integrity control. In the relational framework, these functions can be uniformly achieved by enforcing rules that specify data manipulation control. Solutions initially designed for handling these functions in centralized systems have been significantly extended and enriched for distributed systems, in particular, support for materialized views and group-based discretionary access control. Semantic integrity control has received less attention and is generally not supported by distributed DBMS products.

Full semantic data control is more complex and costly in terms of performance in distributed systems. The two main issues for efficiently performing data control are the definition and storage of the rules (site selection) and the design of enforcement algorithms which minimize communication costs. The problem is difficult since increased functionality (and generality) tends to increase site communication. The problem is simplified if control rules are fully replicated at all sites and harder if site autonomy is to be preserved. In addition, specific optimizations can be done to minimize the cost of data control but with extra overhead such as managing materialized views or redundant data. Thus the specification of distributed data control must be included in the distributed database design so that the cost of control for update programs is also considered.

5.5 Bibliographic Notes

Semantic data control is well-understood in centralized systems [Ramakrishnan and Gehrke, 2003] and all major DBMSs provide extensive support for it. Research on semantic data control in distributed systems started in the early 1980's with the R* project at IBM Research and has increased much since then to address new important applications such as data warehousing or data integration.

Most of the work on view management has concerned updates through views and support for materialized views. The two basic papers on centralized view management are [Chamberlin et al., 1975] and [Stonebraker, 1975]. The first reference presents an integrated solution for view and authorization management in System R. The second reference describes INGRES's query modification technique for uniformly handling views, authorizations, and semantic integrity control. This method was presented in Section 5.1.

Theoretical solutions to the problem of view updates are given in [Bancilhon and Spyratos, 1981; Dayal and Bernstein, 1978], and [Keller, 1982]. The first of these is the seminal paper on view update semantics [Bancilhon and Spyratos, 1981] where the authors formalize the view invariance property after updating, and show how a large class of views including joins can be updated. Semantic information about the base relations is particularly useful for finding unique propagation of updates. However, the current commercial systems are very restrictive in supporting updates through views.

Materialized views have received much attention. The notion of snapshot for optimizing view derivation in distributed database systems is due to [Adiba and Lindsay, 1980]. Adiba [1981] generalizes the notion of snapshot by that of derived relation in a distributed context. He also proposes a unified mechanism for managing views, and snapshots, as well as fragmented and replicated data. Gupta and Mumick [1999c] have edited a thorough collection of papers on materialized view management in. In [Gupta and Mumick, 1999a], they describe the main techniques to perform incremental maintenance of materialized views. The counting algorithm which we presented in Section 5.1.3 has been proposed in [Gupta et al., 1993].

Security in computer systems in general is presented in [Hoffman, 1977]. Security in centralized database systems is presented in [Lunt and Fernández, 1990; Castano et al., 1995]. Discretionary access control in distributed systems has first received much attention in the context of the R* project. The access control mechanism of System R Griffiths and Wade [1976] is extended in [Wilms and Lindsay, 1981] to handle groups of users and to run in a distributed environment. Multilevel access control for distributed DBMS has recently gained much interest. The seminal paper on multilevel access control is the Bell and Lapaduda model originally designed for operating system security [Bell and Lapuda, 1976]. Multilevel access control for databases is described in [Lunt and Fernández, 1990; Jajodia and Sandhu, 1991]. A good introduction to multilevel security in relational DBMS can be found in [Rjaibi, 2004]. Transaction management in multilevel secure DBMS is addressed in [Ray et al., 2000; Jajodia et al., 2001]. Extensions of multilevel access control for distributed DBMS are proposed in [Thuraisingham, 2001].

The content of Section 5.3 comes largely from the work on semantic integrity control described in [Simon and Valduriez, 1984, 1986] and [Simon and Valduriez, 1987]. In particular, [Simon and Valduriez, 1986] extends a preventive strategy for centralized integrity control based on pretests to run in a distributed environment, assuming global transaction support. The initial idea of declarative methods, that is, to use assertions of predicate logic to specify integrity constraints, is due to [Florentin, 1974]. The most important declarative methods are in [Bernstein et al., 1980a; Blaustein, 1981; Nicolas, 1982; Simon and Valduriez, 1984], and [Stonebraker, 1975]. The notion of concrete views for storing redundant data is described in [Bernstein and Blaustein, 1982]. Note that concrete views are useful in optimizing the enforcement of constraints involving aggregates. [Civelek et al., 1988; Sheth et al., 1988b] and Sheth et al. [1988a] describe systems and tools for semantic data control, particularly view management. Semantic intergrity checking in loosely-coupled multidatabase systems without global transaction support is addressed in [Grefen and Widom, 1997].

Exercises

Problem 5.1. Define in SQL-like syntax a view of the engineering database V(ENO, ENAME, PNO, RESP), where the duration is 24. Is view V updatable? Assume that relations EMP and ASG are horizontally fragmented based on access frequencies as follows:

Site 1 Site 2 Site 3
EMP_1 EMP_2
         ASG_1 ASG_2

where

$EMP_1 = \sigma_{TITLE \neq \text{"Engineer"}}(EMP)$
$EMP_2 = \sigma_{TITLE = \text{"Engineer"}}(EMP)$
$ASG_1 = \sigma_{0 < DUR < 36}(ASG)$
$ASG_2 = \sigma_{DUR \geq 36}(ASG)$

At which site(s) should the definition of V be stored without being fully replicated, to increase locality of reference?

Problem 5.2. Express the following query: names of employees in view V who work on the CAD project.

Problem 5.3 (*). Assume that relation PROJ is horizontally fragmented as

$$PROJ_1 = \sigma_{PNAME = \text{"CAD"}}(PROJ)$$
$$PROJ_2 = \sigma_{PNAME \neq \text{"CAD"}}(PROJ)$$

Modify the query obtained in Exercise 5.2 to a query expressed on the fragments.

Problem 5.4 (**). Propose a distributed algorithm to efficiently refresh a snapshot at one site derived by projection from a relation horizontally fragmented at two other sites. Give an example query on the view and base relations which produces an inconsistent result.

Problem 5.5 (*). Consider the view EG of Example 5.5 which uses relations EMP and ASG as base data and assume its state is derived from that of Example 3.1, so that EG has 9 tuples (see Figure 5.4). Assume that tuple $\langle$E3, P3, Consultant, 10$\rangle$ from ASG is updated to $\langle$E3, P3, Engineer, 10$\rangle$. Apply the basic counting algorithm for refreshing the view EG. What projected attributes should be added to view EG to make it self-maintainable?

Problem 5.6. Propose a relation schema for storing the access rights associated with user groups in a distributed database catalog, and give a fragmentation scheme for that relation, assuming that all members of a group are at the same site.

Problem 5.7 (**). Give an algorithm for executing the REVOKE statement in a distributed DBMS, assuming that the GRANT privilege can be granted only to a group of users where all its members are at the same site.

Problem 5.8 (**). Consider the multilevel relation PROJ** in Figure 5.8. Assuming that there are only two classification levels for attributes (S and C), propose an allocation of PROJ** on two sites using fragmentation and replication that avoids covert channels on read queries. Discuss the constraints on updates for this allocation to work.

Problem 5.9. Using the integrity constraint specification language of this chapter, express an integrity constraint which states that the duration spent in a project cannot exceed 48 months.

Problem 5.10 (*). Define the pretests associated with integrity constraints covered in Examples 5.11 to 5.14.

Problem 5.11. Assume the following vertical fragmentation of relations EMP, ASG and PROJ:

Site 1	Site 2	Site 3	Site 4
EMP_1	EMP_2		
	$PROJ_1$	$PROJ_2$	
		ASG_1	ASG_2

where

$EMP_1 = \Pi_{ENO, ENAME}(EMP)$
$EMP_2 = \Pi_{ENO, TITLE}(EMP)$
$PROJ_1 = \Pi_{PNO, PNAME}(PROJ)$
$PROJ_2 = \Pi_{PNO, BUDGET}(PROJ)$
$ASG_1 = \Pi_{ENO, PNO, RESP}(ASG)$
$ASG_2 = \Pi_{ENO, PNO, DUR}(ASG)$

Where should the pretests obtained in Exercise 5.9 be stored?

Problem 5.12 (**). Consider the following set-oriented constraint:

```
CHECK ON e:EMP, a:ASG
    (e.ENO = a.ENO and (e.TITLE = "Programmer")
    IF a.RESP = "Programmer")
```

What does it mean? Assuming that EMP and ASG are allocated as in the previous exercice, define the corresponding pretests and theri storage. Apply algorithm ENFORCE for an update of type INSERT in ASG.

Problem 5.13 (**). Assume a distributed multidatabase system with no global transaction support. Assume also that there are two sites, each with a (different) EMP relation and a integrity manager that communicates with the component DBMS. Suppose that we want to have a global unique key constraint on EMP. Propose a simple strategy using differential relations to check this constraint. Discuss the possible actions when a constraint is violated.

Chapter 6
Overview of Query Processing

The success of relational database technology in data processing is due, in part, to the availability of non-procedural languages (i.e., SQL), which can significantly improve application development and end-user productivity. By hiding the low-level details about the physical organization of the data, relational database languages allow the expression of complex queries in a concise and simple fashion. In particular, to construct the answer to the query, the user does not precisely specify the procedure to follow. This procedure is actually devised by a DBMS module, usually called a *query processor*. This relieves the user from query optimization, a time-consuming task that is best handled by the query processor, since it can exploit a large amount of useful information about the data.

Because it is a critical performance issue, query processing has received (and continues to receive) considerable attention in the context of both centralized and distributed DBMSs. However, the query processing problem is much more difficult in distributed environments than in centralized ones, because a larger number of parameters affect the performance of distributed queries. In particular, the relations involved in a distributed query may be fragmented and/or replicated, thereby inducing communication overhead costs. Furthermore, with many sites to access, query response time may become very high.

In this chapter we give an overview of query processing in distributed DBMSs, leaving the details of the important aspects of distributed query processing to the next two chapters. The context chosen is that of relational calculus and relational algebra, because of their generality and wide use in distributed DBMSs. As we saw in Chapter 3, distributed relations are implemented by fragments. Distributed database design is of major importance for query processing since the definition of fragments is based on the objective of increasing reference locality, and sometimes parallel execution for the most important queries. The role of a distributed query processor is to map a high-level query (assumed to be expressed in relational calculus) on a distributed database (i.e., a set of global relations) into a sequence of database operators (of relational algebra) on relation fragments. Several important functions characterize this mapping. First, the *calculus query* must be *decomposed* into a sequence of relational operators called an *algebraic query*. Second, the data accessed by the

M.T. Özsu and P. Valduriez, *Principles of Distributed Database Systems: Third Edition*, DOI 10.1007/978-1-4419-8834-8_6, © Springer Science+Business Media, LLC 2011

query must be *localized* so that the operators on relations are translated to bear on local data (fragments). Finally, the algebraic query on fragments must be extended with communication operators and *optimized* with respect to a cost function to be minimized. This cost function typically refers to computing resources such as disk I/Os, CPUs, and communication networks.

The chapter is organized as follows. In Section 6.1 we illustrate the query processing problem. In Section 6.2 we define precisely the objectives of query processing algorithms. The complexity of relational algebra operators, which affect mainly the performance of query processing, is given in Section 6.3. In Section 6.4 we provide a characterization of query processors based on their implementation choices. Finally, in Section 6.5 we introduce the different layers of query processing starting from a distributed query down to the execution of operators on local sites and communication between sites. The layers introduced in Section 6.5 are described in detail in the next two chapters.

6.1 Query Processing Problem

The main function of a relational query processor is to transform a high-level query (typically, in relational calculus) into an equivalent lower-level query (typically, in some variation of relational algebra). The low-level query actually implements the execution strategy for the query. The transformation must achieve both correctness and efficiency. It is correct if the low-level query has the same semantics as the original query, that is, if both queries produce the same result. The well-defined mapping from relational calculus to relational algebra (see Chapter 2) makes the correctness issue easy. But producing an efficient execution strategy is more involved. A relational calculus query may have many equivalent and correct transformations into relational algebra. Since each equivalent execution strategy can lead to very different consumptions of computer resources, the main difficulty is to select the execution strategy that minimizes resource consumption.

Example 6.1. We consider the following subset of the engineering database schema given in Figure 2.3:

    EMP(ENO, ENAME, TITLE)
    ASG(ENO, PNO, RESP, DUR)

and the following simple user query:

    "Find the names of employees who are managing a project"

The expression of the query in relational calculus using the SQL syntax is

```
SELECT ENAME
FROM    EMP,ASG
WHERE   EMP.ENO = ASG.ENO
AND     RESP = ``Manager''
```

Two equivalent relational algebra queries that are correct transformations of the query above are

$$\Pi_{ENAME}(\sigma_{RESP=\text{``Manager''} \wedge EMP.ENO=ASG.ENO} (EMP \times ASG))$$

and

$$\Pi_{ENAME}(EMP \bowtie_{ENO} (\sigma_{RESP=\text{``Manager''}} (ASG)))$$

It is intuitively obvious that the second query, which avoids the Cartesian product of EMP and ASG, consumes much less computing resources than the first, and thus should be retained. ◆

In a centralized context, query execution strategies can be well expressed in an extension of relational algebra. The main role of a centralized query processor is to choose, for a given query, the best relational algebra query among all equivalent ones. Since the problem is computationally intractable with a large number of relations [Ibaraki and Kameda, 1984], it is generally reduced to choosing a solution close to the optimum.

In a distributed system, relational algebra is not enough to express execution strategies. It must be supplemented with operators for exchanging data between sites. Besides the choice of ordering relational algebra operators, the distributed query processor must also select the best sites to process data, and possibly the way data should be transformed. This increases the solution space from which to choose the distributed execution strategy, making distributed query processing significantly more difficult.

Example 6.2. This example illustrates the importance of site selection and communication for a chosen relational algebra query against a fragmented database. We consider the following query of Example 6.1:

$$\Pi_{ENAME} (EMP \bowtie_{ENO} (\sigma_{RESP=\text{``Manager''}} (ASG)))$$

We assume that relations EMP and ASG are horizontally fragmented as follows:

$EMP_1 = \sigma_{ENO \leq \text{``E3''}} (EMP)$

$EMP_2 = \sigma_{ENO > \text{``E3''}}(EMP)$

$ASG_1 = \sigma_{ENO \leq \text{``E3''}}(ASG)$

$ASG_2 = \sigma_{ENO > \text{``E3''}}(ASG)$

Fragments ASG_1, ASG_2, EMP_1, and EMP_2 are stored at sites 1, 2, 3, and 4, respectively, and the result is expected at site 5.

For the sake of pedagogical simplicity, we ignore the project operator in the following. Two equivalent distributed execution strategies for the above query are shown in Figure 6.1. An arrow from site i to site j labeled with R indicates that relation R is transferred from site i to site j. Strategy A exploits the fact that relations EMP and ASG are fragmented the same way in order to perform the select and join operator in parallel. Strategy B centralizes all the operand data at the result site before processing the query.

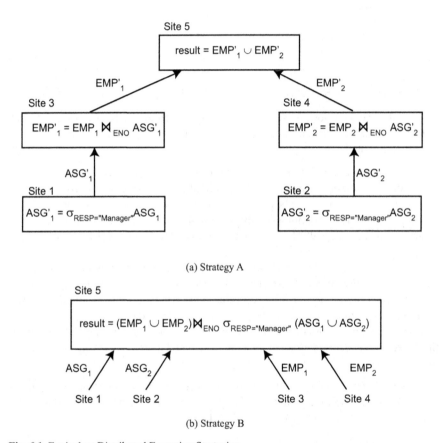

Fig. 6.1 Equivalent Distributed Execution Strategies

To evaluate the resource consumption of these two strategies, we use a simple cost model. We assume that a tuple access, denoted by *tupacc*, is 1 unit (which we leave unspecified) and a tuple transfer, denoted *tuptrans*, is 10 units. We assume that relations EMP and ASG have 400 and 1000 tuples, respectively, and that there are 20 managers in relation ASG. We also assume that data is uniformly distributed among sites. Finally, we assume that relations ASG and EMP are locally clustered on attributes RESP and ENO, respectively. Therefore, there is direct access to tuples of ASG (respectively, EMP) based on the value of attribute RESP (respectively, ENO).

The total cost of strategy A can be derived as follows:

1. Produce ASG′ by selecting ASG requires $(10+10) * tupacc$ = 20
2. Transfer ASG′ to the sites of EMP requires $(10+10) * tuptrans$ = 200
3. Produce EMP′ by joining ASG′ and EMP requires
   $(10+10) * tupacc * 2$ = 40
4. Transfer EMP′ to result site requires $(10+10) * tuptrans$ = 200

   The total cost is $\overline{460}$

The cost of strategy B can be derived as follows:

1. Transfer EMP to site 5 requires $400 * tuptrans$ = 4,000
2. Transfer ASG to site 5 requires $1000 * tuptrans$ = 10,000
3. Produce ASG′ by selecting ASG requires $1000 * tupacc$ = 1,000
4. Join EMP and ASG′ requires $400 * 20 * tupacc$ = 8,000

   The total cost is $\overline{23,000}$

In strategy A, the join of ASG′ and EMP (step 3) can exploit the cluster index on ENO of EMP. Thus, EMP is accessed only once for each tuple of ASG′. In strategy B, we assume that the access methods to relations EMP and ASG based on attributes RESP and ENO are lost because of data transfer. This is a reasonable assumption in practice. We assume that the join of EMP and ASG′ in step 4 is done by the default nested loop algorithm (that simply performs the Cartesian product of the two input relations). Strategy A is better by a factor of 50, which is quite significant. Furthermore, it provides better distribution of work among sites. The difference would be even higher if we assumed slower communication and/or higher degree of fragmentation.   ◆

6.2 Objectives of Query Processing

As stated before, the objective of query processing in a distributed context is to transform a high-level query on a distributed database, which is seen as a single database by the users, into an efficient execution strategy expressed in a low-level language on local databases. We assume that the high-level language is relational calculus, while the low-level language is an extension of relational algebra with communication operators. The different layers involved in the query transformation are detailed in Section 6.5. An important aspect of query processing is query optimization. Because many execution strategies are correct transformations of the same high-level query, the one that optimizes (minimizes) resource consumption should be retained.

A good measure of resource consumption is the *total cost* that will be incurred in processing the query [Sacco and Yao, 1982]. Total cost is the sum of all times incurred in processing the operators of the query at various sites and in intersite communication. Another good measure is the *response time* of the query [Epstein et al., 1978], which is the time elapsed for executing the query. Since operators can be executed in parallel at different sites, the response time of a query may be significantly less than its total cost.

In a distributed database system, the total cost to be minimized includes CPU, I/O, and communication costs. The CPU cost is incurred when performing operators on data in main memory. The I/O cost is the time necessary for disk accesses. This cost can be minimized by reducing the number of disk accesses through fast access methods to the data and efficient use of main memory (buffer management). The communication cost is the time needed for exchanging data between sites participating in the execution of the query. This cost is incurred in processing the messages (formatting/deformatting), and in transmitting the data on the communication network.

The first two cost components (I/O and CPU cost) are the only factors considered by centralized DBMSs. The communication cost component is equally important factor considered in distributed databases. Most of the early proposals for distributed query optimization assume that the communication cost largely dominates local processing cost (I/O and CPU cost), and thus ignore the latter. This assumption is based on very slow communication networks (e.g., wide area networks that used to have a bandwidth of a few kilobytes per second) rather than on networks with bandwidths that are comparable to disk connection bandwidth. Therefore, the aim of distributed query optimization reduces to the problem of minimizing communication costs generally at the expense of local processing. The advantage is that local optimization can be done independently using the known methods for centralized systems. However, modern distributed processing environments have much faster communication networks, as discussed in Chapter 2, whose bandwidth is comparable to that of disks. Therefore, more recent research efforts consider a weighted combination of these three cost components since they all contribute significantly to the total cost of evaluating a query[1] [Page and Popek, 1985]. Nevertheless, in distributed environments with high bandwidths, the overhead cost incurred for communication between sites (e.g., software protocols) makes communication cost still an important factor.

6.3 Complexity of Relational Algebra Operations

In this chapter we consider relational algebra as a basis to express the output of query processing. Therefore, the complexity of relational algebra operators, which directly affects their execution time, dictates some principles useful to a query processor. These principles can help in choosing the final execution strategy.

The simplest way of defining complexity is in terms of relation cardinalities independent of physical implementation details such as fragmentation and storage

---

[1] There are some studies that investigate the feasibility of retrieving data from a neighboring nodes' main memory cache rather than accessing them from a local disk [Franklin et al., 1992; Dahlin et al., 1994; Freeley et al., 1995]. These approaches would have a significant impact on query optimization.

structures. Figure 6.2 shows the complexity of unary and binary operators in the order of increasing complexity, and thus of increasing execution time. Complexity is $O(n)$ for unary operators, where n denotes the relation cardinality, if the resulting tuples may be obtained independently of each other. Complexity is $O(n*\log n)$ for binary operators if each tuple of one relation must be compared with each tuple of the other on the basis of the equality of selected attributes. This complexity assumes that tuples of each relation must be sorted on the comparison attributes. However, using hashing and enough memory to hold one hashed relation can reduce the complexity of binary operators $O(n)$ [Bratbergsengen, 1984]. Projects with duplicate elimination and grouping operators require that each tuple of the relation be compared with each other tuple, and thus also have $O(n*\log n)$ complexity. Finally, complexity is $O(n^2)$ for the Cartesian product of two relations because each tuple of one relation must be combined with each tuple of the other.

Operation	Complexity
Select Project (without duplicate elimination)	$O(n)$
Project (with duplicate elimination) Group by	$O(n*\log n)$
Join Semijoin Division Set Operators	$O(n*\log n)$
Cartesian Product	$O(n^2)$

Fig. 6.2 Complexity of Relational Algebra Operations

This simple look at operator complexity suggests two principles. First, because complexity is relative to relation cardinalities, the most selective operators that reduce cardinalities (e.g., selection) should be performed first. Second, operators should be ordered by increasing complexity so that Cartesian products can be avoided or delayed.

6.4 Characterization of Query Processors

It is quite difficult to evaluate and compare query processors in the context of both centralized systems [Jarke and Koch, 1984] and distributed systems [Sacco and

Yao, 1982; Apers et al., 1983; Kossmann, 2000] because they may differ in many aspects. In what follows, we list important characteristics of query processors that can be used as a basis for comparison. The first four characteristics hold for both centralized and distributed query processors while the next four characteristics are particular to distributed query processors in tightly-integrated distributed DBMSs. This characterization is used in Chapter 8 to compare various algorithms.

6.4.1 Languages

Initially, most work on query processing was done in the context of relational DBMSs because their high-level languages give the system many opportunities for optimization. The input language to the query processor is thus based on relational calculus. With object DBMSs, the language is based on object calculus which is merely an extension of relational calculus. Thus, decomposition to object algebra is also needed (see Chapter 15). XML, another data model that we consider in this book, has its own languages, primarily in XQuery and XPath. Their execution requires special care that we discuss in Chapter 17.

The former requires an additional phase to decompose a query expressed in relational calculus into relational algebra. In a distributed context, the output language is generally some internal form of relational algebra augmented with communication primitives. The operators of the output language are implemented directly in the system. Query processing must perform efficient mapping from the input language to the output language.

6.4.2 Types of Optimization

Conceptually, query optimization aims at choosing the "best" point in the solution space of all possible execution strategies. An immediate method for query optimization is to search the solution space, exhaustively predict the cost of each strategy, and select the strategy with minimum cost. Although this method is effective in selecting the best strategy, it may incur a significant processing cost for the optimization itself. The problem is that the solution space can be large; that is, there may be many equivalent strategies, even with a small number of relations. The problem becomes worse as the number of relations or fragments increases (e.g., becomes greater than 5 or 6). Having high optimization cost is not necessarily bad, particularly if query optimization is done once for many subsequent executions of the query. Therefore, an "exhaustive" search approach is often used whereby (almost) all possible execution strategies are considered [Selinger et al., 1979].

To avoid the high cost of exhaustive search, *randomized* strategies, such as *iterative improvement* [Swami, 1989] and *simulated annealing* [Ioannidis and Wong, 1987] have been proposed. They try to find a very good solution, not necessarily the best one, but avoid the high cost of optimization, in terms of memory and time consumption.

Another popular way of reducing the cost of exhaustive search is the use of heuristics, whose effect is to restrict the solution space so that only a few strategies are considered. In both centralized and distributed systems, a common heuristic is to minimize the size of intermediate relations. This can be done by performing unary operators first, and ordering the binary operators by the increasing sizes of their intermediate relations. An important heuristic in distributed systems is to replace join operators by combinations of semijoins to minimize data communication.

6.4.3 Optimization Timing

A query may be optimized at different times relative to the actual time of query execution. Optimization can be done *statically* before executing the query or *dynamically* as the query is executed. Static query optimization is done at query compilation time. Thus the cost of optimization may be amortized over multiple query executions. Therefore, this timing is appropriate for use with the exhaustive search method. Since the sizes of the intermediate relations of a strategy are not known until run time, they must be estimated using database statistics. Errors in these estimates can lead to the choice of suboptimal strategies.

Dynamic query optimization proceeds at query execution time. At any point of execution, the choice of the best next operator can be based on accurate knowledge of the results of the operators executed previously. Therefore, database statistics are not needed to estimate the size of intermediate results. However, they may still be useful in choosing the first operators. The main advantage over static query optimization is that the actual sizes of intermediate relations are available to the query processor, thereby minimizing the probability of a bad choice. The main shortcoming is that query optimization, an expensive task, must be repeated for each execution of the query. Therefore, this approach is best for ad-hoc queries.

Hybrid query optimization attempts to provide the advantages of static query optimization while avoiding the issues generated by inaccurate estimates. The approach is basically static, but dynamic query optimization may take place at run time when a high difference between predicted sizes and actual size of intermediate relations is detected.

6.4.4 Statistics

The effectiveness of query optimization relies on *statistics* on the database. Dynamic query optimization requires statistics in order to choose which operators should be done first. Static query optimization is even more demanding since the size of intermediate relations must also be estimated based on statistical information. In a distributed database, statistics for query optimization typically bear on fragments, and include fragment cardinality and size as well as the size and number of distinct values of each attribute. To minimize the probability of error, more detailed statistics such as histograms of attribute values are sometimes used at the expense of higher management cost. The accuracy of statistics is achieved by periodic updating. With static optimization, significant changes in statistics used to optimize a query might result in query reoptimization.

6.4.5 Decision Sites

When static optimization is used, either a single site or several sites may participate in the selection of the strategy to be applied for answering the query. Most systems use the centralized decision approach, in which a single site generates the strategy. However, the decision process could be distributed among various sites participating in the elaboration of the best strategy. The centralized approach is simpler but requires knowledge of the entire distributed database, while the distributed approach requires only local information. Hybrid approaches where one site makes the major decisions and other sites can make local decisions are also frequent. For example, System R* [Williams et al., 1982] uses a hybrid approach.

6.4.6 Exploitation of the Network Topology

The network topology is generally exploited by the distributed query processor. With wide area networks, the cost function to be minimized can be restricted to the data communication cost, which is considered to be the dominant factor. This assumption greatly simplifies distributed query optimization, which can be divided into two separate problems: selection of the global execution strategy, based on intersite communication, and selection of each local execution strategy, based on a centralized query processing algorithm.

With local area networks, communication costs are comparable to I/O costs. Therefore, it is reasonable for the distributed query processor to increase parallel execution at the expense of communication cost. The broadcasting capability of some local area networks can be exploited successfully to optimize the processing of join operators [Özsoyoglu and Zhou, 1987; Wah and Lien, 1985]. Other algorithms specialized to take advantage of the network topology are discussed by Kerschberg et al. [1982] for star networks and by LaChimia [1984] for satellite networks.

In a client-server environment, the power of the client workstation can be exploited to perform database operators using *data shipping* [Franklin et al., 1996]. The optimization problem becomes to decide which part of the query should be performed on the client and which part on the server using query shipping.

6.4.7 Exploitation of Replicated Fragments

A distributed relation is usually divided into relation fragments as described in Chapter 3. Distributed queries expressed on global relations are mapped into queries on physical fragments of relations by translating relations into fragments. We call this process *localization* because its main function is to localize the data involved in the query. For higher reliability and better read performance, it is useful to have fragments replicated at different sites. Most optimization algorithms consider the localization process independently of optimization. However, some algorithms exploit the existence of replicated fragments at run time in order to minimize communication times. The optimization algorithm is then more complex because there are a larger number of possible strategies.

6.4.8 Use of Semijoins

The semijoin operator has the important property of reducing the size of the operand relation. When the main cost component considered by the query processor is communication, a semijoin is particularly useful for improving the processing of distributed join operators as it reduces the size of data exchanged between sites. However, using semijoins may result in an increase in the number of messages and in the local processing time. The early distributed DBMSs, such as SDD-1 [Bernstein et al., 1981], which were designed for slow wide area networks, make extensive use of semijoins. Some later systems, such as R* [Williams et al., 1982], assume faster networks and do not employ semijoins. Rather, they perform joins directly since using joins leads to lower local processing costs. Nevertheless, semijoins are still beneficial in the context of fast networks when they induce a strong reduction of the join operand. Therefore, some query processing algorithms aim at selecting an optimal combination of joins and semijoins [Özsoyoglu and Zhou, 1987; Wah and Lien, 1985].

6.5 Layers of Query Processing

In Chapter 1 we have seen where query processing fits within the distributed DBMS architecture. The problem of query processing can itself be decomposed into several subproblems, corresponding to various layers. In Figure 6.3 a generic layering scheme for query processing is shown where each layer solves a well-defined subproblem. To simplify the discussion, let us assume a static and semicentralized query processor that does not exploit replicated fragments. The input is a query on global data expressed in relational calculus. This query is posed on global (distributed) relations, meaning that data distribution is hidden. Four main layers are involved in distributed query processing. The first three layers map the input query into an optimized

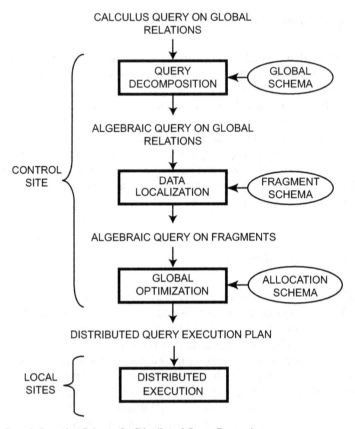

Fig. 6.3 Generic Layering Scheme for Distributed Query Processing

distributed query execution plan. They perform the functions of *query decomposition*, *data localization*, and *global query optimization*. Query decomposition and data localization correspond to query rewriting. The first three layers are performed by a central control site and use schema information stored in the global directory. The fourth layer performs *distributed query execution* by executing the plan and returns the answer to the query. It is done by the local sites and the control site. The first two layers are treated extensively in Chapter 7, while the two last layers are detailed in Chapter 8. In the remainder of this chapter we present an overview of these four layers.

6.5.1 Query Decomposition

The first layer decomposes the calculus query into an algebraic query on global relations. The information needed for this transformation is found in the global conceptual schema describing the global relations. However, the information about data distribution is not used here but in the next layer. Thus the techniques used by this layer are those of a centralized DBMS.

Query decomposition can be viewed as four successive steps. First, the calculus query is rewritten in a *normalized* form that is suitable for subsequent manipulation. Normalization of a query generally involves the manipulation of the query quantifiers and of the query qualification by applying logical operator priority.

Second, the normalized query is *analyzed* semantically so that incorrect queries are detected and rejected as early as possible. Techniques to detect incorrect queries exist only for a subset of relational calculus. Typically, they use some sort of graph that captures the semantics of the query.

Third, the correct query (still expressed in relational calculus) is *simplified*. One way to simplify a query is to eliminate redundant predicates. Note that redundant queries are likely to arise when a query is the result of system transformations applied to the user query. As seen in Chapter 5, such transformations are used for performing semantic data control (views, protection, and semantic integrity control).

Fourth, the calculus query is *restructured* as an algebraic query. Recall from Section 6.1 that several algebraic queries can be derived from the same calculus query, and that some algebraic queries are "better" than others. The quality of an algebraic query is defined in terms of expected performance. The traditional way to do this transformation toward a "better" algebraic specification is to start with an initial algebraic query and transform it in order to find a "good" one. The initial algebraic query is derived immediately from the calculus query by translating the predicates and the target statement into relational operators as they appear in the query. This directly translated algebra query is then restructured through transformation rules. The algebraic query generated by this layer is good in the sense that the worse executions are typically avoided. For instance, a relation will be accessed only once, even if there are several select predicates. However, this query is generally far from providing an optimal execution, since information about data distribution and fragment allocation is not used at this layer.

6.5.2 Data Localization

The input to the second layer is an algebraic query on global relations. The main role of the second layer is to localize the query's data using data distribution information in the fragment schema. In Chapter 3 we saw that relations are fragmented and stored in disjoint subsets, called fragments, each being stored at a different site. This layer determines which fragments are involved in the query and transforms the distributed query into a query on fragments. Fragmentation is defined by fragmentation predicates that can be expressed through relational operators. A global relation can be reconstructed by applying the fragmentation rules, and then deriving a program, called a *localization program*, of relational algebra operators, which then act on fragments. Generating a query on fragments is done in two steps. First, the query is mapped into a fragment query by substituting each relation by its reconstruction program (also called *materialization program*), discussed in Chapter 3. Second, the fragment query is simplified and restructured to produce another "good" query. Simplification and restructuring may be done according to the same rules used in the decomposition layer. As in the decomposition layer, the final fragment query is generally far from optimal because information regarding fragments is not utilized.

6.5.3 Global Query Optimization

The input to the third layer is an algebraic query on fragments. The goal of query optimization is to find an execution strategy for the query which is close to optimal. Remember that finding the optimal solution is computationally intractable. An execution strategy for a distributed query can be described with relational algebra operators and *communication primitives* (send/receive operators) for transferring data between sites. The previous layers have already optimized the query, for example, by eliminating redundant expressions. However, this optimization is independent of fragment characteristics such as fragment allocation and cardinalities. In addition, communication operators are not yet specified. By permuting the ordering of operators within one query on fragments, many equivalent queries may be found.

Query optimization consists of finding the "best" ordering of operators in the query, including communication operators that minimize a cost function. The cost function, often defined in terms of time units, refers to computing resources such as disk space, disk I/Os, buffer space, CPU cost, communication cost, and so on. Generally, it is a weighted combination of I/O, CPU, and communication costs. Nevertheless, a typical simplification made by the early distributed DBMSs, as we mentioned before, was to consider communication cost as the most significant factor. This used to be valid for wide area networks, where the limited bandwidth made communication much more costly than local processing. This is not true anymore today and communication cost can be lower than I/O cost. To select the ordering of operators it is necessary to predict execution costs of alternative candidate orderings. Determining execution costs before query execution (i.e., static optimization) is based on fragment statistics and the formulas for estimating the cardinalities of results of relational operators. Thus the optimization decisions depend on the allocation of fragments and available statistics on fragments which are recorder in the allocation schema.

An important aspect of query optimization is *join ordering*, since permutations of the joins within the query may lead to improvements of orders of magnitude. One basic technique for optimizing a sequence of distributed join operators is through the semijoin operator. The main value of the semijoin in a distributed system is to reduce the size of the join operands and then the communication cost. However, techniques which consider local processing costs as well as communication costs may not use semijoins because they might increase local processing costs. The output of the query optimization layer is a optimized algebraic query with communication operators included on fragments. It is typically represented and saved (for future executions) as a *distributed query execution plan* .

6.5.4 Distributed Query Execution

The last layer is performed by all the sites having fragments involved in the query. Each subquery executing at one site, called a *local query*, is then optimized using the local schema of the site and executed. At this time, the algorithms to perform the relational operators may be chosen. Local optimization uses the algorithms of centralized systems (see Chapter 8).

6.6 Conclusion

In this chapter we provided an overview of query processing in distributed DBMSs. We first introduced the function and objectives of query processing. The main assumption is that the input query is expressed in relational calculus since that is the case with most current distributed DBMS. The complexity of the problem is proportional to the expressive power and the abstraction capability of the query language. For instance, the problem is even harder with important extensions such as the transitive closure operator [Valduriez and Boral, 1986].

The goal of distributed query processing may be summarized as follows: given a calculus query on a distributed database, find a corresponding execution strategy that minimizes a system cost function that includes I/O, CPU, and communication costs. An execution strategy is specified in terms of relational algebra operators and communication primitives (send/receive) applied to the local databases (i.e., the relation fragments). Therefore, the complexity of relational operators that affect the performance of query execution is of major importance in the design of a query processor.

We gave a characterization of query processors based on their implementation choices. Query processors may differ in various aspects such as type of algorithm, optimization granularity, optimization timing, use of statistics, choice of decision site(s), exploitation of the network topology, exploitation of replicated fragments, and use of semijoins. This characterization is useful for comparing alternative query processor designs and to understand the trade-offs between efficiency and complexity.

The query processing problem is very difficult to understand in distributed environments because many elements are involved. However, the problem may be divided into several subproblems which are easier to solve individually. Therefore, we have proposed a generic layering scheme for describing distributed query processing. Four main functions have been isolated: query decomposition, data localization, global query optimization, and distributed query execution. These functions successively refine the query by adding more details about the processing environment. Query decomposition and data localization are treated in detail in Chapter 7. Distributed query optimization and execution is the topic of Chapter 8.

6.7 Bibliographic Notes

Kim et al. [1985] provide a comprehensive set of papers presenting the results of research and development in query processing within the context of the relational model. After a survey of the state of the art in query processing, the book treats most of the important topics in the area. In particular, there are three papers on distributed query processing.

Ibaraki and Kameda [1984] have formally shown that finding the optimal execution strategy for a query is computationally intractable. Assuming a simplified cost function including the number of page accesses, it is proven that the minimization of this cost function for a multiple-join query is NP-complete.

Ceri and Pelagatti [1984] deal extensively with distributed query processing by treating the problem of localization and optimization separately in two chapters. The main assumption is that the query is expressed in relational algebra, so the decomposition phase that maps a calculus query into an algebraic query is ignored.

There are several survey papers on query processing and query optimization in the context of the relational model. A detailed survey is by Graefe [1993]. An earlier survey is [Jarke and Koch, 1984]. Both of these mainly deal with centralized query processing. The initial solutions to distributed query processing are extensively compiled in [Sacco and Yao, 1982; Yu and Chang, 1984]. Many query processing techniques are compiled in the book [Freytag et al., 1994].

The most complete survey on distributed query processing is by Kossmann [2000] and deals with both distributed DBMSs and multidatabase systems. The paper presents the traditional phases of query processing in centralized and distributed systems, and describes the various techniques for distributed query processing. It also discusses different distributed architectures such as client-server, multi-tier, and multidatabases.

Chapter 7
Query Decomposition and Data Localization

In Chapter 6 we discussed a generic layering scheme for distributed query processing in which the first two layers are responsible for query decomposition and data localization. These two functions are applied successively to transform a calculus query specified on distributed relations (i.e., global relations) into an algebraic query defined on relation fragments. In this chapter we present the techniques for query decomposition and data localization.

Query decomposition maps a distributed calculus query into an algebraic query on global relations. The techniques used at this layer are those of the centralized DBMS since relation distribution is not yet considered at this point. The resultant algebraic query is "good" in the sense that even if the subsequent layers apply a straightforward algorithm, the worst executions will be avoided. However, the subsequent layers usually perform important optimizations, as they add to the query increasing detail about the processing environment.

Data localization takes as input the decomposed query on global relations and applies data distribution information to the query in order to localize its data. In Chapter 3 we have seen that to increase the locality of reference and/or parallel execution, relations are fragmented and then stored in disjoint subsets, called fragments, each being placed at a different site. Data localization determines which fragments are involved in the query and thereby transforms the distributed query into a fragment query. Similar to the decomposition layer, the final fragment query is generally far from optimal because quantitative information regarding fragments is not exploited at this point. Quantitative information is used by the query optimization layer that will be presented in Chapter 8.

This chapter is organized as follows. In Section 7.1 we present the four successive phases of query decomposition: normalization, semantic analysis, simplification, and restructuring of the query. In Section 7.2 we describe data localization, with emphasis on reduction and simplification techniques for the four following types of fragmentation: horizontal, vertical, derived, and hybrid.

M.T. Özsu and P. Valduriez, *Principles of Distributed Database Systems: Third Edition*,
DOI 10.1007/978-1-4419-8834-8_7, © Springer Science+Business Media, LLC 2011

7.1 Query Decomposition

Query decomposition (see Figure 6.3) is the first phase of query processing that transforms a relational calculus query into a relational algebra query. Both input and output queries refer to global relations, without knowledge of the distribution of data. Therefore, query decomposition is the same for centralized and distributed systems. In this section the input query is assumed to be syntactically correct. When this phase is completed successfully the output query is semantically correct and good in the sense that redundant work is avoided. The successive steps of query decomposition are (1) normalization, (2) analysis, (3) elimination of redundancy, and (4) rewriting. Steps 1, 3, and 4 rely on the fact that various transformations are equivalent for a given query, and some can have better performance than others. We present the first three steps in the context of tuple relational calculus (e.g., SQL). Only the last step rewrites the query into relational algebra.

7.1.1 Normalization

The input query may be arbitrarily complex, depending on the facilities provided by the language. It is the goal of normalization to transform the query to a normalized form to facilitate further processing. With relational languages such as SQL, the most important transformation is that of the query qualification (the WHERE clause), which may be an arbitrarily complex, quantifier-free predicate, preceded by all necessary quantifiers ($\forall$ or $\exists$). There are two possible normal forms for the predicate, one giving precedence to the AND ($\wedge$) and the other to the OR ($\vee$). The *conjunctive normal form* is a conjunction ($\wedge$ predicate) of disjunctions ($\vee$ predicates) as follows:

$$(p_{11} \vee p_{12} \vee \cdots \vee p_{1n}) \wedge \cdots \wedge (p_{m1} \vee p_{m2} \vee \cdots \vee p_{mn})$$

where p_{ij} is a simple predicate. A qualification in *disjunctive normal form*, on the other hand, is as follows:

$$(p_{11} \wedge p_{12} \wedge \cdots \wedge p_{1n}) \vee \cdots \vee (p_{m1} \wedge p_{m2} \wedge \cdots \wedge p_{mn})$$

The transformation of the quantifier-free predicate is straightforward using the well-known equivalence rules for logical operations ($\wedge$, $\vee$, and $\neg$):

1. $p_1 \wedge p_2 \Leftrightarrow p_2 \wedge p_1$
2. $p_1 \vee p_2 \Leftrightarrow p_2 \vee p_1$
3. $p_1 \wedge (p_2 \wedge p_3) \Leftrightarrow (p_1 \wedge p_2) \wedge p_3$
4. $p_1 \vee (p_2 \vee p_3) \Leftrightarrow (p_1 \vee p_2) \vee p_3$
5. $p_1 \wedge (p_2 \vee p_3) \Leftrightarrow (p_1 \wedge p_2) \vee (p_1 \wedge p_3)$
6. $p_1 \vee (p_2 \wedge p_3) \Leftrightarrow (p_1 \vee p_2) \wedge (p_1 \vee p_3)$

7. $\neg(p_1 \wedge p_2) \Leftrightarrow \neg p_1 \vee \neg p_2$

8. $\neg(p_1 \vee p_2) \Leftrightarrow \neg p_1 \wedge \neg p_2$

9. $\neg(\neg p) \Leftrightarrow p$

In the disjunctive normal form, the query can be processed as independent conjunctive subqueries linked by unions (corresponding to the disjunctions). However, this form may lead to replicated join and select predicates, as shown in the following example. The reason is that predicates are very often linked with the other predicates by AND. The use of rule 5 mentioned above, with p_1 as a join or select predicate, would result in replicating p_1. The conjunctive normal form is more practical since query qualifications typically include more AND than OR predicates. However, it leads to predicate replication for queries involving many disjunctions and few conjunctions, a rare case.

Example 7.1. Let us consider the following query on the engineering database that we have been referring to:

"Find the names of employees who have been working on project P1 for 12 or 24 months"

The query expressed in SQL is

```
SELECT ENAME
FROM    EMP, ASG
WHERE   EMP.ENO = ASG.ENO
AND     ASG.PNO = "P1"
AND     DUR = 12 OR DUR = 24
```

The qualification in conjunctive normal form is

EMP.ENO = ASG.ENO $\wedge$ ASG.PNO = "P1" $\wedge$ (DUR = 12 $\vee$ DUR = 24)

while the qualification in disjunctive normal form is

(EMP.ENO = ASG.ENO $\wedge$ ASG.PNO = "P1" $\wedge$ DUR = 12) $\vee$

(EMP.ENO = ASG.ENO $\wedge$ ASG.PNO = "P1" $\wedge$ DUR = 24)

In the latter form, treating the two conjunctions independently may lead to redundant work if common subexpressions are not eliminated.   ◆

7.1.2 Analysis

Query analysis enables rejection of normalized queries for which further processing is either impossible or unnecessary. The main reasons for rejection are that the query is *type incorrect* or *semantically incorrect*. When one of these cases is detected, the query is simply returned to the user with an explanation. Otherwise, query processing is continued. Below we present techniques to detect these incorrect queries.

A query is type incorrect if any of its attribute or relation names are not defined in the global schema, or if operations are being applied to attributes of the wrong type. The technique used to detect type incorrect queries is similar to type checking for programming languages. However, the type declarations are part of the global schema rather than of the query, since a relational query does not produce new types.

Example 7.2. The following SQL query on the engineering database is type incorrect for two reasons. First, attribute E# is not declared in the schema. Second, the operation ">200" is incompatible with the type string of ENAME.

```
SELECT E#
FROM    EMP
WHERE   ENAME > 200
```
                                                                                    ◆

A query is semantically incorrect if its components do not contribute in any way to the generation of the result. In the context of relational calculus, it is not possible to determine the semantic correctness of general queries. However, it is possible to do so for a large class of relational queries, those which do not contain disjunction and negation [Rosenkrantz and Hunt, 1980]. This is based on the representation of the query as a graph, called a *query graph* or *connection graph* [Ullman, 1982]. We define this graph for the most useful kinds of queries involving select, project, and join operators. In a query graph, one node indicates the result relation, and any other node indicates an operand relation. An edge between two nodes one of which does not correspond to the result represents a join, whereas an edge whose destination node is the result represents a project. Furthermore, a non-result node may be labeled by a select or a self-join (join of the relation with itself) predicate. An important subgraph of the query graph is the *join graph*, in which only the joins are considered. The join graph is particularly useful in the query optimization phase.

Example 7.3. Let us consider the following query:

"Find the names and responsibilities of programmers who have been working on the CAD/CAM project for more than 3 years."

The query expressed in SQL is
```
SELECT ENAME, RESP
FROM    EMP, ASG, PROJ
WHERE   EMP.ENO = ASG.ENO
AND     ASG.PNO = PROJ.PNO
AND     PNAME = "CAD/CAM"
AND     DUR ≥ 36
AND     TITLE = "Programmer"
```

The query graph for the query above is shown in Figure 7.1a. Figure 7.1b shows the join graph for the graph in Figure 7.1a.   ◆

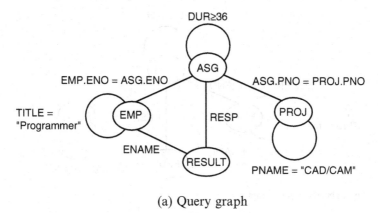

(a) Query graph

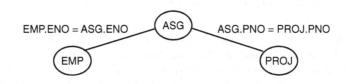

(b) Corresponding join graph

Fig. 7.1 Relation Graphs

The query graph is useful to determine the semantic correctness of a conjunctive multivariable query without negation. Such a query is semantically incorrect if its query graph is not connected. In this case one or more subgraphs (corresponding to subqueries) are disconnected from the graph that contains the result relation. The query could be considered correct (which some systems do) by considering the missing connection as a Cartesian product. But, in general, the problem is that join predicates are missing and the query should be rejected.

Example 7.4. Let us consider the following SQL query:

```
SELECT ENAME, RESP
FROM    EMP, ASG, PROJ
WHERE   EMP.ENO = ASG.ENO
AND     PNAME = "CAD/CAM"
AND     DUR ≥ 36
AND     TITLE = "Programmer"
```

Its query graph, shown in Figure 7.2, is disconnected, which tells us that the query is semantically incorrect. There are basically three solutions to the problem: (1) reject the query, (2) assume that there is an implicit Cartesian product between relations ASG and PROJ, or (3) infer (using the schema) the missing join predicate ASG.PNO = PROJ.PNO which transforms the query into that of Example 7.3.   ◆

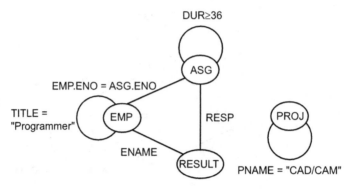

Fig. 7.2 Disconnected Query Graph

7.1.3 Elimination of Redundancy

As we saw in Chapter 5, relational languages can be used uniformly for semantic data control. In particular, a user query typically expressed on a view may be enriched with several predicates to achieve view-relation correspondence, and ensure semantic integrity and security. The enriched query qualification may then contain redundant predicates. A naive evaluation of a qualification with redundancy can well lead to duplicated work. Such redundancy and thus redundant work may be eliminated by simplifying the qualification with the following well-known idempotency rules:

1. $p \land p \Leftrightarrow p$
2. $p \lor p \Leftrightarrow p$
3. $p \land true \Leftrightarrow p$
4. $p \lor false \Leftrightarrow p$
5. $p \land false \Leftrightarrow false$
6. $p \lor true \Leftrightarrow true$
7. $p \land \neg p \Leftrightarrow false$
8. $p \lor \neg p \Leftrightarrow true$
9. $p_1 \land (p_1 \lor p_2) \Leftrightarrow p_1$
10. $p_1 \lor (p_1 \land p_2) \Leftrightarrow p_1$

Example 7.5. The SQL query

```
SELECT TITLE
FROM    EMP
WHERE   (NOT (TITLE = "Programmer")
AND     (TITLE = "Programmer"
OR      TITLE = "Elect. Eng.")
AND     NOT (TITLE = "Elect. Eng."))
OR      ENAME = "J. Doe"
```

can be simplified using the previous rules to become

```
SELECT TITLE
FROM    EMP
WHERE   ENAME = "J. Doe"
```

The simplification proceeds as follows. Let p_1 be TITLE = "Programmer", p_2 be TITLE = "Elect. Eng.", and p_3 be ENAME = "J. Doe". The query qualification is

$$(\neg p_1 \wedge (p_1 \vee p_2) \wedge \neg p_2) \vee p_3$$

The disjunctive normal form for this qualification is obtained by applying rule 5 defined in Section 7.1.1, which yields

$$(\neg p_1 \wedge ((p_1 \wedge \neg p_2) \vee (p_2 \wedge \neg p_2))) \vee p_3$$

and then rule 3 defined in Section 7.1.1, which yields

$$(\neg p_1 \wedge p_1 \wedge \neg p_2) \vee (\neg p_1 \wedge p_2 \wedge \neg p_2) \vee p_3$$

By applying rule 7 defined above, we obtain

$$(false \wedge \neg p_2) \vee (\neg p_1 \wedge false) \vee p_3$$

By applying the same rule, we get

$$false \vee false \vee p_3$$

which is equivalent to p_3 by rule 4. ◆

7.1.4 Rewriting

The last step of query decomposition rewrites the query in relational algebra. For the sake of clarity it is customary to represent the relational algebra query graphically by an *operator tree*. An operator tree is a tree in which a leaf node is a relation stored in the database, and a non-leaf node is an intermediate relation produced by a relational algebra operator. The sequence of operations is directed from the leaves to the root, which represents the answer to the query.

The transformation of a tuple relational calculus query into an operator tree can easily be achieved as follows. First, a different leaf is created for each different tuple variable (corresponding to a relation). In SQL, the leaves are immediately available in the FROM clause. Second, the root node is created as a project operation involving the result attributes. These are found in the SELECT clause in SQL. Third, the qualification (SQL WHERE clause) is translated into the appropriate sequence of relational operations (select, join, union, etc.) going from the leaves to the root. The sequence can be given directly by the order of appearance of the predicates and operators.

Example 7.6. The query

"Find the names of employees other than J. Doe who worked on the CAD/CAM project for either one or two years" whose SQL expression is

```
SELECT ENAME
FROM   PROJ, ASG, EMP
WHERE  ASG.ENO = EMP.ENO
AND    ASG.PNO = PROJ.PNO
AND    ENAME != "J. Doe"
AND    PROJ.PNAME = "CAD/CAM"
AND    (DUR = 12 OR DUR = 24)
```

can be mapped in a straightforward way in the tree in Figure 7.3. The predicates have been transformed in order of appearance as join and then select operations.   ◆

By applying *transformation rules*, many different trees may be found equivalent to the one produced by the method described above [Smith and Chang, 1975]. We now present the six most useful equivalence rules, which concern the basic relational algebra operators. The correctness of these rules has been proven [Ullman, 1982].

In the remainder of this section, R, S, and T are relations where R is defined over attributes $A = \{A_1, A_2, \ldots, A_n\}$ and S is defined over $B = \{B_1, B_2, \ldots, B_n\}$.

1. **Commutativity of binary operators.** The Cartesian product of two relations R and S is commutative:

    $$R \times S \Leftrightarrow S \times R$$

    Similarly, the join of two relations is commutative:

    $$R \bowtie S \Leftrightarrow S \bowtie R$$

    This rule also applies to union but not to set difference or semijoin.

2. **Associativity of binary operators.** The Cartesian product and the join are associative operators:

    $$(R \times S) \times T \Leftrightarrow R \times (S \times T)$$
    $$(R \bowtie S) \bowtie T \Leftrightarrow R \bowtie (S \bowtie T)$$

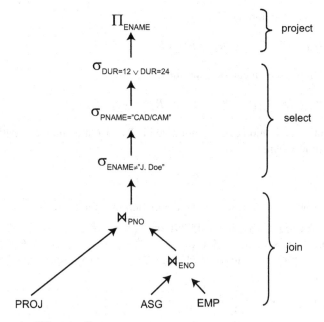

Fig. 7.3 Example of Operator Tree

3. **Idempotence of unary operators.** Several subsequent projections on the same relation may be grouped. Conversely, a single projection on several attributes may be separated into several subsequent projections. If R is defined over the attribute set A, and $A' \subseteq A, A'' \subseteq A$, and $A' \subseteq A''$, then

$$\Pi_{A'}(\Pi_{A''}(R)) \Leftrightarrow \Pi_{A'}(R)$$

Several subsequent selections $\sigma_{p_i(A_i)}$ on the same relation, where p_i is a predicate applied to attribute A_i, may be grouped as follows:

$$\sigma_{p_1(A_1)}(\sigma_{p_2(A_2)}(R)) = \sigma_{p_1(A_1) \wedge p_2(A_2)}(R)$$

Conversely, a single selection with a conjunction of predicates may be separated into several subsequent selections.

4. **Commuting selection with projection.** Selection and projection on the same relation can be commuted as follows:

$$\Pi_{A_1,\dots,A_n}(\sigma_{p(A_p)}(R)) \Leftrightarrow \Pi_{A_1,\dots,A_n}(\sigma_{p(A_p)}(\Pi_{A_1,\dots,A_n,A_p}(R)))$$

Note that if A_p is already a member of $\{A_1,\dots,A_n\}$, the last projection on $[A_1,\dots,A_n]$ on the right-hand side of the equality is useless.

5. **Commuting selection with binary operators.** Selection and Cartesian product can be commuted using the following rule (remember that attribute A_i

belongs to relation R):

$$\sigma_{p(A_i)}(R \times S) \Leftrightarrow (\sigma_{p(A_i)}(R)) \times S$$

Selection and join can be commuted:

$$\sigma_{p(A_i)}(R \bowtie_{p(A_j,B_k)} S) \Leftrightarrow \sigma_{p(A_i)}(R) \bowtie_{p(A_j,B_k)} S$$

Selection and union can be commuted if R and T are union compatible (have the same schema):

$$\sigma_{p(A_i)}(R \cup T) \Leftrightarrow \sigma_{p(A_i)}(R) \cup \sigma_{p(A_i)}(T)$$

Selection and difference can be commuted in a similar fashion.

6. **Commuting projection with binary operators.** Projection and Cartesian product can be commuted. If $C = A' \cup B'$, where $A' \subseteq A$, $B' \subseteq B$, and A and B are the sets of attributes over which relations R and S, respectively, are defined, we have

$$\Pi_C(R \times S) \Leftrightarrow \Pi_{A'}(R) \times \Pi_{B'}(S)$$

Projection and join can also be commuted.

$$\Pi_C(R \bowtie_{p(A_i,B_j)} S) \Leftrightarrow \Pi_{A'}(R) \bowtie_{p(A_i,B_j)} \Pi_{B'}(S)$$

For the join on the right-hand side of the implication to hold we need to have $A_i \in A'$ and $B_j \in B'$. Since $C = A' \cup B'$, A_i and B_j are in C and therefore we don't need a projection over C once the projections over A' and B' are performed. Projection and union can be commuted as follows:

$$\Pi_C(R \cup S) \Leftrightarrow \Pi_C(R) \cup \Pi_C(S)$$

Projection and difference can be commuted similarly.

The application of these six rules enables the generation of many equivalent trees. For instance, the tree in Figure 7.4 is equivalent to the one in Figure 7.3. However, the one in Figure 7.4 requires a Cartesian product of relations EMP and PROJ, and may lead to a higher execution cost than the original tree. In the optimization phase, one can imagine comparing all possible trees based on their predicted cost. However, the excessively large number of possible trees makes this approach unrealistic. The rules presented above can be used to restructure the tree in a systematic way so that the "bad" operator trees are eliminated. These rules can be used in four different ways. First, they allow the separation of the unary operations, simplifying the query expression. Second, unary operations on the same relation may be grouped so that access to a relation for performing unary operations can be done only once. Third, unary operations can be commuted with binary operations so that some operations (e.g., selection) may be done first. Fourth, the binary operations can be ordered. This last rule is used extensively in query optimization. A simple restructuring algorithm uses a single heuristic that consists of applying unary operations (select/project) as soon as possible to reduce the size of intermediate relations [Ullman, 1982].

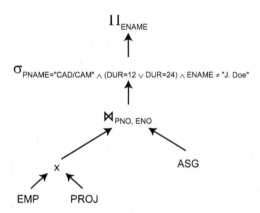

Fig. 7.4 Equivalent Operator Tree

Example 7.7. The restructuring of the tree in Figure 7.3 leads to the tree in Figure 7.5. The resulting tree is good in the sense that repeated access to the same relation (as in Figure 7.3) is avoided and that the most selective operations are done first. However, this tree is far from optimal. For example, the select operation on EMP is not very useful before the join because it does not greatly reduce the size of the operand relation.   ♦

7.2 Localization of Distributed Data

In Section 7.1 we presented general techniques for decomposing and restructuring queries expressed in relational calculus. These global techniques apply to both centralized and distributed DBMSs and do not take into account the distribution of data. This is the role of the localization layer. As shown in the generic layering scheme of query processing described in Chapter 6, the localization layer translates an algebraic query on global relations into an algebraic query expressed on physical fragments. Localization uses information stored in the fragment schema.

Fragmentation is defined through fragmentation rules, which can be expressed as relational queries. As we discussed in Chapter 3, a global relation can be reconstructed by applying the reconstruction (or reverse fragmentation) rules and deriving a relational algebra program whose operands are the fragments. We call this a *localization program*. To simplify this section, we do not consider the fact that data

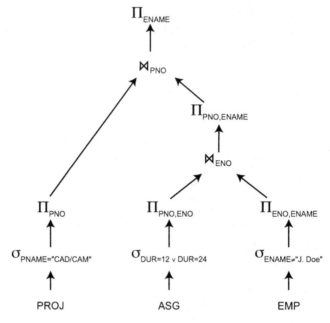

Fig. 7.5 Rewritten Operator Tree

fragments may be replicated, although this can improve performance. Replication is considered in Chapter 8.

A naive way to localize a distributed query is to generate a query where each global relation is substituted by its localization program. This can be viewed as replacing the leaves of the operator tree of the distributed query with subtrees corresponding to the localization programs. We call the query obtained this way the *localized query*. In general, this approach is inefficient because important restructurings and simplifications of the localized query can still be made [Ceri and Pelagatti, 1983; Ceri et al., 1986]. In the remainder of this section, for each type of fragmentation we present *reduction techniques* that generate simpler and optimized queries. We use the transformation rules and the heuristics, such as pushing unary operations down the tree, that were introduced in Section 7.1.4.

7.2.1 Reduction for Primary Horizontal Fragmentation

The horizontal fragmentation function distributes a relation based on selection predicates. The following example is used in subsequent discussions.

Example 7.8. Relation EMP(ENO, ENAME, TITLE) of Figure 2.3 can be split into three horizontal fragments EMP_1, EMP_2, and EMP_3, defined as follows:

$$EMP_1 = \sigma_{ENO \leq "E3"}(EMP)$$
$$EMP_2 = \sigma_{"E3" < ENO \leq "E6"}(EMP)$$
$$EMP_3 = \sigma_{ENO > "E6"}(EMP)$$

Note that this fragmentation of the EMP relation is different from the one discussed in Example 3.12.

The localization program for an horizontally fragmented relation is the union of the fragments. In our example we have

$$EMP = EMP_1 \cup EMP_2 \cup EMP_3$$

Thus the localized form of any query specified on EMP is obtained by replacing it by $(EMP_1 \cup EMP_2 \cup EMP_3$. ◆

The reduction of queries on horizontally fragmented relations consists primarily of determining, after restructuring the subtrees, those that will produce empty relations, and removing them. Horizontal fragmentation can be exploited to simplify both selection and join operations.

7.2.1.1 Reduction with Selection

Selections on fragments that have a qualification contradicting the qualification of the fragmentation rule generate empty relations. Given a relation R that has been horizontally fragmented as $R_1, R_2, \ldots, R_w$, where $R_j = \sigma_{p_j}(R)$, the rule can be stated formally as follows:

Rule 1: $\sigma_{p_i}(R_j) = \phi$ if $\forall x$ in $R : \neg(p_i(x) \wedge p_j(x))$

where p_i and p_j are selection predicates, x denotes a tuple, and $p(x)$ denotes "predicate p holds for x."

For example, the selection predicate ENO="E1" conflicts with the predicates of fragments EMP_2 and EMP_3 of Example 7.8 (i.e., no tuple in EMP_2 and EMP_3 can satisfy this predicate). Determining the contradicting predicates requires theorem-proving techniques if the predicates are quite general [Hunt and Rosenkrantz, 1979]. However, DBMSs generally simplify predicate comparison by supporting only simple predicates for defining fragmentation rules (by the database administrator).

Example 7.9. We now illustrate reduction by horizontal fragmentation using the following example query:

```
SELECT *
FROM    EMP
WHERE   ENO = "E5"
```

Applying the naive approach to localize EMP from EMP_1, EMP_2, and EMP_3 gives the localized query of Figure 7.6a. By commuting the selection with the union operation, it is easy to detect that the selection predicate contradicts the predicates of

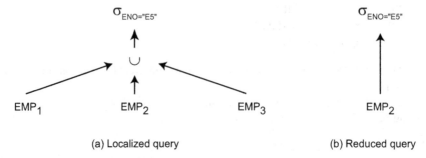

(a) Localized query   (b) Reduced query

Fig. 7.6 Reduction for Horizontal Fragmentation (with Selection)

EMP_1 and EMP_3, thereby producing empty relations. The reduced query is simply applied to EMP_2 as shown in Figure 7.6b.   ◆

7.2.1.2 Reduction with Join

Joins on horizontally fragmented relations can be simplified when the joined relations are fragmented according to the join attribute. The simplification consists of distributing joins over unions and eliminating useless joins. The distribution of join over union can be stated as:

$$(R_1 \cup R_2) \bowtie S = (R_1 \bowtie S) \cup (R_2 \bowtie S)$$

where R_i are fragments of R and S is a relation.

With this transformation, unions can be moved up in the operator tree so that all possible joins of fragments are exhibited. Useless joins of fragments can be determined when the qualifications of the joined fragments are contradicting, thus yielding an empty result. Assuming that fragments R_i and R_j are defined, respectively, according to predicates p_i and p_j on the same attribute, the simplification rule can be stated as follows:

Rule 2: $R_i \bowtie R_j = \phi$ if $\forall x$ in $R_i, \forall y$ in $R_j : \neg(p_i(x) \wedge p_j(y))$

The determination of useless joins and their elimination using rule 2 can thus be performed by looking only at the fragment predicates. The application of this rule permits the join of two relations to be implemented as parallel partial joins of fragments [Ceri et al., 1986]. It is not always the case that the reduced query is better (i.e., simpler) than the localized query. The localized query is better when there are a large number of partial joins in the reduced query. This case arises when there are few contradicting fragmentation predicates. The worst case occurs when each fragment of one relation must be joined with each fragment of the other relation. This is tantamount to the Cartesian product of the two sets of fragments, with each set corresponding to one relation. The reduced query is better when the number of partial joins is small. For example, if both relations are fragmented using the same predicates, the number of partial joins is equal to the number of fragments of each relation. One advantage of the reduced query is that the partial joins can be done in parallel, and thus increase response time.

Example 7.10. Assume that relation EMP is fragmented between EMP_1, EMP_2, and EMP_3, as above, and that relation ASG is fragmented as

$$ASG_1 = \sigma_{ENO \leq "E3"}(ASG)$$
$$ASG_2 = \sigma_{ENO > "E3"}(ASG)$$

EMP_1 and ASG_1 are defined by the same predicate. Furthermore, the predicate defining ASG_2 is the union of the predicates defining EMP_2 and EMP_3. Now consider the join query

```
SELECT *
FROM    EMP, ASG
WHERE   EMP.ENO = ASG.ENO
```

The equivalent localized query is given in Figure 7.7a. The query reduced by distributing joins over unions and applying rule 2 can be implemented as a union of three partial joins that can be done in parallel (Figure 7.7b). ◆

7.2.2 Reduction for Vertical Fragmentation

The vertical fragmentation function distributes a relation based on projection attributes. Since the reconstruction operator for vertical fragmentation is the join, the localization program for a vertically fragmented relation consists of the join of the fragments on the common attribute. For vertical fragmentation, we use the following example.

Example 7.11. Relation EMP can be divided into two vertical fragments where the key attribute ENO is duplicated:

$$EMP_1 = \Pi_{ENO,ENAME}(EMP)$$
$$EMP_2 = \Pi_{ENO,TITLE}(EMP)$$

The localization program is

$$EMP = EMP_1 \bowtie_{ENO} EMP_2$$

◆

Similar to horizontal fragmentation, queries on vertical fragments can be reduced by determining the useless intermediate relations and removing the subtrees that produce them. Projections on a vertical fragment that has no attributes in common

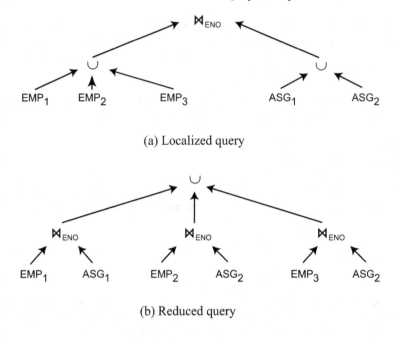

(a) Localized query

(b) Reduced query

Fig. 7.7 Reduction by Horizontal Fragmentation (with Join)

with the projection attributes (except the key of the relation) produce useless, though not empty relations. Given a relation R, defined over attributes $A = \{A_1,\ldots,A_n\}$, which is vertically fragmented as $R_i = \Pi_{A'}(R)$, where $A' \subseteq A$, the rule can be formally stated as follows:

Rule 3: $\Pi_{D,K}(R_i)$ is useless if the set of projection attributes D is not in A'.

Example 7.12. Let us illustrate the application of this rule using the following example query in SQL:

```
SELECT ENAME
FROM    EMP
```

The equivalent localized query on EMP_1 and EMP_2 (as obtained in Example 7.10) is given in Figure 7.8a. By commuting the projection with the join (i.e., projecting on ENO, ENAME), we can see that the projection on EMP_2 is useless because ENAME is not in EMP_2. Therefore, the projection needs to apply only to EMP_1, as shown in Figure 7.8b.   ◆

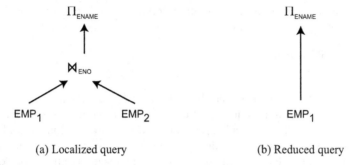

Fig. 7.8 Reduction for Vertical Fragmentation

7.2.3 Reduction for Derived Fragmentation

As we saw in previous sections, the join operation, which is probably the most important operation because it is both frequent and expensive, can be optimized by using primary horizontal fragmentation when the joined relations are fragmented according to the join attributes. In this case the join of two relations is implemented as a union of partial joins. However, this method precludes one of the relations from being fragmented on a different attribute used for selection. Derived horizontal fragmentation is another way of distributing two relations so that the joint processing of select and join is improved. Typically, if relation R is subject to derived horizontal fragmentation due to relation S, the fragments of R and S that have the same join attribute values are located at the same site. In addition, S can be fragmented according to a selection predicate.

Since tuples of R are placed according to the tuples of S, derived fragmentation should be used only for one-to-many (hierarchical) relationships of the form $S \to R$, where a tuple of S can match with n tuples of R, but a tuple of R matches with exactly one tuple of S. Note that derived fragmentation could be used for many-to-many relationships provided that tuples of S (that match with n tuples of R) are replicated. Such replication is difficult to maintain consistently. For simplicity, we assume and advise that derived fragmentation be used only for hierarchical relationships.

Example 7.13. Given a one-to-many relationship from EMP to ASG, relation ASG(ENO, PNO, RESP, DUR) can be indirectly fragmented according to the following rules:

$$ASG_1 = ASG \ltimes_{ENO} EMP_1$$
$$ASG_2 = ASG \ltimes_{ENO} EMP_2$$

Recall from Chapter 3 that the predicate on

$$EMP_1 = \sigma_{TITLE="Programmer"}(EMP)$$
$$EMP_2 = \sigma_{TITLE \neq "Programmer"}(EMP)$$

The localization program for a horizontally fragmented relation is the union of the fragments. In our example, we have

$$ASG = ASG_1 \cup ASG_2$$

♦

Queries on derived fragments can also be reduced. Since this type of fragmentation is useful for optimizing join queries, a useful transformation is to distribute joins over unions (used in the localization programs) and to apply rule 2 introduced earlier. Because the fragmentation rules indicate what the matching tuples are, certain joins will produce empty relations if the fragmentation predicates conflict. For example, the predicates of ASG_1 and EMP_2 conflict; thus we have

$$ASG_1 \bowtie EMP_2 = \phi$$

Contrary to the reduction with join discussed previously, the reduced query is always preferable to the localized query because the number of partial joins usually equals the number of fragments of R.

Example 7.14. The reduction by derived fragmentation is illustrated by applying it to the following SQL query, which retrieves all attributes of tuples from EMP and ASG that have the same value of ENO and the title "Mech. Eng.":

```
SELECT *
FROM    EMP, ASG
WHERE   ASG.ENO = EMP.ENO
AND     TITLE = "Mech. Eng."
```

The localized query on fragments EMP_1, EMP_2, ASG_1, and ASG_2, defined previously is given in Figure 7.9a. By pushing selection down to fragments EMP_1 and EMP_2, the query reduces to that of Figure 7.9b. This is because the selection predicate conflicts with that of EMP_1, and thus EMP_1 can be removed. In order to discover conflicting join predicates, we distribute joins over unions. This produces the tree of Figure 7.9c. The left subtree joins two fragments, ASG_1 and EMP_2, whose qualifications conflict because of predicates TITLE = "Programmer" in ASG_1, and TITLE $\neq$ "Programmer" in EMP_2. Therefore the left subtree which produces an empty relation can be removed, and the reduced query of Figure 7.9d is obtained. This example illustrates the value of fragmentation in improving the execution performance of distributed queries.   ♦

7.2.4 Reduction for Hybrid Fragmentation

Hybrid fragmentation is obtained by combining the fragmentation functions discussed above. The goal of hybrid fragmentation is to support, efficiently, queries involving projection, selection, and join. Note that the optimization of an operation or of a

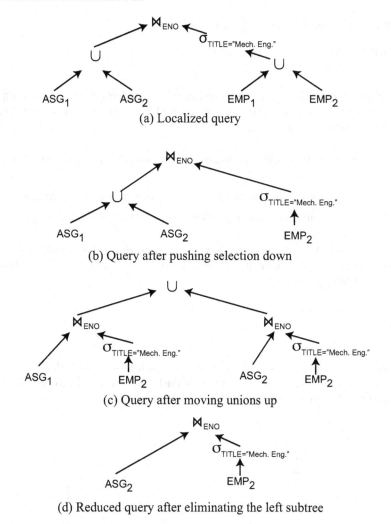

Fig. 7.9 Reduction for Indirect Fragmentation

combination of operations is always done at the expense of other operations. For example, hybrid fragmentation based on selection-projection will make selection only, or projection only, less efficient than with horizontal fragmentation (or vertical fragmentation). The localization program for a hybrid fragmented relation uses unions and joins of fragments.

Example 7.15. Here is an example of hybrid fragmentation of relation EMP:

$$\text{EMP}_1 = \sigma_{\text{ENO}\leq\text{"E4"}}(\Pi_{\text{ENO,ENAME}}(\text{EMP}))$$
$$\text{EMP}_2 = \sigma_{\text{ENO}>\text{"E4"}}(\Pi_{\text{ENO,ENAME}}(\text{EMP}))$$
$$\text{EMP}_3 = \Pi_{\text{ENO,TITLE}}(\text{EMP})$$

In our example, the localization program is

$$EMP = (EMP_1 \cup EMP_2) \bowtie_{ENO} EMP_3$$

♦

Queries on hybrid fragments can be reduced by combining the rules used, respectively, in primary horizontal, vertical, and derived horizontal fragmentation. These rules can be summarized as follows:

1. Remove empty relations generated by contradicting selections on horizontal fragments.

2. Remove useless relations generated by projections on vertical fragments.

3. Distribute joins over unions in order to isolate and remove useless joins.

Example 7.16. The following example query in SQL illustrates the application of rules (1) and (2) to the horizontal-vertical fragmentation of relation EMP into EMP_1, EMP_2 and EMP_3 given above:

```
SELECT ENAME
FROM   EMP
WHERE  ENO="E5"
```

The localized query of Figure 7.10a can be reduced by first pushing selection down, eliminating fragment EMP_1, and then pushing projection down, eliminating fragment EMP_3. The reduced query is given in Figure 7.10b.   ♦

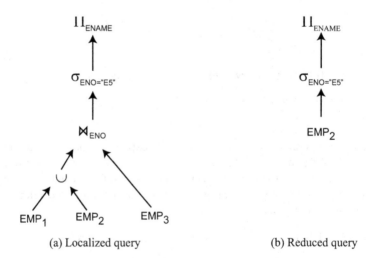

(a) Localized query   (b) Reduced query

Fig. 7.10 Reduction for Hybrid Fragmentation

7.3 Conclusion

In this chapter we focused on the techniques for query decomposition and data localization layers of the localized query processing scheme that was introduced in Chapter 6. Query decomposition and data localization are the two successive functions that map a calculus query, expressed on distributed relations, into an algebraic query (query decomposition), expressed on relation fragments (data localization).

These two layers can produce a localized query corresponding to the input query in a naive way. Query decomposition can generate an algebraic query simply by translating into relational operations the predicates and the target statement as they appear. Data localization can, in turn, express this algebraic query on relation fragments, by substituting for each distributed relation an algebraic query corresponding to its fragmentation rules.

Many algebraic queries may be equivalent to the same input query. The queries produced with the naive approach are inefficient in general, since important simplifications and optimizations have been missed. Therefore, a localized query expression is restructured using a few transformation rules and heuristics. The rules enable separation of unary operations, grouping of unary operations on the same relation, commuting of unary operations with binary operations, and permutation of the binary operations. Examples of heuristics are to push selections down the tree and do projection as early as possible. In addition to the transformation rules, data localization uses reduction rules to simplify the query further, and therefore optimize it. Two main types of rules may be used. The first one avoids the production of empty relations which are generated by contradicting predicates on the same relation(s). The second type of rule determines which fragments yield useless attributes.

The query produced by the query decomposition and data localization layers is good in the sense that the worse executions are avoided. However, the subsequent layers usually perform important optimizations, as they add to the query increasing detail about the processing environment. In particular, quantitative information regarding fragments has not yet been exploited. This information will be used by the query optimization layer for selecting an "optimal" strategy to execute the query. Query optimization is the subject of Chapter 8.

7.4 Bibliographic NOTES

Traditional techniques for query decomposition are surveyed in [Jarke and Koch, 1984]. Techniques for semantic analysis and simplification of queries have their origins in [Rosenkrantz and Hunt, 1980]. The notion of query graph or connection graph is introduced in [Ullman, 1982]. The notion of query tree, which we called operator tree in this chapter, and the transformation rules to manipulate algebraic expressions have been introduced by Smith and Chang [1975] and developed in [Ullman, 1982]. Proofs of completeness and correctness of the rules are given in the latter reference.

Data localization is treated in detail in [Ceri and Pelagatti, 1983] for horizontally partitioned relations which are referred to as multirelations. In particular, an algebra of qualified relations is defined as an extension of relation algebra, where a qualified relation is a relation name and the qualification of the fragment. Proofs of correctness and completeness of equivalence transformations between expressions of algebra of qualified relations are also given. The formal properties of horizontal and vertical fragmentation are used in [Ceri et al., 1986] to characterize distributed joins over fragmented relations.

Exercises

Problem 7.1. Simplify the following query, expressed in SQL, on our example database using idempotency rules:

```
SELECT ENO
FROM    ASG
WHERE   RESP = "Analyst"
AND     NOT(PNO="P2" OR DUR=12)
AND     PNO != "P2"
AND     DUR=12
```

Problem 7.2. Give the query graph of the following query, in SQL, on our example database:

```
SELECT ENAME, PNAME
FROM    EMP, ASG, PROJ
WHERE   DUR > 12
AND     EMP.ENO = ASG.ENO
AND     PROJ.PNO = ASG.PNO
```

and map it into an operator tree.

Problem 7.3 (*). Simplify the following query:

```
SELECT ENAME, PNAME
FROM    EMP, ASG, PROJ
WHERE   (DUR > 12 OR RESP = "Analyst")
AND     EMP.ENO = ASG.ENO
AND     (TITLE = "Elect. Eng."
OR      ASG.PNO < "P3")
AND     (DUR > 12 OR RESP NOT= "Analyst")
AND     ASG.PNO = PROJ.PNO
```

and transform it into an optimized operator tree using the restructuring algorithm (Section 7.1.4) where select and project operations are applied as soon as possible to reduce the size of intermediate relations.

Problem 7.4 (*). Transform the operator tree of Figure 7.5 back to the tree of Figure 7.3 using the restructuring algorithm. Describe each intermediate tree and show which rule the transformation is based on.

Problem 7.5 (**). Consider the following query on our Engineering database:

```
SELECT ENAME,SAL
FROM   EMP,PROJ,ASG,PAY
WHERE  EMP.ENO = ASG.ENO
AND    EMP.TITLE = PAY.TITLE
AND    (BUDGET>200000 OR DUR>24)
AND    ASG.PNO = PROJ.PNO
AND    (DUR>24 OR PNAME = "CAD/CAM")
```

Compose the selection predicate corresponding to the WHERE clause and transform it, using the idempotency rules, into the simplest equivalent form. Furthermore, compose an operator tree corresponding to the query and transform it, using relational algebra transformation rules, to three equivalent forms.

Problem 7.6. Assume that relation PROJ of the sample database is horizontally fragmented as follows:

$$PROJ_1 = \sigma_{PNO \leq "P2"} (PROJ)$$
$$PROJ_2 = \sigma_{PNO > "P2"} (PROJ)$$

Transform the following query into a reduced query on fragments:

```
SELECT ENO, PNAME
FROM   PROJ,ASG
WHERE  PROJ.PNO = ASG.PNO
AND    PNO = "P4"
```

Problem 7.7 (*). Assume that relation PROJ is horizontally fragmented as in Problem 7.6, and that relation ASG is horizontally fragmented as

$$ASG_1 = \sigma_{PNO \leq "P2"} (ASG)$$
$$ASG_2 = \sigma_{"P2" < PNO \leq "P3"} (ASG)$$
$$ASG_3 = \sigma_{PNO > "P3"} (ASG)$$

Transform the following query into a reduced query on fragments, and determine whether it is better than the localized query:

```
SELECT RESP, BUDGET
FROM   ASG, PROJ
WHERE  ASG.PNO = PROJ.PNO
AND    PNAME = "CAD/CAM"
```

Problem 7.8 (**). Assume that relation PROJ is fragmented as in Problem 7.6. Furthermore, relation ASG is indirectly fragmented as

$$ASG_1 = ASG \ltimes_{PNO} PROJ_1$$
$$ASG_2 = ASG \ltimes_{PNO} PROJ_2$$

and relation EMP is vertically fragmented as

$EMP_1 = \Pi_{ENO,ENAME} (EMP)$

$EMP_2 = \Pi_{ENO,TITLE} (EMP)$

Transform the following query into a reduced query on fragments:

```
SELECT ENAME
FROM    EMP,ASG,PROJ
WHERE   PROJ.PNO = ASG.PNO
AND     PNAME = "Instrumentation"
AND     EMP.ENO = ASG.ENO
```

Chapter 8
Optimization of Distributed Queries

Chapter 7 shows how a calculus query expressed on global relations can be mapped into a query on relation fragments by decomposition and data localization. This mapping uses the global and fragment schemas. During this process, the application of transformation rules permits the simplification of the query by eliminating common subexpressions and useless expressions. This type of optimization is independent of fragment characteristics such as cardinalities. The query resulting from decomposition and localization can be executed in that form simply by adding communication primitives in a systematic way. However, the permutation of the ordering of operations within the query can provide many equivalent strategies to execute it. Finding an "optimal" ordering of operations for a given query is the main role of the query optimization layer, or *optimizer* for short.

Selecting the optimal execution strategy for a query is NP-hard in the number of relations [Ibaraki and Kameda, 1984]. For complex queries with many relations, this can incur a prohibitive optimization cost. Therefore, the actual objective of the optimizer is to find a strategy close to optimal and, perhaps more important, to avoid bad strategies. In this chapter we refer to the strategy (or operation ordering) produced by the optimizer as the *optimal strategy* (or *optimal ordering*). The output of the optimizer is an optimized *query execution plan* consisting of the algebraic query specified on fragments and the communication operations to support the execution of the query over the fragment sites.

The selection of the optimal strategy generally requires the prediction of execution costs of the alternative candidate orderings prior to actually executing the query. The execution cost is expressed as a weighted combination of I/O, CPU, and communication costs. A typical simplification of the earlier distributed query optimizers was to ignore local processing cost (I/O and CPU costs) by assuming that the communication cost is dominant. Important inputs to the optimizer for estimating execution costs are fragment statistics and formulas for estimating the cardinalities of results of relational operations. In this chapter we focus mostly on the ordering of join operations for two reasons: it is a well-understood problem, and queries involving joins, selections, and projections are usually considered to be the most frequent type. Furthermore, it is easier to generalize the basic algorithm for other

M.T. Özsu and P. Valduriez, *Principles of Distributed Database Systems: Third Edition*, DOI 10.1007/978-1-4419-8834-8_8, © Springer Science+Business Media, LLC 2011

binary operations, such as union, intersection and difference. We also discuss how the semijoin operation can help to process join queries efficiently.

This chapter is organized as follows. In Section 8.1 we introduce the main components of query optimization, including the search space, the search strategy and the cost model. Query optimization in centralized systems is described in Section 8.2 as a prerequisite to understand distributed query optimization, which is more complex. In Section 8.3 we discuss the major optimization issue, which deals with the join ordering in distributed queries. We also examine alternative join strategies based on semijoin. In Section 8.4 we illustrate the use of the techniques and concepts in four basic distributed query optimization algorithms.

8.1 Query Optimization

This section introduces query optimization in general, i.e., independent of whether the environment is centralized or distributed. The input query is supposed to be expressed in relational algebra on database relations (which can obviously be fragments) after query rewriting from a calculus expression.

Query optimization refers to the process of producing a query execution plan (QEP) which represents an execution strategy for the query. This QEP minimizes an objective cost function. A query optimizer, the software module that performs query optimization, is usually seen as consisting of three components: a search space, a cost model, and a search strategy (see Figure 8.1). The *search space* is the set of alternative execution plans that represent the input query. These plans are equivalent, in the sense that they yield the same result, but they differ in the execution order of operations and the way these operations are implemented, and therefore in their performance. The search space is obtained by applying transformation rules, such as those for relational algebra described in Section 7.1.4. The *cost model* predicts the cost of a given execution plan. To be accurate, the cost model must have good knowledge about the distributed execution environment. The *search strategy* explores the search space and selects the best plan, using the cost model. It defines which plans are examined and in which order. The details of the environment (centralized versus distributed) are captured by the search space and the cost model.

8.1.1 Search Space

Query execution plans are typically abstracted by means of operator trees (see Section 7.1.4), which define the order in which the operations are executed. They are enriched with additional information, such as the best algorithm chosen for each operation. For a given query, the search space can thus be defined as the set of equivalent operator trees that can be produced using transformation rules. To characterize query optimizers, it is useful to concentrate on *join trees*, which are operator trees whose

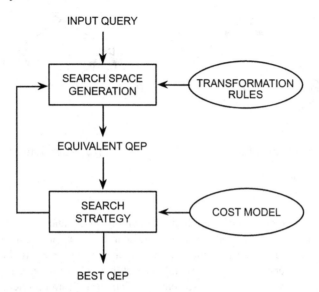

Fig. 8.1 Query Optimization Process

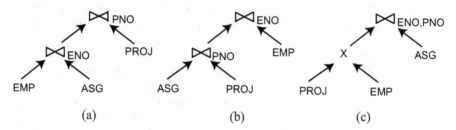

Fig. 8.2 Equivalent Join Trees

operators are join or Cartesian product. This is because permutations of the join order have the most important effect on performance of relational queries.

Example 8.1. Consider the following query:

```
SELECT ENAME, RESP
FROM   EMP, ASG, PROJ
WHERE  EMP.ENO=ASG.ENO
AND    ASG.PNO=PROJ.PNO
```

Figure 8.2 illustrates three equivalent join trees for that query, which are obtained by exploiting the associativity of binary operators. Each of these join trees can be assigned a cost based on the estimated cost of each operator. Join tree (c) which starts with a Cartesian product may have a much higher cost than the other join trees. ◆

For a complex query (involving many relations and many operators), the number of equivalent operator trees can be very high. For instance, the number of alternative

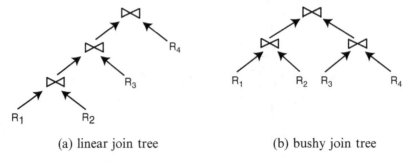

(a) linear join tree   (b) bushy join tree

Fig. 8.3 The Two Major Shapes of Join Trees

join trees that can be produced by applying the commutativity and associativity rules
is $O(N!)$ for N relations. Investigating a large search space may make optimization time prohibitive, sometimes much more expensive than the actual execution
time. Therefore, query optimizers typically restrict the size of the search space they
consider. The first restriction is to use heuristics. The most common heuristic is to
perform selection and projection when accessing base relations. Another common
heuristic is to avoid Cartesian products that are not required by the query. For instance,
in Figure 8.2, operator tree (c) would not be part of the search space considered by
the optimizer.

Another important restriction is with respect to the shape of the join tree. Two
kinds of join trees are usually distinguished: linear versus bushy trees (see Figure
8.3). A *linear tree* is a tree such that at least one operand of each operator node is
a base relation. A *bushy tree* is more general and may have operators with no base
relations as operands (i.e., both operands are intermediate relations). By considering
only linear trees, the size of the search space is reduced to $O(2^N)$. However, in a
distributed environment, bushy trees are useful in exhibiting parallelism. For example,
in join tree (b) of Figure 8.3, operations $R_1 \bowtie R_2$ and $R_3 \bowtie R_4$ can be done in parallel.

8.1.2 Search Strategy

The most popular search strategy used by query optimizers is *dynamic programming*,
which is *deterministic*. Deterministic strategies proceed by *building* plans, starting
from base relations, joining one more relation at each step until complete plans are
obtained, as in Figure 8.4. Dynamic programming builds all possible plans, breadth-
first, before it chooses the "best" plan. To reduce the optimization cost, partial plans
that are not likely to lead to the optimal plan are *pruned* (i.e., discarded) as soon as
possible. By contrast, another deterministic strategy, the greedy algorithm, builds
only one plan, depth-first.

Dynamic programming is almost exhaustive and assures that the "best" of all
plans is found. It incurs an acceptable optimization cost (in terms of time and space)

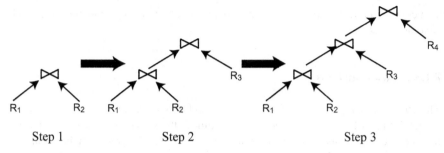

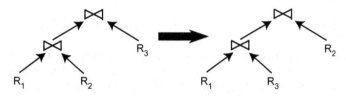

Fig. 8.4 Optimizer Actions in a Deterministic Strategy

Fig. 8.5 Optimizer Action in a Randomized Strategy

when the number of relations in the query is small. However, this approach becomes too expensive when the number of relations is greater than 5 or 6. For more complex queries, *randomized* strategies have been proposed, which reduce the optimization complexity but do not guarantee the best of all plans. Unlike deterministic strategies, *randomized* strategies allow the optimizer to trade optimization time for execution time [Lanzelotte et al., 1993].

Randomized strategies, such as Simulated Annealing [Ioannidis and Wong, 1987] and Iterative Improvement [Swami, 1989] concentrate on searching for the optimal solution around some particular points. They do not guarantee that the best solution is obtained, but avoid the high cost of optimization, in terms of memory and time consumption. First, one or more *start* plans are built by a greedy strategy. Then, the algorithm tries to improve the start plan by visiting its *neighbors*. A neighbor is obtained by applying a random *transformation* to a plan. An example of a typical transformation consists in exchanging two randomly chosen operand relations of the plan, as in Figure 8.5. It has been shown experimentally that randomized strategies provide better performance than deterministic strategies as soon as the query involves more than several relations[Lanzelotte et al., 1993].

8.1.3 Distributed Cost Model

An optimizer's cost model includes cost functions to predict the cost of operators, statistics and base data, and formulas to evaluate the sizes of intermediate results.

The cost is in terms of execution time, so a cost function represents the execution time of a query.

8.1.3.1 Cost Functions

The cost of a distributed execution strategy can be expressed with respect to either the total time or the response time. The total time is the sum of all time (also referred to as cost) components, while the response time is the elapsed time from the initiation to the completion of the query. A general formula for determining the total time can be specified as follows [Lohman et al., 1985]:

$$Total\_time = T_{CPU} * \#insts + T_{I/O} * \#I/Os + T_{MSG} * \#msgs + T_{TR} * \#bytes$$

The two first components measure the local processing time, where T_{CPU} is the time of a CPU instruction and $T_{I/O}$ is the time of a disk I/O. The communication time is depicted by the two last components. T_{MSG} is the fixed time of initiating and receiving a message, while T_{TR} is the time it takes to transmit a data unit from one site to another. The data unit is given here in terms of bytes (#bytes is the sum of the sizes of all messages), but could be in different units (e.g., packets). A typical assumption is that T_{TR} is constant. This might not be true for wide area networks, where some sites are farther away than others. However, this assumption greatly simplifies query optimization. Thus the communication time of transferring #bytes of data from one site to another is assumed to be a linear function of #bytes:

$$CT(\#bytes) = T_{MSG} + T_{TR} * \#bytes$$

Costs are generally expressed in terms of time units, which in turn, can be translated into other units (e.g., dollars).

The relative values of the cost coefficients characterize the distributed database environment. The topology of the network greatly influences the ratio between these components. In a wide area network such as the Internet, the communication time is generally the dominant factor. In local area networks, however, there is more of a balance among the components. Earlier studies cite ratios of communication time to I/O time for one page to be on the order of 20:1 for wide area networks [Selinger and Adiba, 1980] while it is 1:1.6 for a typical early generation Ethernet (10Mbps) [Page and Popek, 1985]. Thus, most early distributed DBMSs designed for wide area networks have ignored the local processing cost and concentrated on minimizing the communication cost. Distributed DBMSs designed for local area networks, on the other hand, consider all three cost components. The new faster networks, both at the wide area network and at the local area network levels, have improved the above ratios in favor of communication cost when all things are equal. However, communication is still the dominant time factor in wide area networks such as the Internet because of the longer distances that data are retrieved from (or shipped to).

When the response time of the query is the objective function of the optimizer, parallel local processing and parallel communications must also be considered

[Khoshafian and Valduriez, 1987]. A general formula for response time is

$$Response\_time = T_{CPU} * seq\_\#insts + T_{I/O} * seq\_\#I/Os$$
$$+ T_{MSG} * seq\_\#msgs + T_{TR} * seq\_\#bytes$$

where $seq\_\#x$, in which x can be instructions (*insts*), I/O, messages (*msgs*) or *bytes*, is the maximum number of x which must be done sequentially for the execution of the query. Thus any processing and communication done in parallel is ignored.

Example 8.2. Let us illustrate the difference between total cost and response time using the example of Figure 8.6, which computes the answer to a query at site 3 with data from sites 1 and 2. For simplicity, we assume that only communication cost is considered.

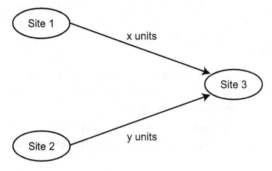

Fig. 8.6 Example of Data Transfers for a Query

Assume that T_{MSG} and T_{TR} are expressed in time units. The total time of transferring x data units from site 1 to site 3 and y data units from site 2 to site 3 is

$$Total\_time = 2\,T_{MSG} + T_{TR} * (x+y)$$

The response time of the same query can be approximated as

$$Response\_time = max\{T_{MSG} + T_{TR} * x, T_{MSG} + T_{TR} * y\}$$

since the transfers can be done in parallel. ♦

Minimizing response time is achieved by increasing the degree of parallel execution. This does not, however, imply that the total time is also minimized. On the contrary, it can increase the total time, for example, by having more parallel local processing and transmissions. Minimizing the total time implies that the utilization of the resources improves, thus increasing the system throughput. In practice, a compromise between the two is desired. In Section 8.4 we present algorithms that can optimize a combination of total time and response time, with more weight on one of them.

8.1.3.2 Database Statistics

The main factor affecting the performance of an execution strategy is the size of the intermediate relations that are produced during the execution. When a subsequent operation is located at a different site, the intermediate relation must be transmitted over the network. Therefore, it is of prime interest to estimate the size of the intermediate results of relational algebra operations in order to minimize the size of data transfers. This estimation is based on statistical information about the base relations and formulas to predict the cardinalities of the results of the relational operations. There is a direct trade-off between the precision of the statistics and the cost of managing them, the more precise statistics being the more costly [Piatetsky-Shapiro and Connell, 1984]. For a relation R defined over the attributes $A = \{A_1, A_2, \ldots, A_n\}$ and fragmented as $R_1, R_2, \ldots, R_r$, the statistical data typically are the following:

1. For each attribute A_i, its length (in number of bytes), denoted by $length(A_i)$, and for each attribute A_i of each fragment R_j, the number of distinct values of A_i, with the cardinality of the projection of fragment R_j on A_i, denoted by $card(\Pi_{A_i}(R_j))$.

2. For the domain of each attribute A_i, which is defined on a set of values that can be ordered (e.g., integers or reals), the minimum and maximum possible values, denoted by $min(A_i)$ and $max(A_i)$.

3. For the domain of each attribute A_i, the cardinality of the domain of A_i, denoted by $card(dom[A_i])$. This value gives the number of unique values in the $dom[A_i]$.

4. The number of tuples in each fragment R_j, denoted by $card(R_j)$.

In addition, for each attribute A_i, there may be a histogram that approximates the frequency distribution of the attribute within a number of buckets, each corresponding to a range of values.

Sometimes, the statistical data also include the join selectivity factor for some pairs of relations, that is the proportion of tuples participating in the join. The *join selectivity factor*, denoted SF_J, of relations R and S is a real value between 0 and 1:

$$SF_J(R,S) = \frac{card(R \bowtie S)}{card(R) * card(S)}$$

For example, a join selectivity factor of 0.5 corresponds to a very large joined relation, while 0.001 corresponds to a small one. We say that the join has bad (or low) selectivity in the former case and good (or high) selectivity in the latter case.

These statistics are useful to predict the size of intermediate relations. Remember that in Chapter 3 we defined the size of an intermediate relation R as follows:

$$size(R) = card(R) * length(R)$$

where $length(R)$ is the length (in bytes) of a tuple of R, computed from the lengths of its attributes. The estimation of $card(R)$, the number of tuples in R, requires the use of the formulas given in the following section.

8.1.3.3 Cardinalities of Intermediate Results

Database statistics are useful in evaluating the cardinalities of the intermediate results of queries. Two simplifying assumptions are commonly made about the database. The distribution of attribute values in a relation is supposed to be uniform, and all attributes are independent, meaning that the value of an attribute does not affect the value of any other attribute. These two assumptions are often wrong in practice, but they make the problem tractable. In what follows we give the formulas for estimating the cardinalities of the results of the basic relational algebra operations (selection, projection, Cartesian product, join, semijoin, union, and difference). The operand relations are denoted by R and S. The *selectivity factor* of an operation, that is, the proportion of tuples of an operand relation that participate in the result of that operation, is denoted SF_{OP}, where OP denotes the operation.

Selection.

The cardinality of selection is

$$card(\sigma_F(R)) = SF_S(F) * card(R)$$

where $SF_S(F)$ is dependent on the selection formula and can be computed as follows [Selinger et al., 1979], where $p(A_i)$ and $p(A_j)$ indicate predicates over attributes A_i and A_j, respectively:

$$SF_S(A = value) = \frac{1}{card(\Pi_A(R))}$$

$$SF_S(A > value) = \frac{max(A) - value}{max(A) - min(A)}$$

$$SF_S(A < value) = \frac{value - min(A)}{max(A) - min(A)}$$

$$SF_S(p(A_i) \wedge p(A_j)) = SF_S(p(A_i)) * SF_S(p(A_j))$$

$$SF_S(p(A_i) \vee p(A_j)) = SF_S(p(A_i)) + SF_S(p(A_j)) - (SF_S(p(A_i)) * SF_S(p(A_j)))$$

$$SF_S(A \in \{values\}) = SF_S(A = value) * card(\{values\})$$

Projection.

As indicated in Section 2.1, projection can be with or without duplicate elimination. We consider projection with duplicate elimination. An arbitrary projection is difficult to evaluate precisely because the correlations between projected attributes are usually unknown [Gelenbe and Gardy, 1982]. However, there are two particularly useful cases where it is trivial. If the projection of relation R is based on a single attribute A, the cardinality is simply the number of tuples when the projection is performed. If one of the projected attributes is a key of R, then

$$card(\Pi_A(R)) = card(R)$$

Cartesian product.

The cardinality of the Cartesian product of R and S is simply

$$card(R \times S) = card(R) * card(S)$$

Join.

There is no general way to estimate the cardinality of a join without additional information. The upper bound of the join cardinality is the cardinality of the Cartesian product. It has been used in the earlier distributed DBMS (e.g. [Epstein et al., 1978]), but it is a quite pessimistic estimate. A more realistic solution is to divide this upper bound by a constant to reflect the fact that the join result is smaller than that of the Cartesian product [Selinger and Adiba, 1980]. However, there is a case, which occurs frequently, where the estimation is simple. If relation R is equijoined with S over attribute A from R, and B from S, where A is a key of relation R, and B is a foreign key of relation S, the cardinality of the result can be approximated as

$$card(R \bowtie_{A=B} S) = card(S)$$

because each tuple of S matches with at most one tuple of R. Obviously, the same thing is true if B is a key of S and A is a foreign key of R. However, this estimation is an upper bound since it assumes that each tuple of R participates in the join. For other important joins, it is worthwhile to maintain their join selectivity factor SF_J as part of statistical information. In that case the result cardinality is simply

$$card(R \bowtie S) = SF_J * card(R) * card(S)$$

Semijoin.

The selectivity factor of the semijoin of R by S gives the fraction (percentage) of tuples of R that join with tuples of S. An approximation for the semijoin selectivity factor is given by Hevner and Yao [1979] as

$$SF_{SJ}(R \ltimes_A S) = \frac{card(\Pi_A(S))}{card(dom[A])}$$

This formula depends only on attribute A of S. Thus it is often called the selectivity factor of attribute A of S, denoted $SF_{SJ}(S.A)$, and is the selectivity factor of $S.A$ on any other joinable attribute. Therefore, the cardinality of the semijoin is given by

$$card(R \ltimes_A S) = SF_{SJ}(S.A) * card(R)$$

This approximation can be verified on a very frequent case, that of $R.A$ being a foreign key of S ($S.A$ is a primary key). In this case, the semijoin selectivity factor is 1 since $\Pi_A(S)) = card(dom[A])$ yielding that the cardinality of the semijoin is $card(R)$.

Union.

It is quite difficult to estimate the cardinality of the union of R and S because the duplicates between R and S are removed by the union. We give only the simple formulas for the upper and lower bounds, which are, respectively,

$$card(R) + card(S)$$
$$max\{card(R), card(S)\}$$

Note that these formulas assume that R and S do not contain duplicate tuples.

Difference.

Like the union, we give only the upper and lower bounds. The upper bound of $card(R - S)$ is $card(R)$, whereas the lower bound is 0.

More complex predicates with conjunction and disjunction can also be handled by using the formulas given above.

8.1.3.4 Using Histograms for Selectivity Estimation

The formulae above for estimating the cardinalities of intermediate results of queries rely on the strong assumption that the distribution of attribute values in a relation is uniform. The advantage of this assumption is that the cost of managing the statistics is minimal since only the number of distinct attribute values is needed. However, this assumption is not practical. In case of skewed data distributions, it can result in fairly inaccurate estimations and QEPs which are far from the optimal.

An effective solution to accurately capture data distributions is to use histograms. Today, most commercial DBMS optimizers support histograms as part of their cost model. Various kinds of histograms have been proposed for estimating the selectivity of query predicates with different trade-offs between accuracy and maintenance cost [Poosala et al., 1996]. To illustrate the use of histograms, we use the basic definition by Bruno and Chaudhuri [2002]. A *histogram* on attribute A from R is a set of buckets. Each bucket b_i describes a range of values of A, denoted by $range_i$, with its associated frequency f_i and number of distinct values d_i. f_i gives the number of tuples of R where $R.A \in range_i$. d_i gives the number of distinct values of A where $R.A \in range_i$. This representation of a relation's attribute can capture non-uniform distributions of values, with the buckets adapted to the different ranges. However, within a bucket, the distribution of attribute values is assumed to be uniform.

Histograms can be used to accurately estimate the selectivity of selection operations. They can also be used for more complex queries including selection, projection and join. However, the precise estimation of join selectivity remains difficult and depends on the type of the histogram [Poosala et al., 1996]. We now illustrate the use of histograms with two important selection predicates: equality and range predicate.

Equality predicate.

With $value \in range_i$, we simply have: $SF_S(A = value) = 1/d_i$.

Range predicate.

Computing the selectivity of range predicates such as $A \leq value$, $A < value$ and $A > value$ requires identifying the relevant buckets and summing up their frequencies. Let us consider the range predicate $R.A \leq value$ with $value \in range_i$. To estimate the numbers of tuples of R that satisfy this predicate, we must sum up the frequencies of all buckets which precede bucket i and the estimated number of tuples that satisfy the predicate in bucket b_i. Assuming uniform distribution of attribute values in b_i, we have:

$$card(\sigma_{A \leq value}(R)) = \sum_{j=1}^{i-1} f_j + \left(\frac{value - min(range_i)}{min(range_i)} - min(range_i) * f_i \right)$$

The cardinality of other range predicates can be computed in a similar way.

Example 8.3. Figure 8.7 shows a possible 4-bucket histogram for attribute DUR of a relation ASG with 300 tuples. Let us consider the equality predicate ASG.DUR=18. Since the value "18" fits in bucket b_3, the selectivity factor is 1/12. Since the cardinalty of b_3 is 50, the cardinality of the selection is 50/12 which is approximately 5 tuples. Let us now consider the range predicate ASG.DUR $\leq$ 18. We have $min(range_3) =$ 12 and $max(range_3) = 24$. The cardinality of the selection is: $100 + 75 + (((18 - 12)/(24 - 12)) * 50) = 200$ tuples. ♦

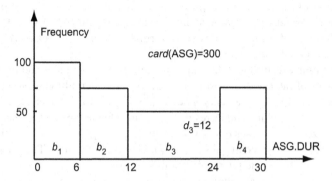

Fig. 8.7 Histogram of Attribute ASG.DUR

8.2 Centralized Query Optimization

In this section we present the main query optimization techniques for centralized systems. This presentation is a prerequisite to understanding distributed query optimization for three reasons. First, a distributed query is translated into local queries, each of which is processed in a centralized way. Second, distributed query optimization techniques are often extensions of the techniques for centralized systems. Finally, centralized query optimization is a simpler problem; the minimization of communication costs makes distributed query optimization more complex.

As discussed in Chapter 6, the optimization timing, which can be dynamic, static or hybrid, is a good basis for classifying query optimization techniques. Therefore, we present a representative technique of each class.

8.2.1 Dynamic Query Optimization

Dynamic query optimization combines the two phases of query decomposition and optimization with execution. The QEP is dynamically constructed by the query optimizer which makes calls to the DBMS execution engine for executing the query's operations. Thus, there is no need for a cost model.

The most popular dynamic query optimization algorithm is that of INGRES [Stonebraker et al., 1976], one of the first relational DBMS. In this section, we present this algorithm based on the detailed description by Wong and Youssefi [1976]. The algorithm recursively breaks up a query expressed in relational calculus (i.e., SQL) into smaller pieces which are executed along the way. The query is first decomposed into a sequence of queries having a unique relation in common. Then each monorelation query is processed by selecting, based on the predicate, the best access method to that relation (e.g., index, sequential scan). For example, if the predicate is of the form $A = value$, an index available on attribute A would be used if it exists. However, if the predicate is of the form $A \neq value$, an index on A would not help, and sequential scan should be used.

The algorithm executes first the unary (monorelation) operations and tries to minimize the sizes of intermediate results in ordering binary (multirelation) operations. Let us denote by $q_{i-1} \rightarrow q_i$ a query q decomposed into two subqueries, q_{i-1} and q_i, where q_{i-1} is executed first and its result is consumed by q_i. Given an n-relation query q, the optimizer decomposes q into n subqueries $q_1 \rightarrow q_2 \rightarrow \cdots \rightarrow q_n$. This decomposition uses two basic techniques: *detachment* and *substitution*. These techniques are presented and illustrated in the rest of this section.

Detachment is the first technique employed by the query processor. It breaks a query q into $q' \rightarrow q''$, based on a common relation that is the result of q'. If the query q expressed in SQL is of the form

```
SELECT  R₂.A₂,R₃.A₃,...,Rₙ.Aₙ
FROM    R₁,R₂,...,Rₙ
WHERE   P₁(R₁.A₁')
AND     P₂(R₁.A₁,R₂.A₂,...,Rₙ.Aₙ)
```

where A_i and A_i' are lists of attributes of relation R_i, P_1 is a predicate involving attributes from relation R_1, and P_2 is a multirelation predicate involving attributes of relations $R_1, R_2, \ldots, R_n$. Such a query may be decomposed into two subqueries, q' followed by q'', by detachment of the common relation R_1:

```
q': SELECT  R₁.A₁ INTO R₁'
    FROM    R₁
    WHERE   P₁(R₁.A₁')
```

where R_1' is a temporary relation containing the information necessary for the continuation of the query:

```
q'': SELECT  R₂.A₂,...,Rₙ.Aₙ
     FROM    R₁',R₂,...,Rₙ
     WHERE   P₂(R₁'.A₁,...,Rₙ.Aₙ)
```

This step has the effect of reducing the size of the relation on which the query q'' is defined. Furthermore, the created relation R_1' may be stored in a particular structure to speed up the following subqueries. For example, the storage of R_1' in a hashed file on the join attributes of q'' will make processing the join more efficient. Detachment extracts the select operations, which are usually the most selective ones. Therefore, detachment is systematically done whenever possible. Note that this can have adverse effects on performance if the selection has bad selectivity.

Example 8.4. To illustrate the detachment technique, we apply it to the following query:

"Names of employees working on the CAD/CAM project"

This query can be expressed in SQL by the following query q_1 on the engineering database of Chapter 2:

```
q1: SELECT EMP.ENAME
    FROM    EMP, ASG, PROJ
    WHERE   EMP.ENO=ASG.ENO
    AND     ASG.PNO=PROJ.PNO
    AND     PNAME="CAD/CAM"
```

After detachment of the selections, query q_1 is replaced by q_{11} followed by q', where JVAR is an intermediate relation.

```
q11: SELECT PROJ.PNO INTO JVAR
     FROM    PROJ
     WHERE   PNAME="CAD/CAM"
q': SELECT EMP.ENAME
    FROM    EMP, ASG, JVAR
    WHERE   EMP.ENO=ASG.ENO
    AND     ASG.PNO=JVAR.PNO
```

The successive detachments of q' may generate

```
q12: SELECT ASG.ENO INTO GVAR
     FROM    ASG, JVAR
     WHERE   ASG.PNO=JVAR.PNO
q13: SELECT EMP.ENAME
     FROM    EMP, GVAR
     WHERE   EMP.ENO=GVAR.ENO
```

Note that other subqueries are also possible.

Thus query q_1 has been reduced to the subsequent queries $q_{11} \rightarrow q_{12} \rightarrow q_{13}$. Query q_{11} is monorelation and can be executed. However, q_{12} and q_{13} are not monorelation and cannot be reduced by detachment. ◆

Multirelation queries, which cannot be further detached (e.g., q_{12} and q_{13}), are *irreducible*. A query is irreducible if and only if its query graph is a chain with two nodes or a cycle with k nodes where $k > 2$. Irreducible queries are converted into monorelation queries by tuple substitution. Given an n-relation query q, the tuples of one relation are substituted by their values, thereby producing a set of $(n-1)$-relation queries. Tuple substitution proceeds as follows. First, one relation in q is chosen for tuple substitution. Let R_1 be that relation. Then for each tuple t_{1i} in R_1, the attributes referred to by in q are replaced by their actual values in t_{1i}, thereby generating a query q' with $n-1$ relations. Therefore, the total number of queries q' produced by tuple substitution is $card(R_1)$. Tuple substitution can be summarized as follows:

$$q(R_1, R_2, \ldots, R_n) \text{ is replaced by } \{q'(t_{1i}, R_2, R_3, \ldots, R_n), t_{1i} \in R_1\}$$

For each tuple thus obtained, the subquery is recursively processed by substitution if it is not yet irreducible.

Example 8.5. Let us consider the query q_{13}:

```
SELECT EMP.ENAME
FROM    EMP, GVAR
WHERE   EMP.ENO=GVAR.ENO
```

The relation GVAR is over a single attribute (ENO). Assume that it contains only two tuples: $\langle E1 \rangle$ and $\langle E2 \rangle$. The substitution of GVAR generates two one-relation subqueries:

```
q131: SELECT EMP.ENAME
      FROM    EMP
      WHERE   EMP.ENO="E1"
q132: SELECT EMP.ENAME
      FROM    EMP
      WHERE   EMP.ENO="E2"
```

These queries may then be executed.   ◆

This dynamic query optimization algorithm (called Dynamic-QOA) is depicted in Algorithm 8.1. The algorithm works recursively until there remain no more monorelation queries to be processed. It consists of applying the selections and projections as soon as possible by detachment. The results of the monorelation queries are stored in data structures that are capable of optimizing the later queries (such as joins). The irreducible queries that remain after detachment must be processed by tuple substitution. For the irreducible query, denoted by MRQ', the smallest relation whose cardinality is known from the result of the preceding query is chosen for substitution. This simple method enables one to generate the smallest number of subqueries. Monorelation queries generated by the reduction algorithm are executed after choosing the best existing access path to the relation, according to the query qualification.

Algorithm 8.1: Dynamic-QOA

Input: *MRQ*: multirelation query with n relations
Output: *output*: result of execution
begin
> $output \leftarrow \phi$;
> **if** $n = 1$ **then**
>> $output \leftarrow run(MRQ)$ {execute the one relation query}
>
> {detach *MRQ* into m one-relation queries (ORQ) and one multirelation
> query} $ORQ_1, \ldots, ORQ_m, MRQ' \leftarrow MRQ$;
> **for** i *from 1 to m* **do**
>> $output' \leftarrow run(ORQ_i)$;   {execute ORQ_i}
>> $output \leftarrow output \cup output'$ {merge all results}
>
> $R \leftarrow$ CHOOSE_RELATION(MRQ') ;   {R chosen for tuple substitution}
> **for** *each tuple* $t \in R$ **do**
>> $MRQ'' \leftarrow$ substitute values for t in MRQ' ;
>> $output' \leftarrow$ Dynamic-QOA(MRQ'') ;   {recursive call}
>> $output \leftarrow output \cup output'$ {merge all results}

end

8.2.2 Static Query Optimization

With static query optimization, there is a clear separation between the generation of the QEP at compile-time and its execution by the DBMS execution engine. Thus, an accurate cost model is key to predict the costs of candidate QEPs.

The most popular static query optimization algorithm is that of System R [Astrahan et al., 1976], also one of the first relational DBMS. In this section, we present this algorithm based on the description by Selinger et al. [1979]. Most commercial relational DBMSs have implemented variants of this algorithm due to its efficiency and compatibility with query compilation.

The input to the optimizer is a relational algebra tree resulting from the decomposition of an SQL query. The output is a QEP that implements the "optimal" relational algebra tree.

The optimizer assigns a cost (in terms of time) to every candidate tree and retains the one with the smallest cost. The candidate trees are obtained by a permutation of the join orders of the n relations of the query using the commutativity and associativity rules. To limit the overhead of optimization, the number of alternative trees is reduced using dynamic programming. The set of alternative strategies is constructed dynamically so that, when two joins are equivalent by commutativity, only the cheapest one is kept. Furthermore, the strategies that include Cartesian products are eliminated whenever possible.

The cost of a candidate strategy is a weighted combination of I/O and CPU costs (times). The estimation of such costs (at compile time) is based on a cost model that provides a cost formula for each low-level operation (e.g., select using a B-tree index with a range predicate). For most operations (except exact match select), these cost formulas are based on the cardinalities of the operands. The cardinality information for the relations stored in the database is found in the database statistics. The cardinality of the intermediate results is estimated based on the operation selectivity factors discussed in Section 8.1.3.

The optimization algorithm consists of two major steps. First, the best access method to each individual relation based on a select predicate is predicted (this is the one with the least cost). Second, for each relation R, the best join ordering is estimated, where R is first accessed using its best single-relation access method. The cheapest ordering becomes the basis for the best execution plan.

In considering the joins, there are two basic algorithms available, with one of them being optimal in a given context. For the join of two relations, the relation whose tuples are read first is called the *external*, while the other, whose tuples are found according to the values obtained from the external relation, is called the *internal relation*. An important decision with either join method is to determine the cheapest access path to the internal relation.

The first method, called *nested-loop*, performs two loops over the relations. For each tuple of the external relation, the tuples of the internal relation that satisfy the join predicate are retrieved one by one to form the resulting relation. An index or a hashed table on the join attribute is a very efficient access path for the internal relation. In the absence of an index, for relations of n_1 and n_2 tuples, respectively, this algorithm has a cost proportional to $n_1 * n_2$, which may be prohibitive if n_1 and n_2 are high. Thus, an efficient variant is to build a hashed table on the join attribute for the internal relation (chosen as the smallest relation) before applying nested-loop. If the internal relation is itself the result of a previous operation, then the cost of building the hashed table can be shared with that of producing the previous result.

The second method, called *merge-join*, consists of merging two sorted relations on the join attribute. Indices on the join attribute may be used as access paths. If the join criterion is equality, the cost of joining two relations of n_1 and n_2 tuples, respectively, is proportional to $n_1 + n_2$. Therefore, this method is always chosen when there is an equijoin, and when the relations are previously sorted. If only one or neither of the relations are sorted, the cost of the nested-loop algorithm is to be compared with the combined cost of the merge join and of the sorting. The cost of sorting n pages is proportional to $n \log n$. In general, it is useful to sort and apply the merge join algorithm when large relations are considered.

The simplified version of the static optimization algorithm, for a select-project-join query, is shown in Algorithm 8.2. It consists of two loops, the first of which selects the best single-relation access method to each relation in the query, while the second examines all possible permutations of join orders (there are $n!$ permutations with n relations) and selects the best access strategy for the query. The permutations are produced by the dynamic construction of a tree of alternative strategies. First, the join of each relation with every other relation is considered, followed by joins of three relations. This continues until joins of n relations are optimized. Actually, the algorithm does not generate all possible permutations since some of them are useless.

As we discussed earlier, permutations involving Cartesian products are eliminated, as are the commutatively equivalent strategies with the highest cost. With these two heuristics, the number of strategies examined has an upper bound of 2^n rather than $n!$.

Algorithm 8.2: Static-QOA

Input: QT: query tree with n relations
Output: *output*: best QEP
begin
    for *each relation $R_i \in QT$* **do**
        for *each access path AP_{ij} to R_i* **do**
             compute cost(AP_{ij})
        best_AP$_i$ $\leftarrow AP_{ij}$ with minimum cost ;
        for *each order $(R_{i1}, R_{i2}, \cdots, R_{in})$ with $i = 1, \cdots, n!$* **do**
             build QEP $(\ldots((best\ AP_{i1} \bowtie R_{i2}) \bowtie R_{i3}) \bowtie \ldots \bowtie R_{in})$;
             compute cost (QEP)
        output $\leftarrow$ QEP with minimum cost
end

Example 8.6. Let us illustrate this algorithm with the query q_1 (see Example 8.4) on the engineering database. The join graph of q_1 is given in Figure 8.8. For short, the label ENO on edge EMP–ASG stands for the predicate EMP.ENO=ASG.ENO and the label PNO on edge ASG–PROJ stands for the predicate ASG.PNO=PROJ.PNO. We assume the following indices:

    EMP has an index on ENO
    ASG has an index on PNO
    PROJ has an index on PNO and an index on PNAME

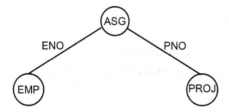

Fig. 8.8 Join Graph of Query q_1

We assume that the first loop of the algorithm selects the following best single-relation access paths:

EMP: sequential scan (because there is no selection on EMP)
ASG: sequential scan (because there is no selection on ASG)
PROJ: index on PNAME (because there is a selection on PROJ
      based on PNAME)

The dynamic construction of the tree of alternative strategies is illustrated in Figure 8.9. Note that the maximum number of join orders is 3!; dynamic search considers fewer alternatives, as depicted in Figure 8.9. The operations marked "pruned" are dynamically eliminated. The first level of the tree indicates the best single-relation access method. The second level indicates, for each of these, the best join method with any other relation. Strategies (EMP × PROJ) and (PROJ × EMP) are pruned because they are Cartesian products that can be avoided (by other strategies). We assume that (EMP ⋈ ASG) and (ASG ⋈ PROJ) have a cost higher than (ASG ⋈ EMP) and (PROJ ⋈ ASG), respectively. Thus they can be pruned because there are better join orders equivalent by commutativity. The two remaining possibilities are given at the third level of the tree. The best total join order is the least costly of ((ASG ⋈ EMP) ⋈ PROJ) and ((PROJ ⋈ ASG) ⋈ EMP). The latter is the only one that has a useful index on the select attribute and direct access to the joining tuples of ASG and EMP. Therefore, it is chosen with the following access methods:

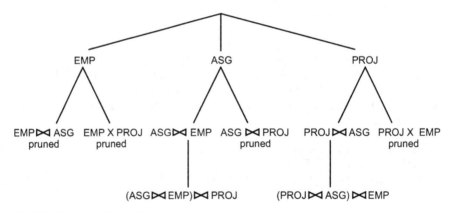

Fig. 8.9 Alternative Join Orders

Select PROJ using index on PNAME

Then join with ASG using index on PNO

Then join with EMP using index on ENO

                                                    ◆

The performance measurements substantiate the important contribution of the CPU time to the total time of the query[Mackert and Lohman, 1986]. The accuracy of the optimizer's estimations is generally good when the relations can be contained in the main memory buffers, but degrades as the relations increase in size and are written to disk. An important performance parameter that should also be considered for better predictions is buffer utilization.

8.2.3 Hybrid Query Optimization

Dynamic and static query optimimization both have advantages and drawbacks. Dynamic query optimization mixes optimization and execution and thus can make accurate optimization choices at run-time. However, query optimization is repeated for each execution of the query. Therefore, this approach is best for ad-hoc queries. Static query optimization, done at compilation time, amortizes the cost of optimization over multiple query executions. The accuracy of the cost model is thus critical to predict the costs of candidate QEPs. This approach is best for queries embedded in stored procedures, and has been adopted by all commercial DBMSs.

However, even with a sophisticated cost model, there is an important problem that prevents accurate cost estimation and comparison of QEPs at compile-time. The problem is that the actual bindings of parameter values in embedded queries is not known until run-time. Consider for instance the selection predicate "WHERE $R.A = \$a$" where "$\$a$" is a parameter value. To estimate the cardinality of this selection, the optimizer must rely on the assumption of uniform distribution of A values in R and cannot make use of histograms. Since there is a runtime binding of the parameter a, the accurate selectivity of $\sigma_{A=\$a}(R)$ cannot be estimated until runtime.

Thus, it can make major estimation errors that can lead to the choice of suboptimal QEPs.

Hybrid query optimization attempts to provide the advantages of static query optimization while avoiding the issues generated by inaccurate estimates. The approach is basically static, but further optimization decisions may take place at run time. This approach was pionnered in System R by adding a conditional runtime reoptimization phase for execution plans statically optimized [Chamberlin et al., 1981]. Thus, plans that have become infeasible (e.g., because indices have been dropped) or suboptimal (e.g. because of changes in relation sizes) are reoptimized. However, detecting suboptimal plans is hard and this approach tends to perform much more reoptimization than necessary. A more general solution is to produce *dynamic QEPs* which include carefully selected optimization decisions to be made at runtime using "choose-plan" operators [Cole and Graefe, 1994]. The choose-plan operator links two or more equivalent subplans of a QEP that are incomparable at compile-time because important runtime information (e.g. parameter bindings) is missing to estimate costs. The execution of a choose-plan operator yields the comparison of the subplans based on actual costs and the selection of the best one. Choose-plan nodes can be inserted anywhere in a QEP.

Example 8.7. Consider the following query expressed in relational algebra:

$$\sigma_{A \leq \$a}(R_1) \bowtie R_2 \bowtie R_3$$

Figure 8.10 shows a dynamic execution plan for this query. We assume that each join is performed by nested-loop, with the left operand relation as external and the right operand relation as internal. The bottom choose-plan operator compares the cost of two alternative subplans for joining R_1 and R_2, the left subplan being better than the right one if the selection predicate has high selectivity. As stated above, since there is a runtime binding of the parameter $a, the accurate selectivity of $\sigma_{A \leq \$a}(R_1)$ cannot be estimated until runtime. The top choose-plan operator compares the cost of two alternative subplans for joining the result of the bottom choose-plan operation with R_3. Depending on the estimated size of the join of R_1 and R_2, which indirectly depends on the selectivity of the selection on R_1 it may be better to use R_3 as external or internal relation.   ◆

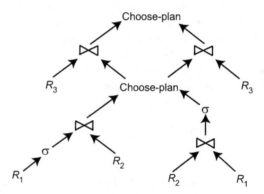

Fig. 8.10 A Dynamic Execution Plan

Dynamic QEPs are produced at compile-time using any static algorithm such as the one presented in Section 8.2.2. However, instead of producing a total order of operations, the optimizer must produce a partial order by introducing choose-node operators anywhere in the QEP. The main modification necessary to a static query optimizer to handle dynamic QEPs is that the cost model supports *incomparable* costs of plans in addition to the standard values "greater than", "less than" and "equal to". Costs may be incomparable because the costs of some subplans are unknown at compile-time. Another reason for cost incomparability is when cost is modeled as an interval of possible cost values rather than a single value [Cole and Graefe, 1994]. Therefore, if two plan costs have overlapping intervals, it is not possible to decide which one is better and they should be considered as incomparable.

Given a dynamic QEP, produced by a static query optimizer, the choose-plan decisions must be made at query startup time. The most effective solution is to simply evaluate the costs of the participating subplans and compare them. In Algorithm 8.3, we describe the startup procedure (called Hybrid-QOA) which makes the optimization decisions to produce the final QEP and run it. The algorithm executes the choose-plan operators in bottom-up order and propagates cost information upward in the QEP.

Algorithm 8.3: Hybrid-QOA

Input: *QEP*: dynamic QEP; *B*: Query parameter bindinds
Output: *output*: result of execution
begin
   | *best_QEP* ← *QEP* ;
   | **for** *each choose-plan operator CP in bottom-up order* **do**
   | **for** *each alternative subplan SP* **do**
   | ⌊ compute cost(*CP*) using *B*
   | ⌊ *best_QEP* ← *best_QEP* without *CP* and *SP* of highest cost
   | *output* ← execute *best_QEP*
end

Experimentation with the Volcano query optimizer [Graefe, 1994] has shown that this hybrid query optimization outperforms both dynamic and static query optimization. In particular, the overhead of dynamic QEP evaluation at startup time is significantly less than that of dynamic optimization, and the reduced execution time of dynamic QEPs relative to static QEPs more than offsets the startup time overhead.

8.3 Join Ordering in Distributed Queries

As we have seen in Section 8.2, ordering joins is an important aspect of centralized query optimization. Join ordering in a distributed context is even more important since joins between fragments may increase the communication time. Two basic approaches exist to order joins in distributed queries. One tries to optimize the ordering of joins directly, whereas the other replaces joins by combinations of semijoins in order to minimize communication costs.

8.3.1 Join Ordering

Some algorithms optimize the ordering of joins directly without using semijoins. The purpose of this section is to stress the difficulty that join ordering presents and to motivate the subsequent section, which deals with the use of semijoins to optimize join queries.

A number of assumptions are necessary to concentrate on the main issues. Since the query is localized and expressed on fragments, we do not need to distinguish between fragments of the same relation and fragments of different relations. To simplify notation, we use the term *relation* to designate a fragment stored at a particular site. Also, to concentrate on join ordering, we ignore local processing time, assuming that reducers (selection, projection) are executed locally either before or during the join (remember that doing selection first is not always efficient). Therefore, we consider only join queries whose operand relations are stored at different sites. We assume that relation transfers are done in a set-at-a-time mode rather than in a tuple-at-a-time mode. Finally, we ignore the transfer time for producing the data at a result site.

Let us first concentrate on the simpler problem of operand transfer in a single join. The query is $R \bowtie S$, where R and S are relations stored at different sites. The obvious choice of the relation to transfer is to send the smaller relation to the site of the larger one, which gives rise to two possibilities, as shown in Figure 8.11. To make this choice we need to evaluate the sizes of R and S. We now consider the case where there are more than two relations to join. As in the case of a single join, the objective of the join-ordering algorithm is to transmit smaller operands. The difficulty stems from the fact that the join operations may reduce or increase the size of the intermediate results. Thus, estimating the size of join results is mandatory, but also difficult. A solution is to estimate the communication costs of all alternative strategies and to choose the best one. However, as discussed earlier, the number of strategies grows rapidly with the number of relations. This approach makes optimization costly, although this overhead is amortized rapidly if the query is executed frequently.

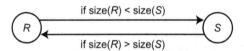

Fig. 8.11 Transfer of Operands in Binary Operation

Example 8.8. Consider the following query expressed in relational algebra:

PROJ $\bowtie_{\mathrm{PNO}}$ ASG $\bowtie_{\mathrm{ENO}}$ EMP

whose join graph is given in Figure 8.12. Note that we have made certain assumptions about the locations of the three relations. This query can be executed in at least five different ways. We describe these strategies by the following programs, where (R $\rightarrow$ site j) stands for "relation R is transferred to site j."

1. EMP $\rightarrow$ site 2; Site 2 computes EMP$'$ = EMP $\bowtie$ ASG; EMP$'$ $\rightarrow$ site 3; Site 3 computes EMP$'$ $\bowtie$ PROJ.

2. ASG $\rightarrow$ site 1; Site 1 computes EMP$'$ = EMP $\bowtie$ ASG; EMP$'$ $\rightarrow$ site 3; Site 3 computes EMP$'$ $\bowtie$ PROJ.

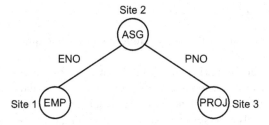

Fig. 8.12 Join Graph of Distributed Query

3. ASG $\rightarrow$ site 3; Site 3 computes ASG$'$ = ASG $\bowtie$ PROJ; ASG$'$ $\rightarrow$ site 1; Site 1 computes ASG$'$ $\bowtie$ EMP.

4. PROJ $\rightarrow$ site 2; Site 2 computes PROJ$'$ = PROJ $\bowtie$ ASG; PROJ$'$ $\rightarrow$ site 1; Site 1 computes PROJ$'$ $\bowtie$ EMP.

5. EMP $\rightarrow$ site 2; PROJ $\rightarrow$ site 2; Site 2 computes EMP $\bowtie$ PROJ $\bowtie$ ASG

To select one of these programs, the following sizes must be known or predicted: *size*(EMP), *size*(ASG), *size*(PROJ), *size*(EMP $\bowtie$ ASG), and *size*(ASG $\bowtie$ PROJ). Furthermore, if it is the response time that is being considered, the optimization must take into account the fact that transfers can be done in parallel with strategy 5. An alternative to enumerating all the solutions is to use heuristics that consider only the sizes of the operand relations by assuming, for example, that the cardinality of the resulting join is the product of operand cardinalities. In this case, relations are ordered by increasing sizes and the order of execution is given by this ordering and the join graph. For instance, the order (EMP, ASG, PROJ) could use strategy 1, while the order (PROJ, ASG, EMP) could use strategy 4.   ◆

8.3.2 Semijoin Based Algorithms

In this section we show how the semijoin operation can be used to decrease the total time of join queries. The theory of semijoins was defined by Bernstein and Chiu [1981]. We are making the same assumptions as in Section 8.3.1. The main shortcoming of the join approach described in the preceding section is that entire operand relations must be transferred between sites. The semijoin acts as a size reducer for a relation much as a selection does.

The join of two relations R and S over attribute A, stored at sites 1 and 2, respectively, can be computed by replacing one or both operand relations by a semijoin with the other relation, using the following rules:

$$R \bowtie_A S \Leftrightarrow (R \ltimes_A S) \bowtie_A S$$
$$\Leftrightarrow R \bowtie_A (S \ltimes_A R)$$

$$\Leftrightarrow (R \ltimes_A S) \bowtie_A (S \ltimes_A R)$$

The choice between one of the three semijoin strategies requires estimating their respective costs.

The use of the semijoin is beneficial if the cost to produce and send it to the other site is less than the cost of sending the whole operand relation and of doing the actual join. To illustrate the potential benefit of the semijoin, let us compare the costs of the two alternatives: $R \bowtie_A S$ versus $(R \ltimes_A S) \bowtie_A S$, assuming that $size(R) < size(S)$.

The following program, using the notation of Section 8.3.1, uses the semijoin operation:

1. $\Pi_A(S) \rightarrow$ site 1
2. Site 1 computes $R' = R \ltimes_A S$
3. $R' \rightarrow$ site 2
4. Site 2 computes $R' \bowtie_A S$

For the sake of simplicity, let us ignore the constant T_{MSG} in the communication time assuming that the term $T_{TR} * size(R)$ is much larger. We can then compare the two alternatives in terms of the amount of transmitted data. The cost of the join-based algorithm is that of transferring relation R to site 2. The cost of the semijoin-based algorithm is the cost of steps 1 and 3 above. Therefore, the semijoin approach is better if

$$size(\Pi_A(S)) + size(R \ltimes_A S) < size(R)$$

The semijoin approach is better if the semijoin acts as a sufficient reducer, that is, if a few tuples of R participate in the join. The join approach is better if almost all tuples of R participate in the join, because the semijoin approach requires an additional transfer of a projection on the join attribute. The cost of the projection step can be minimized by encoding the result of the projection in bit arrays [Valduriez, 1982], thereby reducing the cost of transferring the joined attribute values. It is important to note that neither approach is systematically the best; they should be considered as complementary.

More generally, the semijoin can be useful in reducing the size of the operand relations involved in multiple join queries. However, query optimization becomes more complex in these cases. Consider again the join graph of relations EMP, ASG, and PROJ given in Figure 8.12. We can apply the previous join algorithm using semijoins to each individual join. Thus an example of a program to compute EMP $\bowtie$ ASG $\bowtie$ PROJ is EMP$'$ $\bowtie$ ASG$'$ $\bowtie$ PROJ, where EMP$'$ = EMP $\ltimes$ ASG and ASG$'$ = ASG $\ltimes$ PROJ.

However, we may further reduce the size of an operand relation by using more than one semijoin. For example, EMP$'$ can be replaced in the preceding program by EMP$''$ derived as

$$EMP'' = EMP \ltimes (ASG \ltimes PROJ)$$

since if $size(\text{ASG} \ltimes \text{PROJ}) \leq size(\text{ASG})$, we have $size(\text{EMP}'') \leq size(\text{EMP}')$. In this way, EMP can be reduced by the sequence of semijoins: EMP $\ltimes$ (ASG $\ltimes$ PROJ). Such a sequence of semijoins is called a *semijoin program* for EMP. Similarly, semijoin programs can be found for any relation in a query. For example, PROJ could be reduced by the semijoin program PROJ $\ltimes$ (ASG $\ltimes$ EMP). However, not all of the relations involved in a query need to be reduced; in particular, we can ignore those relations that are not involved in the final joins.

For a given relation, there exist several potential semijoin programs. The number of possibilities is in fact exponential in the number of relations. But there is one optimal semijoin program, called the *full reducer*, which for each relation R reduces R more than the others [Chiu and Ho, 1980]. The problem is to find the full reducer. A simple method is to evaluate the size reduction of all possible semijoin programs and to select the best one. The problems with the enumerative method are twofold:

1. There is a class of queries, called *cyclic queries*, that have cycles in their join graph and for which full reducers cannot be found.

2. For other queries, called *tree queries*, full reducers exist, but the number of candidate semijoin programs is exponential in the number of relations, which makes the enumerative approach NP-hard.

In what follows we discuss solutions to these problems.

Example 8.9. Consider the following relations, where attribute CITY has been added to relations EMP (renamed ET), PROJ (renamed PT) and ASG (renamed AT) of the engineering database. Attribute CITY of AT corresponds to the city where the employee identified by ENO lives.

ET(ENO, ENAME, TITLE, CITY)
AT(ENO, PNO, RESP, DUR)
PT(PNO, PNAME, BUDGET, CITY)

The following SQL query retrieves the names of all employees living in the city in which their project is located together with the project name.

```
SELECT ENAME, PNAME
FROM   ET, AT, PT
WHERE  ET.ENO = AT.ENO
AND    AT.ENO = PT.ENO
AND    ET.CITY = PT.CITY
```

As illustrated in Figure 8.13a, this query is cyclic. ♦

No full reducer exists for the query in Example 8.9. In fact, it is possible to derive semijoin programs for reducing it, but the number of operations is multiplied by the number of tuples in each relation, making the approach inefficient. One solution consists of transforming the cyclic graph into a tree by removing one arc of the graph and by adding appropriate predicates to the other arcs such that the removed

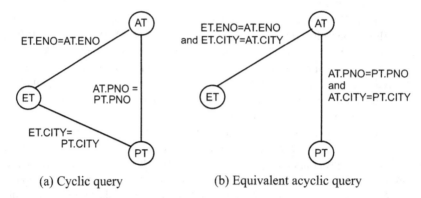

(a) Cyclic query   (b) Equivalent acyclic query

Fig. 8.13 Transformation of Cyclic Query

predicate is preserved by transitivity [Kambayashi et al., 1982]. In the example of Figure 8.13b, where the arc (ET, PT) is removed, the additional predicate ET.CITY = AT.CITY and AT.CITY = PT.CITY imply ET.CITY = PT.CITY by transitivity. Thus the acyclic query is equivalent to the cyclic query.

Although full reducers for tree queries exist, the problem of finding them is NP-hard. However, there is an important class of queries, called *chained queries*, for which a polynomial algorithm exists [Chiu and Ho, 1980; Ullman, 1982]). A chained query has a join graph where relations can be ordered, and each relation joins only with the next relation in the order. Furthermore, the result of the query is at the end of the chain. For instance, the query in Figure 8.12 is a chain query. Because of the difficulty of implementing an algorithm with full reducers, most systems use single semijoins to reduce the relation size.

8.3.3 Join versus Semijoin

Compared with the join, the semijoin induces more operations but possibly on smaller operands. Figure 8.14 illustrates these differences with an equivalent pair of join and semijoin strategies for the query whose join graph is given in Figure 8.12. The join of two relations, EMP ⋈ ASG in Figure 8.12, is done by sending one relation, ASG, to the site of the other one, EMP, to complete the join locally. When a semijoin is used, however, the transfer of relation ASG is avoided. Instead, it is replaced by the transfer of the join attribute values of relation EMP to the site of relation ASG, followed by the transfer of the matching tuples of relation ASG to the site of relation EMP, where the join is completed. If the join attribute length is smaller than the length of an entire tuple and the semijoin has good selectivity, then the semijoin approach can result in significant savings in communication time. Using semijoins may well increase the local processing time, since one of the two joined relations must be accessed twice. For example, relations EMP and PROJ are accessed twice in Figure

8.14. Furthermore, the join of two intermediate relations produced by semijoins cannot exploit the indices that were available on the base relations. Therefore, using semijoins might not be a good idea if the communication time is not the dominant factor, as is the case with local area networks [Lu and Carey, 1985].

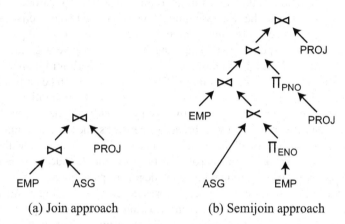

(a) Join approach   (b) Semijoin approach

Fig. 8.14 Join versus Semijoin Approaches

Semijoins can still be beneficial with fast networks if they have very good selectivity and are implemented with bit arrays [Valduriez, 1982]. A bit array $BA[1:n]$ is useful in encoding the join attribute values present in one relation. Let us consider the semijoin $R \ltimes S$. Then $BA[i]$ is set to 1 if there exists a join attribute value $A = val$ in relation S such that $h(val) = i$, where h is a hash function. Otherwise, $BA[i]$ is set to 0. Such a bit array is much smaller than a list of join attribute values. Therefore, transferring the bit array instead of the join attribute values to the site of relation R saves communication time. The semijoin can be completed as follows. Each tuple of relation R, whose join attribute value is val, belongs to the semijoin if $BA[h(val)] = 1$.

8.4 Distributed Query Optimization

In this section we illustrate the use of the techniques presented in earlier sections within the context of four basic query optimization algorithms. First, we present the dynamic and static approaches which extend the centralized algorithms presented in Section 8.2. Then, we describe a popular semijoin-based optimization algorithm. Finally, we present a hybrid approach.

8.4.1 Dynamic Approach

We illustrate the dynamic approach with the algorithm of Distributed INGRES [Epstein et al., 1978] that is derived from the algorithm described in Section 8.2.1. The objective function of the algorithm is to minimize a combination of both the communication time and the response time. However, these two objectives may be conflicting. For instance, increasing communication time (by means of parallelism) may well decrease response time. Thus, the function can give a greater weight to one or the other. Note that this query optimization algorithm ignores the cost of transmitting the data to the result site. The algorithm also takes advantage of fragmentation, but only horizontal fragmentation is handled for simplicity.

Since both general and broadcast networks are considered, the optimizer takes into account the network topology. In broadcast networks, the same data unit can be transmitted from one site to all the other sites in a single transfer, and the algorithm explicitly takes advantage of this capability. For example, broadcasting is used to replicate fragments and then to maximize the degree of parallelism.

The input to the algorithm is a query expressed in tuple relational calculus (in conjunctive normal form) and schema information (the network type, as well as the location and size of each fragment). This algorithm is executed by the site, called the *master site*, where the query is initiated. The algorithm, which we call Dynamic*-QOA, is given in Algorithm 8.4.

Algorithm 8.4: Dynamic*-QOA

Input: *MRQ*: multirelation query
Output: result of the last multirelation query
begin
    for *each detachable ORQ$_i$ in MRQ* **do**   {*ORQ* is monorelation query}
        run(*ORQ$_i$*)   (1)
    MRQ'_list ← REDUCE(*MRQ*)   {MRQ repl. by n irreducible queries} (2)
    while $n \neq 0$ **do**   {n is the number of irreducible queries} (3)
        {choose next irreducible query involving the smallest fragments}
        MRQ' ← SELECT_QUERY(*MRQ'_list*);   (3.1)
        {determine fragments to transfer and processing site for *MRQ'*}
        Fragment-site-list ← SELECT_STRATEGY(*MRQ'*);   (3.2)
        {move the selected fragments to the selected sites}
        for *each pair* (F, S) *in Fragment-site-list* **do**
            move fragment F to site S (3.3)
        execute *MRQ'*;   (3.4)
        $n \leftarrow n - 1$
    {output is the result of the last *MRQ'*}
end

All monorelation queries (e.g., selection and projection) that can be detached are first processed locally [Step (1)]. Then the reduction algorithm [Wong and Youssefi, 1976] is applied to the original query [Step (2)]. Reduction is a technique that isolates all irreducible subqueries and monorelation subqueries by detachment (see Section 8.2.1). Monorelation subqueries are ignored because they have already been processed in step (1). Thus the REDUCE procedure produces a sequence of irreducible subqueries $q_1 \rightarrow q_2 \rightarrow \cdots \rightarrow q_n$, with at most one relation in common between two consecutive subqueries. Wong and Youssefi [1976] have shown that such a sequence is unique. Example 8.4 (in Section 8.2.1), which illustrated the detachment technique, also illustrates what the REDUCE procedure would produce.

Based on the list of irreducible queries isolated in step (2) and the size of each fragment, the next subquery, MRQ', which has at least two variables, is chosen at step (3.1) and steps (3.2), (3.3), and (3.4) are applied to it. Steps (3.1) and (3.2) are discussed below. Step (3.2) selects the best strategy to process the query MRQ'. This strategy is described by a list of pairs (F, S), in which F is a fragment to transfer to the processing site S. Step (3.3) transfers all the fragments to their processing sites. Finally, step (3.4) executes the query MRQ'. If there are remaining subqueries, the algorithm goes back to step (3) and performs the next iteration. Otherwise, it terminates.

Optimization occurs in steps (3.1) and (3.2). The algorithm has produced subqueries with several components and their dependency order (similar to the one given by a relational algebra tree). At step (3.1) a simple choice for the next subquery is to take the next one having no predecessor and involving the smaller fragments. This minimizes the size of the intermediate results. For example, if a query q has the subqueries q_1, q_2, and q_3, with dependencies $q_1 \rightarrow q_3, q_2 \rightarrow q_3$, and if the fragments referred to by q_1 are smaller than those referred to by q_2, then q_1 is selected. Depending on the network, this choice can also be affected by the number of sites having relevant fragments.

The subquery selected must then be executed. Since the relation involved in a subquery may be stored at different sites and even fragmented, the subquery may nevertheless be further subdivided.

Example 8.10. Assume that relations EMP, ASG, and PROJ of the query of Example 8.4 are stored as follows, where relation EMP is fragmented.

Site 1	Site 2
EMP_1	EMP_2
ASG	PROJ

There are several possible strategies, including the following:

1. Execute the entire query (EMP ⋈ ASG ⋈ PROJ) by moving EMP_1 and ASG to site 2.

2. Execute (EMP ⋈ ASG) ⋈ PROJ by moving (EMP_1 ⋈ ASG) and ASG to site 2, and so on.

The choice between the possible strategies requires an estimate of the size of the intermediate results. For example, if $size(\text{EMP}_1 \bowtie \text{ASG}) > size(\text{EMP}_1)$, strategy 1 is preferred to strategy 2. Therefore, an estimate of the size of joins is required. ◆

At step (3.2), the next optimization problem is to determine how to execute the subquery by selecting the fragments that will be moved and the sites where the processing will take place. For an n-relation subquery, fragments from $n-1$ relations must be moved to the site(s) of fragments of the remaining relation, say R_p, and then replicated there. Also, the remaining relation may be further partitioned into k "equalized" fragments in order to increase parallelism. This method is called *fragment-and-replicate* and performs a substitution of fragments rather than of tuples. The selection of the remaining relation and of the number of processing sites k on which it should be partitioned is based on the objective function and the topology of the network. Remember that replication is cheaper in broadcast networks than in point-to-point networks. Furthermore, the choice of the number of processing sites involves a trade-off between response time and total time. A larger number of sites decreases response time (by parallel processing) but increases total time, in particular increasing communication costs.

Epstein et al. [1978] give formulas to minimize either communication time or processing time. These formulas use as input the location of fragments, their size, and the network type. They can minimize both costs but with a priority to one. To illustrate these formulas, we give the rules for minimizing communication time. The rule for minimizing response time is even more complex. We use the following assumptions. There are n relations $R_1, R_2, \ldots, R_n$ involved in the query. R_i^j denotes the fragment of R_i stored at site j. There are m sites in the network. Finally, $CT_k(\#bytes)$ denotes the communication time of transferring #bytes to k sites, with $1 \leq k \leq m$.

The rule for minimizing communication time considers the types of networks separately. Let us first concentrate on a broadcast network. In this case we have

$$CT_k(\#bytes) = CT_1(\#bytes)$$

The rule can be stated as

if $\max_{j=1,m}\left(\sum_{i=1}^{n} size(R_i^j)\right) > \max_{i=1,n}(size(R_i))$
then
    the processing site is the j that has the largest amount of data
else
    R_p is the largest relation and site of R_p is the processing site

If the inequality predicate is satisfied, one site contains an amount of data useful to the query larger than the size of the largest relation. Therefore, this site should be the processing site. If the predicate is not satisfied, one relation is larger than the maximum useful amount of data at one site. Therefore, this relation should be the R_p, and the processing sites are those which have its fragments.

Let us now consider the case of the point-to-point networks. In this case we have

$$CT_k(\#bytes) = k * CT_1(\#bytes)$$

The choice of R_p that minimizes communication is obviously the largest relation. Assuming that the sites are arranged by decreasing order of amounts of useful data for the query, that is,

$$\sum_{i=1}^{n} size(R_i^j) > \sum_{i=1}^{n} size(R_i^{j+1})$$

the choice of k, the number of sites at which processing needs to be done, is given as

if $\sum_{i \neq p}(size(R_i) - size(R_i^1)) > size(R_p^1)$
then
    $k = 1$
else
    k is the largest j such that $\sum_{i \neq p}(size(R_i) - size(R_i^j)) \leq size(R_p^j)$

This rule chooses a site as the processing site only if the amount of data it must receive is smaller than the additional amount of data it would have to send if it were not a processing site. Obviously, the then-part of the rule assumes that site 1 stores a fragment of R_p.

Example 8.11. Let us consider the query PROJ ⋈ ASG, where PROJ and ASG are fragmented. Assume that the allocation of fragments and their sizes are as follows (in kilobytes):

	Site 1	Site 2	Site 3	Site 4
PROJ	1000	1000	1000	1000
ASG			2000	

With a point–to–point network, the best strategy is to send each $PROJ_i$ to site 3, which requires a transfer of 3000 kbytes, versus 6000 kbytes if ASG is sent to sites 1, 2, and 4. However, with a broadcast network, the best strategy is to send ASG (in a single transfer) to sites 1, 2, and 4, which incurs a transfer of 2000 kbytes. The latter strategy is faster and maximizes response time because the joins can be done in parallel.   ◆

This dynamic query optimization algorithm is characterized by a limited search of the solution space, where an optimization decision is taken for each step without concerning itself with the consequences of that decision on global optimization. However, the algorithm is able to correct a local decision that proves to be incorrect.

8.4.2 Static Approach

We illustrate the static approach with the algorithm of R* [Selinger and Adiba, 1980; Lohman et al., 1985] which is a substantial extension of the techniques we described in Section 8.2.2. This algorithm performs an exhaustive search of all alternative strategies in order to choose the one with the least cost. Although predicting and enumerating these strategies may be costly, the overhead of exhaustive search is rapidly amortized if the query is executed frequently. Query compilation is a distributed task, coordinated by a *master site*, where the query is initiated. The optimizer of the master site makes all intersite decisions, such as the selection of the execution sites and the fragments as well as the method for transferring data. The *apprentice sites*, which are the other sites that have relations involved in the query, make the remaining local decisions (such as the ordering of joins at a site) and generate local access plans for the query. The objective function of the optimizer is the general total time function, including local processing and communications costs (see Section 8.1.1).

We now summarize this query optimization algorithm. The input to the algorithm is a localized query expressed as a relational algebra tree (the query tree), the location of relations, and their statistics. The algorithm is described by the procedure Static*-QOA in Algorithm 8.5.

Algorithm 8.5: Static*-QOA

Input: QT: query tree
Output: $strat$: minimum cost strategy
begin
    for *each relation $R_i \in QT$* **do**
        for *each access path AP_{ij} to R_i* **do**
             compute $cost(AP_{ij})$
        $best\_AP_i \leftarrow AP_{ij}$ with minimum cost
    for *each order $(R_{i1}, R_{i2}, \cdots, R_{in})$ with $i = 1, \cdots, n!$* **do**
        build strategy $(\ldots((best\ AP_{i1} \bowtie R_{i2}) \bowtie R_{i3}) \bowtie \ldots \bowtie R_{in})$;
        compute the cost of strategy
    $strat \leftarrow$ strategy with minimum cost ;
    for *each site k storing a relation involved in QT* **do**
        $LS_k \leftarrow$ local strategy (strategy, k) ;
        send $(LS_k$, site $k)$ {each local strategy is optimized at site k}
end

As in the centralized case, the optimizer must select the join ordering, the join algorithm (nested-loop or merge-join), and the access path for each fragment (e.g., clustered index, sequential scan, etc.). These decisions are based on statistics and formulas used to estimate the size of intermediate results and access path information. In addition, the optimizer must select the sites of join results and the method of transferring data between sites. To join two relations, there are three candidate sites: the site of the first relation, the site of the second relation, or a third site (e.g., the site of a third relation to be joined with). Two methods are supported for intersite data transfers.

1. *Ship-whole*. The entire relation is shipped to the join site and stored in a temporary relation before being joined. If the join algorithm is merge join, the relation does not need to be stored, and the join site can process incoming tuples in a pipeline mode, as they arrive.

2. *Fetch-as-needed*. The external relation is sequentially scanned, and for each tuple the join value is sent to the site of the internal relation, which selects the internal tuples matching the value and sends the selected tuples to the site of the external relation. This method is equivalent to the semijoin of the internal relation with each external tuple.

The trade-off between these two methods is obvious. Ship-whole generates a larger data transfer but fewer messages than fetch-as-needed. It is intuitively better to ship whole relations when they are small. On the contrary, if the relation is large and the join has good selectivity (only a few matching tuples), the relevant tuples should be fetched as needed. The optimizer does not consider all possible combinations of join methods with transfer methods since some of them are not worthwhile. For example, it would be useless to transfer the external relation using fetch-as-needed in the nested-loop join algorithm, because all the outer tuples must be processed anyway and therefore should be transferred as a whole.

Given the join of an external relation R with an internal relation S on attribute A, there are four join strategies. In what follows we describe each strategy in detail and provide a simplified cost formula for each, where LT denotes local processing time (I/O + CPU time) and CT denotes communication time. For simplicity, we ignore the cost of producing the result. For convenience, we denote by s the average number of tuples of S that match one tuple of R:

$$s = \frac{card(S \ltimes_A R)}{card(R)}$$

Strategy 1.

Ship the entire external relation to the site of the internal relation. In this case the external tuples can be joined with S as they arrive. Thus we have

$$Total\_cost = LT(\text{retrieve } card(R) \text{ tuples from } R)$$
$$+ CT(size(R))$$
$$+ LT(\text{retrieve } s \text{ tuples from } S) * card(R)$$

Strategy 2.

Ship the entire internal relation to the site of the external relation. In this case, the internal tuples cannot be joined as they arrive, and they need to be stored in a temporary relation T. Thus we have

$Total\_cost = LT$ (retrieve $card(S)$ tuples from S)
$\qquad + CT(size(S))$
$\qquad + LT$ (store $card(S)$ tuples in T)
$\qquad + LT$ (retrieve $card(R)$ tuples from R)
$\qquad + LT$ (retrieve s tuples from T) $* card(R)$

Strategy 3.

Fetch tuples of the internal relation as needed for each tuple of the external relation.
In this case, for each tuple in R, the join attribute value is sent to the site of S. Then
the s tuples of S which match that value are retrieved and sent to the site of R to be
joined as they arrive. Thus we have

$Total\_cost = LT$ (retrieve $card(R)$ tuples from R)
$\qquad + CT(length(A)) * card(R)$
$\qquad + LT$ (retrieve s tuples from S) $* card(R)$
$\qquad + CT(s * length(S)) * card(R)$

Strategy 4.

Move both relations to a third site and compute the join there. In this case the internal
relation is first moved to a third site and stored in a temporary relation T. Then the
external relation is moved to the third site and its tuples are joined with T as they
arrive. Thus we have

$Total\_cost = LT$ (retrieve $card(S)$ tuples from S)
$\qquad + CT(size(S))$
$\qquad + LT$ (store $card(S)$ tuples in T)
$\qquad + LT$ (retrieve $card(R)$ tuples from R)
$\qquad + CT(size(R))$
$\qquad + LT$ (retrieve s tuples from T) $* card(R)$

Example 8.12. Let us consider a query that consists of the join of relations PROJ, the
external relation, and ASG, the internal relation, on attribute PNO. We assume that
PROJ and ASG are stored at two different sites and that there is an index on attribute
PNO for relation ASG. The possible execution strategies for the query are as follows:

1. Ship whole PROJ to site of ASG.
2. Ship whole ASG to site of PROJ.
3. Fetch ASG tuples as needed for each tuple of PROJ.

4. Move ASG and PROJ to a third site.

The optimization algorithm predicts the total time of each strategy and selects the cheapest. Given that there is no operation following the join PROJ ⋈ ASG, strategy 4 obviously incurs the highest cost since both relations must be transferred. If size(PROJ) is much larger than size(ASG), strategy 2 minimizes the communication time and is likely to be the best if local processing time is not too high compared to strategies 1 and 3. Note that the local processing time of strategies 1 and 3 is probably much better than that of strategy 2 since they exploit the index on the join attribute.

If strategy 2 is not the best, the choice is between strategies 1 and 3. Local processing costs in both of these alternatives are identical. If PROJ is large and only a few tuples of ASG match, strategy 3 probably incurs the least communication time and is the best. Otherwise, that is, if PROJ is small or many tuples of ASG match, strategy 1 should be the best.   ♦

Conceptually, the algorithm can be viewed as an exhaustive search among all alternatives that are defined by the permutation of the relation join order, join methods (including the selection of the join algorithm), result site, access path to the internal relation, and intersite transfer mode. Such an algorithm has a combinatorial complexity in the number of relations involved. Actually, the algorithm significantly reduces the number of alternatives by using dynamic programming and the heuristics, as does the System R's optimizer (see Section 8.2.2). With dynamic programming, the tree of alternatives is dynamically constructed and pruned by eliminating the inefficient choices.

Performance evaluation of the algorithm in the context of both high-speed networks (similar to local networks) and medium-speed wide area networks confirm the significant contribution of local processing costs, even for wide area networks[Lohman and Mackert, 1986; Mackert and Lohman, 1986]. It is shown in particular that for the distributed join, transferring the entire internal relation outperforms the fetch-as-needed method.

8.4.3 Semijoin-based Approach

We illustrate the semijoin-based approach with the algorithm of SDD-1 [Bernstein et al., 1981] which takes full advantage of the semijoin to minimize communication cost. The query optimization algorithm is derived from an earlier method called the "hill-climbing" algorithm [Wong, 1977], which has the distinction of being the first distributed query processing algorithm. In the hill-climbing algorithm, refinements of an initial feasible solution are recursively computed until no more cost improvements can be made. The algorithm does not use semijoins, nor does it assume data replication and fragmentation. It is devised for wide area point-to-point networks. The cost of transferring the result to the final site is ignored. This algorithm is quite general in that it can minimize an arbitrary objective function, including the total time and response time.

The hill-climbing algorithm proceeds as follows. The input to the algorithm includes the query graph, location of relations, and relation statistics. Following the completion of initial local processing, an initial feasible solution is selected which is a global execution schedule that includes all intersite communication. It is obtained by computing the cost of all the execution strategies that transfer all the required relations to a single candidate result site, and then choosing the least costly strategy. Let us denote this initial strategy as ES_0. Then the optimizer splits ES_0 into two strategies, ES_1 followed by ES_2, where ES_1 consists of sending one of the relations involved in the join to the site of the other relation. The two relations are joined locally and the resulting relation is transmitted to the chosen result site (specified as schedule ES_2). If the cost of executing strategies ES_1 and ES_2, plus the cost of local join processing, is less than that of ES_0, then ES_0 is replaced in the schedule by ES_1 and ES_2. The process is then applied recursively to ES_1 and ES_2 until no more benefit can be gained. Notice that if n-way joins are involved, ES_0 will be divided into n subschedules instead of just two.

The hill-climbing algorithm is in the class of greedy algorithms, which start with an initial feasible solution and iteratively improve it. The main problem is that strategies with higher initial cost, which could nevertheless produce better overall benefits, are ignored. Furthermore, the algorithm may get stuck at a local minimum cost solution and fail to reach the global minimum.

Example 8.13. Let us illustrate the hill-climbing algorithm using the following query involving relations EMP, PAY, PROJ, and ASG of the engineering database:

"Find the salaries of engineers who work on the CAD/CAM project"

The query in relational algebra is

$$\Pi_{SAL} (PAY \bowtie_{TITLE} (EMP \bowtie_{ENO} (ASG \bowtie_{PNO} (\sigma_{PNAME = \text{``CAD/CAM''}}(PROJ)))))$$

We assume that $T_{MSG} = 0$ and $T_{TR} = 1$. Furthermore, we ignore the local processing, following which the database is

Relation	Size	Site
EMP	8	1
PAY	4	2
PROJ	1	3
ASG	10	4

To simplify this example, we assume that the length of a tuple (of every relation) is 1, which means that the size of a relation is equal to its cardinality. Furthermore, the placement of the relation is arbitrary. Based on join selectivities, we know that $size(EMP \bowtie PAY) = size(EMP)$, $size(PROJ \bowtie ASG) = 2 * size(PROJ)$, and $size(ASG \bowtie EMP) = size(ASG)$.

Considering only data transfers, the initial feasible solution is to choose site 4 as the result site, producing the schedule

ES_0 : EMP $\rightarrow$ site 4
      PAY $\rightarrow$ site 4
      PROJ $\rightarrow$ site 4
      $Total\_cost(ES_0) = 4 + 8 + 1 = 13$

This is true because the cost of any other solution is greater than the foregoing alternative. For example, if one chooses site 2 as the result site and transmits all the relations to that site, the total cost will be

$$Total\_cost = cost(\text{EMP} \rightarrow \text{site 2}) + cost(\text{ASG} \rightarrow \text{site 2})$$
$$+ cost(\text{PROJ} \rightarrow \text{site 2})$$
$$= 19$$

Similarly, the total cost of choosing either site 1 or site 3 as the result site is 15 and 22, respectively.

One way of splitting this schedule (call it ES') is the following:

ES_1 : EMP $\rightarrow$ site 2
ES_2 : (EMP $\bowtie$ PAY) $\rightarrow$ site 4
ES_3 : PROJ $\rightarrow$ site 4
$Total\_cost(ES') = 8 + 8 + 1 = 17$

A second splitting alternative (ES'') is as follows:

ES_1 : PAY $\rightarrow$ site 1
ES_2 : (PAY $\bowtie$ EMP) $\rightarrow$ site 4
ES_3 : PROJ $\rightarrow$ site 4
$Total\_cost(ES'') = 4 + 8 + 1 = 13$

Since the cost of either of the alternatives is greater than or equal to the cost of ES_0, ES_0 is kept as the final solution. A better solution (ignored by the algorithm) is

B : PROJ $\rightarrow$ site 4
    ASG$' = $ (PROJ $\bowtie$ ASG) $\rightarrow$ site 1
    (ASG$'$ $\bowtie$ EMP) $\rightarrow$ site 2
    $Total\_cost(B) = 1 + 2 + 2 = 5$

                                                                    ◆

The semijoin-based algorithm extends the hill-climbing algorithm in a number of ways [Bernstein et al., 1981]. In addition to the extensive use of semijoins, the objective function is expressed in terms of total communication time (local time and response time are not considered). Furthermore, the algorithm uses statistics on the database, called *database profiles*, where a profile is associated with a relation. The algorithm also selects an initial feasible solution that is iteratively refined. Finally, a postoptimization step is added to improve the total time of the solution selected. The main step of the algorithm consists of determining and ordering beneficial semijoins, that is semijoins whose cost is less than their benefit.

The cost of a semijoin is that of transferring the semijoin attributes A,

$$Cost(R \ltimes_A S) = T_{MSG} + T_{TR} * size(\Pi_A(S))$$

while its benefit is the cost of transferring irrelevant tuples of R (which is avoided by the semijoin):

$$Benefit(R \ltimes_A S) = (1 - SF_{SJ}(S.A)) * size(R) * T_{TR}$$

The semijoin-based algorithm proceeds in four phases: initialization, selection of beneficial semijoins, assembly site selection, and postoptimization. The output of the algorithm is a global strategy for executing the query (Algorithm 8.6).

Algorithm 8.6: Semijoin-based-QOA

Input: QG: query graph with n relations; statistics for each relation
Output: ES: execution strategy
begin
  ES $\leftarrow$ local-operations (QG) ;
  modify statistics to reflect the effect of local processing ;
  BS $\leftarrow \phi$;   {set of beneficial semijoins}
  for *each semijoin SJ in QG* **do**
    if $cost(SJ) < benefit(SJ)$ **then**
      $BS \leftarrow BS \cup SJ$

  while $BS \neq \phi$ **do**
           {selection of beneficial semijoins}
    $SJ \leftarrow most\_beneficial(BS)$;   {$SJ$: semijoin with $max(benefit - cost)$}
    $BS \leftarrow BS - SJ$;   {remove SJ from BS}
    $ES \leftarrow ES + SJ$;   {append SJ to execution strategy}
    modify statistics to reflect the effect of incorporating SJ ;
    $BS \leftarrow BS-$ non-beneficial semijoins ;
    $BS \leftarrow BS \cup$ new beneficial semijoins ;
  {assembly site selection}
  $AS(ES) \leftarrow$ select site i such that i stores the largest amount of data after all local operations ;
  $ES \leftarrow ES \cup$ transfers of intermediate relations to $AS(ES)$;
  {postoptimization}
  for *each relation R_i at $AS(ES)$* **do**
    for *each semijoin SJ of R_i by R_j* **do**
      if $cost(ES) > cost(ES - SJ)$ **then**
        $ES \leftarrow ES - SJ$

end

The initialization phase generates a set of beneficial semijoins, $BS = \{SJ_1, SJ_2, \ldots, SJ_k\}$, and an execution strategy ES that includes only local processing. The next phase selects the beneficial semijoins from BS by iteratively choosing the most beneficial semijoin, SJ_i, and modifying the database statistics and BS accordingly. The modification affects the statistics of relation R involved in SJ_i and the remaining semijoins in BS that use relation R. The iterative phase terminates when all semijoins in BS have been appended to the execution strategy. The order in which semijoins are appended to ES will be the execution order of the semijoins.

The next phase selects the assembly site by evaluating, for each candidate site, the cost of transferring to it all the required data and taking the one with the least cost. Finally, a postoptimization phase permits the removal from the execution strategy of those semijoins that affect only relations stored at the assembly site. This phase is necessary because the assembly site is chosen after all the semijoins have been ordered. The SDD-1 optimizer is based on the assumption that relations can be transmitted to another site. This is true for all relations except those stored at the assembly site, which is selected after beneficial semijoins are considered. Therefore, some semijoins may incorrectly be considered beneficial. It is the role of postoptimization to remove them from the execution strategy.

Example 8.14. Let us consider the following query:

```
SELECT  R₃.C
FROM    R₁,R₂,R₃
WHERE   R₁.A = R₂.A
AND     R₂.B = R₃.B
```

Figure 8.15 gives the join graph of the query and of relation statistics. We assume that $T_{MSG} = 0$ and $T_{TR} = 1$. The initial set of beneficial semijoins will contain the following two:

SJ_1: $R_2 \ltimes R_1$, whose benefit is $2100 = (1 - 0.3) * 3000$ and cost is 36
SJ_2: $R_2 \ltimes R_3$, whose benefit is $1800 = (1 - 0.4) * 3000$ and cost is 80

Furthermore there are two non-beneficial semijoins:

SJ_3: $R_1 \ltimes R_2$, whose benefit is $300 = (1 - 0.8) * 1500$ and cost is 320
SJ_4: $R_3 \ltimes R_2$, whose benefit is 0 and cost is 400.

At the first iteration of the selection of beneficial semijoins, SJ_1 is appended to the execution strategy ES. One effect on the statistics is to change the size of R_2 to $900 = 3000 * 0.3$. Furthermore, the semijoin selectivity factor of attribute $R_2.A$ is reduced because $card(\Pi_A(R_2))$ is reduced. We approximate $SF_{SJ}(R_2.A)$ by $0.8 * 0.3 = 0.24$. Finally, size of $\Pi_{R_2.A}$ is also reduced to $96 = 320 * 0.3$. Similarly, the semijoin selectivity factor of attribute $R_2.B$ and $\Pi_{R_2.B}$ should also be reduced (but they not needed in the rest of the example).

At the second iteration, there are two beneficial semijoins:

SJ_2 : $R_2' \ltimes R_3$, whose benefit is $540 = 900 * (1 - 0.4)$ and cost is 80
          (here $R_2' = R_2 \ltimes R_1$, which is obtained by SJ_1
SJ_3: $R_1 \ltimes R_2'$, whose benefit is $1140 = (1 - 0.24) * 1500$ and cost is 96

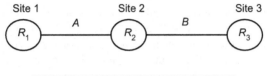

relation	card	tuple size	relation size
R_1	30	50	1500
R_2	100	30	3000
R_3	50	40	2000

attribute	SF_{SJ}	$size(\Pi_{attribute})$
$R_1.A$	0.3	36
$R_2.A$	0.8	320
$R_2.B$	1.0	400
$R_3.B$	0.4	80

Fig. 8.15 Example Query and Statistics

The most beneficial semijoin is SJ_3 and is appended to ES. One effect on the statistics of relation R_1 is to change the size of R_1 to $360(= 1500 * 0.24)$. Another effect is to change the selectivity of R_1 and size of $\Pi_{R_1.A}$.

At the third iteration, the only remaining beneficial semijoin, SJ_2, is appended to ES. Its effect is to reduce the size of relation R_2 to $360(= 900 * 0.4)$. Again, the statistics of relation R_2 may also change.

After reduction, the amount of data stored is 360 at site 1, 360 at site 2, and 2000 at site 3. Site 3 is therefore chosen as the assembly site. The postoptimization does not remove any semijoin since they all remain beneficial. The strategy selected is to send $(R_2 \ltimes R_1) \ltimes R_3$ and $R_1 \ltimes R_2$ to site 3, where the final result is computed. ◆

Like its predecessor hill-climbing algorithm, the semijoin-based algorithm selects locally optimal strategies. Therefore, it ignores the higher-cost semijoins which would result in increasing the benefits and decreasing the costs of other semijoins. Thus this algorithm may not be able to select the global minimum cost solution.

8.4.4 Hybrid Approach

The static and dynamic distributed optimization approaches have the same advantages and disadvantages as in centralized systems (see Section 8.2.3). However, the problems of accurate cost estimation and comparison of QEPs at compile-time are much more severe in distributed systems. In addition to unknown bindings of parameter values in embedded queries, sites may become unavailable or overloaded at runtime. In addition, relations (or relation fragments) may be replicated at several sites. Thus, site and copy selection should be done at runtime to increase availability and load balancing of the system.

The hybrid query optimization technique using dynamic QEPs (see Section 8.2.3) is general enough to incorporate site and copy selection decisions. However, the search space of alternative subplans linked by choose-plan operators becomes much larger and may result in heavy static plans and much higher startup time. Therefore, several hybrid techniques have been proposed to optimize queries in distributed systems [Carey and Lu, 1986; Du et al., 1995; Evrendilek et al., 1997]. They essentially rely on the following two-step approach:

1. At compile time, generate a static plan that specifies the ordering of operations and the access methods, without considering where relations are stored.

2. At startup time, generate an execution plan by carrying out site and copy selection and allocating the operations to the sites.

Example 8.15. Consider the following query expressed in relational algebra:

$$\sigma(R_1) \bowtie R_2 \bowtie R_3$$

Figure 8.16 shows a 2-step plan for this query. The static plan shows the relational operation ordering as produced by a centralized query optimizer. The run-time plan extends the static plan with site and copy selection and communication between sites. For instance, the first selection is allocated at site s_1 on copy R_{11} of relation R_1 and sends its result to site s_3 to be joined with R_{23} and so on. ◆

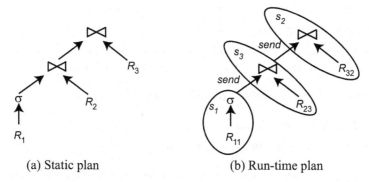

(a) Static plan   (b) Run-time plan

Fig. 8.16 A 2-Step Plan

The first step can be done by a centralized query optimizer. It may also include choose-plan operators so that runtime bindings can be used at startup time to make accurate cost estimations. The second step carries out site and copy selection, possibly in addition to choose-plan operator execution. Furthermore, it can optimize the load balancing of the system. In the rest of this section, we illustrate this second step based on the seminal paper by Carey and Lu [1986] on two-step query optimization.

We consider a distributed database system with a set of sites $S = \{s_1, .., s_n\}$. A query Q is represented as an ordered sequence of subqueries $Q = \{q_1, .., q_m\}$. Each subquery q_i is the maximum processing unit that accesses a single base relation and communicates with its neighboring subqueries. For instance, in Figure 8.16, there are three subqueries, one for R_1, one for R_2, and one for R_3. Each site s_i has a load, denoted by $load(s_i)$, which reflects the number of queries currently submitted. The load can be expressed in different ways, e.g. as the number of I/O bound and CPU bound queries at the site [Carey and Lu, 1986]. The average load of the system is defined as:

$$Avg\_load(S) = \frac{\sum_{i=1}^{n} load(s_i)}{n}$$

The balance of the system for a given allocation of subqueries to sites can be measured as the variance of the site loads using the following *unbalance factor* [Carey and Lu, 1986]:

$$UF(S) = \frac{1}{n} \sum_{i=1}^{n} (load(s_i) - Avg\_load(S))^2$$

As the system gets balanced, its unbalance factor approaches 0 (perfect balance). For example, with $load(s_1)=10$ and $load(s_1)=30$, the unbalance factor of s_1, s_2 is 100 while with $load(s_1)=20$ and $load(s_1)=20$, it is 0.

The problem addressed by the second step of two-step query optimization can be formalized as the following subquery allocation problem. Given

1. a set of sites $S = \{s_1, .., s_n\}$ with the load of each site;

2. a query $Q = \{q_1, .., q_m\}$; and

3. for each subquery q_i in Q, a feasible allocation set of sites $S_q = \{s_1, ..., s_k\}$ where each site stores a copy of the relation involved in q_i;

the objective is to find an optimal allocation on Q to S such that

1. $UF(S)$ is minimized, and

2. the total communication cost is minimized.

Carey and Lu [1986] propose an algorithm that finds near-optimal solutions in a reasonable amount of time. The algorithm, which we describe in Algorithm 8.7 for linear join trees, uses several heuristics. The first heuristic (step 1) is to start by allocating subqueries with least allocation flexibility, i.e. with the smaller feasible allocation sets of sites. Thus, subqueries with a few candidate sites are allocated earlier. Another heuristic (step 2) is to consider the sites with least load and best benefit. The benefit of a site is defined as the number of subqueries already allocated to the site and measures the communication cost savings from allocating the subquery to the site. Finally, in step 3 of the algorithm, the load information of any unallocated subquery that has a selected site in its feasible allocation set is recomputed.

Algorithm 8.7: SQAllocation

Input: Q: $q_1, \ldots, q_m$;
  Feasible allocation sets: $S_{q_1}, \ldots, S_{q_m}$;
  Loads: $load(S_1), \ldots, load(S_m)$;
Output: an allocation of Q to S
begin

  for *each q in Q* **do**
  $\quad \lfloor$ compute($load(S_q)$)

  while *Q not empty* **do**
  $\quad a \leftarrow q \in Q$ with least allocation flexibility; {select subquery a for
  $\quad$ allocation} $\qquad\qquad\qquad\qquad\qquad\qquad\qquad\qquad\qquad$ (1)
  $\quad b \leftarrow s \in S_a$ with least load and best benefit; {select best site b for a} (2)
  $\quad Q \leftarrow Q - a$;
  $\quad$ {recompute loads of remaining feasible allocation sets if necessary} (3)
  $\quad$ **for** *each* $q \in Q$ *where* $b \in S_q$ **do**
  $\quad\quad \lfloor$ compute($load(S_q)$

end

Example 8.16. Consider the following query Q expressed in relational algebra:

$$\sigma(R_1) \bowtie R_2 \bowtie R_3 \bowtie R_4$$

Figure 8.17 shows the placement of the copies of the 4 relations at the 4 sites, and the site loads. We assume that Q is decomposed as $Q = \{q_1, q_2, q_3, q_4\}$ where q_1 is associated with R_1, q_2 with R_2 joined with the result of q_1, q_3 with R_3 joined with the result of q_2, and q_4 with R_4 joined with the result of q_3. The SQAllocation algorithm performs 4 iterations. At the first one, it selects q_4 which has the least allocation flexibility, allocates it to s_1 and updates the load of s_1 to 2. At the second iteration, the next set of subqueries to be selected are either q_2 or q_3 since they have the same allocation flexibility. Let us choose q_2 and assume it gets allocated to s_2 (it could be allocated to s_4 which has the same load as s_2). The load of s_2 is increased to 3. At the third iteration, the next subquery selected is q_3 and it is allocated to s_1 which has the same load as s_3 but a benefit of 1 (versus 0 for s_3) as a result of the allocation of q_4. The load of s_1 is increased to 3. Finally, at the last iteration, q_1 gets allocated to either s_3 or s_4 which have the least loads. If in the second iteration q_2 were allocated to s_4 instead of to s_2, then the fourth iteration would have allocated q_1 to s_4 because of a benefit of 1. This would have produced a better execution plan with less communication. This illustrates that two-step optimization can still miss optimal plans. $\qquad\qquad\blacklozenge$

sites	load	R_1	R_2	R_3	R_4
s_1	1	R_{11}		R_{31}	R_{41}
s_2	2		R_{22}		
s_3	2	R_{13}		R_{33}	
s_4	2	R_{14}	R_{24}		

Fig. 8.17 Example Data Placement and Load

This algorithm has reasonable complexity. It considers each subquery in turn, considering each potential site, selects a current one for allocation, and sorts the list of remaining subqueries. Thus, its complexity can be expressed as $O(max(m*n, m^2 * log_2 m))$.

Finally, the algorithm includes a refining phase to further optimize join processing and decide whether or not to use semijoins. Although it minimizes communication given a static plan, two-step query optimization may generate runtime plans that have higher communication cost than the optimal plan. This is because the first step is carried out ignoring data location and its impact on communication cost. For instance, consider the runtime plan in 8.16 and assume that the third subquery on R_3 is allocated to site s_1 (instead of site s_2). In this case, the plan that does the join (or Cartesian product) of the result of the selection of R_1 with R_3 first at site s_1 may be better since it minimizes communication. A solution to this problem is to perform plan reorganization using operation tree transformations at startup time [Du et al., 1995].

8.5 Conclusion

In this chapter we have presented the basic concepts and techniques for distributed query optimization. We first introduced the main components of query optimization, including the search space, the cost model and the search strategy. The details of the environment (centralized versus distributed) are captured by the search space and the cost model. The search space describes the equivalent execution plans for the input query. These plans differ on the execution order of operations and their implementation, and therefore on performance. The search space is obtained by applying transformation rules, such as those described in Section 7.1.4.

The cost model is key to estimating the cost of a given execution plan. To be accurate, the cost model must have good knowledge about the distributed execution environment. Important inputs are the database statistics and the formulas used to estimate the size of intermediate results. For simplicity, earlier cost models relied on the strong assumption that the distribution of attribute values in a relation is uniform. However, in case of skewed data distributions, this can result in fairly inaccurate estimations and execution plans which are far from the optimal. An effective solution to accurately capture data distributions is to use histograms. Today, most commercial DBMS optimizers support histograms as part of their cost model. A difficulty remains to estimate the selectivity of the join operation when it is not on foreign key. In this case, maintaining join selectivity factors is of great benefit [Mackert and Lohman, 1986]. Earlier distributed DBMSs considered transmission costs only. With the availability of faster communication networks, it is important to consider local processing costs as well.

The search strategy explores the search space and selects the best plan, using the cost model. It defines which plans are examined and in which order. The most popular search strategy is dynamic programming which enumerates all equivalent execution plans with some pruning. However, it may incur a high optimization cost for queries involving large number of relations. Thus, it is best suited when optimization is static (done at compile time) and amortized over multiple executions. Randomized strategies, such as Iterative Improvement and Simulated Annealing, have received much attention. They do not guarantee that the best solution is obtained, but avoid the high cost of optimization. Thus, they are appropriate for ad-hoc queries which are not repetitive.

As a prerequisite to understanding distributed query optimization, we have introduced centralized query optimization with the three basic techniques: dynamic, static and hybrid. Dynamic and static query optimimization both have advantages and drawbacks. Dynamic query optimization can make accurate optimization choices at run-time. but optimization is repeated for each query execution. Therefore, this approach is best for ad-hoc queries. Static query optimization, done at compilation time, is best for queries embedded in stored procedures, and has been adopted by all commercial DBMSs. However, it can make major estimation errors, in particular, in the case of parameter values not known until runtime, which can lead to the choice of suboptimal execution plans. Hybrid query optimization attempts to provide the advantages of static query optimization while avoiding the issues generated by inaccurate estimates. The approach is basically static, but further optimization decisions may take place at run time.

Next, we have seen two approaches to solve distributed join queries, which are the most important type of queries. The first one considers join ordering. The second one computes joins with semijoins. Semijoins are beneficial only when a join has good selectivity, in which case the semijoins act as powerful size reducers. The first systems that make extensive use of semijoins assumed a slow network and therefore concentrated on minimizing only the communication time at the expense of local processing time. However, with faster networks, the local processing time is as important as the communication time and sometimes even more important. Therefore, semijoins should be employed carefully since they tend to increase the local processing time. Join and semijoin techniques should be considered complementary, not alternative [Valduriez and Gardarin, 1984], because each technique may be better under certain database-dependent parameters. For instance, if a relation has very large tuples, as is the case with multimedia data, semijoin is useful to minimize data transfers. Finally, semijoins implemented by hashed bit arrays [Valduriez, 1982] can be made very efficient [Mackert and Lohman, 1986].

We illustrated the use of the join and semijoin techniques in four basic distributed query optimization algorithms: dynamic, static, semijoin-based and hybrid. The static and dynamic distributed optimization approaches have the same advantages and disadvantages as in centralized systems. The semijoin-based approach is best for slow networks. The hybrid approach is best in today's dynamic environments as it delays important decisions such as copy selection and allocation of subqueries to sites at query startup time. Thus, it can better increase availability and load balancing of the system. We illustrated the hybrid approach with two-step query optimization which first generates a static plan that specifies the operations ordering as in a centralized system and then generates an execution plan at startup time, by carrying out site and copy selection and allocating the operations to the sites.

In this chapter we focused mostly on join queries for two reasons: join queries are the most frequent queries in the relational framework and they have been studied extensively. Furthermore, the number of joins involved in queries expressed in languages of higher expressive power than relational calculus (e.g., Horn clause logic) can be extremely large, making the join ordering more crucial [Krishnamurthy et al., 1986]. However, the optimization of general queries containing joins, unions, and aggregate functions is a harder problem [Selinger and Adiba, 1980]. Distributing unions over joins is a simple and good approach since the query can be reduced as a union of join subqueries, which are optimized individually. Note also that the unions are more frequent in distributed DBMSs because they permit the localization of horizontally fragmented relations.

8.6 Bibliographic Notes

Good surveys of query optimization are provided in [Graefe, 1993], [Ioannidis, 1996] and [Chaudhuri, 1998]. Distributed query optimization is surveyed in [Kossmann, 2000].

The three basic algorithms for query optimization in centralized systems are: the dynamic algorithm of INGRES [Wong and Youssefi, 1976] which performs query reduction, the static algorithm of System R [Selinger et al., 1979] which uses dynamic programming and a cost model and the hybrid algorithm of Volcano [Cole and Graefe, 1994] which uses choose-plan operators.

The theory of semijoins and their value for distributed query processing has been covered in [Bernstein and Chiu, 1981], [Chiu and Ho, 1980], and [Kambayashi et al., 1982]. Algorithms for improving the processing of semijoins in distributed systems are proposed in [Valduriez, 1982]. The value of semijoins for multiprocessor database machines having fast communication networks is also shown in [Valduriez and Gardarin, 1984]. Parallel execution strategies for horizontally fragmented databases is treated in [Ceri and Pelagatti, 1983] and [Khoshafian and Valduriez, 1987]. The solutions in [Shasha and Wang, 1991] are also applicable to parallel systems.

The dynamic approach to distributed query optimization was was first proposed for Distributed INGRES in [Epstein et al., 1978]. It extends the dynamic algorithm of INGRES, with a heuristic approach. The algorithm takes advantage of the network topology (general or broadcast networks). Improvements on this method based on the enumeration of all possible solutions are given and analyzed in [Epstein and Stonebraker, 1980].

The static approach to distributed query optimization was first proposed for R* in [Selinger and Adiba, 1980] as an extension of the static algorithm of System R. It is one of the first papers to recognize the significance of local processing on the performance of distributed queries. Experimental validation in [Lohman and Mackert, 1986] have confirmed this important statement.

The semijoin-based approach to distributed query optimization was proposed in [Bernstein et al., 1981] for SDD-1 [Wong, 1977]. It is one of the most complete algorithms which make full use of semijoins.

Several hybrid approaches based on two-step query optimization have been proposed for distributed systems [Carey and Lu, 1986; Du et al., 1995; Evrendilek et al., 1997]. The content of Section 8.4.4 is based on [Carey and Lu, 1986] which is the first paper on two-step query optimization. In [Du et al., 1995], efficient operations to transform linear join trees (produced by the first step) into bushy trees which exhibit more parallelism are proposed. In [Evrendilek et al., 1997], a solution to maximize intersite join parallelism in the second step is proposed.

Exercises

Problem 8.1 (*). Apply the dynamic query optimization algorithm in Section 8.2.1 to the query of Exercise 7.3, and illustrate the successive detachments and substitutions by giving the monorelation subqueries generated.

Problem 8.2. Consider the join graph of Figure 8.12 and the following information: $size(EMP) = 100$, $size(ASG) = 200$, $size(PROJ) = 300$, $size(EMP \bowtie ASG) = 300$, and $size(ASG \bowtie PROJ) = 200$. Describe an optimal join program based on the objective function of total transmission time.

Problem 8.3. Consider the join graph of Figure 8.12 and make the same assumptions as in Problem 8.2. Describe an optimal join program that minimizes response time (consider only communication).

Problem 8.4. Consider the join graph of Figure 8.12, and give a program (possibly not optimal) that reduces each relation fully by semijoins.

Problem 8.5 (*). Consider the join graph of Figure 8.12 and the fragmentation depicted in Figure 8.18. Also assume that $size(EMP \bowtie ASG) = 2000$ and $size(ASG \bowtie PROJ) = 1000$. Apply the dynamic distributed query optimization algorithm in Section 8.4.1 in two cases, general network and broadcast network, so that communication time is minimized.

Rel.	Site 1	Site 2	Site 3
EMP	1000	1000	1000
ASG		2000	
PROJ	1000		

Fig. 8.18 Fragmentation

Problem 8.6. Consider the join graph of Figure 8.19 and the statistics given in Figure 8.20. Apply the semijoin-based distributed query optimization algorithm in Section 8.4.3 with $T_{MSG} = 20$ and $T_{TR} = 1$.

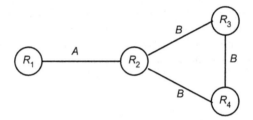

Fig. 8.19 Join Graph

relation	size
R_1	1000
R_2	1000
R_3	2000
R_3	1000

attribute	size	SF_{SJ}
$R_1.A$	200	0.5
$R_2.A$	100	0.1
$R_2.A$	100	0.2
$R_3.B$	300	0.9
$R_4.B$	150	0.4

(a)   (b)

Fig. 8.20 Relation Statistics

Problem 8.7 (**). Consider the query in Problem 7.5. Assume that relations EMP, ASG, PROJ and PAY have been stored at sites 1, 2, and 3 according to the table in Figure 8.21. Assume also that the transfer rate between any two sites is equal and that data transfer is 100 times slower than data processing performed by any site. Finally, assume that $size(R \bowtie S) = max(size(R), size(S))$ for any two relations R and S, and the selectivity factor of the disjunctive selection of the query in Exercise 7.5 is

0.5. Compose a distributed program which computes the answer to the query and minimizes total time.

Rel.	Site 1	Site 2	Site 3
EMP	2000		
ASG		3000	
PROJ			1000
PAY			500

Fig. 8.21 Fragmentation Statistics

Problem 8.8 (**). In Section 8.4.4, we described Algorithm 8.7 for linear join trees. Extend this algorithm to support bushy join trees. Apply it to the bushy join tree in Figure 8.3 using the data placement and site loads shown in Figure 8.17.

Chapter 9
Multidatabase Query Processing

In the previous three chapters, we have considered query processing in tighly-coupled homogeneous distributed database systems. As we discussed in Chapter 1, these systems are logically integrated and provide a single image of the database, even though they are physically distributed. In this chapter, we concentrate on query processing in multidatabase systems that provide interoperability among a set of DBMSs. This is only one part of the more general *interoperability* problem. Distributed applications pose major requirements regarding the databases they access, in particular, the ability to access legacy data as well as newly developed databases. Thus, providing integrated access to multiple, distributed databases and other heterogeneous data sources has become a topic of increasing interest and focus.

Many of the distributed query processing and optimization techniques carry over to multidatabase systems, but there are important differences. Recall from Chapter 6 that we characterized distributed query processing in four steps: query decomposition, data localization, global optimization, and local optimization. The nature of multidatabase systems requires slightly different steps and different techniques. The component DBMSs may be autonomous and have different database languages and query processing capabilities. Thus, a multi-DBMS layer (see Figure 1.17) is necessary to communicate with component DBMSs in an effective way, and this requires additional query processing steps (Figure 9.1). Furthermore, there may be many component DBMSs, each of which may exhibit different behavior, thereby posing new requirements for more adaptive query processing techniques.

This chapter is organized as follows. In Section 9.1 we introduce in more detail the main issues in multidatabase query processing. Assuming the mediator/wrapper architecture, we describe the multidatabase query processing architecture in Section 9.2. Section 9.3 describes the techniques for rewriting queries using multidatabase views. Section 9.4 describes multidatabase query optimization and execution, in particular, heterogeneous cost modeling, heterogeneous query optimization, and adaptive query processing. Section 9.5 describes query translation and execution at the wrappers, in particular, the techniques for translating queries for execution by the component DBMSs and for generating and managing wrappers.

M.T. Özsu and P. Valduriez, *Principles of Distributed Database Systems: Third Edition*,   297
DOI 10.1007/978-1-4419-8834-8_9, © Springer Science+Business Media, LLC 2011

9.1 Issues in Multidatabase Query Processing

Query processing in a multidatabase system is more complex than in a distributed DBMS for the following reasons [Sheth and Larson, 1990]:

1. The computing capabilities of the component DBMSs may be different, which prevents uniform treatment of queries across multiple DBMSs. For example, some DBMSs may be able to support complex SQL queries with join and aggregation while some others cannot. Thus the multidatabase query processor should consider the various DBMS capabilities.

2. Similarly, the cost of processing queries may be different on different DBMSs, and the local optimization capability of each DBMS may be quite different. This increases the complexity of the cost functions that need to be evaluated.

3. The data models and languages of the component DBMSs may be quite different, for instance, relational, object-oriented, XML, etc. This creates difficulties in translating multidatabase queries to component DBMS and in integrating heterogeneous results.

4. Since a multidatabase system enables access to very different DBMSs that may have different performance and behavior, distributed query processing techniques need to adapt to these variations.

The autonomy of the component DBMSs poses problems. DBMS autonomy can be defined along three main dimensions: communication, design and execution [Lu et al., 1993]. Communication autonomy means that a component DBMS communicates with others at its own discretion,and, in particular, it may terminate its services at any time. This requires query processing techniques that are tolerant to system unavailability. The question is how the system answers queries when a component system is either unavailable from the beginning or shuts down in the middle of query execution. Design autonomy may restrict the availability and accuracy of cost information that is needed for query optimization. The difficulty of determining local cost functions is an important issue. The execution autonomy of multidatabase systems makes it difficult to apply some of the query optimization strategies we discussed in previous chapters. For example, semijoin-based optimization of distributed joins may be difficult if the source and target relations reside in different component DBMSs, since, in this case, the semijoin execution of a join translates into three queries: one to retrieve the join attribute values of the target relation and to ship it to the source relation's DBMS, the second to perform the join at the source relation, and the third to perform the join at the target relation's DBMS. The problem arises because communication with component DBMSs occurs at a high level of the DBMS API.

In addition to these difficulties, the architecture of a distributed multidatabase system poses certain challenges. The architecture depicted in Figure 1.17 points to an additional complexity. In distributed DBMSs, query processors have to deal only with data distribution across multiple sites. In a distributed multidatabase environment, on the other hand, data are distributed not only across sites but also across multiple databases, each managed by an autonomous DBMS. Thus, while there are two parties that cooperate in the processing of queries in a distributed DBMS (the control site and local sites), the number of parties increases to three in the case of a distributed multi-DBMS: the multi-DBMS layer at the control site (i.e., the mediator) receives the global query, the multi-DBMS layers at the sites (i.e., the wrappers) participate in processing the query, and the component DBMSs ultimately optimize and execute the query.

9.2 Multidatabase Query Processing Architecture

Most of the work on multidatabase query processing has been done in the context of the mediator/wrapper architecture (see Figure 1.18). In this architecture, each component database has an associated wrapper that exports information about the source schema, data and query processing capabilities. A mediator centralizes the information provided by the the wrappers in a unified view of all available data (stored in a global data dictionary) and performs query processing using the wrappers to access the component DBMSs. The data model used by the mediator can be relational, object-oriented or even semi-structured (based on XML). In this chapter, for consistency with the previous chapters on distributed query processing, we continue to use the relational model, which is quite sufficient to explain the multidatabase query processing techniques.

The mediator/wrapper architecture has several advantages. First, the specialized components of the architecture allow the various concerns of different kinds of users to be handled separately. Second, mediators typically specialize in a related set of component databases with "similar" data, and thus export schemas and semantics related to a particular domain. The specialization of the components leads to a flexible and extensible distributed system. In particular, it allows seamless integration of different data stored in very different components, ranging from full-fledged relational DBMSs to simple files.

Assuming the mediator/wrapper architecture, we can now discuss the various layers involved in query processing in distributed multidatabase systems as shown in Figure 9.1. As before, we assume the input is a query on global relations expressed in relational calculus. This query is posed on global (distributed) relations, meaning that data distribution and heterogeneity are hidden. Three main layers are involved in multidatabase query processing. This layering is similar to that of query processing in homogeneous distributed DBMSs (see Figure 6.3). However, since there is no fragmentation, there is no need for the data localization layer.

The first two layers map the input query into an optimized distributed query execution plan (QEP). They perform the functions of query rewriting, query optimization and some query execution. The first two layers are performed by the mediator and use meta-information stored in the global directory (global schema, allocation and capability schema). Query rewriting transforms the input query into a query on local relations, using the global schema. Recall from Chapter 4 that there are two main

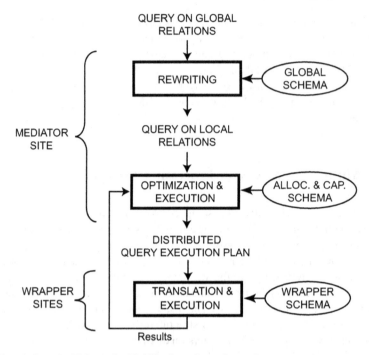

Fig. 9.1 Generic Layering Scheme for Multidatabase Query Processing

approaches for database integration: global-as-view (GAV) and local-as-view (LAV). Thus, the global schema provides the view definitions (i.e., mappings between the global relations and the local relations stored in the component databases) and the query is rewritten using the views.

Rewriting can be done at the relational calculus or algebra levels. In this chapter, we will use a generalized form of relational calculus called Datalog [Ullman, 1988] which is well suited for such rewriting. Thus, there is an additional step of calculus to algebra translation that is similar to the decomposition step in homogeneous distributed DBMSs.

The second layer performs query optimization and (some) execution by considering the allocation of the local relations and the different query processing capabilities of the component DBMSs exported by the wrappers. The allocation and capability schema used by this layer may also contain heterogeneous cost information. The distributed QEP produced by this layer groups within subqueries the operations that can be performed by the component DBMSs and wrappers. Similar to distributed DBMSs, query optimization can be static or dynamic. However, the lack of homogeneity in multidatabase systems (e.g., some component DBMSs may have unexpectedly long delays in answering) make dynamic query optimization more critical. In the case of dynamic optimization, there may be subsequent calls to this layer after execution by the next layer. This is illustrated by the arrow showing results coming from the next layer. Finally, this layer integrates the results coming from the different wrappers to provide a unified answer to the user's query. This requires the capability of executing some operations on data coming from the wrappers. Since the wrappers may provide very limited execution capabilities, e.g., in the case of very simple component DBMSs, the mediator must provide the full execution capabilities to support the mediator interface.

The third layer performs *query translation and execution* using the wrappers. Then it returns the results to the mediator that can perform result integration from different wrappers and subsequent execution. Each wrapper maintains a *wrapper schema* that includes the local export schema (see Chapter 4) and mapping information to facilitate the translation of the input subquery (a subset of the QEP) expressed in a common language into the language of the component DBMS. After the subquery is translated, it is executed by the component DBMS and the local result is translated back to the common format.

The wrapper schema contains information describing how mappings from/to participating local schemas and global schema can be performed. It enables conversions between components of the database in different ways. For example, if the global schema represents temperatures in Fahrenheit degrees, but a participating database uses Celsius degrees, the wrapper schema must contain a conversion formula to provide the proper presentation to the global user and the local databases. If the conversion is across types and simple formulas cannot perform the translation, complete mapping tables could be used in the wrapper schema.

9.3 Query Rewriting Using Views

Query rewriting reformulates the input query expressed on global relations into a query on local relations. It uses the global schema, which describes in terms of views the correspondences between the global relations and the local relations. Thus, the query must be rewritten using views. The techniques for query rewriting differ in major ways depending on the database integration approach that is used, i.e., global-as-view (GAV) or local-as-view (LAV). In particular, the techniques for LAV (and its extension GLAV) are much more involved [Halevy, 2001]. Most of the work on query rewriting using views has been done using Datalog [Ullman, 1988], which is a logic-based database language. Datalog is more concise than relational calculus and thus more convenient for describing complex query rewriting algorithms. In this section, we first introduce Datalog terminology. Then, we describe the main techniques and algorithms for query rewriting in the GAV and LAV approaches.

9.3.1 Datalog Terminology

Datalog can be viewed as an in-line version of domain relational calculus. Let us first define *conjunctive queries*, i.e., select-project-join queries, which are the basis for more complex queries. A conjuntive query in Datalog is expressed as a rule of the form:

$$Q(T) : -R_1(T_1), \ldots, R_n(T_n)$$

The atom $Q(T)$ is the *head* of the query and denotes the result relation. The atoms $R_1(T_1), \ldots, R_n(T_n)$ are the *subgoals* in the body of the query and denote database relations. Q and $R_1, \ldots, R_n$ are predicate names and correspond to relation names. $T, T_1, \ldots, T_n$ refer to the relation tuples and contain variables or constants. The variables are similar to domain variables in domain relational calculus. Thus, the use of the same variable name in multiple predicates expresses equijoin predicates. Constants correspond to equality predicates. More complex comparison predicates (e.g., using comparators such as $\neq$, $\leq$ and $<$) must be expressed as other subgoals. We consider queries which are *safe*, i.e., those where each variable in the head also appears in the body. Disjunctive queries can also be expressed in Datalog using unions, by having several conjuntive queries with the same head predicate.

Example 9.1. Let us consider relations EMP(ENO, ENAME, TITLE, CITY) and ASG(ENO, PNO, DUR) assuming that ENO is the primary key of EMP and (ENO, PNO) is the primary key of ASG. Consider the following SQL query:

```
SELECT ENO, TITLE, PNO
FROM   EMP, ASG
WHERE  EMP.ENO = ASG.ENO
AND    TITLE = "Programmer" OR DUR = 24
```

The corresponding query in Datalog can be expressed as:

$$Q(\text{ENO}, \text{TITLE}, \text{PNO}) : - \text{EMP}(\text{ENO}, \text{ENAME}, \text{"Programmer"}, \text{CITY}),$$
$$\text{ASG}(\text{ENO}, \text{PNO}, \text{DUR})$$
$$Q(\text{ENO}, \text{TITLE}, \text{PNO}) : - \text{EMP}(\text{ENO}, \text{ENAME}, \text{TITLE}, \text{CITY}),$$
$$\text{ASG}(\text{ENO}, \text{PNO}, 24)$$

$\blacklozenge$

9.3.2 Rewriting in GAV

In the GAV approach, the global schema is expressed in terms of the data sources and each global relation is defined as a view over the local relations. This is similar to the global schema definition in tightly-integrated distributed DBMS. In particular, the local relations (i.e., relations in a component DBMS) can correspond to fragments. However, since the local databases pre-exist and are autonomous, it may happen that tuples in a global relation do not exist in local relations or that a tuple in a global relation appears in different local relations. Thus, the properties of completeness and disjointness of fragmentation cannot be guaranteed. The lack of completeness may yield incomplete answers to queries. The lack of disjointness may yield duplicate results that may still be useful information and may not need to be eliminated. Similar to queries, view definitions can use Datalog notation.

Example 9.2. Let us consider the local relations EMP1(ENO, ENAME, TITLE, CITY), EMP2(ENO, ENAME, TITLE, CITY) and ASG1(ENO, PNO, DUR). The global relations EMP(ENO, ENAME, CITY) and ASG(ENO, PNO, TITLE, DUR) can be simply defined with the following Datalog rules:

$$\text{EMP(ENO, ENAME, CITY)} : -\text{EMP1(ENO, ENAME, TITLE, CITY)} \quad (r_1)$$

$$\text{EMP(ENO, ENAME, CITY)} : -\text{EMP2(ENO, ENAME, TITLE, CITY)} \quad (r_2)$$

$$\text{ASG(ENO, PNO, TITLE, DUR)} : -\text{EMP1(ENO, ENAME, TITLE, CITY)},$$
$$\text{ASG1(ENO, PNO, DUR)} \quad (r_3)$$

$$\text{ASG(ENO, PNO, TITLE, DUR)} : -\text{EMP2(ENO, ENAME, TITLE, CITY)},$$
$$\text{ASG1(ENO, PNO, DUR)} \quad (r_4)$$

◆

Rewriting a query expressed on the global schema into an equivalent query on the local relations is relatively simple and similar to data localization in tightly-integrated distributed DBMS (see Section 7.2). The rewriting technique using views is called *unfolding* [Ullman, 1997], and it replaces each global relation invoked in the query with its corresponding view. This is done by applying the view definition rules to the query and producing a union of conjunctive queries, one for each rule application. Since a global relation may be defined by several rules (see Example 9.2), unfolding can generate redundant queries that need to be eliminated.

Example 9.3. Let us consider the global schema in Example 9.2 and the following query Q that asks for assignment information about the employees living in "Paris":

$$Q(e, p) : -\text{EMP}(e, \text{ENAME}, \text{"Paris"}), \text{ASG}(e, p, \text{TITLE}, \text{DUR}).$$

Unfolding Q produces Q' as follows:

$$Q'(e, p) : -\text{EMP1}(e, \text{ENAME}, \text{TITLE}, \text{"Paris"}), \text{ASG1}(e, p, \text{DUR}). \quad (q_1)$$

$$Q'(e, p) : -\text{EMP2}(e, \text{ENAME}, \text{TITLE}, \text{"Paris"}), \text{ASG1}(e, p, \text{DUR}). \quad (q_2)$$

Q' is the union of two conjunctive queries labeled as q_1 and q_2. q_1 is obtained by applying rule r_3 or both rules r_1 and r_3. In the latter case, the query obtained is redundant with respect to that obtained with r_3 only. Similarly, q_2 is obtained by applying rule r_4 or both rules r_2 and r_4. ◆

Although the basic technique is simple, rewriting in GAV becomes difficult when local databases have limited access patterns [Calì and Calvanese, 2002]. This is the case for databases accessed over the web where relations can be only accessed using certain binding patterns for their attributes. In this case, simply substituing the global relations with their views is not sufficient, and query rewriting requires the use of recursive Datalog queries.

9.3.3 Rewriting in LAV

In the LAV approach, the global schema is expressed independent of the local databases and each local relation is defined as a view over the global relations. This enables considerable flexibility for defining local relations.

Example 9.4. To facilitate comparison with GAV, we develop an example that is symmetric to Example 9.2 with EMP(ENO, ENAME, CITY) and ASG(ENO, PNO, TITLE, DUR) as global relations. In the LAV approach, the local relations EMP1(ENO, ENAME, TITLE, CITY), EMP2(ENO, ENAME, TITLE, CITY) and ASG1(ENO, PNO, DUR) can be defined with the following Datalog rules:

$$
\begin{aligned}
\text{EMP1(ENO, ENAME, TITLE, CITY)} :&- \text{EMP(ENO, ENAME, CITY)}, && (r_1) \\
& \text{ASG(ENO, PNO, TITLE, DUR)} \\
\text{EMP2(ENO, ENAME, TITLE, CITY)} :&- \text{EMP(ENO, ENAME, CITY)}, && (r_2) \\
& \text{ASG(ENO, PNO, TITLE, DUR)} \\
\text{ASG1(ENO, PNO, DUR)} :&- \text{ASG(ENO, PNO, TITLE, DUR)} && (r_3)
\end{aligned}
$$

$\blacklozenge$

Rewriting a query expressed on the global schema into an equivalent query on the views describing the local relations is difficult for three reasons. First, unlike in the GAV approach, there is no direct correspondence between the terms used in the global schema, (e.g., EMP, ENAME) and those used in the views (e.g., EMP1, EMP2, ENAME). Finding the correspondences requires comparison with each view. Second, there may be many more views than global relations, thus making view comparison time consuming. Third, view definitions may contain complex predicates to reflect the specific contents of the local relations, e.g., view EMP3 containing only programmers. Thus, it is not always possible to find an equivalent rewriting of the query. In this case, the best that can be done is to find a *maximally-contained* query, i.e., a query that produces the maximum subset of the answer [Halevy, 2001]. For instance, EMP3 could only return a subset of all employees, those who are programmers.

Rewriting queries using views has received much attention because of its relevance to both logical and physical data integration problems. In the context of physical integration (i.e., data warehousing), using materialized views may be much more efficient than accessing base relations. However, the problem of finding a rewriting using views is NP-complete in the number of views and the number of subgoals in the query [Levy et al., 1995]. Thus, algorithms for rewriting a query using views essentially try to reduce the numbers of rewritings that need to be considered. Three main algorithms have been proposed for this purpose: the bucket algorithm [Levy et al., 1996b], the inverse rule algorithm [Duschka and Genesereth, 1997], and the MinCon algorithm [Pottinger and Levy, 2000]. The bucket algorithm and the inverse rule algorithm have similar limitations that are addressed by the MinCon algorithm.

The bucket algorithm considers each predicate of the query independently to select only the views that are relevant to that predicate. Given a query Q, the algorithm proceeds in two steps. In the first step, it builds a bucket b for each subgoal q of Q that is not a comparison predicate and inserts in b the heads of the views that are relevant to answer q. To determine whether a view V should be in b, there must be a mapping that unifies q with one subgoal v in V.

For instance, consider query Q in Example 9.3 and the views in Example 9.4. The following mapping unifies the subgoal EMP(e, ENAME, "Paris") of Q with the subgoal EMP(ENO, ENAME, CITY) in view EMP1:

$$e \rightarrow \text{ENO, "Paris"} \rightarrow \text{CITY}$$

In the second step, for each view V of the Cartesian product of the non-empty buckets (i.e., some subset of the buckets), the algorithm produces a conjuntive query and checks whether it is contained in Q. If it is, the conjunctive query is kept as it represents one way to anwer part of Q from V. Thus, the rewritten query is a union of conjunctive queries.

Example 9.5. Let us consider query Q in Example 9.3 and the views in Example 9.4. In the first step, the bucket algorithm creates two buckets, one for each subgoal of Q. Let us denote by b_1 the bucket for the subgoal EMP(e, ENAME, "Paris") and by b_2 the bucket for the subgoal ASG(e, p, TITLE, DUR). Since the algorithm inserts only the view heads in a bucket, there may be variables in a view head that are not in the unifying mapping. Such variables are simply primed. We obtain the following buckets:

$$b_1 = \{\text{EMP1}(\text{ENO, ENAME, TITLE}', \text{CITY}),$$
$$\qquad \text{EMP2}(\text{ENO, ENAME, TITLE}', \text{CITY})\}$$
$$b_2 = \{\text{ASG1}(\text{ENO, PNO, DUR}')\}$$

In the second step, the algorithm combines the elements from the buckets, which produces a union of two conjuntive queries:

$$Q'(e, p) : -\text{EMP1}(e, \text{ENAME, TITLE, "Paris"}), \text{ASG1}(e, p, \text{DUR}) \qquad (q_1)$$
$$Q'(e, p) : -\text{EMP2}(e, \text{ENAME, TITLE, "Paris"}), \text{ASG1}(e, p, \text{DUR}) \qquad (q_2)$$

◆

The main advantage of the bucket algorithm is that, by considering the predicates in the query, it can significantly reduce the number of rewritings that need to be considered. However, considering the predicates in the query in isolation may yield the addition of a view in a bucket that is irrelevant when considering the join with other views. Furthermore, the second step of the algorithm may still generate a large number of rewritings as a result of the Cartesian product of the buckets.

Example 9.6. Let us consider query Q in Example 9.3 and the views in Example 9.4 with the addition of the following view that gives the projects for which there are employees who live in Paris.

$$\text{PROJ1}(PNO) : -\text{EMP1}(ENO, ENAME, \text{"Paris"}),$$
$$\text{ASG}(ENO, PNO, TITLE, DUR) \qquad\qquad (r_4)$$

Now, the following mapping unifies the subgoal ASG(e, p, TITLE, DUR) of Q with the subgoal ASG(ENO, PNO, TITLE, DUR) in view PROJ1:

$p \rightarrow PNAME$

Thus, in the first step of the bucket algorithm, PROJ1 is added to bucket b_2. However, PROJ1 cannot be useful in a rewriting of Q since the variable ENAME is not in the head of PROJ1 and thus makes it impossible to join PROJ1 on the variable e of Q. This can be discovered only in the second step when building the conjunctive queries.   ♦

The MinCon algorithm addresses the limitations of the bucket algorithm (and the inverse rule algorithm) by considering the query globally and considering how each predicate in the query interacts with the views. It proceeds in two steps like the bucket algorithm. The first step starts similar to that of the bucket algorithm, selecting the views that contain subgoals corresponding to subgoals of query Q. However, upon finding a mapping that unifies a subgoal q of Q with a subgoal v in view V, it considers the join predicates in Q and finds the minimum set of additional subgoals of Q that must be mapped to subgoals in V. This set of subgoals of Q is captured by a *MinCon description* (MCD) associated with V. The second step of the algorithm produces a rewritten query by combining the different MCDs. In this second step, unlike in the bucket algorithm, it is not necessary to check that the proposed rewritings are contained in the query because the way the MCDs are created guarantees that the resulting rewritings will be contained in the original query.

Applied to Example 9.6, the algorithm would create 3 MCDs: two for the views EMP1 and EMP2 containing the subgoal EMP of Q and one for ASG1 containing the subgoal ASG. However, the algorithm cannot create an MCD for PROJ1 because it cannot apply the join predicate in Q. Thus, the algorithm would produce the rewritten query Q' of Example 9.5. Compared with the bucket algorithm, the second step of the MinCon algorithm is much more efficient since it performs fewer combinations of MCDs than buckets.

9.4 Query Optimization and Execution

The three main problems of query optimization in multidatabase systems are heterogeneous cost modeling, heterogeneous query optimization (to deal with different capabilities of component DBMSs), and adaptive query processing (to deal with strong variations in the environment – failures, unpredictable delays, etc.). In this section, we describe the techniques for these three problems. We note that the result is a distributed execution plan to be executed by the wrappers and the mediator.

9.4.1 Heterogeneous Cost Modeling

Global cost function definition, and the associated problem of obtaining cost-related information from component DBMSs, is perhaps the most-studied of the three problems. A number of possible solutions have emerged, which we discuss below.

The first thing to note is that we are primarily interested in determining the cost of the lower levels of a query execution tree that correspond to the parts of the query executed at component DBMSs. If we assume that all local processing is "pushed down" in the tree, then we can modify the query plan such that the leaves of the tree correspond to subqueries that will be executed at individual component DBMSs. In this case, we are talking about the determination of the costs of these subqueries that are input to the first level (from the bottom) operators. Cost for higher levels of the query execution tree may be calculated recursively, based on the leaf node costs.

Three alternative approaches exist for determining the cost of executing queries at component DBMSs [Zhu and Larson, 1998]:

1. **Black Box Approach.** This approach treats each component DBMS as a black box, running some test queries on it, and from these determines the necessary cost information [Du et al., 1992; Zhu and Larson, 1994].

2. **Customized Approach.** This approach uses previous knowledge about the component DBMSs, as well as their external characteristics, to subjectively determine the cost information [Zhu and Larson, 1996a; Roth et al., 1999; Naacke et al., 1999].

3. **Dynamic Approach.** This approach monitors the run-time behavior of component DBMSs, and dynamically collects the cost information [Lu et al., 1992; Zhu et al., 2000, 2003; Rahal et al., 2004].

We discuss each approach, focusing on the proposals that have attracted the most attention.

9.4.1.1 Black box approach

In the black box approach, which is used in the Pegasus project [Du et al., 1992], the cost functions are expressed logically (e.g., aggregate CPU and I/O costs, selectivity factors), rather than on the basis of physical characteristics (e.g., relation cardinalities, number of pages, number of distinct values for each column). Thus, the cost functions for component DBMSs are expressed as

$$Cost = initialization\ cost + cost\ to\ find\ qualifying\ tuples$$
$$+ \ cost\ to\ process\ selected\ tuples$$

The individual terms of this formula will differ for different operators. However, these differences are not difficult to specify a priori. The fundamental difficulty is the determination of the term coefficients in these formulae, which change with different component DBMSs. The approach taken in the Pegasus project is to construct a synthetic database (called a *calibrating database*), run queries against it in isolation, and measure the elapsed time to deduce the coefficients.

A problem with this approach is that the calibration database is synthetic, and the results obtained by using it may not apply well to real DBMSs [Zhu and Larson, 1994]. An alternative is proposed in the CORDS project [Zhu and Larson, 1996b], that is based on running probing queries on component DBMSs to determine cost information. Probing queries can, in fact, be used to gather a number of cost information factors. For example, probing queries can be issued to retrieve data from component DBMSs to construct and update the multidatabase catalog. Statistical probing queries can be issued that, for example, count the number of tuples of a relation. Finally, performance measuring probing queries can be issued to measure the elapsed time for determining cost function coefficients.

A special case of probing queries is sample queries [Zhu and Larson, 1998]. In this case, queries are classified according to a number of criteria, and sample queries from each class are issued and measured to derive component cost information. Query classification can be performed according to query characteristics (e.g., unary operation queries, two-way join queries), characteristics of the operand relations (e.g., cardinality, number of attributes, information on indexed attributes), and characteristics of the underlying component DBMSs (e.g., the access methods that are supported and the policies for choosing access methods).

Classification rules are defined to identify queries that execute similarly, and thus could share the same cost formula. For example, one may consider that two queries that have similar algebraic expressions (i.e., the same algebraic tree shape), but different operand relations, attributes, or constants, are executed the same way if their attributes have the same physical properties. Another example is to assume that join order of a query has no effect on execution since the underlying query optimizer applies reordering techniques to choose an efficient join ordering. Thus, two queries that join the same set of relations belong to the same class, whatever ordering is expressed by the user. Classification rules are combined to define query classes. The classification is performed either top-down by dividing a class into more specific ones, or bottom-up by merging two classes into a larger one. In practice, an efficient classification is obtained by mixing both approaches. The global cost function is similar to the Pegasus cost function in that it consists of three components: initialization cost, cost of retrieving a tuple, and cost of processing a tuple. The difference is in the way the parameters of this function are determined. Instead of using a calibrating database, sample queries are executed and costs are measured. The global cost equation is treated as a regression equation, and the regression coefficients are calculated using the measured costs of sample queries [Zhu and Larson, 1996a]. The regression coefficients are the cost function parameters. Eventually, the cost model quality is controlled through statistical tests (e.g., F-test): if the tests fail, the query classification is refined until quality is sufficient. This approach has been validated over various DBMS and has been shown to yield good results [Zhu and Larson, 2000].

The above approaches require a preliminary step to instantiate the cost model (either by calibration or sampling). This may not be appropriate in MDBMSs because it would slow down the system each time a new DBMS component is added. One way to address this problem, as proposed in the Hermes project, is to progressively learn the cost model from queries [Adali et al., 1996b]. The cost model designed in the Hermes mediator assumes that the underlying component DBMSs are invoked by a function call. The cost of a call is composed of three values: the response time to access the first tuple, the whole result response time, and the result cardinality. This allows the query optimizer to minimize either the time to receive the first tuple or the time to process the whole query, depending on end-user requirements. Initially the query processor does not know any statistics about components DBMSs. Then it monitors on-going queries: it collects processing time of every call and stores it for future estimation. To manage the large amount of collected statistics, the cost manager summarizes them, either without loss of precision or with less precision at the benefit of lower space use and faster cost estimation. Summarization consists of aggregating statistics: the average response time is computed of all the calls that match the same pattern, i.e., those with identical function name and zero or more identical argument values. The cost estimator module is implemented in a declarative language. This allows adding new cost formulae describing the behavior of a particular component DBMS. However, the burden of extending the mediator cost model remains with the mediator developer.

The major drawback of the black box approach is that the cost model, although adjusted by calibration, is common for all component DBMSs and may not capture their individual specifics. Thus it might fail to estimate accurately the cost of a query executed at a component DBMS that exposes unforeseen behavior.

9.4.1.2 Customized Approach

The basis of this approach is that the query processors of the component DBMSs are too different to be represented by a unique cost model as used in the black-box approach. It also assumes that the ability to accurately estimate the cost of local subqueries will improve global query optimization. The approach provides a framework to integrate the component DBMSs' cost model into the mediator query optimizer. The solution is to extend the wrapper interface such that the mediator gets some specific cost information from each wrapper. The wrapper developer is free to provide a cost model, partially or entirely. Then, the challenge is to integrate this (potentially partial) cost description into the mediator query optimizer. There are two main solutions.

A first solution is to provide the logic within the wrapper to compute three cost estimates: the time to initiate the query process and receive the first result item (called *reset_cost*), the time to get the next item (called *advance_cost*), and the result cardinality. Thus, the total query cost is:

$$Total\_access\_cost = reset\_cost + (cardinality - 1) * advance\_cost$$

This solution can be extended to estimate the cost of database procedure calls. In that case, the wrapper provides a cost formula that is a linear equation depending on the procedure parameters. This solution has been successfully implemented to model a wide range of heterogeneous components DBMSs, ranging from a relational DBMS to an image server [Roth et al., 1999]. It shows that a little effort is sufficient to implement a rather simple cost model and this significantly improves distributed query processing over heterogeneous sources.

A second solution is to use a hierarchical generic cost model. As shown in Figure 9.2, each node represents a cost rule that associates a query pattern with a cost function for various cost parameters.

The node hierarchy is divided into five levels depending on the genericity of the cost rules (in Figure 9.2, the increasing width of the boxes shows the increased focus of the rules). At the top level, cost rules apply by default to any DBMS. At the underlying levels, the cost rules are increasingly focused on: specific DBMS, relation, predicate or query. At the time of wrapper registration, the mediator receives wrapper metadata including cost information, and completes its built-in cost model by adding new nodes at the appropriate level of the hierarchy. This framework is sufficiently general to capture and integrate both general cost knowledge declared as rules given by wrapper developers and specific information derived from recorded past queries that were previously executed. Thus, through an inheritance hierarchy , the mediator cost-based optimizer can support a wide variety of data sources. The mediator benefits from specialized cost information about each component DBMS, to accurately estimate the cost of queries and choose a more efficient QEP [Naacke et al., 1999].

Example 9.7. Consider the following relations:

EMP(ENO, ENAME, TITLE)
ASG(ENO, PNO, RESP, DUR)

EMP is stored at component DBMS db_1 and contains 1,000 tuples. ASG is stored at component DBMS db_2 and contains 10,000 tuples. We assume uniform distribution

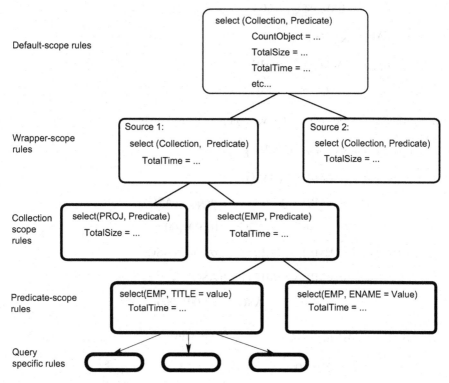

Fig. 9.2 Hierarchical Cost Formula Tree

of attribute values. Half of the ASG tuples have a duration greater than 6. We detail below some parts of the mediator generic cost model (we use superscripts to indicate the access method):

$cost(R) = |R|$

$cost(\sigma_{predicate}(R)) = cost(R)$ (access to R by sequential scan (by default))

$cost(R \bowtie_A^{ind} S) = cost(R) + |R| * cost(\sigma_{A=v}(S))$ (using an index-based (*ind*) join with

the index on $S.A$)

$cost(R \bowtie_A^{nl} S) = cost(R) + |R| * cost(S)$ (using a nested-loop (*nl*) join)

Consider the following global query Q:

```
SELECT *
FROM   EMP, ASG
WHERE  EMP.ENO=ASG.ENO
AND    ASG.DUR>6
```

The cost-based query optimizer generates the following plans to process Q:

$$P_1 = \sigma_{DUR>6}(EMP \bowtie_{ENO}^{ind} ASG)$$

$$P_2 = EMP \bowtie_{ENO}^{nl} \sigma_{DUR>6}(ASG)$$

$$P_3 = \sigma_{DUR>6}(ASG) \bowtie_{ENO}^{ind} EMP$$

$$P_4 = \sigma_{DUR>6}(ASG) \bowtie_{ENO}^{nl} EMP$$

Based on the generic cost model, we compute their cost as:

$$
\begin{aligned}
cost(P_1) &= cost(\sigma_{DUR>6}(EMP \bowtie_{ENO}^{ind} ASG) \\
&= cost(EMP \bowtie_{ENO}^{ind} ASG) \\
&= cost(EMP) + |EMP| * cost(\sigma_{ENO=v}(ASG)) \\
&= |EMP| + |EMP| * |ASG| = 10,001,000 \\
cost(P_2) &= cost(EMP) + |EMP| * cost(\sigma_{DUR>6}(ASG)) \\
&= cost(EMP) + |EMP| * cost(ASG) \\
&= |EMP| + |EMP| * |ASG| = 10,001,000 \\
cost(P_3) &= cost(P_4) = |ASG| + \frac{|ASG|}{2} * |EMP| \\
&= 5,010,000
\end{aligned}
$$

Thus, the optimizer discards plans P_1 and P_2 to keep either P_3 or P_4 for processing Q. Let us assume now that the mediator imports specific cost information about component DBMSs. db_1 exports the cost of accessing EMP tuples as:

$$cost(\sigma_{A=v}(R)) = |\sigma_{A=v}(R)|$$

db_2 exports the specific cost of selecting ASG tuples that have a given ENO as:

$$cost(\sigma_{ENO=v}(ASG)) = |\sigma_{ENO=v}(ASG)|$$

The mediator integrates these cost functions in its hierarchical cost model, and can now estimate more accurately the cost of the QEPs:

$$
\begin{aligned}
cost(P_1) &= |EMP| + |EMP| * |\sigma_{ENO=v}(ASG)| \\
&= 1,000 + 1,000 * 10 \\
&= 11,000 \\
cost(P_2) &= |EMP| + |EMP| * |\sigma_{DUR>6}(ASG)|
\end{aligned}
$$

$$= |EMP| + |EMP| * \frac{|ASG|}{2}$$

$$= 5,001,000$$

$$cost(P_3) = |ASG| + \frac{|ASG|}{2} * |\sigma_{ENO=v}(EMP)|$$

$$= 10,000 + 5,000 * 1$$

$$= 15,000$$

$$cost(P_4) = |ASG| + \frac{|ASG|}{2} * |EMP|$$

$$= 10,000 + 5,000 * 1,000$$

$$= 5,010,000$$

The best QEP is now P_1 which was previously discarded because of lack of cost information about component DBMSs. In many situations P_1 is actually the best alternative to process Q_1. ♦

The two solutions just presented are well suited to the mediator/wrapper architecture and offer a good tradeoff between the overhead of providing specific cost information for diverse component DBMSs and the benefit of faster heterogeneous query processing.

9.4.1.3 Dynamic Approach

The above approaches assume that the execution environment is stable over time. However, in most cases, the execution environment factors are frequently changing. Three classes of environmental factors can be identified based on their dynamicity [Rahal et al., 2004]. The first class for frequently changing factors (every second to every minute) includes CPU load, I/O throughput, and available memory. The second class for slowly changing factors (every hour to every day) includes DBMS configuration parameters, physical data organization on disks, and database schema. The third class for almost stable factors (every month to every year) includes DBMS type, database location, and CPU speed. We focus on solutions that deal with the first two classes.

One way to deal with dynamic environments where network contention, data storage or available memory change over time is to extend the sampling method [Zhu, 1995] and consider user queries as new samples. Query response time is measured to adjust the cost model parameters at run time for subsequent queries. This avoids the overhead of processing sample queries periodically, but still requires heavy computation to solve the cost model equations and does not guarantee that cost model precision improves over time. A better solution, called qualitative [Zhu et al., 2000], defines the system contention level as the combined effect of frequently changing factors on query cost. The system contention level is divided into several discrete categories: high, medium, low, or no system contention. This allows for defining a multi-category cost model that provides accurate cost estimates while dynamic factors are varying. The cost model is initially calibrated using probing queries. The current system contention level is computed over time, based on the most significant system parameters. This approach assumes that query executions are short, so the environment factors remain rather constant during query execution. However, this solution does not apply to long running queries, since the environment factors may change rapidly during query execution.

To manage the case where the environment factor variation is predictable (e.g., the daily DBMS load variation is the same every day), the query cost is computed for successive date ranges [Zhu et al., 2003]. Then, the total cost is the sum of the costs for each range. Furthermore, it may be possible to learn the pattern of the available network bandwidth between the MDBMS query processor and the component DBMS [Vidal et al., 1998]. This allows adjusting the query cost depending on the actual date.

9.4.2 Heterogeneous Query Optimization

In addition to heterogeneous cost modeling, multidatabase query optimization must deal with the issue of the heterogeneous computing capabilities of component DBMSs. For instance, one component DBMS may support only simple select operations while another may support complex queries involving join and aggregate. Thus, depending on how the wrappers export such capabilities, query processing at the mediator level can be more or less complex. There are two main approaches to deal with this issue depending on the kind of interface between mediator and wrapper: query-based and operator-based.

1. **Query-based.** In this approach, the wrappers support the same query capability, e.g., a subset of SQL, which is translated to the capability of the component DBMS. This approach typically relies on a standard DBMS interface such as Open Database Connectivity (ODBC) and its extensions for the wrappers or SQL Management of External Data (SQL/MED) [Melton et al., 2001]. Thus, since the component DBMSs appear homogeneous to the mediator, query processing techniques designed for homogeneous distributed DBMS can be reused. However, if the component DBMSs have limited capabilities, the additional capabilities must be implemented in the wrappers, e.g., join queries may need to be handled at the wrapper, if the component DBMS does not support join.

2. **Operator-based.** In this approach, the wrappers export the capabilities of the component DBMSs through compositions of relational operators. Thus, there is more flexibility in defining the level of functionality between the mediator

and the wrapper. In particular, the different capabilities of the component DBMSs can be made available to the mediator. This makes wrapper construction easier at the expense of more complex query processing in the mediator. In particular, any functionality that may not be supported by component DBMSs (e.g., join) will need to be implemented at the mediator.

In the rest of this section, we present, in more detail, the approaches to query optimization.

9.4.2.1 Query-based Approach

Since the component DBMSs appear homogeneous to the mediator, one approach is to use a distributed cost-based query optimization algorithm (see Chapter 8) with a heterogeneous cost model (see Section 9.4.1). However, extensions are needed to convert the distributed execution plan into subqueries to be executed by the component DBMSs and into subqueries to be executed by the mediator. The hybrid two-step optimization technique is useful in this case (see Section 8.4.4): in the first step, a static plan is produced by a centralized cost-based query optimizer; in the second step, at startup time, an execution plan is produced by carrying out site selection and allocating the subqueries to the sites. However, centralized optimizers restrict their search space by eliminating bushy join trees from consideration. Almost all the systems use left linear join orders where the right subtree of a join node is always a leaf node corresponding to a base relation (Figure 9.3a). Consideration of only left linear join trees gives good results in centralized DBMSs for two reasons: it reduces the need to estimate statistics for at least one operand, and indexes can still be exploited for one of the operands. However, in multidatabase systems, these types of join execution plans are not necessarily the preferred ones as they do not allow any parallelism in join execution. As we discussed in earlier chapters, this is also a problem in homogeneous distributed DBMSs, but the issue is more serious in the case of multidatabase systems, because we wish to push as much processing as possible to the component DBMSs.

A way to resolve this problem is to somehow generate bushy join trees and consider them at the expense of left linear ones. One way to achieve this is to apply a cost-based query optimizer to first generate a left linear join tree, and then convert it to a bushy tree [Du et al., 1995]. In this case, the left linear join execution plan can be optimal with respect to total time, and the transformation improves the query response time without severely impacting the total time. A hybrid algorithm that concurrently performs a bottom-up and top-down sweep of the left linear join execution tree, transforming it, step-by-step, to a bushy one has been proposed [Du et al., 1995]. The algorithm maintains two pointers, called *upper anchor nodes* (UAN) on the tree. At the beginning, one of these, called the bottom UAN (UAN_B), is set to the grandparent of the leftmost root node (join with R_3 in Figure 9.3a), while the second one, called the top UAN (UAN_T), is set to the root (join with R_5). For each UAN the algorithm selects a *lower anchor node* (LAN). This is the node closest to the UAN and whose

right child subtree's response time is within a designer-specified range, relative to
that of the UAN's right child subtree. Intuitively, the LAN is chosen such that its
right child subtree's response time is **close** to the corresponding UAN's right child
subtree's response time. As we will see shortly, this helps in keeping the transformed
bushy tree balanced, which reduces the response time.

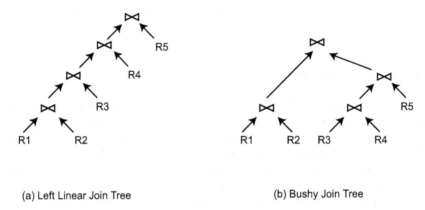

(a) Left Linear Join Tree   (b) Bushy Join Tree

Fig. 9.3 Left Linear versus Bushy Join Tree

At each step, the algorithm picks one of the UAN/LAN pairs (strictly speaking, it
picks the UAN and selects the appropriate LAN, as discussed above), and performs
the following translation for the segment between that LAN and UAN pair:

1. The left child of UAN becomes the new UAN of the transformed segment.
2. The LAN remains unchanged, but its right child node is replaced with a new
   join node of two subtrees, which were the right child subtrees of the input
   UAN and LAN.

The UAN mode that will be considered in that particular iteration is chosen
according to the following heuristic: choose UAN_B if the response time of its left
child subtree is smaller than that of UAN_T's subtree; otherwise choose UAN_T. If the
response times are the same, choose the one with the more unbalanced child subtree.
   At the end of each transformation step, the UAN_B and UAN_T are adjusted. The
algorithm terminates when $UAN_B = UAN_T$, since this indicates that no further transformations are possible. The resulting join execution tree will be almost balanced,
producing an execution plan whose response time is reduced due to parallel execution
of the joins.
   The algorithm described above starts with a left linear join execution tree that is
generated by a commercial DBMS optimizer. While this is a good starting point, it
can be argued that the original linear execution plan may not fully account for the
peculiarities of the distributed multidatabase characteristics, such as data replication.
A special global query optimization algorithm [Evrendilek et al., 1997] can take

these into consideration. Starting from an initial join graph, the algorithm checks for different parenthesizations of this linear join execution order and produces a parenthesized order, which is optimal with respect to response time. The result is an (almost) balanced join execution tree. Performance evaluations indicate that this approach produces better quality plans at the expense of longer optimization time.

9.4.2.2 Operator-based Approach

Expressing the capabilities of the component DBMSs through relational operators allows tight integration of query processing between mediator and wrappers. In particular, the mediator/wrapper communication can be in terms of subplans. We illustrate the operator-based approach with planning functions proposed in the Garlic project [Haas et al., 1997a]. In this approach, the capabilities of the component DBMSs are expressed by the wrappers as planning functions that can be directly called by a centralized query optimizer. It extends the rule-based optimizer proposed by Lohman [1988] with operators to create temporary relations and retrieve locally-stored data. It also creates the *PushDown* operator that pushes a portion of the work to the component DBMSs where it will be executed. The execution plans are represented, as usual, as operator trees, but the operator nodes are annotated with additional information that specifies the source(s) of the operand(s), whether the results are materialized, and so on. The Garlic operator trees are then translated into operators that can be directly executed by the execution engine.

Planning functions are considered by the optimizer as enumeration rules. They are called by the optimizer to construct subplans using two main functions: *accessPlan* to access a relation, and *joinPlan* to join two relations using the access plans. These functions precisely reflect the capabilities of the component DBMSs with a common formalism.

Example 9.8. We consider three component databases, each at a different site. Component database db_1 stores relation EMP(ENO, ENAME, CITY). Component database db_2 stores relation ASG(ENO, PNAME, DUR). Component database db_3 stores only employee information with a single relation of schema EM-PASG(ENAME, CITY, PNAME, DUR), whose primary key is (ENAME, PNAME). Component databases db_1 and db_2 have the same wrapper w_1 whereas db_3 has a different wrapper w_2.

Wrapper w_1 provides two planning functions typical of a relational DBMS. The accessPlan rule

accessPlan(R: relation, A: attribute list, P: select predicate) =
    scan($R, A, P, db(R)$)

produces a scan operator that accesses tuples of R from its component database $db(R)$ (here we can have $db(R) = db_1$ or $db(R) = db_2$), applies select predicate P, and projects on the attribute list A. The joinPlan rule

joinPlan(R_1, R_2: relations, A: attribute list, P: join predicate) =
    join (R_1, R_2, A, P)
condition: $db(R_1) \neq db(R_2)$

produces a join operator that accesses tuples of relations R_1 and R_2 and applies join predicate P and projects on attribute list A. The condition expresses that R_1 and R_2 are stored in different component databases (i.e., db_1 and db_2). Thus, the join operator is implemented by the wrapper.

Wrapper w_2 also provides two planning functions. The accessPlan rule

accessPlan(R: relation, A: attribute list, P: select predicate) =
    fetch(CITY="c")
condition: (CITY="c") $\subseteq P$

produces a fetch operator that directly accesses (entire) employee tuples in component database db_3 whose CITY value is "c". The accessPlan rule

accessPlan(R: relation, A: attribute list, P: select predicate) =
    scan(R, A, P)

produces a scan operator that accesses tuples of relation R in the wrapper and applies select predicate P and attribute project list A. Thus, the scan operator is implemented by the wrapper, not the component DBMS.

Consider the following SQL query submitted to mediator m:

```
SELECT ENAME, PNAME, DUR
FROM    EMPASG
WHERE   CITY = "Paris" AND DUR > 24
```

Assuming the GAV approach, the global view EMPASG(ENAME, CITY, PNAME, DUR) can be defined as follows (for simplicity, we prefix each relation by its component database name):

EMPASG = (db_1.EMP $\bowtie$ db_2.ASG) $\cup$ db_3.EMPASG

After query rewriting in GAV and query optimization, the operator-based approach could produce the QEP shown in Figure 9.4. This plan shows that the operators that are not supported by the component DBMS are to be implemented by the wrappers or the mediator.   ♦

Using planning functions for heterogeneous query optimization has several advantages in multi-DBMSs. First, planning functions provide a flexible way to express precisely the capabilities of component data sources. In particular, they can be used to model non-relational data sources such as web sites. Second, since these rules are declarative, they make wrapper development easier. The only important development for wrappers is the implementation of specific operators, e.g., the scan operator of db_3 in Example 9.8. Finally, this approach can be easily incorporated in an existing, centralized query optimizer.

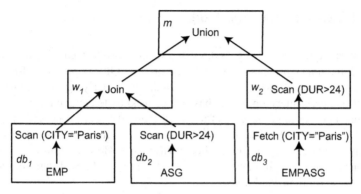

Fig. 9.4 Heterogeneous Query Execution Plan

The operator-based approach has also been successfully used in DISCO, a multi-DBMS designed to access multiple databases over the web [Tomasic et al., 1996, 1997, 1998]. DISCO uses the GAV approach and supports an object data model to represent both mediator and component database schemas and data types. This allows easy introduction of new component databases, easily handling potential type mismatches. The component DBMS capabilities are defined as a subset of an algebraic machine (with the usual operators such as scan, join and union) that can be partially or entirely supported by the wrappers or the mediator. This gives much flexibility for the wrapper implementors in deciding where to support component DBMS capabilities (in the wrapper or in the mediator). Furthermore, compositions of operators, including specific data sets, can be specified to reflect component DBMS limitations. However, query processing is more complicated because of the use of an algrebraic machine and compositions of operators. After query rewriting on the component schemas, there are three main steps [Kapitskaia et al., 1997].

1. **Search space generation.** The query is decomposed into a number of QEPs, which constitutes the search space for query optimization. The search space is generated using a traditional search strategy such as dynamic programming.

2. **QEP decomposition.** Each QEP is decomposed into a forest of *n wrapper QEPs* and a *composition QEP*. Each wrapper QEP is the largest part of the initial QEP that can be entirely executed by the wrapper. Operators that cannot be performed by a wrapper are moved up to the composition QEP. The composition QEP combines the results of the wrapper QEPs in the final answer, typically through unions and joins of the intermediate results produced by the wrappers.

3. **Cost evaluation.** The cost of each QEP is evaluated using a hierarchical cost model discussed in Section 9.4.1.

9.4.3 Adaptive Query Processing

Multidatabase query processing, as discussed so far, follows essentially the principles of traditional query processing whereby an optimal QEP is produced for a query based on a cost model, which is then executed. The underlying assumption is that the multidatabase query optimizer has sufficient knowledge about query runtime conditions in order to produce an efficient QEP and the runtime conditions remain stable during execution. This is a fair assumption for multidatabase queries with few data sources running in a controlled environment. However, this assumption is inappropriate for changing environments with large numbers of data sources and unpredictable runtime conditions.

Example 9.9. Consider the QEP in Figure 9.5 with relations EMP, ASG, PROJ and PAY at sites s_1, s_2, s_3, s_4, respectively. The crossed arrow indicates that, for some reason (e.g., failure), site s_2 (where ASG is stored) is not available at the beginning of execution. Let us assume, for simplicity, that the query is to be executed according to the iterator execution model [Graefe and McKenna, 1993], such that tuples flow from the left most relation,

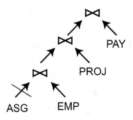

Fig. 9.5 Query Execution Plan with Blocked Data Source

Because of the unavailability of s_2, the entire pipeline is blocked, waiting for ASG tuples to be produced. However, with some reoganization of the plan, some other operators could be evaluated while waiting for s_2, for instance, to evaluate the join of EMP and PAY.   ♦

This simple example illustrates that a typical static plan cannot cope with unpredictable data source unavailability [Amsaleg et al., 1996a]. More complex examples involve continuous queries [Madden et al., 2002b], expensive predicates [Porto et al., 2003] and data skew [Shah et al., 2003]. The main solution is to have some adaptive behavior during query processing, i.e., *adaptive query processing*. Adaptive query processing is a form of dynamic query processing, with a feedback loop between the execution environment and the query optimizer in order to react to unforeseen variations of runtime conditions. A query processing system is defined as adaptive if it receives information from the execution environment and determines its behavior according to that information in an iterative manner [Hellerstein et al., 2000; Gounaris et al., 2002b]. In the context of multidatabase systems, the execution environment includes the mediator, wrappers and component DBMSs. In particular, wrappers should be able to collect information regarding execution within the component DBMSs. Obviously, this is harder to do with legacy DBMSs.

In this section, we first provide a general presentation of the adaptive query processing process. Then, we present, in more detail, the Eddy approach [Avnur and Hellerstein, 2000] that provides a powerful framework for adaptive query processing techniques. Finally, we discuss major extensions to Eddy.

9.4.3.1 Adaptive Query Processing Process

Adaptive query processing adds to the traditional query processing process the following activities: monitoring, assessing and reacting. These activities are logically implemented in the query processing system by sensors, assessment components, and reaction components, respectively. These components may be embedded into control operators of the QEP, e.g., the *Exchange* operator [Graefe and McKenna, 1993]. Monitoring involves measuring some environment parameters within a time window, and reporting them to the assessment component. The latter analyzes the reports and considers thresholds to arrive at an adaptive reaction plan. Finally, the reaction plan is communicated to the reaction component that applies the reactions to query execution.

Typically, an adaptive process specifies the frequency with which each component will be executed. There is a tradeoff between reactiveness, in which higher values lead to eager reactions, and the overhead caused by the adaptive process. A generic representation of the adaptive process is given by the function $f_{adapt}(E, T) \rightarrow Ad$, where E is a set of monitored environment parameters, T is a set of threshold values and Ad is a possibly empty set of adaptive reactions. The elements of E, T and Ad, called adaptive elements, obviously may vary in a number of ways depending on the application. The most important elements are the monitoring parameters and the adaptive reactions. We now describe them, following the presentation in [Gounaris et al., 2002b].

Monitoring parameters.

Monitoring query runtime parameters involves placing sensors at key places of the QEP and defining observation windows, during which sensors collect information. It also requires the specification of a communication mechanism to pass collected information to the assessment component. Examples of candidates for monitoring are:

- Memory size. Monitoring available memory size allows, for instance, operators to react to memory shortage or memory increase [Shah et al., 2003].

- Data arrival rates. Monitoring the variations in data arrival rates may enable the query processor to do useful work while waiting for a blocked data source.

- Actual statistics. Database statistics in a multidatabase environment tend to be inaccurate, if at all available. Monitoring the actual size of relations and intermediate results may lead to important modifications in the QEP. Furthermore, the usual data assumptions, in which the selectivity of predicates over attributes in a relation are considered to be mutually independent, can be abandoned and real selectivity values can be computed.

- Operator execution cost. Monitoring the actual cost of operator execution, including production rates, is useful for better operator scheduling. Furthermore, monitoring the size of the queues placed before operators may avoid overload situations [Tian and DeWitt, 2003b].

- Network throughput. In multidatabase query evaluation with remote data sources, monitoring network throughput may be helpful to define the data retrieval block size. In a lower throughput network, the system may react with larger block sizes to reduce network penalty.

Adaptive reactions.

Adaptive reactions modify query execution behavior according to the decisions taken by the assessment component. Important adaptive reactions are the following:

- Change schedule: modifies the order in which operators in the QEP get scheduled. *Query Scrambling* [Amsaleg et al., 1996a; Urhan et al., 1998a] reacts by a *change schedule* of the plan, e.g., to reorganize the QEP in Example 9.9, to avoid stalling on a blocked data source during query evaluation. Eddy adopts finer reaction where operator scheduling can be decided on a tuple basis.

- Operator replacement: replaces a physical operator by an equivalent one. For example, depending on the available memory, the system may choose between a nested loop join or a hash join. Operator replacement may also change the plan by introducing a new operator to join the intermediate results produced by a previous adaptive reaction. Query Scrambling, for instance, may introduce new operators to evaluate joins between the results of *change schedule* reactions.

- Operator behavior: modifies the physical behavior of an operator. For example, the symmetric hash join [Wilschut and Apers, 1991] or ripple join algorithms [Haas and Hellerstein, 1999b] constantly alternate the inner/outer relation roles between their input tuples.

- Data repartitioning: considers the dynamic repartitioning of a relation through multiple nodes using intra-operator parallelism [Shah et al., 2003]. Static partitioning of a relation tends to produce load imbalance between nodes. For example, information partitioned according to their associated geographical region (i.e., continent) may exhibit different access rates during the day because of the time differences in users' locations.

- Plan reformulation: computes a new QEP to replace an inefficient one. The optimizer considers actual statistics and state information, collected on the fly, to produce a new plan.

9.4.3.2 Eddy Approach

Eddy is a general framework for adaptive query processing. It was developed in the context of the Telegraph project with the goal of running queries on large volumes of online data with unpredictable input rates and fluctuations in the running environment.

For simplicity, we only consider select-project-join (SPJ) queries. Select operators can include expensive predicates [Hellerstein and Stonebraker, 1993]. The process of generating a QEP from an input SPJ query begins by producing a spanning tree of the query graph G modeling the input query. The choice among join algorithms and relation access methods favors adaptiveness. A QEP can be modeled as a tuple $Q = \langle D, P, C \rangle$, where D is a set of data sources, P is a set of query predicates with associated algorithms, and C is a set of ordering constraints that must be followed during execution. Observe that multiple valid spanning trees can be derived from G that obey the constraints in C, by exploring the search space composed of equivalent plans with different predicate orders. There is no need to find an optimal QEP during query compilation. Instead, operator ordering is done on the fly on a tuple-per-tuple basis (i.e., tuple routing). The process of QEP compilation is completed by adding the *Eddy operator* which is an n-ary physical operator placed between data sources in D and query predicates in P.

Example 9.10. Consider a three-relation query $Q = \sigma_p(R) \bowtie S \bowtie T$, where joins are equi-joins. Assume that the only access method to relation T is through an index on join attribute $T.A$, i.e., the second join can only be an index join over $T.A$. Assume also that σ_p is an expensive predicate (e.g., a predicate over the results of running a program over values of $R.B$). Under these assumptions, the QEP is defined as $D = \{R, S, T\}$, $P = \{\sigma_p(R), R \bowtie_1 S, S \bowtie_2 T\}$ and $C = \{S \prec T\}$. The constraint $\prec$ imposes S tuples to probe T tuples, based on the index on $T.A$.

Figure 9.6 shows a QEP produced by the compilation of query Q with Eddy. An ellipse corresponds to a physical operator (i.e., either the Eddy operator or an algorithm implementing a predicate $p \in P$). As usual, the bottom of the plan presents the data sources. In the absence of a scan access method, relation T access is wrapped by the index join implementing the second join, and, thus, does not appear as a data source. The arrows specify pipeline dataflow following a producer-consumer relationship. Finally, an arrow departing from the Eddy models the production of output tuples.					♦

Eddy provides fine-grain adaptiveness by deciding on the fly how to route tuples through predicates according to a scheduling policy. During query execution, tuples in data sources are retrieved and staged into an input buffer managed by the Eddy operator. Eddy responds to data source unavailability by simply reading from another data source and staging tuples in the buffer pool.

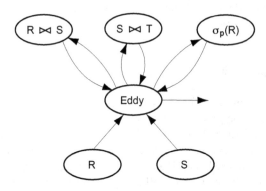

Fig. 9.6 A Query Execution Plan with Eddy.

The flexibility of choosing the currently available data source is obtained by relaxing the fixed order of predicates in a QEP. In Eddy, there is no fixed QEP and each tuple follows its own path through predicates according to the constraints in the plan and its own history of predicate evaluation.

The tuple-based routing strategy produces a new QEP topology. The Eddy operator together with its managed predicates form a circular dataflow in which tuples leave the Eddy operator to be evaluated by the predicates, which in turn bounce back output tuples to the Eddy operator. A tuple leaves the circular dataflow either when it is eliminated by a predicate evaluation or the Eddy operator realizes that the tuple has passed through all the predicates in its list. The lack of a fixed QEP requires each tuple to register the set of predicates it is eligible for. For example, in Figure 9.6, S tuples are eligible for the two join predicates but are not eligible for predicate $\sigma_p(R)$.

Let us now present, in more detail, how Eddy adaptively performs join ordering and scheduling.

Adaptive join ordering.

A fixed QEP (produced at compile time) dictates the join ordering and specifies which relations can be pipelined through the join operators. This makes query execution simple. When, as in Eddy, there is no fixed QEP, the challenge is to dynamically order pipelined join operators at run time, while tuples from different relations are flowing in. Ideally, when a tuple of a relation participating in a join arrives, it should be sent to a join operator (chosen by the scheduling policy) to be processed on the fly. However, most join algorithms cannot process some incoming tuples on the fly because they are asymmetric with respect to the way inner and outer tuples are processed. Consider the basic hash-based join algorithm, for instance: the inner relation is fully read during the build phase to construct a hash table, whereas tuples in the outer relation are pipelined during the probe phase. Thus, an incoming inner tuple cannot be processed on the fly as it must be stored in the hash table and the processing will be possible when the entire hash table has been built. Similarly, the nested loop join algorithm is asymmetric as only the inner relation must be read entirely for each tuple of the outer relation. Join algorithms with some kind of asymmetry offer few opportunities for alternating input relations between inner and outer roles. Thus, to relax the order in which join inputs are consumed, symmetric join algorithms are needed where the role played by the relations in a join may change without producing incorrect results.

The earliest example of a symmetric join algorithm is the symmetric hash join [Wilschut and Apers, 1991], which uses two hash tables, one for each input relation. The traditional build and probe phases of the basic hash join algorithm are simply interleaved. When a tuple arrives, it is used to probe the hash table corresponding to the other relation and find matching tuples. Then, it is inserted in its corresponding hash table so that tuples of the other relation arriving later can be joined. Thus, each arriving tuple can be processed on the fly. Another popular symmetric join algorithm is the ripple join [Haas and Hellerstein, 1999b], which can be viewed as a generalization of the nested loop join algorithm where the roles of inner and outer relation continually alternate during query execution. The main idea is to keep the probing state of each input relation, with a pointer that indicates the last tuple used to probe the other relation. At each toggling point, a change of roles between inner and outer relations occurs. At this point, the new outer relation starts to probe the inner input from its pointer position onwards, to a specified number of tuples. The inner relation, in turn, is scanned from its first tuple to its pointer position minus 1. The number of tuples processed at each stage in the outer relation gives the toggling rate and can be adaptively monitored.

Using symmetric join algorithms, Eddy can achieve flexible join ordering by controlling the history and constraints regarding predicate evaluation on a tuple basis. This control is implemented using two sets of *progress bits* carried by each tuple, which indicate, respectively, the predicates to which the tuple is ready to be evaluated by (i.e., the "ready bits") and the set of predicates already evaluated (i.e., the "done bits"). When a tuple t is read into an Eddy operator, all done bits are zeroed and the predicates without ordering constraints, and to which t is eligible for, have their corresponding ready bits set. After each predicate evaluation, the corresponding done bit is set and the ready bits are updated, accordingly. When a join concatenates a pair of tuples, their done bits are ORed and a new set of ready bits are turned on. Combining progress bits and symmetric join algorithms allows Eddy to schedule predicates in an adaptive way.

Adaptive scheduling.

Given a set of candidate predicates, Eddy must adaptively select the one to which each tuple will be sent. Two main principles drive the choice of a predicate in Eddy: cost and selectivity. Predicate costs are measured as a function of the consumption rate of each predicate. Remember that the Eddy operator holds tuples in its internal buffer, which is shared by all predicates. Low cost (i.e., fast) predicates finish their work quicker and request new tuples from the Eddy. As a result, low cost predicates get allocated more tuples than high cost predicates. This strategy, however, is agnostic with respect to predicate selectivity. Eddy's tuple routing strategy is complemented by a simple *lottery scheduling* mechanism that learns about predicate selectivity [Arpaci-Dusseau et al., 1999]. The strategy credits a ticket to a predicate whenever the latter gets scheduled a tuple. Once a tuple has been processed and is bounced back to the Eddy, the corresponding predicate gets its ticket amount decremented. Combining cost and selectivity criteria becomes easy. Eddy continuously runs a lottery among predicates currently requesting tuples. The predicate with higher count of tickets wins the lottery and gets scheduled.

Another interesting issue is the choice of the running tuple from the input buffer. In order to end query processing, all tuples in the input buffer must be evaluated. Thus, a difference in tuple scheduling may reflect user preferences with respect to tuple output. For example, Eddy may favor tuples with higher number of done bits set, so that the user receives first results earlier.

9.4.3.3 Extensions to Eddy

The Eddy approach has been extended in various directions. In the cherry picking approach [Porto et al., 2003], context is used instead of simple ticket-based scheduling. The relationship among expensive predicate input attribute values are discovered at runtime and used as the basis for adaptive tuple scheduling. Given a query Q with $D = \{R[A, B, C]\}$, $P = \{\sigma_p^1(R.A), \sigma_p^2(R.B), \sigma_p^3(R.C)\}$ and $C = \emptyset$, the main idea is to model the input attribute values of the expensive predicates in P as a hypergraph $G = (V, E)$, where V is a set of n node partitions, with n being the number of expensive predicates. Each partition corresponds to a single attribute of the input relation R that are input to a predicate in P and each node corresponds to a distinct value of that attribute. An hyperedge $e = \{a_i, b_j, c_k\}$ corresponds to a tuple of relation R. The degree of a node v_i corresponds to the number of hyperedges in which v_i takes part. With this modeling, efficiently evaluating query Q corresponds to eliminating as quickly as possible the hyperedges in G. An hyperedge is eliminated whenever a value associated with one of its nodes is evaluated by a predicate in P and returns false. Furthermore, node degrees model hidden attribute dependencies, so that when the result of a predicate evaluation over a value v_i returns false, all hyperedges (i.e., tuples) that v_i takes part in are also eliminated. An adaptive content-sensitive strategy to evaluate a query Q is proposed for this model. It schedules values to be evaluated by a predicate according to the *Fanout* of its corresponding node, computed as the product of the node degree in the hypergraph G with the ratio between the corresponding predicate selectivity and predicate unitary evaluation cost.

Another interesting extension is distributed Eddies [Tian and DeWitt, 2003b] to deal with distributed input data streams. Since a centralized Eddy operator may quickly become a bottleneck, a distributed approach is proposed for tuple routing.

Each operator decides on the next operator to route a tuple to based on its history of operator's evaluation (i.e., done bits) and statistics collected from the remaining operators. In a distributed setting, each operator may run at a different node in the network with a queue holding input tuples. The query optimization problem is specified by considering two new metrics for measuring stream query performance: average response time and maximum data rate. The former corresponds to the average time tuples take to traverse the operators in a plan, whereas the latter measures the maximum throughput the system can withstand without overloading. Routing strategies use the following parameters: operator's cost, selectivity, length of operator's input queue and probability of an operator being routed a tuple. The combination of these parameters yields efficient query evaluation. Using operator's cost and selectivity guarantee that low-cost and highly selective operators are given higher routing priority. Queue length provides information on the average time tuples are staged in queues. Managing operator's queue length allows the routing decision to avoid overloaded operators. Thus, by supporting routing policies, each operator is able to individually make routing decisions, thereby avoiding the bottlneck of a centralized router.

9.5 Query Translation and Execution

Query translation and execution is performed by the wrappers using the component DBMSs. A wrapper encapsulates the details of one or more component databases, each supported by the same DBMS (or file system). It also exports to the mediator the component DBMS capabilities and cost functions in a common interface. One of the major practical uses of wrappers has been to allow an SQL-based DBMS to access non-SQL databases [Roth and Schwartz, 1997].

The main function of a wrapper is conversion between the common interface and the DBMS-dependent interface. Figure 9.7 shows these different levels of interfaces between the mediator, the wrapper and the component DBMSs. Note that, depending on the level of autonomy of the component DBMSs, these three components can be located differently. For instance, in the case of strong autonomy, the wrapper should be at the mediator site, possibly on the same server. Thus, communication between a wrapper and its component DBMS incurs network cost. However, in the case of a cooperative component database (e.g., within the same organization), the wrapper could be installed at the component DBMS site, much like an ODBC driver. Thus, communication between the wrapper and the component DBMS is much more efficient.

The information necessary to perform conversion is stored in the wrapper schema that includes the local schema exported to the mediator in the common interface (e.g., relational) and the schema mappings to transform data between the local schema and the component database schema and vice-versa. We discussed schema mappings in Chapter 4. Two kinds of conversion are needed. First, the wrapper must translate the input QEP generated by the mediator and expressed in a common interface into calls to the component DBMS using its DBMS-dependent interface. These calls yield query execution by the component DBMS that return results expressed in the DBMS-dependent interface. Second, the wrapper must translate the results to the common interface format so that they can be returned to the mediator for integration. In addition, the wrapper can execute operations that are not supported by the component DBMS (e.g., the scan operation by wrapper w_2 in Figure 9.4).

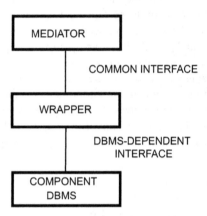

Fig. 9.7 Wrapper interfaces

As discussed in Section 9.4.2, the common interface to the wrappers can be query-based or operator-based. The problem of translation is similar in both approaches. To illustrate query translation in the following example, we use the query-based approach with the SQL/MED standard that allows a relational DBMS to access external data represented as foreign relations in the wrapper's local schema. This example, borrowed from [Melton et al., 2001], illustrates how a very simple data source can be wrapped to be accessed through SQL.

Example 9.11. We consider relation EMP(ENO, ENAME, CITY) stored in a very simple component database, in server *ComponentDB*, built with Unix text files. Each EMP tuple can then be stored as a line in a file, e.g., with the attributes separated by ":". In SQL/MED, the definition of the local schema for this relation together with the mapping to a Unix file can be declared as a foreign relation with the following statement:

```
CREATE  FOREIGN TABLE EMP
        ENO INTEGER,
        ENAME VARCHAR(30),
        CITY VARCHAR(20)
SERVER  ComponentDB
OPTIONS (Filename '/usr/EngDB/emp.txt', Delimiter ':')
```

Then, the mediator can send the wrapper supporting access to this relation SQL statements. For instance, the query:

```
SELECT ENAME
FROM   EMP
```

can be translated by the wrapper using the following Unix shell command to extract the relevant attribute:

```
cut -d: -f2 /usr/EngDB/emp
```

Additional processing, e.g., for type conversion, can then be done using programming code.   ♦

Wrappers are mostly used for read-only queries, which makes query translation and wrapper construction relatively easy. Wrapper construction typically relies on CASE tools with reusable components to generate most of the wrapper code [Tomasic et al., 1997]. Furthermore, DBMS vendors provide wrappers for transparently accessing their DBMS using standard interfaces. However, wrapper construction is much more difficult if updates to component databases are to be supported through wrappers (as opposed to directly updating the component databases through their DBMS). The main problem is due to the heterogeneity of integrity constraints between the common interface and the DBMS-dependent interface. As discussed in Chapter 5, integrity constraints are used to reject updates that violate database consistency. In modern DBMSs, integrity constraints are explicit and specified as rules as part of the database schema. However, in older DBMSs or simpler data sources (e.g., files), integrity constraints are implicit and implemented by specific code in the applications. For instance, in Example 9.11, there could be applications with some embedded code that rejects insertions of new lines with an existing ENO in the EMP text file. This code corresponds to a unique key constraint on ENO in relation EMP but is not readily available to the wrapper. Thus, the main problem of updating through a wrapper is to guarantee component database consistency by rejecting all updates that violate integrity constraints, whether they are explicit or implicit. A software engineering solution to this problem uses a CASE tool with reverse engineering techniques to identify within application code the implicit integrity constraints which are then translated into validation code in the wrappers [Thiran et al., 2006].

Another major problem is wrapper maintenance. Query translation relies heavily on the mappings between the component database schema and the local schema. If the component database schema is changed to reflect the evolution of the component database, then the mappings can become invalid. For instance, in Example 9.11, the administrator may switch the order of the fields in the EMP file. Using invalid mappings may prevent the wrapper from producing correct results. Since the component databases are autonomous, detecting and correcting invalid mappings is important. The techniques to do so are those for mapping maintenance that we presented in Chapter 4.

9.6 Conclusion

Query processing in multidatabase systems is significantly more complex than in tightly-integrated and homogeneous distributed DBMSs. In addition to being distributed, component databases may be autonomous, have different database languages and query processing capabilities, and exhibit varying behavior. In particular, component databases may range from full-fledged SQL databases to very simple data sources (e.g., text files).

In this chapter, we addressed these issues by extending and modifying the distributed query processing architecture presented in Chapter 6. Assuming the popular mediator/wrapper architecture, we isolated the three main layers by which a query is successively rewritten (to bear on local relations) and optimized by the mediator, and then translated and executed by the wrappers and component DBMSs. We also discussed how to support OLAP queries in a multidatabase, an important requirement of decision-support applications. This requires an additional layer of translation from OLAP multidimensional queries to relational queries. This layered architecture for multidatabase query processing is general enough to capture very different variations. This has been useful to describe various query processing techniques, typically designed with different objectives and assumptions.

The main techniques for multidatabase query processing are query rewriting using multidatabase views, multidatabase query optimization and execution, and query translation and execution. The techniques for query rewriting using multidatabase views differ in major ways depending on whether the GAV or LAV integration approach is used. Query rewriting in GAV is similar to data localization in homogeneous distributed database systems. But the techniques for LAV (and its extension GLAV) are much more involved and it is often not possible to find an equivalent rewriting for a query, in which case a query that produces a maximum subset of the answer is necessary. The techniques for multidatabase query optimization include cost modeling and query optimization for component databases with different computing capabilities. These techniques extend traditional distributed query processing by focusing on heterogeneity. Besides heterogeneity, an important problem is to deal with the dynamic behavior of the component DBMSs. Adaptive query processing addresses this problem with a dynamic approach whereby the query optimizer communicates at run time with the execution environment in order to react to unforeseen variations of runtime conditions. Finally, we discussed the techniques for translating queries for execution by the components DBMSs and for generating and managing wrappers.

The data model used by the mediator can be relational, object-oriented or even semi-structured (based on XML). In this chapter, for simplicity, we assumed a mediator with a relational model that is sufficient to explain the multidatabase query processing techniques. However, when dealing with data sources on the Web, a richer mediator model such as object-oriented or semi-structured (e.g., XML-based) may be preferred. This requires significant extensions to query processing techniques.

9.7 Bibliographic Notes

Work on multidatabase query processing started in the early 1980's with the first multidatabase systems (e.g., [Brill et al., 1984; Dayal and Hwang, 1984] and [Landers and Rosenberg, 1982]). The objective then was to access different databases within an organization. In the 1990's, the increasing use of the Web for accessing all kinds of data sources triggered renewed interest and much more work in multidatabase query processing, following the popular mediator/wrapper architecture [Wiederhold, 1992]. A brief overview of multidatabase query optimization issues can be found in [Meng et al., 1993]. Good discussions of multidatabase query processing can be found in [Lu et al., 1992, 1993], in Chapter 4 of [Yu and Meng, 1998] and in [Kossmann, 2000].

Query rewriting using views is surveyed in [Halevy, 2001]. In [Levy et al., 1995], the general problem of finding a rewriting using views is shown to be NP-complete in the number of views and the number of subgoals in the query The unfolding technique for rewriting a query expressed in Datalog in GAV was proposed in [Ullman, 1997]. The main techniques for query rewriting using views in LAV are the bucket algorithm [Levy et al., 1996b], the inverse rule algorithm [Duschka and Genesereth, 1997], and the MinCon algorithm [Pottinger and Levy, 2000].

The three main approaches for heterogeneous cost modeling are discussed in [Zhu and Larson, 1998]. The black-box approach is used in [Du et al., 1992; Zhu and Larson, 1994]. The customized approach is developped in [Zhu and Larson, 1996a; Roth et al., 1999; Naacke et al., 1999]. The dynamic approach is used in [Zhu et al., 2000], [Zhu et al., 2003] and [Rahal et al., 2004].

The algorithm we described to illustrate the query-based approach to heterogeneous query optimization has been proposed in [Du et al., 1995]. To illustrate the operator-based approach, we described the popular solution with planning functions proposed in the Garlic project [Haas et al., 1997a]. The operator-based approach has been also used in DISCO, a multidatabase system to access component databases over the web [Tomasic et al., 1996, 1998].

Adaptive query processing is surveyed in [Hellerstein et al., 2000; Gounaris et al., 2002b]. The seminal paper on the Eddy approach which we used to illustrate adaptive query processing is [Avnur and Hellerstein, 2000]. Other important techniques for adaptive query processing are query scrambling [Amsaleg et al., 1996a; Urhan et al., 1998a], Ripple joins [Haas and Hellerstein, 1999b], adaptive partitioning [Shah et al., 2003] and Cherry picking [Porto et al., 2003]. Major extensions to Eddy are state modules [Raman et al., 2003] and distributed Eddies [Tian and DeWitt, 2003b].

A software engineering solution to the problem of wrapper creation and maintenance, considering integrity control, is proposed in [Thiran et al., 2006].

Exercises

Problem 9.1 (**). Can any type of global optimization be performed on global queries in a multidatabase system? Discuss and formally specify the conditions under which such optimization would be possible.

Problem 9.2 (*). Consider a marketing application with a ROLAP server at site s_1 which needs to integrate information from two customer databases, each at site s_2 within the corporate network. Assume also that the application needs to combine customer information with information extracted from Web data sources about cities in 10 different countries. For security reasons, a web server at site s_3 is dedicated to Web access outside the corporate network. Propose a multidatabase system architecture with mediator and wrappers to support this application. Discuss and justify design choices.

Problem 9.3 (**). Consider the global relations EMP(ENAME, TITLE, CITY) and ASG(ENAME, PNAME, CITY, DUR). City in ASG is the location of the project of name PNAME (i.e., PNAME functionnally determines CITY). Consider the local relations EMP1(ENAME, TITLE, CITY), EMP2(ENAME, TITLE, CITY), PROJ1(PNAME, CITY), PROJ2(PNAME, CITY) and ASG1(ENAME, PNAME, DUR). Consider query Q which selects the names of the employees assigned to a project in Rio de Janeiro for more than 6 months and the duration of their assignment.

(a)   Assuming the GAV approach, perform query rewriting.
(b)   Assuming the LAV approach, perform query rewriting using the bucket algorithm.
(c)   Same as (b) using the MinCon algorithm.

Problem 9.4 (*). Consider relations EMP and ASG of Example 9.7. We denote by $|R|$ the number of pages to store R on disk. Consider the following statistics about the data:

$$|EMP| = 1\,000$$
$$\|EMP\| = 100$$
$$|ASG| = 10\,000$$
$$\|ASG\| = 2\,000$$
$$selectivity(ASG.DUR > 36) = 1\%$$

The mediator generic cost model is:

$$cost(\sigma_{A=v}(R)) = |R|$$
$cost(\sigma(X)) = cost(X)$ where X contains at least one operator.
$cost(R \bowtie_A^{ind} S) = cost(R) + |R| * cost(\sigma_{A=v}(S))$ using an indexed join algorithm.
$cost(R \bowtie_A^{nl} S) = cost(R) + |R| * cost(S)$ using a nested loop join algorithm.

Consider the MDBMS input query Q:

```
SELECT *
FROM    EMP, ASG
WHERE   EMP.ENO=ASG.ENO
AND     ASG.DUR>36
```

Consider four plans to process Q:

$$P_1 = EMP \bowtie_{ENO}^{ind} \sigma_{DUR>36}(ASG)$$
$$P_2 = EMP \bowtie_{ENO}^{nl} \sigma_{DUR>36}(ASG)$$
$$P_3 = \sigma_{DUR>36}(ASG) \bowtie_{ENO}^{ind} EMP$$
$$P_4 = \sigma_{DUR>36}(ASG) \bowtie_{ENO}^{nl} EMP$$

(a)   What is the cost of plans P_1 to P_4?
(b)   Which plan has the minimal cost?

Problem 9.5 (*). Consider relations EMP and ASG of the previous exercice. Suppose now that the mediator cost model is completed with the following cost information issued from the component DBMSs.

The cost of accessing EMP tuples at db_1 is:

$$cost(\sigma_{A=v}(R)) = |\sigma_{A=v}(R)|$$

The specific cost of selecting ASG tuples that have a given ENO at D_2 is:

$$cost(\sigma_{ENO=v}(ASG)) = |\sigma_{ENO=v}(ASG)|$$

(a)   What is the cost of plans P_1 to P_4?
(b)   Which plan has the minimal cost?

Problem 9.6 (**). What are the respective advantages and limitations of the query-based and operator-based approaches to heterogeneous query optimization from the points of view of query expressiveness, query performance, development cost of wrappers, system (mediator and wrappers) maintenance and evolution?

Problem 9.7 (**). Consider Example 9.8 by adding, at a new site, component database db_4 which stores relations EMP(ENO, ENAME, CITY) and ASG(ENO, PNAME, DUR). db_4 exports through its wrapper w_3 join and scan capabilities. Let us assume that there can be employees in db_1 with corresponding assignments in db_4 and employees in db_4 with corresponding assignments in db_2.

(a)   Define the planning functions of wrapper w_3.
(b)   Give the new definition of global view EMPASG(ENAME, CITY, PNAME, DUR).
(c)   Give a QEP for the same query as in Example 9.8.

Problem 9.8 (**). Consider three relations $R(A,B)$, $S(B,C)$ and $T(C,D)$ and query $Q(\sigma_p^1(R) \bowtie_1 S \bowtie_2 T)$, where $\bowtie_1$ and $\bowtie_2$ are natural joins. Assume that S has an index on attribute B and T has an index on attribute C. Furthermore, σ_p^1 is an expensive predicate (i.e., a predicate over the results of running a program over values of $R.A$). Using the Eddy approach for adaptive query processing, answer the following questions:

(a)   Propose the set C of constraints on Q to produce an Eddy-based QEP.
(b)   Give a query graph G for Q.
(c)   Using C and G, propose an Eddy-based QEP.
(d)   Propose a second QEP that uses State Modules. Discuss the advantages obtained by using state modules in this QEP.

Problem 9.9 (**). Propose a data structure to store tuples in the Eddy buffer pool to help choosing quickly the next tuple to be evaluated according to user specified preference, for instance, produce first results earlier.

Problem 9.10 (**). Propose a predicate scheduling algorithm based on the Cherry picking approach introduced in Section 9.4.3.3.

Chapter 10
Introduction to Transaction Management

Up to this point the basic access primitive that we have considered has been a query. Our focus has been on retrieve-only (or read-only) queries that read data from a distributed database. We have not yet considered what happens if, for example, two queries attempt to update the same data item, or if a system failure occurs during execution of a query. For retrieve-only queries, neither of these conditions is a problem. One can have two queries reading the value of the same data item concurrently. Similarly, a read-only query can simply be restarted after a system failure is handled. On the other hand, it is not difficult to see that for update queries, these conditions can have disastrous effects on the database. We cannot, for example, simply restart the execution of an update query following a system failure since certain data item values may already have been updated prior to the failure and should not be updated again when the query is restarted. Otherwise, the database would contain incorrect data.

The fundamental point here is that there is no notion of "consistent execution" or "reliable computation" associated with the concept of a query. The concept of a *transaction* is used in database systems as a basic unit of consistent and reliable computing. Thus queries are executed as transactions once their execution strategies are determined and they are translated into primitive database operations.

In the discussion above, we used the terms *consistent* and *reliable* quite informally. Due to their importance in our discussion, we need to define them more precisely. We differentiate between *database consistency* and *transaction consistency*.

A database is in a *consistent state* if it obeys all of the consistency (integrity) constraints defined over it (see Chapter 5). State changes occur due to modifications, insertions, and deletions (together called *updates*). Of course, we want to ensure that the database never enters an inconsistent state. Note that the database can be (and usually is) temporarily inconsistent during the execution of a transaction. The important point is that the database should be consistent when the transaction terminates (Figure 10.1).

Transaction consistency, on the other hand, refers to the actions of concurrent transactions. We would like the database to remain in a consistent state even if there are a number of user requests that are concurrently accessing (reading or updating)

M.T. Özsu and P. Valduriez, *Principles of Distributed Database Systems: Third Edition*, DOI 10.1007/978-1-4419-8834-8_10, © Springer Science+Business Media, LLC 2011

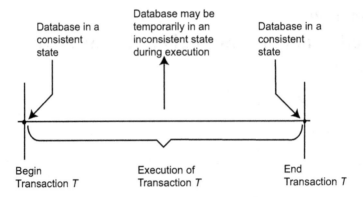

Fig. 10.1 A Transaction Model

the database. A complication arises when replicated databases are considered. A replicated database is in a *mutually consistent state* if all the copies of every data item in it have identical values. This is referred to as *one-copy equivalence* since all replica copies are forced to assume the same state at the end of a transaction's execution. There are more relaxed notions of replica consistency that allow replica values to diverge. These will be discussed later in Chapter 13.

Reliability refers to both the *resiliency* of a system to various types of failures and its capability to *recover* from them. A resilient system is tolerant of system failures and can continue to provide services even when failures occur. A recoverable DBMS is one that can get to a consistent state (by moving back to a previous consistent state or forward to a new consistent state) following various types of failures.

Transaction management deals with the problems of always keeping the database in a consistent state even when concurrent accesses and failures occur. In the upcoming two chapters, we investigate the issues related to managing transactions. A third chapter will address issues related to keeping replicated databases consistent. The purpose of the current chapter is to define the fundamental terms and to provide the framework within which these issues can be discussed. It also serves as a concise introduction to the problem and the related issues. We will therefore discuss the concepts at a high level of abstraction and will not present any management techniques.

The organization of this chapter is as follows. In the next section we formally and intuitively define the concept of a transaction. In Section 10.2 we discuss the properties of transactions and what the implications of each of these properties are in terms of transaction management. In Section 10.3 we present various types of transactions. In Section 10.4 we revisit the architectural model defined in Chapter 1 and indicate the modifications that are necessary to support transaction management.

10.1 Definition of a Transaction

Gray [1981] indicates that the transaction concept has its roots in contract law. He states, "In making a contract, two or more parties negotiate for a while and then make a deal. The deal is made binding by the joint signature of a document or by some other act (as simple as a handshake or a nod). If the parties are rather suspicious of one another or just want to be safe, they appoint an intermediary (usually called an escrow officer) to coordinate the commitment of the transaction." The nice aspect of this historical perspective is that it does indeed encompass *some* of the fundamental properties of a transaction (atomicity and durability) as the term is used in database systems. It also serves to indicate the differences between a transaction and a query.

As indicated before, a transaction is a unit of consistent and reliable computation. Thus, intuitively, a transaction takes a database, performs an action on it, and generates a new version of the database, causing a state transition. This is similar to what a query does, except that if the database was consistent before the execution of the transaction, we can now guarantee that it will be consistent at the end of its execution regardless of the fact that (1) the transaction may have been executed concurrently with others, and (2) failures may have occurred during its execution.

In general, a transaction is considered to be made up of a sequence of read and write operations on the database, together with computation steps. In that sense, a transaction may be thought of as a program with embedded database access queries [Papadimitriou, 1986]. Another definition of a transaction is that it is a single execution of a program [Ullman, 1988]. A single query can also be thought of as a program that can be posed as a transaction.

Example 10.1. Consider the following SQL query for increasing by 10% the budget of the CAD/CAM project that we discussed (in Example 5.20):

```
UPDATE PROJ
SET     BUDGET = BUDGET*1.1
WHERE  PNAME= "CAD/CAM"
```

This query can be specified, using the embedded SQL notation, as a transaction by giving it a name (e.g., BUDGET_UPDATE) and declaring it as follows:

Begin_transaction BUDGET_UPDATE
begin
    EXEC SQL   UPDATE   PROJ
          SET   BUDGET = BUDGET*1.1
         WHERE   PNAME= "CAD/CAM"
end.

♦

The **Begin_transaction** and **end** statements delimit a transaction. Note that the use of delimiters is not enforced in every DBMS. If delimiters are not specified, a DBMS may simply treat as a transaction the entire program that performs a database access.

Example 10.2. In our discussion of transaction management concepts, we will use an airline reservation system example instead of the one used in the first nine chapters. The real-life implementation of this application almost always makes use of the transaction concept. Let us assume that there is a FLIGHT relation that records the data about each flight, a CUST relation for the customers who book flights, and an FC relation indicating which customers are on what flights. Let us also assume that the relation definitions are as follows (where the underlined attributes constitute the keys):

FLIGHT(<u>FNO, DATE</u>, SRC, DEST, STSOLD, CAP)

CUST(<u>CNAME</u>, ADDR, BAL)

FC(<u>FNO, DATE, CNAME</u>, SPECIAL)

The definition of the attributes in this database schema are as follows: FNO is the flight number, DATE denotes the flight date, SRC and DEST indicate the source and destination for the flight, STSOLD indicates the number of seats that have been sold on that flight, CAP denotes the passenger capacity on the flight, CNAME indicates the customer name whose address is stored in ADDR and whose account balance is in BAL, and SPECIAL corresponds to any special requests that the customer may have for a booking.

Let us consider a simplified version of a typical reservation application, where a travel agent enters the flight number, the date, and a customer name, and asks for a reservation. The transaction to perform this function can be implemented as follows, where database accesses are specified in embedded SQL notation:

```
Begin_transaction Reservation
begin
    input(flight_no, date, customer_name);                          (1)
    EXEC SQL UPDATE FLIGHT                                          (2)
              SET      STSOLD = STSOLD + 1
              WHERE FNO = flight_no
              AND      DATE = date;
    EXEC SQL INSERT                                                 (3)
              INTO     FC(FNO,DATE,CNAME,SPECIAL)
              VALUES (flight_no,date,customer_name, null);
    output("reservation completed")                                (4)
end.
```

Let us explain this example. First a point about notation. Even though we use embedded SQL, we do not follow its syntax very strictly. The lowercase terms are the program variables; the uppercase terms denote database relations and attributes as well as the SQL statements. Numeric constants are used as they are, whereas character constants are enclosed in quotes. Keywords of the host language are written in boldface, and *null* is a keyword for the null string.

The first thing that the transaction does [line (1)], is to input the flight number, the date, and the customer name. Line (2) updates the number of sold seats on the requested flight by one. Line (3) inserts a tuple into the FC relation. Here we assume that the customer is an old one, so it is not necessary to have an insertion into the CUST relation, creating a record for the client. The keyword *null* in line (3) indicates that the customer has no special requests on this flight. Finally, line (4) reports the result of the transaction to the agent's terminal. ◆

10.1.1 Termination Conditions of Transactions

The reservation transaction of Example 10.2 has an implicit assumption about its termination. It assumes that there will always be a free seat and does not take into consideration the fact that the transaction may fail due to lack of seats. This is an unrealistic assumption that brings up the issue of termination possibilities of transactions.

A transaction always terminates, even when there are failures as we will see in Chapter 12. If the transaction can complete its task successfully, we say that the transaction *commits*. If, on the other hand, a transaction stops without completing its task, we say that it *aborts*. Transactions may abort for a number of reasons, which are discussed in the upcoming chapters. In our example, a transaction aborts itself because of a condition that would prevent it from completing its task successfully. Additionally, the DBMS may abort a transaction due to, for example, deadlocks or other conditions. When a transaction is aborted, its execution is stopped and all of its already executed actions are *undone* by returning the database to the state before their execution. This is also known as *rollback*.

The importance of commit is twofold. The commit command signals to the DBMS that the effects of that transaction should now be reflected in the database, thereby making it visible to other transactions that may access the same data items. Second, the point at which a transaction is committed is a "point of no return." The results of the committed transaction are now *permanently* stored in the database and cannot be undone. The implementation of the commit command is discussed in Chapter 12.

Example 10.3. Let us return to our reservation system example. One thing we did not consider is that there may not be any free seats available on the desired flight. To cover this possibility, the reservation transaction needs to be revised as follows:

```
Begin_transaction Reservation
begin
    input(flight_no, date, customer_name);
    EXEC SQL   SELECT  STSOLD,CAP
               INTO    temp1,temp2
               FROM    FLIGHT
               WHERE   FNO = flight_no
               AND     DATE = date;
```

```
          if temp1 = temp2 then
          begin
             output("no free seats");
             Abort
          end
          else begin
             EXEC SQL UPDATE FLIGHT
                          SET       STSOLD = STSOLD + 1
                          WHERE  FNO = flight_no
                          AND      DATE = date;
             EXEC SQL INSERT
                          INTO      FC(FNO,DATE,CNAME,SPECIAL)
                          VALUES (flight_no, date, customer_name, null);
             Commit;
             output("reservation completed")
             end
          end-if
       end.
```

In this version the first SQL statement gets the STSOLD and CAP into the two variables temp1 and temp2. These two values are then compared to determine if any seats are available. The transaction either aborts if there are no free seats, or updates the STSOLD value and inserts a new tuple into the FC relation to represent the seat that was sold.   ♦

Several things are important in this example. One is, obviously, the fact that if no free seats are available, the transaction is aborted[1]. The second is the ordering of the output to the user with respect to the abort and commit commands. Transactions can be aborted either due to application logic, as is the case here, or due to deadlocks or system failures. If the transaction is aborted, the user can be notified before the DBMS is instructed to abort it. However, in case of commit, the user notification has to follow the successful servicing (by the DBMS) of the commit command, for reliability reasons. These are discussed further in Section 10.2.4 and in Chapter 12.

10.1.2 Characterization of Transactions

Observe in the preceding examples that transactions read and write some data. This has been used as the basis for characterizing a transaction. The data items that a transaction reads are said to constitute its *read set* (*RS*). Similarly, the data items that a transaction writes are said to constitute its *write set* (*WS*). The read set and write

---

[1] We will be kind to the airlines and assume that they never overbook. Thus our reservation transaction does not need to check for that condition.

set of a transaction need not be mutually exclusive. The union of the read set and write set of a transaction constitutes its *base set* ($BS = RS \cup WS$).

Example 10.4. Considering the reservation transaction as specified in Example 10.3 and the insert to be a number of write operations, the above-mentioned sets are defined as follows:

RS[Reservation] = {FLIGHT.STSOLD, FLIGHT.CAP}

WS[Reservation] = {FLIGHT.STSOLD, FC.FNO, FC.DATE,
FC.CNAME, FC.SPECIAL}

BS[Reservation] = {FLIGHT.STSOLD, FLIGHT.CAP,
FC.FNO, FC.DATE, FC.CNAME, FC.SPECIAL}

Note that it may be appropriate to include FLIGHT.FNO and FLIGHT.DATE in the read set of Reservation since they are accessed during execution of the SQL query. We omit them to simplify the example. ◆

We have characterized transactions only on the basis of their read and write operations, without considering the insertion and deletion operations. We therefore base our discussion of transaction management concepts on *static* databases that do not grow or shrink. This simplification is made in the interest of simplicity. Dynamic databases have to deal with the problem of *phantoms*, which can be explained using the following example. Consider that transaction T_1, during its execution, searches the FC table for the names of customers who have ordered a special meal. It gets a set of CNAME for customers who satisfy the search criteria. While T_1 is executing, transaction T_2 inserts new tuples into FC with the special meal request, and commits. If T_1 were to re-issue the same search query later in its execution, it will get back a set of CNAME that is different than the original set it had retrieved. Thus, "phantom" tuples have appeared in the database. We do not discuss phantoms any further in this book; the topic is discussed at length by Eswaran et al. [1976] and Bernstein et al. [1987].

We should also point out that the read and write operations to which we refer are abstract operations that do not have one-to-one correspondence to physical I/O primitives. One read in our characterization may translate into a number of primitive read operations to access the index structures and the physical data pages. The reader should treat each read and write as a language primitive rather than as an operating system primitive.

10.1.3 Formalization of the Transaction Concept

By now, the meaning of a transaction should be intuitively clear. To reason about transactions and about the correctness of the management algorithms, it is necessary to define the concept formally. We denote by $O_{ij}(x)$ some *operation* O_j of transaction T_i that operates on a database entity x. Following the conventions adopted in the preceding section, $O_{ij} \in \{read, write\}$. Operations are assumed to be *atomic* (i.e., each is executed as an indivisible unit). We let OS_i denote the set of all operations in T_i (i.e., $OS_i = \bigcup_j O_{ij}$). We denote by N_i the termination condition for T_i, where $N_i \in \{abort, commit\}$[2].

With this terminology we can define a transaction T_i as a partial ordering over its operations and the termination condition. A partial order $P = \{\Sigma, \prec\}$ defines an ordering among the elements of Σ (called the *domain*) according to an irreflexive and transitive binary relation $\prec$ defined over Σ. In our case Σ consists of the operations and termination condition of a transaction, whereas $\prec$ indicates the execution order of these operations (which we will read as "precedes in execution order"). Formally, then, a transaction T_i is a partial order $T_i = \{\Sigma_i, \prec_i\}$, where

1. $\Sigma_i = OS_i \cup \{N_i\}$.

2. For any two operations $O_{ij}, O_{ik} \in OS_i$, if $O_{ij} = \{R(x) \text{ or } W(x)\}$ and $O_{ik} = W(x)$ for any data item x, then either $O_{ij} \prec_i O_{ik}$ or $O_{ik} \prec_i O_{ij}$.

3. $\forall O_{ij} \in OS_i, O_{ij} \prec_i N_i$.

The first condition formally defines the domain as the set of read and write operations that make up the transaction, plus the termination condition, which may be either commit or abort. The second condition specifies the ordering relation between the conflicting read and write operations of the transaction, while the final condition indicates that the termination condition always follows all other operations.

There are two important points about this definition. First, the ordering relation $\prec$ is given and the definition does not attempt to construct it. The ordering relation is actually application dependent. Second, condition two indicates that the ordering between conflicting operations has to exist within $\prec$. Two operations, $O_i(x)$ and $O_j(x)$, are said to be in *conflict* if $O_i = \text{Write}$ or $O_j = \text{Write}$ (i.e., at least one of them is a Write and they access the same data item).

Example 10.5. Consider a simple transaction T that consists of the following steps:

    Read(x)
    Read(y)
    $x \leftarrow x + y$
    Write(x)
    Commit

The specification of this transaction according to the formal notation that we have introduced is as follows:

$$\Sigma = \{R(x), R(y), W(x), C\}$$
$$\prec = \{(R(x), W(x)), (R(y), W(x)), (W(x), C), (R(x), C), (R(y), C)\}$$

where (O_i, O_j) as an element of the $\prec$ relation indicates that $O_i \prec O_j$.   ◆

---

[2] From now on, we use the abbreviations R, W, A and C for the Read, Write, Abort, and Commit operations, respectively.

Notice that the ordering relation specifies the relative ordering of all operations with respect to the termination condition. This is due to the third condition of transaction definition. Also note that we do not specify the ordering between every pair of operations. That is why it is a *partial* order.

Example 10.6. The reservation transaction developed in Example 10.3 is more complex. Notice that there are two possible termination conditions, depending on the availability of seats. It might first seem that this is a contradiction of the definition of a transaction, which indicates that there can be only one termination condition. However, remember that a transaction is the execution of a program. It is clear that in any execution, only one of the two termination conditions can occur. Therefore, what exists is one transaction that aborts and another one that commits. Using this formal notation, the former can be specified as follows:

$$\Sigma = \{R(\text{STSOLD}), R(\text{CAP}), A\}$$
$$\prec = \{(O_1, A), (O_2, A)\}$$

and the latter can be specified as

$$\Sigma = \{R(\text{STSOLD}), R(\text{CAP}), W(\text{STSOLD}),$$
$$\qquad W(\text{FNO}), W(\text{DATE}), W(\text{CNAME}), W(\text{SPECIAL}), C\}$$
$$\prec = \{(O_1, O_3), (O_2, O_3), (O_1, O_4), (O_1, O_5), (O_1, O_6), (O_1, O_7), (O_2, O_4),$$
$$\qquad (O_2, O_5), (O_2, O_6), (O_2, O_7), (O_1, C), (O_2, C), (O_3, C), (O_4, C),$$
$$\qquad (O_5, C), (O_6, C), (O_7, C)\}$$

where $O_1 = R(\text{STSOLD})$, $O_2 = R(\text{CAP})$, $O_3 = W(\text{STSOLD})$, $O_4 = W(\text{FNO})$, $O_5 = W(\text{DATE})$, $O_6 = W(\text{CNAME})$, and $O_7 = W(\text{SPECIAL})$. ◆

One advantage of defining a transaction as a partial order is its correspondence to a directed acyclic graph (DAG). Thus a transaction can be specified as a DAG whose vertices are the operations of a transaction and whose arcs indicate the ordering relationship between a given pair of operations. This will be useful in discussing the concurrent execution of a number of transactions (Chapter 11) and in arguing about their correctness by means of graph-theoretic tools.

Example 10.7. The transaction discussed in Example 10.5 can be represented as a DAG as depicted in Figure 10.2. Note that we do not draw the arcs that are implied by transitivity even though we indicate them as elements of $\prec$. ◆

In most cases we do not need to refer to the domain of the partial order separately from the ordering relation. Therefore, it is common to drop Σ from the transaction definition and use the name of the partial order to refer to both the domain and the name of the partial order. This is convenient since it allows us to specify the ordering of the operations of a transaction in a more straightforward manner by making use of their relative ordering in the transaction definition. For example, we can define the transaction of Example 10.5 as follows:

$$T = \{R(x), R(y), W(x), C\}$$

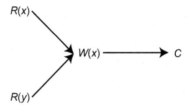

Fig. 10.2 DAG Representation of a Transaction

instead of the longer specification given before. We will therefore use the modified definition in this and subsequent chapters.

10.2 Properties of Transactions

The previous discussion clarifies the concept of a transaction. However, we have not yet provided any justification of our earlier claim that it is a unit of consistent and reliable computation. We do that in this section. The consistency and reliability aspects of transactions are due to four properties: (1) atomicity, (2) consistency, (3) isolation, and (4) durability. Together, these are commonly referred to as the ACID properties of transactions. They are not entirely independent of each other; usually there are dependencies among them as we will indicate below. We discuss each of these properties in the following sections.

10.2.1 Atomicity

Atomicity refers to the fact that a transaction is treated as a unit of operation. Therefore, either all the transaction's actions are completed, or none of them are. This is also known as the "all-or-nothing property." Notice that we have just extended the concept of atomicity from individual operations to the entire transaction. Atomicity requires that if the execution of a transaction is interrupted by any sort of failure, the DBMS will be responsible for determining what to do with the transaction upon recovery from the failure. There are, of course, two possible courses of action: it can either be terminated by completing the remaining actions, or it can be terminated by undoing all the actions that have already been executed.

One can generally talk about two types of failures. A transaction itself may fail due to input data errors, deadlocks, or other factors. In these cases either the transaction aborts itself, as we have seen in Example 10.2, or the DBMS may abort it while handling deadlocks, for example. Maintaining transaction atomicity in the presence of this type of failure is commonly called the *transaction recovery*. The second type of failure is caused by system crashes, such as media failures, processor failures, communication link breakages, power outages, and so on. Ensuring transaction atomicity in the presence of system crashes is called *crash recovery*. An important difference between the two types of failures is that during some types of system crashes, the information in volatile storage may be lost or inaccessible. Both types of recovery are parts of the reliability issue, which we discuss in considerable detail in Chapter 12.

10.2.2 Consistency

The *consistency* of a transaction is simply its correctness. In other words, a transaction is a correct program that maps one consistent database state to another. Verifying that transactions are consistent is the concern of integrity enforcement, covered in Chapter 5. Ensuring transaction consistency as defined at the beginning of this chapter, on the other hand, is the objective of concurrency control mechanisms, which we discuss in Chapter 11.

There is an interesting classification of consistency that parallels our discussion above and is equally important. This classification groups databases into four levels of consistency [Gray et al., 1976]. In the following definition (which is taken verbatim from the original paper), *dirty* data refers to data values that have been updated by a transaction prior to its commitment. Then, based on the concept of dirty data, the four levels are defined as follows:

"Degree 3: Transaction T sees *degree 3 consistency* if:

1. T does not overwrite dirty data of other transactions.
2. T does not commit any writes until it completes all its writes [i.e., until the end of transaction (EOT)].
3. T does not read dirty data from other transactions.
4. Other transactions do not dirty any data read by T before T completes.

Degree 2: Transaction T sees *degree 2 consistency* if:

1. T does not overwrite dirty data of other transactions.
2. T does not commit any writes before EOT.
3. T does not read dirty data from other transactions.

Degree 1: Transaction T sees *degree 1 consistency* if:

1. T does not overwrite dirty data of other transactions.
2. T does not commit any writes before EOT.

Degree 0: Transaction T sees *degree 0 consistency* if:

1. T does not overwrite dirty data of other transactions."

Of course, it is true that a higher degree of consistency encompasses all the lower degrees. The point in defining multiple levels of consistency is to provide application programmers the flexibility to define transactions that operate at different levels. Consequently, while some transactions operate at Degree 3 consistency level, others may operate at lower levels and may see, for example, dirty data.

10.2.3 Isolation

Isolation is the property of transactions that requires each transaction to see a consistent database at all times. In other words, an executing transaction cannot reveal its results to other concurrent transactions before its commitment.

There are a number of reasons for insisting on isolation. One has to do with maintaining the interconsistency of transactions. If two concurrent transactions access a data item that is being updated by one of them, it is not possible to guarantee that the second will read the correct value.

Example 10.8. Consider the following two concurrent transactions (T_1 and T_2), both of which access data item x. Assume that the value of x before they start executing is 50.

T_1: Read(x)	T_2: Read(x)
$x \leftarrow x+1$	$x \leftarrow x+1$
Write(x)	Write(x)
Commit	Commit

The following is one possible sequence of execution of the actions of these transactions:

T_1: Read(x)
T_1: $x \leftarrow x+1$
T_1: Write(x)
T_1: Commit
T_2: Read(x)
T_2: $x \leftarrow x+1$
T_2: Write(x)
T_2: Commit

In this case, there are no problems; transactions T_1 and T_2 are executed one after the other and transaction T_2 reads 51 as the value of x. Note that if, instead, T_2 executes before T_1, T_2 reads 51 as the value of x. So, if T_1 and T_2 are executed one after the other (regardless of the order), the second transaction will read 51 as the value of x and x will have 52 as its value at the end of execution of these two transactions. However, since transactions are executing concurrently, the following execution sequence is also possible:

T_1: Read(x)
T_1: $x \leftarrow x + 1$
T_2: Read(x)
T_1: Write(x)
T_2: $x \leftarrow x + 1$
T_2: Write(x)
T_1: Commit
T_2: Commit

In this case, transaction T_2 reads 50 as the value of x. This is incorrect since T_2 reads x while its value is being changed from 50 to 51. Furthermore, the value of x is 51 at the end of execution of T_1 and T_2 since T_2's Write will overwrite T_1's Write. ◆

Ensuring isolation by not permitting incomplete results to be seen by other transactions, as the previous example shows, solves the *lost updates* problem. This type of isolation has been called *cursor stability*. In the example above, the second execution sequence resulted in the effects of T_1 being lost[3]. A second reason for isolation is *cascading aborts*. If a transaction permits others to see its incomplete results before committing and then decides to abort, any transaction that has read its incomplete values will have to abort as well. This chain can easily grow and impose considerable overhead on the DBMS.

It is possible to treat consistency levels discussed in the preceding section from the perspective of the isolation property (thus demonstrating the dependence between isolation and consistency). As we move up the hierarchy of consistency levels, there is more isolation among transactions. Degree 0 provides very little isolation other than preventing lost updates. However, since transactions commit write operations before the entire transaction is completed (and committed), if an abort occurs after some writes are committed to disk, the updates to data items that have been committed will need to be undone. Since at this level other transactions are allowed to read the dirty data, it may be necessary to abort them as well. Degree 2 consistency avoids cascading aborts. Degree 3 provides full isolation which forces one of the conflicting transactions to wait until the other one terminates. Such execution sequences are called *strict* and will be discussed further in the next chapter. It is obvious that the issue of isolation is directly related to database consistency and is therefore the topic of concurrency control.

---

[3] A more dramatic example may be to consider x to be your bank account and T_1 a transaction that executes as a result of your *depositing* money into your account. Assume that T_2 is a transaction that is executing as a result of your spouse *withdrawing* money from the account at another branch. If the same problem as described in Example 10.8 occurs and the results of T_1 are lost, you will be terribly unhappy. If, on the other hand, the results of T_2 are lost, the bank will be furious. A similar argument can be made for the reservation transaction example we have been considering.

ANSI, as part of the SQL2 (also known as SQL-92) standard specification, has defined a set of isolation levels [ANSI, 1992]. SQL isolation levels are defined on the basis of what ANSI call *phenomena* which are situations that can occur if proper isolation is not maintained. Three phenomena are specified:

Dirty Read: As defined earlier, dirty data refer to data items whose values have been modified by a transaction that has not yet committed. Consider the case where transaction T_1 modifies a data item value, which is then read by another transaction T_2 before T_1 performs a Commit or Abort. In case T_1 aborts, T_2 has read a value which never exists in the database.

A precise specification[4] of this phenomenon is as follows (where subscripts indicate the transaction identifiers)

$$\ldots, W_1(x), \ldots, R_2(x), \ldots, C_1(\text{or } A_1), \ldots, C_2(\text{or } A_2)$$

or

$$\ldots, W_1(x), \ldots, R_2(x), \ldots, C_2(\text{or } A_2), \ldots, C_1(\text{or } A_1)$$

Non-repeatable or Fuzzy read: Transaction T_1 reads a data item value. Another transaction T_2 then modifies or deletes that data item and commits. If T_1 then attempts to reread the data item, it either reads a different value or it can't find the data item at all; thus two reads within the same transaction T_1 return different results.

A precise specification of this phenomenon is as follows:

$$\ldots, R_1(x), \ldots, W_2(x), \ldots, C_1(\text{or } A_1), \ldots, C_2(\text{or } A_2)$$

or

$$\ldots, R_1(x), \ldots, W_2(x), \ldots, C_2(\text{or } A_2), \ldots, C_1(\text{or } A_1)$$

Phantom: The phantom condition that was defined earlier occurs when T_1 does a search with a predicate and T_2 inserts new tuples that satisfy the predicate. Again, the precise specification of this phenomenon is (where P is the search predicate)

$$\ldots, R_1(P), \ldots, W_2(y \text{ in } P), \ldots, C_1(\text{or } A_1), \ldots, C_2(\text{or } A_2)$$

or

$$\ldots, R_1(P), \ldots, W_2(y \text{ in } P), \ldots, C_2(\text{ or } A_2), \ldots, C_1(\text{or } A_1)$$

---

[4] The precise specifications of these phenomena are due to Berenson et al. [1995] and correspond to their *loose interpretations* which they indicate are the more appropriate interpretations.

Based on these phenomena, the isolation levels are defined as follows. The objective of defining multiple isolation levels is the same as defining multiple consistency levels.

Read uncommitted: For transactions operating at this level all three phenomena are possible.

Read committed: Fuzzy reads and phantoms are possible, but dirty reads are not.

Repeatable read: Only phantoms are possible.

Anomaly serializable: None of the phenomena are possible.

ANSI SQL standard uses the term "serializable" rather than "anomaly serializable." However, a serializable isolation level, as precisely defined in the next chapter, cannot be defined solely in terms of the three phenomena identified above; thus this isolation level is called "anomaly serializable" [Berenson et al., 1995]. The relationship between SQL isolation levels and the four levels of consistency defined in the previous section are also discussed in [Berenson et al., 1995].

One non-serializable isolation level that is commonly implemented in commercial products is *snapshot isolation* [Berenson et al., 1995]. Snapshot isolation provides repeatable reads, but not serializable isolation. Each transaction "sees" a snapshot of the database when it starts and its reads and writes are performed on this snapshot – thus the writes are not visible to other transactions and it does not see the writes of other transactions.

10.2.4 Durability

Durability refers to that property of transactions which ensures that once a transaction commits, its results are permanent and cannot be erased from the database. Therefore, the DBMS ensures that the results of a transaction will survive subsequent system failures. This is exactly why in Example 10.2 we insisted that the transaction commit before it informs the user of its successful completion. The durability property brings forth the issue of *database recovery*, that is, how to recover the database to a consistent state where all the committed actions are reflected. This issue is discussed further in Chapter 12.

10.3 Types of Transactions

A number of transaction models have been proposed in literature, each being appropriate for a class of applications. The fundamental problem of providing "ACID"ity usually remains, but the algorithms and techniques that are used to address them may be considerably different. In some cases, various aspects of ACID requirements are relaxed, removing some problems and adding new ones. In this section we provide an overview of some of the transaction models that have been proposed and then identify our focus in Chapters 11 and 12.

Transactions have been classified according to a number of criteria. One criterion is the duration of transactions. Accordingly, transactions may be classified as *online* or *batch* [Gray, 1987]. These two classes are also called *short-life* and *long-life* transactions, respectively. Online transactions are characterized by very short execution/response times (typically, on the order of a couple of seconds) and by access to a relatively small portion of the database. This class of transactions probably covers a large majority of current transaction applications. Examples include banking transactions and airline reservation transactions.

Batch transactions, on the other hand, take longer to execute (response time being measured in minutes, hours, or even days) and access a larger portion of the database. Typical applications that might require batch transactions are design databases, statistical applications, report generation, complex queries, and image processing. Along this dimension, one can also define a *conversational* transaction, which is executed by interacting with the user issuing it.

Another classification that has been proposed is with respect to the organization of the read and write actions. The examples that we have considered so far intermix their read and write actions without any specific ordering. We call this type of transactions *general*. If the transactions are restricted so that all the read actions are performed before any write action, the transaction is called a *two-step* transaction [Papadimitriou, 1979]. Similarly, if the transaction is restricted so that a data item has to be read before it can be updated (written), the corresponding class is called *restricted* (or *read-before-write*) [Stearns et al., 1976]. If a transaction is both two-step and restricted, it is called a *restricted two-step* transaction. Finally, there is the *action* model of transactions [Kung and Papadimitriou, 1979], which consists of the restricted class with the further restriction that each ⟨read, write⟩ pair be executed atomically. This classification is shown in Figure 10.3, where the generality increases upward.

Example 10.9. The following are some examples of the above-mentioned models. We omit the declaration and commit commands.
General:

$$T_1 : \{R(x), R(y), W(y), R(z), W(x), W(z), W(w), C\}$$

Two-step:

$$T_2 : \{R(x), R(y), R(z), W(x), W(z), W(y), W(w), C\}$$

Restricted:

$$T_3 : \{R(x), R(y), W(y), R(z), W(x), W(z), R(w), W(w), C\}$$

Note that T_3 has to read w before writing.
Two-step restricted:

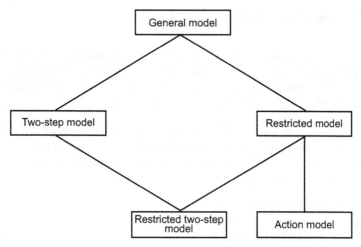

Fig. 10.3 Various Transaction Models (From: C.H. Papadimitriou and P.C. Kanellakis, ON CON-CURRENCY CONTROL BY MULTIPLE VERSIONS. ACM Trans. Database Sys.; December 1984; 9(1): 89–99.)

$$T_4 : \{R(x), R(y), R(z), R(w), W(x), W(z), W(y), W(w), C\}$$

Action:

$$T_5 : \{[R(x), W(x)], [R(y), W(y)], [R(z), W(z)], [R(w), W(w)], C\}$$

Note that each pair of actions within square brackets is executed atomically. ◆

Transactions can also be classified according to their structure. We distinguish four broad categories in increasing complexity: *flat transactions*, *closed nested transactions* as in [Moss, 1985], and *open nested transactions* such as sagas [Garcia-Molina and Salem, 1987], and *workflow models* which, in some cases, are combinations of various nested forms. This classification is arguably the most dominant one and we will discuss it at some length.

10.3.1 Flat Transactions

Flat transactions have a single start point (**Begin_transaction**) and a single termination point (**End_transaction**). All our examples in this section are of this type. Most of the transaction management work in databases has concentrated on flat transactions. This model will also be our main focus in this book, even though we discuss management techniques for other transaction types, where appropriate.

10.3.2 Nested Transactions

An alternative transaction model is to permit a transaction to include other transactions with their own begin and commit points. Such transactions are called *nested* transactions. These transactions that are embedded in another one are usually called *subtransactions*.

Example 10.10. Let us extend the reservation transaction of Example 10.2. Most travel agents will make reservations for hotels and car rentals in addition to the flights. If one chooses to specify all of this as one transaction, the reservation transaction would have the following structure:

Begin_transaction Reservation
begin
   Begin_transaction Airline
        . . .
   end. {Airline}
   Begin_transaction Hotel
        . . .
   end. {Hotel}
   Begin_transaction Car
        . . .
   end. {Car}
end.

                                               ◆

Nested transactions have received considerable interest as a more generalized transaction concept. The level of nesting is generally open, allowing subtransactions themselves to have nested transactions. This generality is necessary to support application areas where transactions are more complex than in traditional data processing.

In this taxonomy, we differentiate between *closed* and *open* nesting because of their termination characteristics. Closed nested transactions [Moss, 1985] commit in a bottom-up fashion through the root. Thus, a nested subtransaction begins *after* its parent and finishes *before* it, and the commitment of the subtransactions is conditional upon the commitment of the parent. The semantics of these transactions enforce atomicity at the top-most level. Open nesting relaxes the top-level atomicity restriction of closed nested transactions. Therefore, an open nested transaction allows its partial results to be observed outside the transaction. Sagas [Garcia-Molina and Salem, 1987; Garcia-Molina et al., 1990] and split transactions [Pu, 1988] are examples of open nesting.

A saga is a "sequence of transactions that can be interleaved with other transactions" [Garcia-Molina and Salem, 1987]. The DBMS guarantees that either all the transactions in a saga are successfully completed or *compensating transactions* [Garcia-Molina, 1983; Korth et al., 1990] are run to recover from a partial execution. A compensating transaction effectively does the inverse of the transaction that it is associated with. For example, if the transaction adds $100 to a bank account, its compensating transaction deducts $100 from the same bank account. If a transaction is viewed as a function that maps the old database state to a new database state, its compensating transaction is the inverse of that function.

Two properties of sagas are: (1) only two levels of nesting are allowed, and (2) at the outer level, the system does not support full atomicity. Therefore, a saga differs from a closed nested transaction in that its level structure is more restricted (only 2) and that it is open (the partial results of component transactions or sub-sagas are visible to the outside). Furthermore, the transactions that make up a saga have to be executed sequentially.

The saga concept is extended and placed within a more general model that deals with long-lived transactions and with activities that consist of multiple steps [Garcia-Molina et al., 1990] . The fundamental concept of the model is that of a module that captures code segments each of which accomplishes a given task and access a database in the process. The modules are modeled (at some level) as sub-sagas that communicate with each other via messages over ports. The transactions that make up a saga can be executed in parallel. The model is multi-layer where each subsequent layer adds a level of abstraction.

The advantages of nested transactions are the following. First, they provide a higher-level of concurrency among transactions. Since a transaction consists of a number of other transactions, more concurrency is possible within a single transaction. For example, if the reservation transaction of Example 10.10 is implemented as a flat transaction, it may not be possible to access records about a specific flight concurrently. In other words, if one travel agent issues the reservation transaction for a given flight, any concurrent transaction that wishes to access the same flight data will have to wait until the termination of the first, which includes the hotel and car reservation activities in addition to flight reservation. However, a nested implementation will permit the second transaction to access the flight data as soon as the Airline subtransaction of the first reservation transaction is completed. In other words, it may be possible to perform a finer level of synchronization among concurrent transactions.

A second argument in favor of nested transactions is related to recovery. It is possible to recover independently from failures of each subtransaction. This limits the damage to a smaller part of the transaction, making it less costly to recover. In a flat transaction, if any operation fails, the entire transaction has to be aborted and restarted, whereas in a nested transaction, if an operation fails, only the subtransaction containing that operation needs to be aborted and restarted.

Finally, it is possible to create new transactions from existing ones simply by inserting the old one inside the new one as a subtransaction.

10.3.3 Workflows

Flat transactions model relatively simple and short activities very well. However, they are less appropriate for modeling longer and more elaborate activities.That is the reason for the development of the various nested transaction models discussed above. It has been argued that these extensions are not sufficiently powerful to model business activities: "after several decades of data processing, we have learned that we have not won the battle of modeling and automating complex enterprises" [Medina-Mora et al., 1993]. To meet these needs, more complex transaction models which are combinations of open and nested transactions have been proposed. There are well-justified arguments for not calling these transactions, since they hardly follow any of the ACID properties; a more appropriate name that has been proposed is a *workflow* [Dogac et al., 1998b; Georgakopoulos et al., 1995].

The term "workflow," unfortunately, does not have a clear and uniformly accepted meaning. A working definition is that a workflow is "a collection of *tasks* organized to accomplish some business process." [Georgakopoulos et al., 1995]. This definition, however, leaves a lot undefined. This is perhaps unavoidable given the very different contexts where this term is used. Three types of workflows are identified [Georgakopoulos et al., 1995]:

1. *Human-oriented workflows*, which involve humans in performing the tasks. The system support is provided to facilitate collaboration and coordination among humans, but it is the humans themselves who are ultimately responsible for the consistency of the actions.

2. *System-oriented workflows* are those that consist of computation-intensive and specialized tasks that can be executed by a computer. The system support in this case is substantial and involves concurrency control and recovery, automatic task execution, notification, etc.

3. *Transactional workflows* range in between human-oriented and system-oriented workflows and borrow characteristics from both. They involve "coordinated execution of multiple tasks that (a) may involve humans, (b) require access to HAD [heterogeneous, autonomous, and/or distributed] systems, and (c) support selective use of transactional properties [i.e., ACID properties] for individual tasks or entire workflows." [Georgakopoulos et al., 1995].
   Among the features of transactional workflows, the selective use of transactional properties is particularly important as it characterizes possible relaxations of ACID properties.

In this book, our primary interest is with transactional workflows. There have been many transactional workflow proposals [Elmagarmid et al., 1990; Nodine and Zdonik, 1990; Buchmann et al., 1982; Dayal et al., 1991; Hsu, 1993], and they differ in a number of ways. The common point among them is that a workflow is defined as an *activity* consisting of a set of tasks with well-defined precedence relationship among them.

Example 10.11. Let us further extend the reservation transaction of Example 10.3. The entire reservation activity consists of the following taks and involves the following data:

- Customer request is obtained (task T_1) and Customer Database is accessed to obtain customer information, preferences, etc.;

- Airline reservation is performed (T_2) by accessing the Flight Database;

- Hotel reservation is performed (T_3), which may involve sending a message to the hotel involved;

- Auto reservation is performed (T_4), which may also involve communication with the car rental company;

- Bill is generated (T_5) and the billing info is recorded in the billing database.

Figure 10.4 depicts this workflow where there is a serial dependency of T_2 on T_1, and T_3, T_4 on T_2; however, T_3 and T_4 (hotel and car reservations) are performed in parallel and T_5 waits until their completion.   ◆

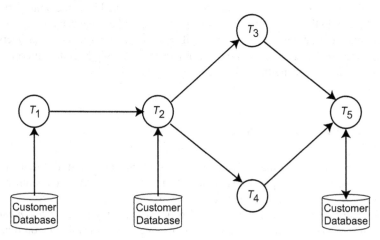

Fig. 10.4 Example Workflow

A number of workflow models go beyond this basic model by both defining more precisely what tasks can be and by allocating different relationships among the tasks. In the following, we define one model that is similar to the models of Buchmann et al. [1982] and Dayal et al. [1991].

A workflow is modeled as an *activity* with open nesting semantics in that it permits partial results to be visible outside the activity boundaries. Thus, tasks that make up the activity are allowed to commit individually. Tasks may be other activities (with the same open transaction semantics) or closed nested transactions that make their results visible to the entire system when they commit. Even though an activity can have both other activities and closed nested transactions as its component, a closed nested transaction task can only be composed of other closed nested transactions (i.e., once closed nesting semantics begins, it is maintained for all components).

An activity commits when its components are ready to commit. However, the components commit individually, without waiting for the root activity to commit.

This raises problems in dealing with aborts since when an activity aborts, all of its components should be aborted. The problem is dealing with the components that have already committed. Therefore, compensating transactions are defined for the components of an activity. Thus, if a component has already committed when an activity aborts, the corresponding compensating transaction is executed to "undo" its effects.

Some components of an activity may be marked as *vital*. When a vital component aborts, its parent must also abort. If a non-vital component of a workflow model aborts, it may continue executing. A workflow, on the other hand, always aborts when one of its components aborts. For example, in the reservation workflow of Example 10.11, T_2 (airline reservation) and T_3 (hotel reservation) may be declared as vital so that if an airline reservation or a hotel reservation cannot be made, the workflow aborts and the entire trip is canceled. However, if a car reservation cannot be committed, the workflow can still successfully terminate.

It is possible to define *contingency tasks* that are invoked if their counterparts fail. For example, in the Reservation example presented earlier, one can specify that the contingency to making a reservation at Hilton is to make a reservation at Sheraton. Thus, if the hotel reservation component for Hilton fails, the Sheraton alternative is tried rather than aborting the task and the entire workflow.

10.4 Architecture Revisited

With the introduction of the transaction concept, we need to revisit the architectural model introduced in Chapter 1. We do not need to revise the model but simply need to expand the role of the distributed execution monitor.

The distributed execution monitor consists of two modules: a *transaction manager* (TM) and a *scheduler* (SC). The transaction manager is responsible for coordinating the execution of the database operations on behalf of an application. The scheduler, on the other hand, is responsible for the implementation of a specific concurrency control algorithm for synchronizing access to the database.

A third component that participates in the management of distributed transactions is the local recovery managers (LRM) that exist at each site. Their function is to implement the local procedures by which the local database can be recovered to a consistent state following a failure.

Each transaction originates at one site, which we will call its *originating site*. The execution of the database operations of a transaction is coordinated by the TM at that transaction's originating site.

The transaction managers implement an interface for the application programs which consists of five commands: begin_transaction, read, write, commit, and abort. The processing of each of these commands in a non-replicated distributed DBMS is discussed below at an abstract level. For simplicity, we ignore the scheduling of concurrent transactions as well as the details of how data is physically retrieved by the data processor. These assumptions permit us to concentrate on the interface to the TM. The details are presented in the Chapters 11 and 12, while the execution of these commands in a replicated distributed database is discussed in Chapter 13.

1. *Begin_transaction.* This is an indicator to the TM that a new transaction is starting. The TM does some bookkeeping, such as recording the transaction's name, the originating application, and so on, in coordination with the data processor.

2. *Read.* If the data item to be read is stored locally, its value is read and returned to the transaction. Otherwise, the TM finds where the data item is stored and requests its value to be returned (after appropriate concurrency control measures are taken).

3. *Write.* If the data item is stored locally, its value is updated (in coordination with the data processor). Otherwise, the TM finds where the data item is located and requests the update to be carried out at that site after appropriate concurrency control measures are taken).

4. *Commit.* The TM coordinates the sites involved in updating data items on behalf of this transaction so that the updates are made permanent at every site.

5. *Abort.* The TM makes sure that no effects of the transaction are reflected in any of the databases at the sites where it updated data items.

In providing these services, a TM can communicate with SCs and data processors at the same or at different sites. This arrangement is depicted in Figure 10.5.

As we indicated in Chapter 1, the architectural model that we have described is only an abstraction that serves a pedagogical purpose. It enables the separation of many of the transaction management issues and their independent and isolated discussion. In Chapter 11 we focus on the interface between a TM and an SC and between an SC and a data processor, in addition to the scheduling algorithms. In Chapter 12 we consider the execution strategies for the commit and abort commands in a distributed environment, in addition to the recovery algorithms that need to be implemented for the recovery manager. In Chapter 13, we extend this discussion to the case of replicated databases. We should point out that the computational model that we described here is not unique. Other models have been proposed such as, for example, using a private workspace for each transaction.

10.5 Conclusion

In this chapter we introduced the concept of a transaction as a unit of consistent and reliable access to the database. The properties of transactions indicate that they are larger atomic units of execution which transform one consistent database to another consistent database. The properties of transactions also indicate what the requirements for managing them are, which is the topic of the next two chapters. Consistency requires a definition of integrity enforcement (which we did in Chapter

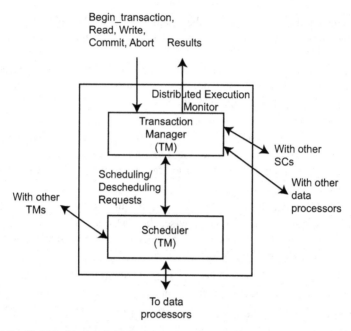

Fig. 10.5 Detailed Model of the Distributed Execution Monitor

5), as well as concurrency control algorithms (which is the topic of Chapter 11). Concurrency control also deals with the issue of isolation. Durability and atomicity properties of transactions require a discussion of reliability, which we cover in Chapter 12. Specifically, durability is supported by various commit protocols and commit management, whereas atomicity requires the development of appropriate recovery protocols.

10.6 Bibliographic Notes

Transaction management has been the topic of considerable study since DBMSs have become a significant research area. There are two excellent books on the subject: [Gray and Reuter, 1993] and [Weikum and Vossen, 2001]. An excellent companion to these is [Bernstein and Newcomer, 1997] which provides an in-depth discussion of transaction processing principles. It also gives a view of transaction processing and transaction monitors which is more general than the database-centric view that we provide in this book. A good collection of papers that focus on the concurrency control and reliability aspects of distributed systems is [Bhargava, 1987]. Two books focus on the performance of concurrency control mechanisms with a focus on centralized systems [Kumar, 1996; Thomasian, 1996]. Distributed concurrency control is the topic of [Cellary et al., 1988].

Advanced transaction models are discussed and various examples are given in [Elmagarmid, 1992]. Nested transactions are also covered in [Lynch et al., 1993]. A good introduction to workflow systems is [Georgakopoulos et al., 1995]. The same topic is covered in detail in [Dogac et al., 1998b].

A very important work is a set of notes on database operating systems by Gray [1979]. These notes contain valuable information on transaction management, among other things.

The discussion concerning transaction classification in Section 10.3 comes from a number of sources. Part of it is from [Farrag, 1986]. The structure discussion is from [Özsu, 1994] and [Buchmann et al., 1982], where the authors combine transaction structure with the structure of the objects that these transactions operate upon to develop a more complete classification.

There are numerous papers dealing with various transaction management issues. The ones referred to in this chapter are those that deal with the concept of a transaction. More detailed references on their management are left to Chapters 11 and 12.

Chapter 11
Distributed Concurrency Control

As we discussed in Chapter 10, concurrency control deals with the isolation and consistency properties of transactions. The distributed concurrency control mechanism of a distributed DBMS ensures that the consistency of the database, as defined in Section 10.2.2, is maintained in a multiuser distributed environment. If transactions are internally consistent (i.e., do not violate any consistency constraints), the simplest way of achieving this objective is to execute each transaction alone, one after another. It is obvious that such an alternative is only of theoretical interest and would not be implemented in any practical system, since it minimizes the system throughput. The level of concurrency (i.e., the number of concurrent transactions) is probably the most important parameter in distributed systems [Balter et al., 1982]. Therefore, the concurrency control mechanism attempts to find a suitable trade-off between maintaining the consistency of the database and maintaining a high level of concurrency.

In this chapter, we make two major assumptions: the distributed system is fully reliable and does not experience any failures (of hardware or software), and the database is not replicated. Even though these are unrealistic assumptions, they permit us to delineate the issues related to the management of concurrency from those related to the operation of a reliable distributed system and those related to maintaining replicas. In Chapter 12, we discuss how the algorithms that are presented in this chapter need to be enhanced to operate in an unreliable environment. In Chapter 13 we address the issues related to replica management.

We start our discussion of concurrency control with a presentation of serializability theory in Section 11.1. Serializability is the most widely accepted correctness criterion for concurrency control algorithms. In Section 11.2 we present a taxonomy of algorithms that will form the basis for most of the discussion in the remainder of the chapter. Sections 11.3 and 11.4 cover the two major classes of algorithms: locking-based and timestamp ordering-based. Both locking and timestamp ordering classes cover what is called pessimistic algorithms; optimistic concurrency control is discussed in Section 11.5. Any locking-based algorithm may result in deadlocks, requiring special management methods. Various deadlock management techniques are therefore the topic of Section 11.6. In Section 11.7, we discuss "relaxed" concurrency control approaches. These are mechanisms which use weaker correctness criteria than serializability, or relax the isolation property of transactions.

11.1 Serializability Theory

In Section 10.1.3 we discussed the issue of isolating transactions from one another in terms of their effects on the database. We also pointed out that if the concurrent execution of transactions leaves the database in a state that can be achieved by their serial execution in some order, problems such as lost updates will be resolved. This is exactly the point of the serializability argument. The remainder of this section addresses serializability issues more formally.

A *history R* (also called a *schedule*) is defined over a set of transactions $T = \{T_1, T_2, \ldots, T_n\}$ and specifies an interleaved order of execution of these transactions' operations. Based on the definition of a transaction introduced in Section 10.1, the history can be specified as a partial order over T. We need a few preliminaries, though, before we present the formal definition.

Recall the definition of conflicting operations that we gave in Chapter 10. Two operations $O_{ij}(x)$ and $O_{kl}(x)$ (i and k representing transactions and are not necessarily distinct) accessing the same database entity x are said to be in *conflict* if at least one of them is a write operation. Note two things in this definition. First, read operations do not conflict with each other. We can, therefore, talk about two types of conflicts: *read-write* (or *write-read*), and *write-write*. Second, the two operations can belong to the same transaction or to two different transactions. In the latter case, the two transactions are said to be *conflicting*. Intuitively, the existence of a conflict between two operations indicates that their order of execution is important. The ordering of two read operations is insignificant.

We first define a *complete history*, which defines the execution order of all operations in its domain. We will then define a history as a prefix of a complete history. Formally, a complete history H_T^c defined over a set of transactions $T = \{T_1, T_2, \ldots, T_n\}$ is a partial order $H_T^c = \{\Sigma_T, \prec_H\}$ where

1. $\Sigma_T = \bigcup_{i=1}^{n} \Sigma_i$.
2. $\prec_H \supseteq \bigcup_{i=1}^{n} \prec_{T_i}$.
3. For any two conflicting operations $O_{ij}, O_{kl} \in \Sigma_T$, either $O_{ij} \prec_H O_{kl}$, or $O_{kl} \prec_H O_{ij}$.

The first condition simply states that the domain of the history is the union of the domains of individual transactions. The second condition defines the ordering relation of the history as a superset of the ordering relations of individual transactions. This maintains the ordering of operations within each transaction. The final condition simply defines the execution order among conflicting operations in H.

Example 11.1. Consider the two transactions from Example 10.8, which were as follows:

T_1: Read(x) T_2: Read(x)
    $x \leftarrow x + 1$ $x \leftarrow x + 1$
    Write(x)   Write(x)
    Commit   Commit

A possible complete history H_T^c over $T = \{T_1, T_2\}$ is the partial order $H_T^c = \{\Sigma_T, \prec_T\}$ where

$$\Sigma_1 = \{R_1(x), W_1(x), C_1\}$$
$$\Sigma_2 = \{R_2(x), W_2(x), C_2\}$$

Thus

$$\Sigma_T = \Sigma_1 \cup \Sigma_2 = \{R_1(x), W_1(x), C_1, R_2(x), W_2(x), C_2\}$$

and

$$\prec_H = \{(R_1, R_2), (R_1, W_1), (R_1, C_1), (R_1, W_2), (R_1, C_2), (R_2, W_1), (R_2, C_1), (R_2, W_2),$$
$$(R_2, C_2), (W_1, C_1), (W_1, W_2), (W_1, C_2), (C_1, W_2), (C_1, C_2), (W_2, C_2)\}$$

which can be specified as a DAG as depicted in Figure 11.1. Note that consistent with our earlier adopted convention (see Example 10.7), we do not draw the arcs that are implied by transitivity [e.g., (R_1, C_1)].

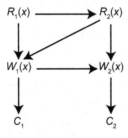

Fig. 11.1 DAG Representation of a Complete History

It is quite common to specify a history as a listing of the operations in Σ_T, where their execution order is relative to their order in this list. Thus H_T^c can be specified as

$$H_T^c = \{R_1(x), R_2(x), W_1(x), C_1, W_2(x), C_2\}$$

♦

A history is defined as a prefix of a complete history. A prefix of a partial order can be defined as follows. Given a partial order $P = \{\Sigma, \prec\}$, $P' = \{\Sigma', \prec'\}$ is a *prefix* of P if

1. $\Sigma' \subseteq \Sigma$;
2. $\forall e_i \in \Sigma', e_1 \prec' e_2$ if and only if $e_1 \prec e_2$; and
3. $\forall e_i \in \Sigma'$, if $\exists e_j \in \Sigma$ and $e_j \prec e_i$, then $e_j \in \Sigma'$.

The first two conditions define P' as a *restriction* of P on domain Σ', whereby the ordering relations in P are maintained in P'. The last condition indicates that for any element of Σ', all its predecessors in Σ have to be included in Σ' as well.

What does this definition of a history as a prefix of a partial order provide for us? The answer is simply that we can now deal with incomplete histories. This is useful for a number of reasons. From the perspective of the serializability theory, we deal only with conflicting operations of transactions rather than with all operations. Furthermore, and perhaps more important, when we introduce failures, we need to be able to deal with incomplete histories, which is what a prefix enables us to do.

The history discussed in Example 11.1 is special in that it is complete. It needs to be complete in order to talk about the execution order of these two transactions' operations. The following example demonstrates a history that is not complete.

Example 11.2. Consider the following three transactions:

T_1: Read(x)	T_2: Write(x)	T_3: Read(x)
Write(x)	Write(y)	Read(y)
Commit	Read(z)	Read(z)
	Commit	Commit

A complete history H^c for these transactions is given in Figure 11.2, and a history H (as a prefix of H^c) is depicted in Figure 11.3. ♦

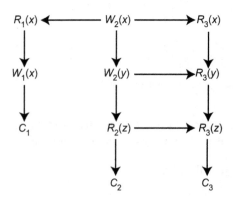

Fig. 11.2 A Complete History

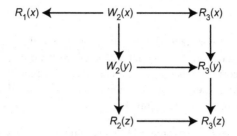

Fig. 11.3 Prefix of Complete History in Figure 11.2

If in a complete history H, the operations of various transactions are not interleaved (i.e., the operations of each transaction occur consecutively), the history is said to be *serial*. As we indicated before, the serial execution of a set of transactions maintains the consistency of the database. This follows naturally from the consistency property of transactions: each transaction, when executed alone on a consistent database, will produce a consistent database.

Example 11.3. Consider the three transactions of Example 11.2. The following history is serial since all the operations of T_2 are executed before all the operations of T_1 and all operations of T_1 are executed before all operations of T_3[1].

$$H = \{\underbrace{W_2(x), W_2(y), R_2(z)}_{T_2}, \underbrace{R_1(x), W_1(x)}_{T_1}, \underbrace{R_3(x), R_3(y), R_3(z)}_{T_3}\}$$

One common way to denote this precedence relationship between transaction executions is $T_2 \rightarrow T_1 \rightarrow T_3$ rather than the more formal $T_2 \prec_H T_1 \prec_H T_3$. ◆

Based on the precedence relationship introduced by the partial order, it is possible to discuss the equivalence of histories with respect to their effects on the database. Intuitively, two histories H_1 and H_2, defined over the same set of transactions T, are *equivalent* if they have the same effect on the database. More formally, two histories, H_1 and H_2, defined over the same set of transactions T, are said to be *equivalent* if for each pair of conflicting operations O_{ij} and O_{kl} $(i \neq k)$, whenever $O_{ij} \prec_{H_1} O_{kl}$, then $O_{ij} \prec_{H_2} O_{kl}$. This is called *conflict equivalence* since it defines equivalence of two histories in terms of the relative order of execution of the conflicting operations in those histories. Here, for the sake of simplicity, we assume that T does not include any aborted transaction. Otherwise, the definition needs to be modified to specify only those conflicting operations that belong to unaborted transactions.

Example 11.4. Again consider the three transactions given in Example 11.2. The following history H' defined over them is conflict equivalent to H given in Example 11.3:

$$H' = \{W_2(x), R_1(x), W_1(x), R_3(x), W_2(y), R_3(y), R_2(z), R_3(z)\}$$

---

[1] From now on we will generally omit the Commit operation from histories.

◆

We are now ready to define serializability more precisely. A history H is said to be *serializable* if and only if it is conflict equivalent to a serial history. Note that serializability roughly corresponds to degree 3 consistency, which we defined in Section 10.2.2. Serializability so defined is also known as *conflict-based serializability* since it is defined according to conflict equivalence.

Example 11.5. History H' in Example 11.4 is serializable since it is equivalent to the serial history H of Example 11.3. Also note that the problem with the uncontrolled execution of transactions T_1 and T_2 in Example 10.8 was that they could generate an unserializable history.   ◆

Now that we have formally defined serializability, we can indicate that the primary function of a concurrency controller is to generate a serializable history for the execution of pending transactions. The issue, then, is to devise algorithms that are guaranteed to generate only serializable histories.

Serializability theory extends in a straightforward manner to the non-replicated (or partitioned) distributed databases. The history of transaction execution at each site is called a *local history*. If the database is not replicated and each local history is serializable, their union (called the *global history*) is also serializable as long as local serialization orders are identical.

Example 11.6. We will give a very simple example to demonstrate the point. Consider two bank accounts, x (stored at Site 1) and y (stored at Site 2), and the following two transactions where T_1 transfers \$100 from x to y, while T_2 simply reads the balances of x and y:

T_1: Read(x) T_2: Read(x)
    $x \leftarrow x - 100$ Read(y)
    Write(x)   Commit
    Read(y)
    $y \leftarrow y + 100$
    Write(y)
    Commit

Obviously, both of these transactions need to run at both sites. Consider the following two histories that may be generated locally at the two sites (H_i is the history at Site i):

$$H_1 = \{R_1(x), W_1(x), R_2(x)\}$$
$$H_2 = \{R_1(y), W_1(y), R_2(y)\}$$

Both of these histories are serializable; indeed, they are serial. Therefore, each represents a correct execution order. Furthermore, the serialization order for both are the same $T_1 \rightarrow T_2$. Therefore, the global history that is obtained is also serializable with the serialization order $T_1 \rightarrow T_2$.

However, if the histories generated at the two sites are as follows, there is a problem:

$$H_1' = \{R_1(x), W_1(x), R_2(x)\}$$
$$H_2' = \{R_2(y), R_1(y), W_1(y)\}$$

Although each local history is still serializable, the serialization orders are different: H_1' serializes T_1 before T_2 while H_2' serializes T_2 before T_1. Therefore, there can be no global history that is serializable. ◆

A weaker version of serializability that has gained importance in recent years is *snapshot isolation* [Berenson et al., 1995] that is now provided as a standard consistency criterion in a number of commercial systems. Snapshot isolation allows read transactions (queries) to read stale data by allowing them to read a snapshot of the database that reflects the committed data at the time the read transaction starts. Consequently, the reads are never blocked by writes, even though they may read old data that may be dirtied by other transactions that were still running when the snapshot was taken. Hence, the resulting histories are not serializable, but this is accepted as a reasonable tradeoff between a lower level of isolation and better performance.

11.2 Taxonomy of Concurrency Control Mechanisms

There are a number of ways that the concurrency control approaches can be classified. One obvious classification criterion is the mode of database distribution. Some algorithms that have been proposed require a fully replicated database, while others can operate on partially replicated or partitioned databases. The concurrency control algorithms may also be classified according to network topology, such as those requiring a communication subnet with broadcasting capability or those working in a star-type network or a circularly connected network.

The most common classification criterion, however, is the synchronization primitive. The corresponding breakdown of the concurrency control algorithms results in two classes [Bernstein and Goodman, 1981]: those algorithms that are based on mutually exclusive access to shared data (locking), and those that attempt to order the execution of the transactions according to a set of rules (protocols). However, these primitives may be used in algorithms with two different viewpoints: the pessimistic view that many transactions will conflict with each other, or the optimistic view that not too many transactions will conflict with one another.

We will thus group the concurrency control mechanisms into two broad classes: pessimistic concurrency control methods and optimistic concurrency control methods. *Pessimistic* algorithms synchronize the concurrent execution of transactions early in their execution life cycle, whereas *optimistic* algorithms delay the synchronization of transactions until their termination. The pessimistic group consists of *locking-*

based algorithms, *ordering* (or *transaction ordering*) *based* algorithms, and *hybrid* algorithms. The optimistic group can, similarly, be classified as locking-based or timestamp ordering-based. This classification is depicted in Figure 11.4.

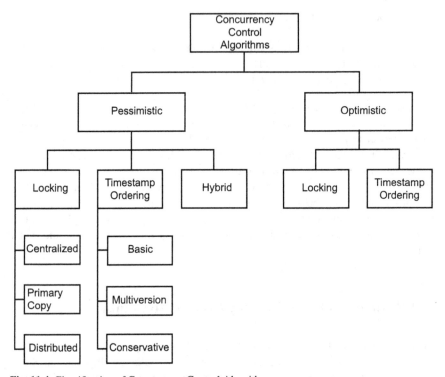

Fig. 11.4 Classification of Concurrency Control Algorithms

In the *locking-based* approach, the synchronization of transactions is achieved by employing physical or logical locks on some portion or granule of the database. The size of these portions (usually called *locking granularity*) is an important issue. However, for the time being, we will ignore it and refer to the chosen granule as a *lock unit*. This class is subdivided further according to where the lock management activities are performed: *centralized* and *decentralized* (or *distributed*) *locking*.

The *timestamp ordering* (TO) class involves organizing the execution order of transactions so that they maintain transaction consistency. This ordering is maintained by assigning timestamps to both the transactions and the data items that are stored in the database. These algorithms can be *basic TO*, *multiversion TO*, or *conservative TO*.

We should indicate that in some locking-based algorithms, timestamps are also used. This is done primarily to improve efficiency and the level of concurrency. We call these *hybrid* algorithms. We will not discuss these algorithms in this chapter since they have not been implemented in any commercial or research prototype distributed

DBMS. The rules for integrating locking and timestamp ordering protocols are discussed by Bernstein and Goodman [1981].

11.3 Locking-Based Concurrency Control Algorithms

The main idea of locking-based concurrency control is to ensure that a data item that is shared by conflicting operations is accessed by one operation at a time. This is accomplished by associating a "lock" with each lock unit. This lock is set by a transaction before it is accessed and is reset at the end of its use. Obviously a lock unit cannot be accessed by an operation if it is already locked by another. Thus a lock request by a transaction is granted only if the associated lock is not being held by any other transaction.

Since we are concerned with synchronizing the conflicting operations of conflicting transactions, there are two types of locks (commonly called *lock modes*) associated with each lock unit: *read lock* (*rl*) and *write lock* (*wl*). A transaction T_i that wants to read a data item contained in lock unit x obtains a read lock on x [denoted $rl_i(x)$]. The same happens for write operations. Two lock modes are *compatible* if two transactions that access the same data item can obtain these locks on that data item at the same time. As Figure 11.5 shows, read locks are compatible, whereas read-write or write-write locks are not. Therefore, it is possible, for example, for two transactions to read the same data item concurrently.

	$rl_j(x)$	$wl_j(x)$
$rl_j(x)$	compatible	not compatible
$wl_j(x)$	not compatible	not compatible

Fig. 11.5 Compatibility Matrix of Lock Modes

The distributed DBMS not only manages locks but also handles the lock management responsibilities on behalf of the transactions. In other words, users do not need to specify when a data item needs to be locked; the distributed DBMS takes care of that every time the transaction issues a read or write operation.

In locking-based systems, the scheduler (see Figure 10.5) is a *lock manager* (LM). The transaction manager passes to the lock manager the database operation (read or write) and associated information (such as the item that is accessed and the identifier of the transaction that issues the database operation). The lock manager then checks if the lock unit that contains the data item is already locked. If so, and if the existing lock mode is incompatible with that of the current transaction, the current operation is delayed. Otherwise, the lock is set in the desired mode and the database operation is passed on to the data processor for actual database access. The transaction manager is then informed of the results of the operation. The termination of a transaction results in the release of its locks and the initiation of another transaction that might be waiting for access to the same data item.

The locking algorithm as described above will not, unfortunately, properly synchronize transaction executions. This is because to generate serializable histories, the locking and releasing operations of transactions also need to be coordinated. We demonstrate this by an example.

Example 11.7. Consider the following two transactions:

T_1: Read(x) T_2: Read(x)
     $x \leftarrow x + 1$ $x \leftarrow x * 2$
     Write(x)   Write(x)
     Read(y)   Read(y)
     $y \leftarrow y - 1$ $y \leftarrow y * 2$
     Write(y)   Write(y)
     Commit   Commit

The following is a valid history that a lock manager employing the locking algorithm may generate:

$$H = \{wl_1(x), R_1(x), W_1(x), lr_1(x), wl_2(x), R_2(x), w_2(x), lr_2(x), wl_2(y),$$
$$R_2(y), W_2(y), lr_2(y), wl_1(y), R_1(y), W_1(y), lr_1(y)\}$$

where $lr_i(z)$ indicates the release of the lock on z that transaction T_i holds.

Note that H is not a serializable history. For example, if prior to the execution of these transactions, the values of x and y are 50 and 20, respectively, one would expect their values following execution to be, respectively, either 102 and 38 if T_1 executes before T_2, or 101 and 39 if T_2 executes before T_1. However, the result of executing H would give x and y the values 102 and 39. Obviously, H is not serializable.   ◆

The problem with history H in Example 11.7 is the following. The locking algorithm releases the locks that are held by a transaction (say, T_i) as soon as the associated database command (read or write) is executed, and that lock unit (say x) no longer needs to be accessed. However, the transaction itself is locking other items (say, y), after it releases its lock on x. Even though this may seem to be advantageous from the viewpoint of increased concurrency, it permits transactions to interfere with one another, resulting in the loss of isolation and atomicity. Hence the argument for *two-phase locking* (2PL).

The two-phase locking rule simply states that no transaction should request a lock after it releases one of its locks. Alternatively, a transaction should not release a lock until it is certain that it will not request another lock. 2PL algorithms execute transactions in two phases. Each transaction has a *growing phase*, where it obtains locks and accesses data items, and a *shrinking phase*, during which it releases locks (Figure 11.6). The *lock point* is the moment when the transaction has achieved all its locks but has not yet started to release any of them. Thus the lock point determines the end of the growing phase and the beginning of the shrinking phase of a transaction. It has been proven that any history generated by a concurrency control algorithm that obeys the 2PL rule is serializable [Eswaran et al., 1976].

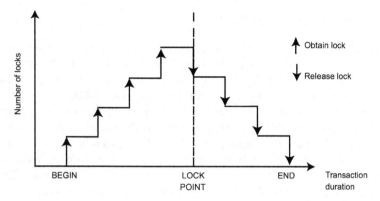

Fig. 11.6 2PL Lock Graph

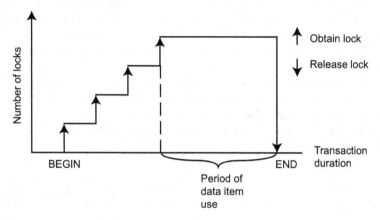

Fig. 11.7 Strict 2PL Lock Graph

Figure 11.6 indicates that the lock manager releases locks as soon as access to that data item has been completed. This permits other transactions awaiting access to go ahead and lock it, thereby increasing the degree of concurrency. However, this is difficult to implement since the lock manager has to know that the transaction has obtained all its locks and will not need to lock another data item. The lock manager also needs to know that the transaction no longer needs to access the data item in question, so that the lock can be released. Finally, if the transaction aborts after it releases a lock, it may cause other transactions that may have accessed the unlocked data item to abort as well. This is known as *cascading aborts*. These problems may be overcome by *strict two-phase locking*, which releases all the locks together when the transaction terminates (commits or aborts). Thus the lock graph is as shown in Figure 11.7.

We should note that even though a 2PL algorithm enforces conflict serializability, it does not allow all histories that are conflict serializable. Consider the following history discussed by Agrawal and El-Abbadi [1990]:

$$H = \{W_1(x), R_2(x), W_3(y), W_1(y)\}$$

H is not allowed by 2PL algorithm since T_1 would need to obtain a write lock on y after it releases its write lock on x. However, this history is serializable in the order $T_3 \rightarrow T_1 \rightarrow T_2$. The order of locking can be exploited to design locking algorithms that allow histories such as these [Agrawal and El-Abbadi, 1990].

The main idea is to observe that in serializability theory, the order of serialization of conflicting operations is as important as detecting the conflict in the first place and this can be exploited in defining locking modes. Consequently, in addition to read (shared) and write (exclusive) locks, a third lock mode is defined: *ordered shared*. Ordered shared locking of an object x by transactions T_i and T_j has the following meaning: Given a history H that allows ordered shared locks between operations $o \in T_i$ and $p \in T_j$, if T_i acquires o-lock before T_j acquires p-lock, then o is executed before p. Consider the compatibility table between read and write locks given in Figure 11.5. If the ordered shared mode is added, there are eight variants of this table. Figure 11.5 depicts one of them and two more are shown in Figure 11.8. In Figure 11.8(b), for example, there is an ordered shared relationship between $rl_j(x)$ and $wl_i(x)$ indicating that T_i can acquire a write lock on x while T_j holds a read lock on x as long as the ordered shared relationship from $rl_j(x)$ to $wl_i(x)$ is observed. The eight compatibility tables can be compared with respect to their permissiveness (i.e., with respect to the histories that can be produced using them) to generate a lattice of tables such that the one in Figure 11.5 is the most restrictive and the one in Figure 11.8(b) is the most liberal.

	$rl_j(x)$	$wl_j(x)$		$rl_j(x)$	$wl_j(x)$
$rl_i(x)$	compatible	not compatible	$rl_i(x)$	compatible	ordered shared
$wl_i(x)$	ordered shared	not compatible	$wl_i(x)$	ordered shared	ordered shared
	(a)			(b)	

Fig. 11.8 Commutativity Table with Ordered Shared Lock Mode

The locking protocol that enforces a compatibility matrix involving ordered shared lock modes is identical to 2PL, except that a transaction may not release any locks as long as any of its locks are on hold. Otherwise circular serialization orders can exist.

Locking-based algorithms may cause deadlocks since they allow exclusive access to resources. It is possible that two transactions that access the same data items may lock them in reverse order, causing each to wait for the other to release its locks causing a deadlock. We discuss deadlock management in Section 11.6.

11.3.1 Centralized 2PL

The 2PL algorithm discussed in the preceding section can easily be extended to the distributed DBMS environment. One way of doing this is to delegate lock management responsibility to a single site only. This means that only one of the sites has a lock manager; the transaction managers at the other sites communicate with it rather than with their own lock managers. This approach is also known as the *primary site* 2PL algorithm [Alsberg and Day, 1976].

The communication between the cooperating sites in executing a transaction according to a centralized 2PL (C2PL) algorithm is depicted in Figure 11.9. This communication is between the transaction manager at the site where the transaction is initiated (called the *coordinating* TM), the lock manager at the central site, and the data processors (DP) at the other participating sites. The participating sites are those that store the data item and at which the operation is to be carried out. The order of messages is denoted in the figure.

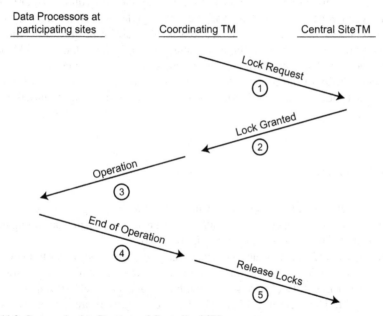

Fig. 11.9 Communication Structure of Centralized 2PL

The centralized 2PL transaction management algorithm (C2PL-TM) that incorporates these changes is given at a very high level in Algorithm 11.1, while the centralized 2PL lock management algorithm (C2PL-LM) is shown in Algorithm 11.2. A highly simplified data processor algorithm (DP) is given in Algorithm 11.3; this is the algorithm that will see major changes when we discuss reliability issues in Chapter 12. For the time being, this is sufficient for our purposes.

There is one important data structure that is used in these algorithms and that is the operation that is defined as a 5-tuple: $Op : \langle Type = \{BT,R,W,A,C\}, arg :$ Data item, val : Value, tid : Transaction identifier, res : Result$\rangle$. The meaning of the components is as follows: for an operation $o : Op$, $o.Type \in \{BT,R,W,A,C\}$ specifies its type where BT = Begin_transaction, R = Read, W = Write, A = Abort, and C = Commit, arg is the data item that the operation accesses (reads or writes; for other operations this field is null), val is also used in case of Read and Write operations to specify the value that has been read or the value to be written for data item arg (otherwise it is null), tid is the transaction that this operation belongs to (strictly speaking, this is the transaction identifier), and res indicates the completion code of operations requested of DP. In the high level descriptions of the algorithms in this chapter, res may seem unnecessary, but we will see in Chapter 12 that these return codes will be important.

The transaction manager (C2PL-TM) algorithm is written as a process that runs forever and waits until a message arrives from either an application (with a transaction operation) or from a lock manager, or from a data processor. The lock manager (C2PL-LM) and data processor (DP) algorithms are written as procedures that are called when needed. Since the algorithms are given at a high level of abstraction, this is not a major concern, but actual implementations may, naturally, be quite different.

One common criticism of C2PL algorithms is that a bottleneck may quickly form around the central site. Furthermore, the system may be less reliable since the failure or inaccessibility of the central site would cause major system failures. There are studies that indicate that the bottleneck will indeed form as the transaction rate increases.

11.3.2 Distributed 2PL

Distributed 2PL (D2PL) requires the availability of lock managers at each site. The communication between cooperating sites that execute a transaction according to the distributed 2PL protocol is depicted in Figure 11.10.

The distributed 2PL transaction management algorithm is similar to the C2PL-TM, with two major modifications. The messages that are sent to the central site lock manager in C2PL-TM are sent to the lock managers at all participating sites in D2PL-TM. The second difference is that the operations are not passed to the data processors by the coordinating transaction manager, but by the participating lock managers. This means that the coordinating transaction manager does not wait for a "lock request granted" message. Another point about Figure 11.10 is the following. The participating data processors send the "end of operation" messages to the coordinating TM. The alternative is for each DP to send it to its own lock manager who can then release the locks and inform the coordinating TM. We have chosen to describe the former since it uses an LM algorithm identical to the strict 2PL lock manager that we have already discussed and it makes the discussion of the commit protocols simpler (see Chapter 12). Owing to these similarities, we do not

---

Algorithm 11.1: Centralized 2PL Transaction Manager (C2PL-TM) Algorithm

---

Input: *msg* : a message
begin
   repeat
      wait for a *msg* ;
      switch *msg* **do**
         case *transaction operation*
            let *op* be the operation ;
            if *op.Type = BT* **then** DP(*op*)   {call DP with operation}
            else C2PL-LM(*op*)   {call LM with operation}
         case *Lock Manager response*   {lock request granted or locks released}
            if *lock request granted* **then**
               find site that stores the requested data item (say H_i) ;
               DP_{Si}(*op*)   {call DP at site S_i with operation}
            else   {must be lock release message}
             inform user about the termination of transaction

         case *Data Processor response*   {operation completed message}
            switch *transaction operation* **do**
               let *op* be the operation ;
            case *R*
               return *op.val* (data item value) to the application
            case *W*
               inform application of completion of the write
            case *C*
               if *commit msg has been received from all participants*
               then
                  inform application of successful completion of
                  transaction ;
                  C2PL-LM(*op*)   {need to release locks}
               else   {wait until commit messages come from all}
               record the arrival of the commit message

            case *A*
               inform application of completion of the abort ;
               C2PL-LM(*op*)   {need to release locks}
   until *forever* ;
end

Algorithm 11.2: Centralized 2PL Lock Manager (C2PL-LM) Algorithm

---

Input: *op* : *Op*
begin
    switch *op.Type* **do**
        case *R or W*   {lock request; see if it can be granted}
            find the lock unit *lu* such that *op.arg* $\subseteq$ *lu* ;
            if *lu is unlocked or lock mode of lu is compatible with op.Type*
            then
                set lock on *lu* in appropriate mode on behalf of transaction
                op.tid ;
                send "Lock granted" to coordinating TM of transaction
            else
                put *op* on a queue for *lu*

        case *C or A*   {locks need to be released}
            foreach *lock unit lu held by transaction* **do**
                release lock on *lu* held by transaction ;
                if *there are operations waiting in queue for lu* **then**
                    find the first operation *O* on queue ;
                    set a lock on *lu* on behalf of *O* ;
                    send "Lock granted" to coordinating TM of transaction
                    O.tid
            send "Locks released" to coordinating TM of transaction
end

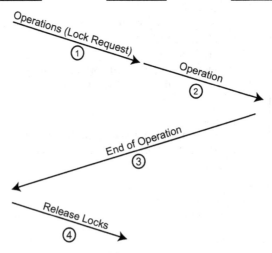

Fig. 11.10 Communication Structure of Distributed 2PL

Algorithm 11.3: Data Processor (DP) Algorithm

Input: $op : Op$
begin

    switch $op.Type$ **do**   {check the type of operation}

        case BT {details to be discussed in Chapter 12}

           do some bookkeeping

        case R

           $op.res \leftarrow$ READ($op.arg$) ;   {database READ operation}

           $op.res \leftarrow$ "Read done"

        case W {database WRITE of val into data item arg}

           WRITE($op.arg, op.val$) ;

           $op.res \leftarrow$ "Write done"

        case C

           COMMIT ;   {execute COMMIT }

           $op.res \leftarrow$ "Commit done"

        case A

           ABORT ;   {execute ABORT }

           $op.res \leftarrow$ "Abort done"

    return op

end

---

give the distributed TM and LM algorithms here. Distributed 2PL algorithms have been used in System R* [Mohan et al., 1986] and in NonStop SQL ([Tandem, 1987, 1988] and [Borr, 1988]).

11.4 Timestamp-Based Concurrency Control Algorithms

Unlike locking-based algorithms, timestamp-based concurrency control algorithms do not attempt to maintain serializability by mutual exclusion. Instead, they select, a priori, a serialization order and execute transactions accordingly. To establish this ordering, the transaction manager assigns each transaction T_i a unique *timestamp*, $ts(T_i)$, at its initiation.

A timestamp is a simple identifier that serves to identify each transaction uniquely and is used for ordering. *Uniqueness* is only one of the properties of timestamp generation. The second property is *monotonicity*. Two timestamps generated by the same transaction manager should be monotonically increasing. Thus timestamps are values derived from a totally ordered domain. It is this second property that differentiates a timestamp from a transaction identifier.

There are a number of ways that timestamps can be assigned. One method is to use a global (system-wide) monotonically increasing counter. However, the maintenance of global counters is a problem in distributed systems. Therefore, it is preferable that each site autonomously assigns timestamps based on its local counter. To maintain uniqueness, each site appends its own identifier to the counter value. Thus the timestamp is a two-tuple of the form ⟨local counter value, site identifier⟩. Note that the site identifier is appended in the least significant position. Hence it serves only to order the timestamps of two transactions that might have been assigned the same local counter value. If each system can access its own system clock, it is possible to use system clock values instead of counter values.

With this information, it is simple to order the execution of the transactions' operations according to their timestamps. Formally, the timestamp ordering (TO) rule can be specified as follows:

TO Rule. Given two conflicting operations O_{ij} and O_{kl} belonging, respectively, to transactions T_i and T_k, O_{ij} is executed before O_{kl} if and only if $ts(T_i) < ts(T_k)$. In this case T_i is said to be the *older* transaction and T_k is said to be the *younger* one.

A scheduler that enforces the TO rule checks each new operation against conflicting operations that have already been scheduled. If the new operation belongs to a transaction that is younger than all the conflicting ones that have already been scheduled, the operation is accepted; otherwise, it is rejected, causing the entire transaction to restart with a *new* timestamp.

A timestamp ordering scheduler that operates in this fashion is guaranteed to generate serializable histories. However, this comparison between the transaction timestamps can be performed only if the scheduler has received all the operations to be scheduled. If operations come to the scheduler one at a time (which is the realistic case), it is necessary to be able to detect, in an efficient manner, if an operation has arrived out of sequence. To facilitate this check, each data item x is assigned two timestamps: a *read timestamp* $[rts(x)]$, which is the largest of the timestamps of the transactions that have read x, and a *write timestamp* $[wts(x)]$, which is the largest of the timestamps of the transactions that have written (updated) x. It is now sufficient to compare the timestamp of an operation with the read and write timestamps of the data item that it wants to access to determine if any transaction with a larger timestamp has already accessed the same data item.

Architecturally (see Figure 10.5), the transaction manager is responsible for assigning a timestamp to each new transaction and attaching this timestamp to each database operation that it passes on to the scheduler. The latter component is responsible for keeping track of read and write timestamps as well as performing the serializability check.

11.4.1 Basic TO Algorithm

The basic TO algorithm is a straightforward implementation of the TO rule. The coordinating transaction manager assigns the timestamp to each transaction, determines the sites where each data item is stored, and sends the relevant operations to these sites. The basic TO transaction manager algorithm (BTO-TM) is depicted in Algorithm 11.4. The histories at each site simply enforce the TO rule. The scheduler algorithm is given in Algorithm 11.5. The data manager is still the one given in Algorithm 11.3. The same data structures and assumptions we used for centralized 2PL algorithms apply to these algorithms as well.

As indicated before, a transaction one of whose operations is rejected by a scheduler is restarted by the transaction manager with a new timestamp. This ensures that the transaction has a chance to execute in its next try. Since the transactions never wait while they hold access rights to data items, the basic TO algorithm never causes deadlocks. However, the penalty of deadlock freedom is potential restart of a transaction numerous times. There is an alternative to the basic TO algorithm that reduces the number of restarts, which we discuss in the next section.

Another detail that needs to be considered relates to the communication between the scheduler and the data processor. When an accepted operation is passed on to the data processor, the scheduler needs to refrain from sending another conflicting, but acceptable operation to the data processor until the first is processed and acknowledged. This is a requirement to ensure that the data processor executes the operations in the order in which the scheduler passes them on. Otherwise, the read and write timestamp values for the accessed data item would not be accurate.

Example 11.8. Assume that the TO scheduler first receives $W_i(x)$ and then receives $W_j(x)$, where $ts(T_i) < ts(T_j)$. The scheduler would accept both operations and pass them on to the data processor. The result of these two operations is that $wts(x) = ts(T_j)$, and we then expect the effect of $W_j(x)$ to be represented in the database. However, if the data processor does not execute them in that order, the effects on the database will be wrong. ♦

The scheduler can enforce the ordering by maintaining a queue for each data item that is used to delay the transfer of the accepted operation until an acknowledgment is received from the data processor regarding the previous operation on the same data item. This detail is not shown in Algorithm 11.5.

Such a complication does not arise in 2PL-based algorithms because the lock manager effectively orders the operations by releasing the locks only after the operation is executed. In one sense the queue that the TO scheduler maintains may be thought of as a lock. However, this does not imply that the history generated by a TO scheduler and a 2PL scheduler would always be equivalent. There are some histories that a TO scheduler would generate that would not be admissible by a 2PL history.

Remember that in the case of strict 2PL algorithms, the releasing of locks is delayed further, until the commit or abort of a transaction. It is possible to develop a strict TO algorithm by using a similar scheme. For example, if $W_i(x)$ is accepted and released to the data processor, the scheduler delays all $R_j(x)$ and $W_j(x)$ operations (for all T_j) until T_i terminates (commits or aborts).

Algorithm 11.4: Basic Timestamp Ordering (BTO-TM) Algorithm

Input: *msg* : a message
begin
  repeat
    wait for a *msg* ;
    switch *msg type* **do**
      case *transaction operation* {operation from application program }
        let *op* be the operation ;
        switch *op.Type* **do**
          case *BT*
            $S \leftarrow \emptyset$; {S is the set of sites where transaction executes
            }
            assign a timestamp to transaction – call it $ts(T)$;
            DP(*op*)   {call DP with operation}
          case *R, W*
            find site that stores the requested data item (say S_i) ;
            BTO-SC$_{S_i}(op, ts(T))$;   {send *op* and *ts* to SC at H_i}
            $S \leftarrow S \cup S_i$ {build list of sites where transaction runs}
          case *A, C*   {send *op* to DPs at all sites where transaction
          runs}
            DP$_S$(*op*)
      case *SC response*   {operation must have been rejected by one
      SC}
        op.Type $\leftarrow$ A;   {prepare an abort message}
        BTO-SC$_S$(*op*, −) ;   {ask other SCs where transaction runs to
        abort}
        restart transaction with a new timestamp
      case *DP response*   {operation completed message}
        switch *transaction operation type* **do**
          let *op* be the operation ;
          case *R* return *op.val* to the application ;
          case *W* inform application of completion of the write ;
          case *C*
            if *commit msg has been received from all participants*
            then
              inform application of successful completion of
              transaction
            else   {wait until commit messages come from all}
             record the arrival of the commit message
          case *A*
            inform application of completion of the abort ;
            BTO-SC(*op*) {need to reset read and write timestamps}
  until *forever* ;
end

Algorithm 11.5: Basic Timestamp Ordering Scheduler (BTO-SC) Algorithm

---

Input: $op : Op; ts(T) : Timestamp$
begin
    retrieve $rts(op.arg)$ and $wts(arg)$;
    save $rts(op.arg)$ and $wts(arg)$;   {might be needed if aborted }
    switch $op.arg$ **do**
        case R
            if $ts(T) > wts(op.arg)$ **then**
                $DP(op)$;   {operation can be executed; send it to the data
                processor}
                $rts(op.arg) \leftarrow ts(T)$
            else
                send "Reject transaction" message to coordinating TM
        case W
            if $ts(T) > rts(op.arg)$ and $ts(T) > wts(op.arg)$ **then**
                $DP(op)$;   {operation can be executed; send it to the data
                processor}
                $rts(op.arg) \leftarrow ts(T)$;
                $wts(op.arg) \leftarrow ts(T)$
            else
                send"Reject transaction" message to coordinating TM
        case A
            forall the $op.arg$ *that has been accessed by transaction* **do**
                reset $rts(op.arg)$ and $wts(op.arg)$ to their initial values
end

11.4.2 Conservative TO Algorithm

We indicated in the preceding section that the basic TO algorithm never causes operations to wait, but instead, restarts them. We also pointed out that even though this is an advantage due to deadlock freedom, it is also a disadvantage, because numerous restarts would have adverse performance implications. The conservative TO algorithms attempt to lower this system overhead by reducing the number of transaction restarts.

Let us first present a technique that is commonly used to reduce the probability of restarts. Remember that a TO scheduler restarts a transaction if a younger conflicting transaction is already scheduled or has been executed. Note that such occurrences increase significantly if, for example, one site is comparatively inactive relative to the others and does not issue transactions for an extended period. In this case its timestamp counter indicates a value that is considerably smaller than the counters of other sites. If the TM at this site then receives a transaction, the operations that are sent to the histories at the other sites will almost certainly be rejected, causing the transaction to restart. Furthermore, the same transaction will restart repeatedly until the timestamp counter value at its originating site reaches a level of parity with the counters of other sites.

The foregoing scenario indicates that it is useful to keep the counters at each site synchronized. However, total synchronization is not only costly—since it requires exchange of messages every time a counter changes—but also unnecessary. Instead, each transaction manager can send its remote operations, rather than histories, to the transaction managers at the other sites. The receiving transaction managers can then compare their own counter values with that of the incoming operation. Any manager whose counter value is smaller than the incoming one adjusts its own counter to one more than the incoming one. This ensures that none of the counters in the system run away or lag behind significantly. Of course, if system clocks are used instead of counters, this approximate synchronization may be achieved automatically as long as the clocks are of comparable speeds.

We can now return to our discussion of conservative TO algorithms. The "conservative" nature of these algorithms relates to the way they execute each operation. The basic TO algorithm tries to execute an operation as soon as it is accepted; it is therefore "aggressive" or "progressive." Conservative algorithms, on the other hand, delay each operation until there is an assurance that no operation with a smaller timestamp can arrive at that scheduler. If this condition can be guaranteed, the scheduler will never reject an operation. However, this delay introduces the possibility of deadlocks.

The basic technique that is used in conservative TO algorithms is based on the following idea: the operations of each transaction are buffered until an ordering can be established so that rejections are not possible, and they are executed in that order. We will consider one possible implementation of the conservative TO algorithm due to Herman and Verjus [1979].

Assume that each scheduler maintains one queue for each transaction manager in the system. The scheduler at site i stores all the operations that it receives from the transaction manager at site j in queue Q_{ij}. Scheduler i has one such queue for each j. When an operation is received from a transaction manager, it is placed in its appropriate queue in increasing timestamp order. The histories at each site execute the operations from these queues in increasing timestamp order.

This scheme will reduce the number of restarts, but it will not guarantee that they will be eliminated completely. Consider the case where at site i the queue for site j (Q_{ij}) is empty. The scheduler at site i will choose an operation [say, $R(x)$] with the smallest timestamp and pass it on to the data processor. However, site j may have sent to i an operation [say, $W(x)$] with a smaller timestamp which may still be in transit in the network. When this operation reaches site i, it will be rejected since it violates the TO rule: it wants to access a data item that is currently being accessed (in an incompatible mode) by another operation with a higher timestamp.

It is possible to design an extremely conservative TO algorithm by insisting that the scheduler choose an operation to be sent to the data processor only if there is at least one operation in each queue. This guarantees that every operation that the scheduler receives in the future will have timestamps greater than or equal to those currently in the queues. Of course, if a transaction manager does not have a transaction to process, it needs to send dummy messages periodically to every scheduler in the system, informing them that the operations that it will send in the future will have timestamps greater than that of the dummy message.

The careful reader will realize that the extremely conservative timestamp ordering scheduler actually executes transactions serially at each site. This is very restrictive. One method that has been employed to overcome this restriction is to group transactions into classes. Transaction classes are defined with respect to their read sets and write sets. It is therefore sufficient to determine the class that a transaction belongs to by comparing the transaction's read set and write set, respectively, with the read set and write set of each class. Thus the conservative TO algorithm can be modified so that instead of requiring the existence, at each site, of one queue for each transaction manager, it is only necessary to have one queue for each transaction class. Alternatively, one might mark each queue with the class to which it belongs. With either of these modifications, the conditions for sending an operation to the data processor are changed. It is no longer necessary to wait until there is at least one operation in each queue; it is sufficient to wait until there is at least one operation in each class to which the transaction belongs. This and other weaker conditions that reduce the waiting delay can be defined and are sufficient. A variant of this method is used in the SDD-1 prototype system [Bernstein et al., 1980b].

11.4.3 Multiversion TO Algorithm

Multiversion TO is another attempt at eliminating the restart overhead cost of transactions. Most of the work on multiversion TO has concentrated on centralized databases, so we present only a brief overview. However, we should indicate that multiversion TO algorithm would be a suitable concurrency control mechanism for DBMSs that are designed to support applications that inherently have a notion of versions of database objects (e.g., engineering databases and document databases).

In multiversion TO, the updates do not modify the database; each write operation creates a new version of that data item. Each version is marked by the timestamp of the transaction that creates it. Thus the multiversion TO algorithm trades storage space for time. In doing so, it processes each transaction on a state of the database that it would have seen if the transactions were executed serially in timestamp order.

The existence of versions is transparent to users who issue transactions simply by referring to data items, not to any specific version. The transaction manager assigns a timestamp to each transaction, which is also used to keep track of the timestamps of each version. The operations are processed by the histories as follows:

1. A $R_i(x)$ is translated into a read on one version of x. This is done by finding a version of x (say, x_v) such that $ts(x_v)$ is the largest timestamp less than $ts(T_i)$. $R_i(x_v)$ is then sent to the data processor to read x_v. This case is depicted in

Figure 11.11a, which shows that R_i can read the version (x_v) that it would have read had it arrived in timestamp order.

2. A $W_i(x)$ is translated into $W_i(x_w)$ so that $ts(x_w) = ts(T_i)$ and sent to the data processor if and only if no other transaction with a timestamp greater than $ts(T_i)$ has read the value of a version of x (say, x_r) such that $ts(x_r) > ts(x_w)$. In other words, if the scheduler has already processed a $R_j(x_r)$ such that

$$ts(T_i) < ts(x_r) < ts(T_j)$$

then $W_i(x)$ is rejected. This case is depicted in Figure 11.11b, which shows that if W_i is accepted, it would create a version (x_w) that R_j should have read, but did not since the version was not available when R_j was executed – it, instead, read version x_k, which results in the wrong history.

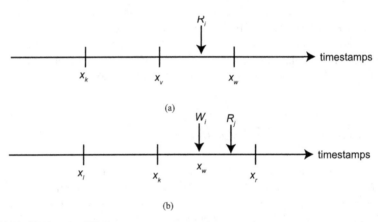

Fig. 11.11 Multiversion TO Cases

A scheduler that processes the read and the write requests of transactions according to the rules noted above is guaranteed to generate serializable histories. To save space, the versions of the database may be purged from time to time. This should be done when the distributed DBMS is certain that it will no longer receive a transaction that needs to access the purged versions.

11.5 Optimistic Concurrency Control Algorithms

The concurrency control algorithms discussed in Sections 11.3 and 11.4 are pessimistic in nature. In other words, they assume that the conflicts between transactions are quite frequent and do not permit a transaction to access a data item if there is a conflicting transaction that accesses that data item. Thus the execution of any operation of a transaction follows the sequence of phases: validation (V), read (R), computation (C), write (W) (Figure 11.12).[2] Generally, this sequence is valid for an update transaction as well as for each of its operations.

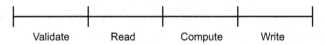

Validate   Read   Compute   Write

Fig. 11.12 Phases of Pessimistic Transaction Execution

Optimistic algorithms, on the other hand, delay the validation phase until just before the write phase (Figure 11.13). Thus an operation submitted to an optimistic scheduler is never delayed. The read, compute, and write operations of each transaction are processed freely without updating the actual database. Each transaction initially makes its updates on local copies of data items. The validation phase consists of checking if these updates would maintain the consistency of the database. If the answer is affirmative, the changes are made global (i.e., written into the actual database). Otherwise, the transaction is aborted and has to restart.

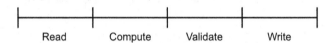

Read   Compute   Validate   Write

Fig. 11.13 Phases of Optimistic Transaction Execution

It is possible to design locking-based optimistic concurrency control algorithms (see [Bernstein et al., 1987]). However, the original optimistic proposals [Thomas, 1979; Kung and Robinson, 1981] are based on timestamp ordering. Therefore, we describe only the optimistic approach using timestamps.

The algorithm that we discuss was proposed by Kung and Robinson [1981] and was later extended for distributed DBMS by Ceri and Owicki [1982]. This is not the only extension of the model to distributed databases, however (see, for example, [Sinha et al., 1985]). It differs from pessimistic TO-based algorithms not only by being optimistic but also in its assignment of timestamps. Timestamps are associated only with transactions, not with data items (i.e., there are no read or write timestamps). Furthermore, timestamps are not assigned to transactions at their initiation but at the beginning of their validation step. This is because the timestamps are needed only during the validation phase, and as we will see shortly, their early assignment may cause unnecessary transaction rejections.

Each transaction T_i is subdivided (by the transaction manager at the originating site) into a number of subtransactions, each of which can execute at many sites. Notationally, let us denote by T_{ij} a subtransaction of T_i that executes at site j. Until

---

[2] We consider only the update transactions in this discussion because they are the ones that cause consistency problems. Read-only transactions do not have the computation and write phases. Furthermore, we assume that the write phase includes the commit action.

the validation phase, each local execution follows the sequence depicted in Figure 11.13. At that point a timestamp is assigned to the transaction which is copied to all its subtransactions. The local validation of T_{ij} is performed according to the following rules, which are mutually exclusive.

Rule 1. If all transactions T_k where $ts(T_k) < ts(T_{ij})$ have completed their write phase before T_{ij} has started its read phase (Figure 11.14a),[3] validation succeeds, because transaction executions are in serial order.

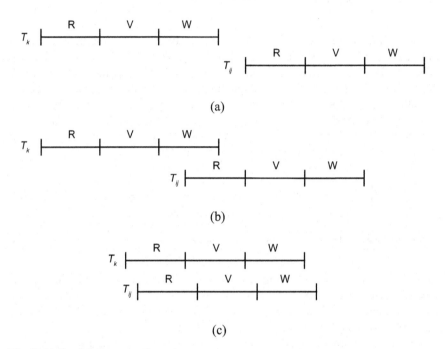

(a)

(b)

(c)

Fig. 11.14 Possible Execution Scenarios

Rule 2. If there is any transaction T_k such that $ts(T_k) < ts(T_{ij})$, and which completes its write phase while T_{ij} is in its read phase (Figure 11.14b), the validation succeeds if $WS(T_k) \cap RS(T_{ij}) = \emptyset$.

Rule 3. If there is any transaction T_k such that $ts(T_k) < ts(T_{ij})$, and which completes its read phase before T_{ij} completes its read phase (Figure 11.14c), the validation succeeds if $WS(T_k) \cap RS(T_{ij}) = \emptyset$, and $WS(T_k) \cap WS(T_{ij}) = \emptyset$.

Rule 1 is obvious; it indicates that the transactions are actually executed serially in their timestamp order. Rule 2 ensures that none of the data items updated by T_k

---

[3] Following the convention we have adopted, we omit the computation step in this figure and in the subsequent discussion. Thus timestamps are assigned at the end of the read phase.

are read by T_{ij} and that T_k finishes writing its updates into the database before T_{ij} starts writing. Thus the updates of T_{ij} will not be overwritten by the updates of T_k. Rule 3 is similar to Rule 2, but does not require that T_k finish writing before T_{ij} starts writing. It simply requires that the updates of T_k not affect the read phase or the write phase of T_{ij}.

Once a transaction is locally validated to ensure that the local database consistency is maintained, it also needs to be globally validated to ensure that the mutual consistency rule is obeyed. Unfortunately, there is no known optimistic method of doing this. A transaction is globally validated if all the transactions that precede it in the serialization order (at that site) terminate (either by committing or aborting). This is a pessimistic method since it performs global validation early and delays a transaction. However, it guarantees that transactions execute in the same order at each site.

An advantage of optimistic concurrency control algorithms is their potential to allow a higher level of concurrency. It has been shown that when transaction conflicts are very rare, the optimistic mechanism performs better than locking [Kung and Robinson, 1981]. A major problem with optimistic algorithms is the higher storage cost. To validate a transaction, the optimistic mechanism has to store the read and the write sets of several other terminated transactions. Specifically, the read and write sets of terminated transactions that were in progress when transaction T_{ij} arrived at site j need to be stored in order to validate T_{ij}. Obviously, this increases the storage cost.

Another problem is starvation. Consider a situation in which the validation phase of a long transaction fails. In subsequent trials it is still possible that the validation will fail repeatedly. Of course, it is possible to solve this problem by permitting the transaction exclusive access to the database after a specified number of trials. However, this reduces the level of concurrency to a single transaction. The exact "mix" of transactions that would cause an intolerable level of restarts is an issue that remains to be studied.

11.6 Deadlock Management

As we indicated before, any locking-based concurrency control algorithm may result in deadlocks, since there is mutual exclusion of access to shared resources (data) and transactions may wait on locks. Furthermore, we have seen that some TO-based algorithms that require the waiting of transactions (e.g., strict TO) may also cause deadlocks. Therefore, the distributed DBMS requires special procedures to handle them.

A deadlock can occur because transactions wait for one another. Informally, a deadlock situation is a set of requests that can never be granted by the concurrency control mechanism.

Example 11.9. Consider two transactions T_i and T_j that hold write locks on two entities x and y [i.e., $wl_i(x)$ and $wl_j(y)$]. Suppose that T_i now issues a $rl_i(y)$ or a $wl_i(y)$. Since y is currently locked by transaction T_j, T_i will have to wait until T_j

releases its write lock on y. However, if during this waiting period, T_j now requests a lock (read or write) on x, there will be a deadlock. This is because, T_i will be blocked waiting for T_j to release its lock on y while T_j will be waiting for T_i to release its lock on x. In this case, the two transactions T_i and T_j will wait indefinitely for each other to release their respective locks.   ♦

A deadlock is a permanent phenomenon. If one exists in a system, it will not go away unless outside intervention takes place. This outside interference may come from the user, the system operator, or the software system (the operating system or the distributed DBMS).

A useful tool in analyzing deadlocks is a *wait-for graph* (WFG). A WFG is a directed graph that represents the wait-for relationship among transactions. The nodes of this graph represent the concurrent transactions in the system. An edge $T_i \to T_j$ exists in the WFG if transaction T_i is waiting for T_j to release a lock on some entity. Figure 11.15 depicts the WFG for Example 11.9.

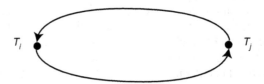

Fig. 11.15 A WFG Example

Using the WFG, it is easier to indicate the condition for the occurrence of a deadlock. A deadlock occurs when the WFG contains a cycle. We should indicate that the formation of the WFG is more complicated in distributed systems, since two transactions that participate in a deadlock condition may be running at different sites. We call this situation a *global deadlock*. In distributed systems, then, it is not sufficient that each local distributed DBMS form a *local wait-for graph* (LWFG) at each site; it is also necessary to form a *global wait-for graph* (GWFG), which is the union of all the LWFGs.

Example 11.10. Consider four transactions T_1, T_2, T_3, and T_4 with the following wait-for relationship among them: $T_1 \to T_2 \to T_3 \to T_4 \to T_1$. If T_1 and T_2 run at site 1 while T_3 and T_4 run at site 2, the LWFGs for the two sites are shown in Figure 11.16a. Notice that it is not possible to detect a deadlock simply by examining the two LWFGs, because the deadlock is global. The deadlock can easily be detected, however, by examining the GWFG where intersite waiting is shown by dashed lines (Figure 11.16b).   ♦

There are three known methods for handling deadlocks: prevention, avoidance, and detection and resolution. In the remainder of this section we discuss each approach in more detail.

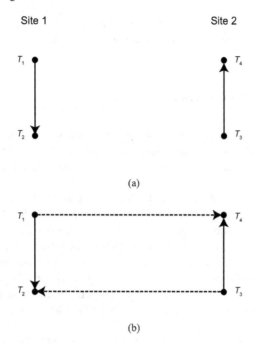

Fig. 11.16 Difference between LWFG and GWFG

11.6.1 Deadlock Prevention

Deadlock prevention methods guarantee that deadlocks cannot occur in the first place. Thus the transaction manager checks a transaction when it is first initiated and does not permit it to proceed if it may cause a deadlock. To perform this check, it is required that all of the data items that will be accessed by a transaction be predeclared. The transaction manager then permits a transaction to proceed if all the data items that it will access are available. Otherwise, the transaction is not permitted to proceed. The transaction manager reserves all the data items that are predeclared by a transaction that it allows to proceed.

Unfortunately, such systems are not very suitable for database environments. The fundamental problem is that it is usually difficult to know precisely which data items will be accessed by a transaction. Access to certain data items may depend on conditions that may not be resolved until run time. For example, in the reservation transaction that we developed in Example 10.3, access to CID and CNAME is conditional upon the availability of free seats. To be safe, the system would thus need to consider the maximum set of data items, even if they end up not being accessed. This would certainly reduce concurrency. Furthermore, there is additional overhead in evaluating whether a transaction can proceed safely. On the other hand, such systems require no run-time support, which reduces the overhead. It has the additional advantage that it is not necessary to abort and restart a transaction due to deadlocks. This not only reduces the overhead but also makes such methods suitable for systems that have no provisions for undoing processes.[4]

11.6.2 Deadlock Avoidance

Deadlock avoidance schemes either employ concurrency control techniques that will never result in deadlocks or require that potential deadlock situations are detected in advance and steps are taken such that they will not occur. We consider both of these cases.

The simplest means of avoiding deadlocks is to order the resources and insist that each process request access to these resources in that order. This solution was long ago proposed for operating systems. A revised version has been proposed for database systems as well [Garcia-Molina, 1979]. Accordingly, the lock units in the distributed database are ordered and transactions always request locks in that order. This ordering of lock units may be done either globally or locally at each site. In the latter case, it is also necessary to order the sites and require that transactions which access data items at multiple sites request their locks by visiting the sites in the predefined order.

Another alternative is to make use of transaction timestamps to prioritize transactions and resolve deadlocks by aborting transactions with higher (or lower) priorities. To implement this type of prevention method, the lock manager is modified as follows. If a lock request of a transaction T_i is denied, the lock manager does not automatically force T_i to wait. Instead, it applies a prevention test to the requesting transaction and the transaction that currently holds the lock (say T_j). If the test is passed, T_i is permitted to wait for T_j; otherwise, one transaction or the other is aborted.

Examples of this approach is the WAIT-DIE and WOUND-WAIT algorithms [Rosenkrantz et al., 1978], also used in the MADMAN DBMS [GE, 1976]. These algorithms are based on the assignment of timestamps to transactions. WAIT-DIE is a non-preemptive algorithm in that if the lock request of T_i is denied because the lock is held by T_j, it never preempts T_j, following the rule:

WAIT-DIE Rule. If T_i requests a lock on a data item that is already locked by T_j, T_i is permitted to wait if and only if T_i is older than T_j. If T_i is younger than T_j, then T_i is aborted and restarted with the same timestamp.

A preemptive version of the same idea is the WOUND-WAIT algorithm, which follows the rule:

---

[4] This is not a significant advantage since most systems have to be able to undo transactions for reliability purposes, as we will see in Chapter 12.

WOUND-WAIT Rule. If T_i requests a lock on a data item that is already locked by T_j, then T_i is permitted to wait if only if it is younger than T_j; otherwise, T_j is aborted and the lock is granted to T_i.

The rules are specified from the viewpoint of T_i: T_i waits, T_i dies, and T_i wounds T_j. In fact, the result of wounding and dying are the same: the affected transaction is aborted and restarted. With this perspective, the two rules can be specified as follows:

if $ts(T_i) < ts(T_j)$ **then** T_i waits **else** T_i dies   (WAIT-DIE)

if $ts(T_i) < ts(T_j)$ **then** T_j is wounded **else** T_i waits   (WOUND-WAIT)

Notice that in both algorithms the younger transaction is aborted. The difference between the two algorithms is whether or not they preempt active transactions. Also note that the WAIT-DIE algorithm prefers younger transactions and kills older ones. Thus an older transaction tends to wait longer and longer as it gets older. By contrast, the WOUND-WAIT rule prefers the older transaction since it never waits for a younger one. One of these methods, or a combination, may be selected in implementing a deadlock prevention algorithm.

Deadlock avoidance methods are more suitable than prevention schemes for database environments. Their fundamental drawback is that they require run-time support for deadlock management, which adds to the run-time overhead of transaction execution.

11.6.3 Deadlock Detection and Resolution

Deadlock detection and resolution is the most popular and best-studied method. Detection is done by studying the GWFG for the formation of cycles. We will discuss means of doing this in considerable detail. Resolution of deadlocks is typically done by the selection of one or more *victim* transaction(s) that will be preempted and aborted in order to break the cycles in the GWFG. Under the assumption that the cost of preempting each member of a set of deadlocked transactions is known, the problem of selecting the minimum total-cost set for breaking the deadlock cycle has been shown to be a difficult (NP-complete) problem [Leung and Lai, 1979]. However, there are some factors that affect this choice [Bernstein et al., 1987]:

1. The amount of effort that has already been invested in the transaction. This effort will be lost if the transaction is aborted.

2. The cost of aborting the transaction. This cost generally depends on the number of updates that the transaction has already performed.

3. The amount of effort it will take to finish executing the transaction. The scheduler wants to avoid aborting a transaction that is almost finished. To do this, it must be able to predict the future behavior of active transactions (e.g., based on the transaction's type).

4. The number of cycles that contain the transaction. Since aborting a transaction breaks all cycles that contain it, it is best to abort transactions that are part of more than one cycle (if such transactions exist).

Now we can return to deadlock detection. There are three fundamental methods of detecting distributed deadlocks, referred as *centralized, distributed*, and *hierarchical deadlock detection*.

11.6.3.1 Centralized Deadlock Detection

In the centralized deadlock detection approach, one site is designated as the deadlock detector for the entire system. Periodically, each lock manager transmits its LWFG to the deadlock detector, which then forms the GWFG and looks for cycles in it. Actually, the lock managers need only send changes in their graphs (i.e., the newly created or deleted edges) to the deadlock detector. The length of intervals for transmitting this information is a system design decision: the smaller the interval, the smaller the delays due to undetected deadlocks, but the larger the communication cost.

Centralized deadlock detection has been proposed for distributed INGRES. This method is simple and would be a very natural choice if the concurrency control algorithm were centralized 2PL. However, the issues of vulnerability to failure, and high communication overhead, must also be considered.

11.6.3.2 Hierarchical Deadlock Detection

An alternative to centralized deadlock detection is the building of a hierarchy of deadlock detectors [Menasce and Muntz, 1979] (see Figure 11.17). Deadlocks that are local to a single site would be detected at that site using the LWFG. Each site also sends its LWFG to the deadlock detector at the next level. Thus, distributed deadlocks involving two or more sites would be detected by a deadlock detector in the next lowest level that has control over these sites. For example, a deadlock at site 1 would be detected by the local deadlock detector (*DD*) at site 1 (denoted DD_{21}, 2 for level 2, 1 for site 1). If, however, the deadlock involves sites 1 and 2, then DD_{11} detects it. Finally, if the deadlock involves sites 1 and 4, DD_{0x} detects it, where x is either one of 1, 2, 3, or 4.

The hierarchical deadlock detection method reduces the dependence on the central site, thus reducing the communication cost. It is, however, considerably more complicated to implement and would involve non-trivial modifications to the lock and transaction manager algorithms.

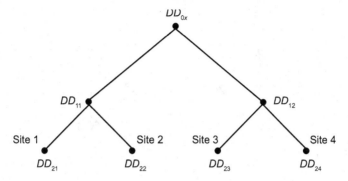

Fig. 11.17 Hierarchical Deadlock Detection

11.6.3.3 Distributed Deadlock Detection

Distributed deadlock detection algorithms delegate the responsibility of detecting deadlocks to individual sites. Thus, as in the hierarchical deadlock detection, there are local deadlock detectors at each site that communicate their LWFGs with one another (in fact, only the potential deadlock cycles are transmitted). Among the various distributed deadlock detection algorithms, the one implemented in System R* [Obermarck, 1982; Mohan et al., 1986] seems to be the more widely known and referenced. We therefore briefly outline that method, basing the discussion on [Obermarck, 1982].

The LWFG at each site is formed and is modified as follows:

1. Since each site receives the potential deadlock cycles from other sites, these edges are added to the LWFGs.

2. The edges in the LWFG which show that local transactions are waiting for transactions at other sites are joined with edges in the LWFGs which show that remote transactions are waiting for local ones.

Example 11.11. Consider the example depicted in Figure 11.16. The local WFG for the two sites are modified as shown in Figure 11.18.   ♦

Local deadlock detectors look for two things. If there is a cycle that does not include the external edges, there is a local deadlock that can be handled locally. If, on the other hand, there is a cycle involving these external edges, there is a potential distributed deadlock and this cycle information has to be communicated to other deadlock detectors. In the case of Example 11.11, the possibility of such a distributed deadlock is detected by both sites.

A question that needs to be answered at this point is to whom to transmit the information. Obviously, it can be transmitted to all deadlock detectors in the system. In the absence of any more information, this is the only alternative, but it incurs a high overhead. If, however, one knows whether the transaction is ahead or behind in the deadlock cycle, the information can be transmitted forward or backward along

Site 1   Site 2

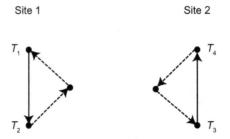

Fig. 11.18 Modified LWFGs

the sites in this cycle. The receiving site then modifies its LWFG as discussed above, and checks for deadlocks. Obviously, there is no need to transmit along the deadlock cycle in both the forward and backward directions. In the case of Example 11.11, site 1 would send it to site 2 in both forward and backward transmission along the deadlock cycle.

The distributed deadlock detection algorithms require uniform modification to the lock managers at each site. This uniformity makes them easier to implement. However, there is the potential for excessive message transmission. This happens, for example, in the case of Example 11.11: site 1 sends its potential deadlock information to site 2, and site 2 sends its information to site 1. In this case the deadlock detectors at both sites will detect the deadlock. Besides causing unnecessary message transmission, there is the additional problem that each site may choose a different victim to abort. Obermack's algorithm solves the problem by using transaction timestamps as well as the following rule. Let the path that has the potential of causing a distributed deadlock in the local WFG of a site be $T_i \rightarrow \cdots \rightarrow T_j$. A local deadlock detector forwards the cycle information only if $ts(T_i) < ts(T_j)$. This reduces the average number of message transmissions by one-half. In the case of Example 11.11, site 1 has a path $T_1 \rightarrow T_2 \rightarrow T_3$, whereas site 2 has a path $T_3 \rightarrow T_4 \rightarrow T_1$. Therefore, assuming that the subscripts of each transaction denote their timestamp, only site 1 will send information to site 2.

11.7 "Relaxed" Concurrency Control

For most of this chapter, we focused only on distributed concurrency control algorithms that are designed for flat transactions and enforce serializability as the correctness criterion. This is the baseline case. There have been studies that (a) relax serializability in arguing for correctness of concurrent execution, and (b) consider other transaction models, primarily nested ones. We will briefly review these in this section.

11.7.1 Non-Serializable Histories

Serializability is a fairly simple and elegant concept which can be enforced with acceptable overhead. However, it is considered to be too "strict" for certain applications since it does not consider as correct certain histories that might be argued as reasonable. We have shown one case when we discussed the ordered shared lock concept. In addition, consider the Reservation transaction of Example 10.10. One can argue that the history generated by two concurrent executions of this transaction can be non-serializable, but correct – one may do the Airline reservation first and then do the Hotel reservation while the other one reverses the order – as long as both executions successfully terminate. The question, however, is how one can generalize these intuitive observations. The solution is to observe and exploit the "semantics" of these transactions.

There have been a number of proposals for exploiting transaction semantics. Of particular interest for distributed DBMS is one class that depends on identifying transaction *steps*, which may consist of a single operation or a set of operations, and establishing how transactions can interleave with each other between steps. Garcia-Molina [1983] classifies transactions into classes such that transactions in the same class are *compatible* and can interleave arbitrarily while transactions in different classes are incompatible and have to be synchronized. The synchronization is based on semantic notions, allowing more concurrency than serializability. The use of the concept of transaction classes can be traced back to SDD-1 [Bernstein et al., 1980b].

The concept of compatibility is refined by Lynch [1983b] and several levels of compatibility among transactions are defined. These levels are structured hierarchically so that interleavings at higher levels include those at lower levels. Furthermore, Lynch [1983b] introduces the concept of *breakpoints* within transactions, which represent points at which other transactions can interleave. This is an alternative to the use of compatibility sets.

Another work along these lines uses breakpoints to indicate the interleaving points, but does not require that the interleavings be hierarchical [Farrag and Özsu, 1989]. A transaction is modeled as consisting of a number of steps. Each step consists of a sequence of atomic operations and a breakpoint at the end of these operations. For each breakpoint in a transaction the set of transaction types that are allowed to interleave at that breakpoint is specified. A correctness criterion called *relative consistency* is defined based on the correct interleavings among transactions. Intuitively, a relatively consistent history is equivalent to a history that is stepwise serial (i.e., the operations and breakpoint of each step appear without interleaving), and in which a step (T_{ik}) of transaction T_i interleaves two consecutive steps $(T_{jm}$ and $T_{jm+1})$ of transaction T_j only if transactions of T_i's type are allowed to interleave T_{jm} at its breakpoint. It can be shown that some of the relatively consistent histories are not serializable, but are still "correct" [Farrag and Özsu, 1989].

A unifying framework that combines the approaches of Lynch [1983b] and Farrag and Özsu [1989] has been proposed by Agrawal et al. [1994]. A correctness criterion called *semantic relative atomicity* is introduced which provides finer interleavings and more concurrency.

The above mentioned relaxed correctness criteria have formal underpinnings similar to serializability, allowing their formal analysis. However, these have not been extended to distributed DBMS even though this possibility exists.

11.7.2 Nested Distributed Transactions

We introduced the nested transaction model in the previous chapter. The concurrent execution of nested transactions is interesting, especially since they are good candidates for distributed execution.

Let us first consider closed nested transactions [Moss, 1985]. The concurrency control of nested transactions have generally followed a locking-based approach. The following rules govern the management of the locks and the completion of transaction execution in the case of closed nested transactions:

1. Each subtransaction executes as a transaction and upon completion transfers its lock to its parent transaction.

2. A parent inherits both the locks and the updates of its committed subtransactions.

3. The inherited state will be visible only to descendants of the inheriting parent transaction. However, to access the sate, a descendant must acquire appropriate locks. Lock conflicts are determined as for flat transactions, except that one ignores inherited locks retained by ancestor's of the requesting subtransaction.

4. If a subtransaction aborts, then all locks and updates that the subtransaction and its descendants are discarded. The parent of an aborted subtransaction need not, but may, choose to abort.

From the perspective of ACID properties, closed nested transactions relax durability since the effects of successfully completed subtransactions can be erased if an ancestor transaction aborts. They also relax the isolation property in a limited way since they share their state with other subtransactions within the same nested transaction.

The distributed execution potential of nested transactions is obvious. After all, nested transactions are meant to improve intra-transaction concurrency and one can view each subtransaction as a potential unit of distribution if data are also appropriately distributed.

However, from the perspective of lock management, some care has to be observed. When subtransactions release their locks to their parents, these lock releases cannot be reflected in the lock tables automatically. The subtransaction commit commands do not have the same semantics as flat transactions.

Open nested transactions are even more relaxed than their closed nested counterparts. They have been called "anarchic" forms of nested transactions [Gray and Reuter, 1993]. The open nested transaction model is best exemplified in the saga model [Garcia-Molina and Salem, 1987; Garcia-Molina et al., 1990] which was discussed in Section 10.3.2.

From the perspective of lock management, open nested transactions are easy to deal with. The locks held by a subtransaction are released as soon as it commits or aborts and this is reflected in the lock tables.

A variant of open nested transactions with precise and formal semantics is the *multilevel transaction* model [Weikum, 1986; Weikum and Schek, 1984; Beeri et al., 1988; Weikum, 1991]. Multilevel transactions "are a variant of open nested transactions in which the subtransactions correspond to operations at different levels of a layered system architecture" [Weikum and Hasse, 1993]. We introduce the concept with an example taken from [Weikum, 1991]. We consider a transaction specification language which allows users to write transactions involving abstract operations so as to be able to exploit application semantics.

Consider two transactions that transfer funds from one bank account to another:

T_1: Withdraw(o,x) T_2: Withdraw(o,y)
     Deposit(p,x)   Deposit(p,y)

The notation here is that each T_i withdraws x (y) amount from account o and deposits that amount to account p. The semantics of Withdraw is test-and-withdraw to ensure that the account balance is sufficient to meet the withdrawal request. In relational systems, each of these abstract operations will be translated to tuple operations Select (*Sel*), and Update (*Upd*) which will, in turn, be translated into page-level Read and Write operations (assuming o is on page r and p is on page w). This results in a layered abstraction of transaction execution as depicted in Figure 11.19.

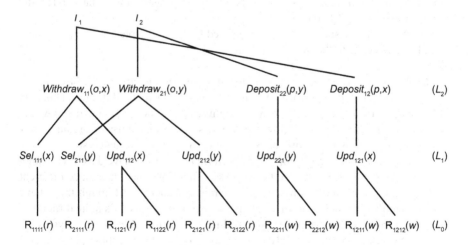

Fig. 11.19 Multilevel Transaction Example (Based on [Weikum, 1991])

The traditional method of dealing with these types of histories is to develop a scheduler that enforces serializability at the lowest level (L_0). This, however, reduces the level of concurrency since it does not take into account application semantics and the granularity of synchronization is too coarse. Abstracting from the lower-level details can provide higher concurrency. For example, the page-level history (L_0) in Figure 11.19 is not serializable with respect to transactions T_1 and T_2, but the tuple-level history L_1 is serializable ($T_2 \rightarrow T_1$). When one goes up to level L_2, it is possible to make use of the semantics of the abstract operations (i.e., their commutativity) to provide even more concurrency. Therefore, *multilevel serializability* is defined to reason about the serializability of multilevel histories and *multilevel histories* are proposed to enforce it [Weikum, 1991].

11.8 Conclusion

In this chapter we discussed distributed currency control algorithms that provide the isolation and consistency properties of transactions. The distributed concurrency control mechanism of a distributed DBMS ensures that the consistency of the distributed database is maintained and is therefore one of the fundamental components of a distributed DBMS. This is evidenced by the significant amount of research that has been conducted in this area.

Our discussion in this chapter assumed that both the hardware and the software components of the computer systems were totally reliable. Even though this assumption is completely unrealistic, it has served a didactic purpose. It has permitted us to focus only on the concurrency control aspects, leaving to another chapter the features that need to be added to a distributed DBMS to make it reliable in an unreliable environment. We have also assumed a non-replicated distributed database, leaving replication issues to Chapter 13.

There are a few issues that we have omitted from this chapter. We mention them here for the benefit of the interested reader.

1. *Performance evaluation of concurrency control algorithms.* We have not explicitly included performance analysis results or methodologies. This may be somewhat surprising given the significant number of papers that have appeared in the literature. However, the reasons for this omission are numerous. First, there is no comprehensive and definitive performance study of concurrency control algorithms. The performance studies have developed rather haphazardly and for specific purposes. Therefore, each has made different assumptions and has measured different parameters. Although these have identified a number of important performance tradeoffs, it is quite difficult, if not impossible, to make meaningful generalizations that extend beyond the obvious. Second, the analytical methods for conducting these performance analysis studies have not been developed sufficiently.
   The relative performance characteristics of distributed concurrency methods is less understood than their centralized counterparts [Thomasian, 1996]. The main reason for this is the complexity of these algorithms. This complexity

has resulted in a number of simplifying assumptions such as a fully replicated database, fully interconnected network, network delays represented by
simplistic queueing models (M/M/1), etc. [Thomasian, 1996].

2. *Other concurrency control methods.* There is another class of concurrency
control algorithms, called "serializability graph testing methods," which we
have not mentioned in this chapter. Such mechanisms work by explicitly
building a *dependency* (or *serializability*) *graph* and checking it for cycles.
The dependency (serializability) graph of a history H, denoted $DG(H)$, is a
directed graph representing the conflict relations among the transactions in H.
The nodes of this graph are the set of transactions in H [i.e., each transaction T_i
in H is represented by a node in $DG(H)$]. An edge (T_i, T_j) exists in $DG(SH)$ if
and only if there is an operation in T_i that conflicts with and precedes another
operation in T_j.
Schedulers update their dependency graphs whenever one of the following
conditions is fulfilled: (1) a new transaction starts in the system, (2) a read or
a write operation is received by the scheduler, (3) a transaction terminates, or
(4) a transaction aborts.
It is now possible to talk about "correct" concurrency control algorithms based
on the dependency graph. Given a history H, if its dependency graph $DG(S)$
is acyclic, then H is serializable. In the distributed case we may use a global
dependency graph, which can be formed by taking the union of the local
dependency graphs and further annotating each transaction by the identifier
of the site where it is executed. It is then necessary to show that the global
dependency graph is acyclic.

Example 11.12. The dependency graph of history H_1 discussed in Example
11.6 is given in Figure 11.20. Since the graph is acyclic, H_1 is serializable. ♦

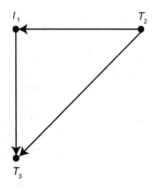

Fig. 11.20 Dependency Graph

3. *Assumptions about transactions.* In our discussions, we did not make any
distinction between read-only transactions and update transactions. It is pos-

sible to improve significantly the performance of transactions that only read data items, or of systems with a high ratio of read-only transactions to update transactions. These issues are beyond the scope of this book.

We have also treated read and write locks in an identical fashion. It is possible to differentiate between them and develop concurrency control algorithms that permit "lock conversion," whereby transactions can obtain locks in one mode and then modify their lock modes as they change their requirements. Typically, the conversion is from read locks to write locks.

4. *More "general" algorithms.* There are some indications which suggest that it should be possible to study the two fundamental concurrency control primitives (i.e., locking and timestamp ordering) using a unifying framework. Three major indications are worth mentioning. First, it is possible to develop both pessimistic and optimistic algorithms based on either one of the primitives. Second, a strict TO algorithm performs similarly to a locking algorithm, since it delays the acceptance of a transaction until all older ones are terminated. This does not mean that all histories which can be generated by a strict TO scheduler would be permitted by a 2PL scheduler. However, this similarity is interesting. Finally, it is possible to develop hybrid algorithms that use both timestamp ordering and locking. Furthermore, it is possible to state precisely rules for their interaction.

One study [Farrag and Özsu, 1985, 1987] has resulted in the development of a theoretical framework for the uniform treatment of both of these primitives. Based on this theoretical foundation, it was shown that 2PL and TO algorithms are two endpoints of a range of algorithms that can be generated by a more general concurrency control algorithm. This study, which is only for centralized database systems, is significant not only because it indicates that locking and timestamp ordering are related, but also because it would be interesting to study the nature and characteristics of the algorithms that lie between these two endpoints. In addition, such a uniform framework may be helpful in conducting comprehensive and internally consistent performance studies.

5. *Transaction execution models.* The algorithms that we have described all assume a computational model where the transaction manager at the originating site of a transaction coordinates the execution of each database operation of that transaction. This is called *centralized execution* [Carey and Livny, 1988]. It is also possible to consider a *distributed execution* model where a transaction is decomposed into a set of subtransactions each of which is allocated to one site where the transaction manager coordinates its execution. This is intuitively more attractive because it may permit load balancing across the multiple sites of a distributed database. However, the performance studies indicate that distributed computation performs better only under light load.

11.9 Bibliographic Notes

As indicated earlier, distributed concurrency control has been a very popular area of study. [Bernstein and Goodman, 1981] is a comprehensive study of the fundamental primitives which also lays down the rules for building hybrid algorithms. The issues that are addressed in this chapter are discussed in much more detail in [Cellary et al., 1988; Bernstein et al., 1987; Papadimitriou, 1986] and [Gray and Reuter, 1993].

Nested transaction models and their specific concurrency control algorithms have been the subjects of some study. Specific results can be found in [Moss, 1985; Lynch, 1983a; Lynch and Merritt, 1986; Fekete et al., 1987a,b; Goldman, 1987; Beeri et al., 1989; Fekete et al., 1989] and more recently in [Lynch et al., 1993].

The work on transaction management with semantic knowledge is presented in [Lynch, 1983b; Garcia-Molina, 1983], and [Farrag and Özsu, 1989]. The processing of read-only transactions is discussed in [Garcia-Molina and Wiederhold, 1982]. Transaction groups [Skarra et al., 1986; Skarra, 1989] also exploit a correctness criterion called *semantic patterns* that is more relaxed than serializability. Further-more, work on the ARIES system [Haderle et al., 1992] is also within this class of algorithms. In particular, [Rothermel and Mohan, 1989] discusses ARIES within the context of nested transactions. Epsilon serializability [Ramamritham and Pu, 1995; Wu et al., 1997] and NT/PV model [Kshemkalyani and Singhal, 1994] are other "relaxed" correctness criteria. An algorithm based on ordering transactions using *serialization numbers* is discussed in [Halici and Dogac, 1989].

There are a number of papers that discuss the results of performance evaluation studies on distributed concurrency control algorithms. These include [Gelenbe and Sevcik, 1978; Garcia-Molina, 1979; Potier and LeBlanc, 1980; Menasce and Nakan-ishi, 1982a,b; Lin, 1981; Lin and Nolte, 1982, 1983; Goodman et al., 1983; Sevcik, 1983; Carey and Stonebraker, 1984; Merrett and Rallis, 1985; Özsu, 1985b,a; Koon and Özsu, 1986; Tsuchiya et al., 1986; Li, 1987; Agrawal et al., 1987; Bhide, 1988; Carey and Livny, 1988], and [Carey and Livny, 1991]. [Liang and Tripathi, 1996] studies the performance of sagas and Thomasian has conducted a series of perfor-mance studies that focus on various aspects of transaction processing in centralized and distributed DBMSs [Thomasian, 1993, 1998; Yu et al., 1989]. [Kumar, 1996] focuses on the performance of centralized DBMSs; the performance of distributed concurrency control methods are discussed in [Thomasian, 1996] and [Cellary et al., 1988]. An early but comprehensive review of deadlock management is [Isloor and Marsland, 1980]. Most of the work on distributed deadlock management has been on detection and resolution (see, e.g., [Obermarck, 1982; Elmagarmid et al., 1988]). Two surveys of the important algorithms are included in [Elmagarmid, 1986] and [Knapp, 1987]. A more recent survey is [Singhal, 1989]. There are two annotated bibliographies on the deadlock problem which do not emphasize the database issues but consider the problem in general: [Newton, 1979; Zobel, 1983]. The research activity on this topic has slowed down in the last years. Some of the recent relevant papers are [Yeung and Hung, 1995; Hofri, 1994; Lee and Kim, 1995; Kshemkalyani and Singhal, 1994; Chen et al., 1996; Park et al., 1995] and [Makki and Pissinou, 1995].

Exercises

Problem 11.1. Which of the following histories are conflict equivalent?

$$H_1 = \{W_2(x), W_1(x), R_3(x), R_1(x), W_2(y), R_3(y), R_3(z), R_2(x)\}$$
$$H_2 = \{R_3(z), R_3(y), W_2(y), R_2(z), W_1(x), R_3(x), W_2(x), R_1(x)\}$$
$$H_3 = \{R_3(z), W_2(x), W_2(y), R_1(x), R_3(x), R_2(z), R_3(y), W_1(x)\}$$
$$H_4 = \{R_2(z), W_2(x), W_2(y), W_1(x), R_1(x), R_3(x), R_3(z), R_3(y)\}$$

Problem 11.2. Which of the above histories $H_1 - H_4$ are serializable?

Problem 11.3. Give a history of two complete transactions which is not allowed by a strict 2PL scheduler but is accepted by the basic 2PL scheduler.

Problem 11.4 (*). One says that history H is *recoverable* if, whenever transaction T_i reads (some item x) from transaction T_j $(i \neq j)$ in H and C_i occurs in H, then $C_j \prec_S C_i$. T_i "reads x from" T_j in H if

1. $W_j(x) \prec_H R_i(x)$, and
2. $A_j \text{not} \prec_H R_i(x)$, and
3. if there is some $W_k(x)$ such that $W_j(x) \prec_H W_k(x) \prec_H R_i(x)$, then $A_k \prec_H R_i(x)$.

Which of the following histories are recoverable?

$$H_1 = \{W_2(x), W_1(x), R_3(x), R_1(x), C_1, W_2(y), R_3(y), R_3(z), C_3, R_2(x), C_2\}$$
$$H_2 = \{R_3(z), R_3(y), W_2(y), R_2(z), W_1(x), R_3(x), W_2(x), R_1(x), C_1, C_2, C_3\}$$
$$H_3 = \{R_3(z), W_2(x), W_2(y), R_1(x), R_3(x), R_2(z), R_3(y), C_3, W_1(x), C_2, C_1\}$$
$$H_4 = \{R_2(z), W_2(x), W_2(y), C_2, W_1(x), R_1(x), A_1, R_3(x), R_3(z), R_3(y), C_3\}$$

Problem 11.5 (*). Give the algorithms for the transaction managers and the lock managers for the distributed two-phase locking approach.

Problem 11.6 (**). Modify the centralized 2PL algorithm to handle phantoms. (See Chapter 10 for a definition of phantoms.)

Problem 11.7. Timestamp ordering-based concurrency control algorithms depend on either an accurate clock at each site or a global clock that all sites can access (the clock can be a counter). Assume that each site has its own clock which "ticks" every 0.1 second. If all local clocks are resynchronized every 24 hours, what is the maximum drift in seconds per 24 hours permissible at any local site to ensure that a timestamp-based mechanism will successfully synchronize transactions?

Problem 11.8 (**). Incorporate the distributed deadlock strategy described in this chapter into the distributed 2PL algorithms that you designed in Problem 11.5.

Problem 11.9. Explain the relationship between transaction manager storage requirement and transaction size (number of operations per transaction) for a transaction manager using an optimistic timestamp ordering for concurrency control.

Problem 11.10 (*). Give the scheduler and transaction manager algorithms for the distributed optimistic concurrency controller described in this chapter.

Problem 11.11. Recall from the discussion in Section 11.7 that the computational model that is used in our descriptions in this chapter is a centralized one. How would the distributed 2PL transaction manager and lock manager algorithms change if a distributed execution model were to be used?

Problem 11.12. It is sometimes claimed that serializability is quite a restrictive correctness criterion. Can you give examples of distributed histories that are correct (i.e., maintain the consistency of the local databases as well as their mutual consistency) but are not serializable?

Chapter 12
Distributed DBMS Reliability

We have referred to "reliability" and "availability" of the database a number of times so far without defining these terms precisely. Specifically, we mentioned these terms in conjunction with data replication, because the principle method of building a reliable system is to provide redundancy in system components. We also claimed in Chapter 1 that the distribution of data enhances system reliability. However, the distribution of the database or the replication of data items is not sufficient to make the distributed DBMS reliable. A number of protocols need to be implemented within the DBMS to exploit this distribution and replication in order to make operations more reliable.

A reliable distributed database management system is one that can continue to process user requests even when the underlying system is unreliable. In other words, even when components of the distributed computing environment fail, a reliable distributed DBMS should be able to continue executing user requests without violating database consistency.

The purpose of this chapter is to discuss the reliability features of a distributed DBMS. From Chapter 10 the reader will recall that the reliability of a distributed DBMS refers to the atomicity and durability properties of transactions. Two specific aspects of reliability protocols that need to be discussed in relation to these properties are the commit and the recovery protocols. In that sense, in this chapter we relax one of the major assumptions of Chapter 11: that the underlying distributed system is fully reliable and does not experience any hardware or software failures. Furthermore, the commit protocols discussed in this chapter constitute the support provided by the distributed DBMS for the execution of commit commands in transactions.

The organization of this chapter is as follows. We start with a definition of the fundamental reliability concepts and reliability measures in Section 12. In Section 12.2 we discuss the reasons for failures in distributed systems and focus on the types of failures in distributed DBMSs. Section 12.3 focuses on the functions of the local recovery manager and provides an overview of reliability measures in centralized DBMS. This discussion forms the foundation for the distributed commit and recovery protocols, which are introduced in Section 12.4. In Sections 12.5 and 12.6 we present detailed protocols for dealing with site failures and network partitioning, respectively.

M.T. Özsu and P. Valduriez, *Principles of Distributed Database Systems: Third Edition*,
DOI 10.1007/978-1-4419-8834-8_12, © Springer Science+Business Media, LLC 2011

Implementation of these protocols within our architectural model is the topic of Section 12.7.

12.1 Reliability Concepts and Measures

Too often, the terms *reliability* and *availability* are used loosely in literature. Even among the researchers in the area of reliable computer systems, the definitions of these terms sometimes vary. In this section, we give precise definitions of a number of concepts that are fundamental to an understanding and study of reliable systems. Our definitions follow those of Anderson and Lee [1985] and Randell et al. [1978]. Nevertheless, we indicate where these definitions might differ from other usage of the terms.

12.1.1 System, State, and Failure

Reliability refers to a *system* that consists of a set of *components*. The system has a *state*, which changes as the system operates. The behavior of the system in providing response to all the possible external stimuli is laid out in an authoritative *specification* of its behavior. The specification indicates the valid behavior of each system state.

Any deviation of a system from the behavior described in the specification is considered a *failure*. For example, in a distributed transaction manager the specification may state that only serializable schedules for the execution of concurrent transactions should be generated. If the transaction manager generates a non-serializable schedule, we say that it has failed.

Each failure obviously needs to be traced back to its cause. Failures in a system can be attributed to deficiencies either in the components that make it up, or in the design, that is, how these components are put together. Each state that a reliable system goes through is valid in the sense that the state fully meets its specification. However, in an unreliable system, it is possible that the system may get to an internal state that may not obey its specification. Further transitions from this state would eventually cause a system failure. Such internal states are called *erroneous states*; the part of the state that is incorrect is called an *error* in the system. Any error in the internal states of the components of a system or in the design of a system is called a *fault* in the system. Thus, a fault causes an error that results in a system failure (Figure 12.1).

Fig. 12.1 Chain of Events Leading to System Failure

We differentiate between errors (or faults and failures) that are permanent and those that are not permanent. Permanence can apply to a failure, a fault, or an error, although we typically use the term with respect to faults. A *permanent fault*, also commonly called a *hard fault*, is one that reflects an irreversible change in the behavior of the system. Permanent faults cause permanent errors that result in permanent failures. The characteristics of these failures is that recovery from them requires intervention to "repair" the fault. Systems also experience *intermittent* and *transient faults*. In the literature, these two are typically not differentiated; they are jointly called *soft faults*. The dividing line in this differentiation is the repairability of the system that has experienced the fault [Siewiorek and Swarz, 1982]. An intermittent fault refers to a fault that demonstrates itself occasionally due to unstable hardware or varying hardware or software states. A typical example is the faults that systems may demonstrate when the load becomes too heavy. On the other hand, a transient fault describes a fault that results from temporary environmental conditions. A transient fault might occur, for example, due to a sudden increase in the room temperature. The transient fault is therefore the result of environmental conditions that may be impossible to repair. An intermittent fault, on the other hand, can be repaired since the fault can be traced to a component of the system.

Remember that we have also indicated that system failures can be due to design faults. Design faults together with unstable hardware cause intermittent errors that result in system failure. A final source of system failure that may not be attributable to a component fault or a design fault is operator mistakes. These are the sources of a significant number of errors as the statistics included further in this section demonstrate. The relationship between various types of faults and failures is depicted in Figure 12.2.

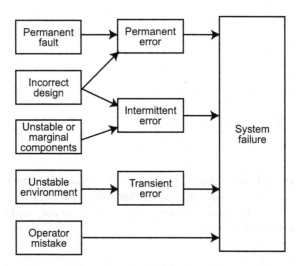

Fig. 12.2 Sources of System Failure (Based on [Siewiorek and Swarz, 1982])

12.1.2 Reliability and Availability

Reliability refers to the probability that the system under consideration does not experience any failures in a given time interval. It is typically used to describe systems that cannot be repaired (as in space-based computers), or where the operation of the system is so critical that no downtime for repair can be tolerated.

Formally, the reliability of a system, $R(t)$, is defined as the following conditional probability:

$$R(t) = \Pr\{0 \text{ failures in time } [0,t] \mid \text{no failures at } t = 0\}$$

If we assume that failures follow a Poisson distribution (which is usually the case for hardware), this formula reduces to

$$R(t) = \Pr\{0 \text{ failures in time } [0,t]\}$$

Under the same assumptions, it is possible to derive that

$$\Pr\{k \text{ failures in time } [0, \, t]\} = \frac{e^{-m(t)}[m(t)]^k}{k!}$$

where $m(t) = \int_0^t z(x) \, dx$. Here $z(t)$ is known as the *hazard function*, which gives the time-dependent failure rate of the specific hardware component under consideration. The probability distribution for $z(t)$ may be different for different electronic components.

The expected (mean) number of failures in time $[0, t]$ can then be computed as

$$E[k] = \sum_{k=0}^{\infty} k \, \frac{e^{-m(t)}[m(t)]^k}{k!} = m(t)$$

and the variance as

$$Var[k] = E[k^2] - (E[k])^2 = m(t)$$

Given these values, $R(t)$ can be written as

$$R(t) = e^{-m(t)}$$

Note that the reliability equation above is written for one component of the system. For a system that consists of n non-redundant components (i.e., they all have to function properly for the system to work) whose failures are independent, the overall system reliability can be written as

$$R_{sys}(t) = \Pi_{i=1}^{n} R_i(t)$$

Availability, $A(t)$, refers to the probability that the system is operational according to its specification at a given point in time t. A number of failures may have occurred prior to time t, but if they have all been repaired, the system is available at time t. Obviously, availability refers to systems that can be repaired.

If one looks at the limit of availability as time goes to infinity, it refers to the expected percentage of time that the system under consideration is available to perform useful computations. Availability can be used as some measure of "goodness" for those systems that can be repaired and which can be out of service for short periods of time during repair. Reliability and availability of a system are considered to be contradictory objectives [Siewiorek and Swarz, 1982]. It is usually accepted that it is easier to develop highly available systems as opposed to highly reliable systems.

If we assume that failures follow a Poisson distribution with a failure rate λ, and that repair time is exponential with a mean repair time of $1/\mu$, the steady-state availability of a system can be written as

$$A = \frac{\mu}{\lambda + \mu}$$

12.1.3 Mean Time between Failures/Mean Time to Repair

Two single-parameter measures have become more popular than the reliability and availability functions given above to model the behavior of systems. These two measures used are *mean time between failures* (MTBF) and *mean time to repair* (MTTR). MTBF is the expected time between subsequent failures in a system with repair.[1] MTBF can be calculated either from empirical data or from the reliability function as

$$\text{MTBF} = \int_0^\infty R(t) \, dt$$

Since $R(t)$ is related to the system failure rate, there is a direct relationship between MTBF and the failure rate of a system. MTTR is the expected time to repair a failed system. It is related to the repair rate as MTBF is related to the failure rate. Using these two metrics, the steady-state availability of a system with exponential failure and repair rates can be specified as

$$A = \frac{\text{MTBF}}{\text{MTBF} + \text{MTTR}}$$

System failures may be *latent*, in that a failure is typically detected some time after its occurrence. This period is called *error latency*, and the average error latency time over a number of identical systems is called *mean time to detect* (MTTD).

---

[1] A distinction is sometimes made between MTBF and MTTF (mean time to fail). MTTF is defined as the expected time of the first system failure given a successful startup at time 0. MTBF is then defined only for systems that can be repaired. An approximation for MTBF is given as MTBF = MTTF + MTTR [McConnel and Siewiorek, 1982]. We do not make this distinction in this book.

Figure 12.3 depicts the relationship of various reliability measures with the actual occurrences of faults.

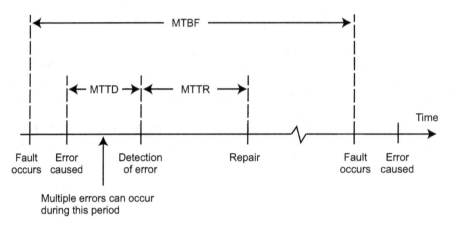

Fig. 12.3 Occurrence of Events over Time

12.2 Failures in Distributed DBMS

Designing a reliable system that can recover from failures requires identifying the types of failures with which the system has to deal. In a distributed database system, we need to deal with four types of failures: transaction failures (aborts), site (system) failures, media (disk) failures, and communication line failures. Some of these are due to hardware and others are due to software. The ratio of hardware failures vary from study to study and range from 18% to over 50%. Soft failures make up more than 90% of all hardware system failures. It is interesting to note that this percentage has not changed significantly since the early days of computing. A 1967 study of the U.S. Air Force indicates that 80% of electronic failures in computers are intermittent [Roth et al., 1967]. A study performed by IBM during the same year concludes that over 90% of all failures are intermittent [Ball and Hardie, 1967]. More recent studies indicate that the occurrence of soft failures is significantly higher than that of hard failures ([Longbottom, 1980; Gray, 1987]). Gray [1987] also mentions that most of the software failures are transient—and therefore soft—suggesting that a dump and restart may be sufficient to recover without any need to "repair" the software.

Software failures are typically caused by "bugs" in the code. The estimates for the number of bugs in software vary considerably. Figures such as 0.25 bug per 1000 instructions to 10 bugs per 1000 instructions have been reported. As stated before, most of the software failures are soft failures. The statistics for software failures are comparable to those we have previously reported on hardware failures. The fundamental reason for the dominance of soft failures in software is the significant amount of design review and code inspection that a typical software project goes through before it gets to the testing stage. Furthermore, most commercial software goes through extensive alpha and beta testing before being released for field use.

12.2.1 Transaction Failures

Transactions can fail for a number of reasons. Failure can be due to an error in the transaction caused by incorrect input data (e.g., Example 10.3) as well as the detection of a present or potential deadlock. Furthermore, some concurrency control algorithms do not permit a transaction to proceed or even to wait if the data that they attempt to access are currently being accessed by another transaction. This might also be considered a failure. The usual approach to take in cases of transaction failure is to *abort* the transaction, thus resetting the database to its state prior to the start of this transaction.[2]

The frequency of transaction failures is not easy to measure. An early study reported that in System R, 3% of the transactions aborted abnormally [Gray et al., 1981]. In general, it can be stated that (1) within a single application, the ratio of transactions that abort themselves is rather constant, being a function of the incorrect data, the available semantic data control features, and so on; and (2) the number of transaction aborts by the DBMS due to concurrency control considerations (mainly deadlocks) is dependent on the level of concurrency (i.e., number of concurrent transactions), the interference of the concurrent applications, the granularity of locks, and so on [Härder and Reuter, 1983].

12.2.2 Site (System) Failures

The reasons for system failure can be traced back to a hardware or to a software failure. The important point from the perspective of this discussion is that a system failure is always assumed to result in the loss of main memory contents. Therefore, any part of the database that was in main memory buffers is lost as a result of a system failure. However, the database that is stored in secondary storage is assumed to be safe and correct. In distributed database terminology, system failures are typically referred to as *site failures*, since they result in the failed site being unreachable from other sites in the distributed system.

We typically differentiate between partial and total failures in a distributed system. *Total failure* refers to the simultaneous failure of all sites in the distributed system; *partial failure* indicates the failure of only some sites while the others remain operational. As indicated in Chapter 1, it is this aspect of distributed systems that makes them more available.

---

[2] Recall that all transaction aborts are not due to failures; in some cases, application logic requires transaction aborts as in Example 10.3.

12.2.3 Media Failures

Media failure refers to the failures of the secondary storage devices that store the database. Such failures may be due to operating system errors, as well as to hardware faults such as head crashes or controller failures. The important point from the perspective of DBMS reliability is that all or part of the database that is on the secondary storage is considered to be destroyed and inaccessible. Duplexing of disk storage and maintaining archival copies of the database are common techniques that deal with this sort of catastrophic problem.

Media failures are frequently treated as problems local to one site and therefore not specifically addressed in the reliability mechanisms of distributed DBMSs. We consider techniques for dealing with them in Section 12.3.5 under local recovery management. We then turn our attention to site failures when we consider distributed recovery functions.

12.2.4 Communication Failures

The three types of failures described above are common to both centralized and distributed DBMSs. Communication failures, however, are unique to the distributed case. There are a number of types of communication failures. The most common ones are the errors in the messages, improperly ordered messages, lost (or undeliverable) messages, and communication line failures. As discussed in Chapter 2, the first two errors are the responsibility of the computer network; we will not consider them further. Therefore, in our discussions of distributed DBMS reliability, we expect the underlying computer network hardware and software to ensure that two messages sent from a process at some originating site to another process at some destination site are delivered without error and in the order in which they were sent.

Lost or undeliverable messages are typically the consequence of communication line failures or (destination) site failures. If a communication line fails, in addition to losing the message(s) in transit, it may also divide the network into two or more disjoint groups. This is called *network partitioning*. If the network is partitioned, the sites in each partition may continue to operate. In this case, executing transactions that access data stored in multiple partitions becomes a major issue.

Network partitions point to a unique aspect of failures in distributed computer systems. In centralized systems the system state can be characterized as all-or-nothing: either the system is operational or it is not. Thus the failures are complete: when one occurs, the entire system becomes non-operational. Obviously, this is not true in distributed systems. As we indicated a number of times before, this is their potential strength. However, it also makes the transaction management algorithms more difficult to design.

If messages cannot be delivered, we will assume that the network does nothing about it. It will not buffer it for delivery to the destination when the service is reestablished and will not inform the sender process that the message cannot be delivered. In short, the message will simply be lost. We make this assumption because it represents the least expectation from the network and places the responsibility of dealing with these failures to the distributed DBMS.

As a consequence, the distributed DBMS is responsible for detecting that a message is undeliverable is left to the application program (in this case the distributed DBMS). The detection will be facilitated by the use of timers and a timeout mechanism that keeps track of how long it has been since the sender site has not received a confirmation from the destination site about the receipt of a message. This timeout interval needs to be set to a value greater than that of the maximum round-trip propagation delay of a message in the network. The term for the failure of the communication network to deliver messages and the confirmations within this period is *performance failure*. It needs to be handled within the reliability protocols for distributed DBMSs.

12.3 Local Reliability Protocols

In this section we discuss the functions performed by the local recovery manager (LRM) that exists at each site. These functions maintain the atomicity and durability properties of local transactions. They relate to the execution of the commands that are passed to the LRM, which are **begin_transaction**, **read**, **write**, **commit**, and **abort**. Later in this section we introduce a new command into the LRM's repertoire that initiates recovery actions after a failure. Note that in this section we discuss the execution of these commands in a centralized environment. The complications introduced in distributed databases are addressed in the upcoming sections.

12.3.1 Architectural Considerations

It is again time to use our architectural model and discuss the specific interface between the LRM and the database buffer manager (BM). First note that the LRM is implemented within the data processor introduced in Chapter 11. The simple DP implementation that was given earlier will be enhanced with the reliability protocols discussed in this section. Also remember that all accesses to the database are via the database buffer manager. The detailed discussion of the algorithms that the buffer manager implements is beyond the scope of this book; we provide a summary later in this subsection. Even without these details, we can still specify the interface and its function, as depicted in Figure 12.4.[3]

In this discussion we assume that the database is stored permanently on secondary storage, which in this context is called the *stable storage* [Lampson and Sturgis, 1976]. The stability of this storage medium is due to its robustness to failures. A

---

[3] This architectural model is similar to that used by Härder and Reuter [1983] and Bernstein et al. [1987].

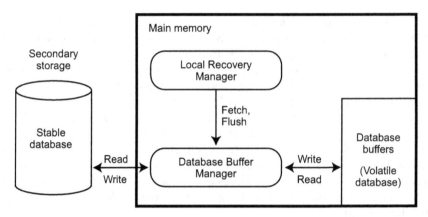

Fig. 12.4 Interface Between the Local Recovery Manager and the Buffer Manager

stable storage device would experience considerably less-frequent failures than would a non-stable storage device. In today's technology, stable storage is typically implemented by means of duplexed magnetic disks which store duplicate copies of data that are always kept mutually consistent (i.e., the copies are identical). We call the version of the database that is kept on stable storage the *stable database*. The unit of storage and access of the stable database is typically a *page*.

The database buffer manager keeps some of the recently accessed data in main memory buffers. This is done to enhance access performance. Typically, the buffer is divided into pages that are of the same size as the stable database pages. The part of the database that is in the database buffer is called the *volatile database*. It is important to note that the LRM executes the operations on behalf of a transaction only on the volatile database, which, at a later time, is written back to the stable database.

When the LRM wants to read a page of data[4] on behalf of a transaction—strictly speaking, on behalf of some operation of a transaction—it issues a **fetch** command, indicating the page that it wants to read. The buffer manager checks to see if that page is already in the buffer (due to a previous fetch command from another transaction) and if so, makes it available for that transaction; if not, it reads the page from the stable database into an empty database buffer. If no empty buffers exist, it selects one of the buffer pages to write back to stable storage and reads the requested stable database page into that buffer. There are a number of different algorithms by which the buffer manager may choose the buffer page to be replaced; these are discussed in standard database textbooks.

The buffer manager also provides the interface by which the LRM can actually force it to write back some of the buffer pages. This can be accomplished by means of the **flush** command, which specifies the buffer pages that the LRM wants to be

---

[4] The LRM's unit of access may be in blocks which have sizes different from a page. However, for simplicity, we assume that the unit of access is the same.

written back. We should indicate that different LRM implementations may or may not use this forced writing. This issue is discussed further in subsequent sections.

As its interface suggests, the buffer manager acts as a conduit for all access to the database via the buffers that it manages. It provides this function by fulfilling three tasks:

1. *Searching* the buffer pool for a given page;

2. If it is not found in the buffer, *allocating* a free buffer page and *loading* the buffer page with a data page that is brought in from secondary storage;

3. If no free buffer pages are available, choosing a buffer page for *replacement.*

Searching is quite straightforward. Typically, the buffer pages are shared among the transactions that execute against the database, so search is global.

Allocation of buffer pages is typically done dynamically. This means that the allocation of buffer pages to processes is performed as processes execute. The buffer manager tries to calculate the number of buffer pages needed to run the process efficiently and attempts to allocate that number of pages. The best known dynamic allocation method is the *working-set algorithm* [Denning, 1968, 1980].

A second aspect of allocation is fetching data pages. The most common technique is *demand paging*, where data pages are brought into the buffer as they are referenced. However, a number of operating systems prefetch a group of data pages that are in close physical proximity to the data page referenced. Buffer managers choose this route if they detect sequential access to a file.

In replacing buffer pages, the best known technique is the least recently used (LRU) algorithm that attempts to determine the *logical reference strings* [Effelsberg and Härder, 1984] of processes to buffer pages and to replace the page that has not been referenced for an extended period. The anticipation here is that if a buffer page has not been referenced for a long time, it probably will not be referenced in the near future.

The techniques discussed above are the most common. Other alternatives are discussed in [Effelsberg and Härder, 1984].

Clearly, these functions are similar to those performed by operating system (OS) buffer managers. However, quite frequently, DBMSs bypass OS buffer managers and manage disks and main memory buffers themselves due to a number of problems (see, e.g., [Stonebraker, 1981]) that are beyond the scope of this book. Basically, the requirements of DBMSs are usually incompatible with the services that OSs provide. The consequence is that DBMS kernels duplicate OS services with an implementation that is more suitable for their needs.

12.3.2 Recovery Information

In this section we assume that only system failures occur. We defer the discussion of techniques for recovering from media failures until later. Since we are dealing with centralized database recovery, communication failures are not applicable.

When a system failure occurs, the volatile database is lost. Therefore, the DBMS has to maintain some information about its state at the time of the failure in order to be able to bring the database to the state that it was in when the failure occurred. We call this information the *recovery information*.

The recovery information that the system maintains is dependent on the method of executing updates. Two possibilities are in-place updating and out-of-place updating. *In-place updating* physically changes the value of the data item in the stable database. As a result, the previous values are lost. *Out-of-place updating*, on the other hand, does not change the value of the data item in the stable database but maintains the new value separately. Of course, periodically, these updated values have to be integrated into the stable database. We should note that the reliability issues are somewhat simpler if in-place updating is not used. However, most DBMSs use it due to its improved performance.

12.3.2.1 In-Place Update Recovery Information

Since in-place updates cause previous values of the affected data items to be lost, it is necessary to keep enough information about the database state changes to facilitate the recovery of the database to a consistent state following a failure. This information is typically maintained in a *database log*. Thus each update transaction not only changes the database but the change is also recorded in the database log (Figure 12.5). The log contains information necessary to recover the database state following a failure.

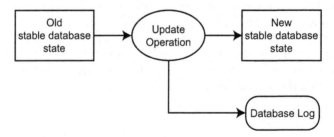

Fig. 12.5 Update Operation Execution

For the following discussion assume that the LRM and buffer manager algorithms are such that the buffer pages are written back to the stable database only when the buffer manager needs new buffer space. In other words, the **flush** command is not used by the LRM and the decision to write back the pages into the stable database is taken at the discretion of the buffer manager. Now consider that a transaction T_1 had completed (i.e., committed) before the failure occurred. The durability property of transactions would require that the effect os T_1 be reflected in the database. However, it is possible that the volatile database pages that have been updated by T_1 may not have been written back to the stable database at the time of the failure. Therefore, upon recovery, it is important to be able to *redo* the operations of T_1. This requires some information to be stored in the database log about the effects of T_1. Given this information, it is possible to recover the database from its "old" state to the "new" state that reflects the effects of T_1 (Figure 12.6).

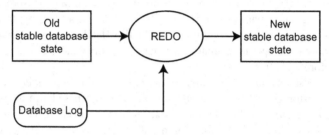

Fig. 12.6 REDO Action

Now consider another transaction, T_2, that was still running when the failure occurred. The atomicity property would dictate that the stable database not contain any effects of T_2. It is possible that the buffer manager may have had to write into the stable database some of the volatile database pages that have been updated by T_2. Upon recovery from failures it is necessary to *undo* the operations of T_2.[5] Thus the recovery information should include sufficient data to permit the undo by taking the "new" database state that reflects partial effects of T_2 and recovers the "old" state that existed at the start of T_2 (Figure 12.7).

We should indicate that the undo and redo actions are assumed to be idempotent. In other words, their repeated application to a transaction would be equivalent to performing them once. Furthermore, the undo/redo actions form the basis of different methods of executing the commit commands. We discuss this further in Section 12.3.3.

The contents of the log may differ according to the implementation. However, the following minimal information for each transaction is contained in almost all

---

[5] One might think that it could be possible to continue with the operation of T_2 following restart instead of undoing its operations. However, in general it may not be possible for the LRM to determine the point at which the transaction needs to be restarted. Furthermore, the failure may not be a system failure but a transaction failure (i.e., T_2 may actually abort itself) after some of its actions have been reflected in the stable database. Therefore, the possibility of undoing is necessary.

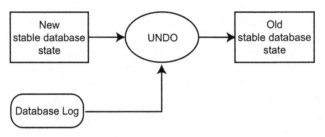

Fig. 12.7 UNDO Action

database logs: a begin_transaction record, the value of the data item before the update (called the *before image*), the updated value of the data item (called the *after image*), and a termination record indicating the transaction termination condition (commit, abort). The granularity of the before and after images may be different, as it is possible to log entire pages or some smaller unit. As an alternative to this form of *state logging*, *operational logging*, as in ARIES [Haderle et al., 1992], may be supported where the operations that cause changes to the database are logged rather than the before and after images.

The log is also maintained in main memory buffers (called *log buffers*) and written back to stable storage (called *stable log*) similar to the database buffer pages (Figure 12.8). The log pages can be written to stable storage in one of two ways. They can be written *synchronously* (more commonly known as *forcing a log*) where the addition of each log record requires that the log be moved from main memory to stable storage. They can also be written *asynchronously*, where the log is moved to stable storage either at periodic intervals or when the buffer fills up. When the log is written synchronously, the execution of the transaction is suspended until the write is complete. This adds some delay to the response-time performance of the transaction. On the other hand, if a failure occurs immediately after a forced write, it is relatively easy to recover to a consistent database state.

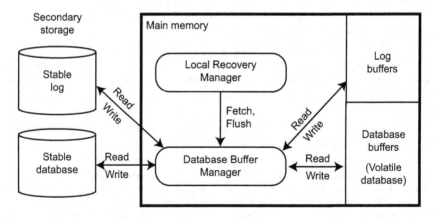

Fig. 12.8 Logging Interface

Whether the log is written synchronously or asynchronously, one very important protocol has to be observed in maintaining logs. Consider a case where the updates to the database are written into the stable storage before the log is modified in stable storage to reflect the update. If a failure occurs before the log is written, the database will remain in updated form, but the log will not indicate the update that makes it impossible to recover the database to a consistent and up-to-date state. Therefore, the stable log is always updated prior to the updating of the stable database. This is known as the *write-ahead logging* (WAL) protocol [Gray, 1979] and can be precisely specified as follows:

1. Before a stable database is updated (perhaps due to actions of a yet uncommitted transaction), the before images should be stored in the stable log. This facilitates undo.

2. When a transaction commits, the after images have to be stored in the stable log prior to the updating of the stable database. This facilitates redo.

12.3.2.2 Out-of-Place Update Recovery Information

As we mentioned above, the most common update technique is in-place updating. Therefore, we provide only a brief overview of the other updating techniques and their recovery information. Details can be found in [Verhofstadt, 1978] and the other references given earlier.

Typical techniques for out-of-place updating are *shadowing* ([Astrahan et al., 1976; Gray, 1979]) and *differential files* [Severence and Lohman, 1976]. Shadowing uses duplicate stable storage pages in executing updates. Thus every time an update is made, the old stable storage page, called the *shadow page*, is left intact and a new page with the updated data item values is written into the stable database. The access path data structures are updated to point to the new page, which contains the current data so that subsequent accesses are to this page. The old stable storage page is retained for recovery purposes (to perform undo).

Recovery based on shadow paging is implemented in System R's recovery manager [Gray et al., 1981]. This implementation uses shadowing together with logging.

The differential file approach was discussed in Chapter 5 within the context of integrity enforcement. In general, the method maintains each stable database file as a read-only file. In addition, it maintains a corresponding read-write differential file that stores the changes to that file. Given a logical database file F, let us denote its read-only part as FR and its corresponding differential file as DF. DF consists of two parts: an insertions part, which stores the insertions to F, denoted DF^+, and a corresponding deletions part, denoted DF^-. All updates are treated as the deletion of the old value and the insertion of a new one. Thus each logical file F is considered to be a view defined as $F = (FR \cup DF^+) - DF^-$. Periodically, the differential file needs to be merged with the read-only base file.

Recovery schemes based on this method simply use private differential files for each transaction, which are then merged with the differential files of each file at commit time. Thus recovery from failures can simply be achieved by discarding the private differential files of non-committed transactions.

There are studies that indicate that the shadowing and differential files approaches may be advantageous in certain environments. One study by Agrawal and DeWitt [1985] investigates the performance of recovery mechanisms based on logging, differential files, and shadow paging, integrated with locking and optimistic (using timestamps) concurrency control algorithms. The results indicate that shadowing, together with locking, can be a feasible alternative to the more common log-based recovery integrated with locking if there are only large (in terms of the base-set size) transactions with sequential access patterns. Similarly, differential files integrated with locking can be a feasible alternative if there are medium-sized and large transactions.

12.3.3 Execution of LRM Commands

Recall that there are five commands that form the interface to the LRM. These are the **begin_transaction, read, write, commit**, and **abort** commands. As we indicated in Chapter 10, some DBMSs do not have an explicit commit command. In this case the end (of transaction) indicator serves as the commit command. For simplicity, we specify commit explicitly.

In this section we introduce a sixth interface command to the LRM: **recover**. The **recover** command is the interface that the operating system has to the LRM. It is used during recovery from system failures when the operating system asks the DBMS to recover the database to the state that existed when the failure occurred.

The execution of some of these commands (specifically, **abort, commit**, and **recover**) is quite dependent on the specific LRM algorithms that are used as well as on the interaction of the LRM with the buffer manager. Others (i.e., **begin_transaction, read**, and **write**) are quite independent of these considerations.

The fundamental design decision in the implementation of the local recovery manager, the buffer manager, and the interaction between the two components is whether or not the buffer manager obeys the local recovery manager's instructions as to when to write the database buffer pages to stable storage. Specifically, two decisions are involved. The first one is whether the buffer manager may write the buffer pages updated by a transaction into stable storage during the execution of that transaction, or it waits for the LRM to instruct it to write them back. We call this the *fix/no-fix* decision. The reasons for the choice of this terminology will become apparent shortly. Note that it is also called the steal/no-steal decision by Härder and Reuter [1983]. The second decision is whether the buffer manager will be forced to flush the buffer pages updated by a transaction into the stable storage at the end of that transaction (i.e., the commit point), or the buffer manager flushes them out whenever it needs to according to its buffer management algorithm. We call this the *flush/no-flush* decision. It is called the force/no-force decision by Härder and Reuter [1983].

Accordingly, four alternatives can be identified: (1) no-fix/no-flush, (2) no-fix/flush, (3) fix/no-flush, and (4) fix/flush. We will consider each of these in more detail. However, first we present the execution methods of the **begin_transaction, read**, and **write** commands, which are quite independent of these considerations. Where modifications are required in these methods due to different LRM and buffer manager implementation strategies, we will indicate them.

12.3.3.1 Begin_transaction, Read, and Write Commands

Begin_transaction.

This command causes various components of the DBMS to carry out some bookkeeping functions. We will also assume that it causes the LRM to write a begin_transaction record into the log. This is an assumption made for convenience of discussion; in reality, writing of the begin_transaction record may be delayed until the first **write** to improve performance by reducing I/O.

Read.

The **read** command specifies a data item. The LRM tries to read the specified data item from the buffer pages that belong to the transaction. If the data item is not in one of these pages, it issues a **fetch** command to the buffer manager in order to make the data available. Upon reading the data, the LRM returns it to the scheduler.

Write.

The **write** command specifies the data item and the new value. As with a read command, if the data item is available in the buffers of the transaction, its value is modified in the database buffers (i.e., the volatile database). If it is not in the private buffer pages, a **fetch** command is issued to the buffer manager, and the data is made available and updated. The before image of the data page, as well as its after image, are recorded in the log. The local recovery manager then informs the scheduler that the operation has been completed successfully.

12.3.3.2 No-fix/No-flush

This type of LRM algorithm is called a redo/undo algorithm by Bernstein et al. [1987] since it requires, as we will see, performing both the redo and undo operations upon recovery. It is called steal/no-force by Härder and Reuter [1983].

Abort.

As we indicated before, abort is an indication of transaction failure. Since the buffer manager may have written the updated pages into the stable database, abort will have to undo the actions of the transaction. Therefore, the LRM reads the log records for that specific transaction and replaces the values of the updated data items in the volatile database with their before images. The scheduler is then informed about the successful completion of the abort action. This process is called the *transaction undo* or *partial undo*.

An alternative implementation is the use of an *abort list*, which stores the identifiers of all the transactions that have been aborted. If such a list is used, the abort action is considered to be complete as soon as the transaction's identifier is included in the abort list.

Note that even though the values of the updated data items in the stable database are not restored to their before images, the transaction is considered to be aborted at this point. The buffer manager will write the "corrected" volatile database pages into the stable database at a future time, thereby restoring it to its state prior to that transaction.

Commit.

The **commit** command causes an end_of_transaction record to be written into the log by the LRM. Under this scenario, no other action is taken in executing a commit command other than informing the scheduler about the successful completion of the commit action.

An alternative to writing an end_of_transaction record into the log is to add the transaction's identifier to a *commit list*, which is a list of the identifiers of transactions that have committed. In this case the commit action is accepted as complete as soon as the transaction identifier is stored in this list.

Recover.

The LRM starts the recovery action by going to the beginning of the log and redoing the operations of each transaction for which both a begin_transaction and an end_of_transaction record is found. This is called *partial redo*. Similarly, it undoes the operations of each transaction for which a begin_transaction record is found in the log without a corresponding end_of_transaction record. This action is called *global undo*, as opposed to the transaction undo discussed above. The difference is that the effects of all incomplete transactions need to be rolled back, not one.

If commit list and abort list implementations are used, the recovery action consists of redoing the operations of all the transactions in the commit list and undoing the operations of all the transactions in the abort list. In the remainder of this chapter we will not make this distinction, but rather will refer to both of these recovery implementations as global undo.

12.3.3.3 No-fix/Flush

The LRM algorithms that use this strategy are called undo/no-redo in Bernstein et al. [1987] and steal/force by Härder and Reuter [1983].

Abort.

The execution of **abort** is identical to the previous case. Upon transaction failure, the LRM initiates a partial undo for that particular transaction.

Commit.

The LRM issues a **flush** command to the buffer manager, forcing it to write back all the updated volatile database pages into the stable database. The commit command is then executed either by placing a record in the log or by insertion of the transaction identifier into the commit list as specified for the previous case. When all of this is complete, the LRM informs the scheduler that the commit has been carried out successfully.

Recover.

Since all the updated pages are written into the stable database at the commit point, there is no need to perform redo; all the effects of successful transactions will have been reflected in the stable database. Therefore, the recovery action initiated by the LRM consists of a global undo.

12.3.3.4 Fix/No-flush

In this case the LRM controls the writing of the volatile database pages into stable storage. The key here is not to permit the buffer manager to write any updated volatile database page into the stable database until at least the transaction commit point. This is accomplished by the **fix** command, which is a modified version of the **fetch** command whereby the specified page is fixed in the database buffer and cannot be written back to the stable database by the buffer manager. Thus any **fetch** command to the buffer manager for a write operation is replaced by a **fix** command.[6] Note

---

[6] Of course, any page that was previously fetched for read but is now being updated also needs to be fixed.

that this precludes the need for a global undo operation and is therefore called a redo/no-undo algorithm by Bernstein et al. [1987] and a no-force/no-steal algorithm by Härder and Reuter [1983].

Abort.

Since the volatile database pages have not been written to the stable database, no special action is necessary. To release the buffer pages that have been fixed by the transaction, however, it is necessary for the LRM to send an **unfix** command to the buffer manager for all such pages. It is then sufficient to carry out the abort action either by writing an abort record in the log or by including the transaction in the abort list, informing the scheduler and then forgetting about the transaction.

Commit.

The LRM sends an **unfix** command to the buffer manager for every volatile database page that was previously fixed by that transaction. Note that these pages may now be written back to the stable database at the discretion of the buffer manager. The commit command is then executed either by placing an end_of_transaction record in the log or by inserting the transaction identifier into the commit list as specified for the preceding case. When all of this is complete, the LRM informs the scheduler that the commit has been successfully carried out.

Recover.

As we mentioned above, since the volatile database pages that have been updated by ongoing transactions are not yet written into the stable database, there is no necessity for global undo. The LRM, therefore, initiates a partial redo action to recover those transactions that may have already committed, but whose volatile database pages may not have yet written into the stable database.

12.3.3.5 Fix/Flush

This is the case where the LRM forces the buffer manager to write the updated volatile database pages into the stable database at precisely the commit point—not before and not after. This strategy is called no-undo/no-redo by Bernstein et al. [1987] and no-steal/force by Härder and Reuter [1983].

Abort.

The execution of **abort** is identical to that of the fix/no-flush case.

Commit.

The LRM sends an **unfix** command to the buffer manager for every volatile database page that was previously fixed by that transaction. It then issues a **flush** command to the buffer manager, forcing it to write back all the unfixed volatile database pages into the stable database.[7] Finally, the **commit** command is processed by either writing an end_of_transaction record into the log or by including the transaction in the commit list. The important point to note here is that all three of these operations have to be executed as an atomic action. One step that can be taken to achieve this atomicity is to issue only a **flush** command, which serves to unfix the pages as well. This eliminates the need to send two messages from the LRM to the buffer manager, but does not eliminate the requirement for the atomic execution of the flush operation and the writing of the database log. The LRM then informs the scheduler that the **commit** has been carried out successfully. Methods for ensuring this atomicity are beyond the scope of our discussion (see [Bernstein et al., 1987]).

Recover.

The **recover** command does not need to do anything in this case. This is true since the stable database reflects the effects of all the successful transactions and none of the effects of the uncommitted transactions.

12.3.4 Checkpointing

In most of the LRM implementation strategies, the execution of the recovery action requires searching the entire log. This is a significant overhead because the LRM is trying to find all the transactions that need to be undone and redone. The overhead can be reduced if it is possible to build a wall which signifies that the database at that point is up-to-date and consistent. In that case, the redo has to start from that point on and the undo only has to go back to that point. This process of building the wall is called *checkpointing*.

Checkpointing is achieved in three steps [Gray, 1979]:

---

[7] Our discussion here gives the impression that two commands (*unfix* and *flush*) need to be sent to the BM by the LRM for each commit action. We have chosen to explain the action in this way only for presentation simplicity. In reality, it is, of course, possible and preferable to implement one command that instructs the BM to both unfix and flush, thereby reducing the message overhead between DBMS components.

1. Write a begin_checkpoint record into the log.

2. Collect the checkpoint data into the stable storage.

3. Write an end_checkpoint record into the log.

The first and the third steps enforce the atomicity of the checkpointing operation. If a system failure occurs during checkpointing, the recovery process will not find an end_checkpoint record and will consider checkpointing not completed.

There are a number of different alternatives for the data that is collected in Step 2, how it is collected, and where it is stored. We will consider one example here, called *transaction-consistent checkpointing* ([Gray, 1979; Gray et al., 1981]). The checkpointing starts by writing the begin_checkpoint record in the log and stopping the acceptance of any new transactions by the LRM. Once the active transactions are all completed, all the updated volatile database pages are flushed to the stable database followed by the insertion of an end_checkpoint record into the log. In this case, the redo action only needs to start from the end_checkpoint record in the log. The undo action can go the reverse direction, starting from the end of the log and stopping at the end_checkpoint record.

Transaction-consistent checkpointing is not the most efficient algorithm, since a significant delay is experienced by all the transactions. There are alternative check-pointing schemes such as action-consistent checkpoints, fuzzy checkpoints, and others ([Gray, 1979; Lindsay, 1979]).

12.3.5 Handling Media Failures

As we mentioned before, the previous discussion on centralized recovery considered non-media failures, where the database as well as the log stored in the stable storage survive the failure. Media failures may either be quite catastrophic, causing the loss of the stable database or of the stable log, or they can simply result in partial loss of the database or the log (e.g., loss of a track or two).

The methods that have been devised for dealing with this situation are again based on duplexing. To cope with catastrophic media failures, an *archive* copy of both the database and the log is maintained on a different (tertiary) storage medium, which is typically the magnetic tape or CD-ROM. Thus the DBMS deals with three levels of memory hierarchy: the main memory, random access disk storage, and magnetic tape (Figure 12.9). To deal with less catastrophic failures, having duplicate copies of the database and log may be sufficient.

When a media failure occurs, the database is recovered from the archive copy by redoing and undoing the transactions as stored in the archive log. The real question is how the archive database is stored. If we consider the large sizes of current databases, the overhead of writing the entire database to tertiary storage is significant. Two methods that have been proposed for dealing with this are to perform the archiving activity concurrent with normal processing and to archive the database incrementally

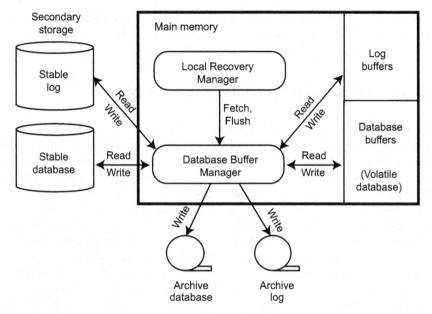

Fig. 12.9 Full Memory Hierarchy Managed by LRM and BM

as changes occur so that each archive version contains only the changes that have occurred since the previous archiving.

12.4 Distributed Reliability Protocols

As with local reliability protocols, the distributed versions aim to maintain the atomicity and durability of distributed transactions that execute over a number of databases. The protocols address the distributed execution of the **begin_transaction, read, write, abort, commit**, and **recover** commands.

At the outset we should indicate that the execution of the **begin_transaction, read,** and **write** commands does not cause any significant problems. **Begin_transaction** is executed in exactly the same manner as in the centralized case by the transaction manager at the originating site of the transaction. The **read** and **write** commands are executed as discussed in Chapter 11. At each site, the commands are executed in the manner described in Section 12.3.3. Similarly, abort is executed by undoing its effects.

The implementation of distributed reliability protocols within the architectural model we have adopted in this book raises a number of interesting and difficult issues. We discuss these in Section 12.7 after we introduce the protocols. For the time being, we adopt a common abstraction: we assume that at the originating site of a transaction there is a *coordinator* process and at each site where the transaction executes there are *participant* processes. Thus, the distributed reliability protocols are implemented between the coordinator and the participants.

12.4.1 Components of Distributed Reliability Protocols

The reliability techniques in distributed database systems consist of commit, termination, and recovery protocols. Recall from the preceding section that the commit and recovery protocols specify how the commit and the recover commands are executed. Both of these commands need to be executed differently in a distributed DBMS than in a centralized DBMS. Termination protocols are unique to distributed systems. Assume that during the execution of a distributed transaction, one of the sites involved in the execution fails; we would like the other sites to terminate the transaction somehow. The techniques for dealing with this situation are called *termination protocols*. Termination and recovery protocols are two opposite faces of the recovery problem: given a site failure, termination protocols address how the operational sites deal with the failure, whereas recovery protocols deal with the procedure that the process (coordinator or participant) at the failed site has to go through to recover its state once the site is restarted. In the case of network partitioning, the termination protocols take the necessary measures to terminate the active transactions that execute at different partitions, while the recovery protocols address the establishment of mutual consistency of replicated databases following reconnection of the partitions of the network.

The primary requirement of commit protocols is that they maintain the atomicity of distributed transactions. This means that even though the execution of the distributed transaction involves multiple sites, some of which might fail while executing, the effects of the transaction on the distributed database is all-or-nothing. This is called *atomic commitment*. We would prefer the termination protocols to be *non-blocking*. A protocol is non-blocking if it permits a transaction to terminate at the operational sites without waiting for recovery of the failed site. This would significantly improve the response-time performance of transactions. We would also like the distributed recovery protocols to be *independent*. Independent recovery protocols determine how to terminate a transaction that was executing at the time of a failure without having to consult any other site. Existence of such protocols would reduce the number of messages that need to be exchanged during recovery. Note that the existence of independent recovery protocols would imply the existence of non-blocking termination protocols, but the reverse is not true.

12.4.2 Two-Phase Commit Protocol

Two-phase commit (2PC) is a very simple and elegant protocol that ensures the atomic commitment of distributed transactions. It extends the effects of local atomic commit actions to distributed transactions by insisting that all sites involved in the execution of a distributed transaction agree to commit the transaction before its effects are made permanent. There are a number of reasons why such synchronization among sites is necessary. First, depending on the type of concurrency control algorithm that is used, some schedulers may not be ready to terminate a transaction. For example, if a transaction has read a value of a data item that is updated by another transaction that has not yet committed, the associated scheduler may not want to commit the former. Of course, strict concurrency control algorithms that avoid cascading aborts would not permit the updated value of a data item to be read by any other transaction until the updating transaction terminates. This is sometimes called the *recoverability condition* ([Hadzilacos, 1988; Bernstein et al., 1987]).

Another possible reason why a participant may not agree to commit is due to deadlocks that require a participant to abort the transaction. Note that, in this case, the participant should be permitted to abort the transaction without being told to do so. This capability is quite important and is called *unilateral abort*.

A brief description of the 2PC protocol that does not consider failures is as follows. Initially, the coordinator writes a begin_commit record in its log, sends a "prepare" message to all participant sites, and enters the WAIT state. When a participant receives a "prepare" message, it checks if it could commit the transaction. If so, the participant writes a ready record in the log, sends a "vote-commit" message to the coordinator, and enters READY state; otherwise, the participant writes an abort record and sends a "vote-abort" message to the coordinator. If the decision of the site is to abort, it can forget about that transaction, since an abort decision serves as a veto (i.e., unilateral abort). After the coordinator has received a reply from every participant, it decides whether to commit or to abort the transaction. If even one participant has registered a negative vote, the coordinator has to abort the transaction globally. So it writes an abort record, sends a "global-abort" message to all participant sites, and enters the ABORT state; otherwise, it writes a commit record, sends a "global-commit" message to all participants, and enters the COMMIT state. The participants either commit or abort the transaction according to the coordinator's instructions and send back an acknowledgment, at which point the coordinator terminates the transaction by writing an end_of_transaction record in the log.

Note the manner in which the coordinator reaches a global termination decision regarding a transaction. Two rules govern this decision, which, together, are called the *global commit rule*:

1. If even one participant votes to abort the transaction, the coordinator has to reach a global abort decision.

2. If all the participants vote to commit the transaction, the coordinator has to reach a global commit decision.

The operation of the 2PC protocol between a coordinator and one participant in the absence of failures is depicted in Figure 12.10, where the circles indicate the states and the dashed lines indicate messages between the coordinator and the participants. The labels on the dashed lines specify the nature of the message.

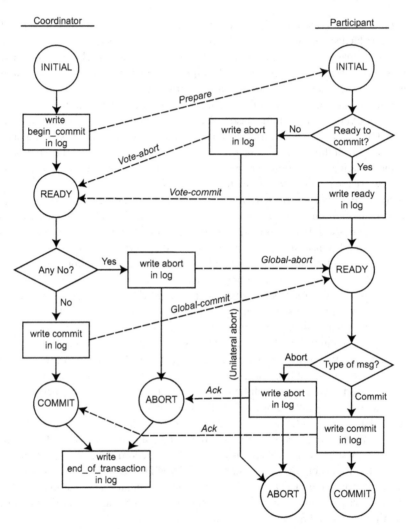

Fig. 12.10 2PC Protocol Actions

A few important points about the 2PC protocol that can be observed from Figure 12.10 are as follows. First, 2PC permits a participant to unilaterally abort a transaction until it has decided to register an affirmative vote. Second, once a participant votes to commit or abort a transaction, it cannot change its vote. Third, while a participant is in the READY state, it can move either to abort the transaction or to commit it, depending on the nature of the message from the coordinator. Fourth, the global termination decision is taken by the coordinator according to the global commit rule. Finally, note that the coordinator and participant processes enter certain states where they have to wait for messages from one another. To guarantee that they can exit from these states and terminate, timers are used. Each process sets its timer when it enters a state, and if the expected message is not received before the timer runs out, the process times out and invokes its timeout protocol (which will be discussed later).

There are a number of different communication paradigms that can be employed in implementing a 2PC protocol. The one discussed above and depicted in Figure 12.10 is called a *centralized 2PC* since the communication is only between the coordinator and the participants; the participants do not communicate among themselves. This communication structure, which is the basis of our subsequent discussions in this chapter, is depicted more clearly in Figure 12.11.

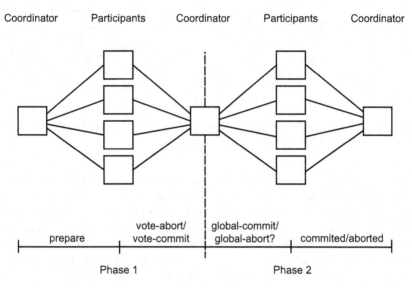

Fig. 12.11 Centralized 2PC Communication Structure

Another alternative is *linear 2PC* (also called *nested 2PC* [Gray, 1979]) where participants can communicate with one another. There is an ordering between the sites in the system for the purposes of communication. Let us assume that the ordering among the sites that participate in the execution of a transaction are $1, \ldots, N$, where the coordinator is the first one in the order. The 2PC protocol is implemented by a forward communication from the coordinator (number 1) to N, during which the first phase is completed, and by a backward communication from N to the coordinator, during which the second phase is completed. Thus linear 2PC operates in the following manner.

The coordinator sends the "prepare" message to participant 2. If participant 2 is not ready to commit the transaction, it sends a "vote-abort" message (VA) to participant 3 and the transaction is aborted at this point (unilateral abort by 2). If, on the other hand, participant 2 agrees to commit the transaction, it sends a "vote-commit" message (VC) to participant 3 and enters the READY state. This process continues until a "vote-commit" vote reaches participant N. This is the end of the first phase. If N decides to commit, it sends back to $N - 1$ "global-commit" (GC); otherwise, it sends a "global-abort" message (GA). Accordingly, the participants enter the appropriate state (COMMIT or ABORT) and propagate the message back to the coordinator.

Linear 2PC, whose communication structure is depicted in Figure 12.12, incurs fewer messages but does not provide any parallelism. Therefore, it suffers from low response-time performance.

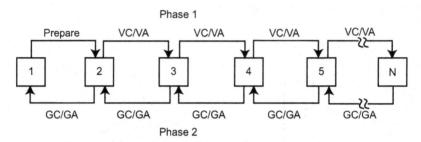

Fig. 12.12 Linear 2PC Communication Structure. VC, vote.commit; VA, vote.abort; GC, global.commit; GA, global.abort.)

Another popular communication structure for implementation of the 2PC protocol involves communication among all the participants during the first phase of the protocol so that they all independently reach their termination decisions with respect to the specific transaction. This version, called *distributed 2PC*, eliminates the need for the second phase of the protocol since the participants can reach a decision on their own. It operates as follows. The coordinator sends the prepare message to all participants. Each participant then sends its decision to all the other participants (and to the coordinator) by means of either a "vote-commit" or a "vote-abort" message. Each participant waits for messages from all the other participants and makes its termination decision according to the global commit rule. Obviously, there is no need for the second phase of the protocol (someone sending the global abort or global commit decision to the others), since each participant has independently reached that decision at the end of the first phase. The communication structure of distributed commit is depicted in Figure 12.13.

One point that needs to be addressed with respect to the last two versions of 2PC implementation is the following. A participant has to know the identity of either the next participant in the linear ordering (in case of linear 2PC) or of all the participants (in case of distributed 2PC). This problem can be solved by attaching the list of participants to the prepare message that is sent by the coordinator. Such an issue does not arise in the case of centralized 2PC since the coordinator clearly knows who the participants are.

The algorithm for the centralized execution of the 2PC protocol by the coordinator is given in Algorithm 12.1, and the algorithm for participants is given in Algorithm 12.2.

Algorithm 12.1: 2PC Coordinator Algorithm (2PC-C)

```
begin
    repeat
        wait for an event ;
        switch event do
            case Msg Arrival
                Let the arrived message be msg ;
                switch msg do
                    case Commit                    {commit command from scheduler}
                        write begin_commit record in the log ;
                        send "Prepared" message to all the involved
                        participants ;
                        set timer
                    case Vote-abort {one participant has voted to abort;
                    unilateral abort}
                        write abort record in the log ;
                        send "Global-abort" message to the other involved
                        participants ;
                        set timer
                    case Vote-commit
                        update the list of participants who have answered ;
                        if all the participants have answered then {all must
                        have voted to commit}
                            write commit record in the log ;
                            send "Global-commit" to all the involved
                            participants ;
                            set timer

                    case Ack
                        update the list of participants who have acknowledged ;
                        if all the participants have acknowledged then
                            write end_of_transaction record in the log
                        else
                            send global decision to the unanswering participants

            case Timeout
                execute the termination protocol
    until forever ;
end
```

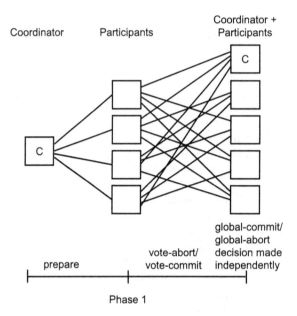

Coordinator   Participants   Coordinator +
                                                 Participants

                                                 global-commit/
                                                 global-abort
                                    vote-abort/   decision made
            prepare   vote-commit independently

                                Phase 1

Fig. 12.13 Distributed 2PC Communication Structure

12.4.3 Variations of 2PC

Two variations of 2PC have been proposed to improve its performance. This is accomplished by reducing (1) the number of messages that are transmitted between the coordinator and the participants, and (2) the number of times logs are written. These protocols are called *presumed abort* and *presumed commit* [Mohan and Lindsay, 1983; Mohan et al., 1986]. Presumed abort is a protocol that is optimized to handle read-only transactions as well as those update transactions, some of whose processes do not perform any updates to the database (called partially read-only). The presumed commit protocol is optimized to handle the general update transactions. We will discuss briefly both of these variations.

12.4.3.1 Presumed Abort 2PC Protocol

In the presumed abort 2PC protocol the following assumption is made. Whenever a prepared participant polls the coordinator about a transaction's outcome and there is no information in virtual storage about it, the response to the inquiry is to abort the transaction. This works since, in the case of a commit, the coordinator does not forget about a transaction until all participants acknowledge, guaranteeing that they will no longer inquire about this transaction.

When this convention is used, it can be seen that the coordinator can forget about a transaction immediately after it decides to abort it. It can write an abort record and

---

Algorithm 12.2: 2PC Participant Algorithm (2PC-P)

---

begin
  repeat
    wait for an *event* ;
    switch *ev* **do**
      case *Msg Arrival*
        Let the arrived message be *msg* ;
        switch *msg* **do**
          case *Prepare*   {Prepare command from the coordinator}
            if *ready to commit* **then**
              write ready record in the log ;
              send "Vote-commit" message to the coordinator ;
              set timer
            else   {unilateral abort}
              write abort record in the log ;
              send "Vote-abort" message to the coordinator ;
              abort the transaction
          case *Global-abort*
            write abort record in the log ;
            abort the transaction
          case *Global-commit*
            write commit record in the log ;
            commit the transaction
      case *Timeout*
        execute the termination protocol
  until *forever* ;
end

---

not expect the participants to acknowledge the abort command. The coordinator does not need to write an end_of_transaction record after an abort record.

The abort record does not need to be forced, because if a site fails before receiving the decision and then recovers, the recovery routine will check the log to determine the fate of the transaction. Since the abort record is not forced, the recovery routine may not find any information about the transaction, in which case it will ask the coordinator and will be told to abort it. For the same reason, the abort records do not need to be forced by the participants either.

Since it saves some message transmission between the coordinator and the participants in case of aborted transactions, presumed abort 2PC is expected to be more efficient.

12.4.3.2 Presumed Commit 2PC Protocol

The presumed abort 2PC protocol, as discussed above, improves performance by forgetting about transactions once a decision is reached to abort them. Since most transactions are expected to commit, it is reasonable to expect that it may be similarly possible to improve performance for commits. Hence the presumed commit 2PC protocol.

Presumed commit 2PC is based on the premise that if no information about the transaction exists, it should be considered committed. However, it is not an exact dual of presumed abort 2PC, since an exact dual would require that the coordinator forget about a transaction immediately after it decides to commit it, that commit records (also the ready records of the participants) not be forced, and that commit commands need not be acknowledged. Consider, however, the following scenario. The coordinator sends prepared messages and starts collecting information, but fails before being able to collect all of them and reach a decision. In this case, the participants will wait until they timeout, and then turn the transaction over to their recovery routines. Since there is no information about the transaction, the recovery routines of each participant will commit the transaction. The coordinator, on the other hand, will abort the transaction when it recovers, thus causing inconsistency.

A simple variation of this protocol, however, solves the problem and that variant is called the *presumed commit 2PC*. The coordinator, prior to sending the prepare message, force-writes a collecting record, which contains the names of all the participants involved in executing that transaction. The participant then enters the COLLECTING state, following which it sends the prepare message and enters the WAIT state. The participants, when they receive the prepare message, decide what they want to do with the transaction, write an abort record, or write a ready record and respond with either a "vote-abort" or a "vote-commit" message. When the coordinator receives decisions from all the participants, it decides to abort or commit the transaction. If the decision is to abort, the coordinator writes an abort record, enters the ABORT state, and sends a "global-abort" message. If it decides to commit the transaction, it writes a commit record, sends a "global-commit" command, and forgets the transaction. When the participants receive a "global-commit" message, they write a commit record and update the database. If they receive a "global-abort" message, they write an abort record and acknowledge. The participant, upon receiving the abort acknowledgment, writes an end_of_transaction record and forgets about the transaction.

12.5 Dealing with Site Failures

In this section we consider the failure of sites in the network. Our aim is to develop non-blocking termination and independent recovery protocols. As we indicated before, the existence of independent recovery protocols would imply the existence of non-blocking recovery protocols. However, our discussion addresses both aspects separately. Also note that in the following discussion we consider only the standard 2PC protocol, not its two variants presented above.

Let us first set the boundaries for the existence of non-blocking termination and independent recovery protocols in the presence of site failures. It can formally be proven that such protocols exist when a single site fails. In the case of multiple site failures, however, the prospects are not as promising. A negative result indicates that it is not possible to design independent recovery protocols (and, therefore, non-blocking termination protocols) when multiple sites fail [Skeen and Stonebraker, 1983]. We first develop termination and recovery protocols for the 2PC algorithm and show that 2PC is inherently blocking. We then proceed to the development of atomic commit protocols which are non-blocking in the case of single site failures.

12.5.1 Termination and Recovery Protocols for 2PC

12.5.1.1 Termination Protocols

The termination protocols serve the timeouts for both the coordinator and the participant processes. A timeout occurs at a destination site when it cannot get an expected message from a source site within the expected time period. In this section we consider that this is due to the failure of the source site.

The method for handling timeouts depends on the timing of failures as well as on the types of failures. We therefore need to consider failures at various points of 2PC execution. This discussion is facilitated by means of the state transition diagram of the 2PC protocol given in Figure 12.14. Note that the state transition diagram is a simplification of Figure 12.10. The states are denoted by circles and the edges represent the state transitions. The terminal states are depicted by concentric circles. The interpretation of the labels on the edges is as follows: the reason for the state transition, which is a received message, is given at the top, and the message that is sent as a result of state transition is given at the bottom.

Coordinator Timeouts.

There are three states in which the coordinator can timeout: WAIT, COMMIT, and ABORT. Timeouts during the last two are handled in the same manner. So we need to consider only two cases:

1. *Timeout in the WAIT state.* In the WAIT state, the coordinator is waiting for the local decisions of the participants. The coordinator cannot unilaterally commit the transaction since the global commit rule has not been satisfied. However, it can decide to globally abort the transaction, in which case it writes an abort record in the log and sends a "global-abort" message to all the participants.

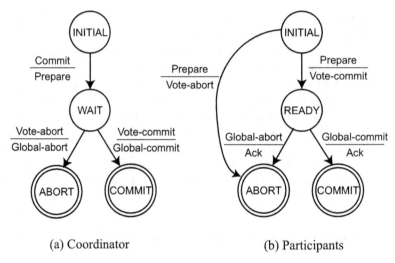

(a) Coordinator   (b) Participants

Fig. 12.14 State Transitions in 2PC Protocol

2. *Timeout in the COMMIT or ABORT states.* In this case the coordinator is
   not certain that the commit or abort procedures have been completed by the
   local recovery managers at all of the participant sites. Thus the coordinator
   repeatedly sends the "global-commit" or "global-abort" commands to the
   sites that have not yet responded, and waits for their acknowledgement.

Participant Timeouts.

A participant can time out[8] in two states: INITIAL and READY. Let us examine
both of these cases.

1. *Timeout in the INITIAL state.* In this state the participant is waiting for a
   "prepare" message. The coordinator must have failed in the INITIAL state.
   The participant can unilaterally abort the transaction following a timeout. If
   the "prepare" message arrives at this participant at a later time, this can be
   handled in one of two possible ways. Either the participant would check its
   log, find the abort record, and respond with a "vote-abort," or it can simply
   ignore the "prepare" message. In the latter case the coordinator would time
   out in the WAIT state and follow the course we have discussed above.

2. *Timeout in the READY state.* In this state the participant has voted to commit
   the transaction but does not know the global decision of the coordinator. The
   participant cannot unilaterally make a decision. Since it is in the READY state,

---

[8] In some discussions of the 2PC protocol, it is assumed that the participants do not use timers and
do not time out. However, implementing timeout protocols for the participants solves some nasty
problems and may speed up the commit process. Therefore, we consider this more general case.

it must have voted to commit the transaction. Therefore, it cannot now change its vote and unilaterally abort it. On the other hand, it cannot unilaterally decide to commit it since it is possible that another participant may have voted to abort it. In this case the participant will remain blocked until it can learn from someone (either the coordinator or some other participant) the ultimate fate of the transaction.

Let us consider a centralized communication structure where the participants cannot communicate with one another. In this case the participant that is trying to terminate a transaction has to ask the coordinator for its decision and wait until it receives a response. If the coordinator has failed, the participant will remain blocked. This is undesirable.

If the participants can communicate with each other, a more distributed termination protocol may be developed. The participant that times out can simply ask all the other participants to help it make a decision. Assuming that participant P_i is the one that times out, each of the other participants (P_j) responds in the following manner:

1. P_j is in the INITIAL state. This means that P_j has not yet voted and may not even have received the "prepare" message. It can therefore unilaterally abort the transaction and reply to P_i with a "vote-abort" message.

2. P_j is in the READY state. In this state P_j has voted to commit the transaction but has not received any word about the global decision. Therefore, it cannot help P_i to terminate the transaction.

3. P_j is in the ABORT or COMMIT states. In these states, either P_j has unilaterally decided to abort the transaction, or it has received the coordinator's decision regarding global termination. It can, therefore, send P_i either a "vote-commit" or a "vote-abort" message.

Consider how the participant that times out (P_i) can interpret these responses. The following cases are possible:

1. P_i receives "vote-abort" messages from all P_j. This means that none of the other participants had yet voted, but they have chosen to abort the transaction unilaterally. Under these conditions, P_i can proceed to abort the transaction.

2. P_i receives "vote-abort" messages from some P_j, but some other participants indicate that they are in the READY state. In this case P_i can still go ahead and abort the transaction, since according to the global commit rule, the transaction cannot be committed and will eventually be aborted.

3. P_i receives notification from all P_j that they are in the READY state. In this case none of the participants knows enough about the fate of the transaction to terminate it properly.

4. P_i receives "global-abort" or "global-commit" messages from all P_j. In this case all the other participants have received the coordinator's decision. Therefore, P_i can go ahead and terminate the transaction according to the messages

it receives from the other participants. Incidentally, note that it is not possible for some of the P_j to respond with a "global-abort" while others respond with "global-commit" since this cannot be the result of a legitimate execution of the 2PC protocol.

5. P_i receives "global-abort" or "global-commit" from some P_j, whereas others indicate that they are in the READY state. This indicates that some sites have received the coordinator's decision while others are still waiting for it. In this case P_i can proceed as in case 4 above.

These five cases cover all the alternatives that a termination protocol needs to handle. It is not necessary to consider cases where, for example, one participant sends a "vote-abort" message while another one sends "global-commit." This cannot happen in 2PC. During the execution of the 2PC protocol, no process (participant or coordinator) is more than one state transition apart from any other process. For example, if a participant is in the INITIAL state, all other participants are in either the INITIAL or the READY state. Similarly, the coordinator is either in the INITIAL or the WAIT state. Thus, all the processes in a 2PC protocol are said to be *synchronous within one state transition* [Skeen, 1981].

Note that in case 3 the participant processes stay blocked, as they cannot terminate a transaction. Under certain circumstances there may be a way to overcome this blocking. If during termination all the participants realize that only the coordinator site has failed, they can elect a new coordinator, which can restart the commit process. There are different ways of electing the coordinator. It is possible either to define a total ordering among all sites and elect the next one in order [Hammer and Shipman, 1980], or to establish a voting procedure among the participants [Garcia-Molina, 1982]. This will not work, however, if both a participant site and the coordinator site fail. In this case it is possible for the participant at the failed site to have received the coordinator's decision and have terminated the transaction accordingly. This decision is unknown to the other participants; thus if they elect a new coordinator and proceed, there is the danger that they may decide to terminate the transaction differently from the participant at the failed site. It is clear that it is not possible to design termination protocols for 2PC that can guarantee non-blocking termination. The 2PC protocol is, therefore, a blocking protocol.

Since we had assumed a centralized communication structure in developing the 2PC algorithms in Algorithms 12.1 and 12.2, we will continue with the same assumption in developing the termination protocols. The portion of code that should be included in the timeout section of the coordinator and the participant 2PC algorithms is given in Algorithms 12.3 and 12.4, respectively.

12.5.1.2 Recovery Protocols

In the preceding section, we discussed how the 2PC protocol deals with failures from the perspective of the operational sites. In this section, we take the opposite viewpoint: we are interested in investigating protocols that a coordinator or participant can use

---

Algorithm 12.3: 2PC Coordinator Terminate

---

begin
    if *in WAIT state* **then**   {coordinator is in ABORT state}
       | write abort record in the log ;
       | send "Global-abort" message to all the participants
    else   {coordinator is in COMMIT state}
       check for the last log record ;
       if *last log record = abort* **then**
        | send "Global-abort" to all participants that have not responded
       else
        | send "Global-commit" to all the participants that have not
        | responded
    set timer ;
end

Algorithm 12.4: 2PC-Participant Terminate

---

begin
    if *in INITIAL state* **then**
    | write abort record in the log
    else
    | send "Vote-commit" message to the coordinator ;
    | reset timer
end

---

to recover their states when their sites fail and then restart. Remember that we would like these protocols to be independent. However, in general, it is not possible to design protocols that can guarantee independent recovery while maintaining the atomicity of distributed transactions. This is not surprising given the fact that the termination protocols for 2PC are inherently blocking.

In the following discussion, we again use the state transition diagram of Figure 12.14. Additionally, we make two interpretive assumptions: (1) the combined action of writing a record in the log and sending a message is assumed to be atomic, and (2) the state transition occurs after the transmission of the response message. For example, if the coordinator is in the WAIT state, this means that it has successfully written the begin_commit record in its log and has successfully transmitted the "prepare" command. This does not say anything, however, about successful completion of the message transmission. Therefore, the "prepare" message may never get to the participants, due to communication failures, which we discuss separately. The first assumption related to atomicity is, of course, unrealistic. However, it simplifies our discussion of fundamental failure cases. At the end of this section we show that the other cases that arise from the relaxation of this assumption can be handled by a combination of the fundamental failure cases.

Coordinator Site Failures.

The following cases are possible:

1. *The coordinator fails while in the INITIAL state.* This is before the coordinator has initiated the commit procedure. Therefore, it will start the commit process upon recovery.

2. *The coordinator fails while in the WAIT state.* In this case, the coordinator has sent the "prepare" command. Upon recovery, the coordinator will restart the commit process for this transaction from the beginning by sending the "prepare" message one more time.

3. *The coordinator fails while in the COMMIT or ABORT states.* In this case, the coordinator will have informed the participants of its decision and terminated the transaction. Thus, upon recovery, it does not need to do anything if all the acknowledgments have been received. Otherwise, the termination protocol is involved.

Participant Site Failures.

There are three alternatives to consider:

1. *A participant fails in the INITIAL state.* Upon recovery, the participant should abort the transaction unilaterally. Let us see why this is acceptable. Note that the coordinator will be in the INITIAL or WAIT state with respect to this transaction. If it is in the INITIAL state, it will send a "prepare" message and then move to the WAIT state. Because of the participant site's failure, it will not receive the participant's decision and will time out in that state. We have already discussed how the coordinator would handle timeouts in the WAIT state by globally aborting the transaction.

2. *A participant fails while in the READY state.* In this case the coordinator has been informed of the failed site's affirmative decision about the transaction before the failure. Upon recovery, the participant at the failed site can treat this as a timeout in the READY state and hand the incomplete transaction over to its termination protocol.

3. *A participant fails while in the ABORT or COMMIT state.* These states represent the termination conditions, so, upon recovery, the participant does not need to take any special action.

Additional Cases.

Let us now consider the cases that may arise when we relax the assumption related to the atomicity of the logging and message sending actions. In particular, we assume that a site failure may occur after the coordinator or a participant has written a log record but before it can send a message. For this discussion, the reader may wish to refer to Figure 12.10.

1. *The coordinator fails after the* begin_commit *record is written in the log but before the "prepare" command is sent.* The coordinator would react to this as a failure in the WAIT state (case 2 of the coordinator failures discussed above) and send the "prepare" command upon recovery.

2. *A participant site fails after writing the* ready *record in the log but before sending the "vote-commit" message.* The failed participant sees this as case 2 of the participant failures discussed before.

3. *A participant site fails after writing the* abort *record in the log but before sending the "vote-abort" message.* This is the only situation that is not covered by the fundamental cases discussed before. However, the participant does not need to do anything upon recovery in this case. The coordinator is in the WAIT state and will time out. The coordinator termination protocol for this state globally aborts the transaction.

4. *The coordinator fails after logging its final decision record* (abort *or* commit), *but before sending its "global-abort" or "global-commit" message to the participants.* The coordinator treats this as its case 3, while the participants treat it as a timeout in the READY state.

5. *A participant fails after it logs an* abort *or a* commit *record but before it sends the acknowledgment message to the coordinator.* The participant can treat this as its case 3. The coordinator will handle this by timeout in the COMMIT or ABORT state.

12.5.2 Three-Phase Commit Protocol

The three-phase commit protocol (3PC) [Skeen, 1981] is designed as a non-blocking protocol. We will see in this section that it is indeed non-blocking when failures are restricted to site failures.

Let us first consider the necessary and sufficient conditions for designing non-blocking atomic commitment protocols. A commit protocol that is synchronous within one state transition is non-blocking if and only if its state transition diagram contains neither of the following:

1. No state that is "adjacent" to both a commit and an abort state.

2. No non-committable state that is "adjacent" to a commit state ([Skeen, 1981; Skeen and Stonebraker, 1983]).

The term *adjacent* here means that it is possible to go from one state to the other with a single state transition.

Consider the COMMIT state in the 2PC protocol (see Figure 12.14). If any process is in this state, we know that all the sites have voted to commit the transaction. Such states are called *committable*. There are other states in the 2PC protocol that are *non-committable*. The one we are interested in is the READY state, which is non-committable since the existence of a process in this state does not imply that all the processes have voted to commit the transaction.

It is obvious that the WAIT state in the coordinator and the READY state in the participant 2PC protocol violate the non-blocking conditions we have stated above. Therefore, one might be able to make the following modification to the 2PC protocol to satisfy the conditions and turn it into a non-blocking protocol.

We can add another state between the WAIT (and READY) and COMMIT states which serves as a buffer state where the process is ready to commit (if that is the final decision) but has not yet committed. The state transition diagrams for the coordinator and the participant in this protocol are depicted in Figure 12.15. This is called the three-phase commit protocol (3PC) because there are three state transitions from the INITIAL state to a COMMIT state. The execution of the protocol between the coordinator and one participant is depicted in Figure 12.16. Note that this is identical to Figure 12.10 except for the addition of the PRECOMMIT state. Observe that 3PC is also a protocol where all the states are synchronous within one state transition. Therefore, the foregoing conditions for non-blocking 2PC apply to 3PC.

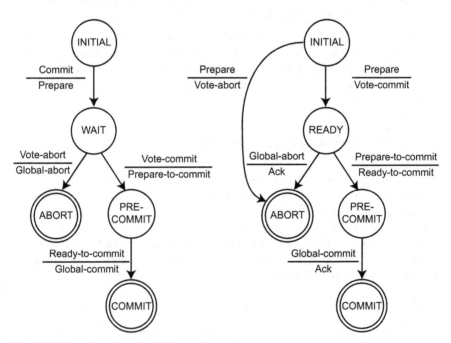

Fig. 12.15 State Transitions in 3PC Protocol

It is possible to design different 3PC algorithms depending on the communication topology. The one given in Figure 12.16 is centralized. It is also straightforward to design a distributed 3PC protocol. A linear 3PC protocol is somewhat more involved, so we leave it as an exercise.

12.5.2.1 Termination Protocol

As we did in discussing the termination protocols for handling timeouts in the 2PC protocol, let us investigate timeouts at each state of the 3PC protocol.

Coordinator Timeouts.

In 3PC, there are four states in which the coordinator can time out: WAIT, PRECOMMIT, COMMIT, or ABORT.

1. *Timeout in the WAIT state.* This is identical to the coordinator timeout in the WAIT state for the 2PC protocol. The coordinator unilaterally decides to abort the transaction. It therefore writes an abort record in the log and sends a "global-abort" message to all the participants that have voted to commit the transaction.

2. *Timeout in the PRECOMMIT state.* The coordinator does not know if the non-responding participants have already moved to the PRECOMMIT state. However, it knows that they are at least in the READY state, which means that they must have voted to commit the transaction. The coordinator can therefore move all participants to PRECOMMIT state by sending a "prepare-to-commit" message go ahead and globally commit the transaction by writing a commit record in the log and sending a "global-commit" message to all the operational participants.

3. *Timeout in the COMMIT (or ABORT) state.* The coordinator does not know whether the participants have actually performed the commit (abort) command. However, they are at least in the PRECOMMIT (READY) state (since the protocol is synchronous within one state transition) and can follow the termination protocol as described in case 2 or case 3 below. Thus the coordinator does not need to take any special action.

Participant Timeouts.

A participant can time out in three states: INITIAL, READY, and PRECOMMIT. Let us examine all of these cases.

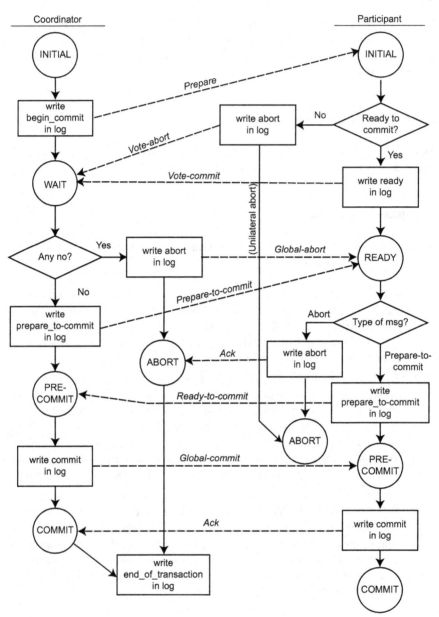

Fig. 12.16 3PC Protocol Actions

1. *Timeout in the INITIAL state.* This can be handled identically to the termination protocol of 2PC.

2. *Timeout in the READY state.* In this state the participant has voted to commit the transaction but does not know the global decision of the coordinator. Since communication with the coordinator is lost, the termination protocol proceeds by electing a new coordinator, as discussed earlier. The new coordinator then terminates the transaction according to a termination protocol that we discuss below.

3. *Timeout in the PRECOMMIT state.* In this state the participant has received the "prepare-to-commit" message and is awaiting the final "global-commit" message from the coordinator. This case is handled identically to case 2 above.

Let us now consider the possible termination protocols that can be adopted in the last two cases. There are various alternatives; let us consider a centralized one [Skeen, 1981]. We know that the new coordinator can be in one of three states: WAIT, PRECOMMIT, COMMIT or ABORT. It sends its own state to all the operational participants, asking them to assume that state. Any participant who has proceeded ahead of the new coordinator (which is possible since it may have already received and processed a message from the old coordinator) simply ignores the new coordinator's message; others make their state transitions and send back the appropriate message. Once the new coordinator gets messages from the participants, it guides the participants toward termination as follows:

1. If the new coordinator is in the WAIT state, it will globally abort the transaction. The participants can be in the INITIAL, READY, ABORT, or PRECOMMIT states. In the first three cases, there is no problem. However, the participants in the PRECOMMIT state are expecting a "global-commit" message, but they get a "global-abort" instead. Their state transition diagram does not indicate any transition from the PRECOMMIT to the ABORT state. This transition is necessary for the termination protocol, so it should be added to the set of legal transitions that can occur during execution of the termination protocol.

2. If the new coordinator is in the PRECOMMIT state, the participants can be in the READY, PRECOMMIT or COMMIT states. No participant can be in ABORT state. The coordinator will therefore globally commit the transaction and send a "global-commit" message.

3. If the new coordinator is in the ABORT state, at the end of the first message all the participants will have moved into the ABORT state as well.

The new coordinator is not keeping track of participant failures during this process. It simply guides the operational sites toward termination. If some participants fail in the meantime, they will have to terminate the transaction upon recovery according to the methods discussed in the next section. Also, the new coordinator may fail during the process; the termination protocol therefore needs to be reentrant in implementation.

This termination protocol is obviously non-blocking. The operational sites can properly terminate all the ongoing transactions and continue their operations. The proof of correctness of the algorithm is given in [Skeen, 1982b].

12.5.2.2 Recovery Protocols

There are some minor differences between the recovery protocols of 3PC and those of 2PC. We only indicate those differences.

1. *The coordinator fails while in the WAIT state.* This is the case we discussed at length in the earlier section on termination protocols. The participants have already terminated the transaction. Therefore, upon recovery, the coordinator has to ask around to determine the fate of the transaction.

2. *The coordinator fails while in the PRECOMMIT state.* Again, the termination protocol has guided the operational participants toward termination. Since it is now possible to move from the PRECOMMIT state to the ABORT state during this process, the coordinator has to ask around to determine the fate of the transaction.

3. *A participant fails while in the PRECOMMIT state.* It has to ask around to determine how the other participants have terminated the transaction.

One property of the 3PC protocol becomes obvious from this discussion. When using the 3PC protocol, we are able to terminate transactions without blocking. However, we pay the price that fewer cases of independent recovery are possible. This also results in more messages being exchanged during recovery.

12.6 Network Partitioning

In this section we consider how the network partitions can be handled by the atomic commit protocols that we discussed in the preceding section. Network partitions are due to communication line failures and may cause the loss of messages, depending on the implementation of the communication subnet. A partitioning is called a *simple partitioning* if the network is divided into only two components; otherwise, it is called *multiple partitioning*.

The termination protocols for network partitioning address the termination of the transactions that were active in each partition at the time of partitioning. If one can develop non-blocking protocols to terminate these transactions, it is possible for the sites in each partition to reach a termination decision (for a given transaction) which is consistent with the sites in the other partitions. This would imply that the sites in each partition can continue executing transactions despite the partitioning.

Unfortunately, it is not in general possible to find non-blocking termination protocols in the presence of network partitions. Remember that our expectations regarding the reliability of the communication subnet are minimal. If a message cannot be delivered, it is simply lost. In this case it can be proven that no non-blocking atomic commitment protocol exists that is resilient to network partitioning [Skeen and Stonebraker, 1983]. This is quite a negative result since it also means that if network partitioning occurs, we cannot continue normal operations in all partitions, which limits the availability of the entire distributed database system. A positive counter result, however, indicates that it is possible to design non-blocking atomic commit protocols that are resilient to simple partitions. Unfortunately, if multiple partitions occur, it is again not possible to design such protocols [Skeen and Stonebraker, 1983].

In the remainder of this section we discuss a number of protocols that address network partitioning in non-replicated databases. The problem is quite different in the case of replicated databases, which we discuss in the next chapter.

In the presence of network partitioning of non-replicated databases, the major concern is with the termination of transactions that were active at the time of partitioning. Any new transaction that accesses a data item that is stored in another partition is simply blocked and has to await the repair of the network. Concurrent accesses to the data items within one partition can be handled by the concurrency control algorithm. The significant problem, therefore, is to ensure that the transaction terminates properly. In short, the network partitioning problem is handled by the commit protocol, and more specifically, by the termination and recovery protocols.

The absence of non-blocking protocols that would guarantee atomic commitment of distributed transactions points to an important design decision. We can either permit all the partitions to continue their normal operations and accept the fact that database consistency may be compromised, or we guarantee the consistency of the database by employing strategies that would permit operation in one of the partitions while the sites in the others remain blocked. This decision problem is the premise of a classification of partition handling strategies. We can classify the strategies as *pessimistic* or *optimistic* [Davidson et al., 1985]. Pessimistic strategies emphasize the consistency of the database, and would therefore not permit transactions to execute in a partition if there is no guarantee that the consistency of the database can be maintained. Optimistic approaches, on the other hand, emphasize the availability of the database even if this would cause inconsistencies.

The second dimension is related to the correctness criterion. If serializability is used as the fundamental correctness criterion, such strategies are called *syntactic* since the serializability theory uses only syntactic information. However, if we use a more abstract correctness criterion that is dependent on the semantics of the transactions or the database, the strategies are said to be *semantic*.

Consistent with the correctness criterion that we have adopted in this book (serializability), we consider only syntactic approaches in this section. The following two sections outline various syntactic strategies for non-replicated databases.

All the known termination protocols that deal with network partitioning in the case of non-replicated databases are pessimistic. Since the pessimistic approaches emphasize the maintenance of database consistency, the fundamental issue that we need to address is which of the partitions can continue normal operations. We consider two approaches.

12.6.1 Centralized Protocols

Centralized termination protocols are based on the centralized concurrency control algorithms discussed in Chapter 11. In this case, it makes sense to permit the operation of the partition that contains the central site, since it manages the lock tables.

Primary site techniques are centralized with respect to each data item. In this case, more than one partition may be operational for different queries. For any given query, only the partition that contains the primary site of the data items that are in the write set of that transaction can execute that transaction.

Both of these are simple approaches that would work well, but they are dependent on the concurrency control mechanism employed by the distributed database manager. Furthermore, they expect each site to be able to differentiate network partitioning from site failures properly. This is necessary since the participants in the execution of the commit protocol react differently to the different types of failures.

12.6.2 Voting-based Protocols

Voting as a technique for managing concurrent data accesses has been proposed by a number of researchers. A straightforward voting with majority was first proposed in [Thomas, 1979] as a concurrency control method for fully replicated databases. The fundamental idea is that a transaction is executed if a majority of the sites vote to execute it.

The idea of majority voting has been generalized to voting with *quorums*. Quorum-based voting can be used as a replica control method (as we discuss in the next chapter), as well as a commit method to ensure transaction atomicity in the presence of network partitioning. In the case of non-replicated databases, this involves the integration of the voting principle with commit protocols. We present a specific proposal along this line [Skeen, 1982b].

Every site in the system is assigned a vote V_i. Let us assume that the total number of votes in the system is V, and the abort and commit quorums are V_a and V_c, respectively. Then the following rules must be obeyed in the implementation of the commit protocol:

1. $V_a + V_c > V$, where $0 \leq V_a, V_c \leq V$.
2. Before a transaction commits, it must obtain a commit quorum V_c.

3. Before a transaction aborts, it must obtain an abort quorum V_a.

The first rule ensures that a transaction cannot be committed and aborted at the same time. The next two rules indicate the votes that a transaction has to obtain before it can terminate one way or the other.

The integration of these rules into the 3PC protocol requires a minor modification of the third phase. For the coordinator to move from the PRECOMMIT state to the COMMIT state, and to send the "global-commit" command, it is necessary for it to have obtained a commit quorum from the participants. This would satisfy rule 2. Note that we do not need to implement rule 3 explicitly. This is due to the fact that a transaction which is in the WAIT or READY state is willing to abort the transaction. Therefore, an abort quorum already exists.

Let us now consider the termination of transactions in the presence of failures. When a network partitioning occurs, the sites in each partition elect a new coordinator, similar to the 3PC termination protocol in the case of site failures. There is a fundamental difference, however. It is not possible to make the transition from the WAIT or READY state to the ABORT state in one state transition, for a number of reasons. First, more than one coordinator is trying to terminate the transaction. We do not want them to terminate differently or the transaction execution will not be atomic. Therefore, we want the coordinators to obtain an abort quorum explicitly. Second, if the newly elected coordinator fails, it is not known whether a commit or abort quorum was reached. Thus it is necessary that participants make an explicit decision to join either the commit or the abort quorum and not change their votes afterward. Unfortunately, the READY (or WAIT) state does not satisfy these requirements. Thus we introduce another state, PREABORT, between the READY and ABORT states. The transition from the PREABORT state to the ABORT state requires an abort quorum. The state transition diagram is given in Figure 12.17.

With this modification, the termination protocol works as follows. Once a new coordinator is elected, it requests all participants to report their local states. Depending on the responses, it terminates the transaction as follows:

1. If at least one participant is in the COMMIT state, the coordinator decides to commit the transaction and sends a "global-commit" message to all the participants.

2. If at least one participant is in the ABORT state, the coordinator decides to abort the transaction and sends a "global-abort" message to all the participants.

3. If a commit quorum is reached by the votes of participants in the PRECOMMIT state, the coordinator decides to commit the transaction and sends a "global-commit" message to all the participants.

4. If an abort quorum is reached by the votes of participants in the PREABORT state, the coordinator decides to abort the transaction and sends a "global-abort" message to all the participants.

5. If case 3 does not hold but the sum of the votes of the participants in the PRECOMMIT and READY states are enough to form a commit quorum, the

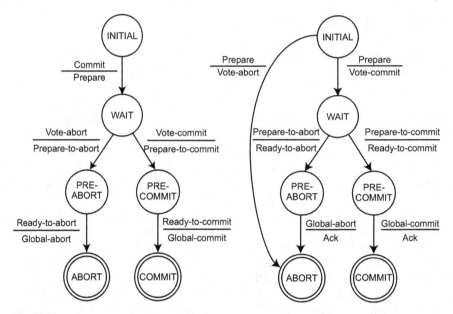

Fig. 12.17 State Transitions in Quorum 3PC Protocol

coordinator moves the participants to the PRECOMMIT state by sending a "prepare-to-commit" message. The coordinator then waits for case 3 to hold.

6. Similarly, if case 4 does not hold but the sum of the votes of the participants in the PREABORT and READY states are enough to form an abort quorum, the coordinator moves the participants to the PREABORT state by sending a "prepare-to-abort" message. The coordinator then waits for case 4 to hold.

Two points are important about this quorum-based commit algorithm. First, it is blocking; the coordinator in a partition may not be able to form either an abort or a commit quorum if messages get lost or multiple partitionings occur. This is hardly surprising given the theoretical bounds that we discussed previously. The second point is that the algorithm is general enough to handle site failures as well as network partitioning. Therefore, this modified version of 3PC can provide more resiliency to failures.

The recovery protocol that can be used in conjunction with the above-discussed termination protocol is very simple. When two or more partitions merge, the sites that are part of the new larger partition simply execute the termination protocol. That is, a coordinator is elected to collect votes from all the participants and try to terminate the transaction.

12.7 Architectural Considerations

In previous sections we have discussed the atomic commit protocols at an abstract level. Let us now look at how these protocols can be implemented within the framework of our architectural model. This discussion involves specification of the interface between the concurrency control algorithms and the reliability protocols. In that sense, the discussions of this chapter relate to the execution of **commit abort**, and **recover** commands.

Unfortunately, it is quite difficult to specify precisely the execution of these commands. The difficulty is twofold. First, a significantly more detailed model of the architecture than the one we have presented needs to be considered for correct implementation of these commands. Second, the overall scheme of implementation is quite dependent on the recovery procedures that the local recovery manager implements. For example, implementation of the 2PC protocol on top of a LRM that employs a no-fix/no-flush recovery scheme is quite different from its implementation on top of a LRM that employs a fix/flush recovery scheme. The alternatives are simply too numerous. We therefore confine our architectural discussion to three areas: implementation of the coordinator and participant concepts for the commit and replica control protocols within the framework of the transaction manager-scheduler-local recovery manager architecture, the coordinator's access to the database log, and the changes that need to be made in the local recovery manager operations.

One possible implementation of the commit protocols within our architectural model is to perform both the coordinator and participant algorithms within the transaction managers at each site. This provides some uniformity in executing the distributed commit operations. However, it entails unnecessary communication between the participant transaction manager and its scheduler; this is because the scheduler has to decide whether a transaction can be committed or aborted. Therefore, it may be preferable to implement the coordinator as part of the transaction manager and the participant as part of the scheduler. Of course, the replica control protocol is implemented as part of the transaction manager as well. If the scheduler implements a strict concurrency control algorithm (i.e., does not allow cascading aborts), it will be ready automatically to commit the transaction when the prepare message arrives. Proof of this claim is left as an exercise. However, even this alternative of implementing the coordinator and the participant outside the data processor has problems. The first issue is database log management. Recall from Section 12.3 that the database log is maintained by the LRM and the buffer manager. However, implementation of the commit protocol as described here requires the transaction manager and the scheduler to access the log as well. One possible solution to this problem is to maintain a commit log (which could be called the *distributed transaction log* [Bernstein et al., 1987; Lampson and Sturgis, 1976]) that is accessed by the transaction manager and is separate from the database log that the LRM and buffer manager maintain. The other alternative is to write the commit protocol records into the same database log. This second alternative has a number of advantages. First, only one log is maintained; this simplifies the algorithms that have to be implemented in order to save log records on stable storage. More important, the recovery from failures in a distributed database requires the cooperation of the local recovery manager and the scheduler (i.e., the participant). A single database log can serve as a central repository of recovery information for both these components.

A second problem associated with implementing the coordinator within the transaction manager and the participant as part of the scheduler has to be with integration with the concurrency control protocols. This implementation is based on the schedulers determining whether a transaction can be committed. This is fine for distributed concurrency control algorithms where each site is equipped with a scheduler. However, in centralized protocols such as the centralized 2PL, there is only one scheduler in the system. In this case, the participants may be implemented as part of the data processors (more precisely, as part of local recovery managers), requiring modification to both the algorithms implemented by the LRM and, possibly, to the execution of the 2PC protocol. We leave the details to exercises.

Storing the commit protocol records in the database log maintained by the LRM and the buffer manager requires some changes to the LRM algorithms. This is the third architectural issue we address. Unfortunately, these changes are dependent on the type of algorithm that the LRM uses. In general, however, the LRM algorithms have to be modified to handle separately the prepare command and global commit (or global abort) decisions. Furthermore, upon recovery, the LRM should be modified to read the database log and to inform the scheduler as to the state of each transaction, in order that the recovery procedures discussed before can be followed. Let us take a more detailed look at this function of the LRM.

The LRM first has to determine whether the failed site is the host of the coordinator or of a participant. This information can be stored together with the begin_transaction record. The LRM then has to search for the last record written in the log record during execution of the commit protocol. If it cannot even find a begin_commit record (at the coordinator site) or an abort or commit record (at the participant sites), the transaction has not started to commit. In this case, the LRM can continue with its recovery procedure as we discussed in Section 12.3.3. However, if the commit process has started, the recovery has to be handed over to the coordinator. Therefore, the LRM sends the last log record to the scheduler.

12.8 Conclusion

In this chapter we discussed the reliability aspects of distributed transaction management. The studied algorithms (2PC and 3PC) guarantee the atomicity and durability of distributed transactions even when failures occur. One of these algorithms (3PC) can be made non-blocking, which would permit each site to continue its operation without waiting for recovery of the failed site. An unfortunate result that we presented relates to network partitioning. It is not possible to design protocols that guarantee the atomicity of distributed transactions and permit each partition of the distributed system to continue its operation under the assumptions made in this chapter with respect to the functionality of the communication subnet. The performance of the distributed commit protocols with respect to the overhead they add to the concurrency control algorithms is an interesting issue. Some studies have addressed this issue [Dwork and Skeen, 1983; Wolfson, 1987].

A final point that should be stressed is the following. We have considered only failures that are attributable to errors. In other words, we assumed that every effort was made to design and implement the systems (hardware and software), but that because of various faults in the components, the design, or the operating environment, they failed to perform properly. Such failures are called *failures of omission*. There is another class of failures, called *failures of commission*, where the systems may not have been designed and implemented so that they would work properly. The difference is that in the execution of the 2PC protocol, for example, if a participant receives a message from the coordinator, it treats this message as correct: the coordinator is operational and is sending the participant a correct message to go ahead and process. The only failure that the participant has to worry about is if the coordinator fails or if its messages get lost. These are failures of omission. If, on the other hand, the messages that a participant receives cannot be trusted, the participant also has to deal with failures of commission. For example, a participant site may pretend to be the coordinator and may send a malicious message. We have not discussed reliability measures that are necessary to cope with these types of failures. The techniques that address failures of commission are typically called *byzantine agreement*.

12.9 Bibliographic Notes

There are numerous books on the reliability of computer systems. These include [Anderson and Lee, 1981; Anderson and Randell, 1979; Avizienis et al., 1987; Longbottom, 1980; Gibbons, 1976; Pradhan, 1986; Siewiorek and Swarz, 1982], and [Shrivastava, 1985]. In addition, the survey paper [Randell et al., 1978] addresses the same issues. Myers [1976] specifically addresses software reliability. An important software fault tolerance technique that we have not discussed in this chapter is exception handling. This issue is treated in [Cristian, 1982, 1985], and [Cristian, 1987]. Jr and Malek [1988] surveys the existing software tools for reliability measurement.

The fundamental principles employed in fault-tolerant systems are *redundancy* in system components and *modularization* of the design. These two concepts are utilized in typical systems by means of *fail-stop modules* (also called *fail-fast* [Gray, 1985]) and *process pairs*. A fail-stop module constantly monitors itself, and when it detects a fault, shuts itself down automatically [Schlichting and Schneider, 1983]. Process pairs provide fault tolerance by duplicating software modules. The idea is to eliminate single points of failure by implementing each system service as two processes that communicate and cooperate in providing the service. One of these processes is called the *primary* and the other the *backup*. Both the primary and the backup are typically implemented as fail-stop modules that cooperate in providing a service. There are a number of different ways of implementing process pairs, depending on the mode of communication between the primary and the backup.

The five common types are *lock-step, automatic checkpointing, state checkpointing, delta checkpointing,* and *persistent* process pairs. With respect to our discussion of process pairs, the lock-step process pair approach is implemented in the Stratus/32 systems ([Computers, 1982; Kim, 1984]) for hardware processes. An automatic checkpointing process pairs approach is used in the Auras (TM) operating system for Aurogen computers ([Borg et al., 1983; Gastonian, 1983]). State checkpointing has been used in earlier versions of the Tandem operating systems [Bartlett, 1978, 1981], which have later utilized the delta checkpointing approach [Borr, 1984]. A review of different implementations appears in [Gray, 1985].

More detailed material on the functions of the local recovery manager discussed in Section 12.3 can be found in [Verhofstadt, 1978; Härder and Reuter, 1983]. Implementation of the local recovery functions in System R is described in [Gray et al., 1981].

Kohler [1981] presents a general discussion of the reliability issues in distributed database systems. Hadzilacos [1988] is a formalization of the reliability concept. The reliability aspects of System R* are given in [Traiger et al., 1982], whereas Hammer and Shipman [1980] describe the same for the SDD-1 system.

The two-phase commit protocol is first described in [Gray, 1979]. Modifications to it are presented in [Mohan and Lindsay, 1983]. The definition of three-phase commit is due to Skeen [1981, 1982a]. Formal results on the existence of non-blocking termination protocols is due to Skeen and Stonebraker [1983].

Replication and replica control protocols have been the subject of significant research in recent years. This work is summarized very well in [Helal et al., 1997]. Replica control protocols that deal with network partitioning are surveyed in [David-son et al., 1985]. Besides the algorithms we have described here, some notable others are given in [Davidson, 1984; Eager and Sevcik, 1983; Herlihy, 1987; Minoura and Wiederhold, 1982; Skeen and Wright, 1984; Wright, 1983]. These algorithms are generally called *static* since the vote assignments and read/write quorums are fixed a priori. An analysis of one such protocol (such analyses are rare) is given in [Kumar and Segev, 1993]. Examples of *dynamic replication protocols* are in [Jajodia and Mutchler, 1987; Barbara et al., 1986, 1989] among others. It is also possible to change the way data are replicated. Such protocols are called *adaptive* and one example is described in [Wolfson, 1987]. An interesting replication algorithm based on economic models is described in [Sidell et al., 1996].

Our discussion of checkpointing has been rather short. Further treatment of the issue can be found in [Bhargava and Lian, 1988; Dadam and Schlageter, 1980; Schlageter and Dadam, 1980; Kuss, 1982; Ng, 1988; Ramanathan and Shin, 1988]. Byzantine agreement is surveyed in [Strong and Dolev, 1983] and is discussed in [Babaoglu, 1987; Pease et al., 1980].

Exercises

Problem 12.1. Briefly describe the various implementations of the process pairs concept. Comment on how process pairs may be useful in implementing a fault-tolerant distributed DBMS.

Problem 12.2 (*). Discuss the site failure termination protocol for 2PC using a distributed communication topology.

Problem 12.3 (*).
Design a 3PC protocol using the linear communication topology.

Problem 12.4 (*). In our presentation of the centralized 3PC termination protocol, the first step involves sending the coordinator's state to all participants. The participants move to new states according to the coordinator's state. It is possible to design the termination protocol such that the coordinator, instead of sending its own state information to the participants, asks the participants to send their state information to the coordinator. Modify the termination protocol to function in this manner.

Problem 12.5 (**). In Section 12.7 we claimed that a scheduler which implements a strict concurrency control algorithm will always be ready to commit a transaction when it receives the coordinator's "prepare" message. Prove this claim.

Problem 12.6 (**). Assuming that the coordinator is implemented as part of the transaction manager and the participant as part of the scheduler, give the transaction manager, scheduler, and the local recovery manager algorithms for a non-replicated distributed DBMS under the following assumptions.

(a) The scheduler implements a distributed (strict) two-phase locking concurrency control algorithm.
(b) The commit protocol log records are written to a central database log by the LRM when it is called by the scheduler.
(c) The LRM may implement any of the protocols that have been discussed in Section 12.3.3. However, it is modified to support the distributed recovery procedures as we discussed in Section 12.7.

Problem 12.7 (*). Write the detailed algorithms for the no-fix/no-flush local recovery manager.

Problem 12.8 (**). Assume that

(a) The scheduler implements a centralized two-phase locking concurrency control,
(b) The LRM implements no-fix/no-flush protocol.

Give detailed algorithms for the transaction manager, scheduler, and local recovery managers.

Chapter 13
Data Replication

As we discussed in previous chapters, distributed databases are typically replicated. The purposes of replication are multiple:

1. **System availability.** As discussed in Chapter 1, distributed DBMSs may remove single points of failure by replicating data, so that data items are accessible from multiple sites. Consequently, even when some sites are down, data may be accessible from other sites.

2. **Performance.** As we have seen previously, one of the major contributors to response time is the communication overhead. Replication enables us to locate the data closer to their access points, thereby localizing most of the access that contributes to a reduction in response time.

3. **Scalability.** As systems grow geographically and in terms of the number of sites (consequently, in terms of the number of access requests), replication allows for a way to support this growth with acceptable response times.

4. **Application requirements.** Finally, replication may be dictated by the applications, which may wish to maintain multiple data copies as part of their operational specifications.

Although data replication has clear benefits, it poses the considerable challenge of keeping different copies synchronized. We will discuss this shortly, but let us first consider the execution model in replicated databases. Each replicated data item x has a number of copies $x_1, x_2, \ldots, x_n$. We will refer to x as the *logical data item* and to its copies (or *replicas*)[1] as *physical data items*. If replication transparency is to be provided, user transactions will issue read and write operations on the logical data item x. The replica control protocol is responsible for mapping these operations to reads and writes on the physical data items $x_1, \ldots, x_n$. Thus, the system behaves as if there is a single copy of each data item – referred to as *single system image* or *one-copy equivalence*. The specific implementation of the Read and Write interfaces

---

[1] In this chapter, we use the terms "replica", "copy", and "physical data item" interchangeably.

M.T. Özsu and P. Valduriez, *Principles of Distributed Database Systems: Third Edition*, DOI 10.1007/978-1-4419-8834-8_13, © Springer Science+Business Media, LLC 2011

of the transaction monitor differ according to the specific replication protocol, and we will discuss these differences in the appropriate sections.

There are a number of decisions and factors that impact the design of replication protocols. Some of these were discussed in previous chapters, while others will be discussed here.

- **Database design.** As discussed in Chapter 3, a distributed database may be fully or partially replicated. In the case of a partially replicated database, the number of physical data items for each logical data item may vary, and some data items may even be non-replicated. In this case, transactions that access only non-replicated data items are *local transactions* (since they can be executed locally at one site) and their execution typically does not concern us here. Transactions that access replicated data items have to be executed at multiple sites and they are *global transactions*.

- **Database consistency.** When global transactions update copies of a data item at different sites, the values of these copies may be different at a given point in time. A replicated database is said to be in a *mutually consistent* state if all the replicas of each of its data items have identical values. What differentiates different mutual consistency criteria is how tightly synchronized replicas have to be. Some ensure that replicas are mutually consistent when an update transaction commits, thus, they are usually called *strong consistency* criteria. Others take a more relaxed approach, and are referred to as *weak consistency* criteria.

- **Where updates are performed.** A fundamental design decision in designing a replication protocol is where the database updates are first performed [Gray et al., 1996]. The techniques can be characterized as *centralized* if they perform updates first on a *master* copy, versus *distributed* if they allow updates over any replica. Centralized techniques can be further identified as *single master* when there is only one master database copy in the system, or *primary copy* where the master copy of each data item may be different[2].

- **Update propagation.** Once updates are performed on a replica (master or otherwise), the next decision is how updates are propagated to the others. The alternatives are identified as *eager* versus *lazy* [Gray et al., 1996]. Eager techniques perform all of the updates within the context of the global transaction that has initiated the write operations. Thus, when the transaction commits, its updates will have been applied to all of the copies. Lazy techniques, on the other hand, propagate the updates sometime after the initiating transaction has committed. Eager techniques are further identified according to when they push each write to the other replicas – some push each write operation individually, others batch the writes and propagate them at the commit point.

---

[2] Centralized techniques are referred to, in the literature, as *single master*, while distributed ones are referred to as *multi-master* or *update anywhere*. These terms, in particular "single master", are confusing, since they refer to alternative architectures for implementing centralized protocols (more on this in Section 13.2.3). Thus, we prefer the more descriptive terms "centralized" and "distributed".

- **Degree of replication transparency.** Certain replication protocols require each user application to know the master site where the transaction operations are to be submitted. These protocols provide only *limited replication transparency* to user applications. Other protocols provide *full replication transparency* by involving the Transaction Manager (TM) at each site. In this case, user applications submit transactions to their local TMs rather than the master site.

We discuss consistency issues in replicated databases in Section 13.1, and analyze centralized versus distributed update application as well as update propagation alternatives in Section 13.2. This will lead us to a discussion of the specific protocols in Section 13.3. In Section 13.4, we discuss the use of group communication primitives in reducing the messaging overhead of replication protocols. In these sections, we will assume that no failures occur so that we can focus on the replication protocols. We will then introduce failures and investigate how protocols are revised to handle failures (Section 13.5). Finally, in Section 13.6, we discuss how replication services can be provided in multidatabase systems (i.e., outside the component DBMSs).

13.1 Consistency of Replicated Databases

There are two issues related to consistency of a replicated database. One is mutual consistency, as discussed above, that deals with the convergence of the values of physical data items corresponding to one logical data item. The second is transaction consistency as we discussed in Chapter 11. Serializability, which we introduced as the transaction consistency criterion needs to be recast in the case of replicated databases. In addition, there are relationships between mutual consistency and transaction consistency. In this section we first discuss mutual consistency approaches and then focus on the redefinition of transaction consistency and its relationship to mutual consistency.

13.1.1 Mutual Consistency

As indicated earlier, mutual consistency criteria for replicated databases can either be strong or weak. Each is suitable for different classes of applications with different consistency requirements.

Strong mutual consistency criteria require that all copies of a data item have the same value at the end of the execution of an update transaction. This is achieved by a variety of means, but the execution of 2PC at the commit point of an update transaction is a common way to achieve strong mutual consistency.

Weak mutual consistency criteria do not require the values of replicas of a data item to be identical when an update transaction terminates. What is required is that, if the update activity ceases for some time, the values *eventually* become identical. This is commonly referred to as *eventual consistency*, which refers to the fact that replica values may diverge over time, but will eventually converge. It is hard to define this concept formally or precisely, although the following definition is probably as precise as one can hope to get [Saito and Shapiro, 2005]:

> "A replicated [data item] is *eventually consistent* when it meets the following conditions, assuming that all replicas start from the same initial state.
>
> - At any moment, for each replica, there is a prefix of the [history] that is equivalent to a prefix of the [history] of every other replica. We call this a *committed prefix* for the replica.
>
> - The committed prefix of each replica grows monotonically over time.
>
> - All non-aborted operations in the committed prefix satisfy their preconditions.
>
> - For every submitted operation α, either α or [its abort] will eventually be included in the committed prefix."

It should be noted that this definition of eventual consistency is rather strong – in particular the requirements that history prefixes are the same at any given moment and that the committed prefix grows monotonically. Many systems that claim to provide eventual consistency would violate these requirements.

Epsilon serializability (ESR) [Pu and Leff, 1991; Ramamritham and Pu, 1995] allows a query to see inconsistent data while replicas are being updated, but requires that the replicas converge to a one-copy serializable state once the updates are propagated to all of the copies. It bounds the error on the read values by an epsilon (ε) value (hence the name), which is defined in terms of the number of updates (write operations) that a query "misses". Given a read-only transaction (query) T_Q, let T_U be all the update transactions that are executing concurrently with T_Q. If $RS(T_Q) \cap WS(T_U) \neq \emptyset$ (T_Q is reading some copy of some data items while T_U is updating (possibly a different) copy of those data items) then there is a read-write conflict and T_Q may be reading inconsistent data. The inconsistency is bounded by the changes performed by T_U. Clearly, ESR does not sacrifice database consistency, but only allows read-only transactions (queries) to read inconsistent data. For this reason, it has been claimed that ESR does not weaken database consistency, but "stretches" it [Wu et al., 1997].

Other looser bounds have also been discussed. It has even been suggested that users should be allowed to specify *freshness constraints* that are suitable for particular applications and the replication protocols should enforce these [Pacitti and Simon, 2000; Röhm et al., 2002b; Bernstein et al., 2006]. The types of freshness constraints that can be specified are the following:

- Time-bound constraints. Users may accept divergence of physical copy values up to a certain time: x_i may reflect the value of an update at time t while x_j may reflect the value at $t - \Delta$ and this may be acceptable.

- Value-bound constraints. It may be acceptable to have values of all physical data items within a certain range of each other. The user may consider the database to be mutually consistent if the values do not diverge more than a certain amount (or percentage).

- Drift constraints on multiple data items. For transactions that read multiple data items, users may be satisfied if the time drift between the update timestamps of two data items is less than a threshold (i.e., they were updated within that threshold) or, in the case of aggregate computation, if the aggregate computed over a data item is within a certain range of the most recent value (i.e., even if the individual physical copy values may be more out of sync than this range, as long as a particular aggregate computation is within range, it may be acceptable).

An important criterion in analyzing protocols that employ criteria that allow replicas to diverge is *degree of freshness*. The degree of freshness of a given replica r_i at time t is defined as the proportion of updates that have been applied at r_i at time t to the total number of updates [Pacitti et al., 1998, 1999].

13.1.2 Mutual Consistency versus Transaction Consistency

Mutual consistency, as we have defined it here, and transactional consistency as we discussed in Chapter 11 are related, but different. Mutual consistency refers to the replicas converging to the same value, while transaction consistency requires that the global execution history be serializable. It is possible for a replicated DBMS to ensure that data items are mutually consistent when a transaction commits, but the execution history may not be globally serializable. This is demonstrated in the following example.

Example 13.1. Consider three sites (A, B, and C) and three data items (x, y, z) that are distributed as follows: Site A hosts x, Site B hosts x, y, Site C hosts x, y, z. We will use site identifiers as subscripts on the data items to refer to a particular replica.

Now consider the following three transactions:

T_1: $x \leftarrow 20$	T_2: Read(x)	T_3: Read(x)
Write(x)	$y \leftarrow x + y$	Read(y)
Commit	Write(y)	$z \leftarrow (x * y)/100$
	Commit	Write(z)
		Commit

Note that T_1's *Write* has to be executed at all three sites (since x is replicated at all three sites), T_2's *Write* has to be executed at B and C, and T_3's *Write* has to be executed only at C. We are assuming a transaction execution model where transactions can read their local replicas, but have to update all of the replicas.

Assume that the following three local histories are generated at the sites:

$$H_A = \{W_1(x_A), C_1\}$$
$$H_B = \{W_1(x_B), C_1, R_2(x_B), W_2(y_B), C_2\}$$
$$H_C = \{W_2(y_C), C_2, R_3(x_C), R_3(y_C), W_3(z_C), C_3, W_1(x_C), C_1\}$$

The serialization order in H_B is $T_1 \rightarrow T_2$ while in H_C it is $T_2 \rightarrow T_3 \rightarrow T_1$. Therefore, the global history is not serializable. However, the database is mutually consistent. Assume, for example, that initially $x_A = x_B = x_C = 10, y_B = y_C = 15$, and $z_C = 7$. With the above histories, the final values will be $x_A = x_B = x_C = 20, y_B = y_C = 35, z_C = 3.5$. All the physical copies (replicas) have indeed converged to the same value.   ◆

Of course, it is possible for both the database to be mutually inconsistent, and the execution history to be globally non-serializable, as demonstrated in the following example.

Example 13.2. Consider two sites (A and B), and one data item (x) that is replicated at both sites (x_A and x_B). Further consider the following two transactions:

T_1: Read(x)	T_2: Read(x)
$x \leftarrow x + 5$	$x \leftarrow x * 10$
Write(x)	Write(x)
Commit	Commit

Assume that the following two local histories are generated at the two sites (again using the execution model of the previous example):

$$H_A = \{R_1(x_A), W_1(x_A), C_1, R_2(x_A), W_2(x_A), C_2\}$$
$$H_B = \{R_2(x_B), W_2(x_B), C_2, R_1(x_B), W_1(x_B), C_1\}$$

Although both of these histories are serial, they serialize T_1 and T_2 in reverse order; thus the global history is not serializable. Furthermore, the mutual consistency is violated as well. Assume that the value of x prior to the execution of these transactions was 1. At the end of the execution of these schedules, the value of x is 60 at site A while it is 15 at site B. Thus, in this example, the global history is non-serializable, **and** the databases are mutually inconsistent.   ◆

Given the above observation, the transaction consistency criterion given in Chapter 11 is extended in replicated databases to define *one-copy serializability*. One-copy serializability (1SR) states that the effects of transactions on replicated data items should be the same as if they had been performed one at-a-time on a single set of data items. In other words, the histories are equivalent to some serial execution over non-replicated data items.

Snapshot isolation that we introduced in Chapter 11 has been extended for replicated databases [Lin et al., 2005] and used as an alternative transactional consistency criterion within the context of replicated databases [Plattner and Alonso, 2004; Daudjee and Salem, 2006]. Similarly, a weaker form of serializability, called *relaxed concurrency (RC-) serializability* has been defined that corresponds to "read committed" isolation level (Section 10.2.3) [Bernstein et al., 2006].

13.2 Update Management Strategies

As discussed earlier, the replication protocols can be classified according to when the updates are propagated to copies (eager versus lazy) and where updates are allowed to occur (centralized versus distributed). These two decisions are generally referred to as *update management* strategies. In this section, we discuss these alternatives before we present protocols in the next section.

13.2.1 Eager Update Propagation

The eager update propagation approaches apply the changes to all the replicas within the context of the update transaction. Consequently, when the update transaction commits, all the copies have the same value. Typically, eager propagation techniques use 2PC at commit point, but, as we will see later, alternatives are possible to achieve agreement. Furthermore, eager propagation may use *synchronous* propagation of each update by applying it on all the replicas at the same time (when the *Write* is issued), or *deferred* propagation whereby the updates are applied to one replica when they are issued, but their application on the other replicas is batched and deferred to the end of the transaction. Deferred propagation can be implemented by including the updates in the "Prepare-to-Commit" message at the start of 2PC execution.

Eager techniques typically enforce strong mutual consistency criteria. Since all the replicas are mutually consistent at the end of an update transaction, a subsequent read can read from any copy (i.e., one can map a $Read(x)$ to $Read(x_i)$ for any x_i). However, a $Write(x)$ has to be applied to all x_i (i.e., $Write(x_i), \forall x_i$). Thus, protocols that follow eager update propagation are known as *read-one/write-all* (ROWA) protocols.

The advantages of eager update propagation are threefold. First, they typically ensure that mutual consistency is enforced using 1SR; therefore, there are no transactional inconsistencies. Second, a transaction can read a local copy of the data item (if a local copy is available) and be certain that an up-to-date value is read. Thus, there is no need to do a remote read. Finally, the changes to replicas are done atomically; thus recovery from failures can be governed by the protocols we have already studied in the previous chapter.

The main disadvantage of eager update propagation is that a transaction has to update all the copies before it can terminate. This has two consequences. First, the response time performance of the update transaction suffers, since it typically has to participate in a 2PC execution, and because the update speed is restricted by the slowest machine. Second, if one of the copies is unavailable, then the transaction cannot terminate since all the copies need to be updated. As discussed in Chapter 12, if it is possible to differentiate between site failures and network failures, then one can terminate the transaction as long as only one replica is unavailable (recall that more than one site unavailability causes 2PC to be blocking), but it is generally not possible to differentiate between these two types of failures.

13.2.2 Lazy Update Propagation

In lazy update propagation the replica updates are not all performed within the context of the update transaction. In other words, the transaction does not wait until its updates are applied to all the copies before it commits – it commits as soon as one replica is updated. The propagation to other copies is done *asynchronously* from the original transaction, by means of *refresh transactions* that are sent to the replica sites some time after the update transaction commits. A refresh transaction carries the sequence of updates of the corresponding update transaction.

Lazy propagation is used in those applications for which strong mutual consistency may be unnecessary and too restrictive. These applications may be able to tolerate some inconsistency among the replicas in return for better performance. Examples of such applications are Domain Name Service (DNS), databases over geographically widely distributed sites, mobile databases, and personal digital assistant databases [Saito and Shapiro, 2005]. In these cases, usually weak mutual consistency is enforced.

The primary advantage of lazy update propagation techniques is that they generally have lower response times for update transactions, since an update transaction can commit as soon as it has updated one copy. The disadvantages are that the replicas are not mutually consistent and some replicas may be out-of-date, and, consequently, a local read may read stale data and does not guarantee to return the up-to-date value. Furthermore, under some scenarios that we will discuss later, transactions may not see their own writes, i.e., $Read_i(x)$ of an update transaction T_i may not see the effects of $Write_i(x)$ that was executed previously. This has been referred to as *transaction inversion*. Strong one-copy serializability (strong 1SR) [Daudjee and Salem, 2004] and strong snapshot isolation (strong SI) [Daudjee and Salem, 2006] prevent all transaction inversions at 1SR and SI isolation levels, respectively, but are expensive to provide. The weaker guarantees of 1SR and global SI, while being much less expensive to provide than their stronger counterparts, do not prevent transaction inversions. Session-level transactional guarantees at the 1SR and SI isolation levels have been proposed that address these shortcomings by preventing transaction inversions within a client session but not necessarily across sessions [Daudjee and Salem, 2004, 2006]. These session-level guarantees are less costly to provide than their strong counterparts while preserving many of the desirable properties of the strong counterparts.

13.2.3 Centralized Techniques

Centralized update propagation techniques require that updates are first applied at a master copy and then propagated to other copies (which are called *slaves*). The site that hosts the master copy is similarly called the *master site*, while the sites that host the slave copies for that data item are called *slave sites*.

In some techniques, there is a single master for all replicated data. We refer to these as *single master* centralized techniques. In other protocols, the master copy for each data item may be different (i.e., for data item x, the master copy may be x_i stored at site S_i, while for data item y, it may be y_j stored at site S_j). These are typically known as *primary copy* centralized techniques.

The advantages of centralized techniques are two-fold. First, application of the updates is easy since they happen at only the master site, and they do not require synchronization among multiple replica sites. Second, there is the assurance that at least one site – the site that holds the master copy – has up-to-date values for a data item. These protocols are generally suitable in data warehouses and other applications where data processing is centralized at one or a few master sites.

The primary disadvantage is that, as in any centralized algorithm, if there is one central site that hosts all of the masters, this site can be overloaded and can become a bottleneck. Distributing the master site responsibility for each data item as in primary copy techniques is one way of reducing this overhead, but it raises consistency issues, in particular with respect to maintaining global serializability in lazy replication techniques since the refresh transactions have to be executed at the replicas in the same serialization order. We discuss these further in relevant sections.

13.2.4 Distributed Techniques

Distributed techniques apply the update on the local copy at the site where the update transaction originates, and then the updates are propagated to the other replica sites. These are called distributed techniques since different transactions can update different copies of the same data item located at different sites. They are appropriate for collaborative applications with distributive decision/operation centers. They can more evenly distribute the load, and may provide the highest system availability if coupled with lazy propagation techniques.

A serious complication that arises in these systems is that different replicas of a data item may be updated at different sites (masters) concurrently. If distributed techniques are coupled by eager propagation methods, then the distributed concurrency control methods can adequately address the concurrent updates problem. However, if lazy propagation methods are used, then transactions may be executed in different orders at different sites causing non-1SR global history. Furthermore, various replicas will get out of sync. To manage these problems, a reconciliation method is applied involving undoing and redoing transactions in such a way that transaction execution is the same at each site. This is not an easy issue since the reconciliation is generally application dependent.

13.3 Replication Protocols

In the previous section, we discussed two dimensions along which update management techniques can be classified. These dimensions are orthogonal; therefore four
combinations are possible: eager centralized, eager distributed, lazy centralized, and
lazy distributed. We discuss each of these alternatives in this section. For simplicity
of exposition, we assume a fully replicated database, which means that all update
transactions are global. We further assume that each site implements a 2PL-based
concurrency control technique.

13.3.1 Eager Centralized Protocols

In eager centralized replica control, a master site controls the operations on a data
item. These protocols are coupled with strong consistency techniques, so that updates
to a logical data item are applied to all of its replicas within the context of the
update transaction, which is committed using the 2PC protocol (although non-2PC
alternatives exist as we discuss shortly). Consequently, once the update transaction
completes, all replicas have the same values for the updated data items (i.e., mutually
consistent), and the resulting global history is 1SR.

The two design parameters that we discussed earlier determine the specific implementation of eager centralized replica protocols: where updates are performed,
and degree of replication transparency. The first parameter, which was discussed in
Section 13.2.3, refers to whether there is a single master site for all data items (single
master), or different master sites for each, or, more likely, for a group of data items
(primary copy). The second parameter indicates whether each application knows
the location of the master copy (limited application transparency) or whether it can
rely on its local TM for determining the location of the master copy (full replication
transparency).

13.3.1.1 Single Master with Limited Replication Transparency

The simplest case is to have a single master for the entire database (i.e., for all
data items) with limited replication transparency so that user applications know the
master site. In this case, global update transactions (i.e., those that contain at least
one $Write(x)$ operation where x is a replicated data item) are submitted directly to
the master site – more specifically, to the transaction manager (TM) at the master
site. At the master, each $Read(x)$ operation is performed on the master copy (i.e.,
$Read(x)$ is converted to $Read(x_M)$, where M signifies master copy) and executed
as follows: a read lock is obtained on x_M, the read is performed, and the result is
returned to the user. Similarly, each $Write(x)$ causes an update of the master copy
(i.e., executed as $Write(x_M)$) by first obtaining a write lock and then performing the
write operation. The master TM then forwards the $Write$ to the slave sites either

synchronously or in a deferred fashion (Figure 13.1). In either case, it is important to propagate updates such that conflicting updates are executed at the slaves in the same order they are executed at the master. This can be achieved by timestamping or by some other ordering scheme.

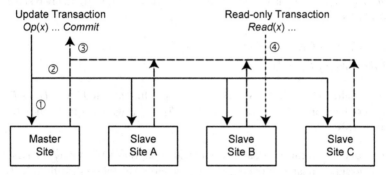

Fig. 13.1 Eager Single Master Replication Protocol Actions. (1) A *Write* is applied on the master copy; (2) *Write* is then propagated to the other replicas; (3) Updates become permanent at commit time; (4) Read-only transaction's *Read* goes to any slave copy.

The user application may submit a read-only transaction (i.e., all operations are *Read*) to any slave site. The execution of read-only transactions at the slaves can follow the process of centralized concurrency control algorithms, such as C2PL (Algorithms 11.1-11.3), where the centralized lock manager resides at the master replica site. Implementations within C2PL require minimal changes to the TM at the non-master sites, primarily to deal with the *Write* operations as described above, and its consequences (e.g., in the processing of Commit command). Thus, when a slave site receives a *Read* operation (from a read-only transaction), it forwards it to the master site to obtain a read lock. The *Read* can then be executed at the master and the result returned to the application, or the master can simply send a "lock granted" message to the originating site, which can then execute the *Read* on the local copy.

It is possible to reduce the load on the master by performing the *Read* on the local copy without obtaining a read lock from the master site. Whether synchronous or deferred propagation is used, the local concurrency control algorithm ensures that the local read-write conflicts are properly serialized, and since the *Write* operations can only be coming from the master as part of update propagation, local write-write conflicts won't occur as the propagation transactions are executed in each slave in the order dictated by the master. However, a *Read* may read data item values at a slave either before an update is installed or after. The fact that a read transaction at one slave site may read the value of one replica before an update while another read transaction reads another replica at another slave after the same update is inconsequential from the perspective of ensuring global 1SR histories. This is demonstrated by the following example.

Example 13.3. Consider a data item x whose master site is at Site A with slaves at sites B and C. Consider the following three transactions:

T_1: Write(x) T_2: Read(x) T_3: Read(x)
    Commit   Commit   Commit

Assume that T_2 is sent to slave at Site B and T_3 to slave at Site C. Assume that T_2 reads x at B [$Read(x_B)$] before T_1's update is applied at B, while T_3 reads x at C [$Read(x_C)$] after T_1's update at C. Then the histories generated at the two slaves will be as follows:

$$H_B = \{R_2(x), C_2, W_1(x), C_1\}$$
$$H_C = \{W_1(x), C_1, R_3(x), C_3\}$$

The serialization order at Site B is $T_2 \rightarrow T_1$, while at Site C it is $T_1 \rightarrow T_3$. The global serialization order, therefore, is $T_2 \rightarrow T_1 \rightarrow T_3$, which is fine. Therefore the history is 1SR.   ◆

Consequently, if this approach is followed, read transactions may read data that are concurrently updated at the master, but the global history will still be 1SR.

In this alternative protocol, when a slave site receives a $Read(x)$, it obtains a local read lock, reads from its local copy (i.e., $Read(x_i)$) and returns the result to the user application; this can only come from a read-only transaction. When it receives a $Write(x)$, if the $Write$ is coming from the master site, then it performs it on the local copy (i.e., $Write(x_i)$). If it receives a $Write$ from a user application, then it rejects it, since this is obviously an error given that update transactions have to be submitted to the master site.

These alternatives of a single master eager centralized protocol are simple to implement. One important issue to address is how one recognizes a transaction as "update" or "read-only" – it may be possible to do this by explicit declaration within the `Begin_Transaction` command.

13.3.1.2 Single Master with Full Replication Transparency

Single master eager centralized protocols require each user application to know the master site, and they put significant load on the master that has to deal with (at least) the $Read$ operations within update transactions as well as acting as the coordinator for these transactions during 2PC execution. These issues can be addressed, to some extent, by involving, in the execution of the update transactions, the TM at the site where the application runs. Thus, the update transactions are not submitted to the master, but to the TM at the site where the application runs (since they don't need to know the master). This TM can act as the coordinating TM for both update and read-only transactions. Applications can simply submit their transactions to their local TM, providing full transparency.

There are alternatives to implementing full transparency – the coordinating TM may only act as a "router", forwarding each operation directly to the master site. The master site can then execute the operations locally (as described above) and return the results to the application. Although this alternative implementation provides full transparency and has the advantage of being simple to implement, it does not address the overloading problem at the master. An alternative implementation may be as follows.

1. The coordinating TM sends each operation, as it gets it, to the central (master) site. This requires no change to the C2PL-TM algorithm (Algorithm 11.1).

2. If the operation is a $Read(x)$, then the centralized lock manager (C2PL-LM in Algorithm 11.2) can proceed by setting a read lock on its copy of x (call it x_M) on behalf of this transaction and informs the coordinating TM that the read lock is granted. The coordinating TM can then forward the $Read(x)$ to any slave site that holds a replica of x (i.e., converts it to a $Read(x_i)$). The read can then be carried out by the data processor (DP) at that slave.

3. If the operation is a $Write(x)$, then the centralized lock manager (master) proceeds as follows:

    (a) It first sets a write lock on its copy of x.

    (b) It then calls its local DP to perform the $Write$ on its own copy of x (i.e., converts the operation to $Write(x_M)$).

    (c) Finally, it informs the coordinating TM that the write lock is granted.

The coordinating TM, in this case, sends the $Write(x)$ to all the slaves where a copy of x exists; the DPs at these slaves apply the $Write$ to their local copies.

The fundamental difference in this case is that the master site does not deal with $Read$s or with the coordination of the updates across replicas. These are left to the TM at the site where the user application runs.

It is straightforward to see that this algorithm guarantees that the histories are 1SR since the serialization orders are determined at a single master (similar to centralized concurrency control algorithms). It is also clear that the algorithm follows the ROWA protocol, as discussed above – since all the copies are ensured to be up-to-date when an update transaction completes, a $Read$ can be performed on any copy.

To demonstrate how eager algorithms combine replica control and concurrency control, we show how the Transaction Management algorithm for the coordinating TM (Algorithm 13.1) and the Lock Management algorithm for the master site (Algorithm 13.2). We show only the revisions to the centralized 2PL algorithms (Algorithms 11.1 and 11.2 in Chapter 11).

Note that in the algorithm fragments that we have given, the LM simply sends back a "Lock granted" message and not the result of the update operation. Consequently, when the update is forwarded to the slaves by the coordinating TM, they need to execute the update operation themselves. This is sometimes referred to as *operation transfer*. The alternative is for the "Lock granted" message to include the result of the update computation, which is then forwarded to the slaves who simply need to apply the result and update their logs. This is referred to as *state transfer*. The distinction may seem trivial if the operations are simply in the form $Write(x)$, but recall that this

---

Algorithm 13.1: Eager Single Master Modifications to C2PL-TM

---

begin
   ⋮
   if *lock request granted* **then**
      if *op.Type* = *W* **then**
       | *S* ← set of **all** sites that are slaves for the data item
      else
       └ *S* ← **any** one site which has a copy of data item
      $DP_S(op)$ {send operation to all sites in set S}
   else
    └ inform user about the termination of transaction
   ⋮
end

Algorithm 13.2: Eager Single Master Modifications to C2PL-LM

---

begin
   ⋮
   switch *op.Type* **do**
      case *R or W*   {lock request; see if it can be granted}
       | find the lock unit *lu* such that *op.arg* ⊆ *lu* ;
       | **if** *lu is unlocked or lock mode of lu is compatible with op.Type*
       | **then**
       | | set lock on *lu* in appropriate mode on behalf of transaction
       | | *op.tid* ;
       | | **if** *op.Type* = *W* **then**
       | | | $DP_M(op)$ {call local DP (M for "master") with operation}
       | | send "Lock granted" to coordinating TM of transaction
       | **else**
       | └ put *op* on a queue for *lu*
      └ ⋮
end

Write operation is an abstraction; each update operation may require the execution of an SQL expression, in which case the distinction is quite important.

The above implementation of the protocol relieves some of the load on the master site and alleviates the need for user applications to know the master. However, its implementation is more complicated than the first alternative we discussed. In particular, now the TM at the site where transactions are submitted has to act as the 2PC coordinator and the master site becomes a participant. This requires some care in revising the algorithms at these sites.

13.3.1.3 Primary Copy with Full Replication Transparency

Let us now relax the requirement that there is one master for all data items; each data item can have a different master. In this case, for each replicated data item, one of the replicas is designated as the *primary copy*. Consequently, there is no single master to determine the global serialization order, so more care is required. In the case of fully replicated databases, any replica can be primary copy for a data item, however for partially replicated databases, limited replication transparency option only makes sense if an update transaction accesses only data items whose primary sites are at the same site. Otherwise, the application program cannot forward the update transactions to one master; it will have to do it operation-by-operation, and, furthermore, it is not clear which primary copy master would serve as the coordinator for 2PC execution. Therefore, the reasonable alternative is the full transparency support, where the TM at the application site acts as the coordinating TM and forwards each operation to the primary site of the data item that it acts on. Figure 13.2 depicts the sequence of operations in this case where we relax our previous assumption of fully replication. Site A is the master for data item *x* and sites B and C hold replicas (i.e., they are slaves); similarly data item *y*'s master is site C with slave sites B and D.

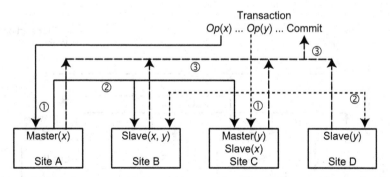

Fig. 13.2 Eager Primary Copy Replication Protocol Actions. (1) Operations (*Read* or *Write*) for each data item are routed to that data item's master and a *Write* is first applied at the master; (2) *Write* is then propagated to the other replicas; (3) Updates become permanent at commit time.

Recall that this version still applies the updates to all the replicas within transactional boundaries, requiring integration with concurrency control techniques. A very early proposal is the *primary copy two-phase locking* (PC2PL) algorithm proposed for the prototype distributed version of INGRES [Stonebraker and Neuhold, 1977]. PC2PL is a straightforward extension of the single master protocol discussed above in an attempt to counter the latter's potential performance problems. Basically, it implements lock managers at a number of sites and makes each lock manager responsible for managing the locks for a given set of lock units for which it is the master site. The transaction managers then send their lock and unlock requests to the lock managers that are responsible for that specific lock unit. Thus the algorithm treats one copy of each data item as its primary copy.

As a combined replica control/concurrency control technique, primary copy approach demands a more sophisticated directory at each site, but it also improves the previously discussed approaches by reducing the load of the master site without causing a large amount of communication among the transaction managers and lock managers.

13.3.2 Eager Distributed Protocols

In eager distributed replica control, the updates can originate anywhere, and they are first applied on the local replica, then the updates are propagated to other replicas. If the update originates at a site where a replica of the data item does not exist, it is forwarded to one of the replica sites, which coordinates its execution. Again, all of these are done within the context of the update transaction, and when the transaction commits, the user is notified and the updates are made permanent. Figure 13.3 depicts the sequence of operations for one logical data item x with copies at sites A, B, C and D, and where two transactions update two different copies (at sites A and D).

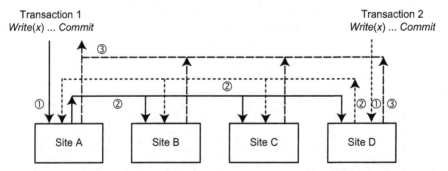

Fig. 13.3 Eager Distributed Replication Protocol Actions. (1) Two *Write* operations are applied on two local replicas of the same data item; (2) The *Write* operations are independently propagated to the other replicas; (3) Updates become permanent at commit time (shown only for Transaction 1).

As can be clearly seen, the critical issue is to ensure that concurrent conflicting *Writes* initiated at different sites are executed in the same order at every site where they execute together (of course, the local executions at each site also have to be serializable). This is achieved by means of the concurrency control techniques that are employed at each site. Consequently, read operations can be performed on any copy, but writes are performed on all copies within transactional boundaries (e.g., ROWA) using a concurrency control protocol.

13.3.3 Lazy Centralized Protocols

Lazy centralized replication algorithms are similar to eager centralized replication ones in that the updates are first applied to a master replica and then propagated to the slaves. The important difference is that the propagation does not take place within the update transaction, but after the transaction commits as a separate refresh transaction. Consequently, if a slave site performs a *Read(x)* operation on its local copy, it may read stale (non-fresh) data, since *x* may have been updated at the master, but the update may not have yet been propagated to the slaves.

13.3.3.1 Single Master with Limited Transparency

In this case, the update transactions are submitted and executed directly at the master site (as in the eager single master); once the update transaction commits, the refresh transaction is sent to the slaves. The sequence of execution steps are as follows: (1) an update transaction is first applied to the master replica, (2) the transaction is committed at the master, and then (3) the refresh transaction is sent to the slaves (Figure 13.4).

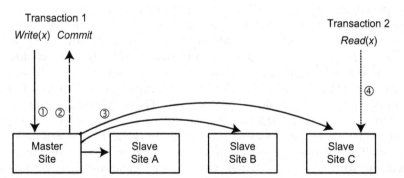

Fig. 13.4 Lazy Single Master Replication Protocol Actions. (1) Update is applied on the local replica; (2) Transaction commit makes the updates permanent at the master; (3) Update is propagated to the other replicas in refresh transactions; (4) Transaction 2 reads from local copy.

When a slave (secondary) site receives a $Read(x)$, it reads from its local copy and returns the result to the user. Notice that, as indicated above, its own copy may not be up-to-date if the master is being updated and the slave has not yet received and executed the corresponding refresh transaction. A $Write(x)$ received by a slave is rejected (and the transaction aborted), as this should have been submitted directly to the master site. When a slave receives a refresh transaction from the master, it applies the updates to its local copy. When it receives a *Commit* or *Abort* (*Abort* can happen for only locally submitted read-only transactions), it locally performs these actions.

The case of primary copy with limited transparency is similar, so we don't discuss it in detail. Instead of going to a single master site, $Write(x)$ is submitted to the primary copy of x; the rest is straightforward.

How can it be ensured that the refresh transactions can be applied at all of the slaves in the same order? In this architecture, since there is a single master copy for all data items, the ordering can be established by simply using timestamps. The master site would attach a timestamp to each refresh transaction according to the commit order of the actual update transaction, and the slaves would apply the refresh transactions in timestamp order.

A similar approach may be followed in the primary copy, limited transparency case. In this case, a site contains slave copies of a number of data items, causing it to get refresh transactions from multiple masters. The execution of these refresh transactions need to be ordered the same way at all of the involved slaves to ensure that the database states eventually converge. There are a number of alternatives that can be followed.

One alternative is to assign timestamps such that refresh transactions issued from different masters have different timestamps (by appending the site identifier to a monotonic counter at each site). Then the refresh transactions at each site can be executed in their timestamp order. However, those that come out of order cause difficulty. In traditional timestamp-based techniques discussed in Chapter 11, these transactions would be aborted; however in lazy replication, this is not possible since the transaction has already been committed at the primary copy site. The only possibility is to run a compensating transaction (which, effectively, aborts the transaction by rolling back its effects) or to perform update reconciliation that will be discussed shortly. The issue can be addressed by a more careful study of the resulting histories. An approach proposed by Breitbart and Korth [1997] uses a serialization graph approach that builds a *replication graph* whose nodes consist of transactions (T) and sites (S) and an edge $\langle T_i, S_j \rangle$ exists in the graph if and only if T_i performs a $Write$ on a (replicated) physical copy that is stored at S_j. When an operation (op_k) is submitted, the appropriate nodes (T_k) and edges are inserted into the replication graph, which is checked for cycles. If there is no cycle, then the execution can proceed. If a cycle is detected and it involves a transaction that has committed at the master, but whose refresh transactions have not yet committed at all of the involved slaves, then the current transaction (T_k) is aborted (to be restarted later) since its execution would cause the history to be non-1SR. Otherwise, T_k can wait until the other transactions in the cycle are completed (i.e., they are committed at their masters and their refresh transactions are committed at all of the slaves). When a transaction is completed in this manner, the corresponding node and all of its incident edges are removed from the replication graph. This protocol is proven to produce 1SR histories. An important issue is the maintenance of the replication graph. If it is maintained by a single site, then this becomes a centralized algorithm. We leave the distributed construction and maintenance of the replication graph as an exercise.

Another alternative is to rely on the group communication mechanism provided by the underlying communication infrastructure (if it can provide it). We discuss this alternative in Section 13.4.

Recall from Section 13.3.1 that, in the case of partially replicated databases, eager primary copy with limited replication transparency approach makes sense if the update transactions access only data items whose master sites are the same, since the update transactions are run completely at a master. The same problem exists in the case of lazy primary copy, limited replication approach. The issue that arises in both cases is how to design the distributed database so that meaningful transactions can be executed. This problem has been studied within the context of lazy protocols [Chundi et al., 1996] and a primary site selection algorithm was proposed that, given a set of transactions, a set of sites, and a set of data items, finds a primary site assignment to these data items (if one exists) such that the set of transactions can be executed to produce a 1SR global history.

13.3.3.2 Single Master or Primary Copy with Full Replication Transparency

We now turn to alternatives that provide full transparency by allowing (both read and update) transactions to be submitted at any site and forwarding their operations to either the single master or to the appropriate primary master site. This is tricky and involves two problems: the first is that, unless one is careful, 1SR global history may not be guaranteed; the second problem is that a transaction may not see its own updates. The following two examples demonstrate these problems.

Example 13.4. Consider the single master scenario and two sites M and B where M holds the master copies of x and y and B holds their slave copies. Now consider the following two transactions: T_1 submitted at site B, while transaction T_2 submitted at site M:

T_1: Read(x)	T_2: Write(x)
Write(y)	Write(y)
Commit	Commit

One way these would be executed under full transparency is as follows. T_2 would be executed at site M since it contains the master copies of both x and y. Sometime after it commits, refresh transactions for its *Writes* are sent to site B to update the slave copies. On the other hand, T_1 would read the local copy of x at site B, but its *Write*(x) would be forwarded to x's master copy, which is at site M. Some time after *Write*$_1$(x) is executed at the master site and commits there, a refresh transaction would be sent back to site B to update the slave copy. The following is a possible sequence of steps of execution (Figure 13.5):

1. $Read_1(x)$ is submitted at site B, where it is performed;

2. $Write_2(x)$ is submitted at site M, and it is executed;

3. $Write_2(y)$ is submitted at site M, and it is executed;

4. T_2 submits its *Commit* at site M and commits there;

5. $Write_1(x)$ is submitted at site B; since the master copy of x is at site M, the *Write* is forwarded to M;

6. $Write_1(x)$ is executed at site M and the confirmation is sent back to site B;

7. T_1 submits *Commit* at site B, which forwards it to site M; it is executed there and B is informed of the commit where T_1 also commits;

8. Site M now sends refresh transaction for T_2 to site B where it is executed and commits;

9. Site M finally sends refresh transaction for T_1 to site B (this is for T_1's *Write* that was executed at the master), it is executed at B and commits.

The following two histories are now generated at the two sites where the superscript r on operations indicate that they are part of a refresh transaction:

$$H_M = \{W_2(x_M), W_2(y_M), C_2, W_1(y_M), C_1\}$$
$$H_B = \{R_1(x_B), C_1, W_2^r(x_B), W_2^r(y_B), C_2^r, W_1^r(x_B), C_1^r\}$$

The resulting global history over the *logical* data items x and y is non-1SR.   ◆

Example 13.5. Again consider a single master scenario, where site M holds the master copy of x and site D holds its slave. Consider the following simple transaction:

T_3: Write(x)
    Read(x)
    Commit

Following the same execution model as in Example 13.4, the sequence of steps would be as follows:

1. $Write_3(x)$ is submitted at site D, which forwards it to site M for execution;

2. The *Write* is executed at M and the confirmation is sent back to site D;

3. $Read_3(x)$ is submitted at site D and is executed on the local copy;

4. T_3 submits commit at D, which is forwarded to M, executed there and a notification is sent back to site D, which also commits the transaction;

5. Site M sends a refresh transaction to site D for the $W_3(x)$ operation;

6. Site D executes the refresh transaction and commits it.

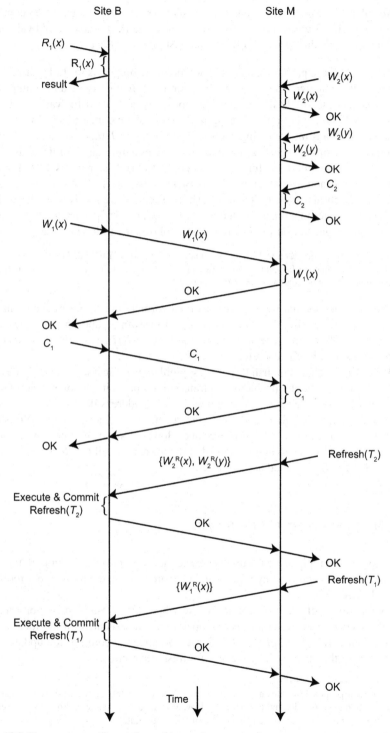

Fig. 13.5 Time sequence of executions of transactions

Note that, since the refresh transaction is sent to site D sometime after T_3 commits at site M, at step 3 when it reads the value of x at site D, it reads the old value and does not see the value of its own *Write* that just precedes *Read*.   ◆

Because of these problems, there are not too many proposals for full transparency in lazy replication algorithms. A notable exception is that by Bernstein et al. [2006] that considers the single master case and provides a method for validity testing by the master site, at commit point, similar to optimistic concurrency control. The fundamental idea is the following. Consider a transaction T that writes a data item x. At commit time of transaction T, the master generates a timestamp for it and uses this timestamp to set a timestamp for the master copy of x (x_M) that records the timestamp of the last transaction that updated it $(last\_modified(x_M))$. This is appended to refresh transactions as well. When refresh transactions are received at slaves they also set their copies to this same value, i.e., $last\_modified(x_i) \leftarrow last\_modified(x_M)$. The timestamp generation for T at the master follows the following rule:

> The timestamp for transaction T should be greater than all previously issued timestamps and should be less than the $last\_modified$ timestamps of the data items it has accessed. If such a timestamp cannot be generated, then T is aborted.[3]

This test ensures that read operations read correct values. For example, in Example 13.4, master site M would not be able to assign an appropriate timestamp to transaction T_1 when it commits, since the $last\_modified(x_M)$ would reflect the update performed by T_2. Therefore, T_1 would be aborted.

Although this algorithm handles the first problem we discussed above, it does not automatically handle the problem of a transaction not seeing its own writes (what we referred to as transaction inversion earlier). To address this issue, it has been suggested that a list be maintained of all the updates that a transaction performs and this list is consulted when a *Read* is executed. However, since only the master knows the updates, the list has to be maintained at the master and all the *Read*s (as well as *Write*s) have to be executed at the master.

13.3.4 Lazy Distributed Protocols

Lazy distributed replication protocols are the most complex ones owing to the fact that updates can occur on any replica and they are propagated to the other replicas lazily (Figure 13.6).

The operation of the protocol at the site where the transaction is submitted is straightforward: both *Read* and *Write* operations are executed on the local copy, and the transaction commits locally. Sometime after the commit, the updates are propagated to the other sites by means of refresh transactions.

---

[3] The original proposal handles a wide range of freshness constraints, as we discussed earlier; therefore, the rule is specified more generically. However, since our discussion primarily focuses on 1SR behavior, this (more strict) recasting of the rule is appropriate.

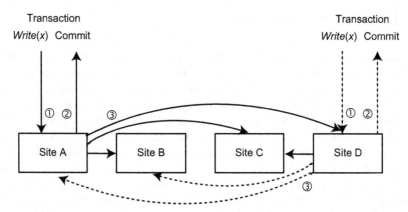

Fig. 13.6 Lazy Distributed Replication Protocol Actions. (1) Two updates are applied on two local replicas; (2) Transaction commit makes the updates permanent; (3) The updates are independently propagated to the other replicas.

The complications arise in processing these updates at the other sites. When the refresh transactions arrive at a site, they need to be locally scheduled, which is done by the local concurrency control mechanism. The proper serialization of these refresh transactions can be achieved using the techniques discussed in previous sections. However, multiple transactions can update different copies of the same data item concurrently at different sites, and these updates may conflict with each other. These changes need to be reconciled, and this complicates the ordering of refresh transactions. Based on the results of reconciliation, the order of execution of the refresh transactions is determined and updates are applied at each site.

The critical issue here is reconciliation. One can design a general purpose reconciliation algorithm based on heuristics. For example, updates can be applied in timestamp order (i.e., those with later timestamps will always win) or one can give preference to updates that originate at certain sites (perhaps there are more important sites). However, these are ad hoc methods and reconciliation is really dependent upon application semantics. Furthermore, whatever reconciliation technique is used, some of the updates are lost. Note that timestamp-based ordering will only work if timestamps are based on local clocks that are synchronized. As we discussed earlier, this is hard to achieve in large-scale distributed systems. Simple timestamp-based approach, which concatenates a site number and local clock, gives arbitrary preference between transactions that may have no real basis in application logic. The reason timestamps work well in concurrency control and not in this case is because in concurrency control we are only interested in determining *some* order; here we are interested in determining a *particular* order that is consistent with application semantics.

13.4 Group Communication

As discussed in the previous section, the overhead of replication protocols can be high – particularly in terms of message overhead. A very simple cost model for the replication algorithms is as follows. If there are n replicas and each transaction consists of m update operations, then each transaction issues $n * m$ messages (if multicast communication is possible, m messages would be sufficient). If the system wishes to maintain a throughput of k transactions-per-second, this results in $k * n * m$ messages per second (or $k * m$ in the case of multicasting). One can add sophistication to this cost function by considering the execution time of each operation (perhaps based on system load) to get a cost function in terms of time. The problem with many of the replication protocols discussed above (in particular the distributed ones) is that their message overhead is high.

A critical issue in efficient implementation of these protocols is to reduce the message overhead. Solutions have been proposed that use group communication protocols [Chockler et al., 2001] together with non-traditional techniques for processing local transactions [Stanoi et al., 1998; Kemme and Alonso, 2000a,b; Patiño-Martínez et al., 2000; Jiménez-Peris et al., 2002]. These solutions introduce two modifications: they do not employ 2PC at commit time, but rely on the underlying group communication protocols to ensure agreement, and they use deferred update propagation rather than synchronous.

Let us first review the group communication idea. A group communication system enables a node to multicast a message to all nodes of a group with a delivery guarantee, i.e., the message is eventually delivered to all nodes. Furthermore, it can provide multicast primitives with different delivery orders only one of which is important for our discussion: total order. In total ordered multicast, all messages sent by different nodes are delivered in the same total order at all nodes. This is important in understanding the following discussion.

We will demonstrate the use of group communication by considering two protocols. The first one is an alternative eager distributed protocol [Kemme and Alonso, 2000a], while the second one is a lazy centralized protocol [Pacitti et al., 1999].

The group communication-based eager distributed protocol due to Kemme and Alonso [2000a] uses a local processing strategy where *Write* operations are carried out on local shadow copies where the transaction is submitted and utilizes total ordered group communication to multicast the set of write operations of the transaction to all the other replica sites. Total ordered communication guarantees that all sites receive the write operations in exactly the same order, thereby ensuring identical serialization order at every site. For simplicity of exposition, in the following discussion, we assume that the database is fully replicated and that each site implements a 2PL concurrency control algorithm.

The protocol executes a transaction T_i in four steps (local concurrency control actions are not indicated):

I. **Local processing phase.** A $Read_i(x)$ operation is performed at the site where it is submitted (this is the master site for this transaction). A $Write_i(x)$ operation is also performed at the master site, but on a shadow copy (see the previous chapter for a discussion of shadow paging).

II. **Communication phase.** If T_i consists only of *Read* operations, then it can be committed at the master site. If it involves *Write* operations (i.e., if it is an update transaction), then the TM at T_i's master site (i.e., the site where T_i is submitted) assembles the writes into one *write message* WM_i[4] and multicasts it to all the replica sites (including itself) using total ordered group communication.

III. **Lock phase.** When WM_i is delivered at a site S_j, it requests all locks in WM_i in an atomic step. This can be done by acquiring a latch (lighter form of a lock) on the lock table that is kept until all the locks are granted or requests are enqueued. The following actions are performed:

1. For each *Write(x)* in WM_i (let x_j refer to the copy of x that exists at site S_j), the following are performed:

    (a) If there are no other transactions that have locked x_j, then the write lock on x_j is granted.

    (b) Otherwise a conflict test is performed:

     - If there is a local transaction T_k that has already locked x_j, but is in its local read or communication phases, then T_k is aborted. Furthermore, if T_k is in its communication phase, a final decision message *Abort* is multicast to all the sites. At this stage, read/write conflicts are detected and local read transactions are simply aborted. Note that only local read operations obtain locks during the local execution phase, since local writes are only executed on shadow copies. Therefore, there is no need to check for write/write conflicts at this stage.

     - Otherwise, $W_i(x_j)$ lock request is put on queue for x_j.

2. If T_i is a local transaction (recall that the message is also sent to the site where T_i originates, in which case $j = i$), then the site can commit the transaction, so it multicasts a *Commit* message. Note that the commit message is sent as soon as the locks are requested and not after writes; thus this is not a 2PC execution.

IV. **Write phase.** When a site is able to obtain the write lock, it applies the corresponding update (for the master site, this means that the shadow copy is made the valid version). The site where T_i is submitted can commit and release all the locks. Other sites have to wait for the decision message and terminate accordingly.

---

[4] What is being sent are the updated data items (i.e., state transfer).

Note that in this protocol, the important thing is to ensure that the lock phases of the concurrent transactions are executed in the same order at each site; that is what total ordered multicasting achieves. Also note that there is no ordering requirement on the decision messages (step III.2) and these may be delivered in any order, even before the delivery of the corresponding *WM*. If this happens, then the sites that receive the decision message before *WM* simply register the decision, but do not take any action. When *WM* message arrives, they can execute the lock and write phases and terminate the transaction according to the previously delivered decision message.

This protocol is significantly better, in terms of performance, than the naive one discussed in Section 13.3.2. For each transaction, the master site sends two messages: one when it sends the *WM* and the second one when it communicates the decision. Thus, if we wish to maintain a system throughput of k transactions-per-second, the total number of messages is $2k$ rather than $k * m$, as is the case with the naive protocol (assuming multicast in both cases). Furthermore, system performance is improved by the use of deferred eager propagation since synchronization among replica sites for all *Write* operations is done once at the end rather than throughout the transaction execution.

The second example of the use of group communication that we will discuss is in the context of lazy centralized algorithms. Recall that an important issue in this case is to ensure that the refresh transactions are ordered the same way at all the involved slaves so that the database states converge. If totally ordered multicasting is available, the refresh transactions sent by different master sites would be delivered in the same order at all the slaves. However, total order multicast has high messaging overhead which may limit its scalability. It is possible to relax the ordering requirement of the communication system and let the replication protocol take responsibility for ordering the execution of refresh transactions. We will demonstrate this alternative by means of a proposal due to Pacitti et al. [1999]. The protocol assumes FIFO ordered multicast communication with a bounded delay for communication (call it *Max*), and assumes that the clocks are loosely synchronized so that they may only be out of sync by up to ε. It further assumes that there is an appropriate transaction management functionality at each site. The result of the replication protocol at each slave is to maintain a "running queue" that holds an ordered list of refresh transactions, which is the input to the transaction manager for local execution. Thus, the protocol ensures that the orders in the running queues at each slave site where a set of refresh transactions run are the same.

At each slave site, a "pending queue" is maintained for each master site of this slave (i.e., if the slave site has replicas of x and y whose master sites are $Site_1$ and $Site_2$, respectively, then there are two pending queues, q_1 and q_2, corresponding to master sites $Site_1$ and $Site_2$, respectively). When a refresh transaction RT_i^k is created at a master site $Site_k$, it is assigned a timestamp $ts(RT_i)$ that corresponds to the real time value at the commit time of the corresponding update transaction T_i. When RT_i arrives at a slave, it is put on queue q_k. At each message arrival the top elements of all pending queues are scanned and the one with the lowest timestamp is chosen as the new RT (*new_RT*) to be handled. If the *new_RT* has changed since the last cycle (i.e., a new RT arrived with a lower timestamp than what was chosen in the previous cycle), then the one with the lower timestamp becomes the *new_RT* and is considered for scheduling.

When a refresh transaction is chosen as the *new_RT*, it is not immediately put on the "running queue" for the transaction manager; the scheduling of a refresh transaction takes into account the maximum delay and the possible drift in local clocks. This is done to ensure that any refresh transaction that may be delayed has a chance of reaching the slave. The time when an RT_i is put into the "running queue" at a slave site is $delivery\_time = ts(new\_RT) + Max + \varepsilon$. Since the communication system guarantees an upper bound of Max for message delivery and since the maximum drift in local clocks (that determine timestamps) is ε, a refresh transaction cannot be delayed by more than the *delivery_time* before reaching all of the intended slaves. Thus, the protocol guarantees that a refresh transaction is scheduled for execution at a slave when the following hold: (1) all the write operations of the corresponding update transaction are performed at the master, (2) according to the order determined by the timestamp of the refresh transaction (which reflects the commit order of the update transaction), and (3) at the earliest at real time equivalent to its *delivery_time*. This ensures that the updates on secondary copies at the slave sites follow the same chronological order in which their primary copies were updated and this order will be the same at all of the involved slaves, assuming that the underlying communication infrastructure can guarantee Max and ε. This is an example of a lazy algorithm that ensures 1SR global history, but weak mutual consistency, allowing the replica values to diverge by up to a predetermined time period.

13.5 Replication and Failures

Up to this point, we have focused on replication protocols in the absence of any failures. What happens to mutual consistency concerns if there are system failures? The handling of failures differs between eager replication and lazy replication approaches.

13.5.1 Failures and Lazy Replication

Let us first consider how lazy replication techniques deal with failures. This case is relatively easy since these protocols allow divergence between the master copies and the replicas. Consequently, when communication failures make one or more sites unreachable (the latter due to network partitioning), the sites that are available can simply continue processing. Even in the case of network partitioning, one can allow operations to proceed in multiple partitions independently and then worry about the convergence of the database states upon repair using the conflict resolution techniques discussed in Section 13.3.4. Before the merge, databases at multiple partitions diverge, but they are reconciled at merge time.

13.5.2 Failures and Eager Replication

Let us now focus on eager replication, which is considerably more involved. As we noted earlier, all eager techniques implement some sort of ROWA protocol, ensuring that, when the update transaction commits, all of the replicas have the same value. ROWA family of protocols is attractive and elegant. However, as we saw during the discussion of commit protocols, it has one significant drawback. Even if one of the replicas is unavailable, then the update transaction cannot be terminated. So, ROWA fails in meeting one of the fundamental goals of replication, namely providing higher availability.

An alternative to ROWA which attempts to address the low availability problem is the Read-One/Write-All Available (ROWA-A) protocol. The general idea is that the write commands are executed on all the available copies and the transaction terminates. The copies that were unavailable at the time will have to "catch up" when they become available.

There have been various versions of this protocol [Helal et al., 1997], two of which will be discussed here. The first one is known as the *available copies protocol* [Bernstein and Goodman, 1984; Bernstein et al., 1987]. The coordinator of an update transaction T_i (i.e., the master where the transaction is executing) sends each $W_i(x)$ to all the slave sites where replicas of x reside, and waits for confirmation of execution (or rejection). If it times out before it gets acknowledgement from all the sites, it considers those which have not replied as unavailable and continues with the update on the available sites. The unavailable slave sites update their databases to the latest state when they recover. Note, however, that these sites may not even be aware of the existence of T_i and the update to x that T_i has made if they had become unavailable before T_i started.

There are two complications that need to be addressed. The first one is the possibility that the sites that the coordinator thought were unavailable were in fact up and running and may have already updated x but their acknowledgement may not have reached the coordinator before its timer ran out. Second, some of these sites may have been unavailable when T_i started and may have recovered since then and have started executing transactions. Therefore, the coordinator undertakes a validation procedure before committing T_i:

1. The coordinator checks to see if all the sites it thought were unavailable are still unavailable. It does this by sending an inquiry message to every one of these sites. Those that are available reply. If the coordinator gets a reply from one of these sites, it aborts T_i since it does not know the state that the previously unavailable site is in: it could have been that the site was available all along and had performed the original $W_i(x)$ but its acknowledgement was delayed (in which case everything is fine), or it could be that it was indeed unavailable when T_i started but became available later on and perhaps even executed $W_j(x)$ on behalf of another transaction T_j. In the latter case, continuing with T_i would make the execution schedule non-serializable.

2. If the coordinator of T does not get any response from any of the sites that it thought were unavailable, then it checks to make sure that all the sites that were available when $W_i(x)$ executed are still available. If they are, then T can proceed to commit. Naturally, this second step can be integrated into a commit protocol.

The second ROWA-A variant that we will discuss is the distributed ROWA-A protocol. In this case, each site S maintains a set, V_S, of sites that it believes to be available; this is the "view" that S has of the system configuration. In particular, when a transaction T_i is submitted, its coordinator's view reflects all the sites that the coordinator knows to be available (let us denote this as $V_C(T_i)$ for simplicity). A $R_i(x)$ is performed on any replica in $V_C(T_i)$ and a $W_i(x)$ updates all copies in $V_C(T_i)$. The coordinator checks its view at the end of T_i, and if the view has changed since T_i's start, then T_i is aborted. To modify V, a special atomic transaction is run at all sites, ensuring that no concurrent views are generated. This can be achieved by assigning timestamps to each V when it is generated and ensuring that a site only accepts a new view if its version number is greater than the version number of that site's current view.

The ROWA-A class of protocols are more resilient to failures, including network partitioning, than the simple ROWA protocol.

Another class of eager replication protocols are those based on voting. The fundamental characteristics of voting were presented in the previous chapter when we discussed network partitioning in non-replicated databases. The general ideas hold in the replicated case. Fundamentally, each read and write operation has to obtain a sufficient number of votes to be able to commit. These protocols can be pessimistic or optimistic. In what follows we discuss only pessimistic protocols. An optimistic version compensates transactions to recover if the commit decision cannot be confirmed at completion [Davidson, 1984]. This version is suitable wherever compensating transactions are acceptable (see Chapter 10).

The initial voting algorithm was proposed by Thomas [1979] and an early suggestion to use quorum-based voting for replica control is due to Gifford [1979]. Thomas's algorithm works on fully replicated databases and assigns an equal vote to each site. For any operation of a transaction to execute, it must collect affirmative votes from a majority of the sites. Gifford's algorithm, on the other hand, works with partially replicated databases (as well as with fully replicated ones) and assigns a vote to each copy of a replicated data item. Each operation then has to obtain a *read quorum* (V_r) or a *write quorum* (V_w) to read or write a data item, respectively. If a given data item has a total of V votes, the quorums have to obey the following rules:

1. $V_r + V_w > V$

2. $V_w > V/2$

As the reader may recall from the preceding chapter, the first rule ensures that a data item is not read and written by two transactions concurrently (avoiding the read-write conflict). The second rule, on the other hand, ensures that two write operations from two transactions cannot occur concurrently on the same data item (avoiding write-write conflict). Thus the two rules ensure that serializability and one-copy equivalence are maintained.

In the case of network partitioning, the quorum-based protocols work well since they basically determine which transactions are going to terminate based on the votes that they can obtain. The vote allocation and threshold rules given above ensure that two transactions that are initiated in two different partitions and access the same data cannot terminate at the same time.

The difficulty with this version of the protocol is that transactions are required to obtain a quorum even to read data. This significantly and unnecessarily slows down read access to the database. We describe below another quorum-based voting protocol that overcomes this serious performance drawback [Abbadi et al., 1985].

The protocol makes certain assumptions about the underlying communication layer and the occurrence of failures. The assumption about failures is that they are "clean." This means two things:

1. Failures that change the network's topology are detected by all sites instanta-neously.

2. Each site has a view of the network consisting of all the sites with which it can communicate.

Based on the presence of a communication network that can ensure these two conditions, the replica control protocol is a simple implementation of the ROWA-A principle. When the replica control protocol attempts to read or write a data item, it first checks if a majority of the sites are in the same partition as the site at which the protocol is running. If so, it implements the ROWA rule within that partition: it reads any copy of the data item and writes all copies that are in that partition.

Notice that the read or the write operation will execute in only one partition. Therefore, this is a pessimistic protocol that guarantees one-copy serializability, *but only within that partition*. When the partitioning is repaired, the database is recovered by propagating the results of the update to the other partitions.

A fundamental question with respect to implementation of this protocol is whether or not the failure assumptions are realistic. Unfortunately, they may not be, since most network failures are not "clean." There is a time delay between the occurrence of a failure and its detection by a site. Because of this delay, it is possible for one site to think that it is in one partition when in fact subsequent failures have placed it in another partition. Furthermore, this delay may be different for various sites. Thus two sites that were in the same partition but are now in different partitions may proceed for a while under the assumption that they are still in the same partition. The violations of these two failure assumptions have significant negative consequences on the replica control protocol and its ability to maintain one-copy serializability.

The suggested solution is to build on top of the physical communication layer another layer of abstraction which hides the "unclean" failure characteristics of the physical communication layer and presents to the replica control protocol a com-munication service that has "clean" failure properties. This new layer of abstraction provides *virtual partitions* within which the replica control protocol operates. A virtual partition is a group of sites that have agreed on a common view of who is in that partition. Sites join and depart from virtual partitions under the control of this new communication layer, which ensures that the clean failure assumptions hold.

The advantage of this protocol is its simplicity. It does not incur any overhead to maintain a quorum for read accesses. Thus the reads can proceed as fast as they would in a non-partitioned network. Furthermore, it is general enough so that the replica control protocol does not need to differentiate between site failures and network partitions.

Given alternative methods for achieving fault-tolerance in the case of replicated databases, a natural question is what the relative advantages of these methods are. There have been a number of studies that analyze these techniques, each with varying assumptions. A comprehensive study suggests that ROWA-A implementations achieve better scalability and availability than quorum techniques [Jiménez-Peris et al., 2003].

13.6 Replication Mediator Service

The replication protocols we have covered so far are suitable for tightly integrated distributed database systems where we can insert the protocols into each component DBMS. In multidatabase systems, replication support has to be supported outside the DBMSs by mediators. In this section we discuss how to provide replication support at the mediator level by means of an example protocol called NODO [Patiño-Martínez et al., 2000].

The NODO (NOn-Disjoint conflict classes and Optimistic multicast) protocol is a hybrid between distributed and primary copy – it permits transactions to be submitted at any site, but it does have the notion of a primary copy for a data item. It uses group communications and optimistic delivery to reduce latency. The optimistic delivery technique delivers a message optimistically as soon as it is received without guaranteeing any order among messages. The message is said to be "opt-delivered". When the total order of the message is established, then the message is to-delivered. Although optimistic delivery does not guarantee any order, most of the time the order will be the same as total ordering. This fact is exploited by NODO to overlap the total ordering of the transaction request with the transaction execution at the master node, thus masking the latency of total ordering. The protocol also executes transactions optimistically (see Section 11.5), and may abort them if necessary.

In the following discussion, we will assume a fully replicated database for simplicity. This allows us to ignore issues such as finding the primary copy site, how to execute a transaction over a set of data items that have different primary copies, etc. In the fully replicated environment, all of the sites in the system form a multicast group.

It is assumed that the data items are grouped into disjoint sets and each set has a primary copy. Each transaction accesses a particular set of items, and, as in all primary copy techniques, it first executes at the primary copy site, and its writes are then propagated to the slave sites. The transaction is said to be *local* to its primary copy site.

Each set of data items is called a *conflict class*, and the protocol exploits the knowledge of transactions' conflict classes to increase concurrency. Two transactions that access the same conflict class have a high probability of conflict, while two transactions that access different conflict classes can run in parallel. A transaction can access several conflict classes and this must be statically known before execution (e.g., by analyzing the transaction code). Thus, conflict classes are further abstracted into conflict class groups. Each conflict class group has a single primary copy (i.e., the primary copy of one of the individual conflict classes in the group) where all transactions on that conflict class group must be executed. The same individual conflict class can be in different conflict class groups. For instance, if S_i be the primary copy site of $\{C_x, C_y\}$ and S_j be the primary copy site of $\{C_y\}$, transactions T_1 on $\{C_x, C_y\}$ and T_2 on $\{C_y\}$ are executed at S_i and S_j, respectively.

Each transaction is associated with a single conflict class group, and therefore, it has a single primary copy. Each site manages a number of queues for its incoming transactions, one per individual conflict class (not one per conflict class group). The processing of a transaction proceeds in the following way:

1. A transaction is submitted by an application at a site.

2. That site multicasts the transaction to the multicast group (which is the entire set of sites since we are assuming full replication).

3. When the transaction is opt-delivered at a site, it is appended to the queue of all the individual classes included in its conflict class group.

4. At the primary copy site, when the transaction becomes the first in the queue of all the individual conflict classes of its conflict class group, it is optimistically executed.

5. When the transaction is to-delivered at a site, it is checked whether its optimistic ordering was the same as the total ordering. If the optimistic order was wrong, the transaction is reordered in all the queues according to the total order. The primary copy site, in addition, aborts the transaction (if it was already executed) and re-executes it when it again gets to the head of all the relevant queues. If the optimistic ordering was correct, the primary copy site extracts the resulting write set of the transaction and multicasts (without total ordering) it to the multicast group.

6. When the write set is received at the primary copy site (remember that in this case the primary copy site is also in the multicast group, so it receives its own transmission), it commits the transaction. When the write set is received at a slave site and the transaction becomes the first in all the relevant queues, its write set is applied, and then the transaction commits.

Example 13.6. Let site S_i, respectively S_j, be the master of the conflict class group $\{C_x, C_y\}$, respectively $\{C_x\}$ and $\{C_y\}$. Let transaction T_1 be on $\{C_x, C_y\}$, T_2 on $\{C_y\}$ and T_3 on $\{C_x\}$. Thus, T_1 is local to S_i while T_2 and T_3 are local to S_j. At S_i and S_j, let transaction T_i be the i-th in the total order (i.e., the total order is $T_1 \rightarrow T_2 \rightarrow T_3$). Consider the following state of the queues C_x and C_y at S_i and S_j after the transactions have been opt-delivered.

$$S_i : C_x = [T_1, T_3]; C_y = [T_1, T_2]$$
$$S_j : C_x = [T_3, T_1]; C_y = [T_1, T_2]$$

At S_i T_1 is the first in the queues C_x and C_y and thus it is executed. Similarly, at S_j T_3 is at the head of C_x and thus, executed. When S_i to-delivers T_1, since the optimistic ordering was correct, it extracts T_1's write set and multicasts it. Upon delivering the write set of T_1 at S_i, T_1 is committed. Upon delivering T_1's write set at S_j, it is realized that T_1 was wrongly ordered after T_3, and T_1 is reordered before T_3 and T_3 is aborted since its optimistic ordering was wrong. T_1's write set is then applied and committed. At both S_i and S_j, T_1 is removed from all the queues. Now T_2 and T_3 are first of their queues at S_j, their primary copy site, and both are executed in parallel. Since they are in disjoint conflict class groups, their relative ordering is irrelevant. Now T_2 is to-delivered and since it is optimistic delivery was correct, its write set is extracted and multicast. Upon delivery of the T_2's write set, S_j commits T_2, while S_i applies the write set and commits it. Finally, T_3 is to-delivered and since its execution was performed according to the total order, S_j extracts T_3's write set and multicasts it. Upon delivery of the T_3's writeset, S_j commits T_3. Similarly, S_i applies the write set and commits T_3. The final ordering is $T_1 \rightarrow T_2 \rightarrow T_3$ at both nodes.   ◆

Interestingly, there are many cases where, in spite of an ordering mismatch between opt and to-delivery, it is possible to commit transactions consistently by using the optimistic rather than total ordering, thus minimizing the number of aborts due to optimism failures. This fact is exploited by the REORDERING protocol [Patiño-Martínez et al., 2005].

The implementation of the NODO protocol combines concurrency control with group communication primitives and what has been traditionally done inside the DBMS. This solution can be implemented outside a DBMS without a negligible overhead, and thus supports DBMS autonomy Jiménez-Peris et al. [2002]. Similar eager replication protocols have been proposed to support *partial replication*, where copies can be stored at subsets of nodes [Sousa et al., 2001; Serrano et al., 2007]. Unlike full replication, partial replication increases access locality and reduces the number of messages for propagating updates to replicas.

13.7 Conclusion

In this chapter we discussed different approaches to data replication and presented protocols that are appropriate under different circumstances. Each of the alternative protocols we have discussed have their advantages and disadvantages. Eager centralized protocols are simple to implement, they do not require update coordination across sites, and they are guaranteed to lead to one-copy serializable histories. However, they put a significant load on the master sites, potentially causing them to become bottlenecks. Consequently, they are harder to scale, in particular in the single master site architecture – primary copy versions have better scalability properties since the master responsibilities are somewhat distributed. These protocols result in long response times (the longest among the four alternatives), since the access to any data has to wait until the commit of any transaction that is currently updating it (using 2PC, which is expensive). Furthermore, the local copies are used sparingly, only for read operations. Thus, if the workload is update-intensive, eager centralized protocols are likely to suffer from bad performance.

Eager distributed protocols also guarantee one-copy serializability and provide an elegant symmetric solution where each site performs the same function. However, unless there is communication system support for efficient multicasting, they result in very high number of messages that increase network load and result in high transaction response times. This also constrains their scalability. Furthermore, naive implementations of these protocols will cause significant number of deadlocks since update operations are executed at multiple sites concurrently.

Lazy centralized protocols have very short response times since transactions execute and commit at the master, and do not need to wait for completion at the slave sites. There is also no need to coordinate across sites during the execution of an update transaction, thus reducing the number of messages. On the other hand, mutual consistency (i.e., freshness of data at all copies) is not guaranteed as local copies can be out of date. This means that it is not possible to do a local read and be assured that the most up-to-date copy is read.

Finally, lazy multi-master protocols have the shortest response times and the highest availability. This is because each transaction is executed locally, with no distributed coordination. Only after they commit are the other replicas updated through refresh transactions. However, this is also the shortcoming of these protocols – different replicas can be updated by different transactions, requiring elaborate reconciliation protocols and resulting in lost updates.

Replication has been studied extensively within the distributed computing community as well as the database community. Although there are considerable similarities in the problem definition in the two environments, there are also important differences. Perhaps the two more important differences are the following. Data replication focuses on data, while replication of computation is equally important in distributed computing. In particular, concerns about data replication in mobile environments that involve disconnected operation have received considerable attention. Secondly, database and transaction consistency is of paramount importance in data replication; in distributed computing, consistency concerns are not as high on the list of priorities. Consequently, considerably weaker consistency criteria have been defined.

Replication has been studied within the context of parallel database systems, in particular within parallel database clusters. We discuss these separately in Chapter 14.

13.8 Bibliographic Notes

Replication and replica control protocols have been the subject of significant investigation since early days of distributed database research. This work is summarized very well in [Helal et al., 1997]. Replica control protocols that deal with network partitioning are surveyed in [Davidson et al., 1985].

A landmark paper that defined a framework for various replication algorithms and argued that eager replication is problematic (thus opening up a torrent of activity on lazy techniques) is [Gray et al., 1996]. The characterization that we use in this chapter is based on this framework. A more detailed characterization is given in [Wiesmann et al., 2000]. A recent survey on optimistic (or lazy) replication techniques is [Saito and Shapiro, 2005]. The entire topic is discussed at length in [Kemme et al., 2010]

Freshness, in particular for lazy techniques, have been a topic of some study. Alternative techniques to ensure "better" freshness are discussed in [Pacitti et al., 1998; Pacitti and Simon, 2000; Röhm et al., 2002a; Pape et al., 2004; Akal et al., 2005].

There are many different versions of quorum-based protocols. Some of these are discussed in [Triantafillou and Taylor, 1995; Paris, 1986; Tanenbaum and van Renesse, 1988]. Besides the algorithms we have described here, some notable others are given in [Davidson, 1984; Eager and Sevcik, 1983; Herlihy, 1987; Minoura and Wiederhold, 1982; Skeen and Wright, 1984; Wright, 1983]. These algorithms are generally called *static* since the vote assignments and read/write quorums are fixed a priori. An analysis of one such protocol (such analyses are rare) is given in [Kumar and Segev, 1993]. Examples of *dynamic replication protocols* are in [Jajodia and Mutchler, 1987; Barbara et al., 1986, 1989] among others. It is also possible to change the way data are replicated. Such protocols are called *adaptive* and one example is described in [Wolfson, 1987].

An interesting replication algorithm based on economic models is described in [Sidell et al., 1996].

Exercises

Problem 13.1. For each of the four replication protocols (eager centralized, eager distributed, lazy centralized, lazy distributed), give a scenario/application where the approach is more suitable than the other approaches. Explain why.

Problem 13.2. A company has several geographically distributed warehouses storing and selling products. Consider the following partial database schema:

ITEM(ID, ItemName, Price, ...)

STOCK(ID, Warehouse, Quantity, ...)

CUSTOMER(ID, CustName, Address, CreditAmt, ...)

CLIENT-ORDER(ID, Warehouse, Balance, ...)

ORDER(ID, Warehouse, CustID, Date)

ORDER-LINE(ID, ItemID, Amount, ...)

The database contains relations with product information (ITEM contains the general product information, STOCK contains, for each product and for each warehouse, the number of pieces currently on stock). Furthermore, the database stores information about the clients/customers, e.g., general information about the clients is stored in the CUSTOMER table. The main activities regarding the clients are the rdering of products, the payment of bills and general information requests. There exist several tables to register the orders of a customer. Each order is regustered in the ORDER and ORDER-LINE tables. For each order/purchase, one entry exists in the order table, having an ID, indicating the customer-id, the warehouse at which the order was submitted, the date of the order, etc. A client can have several orders pending at a warehouse. Within each order, several products can be ordered. ORDER-LINE contains an entry for each product of the order, which may include one or more products. CLIENT-ORDER is a summary table that lists, for each client and for each warehouse, the sum of all existing orders.

(a)   The company has a customer service group consisting of several employees that receive customers' orders and payments, query the data of local customers to write bills or register paychecks, etc. Furthermore, they answer any type of requests which the customers might have. For instance, ordering products changes (update/insert) the CLIENT-ORDER, ORDER, ORDER-LINE, and STOCK tables. To be flexible, each employee must be able to work with any of the clients. The workload is estimated to be 80% queries and 20% updates. Since the workload is query oriented, the management has decided to build a cluster of PCs each equipped with its own database to accelerate queries through fast local access. How would you replicate the data for this purpose? Which replica control protocol(s) wold you use to keep the data consistent?

(b)   The company's management has to decide each fiscal quarter on their product offerings and sales strategies. For this purpose, they must continually observe and analyze the sales of the different products at the different warehouses as well as observe consumer behavior. How would you replicate the data for this purpose? Which replica control protocol(s) would you use to keep the data consistent?

Problem 13.3 (*). An alternative to ensuring that the refresh transactions can be applied at all of the slaves in the same order in lazy single master protocols with limited transparency is the use of a replication graph as discussed in Section 13.3.3. Develop a method for distributed management of the replication graph.

Problem 13.4. Consider data items x and y replicated across the sites as follows:

Site 1	Site 2	Site 3	Site 4
x	x		x
	y	y	y

(a)   Assign votes to each site and give the read and write quorum.
(b)   Determine the possible ways that the network can partition and for each specify in which group of sites a transaction that updates (reads and writes) x can be terminated and what the termination condition would be.
(c)   Repeat **(b)** for y.

Problem 13.5 (**). In the NODO protocol, we have seen that each conflict class group has a master. However, this is not inherent to the protocol. Design a multi-master variation of NODO in which a transaction might be executed by any replica. What condition should be enforced to guarantee that each updated transaction is processed only by one replica?

Problem 13.6 (**). In the NODO protocol, if the DBMS could provide additional introspection functionality, it would be possible to execute in certain circumstances transactions of the same conflict class in parallel. Determine which functionality would be needed from the DBMS. Also characterize formally under which circumstances concurrent execution of transactions in the same conflict class could be allowed to be executed in parallel whilst respecting 1-copy consistency. Extend the NODO protocol with this enhancement.

Chapter 14
Parallel Database Systems

Many data-intensive applications require support for very large databases (e.g., hundreds of terabytes or petabytes). Examples of such applications are e-commerce, data warehousing, and data mining. Very large databases are typically accessed through high numbers of concurrent transactions (e.g., performing on-line orders on an electronic store) or complex queries (e.g., decision-support queries). The first kind of access is representative of On-Line Transaction Processing (OLTP) applications while the second is representative of On-Line Analytical Processing (OLAP) applications. Supporting very large databases efficiently for either OLTP or OLAP can be addressed by combining parallel computing and distributed database management.

As introduced in Chapter 1, a parallel computer, or multiprocessor, is a special kind of distributed system made of a number of nodes (processors, memories and disks) connected by a very fast network within one or more cabinets in the same room. The main idea is to build a very powerful computer out of many small computers, each with a very good cost/performance ratio, at a much lower cost than equivalent mainframe computers. As discussed in Chapter 1, data distribution can be exploited to increase performance (through parallelism) and availability (through replication). This principle can be used to implement *parallel database systems*, i.e., database systems on parallel computers [DeWitt and Gray, 1992; Valduriez, 1993]. Parallel database systems can exploit the parallelism in data management in order to deliver high-performance and high-availability database servers. Thus, they can support very large databases with very high loads.

Most of the research on parallel database systems has been done in the context of the relational model that provides a good basis for data-based parallelism. In this chapter, we present the parallel database system approach as a solution to high-performance and high-availability data management. We discuss the advantages and disadvantages of the various parallel system architectures and we present the generic implementation techniques.

Implementation of parallel database systems naturally relies on distributed database techniques. However, the critical issues are data placement, parallel query processing, and load balancing because the number of nodes may be much higher

M.T. Özsu and P. Valduriez, *Principles of Distributed Database Systems: Third Edition*,   497
DOI 10.1007/978-1-4419-8834-8_14, © Springer Science+Business Media, LLC 2011

than in a distributed DBMS. Furthermore, a parallel computer typically provides reliable, fast communication that can be exploited to efficiently implement distributed transaction management and replication. Therefore, although the basic principles are the same as in distributed DBMS, the techniques for parallel database systems are fairly different.

This chapter is organized as follows. In Section 14.1, we clarify the objectives, and discuss the functional and architectural aspects of parallel database systems. In particular, we discuss the respective advantages and limitations of the parallel system architectures (shared-memory, shared-disk, shared-nothing) along several important dimensions including the perspective of both end-users, database administrators and system developers. Then, we present the techniques for data placement in Section 14.2, query processing in Section 14.3 and load balancing in Section 14.4.

In Section 14.5, we present the use of parallel data management techniques in database clusters, an important type of parallel database system implemented on a cluster of PCs.

14.1 Parallel Database System Architectures

In this section we show the value of parallel systems for efficient database management. We motivate the needs for parallel database systems by reviewing the requirements of very large information systems using current hardware technology trends. We present the functional and architectural aspects of parallel database systems. In particular, we present and compare the main architectures: shared-memory, shared-disk, shared-nothing and hybrid architectures.

14.1.1 Objectives

Parallel processing exploits multiprocessor computers to run application programs by using several processors cooperatively, in order to improve performance. Its prominent use has long been in scientific computing by improving the response time of numerical applications [Kowalik, 1985; Sharp, 1987]. The developments in both general-purpose parallel computers using standard microprocessors and parallel programming techniques [Osterhaug, 1989] have enabled parallel processing to break into the data processing field.

Parallel database systems combine database management and parallel processing to increase performance and availability. Note that performance was also the objective of *database machines* in the 70s and 80s [Hsiao, 1983]. The problem faced by conventional database management has long been known as "I/O bottleneck" [Boral and DeWitt, 1983], induced by high disk access time with respect to main memory access time (typically hundreds of thousands times faster).

Initially, database machine designers tackled this problem through special-purpose hardware, e.g., by introducing data filtering devices within the disk heads. However, this approach failed because of poor cost/performance compared to the software solution, which can easily benefit from hardware progress in silicon technology. A notable exception to these failures was the CAFS-ISP hardware-based filtering device [Babb, 1979] that was bundled within disk controllers for fast associative search. The idea of pushing database functions closer to disk has received renewed interest with the introduction of general-purpose microprocessors in disk controllers, thus leading to intelligent disks [Keeton et al., 1998]. For instance, basic functions that require costly sequential scan, e.g. select operations on tables with fuzzy predicates, can be more efficiently performed at the disk level since they avoid overloading the DBMS memory with irrelevant disk blocks. However, exploiting intelligent disks requires adapting the DBMS, in particular, the query processor to decide whether to use the disk functions. Since there is no standard intelligent disk technology, adapting to different intelligent disk technologies hurts DBMS portability.

An important result, however, is in the general solution to the I/O bottleneck. We can summarize this solution as *increasing the I/O bandwidth through parallelism*. For instance, if we store a database of size D on a single disk with throughput T, the system throughput is bounded by T. On the contrary, if we partition the database across n disks, each with capacity D/n and throughput T' (hopefully equivalent to T), we get an ideal throughput of $n * T'$ that can be better consumed by multiple processors (ideally n). Note that the main memory database system solution [Eich, 1989], which tries to maintain the database in main memory, is complementary rather than alternative. In particular, the "memory access bottleneck" in main memory systems can also be tackled using parallelism in a similar way. Therefore, parallel database system designers have strived to develop software-oriented solutions in order to exploit parallel computers.

A parallel database system can be loosely defined as a DBMS implemented on a parallel computer. This definition includes many alternatives ranging from the straightforward porting of an existing DBMS, which may require only rewriting the operating system interface routines, to a sophisticated combination of parallel processing and database system functions into a new hardware/software architecture. As always, we have the traditional trade-off between portability (to several platforms) and efficiency. The sophisticated approach is better able to fully exploit the opportunities offered by a multiprocessor at the expense of portability. Interestingly, this gives different advantages to computer manufacturers and software vendors. It is therefore important to characterize the main points in the space of alternative parallel system architectures. In order to do so, we will make precise the parallel database system solution and the necessary functions. This will be useful in comparing the parallel database system architectures.

The objectives of parallel database systems are covered by those of distributed DBMS (performance, availability, extensibility). Ideally, a parallel database system should provide the following advantages.

1. **High-performance.** This can be obtained through several complementary solutions: database-oriented operating system support, parallel data management, query optimization, and load balancing. Having the operating system constrained and "aware" of the specific database requirements (e.g., buffer management) simplifies the implementation of low-level database functions and therefore decreases their cost. For instance, the cost of a message can be significantly reduced to a few hundred instructions by specializing the communication protocol. Parallelism can increase throughput, using inter-query parallelism, and decrease transaction response times, using intra-query parallelism. However, decreasing the response time of a complex query through large-scale parallelism may well increase its total time (by additional communication) and hurt throughput as a side-effect. Therefore, it is crucial to optimize and parallelize queries in order to minimize the overhead of parallelism, e.g., by constraining the degree of parallelism for the query. *Load balancing* is the ability of the system to divide a given workload equally among all processors. Depending on the parallel system architecture, it can be achieved statically by appropriate physical database design or dynamically at run-time.

2. **High-availability.** Because a parallel database system consists of many redundant components, it can well increase data availability and fault-tolerance. In a highly-parallel system with many nodes, the probability of a node failure at any time can be relatively high. Replicating data at several nodes is useful to support *failover*, a fault-tolerance technique that enables automatic redirection of transactions from a failed node to another node that stores a copy of the data. This provides uninterupted service to users. However, it is essential that a node failure does not crate load imbalance, e.g., by doubling the load on the available copy. Solutions to this problem require partitioning copies in such a way that they can also be accessed in parallel.

3. **Extensibility.** In a parallel system, accommodating increasing database sizes or increasing performance demands (e.g., throughput) should be easier. Extensibility is the ability to expand the system smoothly by adding processing and storage power to the system. Ideally, the parallel database system should demonstrate two extensibility advantages [DeWitt and Gray, 1992]: *linear speedup* and *linear scaleup* see Figure 14.1. Linear speedup refers to a linear increase in performance for a constant database size while the number of nodes (i.e., processing and storage power) are increased linearly. Linear scaleup refers to a sustained performance for a linear increase in both database size and number of nodes. Furthermore, extending the system should require minimal reorganization of the existing database.

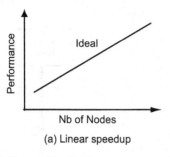
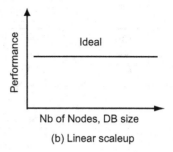

(a) Linear speedup   (b) Linear scaleup

Fig. 14.1 Extensibility Metrics

14.1.2 Functional Architecture

Assuming a client/server architecture, the functions supported by a parallel database system can be divided into three subsystems much like in a typical DBMS. The differences, though, have to do with implementation of these functions, which must now deal with parallelism, data partitioning and replication, and distributed transactions. Depending on the architecture, a processor node can support all (or a subset) of these subsystems. Figure 14.2 shows the architecture using these subsystems due to Bergsten et al. [1991].

1. **Session Manager.** It plays the role of a transaction monitor, providing support for client interactions with the server. In particular, it performs the connections and disconnections between the client processes and the two other subsystems. Therefore, it initiates and closes user sessions (which may contain multiple transactions). In case of OLTP sessions, the session manager is able to trigger the execution of pre-loaded transaction code within data manager modules.

2. **transaction Manager.** It receives client transactions related to query compilation and execution. It can access the database directory that holds all meta-information about data and programs. The directory itself should be managed as a database in the server. Depending on the transaction, it activates the various compilation phases, triggers query execution, and returns the results as well as error codes to the client application. Because it supervises transaction execution and commit, it may trigger the recovery procedure in case of transaction failure. To speed up query execution, it may optimize and parallelize the query at compile-time.

3. **Data Manager.** It provides all the low-level functions needed to run compiled queries in parallel, i.e., database operator execution, parallel transaction support, cache management, etc. If the transaction manager is able to compile dataflow control, then synchronization and communication among data manager modules is possible. Otherwise, transaction control and synchronization must be done by a transaction manager module.

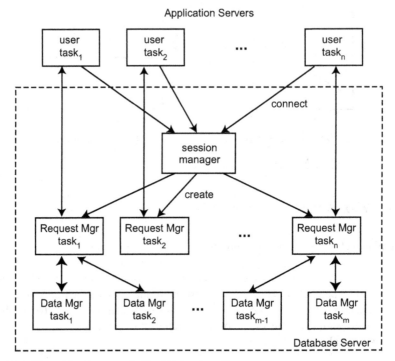

Fig. 14.2 General Architecture of a Parallel Database System

14.1.3 Parallel DBMS Architectures

As any system, a parallel database system represents a compromise in design choices in order to provide the aforementioned advantages with a good cost/performance. One guiding design decision is the way the main hardware elements, i.e., processors, main memory, and disks, are connected through some fast interconnection network. There are three basic parallel computer architectures depending on how main memory or disk is shared: *shared-memory*, *shared-disk* and *shared-nothing*. Hybrid architectures such as NUMA or *cluster* try to combine the benefits of the basic architectures. In the rest of this section, when describing parallel architectures, we focus on the four main hardware elements: interconnect, processors (P), main memory (M) and disks. For simplicity, we ignore other elements such as processor cache and I/O bus.

14.1.3.1 Shared-Memory

In the shared-memory approach (see Figure 14.3), any processor has access to any memory module or disk unit through a fast interconnect (e.g., a high-speed bus or a cross-bar switch). All the processors are under the control of a single operating system.

Current mainframe designs and symmetric multiprocessors (SMP) follow this approach. Examples of shared-memory parallel database systems include XPRS [Hong, 1992], DBS3 [Bergsten et al., 1991], and Volcano [Graefe, 1990], as well as portings of major commercial DBMSs on SMP. In a sense, the implementation of DB2 on an IBM3090 with 6 processors [Cheng et al., 1984] was the first example. All shared-memory parallel database products today can exploit inter-query parallelism to provide high transaction throughput and intra-query parallelism to reduce response time of decision-support queries.

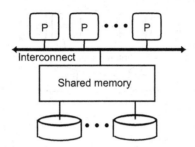

Fig. 14.3 Shared-Memory Architecture

Shared-memory has two strong advantages: simplicity and load balancing. Since meta-information (directory) and control information (e.g., lock tables) can be shared by all processors, writing database software is not very different than for single-processor computers. In particular, inter-query parallelism comes for free. Intra-query parallelism requires some parallelization but remains rather simple. Load balancing is easy to achieve since it can be achieved at run-time using the shared-memory by allocating each new task to the least busy processor.

Shared-memory has three problems: high cost, limited extensibility and low availability. High cost is incurred by the interconnect that requires fairly complex hardware because of the need to link each processor to each memory module or disk. With faster processors (even with larger caches), conflicting accesses to the shared-memory increase rapidly and degrade performance [Thakkar and Sweiger, 1990]. Therefore, extensibility is limited to a few tens of processors, typically up to 16 for the best cost/performance using 4-processor boards. Finally, since the memory space is shared by all processors, a memory fault may affect most processors thereby hurting availability. The solution is to use duplex memory with a redundant interconnect.

14.1.3.2 Shared-Disk

In the shared-disk approach (see Figure 14.4), any processor has access to any disk unit through the interconnect but exclusive (non-shared) access to its main memory. Each processor-memory node is under the control of its own copy of the operating system. Then, each processor can access database pages on the shared disk and cache them into its own memory. Since different processors can access the same page in conflicting update modes, global cache consistency is needed. This is typically achieved using a distributed lock manager that can be implemented using the techniques described in Chapter 11. The first parallel DBMS that used shared-disk is Oracle with an efficient implementation of a distributed lock manager for cache consistency. Other major DBMS vendors such as IBM, Microsoft and Sybase provide shared-disk implementations.

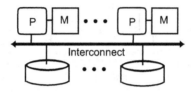

Fig. 14.4 Shared-Disk Architecture

Shared-disk has a number of advantages: lower cost, high extensibility, load balancing, availability, and easy migration from centralized systems. The cost of the interconnect is significantly less than with shared-memory since standard bus technology may be used. Given that each processor has enough main memory, interference on the shared disk can be minimized. Thus, extensibility can be better, typically up to a hundred processors. Since memory faults can be isolated from other nodes, availability can be higher. Finally, migrating from a centralized system to shared-disk is relatively straightforward since the data on disk need not be reorganized.

Shared-disk suffers from higher complexity and potential performance problems. It requires distributed database system protocols, such as distributed locking and two-phase commit. As we have discussed in previous chapters, these can be complex. Furthermore, maintaining cache consistency can incur high communication overhead among the nodes. Finally, access to the shared-disk is a potential bottleneck.

14.1.3.3 Shared-Nothing

In the shared-nothing approach (see Figure 14.5), each processor has exclusive access to its main memory and disk unit(s). Similar to shared-disk, each processor-memory-disk node is under the control of its own copy of the operating system. Then, each node can be viewed as a local site (with its own database and software) in a distributed database system. Therefore, most solutions designed for distributed databases such as database fragmentation, distributed transaction management and distributed query processing may be reused. Using a fast interconnect, it is possible to accommodate large numbers of nodes. As opposed to SMP, this architecture is often called Massively Parallel Processor (MPP).

Many research prototypes have adopted the shared-nothing architecture, e.g., BUBBA [Boral et al., 1990], EDS [Group, 1990], GAMMA [DeWitt et al., 1986], GRACE [Fushimi et al., 1986], and PRISMA [Apers et al., 1992], because it can scale. The first major parallel DBMS product was Teradata's Database Computer that could accommodate a thousand processors in its early version. Other major DBMS vendors such as IBM, Microsoft and Sybase provide shared-nothing implementations.

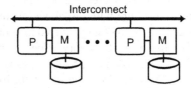

Fig. 14.5 Shared-Nothing Architecture

As demonstrated by the existing products, shared-nothing has three main virtues: lower cost, high extensibility, and high availability. The cost advantage is better than that of shared-disk that requires a special interconnect for the disks. By implementing a distributed database design that favors the smooth incremental growth of the system by the addition of new nodes, extensibility can be better (in the thousands of nodes). With careful partitioning of the data on multiple disks, almost linear speedup and linear scaleup could be achieved for simple workloads. Finally, by replicating data on multiple nodes, high availability can also be achieved.

Shared-nothing is much more complex to manage than either shared-memory or shared-disk. Higher complexity is due to the necessary implementation of distributed database functions assuming large numbers of nodes. In addition, load balancing is more difficult to achieve because it relies on the effectiveness of database partitioning for the query workloads. Unlike shared-memory and shared-disk, load balancing is decided based on data location and not the actual load of the system. Furthermore, the addition of new nodes in the system presumably requires reorganizing the database to deal with the load balancing issues.

14.1.3.4 Hybrid Architectures

Various possible combinations of the three basic architectures are possible to obtain different trade-offs between cost, performance, extensibility, availability, etc. Hybrid architectures try to obtain the advantages of different architectures: typically the efficiency and simplicity of shared-memory and the extensibility and cost of either shared disk or shared nothing. In this section, we discuss two popular hybrid architectures: NUMA and cluster.

NUMA.

With shared-memory, each processor has *uniform memory access* (UMA), with constant access time, since both the virtual memory and the physical memory are shared. One major advantage is that the programming model based on shared virtual memory is simple. With either shared-disk or shared-nothing, both virtual and shared memory are distributed, which yields scalability to large numbers of processors. The objective of NUMA is to provide a shared-memory programming model and all its benefits, in a scalable architecture with distributed memory. The term NUMA reflects the fact that an access to the (virtually) shared memory may have a different cost depending on whether the physical memory is local or remote to the processor. The most successful class of NUMA multiprocessors is Cache Coherent NUMA (CC-NUMA) [Goodman and Woest, 1988; Lenoski et al., 1992]. With CC-NUMA, the main memory is physically distributed among the nodes as with shared-nothing or shared-disk. However, any processor has access to all other processors' memories (see Figure 14.6). Each node can itself be an SMP. Similar to shared-disk, different processors can access the same data in a conflicting update mode, so global cache consistency protocols are needed. In order to make remote memory access efficient, the only viable solution is to have cache consistency done in hardware through a special consistent cache interconnect [Lenoski et al., 1992]. Because shared-memory and cache consistency are supported by hardware, remote memory access is very efficient, only several times (typically between 2 and 3 times) the cost of local access.

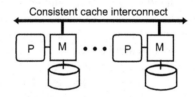

Fig. 14.6 Cache coherent NUMA (CC-NUMA)

Most SMP manufacturers are now offering NUMA systems that can scale up to a hundred processors. The strong argument for NUMA is that it does not require any rewriting of the application software. However some rewriting is still necessary in the database engine (and the operating system) to take full advantage of access locality [Bouganim et al., 1999].

Cluster.

A cluster is a set of independent server nodes interconnected to share resources and form a single system. The shared resources, called *clustered* resources, can be hardware such as disk or software such as data management services. The server nodes are made of off-the-shelf components ranging from simple PC components to more powerful SMP. Using many off-the-shelf components is essential to obtain the best cost/performance ratio while exploiting continuing progress in hardware components. In its cheapest form, the interconnect can be a local network. However, there are now fast standard interconnects for clusters (e.g., Myrinet and Infiniband) that provide high bandwidth (Gigabits/sec) with low latency for message traffic.

Compared to a distributed system, a cluster is geographically concentrated (at a single site) and made of homogeneous nodes. Its architecture can be either shared-nothing or shared-disk. Shared-nothing clusters have been widely used because they can provide the best cost/performance ratio and scale up to very large configurations (thousands of nodes). However, because each disk is directly connected to a computer via a bus, adding or replacing cluster nodes requires disk and data reorganization. Shared-disk avoids such reorganization but requires disks to be globally accessible by the cluster nodes. There are two main technologies to share disks in a cluster: network-attached storage (NAS) and storage-area network (SAN). A NAS is a dedicated device to shared disks over a network (usually TCP/IP) using a distributed file system protocol such as Network File System (NFS). NAS is well suited for low throughput applications such as data backup and archiving from PC's hard disks. However, it is relatively slow and not appropriate for database management as it quickly becomes a bottleneck with many nodes. A storage area network (SAN) provides similar functionality but with a lower level interface. For efficiency, it uses a block-based protocol thus making it easier to manage cache consistency (at the block level). In fact, disks in a SAN are attached to the network instead to the bus as happens in Directly Attached Storage (DAS), but otherwise they are handled as sharable local disks. Existing protocols for SANs extend their local disk counterparts to run over a network (e.g., i-SCSI extends SCSI, and ATA-over-Ethernet extends ATA). As a result, SAN provides high data throughput and can scale up to large numbers of nodes. Its only limitation with respect to shared-nothing is its higher cost of ownership.

A cluster architecture has important advantages. It combines the flexibility and performance of shared-memory at each node with the extensibility and availability of shared-nothing or shared-disk. Furthermore, using off-the-shelf shared-memory nodes with a standard cluster interconnect makes it a cost-effective alternative to proprietary high-end multiprocessors such as NUMA or MPP. Finally, using SAN eases disk management and data placement.

14.1.3.5 Discussion

Let us briefly compare the three basic architectures based on their potential advantages (high-performance, high-availability, and extensibility). It is fair to say that, for a small configuration (e.g., less than 20 processors), shared-memory can provide the highest performance because of better load balancing. Shared-disk and shared-nothing architectures outperform shared-memory in terms of extensibility. Some years ago, shared-nothing was the only choice for high-end systems. However, recent progress in disk connectivity technologies such as SAN make shared-disk a viable alternative with the main advantage of simplifying data administration and DBMS implementation. In particular, shared-disk is now the preferred architecture for OLTP applications because it is easier to support ACID transactions and distributed concurrency control. But for OLAP databases that are typically very large and mostly read-only, shared-nothing is the preferred architecture. Most major DBMS vendors now provide a shared-nothing implementation of their DBMS for OLAP, in addition to a shared-disk version for OLTP. The only execption is Oracle that uses shared-disk for both OLTP and OLAP.

Hybrid architectures, such as NUMA and cluster, can combine the efficiency and simplicity of shared-memory and the extensibility and cost of either shared disk or shared nothing. In particular, they can exploit continous progress in SMP and use shared-memory nodes with excellent cost/performance ratio. Both NUMA and cluster can scale up to large configurations (hundred of nodes). The main advantage of NUMA over a cluster is the simple (shared-memory) programming model that eases database administration and tuning. However, using standard PC nodes and interconnects, clusters provide a better overall cost/performance ratio, and, using shared-nothing, they can scale up to very large configurations (thousands of nodes).

14.2 Parallel Data Placement

In this section, we assume a shared-nothing architecture because it is the most general case and its implementation techniques also apply, sometimes in a simplified form, to other architectures. Data placement in a parallel database system exhibits similarities with data fragmentation in distributed databases (see Chapter 3). An obvious similarity is that fragmentation can be used to increase parallelism. In what follows, we use the terms *partitioning* and *partition* instead of horizontal fragmentation and horizontal fragment, respectively, to contrast with the alternative strategy, which consists of *clustering* a relation at a single node. The term *declustering* is sometimes used to mean partitioning [Livny et al., 1987]. Vertical fragmentation can also be used to increase parallelism and load balancing much as in distributed databases. Another similarity is that since data are much larger than programs, execution should occur, as much as possible, where the data reside. However, there are two important differences with the distributed database approach. First, there is no need to maximize local processing (at each node) since users are not associated with particular nodes. Second, load balancing is much more difficult to achieve in the presence of a large number of nodes. The main problem is to avoid resource contention, which may result in the entire system thrashing (e.g., one node ends up doing all the work while the others remain idle). Since programs are executed where the data reside, data placement is a critical performance issue.

Data placement must be done so as to maximize system performance, which can be measured by combining the total amount of work done by the system and the response time of individual queries. In Chapter 8, we have seen that maximizing response time (through intra-query parallelism) results in increased total work due to communication overhead. For the same reason, inter-query parallelism results in increased total work. On the other hand, clustering all the data necessary to a program minimizes communication and thus the total work done by the system in executing that program. In terms of data placement, we have the following trade-off: maximizing response time or inter-query parallelism leads to partitioning, whereas minimizing the total amount of work leads to clustering. As we have seen in Chapter 3, this problem is addressed in distributed databases in a rather static manner. The database administrator is in charge of periodically examining fragment access frequencies, and when necessary, moving and reorganizing fragments.

An alternative solution to data placement is *full partitioning*, whereby each relation is horizontally fragmented across *all* the nodes in the system. There are three basic strategies for data partitioning: round-robin, hash, and range partitioning (Figure 14.7).

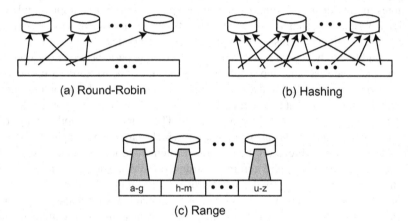

Fig. 14.7 Different Partitioning Schemes

1. *Round-robin partitioning* is the simplest strategy, it ensures uniform data distribution. With n partitions, the ith tuple in insertion order is assigned to partition (i mod n). This strategy enables the sequential access to a relation to be done in parallel. However, the direct access to individual tuples, based on a predicate, requires accessing the entire relation.

2. *Hash partitioning* applies a hash function to some attribute that yields the partition number. This strategy allows exact-match queries on the selection attribute to be processed by exactly one node and all other queries to be processed by all the nodes in parallel.

3. *Range partitioning* distributes tuples based on the value intervals (ranges) of some attribute. In addition to supporting exact-match queries (as in hashing), it is well-suited for range queries. For instance, a query with a predicate "A between A_1 and A_2" may be processed by the only node(s) containing tuples

whose A value is in range $[A_1, A_2]$. However, range partitioning can result in high variation in partition size.

Compared to clustering relations on a single (possibly very large) disk, full partitioning yields better performance [Livny et al., 1987]. Although full partitioning has obvious performance advantages, highly parallel execution might cause a serious performance overhead for complex queries involving joins. Furthermore, full partitioning is not appropriate for small relations that span a few disk blocks. These drawbacks suggest that a compromise between clustering and full partitioning (i.e., *variable partitioning*), needs to be found.

A solution is to do data placement by variable partitioning [Copeland et al., 1988]. The degree of partitioning, i.e., the number of nodes over which a relation is fragmented, is a function of the size and access frequency of the relation. This strategy is much more involved than either clustering or full partitioning because changes in data distribution may result in reorganization. For example, a relation initially placed across eight nodes may have its cardinality doubled by subsequent insertions, in which case it should be placed across 16 nodes.

In a highly parallel system with variable partitioning, periodic reorganizations for load balancing are essential and should be frequent unless the workload is fairly static and experiences only a few updates. Such reorganizations should remain transparent to compiled programs that run on the database server. In particular, programs should not be recompiled because of reorganization. Therefore, the compiled programs should remain independent of data location, which may change rapidly. Such independence can be achieved if the run-time system supports associative access to distributed data. This is different from a distributed DBMS, where associative access is achieved at compile time by the query processor using the data directory.

One solution to associative access is to have a global index mechanism replicated on each node [Khoshafian and Valduriez, 1987]. The global index indicates the placement of a relation onto a set of nodes. Conceptually, the global index is a two-level index with a major clustering on the relation name and a minor clustering on some attribute of the relation. This global index supports variable partitioning, where each relation has a different degree of partitioning. The index structure can be based on hashing or on a B-tree like organization [Bayer and McCreight, 1972]. In both cases, exact match queries can be processed efficiently with a single node access. However, with hashing, range queries are processed by accessing all the nodes that contain data from the r queried elation. Using a B-tree index (usually much larger than a hashed index) enables more efficient processing of range queries, where only the nodes containing data in the specified range are accessed.

Example 14.1. Figure 14.8 provides an example of a global index and a local index for relation EMP(ENO, ENAME, DEPT, TITLE) of the engineering database example we have been using in this book.

Suppose that we want to locate the elements in relation EMP with ENO value "E50". The first-level index on set name maps the name EMP onto the index on attribute ENO for relation EMP. Then the second-level index further maps the cluster value "E50" onto node number j. A local index within each node is also necessary

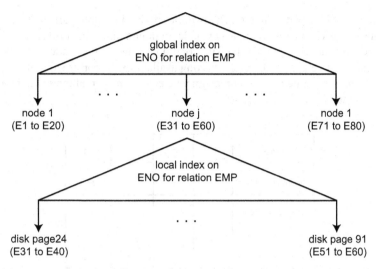

Fig. 14.8 Example of Global and Local Indexes

to map a relation onto a set of disk pages within the node. The local index has two levels, with a major clustering on relation name and a minor clustering on some attribute. The minor clustering attribute for the local index is the *same* as that for the global index. Thus *associative routing* is improved from one node to another based on (relation name, cluster value). This local index further maps the cluster value "E5" onto page number 91.   ◆

Experimental results for variable partitioning of a workload consisting of a mix of short transactions (debit-credit like) and complex ones indicate that as partitioning is increased, throughput continues to increase for short transactions. However, for complex transactions involving several large joins, further partitioning reduces throughput because of communication overhead [Copeland et al., 1988].

A serious problem in data placement is dealing with skewed data distributions that may lead to non-uniform partitioning and hurt load balancing. Range partitioning is more sensitive to skew than either round-robin or hash partitioning. A solution is to treat non-uniform partitions appropriately, e.g., by further fragmenting large partitions. The separation between logical and physical nodes is also useful since a logical node may correspond to several physical nodes.

A final complicating factor is data replication for high availability. The simple solution is to maintain two copies of the same data, a primary and a backup copy, on two separate nodes. This is the *mirrored disks* architecture promoted by many computer manufacturers. However, in case of a node failure, the load of the node with the copy may double, thereby hurting load balancing. To avoid this problem, several high-availability data replication strategies have been proposed for parallel database systems [Hsiao and DeWitt, 1991]. An interesting solution is Teradata's interleaved partitioning that further partitions the backup copy on a number of nodes. Figure 14.9 illustrates the interleaved partitioning of relation R over four nodes, where each primary copy of a partition, e.g., R_1, is futher divided in three partitions, e.g., $r_1 1$, $r_1 2$, and $r_1 3$, each at a different backup node. In failure mode, the load of the primary copy gets balanced among the backup copy nodes. But if two nodes fail, then the relation cannot be accessed thereby hurting availability. Reconstructing the primary copy from its separate backup copies may be costly. In normal mode, maintaining copy consistency may also be costly.

Node	1	2	3	4
Primary copy	R_1	R_2	R_3	R_4
Backup copy		$r_{1.1}$	$r_{1.2}$	$r_{1.3}$
	$r_{2.3}$		$r_{2.1}$	$r_{2.2}$
	$r_{3.2}$	$r_{3.3}$		$r_{3.1}$

Fig. 14.9 Example of Interleaved Partitioning

A better solution is Gamma's *chained partitioning* [Hsiao and DeWitt, 1991], which stores the primary and backup copy on two adjacent nodes (Figure 14.10). The main idea is that the probability that two adjacent nodes fail is much lower than the probability that any two nodes fail. In failure mode, the load of the failed node and the backup nodes are balanced among all remaining nodes by using both primary and backup copy nodes. In addition, maintaining copy consistency is cheaper. An open issue is how to perform data placement taking into account data replication. Similar to the fragment allocation in distributed databases, this should be considered an optimization problem.

Node	1	2	3	4
Primary copy	R_1	R_2	R_3	R_4
Backup copy	r_4	r_1	r_2	r_3

Fig. 14.10 Example of Chained Partitioning

14.3 Parallel Query Processing

The objective of parallel query processing is to transform queries into execution plans that can be efficiently executed in parallel. This is achieved by exploiting parallel data placement and the various forms of parallelism offered by high-level queries. In this section, we first introduce the various forms of query parallelism. Then we derive basic parallel algorithms for data processing. Finally, we discuss parallel query optimization.

14.3.1 Query Parallelism

Parallel query execution can exploit two forms of parallelism: inter- and intra-query. *Inter-query parallelism* enables the parallel execution of multiple queries generated by concurrent transactions, in order to increase the transactional throughput. Within a query (*intra-query parallelism*), *inter-operator* and *intra-operator parallelism* are used to decrease response time. Inter-operator parallelism is obtained by executing in parallel several operators of the query tree on several processors while with intra-operator parallelism, the same operator is executed by many processors, each one working on a subset of the data. Note that these two forms of parallelism also exist in distributed query processing.

14.3.1.1 Intra-operator Parallelism

Intra-operator parallelism is based on the decomposition of one operator in a set of independent sub-operators, called *operator instances*. This decomposition is done using static and/or dynamic partitioning of relations. Each operator instance will then process one relation partition, also called a *bucket*. The operator decomposition frequently benefits from the initial partitioning of the data (e.g., the data are partitioned on the join attribute). To illustrate intra-operator parallelism, let us consider a simple select-join query. The select operator can be directly decomposed into several select operators, each on a different partition, and no redistribution is required (Figure 14.11). Note that if the relation is partitioned on the select attribute, partitioning properties can be used to eliminate some select instances. For example, in an exact-match select, only one select instance will be executed if the relation was partitioned by hashing (or range) on the select attribute. It is more complex to decompose the join operator. In order to have independent joins, each bucket of the first relation R may be joined to the entire relation S. Such a join will be very inefficient (unless S is very small) because it will imply a broadcast of S on each participating processor. A more efficient way is to use partitioning properties. For example, if R and S are partitioned by hashing on the join attribute and if the join is an equijoin, then we can partition the join into independent joins (see Algorithm 14.3 in Section 14.3.2). This is the ideal case that cannot be always used, because it depends on the initial partitioning of R and S. In the other cases, one or two operands may be repartitioned [Valduriez and Gardarin, 1984]. Finally, we may notice that the partitioning function (hash, range, round robin) is independent of the local algorithm (e.g., nested loop, hash, sort merge) used to process the join operator (i.e., on each processor). For instance, a hash join using a hash partitioning needs two hash functions. The first one, h_1, is used to partition the two base relations on the join attribute. The second one, h_2, which can be different for each processor, is used to process the join on each processor.

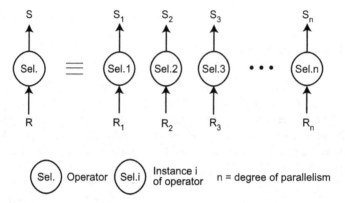

Fig. 14.11 Intra-operator Parallelism

14.3.1.2 Inter-operator Parallelism

Two forms of inter-operator parallelism can be exploited. With *pipeline parallelism*, several operators with a producer-consumer link are executed in parallel. For instance, the select operator in Figure 14.12 will be executed in parallel with the join operator. The advantage of such execution is that the intermediate result is not materialized, thus saving memory and disk accesses. In the example of Figure 14.12, only S may fit in memory. *Independent parallelism* is achieved when there is no dependency between the operators that are executed in parallel. For instance, the two select operators of Figure 14.12 can be executed in parallel. This form of parallelism is very attractive because there is no interference between the processors.

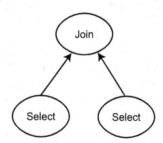

Fig. 14.12 Inter-operator Parallelism

14.3.2 Parallel Algorithms for Data Processing

Partitioned data placement is the basis for the parallel execution of database queries. Given a partitioned data placement, an important issue is the design of parallel algorithms for an efficient processing of database operators (i.e., relational algebra operators) and database queries that combine multiple operators. This issue is difficult because a good trade-off between parallelism and communication cost must be reached since increasing parallelism involves more communication among nodes. Parallel algorithms for relational algebra operators are the building blocks necessary for parallel query processing.

Parallel data processing should exploit intra-operator parallelism. We concentrate our presentation of parallel algorithms for database operators on the select and join operators, since all other binary operators (such as union) can be handled very much like join [Bratbergsengen, 1984]. The processing of the select operator in a partitioned data placement context is identical to that in a fragmented distributed database. Depending on the select predicate, the operator may be executed at a single node (in the case of an exact match predicate) or, in the case of arbitrarily complex predicates, at all the nodes over which the relation is partitioned. If the global index is organized as a B-tree-like structure (see Figure 14.8), a select operator with a range predicate may be executed only by the nodes that store relevant data.

The parallel processing of join is significantly more involved than that of select. The distributed join algorithms designed for high-speed networks (see Chapter 8) can be applied successfully in a partitioned database context. However, the availability of a global index at run time provides more opportunities for efficient parallel execution. In the following, we introduce three basic parallel join algorithms for partitioned databases: the parallel nested loop (PNL) algorithm, the parallel associative join (PAJ) algorithm, and the parallel hash join (PHJ) algorithm. We describe each using a pseudo-concurrent programming language with three main constructs: **parallel-do, send**, and **receive**. **Parallel-do** specifies that the following block of actions is executed in parallel. For example,

for i from 1 to n in parallel do action A

indicates that action A is to be executed by n nodes in parallel. **Send** and **receive** are the basic communication primitives to transfer data between nodes. **Send** enables data to be sent from one node to one or more nodes. The destination nodes are typically obtained from the global index. **Receive** gets the content of the data sent to a particular node. In what follows we consider the join of two relations R and S that are partitioned over m and n nodes, respectively. For the sake of simplicity, we assume that the m nodes are distinct from the n nodes. A node at which a fragment of R (respectively, S) resides is called an R-node (respectively, S-node).

The parallel nested loop algorithm [Bitton et al., 1983] is the simplest one and the most general. It basically composes the Cartesian product of

relations R and S in parallel. Therefore, arbitrarily complex join predicates may be supported. This algorithm has been introduced in Chapter 8 in the context of Distributed INGRES. It is more precisely described in Algorithm 14.1, where the join result is produced at the S-nodes. The algorithm proceeds in two phases.

In the first phase, each fragment of R is sent and replicated at each node containing a fragment of S (there are n such nodes). This phase is done in parallel by m nodes and is efficient if the communication network has a broadcast capability. In this case each fragment of R can be broadcast to n nodes in a single transfer, thereby incurring a total communication cost of m messages. Otherwise, $(m * n)$ messages are necessary.

In the second phase, each S-node j receives relation R entirely, and locally joins R with fragment S_j. This phase is done in parallel by n nodes. The local join can be done as in a centralized DBMS. Depending on the local join algorithm, join processing may or may not start as soon as data are received. If a nested loop join algorithm is used, join processing can be done in a pipelined fashion as soon as a tuple of R arrives. If, on the other hand, a sort-merge join algorithm is used, all the data must have been received before the join of the sorted relations begins.

To summarize, the parallel nested loop algorithm can be viewed as replacing the operator $R \bowtie S$ by $\cup_{i=1}^{n} (R \bowtie S_i)$.

Algorithm 14.1: PNL Algorithm

Input: $R_1, R_2, \ldots, R_m$: fragments of relation R;
$S_1, S_2, \ldots, S_n$: fragments of relation S;
JP: join predicate
Output: $T_1, T_2, \ldots, T_n$: result fragments
begin

    for i *from* 1 *to m in parallel* **do**   {send R entirely to each S-node}
        send R_i to each node containing a fragment of S

    for j *from* 1 *to n in parallel* **do**   {perform the join at each S-node}
        $R \leftarrow \cup_{i=1}^{m} R_i$;   {receive R_i from R-nodes; R is fully replicated at
        S-nodes}
        $T_j \leftarrow R \bowtie_{JP} S_j$

end

Example 14.2. Figure 14.13 shows the application of the parallel nested loop algorithm with $m = n = 2$.   ♦

The parallel associative join algorithm, shown in Algorithm 14.2, applies only in the case of equijoin with one of the operand relations partitioned according to the join attribute. To simplify the description of the algorithm, we assume that the equijoin predicate is on attribute A from R, and B from S. Furthermore, relation S is partitioned according to the hash function h applied to join attribute B, meaning that all the tuples of S that have the same value for $h(B)$ are placed at the same node. No knowledge of how R is partitioned is assumed.

The application of the parallel associative join algorithm will produce the join result at the nodes where S_i exists (i.e., the S-nodes).

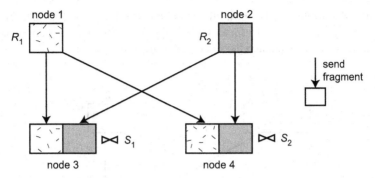

Fig. 14.13 Example of Parallel Nested Loop

Algorithm 14.2: PAJ Algorithm

Input: $R_1, R_2, \ldots, R_m$: fragments of relation R;
$S_1, S_2, \ldots, S_n$: fragments of relation S;
JP: join predicate
Output: $T_1, T_2, \ldots, T_n$: result fragments
begin
> {we assume that JP is $R.A = S.B$ and relation S is fragmented according to the function $h(B)$}
>
> **for** i *from* 1 *to* m *in parallel* **do**   {send R associatively to each S-node}
> $\quad\lfloor\ R_{ij} \leftarrow$ apply $h(A)$ to R_i $(j = 1, \ldots, n)$
>
> **for** j *from* 1 *to* n *in parallel* **do**
> $\quad\lfloor$ send R_{ij} to the node storing S_j
>
> **for** j *from* 1 *to* n *in parallel* **do**   {perform the join at each S-node}
> $\quad\lfloor$ $R_j \leftarrow \bigcup_{i=1}^{m} R_{ij}$;   {receive only the useful subset of R}
> $\quad\ \ T_j \leftarrow R_j \bowtie_{JP} S_j$

end

The algorithm proceeds in two phases. In the first phase, relation R is sent associatively to the S-nodes based on the hash function h applied to attribute A. This guarantees that a tuple of R with hash value v is sent only to the S-node that contains tuples with hash value v. The first phase is done in parallel by m nodes where R_i's exist. Thus, unlike the parallel nested loop join algorithm, the tuples of R get distributed but not replicated across the S-nodes. This is reflected in the first two Parallel-do statements of the algorithm where each node i produces m fragments of R_i and sends each fragment R_{ij} to the node storing S_j.

In the second phase, each S-node j receives in parallel from the different R-nodes the relevant subset of R (i.e., R_j) and joins it locally with the fragments S_j. Local join processing can be done as in the parallel nested loop join algorithm.

To summarize, the parallel associative join algorithm replaces the operator $R \bowtie S$ by $\bigcup_{i=1}^{n} (R_i \bowtie S_i)$.

Example 14.3. Figure 14.14 shows the application of the parallel associative join algorithm with $m = n = 2$. The squares that are hatched with the same pattern indicate fragments whose tuples match the same hash function. ◆

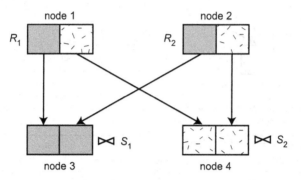

Fig. 14.14 Example of Parallel Associative Join

The parallel hash join algorithm, shown in Algorithm 14.3, can be viewed as a generalization of the parallel associative join algorithm. It also applies in the case of equijoin but does not require any particular partitioning of the operand relations. The basic idea is to partition relations R and S into the same number p of mutually exclusive sets (fragments) $R_1, R_2, \ldots, R_p$, and $S_1, S_2, \ldots, S_p$, such that

$$R \bowtie S = \bigcup_{i=1}^{p} (R_i \bowtie S_i)$$

As in the parallel associative join algorithm, the partitioning of R and S can be based on the same hash function applied to the join attribute. Each individual join $(R_i \bowtie S_i)$ is done in parallel, and the join result is produced at p nodes. These p nodes may actually be selected at run time based on the load of the system. The main difference with the parallel associative join algorithm is that partitioning of S is necessary and the result is produced at p nodes rather than at n S-nodes.

The algorithm can be divided into two main phases, a *build* phase and a *probe* phase [DeWitt and Gerber, 1985]. The build phase hashes R on the join attribute, sends it to the target p nodes that build a hash table for the incoming tuples. The probe phase sends S associatively to the target p nodes that probe the hash table for each incoming tuple. Thus, as soon as the hash tables have been built for R, the S tuples can be sent and processed in pipeline by probing the hash tables.

Example 14.4. Figure 14.15 shows the application of the parallel hash join algorithm with $m = n = 2$. We assumed that the result is produced at nodes 1 and 2. Therefore, an arrow from node 1 to node 1 or node 2 to node 2 indicates a local transfer. ◆

As is common, each parallel join algorithm applies and dominates under different conditions. Join processing is achieved with a degree of parallelism of either n or p.

Algorithm 14.3: PHJ Algorithm

Input: $R_1, R_2, \ldots, R_m$: fragments of relation R ;
$S_1, S_2, \ldots, S_n$: fragments of relation S ;
JP: join predicate $R.A = S.B$;
h: hash function that returns an element of $[1, p]$
Output: $T_1, T_2, \ldots, T_p$: result fragments
begin

    {Build phase}
    for i *from* 1 *to* m *in parallel* **do**
       | $R_{ij} \leftarrow$ apply $h(A)$ to R_i $(j = 1, \ldots, p)$;   {hash R on A)} ;
       | send R_{ij} to node j

    for j *from* 1 *to* p *in parallel* **do**
       | $R_j \leftarrow \bigcup_{i=1}^{m} R_{ij}$ {receive from R-nodes}
    {Probe phase}
    for i *from* 1 *to* n *in parallel* **do**
       | $S_{ij} \leftarrow$ apply $h(B)$ to S_i $(j = 1, \ldots, p)$;   {hash S on B)} ;
       | send S_{ij} to node j

    for j *from* 1 *to* p *in parallel* **do**   {perform the join at each of the p nodes}
       | $S_j \leftarrow \bigcup_{i=1}^{n} S_{ij}$;   {receive from S-nodes} ;
       | $T_j \leftarrow R_j \bowtie_{JP} S_j$

end

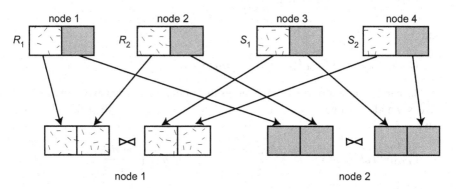

Fig. 14.15 Example of Parallel Hash Join

Since each algorithm requires moving at least one of the operand relations, a good indicator of their performance is total cost. To compare these algorithms, we now give a simple analysis of cost, defined in terms of total communication cost (C_{COM}) and processing cost (C_{PRO}). The total cost of each algorithm is therefore

$$Cost(Alg.) = C_{COM}(Alg.) + C_{PRO}(Alg.)$$

For simplicity, C_{COM} does not include control messages, which are necessary to initiate and terminate local tasks. We denote by $msg(\#tup)$ the cost of transferring a message of $\#tup$ tuples from one node to another. Processing costs (that include total I/O and CPU cost) are based on the function $C_{LOC}(m,n)$ that computes the local processing cost for joining two relations with cardinalities m and n. We assume that the local join algorithm is the same for all three parallel join algorithms. Finally, we assume that the amount of work done in parallel is uniformly distributed over all nodes allocated to the operator.

Without broadcasting capability, the parallel nested loop algorithm incurs a cost of $m*n$ messages, where a message contains a fragment of R of size $card(R)/m$ tuples. Thus we have

$$C_{COM}(PNL) = m*n*msg\left(\frac{card(R)}{m}\right)$$

Each of the S-nodes must join all of R with its S fragments. Thus we have

$$C_{PRO}(PNL) = n*C_{LOC}(card(R),card(S)/n)$$

The parallel associative join algorithm requires that each R-node partitions a fragment of R into n subsets of size $card(R)/(m*n)$ and sends them to n S-nodes. Thus we have

$$C_{COM}(PAJ) = m*n*msg\left(\frac{card(R)}{m*n}\right)$$

and

$$C_{PRO}(PAJ) = n*C_{LOC}(card(R)/n,card(S)/n)$$

The parallel hash join algorithm requires that both relations R and S be partitioned across p nodes in a way similar to the parallel associative join algorithm. Thus we have

$$C_{COM}(PHJ) = m*p*msg\left(\frac{card(R)}{m*p}\right) + n*p*msg\left(\frac{card(S)}{n*p}\right)$$

and

$$C_{PRO}(PHJ) = n*C_{LOC}(card(R)/n,card(S)/n)$$

Let us first assume that $p = n$. In this case, the join processing cost for the PAJ and PHJ algorithms is identical. However, it is higher for the PNL algorithm, because each S-node must perform the join with R entirely. From the equations above, it is clear that the PAJ algorithm incurs the least communication cost. However, the comparison of communication cost between the PNL and PHJ algorithms depends on the values of relation cardinality and degree of partitioning. If we choose $p < n$, the PHJ algorithm incurs the least communication cost but at the expense of increased join processing cost. For example, if $p = 1$, the join is processed in a purely centralized way.

In conclusion, the PAJ algorithm is most likely to dominate and should be used when applicable. Otherwise, the choice between the PNL and PHJ algorithms requires the estimation of their total cost with the optimal value for p. The choice of a parallel join algorithm can be summarized by the procedure CHOOSE_JA shown in Algorithm 14.4, where the profile of a relation indicates whether it is partitioned and on which attribute.

Algorithm 14.4: CHOOSE_JA

Input: $prof(R)$: profile of relation R ;
$prof(S)$: profile of relation S ;
JP: join predicate
Output: JA: join algorithm
begin
    if *JP is equijoin* **then**
        if *one relation is partitioned according to the join attribute* **then**
          | $JA \leftarrow PAJ$
        else
          if $Cost(PNL) < Cost(PHJ)$ **then**
            | $JA \leftarrow PNL$
          else
            ∟ $JA \leftarrow PHJ$
    else
      ∟ $JA \leftarrow PNL$
end

14.3.3 Parallel Query Optimization

Parallel query optimization exhibits similarities with distributed query processing. However, it focuses much more on taking advantage of both intra-operator parallelism (using the algorithms described above) and inter-operator parallelism. As any query optimizer (see Chapter 8), a parallel query optimizer can be seen as three components: a search space, a cost model, and a search strategy. In this section, we describe the techniques for these components.

14.3.3.1 Search Space

Execution plans are abstracted by means of operator trees, which define the order in which the operators are executed. Operator trees are enriched with *annotations*, which indicate additional execution aspects, such as the algorithm of each operator. In a parallel DBMS, an important execution aspect to be reflected by annotations is the fact that two subsequent operators can be executed in *pipeline*. In this case, the second operator can start before the first one is completed. In other words, the second operator starts *consuming* tuples as soon as the first one *produces* them. Pipelined executions do not require temporary relations to be materialized, i.e., a tree node corresponding to an operator executed in pipeline is not *stored*.

Some operators and some algorithms require that one operand is stored. For example, in the parallel hash join algorithm (see Algorithm 14.3), in the build phase, a hash table is constructed in parallel on the join attribute of the smallest relation. In the probe phase, the largest relation is sequentially scanned and the hash table is consulted for each of its tuples. Therefore, pipeline and stored annotations constrain the *scheduling* of execution plans by splitting an operator tree into non-overlapping sub-trees, corresponding to execution phases. Pipelined operators are executed in the same phase, usually called *pipeline chain* whereas a storing indication establishes the boundary between one phase and a subsequent phase.

Example 14.5. Figure 14.16 shows two execution trees, one with no pipeline and one with pipeline. Pipelining a relation is indicated by an arrow with larger head. Figure 14.16(a) shows an execution without pipeline. The temporary relation *Temp1* must be completely produced and the hash table in *Build2* must be built before *Probe2* can start consuming R_3. The same is true for *Temp2*, *Build3* and *Probe3*. Thus, the tree is executed in four consecutive phases: (1) build R_1's hash table, (2) probe it with R_2 and build *Temp1*'s hash table, (3) probe it with R_3 and build *Temp2*'s hash table, (3) probe it with R_3 and produce the result. Figure 14.16(b) shows a pipeline execution. The tree can be executed in two phases if enough memory is available to build the hash tables: (1) build the tables for R_1 R_3 and R_4, (2) execute *Probe1*, *Probe2* and *Probe3* in pipeline. ◆

The set of nodes where a relation is stored is called its *home*. The *home of an operator* is the set of nodes where it is executed and it must be the home of its operands in order for the operator to access its operand. For binary operators such as join, this might imply repartitioning one of the operands. The optimizer might even sometimes find that repartitioning both the operands is of interest. Operator trees bear execution annotations to indicate repartitioning.

Figure 14.17 shows four operator trees that represent execution plans for a three-way join. Large-head arrows indicate that the input relation is consumed in pipeline, i.e., is not locally stored. Operator trees may be *linear*, i.e., at least one operand of each join node is a base relation or *bushy*. It is convenient to represent pipelined relations as the right-hand side input of an operator. Thus, right-deep trees express full pipelining while left-deep trees express full materialization of all intermediate results. Thus, long right-deep trees are more efficient then corresponding left-deep

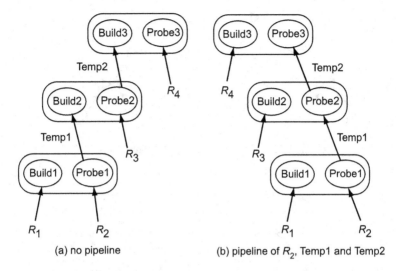

Fig. 14.16 Two hash-join trees with a different scheduling.

trees but tend to consume more memory to store left-hand side relations. In a left-deep tree such as that of Figure 14.17(a), only the last operator can consume its right input relation in pipeline provided that the left input relation can be entirely stored in main memory.

Parallel tree formats other than left or right-deep are also interesting. For example, bushy trees (Figure 14.17(d)) are the only ones to allow independent parallelism and some pipeline parallelism. Independent parallelism is useful when the relations are partitioned on disjoint homes. Suppose that the relations in Figure 14.17(d) are partitioned such that (R_1 and R_2) have the same home h_1 and (R_3 and $R4$ have the same home h_2), disjoint from h_1. Then, the two joins of the base relations could be independently executed in parallel by the set of nodes that constitutes h_1 and h_2.

When pipeline parallelism is beneficial, *zigzag trees*, which are intermediate formats between left-deep and right-deep trees, can sometimes outperform right-deep trees due to a better use of main memory [Ziane et al., 1993]. A reasonable heuristic is to favor right-deep or zigzag trees when relations are partially fragmented on disjoint homes and intermediate relations are rather large. In this case, bushy trees will usually need more phases and take longer to execute. On the contrary, when intermediate relations are small, pipelining is not very efficient because it is difficult to balance the load between the pipeline stages.

14.3.3.2 Cost Model

Recall that the optimizer cost model is responsible for estimating the cost of a given execution plan. It consists of two parts: architecture-dependent and architecture-independent [Lanzelotte et al., 1994]. The architecture-independent part is constituted

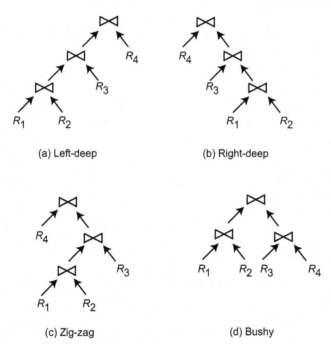

Fig. 14.17 Execution Plans as Operator Trees

of the cost functions for operator algorithms, e.g., nested loop for join and sequential access for select. If we ignore concurrency issues, only the cost functions for data repartitioning and memory consumption differ and constitute the architecture-dependent part. Indeed, repartitioning a relation's tuples in a shared-nothing system implies transfers of data across the interconnect, whereas it reduces to hashing in shared-memory systems. Memory consumption in the shared-nothing case is complicated by inter-operator parallelism. In shared-memory systems, all operators read and write data through a global memory, and it is easy to test whether there is enough space to execute them in parallel, i.e., the sum of the memory consumption of individual operators is less than the available memory. In shared-nothing, each processor has its own memory, and it becomes important to know which operators are executed in parallel on the same processor. Thus, for simplicity, it can be assumed that the set of processors (home) assigned to operators do not overlap, i.e., either the intersection of the set of processors is empty or the sets are identical.

The total time of a plan can be computed by a formula that simply adds all CPU, I/O and communication cost components as in distributed query optimization. The response time is more involved as it must take pipelining into account.

The response time of plan p, scheduled in phases (each denoted by ph), is computed as follows [Lanzelotte et al., 1994]:

$$RT(p) = \sum_{ph \in p} (max_{Op \in ph}(respTime(Op) + pipe\_delay(Op)) + store\_delay(ph))$$

where Op denotes an operator and $respTime(Op)$ is the response time of Op, $pipe\_delay(Op)$ is the waiting period of Op necessary for the producer to deliver the first result tuples (it is equal to 0 if the input relations of O are stored), $store\_delay(ph)$ is the time necessary to store the output result of phase ph (it is equal to 0 if ph is the last phase, assuming that the result are delivered as soon as they are produced).

To estimate the cost of an execution plan, the cost model uses database statistics and organization information, such as relation cardinalities and partitioning, as with distributed query optimization.

14.3.3.3 Search Strategy

The search strategy does not need to be different from either centralized or distributed query optimization. However, the search space tends to be much larger because there are more parameters that impact parallel execution plans, in particular, pipeline and store annotations. Thus, randomized search strategies (see Section 8.1.2) generally outperform deterministic strategies in parallel query optimization.

14.4 Load Balancing

Good load balancing is crucial for the performance of a parallel system. As noted in Chapter 8 the response time of a set of parallel operators is that of the longest one. Thus, minimizing the time of the longest one is important for minimizing response time. Balancing the load of different transactions and queries among different nodes is also essential to maximize throughput. Although the parallel query optimizer incorporates decisions on how to execute a parallel execution plan, load balancing can be hurt by several problems incurring at execution time. Solutions to these problems can be obtained at the intra- and inter-operator levels. In this section, we discuss these parallel execution problems and their solutions.

14.4.1 Parallel Execution Problems

The principal problems introduced by parallel query execution are initialization, interference and skew.

Initialization.

Before the execution takes place, an initialization step is necessary. This first step is generally sequential. It includes process (or thread) creation and initialization, communication initialization, etc. The duration of this step is proportional to the degree of parallelism and can actually dominate the execution time of simple queries, e.g., a select query on a single relation. Thus, the degree of parallelism should be fixed according to query complexity.

A formula can be developed to estimate the maximal speedup reachable during the execution of an operator and to deduce the optimal number of processors [Wilshut and Apers, 1992]. Let us consider the execution of an operator that processes N tuples with n processors. Let c be the average processing time of each tuple and a the initialization time per processor. In the ideal case, the response time of the operator execution is

$$ResponseTime = (a*n) + \frac{c*N}{n}$$

By derivation, we can obtain the optimal number of processors n_0 to allocate and the maximal achievable speedup (S_0).

$$n_0 = \sqrt{\frac{c*N}{a}} \qquad\qquad S_0 = \frac{n_0}{2}$$

The optimal number of processors (n_0) is independent of n and only depends on the total processing time and initialization time. Thus, maximizing the degree of parallelism for an operator, e.g., using all available processors, can hurt speed-up because of the overhead of initialization.

Interferences.

A highly parallel execution can be slowed down by *interference*. Interference occurs when several processors simultaneously access the same resource, hardware or software.

A typical example of hardware interference is the contention created on the bus of a shared-memory system. When the number of processors is increased, the number of conflicts on the bus increases, thus limiting the extensibility of shared-memory systems. A solution to these interferences is to duplicate shared resources. For instance, disk access interference can be eliminated by adding several disks and partitioning the relations.

Software interference occurs when several processors want to access shared data. To prevent incoherence, mutual exclusion variables are used to protect shared data, thus blocking all but one processor that accesses the shared data. This is similar to the locking-based concurrency control algorithms (see Chapter 11).

However, shared variables may well become the bottleneck of query execution, creating hot spots and convoy effects [Blasgen et al., 1979]. A typical example of software interference is the access of database internal structures such as indexes and buffers. For simplicity, the earlier versions of database systems were protected by a unique mutual exclusion variable. Studies have shown the overhead of such strategy: 45% of the query execution time was consumed by interference among 16 processors.

A general solution to software interference is to partition the shared resource into several independent resources, each protected by a different mutual exclusion variable. Thus, two independent resources can be accessed in parallel, which reduces the probability of interference. To further reduce interference on an independent resource (e.g., an index structure), replication can be used. Thus, access to replicated resources can also be parallelized.

Skew.

Load balancing problems can appear with intra-operator parallelism (variation in partition size), namely *data skew*, and inter-operator parallelism (variation in the complexity of operators).

The effects of skewed data distribution on a parallel execution can be classified as follows [Walton et al., 1991]. *Attribute value skew (AVS)* is skew inherent in the dataset (e.g., there are more citizens in Paris than in Waterloo) while *tuple placement skew (TPS)* is the skew introduced when the data are initially partitioned (e.g., with range partitioning). *Selectivity skew (SS)* is introduced when there is variation in the selectivity of select predicates on each node. *Redistribution skew (RS)* occurs in the redistribution step between two operators. It is similar to TPS. Finally *join product skew (JPS)* occurs because the join selectivity may vary between nodes. Figure 14.18 illustrates this classification on a query over two relations R and S that are poorly partitioned. The boxes are proportional to the size of the corresponding partitions. Such poor partitioning stems from either the data (AVS) or the partitioning function (TPS). Thus, the processing times of the two instances Scan1 and Scan2 are not equal. The case of the join operator is worse. First, the number of tuples received is different from one instance to another because of poor redistribution of the partitions of R (RS) or variable selectivity according to the partition of R processed (SS). Finally, the uneven size of S partitions (AVS/TPS) yields different processing times for tuples sent by the scan operator and the result size is different from one partition to the other due to join selectivity (JPS).

14.4.2 Intra-Operator Load Balancing

Good intra-operator load balancing depends on the degree of parallelism and the allocation of processors for the operator. For some algorithms, e.g., the parallel hash join algorithm, these parameters are not constrained by the placement of the data. Thus, the home of the operator (the set of processors where it is executed) must be carefully decided. The skew problem makes it hard for a parallel query optimizer to make this decision statically (at compile-time) as it would require a very accurate and detailed cost model. Therefore, the main solutions rely on adaptive or specialized

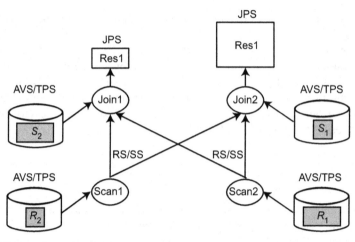

Fig. 14.18 Data skew example

techniques that can be incorporated in a hybrid query optimizer. We describe below these techniques in the context of parallel joins, which has received much attention. For simplicity, we assume that each operator is given a home as decided by the query processor (either statically or just before execution).

Adaptive techniques.

The main idea is to statically decide on an initial allocation of the processors to the operator (using a cost model) and, at execution time, adapt to skew using load reallocation. A simple approach to load reallocation is to detect the oversized partitions and partition them again onto several processors (among the processors already allocated to the operation) to increase parallelism [Kitsuregawa and Ogawa, 1990; Omiecinski, 1991]. This approach is generalized to allow for more dynamic adjustment of the degree of parallelism [Biscondi et al., 1996]. It uses specific *control operators* in the execution plan to detect whether the static estimates for intermediate result sizes will differ from the run-time values. During execution, if the difference between tje estimate and the real value is sufficiently high, the control operator performs relation redistribution in order to prevent join product skew and redistribution skew. Adaptive techniques are useful to improve intra-operator load balancing in all kinds of parallel architectures. However, most of the work has been done in the context of shared-nothing where the effects of load unbalance are more severe on performance. DBS3 [Bergsten et al., 1991; Dageville et al., 1994] has pioneered the use of an adaptive technique based on relation partitioning (as in shared-nothing) for shared-memory. By reducing processor interference, this technique yields excellent load balancing for intra-operator parallelism [Bouganim et al., 1996a,b].

Specialized techniques.

Parallel join algorithms can be specialized to deal with skew. One approach is to use multiple join algorithms, each specialized for a different degree of skew, and to determine, at execution time, which algorithm is best [DeWitt et al., 1992]. It relies on two main techniques: range partitioning and sampling. Range partitioning is used instead of hash partitioning (in the parallel hash join algorithm) to avoid redistribution skew of the building relation. Thus, processors can get partitions of equal numbers of tuples, corresponding to different ranges of join attribute values. To determine the values that delineate the range values, sampling of the building relation is used to produce a histogram of the join attribute values, i.e., the numbers of tuples for each attribute value. Sampling is also useful to determine which algorithm to use and which relation to use for building or probing. Using these techniques, the parallel hash join algorithm can be adapted to deal with skew as follows:

1. Sample the building relation to determine the partitioning ranges.

2. Redistribute the building relation to the processors using the ranges. Each processor builds a hash table containing the incoming tuples.

3. Redistribute the probing relation using the same ranges to the processors. For each tuple received, each processor probes the hash table to perform the join.

This algorithm can be further improved to deal with high skew using additional techniques and different processor allocation strategies [DeWitt et al., 1992]. A similar approach is to modify the join algorithms by inserting a scheduling step that is in charge of redistributing the load at runtime [Wolf et al., 1993].

14.4.3 Inter-Operator Load Balancing

In order to obtain good load balancing at the inter-operator level, it is necessary to choose, for each operator, how many and which processors to assign for its execution. This should be done taking into account pipeline parallelism, which requires inter-operator communication. This is harder to achieve in shared-nothing for the following reasons [Wilshut et al., 1995]. First, the degree of parallelism and the allocation of processors to operators, when decided in the parallel optimization phase, are based on a possibly inaccurate cost model. Second, the choice of the degree of parallelism is subject to errors because both processors and operators are discrete entities. Finally, the processors associated with the latest operators in a pipeline chain may remain idle a significant time. This is called the pipeline delay problem.

The main approach in shared-nothing is to determine dynamically (just before the execution) the degree of parallelism and the localization of the processors for each operator. For instance, the *Rate Match* algorithm [Mehta and DeWitt, 1995]. uses a cost model in order to match the rate at which tuples are produced and consumed. It is the basis for choosing the set of processors that will be used for query execution (based on available memory, CPU, and disk utilization). Many other algorithms are possible for the choice of the number and localization of processors, for instance, by maximizing the use of several resources, using statistics on their usage [Rahm and Marek, 1995; Garofalakis and Ioannidis, 1996].

In shared-disk and shared-memory, there is more flexibility since all processors have equal access to the disks. Since there is no need for physical relation partitioning, any processor can be allocated to any operator [Lu et al., 1991; Shekita et al., 1993]. In particular, a processor can be allocated all the operators in the same pipeline chain, thus, with no inter-operator parallelism. However, inter-operator parallelism is useful for executing independent pipeline chains. The approach proposed by Hong [1992] for shared-memory allows the parallel execution of independent pipeline chains, called tasks. The main idea is to combine I/O-bound and CPU-bound tasks to increase system resource utilization. Before execution, a task is classified as I/O-bound or CPU-bound using cost model information as follows. Let us suppose that, if executed sequentially, task t generates disk accesses at rate $IO - rate(t)$, e.g., in numbers of disk accesses per second. Let us consider a shared-memory system with n processors and a total disk bandwidth of B (numbers of disk accesses per second). Task t is defined as I/O-bound if $IO - rate(t) > B/n$ and CPU-bound otherwise. CPU-bound and I/O-bound talks can then be run in parallel at their optimal I/O-CPU balance point. This is accomplished by dynamically adjusting the degree of intra-operator parallelism of the tasks in order to reach maximum resource utilization.

14.4.4 Intra-Query Load Balancing

Intra-query load balancing must combine intra- and inter-operator parallelism. To some extent, given a parallel architecture, the techniques for either intra- or inter-operator load balancing we just presented can be combined. However, in the important context of hybrid systems such as NUMA or cluster, the problems of load balancing are exacerbated because they must be addressed at two levels, locally among the processors of each shared-memory node (SM-node) and globally among all nodes. None of the approaches for intra- and inter-operator load balancing just discussed can be easily extended to deal with this problem. Load balancing strategies for shared-nothing would experience even more severe problems worsening (e.g., complexity and inaccuracy of the cost model). On the other hand, adapting dynamic solutions developed for shared-memory systems would incur high communication overhead.

A general solution to load balancing in hybrid systems is the execution model called *Dynamic Processing (DP)* [Bouganim et al., 1996c]. The fundamental idea is that the query is decomposed into self-contained units of sequential processing, each of which can be carried out by any processor. Intuitively, a processor can migrate horizontally (intra-operator parallelism) and vertically (inter-operator parallelism) along the query operators. This minimizes the communication overhead of inter-node load balancing by maximizing intra and inter-operator load balancing within shared-memory nodes. The input to the execution model is a parallel execution plan as produced by the optimizer, i.e., an operator tree with operator scheduling and allocation of computing resources to operators. The operator scheduling constraints express a partial order among the operators of the query: $O_1 < O_2$ indicates that operator O_1 cannot start before operator O_2.

Example 14.6. Figure 14.19 shows a join tree with four relations R_1, R_2, R_3 and R_4, and the corresponding operator tree with the pipeline chains clearly identified. Assuming that parallel hash join is used, the operator scheduling constraints are between the associated build and probe operators:

Build1 < Probe1
Build2 < Probe3
Build3 < Probe2

There are also scheduling heuristics between operators of different pipeline chains that follow from the scheduling constraints :

Heuristic1: Build1 < Scan2, Build3 < Scan4, Build2 < Scan3
Heuristic2: Build2 < Scan3

Assuming three SM-nodes i, j and k with R_1 stored at node i, R_2 and R_3 at node j and R_4 at node k, we can have the following operator homes:

home (Scan1) = i
home (Build1, Probe1, Scan2, Scan3) = j
home (Scan4) = Node C
home (Build2, Build3, Probe2, Probe3) = j and k

♦

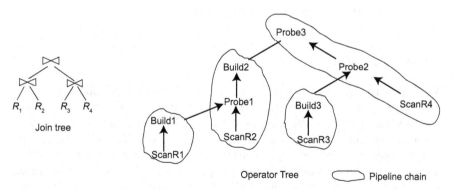

Fig. 14.19 A join tree and associated operator tree

Given such an operator tree, the problem is to produce an execution on a hybrid architecture that minimizes response time. This can be done by using a dynamic load balancing mechanism at two levels: (i) within a SM-node, load balancing is achieved via fast interprocess communication; (ii) between SM-nodes, more expensive message-passing communication is needed. Thus, the problem is to come up with an execution model so that the use of local load balancing is maximized while the use of global load balancing (through message passing) is minimized.

We call *activation* the smallest unit of sequential processing that cannot be further partitioned. The main property of the DP model is to allow any processor to process any activation of its SM-node. Thus, there is no static association between threads and operators. This yields good load balancing for both intra-operator and inter-operator parallelism within a SM-node, and thus reduces to the minimum the need for global load balancing, i.e., when there is no more work to do in a SM-node.

The DP execution model is based on a few concepts: activations, activation queues, and threads.

Activations.

An activation represents a sequential unit of work. Since any activation can be executed by any thread (by any processor), activations must be self-contained and reference all information necessary for their execution: the code to execute and the data to process. Two kinds of activations can be distinguished: trigger activations and data activations. A *trigger activation* is used to start the execution of a leaf operator, i.e., scan. It is represented by an $(Operator, Bucket)$ pair that references the scan operator and the base relation bucket to scan. A *data activation* describes a tuple produced in pipeline mode. It is represented by an $(Operator, Tuple, Bucket)$ triple that references the operator to process. For a build operator, the data activation specifies that the tuple must be inserted in the hash table of the bucket and for a probe operator, that the tuple must be probed with the bucket's hash table. Although activations are self-contained, they can only be executed on the SM-node where the associated data (hash tables or base relations) are.

Activation Queues.

Moving data activations along pipeline chains is done using *activation queues*, also called *table queues* [Pirahesh et al., 1990], associated with operators. If the producer and consumer of an activation are on the same SM-node, then the move is done via shared-memory. Otherwise, it requires message-passing. To unify the execution model, queues are used for trigger activations (inputs for scan operators) as well as tuple activations (inputs for build or probe operators). All threads have unrestricted access to all queues located on their SM-node. Managing a small number of queues (e.g., one for each operator) may yield interference. To reduce interference, one queue is associated with each thread working on an operator. Note that a higher number of queues would likely trade interference for queue management overhead. To further reduce interference without increasing the number of queues, each thread is given priority access to a distinct set of queues, called its primary queues. Thus, a thread always tries to first consume activations in its *primary queues*. During execution, operator scheduling constraints may imply that an operator is to be blocked until the end of some other operators (the blocking operators). Therefore, a queue for a blocked operator is also blocked, i.e., its activations cannot be consumed but they can still be produced if the producing operator is not blocked. When all its blocking operators terminate, the blocked queue becomes consumable, i.e., threads can consume its activations. This is illustrated in Figure 14.20 with an execution snapshot for the operator tree of Figure 14.19.

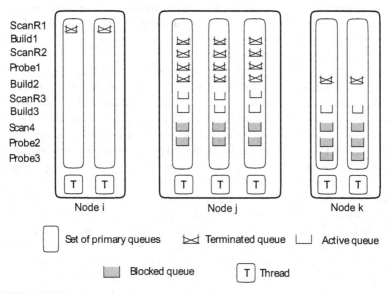

Fig. 14.20 Snapshot of an execution

Threads.

A simple strategy for obtaining good load balancing inside a SM-node is to allocate a number of threads that is much higher than the number of processors and let the operating system do thread scheduling. However, this strategy incurs high numbers of system calls due to thread scheduling, interference, and convoy problems [Pirahesh et al., 1990; Hong, 1992]. Instead of relying on the operating system for load balancing, it is possible to allocate only one thread per processor per query. This is made possible by the fact that any thread can execute any operator assigned to its SM-node. The advantage of this one-thread-per-processor allocation strategy is to significantly reduce the overhead of interference and synchronization, provided that a thread is never blocked.

Load balancing within a SM-node is obtained by allocating all activation queues in a segment of shared-memory and by allowing all threads to consume activations in any queue. To limit thread interference, a thread will consume as much as possible from its set of primary queues before considering the other queues of the SM-node. Therefore, a thread becomes idle only when there is no more activation of any operator, which means that there is no more work to do on its SM-node that is starving.

When a SM-node starves, we can apply load sharing with another SM-node by acquiring some of its workload [Shatdal and Naughton, 1993]. However, acquiring activations (through message-passing) incurs communication overhead. Furthermore, activation acquisition is not sufficient since associated data, i.e., hash tables, must also be acquired. Thus, we need a mechanism that can dynamically estimate the benefit of acquiring activations and data.

Let us call "transactioner," which acquires work, the SM-node and "provider," which gets off-loaded by providing work to the transactioner, the SM-node. The problem is to select a queue to acquire activations and decide how much work to acquire. This is a dynamic optimization problem since there is a trade-off between the potential gain of off-loading the provider and the overhead of acquiring activations and data. This trade-off can be expressed by the following conditions: (i) the transactioner must be able to store in memory the activations and corresponding data; (ii) enough work must be acquired in order to amortize the overhead of acquisition; (iii) acquiring too much work should be avoided; (iv) only probe activations can be acquired since triggered activations require disk accesses and building activations require building hash tables locally; (v) there is no gain in moving activations associated with blocked operators that could not be processed anyway. Finally, to respect the decisions of the optimizer, a SM-node cannot execute activations of an operator that it does not own, i.e., the SM-node is not in the operator home.

The amount of load balancing depends on the number of operators that are concurrently executed, which provides opportunities for finding some work to share in case of idle times. Increasing the number of concurrent operators can be done by allowing concurrent execution of several pipeline chains or by using non-blocking hash-join algorithms, which allows the concurrent execution of all the operators of the bushy tree [Wilshut et al., 1995]. On the other hand, executing more operators concurrently can increase memory consumption. Static operator scheduling as provided by the optimizer should avoid memory overflow and solve this tradeoff.

Performance evaluation of DP with a 72-processor organized as a cluster of SM-nodes has shown that DP performs as well as a dedicated model in shared-memory and can scale up very well [Bouganim et al., 1996c].

14.5 Database Clusters

Clusters of PC servers are another form of parallel computer that provides a cost-effective alternative to supercomputers or tightly-coupled multiprocessors. For instance, they have been used successfully in scientific computing, web information retrieval (e.g., Google search engine) and data warehousing. However, these applications are typically read-intensive, which makes it easier to exploit parallelism. In order to support update-intensive applications that are typical of business data processing, full parallel database capabilities, including transaction support, must be provided. This can be achieved using a parallel DBMS implemented over a cluster. In this case, all cluster nodes are homogeneous, under the full control of the parallel DBMS.

The parallel DBMS solution may be not viable for some businesses such as Application Service Providers (ASP). In the ASP model, customers' applications and databases (including data and DBMS) are hosted at the provider site and need to be available, typically through the Internet, as efficiently as if they were local to the customer site. A major requirement is that applications and databases remain autonomous, i.e., remain unchanged when moved to the provider site's cluster and under the control of the customers. Thus, preserving autonomy is critical to avoid the high costs and problems associated with application code modification. Using a parallel DBMS in this case is not appropriate as it is expensive, requires heavy migration to the parallel DBMS and hurts database autonomy.

A solution is to use a *database cluster*, which is a cluster of autonomous databases, each managed by an off-the-shelf DBMS [Röhm et al., 2000, 2001]. A major difference with a parallel DBMS implemented on a cluster is the use of a "black-box" DBMS at each node. Since the DBMS source code is not necessarily available and cannot be changed to be "cluster-aware", parallel data management capabilities must be implemented via middleware. In its simplest form, a database cluster can be viewed as a multidatabase system on a cluster. However, much research has been devoted to take full advantage of the cluster environment (with fast, reliable communication) in order to improve performance and availability by exploiting data replication. The main results of this research are new techniques for replication, load balancing, query processing, and fault-tolerance. In this section, we present these techniques after introducing a database cluster architecture.

14.5.1 Database Cluster Architecture

As discussed in Section 14.1.3.4, a cluster can have a shared-disk or shared-nothing architecture. Shared-disk requires a special interconnect that provides a shared disk space to all nodes with provision for cache consistency. Shared-nothing can better support database autonomy without the additional cost of a special interconnect and can scale up to very large configurations. This explains why most of the work in database clusters has assumed a shared-nothing architecture. However, techniques designed for shared-nothing can be applied, perhaps in a simpler way, to shared-disk.

Figure 14.21 illustrates a database cluster with a shared-nothing architecture. Parallel data management is done by independent DBMSs orchestrated by a middleware replicated at each node. To improve performance and availability, data can be replicated at different nodes using the local DBMS. Client applications (e.g., at application servers) interact with the middleware in a classical way to submit database transactions, i.e., ad-hoc queries, transactions, or calls to stored procedures. Some nodes can be specialized as access nodes to receive transactions, in which case they share a global directory service that captures information about users and databases. The general processing of a transaction to a single database is as follows. First, the transaction is authenticated and authorized using the directory. If successful, the transaction is routed to a DBMS at some, possibly different, node to be executed. We will see in Section 14.5.4 how this simple model can be extended to deal with parallel query processing, using several nodes to process a single query.

As in a parallel DBMS, the database cluster middleware has several software layers: transaction load balancer, replication manager, query processor and fault-tolerance manager. The transaction load balancer triggers transaction execution at the best node, using load information obtained from node probes. The "best" node is defined as the one with lightest transaction load. The transaction load balancer also ensures that each transaction execution obeys the ACID properties, and then signals to the DBMS to commit or abort the transaction. The replication manager manages access to replicated data and assures strong consistency in such a way that transactions that update replicated data are executed in the same serial order at each node. The query processor exploits both inter- and intra-query parallelism. With inter-query parallelism, the query processor routes each submitted query to one node and, after query completion, sends results to the client application. Intra-query parallelism is more involved. As the black-box DBMSs are not cluster-aware, they cannot interact with one another in order to process the same query. Then, it is up to the query processor to control query execution, final result composition and load balancing. Finally, the fault-tolerance manager provides on-line recovery and failover.

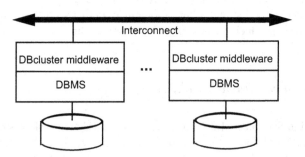

Fig. 14.21 A Database Cluster Shared-nothing Architecture

14.5.2 Replication

As in distributed DBMSs, replication can be used to improve performance and availability. In a database cluster, the fast interconnect and communication system can be exploited to support one-copy serializability while providing scalability (to achieve performance with large numbers of nodes) and autonomy (to exploit black-box DBMS). Unlike a distributed system, a cluster provides a stable environment with little evolution of the topology (e.g., as a result of added nodes or communication link failures). Thus, it is easier to support a group communication system [Chockler et al., 2001] that manages reliable communication between groups of nodes. Group communication primitives can be used with either eager or lazy replication techniques as a means to attain atomic information dissemination (i.e., instead of the expensive 2PC). The NODO protocol (see Chapter 13) is a representative of eager protocol that can be used in a database cluster. We present now another protocol for replication that is lazy and provides support for one-copy serializability and scalability.

Preventive replication protocol.

Preventive replication is a lazy protocol for lazy distributed replication in a database cluster [Pacitti et al., 2003; Coulon et al., 2005; Pacitti et al., 2006]. It also preserves DBMS autonomy. Instead of using total ordered multicast, as in eager protocols such as NODO, it uses FIFO reliable multicast that is simpler and more efficient. The principle is the following. Each incoming transaction T to the system has a chronological timestamp $ts(T) = C$, and is multicast to all other nodes where there is a copy. At each node, a time delay is introduced before starting the execution of T. This delay corresponds to the upper bound of the time needed to multicast a message (a synchronous system with bounded computation and transmission time is assumed). The critical issue is the accurate computation of the upper bounds for messages (i.e., delay). In a cluster system, the upper bound can be computed quite accurately. When the delay expires, all transactions that may have committed before C are guaranteed to be received and executed before T, following the timestamp order (i.e., total order). Hence, this approach prevents conflicts and enforces strong consistency in database clusters. Introducing delay times has also been exploited in several lazy centralized replication protocols for distributed systems [Pacitti et al., 1999; Pacitti and Simon, 2000; Pacitti et al., 2006].

We present the basic refreshment algorithm for updating copies, assuming full replication, for simplicity. The communication system is assumed to provide FIFO multicast [Pacitti et al., 2003]. Max is the upper bound of the time needed to multicast a message from a node i to any other node j. It is essential to have a value of Max that is not over estimated. The computation of Max resorts to scheduling theory [Pinedo, 2001] and takes into account several parameters such as the global reliable network itself, the characteristics of the messages to multicast and the failures to be tolerated. Each node has a local clock. For fairness, clocks are assumed to have a drift and to be ε-synchronized, i.e., the difference between any two correct clocks is not higher that

ε (known as the precision). Inconsistencies may arise whenever the serial orders of two transactions at two nodes are not equal. Therefore, they must be executed in the same serial order at any two nodes. Thus, global FIFO ordering is not sufficient to guarantee the correctness of the refreshment algorithm. Each transaction is associated with a chronological timestamp value C. The principle of the preventive refreshment algorithm is to submit a sequence of transactions in the same chronological order at each node. Before submitting a transaction at node i, it checks whether there is any older transaction en route to node i. To accomplish this, the submission time of a new transaction at node i is delayed by $Max + \varepsilon$. Thus the earliest time a transaction is submitted is $C + Max + \varepsilon$ (henceforth called the delivery_time).

Whenever a transaction T_i is to be triggered at some node i, node i multicasts T_i to all nodes $1, 2, ..., n$, including itself. Once T_i is received at some other node j (i may be equal to j), it is placed in the pending queue in FIFO order with respect to the triggering node i. Therefore, at each node i, there is a set of queues, $q_1, q_2, ..., q_n$, called pending queues, each of which corresponds to a node and is used by the refreshment algorithm to perform chronological ordering with respect to the delivery times. Figure 14.22 shows part of the components necessary to run the algorithm. The Refresher reads transactions from the top of pending queues and performs chronological ordering with respect to the delivery times. Once a transaction is ordered, then the refresher writes it to the running queue in FIFO order, one after the other. Finally the Deliverer keeps checking the top of the running queue to start transaction execution, one after the other, in the local DBMS.

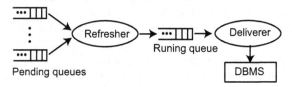

Fig. 14.22 Preventive Refreshment Architecture

Example 14.7. Let us illustrate the algorithm. Suppose we have two nodes i and j, masters of the copy R. So at node i, there are two pending queues: q_i and q_j corresponding to master nodes i and j. T_1 and T_2 are two transactions that update R at nodes i and j, respectively. Let us suppose that $Max = 10$ and $\varepsilon = 1$. So, at node i, we have the following sequence of execution:

- At time 10: T_2 arrives with a timestamp $ts(T_2) = 5$. So $q_i = [T_2(5)], q(j) = []$ and T_2 is chosen by the Refresher to be the next transaction to perform at delivery_time $16 (= 5 + 10 + 1)$, and the time is set to expire at time 16.

- At time 12: T_1 arrives from node j with a timestamp $ts(T_1) = 3$; so $q_i = [T_2(5)], q_j = [T_1(3)]$. T_1 is chosen by the Refresher to be the next transaction to perform at delivery_time $14 (= 3 + 10 + 1)$, and the time is re-set to expire at time 14.

- At time 14: the timeout expires and the Refresher writes T_1 into the running queue. Thus, $q_i = [T_2(5)], q(j) = []$. T_2 is selected to be the next transaction to perform at delivery_time $16(= 5 + 10 + 1)$.

- At time 16: the timeout expires. The Refresher writes T_2 into the running queue. So $q_i = [], q(j) = []$.

Although the transactions are received in the wrong order with respect to their timestamps (T_2 then T_1), they are written into the running queue in chronological order according to their timestamps (T_1 then T_2). Thus, the total order is enforced even if messages are not sent in total order. ◆

The original preventive replication protocol has two limitations. First, it assumes that databases are fully replicated across all cluster nodes and thus propagates each transaction to each cluster node. This makes the algorithm unsuitable for supporting very large databases. Second, it has performance limitations since transactions are performed one after the other, and must endure waiting delays before starting. Thus, refreshment is a potential bottleneck, in particular, in the case of bursty workloads where the arrival rates of transactions are high at times.

The first limitation can be addressed by providing support for partial replication [Coulon et al., 2005]. With partial replication, some of the target nodes may not be able to perform a transaction T because they do not hold all the copies necessary to perform the read set of T. However the write set of T, which corresponds to its refresh transaction, must be ordered using T's timestamp value in order to ensure consistency. So T is scheduled as usual but not submitted for execution. Instead, the involved target nodes wait for the reception of the corresponding write set. Then, at origin node i, when the commitment of T is detected, the corresponding write set is produced and node i multicasts it towards the target nodes. Upon reception of the write set at a target node j, the content of T (still waiting) is replaced with the content of the incoming write set and T can be executed.

The second limitation is addressed by a refreshment algorithm that (potentially) eliminates the delay time [Pacitti et al., 2006]. In a cluster (which is typically fast and reliable), messages are often naturally chronologically ordered [Pedone and Schiper, 1998]. Only a few messages can be received in an order that is different than the sending order. Based on this property, the algorithm can be improved by submitting a transaction for execution as soon as it is received, thus avoiding the delay before submitting transactions. To guarantee strong consistency, the commit order of the transactions is scheduled in such a way that a transaction can be committed only after $Max + \varepsilon$. When a transaction T is received out-of-order, all younger transactions must be aborted and re-submitted according to their correct timestamp order with respect to T. Therefore, all transactions are committed in their timestamp order. To improve response time in bursty workloads, transactions can be triggered concurrently. Using the isolation property of the underlying DBMS, each node can guarantee that each transaction sees a consistent database at all times. To maintain strong consistency at all nodes, transactions are committed in the same order in which they are submitted and written to the running queue. Thus, total order is always enforced. However, without access to the DBMS concurrency controller (for autonomy reasons), one cannot guarantee that two conflicting concurrent transactions obtain a lock in the same order at two different nodes. Therefore, conflicting transactions are not triggered concurrently. Detecting that two transactions are conflicting requires code analysis as for determining conflict classes in the NODO protocol. The validation of the preventive replication protocol using experiments with the TPC-C benchmark over a cluster of 64 nodes running the PostgreSQL DBMS have shown excellent scale-up and speed-up [Pacitti et al., 2006].

14.5.3 Load Balancing

In a database cluster, replication offers good load balancing opportunities. With eager or preventive replication, query load balancing is easy to achieve. Since all copies are mutually consistent, any node that stores a copy of the transactioned data, e.g., the least loaded node, can be chosen at run-time by a conventional load balancing strategy. Transaction load balancing is also easy in the case of lazy distributed replication since all master nodes need to eventually perform the transaction. However, the total cost of transaction execution at all nodes may be high. By relaxing consistency, lazy replication can better reduce transaction execution cost and thus increase performance of both queries and transactions. Thus, depending on the consistency/performance requirements, eager and lazy replication are both useful in database clusters.

Relaxed consistency models have been proposed for controlling replica divergence based on user requirements. User requirements on the desired consistency can be expressed by either the programmers, e.g., within SQL statements [Guo et al., 2004] or the database administrators, e.g., using access rules [Gançarski et al., 2002]. In most approaches, consistency reduces to freshness: update transactions are globally serialized over the different cluster nodes, so that whenever a query is sent to a given node, it reads a consistent state of the database. Global consistency is achieved by ensuring that conflicting transactions are executed at each node in the same relative order. However, the consistent state may not be the latest one, since transactions may be running at other nodes. The *data freshness* of a node reflects the difference between the database state of the node and the state it would have if all the running transactions had already been applied to that node. However, freshness is not easy to define, in particular for perfectly fresh database states. Thus, the opposite concept of *staleness*, is often used since it is always defined (e.g., equal to 0 for perfectly fresh database states). The staleness of a relation copy can then be captured by the quantity of change that has been made to the other copies, as measured by the number of tuples updated [Pape et al., 2004].

Example 14.8. Let us illustrate how lazy distributed replication can introduce staleness, and its impact on query answers. Consider the following query Q:

```
SELECT   PNO
FROM     ASG
WHERE    SUM(DUR) > 200
GROUP BY PNO
```

Let us assume that relation ASG is replicated at nodes i and j, both copies with a staleness of 0 at time t_0. Assume that, for the group of tuples where PNO="P1", we have SUM(DUR)=180. Consider that, at t_0+1, node i, respectively node j, commits a transaction that inserts a tuple for PNO="P1" with DUR=12, respectively DUR=18. Thus, the staleness of both i and j is 1. Now, at t_0+2, executing Q at either i or j would not retrieve "P1" since for the group of tuples where PNO="P1", we have SUM(DUR)=192 at i and 198 at j. The reason is that the two copies, although consistent, are stale. However, after reconciliation, e.g., at t_0+3, we have SUM(DUR)=210 at both nodes and executing Q would retrieve "P1". Thus, the accuracy of Q's answer depends on how much stale the node's copy is.   ♦

With relaxed freshness, load balancing is more complex because the cost of copy reconciliation for enforcing user-defined freshness requirements must be considered when routing transactions and queries to cluster nodes. Röhm et al. [2002b] propose a simple solution for freshness-aware query routing in database clusters. Using single-master replication techniques (i.e., transactions are always routed to the master node), queries are routed to the least loaded node that is fresh enough. If no node is fresh enough, the query simply waits.

Gançarski et al. [2007] propose a more general solution to freshness-aware routing. It works with lazy distributed replication that yields the highest opportunities for transaction load balancing. We summarize this solution. A transaction router generates for each incoming transaction or query an execution plan based on user freshness requirements obtained from the shared directory. Then, it triggers execution at the best nodes, using run-time information on nodes' load. When necessary, it also triggers refresh transactions in order to make some nodes fresher for executing subsequent transactions or queries.

The transaction router takes into account the freshness requirements of queries at the relation level to improve load balancing. It uses cost functions that takes into account not only the cluster load in terms of concurrent transactions and queries, but also the estimated time to refresh replicas to the level required by incoming queries. The transaction router uses two cost-based routing strategies, each well-suited to different application needs. The first strategy, called cost-based only (CB), makes no assumption about the workload and assesses the synchronization cost to respect the staleness accepted by queries and transactions. CB simply evaluates, for each node, the cost of refreshing the node (if necessary) to meet the freshness requirements as well as the cost of executing the transaction itself. Then it chooses the node that minimizes the cost. The second strategy favors update transactions to deal with OLTP workloads. It is a variant of CB with bounded response time (BRT) that dynamically assigns nodes for transaction processing and nodes for query processing. It uses a parameter, $Tmax$, which represents the maximum response time users can accept for update transactions. It dedicates as many cluster nodes as necessary to ensure that updates are executed in less than $Tmax$, and uses the remaining nodes for processing queries. The validation of this approach, using implementation and emulation up to 128 nodes with the TPC-C benchmark, shows that excellent scale up can be obtained [Gançarski et al., 2007].

Other approaches have been proposed for load balancing in database clusters. The approach in [Milán-Franco et al., 2004] adjusts to changes in the load submitted to the different replicas and to the type of workload. It combines load-balancing with feedback-driven adjustments of the number of concurrent transactions. The approach is shown to provide high throughput, good scalability, and low response times for changing loads and workloads with little overhead.

14.5.4 Query Processing

In a database cluster, parallel query processing can be used successfully to yield high performance. Inter-query (or inter-transaction) parallelism is naturally obtained as a result of load balancing and replication as discussed in the previous section. Such parallelism is primarily useful to increase the thoughput of transaction-oriented applications and, to some extent, to reduce the response time of transactions and queries. For OLAP applications that typically use ad-hoc queries, which access large quantities of data, intra-query parallelism is essential to further reduce response time. Intra-query parallelism consists of processing the same query on different partitions of the relations involved in the query.

There are two alternative solutions for partitioning relations in a database cluster: physical and virtual. Physical partitioning defines relation partitions, essentially as horizontal fragments, and allocates them to cluster nodes, possibly with replication. This ressembles fragmentation and allocation design in distributed databases (see Chapter 3) except that the objective is to increase intra-query parallelism, not locality of reference. Thus, depending on the query and relation sizes, the degree of partitioning should be much finer. Physical partitioning in database clusters for decision-support is addressed by Stöhr et al. [2000], using small grain partitions. Under uniform data distribution, this solution is shown to yield good intra-query parallelism and outperform inter-query parallelism. However, physical partitioning is static and thus very sensitive to data skew conditions and the variation of query patterns that may require periodic repartitioning.

Virtual partitioning avoids the problems of static physical partitioning using a dynamic approach and full replication (each relation is replicated at each node). In its simplest form, which we call *simple virtual partitioning(SVP)* , virtual partitions are dynamically produced for each query and intra-query parallelism is obtained by sending sub-queries to different virtual partitions [Akal et al., 2002]. To produce the different subqueries, the database cluster query processor adds predicates to the incoming query in order to restrict access to a subset of a relation, i.e., a virtual partition. It may also do some rewriting to decompose the query into equivalent subqueries followed by a composition query. Then, each DBMS that receives a sub-query is forced to process a different subset of data items. Finally, the partitioned result needs to be combined by an aggregate query.

Example 14.9. Let us illustrate SVP with the following query Q:

```
SELECT    PNO, AVG(DUR)
FROM      ASG
WHERE     SUM(DUR) > 200
GROUP BY PNO
```

A generic subquery on a virtual partition is obtained by adding to Q's where clause the predicate "and PNO $>=$ P1 and PNO $<$ P2". By binding [P1, P2] to n subsequent ranges of PNO values, we obtain n subqueries, each for a different node on a different virtual partition of ASG. Thus, the degree of intra-query parallelism is n. Furthermore, the "AVG(DUR)" operation must be rewriten as "SUM(DUR), COUNT(DUR)" in the subquery. Finally, to obtain the correct result for "AVG(DUR)", the composition query must perform "SUM(DUR)/SUM(COUNT(DUR))" over the n partial results.

The performance of each subquery's execution depends heavily on the access methods available on the partitioning attribute (PNO). In this example, a clustered index on PNO would be best. Thus, it is important for the query processor to know the access methods available to decide, according to the query, which partitioning attribute to use. ♦

SVP allows great flexibility for node allocation during query processing since any node can be chosen for executing a subquery. However, not all kinds of queries can benefit from SVP and be parallelized. Akal et al. [2002] propose a classification of OLAP queries such that queries of the same class have similar parallelization properties. This classification relies on how the largest relations, called fact tables (e.g., Orders and LineItems) in a typical OLAP application, are accessed. The rationale is that such the virtual partitioning of such relations yields much intra-operator parallelism. Three main classes are identified:

1. Queries without subqueries that access a fact table.

2. Queries with a subquery that are equivalent to a query of Class 1.

3. Any other queries.

Queries of Class 2 need to be rewritten into queries of Class 1 in order for SVP to apply, while queries of Class 3 cannot benefit from SVP.

SVP has some limitations. First, determining the best virtual partitioning attributes and value ranges can be difficult since assuming uniform value distribution is not realistic. Second, some DBMSs perform full table scans instead of indexed access when retrieving tuples from large intervals of values. This reduces the benefits of parallel disk access since one node could incidentally read an entire relation to access a virtual partition. This makes SVP dependent on the underlying DBMS query capabilities. Third, as a query cannot be externally modified while being executed, load balancing is difficult to achieve and depends on the initial partitioning.

Fine-grained virtual partitioning addresses these limitations by using a large number of sub-queries instead of one per DBMS [Lima et al., 2004a]. Working with smaller sub-queries avoids full table scans and makes query processing less vulnerable to DBMS idiosyncrasies. However, this approach must estimate the partition sizes, using database statistics and query processing time estimates. In practice, these estimates are hard to obtain with black-box DBMSs.

Adaptive virtual partitioning (AVP) solves this problem by dynamically tuning partition sizes, thus without requiring these estimates [Lima et al., 2004b]. AVP runs independently at each participating cluster node, avoiding inter-node communication (for partition size determination). Initially, each node receives an interval of values to work with. These intervals are determined exactly as for SVP. Then, each node performs the following steps:

1. Start with a very small partition size beginning with the first value of the received interval.

2. Execute a sub-query with this interval.

3. Increase the partition size and execute the corresponding sub-query while the increase in execution time is proportionally smaller than the increase in partition size.

4. Stop increasing. A stable size has been found.

5. If there is performance degradation, i.e., there were consecutive worse executions, decrease size and go to Step 2.

Starting with a very small partition size avoids full table scans at the very beginning of the process. This also avoids having to know the threshold after which the DBMS does not use clustered indices and starts performing full table scans. When partition size increases, query execution time is monitored allowing determination of the point after which the query processing steps that are data-size independent do not influence too much total query execution time. For example, if doubling the partition size yields an execution time that is twice the previous one, this means that such a point has been found. Thus the algorithm stops increasing the size. System performance can deteriorate due to DBMS data cache misses or overall system load increase. It may happen that the size being used is too large and has benefited from previous data cache hits. In this case, it may be better to shrink partition size. That is precisely what step 6 does. It gives a chance to go back and inspect smaller partition sizes. On the other hand, if performance deterioration was due to a casual and temporary increase of system load or data cache misses, keeping a small partition size can lead to poor performance. To avoid such a situation, the algorithm goes back to step 2 and restarts increasing sizes.

AVP and other variants of virtual partitioning have several advantages: flexibility for node allocation, high availability because of full replication, and opportunities for dynamic load balancing. But full replication can lead to high cost in disk usage. To support partial replication, hybrid solutions have been proposed to combine physical and virtual partitioning. The hybrid design by Röhm et al. [2000] uses physical partitioning for the largest and most important relations and fully replicates the small tables. Thus, intra-query parallelism can be achieved with lesser disk space requirements. The hybrid solution due to Furtado et al. [2005, 2006] combines AVP with physical partitioning. It solves the problem of disk usage while keeping the advantages of AVP, i.e., full table scan avoidance and dynamic load balancing.

14.5.5 Fault-tolerance

In the previous sections, the focus has been on how to attain consistency, performance and scalability when the system does not fail. In this section, we discuss what happens in the advent of failures. There are several issues raised by failures. The first is how to maintain consistency despite failures. Second, for outstanding transactions, there is the issue of how to perform failover. Third, when a failed replica is reintroduced (following recovery), or a fresh replica is introduced in the system, the current state of the database needs to be recovered. The main concern is how to cope with failures. To start with, failures need to be detected. In group communication based approaches, failure detection is provided by the underlying group communication (typically based on some kind of heartbeat mechanism). Membership changes are notified as events[1]. By comparing the new membership with the previous one, it becomes possible to learn which replicas have failed. Group communication also guarantees that all the connected replicas share the same membership notion. For approaches that are not based on group communication failure detection can either be delegated to the underlying communication layer (e.g., TCP/IP), or implemented as an additional component of the replication logic. However, some agreement protocol is needed to ensure that all connected replicas share the same membership notion of which replicas are operational and which ones are not. Otherwise, inconsistencies can arise.

Failures should also be detected at the client side by the client API. Clients typically connect through TCP/IP and can suspect of failed nodes via broken connections. Upon a replica failure, the client API must discover a new replica, reestablish a new connection to it, and, in the simplest case, retransmit the last outstanding transaction to the just connected replica. Since retransmissions are needed, duplicate transactions might be delivered. This requires a duplicate transaction detection and removal mechanism. In most cases, it is sufficient to have a unique client identifier, and a unique transaction identifier per client. The latter is incremented for each new submitted transaction. Thus, the cluster can track whether a client transaction has already been processed and if so, discard it.

Once a replica failure has been detected, several actions should be taken at the database cluster. These actions are part of the failover process, which must redirect the transactions from a failed node to another replica node, in a way that is as transparent as possible for the clients. Failover highly depends on whether or not the failed replica was a master. If a non-master replica fails, no action needs to be taken on the cluster side. Clients with outstanding transactions connect to a new replica node and resubmit the last transactions. However, the interesting question is which consistency definition is provided. Recall from Section 13.1 that, in a

---

[1] Group communication literature uses the term *view change* to denote the event of a membership change. Here, we will not use the term to avoid confusion with the database *view* concept.

replicated database, one-copy serializability can be violated as a result of serializing transactions at different nodes in reverse order. Due to failover, the transactions may also be processed in such a way that one-copy serializability is compromised.

In most replication approaches, failover is handled by aborting all ongoing transactions to prevent these situations. However, this way of handling failures has an impact on clients that must resubmit the aborted transaction. Since clients typically do not have transactional capabilities to undo the results of a conversational interaction, this can be very complex. The concept of *highly available transactions* makes failures totally transparent to clients so they do not observe transaction abortions due to failures [Perez-Sorrosal et al., 2006]. It has been applied to the NODO replication protocol (see Chapter 13) as follows. The write set and the transaction response for each update transaction are multicast to the other replicas before answering the client. Thus, any other replica can take over at any point in a transactional interaction.

The actions to be taken in the case of a master replica failure are more involved than for the non-master case. First, a new master should be appointed to take over the failed master. The appointment of a new master should be agreed upon all the replicas in the cluster. In group-based replication, thanks to the membership change notification, it is enough to apply a deterministic function over the new membership to assign masters (all nodes receive exactly the same list of up and connected nodes). For instance, the NODO protocol handles failures in this way. When appointing a new master, it is necessary to take care of consistency.

Another essential aspect of fault-tolerance is recovery after failure. High availability has two faces. One is how to tolerate failures and continue to provide consistent access to data despite failures. However, failures diminish the degree of redundancy in the system, thereby degrading availability and performance. Hence, it is necessary to reintroduce failed or fresh replicas in the system to maintain or improve availability and performance. The main difficulty is that replicas do have state and a failed replica may have missed updates while it was down. Thus, a recovering failed replica needs to receive the lost updates before being able to start processing new transactions. A solution is to stop transaction processing. Thus, a quiescent state is directly attained that can be transferred by any of the working replicas to the recovering one. Once the recovering replica has received all the missed updates, transaction processing can resume and all replicas can process new transactions. However, this *offline recovery* protocol hurts availability, which contradicts the initial goal of replication. Therefore, if high availability and performance should be provided, the only option is to perform *online recovery* [Kemme et al., 2001; Jiménez-Peris et al., 2002].

14.6 Conclusion

Parallel database systems strive to exploit multiprocessor architectures using software-oriented solutions for data management. Their promises are high-performance, high-availability, and extensibility with a good cost/performance ratio. Furthermore, parallelism is the only viable solution for supporting very large databases within a single system.

Parallel database systems can be supported by various parallel architectures among shared-memory, shared-disk, shared-nothing and hybrid architectures. Each architecture has advantages and limitations in terms of performance, availability, and extensibility. For small configurations (e.g., less than 20 processors), shared-memory can provide the highest performance because of better load balancing. Shared-disk and shared-nothing architectures outperform shared-memory in terms of extensibility. Some years ago, shared-nothing was the only choice for high-end systems. However, recent progress in disk connectivity technologies such as SAN make shared-disk a viable alternative with the main advantage of simplifying data administration. Hybrid architectures such as NUMA and cluster can combine the efficiency and simplicity of shared-memory and the extensibility and cost of either shared disk or shared nothing. In particular, they can use shared-memory nodes with excellent performance/cost. Both NUMA and cluster can scale up to large configurations (hundred of nodes). The main advantage of NUMA over a cluster is the simple (shared-memory) programming model that eases database design and administration. However, using standard PC nodes and interconnects, clusters provide a better overall cost/performance ratio and, using shared-nothing, can scale up to very large configurations (thousands of nodes).

Parallel data management techniques extend distributed database techniques in order to obtain high-performance, high-availability, and extensibility. Essentially, the solutions for transaction management, i.e., distributed concurrency control, reliability, atomicity, and replication can be reused. However, the critical issues for such architectures are data placement, parallel query execution, parallel data processing, parallel query optimization and load balancing. The solutions to these issues are more involved than in distributed DBMS because the number of nodes may be much higher. Furthermore, parallel data management techniques use different assumptions such as fast interconnect and homogeneous nodes that provide more opportunities for optimization.

A database cluster is an important kind of parallel database system that uses black-box DBMS at each node. Much research has been devoted to take full advantage of the cluster stable environment in order to improve performance and availability by exploiting data replication. The main results of this research are new techniques for replication, load balancing, query processing, and fault-tolerance.

14.7 Bibliographic Notes

The earlier proposal of a database server or database machine is given in [Canaday et al., 1974]. Comprehensive surveys of parallel database systems are provided in [Graefe, 1993].

Parallel database system architectures are discussed in [Bergsten et al., 1993; Stonebraker, 1986], and compared using a simple simulation model in [Bhide and Stonebraker, 1988]. NUMA architectures are described in [Lenoski et al., 1992;

Goodman and Woest, 1988]. Their influence on query execution and performance can be found in [Bouganim et al., 1999] and [Dageville et al., 1994]. Examples of parallel database prototypes or products are described in [DeWitt et al., 1986; Tandem, 1987; Pirahesh et al., 1990; Graefe, 1990; Group, 1990; Bergsten et al., 1991; Hong, 1992], and [Apers et al., 1992]. Data placement in a parallel database server is treated in [Livny et al., 1987]. Parallel optimization studies appear in [Shekita et al., 1993], [Ziane et al., 1993], and [Lanzelotte et al., 1994].

Load balancing in parallel database systems have been extensively studied. [Walton et al., 1991] presents a taxonomy of intra-operator load balancing problems, namely, data skew. [DeWitt et al., 1992], [Kitsuregawa and Ogawa, 1990], [Shatdal and Naughton, 1993], [Wolf et al., 1993], [Rahm and Marek, 1995], [Mehta and DeWitt, 1995] and [Garofalakis and Ioannidis, 1996] present several aproaches for load balancing in shared-nothing architectures. [Omiecinski, 1991] and [Bouganim et al., 1996b] focus on shared-memory architectures while [Bouganim et al., 1996c] and [Bouganim et al., 1999] consider load balancing in the hybrid architecure context.

The concept of database cluster as a cluster of autonomous DBMS is defined in [Röhm et al., 2000]. Several protocols for scalable eager replication in database clusters using group communication are proposed in [Kemme and Alonso, 2000a,b; Patiño-Martínez et al., 2000; Jiménez-Peris et al., 2002]. Their scalability has been studied analytically in [Jiménez-Peris et al., 2003]. Partial replication is studied in [Sousa et al., 2001]. The presentation of preventive replication in Section 14.5.2 is based on [Pacitti et al., 2003; Coulon et al., 2005; Pacitti et al., 2006]. Most of the content of Section 14.5.3 on freshness-aware load balancing is based on [Gançarski et al., 2002; Pape et al., 2004; Gançarski et al., 2007]. Load balancing in database clusters is also addressed in [Milán-Franco et al., 2004]. The content of Section 14.5.5 on fault tolerance in database clusters is based on [Kemme et al., 2001; Jiménez-Peris et al., 2002; Perez-Sorrosal et al., 2006]. Query processing based on virtual partitioning has been first proposed in [Akal et al., 2002]. Combining physical and virtual partitioning is proposed in [Röhm et al., 2000]. Most of the content of Section 14.5.4 is based on the work on adaptive virtual partitioning [Lima et al., 2004a,b] and hybrid partitioning [Furtado et al., 2005, 2006].

Exercises

Problem 14.1 (*). Consider the centralized server organization with several application servers accessing one database server. Also assume that each application server stores a subset of the data directory that is fully stored on the database server. Assume also that the local data directories at different application servers are not necessarily disjoint. What are the implications on data directory management and query processing for the database server if the local data directories can be updated by the application servers rather than the database server?

Problem 14.2 (**). Propose an architecture for a parallel shared-memory database server and provide a qualitative comparison with shared-nothing architecture on the basis of expected performance, software complexity (in particular, data placement and query processing), extensibility, and availability.

Problem 14.3. Specify the parallel hash join algorithm for the parallel shared-memory database server architecture proposed in Exercise 14.2.

Problem 14.4 (*). Explain the problems associated with clustering and full partitioning in a shared-nothing parallel database system. Propose several solutions and compare them.

Problem 14.5. Propose a parallel semijoin algorithm for a shared-nothing parallel database system. How should the parallel join algorithms be extended to exploit this semijoin algorithm?

Problem 14.6. Consider the following SQL query:

```
SELECT ENAME, DUR
FROM   EMP, ASG, PROJ
WHERE  EMP.ENO=ASG.ENO
AND    ASG.PNO=PROJ.PNO
AND    RESP="Manager"
AND    PNAME="Instrumentation"
```

Give four possible operator trees: right-deep, left-deep, zigzag and bushy. For each one, discuss the opportunities for parallelism.

Problem 14.7. Consider a nine way join (ten relations are to be joined) calculate the number of possible right-deep, left-deep and bushy trees, assuming that each relation can be joined with anyone else. What do you conclude about parallel optimization?

Problem 14.8 (**). Propose a data placement strategy for a cluster architecture that maximizes *intra-node* parallelism (intra-operator parallelism within a shared-memory node).

Problem 14.9 (**). How should the DP execution model presented in Section 14.4.4 be changed to deal with inter-query parallelism?

Problem 14.10 (**). Consider a multi-user centralized database system. Describe the main change to allow inter-query parallelism from the database system developer and administrator's points of view. What are the implications for the end-user in terms of interface and performance?

Problem 14.11 (**). Same question for intra-query parallelism on a shared-memory architecture or for a shared-nothing architecture.

Problem 14.12 (*). Consider the database cluster architecture in Figure 14.21. Assuming that each cluster node can accept incoming transactions, make precise the DBcluster middleware box by describing the different software layers, and their components and relationships in terms of data and control flow. What kind of information need be shared between the cluster nodes? how?

Problem 14.13 (**). Discuss the issues of fault-tolerance for the preventive replication protocol (see Section 14.5.2).

Problem 14.14 (**). Compare the preventive replication protocol with the NODO replication protocol (see Chapter 13) in the context of a cluster system in terms of: replication configurations supported, network requirements, consistency, performance, fault-tolerance.

Problem 14.15 (*). Let us consider a database cluster for an online store application. The database is concurrently accessed by short update transactions (e.g., product orders) and long read-only decision support queries (e.g., stock analysis). Discuss how database replication with freshness control can be useful in improving the response time of the decision support queries. What can be the impact on transaction load?

Problem 14.16 (**). Consider two relations R(A,B,C,D,E) and S(A,F,G,H). Assume there is a clustered index on attribute A for each relation. Assuming a database cluster with full replication, for each of the following queries, determine whether Virtual Partitioning can be used to obtain intra-query parallelism and, if so, write the corresponding subquery and the final result composition query.

(a)   SELECT   B, COUNT(C)
           FROM   R
           GROUP BY   B
(b)   SELECT   C, SUM(D), AVG(E)
           FROM   R
           WHERE   B=:v1
           GROUP BY   C
(c)   SELECT   B, SUM(E)
           FROM   R, S
           WHERE   R.A=S.A
           GROUP BY   B
           HAVING   COUNT(*) > 50
(d)   SELECT   B, MAX(D)
           FROM   R, S
           WHERE   C = (SELECT SUM(G) FROM S WHERE S.A=R.A)
           GROUP BY   B
(e)   SELECT   B, MIN(E)
           FROM   R
           WHERE   D > (SELECT MAX(H) FROM S WHERE G >= :v1)
           GROUP BY   B

Chapter 15
Distributed Object Database Management

In this chapter, we relax another one of the fundamental assumptions we made in Chapter 1 — namely that the system implements the relational data model. Relational databases have proven to be very successful in supporting business data processing applications. However, there are many applications for which relational systems may not be appropriate. Examples include XML data management, computer-aided design (CAD), office information systems (OIS), document management systems, and multimedia information systems. For these applications, different data models and languages are more suitable. Object database management systems (object DBMSs) are better candidates for the development of some of these applications due to the following characteristics [Özsu et al., 1994b]:

1. These applications require explicit storage and manipulation of more abstract data types (e.g., images, design documents) and the ability for the users to define their own application-specific types. Therefore, a rich type system supporting user-defined abstract types is required. Relational systems deal with a single object type, a relation, whose attributes come from simple and fixed data type domains (e.g., numeric, character, string, date). There is no support for explicit definition and manipulation of application-specific types.

2. The relational model structures data in a relatively simple and flat manner. Representing structural application objects in the flat relational model results in the loss of natural structure that may be important to the application. For example, in engineering design applications, it may be preferable to explicitly represent that a vehicle object contains an engine object. Similarly, in a multimedia information system, it is important to note that a hyperdocument object contains a particular video object and a captioned text object. This "containment" relationship between application objects is not easy to represent in the relational model, but is fairly straightforward in object models by means of *composite objects* and *complex objects*, which we discuss shortly.

3. Relational systems provide a declarative and (arguably) simple language for accessing the data – SQL. Since this is not a computationally complete lan-

M.T. Özsu and P. Valduriez, *Principles of Distributed Database Systems: Third Edition,*   551
DOI 10.1007/978-1-4419-8834-8_15, © Springer Science+Business Media, LLC 2011

guage, complex database applications have to be written in general programming languages with embedded query statements. This causes the well-known "impedance mismatch" [Copeland and Maier, 1984] problem, which arises because of the differences in the type systems of the relational languages and the programming languages with which they interact. The concepts and types of the query language, typically set-at-a-time, do not match with those of the programming language, which is typically record-at-a-time. This has resulted in the development of DBMS functions, such as cursor processing, that enable iterating over the sets of data objects retrieved by query languages. In an object system, complex database applications may be written entirely in a single object database programming language.

The main issue in object DBMSs is to improve application programmer productivity by overcoming the impedance mismatch problem with acceptable performance. It can be argued that the above requirements can be met by relational DBMSs, since one can possibly map them to relational data structures. In a strict sense this is true; however, from a modeling perspective, it makes little sense, since it forces programmers to map semantically richer and structurally complex objects that they deal with in the application domain to simple structures in representation.

Another alternative is to extend relational DBMSs with "object-oriented" functionality. This has been done, leading to "object-relational DBMS" [Stonebraker and Brown, 1999; Date and Darwen, 1998]. Many (not all) of the problems in object-relational DBMSs are similar to their counterparts in object DBMSs. Therefore, in this chapter we focus on the issues that need to be addressed in object DBMSs.

A careful study of the advanced applications mentioned above indicates that they are inherently distributed, and require distributed data management support. This gives rise to distributed object DBMSs, which is the subject of this chapter.

In Section 15.1, we provide the necessary background of the fundamental object concepts and issues in developing object models. In Section 15.2, we consider the distribution design of object databases. Section 15.3 is devoted to the discussion of the various distributed object DBMS architectural issues. In Section 15.4, we present the new issues that arise in the management of objects, and in Section 15.5 the focus is on object storage considerations. Sections 15.6 and 15.7 are devoted to fundamental DBMS functions: query processing and transaction management. These issues take interesting twists when considered within the context of this new technology; unfortunately, most of the existing work in these areas concentrate on non-distributed object DBMSs. We, therefore, provide a brief overview and some discussion of distribution issues.

We note that the focus in this chapter is on fundamental object DBMS technology. We do not discuss related issues such as Java Data Objects (JDO), the use of object models in XML work (in particular the DOM object interface), or Service Oriented Architectures (SOA) that use object technology. These require more elaborate treatment than we have room in this chapter.

15.1 Fundamental Object Concepts and Object Models

An object DBMS is a system that uses an "object" as the fundamental modeling and access primitive. There has been considerable discussion on the elements of an object DBMS [Atkinson et al., 1989; Stonebraker et al., 1990] as well as significant amount of work on defining an "object model". Although some have questioned whether it is feasible to define an object model, in the same sense as the relational model [Maier, 1989], a number of object models have been proposed. There are a number of features that are common to most model specifications, but the exact semantics of these features are different in each model. Some standard object model specifications have emerged as part of language standards, the most important of which is that developed by the Object Data Management Group (ODMG) that includes an object model (commonly referred to as the ODMG model), an Object Definition Language (ODL), and an Object Query Language (OQL)[1] [Cattell et al., 2000]. As an alternative, there has been a proposal for extending the relational model in SQL3 (now known as SQL:1999) [Melton, 2002]. There has also been a substantial amount of work on the foundations of object models [Abadi and Cardelli, 1996; Abiteboul and Beeri, 1995; Abiteboul and Kanellakis, 1998a]. In the remainder of this section, we will review some of the design issues and alternatives in defining an object model.

15.1.1 Object

As indicated above, all object DBMSs are built around the fundamental concept of an *object*. An object represents a real entity in the system that is being modeled. Most simply, it is represented as a tiple ⟨OID, state, interface⟩, in which OID is the object identifier, the corresponding state is some representation of the current state of the object, and the interface defines the behavior of the object. Let us consider these in turn.

Object identifier is an invariant property of an object which permanently distinguishes it logically and physically from all other objects, regardless of its state [Khoshafian and Copeland, 1986]. This enables referential object sharing [Khoshafian and Valduriez, 1987], which is the basis for supporting composite and complex (i.e., graph) structures (see Section 15.1.3). In some models, OID equality is the only comparison primitive; for other types of comparisons, the type definer is expected to specify the semantics of comparison. In other models, two objects are said to be *identical* if they have the same OID, and *equal* if they have the same state.

The *state* of an object is commonly defined as either an atomic value or a constructed value (e.g., tuple or set). Let D be the union of the system-defined domains

---

[1] The ODMG was an industrial consortium that completed its work on object data management standards in 2001 and disbanded. There are a number of systems now that conform to the developed standard listed here: http://www.barryandassociates.com/odmg-compliance.html.

(e.g., domain of integers) and of user-defined abstract data type (ADT) domains (e.g., domain of companies), let I be the domain of identifiers used to name objects, and let A be the domain of attribute names. A *value* is defined as follows:

1. An element of D is a value, called an *atomic value*.

2. $[a_1 : v_1, \ldots, a_n : v_n]$, in which a_i is an element of A and v_i is either a value or an element of I, is called a *tuple value*. $[\ ]$ is known as the tuple constructor.

3. $\{v_1, \ldots, v_n\}$, in which v_i is either a value or an element of I, is called a *set value*. $\{\ \}$ is known as the set constructor.

These models consider object identifiers as values (similar to pointers in programming languages). Set and tuple are data constructors that we consider essential for database applications. Other constructors, such as list or array, could also be added to increase the modeling power.

Example 15.1. Consider the following objects:

$(i_1, 231)$
$(i_2, S70)$
$(i_3, \{i_6, i_{11}\})$
$(i_4, \{1, 3, 5\})$
$(i_5, [LF: i_7, RF: i_8, LR: i_9, RR: i_10])$

Objects i_1 and i_2 are atomic objects and i_3 and i_4 are constructed objects. i_3 is the OID of an object whose state consists of a set. The same is true of i_4. The difference between the two is that the state of i_4 consists of a set of values, while that of i_3 consists of a set of OIDs. Thus, object i_3 references other objects. By considering object identifiers (e.g., i_6) as values in the object model, arbitrarily complex objects may be constructed. Object i_5 has a tuple valued state consisting of four attributes (or instance variables), the values of each being another object.   ◆

Contrary to values, objects support a well-defined update operation that changes the object state without changing the object identifier (i.e., the identity of the object), which is immutable. This is analogous to updates in imperative programming languages in which object identifier is implemented by main memory pointers. However, object identifier is more general than pointers in the sense that it persists following the program termination. Another implication of object identifier is that objects may be shared without incurring the problem of data redundancy. We will discuss this further in Section 15.1.3.

Example 15.2. Consider the following objects:

$(i_1, Volvo)$
$(i_2, [name: John, mycar: i_1])$
$(i_3, [name: Mary, mycar: i_1])$

John and Mary share the object denoted by i_1 (they both own Volvo cars). Changing the value of object i_1 from "Volvo" to "Chevrolet" is automatically seen by both objects i_2 and i_3. ◆

The above discussion captures the structural aspects of a model – the state is represented as a set of *instance variables* (or *attributes*) that are values. The behavioral aspects of the model are captured in *methods*, which define the allowable operations on these objects and are used to manipulate them. Methods represent the behavioral side of the model because they define the legal behaviors that the object can assume. A classical example is that of an elevator [Jones, 1979]. If the only two methods defined on an elevator object are "up" and "down", they together define the behavior of the elevator object: it can go up or down, but not sideways, for example.

The *interface* of an object consist of its properties. These properties include instance variables that reflect the state of the object, and the methods that define the operations that can be performed on this object. All instance variables and all methods of an object do not need to be visible to the "outside world". An object's *public interface* may consist of a subset of its instance variables and methods.

Some object models take a uniform and behavioral approach. In these models, the distinction between values and objects are eliminated and everything is an object, providing uniformity, and there is no differentiation between intance variables and methods – there are only methods (usually called behaviors) [Dayal, 1989; Özsu et al., 1995a].

An important distinction emerges from the foregoing discussion between relational model and object models. Relational databases deal with data values in a uniform fashion. Attribute values are the atoms with which structured values (tuples and relations) may be constructed. In a value-based data model, such as the relational model, data are identified by values. A relation is identified by a name, and a tuple is identified by a key, a combination of values. In object models, by contrast, data are identified by its OID. This distinction is crucial; modeling of relationships among data leads to data redundancy or the introduction of foreign keys in the relational model. The automatic management of foreign keys requires the support of integrity constraints (referential integrity).

Example 15.3. Consider Example 15.2. In the relational model, to achieve the same purpose, one would typically set the value of attribute `mycar` to "Volvo", which would require both tuples to be updated when it changes to "Chevrolet". To reduce redundancy, one can still represent i_1 as a tuple in another relation and reference it from i_1 and i_2 using foreign keys. Recall that this is the basis of 3NF and BCNF normalization. In this case, the elimination of redundancy requires, in the relational model, normalization of relations. However, i_1 may be a structured object whose representation in a normalized relation may be awkward. In this case, we cannot assign it as the value of the `mycar` attribute even if we accept the redundancy, since the relational model requires attribute values to be atomic. ◆

15.1.2 Types and Classes

The terms "type" and "class" have caused confusion as they have sometimes been used interchangeably and sometimes to mean different things. In this chapter, we will use the more common term "class" when we refer to the specific object model construct and the term "type" to refer to a domain of objects (e.g., integer, string).

A class is a template for a group of objects, thus defining a common type for these objects that conform to the template. In this case, we don't make a distinction between primitive system objects (i.e., values), structural (tuple or set) objects, and user-defined objects. A class describes the type of data by providing a domain of data with the same structure, as well as methods applicable to elements of that domain. The abstraction capability of classes, commonly referred to as *encapsulation*, hides the implementation details of the methods, which can be written in a general-purpose programming language. As indicated earlier, some (possibly proper) subset of its class structure and methods make up the publicly visible interface of objects that belong to that class.

Example 15.4. In this chapter, we will use an example that demonstrates the power of object models. We will model a car that consists of various parts (engine, bumpers, tires) and will store other information such as make, model, serial number, etc. In our examples, we will use an abstract syntax. ODMG ODL is considerably more powerful than the syntax we use, but it is also more complicated, which is not necessary to demonstrate the concepts. The type definition of Car can be as follows using this abstract syntax:

```
type Car
   attributes
      engine : Engine
      bumpers : {Bumper}
      tires : [lf: Tire, rf: Tire, lr: Tire, rr: Tire]
      make : Manufacturer
      model : String
      year : Date
      serial_no : String
      capacity : Integer
   methods
      age: Real
      replaceTire(place, tire)
```

The class definition specifies that Car has eight attributes and two method. Four of the attributes (model, year, serial_no, capacity) are value-based, while the others (engine, bumpers, tires and make) are object-based (i.e., have other objects as their values). Attribute bumpers is set valued (i.e., uses the set constructor), and attribute tires is tuple-valued where the left front (lf), right front (rf), left rear (lr) and right rear (rr) tires are individually identified. Incidentally, we follow a notation where the attributes are lower case and types are capitalized. Thus, engine is an attribute and Engine is a type in the system.

The method `age` takes the system date, and the `year` attribute value and calculates the date. However, since both of these arguments are internal to the object, they are not shown in the type definition, which is the interface for the user. By contrast, `replaceTire` method requires users to provide two external arguments: place (where the tire replacement was done), and tire (which tire was replaced). ◆

The interface data structure of a class may be arbitrarily complex or large. For example, `Car` class has an operation `age`, which takes today's date and the manufacturing date of a car and calculates its age; it may also have more complex operations that, for example, calculate a promotional price based on the time of year. Similarly, a long document with a complex internal structure may be defined as a class with operations specific to document manipulation.

A class has an *extent* that is the collection of all objects that conform to the class specification. In some cases, a class extent can be materialized and maintained, but this is not a requirement for all classes.

Classes provide two major advantages. First, the primitive types provided by the system can easily be extended with user-defined types. Since there are no inherent constraints on the notion of relational domain, such extensibility can be incorporated in the context of the relational model [Osborn and Heaven, 1986]. Second, class operations capture parts of the application programs that are more closely associated with data. Therefore, it becomes possible to model both data and operations at the same time. This does not imply, however, that operations are stored with the data; they may be stored in an operation library.

We end this section with the introduction of another concept, collection, that appears explicitly in some object models. A *collection* is a grouping of objects. In this sense, a class extent is a particular type of collection – one that gathers all objects that conform to a class. However, collections may be more general and may be based on user-defined predicates. The results of queries, for example, are collections of objects. Most object models do not have an explicit collection concept, but it can be argued that they are useful [Beeri, 1990], in particular since collections provide for a clear closure semantics of the query models and facilitate definition of user views. We will return to the relationship between classes and collections after we introduce subtyping and inheritance 15.1.4.

15.1.3 Composition (Aggregation)

In the examples we have discussed so far, some of the instance variables have been value-based (i.e., their domains are simple values), such as the `model` and `year` in Example 15.3, while others are object-based, such as the `make` attribute, whose domain is the set of objects that are of type `Manufacturer`. In this case, the `Car` type is a *composite type* and its instances are referred to as *composite objects*. Composition is one of the most powerful features of object models. It allows sharing of objects, commonly referred to as *referential sharing*, since objects "refer" to each other by their OIDs as values of object-based attributes.

Example 15.5. Let us revise Example 15.3 as follows. Assume that c_1 is one instance of Car type that is defined in Example 15.3. If the following is true:

(i_2, [name: John, mycar: c_1])
(i_3, [name: Mary, mycar: c_1])

then this indicates that John and Mary own the same car.   ◆

A restriction on composite objects results in *complex objects*. The difference between a composite and a complex object is that the former allows referential sharing while the latter does not[2]. For example, Car type may have an attribute whose domain is type Tire. It is not natural for two instances of type Car, c_1 and c_2, to refer to the same set of instances of Tire, since one would not expect in real life for tires to be used on multiple vehicles at the same time. This distinction between composite and complex objects is not always made, but it is an important one.

The composite object relationship between types can be represented by a *composition (aggregation) graph* (or *composition (aggregation) hierarchy* in the case of complex objects). There is an edge from instance variable I of type T_1 to type T_2 if the domain of I is T_2. The composition graphs give rise to a number of issues that we will discuss in the upcoming sections.

15.1.4 Subclassing and Inheritance

Object systems provide extensibility by allowing user-defined classes to be defined and managed by the system. This is accomplished in two ways: by the definition of classes using type constructors or by the definition of classes based on existing classes through the process of *subclassing*[3]. Subclassing is based on the *specialization* relationship among classes (or types that they define). A class A is a *specialization* of another class B if its interface is a superset of B's interface. Thus, a specialized class is more defined (or more specified) than the class from which it is specialized. A class may be a specialization of a number of classes; it is explicitly specified as a *subclass* of a subset of them. Some object models require that a class is specified as a subclass of only one class, in which case the model supports *single subclassing*; others allow *multiple subclassing*, where a class may be specified as a subclass of more than one class. Subclassing and specialization indicate an **is-a** relationship between classes (types). In the above example, A **is-a** B, resulting in *substitutability*: an instance of a subclass (A) can be substituted in place of an instance of any of its *superclasses* (B) in any expression.

---

[2] This distinction between composite and complex objects is not always made, and the term "composite object" is used to refer to both. Some authors reverse the definition between composite and complex objects. We will use the terms as defined here consistently in this chapter.

[3] This is also referred to as *subtyping*. We use the term "subclassing" to be consistent with our use of terminology. However, recall from Section 15.1.2 that each class defines a type; hence the term "subtyping" is also appropriate.

If multiple subclassing is supported, the class system forms a semilattice that can be represented as a graph. In many cases, there is a single root of the class system, which is the least specified class. However, multiple roots are possible, as in C++ [Stroustrup, 1986], resulting in a class system with multiple graphs. If only single subclasssing is allowed, as in Smalltalk [Goldberg and Robson, 1983], the class system is a tree. Some systems also define a most specified type, which forms the bottom of a full lattice. In these graphs/trees, there is an edge from type (class) A to type (class) B if A is a subtype of B.

A class structure establishes the database schema in object databases. It enables one to model the common properties and differences among types in a concise manner.

Declaring a class to be a subclass of another results in *inheritance*. If class A is a subclass of B, then its its properties consist of the properties that it natively defines as well as the properties that it inherits from B. Inheritance allows reuse. A subclass may inherit either the behavior (interface) of its superclass, or its implementation, or both. We talk of single inheritance and multiple inheritance based on the subclass relationship between the types.

Example 15.6. Consider the Car type we defined earlier. A car can be modeled as a special type of Vehicle. Thus, it is possible to define Car as a subtype of Vehicle whose other subtypes may be Motorcycle, Truck, and Bus. In this case, Vehicle would define the common properties of all of these:

```
type Vehicle as Object
   attributes
     engine : Engine
     make : Manufacturer
     model : String
     year : Date
     serial_no : String
   methods
     age: Real
```

Vehicle is defined as a subclass of Object that we assume is the root of the class lattice with common methods such as Put or Store. Vehicle is defined with five attributes and one method that takes the date of manufacture and today's date (both of which are of system-defined type Date) and returns a real value. Obviously, Vehicle is a generalization of Car that we defined in Example 15.3. Car can now be defined as follows:

```
type Car as Vehicle
   attributes
     bumpers : {Bumper}
     tires : [LF: Tire, RF: Tire, LR: Tire, RR: Tire]
     capacity : Integer
```

Even though Car is defined with only two attributes, its interface is the same as the definition given in Example 15.3. This is because Car **is-a** Vehicle, and therefore inherits the attributes and methods of Vehicle.   ◆

Subclassing and inheritance allows us to discuss an issue related to classes and collections. As we defined in Section 15.1.2, each class extent is a collection of objects that conform to that class definition. With subclassing, we need to be careful – the class extent consists of the objects that immediately conform to its definition, which is referred to as (*shallow extent*), along with the extensions of its subtypes (*deep extent*). For example in Example 15.6, the extent of `Vehicle` class consists of all vehicle objects (shallow extent) as well as all car objects (deep extent of `Vehicle`). One consequence of this is that the objects in the extent of a class are homogeneous with respect to subclassing and inheritance – they are all of the superclass's type. In contrast, a user-defined collection may be heterogeneous in that it can contain objects of types unrelated by subclassing.

15.2 Object Distribution Design

Recall from Chapter 3 that the two important aspects of distribution design are fragmentation and allocation. In this section we consider the analogue, in object databases, of the distribution design problem.

Distribution design in the object world brings new complexities due to the encapsulation of methods together with object state. An object is defined by its state and its methods. We can fragment the state, the method definitions, and the method implementation. Furthermore, the objects in a class extent can also be fragmented and placed at different sites. Each of these raise interesting problems and issues. For example, if fragmentation is performed only on state, are the methods duplicated with each fragment, or can one fragment methods as well? The location of objects with respect to their class definition becomes an issue, as does the type of attributes (instance variables). As discussed in Section 15.1.3, the domain of some attributes may be other classes. Thus, the fragmentation of classes with respect to such an attribute may have effects on other classes. Finally, if method definitions are fragmented as well, it is necessary to distinguish between simple methods and complex methods. Simple methods are those that do not invoke other methods, while complex ones can invoke methods of other classes.

Similar to the relational case, there are three fundamental types of fragmentation: horizontal, vertical, and hybrid [Karlapalem et al., 1994]. In addition to these two fundamental cases, derived horizontal partitioning , associated horizontal partitioning , and path partitioning have been defined [Karlapalem and Li, 1995]. Derived horizontal partitioning has similar semantics to its counterpart in relational databases, which we will discuss further in Section 15.2.1. Associated horizontal partitioning, is similar to derived horizontal partitioning except that there is no "predicate clause", like minterm predicate, constraining the object instances. Path partitioning is discussed in Section 15.2.3. In the remainder, for simplicity, we assume a class-based object model that does not distinguish between types and classes.

15.2.1 Horizontal Class Partitioning

There are analogies between horizontal fragmentation of object databases and their relational counterparts. It is possible to identify primary horizontal fragmentation in the object database case identically to the relational case. Derived fragmentation shows some differences, however. In object databases, derived horizontal fragmentation can occur in a number of ways:

1. Partitioning of a class arising from the fragmentation of its subclasses. This occurs when a more specialized class is fragmented, so the results of this fragmentation should be reflected in the more general case. Clearly, care must be taken here, because fragmentation according to one subclass may conflict with those imposed by other subclasses. Because of this dependence, one starts with the fragmentation of the most specialized class and moves up the class lattice, reflecting its effects on the superclasses.

2. The fragmentation of a complex attribute may affect the fragmentation of its containing class.

3. Fragmenation of a class based on a method invocation sequence from one class to another may need to be reflected in the design. This happens in the case of complex methods as defined above.

Let us start the discussion with the simplest case: namely, fragmentation of a class with simple attributes and methods. In this case, primary horizontal partitioning can be performed according to a predicate defined on attributes of the class. Partitioning is easy: given class C for partitioning, we create classes $C_1, \ldots, C_n$, each of which takes the instances of C that satisfy the particular partitioning predicate. If these predicates are mutually exclusive, then classes $C_1, \ldots, C_n$ are disjoint. In this case, it is possible to define $C_1, \ldots, C_n$ as subclasses of C and change C's definition to an *abstract class* – one that does not have an explicit extent (i.e., no instances of its own). Even though this significantly forces the definition of subtyping (since the subclasses are not any more specifically defined than their superclass), it is allowed in many systems.

A complication arises if the partitioning predicates are not mutually exclusive. There are no clean solutions in this case. Some object models allow each object to belong to multiple classes. If this is an option, it can be used to address the problem. Otherwise, "overlap classes" need to be defined to hold objects that satisfy multiple predicates.

Example 15.7. Consider the definition of the Engine class that is referred to in Example 15.6:

```
Class Engine as Object
    attributes
        no_cylinder : Integer
        capacity : Real
        horsepower: Integer
```

In this simple definition of Engine, all the attributes are simple. Consider the partitioning predicates

p_1: horsepower $\leq$ 150
p_2: horsepower $>$ 150

In this case, Engine can be partitioned into two classes, Engine1 and Engine2, which inherit all of their properties from the Engine class, which is redefined as an abstract class (i.e., a class that cannot have any objects in its shallow extent). The objects of Engine class are distributed to the Engine1 and Engine2 classes based on the value of their horsepower attribute value.   ◆

We should first note that this example points to a significant advantage of object models – we can explicitly state that methods in Engine1 class mention only those with horsepower less-than-or-equal-to 150. Consequently, we are able to make distribution explicit (with state and behavior) that is not possible in the relational model.

This primary horizontal fragmentation of classes is applied to all classes in the system that are subject to fragmentation. At the end of this process, one obtains fragmentation schemes for every class. However, these schemes do not reflect the effect of derived fragmentation as a result of subclass fragmentation (as in the example above). Thus, the next step is to produce a set of derived fragments for each superclass using the set of predicates from the previous step. This essentially requires propagation of fragmentation decisions made in the subclasses to the superclasses. The output from this step is the set of primary fragments created in step two and the set of derived fragments from step three.

The final step is to combine these two sets of fragments in a consistent way. The final horizontal fragments of a class are composed of objects accessed by both applications running only on a class and those running on its subclasses. Therefore, we must determine the most appropriate primary fragment to merge with each derived fragment of every class. Several simple heuristics could be used, such as selecting the smallest or largest primary fragment, or the primary fragment that overlaps the most with the derived fragment. But, although these heuristics are simple and intuitive, they do not capture any quantitative information about the distributed object database. Therefore, a more precise approach would be based on an affinity measure between fragments. As a result, fragments are joined with those fragments with which they have the highest affinity.

Let us now consider horizontal partitioning of a class with object-based instance variables (i.e., the domain of some of its instance variables is another class), but all the methods are simple. In this case, the composition relationship between classes comes into effect. In a sense, the composition relationship establishes the owner-member relationship that we discussed in Chapter 3: If class C_1 has an attribute A_1 whose domain is class C_2, then C_1 is the owner and C_2 is the member. Thus, the decomposition of C_2 follows the same principles as derived horizontal partitioning, discussed in Chapter 3.

So far, we have considered fragmentation with respect to attributes only, because the methods were simple. Let us now consider complex methods; these require some care. For example, consider the case where all the attributes are simple, but the methods are complex. In this case, fragmentation based on simple attributes can be performed as described above. However, for methods, it is necessary to determine, at compile time, the objects that are accessed by a method invocation. This can be accomplished with static analysis. Clearly, optimal performance will result if invoked methods are contained within the same fragment as the invoking method. Optimization requires locating objects accessed together in the same fragment because this maximizes local relevant access and minimizes local irrelevant accesses.

The most complex case is where a class has complex attributes and complex methods. In this case, the subtyping relationships, aggregation relationships and relationships of method invocations have to be considered. Thus, the fragmentation method is the union of all of the above. One goes through the classes multiple times, generating a number of fragments, and then uses an affinity-based method to merge them.

15.2.2 Vertical Class Partitioning

Vertical fragmentation is considerably more complicated. Given a class C, fragmenting it vertically into $C_1, \ldots, C_m$ produces a number of classes, each of which contains some of the attributes and some of the methods. Thus, each of the fragments is less defined than the original class. Issues that must be addressed include the subtyping relationship between the original class' superclasses and subclasses and the fragment classes, the relationship of the fragment classes among themselves, and the location of the methods. If all the methods are simple, then methods can be partitioned easily. However, when this is not the case, the location of these methods becomes a problem.

Adaptations of the affinity-based relational vertical fragmentation approaches have been developed for object databases [Ezeife and Barker, 1995, 1998]. However, the break-up of encapsulation during vertical fragmentation has created significant doubts as to the suitability of vertical fragmentation in object DBMSs.

15.2.3 Path Partitioning

The composition graph presents a representation for composite objects. For many applications, it is necessary to access the complete composite object. Path partitioning is a concept describing the clustering of all the objects forming a composite object into a partition. A path partition consists of grouping the objects of all the domain classes that correspond to all the instance variables in the subtree rooted at the composite object.

A path partition can be represented as a hierarchy of nodes forming a structural index. Each node of the index points to the objects of the domain class of the component object. The index thus contains the references to all the component objects of a composite object, eliminating the need to traverse the class composition hierarchy. The instances of the structural index are a set of OIDs pointing to all the component objects of a composite class. The structural index is an orthogonal structure to the object database schema, in that it groups all the OIDs of component objects of a composite object as a structured index class.

15.2.4 Class Partitioning Algorithms

The main issue in class partitioning is to improve the performance of user queries and applications by reducing the irrelevant data access. Thus, class partitioning is a logical database design technique that restructures the object database schema based on the application semantics. It should be noted that class partitioning is more complicated than relation fragmentation, and is also NP-complete. The algorithms for class partitioning are based on affinity-based and cost-driven approaches.

15.2.4.1 Affinity-based Approach

As covered in Section 3.3.2, affinity among attributes is used to vertically fragment relations. Similarly, affinity among instance variables and methods, and affinity among multiple methods can be used for horizontal and vertical class partitioning. Horizontal and vertical class partitioning algorithms have been developed that are based on classifying instance variables and methods as being either simple or complex [Ezeife and Barker, 1995]. A complex instance variable is an object-based instance variable and is part of the class composition hierarchy. An alternative is a method-induced partitioning scheme, which applies the method semantics and appropriately generates fragments that match the methods data requirements [Karlapalem et al., 1996a].

15.2.4.2 Cost-Driven Approach

Though the affinity-based approach provides "intuitively" appealing partitioning schemes, it has been shown that these partitioning schemes do not always result in the greatest reduction of disk accesses required to process a set of applications [Florescu et al., 1997]. Therefore, a cost model for the number of disk accesses for processing both queries [Florescu et al., 1997] and methods [Fung et al., 1996] on an object oriented database has been developed. Further, an heuristic "hill-climbing" approach that uses both the affinity approach (for initial solution) and the cost-driven approach (for further refinement) has been proposed [Fung et al., 1996]. This work also develops structural join index hierarchies for complex object retrieval, and studies its effectiveness against pointer traversal and other approaches, such as join index hierarchies, multi-index and access support relations (see next section). Each structural join index hierarchy is a materialization of path fragment, and facilitates direct access to a complex object and its component objects.

15.2.5 Allocation

The data allocation problem for object databases involves allocation of both methods and classes. The method allocation problem is tightly coupled to the class allocation problem because of encapsulation. Therefore, allocation of classes will imply allocation of methods to their corresponding home classes. But since applications on object-oriented databases invoke methods, the allocation of methods affects the performance of applications. However, allocation of methods that need to access multiple classes at different sites is a problem that has been not yet been tackled. Four alternatives can be identified [Fang et al., 1994]:

1. **Local behavior – local object.** This is the most straightforward case and is included to form the baseline case. The behavior, the object to which it is to be applied, and the arguments are all co-located. Therefore, no special mechanism is needed to handle this case.

2. **Local behavior – remote object.** This is one of the cases in which the behavior and the object to which it is applied are located at different sites. There are two ways of dealing with this case. One alternative is to move the remote object to the site where the behavior is located. The second is to ship the behavior implementation to the site where the object is located. This is possible if the receiver site can run the code.

3. **Remote behavior – local object.** This case is the reverse of case (2).

4. **Remote function – remote argument.** This case is the reverse of case (1).

Affinity-based algorithms for static allocation of class fragments that use a graph partitioning technique have also been proposed [Bhar and Barker, 1995]. However, these algorithms do not address method allocation and do not consider the interdependency between methods and classes. The issue has been addressed by means of an iterative solution for methods and class allocation [Bellatreche et al., 1998].

15.2.6 Replication

Replication adds a new dimension to the design problem. Individual objects, classes of objects, or collections of objects (or all) can be units of replication. Undoubtedly, the decision is at least partially object-model dependent. Whether or not type specifications are located at each site can also be considered a replication problem.

15.3 Architectural Issues

The preferred architectural model for object DBMSs has been client/server. We had discussed the advantages of these systems in Chapter 1. The design issues related to these systems are somewhat more complicated due to the characteristics of object models. The major concerns are listed below.

1. Since data and procedures are encapsulated as objects, the unit of communication between the clients and the server is an issue. The unit can be a page, an object, or a group of objects.

2. Closely related to the above issue is the design decision regarding the functions provided by the clients and the server. This is especially important since objects are not simply passive data, and it is necessary to consider the sites where object methods are executed.

3. In relational client/server systems, clients simply pass queries to the server, which executes them and returns the result tables to the client. This is referred to as *function shipping*. In object client/server DBMSs, this may not be the best approach, as the navigation of composite/complex object structures by the application program may dictate that data be moved to the clients (called *data shipping systems*). Since data are shared by many clients, the management of client cache buffers for data consistency becomes a serious concern. Client cache buffer management is closely related to concurrency control, since data that are cached to clients may be shared by multiple clients, and this has to be controlled. Most commercial object DBMSs use locking for concurrency control, so a fundamental architectural issue is the placement of locks, and whether or not the locks are cached to clients.

4. Since objects may be composite or complex, there may be possibilities for prefetching component objects when an object is requested. Relational client/server systems do not usually prefetch data from the server, but this may be a valid alternative in the case of object DBMSs.

These considerations require revisiting some of the issues common to all DBMSs, along with several new ones. We will consider these issues in three sections: those directly related to architectural design (architectural alternatives, buffer management, and cache consistency) are discussed in this section; those related to object management (object identifier management, pointer swizzling, and object migration) are discussed in Section 15.4; and storage management issues (object clustering and garbage collection) are considered in Section 15.5.

15.3.1 Alternative Client/Server Architectures

Two main types of client/server architectures have been proposed: object servers and page servers. The distinction is partly based on the granularity of data that are shipped between the clients and the servers, and partly on the functionality provided to the clients and servers.

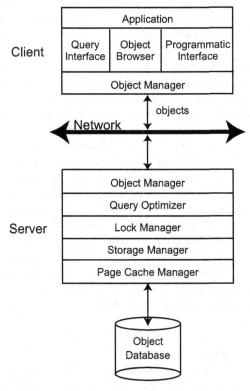

Fig. 15.1 Object Server Architecture

The first alternative is that clients request "objects" from the server, which retrieves them from the database and returns them to the requesting client. These systems are called *object servers* (Figure 15.1). In object servers, the server undertakes most of the DBMS services, with the client providing basically an execution environment for the applications, as well as some level of object management functionality (which will be discussed in Section 15.4). The object management layer is duplicated at both the client and the server in order to allow both to perform object functions. Object manager serves a number of functions. First and foremost, it provides a context for method execution. The replication of the object manager in both the server and the client enables methods to be executed at both the server and the clients. Executing methods in the client may invoke the execution of other methods, which may not have been shipped to the server with the object. The optimization of method executions of this type is an important research problem. Object manager also deals with the implementation of the object identifier (logical, physical, or virtual) and the deletion of objects (either explicit deletion or garbage collection). At the server, it also provides support for object clustering and access methods. Finally, the object managers at the client and the server implement an object cache (in addition to the page cache at the server). Objects are cached at the client to improve system performance by localizing accesses. The client goes to the server only if the needed objects are not in its cache. The optimization of user queries and the synchronization of user transactions are all performed in the server, with the client receiving the resulting objects.

It is not necessary for servers in these architectures to send individual objects to the clients; if it is appropriate, they can send groups of objects. If the clients do not send any prefetching hints then the groups correspond to contiguous space on a disk page [Gerlhof and Kemper, 1994]. Otherwise, the groups can contain objects from different pages. Depending upon the group hit rate, the clients can dynamically either increase or decrease the group size [Liskov et al., 1996]. In these systems, one complication needs to be dealt with: clients return updated objects to clients. These objects have to be installed onto their corresponding data pages (called the *home page*). If the corresponding data page does not exist in the server buffer (such as, for example, if the server has already flushed it out), the server must perform an *installation read* to reload the home page for this object.

An alternative organization is a *page server* client/server architecture, in which the unit of transfer between the servers and the clients is a physical unit of data, such as a page or segment, rather than an object (Figure 15.2). Page server architectures split the object processing services between the clients and the servers. In fact, the servers do not deal with objects anymore, acting instead as "value-added" storage managers.

Early performance studies (e.g., [DeWitt et al., 1990]) favored page server architectures over object server architectures. In fact, these results have influenced an entire generation of research into the optimal design of page server-based object DBMSs. However, these results were not conclusive, since they indicated that page server architectures are better when there is a match between a data clustering pattern[4] and the users' access pattern, and that object server architectures are better when the users' data access pattern is not the same as the clustering pattern. These earlier studies were further limited in their consideration of only single client/single server and multiple client/single server environments. There is clearly a need for further study in this area before a final judgment may be reached.

Page servers simplify the DBMS code, since both the server and the client maintain page caches, and the representation of an object is the same all the way from the disk to the user interface. Thus, updates to the objects occur only in client caches and these updates are reflected on disk when the page is flushed from the client to

---

[4] Clustering is an issue we will discuss later in this chapter. Briefly, it refers to how objects are placed on physical disk pages. Because of composite and complex objects, this becomes an important issue in object DBMSs.

the server. Another advantage of page servers is their full exploitation of the client workstation power in executing queries and applications. Thus, there is less chance of the server becoming a bottleneck. The server performs a limited set of functions and can therefore serve a large number of clients. It is possible to design these systems such that the work distribution between the server and the clients can be determined by the query optimizer. Page servers can also exploit operating systems and even hardware functionality to deal with certain problems, such as pointer swizzling (see Section 15.4.2), since the unit of operation is uniformly a page.

Intuitively, there should be significant performance advantages in having the server understand the "object" concept. One is that the server can apply locking and logging functions to the objects, enabling more clients to access the same page. Of course, this is relevant for small objects less than a page in size.

The second advantage is the potential for savings in the amount of data transmitted to the clients by filtering them at the server, which is possible if the server can perform some of the operations. Note that the concern here is not the relative cost of sending one object versus one page, but that of filtering objects at the server and sending them versus sending all of the pages on which these objects may reside. This is indeed what the relational client/server systems do where the server is responsible for optimizing and executing the entire SQL query passed to it from a client. The situation is not as straightforward in object DBMSs, however, since the applications mix query access with object-by-object navigation. It is generally not a good idea to perform navigation at the server, since doing so would involve continuous interaction between the application and the server, resulting in a remote procedure call (RPC) for each object. In fact, the earlier studies were preferential towards page servers, since they mainly considered workloads involving heavy navigation from object to object.

One possibility of dealing with the navigation problem is to ship the user's application code to the server and execute it there as well. This is what is done in Web access, where the server simply serves as storage. Code shipping may be cheaper than data shipping. This requires significant care, however, since the user code cannot be considered safe and may threaten the safety and reliability of the DBMS. Some systems (e.g., Thor [Liskov et al., 1996]) use a safe language to overcome this problem. Furthermore, since the execution is now divided between the client and the server, data reside in both the server and the client cache, and its consistency becomes a concern. Nevertheless, the "function shipping" approach involving both the clients and the servers in the execution of a query/application must be considered to deal with mixed workloads. The distribution of execution between different machines must also be accommodated as systems move towards peer-to-peer architectures.

Clearly, both of these architectures have important advantages and limitations. There are systems that can shift from one architecture to the other – for example, O_2 would operate as a page server, but if the conflicts on pages increase, would shift to object shipping. Unfortunately, the existing performance studies do not establish clear tradeoffs, even though they provide interesting insights. The issue is complicated further by the fact that some objects, such as multimedia documents, may span multiple pages.

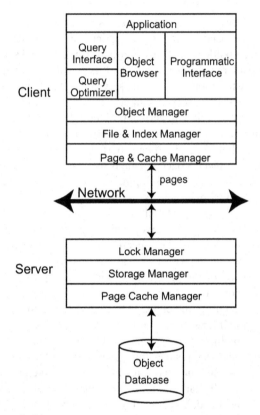

Fig. 15.2 Page Server Architecture

15.3.1.1 Client Buffer Management

The clients can manage either a page buffer, an object buffer, or a dual (i.e., page/object) buffer. If clients have a page buffer, then entire pages are read or written from the server every time a page fault occurs or a page is flushed. Object buffers can read/write individual objects and allow the applications object-by-object access.

Object buffers manage access at a finer granularity and, therefore, can achieve higher levels of concurrency. However, they may experience buffer fragmentation, as the buffer may not be able to accommodate an integral multiple of objects, thereby leaving some unused space. A page buffer does not encounter this problem, but if the data clustering on the disk does not match the application data access pattern, then the pages contain a great deal of unaccessed objects that use up valuable client buffer space. In these situations, buffer utilization of a page buffer will be lower than the buffer utilization of an object buffer.

To realize the benefits of both the page and the object buffers, dual page/object buffers have been proposed [Kemper and Kossmann, 1994; Castro et al., 1997]. In a dual buffer system, the client loads pages into the page buffer. However, when the client flushes out a page, it retains the useful objects from the page by copying the objects into the object buffer. Therefore, the client buffer manager tries to retain well-clustered pages and isolated objects from non-well-clustered pages. The client buffer managers retain the pages and objects across the transaction boundaries (commonly referred to as *inter-transaction caching*). If the clients use a log-based recovery mechanism (see Chapter 12), they also manage an in-memory log buffer in addition to the data buffer. Whereas the data buffers are managed using a variation of the least recently used (LRU) policy, the log buffer typically uses a first-in/first-out buffer replacement policy. As in centralized DBMS buffer management, it is important to decide whether all client transactions at a site should share the cache, or whether each transaction should maintain its own private cache. The recent trend is for systems to have both shared and private buffers [Carey et al., 1994; Biliris and Panagos, 1995].

15.3.1.2 Server Buffer Management

The server buffer management issues in object client/server systems are not much different than their relational counterparts, since the servers usually manage a page buffer. We nevertheless discuss the issues here briefly in the interest of completeness. The pages from the page buffer are, in turn, sent to the clients to satisfy their data requests. A grouped object-server constructs its object groups by copying the necessary objects from the relevant server buffer pages, and sends the object group to the clients. In addition to the page level buffer, the servers can also maintain a modified object buffer (MOB) [Ghemawat, 1995]. A MOB stores objects that have been updated and returned by the clients. These updated objects have to be installed onto their corresponding data pages, which may require installation reads as described earlier. Finally, the modified page has to be written back to the disk. A MOB allows the server to amortize its disk I/O costs by batching the installation read and installation write operations.

In a client/server system, since the clients typically absorb most of the data requests (i.e., the system has a high cache hit rate), the server buffer usually behaves more as a staging buffer than a cache. This, in turn, has an impact on the selection of server buffer replacement policies. Since it is desirable to minimize the duplication of data in the client and the server buffers, the *LRU with hate hints* buffer replacement policy can be used by the server [Franklin et al., 1992]. The server marks the pages that also exist in client caches as *hated*. These pages are evicted first from the server buffer, and then the standard LRU buffer replacement policy is used for the remaining pages.

15.3.2 Cache Consistency

Cache consistency is a problem in any data shipping system that moves data to the clients. So the general framework of the issues discussed here also arise in relational client/server systems. However, the problems arise in unique ways in object DBMSs.

The study of DBMS cache consistency is very tightly coupled with the study of concurrency control (see Chapter 11), since cached data can be concurrently accessed by multiple clients, and locks can also be cached along with data at the clients. The DBMS cache consistency algorithms can be classified as avoidance-based or detection-based [Franklin et al., 1997]. *Avoidance-based algorithms* prevent the access to stale cache data[5] by ensuring that clients cannot update an object if it is being read by other clients. So they ensure that stale data never exists in client caches. *Detection-based algorithms* allow access of stale cache data, because clients can update objects that are being read by other clients. However, the detection-based algorithms perform a validation step at commit time to satisfy data consistency requirements.

Avoidance-based and detection-based algorithms can, in turn, be classified as *synchronous*, *asynchronous* or *deferred*, depending upon when they inform the server that a write operation is being performed. In synchronous algorithms, the client sends a lock escalation message at the time it wants to perform a write operation, and it blocks until the server responds. In asynchronous algorithms, the client sends a lock escalation message at the time of its write operation, but does not block waiting for a server response (it optimistically continues). In deferred algorithms, the client optimistically defers informing the server about its write operation until commit time. In deferred mode, the clients group all their lock escalation requests and send them together to the server at commit time. Thus, communication overhead is lower in a deferred cache consistency scheme, in comparison to synchronous and asynchronous algorithms.

The above classification results in a design space of possible algorithms covering six alternatives. Many performance studies have been conducted to assess the strengths and weaknesses of the various algorithms. In general, for data-caching systems, inter-transaction caching of data and locks is accepted as a performance enhancing optimization [Wilkinson and Neimat, 1990; Franklin and Carey, 1994], because this reduces the number of times a client has to communicate with the server. On the other hand, for most user workloads, invalidation of remote cache copies during updates is preferred over propagation of updated values to the remote client sites [Franklin and Carey, 1994]. Hybrid algorithms that dynamically perform either invalidation or update propagation have been proposed [Franklin and Carey, 1994]. Furthermore, the ability to switch between page and object level locks is generally considered to be better than strictly dealing with page level locks [Carey et al., 1997] because it increases the level of concurrency.

---

[5] An object in a client cache is considered to be *stale* if that object has already been updated and committed into the database by a different client.

We discuss each of the alternatives in the design space and comment on their performance characteristics.

- **Avoidance-based synchronous:** Callback-Read Locking (CBL) is the most common synchronous avoidance-based cache consistency algorithm [Franklin and Carey, 1994]. In this algorithm, the clients retain read locks across transactions, but they relinquish write locks at the end of the transaction. The clients send lock requests to the server and they block until the server responds. If the client requests a write lock on a page that is cached at other clients, the server issues callback messages requesting that the remote clients relinquish their read locks on the page. Callback-Read ensures a low abort rate and generally outperforms deferred avoidance-based, synchronous detection-based, and asynchronous detection-based algorithms.

- **Avoidance-based asynchronous:** Asynchronous avoidance-based cache consistency algorithms (AACC) [Özsu et al., 1998] do not have the message blocking overhead present in synchronous algorithms. Clients send lock escalation messages to the server and continue application processing. Normally, optimistic approaches such as this face high abort rates, which is reduced in avoidance-based algorithms by immediate server actions to invalidate stale cache objects at remote clients as soon as the system becomes aware of the update. Thus, asynchronous algorithms experience lower deadlock abort rates than deferred avoidance-based algorithms, which are discussed next.

- **Avoidance-based deferred:** Optimistic Two-Phase Locking (O2PL) family of cache consistency are deferred avoidance-based algorithms [Franklin and Carey, 1994]. In these algorithms, the clients batch their lock escalation requests and send them to the server at commit time. The server blocks the updating client if other clients are reading the updated objects. As the data contention level increases, O2PL algorithms are susceptible to higher deadlock abort rates than CBL algorithms.

- **Detection-based synchronous:** Caching Two-Phase Locking (C2PL) is a synchronous detection-based cache consistency algorithm [Carey et al., 1991]. In this algorithm, clients contact the server whenever they access a page in their cache to ensure that the page is not stale or being written to by other clients. C2PL's performance is generally worse than CBL and O2PL algorithms, since it does not cache read locks across transactions.

- **Detection-based asynchronous:** No-Wait Locking (NWL) with Notification is an asynchronous detection-based algorithm [Wang and Rowe, 1991]. In this algorithm, the clients send lock escalation requests to the server, but optimistically assume that their requests will be successful. After a client transaction commits, the server propagates the updated pages to all the other clients that have also cached the affected pages. It has been shown that CBL outperforms the NWL algorithm.

- **Detection-based deferred:** Adaptive Optimistic Concurrency Control (AOCC) is a deferred detection-based algorithm. It has been shown that AOCC can outperform callback locking algorithms even while encountering a higher abort rate if the client transaction state (data and logs) completely fits into the client cache, and all application processing is strictly performed at the clients (purely data-shipping architecture) [Adya et al., 1995]. Since AOCC uses deferred messages, its messaging overhead is less than CBL. Furthermore, in a purely data-shipping client/server environment, the impact of an aborting client on the performance of other clients is quite minimal. These factors contribute to AOCC's superior performance.

15.4 Object Management

Object management includes tasks such as object identifier management, pointer swizzling, object migration, deletion of objects, method execution, and some storage management tasks at the server. In this section we will discuss some of these problems; those related to storage management are discussed in the next section.

15.4.1 Object Identifier Management

As indicated in Section 15.1, object identifiers (OIDs) are system-generated and used to uniquely identify every object (transient or persistent, system-created or user-created) in the system. Implementing the identity of persistent objects generally differs from implementing transient objects, since only the former must provide global uniqueness. In particular, transient object identity can be implemented more efficiently.

The implementation of persistent object identifier has two common solutions, based on either physical or logical identifiers, with their respective advantages and shortcomings. The physical identifier (POID) approach equates the OID with the physical address of the corresponding object. The address can be a disk page address and an offset from the base address in the page. The advantage is that the object can be obtained directly from the OID. The drawback is that all parent objects and indexes must be updated whenever an object is moved to a different page.

The logical identifier (LOID) approach consists of allocating a system-wide unique OID (i.e., a surrogate) per object. LOIDs can be generated either by using a system-wide unique counter (called pure LOID) or by concatenating a server identifier with a counter at each server (called pseudo-LOID). Since OIDs are invariant, there is no overhead due to object movement. This is achieved by an OID table associating each OID with the physical object address at the expense of one table look-up per object access. To avoid the overhead of OIDs for small objects that are not referentially shared, both approaches can consider the object value as their identifier. Object-oriented database systems tend to prefer the logical identifier approach, which better supports dynamic environments.

Implementing transient object identifier involves the techniques used in programming languages. As for persistent object identifier, identifiers can be physical or logical. The physical identifier can be the real or virtual address of the object, depending on whether virtual memory is provided. The physical identifier approach is the most efficient, but requires that objects do not move. The logical identifier approach, promoted by object-oriented programming, treats objects uniformly through an indirection table local to the program execution. This table associates a logical identifier, called an *object oriented pointer* (OOP) in Smalltalk, to the physical identifier of the object. Object movement is provided at the expense of one table look-up per object access.

The dilemma for an object manager is a trade-off between generality and efficiency. For example, supporting object-sharing explicitly requires the implementation of object identifiers for all objects within the object manager and maintaining the sharing relationship. However, object identifiers for small objects can make the OID table quite large. If object sharing is not supported at the object manager level, but left to the higher levels of system (e.g., the compiler of the database language), more efficiency may be gained. Object identifier management is closely related to object storage techniques, which we will discuss in Section 15.5.

In distributed object DBMSs, it is more appropriate to use LOIDs, since operations such as reclustering, migration, replication and fragmentation occur frequently. The use of LOIDs raises the following distribution related issues:

- **LOID Generation:** LOIDs must be unique within the scope of the entire distributed domain. It is relatively easy to ensure uniqueness if the LOIDs are generated at a central site. However, a centralized LOID generation scheme is not desirable because of the network latency overhead and the load on the LOID generation site. In multi-server environments, each server site generates LOIDs for the objects stored at that site. The uniqueness of the LOID is ensured by incorporating the server identifier as part of the LOID. Therefore, the LOID consists of both a server identifier part and a sequence number. The sequence number is the logical representation of the disk location of the object and is unique within a particular server. Sequence numbers are usually not re-used to prevent anomalies: an object o_i is deleted, and its sequence number is subsequently assigned to a newly created object o_j, but existing references to o_i now point to the new object o_j, which is not intended.

- **LOID Mapping Location and Data Structures:** The location of the LOID-to-POID mapping information is important. If pure LOIDs are used, and if a client can be directly connected to multiple servers simultaneously, then the LOID-to-POID mapping information must be present at the client. If pseudo-LOIDs are used, the mapping information needs to be present only at the server. The presence of the mapping information at the client is not desirable, because this solution is not scalable (i.e.,the mapping information has to be updated at all the clients that might access the object).

  The LOID-to-POID mapping information is usually stored in hash tables or in B+ trees. There are advantages and disadvantages to both [Eickler et al.,

1995]. Hash tables provide fast access, but are not scalable as the database size increases. B$^+$-trees are scalable, but have logarithmic access time, and require complex concurrency control and recovery strategies. B$^+$-trees also support range queries, facilitating easy access to a collection of objects.

15.4.2 Pointer Swizzling

In object systems, one can navigate from one object to another using *path expressions* that involve attributes with object-based values. For example, if object c is of type Car, then c.engine.manufacturer.name is a path expression[6]. These are basically pointers. Usually on disk, object identifiers are used to represent these pointers. However, in memory, it is desirable to use in-memory pointers for navigating from one object to another. The process of converting a disk version of the pointer to an in-memory version of a pointer is known as "pointer-swizzling". Hardware-based and software-based schemes are two types of pointer-swizzling mechanisms [White and DeWitt, 1992]. In hardware-based schemes, the operating system's page-fault mechanism is used; when a page is brought into memory, all the pointers in it are swizzled, and they point to reserved virtual memory frames. The data pages corresponding to these reserved virtual frames are only loaded into memory when an access is made to these pages. The page access, in turn, generates an operating system page-fault, which must be trapped and processed. In software-based schemes, an object table is used for pointer-swizzling purposes so that a pointer is swizzled to point to a location in the object table – that is LOIDs are used. There are eager and lazy variations to the software-based schemes, depending upon when exactly the pointer is swizzled. Therefore, every object access has a level of indirection associated with it. The advantage of the hardware-based scheme is that it leads to better performance when repeatedly traversing a particular object hierarchy, due to the absence of a level of indirection for each object access. However, in bad clustering situations where only a few objects per page are accessed, the high overhead of the page-fault handling mechanism makes hardware-based schemes unattractive. Hardware-based schemes also do not prevent client applications from accessing deleted objects on a page. Moreover, in badly clustered situations, hardware-based schemes can exhaust the virtual memory address space, because page frames are aggressively reserved regardless of whether the objects in the page are actually accessed. Finally, since the hardware-based scheme is implicitly page-oriented, it is difficult to provide object-level concurrency control, buffer management, data transfer and recovery features. In many cases, it is desirable to manipulate data at the object level rather than the page level.

---

[6] We assume that Engine class is defined with at least one attribute, manufacturer, whose domain is the extent of class Manufacturer. Manufacturer class has an attribute called name.

15.4.3 Object Migration

One aspect of distributed systems is that objects move, from time to time, between sites. This raises a number of issues. First is the unit of migration. It is possible to move the object's state without moving its methods. The application of methods to an object requires the invocation of remote procedures. This issue was discussed above under object distribution. Even if individual objects are units of migration [Dollimore et al., 1994], their relocation may move them away from their type specifications and one has to decide whether types are duplicated at every site where instances reside or the types are accessed remotely when behaviors or methods are applied to objects. Three alternatives can be considered for the migration of classes (types):

1. the source code is moved and recompiled at the destination,

2. the compiled version of a class is migrated just like any other object, or

3. the source code of the class definition is moved, but not its compiled operations, for which a lazy migration strategy is used.

Another issue is that the movements of the objects must be tracked so that they can be found in their new locations. A common way of tracking objects is to leave *surrogates* [Hwang, 1987; Liskov et al., 1994], or *proxy objects* [Dickman, 1994]. These are place-holder objects left at the previous site of the object, pointing to its new location. Accesses to the proxy objects are directed transparently by the system to the objects themselves at the new sites. The migration of objects can be accomplished based on their current state [Dollimore et al., 1994]. Objects can be in one of four states:

1. Ready: Ready objects are not currently invoked, or have not received a message, but are ready to be invoked to receive a message.

2. Active: Active objects are currently involved in an activity in response to an invocation or a message.

3. Waiting: Waiting objects have invoked (or have sent a message to) another object and are waiting for a response.

4. Suspended: Suspended objects are temporarily unavailable for invocation.

Objects in active or waiting state are not allowed to migrate, since the activity they are currently involved in would be broken. The migration involves two steps:

1. shipping the object from the source to the destination, and

2. creating a proxy at the source, replacing the original object.

Two related issues must also be addressed here. One relates to the maintenance of the system directory. As objects move, the system directory must be updated to reflect the new location. This may be done lazily, whenever a surrogate or proxy object redirects an invocation, rather than eagerly, at the time of the movement. The second issue is that, in a highly dynamic environment where objects move frequently, the surrogate or proxy chains may become quite long. It is useful for the system to transparently compact these chains from time to time. However, the result of compaction must be reflected in the directory, and it may not be possible to accomplish that lazily.

Another important migration issue arises with respect to the movement of composite objects. The shipping of a composite object may involve shipping other objects referenced by the composite object. An alternative method of dealing with this is a method called *object assembly* that we will consider under query processing in Section 15.6.3.

15.5 Distributed Object Storage

Among the many issues related to object storage, two are particularly relevant in a distributed system: object clustering and distributed garbage collection. Composite and complex objects provide opportunities, as we mentioned earlier, for clustering data on disk such that the I/O cost of retrieving them is reduced. Garbage collection is a problem that arises in object databases due to reference-based sharing. Indeed, in many object DBMSs, the only way to delete an object is to delete all references to it. Thus, object deletion and subsequent storage reclamation are critical and require special care.

15.5.0.1 Object Clustering

An object model is essentially conceptual, and should provide high physical data independence to increase programmer productivity. The mapping of this conceptual model to a physical storage is a classical database problem. As indicated in Section 15.1, in the case of object DBMSs, two kinds of relationships exist between types: subtyping and composition. By providing a good approximation of object access, these relationships are essential to guide the physical clustering of persistent objects. Object clustering refers to the grouping of objects in physical containers (i.e., disk extents) according to common properties, such as the same value of an attribute or sub-objects of the same object. Thus, fast access to clustered objects can be obtained.

Object clustering is difficult for two reasons. First, it is not orthogonal to object identifier implementation (i.e, LOID vs. POID). LOIDs incur more overhead (an indirection table), but enable vertical partitioning of classes. POIDs yield more efficient direct object access, but require each object to contain all inherited attributes. Second, the clustering of complex objects along the composition relationship is more involved because of object sharing (objects with multiple parents). In this case, the use of POIDs may incur high update overhead as component objects are deleted or change ownership.

Given a class graph, there are three basic storage models for object clustering [Valduriez et al., 1986]:

1. The *decomposition storage model* (DSM) partitions each object class into binary relations (OID, attribute) and therefore relies on logical OID. The advantage of DSM is simplicity.

2. The *normalized storage model* (NSM) stores each class as a separate relation. It can be used with logical or physical OID. However, only logical OID allows the vertical partitioning of objects along the inheritance relationship [Kim et al., 1987].

3. The *direct storage model* (DSM) enables multi-class clustering of complex objects based on the composition relationship. This model generalizes the techniques of hierarchical and network databases, and works best with physical OID [Benzaken and Delobel, 1990]. It can capture object access locality and is therefore potentially superior when access patterns are well-known. The major difficulty, however, is to clustering an object whose parent has been deleted.

In a distributed system, both DSM and NSM are straightforward using horizontal partitioning. Goblin [Kersten et al., 1994] implements DSM as a basis for a distributed object DBMS with large main memory. DSM provides flexibility, and its performance disadvantage is compensated by the use of large main memory and caching. Eos [Gruber and Amsaleg, 1994] implements the direct storage model in a distributed single-level store architecture, where each object has a physical, system-wide OID. The Eos grouping mechanism is based on the concept of most relevant composition links and solves the problem of multiparent shared objects. When an object moves to a different node, it gets a new OID. To avoid the indirection of forwarders, references to the object are subsequently changed as part of the garbage collection process without any overhead. The grouping mechanism is dynamic to achieve load balancing and cope with the evolutions of the object graph.

15.5.0.2 Distributed Garbage Collection

An advantage of object-based systems is that objects can refer to other objects using object identifier. As programs modify objects and remove references, a persistent object may become unreachable from the persistent roots of the system when there is no more reference to it. Such an object is "garbage" and should be de-allocated by the garbage collector. In relational DBMSs, there is no need for automatic garbage collection, since object references are supported by join values. However, cascading updates as specified by referential integrity constraints are a simple form of "manual" garbage collection. In more general operating system or programming language contexts, manual garbage collection is typically error-prone. Therefore, the generality of distributed object-based systems calls for automatic distributed garbage collection.

The basic garbage collection algorithms can be categorized as *reference counting* or tracing-based. In a reference counting system, each object has an associated count of the references to it. Each time a program creates an additional reference that points to an object, the object's count is incremented. When an existing reference to an object is destroyed, the corresponding count is decremented. The memory occupied by an object can be reclaimed when the object's count drops to zero and become unreachable (at which time, the object is garbage). In reference counting, a problem can arise where two objects only refer to each other but not referred to by anyone else; in this case, the two objects are basically unreachable (except from each other) but their reference count has not dropped to zero.

Tracing-based collectors are divided into *mark and sweep* and *copy-based* algorithms. *Mark and sweep* collectors are two-phase algorithms. The first phase, called the "mark" phase, starts from the root and marks every reachable object (for example, by setting a bit associated to each object). This mark is also called a "color", and the collector is said to color the objects it reaches. The mark bit can be embedded in the objects themselves or in *color maps* that record, for every memory page, the colors of the objects stored in that page. Once all live objects are marked, the memory is examined and unmarked objects are reclaimed. This is the "sweep" phase.

Copy-based collectors divide memory into two disjoint areas called *from-space* and *to-space*. Programs manipulate from-space objects, while the to-space is left empty. Instead of marking and sweeping, copying collectors copy (usually in a depth first manner) the from-space objects reachable from the root into the to-space. Once all live objects have been copied, the collection is over, the contents of the from-space are discarded, and the roles of from- and to-spaces are exchanged. The copying process copies objects linearly in the to-space, which compacts memory.

The basic implementations of mark and sweep and copy-based algorithms are "stop-the-world"; i.e., user programs are suspended during the whole collection cycle. For many applications, however, stop-the-world algorithms cannot be used because of their disruptive behavior. Preserving the response time of user applications requires the use of incremental techniques. Incremental collectors must address problems raised by concurrency. The main difficulty with incremental garbage collection is that, while the collector is tracing the object graph, program activity may change other parts of the object graph. Garbage collection algorithms typically avoid the cases where the collector may miss tracing some reachable objects, due to concurrent changes to other parts of the object graph, and may erroneously reclaim them. On the other hand, although not desirable, it is acceptable to miss reclaiming a garbage and believe that it is alive.

Designing a garbage collection algorithm for object DBMSs is very complex. These systems have several features that pose additional problems for incremental garbage collection, beyond those typically addressed by solutions for non-persistent systems. These problems include the ones raised by the resilience to system failures and the semantics of transactions, and, in particular, by the rollbacks of partially completed transactions, by traditional client-server performance optimizations (such as client caching and flexible management of client buffers), and by the huge volume of data to analyze in order to detect garbage objects. There have been a number of proposals starting with [Butler, 1987]. More recent work has investigated fault-tolerant garbage collection techniques for transactional persistent systems in central-ized [Kolodner and Weihl, 1993; O'Toole et al., 1993] and client-server [Yong et al., 1994; Amsaleg, 1995; Amsaleg et al., 1995] architectures.

Distributed garbage collection, however, is even harder than centralized garbage collection. For scalability and efficiency reasons, a garbage collector for a distributed system combines independent per-site collectors with a global inter-site collector. Coordinating local and global collections is difficult because it requires carefully keeping track of reference exchanges between sites. Keeping track of such exchanges is necessary because an object may be referenced from several sites. In addition, an object located at one site may be referenced from live objects at remote sites, but not by any local live object. Such an object must not be reclaimed by the local collector, since it is reachable from the root of a remote site. It is difficult to keep track of inter-site references in a distributed environment where messages can be lost, duplicated or delayed, or where individual sites may crash.

Distributed garbage collectors typically rely either on distributed reference count-ing or distributed tracing. Distributed reference counting is problematic for two reasons. First, reference counting cannot collect unreachable cycles of garbage objects (i.e., mutually-referential garbage objects). Second, reference counting is defeated by common message failures; that is, if messages are not delivered reliably in their causal order, then maintaining the reference counting invariant (i.e., equality of the count with the actual number of references) is problematic. However, several algorithms propose distributed garbage collection solutions based on reference count-ing [Bevan, 1987; Dickman, 1991]. Each solution makes specific assumptions about the failure model, and is therefore incomplete. A variant of a reference counting collection scheme, called "reference listing" [Plainfossé and Shapiro, 1995], is im-plemented in Thor [Maheshwari and Liskov, 1994]. This algorithm tolerates server and client failures, but does not address the problem of reclaiming distributed cycles of garbage.

Distributed tracing usually combines independent per-site collectors with a global inter-site collector. The main problem with distributed tracing is synchronizing the distributed (global) garbage detection phase with independent (local) garbage recla-mation phases. When local collectors and user programs all operate in parallel, enforcing a global, consistent view of the object graph is impossible, especially in an environment where messages are not received instantaneously, and where commu-nications failures are likely. Therefore, distributed tracing-based garbage collection relies on inconsistent information in order to decide if an object is garbage or not. This inconsistent information makes distributed tracing collector very complex, be-cause the collector tries to accurately track the minimal set of reachable objects to at least eventually reclaim some objects that really are garbage. Ladin and Liskov [1992] propose an algorithm that computes, on a central space, the global graph of remote references. Ferreira and Shapiro [1994] present an algorithm that can reclaim cycles of garbage that span several disjoint object spaces. Finally, Fessant et al. [1998] present a complete (i.e., both acyclic and cyclic), asynchronous, distributed garbage collector.

15.6 Object Query Processing

Relational DBMSs have benefitted from the early definition of a precise and formal query model and a set of universally-accepted algebraic primitives. Although object models were not initially defined with a full complement of a query language, there is now a declarative query facility, OQL [Cattell et al., 2000], defined as part of the ODMG standard. In the remainder, we use OQL as the basis of our discussion. As we did earlier with SQL, we will take liberties with the language syntax.

Although there has been significant amount of work on object query processing and optimization, these have primarily focused on centralized systems. Almost all object query processors and optimizers that have been proposed to date use techniques developed for relational systems. Consequently, it is possible to claim that distributed object query processing and optimization techniques require the extension of centralized object query processing and optimization with the distribution approaches we discussed in Chapters 7 and 8. In this section, we will provide a brief review of the object query processing and optimization issues and approaches; the extension we refer to remains an open issue.

Although most object query processing proposals are based on their relational counterparts, there are a number of issues that make query processing and optimization more difficult in object DBMSs [Özsu and Blakeley, 1994]:

1. Relational query languages operate on very simple type systems consisting of a single type: relation. The closure property of relational languages implies that each relational operator takes one or two relations as operands and generates a relation as a result. In contrast, object systems have richer type systems. The results of object algebra operators are usually sets of objects (or collections), which may be of different types. If the object languages are closed under the algebra operators, these heterogeneous sets of objects can be operands to other operators. This requires the development of elaborate type inferencing schemes to determine which methods can be applied to **all** the objects in such a set. Furthermore, object algebras often operate on semantically different collection types (e.g., set, bag, list), which imposes additional requirements on the type inferencing schemes to determine the type of the results of operations on collections of different types.

2. Relational query optimization depends on knowledge of the physical storage of data (access paths) that is readily available to the query optimizer. The encapsulation of methods with the data upon which they operate in object DBMSs raises at least two important issues. First, determining (or estimating) the cost of executing methods is considerably more difficult than calculating

or estimating the cost of accessing an attribute according to an access path. In fact, optimizers have to worry about optimizing method execution, which is not an easy problem because methods may be written using a general-purpose programming language and the evaluation of a particular method may involve some heavy computation (e.g., comparing two DNA sequences). Second, encapsulation raises issues related to the accessibility of storage information by the query optimizer. Some systems overcome this difficulty by treating the query optimizer as a special application that can break encapsulation and access information directly [Cluet and Delobel, 1992]. Others propose a mechanism whereby objects "reveal" their costs as part of their interface [Graefe and Maier, 1988].

3. Objects can (and usually do) have complex structures whereby the state of an object references another object. Accessing such complex objects involves *path expressions*. The optimization of path expressions is a difficult and central issue in object query languages. Furthermore, objects belong to types related through inheritance hierarchies. Optimizing the access to objects through their inheritance hierarchies is also a problem that distinguishes object-oriented from relational query processing.

Object query processing and optimization has been the subject of significant research activity. Unfortunately, most of this work has not been extended to distributed object systems. Therefore, in the remainder of this chapter, we will restrict ourselves to a summary of the important issues: object query processing architectures (Section 15.6.1), object query optimization (Section 15.6.2), and query execution strategies (Section 15.6.3).

15.6.1 Object Query Processor Architectures

As indicated in Chapter 6, query optimization can be modeled as an optimization problem whose solution is the choice, based on a *cost function*, of the "optimum" *state*, which corresponds to an algebraic query, in a *search space* that represents a family of equivalent algebraic queries. Query processors differ, architecturally, according to how they model these components.

Many existing object DBMS optimizers are either implemented as part of the object manager on top of a storage system, or as client modules in a client/server architecture. In most cases, the above-mentioned components are "hardwired" into the query optimizer. Given that extensibility is a major goal of object DBMSs, one would hope to develop an extensible optimizer that accommodates different search strategies, algebra specifications (with their different transformation rules), and cost functions. Rule-based query optimizers [Freytag, 1987; Graefe and DeWitt, 1987] provide some amount of extensibility by allowing the definition of new transformation rules. However, they do not allow extensibility in other dimensions.

It is possible to make the query optimizer extensible with respect to algebraic operators, logical transformation rules, execution algorithms, implementation rules (i.e., logical operator-to-execution algorithm mappings), cost estimation functions, and physical property enforcement functions (e.g., presence of objects in memory). This can be achieved by means of modularization that separates of a number of concerns [Blakeley et al., 1993]. For example, the user query language parsing structures can be separated from the operator graph on which the optimizer operates, allowing the replacement of the user language (i.e., using something other than OQL at the top) or making changes to the optimizer without modifying the parse structures. Similarly, the algebraic operator manipulation (logical optimization, or re-writing) can be separated from the execution algorithms, allowing exploration with alternative methods for implementing algebraic operators. These are extensions that may be achieved by means of well-considered modularization and structuring of the optimizer.

An approach to providing search space extensibility is to consider it as a group of *regions* where each region corresponds to an equivalent family of query expressions that are reachable from each other [Mitchell et al., 1993]. The regions are not necessarily mutually exclusive and differ in the queries they manipulate, the control (search) strategies they use, the query transformation rules they incorporate (e.g., one region may cover transformation rules dealing with simple select queries, while another region may deal with transformations for nested queries), and the optimization objectives they achieve (e.g., one region may have the objective of minimizing a cost function, while another region may attempt to transform queries to some desirable form).

The ultimate extensibility can be achieved by using object-oriented approach to develop the query processor and optimizer. In this case, everything (queries, classes, operators, operator implementations,, meta-information, etc) are all first-class objects [Peters et al., 1993]. The search space, the search strategy and the cost function are modeled as objects. Consequently, using object-oriented techniques, it is easy to add new operators, new re-write rules, or new operator implementations [Özsu et al., 1995b; Lanzelotte and Valduriez, 1991].

15.6.2 *Query Processing Issues*

As indicated earlier, query processing methodology in object DBMSs is similar to its relational counterpart, but with differences in details as a result of the object model and query model characteristics. In this section we will highlight these differences as they apply to algebraic optimization. We will also discuss a particular problem unique to object query models — namely, the execution of path expressions.

15.6.2.1 Algebraic Optimization

Search Space and Transformation Rules.

The transformation rules are very much dependent upon the specific object algebra, since they are defined individually for each object algebra and for their combinations. The general considerations for the definition of transformation rules and the manipulation of query expressions is quite similar to relational systems, with one particularly important difference. Relational query expressions are defined on flat relations, whereas object queries are defined on classes (or collections or sets of objects) that have subclass and composition relationships among them. It is, therefore, possible to use the semantics of these relationships in object query optimizers to achieve some additional transformations.

Consider, for example, three object algebra operators [Straube and Özsu, 1990a]: union (denoted $\cup$), intersection (denoted $\cap$) and parameterized select (denoted $P\sigma_F < Q_1 \ldots Q_k >$), where union and intersection have the usual set-theoretic semantics, and select selects objects from one set P using the sets of objects $Q_1 \ldots Q_k$ as parameters (in a sense, a generalized form of semijoin). The results of these operators are sets of objects as well. It is, of course, possible to specify the usual set-theoretic, syntactic rewrite rules for these operators as we discussed in Chapter 7.

What is more interesting is that the relationships mentioned above allow us to define semantic rules that depend on the object model and the query model. Consider the following rules where C_i denotes the set of objects in the extent of class c_i and C_j^* denotes the deep extent of class c_j (i.e., the set of objects in the extent of c_j, as well as in the extents of all those which are subclasses of c_j):

$$C_1 \cap C_2 = \phi \ \text{ if } \ c_1 \neq c_2$$
$$C_1 \cup C_2^* = C_2^* \ \text{ if } c_1 \text{ is a subclass of } c_2$$
$$(P\sigma_F \langle QSet \rangle) \cap R \overset{c}{\Leftrightarrow} (P\sigma_F \langle QSet \rangle) \cap (R\sigma_{F'} \langle QSet \rangle)$$
$$\overset{c}{\Leftrightarrow} P \cap (R\sigma_{F'} < QSet >)$$

The first rule, for example, is true because the object model restricts each object to belong to only one class. The second rule holds because the query model permits retrieval of objects in the deep extent of the target class. Finally, the third rule relies on type consistency rules [Straube and Özsu, 1990b] for its applicability, as well as a condition (denoted by the c over the $\Leftrightarrow$) that F' is identical to F, except that each occurrence of p is replaced by r.

Since the idea of query transformation is well-known, we will not elaborate on the techniques. The above discussion only demonstrates the general idea and highlights the unique aspects that must be considered in object algebras.

Search Algorithm.

Enumerative algorithms based on dynamic programming with various optimizations are typically used for search [Selinger et al., 1979; Lee et al., 1988; Graefe and McKenna, 1993]. The combinatorial nature of enumerative search algorithms is perhaps more important in object DBMSs than in relational ones. It has been argued that if the number of joins in a query exceeds ten, enumerative search strategies become infeasible [Ioannidis and Wong, 1987]. In applications such as decision support systems, which object DBMSs are well-suited to support, it is quite common to find queries of this complexity. Furthermore, as we will address in Section 15.6.2.2, one method of executing path expressions is to represent them as explicit joins, and then use the well-known join algorithms to optimize them. If this is the case, the number of joins and other operations with join semantics in a query is quite likely to be higher than the empirical threshold of ten.

In these cases, *randomized search algorithms* (that we introduced in Chapters 7 and 8) have been suggested as alternatives to restrict the region of the search space being analyzed. Unfortunately, there has not been any study of randomized search algorithms within the context of object DBMSs. The general strategies are not likely to change, but the tuning of the parameters and the definition of the space of acceptable solutions should be expected to change. Unfortunately, the distributed versions of these algorithms are not available, and their development remains a challenge.

Cost Function.

As we have already seen, the arguments to cost functions are based on various information regarding the storage of the data. Typically, the optimizer considers the number of data items (cardinality), the size of each data item, its organization (e.g., whether there are indexes on it or not), etc. This information is readily available to the query optimizer in relational systems (through the system catalog), but may not be in object DBMSs due to encapsulation. If the query optimizer is considered "special" and allowed to look at the data structures used to implement objects, the cost functions can be specified similar to relational systems [Blakeley et al., 1993; Cluet and Delobel, 1992; Dogac et al., 1994; Orenstein et al., 1992]. Otherwise, an alternative specification must be considered.

The cost function can be defined recursively based on the algebraic processing tree. If the internal structure of objects is not visible to the query optimizer, the cost of each node (representing an algebraic operation) has to be defined. One way to define it is to have objects "reveal" their costs as part of their interface [Graefe and Maier, 1988]. In systems that uniformly implement everything as first-class objects, the cost of an operator can be a method defined on an operator implemented as a function of (a) the execution algorithm and (b) the collection over which they operate. In both cases, more abstract cost functions for operators are specified at type definition time from which the query optimizer can calculate the cost of the entire processing tree.

The definition of cost functions, especially in the approaches based on the objects revealing their costs, must be investigated further before satisfactory conclusions can be reached.

15.6.2.2 Path Expressions

Most object query languages allow queries whose predicates involve conditions on object access along reference chains. These reference chains are called *path expressions* [Zaniolo, 1983] (sometimes also referred to as *complex predicates* or *implicit joins* [Kim, 1989]). The example path expresion c.engine.manufacturer.name that we used in Section 15.4.2 retrieves the value of the name attribute of the object that is the value of the manufacturer attribute of the object that is the value of the engine attribute of object c, which was defined to be of type Car. It is possible to form path expressions involving attributes as well as methods. Optimizing the computation of path expressions is a problem that has received substantial attention in object-query processing.

Path expressions allow a succinct, high-level notation for expressing navigation through the object composition (aggregation) graph, which enables the formulation of predicates on values deeply nested in the structure of an object. They provide a uniform mechanism for the formulation of queries that involve object composition and inherited member functions. Path expressions may be *single-valued* or *set-valued*, and may appear in a query as part of a predicate, a target to a query (when set-valued), or part of a projection list. A path expression is single-valued if every component of a path expression is single-valued; if at least one component is set-valued, then the whole path expression is set-valued. Techniques have been developed to traverse path expressions forward and backward [Jenq et al., 1990].

The problem of optimizing path expressions spans the entire query-compilation process. During or after parsing of a user query, but before algebraic optimization, the query compiler must recognize which path expressions can potentially be optimized. This is typically achieved through *rewriting* techniques, which transform path expressions into equivalent logical algebra expressions [Cluet and Delobel, 1992]. Once path expressions are represented in algebraic form, the query optimizer explores the space of *equivalent algebraic* and execution plans, searching for one of minimal cost [Lanzelotte and Valduriez, 1991; Blakeley et al., 1993]. Finally, the optimal execution plan may involve algorithms to efficiently compute path expressions, including hash-join [Shapiro, 1986], complex-object assembly [Keller et al., 1991], or indexed scan through path indexes [Maier and Stein, 1986; Valduriez, 1987; Kemper and Moerkotte, 1990a,b].

Rewriting and Algebraic Optimization.

Consider again the path expression we used earlier: c.engine.manufacturer.name. Assume every car instance has a reference to an Engine object, each engine has a reference to a `Manufacturer` object, and each manufacturer instance has a `name` field. Also, assume that `Engine` and `Manufacturer` types have a corresponding type extent. The first two links of the above path may involve the retrieval of engine and manufacturer objects from disk. The third path involves only a lookup of a field within a manufacturer object. Therefore, only the first two links present opportunities for query optimization in the computation of that path. An object-query compiler needs a mechanism to distinguish these links in a path representing possible optimizations. This is typically achieved through a *rewriting* phase.

One possibility is to use a type-based rewriting technique [Cluet and Delobel, 1992]. This approach "unifies" algebraic and type-based rewriting techniques, permits factorization of common subexpressions, and supports heuristics to limit rewriting. Type information is exploited to decompose initial complex arguments of a query into a set of simpler operators, and to rewrite path expressions into joins. A similar attempt to optimizing path expressions within an algebraic framework has been devised based on joins, using an operator called *implicit join* [Lanzelotte and Valduriez, 1991]. Rules are defined to transform a series of implicit join operators into an indexed scan using a path index (see below) when it is available.

An alternative operator that has been proposed for optimizing path expressions is *materialize* (Mat) [Blakeley et al., 1993], which represents the computation of each inter-object reference (i.e., path link) explicitly. This enables a query optimizer to express the materialization of multiple components as a group using a single `Mat` operator, or individually using a Mat operator per component. Another way to think of this operator is as a "scope definition," because it brings elements of a path expression into scope so that these elements can be used in later operations or in predicate evaluation. The scoping rules are such that an object component gets into scope either by being scanned (captured using the logical Get operator in the leaves of expressions trees) or by being referenced (captured in the Mat operator). Components remain in scope until a projection discards them. The materialize operator allows a query processor to aggregate all component materializations required for the computation of a query, regardless of whether the components are needed for predicate evaluation or to produce the result of a query. The purpose of the materialize operator is to indicate to the optimizer where path expressions are used and where algebraic transformations can be applied. A number of transformation rules involving Mat are defined.

Path Indexes.

Substantial research on object query optimization has been devoted to the design of index structures to speed up the computation of path expressions [Maier and Stein, 1986; Bertino and Kim, 1989; Valduriez, 1987; Kemper and Moerkotte, 1994].

Computation of path expressions via indexes represents just one class of query-execution algorithms used in object-query optimization. In other words, efficient computation of path expressions through path indexes represents only one collection of implementation choices for algebraic operators, such as materialize and join, used to represent inter-object references. Section 15.6.3 describes a representative collection of query-execution algorithms that promise to provide a major benefit to the efficient execution of object queries. We will defer a discussion of some representative path index techniques to that section.

15.6.3 Query Execution

The relational DBMSs benefit from the close correspondence between the relational algebra operations and the access primitives of the storage system. Therefore, the generation of the execution plan for a query expression basically concerns the choice and implementation of the most efficient algorithms for executing individual algebra operators and their combinations. In object DBMSs, the issue is more complicated due to the difference in the abstraction levels of behaviorally-defined objects and their storage. Encapsulation of objects, which hides their implementation details, and the storage of methods with objects pose a challenging design problem, which can be stated as follows: "At what point in query processing should the query optimizer access information regarding the storage of objects?" One alternative is to leave this to the object manager [Straube and Özsu, 1995]. Consequently, the query-execution plan is generated from the query expression is obtained at the end of the query-rewrite step by mapping the query expression to a well-defined set of object-manager interface calls. The object-manager interface consists of a set of execution algorithms. This section reviews some of the execution algorithms that are likely to be part of future high-performance object-query execution engines.

A query-execution engine requires three basic classes of algorithms on collections of objects: *collection scan*, *indexed scan*, and *collection matching*. Collection scan is a straightforward algorithm that sequentially accesses all objects in a collection. We will not discuss this algorithm further due to its simplicity. Indexed scan allows efficient access to selected objects in a collection through an index. It is possible to use an object's field or the values returned by some method as a key to an index. Also, it is possible to define indexes on values deeply nested in the structure of an object (i.e., path indexes). In this section we mention a representative sample of path-index proposals. Set-matching algorithms take multiple collections of objects as input and produce aggregate objects related by some criteria. Join, set intersection, and assembly are examples of algorithms in this category.

15.6.3.1 Path Indexes

As indicated earlier, support for path expressions is a feature that distinguishes object queries from relational ones. Many indexing techniques designed to accelerate the computation of path expressions have been proposed [Maier and Stein, 1986; Bertino and Kim, 1989] based on the concept of join index [Valduriez, 1987].

One such path indexing technique creates an index on each class traversed by a path [Maier and Stein, 1986; Bertino and Kim, 1989]. In addition to indexes on path expressions, it is possible to define indexes on objects across their type inheritance.

Access support relations [Kemper and Moerkotte, 1994] are an alternative general technique to represent and compute path expressions. An access support relation is a data structure that stores selected path expressions. These path expressions are chosen to be the most frequently navigated ones. Studies provide initial evidence that the performance of queries executed using access support relations improves by about two orders of magnitude over queries that do not use access support relations. A system using access support relations must also consider the cost of maintaining them in the presence of updates to the underlying base relations.

15.6.3.2 Set Matching

As indicated earlier, path expressions are traversals along the composite object composition relationship. We have already seen that a possible way of executing a path expression is to transform it into a join between the source and target sets of objects. A number of different join algorithms have been proposed, such as hybrid-hash join or pointer-based hash join [Shekita and Carey, 1990]. The former uses the divide-and-conquer principle to recursively partition the two operand collections into buckets using a hash function on the join attribute. Each of these buckets may fit entirely in memory. Each pair of buckets is then joined in memory to produce the result. The pointer-based hash join is used when each object in one operand collection (call R) has a pointer to an object in the other operand collection (call S). The algorithm follows three steps, the first one being the partitioning of R in the same way as in the hybrid hash algorithm, except that it is partitioned by OID values rather than by join attribute. The set of objects S is not partitioned. In the second step, each partition R_i of R is joined with S by taking R_i and building a hash table for it in memory. The table is built by hashing each object $r \in R$ on the value of its pointer to its corresponding object in S. As a result, all R objects that reference the same page in S are grouped together in the same hash-table entry. Third, after the hash table for R_i is built, each of its entries is scanned. For each hash entry, the corresponding page in S is read, and all objects in R that reference that page are joined with the corresponding objects in S. These two algorithms are basically centralized algorithms, without any distributed counterparts. So we will not discuss them further.

An alternative method of join execution algorithm, *assembly* [Keller et al., 1991], is a generalization of the pointer-based hash-join algorithm for the case when a multi-way join needs to be computed. Assembly has been proposed as an additional object algebra operator. This operation efficiently assembles the fragments of objects' states required for a particular processing step, and returns them as a complex object in memory. It translates the disk representations of complex objects into readily traversable memory representations.

Assembling a complex object rooted at objects of type R containing object components of types S, U, and T, is analogous to computing a four-way join of these sets.

There is a difference between assembly and *n*-way pointer joins in that assembly does not need the entire collection of root objects to be scanned before producing a single result.

Instead of assembling a single complex object at a time, the assembly operator assembles a *window*, of size *W*, of complex objects simultaneously. As soon as any of these complex objects becomes assembled and passed up the query-execution tree, the assembly operator retrieves another one to work on. Using a window of complex objects increases the pool size of unresolved references and results in more options for optimization of disk accesses. Due to the randomness with which references are resolved, the assembly operator delivers assembled objects in random order up the query execution tree. This behavior is correct in set-oriented query processing, but may not be for other collection types, such as lists.

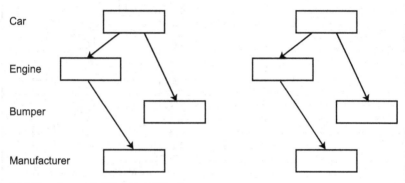

Fig. 15.3 Two Assembled Complex Objects

Example 15.8. Consider the example given in Figure 15.3, which assembles a set of Car objects. The boxes in the figure represent instances of types indicated at the left, and the edges denote the composition relationships (e.g., there is an attribute of every object of type `Car` that points to an object of type `Engine`). Suppose that assembly is using a window of size 2. The assembly operator begins by filling the window with two (since *W* = 2) `Car` object references from the set (Figure 15.4a). The assembly operator begins by choosing among the current outstanding references, say *C*1. After resolving (fetching) *C*1, two new unresolved references are added to the list (Figure 15.4b). Resolving *C*2 results in two more references added to the list (Figure 15.4c), and so on until the first complex object is assembled (Figure 15.4g). At this point, the assembled object is passed up the query-execution tree, freeing some window space. A new `Car` object reference, *C*3, is added to the list and then resolved, bringing two new references *E*3, *B*3 (Figure 15.4h). ◆

The objective of the assembly algorithm is to simultaneously assemble a window of complex objects. At each point in the algorithm, the outstanding reference that optimizes disk accesses is chosen. There are different orders, or schedules, in which references may be resolved, such as depth-first, breath-first, and elevator. Performance

Outstanding References   **Partally Assembled Objects**

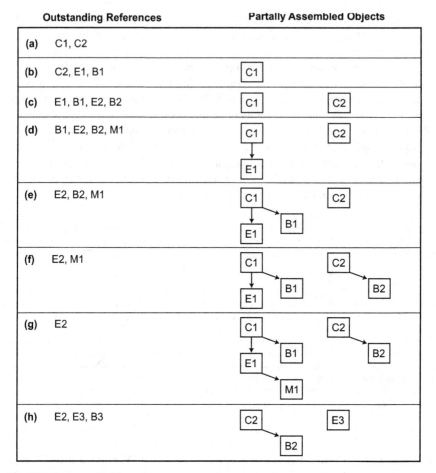

Fig. 15.4 An Assembly Example

results indicate that elevator outperforms depth-first and breath-first under several data-clustering situations [Keller et al., 1991].

A number of possibilities exist in implementing a distributed version of this operation [Maier et al., 1994]. One strategy involves shipping all data to a central site for processing. This is straightforward to implement, but could be inefficient in general. A second strategy involves doing simple operations (e.g., selections, local assembly) at remote sites, then shipping all data to a central site for final assembly. This strategy also requires fairly simple control, since all communication occurs through the central site. The third strategy is significantly more complicated: perform complex operations (e.g., joins, complete assembly of remote objects) at remote sites, then ship the results to the central site for final assembly. A distributed object DBMS may include all or some of these strategies.

15.7 Transaction Management

Transaction management in *distributed* object DBMSs have not been studied except in relation to the cashing problem discussed earlier. However, transactions on objects raise a number of interesting issues, and their execution in a distributed environment can be quite challenging. This is an area that clearly requires more work. In this section we will briefly discuss the particular problems that arise in extending the transaction concept to object DBMSs.

Most object DBMSs maintain page level locks for concurrency control and support the traditional flat transaction model. It has been argued that the traditional flat transaction model would not meet the requirements of the advanced application domains that object data management technology would serve. Some of the considerations are that transactions in these domains are longer in duration, requiring interactions with the user or the application program during their execution. In the case of object systems, transactions do not consist of simple read/write operations, necessitating, instead, synchronization algorithms that deal with complex operations on abstract (and possibly complex) objects. In some application domains, the fundamental transaction synchronization paradigm based on competition among transactions for access to resources must change to one of cooperation among transactions in accomplishing a common task. This is the case, for example, in cooperative work environments.

The more important requirements for transaction management in object DBMSs can be listed as follows [Buchmann et al., 1982; Kaiser, 1989; Martin and Pedersen, 1994]:

1. Conventional transaction managers synchronize simple Read and Write operations. However, their counterparts for object DBMSs must be able to deal with *abstract operations*. It may even be possible to improve concurrency by using semantic knowledge about the objects and their abstract operations.

2. Conventional transactions access "flat" objects (e.g., pages, tuples), whereas transactions in object DBMSs require synchronization of access to composite and complex objects. Synchronization of access to such objects requires synchronization of access to the component objects.

3. Some applications supported by object DBMSs have different database access patterns than conventional database applications, where the access is competitive (e.g., two users accessing the same bank account). Instead, sharing is more cooperative, as in the case of, for example, multiple users accessing and working on the same design document. In this case, user accesses must be synchronized, but users are willing to cooperate rather than compete for access to shared objects.

4. These applications require the support of *long-running activities* spanning hours, days or even weeks (e.g., when working on a design object). Therefore, the transaction mechanism must support the sharing of partial results. Furthermore, to avoid the failure of a partial task jeopardizing a long activity, it is necessary to distinguish between those activities that are essential for

the completion of a transaction and those that are not, and to provide for alternative actions in case the primary activity fails.

5. It has been argued that many of these applications would benefit from *active capabilities* for timely response to events and changes in the environment. This new database paradigm requires the monitoring of events and the execution of system-triggered activities within running transactions.

These requirements point to a need to extend the traditional transaction management functions in order to capture application and data semantics, and to a need to relax isolation properties. This, in turn, requires revisiting every aspect of transaction management that we discussed in Chapters 10–12.

15.7.1 Correctness Criteria

In Chapter 11, we introduced serializability as the fundamental correctness criteria for concurrent execution of database transactions. There are a number of different ways in which serializability can be defined, even though we did not elaborate on this point before. These differences are based on how a *conflict* is defined. We will concentrate on three alternatives: *commutativity* [Weihl, 1988, 1989; Fekete et al., 1989], *invalidation* [Herlihy, 1990], and *recoverability* [Badrinath and Ramamritham, 1987].

15.7.1.1 Commutativity

Commutativity states that two operations conflict if the results of different serial executions of these operations are not equivalent. We had briefly introduced commutativity within the context of ordered-shared locks in Chapter 11 (see Figure 11.8). The traditional conflict definition discussed in Chapter 11 is a special case. Consider the simple operations $R(x)$ and $W(x)$. If nothing is known about the abstract semantics of the Read and Write operations or the object x upon which they operate, it has to be accepted that a $R(x)$ **following** a $W(x)$ does not retrieve the same value as it would **prior** to the $W(x)$. Therefore, a Write operation always conflicts with other Read or Write operations. The conflict table (or the compatibility matrix) given in Figure 11.5 for Read and Write operations is, in fact, derived from the commutativity relationship between these two operations. This table was called the compatibility matrix in Chapter 11, since two operations that do not conflict are said to be compatible. Since this type of commutativity relies only on syntactic information about operations (i.e., that they are Read and Write), we call this *syntactic commutativity* [Buchmann et al., 1982].

In Figure 11.5, Read and Write operations and Write and Write operations do not commute. Therefore, they conflict, and serializability maintains that either all conflicting operations of transaction T_i precede all conflicting operations of T_k, or vice versa.

If the semantics of the operations are taken into account, however, it may be possible to provide a more relaxed definition of conflict. Specifically, some concurrent executions of Write-Write and Read-Write may be considered non-conflicting. *Semantic commutativity* (e.g., [Weihl, 1988, 1989]) makes use of the semantics of operations and their termination conditions.

Example 15.9. Consider, for example, an abstract data type **set** and three operations defined on it: Insert and Delete, which correspond to a Write, and Member, which tests for membership and corresponds to a Read. Due to the semantics of these operations, two Insert operations on an instance of set type would commute, allowing them to be executed concurrently. The commutativity of Insert with Member and the commutativity of Delete with Member depends upon whether or not they reference the same argument and their results[7].   ◆

It is also possible to define commutativity with reference to the database state. In this case, it is usually possible to permit more operations to commute.

Example 15.10. In Example 15.7, we indicated that an Insert and a Member would commute if they do not refer to the same argument. However, if the set already contains the referred element, these two operations would commute even if their arguments are the same.   ◆

15.7.1.2 Invalidation

Invalidation [Herlihy, 1990] defines a conflict between two operations not on the basis of whether they commute or not, but according to whether or not the execution of one invalidates the other. An operation P invalidates another operation Q if there are two histories H_1 and H_2 such that $H_1 \bullet P \bullet H_2$ and $H_1 \bullet H_2 \bullet Q$ are legal, but $H_1 \bullet P \bullet H_2 \bullet Q$ is not. In this context, a *legal history* represents a correct history for the set object and is determined according to its semantics. Accordingly, an *invalidated-by* relation is defined as consisting of all operation pairs (P, Q) such that P invalidates Q. The invalidated-by relation establishes the conflict relation that forms the basis of establishing serializability. Considering the Set example, an Insert cannot be invalidated by any other operation, but a Member can be invalidated by a Delete if their arguments are the same.

---

[7] Depending upon the operation, the result may either be a flag that indicates whether the operation was successful (for example, the result of Insert may be "OK") or the value that the operation returns (as in the case of a Read).

15.7.1.3 Recoverability

Recoverability [Badrinath and Ramamritham, 1987] is another conflict relation that has been defined to determine serializable histories[8]. Intuitively, an operation P is said to be *recoverable with respect to* operation Q if the value returned by P is independent of whether Q executed before P or not. The conflict relation established on the basis of recoverability seems to be identical to that established by invalidation. However, this observation is based on only a few examples, and there is no formal proof of this equivalence. In fact, the absence of a formal theory to reason about these conflict relations is a serious deficiency that must be addressed.

15.7.2 Transaction Models and Object Structures

In Chapter 10, we considered a number of transaction models ranging from flat transactions to workflow systems. All of these alternatives access simple database objects (sets of tuples or a physical page). In the case of object databases, however, the database objects are not simple; they can be objects with state and properties, they can be complex objects, or even active objects (i.e., objects that are capable of responding to events by triggering the execution of actions when certain conditions are satisfied). The complications added by the complexity of objects is significant, as we highlight in subsequent sections.

15.7.3 Transactions Management in Object DBMSs

Transaction management techniques that are developed for object DBMSs need to take into consideration the complications we discussed earlier: they need to employ more sophisticated correctness criteria that take into account method semantics, they need to consider the object structure, they need to be cognizant of the composition and inheritance relationships. In addition to these structures, object DBMSs store methods together with data. Synchronization of shared access to objects must take into account method executions. In particular, transactions invoke methods which may, in turn, invoke other methods. Thus, even if the transaction model is flat, the execution of these transactions may be dynamically nested.

---

[8] Recoverability as used in [Badrinath and Ramamritham, 1987] is different from the notion of recoverability as we defined it in Chapter 12 and as found in [Bernstein et al., 1987] and [Hadzilacos, 1988].

15.7.3.1 Synchronizing Access to Objects

The inherent nesting in method invocations can be used to develop algorithms based on the well-known nested 2PL and nested timestamp ordering algorithms [Hadzilacos and Hadzilacos, 1991]. In the process, intra-object parallelism may be exploited to improve concurrency. In other words, attributes of an object can be modeled as data elements in the database, whereas the methods are modeled as transactions enabling multiple invocations of an object's methods to be active simultaneously. This can provide more concurrency if special intra-object synchronization protocols can be devised that maintain the compatibility of synchronization decisions at each object.

Consequently, a method execution (modeled as a transaction) on an object consists of *local steps*, which correspond to the execution of local operations together with the results that are returned, and *method steps*, which are the method invocations together with the return values. A local operation is an atomic operation (such as Read, Write, Increment) that affects the object's variables. A method execution defines the partial order among these steps in the usual manner.

One of the fundamental directions of this work is to provide total freedom to objects in how they achieve intra-object synchronization. The only requirement is that they be "correct" executions, which, in this case, means that they should be serializable based on commutativity. As a result of the delegation of intra-object synchronization to individual objects, the concurrency control algorithm concentrates on inter-object synchronization.

An alternative approach is multigranularity locking [Garza and Kim, 1988; Cart and Ferrie, 1990]. Multigranularity locking defines a hierarchy of lockable database granules (thus the name "granularity hierarchy") as depicted in Figure 15.5. In relational DBMSs, files correspond to relations and records correspond to tuples. In object DBMSs, the correspondence is with classes and instance objects, respectively. The advantage of this hierarchy is that it addresses the tradeoff between coarse granularity locking and fine granularity locking. Coarse granularity locking (at the file level and above) has low locking overhead, since a small number of locks are set, but it significantly reduces concurrency. The reverse is true for fine granularity locking.

The main idea behind multigranularity locking is that a transaction that locks at a coarse granularity implicitly locks all the corresponding objects of finer granularities. For example, explicit locking at the file level involves implicit locking of all the records in that file. To achieve this, two more lock types in addition to shared (S) and exclusive (X) are defined: *intention* (or *implicit*) *shared* (IS) and *intention* (or *implicit*) *exclusive* (IX). A transaction that wants to set an S or an IS lock on an object has to first set IS or IX locks on its ancestors (i.e., related objects of coarser granularity). Similarly, a transaction that wants to set an X or an IX lock on an object must set IX locks on all of its ancestors. Intention locks cannot be released on an object if the descendants of that object are currently locked.

One additional complication arises when a transaction wants to read an object at some granularity and modify some of its objects at a finer granularity. In this case, both an S lock and an IX lock must be set on that object. For example, a transaction

Fig. 15.5 Multiple Granularities

may read a file and update some records in that file (similarly, a transaction in object DBMSs may want to read the class definition and update some of the instance objects belonging to that class). To deal with these cases, a *shared intention exclusive* (SIX) lock is introduced, which is equivalent to holding an S and an IX lock on that object. The lock compatibility matrix for multigranularity locking is shown in Figure 15.6.

A possible granularity hierarchy is shown in Figure 15.7. The lock modes that are supported and their compatibilities are exactly those given in Figure 15.6. Instance objects are locked only in S or X mode, while class objects can be locked in all five modes. The interpretation of these locks on class objects is as follows:

- S mode: Class definition is locked in S mode, and all its instances are implicitly locked in S mode. This prevents another transaction from updating the instances.

	S	X	IS	IX	SIX
S	+	-	+	-	-
X	-	-	-	-	-
IS	+	-	+	+	+
IX	-	-	+	+	-
SIX	-	-	+	-	-

Fig. 15.6 Compatibility Table for Multigranularity Locking

- X mode: Class definition is locked in X mode, and all its instances are implicitly locked in X mode. Therefore, the class definition and all instances of the class may be read or updated.

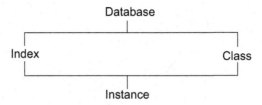

Fig. 15.7 Granularity Hierarchy

- IS mode: Class definition is locked in IS mode, and the instances are to be locked in S mode as necessary.

- IX mode: Class definition is locked in IX mode, and the instances will be locked in either S or X mode as necessary.

- SIX mode: Class definition is locked in S mode, and all the instances are implicitly locked in S mode. Those instances that are to be updated are explicitly locked in X mode as the transaction updates them.

15.7.3.2 Management of Class Lattice

One of the important requirements of object DBMSs is dynamic schema evolution. Consequently, systems must deal with transactions that access schema objects (i.e., types, classes, etc.), as well as instance objects. The existence of schema change operations intermixed with regular queries and transactions, as well as the (multiple) inheritance relationship defined among classes, complicates the picture. First, a query/transaction may not only access instances of a class, but may also access instances of subclasses of that class (i.e., *deep extent*). Second, in a composite object, the domain of an attribute is itself a class. So accessing an attribute of a class may involve accessing the objects in the sublattice rooted at the domain class of that attribute.

One way to deal with these two problems is, again, by using multigranularity locking. The straightforward extension of multigranularity locking where the accessed class and all its subclasses are locked in the appropriate mode does not work very well. This approach is inefficient when classes close to the root are accessed, since it involves too many locks. The problem may be overcome by introducing *read-lattice* (R) and *write-lattice* (W) lock modes, which not only lock the target class in S or X modes, respectively, but also implicitly lock all subclasses of that class in S and X modes, respectively. However, this solution does not work with multiple inheritance (which is the third problem).

The problem with multiple inheritance is that a class with multiple supertypes may be implicitly locked in incompatible modes by two transactions that place R and W locks on different superclasses. Since the locks on the common class are implicit, there is no way of recognizing that there is already a lock on the class. Thus, it is necessary to check the superclasses of a class that is being locked. This can be

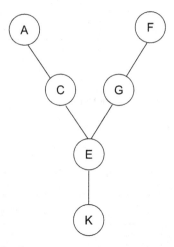

Fig. 15.8 An Example Class Lattice

handled by placing *explicit* locks, rather than implicit ones, on subclasses. Consider the type lattice of Figure 15.8, which is simplified from [Garza and Kim, 1988]. If transaction T_1 sets an IR lock on class A and an R lock on C, it also sets an explicit R lock on E. When another transaction T_2 places an IW lock on F and a W lock on G, it will attempt to place an explicit W lock on E. However, since there is already an R lock on E, this request will be rejected.

An alternative to setting explicit locks is to set locks at a finer granularity, uses ordered sharing, as discussed in Chapter 11 [Agrawal and El-Abbadi, 1994]. In a sense, the algorithm is an extension of Weihl's commutativity-based approach to object DBMSs using a nested transaction model.

Classes are modeled as objects in the system similar to reflective systems that represent schema objects as first-class objects. Consequently, methods can be defined that operate on class objects: $add(m)$ to add method m to the class, $del(m)$ to delete method m from the class, $rep(m)$ to replace the implementation of method m with another one, and $use(m)$ to execute method m. Similarly, atomic operations are defined for accessing attributes of a class. These are identical to the method operations with the appropriate change in semantics to reflect attribute access. The interesting point to note here is that the definition of the $use(a)$ operation for attribute a indicates that the access of a transaction to attribute a within a method execution is through the use operation. This requires that each method explicitly list all the attributes that it accesses. Thus, the following is the sequence of steps that are followed by a transaction, T, in executing a method m:

1. Transaction T issues operation $use(m)$.
2. For each attribute a that is accessed by method m, T issues operation $use(a)$.
3. Transaction T invokes method m.

Commutativity tables are defined for the method and attribute operations. Based on the commutativity tables, ordered sharing lock tables for each atomic operation are determined (see Figure 11.8). Specifically, a lock for an atomic operation p has a shared relationship with all the locks associated with operations with which p has a non-conflicting relationship, whereas it has an ordered shared relationship with respect to all the locks associated with operations with which p has a conflicting relation.

Based on these lock tables, a nested 2PL locking algorithm is used with the following considerations:

1. Transactions observe the strict 2PL rule and hold on to their locks until termination.

2. When a transaction aborts, it releases all of its locks.

3. The termination of a transaction awaits the termination of its children (closed nesting semantics). When a transaction commits, its locks are inherited by its parent.

4. *Ordered commitment rule.* Given two transactions T_i and T_j such that T_i is *waiting for* T_j, T_i cannot commit its operations on any object until T_j terminates (commits or aborts). T_i is said to be *waiting-for* T_j if:

   • T_i is not the root of the nested transaction and T_i was granted a lock in ordered shared relationship with respect to a lock held by T_j on an object such that T_j is a descendent of the parent of T_i; or

   • T_i is the root of the nested transaction and T_i holds a lock (that it has inherited or it was granted) on an object in ordered shared relationship with respect to a lock held by T_j or its descendants.

15.7.3.3 Management of Composition (Aggregation) Graph

Studies dealing with the composition graph are more prevalent. The requirement for object DBMSs to model composite objects in an efficient manner has resulted in considerable interest in this problem.

One approach is based on multigranularity locking where one can lock a composite object and all the classes of the component objects. This is clearly unacceptable, since it involves locking the entire composite object hierarchy, thereby restricting performance significantly. An alternative is to lock the component object instances within a composite object. In this case, it is necessary to chase all the references and lock all those objects. This is quite cumbersome, since it involves locking so many objects.

The problem is that the multigranularity locking protocol does not recognize the composite object as one lockable unit. To overcome this problem, three new lock modes are introduced: ISO, IXO, and SIXO, corresponding to the IS, IX, and SIX modes, respectively. These lock modes are used for locking component classes of

	S	X	IS	IX	SIX	ISO	IXO	SIXO
S	+	-	+	-	-	+	-	-
X	-	-	-	-	-	-	-	-
IS	+	-	+	+	+	+	-	-
IX	-	-	+	+	-	-	-	-
SIX	-	-	+	-	-	-	-	-
ISO	+	-	+	+	-	+	+	+
IXO	-	-	-	-	-	+	+	-
SIXO	N	N	N	N	N	Y	N	N

Fig. 15.9 Compatibility Matrix for Composite Objects

a composite object. The compatibility of these modes is shown in Figure 15.9. The protocol is then as follows: to lock a composite object, the root class is locked in X, IS, IX, or SIX mode, and each of the component classes of the composite object hierarchy is locked in the X, ISO, IXO, and SIXO mode, respectively.

Another approach extends multigranularity locking by replacing the single static lock graph with a hierarchy of graphs associated with each type and query [Herrmann et al., 1990]. There is a "general lock graph" that controls the entire process (Figure 15.10). The smallest lockable units are called *basic lockable units* (BLU). A number of BLUs can make up a *homogeneous lockable unit* (HoLU), which consists of data of the same type. Similarly, they can make up a *heterogeneous lockable unit* (HeLU), which is composed of objects of different types. HeLUs can contain other HeLUs or HoLUs, indicating that component objects do not all have to be atomic. Similarly, HoLUs can consist of other HoLUs or HeLUs, as long as they are of the same type. The separation between HoLUs and HeLUs is meant to optimize lock requests. For example, a set of lists of integers is, from the viewpoint of lock managers, treated as a HoLU composed of HoLUs, which, in turn, consist of BLUs. As a result, it is possible to lock the whole set, exactly one of the lists, or even just one integer.

At type definition time, an object-specific lock graph is created that obeys the general lock graph. As a third component, a query-specific lock graph is generated during query (transaction) analysis. During the execution of the query (transaction), the query-specific lock graph is used to request locks from the lock manager, which uses the object-specific lock graph to make the decision. The lock modes used are the standard ones (i.e., IS, IX, S, X).

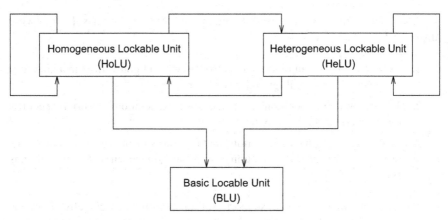

Fig. 15.10 General Lock Graph

Badrinath and Ramamritham [1987] discuss an alternative to dealing with composite object hierarchy based on commutativity. A number of different operations are defined on the aggregation graph:

1. Examine the contents of a vertex (which is a class).
2. Examine an edge (composed-of relationship).
3. Insert a vertex and the associated edge.
4. Delete a vertex and the associated edge.
5. Insert an edge.

Note that some of these operations (1 and 2) correspond to existing object operators, while others (3—5) represent schema operations.

Based on these operations, an *affected-set* can be defined for granularity graphs to form the basis for determining which operations can execute concurrently. The affected-set of a granularity graph consists of the union of:

- *edge-set*, which is the set of pairs (e, a) where e is an edge and a is an operation affecting e and can be one of *insert, delete, examine*; and
- *vertex-set*, which is the set of pairs (v, a), where v is a vertex and a is an operation affecting v and can be one of *insert, delete, examine*, or *modify*.

Using the affected-set generated by two transactions T_i and T_j of an aggregation graph, one may define whether T_i and T_j can execute concurrently or not. Commutativity is used as the basis of the conflict relation. Thus, two transactions T_i and T_j commute on object K if $affected\text{-}set(T_i) \cap_K affected\text{-}set(T_j) = \phi$.

These protocols synchronize on the basis of objects, not operations on objects. It may be possible to improve concurrency by developing techniques that synchronize operation invocations rather than locking entire objects.

Another semantics-based approach due to Muth et al. [1993] has the following distinguishing characteristics:

1. Access to component objects are permitted without going through a hierarchy of objects (i.e., no multigranularity locking).

2. The semantics of operations are taken into consideration by a priori specification of method commutativities[9].

3. Methods invoked by a transaction can themselves invoke other methods. This results in a (dynamic) nested transaction execution, even if the transaction is syntactically flat.

The transaction model used to support (3) is open nesting, specifically multilevel transactions as described in Chapter 10. The restrictions imposed on the dynamic transaction nesting are:

• All pairs (p,g) of potentially conflicting operations on the same object have the same depth in their invocation trees; and

• For each pair (f',g') of ancestors of f and g whose depth of invocation trees are the same, f' and g' operate on the same object.

With these restrictions, the algorithm is quite straightforward. A semantic lock is associated with each method, and a commutativity table defines whether or not the various semantic locks are compatible. Transactions acquire these semantic locks before the invocation of methods, and they are released at the end of the execution of a subtransaction (method), exposing their results to others. However, the parents of committed subtransactions have a higher-level semantic lock, which restricts the results of committed subtransactions only to those that commute with the root of the subtransaction. This requires the definition of a semantic conflict test, which operates on the invocation hierarchies using the commutativity tables.

An important complication arises with respect to the two conditions outlined above. It is not reasonable to restrict the applicability of the protocol to only those for which those conditions hold. What has been proposed to resolve the difficulty is to give up some of the openness and convert the locks that were to be released at the end of a subtransaction into *retained locks* held by the parent. A number of conditions under which retained locks can be discarded for additional concurrency.

A very similar, but more restrictive, approach is discussed by Weikum and Hasse [1993]. The multilevel transaction model is used, but restricted to only two levels: the object level and the underlying page level. Therefore, the dynamic nesting that occurs when transactions invoke methods that invoke other methods is not considered. The similarity with the above work is that page level locks are released at the end of the subtransaction, whereas the object level locks (which are semantically richer) are retained until the transaction terminates.

---

[9] The commutativity test employed in this study is state-independent. It takes into account the actual parameters of operations, but not the states. This is in contrast to Weihl's work [Weihl, 1988].

In both of the above approaches [Muth et al., 1993; Weikum and Hasse, 1993], recovery cannot be performed by page-level state-oriented protocols. Since subtransactions release their locks and make their results visible, compensating transactions must be run to "undo" actions of committed subtransactions.

15.7.4 Transactions as Objects

One important characteristic of relational data model is its lack of a clear update semantics. The model, as it was originally defined, clearly spells out how the data in a relational database is to be retrieved (by means of the relational algebra operators), but does not specify what it really means to update the database. The consequence is that the consistency definitions and the transaction management techniques are orthogonal to the data model. It is possible – and indeed it is common – to apply the same techniques to non-relational DBMSs, or even to non-DBMS storage systems.

The independence of the developed techniques from the data model may be considered an advantage, since the effort can be amortized over a number of different applications. Indeed, the existing transaction management work on object DBMSs have exploited this independence by porting the well-known techniques over to the new system structures. During this porting process, the peculiarities of object DBMSs, such as class (type) lattice structures, composite objects and object groupings (class extents) are considered, but the techniques are essentially the same.

It may be argued that in object DBMSs, it is not only desirable but indeed essential to model update semantics within the object model. The arguments are as follows:

1. In object DBMSs, what is stored are not only data, but operations on data (which are called methods, behaviors, operations in various object models). Queries that access an object database refer to these operations as part of their predicates. In other words, the execution of these queries invokes various operations defined on the classes (types). To guarantee the safety of the query expressions, existing query processing approaches restrict these operations to be side-effect free, in effect disallowing them to update the database. This is a severe restriction that should be relaxed by the incorporation of update semantics into the query safety definitions.

2. As we discussed in Section 15.7.3, transactions in object DBMSs affect the class (type) lattices. Thus, there is a direct relationship between dynamic schema evolution and transaction management. Many of the techniques that we discussed employ locking on this lattice to accommodate these changes. However, locks (even multi-granularity locks) severely restrict concurrency. A definition of what it means to update a database, and a definition of conflicts based on this definition of update semantics, would allow more concurrency. It is interesting to note again the relationship between changes to the class (type) lattice and query processing. In the absence of a clear definition of update semantics and its incorporation into the query processing methodology,

most of the current query processors assume that the database schema (i.e., the class (type) lattice) is static during the execution of a query.

3. There are a few object models (e.g., OODAPLEX [Dayal, 1989] and TIGUKAT [Özsu et al., 1995a]) that treat all system entities as objects. Following this approach, it is only natural to model transactions as objects. However, since transactions are basically constructs that change the state of the database, their effects on the database must be clearly specified.

   Within this context, it should also be noted that the application domains that require the services of object DBMSs tend to have somewhat different transaction management requirements, both in terms of transaction models and consistency constraints. Modeling transactions as objects enables the application of the well-known object techniques of specialization and subtyping to create various different types of TMSs. This gives the system extensibility.

4. Some of the requirements require rule support and active database capabilities. Rules themselves execute as transactions, which may spawn other transactions. It has been argued that rules should be modeled as objects [Dayal et al., 1988]. If that is the case, then certainly transactions should be modeled as objects too.

As a result of these points, it seems reasonable to argue for an approach to transaction management systems that is quite different from what has been done up to this point. This is a topic of some research potential.

15.8 Conclusion

In this chapter we considered the effect of object technology on database management and focused on the distribution aspects when possible. Research into object technologies was widespread in the 1980's and the first half of 1990's. Interest in the topic died down primarily as a result of two factors. The first was that object DBMSs were claimed to be replacements for relational ones, rather than specialized systems that better fit certain application requirements. The object DBMSs, however, were not able to deliver the performance of relational systems for those applications that really fit the relational model well. Consequently, they were easy targets for the relational proponents, which is the second factor. The relational vendors adopted many of the techniques developed for object DBMSs into their products and released "object-relational DBMSs", as noted earlier, allowing them to claim that there is no reason for a new class of systems. The object extensions to relational DBMSs work with varying degrees of success. They allow the attributes to be structured, allowing non-normalized relations. They are also extensible by enabling the insertion of new data types into the system by means of *data blades*, *cartridges*, or *extenders* (each commercial system uses a different name). However, this extensibility is limited, as it requires significant effort to write a data blade/cartridge/extender, and their robustness is a considerable issue.

In recent years, there has been a re-emergence of object technology. This is spurred by the recognition of the advantages of these systems in particular applications that are gaining importance. For example, the DOM interface of XML, the Java Data Objects (JDO) API are all object-oriented and they are crucial technologies. JDO has been critically important in resolving the mapping problems between Java Enterprice Edition (J2EE) and relational systems. Object-oriented middleware architectures such as CORBA Siegel [1996] have not been as influential as they could be in their first incarnation, but they have been demonstrated to contribute to database interoperability [Dogac et al., 1998a], and there is continuing work in improving them.

15.9 Bibliographic Notes

There are a number of good books on object DBMSs such as [Kemper and Moerkotte, 1994; Bertino and Martino, 1993; Cattell, 1994] and [Dogac et al., 1994]. An early collection of readings in object DBMSs is [Zdonik and Maier, 1990]. In addition, object DBMS concepts are discussed in [Kim and Lochovsky, 1989; Kim, 1994]. These are, unfortunately, somewhat dated. [Orfali et al., 1996] is considered the classical book on distributed objects, but the emphasis is mostly on the distributed object platforms (CORBA and COM), not on the fundamental DBMS functionality. Considerable work has been done on the formalization of object models, some of which are discussed in [Abadi and Cardelli, 1996; Maier, 1986; Chen and Warren, 1989; Kifer and Wu, 1993; Kifer et al., 1995; Abiteboul and Kanellakis, 1998b; Guerrini et al., 1998].

Our discussion of the architectural issues is mostly based on [Özsu et al., 1994a] but largely extended. The object distribution design issues are discussed in significant more detail in [Ezeife and Barker, 1995], [Bellatreche et al., 2000a], and [Bellatreche et al., 2000b]. A formal model for distributed objects is given in [Abiteboul and dos Santos, 1995]. The query processing and optimization section is based on [Özsu and Blakeley, 1994] and the transaction management issues are from [Özsu, 1994]. Related work on indexing techniques for query optimization have been discussed in [Bertino et al., 1997; Kim and Lochovsky, 1989]. Several techniques for distributed garbage collection have been classified in a survey article by Plainfossé and Shapiro [1995]. These sources contain more detail than can be covered in one chapter. Object-relational DBMSs are discussed in detail in [Stonebraker and Brown, 1999] and [Date and Darwen, 1998].

Exercises

Problem 15.1. Explain the mechanisms used to support encapsulation in distributed object DBMSs. In particular:

(a) Describe how the encapsulation is hidden from the end users when both the objects and the methods are distributed.

(b) How does a distributed object DBMS present a single global schema to end users? How is this different from supporting fragmentation transparency in relational database systems?

Problem 15.2. List the new data distribution problems that arise in object DBMSs, that are not present in relational DBMSs, with respect to fragmentation, migration and replication.

Problem 15.3 (**). Partitioning of object databases has the premise of reducing the irrelevant data access for user applications. Develop a cost model to execute queries on unpartitioned object databases, and horizontally or vertically partitioned object databases. Use your cost model to illustrate the scenarios under which partitioning does in fact reduce the irrelevant data access.

Problem 15.4. Show the relationship between clustering and partitioning. Illustrate how clustering can deteriorate/improve the performance of queries on a partitioned object database system.

Problem 15.5. Why do client-server object DBMSs primarily employ data shipping architecture while relational DBMSs emply function shipping?

Problem 15.6. Discuss the strengths and weaknesses of page and object servers with respect to data transfer, buffer management, cache consistency, and pointer swizzling mechanims.

Problem 15.7. What is the difference between caching information at the clients and data replication?

Problem 15.8 (*). A new class of applications that object DBMSs support are interactive and deal with large objects (e.g., interactive multimedia systems). Which one of the cache consistency algorithms presented in this chapter are suitable for this class of applications operating across wide area networks?

Problem 15.9 (**). Hardware and software pointer swizzling mechanisms have complementary strengths and weaknesses. Propose a hybrid pointer swizzling mechanism that incorporates the strengths of both.

Problem 15.10 (**). Explain how derived horizontal fragmentation can be exploited to facilitate efficient path queries in distributed object DBMSs. Give examples.

Problem 15.11 (**). Give some heuristics that an object DBMS query optimizer that accepts OQL queries may use to determine how to decompose a query so that parts can be function shipped and other parts have to be executed at the originating client by data shipping.

Problem 15.12 (**). Three alternative ways of performing *distributed* complex object assembly are discussed in this chapter. Give an algorithm for the alternative where complex operations, such as joins and complete assembly of remote objects, are performed at remote sites and the partial results are shipped to the central site for final assembly.

Problem 15.13 (*). Consider the airline reservation example of Chapter 10. Define a Reservation class (type) and give the forward and backward commutativity matrixes for it.

Chapter 16
Peer-to-Peer Data Management

In this chapter, we discuss the data management issues in the "modern" peer-to-peer (P2P) data management systems. We intentionally use the phrase "modern" to differentiate these from the early P2P systems that were common prior to client/server computing. As indicated in Chapter 1, early work on distributed DBMSs had primarily focused on P2P architectures where there was no differentiation between the functionality of each site in the system. So, in one sense, P2P data management is quite old – if one simply interprets P2P to mean that there are no identifiable "servers" and "clients" in the system. However, the "modern" P2P systems go beyond this simple characterization and differ from the old systems that are referred to by the same name in a number of important ways, as mentioned in Chapter 1.

The first difference is the massive distribution in current systems. While the early systems focused on a few (perhaps at most tens of) sites, current systems consider thousands of sites. Furthermore, these sites are geographically very distributed, with possible clusters forming at certain locations.

The second is the inherent heterogeneity of every aspect of the sites and their autonomy. While this has always been a concern of distributed databases, coupled with massive distribution, site heterogeneity and autonomy take on added significance, disallowing some of the approaches from consideration.

The third major difference is the considerable volatility of these systems. Distributed DBMSs are well-controlled environments, where additions of new sites or the removal of existing sites is done very carefully and rarely. In modern P2P systems, the sites are (quite often) people's individual machines and they join and leave the P2P system at will, creating considerable hardship in the management of data.

In this chapter, we focus on this modern incarnation of P2P systems. In these systems, the following requirements are typically cited [Daswani et al., 2003]:

- **Autonomy.** An autonomous peer should be able to join or leave the system at any time without restriction. It should also be able to control the data it stores and which other peers can store its data (e.g., some other trusted peers).

- **Query expressiveness.** The query language should allow the user to describe the desired data at the appropriate level of detail. The simplest form of query

M.T. Özsu and P. Valduriez, *Principles of Distributed Database Systems: Third Edition*, DOI 10.1007/978-1-4419-8834-8_16, © Springer Science+Business Media, LLC 2011

is key look-up, which is only appropriate for finding files. Keyword search with ranking of results is appropriate for searching documents, but for more structured data, an SQL-like query language is necessary.

- **Efficiency.** The efficient use of the P2P system resources (bandwidth, computing power, storage) should result in lower cost, and, thus, higher throughput of queries, i.e., a higher number of queries can be processed by the P2P system in a given time interval.

- **Quality of service.** This refers to the user-perceived efficiency of the system, such as completeness of query results, data consistency, data availability, query response time, etc.

- **Fault-tolerance.** Efficiency and quality of service should be maintained despite the failures of peers. Given the dynamic nature of peers that may leave or fail at any time, it is important to properly exploit data replication.

- **Security.** The open nature of a P2P system gives rise to serious security challenges since one cannot rely on trusted servers. With respect to data management, the main security issue is access control which includes enforcing intellectual property rights on data contents.

A number of different uses of P2P systems have been developed [Valduriez and Pacitti, 2004]: they have been successfully used for sharing computation (e.g., SETI@home – http://www.setiathome.ssl.berkeley.edu), communication (e.g., ICQ – http://www.icq.com), or data sharing (e.g., Gnutella – http://www.gnutelliums.com – and Kazaa – http://www.kazaa.com). Our interest, naturally, is on data sharing systems. The commercial systems (such as Gnutella, Kazaa and others) are quite limited when viewed from the perspective of database functionality. Two important limitations are that they provide only file level sharing with no sophisticated content-based search/query facilities, and they are single-application systems that focus on performing one task, and it is not straightforward to extend them for other applications/functions [Ooi et al., 2003b]. In this chapter, we discuss the research activities towards providing proper database functionality over P2P infrastructures. Within this context, data management issues that must be addressed include the following:

- Data location: peers must be able to refer to and locate data stored in other peers.

- Query processing: given a query, the system must be able to discover the peers that contribute relevant data and efficiently execute the query.

- Data integration: when shared data sources in the system follow different schemas or representations, peers should still be able to access that data, ideally using the data representation used to model their own data.

- Data consistency: if data are replicated or cached in the system, a key issue is to maintain the consistency between these duplicates.

Figure 16.1 shows a reference architecture for a peer participating in a data sharing P2P system. Depending on the functionality of the P2P system, one or more

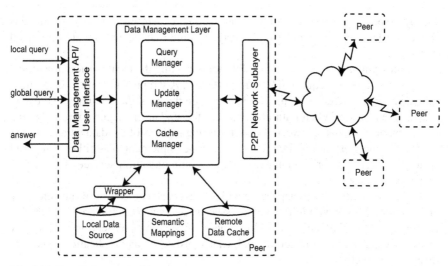

Fig. 16.1 Peer Reference Architecture

of the components in the reference architecture may not exist, may be combined together, or may be implemented by specialized peers. The key aspect of the proposed architecture is the separation of the functionality into three main components: (1) an interface used for submitting the queries; (2) a data management layer that handles query processing and metadata information (e.g., catalogue services); and (3) a P2P infrastructure, which is composed of the P2P network sublayer and P2P network. In this chapter, we focus on the P2P data management layer and P2P infrastructure.

Queries are submitted using a user interface or data management API and handled by the data management layer. Queries may refer to data stored locally or globally in the system. The query request is processed by a query manager module that retrieves semantic mapping information from a repository when the system integrates heterogeneous data sources. This semantic mapping repository contains meta-information that allows the query manager to identify peers in the system with data relevant to the query and to reformulate the original query in terms that other peers can understand. Some P2P systems may store the semantic mapping in specialized peers. In this case, the query manager will need to contact these specialized peers or transmit the query to them for execution. If all data sources in the system follow the same schema, neither the semantic mapping repository nor its associated query reformulation functionality are required.

Assuming a semantic mapping repository, the query manager invokes services implemented by the P2P network sublayer to communicate with the peers that will be involved in the execution of the query. The actual execution of the query is influenced by the implementation of the P2P infrastructure. In some systems, data are sent to the peer where the query was initiated and then combined at this peer. Other systems provide specialized peers for query execution and coordination. In either case, result data returned by the peers involved in the execution of the query may be cached locally to speed up future executions of similar queries. The cache manager maintains the local cache of each peer. Alternatively, caching may occur only at specialized peers.

The query manager is also responsible for executing the local portion of a global query when data are requested by a remote peer. A wrapper may hide data, query language, or any other incompatibilities between the local data source and the data management layer. When data are updated, the update manager coordinates the execution of the update between the peers storing replicas of the data being updated.

The P2P network infrastructure, which can be implemented as either structured or unstructured network topology, provides communication services to the data management layer.

In the remainder of this chapter, we will address each component of this reference architecture, starting with infrastructure issues in Section 16.1. The problems of data mapping and the approaches to address them are the topics of Section 16.2. Query processing is discussed in Section 16.3. Data consistency and replication issues are discussed in Section 16.4.

16.1 Infrastructure

The infrastructure of all P2P systems is a P2P network, which is built on top of a physical network (usually the Internet); thus it is commonly referred to as the *overlay network*. The overlay network may (and usually does) have a different topology than the physical network and all the algorithms focus on optimizing communication over the overlay network (usually in terms of minimizing the number of "hops" that a message needs to go through from a source node to a destination node – both in the overlay network). The possible disconnect between the overlay network and the physical network may be a problem in that two nodes that are neighbors in the overlay network may, in some cases, be considerably far apart in the physical network. Therefore, the cost of communication within the overlay network may not reflect the actual cost of communication in the physical network. We address this issue at the appropriate points during the infrastructure discussion.

Overlay networks can be of two general types: pure and hybrid. *Pure overlay networks* (more commonly referred to as *pure P2P networks*) are those where there is no differentiation between any of the network nodes – they are all equal. In *hybrid P2P networks*, on the other hand, some nodes are given special tasks to perform. Hybrid networks are commonly known as *super-peer systems*, since some of the peers are responsible for "controlling" a set of other peers in their domain. The pure networks can be further divided into structured and unstructured networks. *Structured networks* tightly control the topology and message routing, whereas in *unstructured networks* each node can directly communicate with its neighbors and can join the network by attaching themselves to any node.

16.1.1 Unstructured P2P Networks

Unstructured P2P networks refer to those with no restriction on data placement in the overlay topology. The overlay network is created in a nondeterministic (ad hoc) manner and the data placement is completely unrelated to the overlay topology. Each peer knows its neighbors, but does not know the resources that they have. Figure 16.2 shows an example unstructured P2P network.

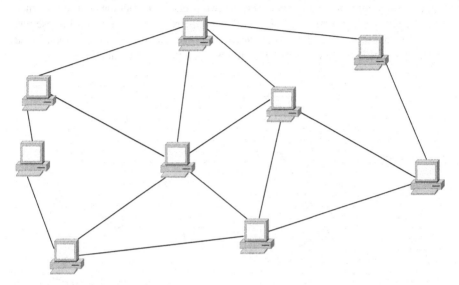

Fig. 16.2 Unstructured P2P Network

Unstructured networks are the earliest examples of P2P systems whose core functionality was (and remains) file sharing. In these systems replicated copies of popular files are shared among peers, without the need to download them from a centralized server. Examples of these systems are Napster (http://www.napster.com), Gnutella, Freenet [Clarke et al., 2000, 2002], Kazaa, and BitTorrent (http://www.bittorrent.com).

A fundamental issue in all P2P networks is the type of index to the resources that each peer holds, since this determines how resources are searched. Note that what is called "index management" in the context of P2P systems is very similar to catalog management that we studied in Chapter 3. Indexes are stored metadata that the system maintains. The exact content of the metadata differs in different P2P systems. In general, it includes, at a minimum, information on the resources and sizes.

There are two alternatives to maintaining indices: centralized, where one peer stores the metadata for the entire P2P system, and distributed, where each peer maintains metadata for resources that it holds. Again, the alternatives are identical to those for directory management. Napster is an example of a system that maintains a centralized index, while Gnutella maintains a distributed one.

The type of index supported by a P2P system (centralized or distributed) impacts how resources are searched. Note that we are not, at this point, referring to running queries; we are merely discussing how, given a resource identifier, the underlying P2P infrastructure can locate the relevant resource. In systems that maintain a centralized index, the process involves consulting the central peer to find the location of the resource, followed by directly contacting the peer where the resource is located (Figure 16.3). Thus, the system operates similar to a client/server one up to the point of obtaining the necessary index information (i.e., the metadata), but from that point on, the communication is only between the two peers. Note that the central peer may return a set of peers who hold the resource and the requesting peer may choose one among them, or the central peer may make the choice (taking into account loads and network conditions, perhaps) and return only a single recommended peer.

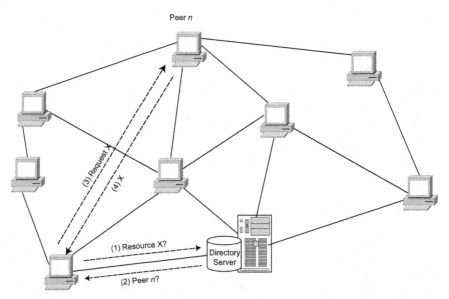

Fig. 16.3 Search over a Centralized Index. (1) A peer asks the central index manager for resource, (2) The response identifies the peer with the resource, (3) The peer is asked for the resource, (4) It is transferred.

In systems that maintain a distributed index, there are a number of search alternatives. The most popular one is flooding, where the peer looking for a resource sends the search request to all of its neighbors on the overlay network. If any of these neighbors have the resource, they respond; otherwise, each of them forwards the request to its neighbors until the resource is found or the overlay network is fully spanned (Figure 16.4).

Naturally, flooding puts very heavy demands on network resources and is not scalable – as the overlay network gets larger, more communication is initiated. This has been addressed by establishing a Time-to-Live (TTL) limit that restricts the

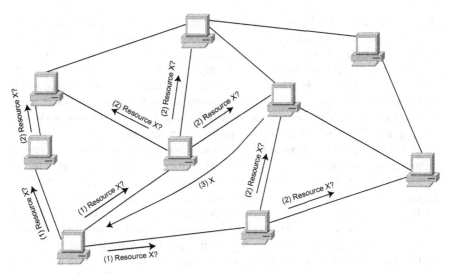

Fig. 16.4 Search over a Decentralized Index. (1) A peer sends the request for resource to all its neighbors, (2) Each neighbor propagates to its neighbors if it doesn't have the resource, (3) The peer who has the resource responds by sending the resource.

number of hops that a request message makes before it is dropped from the network. However, TTL also restricts the number of nodes that are reachable.

There have been other approaches to address this problem. A straightforward method is for each peer to choose a subset of its neighbors and forward the request only to those [Kalogeraki et al., 2002]. How this subset can be determined may vary. For example, the concept of random walks can be used [Lv et al., 2002] where each peer chooses a neighbor at random and propagates the request only to it. Alternatively, each neighbor can maintain not only indices for local resources, but also for resources that are on peers within a radius of itself and use the historical information about their performance in routing queries [Yang and Garcia-Molina, 2002]. Still another alternative is to use similar indices based on resources at each node to provide a list of neighbors that are most likely to be in the direction of the peer holding the requested resources [Crespo and Garcia-Molina, 2002]. These are referred to as routing indices and are used more commonly in structured networks, where we discuss them in more detail.

Another approach is to exploit *gossip protocols*, also known as *epidemic protocols* [Kermarrec and van Steen, 2007]. Gossiping has been initially proposed to maintain the mutual consistency of replicated data by spreading replica updates to all nodes over the network [Demers et al., 1987]. It has since been successfully used in P2P networks for data dissemination. Basic gossiping is simple. Each node in the network has a complete view of the network (i.e., a list of all nodes' addresses) and chooses a node at random to spread the request. The main advantage of gossiping is robustness over node failures since, with very high probability, the request is eventually propagated to all the nodes in the network. In large P2P networks, however, the basic gossiping model does not scale as maintaining the complete view of the network at each node would generate very heavy communication traffic. A solution to scalable gossiping is to maintain at each node only a partial view of the network, e.g., a list of tens of neighbour nodes [Voulgaris et al., 2003]. To gossip a request, a node chooses, at random, a node in its partial view and sends it the request. In addition, the nodes involved in a gossip exchange their partial views to reflect network changes in their own views. Thus, by continuously refreshing their partial views, nodes can self-organize into randomized overlays that scale up very well.

The final issue that we would like to discuss with respect to unstructured networks is how peers join and leave the network. The process is different for centralized versus distributed index approaches. In a centralized index system, a peer that wishes to join simply notifies the central index peer and informs it of the resources that it wishes to contribute to the P2P system. In the case of a distributed index, the joining peer needs to know one other peer in the system to which it "attaches" itself by notifying it and receiving information about its neighbors. At that point, the peer is part of the system and starts building its own neighbors. Peers that leave the system do not need to take any special action, they simply disappear. Their disappearance will be detected in time, and the overlay network will adjust itself.

16.1.2 Structured P2P Networks

Structured P2P networks have emerged to address the scalability issues faced by unstructured P2P networks [Ritter, 2001; Ratnasamy et al., 2001b; Stoica et al., 2001a]. They achieve this goal by tightly controlling the overlay topology and the placement of resources. Thus, they achieve higher scalability at the expense of lower autonomy as each peer that joins the network allows its resources to be placed on the network based on the particular control method that is used.

As with unstructured P2P networks, there are two fundamental issues to be addressed: how are the resources indexed, and how are they searched. The most popular indexing and data location mechanism that is used in structured P2P networks is *dynamic hash table* (DHT). DHT-based systems provide two API's: `put(key, data)` and `get(key)`, where key is an object identifier. The key is hashed to generate a peer id, which stores the data corresponding to object contents (Figure 16.5). Dynamic hashing has also been successfully used to address the scalability issues of very large distributed file structures [Devine, 1993; Litwin et al., 1993].

A straightforward approach could be to use the URI of the resource as the IP address of the peer that would hold the resource [Harvey et al., 2003]. However, one of the important design requirements is to provide a uniform distribution of resources over the overlay network and URIs/IP addresses do not provide sufficient flexibility. Consequently, *consistent hashing* techniques that provide uniform hashing of values are used to evenly place the data on the overlay. Although many hash functions may be employed for generating *virtual address mappings* for the resource, SHA-1 has

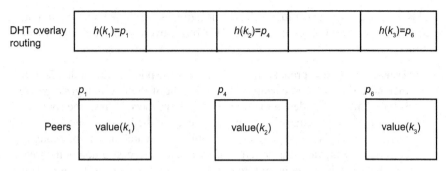

Fig. 16.5 DHT-based P2P Network

become the most widely accepted *base*[1] hash function that supports both uniformity as well as security (by supporting data-integrity for the keys). The actual design of the hash function may be implementation dependent and we won't discuss that issue any further.

Search (commonly called "lookup") over a DHT-based structured P2P network also involves the hash function: the key of the resource is hashed to get the id of the peer in the overlay network that is responsible for that key. The lookup is then initiated on the overlay network to locate the target node in question. This is referred to as the *routing protocol*, and it differs between different implementations and is closely associated with the overlay structure used. We will discuss one example approach shortly.

While all routing protocols aim to provide efficient lookups, they also try to minimize the *routing information* (also called *routing state*) that needs to be maintained in a routing table at each peer in the overlay. This information differs between various routing protocols and overlay structures, but it needs to provide sufficient directory-type information to route the put and get requests to the appropriate peer on the overlay. All routing table implementations require the use of maintenance algorithms in order to keep the routing state up-to-date and consistent. In contrast to routers on the Internet that also maintain routing databases, P2P systems pose a greater challenge since they are characterized by high node volatility and undependable network links. Since DHTs also need to support perfect recall (i.e., all the resources that are accessible through a given key have to be found), routing state consistency becomes a key challenge. Therefore, the maintenance of consistent routing state in the face of concurrent lookups and during periods of high network volatility is essential.

Many DHT-based overlays have been proposed. These can be categorized according to their *routing geometry* and *routing algorithm* [Gummadi et al., 2003]. Routing geometry essentially defines the manner in which neighbors and routes are arranged. The routing algorithm corresponds to the routing protocol discussed above

---

[1] A base hash function is defined as a function that is used as a basis for the design of another hash function.

and is defined as the manner in which next-hops/routes are chosen on a given routing geometry. The more important existing DHT-based overlays can be categorized as follows:

- **Tree.** In the tree approach, the leaf nodes correspond to the node identifiers that store the keys to be searched. The height of the tree is $\log(n)$, where n is the number of nodes in the tree. The search proceeds from the root to the leaves by doing a longest prefix match at each of the intermediate nodes until the target node is found. Therefore, in this case, matching can be thought of as correcting bit values from left-to-right at each successive hop in the tree. A popular DHT implementation that falls into this category is Tapestry [Zhao et al., 2004], which uses *surrogate routing* in order to forward requests at each node to the closest digit in the routing table. Surrogate routing is defined as routing to the *closest* digit when an exact match in the longest prefix cannot be found. In Tapestry, each unique identifier is associated with a node that is the root of a unique spanning tree used to route messages for the given identifier. Therefore, lookups proceed from the base of the spanning tree all the way to the root node of the identifier. Although this is somewhat different from traditional tree structures, Tapestry routing geometry is very closely associated to a tree structure and we classify it as such.

  In tree structures, a node in the system has 2^{i-1} nodes to choose from as its neighbor from the subtree with whom it has $\log(n-i)$ prefix bits in common. The number of potential neighbors increases exponentially as we proceed further up in the tree. Thus, in total there are $n^{\log(n)/2}$ possible routing tables per node (note, however that, only one such routing table can be selected for a node). Therefore, the tree geometry has good neighbor selection characteristics that would provide it with fault tolerance. However, routing can only be done through one neighboring node when sending to a particular destination. Consequently, the tree-structured DHTs do not provide any flexibility in the selection of routes.

- **Hypercube.** The hypercube routing geometry is based on d-dimensional Cartesian coordinate space that is partitioned into an individual set of zones such that each node maintains a separate zone of the coordinate space. An example of hypercube-based DHT is the Content Addressable Network (CAN) [Ratnasamy et al., 2001a]. The number of neighbors that a node may have in a d-dimensional coordinate space is $2d$ (for the sake of discussion, we consider $d = \log(n)$). If we consider each coordinate to represent a set of bits, then each node identifier can be represented as a bit string of length $\log(n)$. In this way, the hypercube geometry is very similar to the tree since it also simply *fixes* the bits at each hop to reach the destination. However, in the hypercube, since the bits of neighboring nodes only differ in *exactly* one bit, each forwarding node needs to modify only a single bit in the bit string, which can be done in any order. Thus, if we consider the correction of the bit string, the first correction can be applied to any $\log(n)$ nodes, the next correction can be applied to any $\log(n) - 1$ nodes, etc. Therefore, we have $\log(n)!$ possible routes between nodes which provides high route flexibility in the hypercube routing geometry. However, a node in the coordinate space does not have any choice over its neighbors' coordinates since adjacent coordinate zones in the coordinate space can't change. Therefore, hypercubes have poor neighbor selection flexibility.

- **Ring.** The ring geometry is represented as a one-dimensional circular identifier space where the nodes are placed at different locations on the circle. The distance between any two nodes on the circle is the numeric identifier difference (clockwise) around the circle. Since the circle is one-dimensional, the data identifiers can be represented as single decimal digits (represented as binary bit strings) that map to a node that is closest in the identifier space to the given decimal digit. Chord [Stoica et al., 2001b] is a popular example of the ring geometry. Specifically, in Chord, a node whose identifier is a maintains information about $\log(n)$ other neighbors on the ring where the ith neighbor is the node closest to $a + 2^{i-1}$ on the circle. Using these links (called *fingers*), Chord is able to route to any other node in $\log(n)$ hops.

  A careful analysis of Chord's structure reveals that a node does not necessarily need to maintain the node closest to $a + 2^{i-1}$ as its neighbor. In fact, it can still maintain the $\log(n)$ lookup upper bound if any node from the range $[(a + 2^{i-1}), (a + 2^i)]$ is chosen. Therefore, in terms of route flexibility, it is able to select between $n^{\log(n)/2}$ routing tables for each node. This provides a great deal of neighbor selection flexibility. Moreover, for routing to any node, the first hop has $\log(n)$ neighbors that can route the search to the destination and the next node has $\log(n) - 1$ nodes, and so on. Therefore, there are typically $\log(n)!$ possible routes to the destination. Consequently, ring geometry also provides good route selection flexibility.

In addition to these most popular geometries, there have been many other DHT-based structured overlays that have been proposed that use different topologies. Some of these are Viceroy [Malkhi et al., 2002], Kademlia [Maymounkov and Mazières, 2002], and Pastry [Rowstron and Druschel, 2001].

DHT-based overlays are efficient in that they guarantee finding the node on which to place or find the data in $\log(n)$ hops where n is the number of nodes in the system. However, they have a number of problems, in particular when viewed from the data management perspective. One of the issues with DHTs that employ consistent hashing functions for better distribution of resources is that two peers that are "neighbors" in the overlay network because of the proximity of their hash values may be geographically quite apart in the actual network. Thus, communicating with a neighbor in the overlay network may incur high transmission delays in the actual network. There have been studies to overcome this difficulty by designing *proximity-aware* or *locality-aware* hash functions. Another difficulty is that they do not provide any flexibility in the placement of data – a data item has to be placed on the node that is determined by the hash function. Thus, if there are P2P nodes that contribute their own data, they need to be willing to have data moved to other nodes. This is problematic from the perspective of node autonomy. The third difficulty is in that it is hard to run range queries over DHT-based architectures since, as is well-known, it is hard to run range queries over hash indices. There have been studies to overcome this difficulty that we discuss later.

These concerns have caused the development of structured overlays that do not use DHT for routing. In these systems, peers are mapped into the data space rather than the hash key space. There are multiple ways to partition the data space among multiple peers.

- **Hierarchical structure.** Many systems employ hierarchical overlay structures, including trie, balanced trees, randomized balance trees (e.g., skip list [Pugh, 1989]), and others. Specifically PHT [Ramabhadran et al., 2004] and P-Grid [Aberer, 2001; Aberer et al., 2003a] employ a binary trie structure, where peers whose data share common prefixes cluster under common branches. Balanced trees are also widely used due to their guaranteed routing efficiency (the expected "hop length" between arbitrary peers is proportional to the tree height). For instance, BATON [Jagadish et al., 2005], VBI-tree [Jagadish et al., 2005], and BATON* [Jagadish et al., 2006] employ k-way balanced tree structure to manage peers, and data are evenly partitioned among peers at the leaf-level. In comparison, P-Tree [Crainiceanu et al., 2004] uses a B-tree structure with better flexibility on tree structural changes. SkipNet [Harvey et al., 2003] and Skip Graph [Aspnes and Shah, 2003] are based on the skip list, and they link peers according to a randomized balanced tree structure where the node order is determined by each node's data values.

- **Space-filling curve.** This architecture is usually used to linearize sort data in multi-dimensional data space. Peers are arranged along the space-filling curve (e.g., Hilbert curve) so that sorted traversal of peers according to data order is possible [Schmidt and Parashar, 2004].

- **Hyper-rectangle structure.** In these systems, each dimension of the hyper-rectangle corresponds to one attribute of the data according to which an organization is desired. Peers are distributed in the data space either uniformly or based on data locality (e.g., through data intersection relationship). The hyper-rectangle space is then partitioned by peers based on their geometric positions in the space, and neighboring peers are interconnected to form the overlay network [Ganesan et al., 2004].

16.1.3 Super-peer P2P Networks

Super-peer P2P systems are hybrid between pure P2P systems and the traditional client-server architectures. They are similar to client-server architectures in that not all peers are equal; some peers (called *super-peers*) act as dedicated serves for some other peers and can perform complex functions such as indexing, query processing, access control, and meta-data management. If there is only one super-peer in the system, then this reduces to the client-server architecture. They are considered P2P systems, however, since the organization of the super-peers follow P2P organization, and super-peers can communicate with each other in sophisticated ways. Thus, unlike client-server systems, global information is not necessarily centralized and can be partitioned or replicated across super-peers.

In a super-peer network, a requesting peer sends the request, which can be expressed in a high-level language, to its responsible super-peer. The super-peer can then find the relevant peers either directly through its index or indirectly using its neighbor super-peers. More precisely, the search for a resource proceeds as follows (see Figure 16.6):

1. A peer, say Peer 1, asks for a resource by sending a request to its super-peer.

2. If the resource exists at one of the peers controlled by this super-peer, it notifies Peer 1, and the two peers then communicate to retrieve the resource. Otherwise, the super-peer sends the request to the other super-peers.

3. If the resource does not exist at one of the peers controlled by this super-peer, the super-peer asks the other super-peers. The super-peer of the node that contains the resource (say Peer n) responds to the requesting super-peer.

4. Peer n's identity is sent to Peer 1, after which the two peers can communicate directly to retrieve the resource.

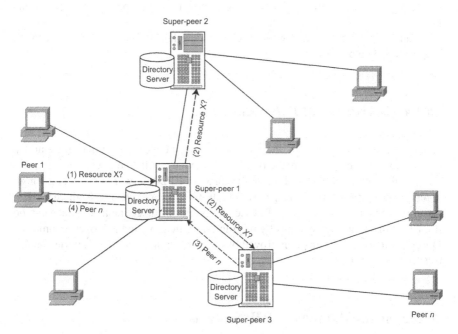

Fig. 16.6 Search over a Super-peer System. (1) A peer sends the request for resource to all its super-peer, (2) The super-peer sends the request to other super-peers if necessary, (3) The super-peer one of whose peers has the resource responds by indicating that peer, (4) The super-peer notifies the original peer.

Requirements	Unstructured	Structured	Super-peer
Autonomy	Low	Low	Moderate
Query expressiveness	High	Low	High
Efficiency	Low	High	High
QoS	Low	High	High
Fault-tolerance	High	High	Low
Security	Low	Low	High

Fig. 16.7 Comparison of Approaches.

The main advantages of super-peer networks are efficiency and quality of service (e.g., completeness of query results, query response time, etc.). The time needed to find data by directly accessing indices in a super-peer is very small compared with flooding. In addition, super-peer networks exploit and take advantage of peers' different capabilities in terms of CPU power, bandwidth, or storage capacity as super-peers take on a large portion of the entire network load. Access control can also be better enforced since directory and security information can be maintained at the super-peers. However, autonomy is restricted since peers cannot log in freely to any super-peer. Fault-tolerance is typically lower since super-peers are single points of failure for their sub-peers (dynamic replacement of super-peers can alleviate this problem).

Examples of super-peer networks include Edutella [Nejdl et al., 2003] and JXTA (http://www.jxta.org).

16.1.4 Comparison of P2P Networks

Figure 16.7 summarizes how the requirements for data management (autonomy, query expressiveness, efficiency, quality of service, fault-tolerance, and security) are possibly attained by the three main classes of P2P networks. This is a rough comparison to understand the respective merits of each class. Obviously, there is room for improvement in each class of P2P networks. For instance, fault-tolerance can be improved in super-peer systems by relying on replication and fail-over techniques. Query expressiveness can be improved by supporting more complex queries on top of structured networks.

16.2 Schema Mapping in P2P Systems

We discussed the importance of, and the techniques for, designing database integration systems in Chapter 4. Similar issues arise in data sharing P2P systems.

Due to specific characteristics of P2P systems, e.g., the dynamic and autonomous nature of peers, the approaches that rely on centralized global schemas no longer apply. The main problem is to support decentralized schema mapping so that a query expressed on one peer's schema can be reformulated to a query on another peer's schema. The approaches which are used by P2P systems for defining and creating the mappings between peers' schemas can be classified as follows: pairwise schema mapping, mapping based on machine learning techniques, common agreement mapping, and schema mapping using information retrieval (IR) techniques.

16.2.1 Pairwise Schema Mapping

In this approach, each user defines the mapping between the local schema and the schema of any other peer that contains data that are of interest. Relying on the transitivity of the defined mappings, the system tries to extract mappings between schemas that have no defined mapping.

Piazza [Tatarinov et al., 2003] follows this approach (see Figure 16.8). The data are shared as XML documents, and each peer has a schema that defines the terminology and the structural constraints of the peer. When a new peer (with a new schema) joins the system for the first time, it maps its schema to the schema of some other peers in the system. Each mapping definition begins with an XML template that matches some path or subtree of an instance of the target schema. Elements in the template may be annotated with query expressions that bind variables to XML nodes in the source. Active XML [Abiteboul et al., 2002, 2008b] also relies on XML documents for data sharing. The main innovation is that XML documents are active in the sense that they can include Web service calls. Therefore, data and queries can be seamlessly integrated. We discuss this further in Chapter 17.

The Local Relational Model (LRM) [Bernstein et al., 2002] is another example that follows this approach. LRM assumes that the peers hold relational databases, and each peer knows a set of peers with which it can exchange data and services. This set of peers is called peer's *acquaintances*. Each peer must define semantic dependencies and translation rules between its data and the data shared by each of its acquaintances. The defined mappings form a semantic network, which is used for query reformulation in the P2P system. Hyperion [Kementsietsidis et al., 2003] generalizes this approach to deal with autonomous peers that form acquaintances at run-time, using mapping tables to define value correspondences among heterogeneous databases. Peers perform local querying and update processing, and also propagate queries and updates to their acquainted peers.

PGrid [Aberer et al., 2003b] also assumes the existence of pairwise mappings between peers, initially constructed by skilled experts. Relying on the transitivity of these mappings and using a gossip algorithm, PGrid extracts new mappings that relate the schemas of the peers between which there is no predefined schema mapping.

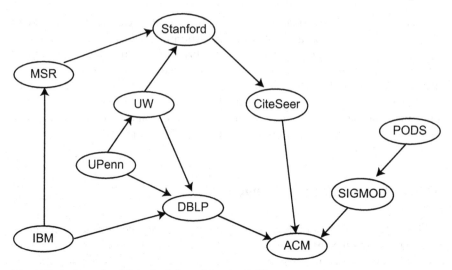

Fig. 16.8 An Example of Pairwise Schema Mapping in Piazza

16.2.2 Mapping based on Machine Learning Techniques

This approach is generally used when the shared data are defined based on ontologies and taxonomies as proposed for the semantic web. It uses machine learning techniques to automatically extract the mappings between the shared schemas. The extracted mappings are stored over the network, in order to be used for processing future queries. GLUE [Doan et al., 2003b] uses this approach. Given two ontologies, for each concept in one, GLUE finds the most similar concept in the other. It gives well founded probabilistic definitions to several practical similarity measures, and uses multiple learning strategies, each of which exploits a different type of information either in the data instances or in the taxonomic structure of the ontologies. To further improve mapping accuracy, GLUE incorporates commonsense knowledge and domain constraints into the schema mapping process. The basic idea is to provide classifiers for the concepts. To decide the similarity between two concepts A and B, the data of concept B are classified using A's classifier and vice versa. The amount of values that can be successfully classified into A and B represent the similarity between A and B.

16.2.3 Common Agreement Mapping

In this approach, the peers that have a common interest agree on a common schema description for data sharing. The common schema is usually prepared and maintained by expert users. APPA [Akbarinia et al., 2006a; Akbarinia and Martins, 2007] makes the assumption that peers wishing to cooperate, e.g., for the duration of an experiment, agree on a Common Schema Description (CSD). Given a CSD, a peer schema can be specified using views. This is similar to the LAV approach in data integration systems, except that queries at a peer are expressed in terms of the local views, not the CSD. Another difference between this approach and LAV is that the CSD is not a global schema, i.e., it is common to a limited set of peers with a common interest (see Figure 16.9). Thus, the CSD does not pose scalability challenges. When a peer decides to share data, it needs to map its local schema to the CSD.

Example 16.1. Given two CSD relation definitions r_1 and r_2, an example of peer mapping at peer p is:

$$p : r(A,B,D) \subseteq csd : r_1(A,B,C), csd : r_2(C,D,E)$$

In this example, the relation $r(A,B,D)$ that is shared by peer p is mapped to relations $r_1(A,B,C)$, $r_2(C,D,E)$ both of which are involved in the CSD. In APPA, the mappings between the CSD and each peer's local schema are stored locally at the peer. Given a query Q on the local schema, the peer reformulates Q to a query on the CSD using locally stored mappings.   ◆

AutoMed [McBrien and Poulovassilis, 2003] is another system that relies on common agreements for schema mapping. It defines the mappings by using primitive bidirectional transformations defined in terms of a low-level data model.

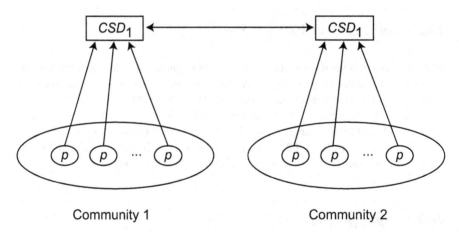

Fig. 16.9 Common Agreement Schema Mapping in APPA

16.2.4 Schema Mapping using IR Techniques

This approach extracts the schema mappings at query execution time using IR techniques by exploring the schema descriptions provided by users. PeerDB [Ooi et al., 2003a] follows this approach for query processing in unstructured P2P networks. For each relation that is shared by a peer, the description of the relation and its attributes is maintained at that peer. The descriptions are provided by users upon creation of relations, and serve as a kind of synonymous names of relation names and attributes. When a query is issued, a request to find out potential matches is produced and flooded to the peers that return the corresponding metadata. By matching keywords from the metadata of the relations, PeerDB is able to find relations that are potentially similar to the query relations. The relations that are found are presented to the issuer of the query who decides whether or not to proceed with the execution of the query at the remote peer that owns the relations.

Edutella [Nejdl et al., 2003] also follows this approach for schema mapping in super-peer networks. Resources in Edutella are described using the RDF metadata model, and the descriptions are stored at super-peers. When a user issues a query at a peer p, the query is sent to p's super-peer where the stored schema descriptions are explored and the addresses of the relevant peers are returned to the user. If the super-peer does not find relevant peers, it sends the query to other super-peers such that they search relevant peers by exploring their stored schema descriptions. In order to explore stored schemas, super-peers use the RDF-QEL query language, which is based on Datalog semantics and thus compatible with all existing query languages, supporting query functionalities that extend the usual relational query languages.

16.3 Querying Over P2P Systems

P2P networks provide basic techniques for routing queries to relevant peers and this is sufficient for supporting simple, exact-match queries. For instance, as noted earlier, a DHT provides a basic mechanism to efficiently look up data based on a key value. However, supporting more complex queries in P2P systems, particularly in DHTs, is difficult and has been the subject of much recent research. The main types of complex queries which are useful in P2P systems are top-k queries, join queries, and range queries. In this section, we discuss the techniques for processing them.

16.3.1 Top-k Queries

Top-k queries have been used in many domains such as network and system monitoring, information retrieval, and multimedia databases [Ilyas et al., 2008]. With a top-k query, the user requests k most relevant answers to be returned by the system. The degree of relevance (score) of the answers to the query is determined by a scoring function. Top-k queries are very useful for data management in P2P systems, in particular when the number of all the answers is very large [Akbarinia et al., 2006b].

Example 16.2. Consider a P2P system with medical doctors who want to share some (restricted) patient data for an epidemiological study. Assume that all doctors agreed on a common Patient description in relational format. Then, one doctor may want to submit the following query to obtain the top 10 answers ranked by a scoring function over height and weight:

```
SELECT      *
FROM        Patient P
WHERE       P.disease = ''diabetes''
AND         P.height < 170
AND         P.weight > 160
ORDER BY    scoring-function(height,weight)
STOP AFTER 10
```

The scoring function specifies how closely each data item matches the conditions. For instance, in the query above, the scoring function could compute the ten most overweight people. ◆

Efficient execution of top-k queries in large-scale P2P systems is difficult. In this section, we first discuss the most efficient techniques proposed for top-k query processing in distributed systems. Then, we present the techniques proposed for P2P systems.

16.3.1.1 Basic Techniques

An efficient algorithm for top-k query processing in centralized and distributed systems is the Threshold Algorithm (TA) [Nepal and Ramakrishna, 1999; Güntzer et al., 2000; Fagin et al., 2003]. TA is applicable for queries where the scoring function is monotonic, i.e., any increase in the value of the input does not decrease the value of the output. Many of the popular aggregation functions such as Min, Max, and Average are monotonic. TA has been the basis for several algorithms, and we discuss these in this section.

Threshold Algorithm (TA).

TA assumes a model based on lists of data items sorted by their local scores [Fagin, 1999]. The model is as follows. Suppose we have m lists of n data items such that each data item has a local score in each list and the lists are sorted according to the local scores of their data items. Furthermore, each data item has an overall score that is computed based on its local scores in all lists using a given scoring function. For example, consider the database (i.e., three sorted lists) in Figure 16.10. Assuming the scoring function computes the sum of the local scores of the same data item in all lists, the overall score of item d_1 is $30 + 21 + 14 = 65$.

Then the problem of top-k query processing is to find the k data items whose overall scores are the highest. This problem model is simple and general. Suppose we want to find the top-k tuples in a relational table according to some scoring function over its attributes. To answer this query, it is sufficient to have a sorted (indexed) list of the values of each attribute involved in the scoring function, and return the k tuples whose overall scores in the lists are the highest. As another example, suppose we want to find the top-k documents whose aggregate rank is the highest with respect to some given set of keywords. To answer this query, the solution is to have, for each keyword, a ranked list of documents, and return the k documents whose aggregate rank over all lists are the highest.

TA considers two modes of access to a sorted list. The first mode is sorted (or sequential) access that accesses each data item in their order of appearance in the list. The second mode is random access by which a given data item in the list is directly looked up, for example, by using an index on item id.

Given the m sorted lists of n data items, TA (see Algorithm 16.1), goes down the sorted lists in parallel, and, for each data item, retrieves its local scores in all lists through random access and computes the overall score. It also maintains in a set Y the k data items whose overall scores are the highest so far. The stopping mechanism of TA uses a threshold that is computed using the last local scores seen under sorted access in the lists. For example, consider the database in Figure 16.10. At position 1 for all lists (i.e., when only the first data items have been seen under sorted access) assuming that the scoring function is the sum of the scores, the threshold is $30 + 28 + 30 = 88$. At position 2, it is 84. Since data items are sorted in the lists in decreasing order of local score, the threshold decreases as one moves down the list. This process continues until k data items are found whose overall scores are greater than a threshold.

Example 16.3. Consider again the database (i.e., three sorted lists) shown in Figure 16.10. Assume a top-3 query Q (i.e., $k = 3$), and suppose the scoring function computes the sum of the local scores of the data item in all lists. TA first looks at the data items which are at position 1 in all lists, i.e., d_1, d_2, and d_3. It looks up the local scores of these data items in other lists using random access and computes their overall scores (which are 65, 63 and 70, respectively). However, none of them has an overall score that is as high as the threshold of position 1 (which is 88). Thus, at position 1, TA does not stop. At this position, we have $Y = \{d_1, d_2, d_3\}$, i.e., the k highest scored data items seen so far. At positions 2 and 3, Y is set to $\{d_3, d_4, d_5\}$ and $\{d_3, d_5, d_8\}$ respectively. Before position 6, none of the data items involved in Y has an overall score higher than or equal to the threshold value. At position 6, the threshold value is 63, which is less than the overall score of the three data items involved in Y, i.e., $Y = \{d_3, d_5, d_8\}$. Thus, TA stops. Note that the contents of Y at position 6 is exactly the same as at position 3. In other words, at position 3, Y already contains all top-k answers. In this example, TA does three additional sorted accesses in each list that do not contribute to the final result. This is a characteristic of TA algorithm in that it has a conservative stopping condition that causes it to stop later than necessary – in this example, it performs 9 sorted accesses and $18 = (9 * 2)$ random accesses that do not contribute to the final result. ♦

Algorithm 16.1: Threshold Algorithm (TA)

Input: $L_1, L_2, \ldots, L_m$: m sorted lists of n data items ;
f: scoring function
Output: Y: list of top-k data items
begin

    $j \leftarrow 1$;
    threshold $\leftarrow 1$;
    min_overall_score $\leftarrow 0$;
    while $j \neq n+1$ *and min_overall_score* $<$ *threshold* **do**
        {Do sorted access in parallel to each of the m sorted lists}
        for i *from* 1 *to* m *in parallel* **do**
            {Process each data item at position j}
            for *each data item* d *at position* j *in* L_i **do**
                {access the local scores of d in the other lists through random access}
                overall_score$(d) \leftarrow f$(scores of d in each L_i)
        $Y \leftarrow k$ data items with highest score so far ;
        min_overall_score $\leftarrow$ smallest overall score of data items in Y ;
        threshold $\leftarrow f$(local scores at position j in each L_i) ;
        $j \leftarrow j+1$

end

TA-Style Algorithms.

Several TA-style algorithms, i.e., extensions of TA, have been proposed for distributed top-k query processing. We illustrate these by means of the Three Phase Uniform Threshold (TPUT) algorithm that executes top-k queries in three round trips [Cao and Wang, 2004], assuming that each list is held by one node (which we call the *list holder*) and that the scoring function is sum. The TPUT algorithm (see Algorithm 16.2 executed by the query originator) works as follows.

1. The query originator first gets from each list holder its k top data items. Let f be the scoring function, d be a received data item, and $s_i(d)$ be the local score of d in list L_i. Then the partial sum of d is defined as $psum(d) = \sum_{i=1}^{m} s_i'(d)$ where $s_i'(d) = s_i(d)$ if d has been sent to the coordinator by the holder of L_i, else $s_i'(d) = 0$. The query originator computes the partial sums for all received data items and identifies the items with the k highest partial sums. The partial sum of the k−th data item (called *phase-1 bottom*) is denoted by λ_1.

2. The query originator sends a threshold value $\tau = \lambda_1/m$ to every list holder. In response, each list holder sends back all its data items whose local scores are not less than τ. The intuition is that if a data item is not reported by any node in this phase, its score must be less than λ_1, so it cannot be one of the

Position	List 1		List 2		List 3	
	Data Item	Local score S_1	Data Item	Local score S_2	Data Item	Local score S_3
1	d_1	30	d_2	28	d_3	30
2	d_4	28	d_6	27	d_5	29
3	d_9	27	d_7	25	d_8	28
4	d_3	26	d_5	24	d_4	25
5	d_7	25	d_9	23	d_2	24
6	d_8	23	d_1	21	d_6	19
7	d_5	17	d_8	20	d_{13}	15
8	d_6	14	d_3	14	d_1	14
9	d_2	11	d_4	13	d_9	12
10	d_{11}	10	d_{14}	12	d_7	11
...	...	...	...	...	...	...

Fig. 16.10 Example database with 3 sorted lists

top-k data items. Let Y be the set of data items received from list holders. The query originator computes the new partial sums for the data items in Y, and identifies the items with the k highest partial sums. The partial sum of the k-th data item (called phase-2 bottom) is denoted by λ_2. Let the upper bound score of a data item d be defined as $u(d) = \sum_{i=1}^{m} u_i(d)$ where $u_i(d) = s_i(d)$ if d has been received, else $u_i(d) = \tau$. For each data item $d \in D$, if $u(d)$ is less than λ_2, it is removed from Y. The data items that remain in Y are called top-k candidates because there may be some data items in Y that have not been obtained from all list holders. A third phase is necessary to retrieve those.

3. The query originator sends the set of top-k candidate data items to each list holder that returns their scores. Then, it computes the overall score, extracts the k data items with highest scores, and returns the answer to the user.

Example 16.4. Consider the first two sorted lists (List 1 and List 2) in Figure 16.10. Assume a top-2 query Q, i.e., $k = 2$, where the scoring function is sum. Phase 1 produces the sets $Y = \{d_1, d_2, d_4, d_6\}$ and $Z = \{d_1, d_2\}$. Thus we get $\lambda_1/2 = 28/2 = 14$. Let us now denote each data item d in Y as $(d, scoreinList1, scoreinList2)$. Phase 2 produces $Y = \{(d_1, 30, 21), (d_2, 0, 28), (d_3, 26, 14), (d_4, 28, 0), (d_5, 17, 24), (d_6, 14, 27), (d_7, 25, 25), (d_8, 23, 20), (d_9, 27, 23)\}$ and $Z = \{(d_1, 30, 21), (d_7, 25, 25)\}$. Note that d_9 could also have been picked instead of d_7 because it has same partial sum. Thus we get $\lambda_2/2=50$. The upper bound scores of the data items in Y are obtained as:

$$u(d_1) = 30 + 21 = 51$$
$$u(d_2) = 14 + 28 = 42$$
$$u(d_3) = 26 + 14 = 40$$

Algorithm 16.2: Three Phase Uniform Threshold(TPUT)

Input: $L_1, L_2, \ldots, L_m$: m sorted lists of n data items, each at a different list holder;

f: scoring function

Output: Y: list of top-k data items

begin

    {Phase 1}

    for i *from* 1 *to* m *in parallel* **do**

        $Y \leftarrow$ receive top-k data items from L_i holder

    $Z \leftarrow$ data items with the k highest partial sum in Y ;

    $\lambda_1 \leftarrow$ partial sum of k-th data item in Z ;

    {Phase 2}

    for i *from* 1 *to* m *in parallel* **do**

        send λ_1/m to L_i's holder ;

        $Y \leftarrow$ all data items from L_i's holder whose local scores are not less than λ_1/m

    $Z \leftarrow$ data items with the k highest partial sum in Y ;

    $\lambda_2 \leftarrow$ partial sum of k-th data item in Z ;

    $Y \leftarrow Y - \{$data items in Y whose upper bound score is less than $\lambda_2\}$;

    {Phase 3}

    for i *from* 1 *to* m *in parallel* **do**

        send Y to L_i holder ;

        $Z \leftarrow$ data items from L_i's holder that are in both Y and L_i

    $Y \leftarrow k$ data items with highest overall score in Z

end

$$u(d_4) = 28 + 14 = 42$$
$$u(d_5) = 17 + 24 = 41$$
$$u(d_6) = 14 + 27 = 41$$
$$u(d_7) = 25 + 25 = 50$$
$$u(d_8) = 23 + 20 = 43$$
$$u(d_9) = 27 + 23 = 50$$

After removal of the data items in Y whose upper bound score is less than λ_2, we have $Y = \{d_1, d_7, d_9\}$. The third phase is not necessary in this case as all data items have all their local scores. Thus the final result is $Y = \{d_1, d_7\}$ or $Y = \{d_1, d_9\}$. ♦

When the number of lists (i.e., m) is high, the response time of TPUT is much better than that of the basic TA algorithm [Cao and Wang, 2004].

Best Position Algorithm (BPA).

There are many database instances over which TA keeps scanning the lists although it has seen all top-k answers (as in Example 16.3). Thus, it is possible to stop much sooner. Based on this observation, best position algorithms (BPA) that execute top-k queries much more efficiently than TA have been proposed [Akbarinia et al., 2007a]. The key idea of BPA is that the stopping mechanism takes into account special seen positions in the lists, called the *best positions*. Intuitively, the best position in a list is the highest position such that any position before it has also been seen. The stopping condition is based on the overall score computed using the best positions in all lists.

The basic version of BPA (see Algorithm 16.3) works like TA, except that it keeps track of all positions that are seen under sorted or random access, computes best positions, and has a different stopping condition. For each list L_i, let P_i be the set of positions that are seen under sorted or random access in L_i. Let bp_i, the best position in L_i, be the highest position in P_i such that any position of L_i between 1 and bp_i is also in P_i. In other words, bp_i is best because we are sure that all positions of L_i between 1 and bpi have been seen under sorted or random access. Let $s_i(bp_i)$ be the local score of the data item that is at position bp_i in list L_i. Then, BPA's threshold is $f(s_1(bp_1), s_2(bp_2), \ldots, s_m(bp_m))$ for some function f.

Example 16.5. To illustrate basic BPA, consider again the three sorted lists shown in Figure 16.10 and the query Q in Example 16.3.

1. At position 1, BPA sees the data items d_1, d_2, and d_3. For each seen data item, it does random access and obtains its local score and position in all the lists. Therefore, at this step, the positions that are seen in list L_1 are positions 1, 4, and 9, which are respectively the positions of d_1, d_3 and d_2. Thus, we have $P_1 = \{1, 4, 9\}$ and the best position in L_1 is $bp_1 = 1$ (since the next position is 4 meaning that positions 2 and 3 have not been seen). For L_2 and L_3 we have $P_2 = \{1, 6, 8\}$ and $P_3 = \{1, 5, 8\}$, so $bp_2 = 1$ and $bp_3 = 1$. Therefore, the best positions overall score is $\lambda = f(s_1(1), s_2(1), s_3(1)) = 30 + 28 + 30 = 88$. At position 1, the set of the three highest scored data items is $Y = \{d_1, d_2, d_3\}$, and since the overall score of these data items is less than λ , BPA cannot stop.

2. At position 2, BPA sees d_4, d_5, and d_6. Thus, we have $P_1 = \{1, 2, 4, 7, 8, 9\}$, $P_2 = \{1, 2, 4, 6, 8, 9\}$ and $P_3 = \{1, 2, 4, 5, 6, 8\}$. Therefore, we have $bp_1 = 2$, $bp_2 = 2$ and $bp_3 = 2$, so $\lambda = f(s_1(2), s_2(2), s_3(2)) = 28 + 27 + 29 = 84$. The overall score of the data items involved in $Y = \{d_3, d_4, d_5\}$ is less than 84, so BPA does not stop.

3. At position 3, BPA sees d_7, d_8, and d_9. Thus, we have $P_1 = P_2 = \{1, 2, 3, 4, 5, 6, 7, 8, 9\}$, and $P_3 = \{1, 2, 3, 4, 5, 6, 7, 8, 10\}$. Thus, we have $bp_1 = 9$, $bp_2 = 9$ and $bp_3 = 8$. The best positions overall score is $\lambda = f(s_1(9), s_2(9), s_3(8)) = 11 + 13 + 14 = 38$. At this position, we have $Y = \{d_3, d_5, d_8\}$. Since the score of all data items involved in Y is higher than λ, BPA stops, i.e., exactly at the first position where BPA has all top-k answers.

Algorithm 16.3: Best Position Algorithm (BPA)

Input: $L_1, L_2, \ldots, L_m$: m sorted lists of n data items ;
f: scoring function
Output: Y: list of top-k data items
begin

     $j \leftarrow 1$;
     $threshold \leftarrow 1$;
     $min\_overall\_score \leftarrow 0$;
     for i *from* 1 *to* m *in parallel* **do**
        $P_i \leftarrow \emptyset$

     while $j \neq n+1$ *and* $min\_overall\_score < threshold$ **do**
        {Do sorted access in parallel to each of the m sorted lists}
        for i *from* 1 *to* m *in parallel* **do**
           {Process each data item at position j}
           for *each data item d at position j in L_i* **do**
              {access the local scores of d in the other lists through random access}
              $overall\_score(d) \leftarrow f(\text{scores of } d \text{ in each } L_i)$
           $P_i \leftarrow P_i \cup \{\text{positions seen under sorted or random access}\}$;
           $bp_i \leftarrow$ best position in L_i
        $Y \leftarrow k$ data items with highest score so far ;
        $min\_overall\_score \leftarrow$ smallest overall score of data items in Y ;
        $threshold \leftarrow f(\text{local scores at position } bp_i \text{ in each } L_i)$;
        $j \leftarrow j+1$

end

Recall that over this database, TA stops at position 6.   ◆

It has been proven that, for any set of sorted lists, BPA stops as early as TA, and its execution cost is never higher than TA [Akbarinia et al., 2007a]. It has also been shown that the execution cost of BPA can be $(m-1)$ times lower than that of TA. Although BPA is quite efficient, it still does redundant work. One of the redundancies with BPA (and also TA) is that it may access some data items several times under sorted access in different lists. For example, a data item that is accessed at a position in a list through sorted access and thus accessed in other lists via random access, may be accessed again in the other lists by sorted access at the next positions. An improved algorithm, BPA2 [Akbarinia et al., 2007a], avoids this and is therefore much more efficient than BPA. It does not transfer the seen positions from list owners to the query originator. Thus, the query originator does not need to maintain the seen positions and their local scores. It also accesses each position in a list at most once. The number of accesses to the lists done by BPA2 can be about $(m-1)$ times lower than that of BPA.

16.3.1.2 Top-k Queries in Unstructured Systems

One possible approach for processing top-k queries in unstructured systems is to route the query to all the peers, retrieve all available answers, score them using the scoring function, and return to the user the k highest scored answers. However, this approach is not efficient in terms of response time and communication cost.

The first efficient solution that has been proposed is that of PlanetP [Cuenca-Acuna et al., 2003], which is an unstructured P2P system. In PlanetP, a content-addressable publish/subscribe service replicates data across P2P communities of up to ten thousand peers. The top-k query processing algorithm works as follows. Given a query Q, the query originator computes a relevance ranking of peers with respect to Q, contacts them one by one in decreasing rank order and asks them to return a set of their top-scored data items together with their scores. To compute the relevance of peers, a global fully replicated index is used that contains term-to-peer mappings. This algorithm has very good performance in moderate-scale systems. However, in a large P2P system, keeping the replicated index up-to-date may hurt scalability.

We describe another solution that was developed within the context of APPA, which is a P2P network-independent data management system [Akbarinia et al., 2006a]. A fully distributed framework to execute top-k queries has been proposed that also addresses the volatility of peers during query execution, and deals with situations where some peers leave the system before finishing query processing. Given a top-k query Q with a specified TTL, the basic algorithm called Fully Decentralized Top-k (FD) proceeds as follows (see Algorithm 16.4).

1. **Query forward.** The query originator forwards Q to the accessible peers whose hop-distance from the query originator is less than TTL.

2. **Local query execution and wait.** Each peer p that receives Q executes it locally: it accesses the local data items that match the query predicate, scores them using a scoring function, selects the k top data items and saves them as well as their scores locally. Then p waits to receive its neighbors' results. However, since some of the neighbors may leave the P2P system and never send a score-list to p, the wait time has a limit that is computed for each peer based on the received TTL, network parameters and peer's local processing parameters.

3. **Merge-and-backward.** In this phase, the top scores are bubbled up to the query originator using a tree-based algorithm as follows. After its wait time has expired, p merges its k local top scores with those received from its neighbors and sends the result to its parent (the peer from which it received Q) in the form of a score-list. In order to minimize network traffic, FD does not bubble up the top data items (which could be large), only their scores and addresses. A score-list is simply a list of k pairs (a, s) where a is the address of the peer owning the data item and s its score.

4. **Data retrieval.** After receiving the score-lists from its neighbors, the query originator forms the final score-list by merging its k local top scores with the

merged score-lists received from its neighbors. Then it directly retrieves the k top data items from the peers that hold them.

Algorithm 16.4: Fully Decentralized Top-k (FD)

Input: Q: top-k query ;
f: scoring function;
TTL: time to live;
w: wait time
Output: Y: list of top-k data items
begin

    At query originator peer
    begin
        send Q to neighbors ;
        Final_score_list ← merge local score lists received from neighbors
        for *each peer p in Final_score_list* **do**
          ⌊ Y ← retrieve top-k data items in p
    end
    for *each peer that receives Q from a peer p* **do**
        $TTL \leftarrow TTL - 1$;
        if $TTL > 0$ **then**
          ⌊ send Q to neighbors
        Local_score_list ← extract top-k local scores;
        Wait a time w;
        Local_score_list ← *Local_score_list* ∪ top-k received scores;
        Send *Local_score_list* to p

end

The algorithm is completely distributed and does not depend on the existence of certain peers, and this makes it possible to address the volatility of peers during query execution. In particular, the following problems are addressed: peers becoming inaccessible in the merge-and-backward phase; peers that hold top data items becoming inaccessible in the data retrieval phase; late reception of score-lists by a peer after its wait time has expired. The performance evaluation of FD shows that it can achieve major performance gains in terms of communication cost and response time [Akbarinia et al., 2006b].

16.3.1.3 Top-k Queries in DHTs

As we discussed earlier, the main functionality of a DHT is to map a set of keys to the peers of the P2P system and lookup efficiently the peer that is responsible for a given key. This offers efficient and scalable support for exact-match queries.

However, supporting top-k queries on top of DHTs is not easy. A simple solution is to retrieve all tuples of the relations involved in the query, compute the score of each retrieved tuple, and finally return the k tuples whose scores are the highest. However, this solution cannot scale up to a large number of stored tuples. Another solution is to store all tuples of each relation using the same key (e.g., relation's name), so that all tuples are stored at the same peer. Then, top-k query processing can be performed at that central peer using well-known centralized algorithms. However, the peer becomes a bottleneck and a single point of failure.

A solution has been proposed as part of APPA project that is based on TA (see Section 16.3.1.1) and a mechanism that stores the shared data in the DHT in a fully distributed fashion [Akbarinia et al., 2007c]. In APPA, peers can store their tuples in the DHT using two complementary methods: tuple storage and attribute-value storage. With tuple storage, each tuple is stored in the DHT using its identifier (e.g., its primary key) as the storage key. This enables looking up a tuple by its identifier similar to a primary index. Attribute value storage individually stores in the DHT the attributes that may appear in a query's equality predicate or in a query's scoring function. Thus, as in secondary indices, it allows looking up the tuples using their attribute values. Attribute value storage has two important properties: (1) after retrieving an attribute value from the DHT, peers can retrieve easily the corresponding tuple of the attribute value; (2) attribute values that are relatively "close" are stored at the same peer. To provide the first property, the key, which is used for storing the entire tuple, is stored along with the attribute value. The second property is provided using the concept of domain partitioning as follows. Consider an attribute a and let D_a be its domain of values. Assume that there is a total order $<$ on D_a (e.g., D_a is numeric). D_a is partitioned into n non-empty sub-domains $d_1, d_2, \ldots, d_n$ such that their union is equal to D_a, the intersection of any two different sub-domains is empty, and for each $v_1 \in d_i$ and $v_2 \in d_j$, if $i < j$ then we have $v_1 < v_2$. The hash function is applied on the sub-domain of the attribute value. Thus, for the attribute values that fall in the same sub-domain, the storage key is the same and they are stored at the same peer. To avoid attribute storage skew (i.e., skewed distribution of attribute values within sub-domains), domain partitioning is done in such a way that attribute values are uniformly distributed in sub-domains. This technique uses histogram-based information that describes the distribution of values of the attribute.

Using this storage model, the top-k query processing algorithm, called DHTop (see Algorithm 16.5), works as follows. Let Q be a given top-k query, f be its scoring function, and p_0 be the peer at which Q is issued. For simplicity, let us assume that f is a monotonic scoring function. Let scoring attributes be the set of attributes that are passed to the scoring function as arguments. DHTop starts at p_0 and proceeds in two phases: first it prepares ordered lists of candidate sub-domains, and then it continuously retrieves candidate attribute values and their tuples until it finds k top tuples. The details of the two steps are as follows:

1. For each scoring attribute a, p_0 prepares the list of sub-domains and sorts them in descending order of their positive impact on the scoring function. For each list, p_0 removes from the list the sub-domains in which no member can

satisfy Q's conditions. For instance, if there is a condition that enforces the scoring attribute to be equal to a constant, (e.g., $a = 10$), then p_0 removes from the list all the sub-domains except the sub-domain to which the constant value belongs. Let us denote by L_a the list prepared in this phase for a scoring attribute a.

2. For each scoring attribute a, in parallel, p_0 proceeds as follows. It sends Q and a to the peer, say p, that is responsible for storing the values of the first sub-domain of L_a, and requests it to return the values of a at p. The values are returned to p_0 in order of their positive impact on the scoring function. After receiving each attribute value, p_0 retrieves its corresponding tuple, computes its score, and keeps it if the score is one of the k highest scores yet computed. This process continues until k tuples are obtained whose scores are higher than a threshold that is computed based on the attribute values retrieved so far. If the attribute values that p returns to p_0 are not sufficient for determining the k top tuples, p_0 sends Q and a to the site that is responsible for the second sub-domain of L_a and so on until k top tuples are found.

Let $a_1, a_2, \ldots, a_m$ be the scoring attributes and $v_1, v_2, \ldots, v_m$ be the last values retrieved respectively for each of them. The threshold is defined to be $\tau = f(v_1, v_2, \ldots, v_m)$. A main feature of DHTop is that after retrieving each new attribute value, the value of the threshold decreases. Thus, after retrieving a certain number of attribute values and their tuples, the threshold becomes less than k of the retrieved data items and the algorithm stops. It has been analytically proven that DHTop works correctly for monotonic scoring functions and also for a large group of non-monotonic functions.

16.3.1.4 Top-k Queries in Super-peer Systems

A typical algorithm for top-k query processing in super-peer systems is that of Edutella [Balke et al., 2005]. In Edutella, a small percentage of nodes are super-peers and are assumed to be highly available with very good computing capacity. The super-peers are responsible for top-k query processing and the other peers only execute the queries locally and score their resources. The algorithm is quite simple and works as follows. Given a query Q, the query originator sends Q to its super-peer, which then sends it to the other super-peers. The super-peers forward Q to the relevant peers connected to them. Each peer that has some data items relevant to Q scores them and sends its maximum scored data item to its super-peer. Each super-peer chooses the overall maximum scored item from all received data items. For determining the second best item, it only asks one peer, one that has returned the first top item, to return its second top scored item. The super-peer selects the overall second top item from the previously received items and the newly received item. Then, it asks the peer which has returned the second top item and so on until all k top items are retrieved. Finally the super-peers send their top items to the super-peer of the query originator, to extract the overall k top items, and send them to the query originator.

Algorithm 16.5: DHT Top-k (DHTop)

Input: Q: top-k query;

f: scoring function;

A: set of m attributes used in f

Output: Y: list of top-k tuples

begin

> {Phase 1: prepare lists of attributes' subdomains}
>
> **for** *each scoring attribute a in A* **do**
>
> > $L_a \leftarrow$ all sub-domains of a;
> >
> > $L_a \leftarrow L_a -$ sub-domains which do not satisfy Q's condition;
> >
> > Sort L_a in descending order of its sub-domains
>
> {Phase 2: continuously retrieve attribute values and their tuples until finding k top tuples}
>
> $Done \leftarrow$ false;
>
> **for** *each scoring attribute a in A in parallel* **do**
>
> > $i \leftarrow 1$
> >
> > **while** *(i < number of sub-domains of a) and not Done* **do**
> >
> > > send Q to peer p that maintains the attribute values of sub-domain i in L_a;
> > >
> > > $Z \leftarrow a$ values (in descending order) from p that satisfy Q's condition, along with their corresponding data storage keys ;
> > >
> > > **for** *each received value v* **do**
> > >
> > > > get the tuple of v;
> > > >
> > > > $Y \leftarrow k$ tuples with highest score so far;
> > > >
> > > > *threshold* $\leftarrow f(v_1, v_2, \ldots, v_m)$ such that v_i is the last value received for attribute a_i in A;
> > > >
> > > > *min_overall_score* $\leftarrow$ smallest overall score of tuples in Y;
> > > >
> > > > **if** *min_overall_score* $\leq$ *threshold* **then**
> > > >
> > > > > $Done \leftarrow$ true
> > > >
> > > > $i \leftarrow i + 1$

end

This algorithm minimizes communication between peers and super-peers since, after having received the maximum scored data items from each peer connected to it, each super-peer asks only one peer for the next top item.

16.3.2 Join Queries

The most efficient join algorithms in distributed and parallel databases are hash-based. Thus, the fact that a DHT relies on hashing to store and locate data can be naturally exploited to support join queries efficiently. A basic solution has been proposed in the context of the PIER P2P system [Huebsch et al., 2003] that provides support for complex queries on top of DHTs. The solution is a variation of the parallel hash join algorithm (PHJ) (see Section 14.3.2) which we call PIERjoin. As in the PHJ algorithm, PIERjoin assumes that the joined relations and the result relations have a home (called *namespace* in PIER), which are the nodes that store horizontal fragments of the relation. Then it makes use of the put method for distributing tuples onto a set of peers based on their join attribute so that tuples with the same join attribute values are stored at the same peers. To perform joins locally, PIER implements a version of the symmetric hash join algorithm [Wilschut and Apers, 1991] that provides efficient support for pipelined parallelism. In symmetric hash join, with two joining relations, each node that receives tuples to be joined maintains two hash tables, one per relation. Thus, upon receiving a new tuple from either relation, the node adds the tuple into the corresponding hash table and probes it against the opposite hash table based on the tuples received so far. PIER also relies on the DHT to deal with the dynamic behavior of peers (joining or leaving the network during query execution) and thus does not give guarantees on result completeness.

For a binary join query Q (which may include select predicates), PIERjoin works in three phases (see Algorithm 16.6): multicast, hash and probe/join.

1. **Multicast phase.** The query originator peer multicasts Q to all peers that store tuples of the join relations R and S, i.e., their homes.

2. **Hash phase.** Each peer that receives Q scans its local relation, searching for the tuples that satisfy the select predicate (if any). Then, it sends the selected tuples to the home of the result relation, using put operations. The DHT key used in the put operation is calculated using the home of the result relation and the join attribute.

3. **Probe/join phase.** Each peer in the home of the result relation, upon receiving a new tuple, inserts it in the corresponding hash table, probes the opposite hash table to find tuples that match the join predicate (and a select predicate if any) and constructs the result joined tuples. Recall that the "home" of a (horizontally partitioned) relation was defined in Chapter 8 as a set of peers where each peer has a different partition. In this case, the partitioning is by hashing on the join attribute. The home of the result relation is also a partitioned relation (using put operations) so it is also at multiple peers.

This basic algorithm can be improved in several ways. For instance, if one of the relations is already hashed on the join attributes, we may use its home as result home, using a variation of the parallel associative join algorithm (PAJ) (see Section 14.3.2), where only one relation needs to be hashed and sent over the DHT.

To avoid multicasting the query to large numbers of peers, another approach is to allocate a limited number of special powerful peers, called *range guards*, for the task of join query processing [Triantafillou and Pitoura, 2003]. The domains of the join attributes are divided, and each partition is dedicated to a range guard. Then, join queries are sent only to range guards, where the query is executed.

Algorithm 16.6: PIERjoin

Input: Q: join query over relations R and S on attribute A;
h: hash function;
H_R, H_S: homes of R and S
Output: T: join result relation;
H_T: home of T
begin
   {Multicast phase}
   At query originator peer send Q to all peers in H_R and H_S ;
   {Hash phase}
   for *each peer p in H_R that received Q in parallel* **do**
      for *each tuple r in R_p that satisfies the select predicate* **do**
          place r using $h(H_T, A)$

   for *each peer p in H_S that received Q in parallel* **do**
      for *each tuple s in S_p that satisfies the select predicate* **do**
          place s using $h(H_T, A)$

   {Probe/join phase}
   for *each peer p in H_T in parallel* **do**
      if *a new tuple i has arrived* **then**
         if *i is an r tuple* **then**
             probe s tuples in S_p using $h(A)$
         else
             probe r tuples in R_p using $h(A)$
          $T_p \leftarrow r \bowtie s$

end

16.3.3 Range Queries

Recall that range queries have a WHERE clause of the form "attribute A in range $[a,b]$", with a and b being numerical values. Structured P2P systems, in particular, DHTs are very efficient at supporting exact-match queries (of the form "$A = a$") but have difficuties with range queries. The main reason is that hashing tends to destroy the ordering of data that is useful in finding ranges quickly.

There are two main approaches for supporting range queries in structured P2P systems: extend a DHT with proximity or order-preserving properties, or maintain the key ordering with a tree-based structure. The first approach has been used in several systems. Locality sentitive hashing [Gupta et al., 2003] is an extension to DHTs that hashes similar ranges to the same DHT node with high probability. However, this method can only obtain approximate answers and may cause unbalanced loads in large networks. SkipNet [Harvey et al., 2003] is a lexicographic order-preserving DHT that allows data items with similar values to be placed on contiguous peers. It uses names rather than hashed identifiers to order peers in the overlay network, and each peer is responsible for a range of strings. This facilitates the execution of range queries. However, the number of peers to be visited is linear in the query range.

The Prefix Hash Tree (PHT) [Ramabhadran et al., 2004] is a trie-based distributed data structure that supports range queries over a DHT, by simply using the DHT lookup operation. The data being indexed are binary strings of length D. Each node has either 0 or 2 children, and a key k is stored at a leaf node whose label is a prefix of k. Furthermore, leaf nodes are linked to their neighbors. PHT's lookup operation on key k must return the unique leaf node $leaf(k)$ whose label is a prefix of k. Given a key k of length D, there are $D+1$ distinct prefixes of k. Obtaining $leaf(k)$ can be performed by a linear scan of these potential $D+1$ nodes. However, since a PHT is a binary trie, the linear scan can be improved using a binary search on prefix length. This reduces the number of DHT lookups from $(D+1)$ to $(\log D)$. Given two keys a and b such as $a \leq b$, two algorithms for range queries are supported, using PHT's lookup. The first one is sequential: it searches $leaf(a)$ and then scans sequentially the linked list of leaf nodes until the node $leaf(b)$ is reached. The second algorithm is parallel: it first identifies the node which corresponds to the smallest prefix range that completely covers the range $[a,b]$. To reach this node, a simple DHT lookup is used and the query is forwarded recursively to those children that overlap with the range $[a,b]$.

As in all hashing schemes, the first approach suffers from data skew that can result in peers with unbalanced ranges, which hurts load balancing. To overcome this problem, the second approach exploits tree-based structures to maintain balanced ranges of keys. The first attempt to build a P2P network based on a balanced tree structure is BATON (BAlanced Tree Overlay Network) [Jagadish et al., 2005]. We now present BATON and its support for range queries in more detail.

BATON organizes peers as a balanced binary tree (each node of the tree is maintained by a peer). The position of a node in BATON is determined by a (level,number) tuple, with level starting from 0 at the root, number starting from 1 at the root and sequentially assigned using in-order traversal. Each tree node stores links to its parent, children, adjacent nodes and selected neighbor nodes that are nodes at the same level. Two routing tables: a *left routing table* and a *right routing table* store links to the selected neighbor nodes. For a node numbered i, these routing tables contain links to nodes located at the same level with numbers that are less (left routing table) and greater (right routing table) than i by a power of 2. The jth element in the left (right) routing table at node i contains a link to the node numbered $i - 2^{j-1}$ (respectively $i + 2^{j-1}$) at the same level in the tree. Figure 16.11 shows the routing table of node 6.

In BATON, each leaf and internal node (or peer) is assigned a range of values. For each link this range is stored at the routing table and when its range changes, the link is modified to record the change. The range of values managed by a peer is required to be to the right of the range managed by its left subtree and less than the range managed by its right subtree (see Figure 16.12). Thus, BATON builds an effective distributed index structure. The joining and departure of peers are processed such that the tree remains balanced by forwarding the request upward in the tree for joins

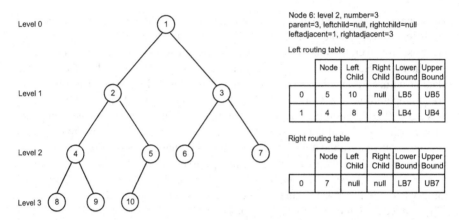

Fig. 16.11 BATON structure-tree index and routing table of node 6

and downward in the tree for leaves, thus with no more than $O(\log n)$ steps for a tree of n nodes.

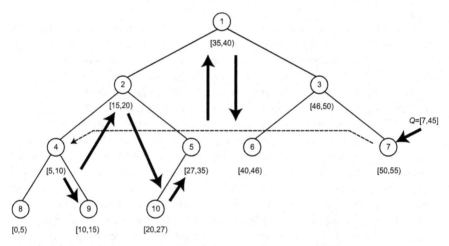

Fig. 16.12 Range query processing in BATON

A range query is processed as follows (Algorithm 16.7). For a range query Q with range $[a,b]$ submitted by node i, it looks for a node that intersects with the lower bound of the searched range. The peer that stores the lower bound of the range checks locally for tuples belonging to the range and forwards the query to its right adjacent node. In general, each node receiving the query checks for local tuples and contacts its right adjacent node until the node containing the upper bound of the range is reached. Partial answers obtained when an intersection is found are sent to the node that submits the query. The first intersection is found in $O(\log n)$ steps using an algorithm for exact match queries. Therefore, a range query with X nodes covering the range is answered in $O(\log n + X)$ steps.

Algorithm 16.7: BatonRange

Input: Q: a range query in the form $[a, b]$
Output: T: result relation
begin
    {Search for the peer storing the lower bound of the range}
    At query originator peer
    begin
        find peer p that holds value a ;
        send Q to p;
    end
    for *each peer p that receives Q* **do**
        $T_p \leftarrow Range(p) \cap [a, b]$;
        send T_p to query originator ;
        if $Range(RightAdjacent(p)) \cap [a, b] \neq \emptyset$ **then**
            let p be right adjacent peer of p ;
            send Q to p
end

Example 16.6. Consider the query Q with range $[7, 45]$ issued at node 7 in Figure 16.12. First, BATON executes an exact match query looking for a node containing the lower bound of the range (see dashed line in the figure). Since the lower bound is in the range assigned to node 4, it checks locally for tuples belonging to the range and forwards the query to its adjacent right node (node 9). Node 9 checks for local tuples belonging to the range and forwards the query to node 2. Nodes 10, 5, 1 and 6 receive the query, they check for local tuples and contact their respective right adjacent node until the node containing the upper bound of the range is reached. ◆

16.4 Replica Consistency

To increase data availability and access performance, P2P systems replicate data. However, different P2P systems provide very different levels of replica consistency. The earlier, simple P2P systems such as Gnutella and Kazaa deal only with static data (e.g., music files) and replication is "passive" as it occurs naturally as peers request and copy files from one another (basically, caching data). In more advanced P2P systems where replicas can be updated, there is a need for proper replica management techniques. Unfortunately, most of the work on replica consistency has been done only in the context of DHTs. We can distinguish three approaches to deal with replica consistency: basic support in DHTs, data currency in DHTs, and replica reconciliation. In this section, we introduce the main techniques used in these approaches.

16.4.1 Basic Support in DHTs

To improve data availability, most DHTs rely on data replication by storing $(key, data)$ pairs at several peers by, for example, using several hash functions. If one peer is unavailable, its data can still be retrieved from the other peers that hold a replica. Some DHTs provide basic support for the application to deal with replica consistency. In this section, we describe the techniques used in two popular DHTs: CAN and Tapestry.

CAN provides two approaches for supporting replication [Ratnasamy et al., 2001a]. The first one is to use m hash functions to map a single key onto m points in the coordinate space, and, accordingly, replicate a single $(key, data)$ pair at m distinct nodes in the network. The second approach is an optimization over the basic design of CAN that consists of a node proactively pushing out popular keys towards its neighbors when it finds it is being overloaded by requests for these keys. In this approach, replicated keys should have an associated TTL field to automatically undo the effect of replication at the end of the overloaded period. In addition, the technique assumes immutable (read-only) data.

Tapestry [Zhao et al., 2004] is an extensible P2P system that provides decentralized object location and routing on top of a structured overlay network. It routes messages to logical end-points (i.e., endpoints whose identifiers are not associated with physical location), such as nodes or object replicas. This enables message delivery to mobile or replicated endpoints in the presence of instability of the underlying infrastructure. In addition, Tapestry takes latency into account to establish each node's neighborhood. The location and routing mechanisms of Tapestry work as follows. Let o be an object identified by $id(o)$; the insertion of o in the P2P network involves two nodes: the server node (noted n_s) that holds o and the root node (noted n_r) that holds a mapping in the form $(id(o), n_s)$ indicating that the object identified by $id(o)$ is stored at node n_s. The root node is dynamically determined by a globally consistent deterministic algorithm. Figure 16.13a shows that when o is inserted into n_s, n_s publishes $id(o)$ at its root node by routing a message from n_s to n_r containing the mapping $(id(o), n_s)$. This mapping is stored at all nodes along the message path. During a location query (e.g., "$id(o)$?" in Figure 16.13a, the message that looks for $id(o)$ is initially routed towards n_r, but it may be stopped before reaching it once a node containing the mapping $(id(o), n_s)$ is found. For routing a message to $id(o)$'s root, each node forwards this message to its neighbor whose logical identifier is the most similar to $id(o)$ [Plaxton et al., 1997].

Tapestry offers the entire infrastructure needed to take advantage of replicas, as shown in Figure 16.13b. Each node in the graph represents a peer in the P2P network and contains the peer's logical identifier in hexadecimal format. In this example, two replicas O_1 and O_2 of object O (e.g., a book file) are inserted into distinct peers

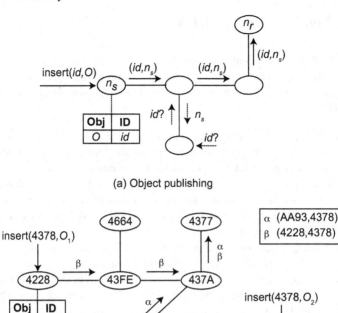

(a) Object publishing

(b) Replica management

Fig. 16.13 Tapestry (a) Object publishing (b) Replica management.

($O_1 \rightarrow$ peer 4228 and $O_2 \rightarrow$ peer AA93). The identifier of O_1 is equal to that of O_2 (i.e., 4378 in hexadecimal) as O_1 and O_2 are replicas of the same object O. When O_1 is inserted into its server node (peer 4228), the mapping $(4378, 4228)$ is routed from peer 4228 to peer 4377 (the root node for O_1's identifier). As the message approaches the root node, the object and the node identifiers become increasingly similar. In addition, the mapping $(4378, 4228)$ is stored at all peers along the message path. The insertion of O_2 follows the same procedure. In Figure 16.13b, if peer E791 looks for a replica of O, the associated message routing stops at peer 4361. Therefore, applications can replicate data across multiple server nodes and rely on Tapestry to direct requests to nearby replicas.

16.4.2 Data Currency in DHTs

Although DHTs provide basic support for replication, the mutual consistency of the replicas after updates can be compromised as a result of peers leaving the network or concurrent updates. Let us illustrate the problem with a simple update scenario in a typical DHT.

Example 16.7. Let us assume that the operation put (k, d_0) (issued by some peer) maps onto peers p_1 and p_2 both of which get to store data d_0. Now consider an update (from the same or another peer) with the operation put (k, d_1) that also maps onto peers p_1 and p_2. Assuming that p_2 cannot be reached (e.g., because it has left the network), only p_1 gets updated to store d_1. When p_2 rejoins the network later on, the replicas are not consistent: p_1 holds the current state of the data associated with k while p_2 holds a stale state.

Concurrent updates also cause problems. Consider now two updates put (k, d_2) and put (k, d_3) (issued by two different peers) that are sent to p_1 and p_2 in reverse order, so that p_1's last state is d_2 while p_2's last state is d_3. Thus, a subsequent get (k) operation will return either stale or current data depending on which peer is looked up, and there is no way to tell whether it is current or not.   ◆

For some applications (e.g., agenda management, bulletin boards, cooperative auction management, reservation management, etc.) that could take advantage of a DHT, the ability to get the current data are very important. Supporting data currency in replicated DHTs requires the ability to return a current replica despite peers leaving the network or concurrent updates. Of course, replica consistency is a more general problem, as discussed in Chapter 13, but the issue is particularly difficult and important in P2P systems, since there is considerable dynamism in the peers joining and leaving the system. The problem can be partially addressed by using data versioning [Knezevic et al., 2005]. Each replica has a version number that is increased after each update. To return a current replica, all replicas need to be retrieved in order to select the latest version. However, because of concurrent updates, it may happen that two different replicas have the same version number, thus making it impossible to decide which one is the current replica.

A more complete solution has been proposed that considers both data availability and data currency [Akbarinia et al., 2007b]. To provide high data availability, data are replicated in the DHT using a set of independent hash functions H_r, called *replication hash functions*. The peer that is responsible for key k with respect to hash function h at the current time is denoted by $rsp(k, h)$. To be able to retrieve a current replica, each pair $(k, data)$ is stamped with a logical timestamp, and for each $h \in H_r$, the pair $(k, newData)$ is replicated at $rsp(k, h)$ where $newData = \{data, timestamp\}$, i.e., newdata is composed of the initial data and the timestamp. Upon a request for the data associated with a key, we can return one of the replicas that are stamped with the latest timestamp. The number of replication hash functions, i.e., H_r, can be different for different DHTs. For instance, if in a DHT the availability of peers is low, a high value of H_r (e.g., 30) can be used to increase data availability.

This solution is the basis for a service called *Update Management Service* (UMS) that deals with efficient insertion and retrieval of current replicas based on timestamping. Experimental validation has shown that UMS incurs very little overhead in terms of communication cost. After retrieving a replica, UMS detects whether it is current or not, i.e., without having to compare with the other replicas, and returns it as output. Thus, UMS does not need to retrieve all replicas to find a current one; it only requires the DHT's lookup service with `put` and `get` operations.

To generate timestamps, UMS uses a distributed service called *Key-based Timestamping Service* (KTS). The main operation of KTS is `gen_ts(`k`)`, which, given a key k, generates a real number as a timestamp for k. The timestamps generated by KTS are *monotonic* such that if ts_i and ts_j are two timestamps generated for the same key at times t_i and t_j, respectively, $ts_j > ts_i$ if t_j is later than t_i. This property allows ordering the timestamps generated for the same key according to the time at which they have been generated. KTS has another operation denoted by *last_ts(k)*, which, given a key k, returns the last timestamp generated for k by KTS. At anytime, `gen_ts(`k`)` generates at most one timestamp for k, and different timestamps for k are monotonic. Thus, in the case of concurrent calls to insert a pair $(k, data)$, i.e., from different peers, only the one that obtains the latest timestamp will succeed to store its data in the DHT.

16.4.3 Replica Reconciliation

Replica reconciliation goes one step further than data currency by enforcing mutual consistency of replicas. Since a P2P network is typically very dynamic, with peers joining or leaving the network at will, eager replication solutions (see Chapter 13) are not appropriate; lazy replication is preferred. In this section, we describe the reconciliation techniques used in OceanStore, P-Grid and APPA to provide a spectrum of proposed solutions.

16.4.3.1 OceanStore

OceanStore [Kubiatowicz et al., 2000] is a data management system designed to provide continuous access to persistent information. It relies on Tapestry and assumes an infrastructure composed of untrusted powerful servers that are connected by high-speed links. For security reasons, data are protected through redundancy and cryptographic techniques. To improve performance, data are allowed to be cached anywhere, anytime.

OceanStore allows concurrent updates on replicated objects; it relies on reconciliation to assure data consistency. Figure 16.14 illustrates update management in OceanStore. In this example, R is a replicated object whereas R_i and r_i denote, respectively, a primary and a secondary copy of R. Nodes n_1 and n_2 are concurrently updating R. Such updates are managed as follows. Nodes that hold primary copies of

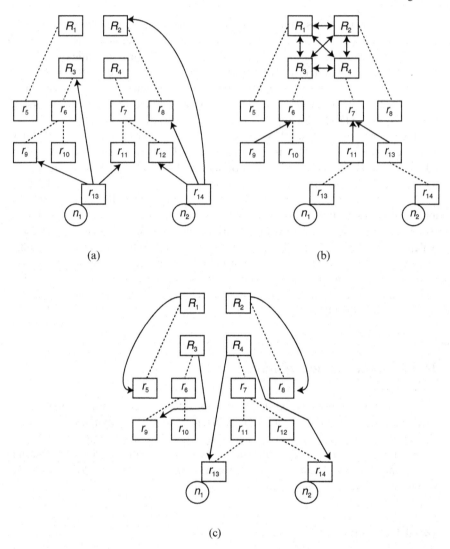

(a)   (b)

(c)

Fig. 16.14 OceanStore reconciliation. (a) Nodes n_1 and n_2 send updates to the master group of R and to several random secondary replicas. (b) The master group of R orders updates while secondary replicas propagate them epidemically. (c) After the master group agreement, the result of updates is multicast to secondary replicas.

R, called the *master group of R*, are responsible for ordering updates. So, n_1 and n_2 perform tentative updates on their local secondary replicas and send these updates to the master group of R as well as to other random secondary replicas (see Figure 16.14a). The tentative updates are ordered by the master group based on timestamps assigned by n_1 and n_2; at the same time, these updates are epidemically propagated among secondary replicas (Figure 16.14b). Once the master group obtains an agreement, the result of updates is multicast to secondary replicas (Figure 16.14c), which contain both tentative[2] and committed data.

Replica management adjusts the number and location of replicas in order to service requests more efficiently. By monitoring the system load, OceanStore detects when a replica is overwhelmed and creates additional replicas on nearby nodes to alleviate load. Conversely, these additional replicas are eliminated when they are no longer needed.

16.4.3.2 P-Grid

P-Grid [Aberer et al., 2003a] is a structured P2P network based on a binary trie structure. A decentralized and self-organizing process builds P-Grid's routing infrastructure which is adapted to a given distribution of data keys stored by peers. This process addresses uniform load distribution of data storage and uniform replication of data to support availability.

To address updates of replicated objects, P-Grid employs gossiping, without strong consistency guarantees. P-Grid assumes that quasi-consistency of replicas (instead of full consistency which is too hard to provide in a dynamic environment) is enough.

The update propagation scheme has a push phase and a pull phase. When a peer p receives a new update to a replicated object R, it pushes the update to a subset of peers that hold replicas of R, which, in turn, propagate it to other peers holding replicas of R, and so on. Peers that have been disconnected and get connected again, peers that do not receive updates for a long time, or peers that receive a pull request but are not sure whether they have the latest update, enter the pull phase to reconcile. In this phase, multiple peers are contacted and the most up-to-date among them is chosen to provide the object content.

16.4.3.3 APPA

APPA provides a general lazy distributed replication solution that assures eventual consistency of replicas [Martins et al., 2006a; Martins and Pacitti, 2006; Martins et al., 2008]. It uses the action-constraint framework [Kermarrec et al., 2001] to capture the application semantics and resolve update conflicts.

The application semantics is described by means of constraints between update actions. An *action* is defined by the application programmer and represents an application-specific operation (e.g., a write operation on a file or document, or a database transaction). A *constraint* is the formal representation of an application invariant. For instance, the *predSucc*(a_1, a_2) constraint establishes causal ordering between actions (i.e., action a_2 executes only after a_1 has succeeded); the *mutuallyExclusive*(a_1, a_2) constraint states that either a_1 or a_2 can be executed. The aim of reconciliation is to take a set of actions with the associated constraints and produce

---

[2] Tentative data are data that the primary replicas have not yet committed.

a *schedule*, i.e., a list of ordered actions that do not violate constraints. In order to reduce the schedule production complexity, the set of actions to be ordered is divided into subsets called *clusters*. A cluster is a subset of actions related by constraints that can be ordered independently of other clusters. Therefore, the *global schedule* is composed by the concatenation of clusters' ordered actions.

Data managed by the APPA reconciliation algorithm are stored in data structures called *reconciliation objects*. Each reconciliation object has a unique identifier in order to enable its storage and retrieval in the DHT. Data replication proceeds as follows. First, nodes execute local actions to update a replica of an object while respecting user-defined constraints. Then, these actions (with the associated constraints) are stored in the DHT based on the object's identifier. Finally, reconciler nodes retrieve actions and constraints from the DHT and produce the global schedule, by reconciling conflicting actions based on the application semantics. This schedule is locally executed at every node, thereby assuring eventual consistency.

Any connected node can try to start reconciliation by inviting other available nodes to engage with it. Only one reconciliation can run at-a-time. The reconciliation of update actions is performed in 6 distributed steps as follows. Nodes at step 2 start reconciliation. The outputs produced at each step become the input to the next one.

- **Step 1 - node allocation:** a subset of connected replica nodes is selected to proceed as reconcilers based on communication costs.

- **Step 2 - action grouping:** reconcilers take actions from the action logs and put actions that try to update common objects into the same group since these actions are potentially in conflict. Groups of actions that try to update object R are stored in the *action log R* reconciliation object (L_R).

- **Step 3 - cluster creation:** reconcilers take action groups from the action logs and split them into clusters of semantically dependent conflicting actions (two actions a_1 and a_2 are semantically independent if the application judges it safe to execute them together, in any order, even if they update a common object; otherwise, a_1 and a_2 are semantically dependent. Clusters produced in this step are stored in the cluster set reconciliation object.

- **Step 4 - clusters extension:** user-defined constraints are not taken into account in cluster creation. Thus, in this step, reconcilers extend clusters by adding to them new conflicting actions, according to user-defined constraints.

- **Step 5 - cluster integration:** cluster extensions lead to cluster overlapping (an overlap occurs when the intersection of two clusters results in a non-null set of actions). In this step, reconcilers bring together overlapping clusters. At this point, clusters become mutually-independent, i.e., there are no constraints involving actions of distinct clusters.

- **Step 6 - cluster ordering:** in this step, reconcilers take each cluster from the cluster set and order the cluster's actions. The ordered actions associated with each cluster are stored in the *schedule* reconciliation object. The concatenation of all clusters' ordered actions makes up the global schedule that is executed by all replica nodes.

At every step, the reconciliation algorithm takes advantage of data parallelism, i.e., several nodes per-form simultaneously independent activities on a distinct subset of actions (e.g., ordering of different clusters).

16.5 Conclusion

By distributing data storage and processing across autonomous peers in the network, "modern" P2P systems can scale without the need for powerful servers. Advanced P2P applications such as scientific cooperation must deal with semantically rich data (e.g., XML documents, relational tables, etc.). Supporting such applications requires significant revisiting of distributed database techniques (schema management, access control, query processing, transaction management, consistency management, reliability and replication). When considering data management, the main requirements of a P2P system are autonomy, query expressiveness, efficiency, quality of service, and fault-tolerance. Depending on the P2P network architecture (unstructured, structured DHT, or hybrid super-peer), these requirements can be achieved to varying degrees. Unstructured networks have better fault-tolerance but can be quite inefficient because they rely on flooding for query routing. Hybrid systems have better potential to satisfy high-level data management requirements. However, DHT systems are best for key-based search and could be combined with super-peer networks for more complex searching.

Most of the work on sharing semantically rich data in P2P systems has focused on schema management and query processing. However, there has been very little work on update management, replication, transactions and access control. Much more work is needed to revisit distributed database techniques for large-scale P2P systems. The main issues that have to be dealt with include schema management, complex query processing, transaction support and replication, and privacy. Furthermore, it is unlikely that all kinds of data management applications are suited for P2P systems. Typical applications that can take advantage of P2P systems are probably light-weight and involve some sort of cooperation. Characterizing carefully these applications is important and will be useful to produce performance benchmarks.

16.6 Bibliographic Notes

Data management in "modern" P2P systems, those characterized by massive distribution, inherent heterogeneity, and high volatility, has become an important research topic. The topic is fully covered in a recent book [Vu et al., 2009]. A shorter survey can be found in [Ulusoy, 2007]. Discussions on the requirements, architectures, and issues faced by P2P data management systems are provided in [Bernstein et al., 2002; Daswani et al., 2003; Valduriez and Pacitti, 2004]. A number of P2P data management systems are presented in [Aberer, 2003].

An extensive survey of query processing in P2P systems is provided in [Akbarinia et al., 2007d] and has been the basis for writing Sections 16.2 and 16.3. A good discussion of the issues of schema mapping in P2P systems can be found in [Tatarinov et al., 2003]. An important kind of query in P2P systems is top-k queries. A survey of top-k query processing techniques in relational database systems is provided in [Ilyas et al., 2008]. An efficient algorithm for top-k query processing is the Threshold Algorithm (TA) which was proposed independently by several researchers [Nepal and Ramakrishna, 1999; Güntzer et al., 2000; Fagin et al., 2003]. TA has been the basis for several algorithms in P2P systems, in particular in DHTs [Akbarinia et al., 2007c]. A more efficient algorithm than TA is the Best Position Algorithm [Akbarinia et al., 2007a]. A survey of ranking algorithms in databases (not necessarily in P2P systems) is given in [Ilyas et al., 2008].

The survey of replication in P2P systems by Martins et al. [2006b] has been the basis for Section 16.4. A complete solution to data currency in replicated DHTs, i.e., providing the ability to find the most current replica, is given in [Akbarinia et al., 2007b]. Reconciliation of replicated data are addressed in OceanStore [Kubiatowicz et al., 2000], P-Grid [Aberer et al., 2003a] and APPA [Martins et al., 2006a; Martins and Pacitti, 2006].

P2P techniques have recently received attention to help scaling up data management in the context of Grid Computing. This triggered open problems and new issues which are discussed in [Pacitti et al., 2007a].

Exercises

Problem 16.1. What is the fundamental difference between P2P and client-server architectures? Is a P2P system with a centralized index equivalent to a client-server system? List the main advantages and drawbacks of P2P file sharing systems from different points of view:

- end-users;
- file owners;
- network administrators.

Problem 16.2 (**). A P2P overlay network is built as a layer on top of a physical network, typically the Internet. Thus, they have different topologies and two nodes that are neighbors in the P2P network may be far apart in the physical network. What are the advantages and drawbacks of this layering? What is the impact of this layering on the design of the three main types of P2P networks (unstructured, structured and superpeer)?

Problem 16.3 (*). Consider the unstructured P2P network in Figure 16.4 and the bottom-left peer that sends a request for resource. Illustrate and discuss the two following search strategies in terms of result completeness:

- flooding with TTL=3;
- gossiping with each peer has a partial view of at most 3 neighbours.

Problem 16.4 (*). Consider Figure 16.7, focusing on structured networks. Refine the comparison using the scale 1-5 (instead of low - moderate - high) by considering the three main types of DHTs: tree, hypercube and ring.

Problem 16.5 (**). The objective is to design a P2P social network application, on top of a DHT. The application should provide basic functions of social networks: register a new user with her profile; invite or retrieve friends; create lists of friends; post a message to friends; read friends' messages; post a comment on a message. Assume a generic DHT with put and get operations, where each user is a peer in the DHT.

Problem 16.6 (**). Propose a P2P architecture of the social network application, with the (key, data) pairs for the different entities which need be distributed. Describe how the following operations: create or remove a user; create or remove a friendship; read messages from a list of friends. Discuss the advantages and drawbacks of the design.

Problem 16.7 (**). Same question, but with the additional requirement that private data (e.g., user profile) must be stored at the user peer.

Problem 16.8. Discuss the commonalities and differences of schema mapping in multidatabase systems and P2P systems. In particular, compare the local-as-view approach presented in Chapter 4 with the pairwise schema mapping approach in Section 16.2.1.

Problem 16.9 (*). The FD algorithm for top-k query processing in unstructured P2P networks (see Algorithm 16.4) relies on flooding. Propose a variation of FD where, instead of flooding, random walk or gossiping is used. What are the advantages and drawbacks?

Problem 16.10 (*). Apply the TPUT algorithm (Algorithm 16.2) to the three lists of the database in Figure 16.10 witk k=3. For each step of the algorithm, show the intermediate results.

Problem 16.11 (*). Same question applied to Algorithm DHTop (see Algorithm 16.5.

Problem 16.12 (*). Algorithm 16.6 assumes that the input relations to be joined are placed arbitrarily in the DHT. Assuming that one of the relations is already hashed on the join attributes, propose an improvement of Algorithm 16.6.

Problem 16.13 (*). To improve data availability in DHTs, a common solution is to replicate $(k, data)$ pairs at several peers using several hash functions. This produces the problem illustrated in Example 16.7. An alternative solution is to use a non-replicated DHT (with a single hash function) and have the nodes replicating (k, data) pairs at some of their neighbors. What is the effect on the scenario in Example 16.7? What are the advantages and drawbacks of this approach, in terms of availability and load balancing?

Chapter 17
Web Data Management

The World Wide Web ("WWW" or "web" for short) has become a major repository of data and documents. Although measurements differ and change, the web has grown at a phenomenal rate. According to two studies in 1998, there were 200 million [Bharat and Broder, 1998] to upwards of 320 million [Lawrence and Giles, 1998] static web pages. A 1999 study reported the size of the web as 800 million pages [Lawrence and Giles, 1999]. By 2005, the number of pages were reported to be 11.5 billion [Gulli and Signorini, 2005]. Today it is estimated that the web contains over 25 billion pages[1] and growing. These are numbers for the "static" web pages, i.e., those whose content do not change unless the page owners make explicit changes. The size of the web is much larger when "dynamic" web pages (i.e., pages whose content changes based on the context of user requests) are considered. A 2005 study reported the size to be over 53 billion pages [Hirate et al., 2006]. Additionally, it was estimated that, as of 2001, over 500 billion documents existed in the *deep web* (which we define below) [Bergman, 2001]. Besides its size, the web is very dynamic and changes rapidly. Thus, for all practical purposes, the web represents a very large, dynamic and distributed data store and there are the obvious distributed data management issues in accessing web data.

The web, in its present form, can be viewed as two distinct yet related components. The first of these components is what is known as the *publicly indexable web* (PIW) [Lawrence and Giles, 1998]. This is composed of all static (and cross-linked) web pages that exist on web servers. The other component, which is known as the *hidden web* [Florescu et al., 1998] (or the *deep web* [Raghavan and Garcia-Molina, 2001]), is composed of a huge number of databases that encapsulate the data, hiding it from the outside world. The data in the hidden web are usually retrieved by means of search interfaces where the user enters a query that is passed to the database server, and the results are returned to the user as a dynamically generated web page.

The difference between the two is basically in the way they are handled for searching and/or querying. Searching the PIW depends mainly on crawling its pages using the link structure between them, indexing the crawled pages, and then

---

[1] See http://www.worldwidewebsize.com/

searching the indexed data (as we discuss at length in Section 17.2). It is not possible to apply this approach to the hidden web directly since it is not possible to crawl and index those data (the techniques for searching the hidden web are discussed in Section 17.3.4).

Research on web data management has followed different threads. Most of the earlier work focused on keyword search and search engines. The subsequent work in the database community focused on declarative querying of web data. There is an emerging trend that combines search/browse mode of access with declarative querying, but this work has not yet reached its full potential. Along another front, XML has emerged as an important data format for representing data on the web. Thus, XML data management, and more recently *distributed* XML data management, have been topics of interest. The result of these different threads of development is that there is little in the way of a unifying architecture or framework for discussing web data management, and the different lines of research have to be considered somewhat separately. Furthermore, the full coverage of all the web-related topics requires far deeper and far more extensive treatment than is possible within a chapter. Therefore, we focus on issues that are directly related to data management.

We start by discussing how web data can be modelled as a graph. Both the structure of this graph and its management are important. This is discussed in Section 17.1. Web search is discussed in Section 17.2 and web querying is covered in Section 17.3. These are fundamental topics in web data management. We then discuss distributed XML data management (Section 17.4). Although the web pages were originally encoded using HTML, the use of XML and the prevalence of XML-encoded data are increasing, particularly in the data repositories available on the web. Therefore, the distributed management of XML data is increasingly important.

17.1 Web Graph Management

The web consists of "pages" that are connected by hyperlinks, and this structure can be modelled as a directed graph that reflects the hyperlink structure. In this graph, commonly referred to as the *web graph*, static HTML web pages are the nodes and the links between them are represented as directed edges [Kumar et al., 2000; Raghavan and Garcia-Molina, 2003; Kleinberg et al., 1999]. Studying the web graph is obviously of interest to theoretical computer scientists, because it exhibits a number of interesting characteristics, but it is also important for studying data management issues since the graph structure is exploited in web search [Kleinberg et al., 1999; Brin and Page, 1998; Kleinberg, 1999], categorization and classification of web content [Chakrabarti et al., 1998], and other web-related tasks. The important characteristics of the web graph are the following [Bonato, 2008]:

(a) It is quite volatile. We already discussed the speed with which the graph is growing. In addition, a significant proportion of the web pages experience frequent updates.

(b) It is sparse. A graph is considered sparse if its average degree is less than the number of vertices. This means that the each node of the graph has a limited number of neighbors, even if the nodes are in general connected. The sparseness of the web graph implies an interesting graph structure that we discuss shortly.

(c) It is "self-organizing." The web contains a number of communities, each of which consist of a set of pages that focus on a particular topic. These communities get organized on their own without any "centralized control," and give rise to the particular subgraphs in the web graph.

(d) It is a "small-world network." This property is related to sparseness – each node in the graph may not have many neighbors (i.e., its degree may be small), but many nodes are connected through intermediaries. Small-world networks were first identified in social sciences where it was noted that many people who are strangers to each other are connected by intermediaries. This holds true in web graphs as well in terms of the connectedness of the graph.

(e) It is a power law network. The in- and out-degree distributions of the web graph follow power law distributions. This means that the probability that a node has in- (out-) degree i is proportional to $1/i^{\alpha}$ for some $\alpha > 1$. The value of α is about 2.1 for in-degree and about 7.2 for out-degree [Broder et al., 2000].

This brings us to a discussion of the structure of the web graph, which has a "bowtie" shape (Figure 17.1) [Broder et al., 2000]. It has a strongly connected component (the knot in the middle) in which there is a path between each pair of pages. The strongly connected component (SCC) accounts for about 28% of the web pages. A further 21% of the pages constitute the "IN" component from which there are paths to pages in SCC, but to which no paths exist from pages in SCC. Symmetrically, "OUT" component has pages to which paths exists from pages in SCC but not vice versa, and these also constitute 21% of the pages. What is referred to as "tendrils" consist of pages that cannot be reached from SCC and from which SCC pages cannot be reached either. These constitute about 22% of the web pages. These are pages that have not yet been "discovered" and have not yet been connected to the better known parts of the web. Finally, there are disconnected components that have no links to/from anything except their own small communities. This makes up about 8% of the web. This structure is interesting in that it determines the results that one gets from web searches and from querying the web. Furthermore, this graph structure is different than many other graphs that are normally studied, requiring special algorithms and techniques for its management.

A particularly relevant issue that needs to be addressed is the management of the very large, dynamic, and volatile web graph. In the remainder, we discuss two methods that have been proposed to deal with this issue. The first one compresses the web graph for more efficient storage and manipulation, while the second one suggests a special representation for the web graph.

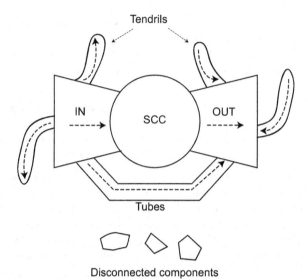

Fig. 17.1 The Structure of the web as a Bowtie (Based on [Kumar et al., 2000].)

17.1.1 Compressing Web Graphs

Compressing a large graph is well-studied, and a number of techniques have been proposed. However, the web graph structure is different from the graphs that are addressed by these techniques, which makes it difficult (if not impossible) to apply the well-known graph compression algorithms to web graphs. Thus, new approaches are needed.

A specific proposal for compressing the web graph takes advantage of the fact that we can attempt to find nodes that share several common *out-edges*, corresponding to the case where one node might have copied links from another node [Adler and Mitzenmacher, 2001]. The main idea behind this technique is that when a new node is added to the graph, it takes an existing page and copies some of the links from that page to itself. For example, a new page v might examine the out-edges from a page w and link to a subset of the pages that w links to. This intuition is based on the idea that the creator of a new page decides what pages to link to based on an existing page or pages that the page creator already likes [Kumar et al., 1999]. In this case, node w is called the *reference* for node v.

Given that the in-degree and out-degree of the web graph follow a Zipfian distribution, there is a large variance in the degrees. Thus, a Huffman-based compression scheme can be used. There are alternative compression methods in this class, but a simple one that demonstrates the idea is as follows.

Once the node from which links were copied has been identified, the difference between the out-edges of the two nodes can be identified. If node w is labelled as a reference of node v, a 0/1 bit vector can be generated that denotes which out-edges of w are also out-edges of node v. Other out-edges of v can be separately identified using another bit vector. Then, the cost of compressing node v using node w as a reference can be expressed as follows:

$$Cost(v, w) = out\_deg(w) + \lceil \log n \rceil * (|N(v) - N(w)| + 1)$$

where $N(v)$ and $N(w)$ represent the set of out-edges for nodes v and w, respectively, and n is the number of nodes in the graph. The first term identifies the cost of representing the out-edges of the reference node w, $\lceil \log n \rceil$ is the number of bits required to identify a node in a web graph with n nodes, and $(|N(v) - N(w)| + 1)$ represents the difference between the out-edges of the two nodes.

Given a description of a graph in this compressed format, let us consider how it could be determined where a link from node v encoded using node w as a reference actually points. If the corresponding link from node w is encoded using another node u as a reference, then it needs to be determined where the corresponding link from node u points. Eventually, a link is reached that is encoded without using a reference node (in order to satisfy this requirement, no cycles among references are allowed) at which point the search stops.

17.1.2 Storing Web Graphs as S-Nodes

An alternative to compressing the web graph is to develop special storage structures that allow efficient storage and querying. *S-Nodes* [Raghavan and Garcia-Molina, 2003] is one such structure that provides a two-level representation of the web graph. In this scheme, the web graph is represented by a set of smaller directed sub-graphs. Each of these smaller sub-graphs encodes the interconnections within a small subset of pages. A top-level directed graph, consisting of *supernodes* and *superedges* contains links to these smaller sub-graphs.

Given a web graph W_G, the S-Node representation can be constructed as follows. Let $P = N_1, N_2, ..., N_n$ be a partition on the vertex set of W_G. The following types of directed graphs can be defined (Figure 17.2):

Supernode graph: A supernode graph contains n vertices, one for each partition in P. In Figure 17.2, there is a supernode for each of the partitions N_1, N_2 and N_3. Supernodes are linked using superedges. A superedge E_{ij} is created from N_i to N_j if there is at least one page in N_i that points to some page in N_j.

Intranode graph: Each partition N_i is associated with an intranode graph *IntraNode_i* that represents all the interconnections between the pages that belong to N_i. For example, in Figure 17.2, *IntraNode_1* represents the hyperlinks between pages P_1 and P_2.

Positive superedge graph: A positive superedge graph $SEdgePos_{i,j}$ is a directed bipartite graph representing all links from N_i to N_j. In Figure 17.2, $SEdgePos_{1,2}$

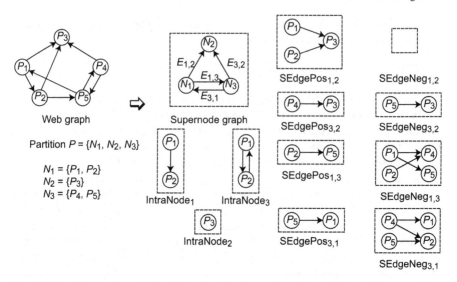

Fig. 17.2 Partitioning the web graph (Based on [Raghavan and Garcia-Molina, 2003].)

contains two edges that represent the two links from P_1 and P_2 to P_3. There is an $SEdgePos_{i,j}$ if there exists a corresponding superedge $E_{i,j}$.

Negative superedge graph: A negative superedge graph $SEdgeNeg_{i,j}$ is a directed bipartite graph that represents all links between N_i and N_j that do not exist in the actual web graph. Similar to $SEdgePos$, an $SEdgeNeg_{i,j}$ exists if and only if there exists a corresponding superedge $E_{i,j}$.

Given a partition P on the vertex set of W_G, an S-Node representation $SNode$ (W_G, P) can be constructed by using the supernode graph that points to the intranode graph and a set of positive and negative supernode graphs. The decision as to whether to use the positive or the negative supernode graph depends on which representation has the lower number of edges. Figure 17.3 shows the specific representation of an S-Node for the example given in Figure 17.2.

S-node representation exploits empirically observed properties of web graphs to guide the grouping of pages into super-nodes and uses compressed encodings for the lower level directed graphs. This compression allows the reduction of the number of bits needed to encode a hyperlink from 15 to 5 [Raghavan and Garcia-Molina, 2003], which in turn allows large web graphs to be loaded into main memory for processing. Furthermore, since the web graph is represented in terms of smaller directed graphs, it is possible to naturally isolate and locally explore portions of the web graph that are relevant to a particular query.

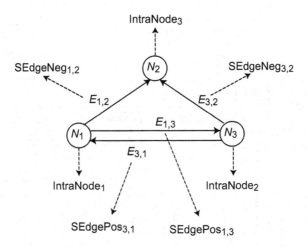

Fig. 17.3 S-node representation (Based on [Raghavan and Garcia-Molina, 2003].)

17.2 Web Search

Web search involves finding "all" the web pages that are relevant (i.e., have content related) to keyword(s) that a user specifies. Naturally, it is not possible to find all the pages, or even to know if one has retrieved all the pages; thus the search is performed on a database of web pages that have been collected and indexed. Since there are usually multiple pages that are relevant to a query, these pages are presented to the user in ranked order of relevance as determined by the search engine.

The abstract architecture of a generic search engine is shown in Figure 17.4 [Arasu et al., 2001]. We discuss the components of this architecture in some detail.

In every search engine the *crawler* plays one of the most crucial roles. A crawler is a program used by a search engine to scan the web on its behalf and collect data about web pages. A crawler is given a starting set of pages – more accurately, it is given a set of Uniform Resource Locators (URLs) that identify these pages. The crawler retrieves and parses the page corresponding to that URL, extracts any URLs in it, and adds these URLs to a queue. In the next cycle, the crawler extracts a URL from the queue (based on some order) and retrieves the corresponding page. This process is repeated until the crawler stops. A control module is responsible for deciding which URLs should be visited next. The retrieved pages are stored in a page repository. Section 17.2.1 examines crawling operations in more detail.

The *indexer module* is responsible for constructing indexes on the pages that have been downloaded by the crawler. While many different indexes can be built, the two most common ones are *text indexes* and *link indexes*. In order to construct a text index, the indexer module constructs a large "lookup table" that can provide all the URLs that point to the pages where a given word occurs. A link index describes the link structure of the web and provides information on the in-link and out-link state

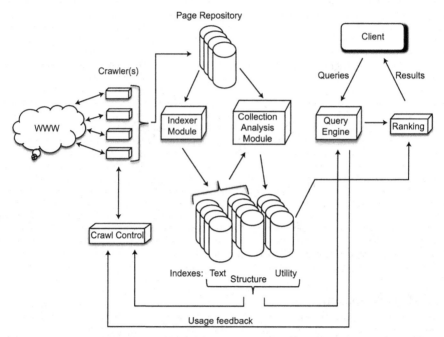

Fig. 17.4 Search Engine Architecture (Based on [?]

of pages. Section 17.2.2 explains current indexing technology and concentrates on ways indexes can be efficiently stored.

The *ranking module* is responsible for sorting the large number of results so that those that are considered to be most relevant to the user's search are presented first. The problem of ranking has drawn increased interest in order to go beyond traditional information retrieval (IR) techniques to address the special characteristics of the web — web queries are usually small and they are executed over a vast amount of data. Section 17.2.3 introduces algorithms for ranking and describes approaches that exploit the link structure of the web to obtain improved ranking results.

17.2.1 Web Crawling

As indicated above, a crawler scans the web on behalf of a search engine to extract information about the visited web pages. Given the size of the web, the changing nature of web pages, and the limited computing and storage capabilities of crawlers, it is impossible to crawl the entire web. Thus, a crawler must be designed to visit "most important" pages before others. The issue, then, is to visit the pages in some ranked order of importance.

There are a number of issues that need to be addressed in designing a crawler [Cho et al., 1998]. Since the primary goal is to access more important pages before others, there needs to be some way of determining the importance of a page. This can be done by means of a measure that reflects the importance of a given page. These measures can be static, such that the importance of a page is determined independent of retrieval queries that will run against it, or dynamic in that they take the queries into consideration. Examples of static measures are those that determine the importance of a page P with respect to the number of pages that point to P (referred to as *backlink*), or those that additionally take into account the importance of the backlink pages as is done in the popular PageRank metric [Page et al., 1998] that is used by Google and others. A possible dynamic measure may be one that calculates the importance of a page P with respect its textual similarity to the query that is being evaluated using some of the well-known information retrieval similarity measures.

Let us briefly discuss the PageRank measure. The PageRank of a page P_i (denoted $r(P_i)$) is simply the normalized sum of the PageRank of all P_i's backlink pages (denoted as B_{P_i}):

$$r(P_i) = \sum_{P_j \in B_{P_i}} \frac{r(P_j)}{|P_j|}$$

This formula calculates the rank of a page based on the backlinks, but normalizes the contribution of each backlinking page P_j using the number of links that P_j has to other pages. The idea here is that it is more important to be pointed at by pages conservatively link to other pages than by those who link to others indiscriminately.

A second issue is how the crawler chooses the next page to visit once it has crawled a particular page. As noted earlier, the crawler maintains a queue in which it stores the URLs for the pages that it discovers as it analyzes each page. Thus, the issue is one of ordering the URLs in this queue. A number of strategies are possible. One possibility is to visit the URLs in the order in which they were discovered; this is referred to as the *breadth-first approach* [Cho et al., 1998; Najork and Wiener, 2001]. Another alternative is to use random ordering whereby the crawler chooses a URL randomly from among those that are in its queue of unvisited pages. Other alternatives are to use metrics that combine ordering with importance ranking discussed above, such as backlink counts or PageRank.

Let us discuss how PageRank can be used for this purpose. A slight revision is required to the PageRank formula given above. We are now modelling a random surfer: when landed on a page P, a random surfer is likely to choose one of the URLs on this page as the next one to visit with some (equal) probability d or will jump to a random page with probability $1 - d$. Then the above formula for PageRank is revised as follows [Langville and Meyer, 2006]:

$$r(P_i) = (1 - d) + d \sum_{P_j \in B_{P_i}} \frac{r(P_j)}{|P_j|}$$

The ordering of the URLs according to this formula allows the importance of a page to be incorporated into the order in which the corresponding page is visited. In some formulations, the first term is normalized with respect to the total number of pages in the web.

In addition to the fundamental design issues discussed above, there are a number of additional concerns that need to be addressed for efficient implementation of crawlers. We discuss these briefly.

Since many web pages change over time, crawling is a continuous activity and pages need to be re-visited. Instead of restarting from scratch each time, it is preferable to selectively re-visit web pages and update the gathered information. Crawlers that follow this approach are called *incremental crawlers*. They ensure that the information in their repositories are as fresh as possible. Incremental crawlers can determine the pages that they re-visit based on the change frequency of the pages or by sampling a number of pages. *Change frequency-based* approaches use an estimate of the change frequency of a page to determine how frequently it should be re-visited [Cho and Garcia-Molina, 2000]. One might intuitively assume that pages with high change frequency should be visited more often, but this is not always true – any information extracted from a page that changes frequently is likely to become obsolete quickly, and it may be better to increase revisit interval to that page. It is also possible to develop an adaptive incremental crawler such that the crawling in one cycle is affected by the information collected in the previous cycle [Edwards et al., 2001]. *Sampling-based approaches* [Cho and Ntoulas, 2002] focus on web sites rather than individual web pages. A small number of pages from a web site are sampled to estimate how much change has happened at the site. Based on this sampling estimate, the crawler determines how frequently it should visit that site.

Some search engines specialize in searching pages belonging to a particular topic. These engines use crawlers optimized for the target topic, and are referred to as *focused crawlers*. A focused crawler ranks pages based on their relevance to the target topic, and uses them to determine which pages it should visit next. Classification techniques that are widely used in information retrieval are used in evaluating relevance. They use learning techniques to identify the topic of a given page. Learning techniques are beyond our scope, but a number of them have been developed for this purpose, such as naïve Bayes classifier [Mitchell, 1997; Chakrabarti et al., 2002], and its extensions [Passerini et al., 2001; Altingövde and Ulusoy, 2004], reinforcement learning [McCallum et al., 1999; Kaelbling et al., 1996], and others.

To achieve reasonable scale-up, crawling can be parallelized by running *parallel crawlers*. Any design for parallel crawlers must use schemes to minimize the overhead of parallelization. For instance, two crawlers running in parallel may download the same set of pages. Clearly, such overlap needs to be prevented through coordination of the crawlers' actions. One method of coordination uses a *central coordinator* to dynamically assign each crawler a set of pages to download. Another coordination scheme is to logically partition the web. Each crawler knows its partition, and there is no need for central coordination. This scheme is referred to as the *static assignment* [Cho and Garcia-Molina, 2002].

17.2.2 Indexing

In order to efficiently search the crawled pages and the gathered information, a number of indexes are built as shown in Figure 17.4. The two more important indexes are the *structure* (or *link*) *index* and a *text* (or *content*) *index*. We discuss these in this section.

17.2.2.1 Structure Index

The structure index is based on the graph model that we discussed in Section 17.1, with the graph representing the structure of the crawled portion of the web. The efficient storage and retrieval of these pages is important and two techniques to address these issues were discussed in Section 17.1. The structure index can be used to obtain important information about the linkage of web pages such as information regarding the *neighborhood* of a page and the siblings of a page.

17.2.2.2 Text Index

The most important and mostly used index is the *text index*. Indexes to support text-based retrieval can be implemented using any of the access methods traditionally used to search over text document collections. Examples include *suffix arrays* [Manber and Myers, 1990], *inverted files* or *inverted indexes* [Hersh, 2001], and *signature files* [Faloutsos and Christodoulakis, 1984]. Although a full treatment of all of these indexes is beyond our scope, we will discuss how inverted indexes are used in this context since these are the most popular type of text indexes.

An inverted index is a collection of inverted lists, where each list is associated with a particular word. In general, an inverted list for a given word is a list of document identifiers in which the particular word occurs [Lim et al., 2003]. If needed, the location of the word in a particular page can also be saved as part of the inverted list. This information is usually needed in proximity queries and query result ranking [Brin and Page, 1998]. Search algorithms also often make use of additional information about the occurrence of terms in a web page. For example, terms occurring in bold face (within $\langle B \rangle$ tags), in section headings (within $\langle H1 \rangle$ or $\langle H2 \rangle$ tags), or as anchor text might be weighted differently in the ranking algorithms [Arasu et al., 2001].

In addition to the inverted list, many text indexes also keep a *lexicon*, which is a list of all terms that occur in the index. The lexicon can also contain some term-level statistics that can be used by ranking algorithms [Salton, 1989].

Constructing and maintaining an inverted index has three major difficulties that need to be addressed [Arasu et al., 2001]:

1. In general, building an inverted index involves processing each page, reading all words and storing the location of each word. In the end, the inverted files are written to disk. This process, while trivial for small and static collections,

becomes hard to manage when dealing with a vast and non-static collection like the web.

2. The rapid change of the web poses the second challenge for maintaining the "freshness" of the index. Although we argued in the previous section that incremental crawlers should be deployed to ensure freshness, it has also been argued that periodic index rebuilding is still necessary because most incremental update techniques do not perform well when dealing with the large changes often observed between successive crawls [Melnik et al., 2001].

3. Storage formats of inverted indexes must be carefully designed. There is a tradeoff between a performance gain through a compressed index that allows portions of the index to be cached in memory, and the overhead of decompression at query time. Achieving the right balance becomes a major concern when dealing with web-scale collections.

Addressing these challenges and developing a highly scalable text index can be achieved by distributing the index by either building a *local inverted index* at each machine where the search engine runs or building a *global inverted index* that is then shared [Ribeiro-Neto and Barbosa, 1998]. We don't discuss these further, as the issues are similar to the distributed data and directory management issues we have already covered in previous chapters.

17.2.3 Ranking and Link Analysis

A typical search engine returns a large number of web pages that are expected to be relevant to a user query. However, these pages are likely to be different in terms of their quality and relevance. The user is not expected to browse through this large collection to find a high quality page. Clearly, there is a need for algorithms to rank these pages thus higher quality web pages appear as part of the top results.

Link-based algorithms can be used to rank a collection of pages. To repeat what we discussed earlier, the intuition is that if a page P_j contains a link to page P_i, then it is likely that the authors of page P_j think that page P_i is of good quality. Thus, a page that has a large number of incoming links is expected to have good quality, and hence the number of incoming links to a page can be used as a ranking criteria. This intuition is the basis of ranking algorithms, but, of course, the each specific algorithm implements this intuition in a different and sophisticated way. We already discussed the PageRank algorithm earlier. We will discuss an alternative algorithm called HITS to highlight different ways of approaching the issue [Kleinberg, 1999].

HITS is also a link-based algorithm. It is based on identifying "authorities" and "hubs". A good authority page receives a high rank. Hubs and authorities have a mutually reinforcing relationship: a good authority is a page that is linked to by many good hubs, and a good hub is a document that links to many authorities. Thus, a page pointed to by many hubs (a good authority page) is likely to be of high quality.

Let us start with a web graph, $G = (V, E)$, where V is the set of pages and E is the set of links among them. Each page P_i in V has a pair of non-negative weights (a_{P_i}, h_{P_i}) that represent the authoritative and hub values of P_i respectively.

The authoritative and hub values are updated as follows. If a page P_i is pointed to by many good hubs, then a_{P_i} is increased to reflect all pages P_j that link to it (the notation $P_j \to P_i$ means that page P_j has a link to page P_i):

$$a_{P_i} = \sum_{\{P_j | P_j \to P_i\}} h_{P_j}$$
$$h_{P_i} = \sum_{\{P_j | P_j \to P_i\}} a_{P_j}$$

Thus, the authoritative value (hub value) of page P_i, is the sum of the hub values (authority values) of all the backlink pages to P_i.

17.2.4 Evaluation of Keyword Search

Keyword-based search engines are the most popular tools to search information on the web. They are simple, and one can specify fuzzy queries that may not have an exact answer, but may only be answered approximately by finding facts that are "similar" to the keywords. However, there are obvious limitations as to how much one can do by simple keyword search. The obvious limitation is that keyword search is not sufficiently powerful to express complex queries. This can be (partially) addressed by employing iterative queries where previous queries by the same user can be used as the context for the subsequent queries. A second limitation is that keyword search does not offer support for a global view of information on the web the way that database querying exploits database schema information. It can, of course, be argued that a schema is meaningless for web data, but the lack of an overall view of the data is an issue nevertheless. A third problem is that it is difficult to capture user's intent by simple keyword search – errors in the choice of keywords may result in retrieving many irrelevant answers.

Category search addresses one of the problems of using keyword search, namely the lack of a global view of the web. Category search is also known as web directory, catalogs, yellow pages, and subject directories. There are a number of public web directories available: dmoz (http://dmoz.org/), LookSmart (http://www.looksmart.com/), and Yahoo (http://www.yahoo.com/). The web directory is a hierarchical taxonomy that classifies human knowledge [Baeza-Yates and Ribeiro-Neto, 1999]. Although, the taxonomy is typically displayed as a tree, it is actually a directed acyclic graph since some categories are cross referenced,.

If a category is identified as the target, then the web directory is a useful tool. However, not all web pages can be classified, so the user can use the directory for searching. Moreover, natural language processing cannot be 100% effective for categorizing web pages. We need to depend on human resource for judging the submitted pages, which may not be efficient or scalable. Finally, some pages change over time, so keeping the directory up-to-date involves significant overhead.

There have also been some attempts to involve multiple search engines in answering a query to improve recall and precision. A metasearcher is a web server that takes a given query from the user and sends it to multiple heterogeneous search engines. The metasearcher then collects the answers and returns a unified result to the user. It has the ability to sort the result by different attributes such as host, keyword, date, and popularity. Examples include Copernic (http://www.copernic.com/), Dogpile (http://www.dogpile.com/), MetaCrawler (http://www.metacrawler.com/), and Mamma (http://www.mamma.com/). Different metasearchers have different ways to unify results and translate the user query to the specific query languages of each search engines. The user can access a metasearcher through client software or a web page. Each search engine covers a smaller percentage of the web. The goal of a metasearcher is to cover more web pages than a single search engine by combining different search engines together.

17.3 Web Querying

Declarative querying and efficient execution of queries has been a major focus of database technology. It would be beneficial if the database techniques can be applied to the web. In this way, accessing the web can be treated, to a certain extent, similar to accessing a large database.

There are difficulties in carrying over traditional database querying concepts to web data. Perhaps the most important difficulty is that database querying assumes the existence of a strict schema. As noted above, it is hard to argue that there is a schema for web data similar to databases[2]. At best, the web data are *semistructured* – data may have some structure, but this may not be as rigid, regular, or complete as that of databases, so that different instances of the data may be similar but not identical (there may be missing or additional attributes or differences in structure). There are, obviously, inherent difficulties in querying schema-less data.

A second issue is that the web is more than the semistructured data (and documents). The links that exist between web data entities (e.g., pages) are important and need to be considered. Similar to search that we discussed in the previous section, links may need to be followed and exploited in executing web queries. This requires links to be treated as first-class objects.

A third major difficulty is that there is no commonly accepted language, similar to SQL, for querying web data. As we noted in the previous section, keyword search has a very simple language, but this is not sufficient for richer querying of web data. Some consensus on the basic constructs of such a language has emerged (e.g., path expressions), but there is no standard language. However, a standardized language

---

[2] We are focusing on the "open" web here; deep web data may have a schema, but it is usually not accessible to users.

for XML has emerged (XQuery), and as XML becomes more prevalent on the web, this language is likely to become dominant and more widely used. We discuss XML data and its management in Section 17.4.

A number of different approaches to web querying have been developed, and we discuss them in this section.

17.3.1 Semistructured Data Approach

One way to approach querying the web data is to treat it as a collection of semistructured data. Then, models and languages that have been developed for this purpose can be used to query the data. Semistructured data models and languages were not originally developed to deal with web data; rather they addressed the requirements of growing data collections that did not have as strict a schema as their relational counterparts. However, since these characteristics are also common to web data, later studies explored their applicability in this domain. We demonstrate this approach using a particular model (OEM) and a language (Lorel), but other approaches such as UnQL [Buneman et al., 1996] are similar.

OEM (Object Exchange Model) [Papakonstantinou et al., 1995] is a self-describing semistructured data model. Self-describing means that each object specifies the schema that it follows.

An OEM object is defined as a four-tuple ⟨label, type, value, oid⟩, where label is a character string describing what the object represents, type specifies the type of the object's value, value is obvious, and oid is the object identifier that distinguishes it from other objects. The type of an object can be atomic, in which case the object is called an *atomic object*, or complex, in which case the object is called a *complex object*. An atomic object contains a primitive value such as an integer, a real, or a string, while a complex object contains a set of other objects, which can themselves be atomic or complex. The value of a complex object is a set of oids. One would immediately recognize the similarity between OEM object definition and the object models that we discussed in Chapter 15.

Example 17.1. Let us consider a bibliographic database that consists of a number of documents. A snapshot of an OEM representation of such a database is given in Figure 17.5. Each line shows one OEM object and the indentation is provided to simplify the display of the object structure. For example, the second line <doc, complex, &o3, &o6, &o7, &o20, &o21, &o2> defines an object whose label is doc, type is complex, oid is &o2, and whose value consists of objects whose oids are &o3, &o6, &o7, &o20, and &o21.

This database contains three documents (&o2, &o22, &o34); the first and third are books and the second is an article. There are commonalities among the two books (and even the article), but there are differences as well. For example, the first book (&o2) has the price information that the second one (&o34) does not have, while the second one has ISBN and publisher information that the first does not have. The object-oriented structure of the database is obvious – complex objects consist of

```
<bib, complex, {&o2, &o22, &o34}, &o1>
   <doc, complex, {&o3, &o6, &o7, &o20, &o22}, &o2>
      <authors, complex, {&o4, &o5}, &o3>
         <author, string, "M. Tamer Ozsu", &o4>
         <author, string, "Patrick Valduriez", &o5>
      <title, string, "Principles of Distributed ...", &o6>
      <chapters, complex, {&o8, &o11, &o14, &o17}, &o7>
         <chapter, complex, {&o9, &o10}, &o8>
            <heading, string, "...", &o9>
            <body, string, "...", &o10>
            ...
         <chapter, complex, {&o18, &o19}, &17>
            <heading, string, "...", &o18>
            <body, string, "...", &o19>
      <what, string, "Book", &o20>
      <price, float, 98.50, &o21>
   <doc, complex, {&o23, &o25, &o26, &o27, &o28}, &o22>
      <authors, complex, {&o24, &o4}, &o23>
         <author, string, "Yingying Tao", &o24>
      <title, string, "Mining data streams ...", &o25>
      <venue, string, "CIKM", &o26>
      <year, integer, 2009, &o27>
      <sections, complex, {&o29, &o30, &o31, &o32, &o33}, &28>
         <section, string, "...", &o29>
         ...
         <section, string, "...", &o33>
   <doc, complex, {&o16,&o17,&o7,&o18,&o19,&o20,&o21},&o34>
      <author, string, "Anthony Bonato", &o35>
      <title, string, "A Course on the Web Graph", &o36>
      <what, string, "Book", &o20>
      <ISBN, string, "TK5105.888.B667", &o37>
      <chapters, complex, {&o39, &o42, &o45}, &o38>
         <chapter, complex, {&o40, &o41}, &o39>
            <heading, string, "...", &o40>
            <body, string, "...", &o41>
         <chapter, complex, {&o43, &o44}, &o42>
            <heading, string, "...", &o43>
            <body, string, "...", &o44>
         <chapter, complex, {&o46, &o47}, &45>
            <heading, string, "...", &o46>
            <body, string, "...", &o47>
      <publisher, string, "AMS", &o48>
```

Fig. 17.5 An Example OEM Specification

subobjects (books consist of chapters in addition to other information), and objects may be shared (e.g., &o4 is shared by both &o3 and &o23).   ◆

As noted earlier, OEM data are self-describing, where each object identifies itself through its type and its label. It is easy to see that the OEM data can be represented as a node-labelled graph where the nodes correspond to each OEM object and the edges correspond to the subobject relationship. The label of a node is the oid and the label of the object corresponding to that node. However, it is quite common in literature to model the data as an edge-labelled graph: if object o_j is a subobject of object o_i, then o_j's label is assigned to the edge connecting o_i to o_j, and the oids are omitted as node labels. In Example 17.2, we use a node and edge-labelled representation that shows oids as node labels and assigns edge labels as described above.

Example 17.2. Figure 17.6 depicts the node and edge-labelled graph representation of the example OEM database given in Example 17.1. Normally, each leaf node also contains the value of that object. To simplify exposition of the idea, we do not show the values.   ◆

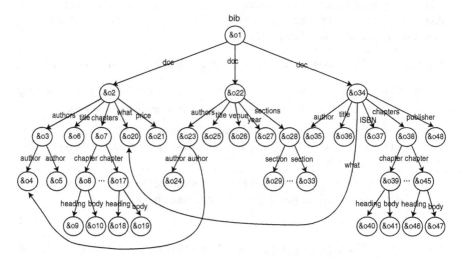

Fig. 17.6 The corresponding OEM graph for the OEM database of Example 17.1

The semistructured approach fits reasonably well for modelling web data that can be represented as a graph. Furthermore, it accepts that data may have some structure, but this may not be as rigid, regular, or complete as that of traditional databases. The users do not need to be aware of the complete structure when they query the data. Therefore, expressing a query should not require full knowledge of the structure. These graph representations of data at each data source are generated by wrappers that we discussed in Chapter 9.

Let us now focus on the languages that have been developed to query semistructured data. As noted above, we will focus our discussion by considering a particular language, Lorel [Papakonstantinou et al., 1995; Abiteboul et al., 1997], but other languages are similar in their basic approaches.

Lorel has changed over its development cycle, and the final version [Abiteboul et al., 1997] is defined as an extension of OQL discussed in Chapter 15. Thus, it has the familiar `SELECT-FROM-WHERE` structure, but path expressions can exist in the `SELECT`, `FROM` and `WHERE` clauses.

The fundamental construct in forming Lorel queries is, therefore, a *path expression*. We discussed path expressions as they appear in object database systems in Section 15.6.2.2, but we give the definition here as it applies to Lore. In its simplest form, a path expression in Lorel is a sequence of labels starting with an object name or a variable denoting an object. For example `bib.doc.title` is a path expression whose interpretation is to start at bib and follow the edge labelled doc and then follow the edge labelled title. Note that there are three paths in Figure 17.6 that would satisfy this expression: (i) `&o1.doc:&o2.title:&o6`, (ii) `&o1.doc:&o22.title:&o25`, and (iii) `&o1.doc:&o34.title:&o36`. Each of these are called a *data path*. In Lorel, path expressions can be more complex regular expressions such that what follows the object name or variable is not only a label, but more general expressions that can be constructed using conjunction, disjunction (|), iteration (? to mean 0 or 1 occurrences, + to mean 1 or more, and * to mean 0 or more), and wildcards (#).

Example 17.3. The following are examples of acceptable path expressions in Lorel:

(a) `bib.doc(.authors)?.author` : start from bib, follow doc edge and the author edge with an optional authors edge in between.

(b) `bib.doc.#.author` : start from bib, follow doc edge, then an arbitrary number of edges with unspecified labels (using the wildcard #), and follow the author edge.

(c) `bib.doc.%price` : start from bib, follow doc edge, then an edge whose label has the string "price" preceded by some characters.

$\blacklozenge$

Example 17.4. The following are example Lorel queries that use some of the path expressions given in Example 17.3:

(a) Find the titles of documents written by Patrick Valduriez.

```
SELECT D.title
FROM   bib.doc D
WHERE  bib.doc(.authors)?.author = "Patrick Valduriez"
```

In this query, the FROM clause restricts the scope to documents (doc), and the SELECT clause specifies the nodes reachable from documents by following the title label. We could have specified the WHERE predicate as

```
D(.authors)?.author = "Patrick Valduriez".
```

(b) Find the authors of all books whose price is under $100.

```
SELECT D(.authors)?.author
FROM   bib.doc D
WHERE  D.what = "Books"
AND    D.price < 100
```

$\blacklozenge$

As can be observed, semistructured data approach to modelling and querying web data is simple and flexible. It also provides a natural way to deal with containment structure of web objects, thereby supporting, to some extent, the link structure of web pages. However, there are also deficiencies of this approach. The data model is too simple – it does not include a record structure (each node is a simple entity) nor does it support ordering as there is no imposed ordering among the nodes of an OEM graph. Furthermore, the support for links is also relatively rudimentary, since the model or the languages do not differentiate between different types of links. The links may show either subpart relationships among objects or connections between different entities that correspond to nodes. These cannot be separately modelled, nor can they be easily queried.

Finally, the graph structure can get quite complicated, making it difficult to query. Although Lorel provides a number of features (such as wildcards) to make querying easier, the examples above indicate that a user still needs to know the general structure of the semistructured data. The OEM graphs for large databases can become quite complicated, and it is hard for users to form the path expressions. The issue, then, is how to "summarize" the graph so that there might be a reasonably small schema-like description that might aid querying. For this purpose, a construct called a DataGuide [Goldman and Widom, 1997] has been proposed. A DataGuide is a graph where each path in the corresponding OEM graph occurs only once. It is dynamic in that as the OEM graph changes, the corresponding DataGuide is updated. Thus, it provides concise and accurate structural summaries of semistructured databases and can be used as a light-weight schema, which is useful for browsing the database structure, formulating queries, storing statistical information, and enabling query optimization.

Example 17.5. The DataGuide corresponding to the OEM graph in Example 17.2 is given in Figure 17.7. ♦

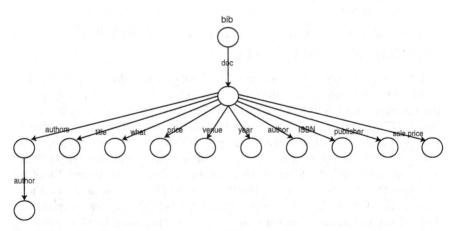

Fig. 17.7 The DataGuide corresponding to the OEM graph of Example 17.2

17.3.2 Web Query Language Approach

The approaches in this category are aimed to directly address the characteristics of web data, particularly focusing on handling *links* properly. Their starting point is to overcome the shortcomings of keyword search by providing proper abstractions for capturing the content structure of documents (as in semistructured data approaches) as well as the external links. They combine the content-based queries (e.g., keyword expressions) and structure-based queries (e.g., path expressions).

A number of languages have been proposed specifically to deal with web data, and these can be categorized as first-generation and second generation [Florescu et al., 1998]. The first generation languages model the web as interconnected collection of *atomic* objects. Consequently, these languages can express queries that search the link structure among web objects and their textual content, but they cannot express queries that exploit the document structure of these web objects. The second generation languages model the web as a linked collection of *structured* objects, allowing them to express queries that exploit the document structure similar to semistructured languages. First generation approaches include WebSQL [Mendelzon et al., 1997], W3QL [Konopnicki and Shmueli, 1995], and WebLog [Lakshmanan et al., 1996], while second generation approaches include WebOQL [Arocena and Mendelzon, 1998], and StruQL [Fernandez et al., 1997]. We will demonstrate the general ideas by considering one first generation language (WebSQL) and one second generation language (WebOQL).

WebSQL is one of the early query languages that combines searching and browsing. It directly addresses web data as captured by web documents (usually in HTML format) that have some content and may include links to other pages or other objects (e.g., PDF files or images). It treats links as first-class objects, and identifies a number of different types of links that we will discuss shortly. As before, the structure can be represented as a graph, but WebSQL captures the information about web objects in two *virtual* relations:

DOCUMENT(URL, TITLE, TEXT, TYPE, LENGTH, MODIF)

ANCHOR(BASE, HREF, LABEL)

DOCUMENT relation holds information about each web document where URL identifies the web object and is the primary key of the relation, TITLE is the title of the web page, TEXT is its text content of the web page, TYPE is the type of the web object (HTML document, image, etc), LENGTH is self-explanatory, and MODIF is the last modification date of the object. Except URL, all other attributes can have null values. ANCHOR relation captures the information about links where BASE is the URL of the HTML document that contains the link, HREF is the URL of the document that is referenced, and LABEL is the label of the link as defined earlier.

WebSQL defines a query language that consists of SQL plus path expressions. The path expressions are more powerful than their counterparts in Lorel; in particular, they identify different types of links:

(a) *interior link* that exists within the same document (#>)

(b) *local link* that is between documents on the same server (->)

(c) *global link* that refers to a document on another server (=>)

(d) *null path* (=)

These link types form the alphabet of the path expressions. Using them, and the usual constructors of regular expressions, different paths can be specified as in Example 17.6.

Example 17.6. The following are examples of possible path expressions that can be specified in WebSQL [Mendelzon et al., 1997].

(a) -> | =>: a path of length one, either local or global

(b) ->*: local path of any length

(c) =>->*: as above, but in other servers

(d) (-> |=>)*: the reachable portion of the web

◆

In addition to path expressions that can appear in queries, WebSQL allows scoping within the FROM clause in the following way:

```
FROM Relation SUCH THAT domain-condition
```

where `domain-condition` can be either a path expression, or can specify a text search using MENTIONS, or can specify that an attribute (in the SELECT clause) is equal to a web object. Of course, following each relation specification, there could be a variable ranging over the relation – this is standard SQL. The following example queries (taken from [Mendelzon et al., 1997] with minor modifications) demonstrate the features of WebSQL.

Example 17.7. Following are some examples of WebSQL:

(a) The first example we consider simply searches for all documents about "hypertext" and demonstrates the use of MENTIONS to scope the query.

```
SELECT D.URL, D.TITLE
FROM   DOCUMENT D
           SUCH THAT D MENTIONS "hypertext"
WHERE  D.TYPE = "text/html"
```

(b) The second example demonstrates two scoping methods as well as a search for links. The query is to find all links to aplets from documents about "Java".

```
SELECT A.LABEL, A.HREF
FROM   DOCUMENT D
           SUCH THAT D MENTIONS "Java",
       ANCHOR A
           SUCH THAT BASE = X
WHERE  A.LABEL = "applet"
```

(c) The third example demonstrates the use of different link types. It searches for documents that have the string "database" in their title that are reachable from the ACM Digital Library home page through paths of length two or less containing only local links.

```
SELECT D.URL, D.TITLE
FROM    DOCUMENT D
            SUCH THAT "http://www.acm.org/dl"=|->|->-> D
WHERE   D.TITLE CONTAINS "database"
```

(d) The final example demonstrates the combination of content and structure specifications in a query. It finds all documents mentioning "Computer Science" and all documents that are linked to them through paths of length two or less containing only local links.

```
SELECT D1.URL, D1.TITLE, D2.URL, D2.TITLE
FROM    DOCUMENT D1
            SUCH THAT D1 MENTIONS "Computer Science",
        DOCUMENT D2
            SUCH THAT D1=|->|->-> D2
```

◆

Careful readers will have recognized that while WebSQL can query web data based on the links and the textual content of web documents, it cannot query the documents based on their structure. This is the consequence of its data model that treats the web as a collection of atomic objects.

As noted earlier, second generation languages, such as WebOQL, address this shortcoming by modelling the web as a graph of structured objects. In a way, they combine some features of semistructured data approaches with those of first generation web query models.

WebOQL's main data structure is a *hypertree*, which is an ordered edge-labelled tree with two types of edges: internal and external. An *internal edge* represents the internal structure of a web document, while an *external edge* represents a reference (i.e., hyperlink) among objects. Each edge is labelled with a record that consists of a number of attributes (fields). An external edge has to have a URL attribute in its record and cannot have descendants (i.e., they are the leaves of the hypertree).

Example 17.8. Let us revisit Example 17.1 and assume that instead of modelling the documents in a bibliography, it models the collection of documents about data management over the web. A possible (partial) hypertree for this example is given in Figure 17.8. Note that we have made one revision to facilitate some of the queries to be discussed later: we added an abstract to each document.

In Figure 17.8, the documents are first grouped along a number of topics as indicated in the records attached to the edges from the root. In this representation, the internal links are shown as solid edges and external links as dashed edges. Recall that in OEM (Figure 17.6), the edges represent both attributes (e.g., author) and document structure (e.g., chapter). In the WebOQL model, the attributes are captured in the records that are associated with each edge, while the (internal) edges represent the document structure.   ◆

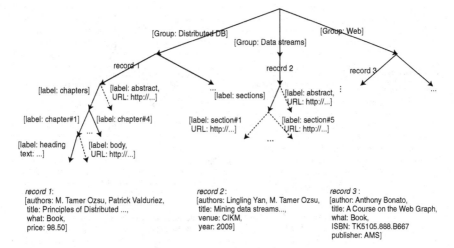

record 1:
[authors: M. Tamer Ozsu, Patrick Valduriez,
title: Principles of Distributed ...,
what: Book,
price: 98.50]

record 2:
[authors: Lingling Yan, M. Tamer Ozsu,
title: Mining data streams...,
venue: CIKM,
year: 2009]

record 3:
[author: Anthony Bonato,
title: A Course on the Web Graph,
what: Book,
ISBN: TK5105.888.B667
publisher: AMS]

Fig. 17.8 The hypertree example

Using this model, WebOQL defines a number of operators over trees:

Prime: returns the first subtree of its argument (denoted ').

Peek: extracts a field from the record that labels the first outgoing edges of its document. This is the straightforward "dot notation" that we have seen multiple times before. For example, if x points to the root of the subtree reached from the "Groups = Distributed DB" edge, x.authors would retrieve "M. Tamer Ozsu, Patrick Valduriez".

Hang: builds an edge-labeled tree with a record formed with the arguments (denoted as []).

Example 17.9.
Let us assume that the tree depicted in Figure 17.9(a) is retrieved as a result of a query (call it Q1). Then the expression ["Label: "Papers by Ozsu" / Q1] results in the tree depicted in Figure 17.9(b). ◆

Concatenate: combines two trees (denoted +).

Example 17.10. Again, assuming that the tree depicted in Figure 17.9(a) is retrieved as a result of query Q1, Q1+Q2 produces tree in Figure 17.9(c). ◆

Head: returns the first simple tree of a tree (denoted &). A simple tree of a tree t are the trees composed of one edge followed by a (possibly null) tree that originates from t's root.

Tail: returns all but the first simple tree of a tree (denoted !).

In addition to these, WebOQL introduces a string pattern matching operator (denoted $\sim$) whose left argument is a string and right argument is a string pattern.

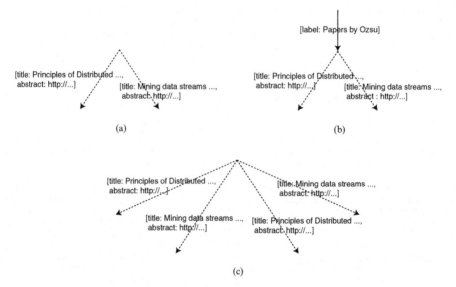

Fig. 17.9 Examples of Hang and Concatenate Operators

Since the only data type supported by the language is string, this is an important operator.

WebOQL is a functional language, so complex queries can be composed by combining these operators. In addition, it allows these operators to be embedded in the usual SQL (or OQL) style queries as demonstrated by the following example.

Example 17.11. Let dbDocuments denote the documents in the database shown in Figure 17.8. Then the following query finds the titles and abstracts of all documents authored by "Ozsu" producing the result depicted in Figure 17.9(a).

```
SELECT [y.title, y'.URL]
FROM   x IN dbDocuments, y IN x'
WHERE  y.authors ~ "Ozsu"
```

The semantics of this query is as follows. The variable x ranges over the simple trees of dbDocuments, and, for a given x value, y iterates over the simple trees of the single subtree of x. It peeks into the record of the edge and if the authors value matches "Ozsu" (using the string matching operator ~), then it constructs a tree whose label is the title attribute of the record that y points to and the URL attribute value of the subtree.   ♦

The web query languages discussed in this section adopt a more powerful data model than the semistructured approaches. The model can capture both the document structure and the connectedness of web documents. The languages can then exploit these different edge semantics. Furthermore, as we have seen from the WebOQL examples, the queries can construct new structures as a result. However, formation of these queries still requires some knowledge about the graph structure.

17.3.3 Question Answering

In this section, we discuss an interesting and unusual (from a database perspective) approach to querying web data: question answering (QA) systems. These systems accept natural language questions that are then analyzed to determine the specific query that is being posed. They, then, conduct a search to find the appropriate answer.

Question answering systems have grown within the context of IR systems where the objective is to determine the answer to posed queries within a well-defined corpus of documents. These are usually referred to as *closed domain* systems. They extend the capabilities of keyword search queries in two fundamental ways. First, they allow users to specify complex queries in natural language that may be difficult to specify as simple keyword search requests. In the context of web querying, they also enable asking questions without a full knowledge of the data organization. Sophisticated natural language processing (NLP) techniques are then applied to these queries to understand the specific query. Second, they search the corpus of documents and return explicit answers rather than links to documents that may be relevant to the query. This does not mean that they return exact answers as traditional DBMSs do, but they may return a (ranked) list of explicit responses to the query, rather than a set of web pages. For example, a keyword search for "President of USA" using a search engine would return the (partial) result in Figure 17.10. The user is expected to find the answer within the pages whose URLs and short descriptions (called snippets) are included on this page (and several more). On the other hand, a similar search using a natural language question "Who is the president of USA?" might return a ranked list of presidents' names (the exact type of answer differs among different systems).

Question answering systems have been extended to operate on the web. In these systems, the web is used as the corpus (hence they are called *open domain* systems). The web data sources are accessed using wrappers that are developed for them to obtain answers to questions. A number of question answering systems have been developed with different objectives and functionalities, such as Mulder [Kwok et al., 2001], WebQA [Lam and Özsu, 2002], Start [Katz and Lin, 2002], and Tritus [Agichtein et al., 2004]. There are also commercial systems with varying capabilities (e.g., Wolfram Alpha http://www.wolframalpha.com/).

We describe the general functionality of these systems using the reference architecture given in Figure 17.11. Preprocessing, which is not employed in all systems, is an offline process to extract and enhance the rules that are used by the systems. In many cases, these are analyses of documents extracted from the web or returned as answers to previously asked questions in order to determine the most effective query structures into which a user question can be transformed. These transformation rules are stored in order to use them at run-time while answering the user questions. For example, Tritus employs a learning-based approach that uses a collection of frequently asked questions and their correct answers as a training data set. In a three-stage process, it attempts to guess the structure of the answer by analyzing the question and searching for the answer in the collection. In the first stage, the question is analyzed to extract the *question phrase* (e.g., in the question "What is a hard disk?", "What is a" is question phrase). This is used to classify the question. In the second phase,

Fig. 17.10 Keyword Search Example

it analyzes the question-answer pairs in the training data and generates *candidate transforms* for each question phrase (e.g., for the question phrase "What is a" , it generates "refers to", "stands for", etc). In the third stage, each candidate transform is applied to the questions in the training data set, and the resulting transformed queries are sent to different search engines. The similarities of the returned answers with the actual answers in the training data are calculated, and, based on these, a ranking is done for candidate transforms. The ranked transformation rules are stored for later use during run-time execution of questions.

The natural language question that is posed by a user first goes through the question analysis process. The objective is to understand the question issued by the user. Most of the systems try to guess the type of the answer in order to categorize the question, which is used in translating the question into queries and also in

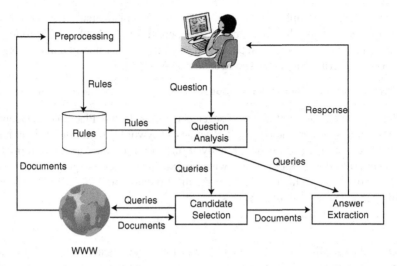

Fig. 17.11 General architecture of QA Systems

answer extraction. If preprocessing has been done, the transformation rules that have been generated are used to assist the process. Although the general goals are the same, the approaches used by different systems vary considerably depending on the sophistication of the NLP techniques employed by the systems (this phase is usually all about NLP). For example, question analysis in Mulder incorporates three phases: question parsing, question classification, and query generation. Query parsing generates a parse tree that is used in query generation and in answer extraction. Question classification, as its name implies, categorizes the question in one of three classes: *nominal* is for nouns, *numerical* is for numbers, and *temporal* is for dates. This type of categorization is done in most of the QA systems because it eases the answer extraction. Finally, query generation phase uses the previously generated parse tree to construct one or more queries that can be executed to obtain the answers to the question. Mulder uses four different methods in this phase.

- Verb conversion: Auxiliary and main verb is replaced by the conjugated verb (e.g., "When did Nixon visit China?" is converted to "Nixon visited China").
- Query expansion: Adjective in the question phrase is replaced by its attribute noun (e.g., "How tall is Mt. Everest?" is converted to "The height of Everest is").
- Noun phrase formation: Some noun phrases are quoted in order to give them together to the search engine in the next stage.
- Transformation: Structure of the question is transformed into the structure of the expected answer type ("Who was the first American in space?" is converted to "The first American in space was").

Mulder is an example of a system that uses a sophisticated NLP approach to question analysis. At the other end of the spectrum is WebQA, which follows a lightweight approach in question parsing. It converts the user question into WebQAL, which is its internal language. The structure of WebQAL is

```
Category [-output Output-Option] -keywords Keyword-List
```

The user question is put in one of seven categories (Name, Place, Time, Quantity, Abbreviation, Weather, and Other). It generates a keyword list after stopword elimination and verb-to-noun conversion. Finally, it further refines the category information and determines the "output option", which is specific to each category. For example, given the question "Which country has the most population in the world?", WebQA would generate the WebQAL expression

```
Place -output country -keywords most population world
```

Once the question is analyzed and one or more queries are generated, the next step is to generate candidate answers. The queries that were generated at question analysis stage are used at this step to perform keyword search for relevant documents. Many of the systems simply use the general purpose search engines in this step, while others also consider additional data sources that are available on the web. For example, CIA's World Factbook (https://www.cia.gov/library/publications/the-world-factbook/) is a very popular source for reliable factual data about countries. Similarly, weather information may be obtained very reliably from a number of weather data sources such as the Weather Network (http://www.theweathernetwork.com/) or Weather Underground (http://www.wunderground.com/). These additional data sources may provide better answers in some cases and different systems take advantage of these to differing degrees (e.g., WebQA uses the data sources extensively in addition to search engines). Since different queries can be better answered by different data sources (and, sometimes, even by different search engines), an important aspect of this processing stage is the choice of the appropriate search engine(s)/data source(s) to consult for a given query. The naive alternative of submitting the queries to all search engines and data sources is not a wise decision, since these operations are quite costly over the web. Usually, the category information is used to assist the choice of the appropriate sources, along with a ranked listing of sources and engines for different categories. For each search engine and data source, wrappers need to be written to convert the query into the format of that data source/search engine and convert the returned result documents into a common format for further analysis.

In response to queries, search engines return links to the documents together with short snippets, while other data sources return results in a variety of formats. The returned results are normalized into what we will call "records". The direct answers need to be extracted from these records, which is the function of the answer extraction phase. Various text processing techniques can be used to match the keywords to (possibly parts of) the returned records. Subsequently, these results need to be ranked using various information retrieval techniques (e.g., word frequencies, inverse document frequency). In this process, the category information that is generated during question analysis is used. Different systems employ different notions of the appropriate answer. Some return a ranked list of direct answers (e.g., if the question is "Who invented the telephone", they would return "Alexander Graham Bell" or "Graham Bell" or "Bell", or all of them in ranked order[3]), while others return a ranked order of the portion of the records that contain the keywords in the query (i.e., a summary of the relevant portion of the document).

Question answering systems are very different than the other web querying approaches we have discussed in previous sections. They are more flexible in what they offer users in terms of querying without any knowledge of the organization of web data. On the other hand, they are constrained by idiosynchrocies of natural language, and the difficulties of natural language processing.

17.3.4 Searching and Querying the Hidden Web

Currently, most general-purpose search engines only operate on the PIW while considerable amount of the valuable data are kept in hidden databases, either as relational data, as embedded documents, or in many other forms. The current trend in web searching is to find ways to search the hidden web as well as the PIW, for two main reasons. First is the size – the size of the hidden web (in terms of generated HTML pages) is considerably larger than the PIW, therefore the probability of finding answers to users' queries is much higher if the hidden web can also be searched. The second is in data quality – the data stored in the hidden web are usually of much higher quality than those found on public web pages since they are properly curated. If they can be accessed, the quality of answers can be improved.

However, searching the hidden web faces many challenges, the most important of which are the following:

1. Ordinary crawlers cannot be used to search the hidden web, since there are neither HTML pages, nor hyperlinks to crawl.

2. Usually, the data in hidden databases can be only accessed through a search interface or a special interface, requiring access to this interface.

3. In most (if not all) cases, the underlying structure of the database is unknown, and the data providers are usually reluctant to provide any information about their data that might help in the search process (possibly due to the overhead of collecting this information and maintaining it). One has to work through the interfaces provided by these data sources.

In the remainder of this section, we describe a number of research efforts that address these issues.

---

[3] The inventor of the telephone is a subject of controversy, with multiple claims to the invention. We'll go with Bell in this example since he was the first one to patent the device.

17.3.4.1 Crawling the Hidden Web

One approach to address the issue of searching the hidden web is to try crawling in a manner similar to that of the PIW. As already mentioned, the only way to deal with hidden web databases is through their search interfaces. A hidden web crawler should be able to perform two tasks: (a) submit queries to the search interface of the database, and (b) analyze the returned result pages and extract relevant information from them.

Querying the Search Interface.

One approach is to analyze the search interface of the database, and build an internal representation for it [Raghavan and Garcia-Molina, 2001]. This internal representation specifies the fields used in the interface, their types (e.g. text boxes, lists, checkboxes, etc.), their domains (e.g. specific values as in lists, or just free text strings as in text boxes), and also the labels associated with these fields. Extracting these labels requires an exhaustive analysis of the HTML structure of the page.

Next, this representation is matched with the system's task-specific database. The matching is based on the labels of the fields. When a label is matched, the field is then populated with the available values for this field. The process is repeated for all possible values of all fields in the search form, and the form is submitted with every combination of values and the results are retrieved.

Another approach is to use agent technology [Lage et al., 2002]. In this case, *hidden web agents* are developed that interact with the search forms and retrieve the result pages. This involves three steps: (a) finding the forms, (b) learning to fill the forms, and (c) identifying and fetching the target (result) pages.

The first step is accomplished by starting from a URL (an entry point), traversing links, and using some heuristics to identify HTML pages that contain forms, excluding those that contain password fields (e.g. login, registration, purchase pages). The form filling task depends on identifying labels and associating them with form fields. This is achieved using some heuristics about the location of the label relative to the field (on the left or above it). Given the identified labels, the agent determines the application domain that the form belongs to, and fills the fields with values from that domain in accordance with the labels (the values are stored in a repository accessible to the agent).

Analyzing the Result Pages.

Once the form is submitted, the returned page has to be analyzed, for example to see if it is a data page or a search-refining page. This can be achieved by matching values in this page with values in the agent's repository [Lage et al., 2002]. Once a data page is found, it is traversed, as well as all pages that it links to (especially pages that have more results), until no more pages can be found that belong to the same domain.

However, the returned pages usually contain a lot of irrelevant data, in addition to the actual results, since most of the result pages follow some template that has a considerable amount of text used only for presentation purposes. A method to identify web page templates is to analyze the textual contents and the adjacent tag structures of a document in order to extract query-related data [Hedley et al., 2004b]. A web page is represented as a sequence of text segments, where a text segment is a piece of tag encapsulated between two tags. The mechanism to detect templates is as follows:

1. Text segments of documents are analyzed based on textual contents and their adjacent tag segments.

2. An initial template is identified by examining the first two sample documents.

3. The template is then generated if matched text segments along with their adjacent tag segments are found from both documents.

4. Subsequent retrieved documents are compared with the generated template. Text segments that are not found in the template are extracted for each document to be further processed.

5. When no matches are found from the existing template, document contents are extracted for the generation of future templates.

17.3.4.2 Metasearching

Metasearching is another approach for querying the hidden web. Given a user's query, a metasearcher performs the following tasks [Ipeirotis and Gravano, 2002]:

1. Database selection: selecting the databases(s) that are most relevant to the user's query. This requires collecting some information about each database. This information is known as a *content summary*, which is statistical information, usually including the *document frequencies* of the words that appear in the database.

2. Query translation: translating the query to a suitable form for each database (e.g. by filling certain fields in the database's search interface).

3. Result merging: collecting the results from the various databases, merging them (and most probably, ordering them), and returning them to the user.

We discuss the important phases of metasearching in more detail below.

Content Summary Extraction.

The first step in metasearching is to compute content summaries. In most of the cases, the data providers are not willing to go through the trouble of providing this information. Therefore, the metasearcher itself extracts this information.

A possible approach is to extract a document sample set from a given database D and compute the frequency of each observed word w in the sample, $SampleDF(w)$ [Callan et al., 1999; Callan and Connell, 2001]. The technique works as follows:

1. Start with an empty content summary where $SampleDF(w) = 0$ for each word w, and a general (i.e., not specific to D), comprehensive word dictionary.

2. Pick a word and send it as a query to database D.

3. Retrieve the top-k documents from among the returned documents.

4. If the number of retrieved documents exceeds a prespecified threshold, stop. Otherwise continue the sampling process by returning to Step 2.

There are two main versions of this algorithm that differ in how Step 2 is executed. One of the algorithms picks a random word from the dictionary. The second algorithm selects the next query from among the words that have been already discovered during sampling. The first constructs better profiles, but is more expensive [Callan and Connell, 2001].

An alternative is to use a focused probing technique that can actually classify the databases into a hierarchical categorization [Ipeirotis and Gravano, 2002]. The idea is to preclassify a set of training documents into some categories, and then extract different terms from these documents and use them as query probes for the database. The single-word probes are used to determine the *actual* document frequencies of these words, while only *sample* document frequencies are computed for other words that appear in longer probes. These are used to estimate the actual document frequencies for these words.

Yet another approach is to start by randomly selecting a term from the search interface itself, assuming that, most probably, this term will be related to the contents of the database [Hedley et al., 2004a]. The database is queried for this term, and the top-k documents are retrieved. A subsequent term is then randomly selected from terms extracted from the retrieved documents. The process is repeated until a pre-defined number of documents are retrieved, and then statistics are calculated based on the retrieved documents.

Database Categorization.

A good approach that can help the database selection process is to categorize the databases into several categories (for example as Yahoo directory). Categorization facilitates locating a database given a user's query, and makes most of the returned results relevant to the query.

If the focused probing technique is used for generating content summaries, then the same algorithm can probe each database with queries from some category and count the number of matches [Ipeirotis and Gravano, 2002]. If the number of matches exceeds a certain threshold, the database is said to belong to this category.

Database Selection.

Database selection is a crucial task in the metasearching process, since it has a critical impact on the efficiency and effectiveness of query processing over multiple databases. A database selection algorithm attempts to find the best set of databases, based on information about the database contents, on which a given query should be executed. Usually this information includes the number of different documents that contain each word (known as the document frequency), as well as some other simple related statistics, such as the number of documents stored in the database. Given these summaries, a database selection algorithm estimates how relevant each database is for a given query (e.g., in terms of the number of matches that each database is expected to produce for the query).

GlOSS [Gravano et al., 1999] is a simple database selection algorithm that assumes that query words are independently distributed over database documents to estimate the number of documents that match a given query. GlOSS is an example of a large family of database selection algorithms that rely on content summaries. Furthermore, database selection algorithms expect such content summaries to be accurate and up to date.

The focused probing algorithm discussed above [Ipeirotis and Gravano, 2002] exploits the database categorization and content summaries for database selection. This algorithm consists of two basic steps: (1) propagate the database content summaries to the categories of the hierarchical classification scheme, and (2) use the content summaries of categories and databases to perform database selection hierarchically by zooming in on the most relevant portions of the topic hierarchy. This results in more relevant answers to the user's query since they only come from databases that belong to the same category as the query itself.

Once the relevant databases are selected, each database is queried, and the returned results are merged and sent back to the user.

17.4 Distributed XML Processing

The predominant encoding for web documents has been HTML (which stands for HyperText Markup Language). A web document encoded in HTML consists of *HTML elements* (e.g., paragraph, heading) that are encapsulated by *tags* (e.g., $< p >$ paragraph $< /p >$). Increasingly, XML (which stands for Extensive Markup Language) [Bray et al., 2009] has emerged as the preferred encoding. Proposed as a simple syntax with flexibility, human-readability, and machine-readability in mind,

XML has been adopted as a standard representation language for data on the Web. Hundreds of XML schemata (e.g., XHTML [XHTML, 2002], DocBook [Walsh, 2006], and MPEG-7 [Martínez, 2004]) are defined to encode data into XML format for specific application domains. Implementing database functionalities over collections of XML documents greatly extends the power to manipulate these data.

In addition to be a data representation language, XML also plays an important role in data exchange between Web-based applications such as Web services. Web services are Web-based autonomous applications that use XML as a *lingua franca* to communicate. A Web service provider describes services using the Web Service Description Language (WSDL) [Christensen et al., 2001], registers services using the Universal Description, Discovery, and the Integration (UDDI) protocol [OASIS UDDI, 2002], and exchanges data with the service requesters using the Simple Object Access Protocol (SOAP) [Gudgin et al., 2007] (a typical workflow can be found in Figure 17.12). All these techniques (WSDL, UDDI, and SOAP) use XML to encode data. Database techniques are also beneficial in this scenario. For example, an XML database can be installed on a UDDI server to store all registered service descriptions. A high-level declarative XML query language, such as XPath [Berglund et al., 2007] or XQuery [Boag et al., 2007] (we will discuss these shortly), can be used to match specific patterns described by a service discovery request.

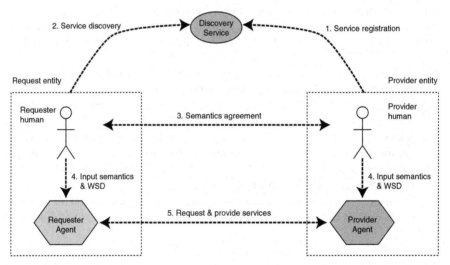

Fig. 17.12 A typical Web Service workflow suggested by the W3C Web Services Architecture (Based on [Booth et al., 2004].)

XML is also used to encode (or annotate) non-Web semistructured or unstructured data. Annotating unstructured data with semantic tags to facilitate queries has been studied in the text community for a long time (e.g., the OED project [Gonnet and Tompa, 1987]). In this scenario, the primary objective is not to share data with others (although one can still do so), but to take advantage of the declarative query languages developed for XML to query the structure that is discovered through the annotation.

As noted above, XML is frequently used to exchange data among a wide variety of systems. Therefore, applications often access data from multiple, independently managed XML data collections. Consequently, a considerable amount of distributed XML processing work has focused on the use of XML in data integration scenarios. The major issues in this conext are similar to those that we have discussed in Chapters 4 and 9.

As the volume of XML data increases along with the workloads that operate on these data, efficient management of these collections become a serious concern. Similar to relational systems, centralized solutions are generally infeasible and distributed solutions are required. The issues here are analogous to the design of tightly-integrated distributed DBMSs that we have discussed in this book. However, the peculiarities of the XML data model and its query languages introduce important differences that we focus on in this section.

We start with a quick overview of XML and the two languages that have been defined for it: XPath and XQuery, particularly focusing on XPath since that has received more attention for its optimization (and since it is an important subset of XQuery). Then we summarize techniques for processing XML queries in a centralized setting as a prelude to the main part of the discussion, which focuses on fragmenting XML data, localizing XML queries by pruning unnecessary fragments, and, finally, their optimization. We should note that our objective is not to provide a complete overview of XML – the topic is much broader than can be covered in a section or a chapter, and there are very good sources, as we note at the end of this chapter, that treat the topic extensively.

17.4.1 Overview of XML

XML tags (also called markups) divide data into pieces called *elements*, with the objective to provide more semantics to the data. Elements can be nested but they cannot be overlapped. Nesting of elements represents hierarchical relationships between them. As an example, Figure 17.13 is the XML representation, with slight revisions, of the bibliography data that we had given earlier.

An XML document can be represented as a tree that contains a *root element*, which has zero or more nested subelements (or *child elements*), which can recursively contain subelements. For each element, there are zero or more *attributes* with atomic values assigned to them. An element also contains an optional value. Due to the textual representation of the tree, a total order, called *document order*, is defined on all elements corresponding to the order in which the first character of the elements occurs in the document.

For instance, the root element in Figure 17.5 is bib, which has three child elements: two book and one article. The first book element has an attribute year with atomic value "1999", and also contains subelements (e.g., the title el-

```
<bib>
   <book year = "1999">
      <author> M. Tamer Ozsu </author>
      <author> Patrick Valduriez </author>
      <title> Principles of Distributed ... </title>
      <chapters>
         <chapter>
            <heading> ... </heading>
            <body> ... </body>
         </chapter>
            ...
         <chapter>
            <heading> ... </heading>
            <body> ... </body>
         </chapter>
      </chapters>
      <price currency= "USD"> 98.50 </price>
   </book>
   <article year = "2009">
      <author> M. Tamer Ozsu </author>
      <author> Yingying Tao </author>
      <title> Mining data streams ... </title>
      <venue> "CIKM" </venue>
      <sections>
         <section> ... </section>
            ...
         <section> ... </section>
      </sections>
   </article>
   <book>
      <author> Anthony Bonato </author>
      <title> A Course on the Web Graph </title>
      <ISBN> TK5105.888.B667 </ISBN>
      <chapters>
         <chapter>
            <heading> ... </heading>
            <body> ... </body>
         </chapter>
         <chapter>
            <heading> ... </heading>
            <body> ... </body>
         </chapter>
         <chapter>
            <heading> ... </heading>
            <body> ... </body>
         </chapter>
      </chapters>
      <publisher> AMS </publisher>
   </book>
</bib>
```

Fig. 17.13 An Example XML Document

ement). An element can contain a value (e.g., "Principles of Distributed Database Systems" for the element title).

Standard XML document definition is a bit more complicated: it can contain ID-IDREFs, which define references between elements in the same document or in another document. In that case, the document representation becomes a graph. However, it is quite common to use the simpler tree representation, and we'll assume the same in this section and we define it more precisely below[4].

An XML document is modelled as an ordered, node-labeled tree $T = (V, E)$, where each node $v \in V$ corresponds to an element or attribute and is characterized by:

- a unique identifier denoted by $ID(v)$;
- a unique *kind* property, denoted as $kind(v)$, assigned from the set {element, attribute, text};
- a label, denoted by $label(v)$, assigned from some alphabet Σ;
- a content, denoted by $content(v)$, which is empty for non-leaf nodes and is a strong for leaf nodes.

A directed edge $e = (u, v)$ is included in E if and only if:

- $kind(u) = kind(v) =$ element, and v is a subelement of u; or
- $kind(u) =$ element $\wedge kind(v) =$ attribute, and v is an attribute of u.

Now that an XML document tree is properly defined, we can define an instance of XML data model as an ordered collection (sequence) of XML document tree nodes or atomic values. A schema may or may not be defined for an XML document, since it is a self-describing format. If a schema is defined for a collection of XML documents, then each document in this collection conforms to that schema; however, the schema allows for variations in each document, since not all elements or attributes may exist in each document. XML schemas can be defined either using the Document Type Definition (DTD) or XMLSchema [Gao et al., 2009]. In this section, we will use a simpler schema definition that exploits the graph structure of XML documents as defined above [Kling et al., 2010].

An XML *schema graph* is defined as a 5-tuple $\langle \Sigma, \Psi, s, m, \rho \rangle$ where Σ is an alphabet of XML document node types, ρ is the root node type, $\Psi \subseteq \Sigma \times \Sigma$ is a set of edges between node types, $s : \Psi \to \{\text{ONCE, OPT, MULT}\}$ and $m : \Sigma \to \{\text{string}\}$. The semantics of this definition are as follows: An edge $\psi = (\sigma_1, \sigma_2) \in \Psi$ denotes that an item of type σ_1 may contain an item of type σ_2. $s(\psi)$ denotes the cardinality of the containment represented by this edge: If $s(\psi) = $ ONCE, then an item of type σ_1 must contain exactly one item of σ_2. If $s(\psi) = $ OPT, then an item of type σ_1 may or may not contain an item of type σ_2. If $s(\psi) = $ MULT, then an item of type σ_1 may contain multiple items of type σ_2. $m(\sigma)$ denotes the domain of the text content of an item of type σ, represented as the set of all strings that may occur inside such an item.

---

[4] In addition, we omit the comment nodes, namespace nodes, and PI nodes from the XQuery Data Model.

Example 17.12. In the remainder of this chapter, we will use a slightly reorganized version of the XML example given in Figure 17.13. This is because that particular XML database consists of a single document, which is not suitable for demonstrating some of the distribution issues. The database definition can be modified by deleting the surrounding `<bib>` `</bib>` tags so that each book is one separate document in the database. However, we will make more changes to have an example that will better assist in the discussion of distribution issues. In this organization, the database will consist of multiple books, but organized by authors (i.e., the root of each document is an `<author>` element). This is given in Figure 17.14.   ◆

Example 17.13. Let us revisit our bibliographic database and make a revision that the entries inside it are organized by authors rather than by publications and the only publications in the collection are books. In this case a (simplified) DTD definition is given below:

```
<?xml version="1.0"?>
<!DOCTYPE            author [
<!ELEMENT            author (name, pubs, agent?)
<!ELEMENT            pubs (book*)
<!ELEMENT            book (title,chapter*)
<!ELEMENT            chapter (reference?)
<!ELEMENT            reference (chapter)
<!ELEMENT            agent (name)
<!ELEMENT            name (first, last)
<!ELEMENT            first (CDATA)
<!ELEMENT            last (CDATA)
<!ATTLIST            book year CDATA #REQUIRED>
<!ATTLIST            book price CDATA #REQUIRED>
<!ATTLIST            author age CDATA #REQUIRED>
]
```

Instead of describing this DTD definition, we give its schema graph in Figure 17.15 using the notation introduced above, and this version clearly shows the semantics. Note that CDATA means that the content of the element is text.   ◆

Using the definition of XML data model and instances of this data model, it is now possible to define the query languages. Expressions in XML query languages take an instance of XML data as input and produce an instance of XML data as output. XPath [Berglund et al., 2007] and XQuery [Boag et al., 2007] are two important query languages proposed by the World Wide Web Consortium (W3C). Path expressions, that we introduced earlier, are present in both query languages and are arguably the most natural way to query the hierarchical XML data. XQuery defines for more powerful constructs in the form of FLWOR expressions and we will briefly touch upon them when appropriate.

Although we have earlier defined path expressions, they take a particular form in the XPath context, so we will define them more carefully. A path expression consists of a list of *steps*, each of which consists of an *axis*, a *name test*, and zero or more *qualifiers*. The last step in the list is called a *return step*. There are in total thirteen

```
<author>
   <name>
      <first>M. Tamer </first>
      <last>Ozsu</last>
      <age>50</age>
   </name>
   <agent>
      <name>
         <first> John </first>
         <last> Doe </last>
      </name>
   </agent>
   <pubs>
      <book year = "1999", price = "$98.50">
         <title> Principles of Distributed ... </title>
         <chapter> ... </chapter>
         ...
         <chapter> ... </chapter>
      </book>
   </pubs>
</author>
<author>
   <name>
      <first>Patrick </first>
      <last>Valduriez</last>
      <age>40</age
   </name>
   <pubs>
      <book year = "1999", price = "$98.50">
         <title> Principles of Distributed ... </title>
         <chapter> ... </chapter>
         ...
         <chapter> ... </chapter>
      </book>
      <book year = "1992", price = "$50.00">
         <title> Data Management and Parallel Processing </title>
         <chapter> ... </chapter>
         ...
         <chapter> ... </chapter>
      </book>
   </pubs>
</author>
<author>
   <name>
      <first> Anthony </first>
      <last> Bonato </last>
      <age>30</age>
   </name>
   <pubs>
      <book year = "2008", price = "$75.00"
         <title> A Course on the Web Graph </title>
         <chapter> ... </chapter>
         ...
         <chapter> ... </chapter>
      </book>
   </pubs>
</author>
```

Fig. 17.14 A Different XML Document Example

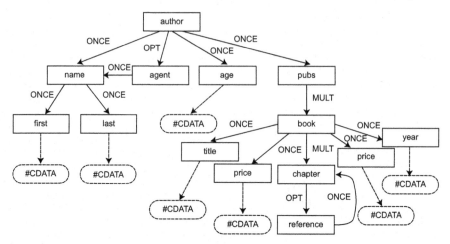

Fig. 17.15 Example XML Schema Graph for Fragmentation

axes, which are listed in Figure 17.16 together with their abbreviations if any. A name test filters nodes by their element or attribute names. Qualifiers are filters testing more complex conditions. The brackets-enclosed expression (which is usually called a *branching predicate*) can be another path expression or a comparison between a path expression and an atomic value (which is a string). The syntax of path expression is as follows:

$$
\begin{aligned}
\text{Path} &::= \text{Step } (\text{"/"Step})^* \\
\text{Step} &::= \text{axis" :: "NameTest (Qualifier)}^* \\
\text{NameTest} &::= \text{ElementName} \mid \text{AttributeName} \mid \text{"} * \text{"} \\
\text{Qualifier} &::= \text{"["Expr"]"} \\
\text{Expr} &::= \text{Path (Comp Atomic)?} \\
\text{Comp} &::= \text{" = "} \mid \text{" > "} \mid \text{" < "} \mid \text{" >= "} \mid \text{" <= "} \mid \text{"! = "} \\
\text{Atomic} &::= \text{"/"String"/"}
\end{aligned}
$$

While the path expression defined here is a fragment of the one defined in XQuery [Boag et al., 2007] (by omitting features related to comments, namespaces, PIs, IDs, and IDREFs, as noted earlier), this definition still covers a significant subset and can express complex queries. As an example, the path expression

```
/author[.//last = "Valduriez"]//book[price < 100]
```

finds all books written by Valduriez with the book price less than 100.

As seen from the above definition, path expressions have three types of constraints: the *tag name constraints*, the *structural relationship constraints*, and the *value constraints*. The tag name, structural relationship, and value constraints correspond to the name tests, axes, and value comparisons in the path expression, respectively. A

Axes	Abbreviations
child	/
descendant	
descendant-or-self	//
parent	
attribute	/@
self	.
ancestor	
ancestor-or-self	
following-sibling	
following	
preceding-sibling	
preceding	
namespace	

Fig. 17.16 Thirteen axes and their abbreviations

path expression can be modeled as a tree, called a *query tree pattern* (QTP) $G(V,E)$ as follows (where V and E are sets of vertices and edges, respectively):

- each step is mapped to an edge in E;
- a special root node is defined as the parent of the tree node corresponding to the first step;
- if one step s_i immediately follows another step s_j, then the node corresponding to s_i is a child of the node corresponding to s_j;
- if step s_i is the first step in the branching predicate of step s_j, then the node corresponding to s_i is a child of the node corresponding to s_j;
- if two nodes represent a parent-child relationship, then the edge in E between them is labeled with the axis between their corresponding steps;
- the node corresponding to the return step is marked as the return node;
- if a branching predicate has a value comparison, then the node corresponding to the last step of the branching predicate is associated with an atomic value and a comparison operator.

For example, the QTP of the path expression

```
/author[last = "Valduriez"]//book[price < 100]
```

is shown in Figure 17.17. In this figure, the node `root` is the root node and the return node (`book`) is identified by two concentric ellipses.

While path expression is an important language component in XQuery, it is only one component of the XQuery language. A major language construct in XQuery is FLWOR expression, which consists of "for", "let", "where", "order by" and "return" clauses. Each clause can reference path expressions or other FLWOR expressions recursively. A FLWOR expression iteration over a list of XML nodes, to bind a list

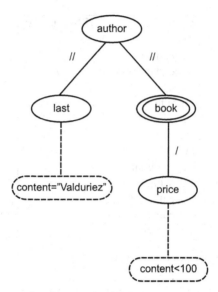

Fig. 17.17 A QTP of expression /author[.//last = "Valduriez"]//book[price
< 100]

of nodes to a variable, to filter a list of nodes based on predicates, to sort the results, and to construct a complex result structure.

In essence, FLWOR is similar to the select-from-where-orderby statement found in SQL, except that the latter operates on a set or bag of tuples while the former manipulates a list of XML document tree nodes. Due to this similarity, FLWOR expressions may be rewritten into SQL statements leveraging existing SQL engines [Liu et al., 2008]. Another approach is to evaluate XQuery using a *native* evaluation engine [Fernández et al., 2003; Brantner et al., 2005]. We will discuss these approaches in the next section.

Example 17.14. The following FLWOR expression returns a list of books with its title and price ordered by their authors names (assuming the database, i.e., the XML document collection, is called "bib").

```
let $col := collection("bib")
for $author in $col/author
   order by $author/name
   for $b in $author/pubs/book
      let $title := $b/title
      let $price := $b/price
      return $title, $price
```
◆

17.4.2 XML Query Processing Techniques

In this section we summarize some of the XML query processing techniques. Again, our objective is not to give an exhaustive coverage of the topic, since that would require an entire book in itself, but only to highlight the major issues.

There are three basic approaches to storing XML documents in a DBMS [Zhang and Özsu, 2010]: (1) the large object (LOB) approach that stores the original XML documents as-is in a LOB column (e.g., [Krishnaprasad et al., 2005; Pal et al., 2005]), (2) the extended relational approach that shreds XML documents into object-relational (OR) tables and columns (e.g., [Zhang et al., 2001; Boncz et al., 2006]), and (3) the native approach that uses a tree-structured data model, and introduces operators that are optimized for tree navigation, insertion, deletion and update (e.g., [Fiebig et al., 2002; Nicola and der Linden, 2005; Zhang et al., 2004]). Each approach has its own advantages and disadvantages.

The LOB approach is very similar to storing the XML documents in a file system, in that there is minimum transformation from the original format to the storage format. It is the simplest one to implement and support. It provides byte-level fidelity (e.g., it preserves extra white spaces that may be ignored by the OR and the native formats) that could be needed for some digital signature schemes. The LOB approach is also efficient for inserting (extracting) the whole documents to (from) the database. However it is slow in processing queries due to unavoidable XML parsing at query execution time.

In the extended relational approach, XML documents are converted to object-relational tables, which are stored in relational databases or in object repositories. This approach can be further divided into two categories based on whether or not the XML-to-relational mapping relies on XML Schema. The OR storage format, if designed and mapped correctly, could perform very well in query processing, thanks to many years of research and development in object-relational database systems. However, insertion, fragment extraction, structural update, and document reconstruction require considerable processing in this approach. For schema-based OR storage, applications need to have a well-structured, rigid XML schema whose relational mapping is tuned by a database administrator in order to take advantage of this storage model. Loosely structured schemas could lead to unmanageable number of tables and joins. Also, applications requiring schema flexibility and schema evolution are limited by those offered by relational tables and columns. The result is that applications encounter a large gap: if they cannot map well to an object-relational way of life due to tradeoffs mentioned above, they suffer a big drop in performance or capabilities.

Native XML storage approach stores XML documents using special data structures and formats that are designed for XML data. There is not, and should not be, a single native format for storing XML documents. Native XML storage techniques treat XML document trees as first class citizens and develop special purpose storage schemes without relying on the existence of an underlying database system. Since it is designed specifically for XML data model, native XML storage usually provides well-balanced tradeoffs among many criteria. Some storage formats may be designed to focus on one set of criteria, while other formats may emphasize another set. For example, some storage schemes are more amenable to fast navigation, and some schemes perform better in fragment extraction and document reconstruction. Therefore, based on their own requirements, different applications adopt different storage schemes to trade off one set of features over another. As an example, Natix [Kanne and Moerkotte, 2000] partitions large XML document trees into small subtrees each of which can fit into a disk page. Inserting a node usually only affects the subtree in which the node is inserted. However, native storage systems may not be efficient in answering certain types of queries (e.g., `/author//book//chapter`) since they require at least one scan of the whole tree. The extended relational storage, on the other hand, may be more efficient for this query due to the special properties of the node encodings. Therefore, a storage system that balances the evaluation and update costs still remains a challenge.

Processing of path queries can also be classified into two categories: join-based approach [Zhang et al., 2001; Al-Khalifa et al., 2002; Bruno et al., 2002; Gottlob et al., 2005; Grust et al., 2003] and navigational approach [Barton et al., 2003; Josifovski et al., 2005; Koch, 2003; Brantner et al., 2005]. Storage systems and query processing techniques are closely related in that the join-based processing techniques are usually based on extended relational storage systems and the navigational approach is based on native storage systems. All techniques in the join-based approach are based on the same idea: each location step in the expression is associated with an input list of elements whose names match with the name test of the step. Two lists of adjacent location steps are joined based on their structural relationships. The differences between different techniques are in their join algorithms, which take into account the special properties of the relational encoding of XML document trees.

The navigational processing techniques, built on top of the native storage systems, match the QTP by traversing the XML document tree. Some navigational techniques (e.g., [Brantner et al., 2005]) are query-driven in that each location step in the path expressions is translated into an algebraic operator which performs the navigation. A data-driven navigational approach (e.g., [Barton et al., 2003; Josifovski et al., 2005; Koch, 2003]) builds an automaton for a path expression and executes the automaton by navigating the XML document tree. Techniques in the data-driven approach guarantee worst case I/O complexity: depending on the expressiveness of the query that can be handled, some techniques (e.g., [Barton et al., 2003; Josifovski et al., 2005]) require only one scan of the data, and the others (e.g., [Koch, 2003]) require two scans.

Both the join-based and navigational approaches have advantages and disadvantages. The join-based approach, while efficient in evaluating expressions having descendent-axes, may not be as efficient as the navigational approach in answering expressions only having child-axes. A specific example is $/*/*$, where all children of the root are returned. As mentioned earlier, each name test ($*$) is associated with an input list, both of which contain all nodes in the XML document (since all element names match with a wildcard). Therefore, the I/O cost of the join-based approach is $2n$, where n is the number of elements. This cost is much higher than the cost of the navigational operator, which only traverses the root and its children. On the other hand, the navigational approach may not be as efficient as the join-based approach for a query such as /author//book//chapter, since the join-based approach only needs to read those elements whose names are book or chapter and join the two lists, but the navigational approach needs to traverse all elements in the tree. Therefore, a technique that combines the best of both approaches would be preferable.

As in relational databases, query processing is significantly aided by the existence of indexes. XML indexing approaches can be categorized into three groups. Some of the indexing techniques are proposed to expedite the execution of existing join-based or navigational approaches (e.g., XB-tree [Bruno et al., 2002] and XR-tree Jiang et al. [2003] for the holistic twig joins). Since these are special-purpose indexes that are designed for a particular baseline operator, their application is quite limited. Another line of research focuses on string-based indexes (e.g., [Wang et al., 2003b; Zezula et al., 2003; Rao and Moon, 2004; Wang and Meng, 2005]). The basic idea is to convert the XML document trees as well as the QTPs into strings and reduce the tree pattern matching problem to string pattern matching. Still other XML indexing techniques focus on the structural similarity of XML document tree nodes and group them accordingly [Milo and Suciu, 1999; Goldman and Widom, 1997; Kaushik et al., 2002]. Although different indexes may be based on different notions of similarity, they are all based on the same idea: similar tree nodes are clustered into equivalence classes (or *index nodes*), which are connected to form a tree or graph. FIX [Zhang et al., 2006b] follows a different approach and indexes the numerical features of subtrees in the data. Features are used as the index keys to a mature index such as B^+-tree. For each incoming query, the features of the query tree are extracted and used as search keys to retrieve the candidate results.

Finally, as we noted a number of times in earlier chapters, a cost-based optimizer is crucial to choosing the "best" query plan. The accuracy of cost estimation is usually dependent on the cardinality estimation. Cardinality estimation techniques for path expressions first summarize an XML document tree (corresponding to a document) into a small synopsis that contains structural information and statistics. The synopsis is usually stored in the database catalog and is used as the basis for estimating cardinality. Depending on how much information is reserved, different synopses cover different types of queries. DataGuide, that we introduced earlier, is on example. Recall that it records all distinct paths from a data set and compresses them into a compact graph. Path tree [Aboulnaga et al., 2001] is another example that follows the same approach (i.e., capturing all distinct paths) and is specifically designed for XML document trees. Path trees can be further compressed if the resulting synopsis is too large. Markov tables [Aboulnaga et al., 2001], on the other hand, do not capture the full paths but sub-paths under a certain length limit. Selectivity of longer paths are calculated using fragments of sub-paths similar to the Markov process. These synopsis structures only support simple linear path queries that may or may not contain descendent-axes. Structural similarity-based synopsis techniques (XSketch [Polyzotis and Garofalakis, 2002] and TreeSketch [Polyzotis et al., 2004]) are proposed to support branching path queries (i.e., those that contain branching predicates as defined earlier). These techniques are very similar to the structural similarity-based indexing techniques: clustering structurally similar nodes into equivalence classes. An extra step is needed for the synopsis: summarize the similarity graph under some memory budget. A common problem of these heuristics is that the synopsis construction (expansion or summarization) time is still prohibitive for structure-rich data. XSEED [Zhang et al., 2006a] also follows the structural similarity approach and constructs a synopsis by first compressing an XML document to a small kernel, and then adds more information to the synopsis to improve accuracy. The amount of additional information is controlled by the memory availability.

Let us now consider XQuery FLWOR expression and introduce possible techniques for its evaluation. As mentioned in the previous subsection, one way to execute FLWOR expressions is to translate them into SQL statements, which can then be evaluated using existing SQL engines. One barrier however is that FLWOR expression works on the XML data model (list of XML nodes) but SQL takes relations as input. The translation has to introduce new operators or functions to convert data between these two data models. One major syntactic construct of this conversion is through the XMLTable function found in SQL/XML [Eisenberg et al., 2008]. XMLTable takes an XML input data source, an XQuery expression to generate rows, and outputs a list of rows with columns specified by the function as well.

Example 17.15. As an example, the following XMLTable function

```
XMLTable('/author/name'
passing collection('bib')
columns
first varchar2(200) PATH '/name/first',
last varchar2(200) PATH '/name/last')
```

takes the input document `bib.xml` from the "passing" clause and applies the path expression `/bib/book` to the input document. For each matching book, there will be one row generated. For each row there are two columns specified by the "columns" clause with its column name and type. A path expression is also given to each column to be used to evaluate its value. The semantics of this XMLTable function is the same as the FLWOR expression:

```
for $a in collection('bib')/author/name
return {$a/first, $a/last}
```
                                                                                    ◆

In fact, almost all FLWOR expressions can be translated to SQL with the help of the XMLTable function. Therefore, the XMLTable function maps XQuery results to relational tables. The result of XMLTable can then be treated as a virtual table and any other SQL construct can be composed on top of that.

Another approach to evaluating XQuery statements is to implement a native XQuery engine that interprets XQuery statements on top of XML data. One example is Galax [Fernández et al., 2003] that first takes an XQuery expression and normalizes it into XQuery core [Draper et al., 2007], which is a covering subset of XQuery. The XQuery core expression is then statically type-checked against the XMLSchema associated with the input data. When the input XML data are parsed and the instance of XML data model (DOM) is generated, the XQuery core expression is dynamically evaluated on the instance of the data model.

Natix [Brantner et al., 2005] is another native approach, but one that defines a set of algebraic operators to which XPath or XQuery queries can be translated. Similar to the relational system, optimization rules can be applied to the operator tree to rewrite it into a more efficient plan. Moreover, Natix defines a native XML storage format based on tree partitioning. Large XML document trees can be partitioned into smaller ones, each of which can fit into a disk page. This native storage format is more scalable than main memory-based DOM representation, and it allows more efficient tree navigation and potentially more efficient path expression evaluation.

In addition to pure relational and pure native XQuery evaluation techniques, there are others that follow a hybrid approach. For example, MonetDB/XQuery [Boncz et al., 2006] stores XML data as a relational table based on the nodes' pre- and post-order position when traversing the tree. XQuery statements are translated into physical relational operators that are designed for efficient evaluation. One particular example is the staircase join operator designed for efficient evaluation of path expressions. In this way, it relies on the SQL engine for most of the relational operations, and expedites XML-specific tree navigations by special purpose operators. In fact, many commercial database vendors also implement special operators in their relational SQL engine to speed up path expression evaluation (e.g., Oracle [Zhang et al., 2009a]). Therefore, while many XQuery engines leverage SQL engines for their ability to efficiently evaluate SQL-like functionalities, many XML specific optimizations and implementations now also penetrate into SQL engine implementations.

17.4.3 Fragmenting XML Data

If we follow the distribution methodology that we introduced earlier in the book, the first step is fragmentation and distribution of data to various sites. In this context, a relevant question is what it means to fragment XML data, and whether we can define horizontal and vertical fragmentation analogous to relational systems. As we will see, this is possible.

Let us first take a detour and consider an interesting case that we refer to as *ad hoc fragmentation*. In this case, there is no explicit, schema-based fragmentation specification; XML data are fragmented by arbitrarily cutting edges in XML document graphs. One example that follows this approach is Active XML [Abiteboul et al., 2008a], which represents cross-fragment edges as calls to remote functions. When such a function call is activated, the data corresponding to the remote fragment are retrieved and made available for local processing. An active XML document, therefore, consists of a static part, which is the XML data, and a dynamic part that includes the function call to web services. When this document is accessed and the service call is invoked, the returned data (i.e., a data fragment) is inserted in place of the call. Although originally designed for easy service integration by allowing calls to various web services, active XML inherently exploits the distribution of data. One way to view this approach is that data fragments are shipped from the source sites to where the XML document is located. When the required data are gathered at this site, and the query is executed on the resulting document.

Example 17.16. Consider the following active XML document where a function call (getPubs) is embedded into a static XML document:

```
<author>
   <name>
      <first> J. </first>
      <last> Doe </last>
   </name>
   ...
   <call fun="getPubs('J. Doe')" />
</author>
```

The resulting document, following the invocation of the function call, would be as follows:

```
<author>
   <name>
      <first> J. </first>
      <last> Doe </last>
   </name>
   ...
   <pubs>
        <book> ... </book>
        ...
   </pubs>
</author>
```
◆

Ad hoc fragmentation works well when the data are already distributed. However, extending it the case where an XML data graph is partitioned arbitrarily is problematic, since it may not be possible to specify the fragmentation predicate clearly. This would decrease the opportunities for distributed query optimization. Remember that distributed optimization in the relational context heavily depends upon the existence of a precise definition of the fragmentation predicate.

The alternative that addresses this issue is *structure-based fragmentation*, which is based on the concept of fragmenting an XML data collection based on some properties of the schema. This is analogous to what we have discussed in the relational setting. The first issue that arises is what types of fragmentations we can define. Similar to relational systems, we can distinguish between horizontal fragmentation where subsets of the data are selected, and vertical fragmentation where fragments are identified based on "projections" over the schema. The specific definitions of these differ among various works; we will follow one line of research to illustrate the concepts [Kling et al., 2010].

A horizontal fragmentation can be defined by a set of fragmentation predicates, such that each fragment consists of the document trees that match the corresponding predicate. For a horizontal fragmentation to be meaningful, the data should consist of multiple document trees; otherwise it makes no sense to have fragments such that each fragment follows the same schema, which is a requirement of horizontal fragmentation. These document trees can either be entire XML documents or they can be the result of a previous vertical fragmentation step. Let $D = \{d_1, d_2, \ldots, d_n\}$ be a collection of document trees such that each $d_i \in D$ follows to the same schema. Then we can define a set of *horizontal fragmentation predicates* $P = \{p_0, p_1, \ldots, p_{l-1}\}$ such that $\forall d \in D : \exists$ unique $p_i \in P$ where $p_i(d)$. If this holds, then $F = \{\{d \in D \mid p_i(d)\} \mid p_i \in P\}$ is a set of horizontal fragments corresponding to collection D and predicates P.

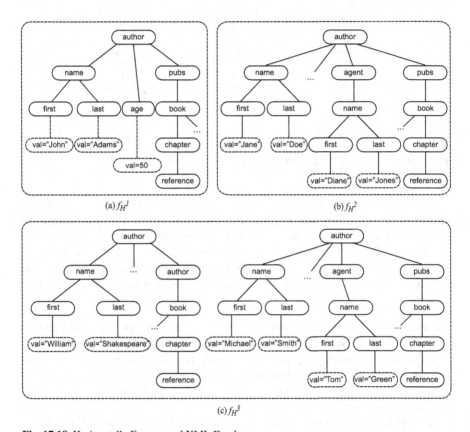

Fig. 17.18 Horizontally Fragmented XML Database

Example 17.17. Consider a bibliographic database that conforms to the schema given in Example 17.13 (and Figure 17.15). A possible horizontal fragmentation of this database based on the first letter of authors' last names is given in Figure 17.18. In this case, we are assuming that there are only four authors in the database whose names are "John Adams", "Jane Doe", "Michael Smith", and "William Shakespeare".

Note that we do not show all of the attributes of elements; in particular, the age attribute of authors, and the price attribute of books are not always shown.

If we assume that, in the example schema, $m(\texttt{last})$ is the set of strings that start with upper-case letters of the English alphabet then the fragmentation predicates are straightforward. Note that the fragmentation predicates can be represented as trees referred to as *fragmentation tree patterns* (FTPs) [Kling et al., 2010] shown in Figure 17.19 where the edges are labelled with the corresponding XPath axis.   ◆

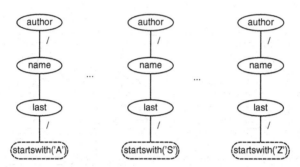

Fig. 17.19 Example Fragmentation Tree Patterns

Definition of vertical fragmentation is more interesting. A vertical fragmentation is defined by fragmenting the schema graph of the collection into disjoint subgraphs. Formally, given a schema as defined earlier, we can define a *vertical fragmentation function* $\phi : \Sigma \rightarrow F_\Sigma$ where F_Σ is a partitioning of Σ (recall that Σ is the set of node types). The fragment that has the root element is called the *root fragment*; the concepts of *parent fragment* and *child fragment* can be defined in a straightforward manner.

Example 17.18. Figure 17.20 shows a fragmented schema graph that corresponds to the schema that we have been considering. The item types have been fragmented into four disjoint subgraphs. Fragment f_V^1 consists of the item types $\texttt{author}$ and $\texttt{agent}$, fragment f_V^2 consists of the item types $\texttt{name}$, $\texttt{first}$ and $\texttt{last}$ along with their text content, fragment f_V^3 consists of $\texttt{pubs}$ and $\texttt{book}$ and fragment f_V^4 includes the item types $\texttt{chapter}$ and $\texttt{reference}$.

The vertical fragment instances of our example database are given in Figure 17.21, where f_V^1 is the root fragment. Again, we do not show all the nodes and we have omitted "val=" from the value nodes to fit the figure (these are done in Figure 17.22 as well).   ◆

As depicted in Figure 17.21, there are document edges that cross fragment boundaries. To facilitate these connections, special nodes are introduced in the fragments: for an edge from fragment f_i to f_j, a *proxy node* is introduced in the originating fragment f_i (denoted $P_k^{i \rightarrow j}$ where k is the ID of the proxy node) and a *root proxy node* is introduced in the target fragment f_j (denoted $RP_k^{i \rightarrow j}$). Since $P_k^{i \rightarrow j}$ and $RP_k^{i \rightarrow j}$

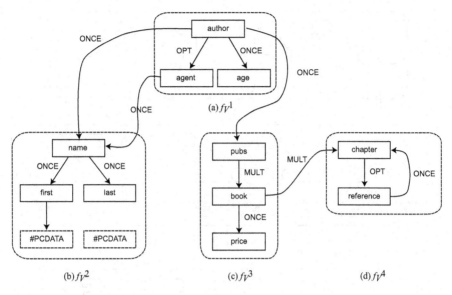

Fig. 17.20 Example Vertical Fragmentation of Schema

share the same ID (k) and reference the same fragments ($i \rightarrow j$), they correspond to each other and together represent a single cross-fragment edge in the collection.

Example 17.19. Figure 17.22 depicts the same fragmentation shown in Figure 17.21 with the proxy nodes inserted.   ◆

Vertical fragments generally consist of multiple unconnected pieces of XML data if the database consists of multiple documents. In this case, each piece comes from one document, and can be referred to as a *document snippet*. In Figure 17.21 (and in Figure 17.22), fragment f_V^1 contains four snippets, each of which consists of the `author` and `agent` nodes of one of the documents in the database.

Based on the above definitions, fragmentation algorithms can be developed. This area is still not fully developed, therefore we will provide a general discussion rather than giving detailed algorithms.

The horizontal fragmentation algorithm for relational systems that we introduced in Chapter 3 can be used for XML databases as well with the appropriate revisions. Recall that the relational fragmentation algorithm is based on minterm predicates, which are conjunctions of simple predicates on individual attributes. Thus, the issue is how to transform the predicates found in QTPs (i.e., trees that correspond to queries) into simple predicates. There may be multiple ways of doing this. Kling et al. [2010] discuss one approach where the mapping is straightforward if the QTP does not contain descendent (//) axes; if they do, then these are "unrolled" into equivalent paths comprised entirely of child axes using schema information.

In the case of vertical fragmentation, the problem is somewhat more complicated. One way to formalize the problem is to use a cost model to estimate the response

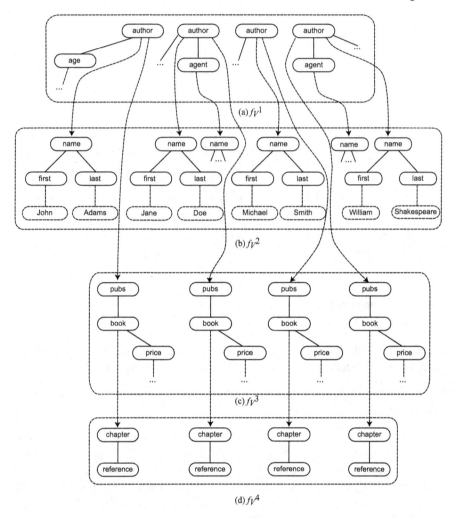

Fig. 17.21 Example Vertical Fragmentation Instances

time of the local query plans corresponding to each fragment. Since these local query plans are evaluated independently of each other in parallel, we can model the overall cost of a query as the maximum local plan cost. In theory, we can then enumerate all possible ways of partitioning the schema. Unfortunately, the large number of partitions to consider makes this approach infeasible for all but the smallest schemas. For a schema with n node types there are B_n partitions to consider where B_n is the nth Bell number, which is exponential in n (this is similar to the relational case). It is, however, possible to use a greedy strategy and still obtain a good fragmentation schema: Starting with a fragmentation schema in which each node type is placed in its own fragment, one can repeatedly merge the fragment corresponding to the most

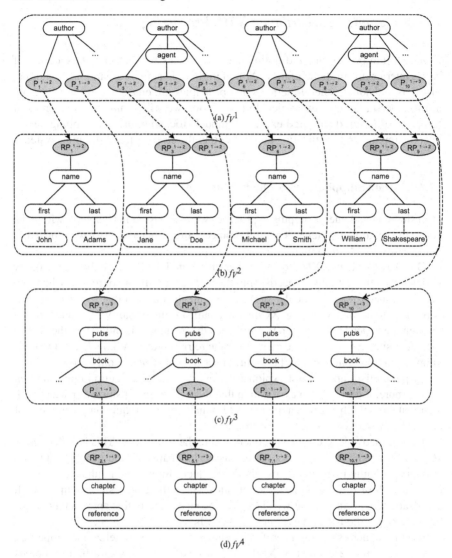

Fig. 17.22 Fragmentation with Proxy Nodes and Numbering

expensive local plan with one of its ancestor fragments until the maximum local plan cost can no longer be reduced.

17.4.4 Optimizing Distributed XML Processing

Research into processing and optimization strategies for distributed execution of
XML queries are in their infancy. Although there is active research on a number
of fronts and some general methods and principles are emerging, we are far from
a full understanding of the issues. In this section we will summarize two areas of
research: different distributed execution models focusing on data shipping versus
query shipping, and localization and pruning in the case of query shipping systems.

17.4.4.1 Data Shipping versus Query Shipping

Data shipping and query shipping approaches were discussed in Chapter 8 within the
context of relational systems. The same choice for distributed query execution exists
in the case of XML data management.

One way to execute XML queries over distributed data is to analyze each query
to determine the data that it needs, ship those data from their sources to where the
query is issued (or to a particular site) and execute the query at that site. This is what
is referred to as *data shipping*. XQuery has built-in functionality for data shipping
through the fn:doc(URI) function that retrieves the document identified by the URI to
the query site and executes the query over the retrieved data. While data shipping is
simple to implement and may be useful in certain situations, it only provides inter-
query parallelism and cannot exploit intra-query parallel execution opportunities.
Furthermore, it relies on the expectation that there is sufficient storage space at each
query site to hold the data that are received. Finally, it may require large amounts of
data to be moved, posing serious overhead.

The alternative is to execute the query where the data reside. This is called *query
shipping* (or *function shipping*). As discussed in Chapter 8, the general approach
to query shipping is to decompose the XML query into a set of subqueries and to
execute each of these subqueries at the sites where the data reside. Coupled with
localization and pruning that we discuss in the next section, this approach provides
intra-query parallelism and executes queries where data are located.

Although query shipping is preferable due to its better parallelization properties,
it is not easy in the context of XML systems. The fundamental difficulty comes
from the fact that, in the most general case, this approach requires shipping both the
function and its parameters to a remote site. It is possible that some of the parameters
may refer to data at the originating site, requiring the "packaging" of these parameter
values and shipping them to a remote site (i.e., call-by-value semantics). If the
parameter and return values are atomic, then this is not a problem, but they may
be more complex, involving element nodes. This issue also arises in the context of
distributed object database systems and we alluded to them in Chapter 15. In the
case of XML systems, the serialization of the subtree rooted at the parameter node is
packaged and shipped. This raises a number of challenges in XML systems [Zhang
et al., 2009b]:

1. In XPath expressions, there may be some axes that are not downward from the parameter node. For example, parent, preceding-sibling (as well as other) axes require accessing data that may not be available in the subtree of the parameter node. A similar problem occurs when certain built-in XQuery functions are executed. For example, root(), id(), idref() functions return nodes that are not descendents of the parameter node, and therefore cannot be executed on the serialization of the subtree rooted at the parameter node.

2. In XML, as in object databases, there is the notion of "identity"; in case of XML, node identity. If two identical nodes are passed as parameters or returned as results, the call-by-value represents them as two different copies, leading to difficulties in node identity comparisons.

3. As noted earlier, in XML there is the notion of document order of nodes and queries are expected to obey this order both in their execution and in their results. The serialization of parameter subtrees in call-by-value organizes nodes with respect to each parameter. Although it is easy to maintain the document order within the serialization of the subtree of each parameter, the relative order of nodes that occur in serializations of different parameters may be different than their order in the original document.

4. There are difficulties with the interaction between different subqueries that access the same document on a given peer. The results of these subqueries would contain nodes from the same document, but ordered differently in the global result.

These problems are still being worked on and general solutions do not yet exist. We describe three quite different approaches to query shipping as indicative of some of the current work.

A proposal to achieve query shipping is to use the theory of partial function evaluation [Buneman et al., 2006; Cong et al., 2007]. Given a function $f(x,y)$, partial evaluation would compute f on one of the inputs (say x) and generate a partial answer, which would be another function f' that is only dependent on the second input y. The way partial evaluation is used to address the issue is to consider the query as a function and the data fragments as its inputs. Then the query can be decomposed into multiple sub-queries, each operating on one fragment. The results of these sub-queries (i.e., functions) are then combined by taking into account the structural relationships between fragments. The overall process, considering an XPath query Q, proceeds as follows:

1. The coordinating site where Q is submitted determines the sites that hold a fragment of the database. Each fragment site and the coordinating site evaluate the query in parallel. At the end of this stage, for some data nodes, the value of each query qualifier is known, while for other nodes, the value of some qualifiers is a Boolean formula whose value is not yet fully determined.

2. In the second phase, the selection part of Q is (partially) evaluated. At the end of this stage, two things are determined for each node n of each fragment: (i)

whether n is part of Q's answer, or (ii) whether or not n is a candidate to be part of Q's answer.

3. In the final phase, the candidate nodes are checked again to determine which ones are indeed part of the answer to Q and any node that is in Q's answer is sent to the coordinating node.

This approach does not decompose the query in the sense that we defined the term. It executes the query over remote fragments, making three passes over each of the fragments. Since it considers only XPath queries, it does not confront the issues related to XQuery that we discussed above.

An alternative that explicitly decomposes the query has been proposed within the context of XRPC project [Zhang and Boncz, 2007; Zhang et al., 2009b]. XRPC extends XQuery by adding remote procedure call functionality through a newly introduced statement execute at {Expr} {FunApp(ParamList)} where Expr is the (explicit or computed) URI of the peer where FunApp() is to be applied.

The target of XRPC is large-scale heterogeneous P2P systems, thus interoperability and efficiency are main design issues. To enable communication between heterogeneous XQuery systems, XRPC also defines an open network protocol called SOAP XRPC that specifies how XDM data types [XDM, 2007] are serialized in XRPC request/response messages. SOAP XRPC protocol encompasses several features to improve efficiency (primarily reducing network latency), by minimizing the number of messages exchanged and the size of message. An important feature of SOAP XRPC is *Bulk RPC* that allows handling of multiple calls to the same function (with different parameters) in a single network interaction. RPC (remote procedure call) is a distributed system functionality that facilitates function calls across different sites. Bulk RPC is exploited when a query contains a function call nested in an XQuery `for`-loop, which, in a naive implementation, would lead to as many RPC network interactions as loop iterations.

The problems with the call-by-value semantics that were discussed above are addressed by a more advanced (but still call-by-copy-based) function parameter passing semantics that is referred to as *call-by-projection* [Zhang et al., 2009b]. Call-by-projection adopts a runtime projection technique to minimize message sizes, which in turn reduces network latency. Basically, it works as follows. A node parameter is first analyzed to see how it is used by the remote function, i.e., a set of *used paths* and a set of *returned paths* of the node parameter are computed. Then, only those descendants of the node parameter, which are actually used by the remote function, are serialized into the request message. At the same time, nodes outside the subtree of the node parameter are added to the request message, if they are needed by the remote function. For instance, if the remote function applies a parent step on the node parameter, the parent node is serialized as well. The same analysis is applied on the function result, so that the remote peer can remove/add nodes into/from the response messages as needed. Thus, the call-by-projection semantics not only preserves node identities and structural properties of XML node parameters (which enables XQuery expressions that access nodes outside the subtrees of remote nodes), but also minimizes message sizes.

Example 17.20. Figure 17.23 shows the impact of the call-by-projection semantics on message sizes and contents.

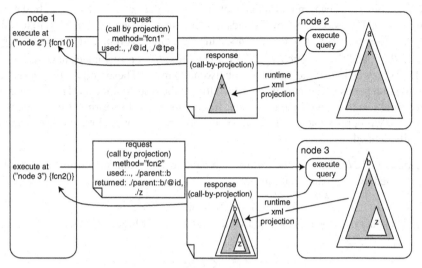

Fig. 17.23 The call-by-projection parameter passing semantics in XPRC

In the upper part of Figure 17.23, node 1 performs an XRPC call to fcn1() on node 2, whose results is the node ⟨x⟩ with a large subtree. With call-by-projection, the query is first analyzed (assuming the call to fcn1() is part of a more complex query) to see how the result of fcn1() is used further in the query. Suppose that only the id and tpe attributes of ⟨x⟩ are used. This information is included in the request message (shown as "used:.,./@id, ./@tpe" in the first request message in the figure). On node 2, before serializing the response message, used paths are applied on the result of fcn1() to compute the projection of ⟨x⟩, which only contains ⟨x id="..." tpe="..."/⟩. Finally, the projected node ⟨x⟩ is serialized, resulting in a much smaller response message (compared to serializing the whole node ⟨x⟩).

In the lower part of Figure 17.23, node 1 performs an XRPC call to fcn2() on node 3, whose result is the node ⟨y⟩ with a large subtree. From the second request message, it can be seen that the query containing this call accesses the parent::b node of ⟨y⟩ (shown as "used:.,./parent::b"), and returns the attributed node parent::b/@id and the ⟨z⟩ child nodes of ⟨y⟩ (shown as "returned:./parent::b/@id, ./z"). Such a call would not be correctly handled using call-by-value, due to the parent step,   ♦

The final query shipping approach that we describe focuses on decomposing queries over horizontally and vertically fragmented XML databases as described above [Kling et al., 2010]. This work only addresses XPath queries, and therefore does not deal with the complications introduced by full XQuery decomposition that we discussed above. We describe it only for the case of vertical fragmentation since that is more interesting (handling horizontal fragmentation is easier). It starts with the QTP representation of the global query (let us call this GQTP) and directly follows the schema graph to get a set of subqueries (i.e., local QTPs – LQTPs), each of which consists of pattern nodes that match items in the same fragment. A child edge from a GQTP node a that corresponds to a document node in fragment f_i to a node b that corresponds to a document node in fragment f_j is replaced by (i) and edge $a \rightarrow P_k^{i \rightarrow j}$, and (ii) an edge $RP_k^{i \rightarrow j} \rightarrow b$. The proxy/root proxy nodes have the same ID, so they establish the connection between a and b. These nodes are marked as extraction points because they are needed to join the results of local QTPs to generate the final result. As with the document fragments, the QTPs form a tree connected by proxy/root proxy nodes. Thus, the usual notions of root/parent/child QTP can be easily defined

Example 17.21. Consider the following XPath query to find references to the books published by "William Shakespeare":

```
/author[name[.//first = 'William' and
     last = 'Shakespeare']]//book//reference
```

This query can be represented by the global QTP of Figure 17.24.

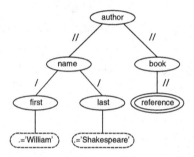

Fig. 17.24 Example QTP

The decomposition of this query based on the vertical fragmentation given in Example 17.18 should result in `author` node being in one subquery (QTP-1), the subtree rooted at `name` being in a second subquery (QTP-2), `book` being in a third subquery (QTP-3), and `reference` in the fourth subquery (QTP-4) as shown in Figure 17.25.   ◆

In this approach, each of the QTPs potentially corresponds to a local query plan that can be executed at one site. The issues that we discuss in the next section address concerns related to the optimization of distributed execution of these local plans.

In addition to pure data shipping and pure query shipping approaches discussed above, it is possible to have a hybrid execution model. Active XML that we discussed earlier is an example. It packages each function with the data that it operates on and when the function is encountered in an Active XML document, it is executed remotely where the data reside. However, the result of the function execution is returned to the original active XML site (i.e., data shipping) for further processing.

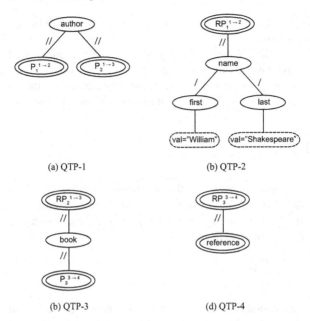

(a) QTP-1   (b) QTP-2

(b) QTP-3   (d) QTP-4

Fig. 17.25 Subqueries after Decomposition

17.4.4.2 Localization and Pruning

As we discussed in Chapter 3, the main objective of localization and pruning is to eliminate unnecessary work by ensuring that the decomposed queries are executed only over the fragments that have data to contribute to the result. Recall that localization was performed by replacing each reference to a global relation with a *localization program* that shows how the global relation can be reconstructed from its fragments. This produces the initial (naïve) query plan. Then, algebraic equivalence rules are used to re-arrange the query plan in order to perform as many operators as possible over each fragment. The localization program is different, of course, for different types of fragmentation. We will follow the same approach here, except that there are further complications in XML databases that are due to the complexity of the XML data model and the XQuery language. As indicated earlier, the general case of distributed execution of XQuery with full power of XML data model is not yet fully solved. To demonstrate localization and pruning more concretely, we will consider a restricted query model and a particular approach proposed by Kling et al. [2010].

In this particular approach, a number of assumptions are made. First, the query plans are represented as QTPs rather than operator trees. Second, queries can have multiple extraction points (i.e., query results are comprised of tuples that consist of multiple nodes), which come from thee same document. Finally, as in XPath, the structural constraints in the queries do not refer to nodes in multiple documents.

Although this is a restricted query model, it is general enough to represent a large class of XPath queries.

Let us first consider a horizontally fragmented XML database. Based on the horizontal fragmentation definition given above, and the query model as specified, the localization program would be the union of fragments – the same as in the relational case. More precisely, given a horizontal fragmentation F_H of database D (i.e., $F_H = f_1, \ldots, f_n$),

$$D = \bigcup_{f_i \in F_H} f_i$$

More interestingly, however, is the definition of the result of a query over a fragmented database, i.e., an initial (or naïve distributed plan). If q is a plan that evaluates the query on an unfragmented database D and F_H is as defined above, then a naïve plan $q(F_H)$ can be defined as

$$q(F_H) := \text{sort}(\bigodot_{f_i \in F_H} q(f_i))$$

where $\odot$ denotes concatenation of results and q_i is the subquery that executes on fragment f_i. It may be necessary to sort the results received from the individual fragments in order to return them in a stable global order as required by the query model.

This naïve plan will access every fragment, which is what pruning attempts to avoid. In this case, since the queries and fragmentation predicates are both represented in the same format (QTP and multiple FTPs, respectively), pruning can be performed by simultaneously traversing these trees and checking for contradictory constraints. If a contradiction is found between the QTP and a FTP_i, there cannot be any result for the query in the fragment corresponding to FTP_i, and the fragment can be eliminated from the distributed plan. This can be achieved by using one of a number of XML tree pattern evaluation algorithms, which we will not get into in this chapter.

Example 17.22. Consider the query given in Example 17.21 and its QTP representation depicted in Figure 17.24.

Assuming the horizontal fragmentation given in Example 17.17, it is clear that this query only needs to run on the fragment that has authors whose last names start with "S" and all other fragments can be eliminated.   ♦

In the case of vertical fragmentation, the localization program is (roughly) the equijoin of the subqueries on fragments where the join predicate is defined on the IDs of the proxy/remote proxy pair. More precisely, given $P = \{p_1, \ldots, p_n\}$ as a set of local query plans corresponding to a query q, and F_V as a vertical fragmentation of a document D (i.e., $F_V = \{f_1, \ldots, f_n\}$) such that f_i denotes the vertical fragments corresponding to p_i, the naïve plan can be defined recursively as follows. If $P' \subseteq P$, then $G_{P'}$ is a vertical execution plan for P' if and only if

1. $P' = \{p_i\}$ and $G'_P = p_i$, or

2. $P' = P'_a \cup P'_b, P_a \cap P_b = \emptyset; p_i \in P_a, p_j \in P_b, p_i = parent(p_j); G_{P'_a}$ and $G_{P'_b}$ are vertical execution plans for P'_a and P'_b, respectively; and $G_{P'} = G_{P'_a} \bowtie_{P_*^{i \to j} = RP_*^{i \to j}} G_{P'_b}$.

If G_P is a vertical execution plan for P (the entire set of local query plans), then $G_q = G_P$ is a vertical execution plan for p.

A vertical execution plan must contain all the local plans corresponding to the query. As shown in the recursive definition above, an execution plan for a single local plan is simply the local plan itself (condition 1). For a set of multiple local plans P', it is assumed that P'_a and P'_b are two non-overlapping subsets of P' such that $P'_a \cup P'_b = P'$. Of course, it is necessary that P'_a contains the parent local plan p_i for some local plan p_j in P'_b. An execution plan for P' is then defined by combining execution plans for P'_a and P'_b using a join whose predicate compares the IDs of proxy nodes in the two fragments (condition 2). This is referred to as the *cross-fragment join* [Kling et al., 2010].

Example 17.23. Let p_a, p_b, p_c and p_d represent local plans that evaluate the QTPs shown in Figures 17.25(a), (b), (c) and (d), respectively. The initial vertical plan is given in Figure 17.26 where QTP_i:P_j refers to the proxy node P_j in QTP_i.   ◆

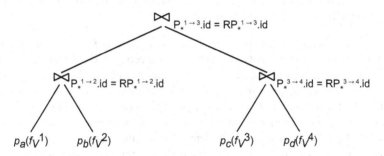

Fig. 17.26 Initial Vertical Plan

If the global QTP does not reach a certain fragment, then the localized plan derived from the local QTPs will not access this fragment. Therefore, the localization technique eliminates some vertical fragments even without further pruning. The partial function execution approach that we introduced earlier works similarly and avoids accessing fragments that are not necessary. However, as demonstrated by Example 17.23, intermediate fragments have to be accessed even if no constraints are evaluated on them. In our example, we have to evaluate QTP_3, and, therefore access fragment f_V^3 (although there is no predicate in the query that refers to any node in that fragment) in order to determine, for example, the root proxy node $RP_3^{1 \to 4}$ instance in fragment f_V^4 that is a descendent of a particular proxy node $P_*^{1 \to 4}$ instance in f_V^1.

A way to prune unnecessary fragments from consideration is to store information in the proxy/root proxy nodes that allow identification of all ancestor proxy nodes for any given root proxy node [Kling et al., 2010]. A simple way of storing this information is by using a Dewey numbering scheme to generate the IDs for each proxy pair. Then it is possible to determine, for any a root proxy node in f_V^4, which proxy node in f_V^1 is its ancestor. This, in turn, would allow answering the query without accessing f_V^3 or evaluating local QTP_3. The benefits of this are twofold: it reduces load on the intermediate fragments (since they are not accessed) and it avoids the cost of computing intermediate results and joining them together.

The numbering scheme works as follows:

1. If a document snippet is in the root fragment, then the proxy nodes in this fragment, and the corresponding root proxy nodes in other fragments are assigned simple numeric IDs.

2. If a document snippet is rooted at a root proxy node, then the ID of each of its proxy nodes is prefixed by the ID of the root proxy node of this document snippet, followed by a numeric identifier that is unique within this snippet.

Example 17.24. Consider the vertical fragmentation given in Figure 17.21. With the introduction of proxy/root proxy pairs and the appropriate numbering as given above, the resulting fragmentation is given in Figure 17.22. The proxy nodes in root fragment f_V^1 are simply numbered. Fragments f_V^2, f_V^3 and f_V^4 consist of document snippets that are rooted at a root proxy. However, of these, only fragment f_V^3 contains proxy nodes, requiring appropriate numbering.   ♦

If all proxy/remote proxy pairs are numbered according to this scheme, a root proxy node in a fragment is the descendant of a proxy node at another fragment precisely when the ID of the proxy node is a prefix of the ID of the root proxy node. When evaluating query patterns, this information can be exploited by removing local QTPs from the distributed query plan if they contain no value or structural constraints and no extraction point nodes other than those corresponding to proxies. These local QTPs are only needed to determine whether a root proxy node in some other fragment is a descendant of a proxy node in a third fragment, which can now be inferred from the IDs.

Example 17.25. The initial query plan in Figure 17.26 is now pruned to the plan in Figure 17.27.   ♦

17.5 Conclusion

The web has become a major repository of data and documents, making it an important topic to study. As noted earlier, there is no unifying framework for many of the topics that fall under web data management. In this chapter, we focused on three major topics, namely, web search, web querying, and distributed XML data management. Even in these areas, many open problems remain.

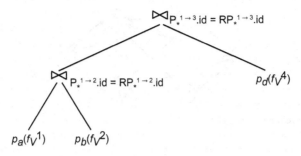

Fig. 17.27 Skipping Vertical Fragments

There are a number of other issues that could be covered. These include service-oriented computing, web data integration, web standards, and others. While some of these have settled, others are still active areas of research. Since it is not possible to cover all of these in detail, we have chosen to focus on the issues related to data management.

17.6 Bibliographic Notes

There are a number of good sources on web topics, each focusing on a different topic. A web data warehousing perspective is given in [Bhowmick et al., 2004]. [Bonato, 2008] primarily focuses on the modelling of the web as a graph and how this graph can be exploited. Early work on the web query languages and approaches are discussed in [Abiteboul et al., 1999]. There are many books on XML, but a good starting point is [Katz et al., 2004].

A very good overview of web search issues is [Arasu et al., 2001], which we also follow in Section 17.2. In construction of Sections 17.4.1 and 17.4.2, we adopted material from Chapter 2 of [Zhang, 2006]. The discussion of distributed XML follows [Kling et al., 2010] and uses material from Chapter 2 of [Zhang, 2010].

Exercises

Problem 17.1 (**). Consider the graph in Figure 17.28. A node P_i is said to be a *reference* for for node P_j iff there exists an edge from P_j to P_i ($P_j \rightarrow P_i$) and there exist a node P_k such that $P_i \rightarrow P_k$ and $P_j \rightarrow P_k$.

(a)   Indicate the reference nodes for each node in the graph.
(b)   Find the cost of compressing each node using the formula given in [Adler and Mitzenmacher, 2001] for each of its reference nodes.

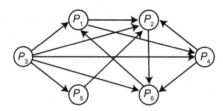

Fig. 17.28 Figure for Problem 17.1

(c) Assuming that (i) for each node we only choose one reference node, and (ii) there must not be cyclic references in the final result, find the optimal set of references that maximizes compression. (Hint: note that this can be systematically done by creating a root node r, and letting all the nodes in the graph point to r, and then finding the minimum spanning tree starting from $r (cost(P_x, r) = \lceil log\ n \rceil * out\_deg(P_x))$.)

Problem 17.2. How does web search differ from web querying?

Problem 17.3 (**). Consider the generic search engine architecture in Figure 17.4. Propose an architecture for a web site with a shared-nothing cluster that implements all the components in this figure as well as web servers in an environment that will support very large sets of web documents and very large indexes, and very high numbers of web users. Define how web pages in the page directory and indexes should be partitioned and replicated. Discuss the main advantages of your architecture with respect to scalability, fault-tolerance and performance.

Problem 17.4 (**). Consider your solution in Problem 17.3. Now consider a keyword search query from a web client to the web search engine. Propose a parallel execution strategy for the query that ranks the result web pages, with a summary of each web page.

Problem 17.5 (*). To increase locality of access and performance in different geographical regions, propose an extension of the web site architecture in Problem 17.4 with multiple sites, with web pages being replicated at all sites. Define how web pages are replicated. Define also how a user query is routed to a web site. Discuss the advantages of your architecture with respect to scalability, availability and performance.

Problem 17.6 (*). Consider your solution in Problem 17.5. Now consider a keyword search query from a web client to the web search engine. Propose a parallel execution strategy for the query that ranks the result web pages, with a summary of each web page.

Problem 17.7 (**). Given an XML document modeled as tree, write an algorithm that matches simple XPath expression that only contains child axes and no branch predicates, For example, /A/B/C should return all C elements who are children of some B elements who are in turn the children of the root element A. Note that A may contain child element other than B, and such is true for B as well.

Problem 17.8 (**). Consider two web data sources that we model as relations EMP1(Name, City, Phone) and EMP2(Firstname, Lastname, City). After schema integration, assume the view EMP(Firstname, Name, City, Phone) defined over EMP1 and EMP2, where each attribute in EMP comes from an attribute of EMP1 or EMP2, with EMP2.Lastname being renamed as Name. Discuss the limitations of such integration. Now consider that the two web data sources are XML. Give a corresponding definition of the XML schemas of EMP1 and EMP2. Propose an XML schema that integrates EMP1 and EMP2, and avoids the problems identified with EMP.

Problem 17.9. Consider the QTP and the set of FTPs shown in Figure 17.29 and the vertical fragmentation schema in Figure 17.20. Determine the fragment(s) that can be excluded from the distributed query plan for this QTP.

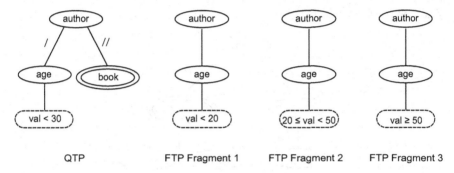

QTP   FTP Fragment 1   FTP Fragment 2   FTP Fragment 3

Fig. 17.29 Figure for Problem 17.9

Problem 17.10 (**). Consider the QTP and the FTP shown in Figure 17.30. Can we exclude the fragment defined by this FTP from a query plan for the QTP? Explain your answer

Problem 17.11 (*). Localize the QTP shown in Figure 17.31 for distributed evaluation based on the vertical fragmentation schema shown in Figure 17.20.

Problem 17.12 (**). When evaluating the query from Problem 17.11, can any of the fragments be skipped using the method based on the Dewey decimal system? Explain your answer.

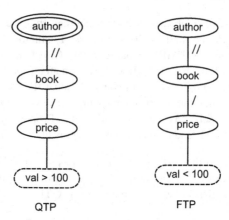

Fig. 17.30 Figure for Problem 17.10

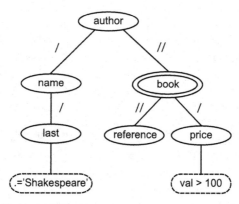

Fig. 17.31 Figure for Problem 17.11

Chapter 18
Current Issues: Streaming Data and Cloud Computing

In this chapter we discuss two topics that are of growing importance in database management. The topics are data stream management (Section 18.1) and cloud data management (Section 18.2). Both of these topics have been topics of considerable interest in the community in recent years. They are still evolving, but there is a possibility that they may have considerable commercial impact. Our objective in this chapter is to give a snapshot of where the field is with respect to these systems at this point, and discuss potential research directions.

18.1 Data Stream Management

The database systems that we have discussed until now consist of a set of unordered objects that are relatively static, with insertions, updates and deletions occurring less frequently than queries. They are sometimes called *snapshot databases* since they show a snapshot of the values of data objects at a given point in time. Queries over these systems are executed when posed and the answer reflects the current state of the database. In these systems, typically, the data are persistent and queries are transient.

However, the past few years have witnessed an emergence of applications that do not fit this data model and querying paradigm. These applications include, among others, sensor networks, network traffic analysis, financial tickers, on-line auctions, and applications that analyze transaction logs (such as web usage logs and telephone call records). In these applications, data are generated in real time, taking the form of an unbounded sequence (stream) of values. These are referred to as the *data stream* applications. In this section, we discuss systems that support these applications; these systems are referred to as *data stream management systems* (DSMS).

A fundamental assumption of the data stream model is that new data are generated continually and in fixed order, although the arrival rates may vary across applications from millions of items per second (e.g., Internet traffic monitoring) down to several items per hour (e.g., temperature and humidity readings from a weather monitoring station). The ordering of streaming data may be implicit (by arrival time at the processing site) or explicit (by generation time, as indicated by a *timestamp* appended to each data item by the source). As a result of these assumptions, DSMSs face the following novel requirements.

1. Much of the computation performed by a DSMS is push-based, or data-driven. Newly arrived stream items are continually (or periodically) pushed into the system for processing. On the other hand, a DBMS employs a mostly pull-based, or query-driven computation model, where processing is initiated when a query is posed.

2. As a consequence of the above, DSMS queries are *persistent* (also referred to as continuous, long-running, or standing queries) in that they are issued once, but remain active in the system for a possibly long period of time. This means that a stream of updated results must be produced as time goes on. In contrast, a DBMS deals with one-time queries (issued once and then "forgotten"), whose results are computed over the current state of the database.

3. The system conditions may not be stable during the *lifetime* of a persistent query. For example, the stream arrival rates may fluctuate and the query workload may change.

4. A data stream is assumed to have unbounded, or at least unknown, length. From the system's point of view, it is infeasible to store an entire stream in a DSMS. From the user's point of view, recently arrived data are likely to be more accurate or useful.

5. New data models, query semantics and query languages are needed for DSMSs in order to reflect the facts that streams are ordered and queries are persistent.

The applications that generate streams of data also have similarities in the type of operations that they perform. We list below a set of fundamental continuous query operations over streaming data.

- **Selection:** All streaming applications require support for complex filtering.

- **Nested aggregation:** Complex aggregates, including nested aggregates (e.g., comparing a minimum with a running average) are needed to compute trends in the data.

- **Multiplexing and demultiplexing:** Physical streams may need to be decomposed into a series of logical streams and conversely, logical streams may need to be fused into one physical stream (similar to group-by and union, respectively).

- **Frequent item queries:** These are also known as *top-k* or *threshold* queries, depending on the cut-off condition.

- **Stream mining:** Operations such as pattern matching, similarity searching, and forecasting are needed for on-line mining of streaming data.

- **Joins:** Support should be included for multi-stream joins and joins of streams with static meta-data.

- **Windowed queries:** All of the above query types may be constrained to return results inside a window (e.g., the last 24 hours or the last one hundred packets).

Proposed data stream systems resemble the abstract architecture shown in Figure 18.1. An input monitor regulates the input rates, perhaps by dropping items if the system is unable to keep up. Data are typically stored in three partitions: temporary working storage (e.g., for window queries that will be discussed shortly), summary storage for stream synopses, and static storage for meta-data (e.g., physical location of each source). Long-running queries are registered in the query repository and placed into groups for shared processing, though one-time queries over the current state of the stream may also be posed. The query processor communicates with the input monitor and may re-optimize the query plans in response to changing input rates. Results are streamed to the users or temporarily buffered. Users may then refine their queries based on the latest results.

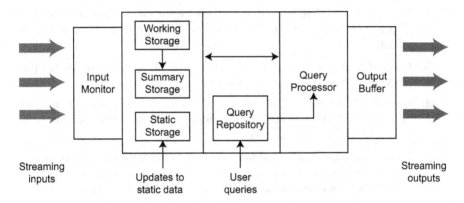

Fig. 18.1 Abstract reference architecture for a data stream management system.

18.1.1 Stream Data Models

A data stream is an append-only sequence of timestamped items that arrive in some order [Guha and McGregor, 2006]. While this is the commonly accepted definition, there are more relaxed versions; for example, *revision tuples*, which are understood to replace previously reported (presumably erroneous) data [Ryvkina et al., 2006], may be considered so that the sequence is not append-only. In publish/subscribe systems, where data are produced by some sources and consumed by those who subscribe to those data feeds, a data stream may be thought of as a sequence of events that are being reported continually [Wu et al., 2006]. Since items may arrive in bursts, a stream may instead be modeled as a sequence of sets (or bags) of elements [Tucker et al., 2003], with each set storing elements that have arrived during the same unit of time (no order is specified among tuplesthat have arrived at the same time). In relation-based stream models (e.g., STREAM [Arasu et al., 2006]), individual items take the form of relational tuples such that all tuples arriving on the same stream have the same schema. In object-based models (e.g., COUGAR [Bonnet et al., 2001] and Tribeca [Sullivan and Heybey, 1998]), sources and item types may be instantiations of (hierarchical) data types with associated methods. Stream items may contain explicit source-assigned timestamps or implicit timestamps assigned by the DSMS upon arrival. In either case, the timestamp attribute may or may not be part of the stream schema, and therefore may or may not be visible to users. Stream items may arrive out of order (if explicit timestamps are used) and/or in pre-processed form. For instance, rather than propagating the header of each IP packet, one value (or several partially pre-aggregated values) may be produced to summarize the length of a connection between two IP addresses and the number of bytes transmitted. This gives rise to the following list of possible models [Gilbert et al., 2001]:

1. *Unordered cash register*: Individual items from various domains arrive in no particular order and without any pre-processing. This is the most general model.

2. *Ordered cash register*: Individual items from various domains are not pre-processed but arrive in some known order, e.g., timestamp order.

3. *Unordered aggregate*: Individual items from the same domain are pre-processed and only one item per domain arrives in no particular order, e.g., one packet per TCP connection.

4. *Ordered aggregate*: Individual items from the same domain are pre-processed and one item per domain arrives in some known order, e.g., one packet per TCP connection in increasing order of the connection end-times.

As discussed earlier, unbounded streams cannot be stored locally in a DSMS, and only a recent excerpt of a stream is usually of interest at any given time. In general, this may be accomplished using a *time-decay model* [Cohen and Kaplan, 2004; Cohen and Strauss, 2003; Douglis et al., 2004], also referred to as an *amnesic* [Palpanas et al., 2004] or *fading* [Aggarwal et al., 2004] model. Time-decay models discount each item in the stream by a scaling factor that is non-decreasing with time. Exponential and polynomial decay are two examples, as are window models where items within the window are given full consideration and items outside the window are ignored. Windows may be classified according the the following criteria.

1. *Direction of movement of the endpoints:* Two fixed endpoints define a *fixed window*, two sliding endpoints (either forward or backward, replacing old items as new items arrive) define a *window!sliding*, and one fixed endpoint and one moving endpoint (forward or backward) define a *window!landmark*. There are a total of nine possibilities as each of the two endpoints could be fixed, moving forward, or moving backward.

2. *Definition of window size:* Logical, or *time-based* windows are defined in terms of a time interval, whereas physical, (also known as *count-based* or *tuple-based*) windows are defined in terms of the number of tuples. Moreover, *partitioned windows* may be defined by splitting a sliding window into groups and defining a separate count-based window on each group [Arasu et al., 2006]. The most general type is a *predicate window*, in which an arbitrary predicate specifies the contents of the window; e.g., all the packets from TCP connections that are currently open [Ghanem et al., 2006]. A predicate window is analogous to a materialized view.

3. *Windows within windows:* In the *elastic window model*, the maximum window size is given, but queries may need to run over any smaller window within the boundaries of the maximum window [Zhu and Shasha, 2003]. In the *n-of-N window model*, the maximum window size is N tuples or time units, but any smaller window of size n and with one endpoint in common with the larger window is also of interest [Lin et al., 2004].

4. *Window update interval:* Eager updating advances the window upon arrival of each new tuple or expiration of an old tuple, but batch processing (lazy updating) induces a *jumping window*. Note that a count-based window may be updated periodically and a time-based window may be updated after some number of new tuples have arrived; these are referred to as *mixed jumping windows* [Ma et al., 2005]. If the update interval is larger than the window size, then the result is a series of non-overlapping *tumbling windows* [Abadi et al., 2003].

As a consequence of the unbounded nature of data streams, DSMS data models may include some notion of change or drift in the underlying distribution that is assumed to generate the attribute values of stream items [Kifer et al., 2004; Dasu et al., 2006; Zhu and Ravishankar, 2004]. We will come back to this issue when we discuss data stream mining in Section 18.1.8. Additionally, it has been observed that in many practical scenarios, the stream arrival rates and distributions of values tend to be bursty or skewed [Kleinberg, 2002; Korn et al., 2006; Leland et al., 1994; Paxson and Floyd, 1995; Zhu and Shasha, 2003].

18.1.2 Stream Query Languages

Earlier we indicated that stream queries are usually persistent. So, one issue to discuss is what the semantics of these queries are, i.e., how do they generate answers. Persistent queries may be monotonic or non-monotonic. A *monotonic query* is one whose results can be updated incrementally. In other words, if $Q(t)$ is the answer to a query at time t, given two executions of the query at t_i and t_j, $Q(t_i) \subseteq Q(t_j)$ for all $t_j > t_i$. For monotonic queries, one can define the following:

$$Q(t) = \bigcup_{t_i=1}^{t} (Q(t_i) - Q(t_{i-1})) \cup Q(0)$$

That is, it is sufficient to re-evaluate the query over newly arrived items and append qualifying tuples to the result [Arasu et al., 2006]. Consequently, the answer of a monotonic persistent query is a continuous, append-only stream of results. Optionally, the output may be updated periodically by appending a batch of new results. It has been proven that a query is monotonic if and only if it is *non-blocking*, which means that it does not need to wait until the end-of-output marker before producing results [Law et al., 2004].

Non-monotonic queries may produce results that cease to be valid as new data are added and existing data changed (or deleted). Consequently, they may need to be re-computed from scratch during every re-evaluation, giving rise to the following semantics:

$$Q(t) = \bigcup_{t_i=0}^{t} Q(t_i)$$

Let us now consider classes of languages that have been proposed for DSMSs. Three querying paradigms can be identified: declarative, object-based, and procedural. *Declarative languages* have SQL-like syntax, but stream-specific semantics, as described above. Similarly, *object-based languages* resemble SQL in syntax, but employ DSMS-specific constructs and semantics, and may include support for streaming abstract data types (ADTs) and associated methods. Finally, *procedural languages* construct queries by defining data flow through various operators.

18.1.2.1 Declarative Languages

The languages in this class include CQL [Arasu et al., 2006; Arasu and Widom, 2004a], GSQL [Cranor et al., 2003], and StreaQuel [Chandrasekaran et al., 2003]. We discuss each of them briefly.

The Continuous Query Language (CQL) is used in the STREAM DSMS and includes three types of operators: relation-to-relation (corresponding to standard relational algebraic operators), stream-to-relation (*sliding windows*), and relation-to-stream. Conceptually, unbounded streams are converted to relations by way of sliding windows, the query is computed over the current state of the sliding windows as if it were a traditional SQL query, and the output is converted back to a stream. There are three relation-to-stream operators—Istream, Dstream, and Rstream—which specify the nature of the output. The Istream operator returns a stream of all those tuples which exist in a relation at the current time, but did not exist at the current time minus one. Thus, Istream suggests incremental evaluation of monotonic queries. Dstream returns a stream of tuples that existed in the given relation in the previous time unit, but not at the current time. Conceptually, Dstream is analogous to generating negative tuples for non-monotonic queries. Finally, the Rstream operator streams the contents of the entire output relation at the current time and corresponds to generating the complete answer of a non-monotonic query. The Rstream operator may also be used in periodic query evaluation to produce an output stream consisting of a sequence of relations, each corresponding to the answer at a different point in time.

Example 18.1. Computing a join of two time-based windows of size one minute each, can be performed by the following query:

```
SELECT Rstream(*)
FROM   S1 [RANGE 1 min], S2 [RANGE 1 min]
WHERE  S1.a = S2.a
```

The RANGE keyword following the name of the input stream specifies a time-based sliding window on that stream, whereas the ROWS keyword may be used to define count-based sliding windows.   ♦

GSQL is used in Gigascope, a stream database for network monitoring and analysis. The input and output of each operator is a stream for reasons of composability. Each stream is required to have an ordering attribute, such as timestamp or packet sequence number. GSQL includes a subset of the operators found in SQL, namely selection, aggregation with group-by, and join of two streams, whose predicate must include ordering attributes that form a join window. The *stream merge* operator, not found in standard SQL, is included and works as an order-preserving union of ordered streams. This operator is useful in network traffic analysis, where flows from multiple links need to be merged for analysis. Only landmark windows are supported directly, but sliding windows may be simulated via user-defined functions.

StreaQuel is used in the TelegraphCQ system and is noteworthy for its windowing capabilities. Each query, expressed in SQL syntax and constructed from SQL's set of relational operators, is followed by a for-loop construct with a variable t that iterates over time. The loop contains a WindowIs statement that specifies the type and size of the window. Let S be a stream and let ST be the start time of a query. To specify a sliding window over S with size five that should run for fifty time units, the following for-loop may be appended to the query.

```
for(t=ST; t<ST+50; t++)
  WindowIs(S, t-4, t)
```

Changing to a landmark window can be done by replacing t-4 with some constant in the WindowIs statement. Changing the for-loop increment condition to t=t+5 would cause the query to re-execute every five time units. The output of a StreaQuel query consists of a time sequence of sets, each set corresponding to the answer set of the query at that time.

18.1.2.2 Object-Based Languages

One approach to object-oriented stream modeling is to classify stream contents according to a type hierarchy. This method is used in the Tribeca network monitoring system, which implements Internet protocol layers as hierarchical data types [Sullivan and Heybey, 1998]. The query language used in Tribeca has SQL-like syntax, but accepts a single stream as input, and returns one or more output streams. Supported operators are limited to projection, selection, aggregation over the entire input stream or over a sliding window, multiplex and demultiplex (corresponding to union and group-by respectively, except that different sets of operators may be applied on each of the demultiplexed sub-streams), as well as a join of the input stream with a fixed window.

Another object-based possibility is to model the sources as ADTs, as in the COUGAR system for managing sensor data [Bonnet et al., 2001]. Each type of sensor is modeled by an ADT, whose interface consists of the supported signal processing methods. The proposed query language has SQL-like syntax and also includes a `$every()` clause that indicates the query re-execution frequency. However, few details on the language are available in the published literature and therefore it is not included in Figure 18.2.

Example 18.2. A simple query that runs every sixty seconds and returns temperature readings from all sensors on the third floor of a building may be specified as follows:

```
SELECT R.s.getTemperature()
FROM   R
WHERE  R.floor = 3 AND $every(60)
```
                                                                              ◆

18.1.2.3 Procedural Languages

An alternative to declarative query languages is to let the user specify how the data should flow through the system. In the Aurora DSMS [Abadi et al., 2003], users construct query plans via a graphical interface by arranging boxes, corresponding to query operators, and joining them with directed arcs to specify data flow, though the system may later re-arrange, add, or remove operators in the optimization phase. SQuAl is the boxes-and-arrows query language used in Aurora, which accepts streams as inputs and returns streams as output (however, static data sets may be incorporated into query plans via *connection points* [Abadi et al., 2003]). There are a total of seven operators in the SQuAl algebra, four of them order-sensitive. The three order-insensitive operators are projection, union, and `map`, the last applying an arbitrary function to each of the tuples in the stream or a window thereof. The other four operators require an order specification, which includes the ordered field and a slack parameter. The latter defines the maximum disorder in the stream, e.g., a slack of 2 means that each tuple in the stream is either in sorted order, or at most two positions or two time units away from being in sorted order. The four order-sensitive operators are buffered sort (which takes an almost-sorted stream and the slack parameter, and outputs the stream in sorted order), windowed aggregates (in which the user can specify how often to advance the window and re-evaluate the aggregate), binary band join (which joins tuples whose timestamps are at most t units apart), and resample (which generates missing stream values by interpolation, e.g., given tuples with timestamps 1 and 3, a new tuple with timestamp 2 can be generated with an attribute value that is an average of the other two tuples' values. Other resampling functions are also possible, e.g., the maximum, minimum, or weighted average of the two neighbouring data values.

18.1.2.4 Summary of DSMS Query Languages

A summary of the proposed DSMS query languages is provided in Figure 18.2 with respect to the allowed inputs and outputs (streams and/or relations), novel operators, supported window types (fixed, landmark or sliding), and supported query re-execution frequency (continuous and/or periodic). With the exception of SQuAl, the surface syntax of DSMS query languages is similar to SQL, but their semantics are considerably different. CQL allows the widest range of semantics with its relation-to-stream operators; note that CQL uses the semantics of SQL during its relation-to-relation phase and incorporates streaming semantics in the stream-to-relation and relation-to-stream components. On the other hand, GSQL, SQuAL, and Tribeca only allow streaming output, whereas StreaQuel continually (or periodically) outputs the entire answer set. In terms of expressive power, CQL closely mirrors SQL as CQL's core set of operators is identical to that of SQL. Additionally, StreaQuel can express a wider range of windows than CQL. GSQL, SQuAl, and Tribeca, which operate in the stream-in-stream-out mode, may be thought of as restrictions of SQL as they focus on incremental, non-blocking computation. In particular, GSQL and Tribeca are application-specific (network monitoring) and have been designed for very fast implementation [Cranor et al., 2003]. However, although SQuAl and GSQL are stream-in/stream-out languages, and, as a result, may have lost some expressive power as compared to SQL, they may regain this power via user-defined functions. Moreover, SQuAl is noteworthy for its attention to issues related to real-time processing such as buffering, out-of-order arrivals and timeouts.

Language/ system	Allowed inputs	Allowed outputs	Novel operators	Supported windows	Execution frequency
CQL/ STREAM	streams and relations	streams and relations	relation-to-stream, stream-to-relation	sliding	continuous or periodic
GSQL/ Gigascope	streams	streams	order-preserving union	landmark	periodic
SQuAl/ Aurora	streams and relations	streams	resample, map, buffered sort	fixed, landmark, sliding	continuous or periodic
StreaQuel/ TelegraphCQ	streams and relations	sequences of relations	WindowIs	fixed, landmark, sliding	continuous or periodic
Tribeca	single stream	streams	multiplex, demultiplex	fixed, landmark, sliding	continuous

Fig. 18.2 Summary of proposed data stream languages

18.1.3 Streaming Operators and their Implementation

While the streaming languages discussed above may resemble standard SQL, their implementation, processing, and optimization present novel challenges. In this section, we highlight the differences between streaming operators and traditional relational operators, including non-blocking behavior, approximations, and sliding windows. Note that simple relational operators such as projection and selection (that do not keep state information) may be used in streaming queries without any modifications.

Some relational operators are blocking. For instance, prior to returning the next tuple, the Nested Loops Join (NLJ) may potentially scan the entire inner relation and compare each tuple therein with the current outer tuple. Some operators have non-blocking counterparts, such as joins [Haas and Hellerstein, 1999a; Urhan and Franklin, 2000; Viglas et al., 2003; Wilschut and Apers, 1991] and simple aggregates [Hellerstein et al., 1997; Wang et al., 2003c]. For example, a pipelined symmetric hash join [Wilschut and Apers, 1991] builds hash tables on-the-fly for each of the participating relations. Hash tables are stored in main memory and when a tuple from one of the relations arrives, it is inserted into its table and the other tables are probed for matches. It is also possible to incrementally output the average of all the items seen so far by maintaining the cumulative sum and item count. When a new item arrives, the item count is incremented, the new item's value is added to the sum, and an updated average is computed by dividing the sum by the count. There remains the issue of memory constraints if an operator requires too much working memory, so a windowing scheme may be needed to bound the memory requirements. Hashing has also been used in developing join execution strategies over DHT-based P2P systems [Palma et al., 2009].

Another way to unblock query operators is to exploit constraints over the input streams. Schema-level constraints include synchronization among timestamps in multiple streams, clustering (duplicates arrive contiguously), and ordering [Babu et al., 2004b]. If two streams have nearly synchronized timestamps, an equi-join on the timestamp can be performed in limited memory: a *scrambling bound B* may be set such that if a tuple with timestamp τ arrives, then no tuple with timestamp greater than $\tau - B$ may arrive later [Motwani et al., 2003].

Constraints at the data level may take the form of control packets inserted into a stream, called *punctuations* [Tucker et al., 2003]. Punctuations are constraints (encoded as data items) that specify conditions for all future items. For instance, a punctuation may arrive asserting that all the items henceforth shall have the A attribute value larger than 10. This punctuation could be used to partially unblock a group-by query on A since all the groups where $A \leq 10$ are guaranteed not to change for the remainder of the stream's lifetime, or until another punctuation arrives and specifies otherwise. Punctuations may also be used to synchronize multiple streams in that a source may send a punctuation asserting that it will not produce any tuples with timestamp smaller than τ [Arasu et al., 2006].

As discussed above, unblocking a query operator may be accomplished by re-implementing it in an incremental form, restricting it to operate over a window (more on this shortly), and exploiting stream constraints. However, there may be cases where an incremental version of an operator does not exist or is inefficient to evaluate, where even a sliding window is too large to fit in main memory, or where no suitable stream constraints are present. In these cases, compact stream summaries may be stored and approximate queries may be posed over the summaries. This implies a trade-off between accuracy and the amount of memory used to store the summaries. An additional restriction is that the processing time per item should be kept small, especially if the inputs arrive at a fast rate.

Counting methods, used mainly to compute quantiles and frequent item sets, typically store frequency counts of selected item types (perhaps chosen by sampling) along with error bounds on their true frequencies. Hashing may also be used to summarize a stream, especially when searching for frequent items—each item type may be hashed to n buckets by n distinct hash functions and may be considered a potentially frequent flow if all of its hash buckets are large. Sampling is a well known data reduction technique and may be used to compute various queries to within a known error bound. However, some queries (e.g., finding the maximum element in a stream) may not be reliably computed by sampling.

Sketches were initially proposed by Alon et al. [1996] and have since then been used in various approximate algorithms. Let $f(i)$ be the number of occurrences of value i in a stream. A sketch of a data stream is created by taking the inner product of f with a vector of random values chosen from some distribution with a known expectation. Moreover, wavelet transforms (that reduce the underlying signal to a small set of coefficients) have been proposed to approximate aggregates over infinite streams.

We end this section with a discussion of window operators. Sliding window operators process two types of events: arrivals of new tuples and expirations of old tuples; the orthogonal problem of determining when tuples expire will be discussed in the next section. The actions taken upon arrival and expiration vary across operators [Hammad et al., 2003b; Vossough and Getta, 2002]. A new tuple may generate new results (e.g., join) or remove previously generated results (e.g., negation). Furthermore, an expired tuple may cause a removal of one or more tuples from the result (e.g., aggregation) or an addition of new tuples to the result (e.g., duplicate elimination and negation). Moreover, operators that must explicitly react to expired tuples (by producing new results or invalidating existing results) perform state purging eagerly (e.g., duplicate elimination, aggregation, and negation), whereas others may do so eagerly or lazily (e.g., join).

In a sliding window join, newly arrived tuples on one of the inputs probe the state of the other input, as in a join of unbounded streams. Additionally, expired tuples are removed from the state [Golab and Özsu, 2003b; Hammad et al., 2003a, 2005; Kang et al., 2003; Wang et al., 2004]. Expiration can be done periodically (lazily), so long as old tuples can be identified and skipped during processing.

Aggregation over a sliding window updates its result when new tuples arrive and when old tuples expire. In many cases, the entire window needs to be stored in order to account for expired tuples, although selected tuples may sometimes be removed early if their expiration is guaranteed not to influence the result. For example, when computing MAX, tuples with value v need not be stored if there is another tuple in the window with value greater than v and a younger timestamp. Additionally, in order to enable incremental computation, the aggregation operator stores the current answer (for distributive and algebraic aggregates) or frequency counters of the distinct values present in the window (for holistic aggregates). For instance, computing COUNT requires storing the current count, incrementing it when a new tuple arrives, and decrementing it when a tuple expires. In this case, in contrast to the join operator, expirations must be dealt with immediately so that an up-to-date aggregate value can be returned right away.

Duplicate elimination over a sliding window may also produce new output when an input tuple expires. This occurs if a tuple with value v was produced on the output stream and later expires from its window, yet there are other tuples with value v still present in the window [Hammad et al., 2003b]. Alternatively, as is the case in the STREAM system, duplicate elimination may produce a single result tuple with a particular value v and retain it on the output stream so long as there is at least one tuple with value v present in the window. In both cases, expirations must be handled eagerly so that the correct result is maintained at all times.

Finally, negation of two sliding windows, $W_1 - W_2$, may produce *negative tuples* (e.g., arrival of a W_2-tuple with value v causes the deletion of a previously reported result with value v), but may also produce new results upon expiration of tuples from W_2 (e.g., if a tuple with value v expires from W_2, then a W_1-tuple with value v may need to be appended to the output stream [Hammad et al., 2003b]). There are methods for implementing duplicate-preserving negation, but those are beyond our scope in this chapter.

18.1.4 Query Processing

Let us now discuss the issues related to processing queries in DSMSs. The overall process is similar to relational systems: declarative queries are translated into execution plans that map logical operators specified in the query into physical implementations. For now, let us assume that the inputs and operator state fit in main memory; we will discuss disk-based processing later.

18.1.4.1 Queuing and Scheduling

DBMS operators are pull-based, whereas DSMS operators consume data pushed into the plan by the sources.

Queues allow sources to push data into the query plan and operators to retrieve data as needed [Abadi et al., 2003; Adamic and Huberman, 2000; Arasu et al., 2006; Madden and Franklin, 2002; Madden et al., 2002a]. A simple scheduling strategy allocates a time slice to each operator, during which the operator extracts tuples from its input queue(s), processes them in timestamp order, and deposits output tuples into the next operator's input queue. The time slice may be fixed or dynamically calculated based upon the size of an operator's input queue and/or processing speed. A possible improvement could be to schedule one or more tuples to be processed by multiple operators at once. In general, there are several possibly conflicting criteria involved in choosing a scheduling strategy, among them queue sizes in the presence of bursty stream arrival patterns [Babcock et al., 2004], average or maximum latency of output tuples [Carney et al., 2003; Jiang and Chakravarthy, 2004; Ou et al., 2005], and average or maximum delay in reporting the answer relative to the arrival of new data [Sharaf et al., 2005].

18.1.4.2 Determining When Tuples Expire

In addition to dequeuing and processing new tuples, sliding window operators must remove old tuples from their state buffers and possibly update their answers, as discussed in Section 18.1.3. Expiration from an individual time-based window is simple: a tuple expires if its timestamp falls out of the range of the window. That is, when a new tuple with timestamp ts arrives, it receives another timestamp, call it exp, that denotes its expiration time as ts plus the window length. In effect, every tuple in the window may be associated with a lifetime interval of length equal to the window size [Krämer and Seeger, 2005]. Now, if this tuple joins with a tuple from another window, whose insertion and expiration timestamps are ts' and exp', respectively, then the expiration timestamp of the result tuple is set to $\min(exp, exp')$. That is, a composite result tuple expires if at least one of its constituent tuples expires from its windows. This means that various join results may have different lifetime lengths and furthermore, the lifetime of a join result may have a lifetime that is shorter than the window size [Cammert et al., 2006]. Moreover, as discussed above, the negation operator may force some result tuples to expire earlier than their exp timestamps by generating negative tuples. Finally, if a stream is not bounded by a sliding window, then the expiration time of each tuple is infinity [Krämer and Seeger, 2005].

In a count-based window, the number of tuples remains constant over time. Therefore, expiration can be implemented by overwriting the oldest tuple with a newly arrived tuple. However, if an operator stores state corresponding to the output of a count-based window join, then the number of tuples in the state may change, depending upon the join attribute values of new tuples. In this case, expirations must be signaled explicitly using negative tuples.

18.1.4.3 Continuous Query Processing over Sliding Windows

There are two techniques for sliding window query processing and state maintenance: the negative tuple approach and the direct approach. In the negative tuple approach [Arasu et al., 2006; Hammad et al., 2003b, 2004], each window referenced in the query is assigned an operator that explicitly generates a negative tuple for every expiration, in addition to pushing newly arrived tuples into the query plan. Thus, each window must be materialized so that the appropriate negative tuples are produced. This approach generalizes the purpose of negative tuples, which are now used to signal all expirations explicitly, rather than only being produced by the negation operator if a result tuple expires because it no longer satisfies the negation condition. Negative tuples propagate through the query plan and are processed by operators in a similar way as regular tuples, but they also cause operators to remove corresponding "real" tuples from their state. The negative tuple approach can be implemented efficiently using hash tables as operator state so that expired tuples can be looked up quickly in response to negative tuples. Conceptually, this is similar to a DBMS indexing a table or materialized view on the primary key in order to speed up insertions and deletions. However, the downside is that twice as many tuples must be processed by the query because every tuple eventually expires from its window and generates a corresponding negative tuple. Furthermore, additional operators must be present in the plan to generate negative tuples as the window slides forward.

Direct approach [Hammad et al., 2003b, 2004] handles negation-free queries over time-based windows. These queries have the property that the expiration times of base tuples and intermediate results can be determined via their *exp* timestamps, as explained in Section 18.1.4.2. Hence, operators can access their state directly and find expired tuples without the need for negative tuples. The direct approach does not incur the overhead of negative tuples and does not have to store the base windows referenced in the query. However, it may be slower than the negative tuple approach for queries over multiple windows [Hammad et al., 2003b]. This is because straightforward implementations of state buffers may require a sequential scan during insertions or deletions. For example, if the state buffer is sorted by tuple arrival time, then insertions are simple, but deletions require a sequential scan of the buffer. On the other hand, sorting the buffer by expiration time simplifies deletions, but insertions may require a sequential scan to ensure that the new tuple is ordered correctly, unless the insertion order is the same as the expiration order.

18.1.4.4 Periodic Query Processing Over Sliding Windows

Query Processing over Windows Stored in Memory.

For reasons of efficiency (reduced expiration and query processing costs) and user preference (users may find it easier to deal with periodic output rather than a continuous output stream [Arasu and Widom, 2004b; Chandrasekaran and Franklin, 2003]), sliding windows may be advanced and queries re-evaluated periodically with a specified frequency [Abadi et al., 2003; Chandrasekaran et al., 2003; Golab et al., 2004; Liu et al., 1999]. As illustrated in Figure 18.3, a periodically-sliding window can be modeled as a circular array of *sub-windows*, each spanning an equal time interval for time-based windows (e.g., a ten-minute window that slides every minute) or an equal number of tuples for tuple-based windows (e.g., a 100-tuple window that slides every ten tuples).

Rather than storing the entire window and re-computing an aggregate after every new tuple arrives or an old tuple expires, a synopsis can be stored that pre-aggregates

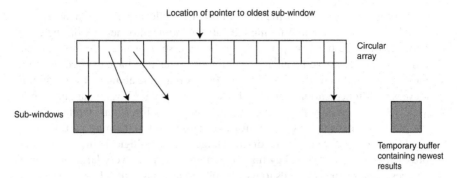

Fig. 18.3 Sliding window implemented as a circular array of pointers to sub-windows

each sub-window and reports updated answers whenever the window slides forward by one sub-window. Thus a "window update" occurs when the oldest sub-window is replaced with newly arrived data (accumulated in a buffer), thereby sliding the window forward by one sub-window. Depending on the type of operator one deals with, it would be necessary to use different types of synopsis (e.g., a *running synopsis* [Arasu and Widom, 2004b] for subtractable aggregates [Cohen, 2006] such as SUM and COUNT or an *interval synopsis* for distributive aggregates that are not subtractable, such as MIN and MAX). An aggregate f is subtractable if, for two multi-sets X and Y such that $X \supseteq Y$, $f(X - Y) = f(X) - f(Y)$.Details are beyond our scope in this chapter.

A disadvantage of periodic query evaluation is that results may be stale. One way to stream new results after each new item arrives is to bound the error caused by delayed expiration of tuples in the oldest sub-window. It has been shown [Datar et al., 2002] that restricting the sizes of the sub-windows (in terms of the number of tuples) to powers of two and imposing a limit on the number of sub-windows of each size yields a space-optimal algorithm (called *exponential histogram*, or EH) that approximates simple aggregates to within ε using logarithmic space (with respect to the sliding window size). Variations of the EH algorithm have been used to approximately compute the sum [Datar et al., 2002; Gibbons and Tirthapura, 2002], variance and k-medians clustering [Babcock et al., 2003], windowed histograms [Qiao et al., 2003], and order statistics [Lin et al., 2004; Xu et al., 2004]. Extensions of the EH algorithm to time-based windows have also been proposed [Cohen and Strauss, 2003].

18.1.4.5 Query Processing over Windows Stored on Disk.

In traditional database applications that use secondary storage, performance may be improved if appropriate indices are built. Consider maintaining an index over a periodically-sliding window stored on disk, e.g., in a data warehousing scenario where new data arrive periodically and decision support queries are executed (offline) over the latest portion of the data. In order to reduce the index maintenance costs, it is desirable to avoid bringing the entire window into memory during every update. This can be done by partitioning the data so as to localize updates (i.e., insertions of newly arrived data and deletion of tuples that have expired from the window) to a small number of disk pages. For example, if an index over a sliding window is partitioned chronologically [Folkert et al., 2005; Shivakumar and García-Molina, 1997], then only the youngest partition incurs insertions, while only the oldest partition needs to be checked for expirations (the remaining partitions "in the middle" are not accessed).The disadvantage of chronological clustering is that records with the same search key may be scattered across a very large number of disk pages, causing index probes to incur prohibitively many disk I/Os.

One way to reduce index access costs is to store a reduced (summarized) version of the data that fits on fewer disk pages [Chandrasekaran and Franklin, 2004], but this does not necessarily improve index update times. In order to balance the access and update times, a *wave index* has been proposed that chronologically divides a sliding window into n equal partitions, each of which is separately indexed and clustered by search key for efficient data retrieval [Shivakumar and García-Molina, 1997]. The window can be partitioned either by insertion time or by expiration time; these are equivalent from the perspective of wave indexes.

18.1.5 DSMS Query Optimization

It is usually the case that a query may be executed in a number of different ways. A DBMS query optimizer is responsible for enumerating (some or all of) the possible query execution strategies and choosing an efficient one using a cost model and/or a set of transformation rules. A DSMS query optimizer has the same responsibility, but it must use an appropriate cost model and rewrite rules. Additionally, DSMS query optimization involves adaptivity, load shedding, and resource sharing among similar queries running in parallel, as summarized below.

18.1.5.1 Cost Metrics and Statistics

Traditional DBMSs use selectivity information and available indices to choose efficient query plans (e.g., those which require the fewest disk accesses). However, this cost metric does not apply to (possibly approximate) persistent queries, where processing cost per-unit-time is more appropriate [Kang et al., 2003]. Alternatively, if the stream arrival rates and output rates of query operators are known, then it may be possible to optimize for the highest output rate or to find a plan that takes the least time to output a given number of tuples [Tao et al., 2005; Urhan and Franklin, 2001; Viglas and Naughton, 2002]. Finally, quality-of-service metrics such as response time may also be used in DSMS query optimization [Abadi et al., 2003; Berthold et al., 2005; Schmidt et al., 2004, 2005].

18.1.5.2 Query Rewriting and Adaptive Query Optimization

Some of the DSMS query languages discussed in Section 18.1.2 introduce rewritings for new operators, e.g., selections and time-based sliding windows commute, but not selections and count-based windows [Arasu et al., 2006]. Other rewritings are similar to those used in relational databases, e.g., re-ordering a sequence of binary joins in order to minimize a particular cost metric. There has been some work in join ordering for data streams in the context of the rate-based model [Viglas and Naughton, 2002; Viglas et al., 2003]. Furthermore, adaptive re-ordering of pipelined stream filters [Babu et al., 2004a] and adaptive materialization of intermediate join results [Babu et al., 2005] have been investigated.

The notion of adaptivity is important in query rewriting; operators may need to be re-ordered on-the-fly in response to changes in system conditions. In particular, the cost of a query plan may change for three reasons: change in the processing time of an operator, change in the selectivity of a predicate, and change in the arrival rate of a stream [Adamic and Huberman, 2000]. Initial efforts on adaptive query plans include mid-query re-optimization [Kabra and DeWitt, 1998] and query scrambling, where the objective was to pre-empt any operators that become blocked and schedule other operators instead [Amsaleg et al., 1996b; Urhan et al., 1998b]. To further increase adaptivity, instead of maintaining a rigid tree-structured query plan, the Eddy approach [Adamic and Huberman, 2000] performs scheduling of each tuple separately by routing it through the operators that make up the query plan. In effect, the query plan is dynamically re-ordered to match current system conditions. This is accomplished by tuple routing policies that attempt to discover which operators are fast and selective, and those operators are scheduled first. A recent extension adds queue length as the third factor for tuple routing strategies in the presence of multiple distributed Eddies [Tian and DeWitt, 2003a]. There is, however, an important trade-off between the resulting adaptivity and the overhead required to route each tuple separately. More details on adaptive query processing may be found in [Babu and Bizarro, 2005; Babu and Widom, 2004; Gounaris et al., 2002a].

Adaptivity involves on-line reordering of a query plan and may therefore require that the internal state stored by some operators be migrated over to the new query plan consisting of a different arrangement of operators [Deshpande and Hellerstein, 2004; Zhu et al., 2004]. We do not discuss this issue further in this chapter.

18.1.6 Load Shedding and Approximation

The stream arrival rates may be so high that not all tuples can be processed, regardless of the (static or run-time) optimization techniques used. In this case, two types of load shedding may be applied—random or semantic—with the latter making use of stream properties or quality-of-service parameters to drop tuples believed to be less significant than others [Tatbul et al., 2003]. For an example of semantic load shedding, consider performing an approximate sliding window join with the objective of attaining the maximum result size. The idea is that tuples that are about to expire or tuples that are not expected to produce many join results should be dropped (in case of memory limitations [Das et al., 2005; Li et al., 2006; Xie et al., 2005]), or inserted into the join state but ignored during the probing step (in case of CPU limitations [Ayad et al., 2006; Gedik et al., 2005; Han et al., 2006]). Note that other objectives are possible, such as obtaining a random sample of the join result [Srivastava and Widom, 2004].

In general, it is desirable to shed load in such a way as to minimize the drop in accuracy. This problem becomes more difficult when multiple queries with many operators are involved, as it must be decided where in the query plan the tuples should be dropped. Clearly, dropping tuples early in the plan is effective because all of the subsequent operators enjoy reduced load. However, this strategy may adversely affect the accuracy of many queries if parts of the plan are shared. On the other hand, load shedding later in the plan, after the shared sub-plans have been evaluated and the only remaining operators are specific to individual queries, may have little or no effect in reducing the overall system load.

One issue that arises in the context of load shedding and query plan generation is whether an optimal plan chosen without load shedding is still optimal if load shedding is used. It has been shown that this is indeed the case for sliding window aggregates, but not for queries involving sliding window joins [Ayad and Naughton, 2004].

Note that instead of dropping tuples during periods of high load, it is also possible to put them aside (e.g., spill to disk) and process them when the load has subsided [Liu et al., 2006; Reiss and Hellerstein, 2005]. Finally, note that in the case of periodic re-execution of persistent queries, increasing the re-execution interval may be thought of as a form of load shedding [Babcock et al., 2002; Cammert et al., 2006; Wu et al., 2005].

18.1.7 Multi-Query Optimization

As seen in Section 18.1.4.4, memory usage may be reduced by sharing internal data structures that store operator state [Denny and Franklin, 2005; Dobra et al., 2004; Zhang et al., 2005]. Additionally, in the context of complex queries containing stateful operators such as joins, computation may be shared by building a common query plan [Chen et al., 2000]. For example, queries belonging to the same group may share a plan, which produces the union of the results needed by the individual queries. A final selection is then applied to the shared result set and new answers are routed to the appropriate queries. An interesting trade-off appears between doing similar work multiple times and doing too much unnecessary work; techniques that balance this trade-off are presented in [Chen et al., 2002; Krishnamurthy et al., 2004; Wang et al., 2006]. For example, suppose that the workload includes several queries referencing a join of the same windows, but having a different selection predicate. If a shared query plan performs the join first and then routes the output to appropriate queries, then too much work is being done because some of the joined tuples may not satisfy any selection predicate (unnecessary tuples are being generated). On the other hand, if each query performs its selection first and then joins the surviving tuples, then the join operator cannot be shared and the same tuples will be probed many times.

For selection queries, a possible multi-query optimization is to index the query predicates and store auxiliary information in each tuple that identifies which queries it satisfies [Chandrasekaran and Franklin, 2003; Demers et al., 2006; Hanson et al., 1999; Krishnamurthy et al., 2006; Lim et al., 2006; Madden et al., 2002a; Wu et al., 2004]. When a new tuple arrives for processing, its attribute values are extracted and matched against the query index to see which queries are satisfied by this tuple. Data and queries may be thought of as duals, in some cases reducing query processing to a multi-way join of the query predicate index and the data tables [Chandrasekaran and Franklin, 2003; Lim et al., 2006].

18.1.8 Stream Mining

In addition to querying as discussed in the previous sections, mining of stream data has been studied for a number of applications. Data mining involves the use of data analysis tools to discover previously unknown relationships and patterns in large data sets. The characteristics of data streams discussed above impose new challenges in performing mining tasks; many of the well-known techniques cannot be used. The major issues are the following:

- **Unbounded data set.** Traditional data mining algorithms are based on the assumption that they can access the full data set. However, this is not possible in data streams, where only a portion of the old data is available and much of the old data are discarded. Hence, data mining techniques that require multiple scan over the entire data set cannot be used.

- **"Messy" data.** Data are never entirely clean, but in traditional data mining applications, they can be cleaned before the application is run. In many stream applications, due to the high arrival rates of data streams, this is not always possible. Given that in many cases the data that are read from sensors and other sources of stream data are already quite noisy, the problem is even more serious.

- **Real-time processing.** Data mining over traditional data is typically a batch process. Although there are obvious efficiency concerns in analyzing these data, they are not as severe as those on data streams. Since data arrival is continuous and potentially at high rate, the mining algorithms have to have real-time performance.

- **Data evolution.** As noted earlier traditional data sets can be assumed to be static, i.e., the data is a sample from a static distribution. However, this is not true for many real-world data streams, since they are generated over long periods of time during which the underlying phenomena can change resulting in significant changes in the distribution of the data values. This means that some mining results that were previously generated may no longer be valid. Therefore, a data stream mining technique must have the ability to detect changes in the stream, and to automatically modify its mining strategy for different distributions.

In the remainder, we will summarize some stream mining techniques. We divide the discussion into two groups: general processing techniques, and specific data mining tasks and their algorithms [Gaber et al., 2005]. Data processing techniques are general approaches to process the stream data before specific tasks can be applied. These consist of the following:

Sampling.   As discussed earlier, data stream sampling is the process of choosing a suitable representative subset from the stream of interest. In addition to the major use of stream sampling to reduce the potentially infinite size of the stream to a bounded set of samples, it can be utilized to clean "messy" data and to preserve representative sets for the historical distributions. However, since some data elements of the stream are not looked at, in general, it is impossible to guarantee that the results produced by the mining application using the samples will be identical to the results returned on the complete stream up to the most recent time. Therefore, one of the most critical tasks for stream sampling techniques is to provide guarantees about how much the results obtained using the samples differ from the non-sampling based results.

Load shedding.   The arrival speed of elements in data streams are usually unstable, and many data stream sources are prone to dramatic spikes in load. Therefore, stream mining applications must cope with the effects of system overload. Maximizing the mining benefits under resource constraints is a challenging task. Load shedding techniques as discussed earlier are helpful.

Synopsis maintenance.   Synopsis maintenance processes create synopses or "sketches" for summarizing the streams and were introduced earlier in this chapter. A synopsis does not represent all characteristics of a stream, but rather some "key features" that might be useful for tuning the stream mining processes and further analyzing the streams. It is especially useful for stream mining applications that are expecting various streams as input, or an input stream with frequent distribution changes. When the stream changes, some re-computation, either from scratch or incrementally, has to be done. An efficient synopsis maintenance process can generate summary of the stream shortly after the change, and the stream mining application can re-adjust its settings or switch to another mining technique based on these precious information.

Change detection.   When the distribution of the stream changes, previous mining results may no longer be valid under the new distribution, and the mining technique must be adjusted to maintain good performance for the new distribution. Hence, it is critical for the distribution changes in a stream to be detected in real-time so that the stream mining application can react promptly.

There are basically two different tracks oftechniques for detecting changes. One track is to look at the natureof the dataset and determine if that set has evolved [Kifer et al., 2004; Aggarwal, 2003, 2005], and the othertrack is to detect if an existing data model is no longer suitablefor recent data, which implies the concept drifting [Hulten et al., 2001; Wang et al., 2003a; Fan, 2004; Gama et al., 2005]belong to the second track.

Now we take a look at some of the popular stream mining tasks and how they can be accomplished in this environment. We focus on clustering, classification, frequency counting and association rule mining, and time series analysis.

Clustering.   Clustering groups together data with similar behavior. It can be thought of as partitioning or segmenting elements into groups (clusters) that may or may not be disjoint. In many cases, the answer to a clustering problem is not unique, i.e., many answers can be found, and interpreting the practical meaning of each cluster may be difficult.

Aggarwal et al. [2003] have proposed a framework for clustering data streams that uses an online component to store summarized information about the streams, and an offline component that performs clustering on the summarized data. This framework has been extended in HPStream in a way that can find projected clusters for high dimensional data streams [Aggarwal et al., 2004] .

The existing clustering algorithms can be categorized into decision tree based ones (e.g., [Domingos and Hulten, 2000; Gama et al., 2005; Hulten et al., 2001; Tao and Özsu, 2009]) and k-mean (or k-median) based approaches (e.g., [Babcock et al., 2002; Charikar et al., 1997, 2003; Guha et al., 2003; Ordonez, 2003]).

Classification.   Classification maps data into predefined groups (classes). Its difference from clustering is that, in classification, the number of groups is predetermined and fixed. Similar to clustering, classification techniques can also adopt the decision tree model (e.g., [Ding et al., 2002; Ganti et al., 2002]). Two decision tree classifiers — Interval Classifier [Agrawal et al., 1992] and SPRINT [Shafer et al., 1996] — can mine databases that do not fit in main memory, and are thus are suitable for data streams. The VFDT [Domingos and Hulten, 2000] and CVFDT [Hulten et al., 2001] systems originally designed for stream clustering can also be adopted for classification tasks.

Frequency counting and association rule mining.   The problem of frequency counting, and mining association rules (frequent itemsets) has long been recognized as an important issue. However, although mining frequent itemsets has been widely studied in data mining and a number of efficient algoirthms exist, extending these to data streams is challenging, especially for streams with non-static distributions [Jiang and Gruenwald, 2006].

Mining frequent itemsets is a continuous process that runs throughout a stream's life span. Since the total number of itemsets is exponential, making it impractical to keep count of each itemset in order to incrementally adjust the frequent itemsets as new data items arrive. Usually only the itemsets that are already known to be frequent are recorded and monitored, and counters of infrequent itemsets are discarded [Chakrabarti et al., 2002; Cormode and Muthukrishnan, 2003; Demaine et al., 2002; Halatchev and Gruenwald, 2005] . However, since data streams can change over time, an itemset that was once infrequent may become frequent if the distribution changes. Such (new) frequent itemsets are difficult to detect, since mining data streams is a one-pass procedure and history information is not retrievable.

Time series analysis.   In general, a time series is a set of attribute values over a period of time. Usually a time series consists of only numeric values, either continuous or discrete. Consequently, it is possible to model data streams that contain only numeric values as time series. This allows one to use analysis techniques that have been developed on time series for some types of stream data. Mining tasks over time series can be briefly classified into two types: pattern detection and trend analysis. A typical mining task for pattern detection is the following: given a sample pattern or a base time series with a certain pattern, find all the time series that contain this pattern. The tasks for trend prediction are detecting trends in time series and predicting the upcoming trends.

18.2 Cloud Data Management

Cloud computing is the latest trend in distributed computing and has been the subject of much hype. The vision encompasses on demand, reliable services provided over the Internet (typically represented as a cloud) with easy access to virtually infinite computing, storage and networking resources. Through very simple web interfaces and at small incremental cost, users can outsource complex tasks, such as data storage, system administration, or application deployment, to very large data centers operated by cloud providers. Thus, the complexity of managing the software/hardware infrastructure gets shifted from the users' organization to the cloud provider.

Cloud computing is a natural evolution, and combination, of different computing models proposed for supporting applications over the web: service oriented architectures (SOA) for high-level communication of applications through web services, utility computing for packaging computing and storage resources as services, cluster and virtualization technologies to manage lots of computing and storage resources, autonomous computing to enable self-management of complex infrastructure, and grid computing to deal with distributed resources over the network. However, what makes cloud computing unique is its ability to provide various levels of functionality such as infrastructure, platform, and application as services that can be combined to best fit the users' requirements [Cusumano, 2010]. From a technical point of view, the grand challenge is to support in a cost-effective way, the very large scale of the infrastructure that has to manage lots of users and resources with high quality of service.

Cloud computing has been developed by web industry giants, such as Amazon, Google, Microsoft and Yahoo, to create a new, huge market. Virtually all computer industry players are interested in cloud computing. Cloud providers have developed new, proprietary technologies (e.g., Google File System), typically with specific, simple applications in mind. There are already open source implementations (e.g., Hadoop Distributed File System) with much contribution from the research community. As the need to support more complex applications increases, the interest of the research community is steadily growing. In particular, data management in cloud computing is becoming a major research direction which we think can capitalize on distributed and parallel database techniques.

The rest of this section is organized as follows. First, we give a general taxonomy of the different kinds of clouds, and a discussion of the advantages and potential disadvantages. Second, we give an overview of grid computing, with which cloud computing is sometimes confused, and point out the main differences. Third, we present the main cloud architectures and associated functions. Fourth, we present the current solutions for data management in the cloud, in particular, data storage, database management and parallel data processing. Finally, we discuss open issues in cloud data management.

18.2.1 Taxonomy of Clouds

In this section, we first give a definition of cloud computing, with the main categories of cloud services. Then, we discuss the main data-intensive applications that are suitable for the cloud and the main issues, in particular, security.

Agreeing on a precise definition of cloud computing is difficult as there are many different perspectives (business, market, technical, research, etc.). However, a good working definition is that a "cloud provides on demand resources and services over the Internet, usually at the scale and with the reliability of a data center" [Grossman and Gu, 2009]. This definition captures well the main objective (providing on-demand resources and services over the Internet) and the main requirements for supporting them (at the scale and with the reliability of a data center).

Since the resources are accessed through services, everything gets delivered as a service. Thus, as in the services industry, this enables cloud providers to propose a pay-as-you-go pricing model, whereby users only pay for the resources they consume. However, implementing a pricing model is complex as users should be charged based on the level of service actually delivered, e.g., in terms of service availability or performance. To govern the use of services by customers and support pricing, cloud providers use the concept of Service Level Agreement (SLA), which is critical in the services industry (e.g., in telecoms), but in a rather simple way. The SLA (between the cloud provider and any customer) typically specifies the responsabilities, guarantees and service commitment. For instance, the service commitment might state that the service uptime during a billing cycle (e.g., a month) should be at least 99%, and if the commitment is not met, the customer should get a service credit.

Cloud services can be divided in three broad categories: Infrastructure-as-a-Service (IaaS), Platform-as-a-Service (PaaS) and Software-as-a-Service (SaaS).

- **Infrastructure-as-a-Service (IaaS).** IaaS is the delivery of a computing infrastructure (i.e., computing, networking and storage resources) as a service. It enables customers to scale up (add more resources) or scale down (release resources) as needed (and only pay for the resources consumed). This important capability is called *elasticity* and is typically achieved through *server virtualization*, a technology that enables multiple applications to run on the same physical server as virtual machines, i.e., as if they would run on distinct physical servers. Customers can then requisition computing instances as virtual machines and add and attach storage as needed. An example of popular IaaS is Amazon web Services.
- **Software-as-a-Service (SaaS).** SaaS is the delivery of application software as a service. It generalizes the earlier Application Service Provider (ASP) model whereby the hosted application is fully owned, operated and maintained by the ASP. With SaaS, the cloud provider allows the customer to use hosted applications (as with ASP) but also provides tools to integrate other applications, from different vendors or even developed by the customer (using the cloud platform). Hosted applications can range from simple ones such as email and calendar to complex applications such as customer relationship management (CRM), data analysis or even social networks. An example of popular SaaS is Safesforce CRM system.
- **Platform-as-a-Service (PaaS).** PaaS is the delivery of a computing platform with development tools and APIs as a service. It enables developers to create and deploy custom applications directly on the cloud infrastructure, in virtual machines, and integrate them with applications provided as SaaS. An example of popular PaaS is Google Apps.

By using a combination of IaaS, SaaS and PaaS, customers could move all or part of their information technology (IT) services to the cloud, with the following main benefits:

- **Cost.** The cost for the customer can be greatly reduced since the IT infrastructure does not need to be owned and managed; billing is only based only on resource consumption. For the cloud provider, using a consolidated infrastructure and sharing costs for multiple customers reduces the cost of ownership and operation.
- **Ease of access and use.** The cloud hides the complexity of the IT infrastructure and makes location and distribution transparent. Thus, customers can have access to IT services anytime, and from anywhere with an Internet connection.
- **Quality of Service (QoS).** The operation of the IT infrastructure by a specialized provider that has extensive experience in running very large infrastructures (including its own infrastructure) increases QoS.
- **Elasticity.** The ability to scale resources out, up and down dynamically to accommodate changing conditions is a major advantage. In particular, it makes it easy for customers to deal with sudden increases in loads by simply creating more virtual machines.

However, not all corporate applications are good candidates for being "cloudified" [Abadi, 2009]. To simplify, we can classify corporate applications between the two main classes of data-intensive applications which we already discussed: OLTP and OLAP. Let us recall their main characteristics. OLTP deals with operational databases of average sizes (up to a few terabytes), that are write-intensive, and require complete ACID transactional properties, strong data protection and response time guarantees. On the other hand, OLAP deals with historical databases of very large sizes (up to petabytes), that are read-intensive, and thus can accept relaxed ACID properties. Furthermore, since OLAP data are typically extracted from operational OLTP databases, sensitive data can be simply hidden for analysis (e.g., using anonymization) so that data protection is not as crucial as in OLTP.

OLAP is more suitable than OLTP for cloud primarily because of two cloud characteristics (see the detailed discussion in [Abadi, 2009]): elasticity and security. To support elasticity in a cost-effective way, the best solution, which most cloud providers adopt, is a shared-nothing cluster architecture. Recall from Section 14.1 that shared-nothing provides high-scalability but requires careful data partitioning. Since OLAP databases are very large and mostly read-only, data partitioning and parallel query processing are effective. However, it is much harder to support OLTP on shared-nothing because of ACID guarantees, which require complex concurrency control. For these reasons and because OLTP databases are not so large, shared-disk is the preferred architecture for OLTP. The second reason that OLTP is not so suitable for cloud is that the corporate data get stored at an untrusted host (the provider site). Storing corporate data at an untrusted third-party, even with a carefully negotiated SLA with a reliable provider, creates resistance from some customers because of security issues. However, this resistance is much reduced for historical data, and with anonymized sensitive data.

There are currently two main solutions to address the security issue in clouds: internal cloud and virtual private cloud. The mainstream cloud approach is generally called *public cloud*, because the cloud is available to anyone on the Internet. An *internal cloud* (or *private cloud*) is the use of cloud technologies for managing a company's data center, but in a private network behind a firewall. This brings much tighter security and many of the advantages of cloud computing. However, the cost advantage tends to be much reduced because the infrastructure is not shared with other customers. Nonetheless, an attractive compromise is the *hybrid cloud* which connects the internal cloud (e.g., for OLTP) with one or more public clouds (e.g., for OLAP). As an alternative to internal clouds, cloud providers such as Amazon and Google have proposed *virtual private clouds* with the promise of a similar level of security as an internal cloud, but within a public cloud. A virtual private cloud provides a Virtual Private Network (VPN) with security services to the customers. Virtual private clouds can also be used to develop hybrid clouds, with tighter security integration with the internal cloud.

One earlier criticism of cloud computing is that customers get locked in proprietary clouds. It is true that most clouds are proprietary and there are no standards for cloud interoperability. But this is changing with open source cloud software such as Hadoop, an Apache project implementing Google's major cloud services such as Google File System and MapReduce, and Eucalyptus, an open source cloud software infrastructure, which are attracting much interest from research and industry.

18.2.2 Grid Computing

Like cloud computing, grid computing enables access to very large compute and storage resources over the web. It has been the subject of much research and development over the last decade. Cloud computing is somewhat more recent and there are similarities but also differences between the two computing models. In this section, we discuss the main aspects of grid computing and end with a comparison with cloud computing.

Grid computing has been initially developed for the scientific community as a generalization of cluster computing, typically to solve very large problems (that require a lot of computing power and/or access to large amounts of data) using many computers over the web. Grid computing has also gained some interest in enterprise information systems. For instance, IBM and Oracle (since Oracle 10g with g standing for grid) have been promoting grid computing with tools and services for both scientific and enterprise applications.

Grid computing enables the virtualization of distributed, heterogeneous resources using web services [Atkinson et al., 2005]. These resources can be data sources (files, databases, web sites, etc.), computing resources (multiprocessors, supercomputers, clusters) and application resources (scientific applications, information management services, etc.). Unlike the web, which is client-server oriented, the grid is demand-oriented: users send requests to the grid which allocates them to the most appropriate resources to handle them. A grid is also an organized, secured environment managed and controlled by administrators. An important unit of control in a grid is the Virtual Organization (VO), i.e., a group of individuals, organizations or companies that share the same resources, with common rules and access rights. A grid can have one or more VOs, and may have different size, duration and goal.

Compared with cluster computing, which only deals with parallelism, the grid is characterized with high heterogeneity, large-scale distribution and large-scale parallelism. Thus, it can offer advanced services on top of very large amounts of distributed data.

Depending on the contributed resources and the targeted applications, many different kinds of grids and architectures are possible. The earlier computational grids typically aggregate very powerful sites (supercomputers, clusters) to provide high-performance computing for scientific applications (e.g., physics, astronomy). Data grids aggregate heterogeneous data sources (like a distributed database) and provide additional services for data discovery, delivery and use to scientific applications. More recently, enterprise grids [Jiménez-Peris et al., 2007] have been proposed to aggregate information system resources, such as web servers, application servers and database servers, in the enterprise.

Figure 18.4 illustrates a typical grid scenario, inspired by the Grid5000 platform in France, with two computing sites (clusters 1 and 2) and one storage site (cluster 3) accessible to authorized users. Each site has one cluster with service nodes and either compute or storage nodes. Service nodes provide common services for users (access, resource reservation, deployment) and administrators (infrastructure services) and are available at each site, through the replication of directories and catalogs.

Compute nodes provide the main computing power while storage nodes provide storage capacity (i.e., lots of disks). The basic communication between grid sites (e.g., to deploy an application or a system image) is through web services (WS) calls (to be discussed shortly). But for distributing computation between compute nodes at two different sites, communication is typically through the standard Message Passing Interface (MPI).

A typical scenario for solving a large scientific problem P is the following. P is initially decomposed (by a scientist programmer User 1) into two subproblems P_1 and P_2, each being solved through a parallel program to be run at one computing site. If P_1 and P_2 are independent then there is no need for communication between the computing sites. If there are computing dependencies, e.g., P_2 consumes results of P_1, communication between P_1 and P_2 must be specified and implemented through MPI. The data produced by P_1 and P_2 could then be sent to the storage site, typically using WS calls. To run P on the grid, a user must first reserve the computing resources (e.g., a needed number of cluster nodes at site 1 and 2) and storage resources (at site 3), deploy the jobs corresponding to the programs, and then start their parallel executions at site 1 and 2, which will produce data and send them to site 3. The resource allocation and the scheduling of job executions at the clusters are done by the grid middleware in a way that guarantees fair access to the reserved resources. More complex scenarios can also involve the distributed execution of workflows. On the other hand, User 2 can simply reserve storage capacity and use it for saving her local data (using the store interface).

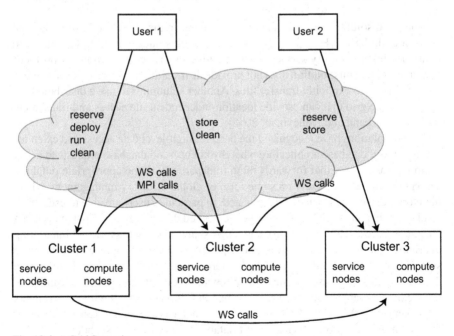

Fig. 18.4 A Grid Scenario

A common need of different kinds of grids is interoperability of heterogeneous resources. To address this need, the Globus Alliance, which represents the grid community, has defined the Open Grid Services Architecture (OGSA) as a standard SOA and a framework to create grid solutions using WS standards. OGSA provides three main layers to build grid applications: (1) resources layer, (2) web services layer, and (3) high-level grid services layer. The first layer provides an abstraction of the physical resources (servers, storage, network) that are managed by logical resources such as database systems, file systems, or workflow managers, all encapsulated by WS. The second layer extends WS, which are typically stateless, to deal with stateful grid services, i.e., those that can retain data between multiple invocations. This capability is useful for instance to access a resources state, e.g., the load of a server, through WS. Stateful grid services can be created and destroyed (using a grid service factory), and have an internal state which can be observed or even changed after notifications from other grid services. The third layer provides high-level grid-specific services such as resource provisioning, data management, security, workflow, and monitoring to ease the development and management of grid applications.

The adoption of WS in enterprise information systems has made OGSA appealing and several offerings for enterprise grids are based on the Globus platform (e.g., Oracle 11g). Web service standards are useful for grid data management: XML for data exchange, XMLSchema for schema description, Simple Object Access Protocol (SOAP) for remote procedure calls, UDDI for directory access, Web Service Definition Language (WSDL) for data source description, WS-Transaction for distributed transactions, Business Process Execution Language (BPEL) for workflow control, etc.

The main solutions for grid data management, in the context of computational grids, are file-based [Pacitti et al., 2007b]. A basic solution, used in Globus, is to combine global directory services to locate files and a secure file transfer protocol. Although simple, this solution does not provide distribution transparency as it requires the application to explicitly transfer files. Another solution is to use a distributed file system for the grid that can provide location-independent file access and transparent replication [Zhang and Honeyman, 2008].

Recent solutions have recognized the need for high-level data access and extended the distributed database architecture whereby clients send database requests to a grid multidatabase server that forwards them transparently to the appropriate database servers. These solutions rely on some form of global directory management, where directories can be distributed and replicated. In particular, users are able to use a high-level query language (SQL) to describe the desired data as with OGSA-DAI (OGSA Database Access and Integration), an OGSA standard for accessing and integrating distributed data [Antonioletti et al., 2005]. OGSA-DAI is a popular multidatabase system that provides uniform access to heterogeneous data sources (e.g., relational databases, XML databases or files) via WS within grids. Its architecture is similar to the mediator/wrapper architecture described in Chapters 1and 9 with the wrappers implemented by WS. The OGSA-DAI mediator includes a distributed query processor which automatically transforms a multidatabase query into a distributed QEP that specifies the WS calls to get the required data from each database wrapper.

We end this section with a discussion of the advantages and disadvantages of grid computing. The main advantages come from the distributed architecture when it uses clusters at each site, as it provides scalability, performance (through parallelism) and availability (through replication). It is also a cost-effective alternative to a huge supercomputer to solve larger, more complex problems in a shorter time. Another advantage is that existing resources are better used and shared with other organizations. The main disadvantages also come from the highly distributed architecture, which is complex for both administrators and developers. In particular, sharing resources across administrative domains is a political challenge for participating organizations as it is hard to assess their cost/benefits.

Compared with cloud computing, there are important differences in terms of objectives and architecture. Grid computing fosters collaboration among participating organizations to leverage existing resources whereas cloud computing provides a rather fixed (distributed) infrastructure to all kinds of users (and customers). Thus, SLA and pay-per-use are essential in cloud computing. The grid architecture is potentially much more distributed than the cloud architecture that typically consists of a few sites in different geographical regions, but each site being a very huge data center. Therefore, the scalability issue at a site (in terms of numbers of users or numbers of server nodes) is much harder in cloud computing. Finally, a major difference is that there are no standards such as OGSA for cloud interoperability.

18.2.3 Cloud architectures

Unlike in grid computing, there is no standard cloud architecture and there will probably never be one, since different cloud providers will provide different cloud services (IaaS, PaaS, SaaS) in different ways (public, private, virtual private, ...) depending on their business models. Thus, in this section, we discuss the main cloud architectures in order to identify the underlying technologies and functions. This is useful to be able to focus on data management (in the next section).

Figure 18.5 illustrates a typical cloud scenario, inspired by that of a popular IaaS/PaaS provider. This scenario is also useful for comparison with the typical grid scenario in Figure 18.4. We assume one cloud provider with two sites, each with the same capabilities and cluster architecture. Thus, any user can access any site to get the needed service as if there were only one site, so the cloud appears "centralized". This is one major difference with grid as distribution can be completely hidden. However, distribution happens under the cover, e.g., to replicate data automatically from one site to the other in order to resist to site failure. Then, to solve the large scientific problem P, User 1 now does not need to decompose it into two subproblems, but she does need to provide a parallel version of P to be run at Site 1. This is done by creating a *virtual machine* (VM) (sometimes called *computing instance*) with executable application code and data, then starting as many VMs as needed for the parallel execution and finally terminating. User 1 is then charged only for the resources (VMs) consumed. The allocation of VMs to physical machines at Site 1 is done by the cloud middleware in a way that optimizes global resource consumption while satisfying the SLA. On the other hand, similar to the grid scenario, User 2 can also reserve storage capacity and use it for saving her local data.

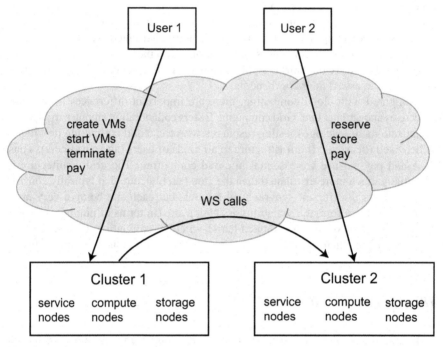

Fig. 18.5 A Cloud Scenario

We can distinguish the cloud architectures between infrastructure (IaaS) and software/platform (SaaS/PaaS). All architectures can be supported by a network of shared-nothing clusters. For IaaS, the preferred architectural model derives from the need to provide computing instances on demand. To support computing instances on demand, as in the scenario in Figure 18.5, the main solution is to rely on server virtualization, which enables VMs to be provisioned and decommissioned as needed. Server virtualization can be well supported by a shared-nothing cluster architecture. For SaaS/PaaS, many different architectural models can be used depending on the targeted services and applications. For instance, to support enterprise applications, a typical architecture is n-tier with web servers, application servers, database servers and storage servers, all organized in a cluster architecture. Server virtualization can also be used in such architecture. For data storage virtualization, SAN can be used to provide shared-disk access to service or compute nodes. As for grids, communication between applications and services is typically done through WS or message passing.

The main functions provided by clouds are similar to those found in grids: security, directory management, resource management (provisioning, allocation, monitoring) and data management (storage, file management, database management, data replication). In addition, clouds provide support for pricing, accounting and SLA management.

18.2.4 Data management in the cloud

For managing data, cloud providers could rely on relational DBMS technology, all of which have distributed and parallel versions. However, relational DBMSs have been lately criticized for their "one size fits all" approach [Stonebraker, 2010]. Although they have been able to integrate support for all kinds of data (e.g., multimedia objects, XML documents) and new functions, this has resulted in a loss of performance, simplicity and flexibility for applications with specific, tight performance requirements. Therefore, it has been argued that more specialized DBMS engines are needed. For instance, column-oriented DBMSs [Abadi et al., 2008], which store column data together rather than rows in traditional row-oriented relational DBMSs, have been shown to perform more than an order of magnitude better on OLAP workloads. Similarly, as discussed in Section 18.1, DSMSs are specifically architected to deal efficiently with data streams which traditional DBMS cannot even support.

The "one size does not fit all" argument generally applies to cloud data management as well. However, internal clouds or virtual private clouds for enterprise information systems, in particular for OLTP, may use traditional relational DBMS technology. On the other hand, for OLAP workloads and web-based applications on the cloud, relational DBMS provide both too much (e.g., ACID transactions, complex query language, lots of tuning parameters), and too little (e.g., specific optimizations for OLAP, flexible programming model, flexible schema, scalability) [Ramakrishnan, 2009]. Some important characteristics of cloud data have been considered for designing data management solutions. Cloud data can be very large (e.g., text-based or scientific applications), unstructured or semi-structured, and typically append-only (with rare updates). And cloud users and application developers may be in high numbers, but not DBMS experts. Therefore, current cloud data management solutions have traded consistency for scalability, simplicity and flexibility.

In this section, we illustrate cloud data management with representative solutions for distributed file management, distributed database management and parallel database programming.

18.2.4.1 Distributed File Management

The Google File System (GFS) [Ghemawat et al., 2003] is a popular distributed file system developed by Google for its internal use. It is used by many Google applications and systems, such as Bigtable and MapReduce, which we discuss next. There are also open source implementations of GFS, such as Hadoop Distributed File System (HDFS), a popular Java product.

Similar to other distributed file systems, GFS aims at providing performance, scalability, fault-tolerance and availability. However, the targeted systems, shared-nothing clusters, are challenging as they are made of many (e.g., thousands of) servers built from inexpensive hardware. Thus, the probability that any server fails at a given time is high, which makes fault-tolerance difficult. GFS addresses this problem. It is also optimized for Google data-intensive applications, such as search engine or data analysis. These applications have the following characteristics. First, their files are very large, typically several gigabytes, containing many objects such as web documents. Second, workloads consist mainly of read and append operations, while random updates are rare. Read operations consist of large reads of bulk data (e.g., 1 MB) and small random reads (e.g., a few KBs). The append operations are also large and there may be many concurrent clients that append the same file. Third, because workloads consist mainly of large read and append operations, high throughput is more important than low latency.

GFS organizes files as a tree of directories and identifies them by pathnames. It provides a file system interface with traditional file operations (create, open, read, write, close, and delete file) and two additional operations: snapshot and record append. Snapshot allows creating a copy of a file or of a directory tree. Record append allows appending data (the record) to a file by concurrent clients in an efficient way. A record is appended atomically, i.e., as a continuous byte string, at a byte location determined by GFS. This avoids the need for distributed lock management that would be necessary with the traditional write operation (which could be used to append data).

The architecture of GFS is illustrated in Figure 18.6. Files are divided into fixed-size partitions, called *chunks*, of large size, i.e., 64 MB. The cluster nodes consist of GFS clients that provide the GFS interface to applications, chunk servers that store chunks and a single GFS master that maintains file metadata such as namespace, access control information, and chunk placement information. Each chunk has a unique id assigned by the master at creation time and, for reliability reasons, is replicated on at least three chunk servers (in Linux files). To access chunk data, a client must first ask the master for the chunk locations, needed to answer the application file access. Then, using the information returned by the master, the client can request the chunk data to one of the replicas.

This architecture using single master is simple. And since the master is mostly used for locating chunks and does not hold chunk data, it is not a bottleneck. Furthermore, there is no data caching at either clients or chunk servers, since it would not benefit large reads. Another simplification is a relaxed consistency model for concurrent writes and record appends. Thus, the applications must deal with relaxed consistency using techniques such as checkpointing and writing self-validating records. Finally, to keep the system highly available in the face of frequent node failures, GFS relies on fast recovery and replication strategies.

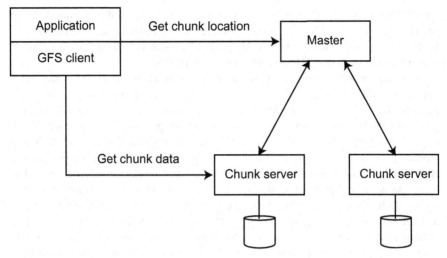

Fig. 18.6 GFS Architecture

18.2.4.2 Distributed Database Management

We can distinguish between two kinds of solutions: online distributed database services and distributed database systems for cloud applications. Online distributed database services such as Amazon SimpleDB and Google Base enable any web user to add and manipulate structured data in a database in a very simple way, without having to define a schema. For instance, SimpleDB provides basic database functionality including scan, filter, join and aggregate operators, caching, replication and transactions, but no complex operators (e.g., union), no query optimizer and no fault-tolerance. Data are structured as (attribute name, value) pairs, all automatically indexed so there is no need for administration. Google Base is a simpler online database service (as a Beta version at the time of this writing) which enables a user to add and retrieve structured data through predefined forms, with predefined attributes (e.g., ingredient for a recipe), thus avoiding the need for schema definition. Data in Google Base can then be searched through other tools, such as the web search engine.

Distributed database systems for cloud applications emphasize scalability, fault-tolerance and availability, sometimes at the expense of consistency or ease of development. We illustrate this approach with two popular solutions: Google Bigtable and Yahoo! PNUTS.

Bigtable.

Bigtable is a database storage system for a shared-nothing cluster [Chang et al., 2008]. It uses GFS for storing structured data in distributed files, which provides fault-tolerance and availability. It also uses a form of dynamic data partitioning for scalability. And like GFS, it is used by popular Google applications, such as Google Earth, Google Analytics and Orkut. There are also open source implementations of Bigtable, such as Hadoop Hbase, which runs on HDFS.

Bigtable supports a simple data model that resembles the relational model, with multi-valued, timestamped attributes. We briefly describe this model as it is the basis for Bigtable implementation that combines aspects of row-store and column-store DBMS. We use the terminology of the original proposal [Chang et al., 2008], in particular, the basic terms "row" and "column" (instead of tuple and attribute). However, for consistency with the concepts we have used so far, we present the Bigtable data model as a slightly extended relational model[1]. Each row in a table (or Bigtable) is uniquely identified by a *row key*, which is an arbitrary string (of up to 64KB in the original system). Thus, a row key is like a mono-attribute key in a relation. A more original concept is that of a *column family* which is a set of columns (of the same type), each identified by a *column key*. A column family is a unit of access control and compression. The syntax for naming column keys is family:qualifier. The column family name is like a relation attribute name. The qualifier is like a relation attribute value, but used as a name as part of the column key to represent a single data item. This allows the equivalent of multi-valued attributes within a relation, but with the capability of naming attribute values. In addition, the data identified by a column key within a row can have multiple versions, each identified by a timestamp (a 64 bit integer).

Figure 18.7 shows an example a row in a Bigtable, as a relational style representation of the example [Chang et al., 2008]. The row key is a reverse URL. The Contents:column family has only one column key that represents the web page contents, with two versions (at timestamps t_1 and t_5). The Language:family has also only one column key that represents the web page language, with one version. The Anchor: column family has two column keys, i.e., Anchor:inria.fr and Anchor:uwaterloo.ca, which represent two anchors. The anchor source site name (e.g., inria.fr) is used as qualifier and the link text as value.

Bigtable provides a basic API for defining and manipulating tables, within a programming language such as C++. The API offers various operators to write and update values, and to iterate over subsets of data, produced by a scan operator. There are various ways to restrict the rows, columns and timestamps produced by a scan, as in a relational select operator. However, there are no complex operators such as join or union, which need to be programmed using the scan operator. Transactional atomicity is supported for single row updates only.

To store a table in GFS, Bigtable uses range partitioning on the row key. Each table is divided into partitions called *tablets*, each corresponding to a row range. Partitioning is dynamic, starting with one tablet (the entire table range) that is subsequently split into multiple tablets as the table grows. To locate the (user) tablets in GFS, Bigtable uses a metadata table, which is itself partitioned in metadata tablets, with a single root tablet stored at a master server, similar to GFSs master. In addition

---

[1] In the original proposal, a Bigtable is defined as a multidimensional map, indexed by a row key, a column key and a timestamp, each cell of the map being a single value (a string).

Row key	Contents:	Anchor:	Language:
"com.google.www"	"<html> ... </html>" t_1 "<html> ... </html>" t_5	inria.fr "google.com" t_2 "Google" t_3 uwaterloo.ca "google.com" t_4	"english" t_1

Fig. 18.7 Example of a Bigtable Row

to exploiting GFS for scalability and availability, Bigtable uses various techniques to optimize data access and minimize the number of disk accesses, such as compression of column families, grouping of column families with high locality of access and aggressive caching of metadata information by clients.

PNUTS.

PNUTS is a parallel and distributed database system for Yahoo!'s cloud applications [Cooper et al., 2008]. It is designed to serve web applications, which typically do not need complex queries, but require good response time, scalability and high availability and can tolerate relaxed consistency guarantees for replicated data. PNUTS is used internally at Yahoo! for various applications such as user database, social networks, content metadata management and shopping listings management.

PNUTS supports the basic relational data model, with tables of flat records. However, arbitrary structures are allowed within attributes of Binary Long Object (Blob) type. Schemas are flexible as new attributes can be added at any time even though the table is being queried or updated, and records need not have values for all attributes. PNUTS provides a simple query language with selection and projection on a single relation. Updates and deletes must specify the primary key.

PNUTS provides a replica consistency model that is between strong consistency and eventual consistency (see Chapter 13 for detailed definitions). This model is motivated by the fact that web applications typically manipulate only one record at a time, but different records may be used under different geographic locations. Thus, PNUTS proposes *per-record timeline consistency*, which guarantees that all replicas of a given record apply all updates to the record in the same order. Using this consistency model, PNUTS supports several API operations with different guarantees. For instance, **Read-any** returns a possibly stale version of the record; **Read-latest** returns the latest copy of the record; **Write** performs a single atomic write operation.

Database tables are horizontally partitioned into tablets, through either range partitioning or hashing, which are distributed across many servers in a cluster (at a site). Furthermore, sites in different geographical regions maintain a complete copy of the system and of each table. An original aspect is the use of a publish/subscribe mechanism, with guaranteed delivery, for both reliability and replication. This avoids the need to keep a traditional database log as the publish/subscribe mechanism is used to replay lost updates.

18.2.4.3 Parallel Data Processing

We illustrate parallel data processing in the cloud with MapReduce, a popular programming framework for processing and generating large datasets [Dean and Ghemawat, 2004]. MapReduce was initially developed by Google as a proprietary product to process large amounts of unstructured or semi-structured data, such as web documents and logs of web page requests, on large shared-nothing clusters of commodity nodes and produce various kinds of data such as inverted indices or URL access frequencies. Different implementations of MapReduce are now available such as Amazon MapReduce (as a cloud service) or Hadoop MapReduce (as open source software).

MapReduce enables programmers to express in a simple, functional style their computations on large data sets and hides the details of parallel data processing, load balancing and fault-tolerance. The programming model includes only two operations, *map* and *reduce*, which we can find in many functional programming languages such as Lisp and ML. The Map operation is applied to each record in the input data set to compute one or more intermediate (key,value) pairs. The Reduce operation is applied to all the values that share the same unique key in order to compute a combined result. Since they work on independent inputs, Map and Reduce can be automatically processed in parallel, on different data partitions using many cluster nodes.

Figure 18.8 gives an overview of MapReduce execution in a cluster. There is one master node (not shown in the figure) in the cluster that assigns Map and Reduce tasks to cluster nodes, i.e., Map and Reduce nodes. The input data set is first automatically split into a number of partitions, each being processed by a different Map node that applies the Map operation to each input record to compute intermediate (key,value) pairs. The intermediate result is divided into n partitions, using a partitioning function applied to the key (e.g., hash(key) mod n). Map nodes periodically write to disk their intermediate data into n regions by applying the partitioning function and indicate the region locations to the master. Reduce nodes are assigned by the master to work on one or more partitions. Each Reduce node first reads the partitions from the corresponding regions on the Map nodes, disks, and groups the values by intermediate key, using sorting. Then, for each unique key and group of values, it calls the user Reduce operation to compute a final result that is written in the output data set.

As in the original description of MapReduce [Dean and Ghemawat, 2004], the favorite examples deal with sets of documents, e.g., counting the occurrences of each word in each document, or matching a given pattern in each document. However,

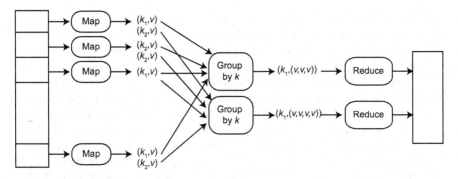

Fig. 18.8 Overview of MapReduce Execution

MapReduce can also be used to process relational data, as in the following example of a Group By select query on a single relation.

Example 18.3. Let us consider relation EMP(ENAME, TITLE, CITY) and the following SQL query that returns for each city, the number of employees whose name is "Smith".

```
SELECT   CITY, COUNT(*)
FROM     EMP
WHERE    ENAME LIKE "%Smith"
GROUP BY CITY
```

Processing this query with MapReduce can be done with the following Map and Reduce functions (which we give in pseudo code).

```
Map (Input (TID,emp), Output: (CITY,1))
    if emp.ENAME like "%Smith" return (CITY,1)
Reduce (Input (CITY,list(1)), Output: (CITY,SUM(list(1)))
    return (CITY,SUM(1*))
```

Map is applied in parallel to every tuple in EMP. It takes one pair (TID,emp), where the key is the EMP tuple identifier (TID) and the value the EMP tuple, and, if applicable, returns one pair (CITY,1). Note that the parsing of the tuple format to extract attributes needs to be done by the Map function. Then all (CITY,1) pairs with the same CITY are grouped together and a pair (CITY,list(1)) is created for each CITY. Reduce is then applied in parallel to compute the count for each CITY and produce the result of the query.   ◆

Fault-tolerance is important as there may be many nodes executing Map and Reduce operations. Input and output data are stored in GFS that already provides high fault-tolerance. Furthermore, all intermediate data are written to disk that helps checkpointing Map operations, and thus provides tolerance to soft failures. However, if one Map node or Reduce node fails during execution (hard failure), the task can be scheduled by the master onto other nodes. It may also be necessary to re-execute completed Map tasks, since the input data on the failed node disk is inaccessible. Overall, fault-tolerance is fine-grained and well suited for large jobs.

MapReduce has been extensively used both within Google and outside, with the Hadoop open source implementation, for many various applications including text processing, machine learning, and graph processing on very large data sets. The often cited advantages of MapReduce are its ability to express various (even complicated) Map and Reduce functions, and its extreme scalability and fault-tolerance. However, the comparison of MapReduce with parallel DBMSs in terms of performance has been the subject of debate between their respective proponents [Stonebraker et al., 2010; Dean and Ghemawat, 2010]. A performance comparison of Hadoop MapReduce and two parallel DBMSs – one row-store and one column-store DBMS – using a benchmark of three queries (a grep query, an aggregation query with a group by clause on a web log, and a complex join of two tables with aggregation and filtering) shows that, once the data has been loaded, the DBMSs are significantly faster, but loading data is very time consuming for the DBMSs [Pavlo et al., 2009]. The study also suggests that MapReduce is less efficient than DBMSs, because it performs repetitive format parsing and does not exploit pipelining and indices. It has been argued that a differentiation needs to be made between the MapReduce model and its implementations, which could be well improved, e.g., by exploiting indices [Dean and Ghemawat, 2010]. Another observation is that MapReduce and parallel DBMSs are complementary as MapReduce could be used to extract-transform-load data in a DBMS for more complex OLAP [Stonebraker et al., 2010].

18.3 Conclusion

In this chapter, we discussed two topics that are currently receiving considerable attention – data stream management, and cloud data management. Both of these have the potential to make considerable impact on distributed data management, but they are still not fully matured and require more research.

Data stream management addresses the requirements of a class of applications that produce data continuously. These systems require a shift in emphasis from traditional DBMSs in that they deal with data that is transient and queries that are (generally) persistent. Thus, they require new solutions and approaches. We discussed the main tenets of data stream management systems (DSMSs) in this chapter. The main challenge in data stream management is that data are produced continually, so it is not possible to store them for processing, as is typically done in traditional DBMSs. This requires unblocking operations, and online algorithms that sometimes have to deal with high data rates. The abstract models, language issues, and windowed query processing of streams are relatively well understood. However, there are a number of interesting research directions including the following:

- **Scaling with data rates.** Some data streams are relatively slow, while others have very high data rates. It is not clear if the strategies that have been developed for processing queries work on the wide range of stream rates. It is probably the case that special processing techniques need to be developed for different classes of streams based on their data rates.

- **Distributed stream processing.** Although there has been some amount of work in considering processing streams in a distributed fashion, most of the existing works consider a single processing site. Distribution, as is usually the case, poses new challenges but also new opportunities that are worth exploring.

- **Stream data warehouses.** Stream data warehouses combine the challenges of standard data warehouses and data streams. This is an area that has recently started to receive attention (e.g., [Golab et al., 2009; Polyzotis et al., 2008]), but there are still many problems that require attention, including update scheduling strategies for optimizing various objectives, and monitoring data consistency and quality as new data arrive [Golab and Özsu, 2010].

- **Uncertain data streams.** In many applications that generate streaming data, there may be uncertainty in the data values. For example, sensors may be faulty and generate data that are not accurate, certain observations may be uncertain, etc. The processing of queries over uncertain data streams poses significant challenges that are still open.

One of the main challenges of cloud data management is to provide ease of programming, consistency, scalability and elasticity at the same time, over cloud data. Current solutions have been quite successful but developed with specific, relatively simple applications in mind. In particular, they have sacrificed consistency and ease of programming for the sake of scalability. This has resulted in a pervasive approach relying on data partitioning and forcing applications to access data partitions individually, with a loss of consistency guarantees across data partitions. As the need to support tighter consistency requirements, e.g., for updating multiple tuples in one or more tables, increases, cloud application developers will be faced with a very difficult problem: providing isolation and atomicity across data partitions through careful engineering. We believe that new solutions are needed that capitalize on the principles of distributed and parallel database systems to raise the level of consistency and abstraction, while retaining the scalability and simplicity advantages of current solutions. Parallel database management techniques such as pipelining, indices and optimization should also be useful to improve the performance of MapReduce-like systems and support more complex data analysis applications. In the context of large-scale shared-nothing clusters, where node failures become the norm rather than the exception, another important problem remains to deal with the trade-off between query performance and fault-tolerance. P2P techniques that do not require centralized query execution control by a master node could also be useful there. Some promising research directions for cloud data management include the following:

- **Declarative programming languages.** Programming large-scale, distributed data management software such as MapReduce remains very hard. One promising solution proposed in the BOOM project [Alvaro et al., 2010] is to adopt a data centric declarative programming language, based on the Overlog data language, in order to improve ease of development and program correctness without sacrificing performance.

- **Autonomic data management.** Self-management of the data by the cloud will be critical to support large numbers of users with no database expertise. Modern database systems already provide good self-administration, self-tuning and self-repairing capabilities which ease application deployment and evolution. However, extending these capabilities to the scale of a cloud is hard. In particular, one problem is the automatic management of replication (definition, allocation, refreshment) to deal with load variations [Doherty and Hurley, 2007].

- **Data security and privacy.** Data security and access control in a cloud typically rely on user authentication and secured communication protocols to exchange encrypted data. However, the semi-open nature of a cloud makes security and privacy a major challenge since users may not trust the providers servers. Thus, the ability to perform relational-like operators directly on encrypted data at the cloud is important [Abadi, 2009]. In some applications, it is important that data privacy be preserved, using high-level mechanisms such as those of Hyppocratic databases [Agrawal et al., 2002].

- **Green data management.** One major problem for large-scale clouds is the energy cost. Harizopoulos et al. [2009] argue that data management techniques will be key in optimizing for energy efficiency. However, current data management techniques for the cloud have focused on scalability and performance, and must be significantly revisited to account for energy costs in query optimization, data structures and algorithms.

Finally there are problems in the intersection of data stream processing and cloud computing. Given the steady increase in data stream volumes, the need to process massive data flows in a scalable way is becoming important. Thus, the potential scalability advantage of a cloud can be exploited for data stream management as in Streamcloud [Gulisano et al., 2010]. This requires new strategies to parallelize continuous queries. And deadling with various trade-offs.

18.4 Bibliographic Notes

Data streams have received a lot of attention in recent years, so the literature on the topic is extensive. Good early overviews are given in [Babcock et al., 2002; Golab and Özsu, 2003a]. A more recent edited volume [Aggarwal, 2007] includes a number of articles on various aspects of these systems. An volume [Golab and Özsu, 2010] gives a full treatment of many of the issues that are discussed here. Mining data streams is reviewed in [Gaber et al., 2005] and issues in mining data streams with underlying distribution changes is discussed in [Hulten et al., 2001].

Our discussion of data stream systems follows [Golab and Özsu, 2003a], Chapter 2 of [Golab, 2006] and [Golab and Özsu, 2010]. The discussion on mining data streams borrows from Chapter 2 of [Tao, 2010].

Cloud computing has recently gained a lot of attention from the professional press as a new platform for enterprise and personal computing (see [Cusumano, 2010] for a good discussion of the trend). However, the research literature on cloud computing in general, and cloud data management in particular, is rather small, but as the number of international conferences and workshops grow, this should change quickly to become a major research domain. Our cloud taxonomy in Section 18.2.1 is based on our compilation of many professional articles and white papers. The discussion on grid computing in Section 18.2.2 is based on [Atkinson et al., 2005; Pacitti et al., 2007b]. The section on data management in the cloud (Section 18.2.4) has been inspired by several keynotes on the topic, e.g., [Ramakrishnan, 2009]. The technical details can be found in the research papers on GFS [Ghemawat et al., 2003], Bigtable [Chang et al., 2008], PNUTS [Cooper et al., 2008] and MapReduce [Dean and Ghemawat, 2004]. The discussion of MapReduce versus parallel DBMS can be found in [Stonebraker et al., 2010; Dean and Ghemawat, 2010].

References

Abadi, D., Carney, D., Cetintemel, U., Cherniack, M., Convey, C., Lee, S., Stone-braker, M., Tatbul, N., and Zdonik, S. (2003). Aurora: A new model and architecture for data stream management. *VLDB J.*, 12(2):120–139. 727, 730, 734, 736, 738

Abadi, D. J. (2009). Data management in the cloud: Limitations and opportunities. *Q. Bull. IEEE TC on Data Eng.*, 32(1):3–12. 746, 747, 762

Abadi, D. J., Madden, S., and Hachem, N. (2008). Column-stores vs. row-stores: how different are they really? In *Proc. ACM SIGMOD Int. Conf. on Management of Data*, pages 967–980. 753

Abadi, M. and Cardelli, L. (1996). *A Theory of Objects*. Springer. 553, 607

Abbadi, A. E., Skeen, D., and Cristian, F. (1985). An efficient, fault–tolerant protocol for replicated data management. In *Proc. ACM SIGACT-SIGMOD Symp. on Principles of Database Systems*, pages 215–229. 488

Aberer, K. (2001). P-grid: A self-organizing access structure for p2p information systems. In *Proc. Int. Conf. on Cooperative Information Systems*, pages 179–194. 622

Aberer, K. (2003). Guest editor's introduction. *ACM SIGMOD Rec.*, 32(3):21–22. 653

Aberer, K., Cudré-Mauroux, P., Datta, A., Despotovic, Z., Hauswirth, M., Punceva, M., and Schmidt, R. (2003a). P-grid: a self-organizing structured p2p system. *ACM SIGMOD Rec.*, 32(3):29–33. 622, 651, 654

Aberer, K., Cudré-Mauroux, P., and Hauswirth, M. (2003b). Start making sense: The chatty web approach for global semantic agreements. *J. Web Semantics*, 1(1):89–114. 625

Abiteboul, S. and Beeri, C. (1995). The power of languages for the manipulation of complex values. *VLDB J.*, 4(4):727–794. 553

Abiteboul, S., Benjelloun, O., Manolescu, I., Milo, T., and Weber, R. (2002). Active XML: Peer-to-peer data and web services integration. In *Proc. 28th Int. Conf. on Very Large Data Bases*, pages 1087–1090. 625

Abiteboul, S., Benjelloun, O., and Milo, T. (2008a). The active XML project: an overview. *VLDB J.*, 17(5):1019–1040. 703

M.T. Özsu and P. Valduriez, *Principles of Distributed Database Systems: Third Edition*, DOI 10.1007/978-1-4419-8834-8, © Springer Science+Business Media, LLC 2011

Abiteboul, S., Buneman, P., and Suciu, D. (1999). *Data on the Web: From Relations to Semistructured Data and XML*. Morgan Kaufmann. 719

Abiteboul, S. and dos Santos, C. S. (1995). IQL(2): A model with ubiquitous objects. In *Proc. 5th Int. Workshop on Database Programming Languages*, page 10. 607

Abiteboul, S. and Kanellakis, P. C. (1998a). Object identity as a query language primitive. *J. ACM*, 45(5):798–842. 553

Abiteboul, S. and Kanellakis, P. C. (1998b). Object identity as a query language primitive. *J. ACM*, 45(5):798–842. 607

Abiteboul, S., Manolescu, I., Polyzotis, N., Preda, N., and Sun, C. (2008b). XML processing in DHT networks. In *Proc. 24th Int. Conf. on Data Engineering*, pages 606–615. 625

Abiteboul, S., Quass, D., McHugh, J., Widom, J., and Wiener, J. (1997). The Lorel query language for semistructured data. *Int. J. Digit. Libr.*, 1(1):68–88. 673

Aboulnaga, A., Alameldeen, A. R., and Naughton, J. F. (2001). Estimating the selectivity of XML path expressions for internet scale applications. In *Proc. 27th Int. Conf. on Very Large Data Bases*, pages 591–600. 701

Abramson, N. (1973). The ALOHA system. In Abramson, N. and Kuo, F. F., editors, *Computer Communication Networks*. Prentice-Hall. 64

Adali, S., Candan, K. S., Papakonstantinou, Y., and Subrahmanian, V. S. (1996a). Query caching and optimization in distributed mediator systems. In *Proc. ACM SIGMOD Int. Conf. on Management of Data*, pages 137–148. 160

Adali, S., Candan, K. S., Papakonstantinou, Y., and Subrahmanian, V. S. (1996b). Query caching and optimization in distributed mediator systems. In *Proc. ACM SIGMOD Int. Conf. on Management of Data*, pages 137–148. 309

Adamic, L. and Huberman, B. (2000). The nature of markets in the world wide web. *Quart. J. Electron. Comm.*, 1:5–12. 734, 739

Adiba, M. (1981). Derived relations: A unified mechanism for views, snapshots and distributed data. In *Proc. 7th Int. Conf. on Very Data Bases*, pages 293–305. 176, 177, 201

Adiba, M. and Lindsay, B. (1980). Database snapshots. In *Proc. 6th Int. Conf. on Very Data Bases*, pages 86–91. 176, 201

Adler, M. and Mitzenmacher, M. (2001). Towards compressing web graphs. In *Proc. Data Compression Conf.*, pages 203–212. 660, 719

Adya, A., Gruber, R., Liskov, B., and Maheshwari, U. (1995). Efficient optimistic concurrency control using loosely synchronized clocks. In *Proc. ACM SIGMOD Int. Conf. on Management of Data*, pages 23–34. 574

Aggarwal, C. (2003). A framework for diagnosing changes in evolving data streams. In *Proc. ACM SIGMOD Int. Conf. on Management of Data*, pages 575–586. 743

Aggarwal, C. (2005). On change diagnosis in evolving data streams. *IEEE Trans. Knowl. and Data Eng.*, 17(5). 743

Aggarwal, C., Han, J., Wang, J., and Yu, P. S. (2003). A framework for clustering evolving data streams. In *Proc. 29th Int. Conf. on Very Large Data Bases*, pages 81–92. 743

Aggarwal, C., Han, J., Wang, J., and Yu, P. S. (2004). A framework for projected clustering of high dimensional data streams. In *Proc. 30th Int. Conf. on Very Large Data Bases*, pages 852–863. 726, 743

Aggarwal, C. C., editor (2007). *Data Streams: Models and Algorithms*. Springer. 762

Agichtein, E., Lawrence, S., and Gravano, L. (2004). Learning to find answers to questions on the web. *ACM Trans. Internet Tech.*, 4(3):129—162. 681

Agrawal, D., Bruno, J. L., El-Abbadi, A., and Krishnasawamy, V. (1994). Relative serializability: An approach for relaxing the atomicity of transactions. In *Proc. ACM SIGACT-SIGMOD Symp. on Principles of Database Systems*, pages 139–149. 395

Agrawal, D. and El-Abbadi, A. (1990). Locks with constrained sharing. In *Proc. ACM SIGACT-SIGMOD Symp. on Principles of Database Systems*, pages 85–93. 371, 372

Agrawal, D. and El-Abbadi, A. (1994). A nonrestrictive concurrency control protocol for object-oriented databases. *Distrib. Parall. Databases*, 2(1):7–31. 600

Agrawal, R., Carey, M., and Livney, M. (1987). Concurrency control performance modeling: Alternatives and implications. *ACM Trans. Database Syst.*, 12(4):609–654. 401

Agrawal, R. and DeWitt, D. J. (1985). Integrated concurrency control and recovery mechanisms. *ACM Trans. Database Syst.*, 10(4):529–564. 420

Agrawal, R., Evfimievski, A. V., and Srikant, R. (2003). Information sharing across private databases. In *Proc. ACM SIGMOD Int. Conf. on Management of Data*, pages 86–97. 187

Agrawal, R., Ghosh, S. P., Imielinski, T., Iyer, B. R., and Swami, A. N. (1992). An interval classifier for database mining applications. In *Proc. 18th Int. Conf. on Very Large Data Bases*, pages 560–573. 743

Agrawal, R., Kiernan, J., Srikant, R., and Xu, Y. (2002). Hippocratic databases. In *Proc. 28th Int. Conf. on Very Large Data Bases*, pages 143–154. 762

Akal, F., Böhm, K., and Schek, H.-J. (2002). Olap query evaluation in a database cluster: A performance study on intra-query parallelism. In *Proc. 6th East European Conf. Advances in Databases and Information Systems*, pages 218–231. 542, 543, 548

Akal, F., Türker, C., Schek, H.-J., Breitbart, Y., Grabs, T., and Veen, L. (2005). Fine-grained replication and scheduling with freshness and correctness guarantees. In *Proc. 31st Int. Conf. on Very Large Data Bases*, pages 565–576. 493

Akbarinia, R. and Martins, V. (2007). Data management in the appa system. *J. Grid Comp.*, 5(3):303–317. 626

Akbarinia, R., Martins, V., Pacitti, E., and Valduriez, P. (2006a). Design and implementation of atlas p2p architecture. In Baldoni, R., Cortese, G., and Davide, F., editors, *Global Data Management*, pages 98–123. IOS Press. 626, 636

Akbarinia, R., Pacitti, E., and Valduriez, P. (2006b). Reducing network traffic in unstructured p2p systems using top-k queries. *Distrib. Parall. Databases*, 19(2-3):67–86. 628, 637

Akbarinia, R., Pacitti, E., and Valduriez, P. (2007a). Best position algorithms for top-k queries. In *Proc. 33rd Int. Conf. on Very Large Data Bases*, pages 495–506. 634, 635, 654

Akbarinia, R., Pacitti, E., and Valduriez, P. (2007b). Data currency in replicated dhts. In *Proc. ACM SIGMOD Int. Conf. on Management of Data*, pages 211–222. 648, 654

Akbarinia, R., Pacitti, E., and Valduriez, P. (2007c). Processing top-k queries in distributed hash tables. In *Proc. 13th Int. Euro-Par Conf.*, pages 489–502. 638, 654

Akbarinia, R., Pacitti, E., and Valduriez, P. (2007d). Query processing in P2P systems. Technical Report 6112, INRIA, Rennes, France. 654

Al-Khalifa, S., Jagadish, H. V., Patel, J. M., Wu, Y., Koudas, N., and Srivastava, D. (2002). Structural joins: A primitive for efficient XML query pattern matching. In *Proc. 18th Int. Conf. on Data Engineering*, pages 141–152. 700

Alon, N., Matias, Y., and Szegedy, M. (1996). The space complexity of approximating the frequency moments. In *Proc. 28th Annual ACM Symp. on Theory of Computing*, pages 20–29. 733

Alsberg, P. A. and Day, J. D. (1976). A principle for resilient sharing of distributed resources. In *Proc. 2nd Int. Conf. on Software Engineering*, pages 562–570. 373

Altingövde, I. S. and Ulusoy, Ö. (2004). Exploiting interclass rules for focused crawling. *IEEE Intelligent Systems*, 19(6):66–73. 666

Alvaro, P., Condie, T., Conway, N., Elmeleegy, K., Hellerstein, J. M., and Sears, R. (2010). Boom analytics: exploring data-centric, declarative programming for the cloud. In *Proc. 5th ACM SIGOPS/EuroSys European Conf. on Computer Systems*, pages 223–236. 761

Amsaleg, L. (1995). *Conception et réalisation d'un glaneur de cellules adapté aux SGBDO client-serveur*. Ph.D. thesis, Université Paris 6 Pierre et Marie Curie, Paris, France. 581

Amsaleg, L., Franklin, M., and Gruber, O. (1995). Efficient incremental garbage collection for client-server object database systems. In *Proc. 21th Int. Conf. on Very Large Data Bases*, pages 42–53. 581

Amsaleg, L., Franklin, M. J., Tomasic, A., and Urhan, T. (1996a). Scrambling query plans to cope with unexpected delays. In *Proc. 4th Int. Conf. on Parallel and Distributed Information Systems*, pages 208–219. 320, 322, 331

Amsaleg, L., Franklin, M. J., Tomasic, A., and Urhan, T. (1996b). Scrambling query plans to cope with unexpected delays. In *Proc. 4th Int. Conf. on Parallel and Distributed Information Systems*, pages 208–219. 739

Anderson, T. and Lee, P. A. (1981). *Fault Tolerance: Principles and Practice*. Prentice-Hall. 455

Anderson, T. and Lee, P. A. (1985). Software fault tolerance terminology proposals. In Shrivastava [1985], pages 6–13. 406

Anderson, T. and Randell, B. (1979). *Computing Systems Reliability*. Cambridge University Press. 455

ANSI (1992). *Database Language SQL*, ansi x3.135-1992 edition. 348

ANSI/SPARC (1975). Interim report: ANSI/X3/SPARC study group on data base management systems. *ACM FDT Bull*, 7(2):1–140. 22

Antonioletti, M. et al. (2005). The design and implementation of grid database services in OGSA-DAI. *Concurrency — Practice & Experience*, 17(2-4):357–376. 750

Apers, P., van den Berg, C., Flokstra, J., Grefen, P., Kersten, M., and Wilschut, A. (1992). Prisma/db: a parallel main-memory relational dbms. *IEEE Trans. Knowl. and Data Eng.*, 4:541–554. 505, 548

Apers, P. M. G. (1981). Redundant allocation of relations in a communication network. In *Proc. 5th Berkeley Workshop on Distributed Data Management and Computer Networks*, pages 245–258. 125

Apers, P. M. G., Hevner, A. R., and Yao, S. B. (1983). Optimization algorithms for distributed queries. *IEEE Trans. Softw. Eng.*, 9(1):57–68. 212

Arasu, A., Babu, S., and Widom, J. (2006). The CQL continuous query language: Semantic foundations and query execution. *VLDB J.*, 15(2):121–142. 726, 727, 728, 732, 734, 735, 739

Arasu, A., Cho, J., Garcia-Molina, H., Paepcke, A., and Raghavan, S. (2001). Searching the web. *ACM Trans. Internet Tech.*, 1(1):2–43. 663, 667, 719

Arasu, A. and Widom, J. (2004a). A denotational semantics for continuous queries over streams and relations. *ACM SIGMOD Rec.*, 33(3):6–11. 728

Arasu, A. and Widom, J. (2004b). Resource sharing in continuous sliding-window aggregates. In *Proc. 30th Int. Conf. on Very Large Data Bases*, pages 336–347. 736, 737

Arocena, G. and Mendelzon, A. (1998). Weboql: Restructuring documents, databases and webs. In *Proc. 14th Int. Conf. on Data Engineering*, pages 24–33. 676

Arpaci-Dusseau, R. H., Anderson, E., Treuhaft, N., Culler, D. E., Hellerstein, J. M., Patterson, D., and Yelick, K. (1999). Cluster i/o with river: making the fast case common. In *Proc. Workshop on I/O in Parallel and Distributed Systems*, pages 10–22. 326

Aspnes, J. and Shah, G. (2003). Skip graphs. In *Proc. 14th Annual ACM-SIAM Symp. on Discrete Algorithms*, pages 384–393. 622

Astrahan, M. M., Blasgen, M. W., Chamberlin, D. D., Eswaran, K. P., Gray, J. N., Griffiths, P. P., King, W. F., Lorie, R. A., McJones, P. R., Mehl, J. W., Putzolu, G. R., Traiger, I. L., Wade, B. W., and Watson, V. (1976). System r: A relational database management system. *ACM Trans. Database Syst.*, 1(2):97–137. 190, 261, 419

Atkinson, M., Bancilhon, F., DeWitt, D., Dittrich, K., Maier, D., and Zdonik, S. (1989). The object-oriented database system manifesto. In *Proc. 1st Int. Conf. on Deductive and Object-Oriented Databases*, pages 40–57. 553

Atkinson, M. P. et al. (2005). Web service grids: an evolutionary approach. *Concurrency and Computation — Practice & Experience*, 17(2-4):377–389. 748, 763

Avizienis, A., Kopetz, H., and (eds.), J. C. L. (1987). *The Evolution of Fault-Tolerant Computing*. Springer. 455

Avnur, R. and Hellerstein, J. M. (2000). Eddies: Continuously adaptive query processing. In *Proc. ACM SIGMOD Int. Conf. on Management of Data*, pages 261–272. 321, 331

Ayad, A. and Naughton, J. (2004). Static optimization of conjunctive queries with sliding windows over unbounded streaming information sources. In *Proc. ACM SIGMOD Int. Conf. on Management of Data*, pages 419–430. 740

Ayad, A., Naughton, J., Wright, S., and Srivastava, U. (2006). Approximate streaming window joins under CPU limitations. In *Proc. 22nd Int. Conf. on Data Engineering*, page 142. 740

Babaoglu, Ö. (1987). On the reliability of consensus-based fault-tolerant distributed computing systems. *ACM Trans. Comp. Syst.*, 5(3):394–416. 456

Babb, E. (1979). Implementing a relational database by means of specialized hardware. *ACM Trans. Database Syst.*, 4(1):1–29. 499

Babcock, B., Babu, S., Datar, M., Motwani, R., and Thomas, D. (2004). Operator scheduling in data stream systems. *VLDB J.*, 13(4):333–353. 735

Babcock, B., Babu, S., Datar, M., Motwani, R., and Widom, J. (2002). Models and issues in data stream systems. In *Proc. ACM SIGACT-SIGMOD Symp. on Principles of Database Systems*, pages 1–16. 740, 743, 762

Babcock, B., Datar, M., Motwani, R., and O'Callaghan, L. (2003). Maintaining variance and k-medians over data stream windows. In *Proc. ACM SIGACT-SIGMOD Symp. on Principles of Database Systems*, pages 234–243. 737

Babu, S. and Bizarro, P. (2005). Adaptive query processing in the looking glass. In *Proc. 2nd Biennial Conf. on Innovative Data Systems Research*, pages 238–249. 739

Babu, S., Motwani, R., Munagala, K., Nishizawa, I., and Widom, J. (2004a). Adaptive ordering of pipelined stream filters. In *Proc. ACM SIGMOD Int. Conf. on Management of Data*, pages 407–418. 739

Babu, S., Munagala, K., Widom, J., and Motwani, R. (2005). Adaptive caching for continuous queries. In *Proc. 21st Int. Conf. on Data Engineering*, pages 118–129. 739

Babu, S., Srivastava, U., and Widom, J. (2004b). Exploiting k-constraints to reduce memory overhead in continuous queries over data streams. *ACM Trans. Database Syst.*, 29(3):545–580. 732

Babu, S. and Widom, J. (2004). StreaMon: an adaptive engine for stream query processing. In *Proc. ACM SIGMOD Int. Conf. on Management of Data*, pages 931–932. 739

Badrinath, B. R. and Ramamritham, K. (1987). Semantics-based concurrency control: Beyond commutativity. In *Proc. 3th Int. Conf. on Data Engineering*, pages 04–311. 594, 596, 602

Baeza-Yates, R. and Ribeiro-Neto, B. (1999). *Modern Information Retrieval*. Addison Wesley, New York, USA. 669

Balke, W.-T., Nejdl, W., Siberski, W., and Thaden, U. (2005). Progressive distributed top-k retrieval in peer-to-peer networks. In *Proc. 21st Int. Conf. on Data Engineering*, pages 174–185. 639

Ball, M. O. and Hardie, F. (1967). Effects and detection of intermittent failures in digital systems. Technical Report Internal Report 67-825-2137, IBM. Cited in [Siewiorek and Swarz, 1982]. 410

Balter, R., Berard, P., and Decitre, P. (1982). Why control of concurrency level in distributed systems is more important than deadlock management. In *Proc. ACM SIGACT-SIGOPS 1st Symp. on the Principles of Distributed Computing*, pages 183–193. 361

Bancilhon, F. and Spyratos, N. (1981). Update semantics of relational views. *ACM Trans. Database Syst.*, 6(4):557–575. 175, 201

Barbara, D., Garcia-Molina, H., and Spauster, A. (1986). Policies for dynamic vote reassignment. In *Proc. 6th Int. Conf. on Distributed Computing Systems*, pages 37–44. 456, 493

Barbara, D., Molina, H. G., and Spauster, A. (1989). Increasing availability under mutual exclusion constraints with dynamic voting reassignment. *ACM Trans. Comp. Syst.*, 7(4):394–426. 456, 493

Bartlett, J. (1978). A nonstop operating system. In *Proc. 11th Hawaii Int. Conf. on System Sciences*, pages 103–117. 456

Bartlett, J. (1981). A nonstop kernel. In *Proc. 8th ACM Symp. on Operating System Principles*, pages 22–29. 456

Barton, C., Charles, P., Goyal, D., Raghavachari, M., Fontoura, M., and Josifovski, V. (2003). Streaming XPath processing with forward and backward axes. In *Proc. 19th Int. Conf. on Data Engineering*, pages 455–466. 700

Batini, C. and Lenzirini, M. (1984). A methodology for data schema integration in entity-relationship model. *IEEE Trans. Softw. Eng.*, SE-10(6):650–654. 147

Batini, C., Lenzirini, M., and Navathe, S. B. (1986). A comparative analysis of methodologies for database schema integration. *ACM Comput. Surv.*, 18(4):323–364. 140, 147, 160

Bayer, R. and McCreight, E. (1972). Organization and maintenance of large ordered indexes. *Acta Informatica*, 1:173–189. 510

Beeri, C. (1990). A formal approach to object-oriented databases. *Data & Knowledge Eng*, 5:353–382. 557

Beeri, C., Bernstein, P. A., and Goodman, N. (1989). A model for concurrency in nested transaction systems. *J. ACM*, 36(2):230–269. 401

Beeri, C., Schek, H.-J., and Weikum, G. (1988). Multi-level transaction management, theoretical art or practical need? In *Advances in Database Technology, Proc. 1st Int. Conf. on Extending Database Technology*, pages 134–154. 397

Bell, D. and Grimson, J. (1992). *Distributed Database Systems*. Addison Wesley. Reading. 38

Bell, D. and Lapuda, L. (1976). Secure computer systems: Unified exposition and Multics interpretation. Technical Report MTR-2997 Rev.1, MITRE Corp, Bedford, MA. 183, 201

Bellatreche, L., Karlapalem, K., and Li, Q. (1998). Complex methods and class allocation in distributed object oriented database systems. Technical Report HKUST98-yy, Department of Computer Science, Hong Kong University of Science and Technologyty of Science and Technology. 565

Bellatreche, L., Karlapalem, K., and Li, Q. (2000a). Algorithms and support for horizontal class partitioning in object-oriented databases. *Distrib. Parall. Databases*, 8(2):155 – 179. 607

Bellatreche, L., Karlapalem, K., and Li, Q. (2000b). A framework for class partitioning in object oriented databases. *Distrib. Parall. Databases*, 8(2):333 – 366. 607

Benzaken, V. and Delobel, C. (1990). Enhancing performance in a persistent object store: Clustering strategies in o_2. In *Implementing Persistent Object Bases: Principles and Practice. Proc. 4th Int. Workshop on Persistent Object Systems*, pages 403–412. 579

Berenson, H., Bernstein, P., Gray, J., Melton, J., O'Neil, E., and O'Neil, P. (1995). A critique of ansi sql isolation levels. In *Proc. ACM SIGMOD Int. Conf. on Management of Data*, pages 1–10. 348, 349, 367

Bergamaschi, S., Castano, S., Vincini, M., and Beneventano, D. (2001). Semantic integration of heterogeneous information sources. *Data & Knowl. Eng.*, 36:215–249. 134, 160

Berglund, A., Boag, S., Chamberlin, D., Fernández, M. F., Kay, M., Robie, J., and Siméon, J., editors. XML Path language (XPath) 2.0 (2007). Available from: http://www.w3.org/TR/xpath20/ [Last retrieved: December 2009]. 690, 694

Bergman, M. K. (2001). The deep web: Surfacing hidden value. *J. Electronic Publishing*, 7(1). 657

Bergsten, B., Couprie, M., and Valduriez, P. (1991). Prototyping dbs3, a shared-memory parallel database system. In *Proc. Int. Conf. on Parallel and Distributed Information Systems*, pages 226–234. 501, 503, 528, 548

Bergsten, B., Couprie, M., and Valduriez, P. (1993). Overview of parallel architectures for databases. *The Comp. J.*, 36(8):734–739. 547

Berlin, J. and Motro, A. (2001). Autoplex: Automated discovery of content for virtual databases. In *Proc. Int. Conf. on Cooperative Information Systems*, pages 108–122. 145

Bernstein, P. and Blaustein, B. (1982). Fast methods for testing quantified relational calculus assertions. In *Proc. ACM SIGMOD Int. Conf. on Management of Data*, pages 39–50. 192, 199, 202

Bernstein, P., Blaustein, B., and Clarke, E. M. (1980a). Fast maintenance of semantic integrity assertions using redundant aggregate data. In *Proc. 6th Int. Conf. on Very Data Bases*, pages 126–136. 192, 202

Bernstein, P. and Melnik, S. (2007). Model management: 2.0: Manipulating richer mappings. In *Proc. ACM SIGMOD Int. Conf. on Management of Data*, pages 1–12. 135, 159, 160

Bernstein, P., Shipman, P., and Rothnie, J. B. (1980b). Concurrency control in a system for distributed databases (sdd-1). *ACM Trans. Database Syst.*, 5(1):18–51. 383, 395

Bernstein, P. A. and Chiu, D. M. (1981). Using semi-joins to solve relational queries. *J. ACM*, 28(1):25–40. 269, 292

Bernstein, P. A., Fekete, A., Guo, H., Ramakrishnan, R., and Tamma, P. (2006). Relexed concurrency serializability for middle-tier caching and replication. In *Proc. ACM SIGMOD Int. Conf. on Management of Data*, pages 599–610. 462, 464, 480

Bernstein, P. A., Giunchiglia, F., Kementsietsidis, A., Mylopoulos, J., Serafini, L., and Zaihrayeu, I. (2002). Data management for peer-to-peer computing : A vision. In *Proc. 5th Int. Workshop on the World Wide Web and Databases*, pages 89–94. 625, 653

Bernstein, P. A. and Goodman, N. (1981). Concurrency control in distributed database systems. *ACM Comput. Surv.*, 13(2):185–222. 39, 367, 369, 401

Bernstein, P. A. and Goodman, N. (1984). An algorithm for concurrency control and recovery in replicated distributed databases. *ACM Trans. Database Syst.*, 9(4):596–615. 486

Bernstein, P. A., Goodman, N., Wong, E., Reeve, C. L., and Jr, J. B. R. (1981). Query processing in a system for distributed databases (sdd-1). *ACM Trans. Database Syst.*, 6(4):602–625. 215, 281, 283, 293

Bernstein, P. A., Hadzilacos, V., and Goodman, N. (1987). *Concurrency Control and Recovery in Database Systems*. Addison Wesley. 39, 341, 385, 391, 401, 413, 421, 423, 424, 425, 429, 453, 486, 596

Bernstein, P. A. and Newcomer, E. (1997). *Principles of Transaction Processing for the Systems Professional*. Morgan Kaufmann. 358

Berthold, H., Schmidt, S., Lehner, W., and Hamann, C.-J. (2005). Integrated resource management for data stream systems. In *Proc. 2005 ACM Symp. on Applied Computing*, pages 555–562. 738

Bertino, E., Chin, O. B., Sacks-Davis, R., Tan, K.-L., Zobel, J., Shidlovsky, B., and Andronico, D. (1997). *Indexing Techniques for Advanced Database Systems*. Kluwer Academic Publishers. 607

Bertino, E. and Kim, W. (1989). Indexing techniques for queries on nested objects. *IEEE Trans. Knowl. and Data Eng.*, 1(2):196–214. 588, 589, 590

Bertino, E. and Martino, L. (1993). *Object-Oriented Database Systems*. Addison Wesley. 607

Bevan, D. I. (1987). Distributed garbage collection using reference counting. In de Bakker, J., Nijman, L., and Treleaven, P., editors, *Parallel Architectures and Languages Europe*, Lecture Notes in Computer Science, pages 117–187. Springer. 581

Bhar, S. and Barker, K. (1995). Static allocation in distributed objectbase systems: A graphical approach. In *Proc. 6th Int. Conf. on Information Systems and Data Management*, pages 92–114. 565

Bharat, K. and Broder, A. (1998). A technique for measuring the relative size and overlap of public web search engines. *Comp. Networks and ISDN Syst.*, 30:379 – 388. (Proc. 7th Int. World Wide Web Conf.). 657

Bhargava, B., editor (1987). *Concurrency Control and Reliability in Distributed Systems*. Van Nostrand Reinhold. 358

Bhargava, B. and Lian, S.-R. (1988). Independent checkpointing and concurrent rollback for recovery in distributed systems: An optimistic approach. In *Proc. 7th Symp. on Reliable Distributed Systems*, pages 3–12. 456

Bhide, A. (1988). An analysis of three transaction processing architectures. In *Proc. ACM SIGMOD Int. Conf. on Management of Data*, pages 339–350. 401

Bhide, A. and Stonebraker, M. (1988). A performance comparison of two architectures for fast transaction processing. In *Proc. 4th Int. Conf. on Data Engineering*, pages 536–545. 547

Bhowmick, S. S., Madria, S. K., and Ng, W. K. (2004). *Web Data Management*. Springer. 719

Biliris, A. and Panagos, E. (1995). A high performance configurable storage manager. In *Proc. 11th Int. Conf. on Data Engineering*, pages 35–43. 571

Biscondi, N., Brunie, L., Flory, A., and Kosch, H. (1996). Encapsulation of intra-operation parallelism in a parallel match operator. In *Proc. ACPC Conf.*, volume 1127 of *Lecture Notes in Computer Science*, pages 124–135. 528

Bitton, D., Boral, H., DeWitt, D. J., and Wilkinson, W. K. (1983). Parallel algorithms for the execution of relational database operations. *ACM Trans. Database Syst.*, 8(3):324–353. 515

Blakeley, J., McKenna, W., and Graefe, G. (1993). Experiences building the open oodb query optimizer. In *Proc. ACM SIGMOD Int. Conf. on Management of Data*, pages 287–296. 584, 586, 587, 588

Blakeley, J. A., Larson, P.-A., and Tompa, F. W. (1986). Efficiently updating materialized views. In *Proc. ACM SIGMOD Int. Conf. on Management of Data*, pages 61–71. 177

Blasgen, M., Gray, J., Mitoma, M., and Price, T. (1979). The convoy phenomenon. *Operating Systems Rev.*, 13(2):20–25. 526

Blaustein, B. (1981). *Enforcing Database Assertions: Techniques and Applications*. Ph.D. thesis, Harvard University, Cambridge, Mass. 192, 202

Boag, S., Chamberlin, D., Fernández, M. F., Florescu, D., Robie, J., and Siméon, J., editors. XQuery 1.0: An XML query language (2007). Available from: http://www.w3.org/TR/xquery [Last retrieved: December 2009]. 690, 694, 696

Bonato, A. (2008). *A Course on the Web Graph*. American Mathematical Society. 658, 719

Boncz, P. A., Grust, T., van Keulen, M., Manegold, S., Rittinger, J., and Teubner, J. (2006). MonetDB/XQuery: a fast XQuery processor powered by a relational engine. In *Proc. ACM SIGMOD Int. Conf. on Management of Data*, pages 479–490. 699, 703

Bonnet, P., Gehrke, J., and Seshadri, P. (2001). Towards sensor database systems. In *Proc. 2nd Int. Conf. on Mobile Data Management*, pages 3–14. 726, 730

Booth, D., Haas, H., McCabe, F., Newcomer, E., Champion, M., Ferris, C., and Orchard, D., editors. Web services architecture (2004). Available from: http://www.w3.org/TR/ws-arch/ [Last retrieved: December 2009]. 690

Boral, H., Alexander, W., Clay, L., Copeland, G., Danforth, S., Franklin, M., Hart, B., Smith, M., and Valduriez, P. (1990). Prototyping bubba, a highly parallel database system. *IEEE Trans. Knowl. and Data Eng.*, 2(1):4–24. 505

Boral, H. and DeWitt, D. (1983). Database machines: An idea whose time has passed? a critique of the future of database machines. In *Proc. 3rd Int. Workshop on Database Machines*, pages 166–187. 498

Borg, A., Baumbach, J., and Glazer, S. (1983). A message system supporting fault tolerance. In *Proc. 9th ACM Symp. on Operating System Principles*, pages 90–99, Bretton Woods, N.H. 456

Borr, A. (1984). Robustness to crash in a distributed database: A non shared-memory multiprocessor approach. In *Proc. 10th Int. Conf. on Very Large Data Bases*, pages 445–453. 456

Borr, A. (1988). High performance sql through low-level system integration. In *Proc. ACM SIGMOD Int. Conf. on Management of Data*, pages 342–349. 377

Bouganim, L., Dageville, B., and Florescu, D. (1996a). Skew handling in the dbs3 parallel database system. In *Proc. International Conference on ACPC*. 528

Bouganim, L., Dageville, B., and Valduriez, P. (1996b). Adaptive parallel query execution in dbs3. In *Advances in Database Technology, Proc. 5th Int. Conf. on Extending Database Technology*, pages 481–484. Springer. 528, 548

Bouganim, L., Florescu, D., and Valduriez, P. (1996c). Dynamic load balancing in hierarchical parallel database systems. In *Proc. 22th Int. Conf. on Very Large Data Bases*, pages 436–447. 530, 534, 548

Bouganim, L., Florescu, D., and Valduriez, P. (1999). Multi-join query execution with skew in numa multiprocessors. *Distrib. Parall. Databases*, 7(1). in press. 506, 548

Brantner, M., Helmer, S., Kanne, C.-C., and Moerkotte, G. (2005). Full-fledged algebraic XPath processing in natix. In *Proc. 21st Int. Conf. on Data Engineering*, pages 705–716. 698, 700, 703

Bratbergsengen, K. (1984). Hashing methods and relational algebra operations. In *Proc. 10th Int. Conf. on Very Large Data Bases*, pages 323–333. 211, 515

Bray, T., Paoli, J., Sperberg-McQueen, C. M., Maler, E., and Yergeau, F., editors. Extensible markup language (XML) 1.0 (Fifth edition) (2008). Available from: http://www.w3.org/TR/2008/REC-xml-20081126/ [Last retrieved: December 2009]. 689

Breitbart, Y. and Korth, H. F. (1997). Replication and consistency: Being lazy helps sometimes. In *Proc. ACM SIGACT-SIGMOD Symp. on Principles of Database Systems*, pages 173–184. 476

Breitbart, Y., Olson, P. L., and Thompson, G. R. (1986). Database integration in a distributed heterogeneous database system. In *Proc. 2nd Int. Conf. on Data Engineering*, pages 301–310. 160

Bright, M. W., Hurson, A. R., and Pakzad, S. H. (1994). Automated resolution of semantic heterogeneity in multidatabases. *ACM Trans. Database Syst.*, 19(2):212–253. 160

Brill, D., Templeton, M., and Yu, C. (1984). Distributed query processing strategies in mermaid: A front-end to data management systems. In *Proc. 1st Int. Conf. on Data Engineering*, pages 211–218. 331

Brin, S. and Page, L. (1998). The anatomy of a large-scale hypertextual web search engine. *Comp. Netw.*, 30(1-7):107 – 117. 658, 667

Broder, A., Kumar, R., Maghoul, F., Raghavan, P., Rajagopalan, S., Stata, R., Tomkins, A., and Wiener, J. (2000). Graph structure in the web. *Comp. Netw.*, 33:309–320. 659

Bruno, N. and Chaudhuri, S. (2002). Exploiting statistics on query expressions for optimization. In *Proc. ACM SIGMOD Int. Conf. on Management of Data*, pages 263–274. 256

Bruno, N., Koudas, N., and Srivastava, D. (2002). Holistic twig joins: Optimal XML pattern matching. In *Proc. ACM SIGMOD Int. Conf. on Management of Data*, pages 310–322. 700, 701

Bucci, G. and Golinelli, S. (1977). A distributed strategy for resource allocation in information networks. In *Proc. Int. Computing Symp*, pages 345–356. 125

Buchmann, A., Özsu, M., Hornick, M., Georgakopoulos, D., and Manola, F. A. (1982). A transaction model for active distributed object systems. In [Elmagarmid, 1982]. 354, 355, 359, 593, 594

Buneman, P., Cong, G., Fan, W., and Kementsietsidis, A. (2006). Using partial evaluation in distributed query evaluation. In *Proc. 32nd Int. Conf. on Very Large Data Bases*, pages 211–222. 711

Buneman, P., Davidson, S., Hillebrand, G. G., and Suciu, D. (1996). A query language and optimization techniques for unstructured data. In *Proc. ACM SIGMOD Int. Conf. on Management of Data*, pages 505–516. 671

Butler, M. (1987). Storage reclamation in object oriented database systems. In *Proc. ACM SIGMOD Int. Conf. on Management of Data*, pages 410–425. 581

Calì, A. and Calvanese, D. (2002). Optimized querying of integrated data over the web. In *Engineering Information Systems in the Internet Context*, pages 285–301. 303

Callan, J. P. and Connell, M. E. (2001). Query-based sampling of text databases. *ACM Trans. Information Syst.*, 19(2):97–130. 688

Callan, J. P., Connell, M. E., and Du, A. (1999). Automatic discovery of language models for text databases. In *Proc. ACM SIGMOD Int. Conf. on Management of Data*, pages 479–490. 688

Cammert, M., Krämer, J., Seeger, B., and S.Vaupel (2006). An approach to adaptive memory management in data stream systems. In *Proc. 22nd Int. Conf. on Data Engineering*, page 137. 735, 740

Canaday, R. H., Harrisson, R. D., Ivie, E. L., Rydery, J. L., and Wehr, L. A. (1974). A back-end computer for data base management. *Commun. ACM*, 17(10):575–582. 30, 547

Cao, P. and Wang, Z. (2004). Query processing issues in image (multimedia) databases. In *ACM Symp. on Principles of Distributed Computing (PODC)*, pages 206–215. 631, 633

Carey, M., Franklin, M., and Zaharioudakis, M. (1997). Adaptive, fine-grained sharing in a client-server oodbms: A callback-based approach. *ACM Trans. Database Syst.*, 22(4):570–627. 572

Carey, M. and Lu, H. (1986). Load balancing in a locally distributed database system. In *Proc. ACM SIGMOD Int. Conf. on Management of Data*, pages 108–119. 287, 288, 293

Carey, M. and Stonebraker, M. (1984). The performance of concurrency control algorithms for database management systems. In *Proc. 10th Int. Conf. on Very Large Data Bases*, pages 107–118. 401

Carey, M. J., DeWitt, D. J., Franklin, M. J., Hall, N. E., McAuliffe, M. L., Naughton, J. F., Schuh, D. T., Solomon, M. H., Tan, C. K., Tsatalos, O. G., White, S. J., and Zwilling, M. J. (1994). Shoring up persistent applications. In *Proc. ACM SIGMOD Int. Conf. on Management of Data*, pages 383–394. 571

Carey, M. J., Franklin, M., Livny, M., and Shekita, E. (1991). Data caching trade-offs in client-server dbms architectures. In *Proc. ACM SIGMOD Int. Conf. on Management of Data*, pages 357–366. 573

Carey, M. J. and Livny, M. (1988). Distributed concurrency control performance: A study of algorithms, distribution and replication. In *Proc. 14th Int. Conf. on Very Large Data Bases*, pages 13–25. 400, 401

Carey, M. J. and Livny, M. (1991). Conflict detection tradeoffs for replicated data. *ACM Trans. Database Syst.*, 16(4):703–746. 401

Carney, D., Cetintemel, U., Rasin, A., Zdonik, S., Cherniack, M., and Stonebraker, M. (2003). Operator scheduling in a data stream manager. In *Proc. 29th Int. Conf. on Very Large Data Bases*, pages 838–849. 735

Cart, M. and Ferrie, J. (1990). Integrating concurrency control into an object-oriented database system. In *Advances in Database Technology, Proc. 2nd Int. Conf. on Extending Database Technology*, pages 363–377. Springer. 597

Casey, R. G. (1972). Allocation of copies of a file in an information network. In *Proc. Spring Joint Computer Conf*, pages 617–625. 115

Castano, S. and Antonellis, V. D. (1999). A schema analysis and reconciliation tool environment for heterogeneous databases. In *Proc. Int. Conf. on Database Eng. and Applications*, pages 53–62. 134

Castano, S., Fugini, M. G., Martella, G., and Samarati, P. (1995). *Database Security*. Addison Wesley. 180, 201

Castro, M., Adya, A., Liskov, B., and Myers, A. (1997). Hac: Hybrid adaptive caching for distributed storage systems. In *Proc. ACM Symp. on Operating System Principles*, pages 102–115. 570

Cattell, R. G., Barry, D. K., Berler, M., Eastman, J., Jordan, D., Russell, C., Schadow, O., Stanienda, T., and Velez, F. (2000). *The Object Database Standard: ODMG-3.0*. Morgan Kaufmann. 553, 582

Cattell, R. G. G. (1994). *Object Data Management*. Addison Wesley, 2 edition. 607

Cellary, W., Gelenbe, E., and Morzy, T. (1988). *Concurrency Control in Distributed Database Systems*. North-Holland. 358, 401

Ceri, S., Gottlob, G., and Pelagatti, G. (1986). Taxonomy and formal properties of distributed joins. *Inf. Syst.*, 11(1):25–40. 232, 234, 242

Ceri, S., Martella, G., and Pelagatti, G. (1982a). Optimal file allocation in a computer network: A solution method based on the knapsack problem. *Comp. Netw.*, 6:345–357. 121

Ceri, S. and Navathe, S. B. (1983). A methodology for the distribution design of databases. *Digest of Papers - COMPCON*, pages 426–431. 125

Ceri, S., Navathe, S. B., and Wiederhold, G. (1983). Distribution design of logical database schemes. *IEEE Trans. Softw. Eng.*, SE-9(4):487–503. 81, 82, 121

Ceri, S., Negri, M., and Pelagatti, G. (1982b). Horizontal data partitioning in database design. In *Proc. ACM SIGMOD Int. Conf. on Management of Data*, pages 128–136. 84, 87

Ceri, S. and Owicki, S. (1982). On the use of optimistic methods for concurrency control in distributed databases. In *Proc. 6th Berkeley Workshop on Distributed Data Management and Computer Networks*, pages 117–130. 385

Ceri, S. and Pelagatti, G. (1982). A solution method for the non-additive resource allocation problem in distributed system design. *Inf. Proc. Letters*, 15(4):174–178. 125

Ceri, S. and Pelagatti, G. (1983). Correctness of query execution strategies in distributed databases. *ACM Trans. Database Syst.*, 8(4):577–607. 38, 232, 242, 292

Ceri, S. and Pelagatti, G. (1984). *Distributed Databases: Principles and Systems*. McGraw-Hill. 84, 220

Ceri, S. and Pernici, B. (1985). Dataid–d: Methodology for distributed database design. In Albano, V. d. A. and di Leva, A., editors, *Computer-Aided Database Design*, pages 157–183. North-Holland. 121

Ceri, S., Pernici, B., and Wiederhold, G. (1987). Distributed database design methodologies. *Proc. IEEE*, 75(5):533–546. 38, 73, 125

Ceri, S. and Widom, J. (1993). Managing semantic heterogeneity with production rules and persistent queues. In *Proc. 19th Int. Conf. on Very Large Data Bases*, pages 108–119. 160

Chakrabarti, K., Keogh, E., Mehrotra, S., and Pazzani, M. (2002). Locally adaptive dimensionality reduction for indexing large time series databases. *ACM Trans. Database Syst.*, 27. 666, 743

Chakrabarti, S., Dom, B., and Indyk, P. (1998). Enhanced hypertext classification using hyperlinks. In *Proc. ACM SIGMOD Int. Conf. on Management of Data*, pages 307 – 318. 658

Chamberlin, D., Gray, J., and Traiger, I. (1975). Views, authorization and locking in a relational database system. In *Proc. National Computer Conf*, pages 425–430. 172, 201

Chamberlin, D. D., Astrahan, M. M., King, W. F., Lorie, R. A., Mehl, J. W., Price, T. G., Schkolnick, M., Selinger, P. G., Slutz, D. R., Wade, B. W., and Yost, R. A. (1981). Support for repetitive transactions and ad hoc queries in System R. *ACM Trans. Database Syst.*, 6(1):70–94. 265

Chandrasekaran, S., Cooper, O., Deshpande, A., Franklin, M. J., Hellerstein, J. M., Hong, W., Krishnamurthy, S., Madden, S., Raman, V., Reiss, F., and Shah, M. (2003). TelegraphCQ: Continuous dataflow processing for an uncertain world. In *Proc. 1st Biennial Conf. on Innovative Data Systems Research*, pages 269–280. 728, 736

Chandrasekaran, S. and Franklin, M. J. (2003). PSoup: a system for streaming queries over streaming data. *VLDB J.*, 12(2):140–156. 736, 741

Chandrasekaran, S. and Franklin, M. J. (2004). Remembrance of streams past: overload-sensitive management of archived streams. In *Proc. 30th Int. Conf. on Very Large Data Bases*, pages 348–359. 738

Chang, F., Dean, J., Ghemawat, S., Hsieh, W. C., Wallach, D. A., Burrows, M., Chandra, T., Fikes, A., and Gruber, R. E. (2008). Bigtable: A distributed storage system for structured data. *ACM Trans. Comp. Syst.*, 26(2). 755, 756, 763

Chang, S. K. and Cheng, W. H. (1980). A methodology for structured database decomposition. *IEEE Trans. Softw. Eng.*, SE-6(2):205–218. 123

Chang, S. K. and Liu, A. C. (1982). File allocation in a distributed database. *Int. J. Comput. Inf. Sci*, 11(5):325–340. 121, 123

Charikar, M., Chen, K., and Motwani, R. (1997). Incremental clustering and dynamic information retrieval. In *Proc. 29th Annual ACM Symp. on Theory of Computing*. 743

Charikar, M., O'Callaghan, L., and Panigrahy, R. (2003). Better streaming algorithms for clustering problems. In *Proc. 35th Annual ACM Symp. on Theory of Computing*. 743

Chaudhuri, S. (1998). An overview of query optimization in relational systems. In *Proc. ACM SIGACT-SIGMOD Symp. on Principles of Database Systems*, pages 34–43. 292

Chaudhuri, S., Ganjam, K., Ganti, V., and Motwani, R. (2003). Robust and efficient fuzzy match for online data cleaning. In *Proc. ACM SIGMOD Int. Conf. on Management of Data*, pages 313–324. 158

Chen, J., DeWitt, D., and Naughton, J. (2002). Design and evaluation of alternative selection placement strategies in optimizing continuous queries. In *Proc. 18th Int. Conf. on Data Engineering*, pages 345–357. 740

Chen, J., DeWitt, D. J., Tian, F., and Wang, Y. (2000). NiagaraCQ: A scalable continuous query system for internet databases. In *Proc. ACM SIGMOD Int. Conf. on Management of Data*, pages 379–390. 6, 740

Chen, P. P. S. (1976). The entity-relationship model: Towards a unified view of data. *ACM Trans. Database Syst.*, 1(1):9–36. 81, 136

Chen, S., Deng, Y., Attie, P., and Sun, W. (1996). Optimal deadlock detection in distributed systems based on locally constructed wait-for graphs. In *Proc. IEEE Int. Conf. Dist. Comp. Sys*, pages 613–619. 401

Chen, W. and Warren, D. S. (1989). C-logic of complex objects. In *Proc. 8th ACM SIGACT-SIGMOD-SIGART Symp. on Principles of Database Systems*, pages 369–378. 607

Cheng, J. M. et al. (1984). Ibm database 2 performance : Design, implementation and tuning. *IBM Systems J.*, 23(2):189–210. 503

Chiu, D. M. and Ho, Y. C. (1980). A methodology for interpreting tree queries into optimal semi-join expressions. In *Proc. ACM SIGMOD Int. Conf. on Management of Data*, pages 169–178. 271, 272, 292

Cho, J. and Garcia-Molina, H. (2000). The evolution of the web and implications for an incremental crawler. In *Proc. 26th Int. Conf. on Very Large Data Bases*. 666

Cho, J. and Garcia-Molina, H. (2002). Parallel crawlers. In *Proc. 11th Int. World Wide Web Conf.* 666

Cho, J., Garcia-Molina, H., and Page, L. (1998). Efficient crawling through URL ordering. *Comp. Netw.*, 30(161–172). Proceedings of WWW Conference. 664, 665

Cho, J. and Ntoulas, A. (2002). Effective change detection using sampling. In *Proc. 28th Int. Conf. on Very Large Data Bases*. 666

Chockler, G., Keidar, I., and Vitenberg, R. (2001). Group communication specifications: a comprehensive study. *ACM Comput. Surv.*, 33(4):427–469. 482, 537

Christensen, E., Curbera, F., Meredith, G., and Weerawarana, S., editors. Web services description language (WSDL) 1.1 (2001). Available from: http://www.w3.org/TR/wsdl [Last retrieved: December 2009]. 690

Chu, W. W. (1969). Optimal file allocation in a multiple computer system. *IEEE Trans. Comput.*, C-18(10):885–889. 125

Chu, W. W. (1973). Optimal file allocation in a computer network. In Abramson, N. and Kuo, F. F., editors, *Computer Communication Networks*, pages 82–94. Prentice-Hall. 125

Chu, W. W. (1976). Performance of file directory systems for data bases in star and distributed networks. In *Proc. National Computer Conf*, pages 577–587. 38

Chu, W. W. and Nahouraii, E. E. (1975). File directory design considerations for distributed databases. In *Proc. 1st Int. Conf. on Very Data Bases*, pages 543–545. 38

Chundi, P., Rosenkrantz, D. J., and Ravi, S. S. (1996). Deferred updates and data placement in distributed databases. In *Proc. ACM SIGACT-SIGMOD Symp. on Principles of Database Systems*, pages 469–476. 477

Civelek, F. N., Dogac, A., and Spaccapietra, S. (1988). An expert system approach to view definition and integration. In *Proc. 7th Int'l. Conf. on Entity-Relationship Approach*, pages 229–249. 202

Clarke, I., Miller, S. G., Hong, T. W., Sandberg, O., and Wiley, B. (2002). Protecting free expression online with Freenet. *IEEE Internet Comput.*, 6(1):40–49. 615

Clarke, I., Sandberg, O., Wiley, B., and Hong, T. W. (2000). Freenet: A distributed anonymous information storage and retrieval system. In *Proc. Workshop on Design Issues in Anonymity and Unobservability*, pages 46–66. 615

Cluet, S. and Delobel, C. (1992). A general framework for the optimization of object-oriented queries. In *Proc. ACM SIGMOD Int. Conf. on Management of Data*, pages 383–392. 583, 586, 587, 588

Codd, E. (1995). Twelve rules for on-line analytical processing. *Computerworld*. 132

Codd, E. F. (1970). A relational model for large shared data banks. *Commun. ACM*, 13(6):377–387. 45, 56

Codd, E. F. (1972). Relational completeness of data base sublanguages. In Rustin, R., editor, *Relational Databases*, pages 65–98. Prentice-Hall, Englewood Cliffs, N.J. 45

Codd, E. F. (1974). Recent investigations in relational data base systems. *Proceedings of IFIP Congress, Information Processing 74*, pages 1017–1021. 44

Codd, E. F. (1979). Extending the database relational model to capture more meaning. *ACM Trans. Database Syst.*, 4(4):397–434. 43

Cohen, E. and Kaplan, H. (2004). Spatially-decaying aggregation over a network: Model and algorithms. In *Proc. ACM SIGMOD Int. Conf. on Management of Data*, pages 707–718. 726

Cohen, E. and Strauss, M. (2003). Maintaining time-decaying stream aggregates. In *Proc. ACM SIGACT-SIGMOD Symp. on Principles of Database Systems*, pages 223–233. 726, 737

Cohen, S. (2006). User-defined aggregate functions: bridging theory and practice. In *Proc. ACM SIGMOD Int. Conf. on Management of Data*, pages 49–60. 737

Cole, R. L. and Graefe, G. (1994). Optimization of dynamic query evaluation plans. In *Proc. ACM SIGMOD Int. Conf. on Management of Data*, pages 150–160. 265, 266, 292

Colouris, G., Dollimore, J., and Kindberg, T. (2001). *Distributed Systems: Concepts and Design*. Addison Wesley, 3 edition. 2

Comer, D. E. (2009). *Computer Networks and Internets*. Prentice-Hall, 5 edition. 70

Computers, S. (1982). *Stratus/32 System Overview*. Stratus, Natick, Mass. 456

Cong, G., Fan, W., and Kementsietsidis, A. (2007). Distributed query evaluation with performance guarantees. In *Proc. ACM SIGMOD Int. Conf. on Management of Data*, pages 509–520. 711

Cooper, B. F., Ramakrishnan, R., Srivastava, U., Silberstein, A., Bohannon, P., Jacobsen, H.-A., Puz, N., Weaver, D., and Yerneni, R. (2008). PNUTS: Yahoo!'s hosted data serving platform. *Proc. VLDB*, 1(2):1277–1288. 757, 763

Copeland, G., Alexander, W., Boughter, E., and Keller, T. (1988). Data placement in bubba. In *Proc. ACM SIGMOD Int. Conf. on Management of Data*, pages 99–108. 510, 511

Copeland, G. and Maier, D. (1984). Making smalltalk a database system. In *Proc. ACM SIGMOD Int. Conf. on Management of Data*, pages 316–325. 552

Cormode, G. and Muthukrishnan, S. (2003). What's hot and what's not: Tracking most frequent items dynamically. In *Proc. ACM SIGACT-SIGMOD Symp. on Principles of Database Systems*, pages 296–306. 743

Coulon, C., Pacitti, E., and Valduriez, P. (2005). Consistency management for partial replication in a high performance database cluster. In *Proc. IEEE Int. Conf. on Parallel and Distributed Systems*, pages 809–815. 537, 539, 548

Crainiceanu, A., Linga, P., Gehrke, J., and Shanmugasundaram, J. (2004). Querying peer-to-peer networks using p-trees. In *Proc. 7th Int. Workshop on the World Wide Web and Databases*, pages 25–30. 622

Cranor, C., Johnson, T., Spatscheck, O., and Shkapenyuk, V. (2003). Gigascope: High performance network monitoring with an SQL interface. In *Proc. ACM SIGMOD Int. Conf. on Management of Data*, pages 647–651. 728, 731

Crespo, A. and Garcia-Molina, H. (2002). Routing indices for peer-to-peer systems. In *Proc. 22nd Int. Conf. on Distributed Computing Systems*, pages 23–33. 617

Cristian, F. (1982). Exception handling and software fault tolerance. *IEEE Trans. Comput.*, C-31(6):531–540. 455

Cristian, F. (1985). A rigorous approach to fault–tolerant programming. *IEEE Trans. Softw. Eng.*, SE-11(1):23–31. 455

Cristian, F. (1987). Exception handling. Technical Report RJ 5724, IBM Almaden Research Laboratory, San Jose, Calif. 455

Cuenca-Acuna, F., Peery, C., Martin, R., and Nguyen, T. (2003). Planetp: using gossiping to build content addressable peer-to-peer information sharing communities. In *IEEE Int. Symp. on High Performance Distributed Computing*, pages 236–249. 636

Cusumano, M. A. (2010). Cloud computing and SaaS as new computing platforms. *Commun. ACM*, 53(4):27–29. 744, 763

Dadam, P. and Schlageter, G. (1980). Recovery in distributed databases based on non-synchronized local checkpoints. In *Information Processing '80*, pages 457–462. 456

Dageville, B., Casadessus, P., and Borla-Salamet, P. (1994). The impact of the ksr1 allcache architecture on the behavior of the dbs3 parallel dbms. In *Proc. International Conf. on Parallel Architectures and Language*. 528, 548

Dahlin, M., Wang, R., Anderson, T., and Patterson, D. (1994). Cooperative caching: Using remote client memory to improve file system performance. In *Proc. 1st USENIX Symp. on Operating System Design and Implementation*, pages 267–280. 210

Das, A., Gehrke, J., and Riedewald, M. (2005). Semantic approximation of data stream joins. *IEEE Trans. Knowl. and Data Eng.*, 17(1):44–59. 740

Dasu, T., Krishnan, S., Venkatasubramanian, S., and Yi, K. (2006). An information-theoretic approach to detecting changes in multi-dimensional data streams. In *Proc. 38th Symp. on the Interface of Stats, Comp. Sci., and Applications*. 727

Daswani, N., Garcia-Molina, H., and Yang, B. (2003). Open problems in data-sharing peer-to-peer systems. In *Proc. 9th Int. Conf. on Database Theory*, pages 1–15. 611, 653

Datar, M., Gionis, A., Indyk, P., and Motwani, R. (2002). Maintaining stream statistics over sliding windows. In *Proc. 13th Annual ACM-SIAM Symp. on Discrete Algorithms*, pages 635–644. 737

Date, C. and Darwen, H. (1998). *Foundation for Object/Relational Databases – The Third Manifesto*. Addison Wesley. 552, 607

Date, C. J. (1987). *A Guide to the SQL Standard*. Addison Wesley. 56

Date, C. J. (2004). *An Introduction to Database Systems*. Pearson, 8th edition. 70

Daudjee, K. and Salem, K. (2004). Lazy database replication with ordering guarantees. In *Proc. 20th Int. Conf. on Data Engineering*, pages 424–435. 466

Daudjee, K. and Salem, K. (2006). Lazy database replication with snapshot isolation. In *Proc. 32nd Int. Conf. on Very Large Data Bases*, pages 715–726. 464, 466

Davenport, R. A. (1981). Design of distributed data base systems. *Comp. J.*, 24(1):31–41. 73

Davidson, S. B. (1984). Optimism and consistency in partitioned distributed database systems. *ACM Trans. Database Syst.*, 9(3):456–481. 456, 487, 493

Davidson, S. B., Garcia-Molina, H., and Skeen, D. (1985). Consistency in partitioned networks. *ACM Comput. Surv.*, 17(3):341–370. 449, 456, 493

Dawson, J. L. (1980). A user demand model for distributed database design. In *Digest of Papers – COMPCON*, pages 211–216. 125

Dayal, U. (1989). Queries and views in an object-oriented data model. In *Proc. 2nd Int. Workshop on Database Programming Languages*, pages 80–102. 555, 606

Dayal, U. and Bernstein, P. (1978). On the updatability of relational views. In *Proc. 4th Int. Conf. on Very Data Bases*, pages 368–377. 175, 201

Dayal, U., Buchmann, A., and McCarthy, D. (1988). Rules are objects too: A knowledge model for an active object-oriented database system. In *Advances in Object-Oriented Database Systems. Proc. of the 2nd Int. Workshop on Object-Oriented Database Systems*, pages 129–143. 606

Dayal, U. and Hwang, H. (1984). View definition and generalization for database integration in multibase: A system for heterogeneous distributed database. *IEEE Trans. Softw. Eng.*, SE-10(6):628–644. 147, 160, 331

Dayal, U., M.Hsu, and Ladin, R. (1991). A transactional model for long-running activities. In *Proc. 17th Int. Conf. on Very Large Data Bases*, pages 113–122. 354, 355

Dean, J. and Ghemawat, S. (2004). MapReduce: Simplified data processing on large clusters. In *Proc. 6th USENIX Symp. on Operating System Design and Implementation*, pages 137–150. 758, 763

Dean, J. and Ghemawat, S. (2010). MapReduce: a flexible data processing tool. *Commun. ACM*, 53(1):72–77. 760, 763

Demaine, E., Lopez-Ortiz, A., and Munro, J. I. (2002). Frequency estimation of internet packet streams with limited space. In *Proc. 10th Annual European Symp. on Algorithms*, pages 348–360. 743

Demers, A., Gehrke, J., Hong, M., Riedewald, M., and White, W. (2006). Towards expressive publish/subscribe systems. In *Advances in Database Technology, Proc. 10th Int. Conf. on Extending Database Technology*, pages 627–644. 741

Demers, A. J., Greene, D. H., Hauser, C., Irish, W., Larson, J., Shenker, S., Sturgis, H. E., Swinehart, D. C., and Terry, D. B. (1987). Epidemic algorithms for replicated database maintenance. In *Proc. ACM SIGACT-SIGOPS 6th Symp. on the Principles of Distributed Computing*, pages 1–12. 617

Denning, P. J. (1968). he working set model for program behavior. *Commun. ACM*, 11(5):323–333. 415

Denning, P. J. (1980). Working sets: Past and present. *IEEE Trans. Softw. Eng.*, SE-6(1):64–84. 415

Denny, M. and Franklin, M. (2005). Predicate result range caching for continuous queries. In *Proc. ACM SIGMOD Int. Conf. on Management of Data*, pages 646–657. 740

Deshpande, A. and Hellerstein, J. (2004). Lifting the burden of history from adaptive query processing. In *Proc. 30th Int. Conf. on Very Large Data Bases*, pages 948–959. 739

Devine, R. (1993). Design and implementation of DDH: A distributed dynamic hashing algorithm. In *Proc. 4th Int. Conf. on Foundations of Data Organization and Algorithms*, pages 101–114. 618

DeWitt, D., Naughton, J., Schneider, D., and Seshadri, S. (1992). Practical skew handling in parallel joins. In *Proc. 22th Int. Conf. on Very Large Data Bases*, pages 27–40. 529, 548

DeWitt, D. J., Futtersack, P., Maier, D., and Velez, F. (1990). A study of three alternative workstation-server architectures for object-oriented database systems. In *Proc. 16th Int. Conf. on Very Large Data Bases*, pages 107–12. 568

DeWitt, D. J. and Gerber, R. (1985). Multi processor hash-based join algorithms. In *Proc. 11th Int. Conf. on Very Large Data Bases*, pages 151–164. 518

DeWitt, D. J., Gerber, R. H., Graek, G., Heytens, M. L., Kumar, K. B., and Muralikrishna, M. (1986). Gamma: A high performance dataflow database machine. In *Proc. 12th Int. Conf. on Very Large Data Bases*, pages 228–237. 505, 548

DeWitt, D. J. and Gray, J. (1992). Parallel database systems: The future of high performance database systems. *Commun. ACM*, 35(6):85–98. 497, 500

Dhamankar, R., Lee, Y., Doan, A., Halevy, A. Y., and Domingos, P. (2004). iMAP: Discovering complex mappings between database schemas. In *Proc. ACM SIGMOD Int. Conf. on Management of Data*, pages 383–394. 147

Dickman, P. (1991). *Distributed Object Management in a Non-Small Graph of Autonomous Networks With Few Failures*. Ph.D. thesis, University of Cambridge, England. 581

Dickman, P. (1994). The bellerophon project: A scalable object-support architecture suitable for a large oodbms? In Özsu et al. [1994a], pages 287–299. 577

Diffie, W. and Hellman, M. E. (1976). New directions in cryptography. *IEEE Trans. Information Theory*, IT–22(6):644–654. 180

Ding, Q., Ding, Q., and Perrizo, W. (2002). Decision tree classification of spatial data streams using peano count trees. In *Proc. 2002 ACM Symp. on Applied Computing*, pages 413–417. 743

Do, H. H. and Rahm, E. (2002). COMA - A system for flexible combination of schema matching approaches. In *Proc. 28th Int. Conf. on Very Large Data Bases*, pages 610–621. 134, 142, 144, 160

Doan, A., Domingos, P., and Halevy, A. Y. (2001). Reconciling schemas of disparate data sources: A machine-learning approach. In *Proc. ACM SIGMOD Int. Conf. on Management of Data*, pages 509–520. 145, 147

Doan, A., Domingos, P., and Halevy, A. Y. (2003a). Learning to match the schemas of data sources: A multistrategy approach. *Machine Learning*, 50(3):279–301. 145, 146, 147

Doan, A., Halevy, A., and Ives, Z. (2010). *Principles of Data Integration*. (in preparation). 159, 160

Doan, A. and Halevy, A. Y. (2005). Semantic integration research in the database community: A brief survey. *AI Magazine*, 26(1):83–94. 160

Doan, A., Madhavan, J., Dhamankar, R., Domingos, P., and Halevy, A. Y. (2003b). Learning to match ontologies on the semantic web. *VLDB J.*, 12(4):303–319. 626

Dobra, A., Garofalakis, M., Gehrke, J., and Rastogi, R. (2004). Sketch-based multi-query processing over data streams. In *Advances in Database Technology, Proc. 9th Int. Conf. on Extending Database Technology*, pages 551–568. 740

Dogac, A., Dengi, C., and Özsu, M. T. (1998a). Distributed object computing platforms. *Commun. ACM*, 41(9):95–103. 607

Dogac, A., Kalinichenko, L., Özsu, M. T., and Sheth, A., editors (1998b). *Advances in Workflow Systems and Interoperability*. Springer. 354, 359

Dogac, A., Özsu, M., Biliris, A., and Sellis, T., editors (1994). *Advances in Object-Oriented Database Systems*. Springer. 586, 607, 814

Doherty, C. and Hurley, N. (2007). Autonomic distributed data management with update accesses. In *Proc. 1st Int. Conf. on Autonomic computing and communication systems*, pages 1–8. 762

D'Oliviera, C. R. (1977). An analysis of computer decentralization. Technical Memo TM-90, Laboratory for Computer Science, Massachusetts Institute of Technology, Cambridge, Mass. 7

Dollimore, J., Nascimento, C., and Xu, W. (1994). Fine-grained object migration. In Özsu et al. [1994a], pages 182–186. 577

Domingos, P. and Hulten, G. (2000). Mining high-speed data streams. In *Proc. 6th ACM SIGKDD Int. Conf. on Knowledge Discovery and Data Mining*, pages 71–80. 743

Douglis, F., Palmer, J., Richards, E., Tao, D., Hetzlaff, W., Tracey, J., and Lin, J. (2004). Position: short object lifetimes require a delete-optimized storage system. In *Proc. 11th ACM SIGOPS European Workshop*. 726

Dowdy, L. W. and Foster, D. V. (1982). Comparative models of the file assignment problem. *ACM Comput. Surv.*, 14(2):287–313. 38, 114, 125

Draper, D., Fankhauser, P., Fernández, M., Malhotra, A., Rose, K., Rys, M., Siméon, J., and Wadler, P., editors. Xquery 1.0 and XPath 2.0 formal semantics (2007). Available from: http://www.w3.org/TR/xquery-semantics/ [Last retrieved: January 2010]. 702

Du, W. and Elmagarmid, A. (1989). Quasi-serializability: A correctness criterion for global concurrency control in interbase. In *Proc. 15th Int. Conf. on Very Large Data Bases*, pages 347–355. 26

Du, W., Krishnamurthy, R., and Shan, M. (1992). Query optimization in a heterogeneous dbms. In *Proc. 18th Int. Conf. on Very Large Data Bases*, pages 277–291. 307, 308, 331

Du, W., Shan, M., and Dayal, U. (1995). Reducing multidatabase query response time by tree balancing. In *Proc. ACM SIGMOD Int. Conf. on Management of Data*, pages 293–303. 287, 290, 293, 315, 331

Duschka, O. M. and Genesereth, M. R. (1997). Answering recursive queries using views. In *Proc. ACM SIGACT-SIGMOD Symp. on Principles of Database Systems*, pages 109–116. 160, 305, 331

Dwork, C. and Skeen, D. (1983). The inherent cost of nonblocking commitment. In *Proc. ACM SIGACT-SIGOPS 2nd Symp. on the Principles of Distributed Computing*, pages 1–11. 455

Eager, D. L. and Sevcik, K. C. (1983). Achieving robustness in distributed database systems. *ACM Trans. Database Syst.*, 8(3):354–381. 456, 493

Edwards, J., McCurley, K., and Tomlin, J. (2001). An adaptive model for optimizing performance of an incremental web crawler. In *Proc. 10th Int. World Wide Web Conf.* 666

Effelsberg, W. and Härder, T. (1984). Principles of database buffer management. *ACM Trans. Database Syst.*, 9(4):560–595. 415

Eich, M. H. (1989). Main memory database research directions. In *Int. Workshop on Database Machines*, pages 251–268. 499

Eickler, A., Gerlhof, C., and Kossmann, D. (1995). A performance evaluation of oid mapping techniques. In *Proc. 21th Int. Conf. on Very Large Data Bases*, pages 18–29. 575

Eisenberg et al., 2008 (2008). Information technology – database languages – SQL – Part 14: XML-related specifications (SQL/XML). 702

Eisner, M. J. and Severance, D. G. (1976). Mathematical techniques for efficient record segmentation in large shared databases. *J. ACM*, 23(4):619–635. 98

Elmagarmid, A., Leu, Y., Litwin, W., and Rusinkiewicz, M. (1990). A multidatabase transaction model for interbase. In *Proc. 16th Int. Conf. on Very Large Data Bases*, pages 507–518. 354

Elmagarmid, A., Rusinkiewicz, M., and Sheth, A., editors (1999). *Management of Heterogeneous and Autonomous Database Systems*. Morgan Kaufmann. 160

Elmagarmid, A. K. (1986). A survey of distributed deadlock detection algorithms. *ACM SIGMOD Rec.*, 15(3):37–45. 39, 401

Elmagarmid, A. K., editor (1992). *Transaction Models for Advanced Database Applications*. Morgan Kaufmann. 359

Elmagarmid, A. K., Soundararajan, N., and Liu, M. T. (1988). A distributed deadlock detection and resolution algorithm and its correctness proof. *IEEE Trans. Softw. Eng.*, 14(10):1443–1452. 401

Elmasri, R., Larson, J., and Navathe, S. B. (1987). Integration algorithms for database and logical database design. Technical report, Honeywell Corporate Research Center, Golden Valley, Minn. 149

Elmasri, R. and Navathe, S. B. (2011). *Fundamentals of Database Systems*. Pearson, 6 edition. 70

Embley, D. W., Jackman, D., and Xu, L. (2001). Multifaceted exploitation of metadata for attribute match discovery in information integration. In *Proc. Workshop on Information Integration on the Web*, pages 110–117. 146

Embley, D. W., Jackman, D., and Xu, L. (2002). Attribute match discovery in information integration: exploiting multiple facets of metadata. *Journal of the Brazilian Computing Society*, 8(2):32–43. 146

Epstein, R. and Stonebraker, M. (1980). Analysis of distributed data base processing strategies. In *Proc. 5th Int. Conf. on Very Data Bases*, pages 92–101. 293

Epstein, R., Stonebraker, M., and Wong, E. (1978). Query processing in a distributed relational database system. In *Proc. ACM SIGMOD Int. Conf. on Management of Data*, pages 169–180. 209, 254, 274, 276, 292

Eswaran, K. P. (1974). Placement of records in a file and file allocation in a computer network. In *Information Processing '74*, pages 304–307. 115, 125

Eswaran, K. P., Gray, J. N., Lorie, R. A., and Traiger, I. L. (1976). The notions of consistency and predicate locks in a database system. *Commun. ACM*, 19(11):624–633. 341, 370

Evrendilek, C., Dogac, A., Nural, S., and Ozcan, F. (1997). Multidatabase query optimization. *Distrib. Parall. Databases*, 5(1):77–114. 287, 293, 316

Ezeife, C. I. and Barker, K. (1995). A comprehensive approach to horizontal class fragmentation in a distributed object based system. *Distrib. Parall. Databases*, 3(3):247–272. 563, 564, 607

Ezeife, C. I. and Barker, K. (1998). Distributed object based design: Vertical fragmentation of classes. *Distrib. Parall. Databases*, 6(4):327–360. 563

Fagin, R. (1977). Multivalued dependencies and a new normal form for relational databases. *ACM Trans. Database Syst.*, 2(3):262–278. 44

Fagin, R. (1979). Normal forms and relational database operators. In *Proc. ACM SIGMOD Int. Conf. on Management of Data*, pages 153–160. 44

Fagin, R. (1999). Combining fuzzy information from multiple systems. *Journal of Computer and System Sciences*, 58(1):83–99. 629

Fagin, R. (2002). Combining fuzzy information: an overview. *ACM SIGMOD Rec.*, 31(2):109–118. 147

Fagin, R., Kolaitis, P. G., Miller, R. J., and Popa, L. (2005). Data exchange: semantics and query answering. *TCS*, 336(1):89–124. 159

Fagin, R., Lotem, J., and Naor, M. (2003). Optimal aggregation algorithms for middleware. *Journal of Computer and System Sciences*, 66(4):614–656. 629, 654

Fagin, R. and Vardi, M. Y. (1984). The theory of data dependencies: A survey. Research Report RJ 4321 (47149), IBM Research Laboratory, San Jose, Calif. 189

Faloutsos, C. and Christodoulakis, S. (1984). Signature files: an access method for documents and its analytical performance evaluation. *ACM Trans. Information Syst.*, 2(4):267–288. 667

Fan, W. (2004). Systematic data selection to mine concept-drifting data streams. In *Proc. 10th ACM SIGKDD Int. Conf. on Knowledge Discovery and Data Mining*, pages 128–137. 743

Fang, D., Hammer, J., and McLeod, D. (1994). An approach to behavior sharing in federated database systems. In Özsu et al. [1994a], pages 334–346. 565

Farrag, A. (1986). *Concurrency and Consistency in Database Systems*. Ph.D. thesis, Department of Computing Science, University of Alberta, Edmonton, Canada. 359

Farrag, A. A. and Özsu, M. T. (1985). A general concurrency control for database systems. In *Proc. National Computer Conf*, pages 567–573. 400

Farrag, A. A. and Özsu, M. T. (1987). Towards a general concurrency control algorithm for database systems. *IEEE Trans. Softw. Eng.*, 13(10):1073–1079. 400

Farrag, A. A. and Özsu, M. T. (1989). Using semantic knowledge of transactions to increase concurrency. *ACM Trans. Database Syst.*, 14(4):503–525. 395, 401

Fekete, A., Lynch, N., Merritt, M., and Weihl, W. (1987a). Nested transactions and read/write locking. Technical Memo MIT/LCS/TM–324, Massachusetts Institute of Technology, Cambridge, Mass. 401

Fekete, A., Lynch, N., Merritt, M., and Weihl, W. (1987b). Nested transactions, conflict-based locking, and dynamic atomicity. Technical Memo MIT/LCS/TM–340, Massachusetts Institute of Technology, Cambridge, Mass. 401

Fekete, A., Lynch, N., Merritt, M., and Weihl, W. (1989). Commutativity-based locking for nested transactions. Technical Memo MIT/LCS/TM-370b, Massachusetts Institute of Technology, Cambridge, Mass. 401, 594

Fernandez, E. B., Summers, R. C., and Wood, C. (1981). *Database Security and Integrity*. Addison Wesley. 180

Fernandez, M., Florescu, D., and Levy, A. (1997). A query language for a web-site management system. *ACM SIGMOD Rec.*, 26(3):4–11. 676

Fernández, M. F., Siméon, J., Choi, B., Marian, A., and Sur, G. (2003). Implementing XQuery 1.0: The Galax experience. In *Proc. 29th Int. Conf. on Very Large Data Bases*, pages 1077–1080. 698, 702

Ferreira, P. and Shapiro, M. (1994). Garbage collection and dsm consistency. In *Proc. of the First Symposium on Operating Systems Design and Implementation*, pages 229–241. 581

Fessant, F. L., Piumarta, I., and Shapiro, M. (1998). An implementation of complete, asynchronous, distributed garbage collection. In *Proc. ACM SIGPLAN Conf. on Programming Language Design and Implementation*, pages 152–161. 582

Fiebig, T., Helmer, S., Kanne, C.-C., Moerkotte, G., Neumann, J., Schiele, R., and Westmann, T. (2002). Anatomy of a native XML base management system. *VLDB J.*, 11(4):292–314. 699

Fisher, M. K. and Hochbaum, D. S. (1980). Database location in computer networks. *J. ACM*, 27(4):718–735. 121

Fisher, P. S., Hollist, P., and Slonim, J. (1980). A design methodology for distributed data bases. In *Digest of Papers – COMPCON*, pages 199–202. 125

Florentin, J. J. (1974). Consistency auditing of databases. *Comp. J.*, 17(1):52–58. 188, 202

Florescu, D., Koller, D., and Levy, A. (1997). Using probabilistic information in data integration. In *Proc. 23th Int. Conf. on Very Large Data Bases*, pages 216–225. 564

Florescu, D., Levy, A., and Mendelzon, A. (1998). Database techniques for the World-Wide Web: a survey. *ACM SIGMOD Rec.*, 27(3):59–74. 657, 676

Folkert, N., Gupta, A., Witkowski, A., Subramanian, S., Bellamkonda, S., Shankar, S., Bozkaya, T., and Sheng, L. (2005). Optimizing refresh of a set of materialized views. In *Proc. 31st Int. Conf. on Very Large Data Bases*, pages 1043–1054. 738

Foster, D. V. and Browne, J. C. (1976). File assignment in memory hierarchies. In Gelenbe, I. E., editor, *Modelling and Performance Evaluation of Computer Systems*, pages 119–127. North-Holland. 125

Franklin, M., Livny, M., and Carey, M. (1997). Transactional client-server cache consistency: Alternatives and performance. *ACM Trans. Database Syst.*, 22(3):315–367. 572

Franklin, M. J., Carey, M., and Livny, M. (1992). Global memory management in client-server dbms architectures. In *Proc. 18th Int. Conf. on Very Large Data Bases*, pages 596–609. 210, 571

Franklin, M. J. and Carey, M. J. (1994). Client-server caching revisited. In Özsu et al. [1994a], pages 57–78. 572, 573

Franklin, M. J., Jonsson, B. T., and Kossmann, D. (1996). Performance tradeoffs for client-server query processing. In *Proc. ACM SIGMOD Int. Conf. on Management of Data*, pages 149–160. 214

Freeley, M., Morgan, W., and Pighin, F. (1995). Implementing global memory management in a workstation cluster. In *Proc. 15th ACM Symp. on Operating Syst. Principles*, pages 201–212. 210

Freytag, J. C. (1987). A rule-based view of query optimization. In *Proc. ACM SIGMOD Int. Conf. on Management of Data*, pages 173–180. 583

Freytag, J. C., Maier, D., and Vossen, G. (1994). *Query Processing for Advanced Database Systems*. Morgan Kaufmann. 220

Friedman, M., Levy, A. Y., and Millstein, T. D. (1999). Navigational plans for data integration. In *Proc. 16th National Conf on Artificial Intelligence and 11th Innovative Applications of Artificial Intelligence Conf.*, pages 67–73. 133

Fung, C. W., Karlaplem, K., and Li, Q. (1996). An analytical approach towards evaluating method induced vertical partitioning algorithms. Technical Report HKUST96-33, Department of Computer Science, Hong Kong University of Science and Technology. 564

Furtado, C., Lima, A., Pacitti, E., Valduriez, P., and Mattoso, M. (2005). Physical and virtual partitioning in olap database clusters. In *Proc. Int. Symp. Computer Architecture and High Performance Computing*, pages 143–150. 544, 548

Furtado, C., Lima, A., Pacitti, E., Valduriez, P., and Mattoso, M. (2006). Adaptive hybrid partitioning for olap query processing in a database cluster. *Int. J. High Perf. Comput. and Networking*. To appear. 544, 548

Fushimi, S., Kitsuregawa, M., and Tanaka, H. (1986). An overview of the system software of a parallel relational database machine grace. In *Proc. 12th Int. Conf. on Very Large Data Bases*, pages 209–219. 505

Gaber, M., Zaslavsky, A., and Krishnaswamy, S. (2005). Mining data streams: A review. *ACM SIGMOD Rec.*, 34(2):18–26. 742, 762

Galhardas, H., Florescu, D., Shasha, D., Simon, E., and Saita, C.-A. (2001). Declarative data cleaning: Language, model, and algorithms. In *Proc. 27th Int. Conf. on Very Large Data Bases*, pages 371–380. 158

Gallaire, H., Minker, J., and Nicolas, J.-M. (1984). Logic and databases: A deductive approach. *ACM Comput. Surv.*, 16(2):153–186. 47

Gama, J., Medas, P., and Rodrigues, P. (2005). Learning decision trees from dynamic data streams. In *Proc. 2005 ACM Symp. on Applied Computing*, pages 573–577. 743

Gançarski, S., Naacke, H., Pacitti, E., and Valduriez, P. (2002). Parallel processing with autonomous databases in a cluster system. In *Proc. Int. Conf. on Cooperative Information Systems*, pages 410–428. 540, 548

Gançarski, S., Naacke, H., Pacitti, E., and Valduriez, P. (2007). The leganet system: Freshness-aware transaction routing in a database cluster. *Inf. Syst.*, 32(7):320–343. 541, 548

Ganesan, P., Yang, B., and Garcia-Molina, H. (2004). One torus to rule them all: Multidimensional queries in p2p systems. In *Proc. 7th Int. Workshop on the World Wide Web and Databases*, pages 19–24. 622

Ganti, Gehrke, and Ramakrishnan (2002). Mining data streams under block evolution. *SIGKDD Explorations*, pages 1–10. 743

Gao, S., Sperberg-McQueen, C. M., and Thompson, H. S., editors. W3C XML schema definition language (XSD) 1.1 part 1: Structures (2009). Available from: http://www.w3.org/TR/xmlschema11-1/ [Last retrieved: January 2010]. 693

Garcia-Molina, H. (1979). *Performance of Update Algorithms for Replicated Data in a Distributed Database*. Ph.D. thesis, Department of Computer Science, Stanford University, Stanford, Calif. 390, 401

Garcia-Molina, H. (1982). Elections in distributed computing systems. *IEEE Trans. Comput.*, C-31(1):48–59. 440

Garcia-Molina, H. (1983). Using semantic knowledge for transaction processing in a distributed database. *ACM Trans. Database Syst.*, 8(2):186–213. 352, 395, 401

Garcia-Molina, H., Gawlick, D., Klein, J., Kleissner, K., and Salem, K. (1990). Coordinating multi-transaction activities. Technical Report CS-TR-247-90, Department of Computer Science, Princeton University. 352, 353, 397

Garcia-Molina, H., Papakonstantinou, Y., Quass, D., Rajaraman, A., Sagiv, Y., Ullman, J. D., Vassalos, V., and Widom, J. (1997). The TSIMMIS approach to mediation: Data models and languages. *J. Intell. Information Syst.*, 8(2):117–132. 160

Garcia-Molina, H. and Salem, K. (1987). Sagas. In *Proc. ACM SIGMOD Int. Conf. on Management of Data*, pages 249–259. 351, 352, 397

Garcia-Molina, H., Ullman, J. D., and Widom, J. (2002). *Database Systems – The Complete Book*. Prentice-Hall. 70

Garcia-Molina, H. and Wiederhold, G. (1982). Read–only transactions in a distributed database. *ACM Trans. Database Syst.*, 7(2):209–234. 401

Garofalakis, M. N. and Ioannidis, Y. E. (1996). Multi-dimensional resource scheduling for parallel queries. In *Proc. ACM SIGMOD Int. Conf. on Management of Data*, pages 365–376. 530, 548

Garza, J. F. and Kim, W. (1988). Transaction management in an object-oriented database system. In *Proc. ACM SIGMOD Int. Conf. on Management of Data*, pages 37–45. 597, 600

Gastonian, R. (1983). The auragen system 4000. *Q. Bull. IEEE TC on Data Eng.*, 6(2). 456

Gavish, B. and Pirkul, H. (1986). Computer and database location in distributed computer systems. *IEEE Trans. Comput.*, C-35(7):583–590. 125

GE (1976). *MADMAN User Manual*. General Electric Company, Schenectady, N.Y. 390

Gedik, B., Wu, K.-L., Yu, P. S., and Liu, L. (2005). Adaptive load shedding for windowed stream joins. In *Proc. 14th ACM Int. Conf. on Information and Knowledge Management*, pages 171–178. 740

Gelenbe, E. and Gardy, D. (1982). The size of projections of relations satisfying a functional dependency. In *Proc. 8th Int. Conf. on Very Data Bases*, pages 325–333. 254

Gelenbe, E. and Sevcik, K. (1978). Analysis of update synchronization for multiple copy databases. In *Proc. 3rd Berkeley Workskop on Distributed Data Management and Computer Networks*, pages 69–88. 401

Georgakopoulos, D., Hornick, M., and Sheth, A. (1995). An overview of work-flow management: From process modeling to workflow automation infrastructure. *Distrib. Parall. Databases*, 3:119–153. 354, 359

Gerlhof, C. and Kemper, A. (1994). A multi-threaded architecture for prefetching in object bases. In Jarke, M., Jr., J. A. B., and Jeffery, K. G., editors, *Advances in Database Technology, Proc. 4th Int. Conf. on Extending Database Technology*, volume 779 of *Lecture Notes in Computer Science*, pages 351–364. Springer. 568

Ghanem, T., Aref, W., and Elmagarmid, A. (2006). Exploiting predicate-window semantics over data streams. *ACM SIGMOD Rec.*, 35(1):3–8. 727

Ghemawat, S. (1995). *The Modified Object Buffer: A Storage Management Technique for Object-Oriented Databases*. Ph.D dissertation, Massachusetts Institute of Technology, Cambridge, Mass. 571

Ghemawat, S., Gobioff, H., and Leung, S.-T. (2003). The Google file system. In *Proc. 19th ACM Symp. on Operating System Principles*, pages 29–43. 753, 763

Gibbons, P. and Tirthapura, S. (2002). Distributed streams algorithms for sliding windows. In *Proc. 14th ACM Symp. on Parallel Algorithms and Architectures*, pages 63–72. 737

Gibbons, T. (1976). *Integrity and Recovery in Computer Systems*. NCC Publications. 455

Gifford, D. K. (1979). Weighted voting for replicated data. In *Proc. 7th ACM Symp. on Operating System Principles*, pages 50–159. 487

Gilbert, A. C., Kotidis, Y., Muthukrishnan, S., and Strauss, M. J. (2001). Surfing wavelets on streams: One-pass summaries for approximate aggregate queries. In *Proc. 27th Int. Conf. on Very Large Data Bases*, pages 79–88. 726

Gligor, V. and Popescu-Zeletin, R. (1986). Transaction management in distributed heterogeneous database management systems. *Inf. Syst.*, 11(4):287–297. 25

Gligor, V. D. and Luckenbaugh, G. L. (1984). Interconnecting heterogeneous database management systems. *Comp.*, 17(1):33–43. 40

Golab, L. (2006). *Sliding Window Query Processing over Data Streams*. PhD thesis, University of Waterloo. 763

Golab, L., Garg, S., and Özsu, M. T. (2004). On indexing sliding windows over on-line data streams. In *Advances in Database Technology, Proc. 9th Int. Conf. on Extending Database Technology*, pages 712–729. 736

Golab, L., Johnson, T., Seidel, J. S., and Shkapenyuk, V. (2009). Stream warehousing with DataDepot. In *Proc. ACM SIGMOD Int. Conf. on Management of Data*, pages 847–854. 761

Golab, L. and Özsu, M. T. (2003a). Issues in data stream management. *ACM SIGMOD Rec.*, 32(2):5–14. 762, 763

Golab, L. and Özsu, M. T. (2003b). Processing sliding window multi-joins in continuous queries over data streams. In *Proc. 29th Int. Conf. on Very Large Data Bases*, pages 500–511. 733

Golab, L. and Özsu, M. T. (2010). *Data Stream Systems*. Morgan & Claypool. 761, 762, 763

Goldberg, A. and Robson, D. (1983). *SmallTalk-80: The Language and Its Implementation*. Addison Wesley. 559

Goldman, K. J. (1987). Data replication in nested transaction systems. Technical Report MIT/LCS/TR-390, Massachusetts Institute of Technology, Cambridge, Mass. 401

Goldman, R. and Widom, J. (1997). Dataguides : Enabling query formulation and optimization in semistructured databases. In *Proc. 23th Int. Conf. on Very Large Data Bases*, pages 436–445. 675, 701

Gonnet, G. H. and Tompa, F. W. (1987). Mind your grammar: A new approach to modelling text. In *Proc. 13th Int. Conf. on Very Large Data Bases*, pages 339–346. 690

Goodman, J. R. and Woest, P. J. (1988). The wisconsin multicube: A new large-scale cache-coherent multiprocessor. Technical Report TR766, University of Wisconsin-Madison. 506, 548

Goodman, N., Suri, R., and Tay, Y. C. (1983). A simple analytic model for performance of exclusive locking in database systems. In *Proc. 2nd ACM SIGACT–SIGMOD Symp. on Principles of Database Systems*, pages 203–215. 401

Gottlob, G., Koch, C., and Pichler, R. (2005). Efficient algorithms for processing XPath queries. *ACM Trans. Database Syst.*, 30(2):444–491. 700

Gounaris, A., Paton, N., Fernandes, A., and Sakellariou, R. (2002a). Adaptive query processing: A survey. In *Proc. British National Conf. on Databases*, pages 11–25. 739

Gounaris, A., Paton, N. W., Fernandes, A. A. A., and Sakellariou, R. (2002b). Adaptive query processing: A survey. In *Proc. British National Conf. on Databases*, pages 11–25. 320, 321, 331

Graefe, G. (1990). Encapsulation of parallelism in the volcano query processing systems. In *Proc. ACM SIGMOD Int. Conf. on Management of Data*, pages 102–111. 503, 548

Graefe, G. (1993). Query evaluation techniques for large databases. *ACM Comput. Surv.*, 25(2):73–170. 220, 292, 547

Graefe, G. (1994). Volcano - an extensible and parallel query evaluation system. *IEEE Trans. Knowl. and Data Eng.*, 6(1):120–135. 267

Graefe, G. and DeWitt, D. (1987). The exodus optimizer generator. In *Proc. ACM SIGMOD Int. Conf. on Management of Data*, pages 160–172. 583

Graefe, G. and Maier, D. (1988). Query optimization in object-oriented database systems: The REVELATION project. Technical Report CS/E 88-025, Oregon Graduate Center. 583, 586

Graefe, G. and McKenna, W. (1993). The volcano optimizer generator. In *Proc. 9th Int. Conf. on Data Engineering*, pages 209–218. 320, 321, 586

Grant, J. (1984). Constraint preserving and lossless database transformations. *Inf. Syst.*, 9(2):139–146. 79

Grapa, E. and Belford, G. G. (1977). Some theorems to aid in solving the file allocation problem. *Commun. ACM*, 20(11):878–882. 125

Gravano, L., Garcia-Molina, H., and Tomasic, A. (1999). Gloss: Text-source discovery over the internet. *ACM Trans. Database Syst.*, 24(2):229–264. 689

Gray, J. (1981). The transaction concept: Virtues and limitations. In *Proc. 7th Int. Conf. on Very Data Bases*, pages 144–154. 337

Gray, J. (1985). Why do computers stop and what can be done about it. Technical Report 85-7, Tandem Computers, Cupertino, Calif. 455, 456

Gray, J. (1987). Why do computers stop and what can be done about it. In *CIPS (Canadian Information Processing Society) Edmonton '87 Conf. Tutorial Notes*, Edmonton, Canada. 350, 410

Gray, J. (1989). Transparency in its place – the case against transparent access to geographically distributed data. Technical Report TR89.1, Tandem Computers Inc, Cupertino, Calif. 11

Gray, J., Helland, P., O'Neil, P. E., and Shasha, D. (1996). The dangers of replication and a solution. In *Proc. ACM SIGMOD Int. Conf. on Management of Data*, pages 173–182. 460, 493

Gray, J. and Reuter, A. (1993). *Transaction Processing: Concepts and Techniques*. Morgan Kaufmann. 358, 396, 401

Gray, J. N. (1979). Notes on data base operating systems. In Bayer, R., Graham, R. M., and Seegmüller, G., editors, *Operating Systems: An Advanced Course*, pages 393–481. Springer. 39, 359, 419, 425, 426, 431, 456

Gray, J. N., Lorie, R. A., Putzolu, G. R., and Traiger, I. L. (1976). Granularity of locks and degrees of consistency in a shared data base. In Nijssen, G. M., editor, *Modelling in Data Base Management Systems*, pages 365–394. North-Holland. 345

Gray, J. N., McJones, P., Blasgen, M., Lindsay, B., Lorie, R., Price, T., Putzolu, F., and Traiger, I. (1981). The recovery manager of the system r database manager. *ACM Comput. Surv.*, 13(2):223–242. 411, 419, 426, 456

Grefen, P. and Widom, J. (1997). Protocols for integrity constraint checking in federated databases. *Distrib. Parall. Databases*, 5(4):327–355. 200, 202

Griffiths, P. P. and Wade, B. W. (1976). An authorization mechanism for a relational database system. *ACM Trans. Database Syst.*, 1(3):242–255. 182, 201

Grossman, R. L. and Gu, Y. (2009). On the varieties of clouds for data intensive computing. *Q. Bull. IEEE TC on Data Eng.*, 32(1):44–50. 745

Group, E. D. S. E. D. (1990). Eds-collaborating for a high-performance parallel relational database. In *Proc. ESPRIT Conf*, pages 274–295. 505, 548

Gruber, O. and Amsaleg, L. (1994). Object grouping in eos. In Özsu et al. [1994a], pages 117–131. 579

Grust, T., van Keulen, M., and Teubner, J. (2003). Staircase join: Teach a relational dbms to watch its (axis) steps. In *Proc. 29th Int. Conf. on Very Large Data Bases*, pages 524–525. 700

Gudgin, M., Hadley, M., Mendelsohn, N., Moreau, J.-J., Nielsen, H. F., Karmarkar, A., and Lafon, Y., editors. Simple object protocol (SOAP) version 1.2 (2007). Available from: http://www.w3.org/TR/soap12 [Last retrieved: December 2009]. 690

Guerrini, G., Bertino, E., and Bal, R. (1998). A formal definition of the chimera object-oriented data model. *J. Intell. Information Syst.*, 11(1):5–40. 607

Guha, S. and McGregor, A. (2006). Approximate quantiles and the order of the stream. In *Proc. ACM SIGACT-SIGMOD Symp. on Principles of Database Systems*, pages 273–279. 725

Guha, S., Meyerson, A., Mishra, N., and Motwani, R. (2003). Clustering data streams: Theory and practice. *IEEE Trans. Knowl. and Data Eng.*, 15(3):515–528. 743

Gulisano, V., Jimenez-Peris, R., Patino-Martinez, M., and Valduriez, P. (2010). StreamCloud: A large scale data streaming system. In *Proc. 30th Int. Conf. on Distributed Computing Systems*. 762

Gulli, A. and Signorini, A. (2005). The indexable web is more than 11.5 billion pages. In *Proc. 14th Int. World Wide Web Conf.*, pages 902 – 903. 657

Gummadi, P. K., Gummadi, R., Gribble, S. D., Ratnasamy, S., Shenker, S., and Stoica, I. (2003). The impact of DHT routing geometry on resilience and proximity. In *Proc. ACM Int. Conf. on Data Communication*, pages 381–394. 619

Güntzer, U., Kießling, W., and Balke, W.-T. (2000). Optimizing multi-feature queries for image databases. In *Proc. 26th Int. Conf. on Very Large Data Bases*, pages 419–428. 629, 654

Guo, H., Larson, P.-A., Ramakrishnan, R., and Goldstein, J. (2004). Relaxed currency and consistency: How to say "good enough" in sql. In *Proc. ACM SIGMOD Int. Conf. on Management of Data*, pages 815–826. 540

Gupta, A., Agrawal, D., and Abbadi, A. E. (2003). Approximate range selection queries in peer-to-peer systems. In *Proc. 1st Biennial Conf. on Innovative Data Systems Research*, pages 141–151. 642

Gupta, A., Jagadish, H., and Mumick, I. S. (1996). Data integration using self-maintainable views. In *Advances in Database Technology, Proc. 5th Int. Conf. on Extending Database Technology*, pages 140–144. 179, 180

Gupta, A. and Mumick, I. S. (1999a). Maintenance of materialized views: Problems, techniques, and applications. In Gupta and Mumick [1999c], chapter 11, pages 145–156. 178, 201

Gupta, A. and Mumick, I. S., editors (1999b). *Materialized Views: Techniques, Implementations, and Applications*. M.I.T. Press. 132

Gupta, A. and Mumick, I. S., editors (1999c). *Materialized Views: Techniques, Implementations, and Applications*. M.I.T. Press. 176, 201, 794

Gupta, A., Mumick, I. S., and Subrahmanian, V. S. (1993). Maintaining views incrementally. In *Proc. ACM SIGMOD Int. Conf. on Management of Data*, pages 157–166. 179, 201

Haas, L. (2007). Beauty and the beast: The theory and practice of information integration. In *Proc. 11th Int. Conf. on Database Theory*, pages 28–43. 160

Haas, L., Kossmann, D., Wimmers, E., and Yang, J. (1997a). Optimizing queries across diverse data sources. In *Proc. 23th Int. Conf. on Very Large Data Bases*, pages 276–285. 317, 331

Haas, L. M., Kossmann, D., Wimmers, E. L., and Yang, J. (1997b). Optimizing queries across diverse data sources. In *Proc. 23th Int. Conf. on Very Large Data Bases*, pages 276–285. 160

Haas, P. and Hellerstein, J. (1999a). Ripple joins for online aggregation. In *Proc. ACM SIGMOD Int. Conf. on Management of Data*, pages 287–298. 732

Haas, P. J. and Hellerstein, J. M. (1999b). Ripple joins for online aggregation. In *Proc. ACM SIGMOD Int. Conf. on Management of Data*, pages 287–298. 322, 325, 331

Haderle, C. M. D., Lindsay, B., Pirahesh, H., and Schwarz, P. (1992). Aries: A transaction recovery method supporting fine-granularity locking and partial rollbacks using write-ahead logging. *ACM Trans. Database Syst.*, 17(1):94–162. 401, 418

Hadzilacos, T. and Hadzilacos, V. (1991). Transaction synchroniation in object bases. *J. Comp. and System Sci.*, 43(1):2–24. 597

Hadzilacos, V. (1988). A theory of reliability in database systems. *J. ACM*, 35(1):121–145. 429, 456, 596

Haessig, K. and Jenny, C. J. (1980). An algorithm for allocating computational objects in distributed computing systems. Research Report RZ 1016, IBM Research Laboratory, Zurich. 125

Halatchev, M. and Gruenwald, L. (2005). Estimating missing values in related sensor data streams. In *Proc. ACM SIGMOD Int. Conf. on Management of Data*, pages 83–94. 744

Halevy, A., Rajaraman, A., and Ordille, J. (2006). Data integration: The teenage years. In *Proc. 32nd Int. Conf. on Very Large Data Bases*, pages 9–16. 160

Halevy, A. Y. (2001). Answering queries using views: A survey. *VLDB J.*, 10(4):270–294. 301, 304, 331

Halevy, A. Y., Ashish, N., Bitton, D., Carey, M., Draper, D., Pollock, J., Rosenthal, A., and Sikka, V. (2005). Enterprise information integration: Successes, challenges and controversies. In *Proc. ACM SIGMOD Int. Conf. on Management of Data*, pages 778–787. 131

Halevy, A. Y., Etzioni, O., Doan, A., Ives, Z. G., Madhavan, J., McDowell, L., and Tatarinov, I. (2003). Crossing the structure chasm. In *Proc. 1st Biennial Conf. on Innovative Data Systems Research*. 159

Halici, U. and Dogac, A. (1989). Concurrency control in distributed databases through time intervals and short-term locks. *IEEE Trans. Softw. Eng.*, 15(8):994–995. 401

Hammad, M., Aref, W., and Elmagarmid, A. (2003a). Stream window join: Tracking moving objects in sensor-network databases. In *Proc. 15th Int. Conf. on Scientific and Statistical Database Management*, pages 75–84. 733

Hammad, M., Aref, W., and Elmagarmid, A. (2005). Optimizing in-order execution of continuous queries over streamed sensor data. In *Proc. 17th Int. Conf. on Scientific and Statistical Database Management*, pages 143–146. 733

Hammad, M., Aref, W., Franklin, M., Mokbel, M., and Elmagarmid, A. (2003b). Efficient execution of sliding window queries over data streams. Technical Report CSD TR 03-035, Purdue University. 733, 734, 735, 736

Hammad, M., Mokbel, M., Ali, M., Aref, W., Catlin, A., Elmagarmid, A., Eltabakh, M., Elfeky, M., Ghanem, T., Gwadera, R., Ilyas, I., Marzouk, M., and Xiong, X. (2004). Nile: a query processing engine for data streams. In *Proc. 20th Int. Conf. on Data Engineering*, page 851. 735, 736

Hammer, M. and Niamir, B. (1979). A heuristic approach to attribute partitioning. In *Proc. ACM SIGMOD Int. Conf. on Management of Data*, pages 93–101. 99, 125

Hammer, M. and Shipman, D. W. (1980). Reliability mechanisms for sdd-1: A system for distributed databases. *ACM Trans. Database Syst.*, 5(4):431–466. 440, 456

Han, D., Xiao, C., Zhou, R., Wang, G., Huo, H., and Hui, X. (2006). Load shedding for window joins over streams. In *Proc. 7th Int. Conf. on Web-Age Information Management:*, pages 472–483. 740

Hanson, E., Carnes, C., Huang, L., Konyala, M., and Noronha, L. (1999). Scalable trigger processing. In *Proc. 15th Int. Conf. on Data Engineering*, pages 266–275. 741

Härder, T. and Reuter, A. (1983). Principles of transaction-oriented database recovery. *ACM Comput. Surv.*, 15(4):287–317. 39, 411, 413, 420, 421, 423, 424, 456

Harizopoulos, S., Shah, M. A., Meza, J., and Ranganathan, P. (2009). Energy efficiency: The new holy grail of data management systems research. In *Proc. 4th Biennial Conf. on Innovative Data Systems Research*. 762

Harvey, N. J. A., Jones, M. B., Saroiu, S., Theimer, M., and Wolman, A. (2003). SkipNet: A scalable overlay network with practical locality properties. In *Proc. 4th USENIX Symp. on Internet Tech. and Systems*. 618, 622, 642

He, B., Chang, K. C.-C., and Han, J. (2004). Mining complex matchings across web query interfaces. In *Proc. ACM SIGMOD Workshop on Research Issues in Data Mining and Knowledge Discovery*, pages 3–10. 149

He, Q. and Ling, T. W. (2006). An ontology-based approach to the integration of entity-relationship schemas. *Data & Knowl. Eng.*, 58(3):299–326. 134

Hedley, Y. L., Younas, M., James, A., and Sanderson, M. (2004a). A two-phase sampling technique for information extraction from hidden web databases. In *WIDM04*, pages 1–8. 688

Hedley, Y.-L., Younas, M., James, A. E., and Sanderson, M. (2004b). Query-related data extraction of hidden web documents. In *Proc. 30th Annual Int. ACM SIGIR Conf. on Research and Development in Information Retrieval*, pages 558–559. 687

Heimbigner, D. and McLeod, D. (1985). A federated architecture for information management. *ACM Trans. Information Syst.*, 3(3):253–278. 36

Helal, A. A., Heddaya, A. A., and Bhargava, B. B. (1997). *Replication Techniques in Distributed Systems*. Kluwer Academic Publishers. 456, 486, 493

Hellerstein, J. M., Franklin, M. J., Chandrasekaran, S., Deshpande, A., Hildrum, K., Madden, S., Raman, V., and Shah, M. A. (2000). Adaptive query processing: Technology in evolution. *Q. Bull. IEEE TC on Data Eng.*, 23(2):7–18. 320, 331

Hellerstein, J. M., Haas, P., and Wang, H. (1997). Online aggregation. In *Proc. ACM SIGMOD Int. Conf. on Management of Data*, pages 171–182. 732

Hellerstein, J. M. and Stonebraker, M. (1993). Predicate migration: Optimizing queries with expensive predicates. In *Proc. ACM SIGMOD Int. Conf. on Management of Data*, pages 267–276. 323

Herlihy, M. (1987). Concurrency versus availability: Atomicity mechanisms for replicated data. *ACM Trans. Comp. Syst.*, 5(3):249–274. 456, 493

Herlihy, M. (1990). Apologizing versus asking permission: Optimistic concurrency control for abstract data types. *ACM Trans. Database Syst.*, 15(1):96–124. 594, 595

Herman, D. and Verjus, J. P. (1979). An algorithm for maintaining the consistency of multiple copies. In *Proc. 1st Int. Conf. on Distributed Computing Systems*, pages 625–631. 382

Hernández, M. A. and Stolfo, S. J. (1998). Real-world data is dirty: Data cleansing and the merge/purge problem. *Proc. ACM SIGMOD Workshop on Research Issues in Data Mining and Knowledge Discovery*, 2(1):9–37. 158

Herrmann, U., Dadam, P., Küspert, K., Roman, E. A., and Schlageter, G. (1990). A lock technique for disjoint and non-disjoint complex objects. In *Advances in Database Technology, Proc. 2nd Int. Conf. on Extending Database Technology*, pages 219–237. Springer. 602

Hersh, W. (2001). Managing gigabytes - compressing and indexing documents and images (second edition). *Inf. Ret.*, 4(1):79–80. 667

Hevner, A. R. and Schneider, G. M. (1980). An integrated design system for distributed database networks. In *Digest of Papers - COMPCON*, pages 459–465. 125

Hevner, A. R. and Yao, S. B. (1979). Query processing in distributed database systems. *IEEE Trans. Softw. Eng.*, 5(3):177–182. 255

Hirate, Y., Kato, S., and Yamana, H. (2006). Web structure in 2005. In *Proc. 4th Int. Workshop on Algorithms and Models for the Web-Graph*, pages 36 – 46. 657

Hoffer, H. A. and Severance, D. G. (1975). The use of cluster analysis in physical data base design. In *Proc. 1st Int. Conf. on Very Data Bases*, pages 69–86. 99, 102, 105, 125

Hoffer, J. A. (1975). *A Clustering Approach to the Generation of Subfiles for the Design of a Computer Data Base*. Ph.D. thesis, Department of Operations Research, Cornell University, Ithaca, N.Y. 125

Hoffman, J. L. (1977). *Model Methods for Computer Security and Privacy*. Prentice-Hall. 181, 201

Hofri, M. (1994). On timeout for global deadlock detection in decentralized database systems. *Inf. Proc. Letters*, 51(6):295–302. 401

Hong, W. (1992). Exploiting inter-operation parallelism in xprs. In *Proc. ACM SIGMOD Int. Conf. on Management of Data*, pages 19–28. 503, 530, 533, 548

Hsiao, D., editor (1983). *Advanced Database Machine Architectures*. Prentice-Hall. 498

Hsiao, H. I. and DeWitt, D. (1991). A performance study of three high-availability data replication strategies. In *Proc. Int. Conf. on Parallel and Distributed Information Systems*, pages 18–28. 511, 512

Hsu, M., editor (1993). *IEEE Quart. Bull. Data Eng., Special Issue on Workflow and Extended Transaction Systems*, volume 16. IEEE Computer Society. 354

Huebsch, R., Hellerstein, J., Lanham, N., Loo, B. T., Shenker, S., and Stoica, I. (2003). Querying the internet with pier. In *Proc. 29th Int. Conf. on Very Large Data Bases*, pages 321–332. 641

Hull, R. (1997). Managing semantic heterogeneity in databases: A theoretical perspective. In *Proc. ACM SIGACT-SIGMOD Symp. on Principles of Database Systems*, pages 51–61. 160

Hulten, G., Spencer, L., and Domingos, P. (2001). Mining time-changing data streams. In *Proc. 7th ACM SIGKDD Int. Conf. on Knowledge Discovery and Data Mining*, pages 97–106. 743, 762

Hunt, H. B. and Rosenkrantz, D. J. (1979). The complexity of testing predicate locks. In *Proc. ACM SIGMOD Int. Conf. on Management of Data*, pages 127–133. 233

Hwang, D. J. (1987). Constructing a highly-available location service for a distributed environment. Technical Report MIT/LCS/TR-410, Massachusetts Institute of Technology, Cambridge, Mass. 577

Ibaraki, T. and Kameda, T. (1984). On the optimal nesting order for computing n-relation joins. *ACM Trans. Database Syst.*, 9(3):482–502. 207, 220, 245

Ilyas, I. F., Beskales, G., and Soliman, M. A. (2008). A survey of top-k query processing techniques in relational database systems. *ACM Comput. Surv.*, 40(4):1–58. 628, 654

Inmon, W. (1992). *Building the Data Warehouse*. John Wiley & Sons. 131

Ioannidis, Y. (1996). Query optimization. In Tucker, A., editor, *The Computer Science and Engineering Handbook*, pages 1038–1054. CRC Press. 292

Ioannidis, Y. and Wong, E. (1987). Query optimization by simulated annealing. In *Proc. ACM SIGMOD Int. Conf. on Management of Data*, pages 9–22. 212, 249, 586

Ipeirotis, P. G. and Gravano, L. (2002). Distributed search over the hidden web: Hierarchical database sampling and selection. In *Proc. 28th Int. Conf. on Very Large Data Bases*, pages 394–405. 687, 688, 689

Irani, K. B. and Khabbaz, N. G. (1982). A methodology for the design of communication networks and the distribution of data in distributed computer systems. *IEEE Trans. Comput.*, C-31(5):419–434. 125

Isloor, S. S. and Marsland, T. A. (1980). The deadlock problem: An overview. *Comp.*, 13(9):58–78. 39, 401

Jagadish, H. V., Ooi, B. C., Tan, K.-L., Vu, Q. H., and Zhang, R. (2006). Speeding up search in peer-to-peer networks with a multi-way tree structure. In *Proc. ACM SIGMOD Int. Conf. on Management of Data*, pages 1–12. 622

Jagadish, H. V., Ooi, B. C., and Vu, Q. H. (2005). BATON: A balanced tree structure for peer-to-peer networks. In *Proc. 31st Int. Conf. on Very Large Data Bases*, pages 661–672. 622, 643

Jajodia, S., Atluri, V., Keefe, T. F., McCollum, C. D., and Mukkamala, R. (2001). Multilevel security transaction processing. *J. Computer Security*, 9(3):165–195. 187, 202

Jajodia, S. and Mutchler, D. (1987). Dynamic voting. In *Proc. ACM SIGMOD Int. Conf. on Management of Data*, pages 227–238. 456, 493

Jajodia, S. and Sandhu, R. S. (1991). Towards a multilevel secure relational data model. In *Proc. ACM SIGMOD Int. Conf. on Management of Data*, pages 50–59. 181, 202

Jarke, M. and Koch, J. (1984). Query optimization in database systems. *ACM Comput. Surv.*, 16(2):111–152. 211, 220, 241

Jarke, M., Lenzerini, M., Vassiliou, Y., and Vassiliadis, P. (2003). *Fundamentals of Data Warehouses*. Springer, 2 edition. 131

Jenq, B., Woelk, D., Kom, W., and Lee, W. L. (1990). Query processing in distributed orion. In *Advances in Database Technology, Proc. 2nd Int. Conf. on Extending Database Technology*, pages 169–187. Springer. 587

Jhingran, A. D., Mattos, N., and Pirahesh, H. (2002). Information integration: A research agenda. *IBM Systems J.*, 41(4):555–562. 131

Jiang, H., Lu, H., 0011, W. W., and Ooi, B. C. (2003). Xr-tree: Indexing XML data for efficient structural joins. In *Proc. 19th Int. Conf. on Data Engineering*, pages 253–263. 701

Jiang, N. and Gruenwald, L. (2006). Research issues in data stream association rule mining. *ACM SIGMOD Rec.*, 35(1):14–19. 743

Jiang, Q. and Chakravarthy, S. (2004). Scheduling strategies for processing continuous queries over streams. In *Proc. British National Conf. on Databases*, pages 16–30. 735

Jiménez-Peris, R., Patiño-Martínez, M., and Alonso, G. (2002). Non-intrusive, parallel recovery of replicated data. In *Proc. 21st Symp. on Reliable Distributed Systems*, pages 150–159. 546, 548

Jiménez-Peris, R., Patiño-Martínez, M., Alonso, G., and Kemme, B. (2003). Are quorums an alternative for data replication? *ACM Trans. Database Syst.*, 28(3):257–294. 489, 548

Jiménez-Peris, R., Patiño-Martínez, M., and Kemme, B. (2007). Enterprise grids: Challenges ahead. *J. Grid Comp.*, 5(3):283–294. 748

Jiménez-Peris, R., Patiño-Martínez, M., Kemme, B., and Alonso, G. (2002). Improving the scalability of fault-tolerant database clusters. In *Proc. 22nd Int. Conf. on Distributed Computing Systems*, pages 477–484. 482, 491, 548

Jones, A. K. (1979). The object model: A conceptual tool for structuring software. In Bayer, R., Graham, R. M., and Seegmüller, G., editors, *Operating Systems: An Advanced Course*, pages 7–1. Springer. 555

Josifovski, V., Fontoura, M., and Barta, A. (2005). Querying XML streams. *VLDB J.*, 14(2):197–210. 700

Jr, A. M. J. and Malek, M. (1988). Survey of software tools for evaluating reliability, availability and serviceability. *ACM Comput. Surv.*, 20(4):227–269. 455

Kabra, N. and DeWitt, D. J. (1998). Efficient mid-query re-optimization of sub-optimal query execution plans. In *Proc. ACM SIGMOD Int. Conf. on Management of Data*, pages 106–117. 739

Kaelbling, L. P., Littman, M. L., and Moore, A. P. (1996). Reinforcement learning: A survey. *J. Artificial Intel. Res.*, 4:237–285. 666

Kaiser, G. (1989). Transactions for concurrent object-oriented programming systems. In *Proc. ACM SIGPLAN Workshop on Object-Based Concurrent Programming*, pages 136–138. 593

Kalogeraki, V., Gunopulos, D., and Zeinalipour-Yazti, D. (2002). A local search mechanism for peer-to-peer networks. In *Proc. 11th Int. Conf. on Information and Knowledge Management*, pages 300–307. 617

Kambayashi, Y., Yoshikawa, M., and Yajima, S. (1982). Query processing for distributed databases using generalized semi–joins. In *Proc. ACM SIGMOD Int. Conf. on Management of Data*, pages 151–160. 272, 292

Kang, J., Naughton, J., and Viglas, S. (2003). Evaluating window joins over un-bounded streams. In *Proc. 19th Int. Conf. on Data Engineering*, pages 341–352. 733, 738

Kanne, C.-C. and Moerkotte, G. (2000). Efficient storage of XML data. In *Proc. 16th Int. Conf. on Data Engineering*, page 198. 700

Kapitskaia, O., Tomasic, A., and Valduriez, P. (1997). Dealing with discrepancies in wrapper functionality. Research Report RR-3138, INRIA. 319

Karlapalem, K. and Li, Q. (1995). Partitioning schemes for object oriented databases. In *Proc. 5th Int. Workshop on Research Issues on Data Eng.*, pages 42–49. 560

Karlapalem, K., Li, Q., and Vieweg, S. (1996a). Method induced partitioning schemes for object-oriented databases. In *Proc. 16th Int. Conf. on Distributed Computing Systems*, pages 377–384. 564

Karlapalem, K. and Navathe, S. B. (1994). Materialization of redesigned distributed relational databases. Technical Report HKUST-CS94-14, Hong Kong University of Science and Technology, Department of Computer Science. 124

Karlapalem, K., Navathe, S. B., and Ammar, M. (1996b). Optimal redesign policies to support dynamic processing of applications on a distributed relational database system. *Inf. Syst.*, 21(4):353–367. 124

Karlapalem, K., Navathe, S. B., and Morsi, M. A. (1994). Issues in distribution design of object-oriented databases. In Özsu et al. [1994a], pages 148–164. 560

Kashyap, V. and Sheth, A. P. (1996). Semantic and schematic similarities between database objects: A context-based approach. *VLDB J.*, 5(4):276–304. 140, 160

Katz, B. and Lin, J. (2002). Annotating the world wide web using natural language. In *Proc. 2nd Workshop on NLP and XML*, pages 1–8. 681

Katz, H., Chamberlin, D., Draper, D., Fernández, M., Kay, M., Robie, J., Rys, M., Simeon, J., Tivy, J., and Wadler, P. (2004). *XQuery from the Experts: A Guide to the W3C XML Query Language*. Addison Wesley. 719

Kaushik, R., Bohannon, P., Naughton, J. F., and Korth, H. F. (2002). Covering indexing for branching path queries. In *Proc. ACM SIGMOD Int. Conf. on Management of Data*, pages 133–144. 701

Kazerouni, L. and Karlapalem, K. (1997). Stepwise redesign of distributed relational databases. Technical Report HKUST-CS97-12, Hong Kong University of Science and Technology, Department of Computer Science. 124

Keeton, K., Patterson, D., and Hellerstein, J. M. (1998). A case for intelligent disks (idisks). *ACM SIGMOD Rec.*, 27(3):42–52. 499

Keller, A. M. (1982). Update to relational databases through views involving joins. In *Proc. 2nd Int. Conf. on Databases: Improving Usability and Responsiveness*, pages 363–384. 175, 201

Keller, T., Graefe, G., and Maier, D. (1991). Efficient assembly of complex objects. In *Proc. ACM SIGMOD Int. Conf. on Management of Data*, pages 148–157. 587, 590, 592

Kementsietsidis, A., Arenas, M., and Miller, R. J. (2003). Managing data mappings in the hyperion project. In *Proc. 19th Int. Conf. on Data Engineering*, pages 732–734. 625

Kemme, B. and Alonso, G. (2000a). Don't be lazy, be consistent: Postgres-R, a new way to implement database replication. In *Proc. 26th Int. Conf. on Very Large Data Bases*, pages 134–143. 482, 548

Kemme, B. and Alonso, G. (2000b). A New Approach to Developing and Implementing Eager Database Replication Protocols. *ACM Trans. Database Syst.*, 25(3):333–379. 482, 548

Kemme, B., Bartoli, A., and O.Babaoglu (2001). Online reconfiguration in replicated databases based on group communication. In *Proc. Int. Conf. on Dependable Systems and Networks*, pages 117–130. 546, 548

Kemme, B., Peris, R. J., and Patino-Martinez, M. (2010). *Database Replication*. Morgan & Claypool. 493

Kemper, A. and Kossmann, D. (1994). Dual-buffering strategies in object bases. In *Proc. 20th Int. Conf. on Very Large Data Bases*, pages 427–438. 570

Kemper, A. and Moerkotte, G. (1990a). Access support in object bases. In *Proc. ACM SIGMOD Int. Conf. on Management of Data*, pages 364–374. 587

Kemper, A. and Moerkotte, G. (1990b). Advanced query processing in object bases using access support relations. In *Proc. 16th Int. Conf. on Very Large Data Bases*, pages 290–301. 587

Kemper, A. and Moerkotte, G. (1994). Physical object management. In Kim [1994], pages 175–202. 588, 590, 607

Kermarrec, A.-M., Rowstron, A., Shapiro, M., and Druschel, P. (2001). The icecube approach to the reconciliation of diverging replicas. In *ACM Symp. on Principles of Distributed Computing (PODC)*, pages 210–218. 651

Kermarrec, A.-M. and van Steen, M. (2007). Gossiping in distributed systems. *Operating Systems Rev.*, 41(5):2–7. 617

Kerschberg, L., Ting, P. D., and Yao, S. B. (1982). Query optimization in star computer networks. *ACM Trans. Database Syst.*, 7(4):678–711. 214

Kersten, M. L., Plomp, S., and van den Berg, C. A. (1994). Object storage management in goblin. In Özsu et al. [1994a], pages 100–116. 579

Khoshafian, S. and Copeland, G. (1986). Object identity. In *Proc. Int. Conf. on OOPSLA*, pages 406–416. 553

Khoshafian, S. and Valduriez, P. (1987). Sharing persistence and object-orientation: A database perspective. In *Int. Workshop on Database Programming Languages*, pages 181–205. 251, 292, 510, 553

Kifer, D., Ben-David, S., and Gehrke, J. (2004). Detecting change in data streams. In *Proc. 30th Int. Conf. on Very Large Data Bases*, pages 180–191. 727, 743

Kifer, M., Bernstein, A., and Lewis, P. M. (2006). *Database Systems – An Application-Oriented Approach*. Pearson, 2 edition. 70

Kifer, M., Lausen, G., and Wu, J. (1995). Logical foundations of object-oriented and frame-based languages. *J. ACM*, 42(4):741–843. 607

Kifer, M. and Wu, J. (1993). A logic programming with complex objects. *J. Comp. and System Sci.*, 47(1):77–120. 607

Kim, W. (1984). Highly available systems for database applications. *ACM Comput. Surv.*, 16(1):71–98. 456

Kim, W. (1989). A model of queries for object-oriented databases. In *Proc. 15th Int. Conf. on Very Large Data Bases*, pages 423–432. 587

Kim, W., editor (1994). *Modern Database Management – Object-Oriented and Multidatabase Technologies*. Addison-Wesley/ACM Press. 607, 801

Kim, W., Banerjee, J., Chou, H., Garza, J., and Woelk, D. (1987). Composite objects support in an object-oriented database system. In *Proc. Int. Conf. on OOPSLA*, pages 118–125. 579

Kim, W. and Lochovsky, F., editors (1989). *Object-Oriented Concepts, Databases, and Applications*. Addison Wesley. 607

Kim, W., Reiner, D. S., and Batory, D. S., editors (1985). *Query Processing in Database Systems*. Springer. 220, 807

Kim, W. and Seo, J. (1991). Classifying schematic and data heterogeneity in multi-database systems. *Comp.*, 24(12):12–18. 160

Kitsuregawa, M. and Ogawa, Y. (1990). Bucket spreading parallel hash: A new, robust, parallel hash join method for data skew in the super database computer. In *Proc. 16th Int. Conf. on Very Large Data Bases*, pages 210–221. 528, 548

Kleinberg, J. (2002). Bursty and hierarchical structure in streams. In *Proc. 8th ACM SIGKDD Int. Conf. on Knowledge Discovery and Data Mining*, pages 91–101. 727

Kleinberg, J. M. (1999). Authoritative sources in a hyperlinked environment. *J. ACM*, 46(5):604–632. 658, 668

Kleinberg, J. M., Kumar, R., Raghavan, P., Rajagopalan, S., and Tomkins, A. (1999). The Web as a graph: measurements, models, and methods. In *Proc. 5th Annual Int. Conf. Computing and Combinatorics*, pages 1–17. 658

Kling, P., Özsu, M. T., and Daudjee, K. (2010). Distributed XML query processing: Fragmentation, localization and pruning. Technical Report TR-CS-2010-02, University of Waterloo, Cheriton School of Computer Science. 693, 704, 706, 707, 713, 715, 717, 718, 719

Knapp, E. (1987). Deadlock detection in distributed databases. *ACM Comput. Surv.*, 19(4):303–328. 39, 401

Knezevic, P., Wombacher, A., and Risse, T. (2005). Enabling high data availability in a dht. In *Int. Workshop on Grid and P2P Computing Impacts on Large Scale Heterogeneous Distributed Database Systems (GLOBE)*, pages 363–367. 648

Koch, C. (2001). *Data Integration against Multiple Evolving Autonomous Schemata*. Ph.D. thesis, Technical University of Vienna. 133, 134

Koch, C. (2003). Efficient processing of expressive node-selecting queries on XML data in secondary storage: A tree automata-based approach. In *Proc. 29th Int. Conf. on Very Large Data Bases*, pages 249–260. 700

Kohler, W. H. (1981). A survey of techniques for synchronization and recovery in decentralized computer systems. *ACM Comput. Surv.*, 13(2):149–183. 456

Kollias, J. G. and Hatzopoulos, M. (1981). Criteria to aid in solving the problem of allocating copies of a file in a computer network. *Comp. J.*, 24(1):29–30. 125

Kolodner, E. and Weihl, W. (1993). Atomic incremental garbage collection and recovery for large stable heap. In *Proc. ACM SIGMOD Int. Conf. on Management of Data*, pages 177–185. 581

Konopnicki, D. and Shmueli, O. (1995). W3QS: A query system for the World Wide Web. In *Proc. 21th Int. Conf. on Very Large Data Bases*, pages 54–65. 676

Koon, T. M. and Özsu, M. T. (1986). Performance comparison of resilient concurrency control algorithms for distributed databases. In *Proc. 2nd Int. Conf. on Data Engineering*, pages 565–573. 401

Korn, F., Muthukrishnan, S., and Wu, Y. (2006). Modeling skew in data streams. In *Proc. ACM SIGMOD Int. Conf. on Management of Data*, pages 181–192. 727

Korth, H., Levy, E., and Silberschatz, A. (1990). Compensating transactions: A new recovery paradigm. In *Proc. 16th Int. Conf. on Very Large Data Bases*, pages 95–106. 352

Kossmann, D. (2000). The state of the art in distributed query processing. *ACM Comput. Surv.*, 32(4):422–469. 212, 220, 292, 331

Kowalik, J., editor (1985). *Parallel MIMD Computation : the HEP Supercomputer and its applications*. M.I.T. Press. 498

Krämer, J. and Seeger, B. (2005). A temporal foundation for continuous queries over data streams. In *Proc. 11th Int. Conf. on Management of Data (COMAD)*, pages 70–82. 735

Krishnamurthy, R., Boral, H., and Zaniolo, C. (1986). Optimization of non-recursive queries. In *Proc. 11th Int. Conf. on Very Large Data Bases*, pages 128–137. 292

Krishnamurthy, R., Litwin, W., and Kent, W. (1991). Language features for interoperability of databases with schematic discrepancies. In *Proc. ACM SIGMOD Int. Conf. on Management of Data*, pages 40–49. 160

Krishnamurthy, S., Franklin, M., Hellerstein, J., and Jacobson, G. (2004). The case for precision sharing. In *Proc. 30th Int. Conf. on Very Large Data Bases*, pages 972–986. 740

Krishnamurthy, S., Wu, C., and Franklin, M. (2006). On-the-fly sharing for streamed aggregation. In *Proc. ACM SIGMOD Int. Conf. on Management of Data*, pages 623–634. 741

Krishnaprasad, M., Liu, Z. H., Manikutty, A., Warner, J. W., and Arora, V. (2005). Towards an industrial strength SQL/XML infrastructure. In *Proc. 21st Int. Conf. on Data Engineering*, pages 991–1000. 699

Kshemkalyani, A. and Singhal, M. (1994). On characterization and correctness of distributed deadlocks. *J. Parall. and Distrib. Comput.*, 22(1):44–59. 401

Kubiatowicz, J., Bindel, D., Chen, Y., Czerwinski, S., Eaton, P., Geels, D., Gummadi, R., Rhea, S., Weatherspoon, H., Weimer, W., Wells, C., and Zhao, B. (2000). Oceanstore: an architecture for global-scale persistent storage. In *ACM Int. Conf. on Architectural Support for Programming Languages and Operating Systems (ASPLOS)*, pages 190–201. 649, 654

Kumar, A. and Segev, A. (1993). Cost and availability tradeoffs in replicated data concurrency control. *ACM Trans. Database Syst.*, 18(1):102–131. 456, 493

Kumar, R., Raghavan, P., Rajagopalan, S., Sivakumar, D., Tomkins, A., and Upfal, E. (2000). The Web as a graph. In *Proc. 19th ACM SIGACT-SIGMOD-SIGART Symp. on Principles of Database Systems*, pages 1–10. Available from: http://doi.acm.org/10.1145/335168.335170. 658, 660

Kumar, R., Raghavan, P., Rajagopalan, S., and Tomkins, A. (1999). Extracting large-scale knowledge bases from the web. In *Proc. 25th Int. Conf. on Very Large Data Bases*, pages 639–650. 660

Kumar, V., editor (1996). *Performance of Concurrency Control Mechanisms in Centralized Database Systems*. Prentice-Hall. 358, 401

Kung, H. T. and Papadimitriou, C. H. (1979). An optimality theory of concurrency control for databases. In *Proc. ACM SIGMOD Int. Conf. on Management of Data*, pages 116–125. 350

Kung, H. T. and Robinson, J. T. (1981). On optimistic methods for concurrency control. *ACM Trans. Database Syst.*, 6(2):213–226. 385, 387

Kurose, J. F. and Ross, K. W. (2010). *Computer Networking - A Top-Down Approach Featuring the Internet*. Addison Wesley, 4 edition. 70

Kuss, H. (1982). On totally ordering checkpoint in distributed data bases. In *Proc. ACM SIGMOD Int. Conf. on Management of Data*, pages 174–174. 456

Kwok, C. C. T., Etzioni, O., and Weld, D. S. (2001). Scaling question answering to the web. In *Proc. 10th Int. World Wide Web Conf.*, pages 150–161. 681

LaChimia, J. (1984). Query decomposition in a distributed database system using satellite communications. In *Proc. 3rd Seminar on Distributed Data Sharing Systems*, pages 105–118. 214

Lacroix, M. and Pirotte, A. (1977). Domain-oriented relational languages. In *Proc. 3rd Int. Conf. on Very Data Bases*, pages 370–378. 57

Ladin, R. and Liskov, B. (1992). Garbage collection of a distributed heap. In *Proc. 12th Int. Conf. on Distributed Computing Systems*, pages 708–715. 581

Lage, J. P., da Silva, A. S., Golgher, P. B., and Laender, A. H. F. (2002). Collecting hidden weeb pages for data extraction. In *Proc. 4th Int. Workshop on Web Information and Data Management*, pages 69–75. 686

Lakshmanan, L. V. S., Sadri, F., and Subramanian, I. N. (1996). A declarative language for querying and restructuring the Web. In *Proc. 6th Int. Workshop on Research Issues on Data Eng.*, pages 12–21. 676

Lam, K. and Yu, C. T. (1980). An approximation algorithm for a file allocation problem in a hierarchical distributed system. In *Proc. ACM SIGMOD Int. Conf. on Management of Data*, pages 125–132. 115

Lam, S. S. and Özsu, M. T. (2002). Querying web data – the WebQA approach. In *Proc. 3rd Int. Conf. on Web Information Systems Eng.*, pages 139–148. 681

Lampson, B. and Sturgis, H. (1976). Crash recovery in distributed data storage system. Technical report, Xerox Palo Alto Research Center, Palo Alto, Calif. 413, 453

Landers, T. and Rosenberg, R. L. (1982). An overview of multibase. In Schneider, H.-J., editor, *Distributed Data Bases*, pages 153–184. North-Holland, Amsterdam. 331

Langville, A. N. and Meyer, C. D. (2006). *Google's PageRank and Beyond*. Princeton University Press. 665

Lanzelotte, R. and Valduriez, P. (1991). Extending the search strategy in a query optimizer. In *Proc. 17th Int. Conf. on Very Large Data Bases*, pages 363–373. 584, 587, 588

Lanzelotte, R., Valduriez, P., and Zaït, M. (1993). On the effectiveness of optimization search strategies for parallel execution spaces. In *Proc. 19th Int. Conf. on Very Large Data Bases*, pages 493–504. 249

Lanzelotte, R., Valduriez, P., Zaït, M., and Ziane, M. (1994). Industrial-strength parallel query optimization: issues and lessons. *Inf. Syst.*, 19(4):311–330. 523, 524, 548

Law, Y.-N., Wang, H., and Zaniolo, C. (2004). Query languages and data models for database sequences and data streams. In *Proc. 30th Int. Conf. on Very Large Data Bases*, pages 492–503. 728

Lawrence, S. and Giles, C. L. (1998). Searching the world wide web. *Science*, 280:98 – 100. 657

Lawrence, S. and Giles, C. L. (1999). Accessibility of information on the web. *Nature*, 400(107 – 109). 657

Lee, M., Freytag, J. C., and Lohman, G. (1988). Implementing an interpreter for functional rules in a query optimizer. In *Proc. 14th Int. Conf. on Very Large Data Bases*, pages 218–229. 586

Lee, S. and Kim, J. (1995). An efficient distributed deadlock detection algorithm. In *Proc. 15th Int. Conf. on Distributed Computing Systems*, pages 169–178. 401

Leland, W., Taqqu, M., Willinger, M., and Wilson, D. (1994). On the self-similar nature of ethernet traffic. *IEEE/ACM Trans. Networking*, 2(1):1–15. 727

Lenoski, D., Laudon, J., Gharachorloo, K., Weber, W. D., Gupta, A., Henessy, J., Horowitz, M., and Lam, M. S. (1992). The stanford dash multiprocessor. *Comp.*, 25(3):63–79. 506, 547

Lenzerini, M. (2002). Data integration: a theoretical perspective. In *Proc. ACM SIGACT-SIGMOD Symp. on Principles of Database Systems*, pages 233–246. 133

Leon-Garcia, A. and Widjaja, I. (2004). *Communication Networks - Fundamental Concepts and Key Architectures*. McGraw-Hill, 2 edition. 70

Leung, J. Y. and Lai, E. K. (1979). On minimum cost recovery from system deadlock. *IEEE Trans. Comput.*, 28(9):671–677. 391

Levin, K. D. and Morgan, H. L. (1975). Optimizing distributed data bases: A framework for research. In *Proc. National Computer Conf*, pages 473–478. 38, 71, 125

Levy, A. Y., Mendelzon, A. O., Sagiv, Y., and Srivastava, D. (1995). Answering queries using views. In *Proc. ACM SIGACT-SIGMOD Symp. on Principles of Database Systems*, pages 95–104. 304, 331

Levy, A. Y., Rajaraman, A., and Ordille, J. J. (1996a). Querying heterogeneous information sources using source descriptions. In *Proc. 22th Int. Conf. on Very Large Data Bases*, pages 251–262. 160

Levy, A. Y., Rajaraman, A., and Ordille, J. J. (1996b). Querying heterogeneous information sources using source descriptions. In *Proc. 22th Int. Conf. on Very Large Data Bases*, pages 251–262. 305, 331

Levy, A. Y., Rajaraman, A., and Ordille, J. J. (1996c). The world wide web as a collection of views: Query processing in the information manifold. In *Proc. Workshop on Materialized Views: Techniques and Applications*, pages 43–55. 160

Li, F., Chang, C., Kollios, G., and Bestavros, A. (2006). Characterizing and exploiting reference locality in data stream applications. In *Proc. 22nd Int. Conf. on Data Engineering*, page 81. 740

Li, V. O. K. (1987). Performance models of timestamp-ordering concurrency control algorithms in distributed databases. *IEEE Trans. Comput.*, C-36(9):1041–1051. 401

Li, W.-S. and Clifton, C. (2000). Semint: A tool for identifying attribute correspondences in heterogeneous databases using neural networks. *Data & Knowl. Eng.*, 33(1):49–84. 145

Li, W.-S., Clifton, C., and Liu, S.-Y. (2000). Database integration using neural networks: Implementation and experiences. *Knowl. and Information Syst.*, 2(1):73–96. 145

Liang, D. and Tripathi, S. K. (1996). Performance analysis of long-lived transaction processing systems with rollbacks and aborts. *IEEE Trans. Knowl. and Data Eng.*, 8(5):802–815. 401

Lim, H.-S., Lee, J.-G., Lee, M.-J., Whang, K.-Y., and Song, I.-Y. (2006). Continuous query processing in data streams using duality of data and queries. In *Proc. ACM SIGMOD Int. Conf. on Management of Data*, pages 313–324. 741

Lim, L., Wang, M., Padmanabhan, S., Vitter, J. S., and Agarwal, R. (2003). Dynamic maintenance of web indexes using landmarks. In *Proc. 12th Int. World Wide Web Conf.*, pages 102–111. 667

Lima, A., Mattoso, M., and Valduriez, P. (2004a). Olap query processing in a database cluster. In *Proc. 10th Int. Euro-Par Conf.*, pages 355–362. 543, 548

Lima, A. A. B., Mattoso, M., and Valduriez, P. (2004b). Adaptive virtual partitioning for olap query processing in a database cluster. In *Proc. Brazilian Symposium on Databases*, pages 92–105. 544, 548

Lin, W. K. (1981). Performance evaluation of two concurrency control mechanisms in a distributed database system. In *Proc. ACM SIGMOD Int. Conf. on Management of Data*, pages 84–92. 401

Lin, W. K. and Nolte, J. (1982). Performance of two phase locking. In *Proc. 6th Berkeley Workshop on Distributed Data Management and Computer Networks*, pages 131–160. 401

Lin, W. K. and Nolte, J. (1983). Basic timestamp, multiple version timestamp, and two-phase locking. In *Proc. 9th Int. Conf. on Very Data Bases*, pages 109–119. 401

Lin, X., Lu, H., Xu, J., and Yu, J. X. (2004). Continuously maintaining quantile summaries of the most recent N elements over a data stream. In *Proc. 20th Int. Conf. on Data Engineering*, pages 362–373. 727, 737

Lin, Y., Kemme, B., Patiño-Martínez, M., and Jiménez-Peris, R. (2005). Middleware based data replication providing snapshot isolation. In *Proc. ACM SIGMOD Int. Conf. on Management of Data*, pages 419–430. 464

Lindsay, B. (1979). Notes on distributed databases. Technical Report RJ 2517, IBM San Jose Research Laboratory, San Jose, Calif. 426

Liskov, B., Adya, A., Castro, M., Day, M., Ghemawat, S., Gruber, R., Maheshwari, U., Myers, A., and Shrira, L. (1996). Safe and efficient sharing of persistent objects in thor. In *ACM SIGMOD Int. Conf. on Management of Data*, pages 318–329. 568, 569

Liskov, B., Day, M., and Shirira, L. (1994). Distributed object management in thor. In Özsu et al. [1994a], pages 79–91. 577

Litwin, W. (1988). From database systems to multidatabase systems: Why and how. In *Proc. British National Conference on Databases*, pages 161–188, Cambridge. Cambridge University Press. 40

Litwin, W., Neimat, M.-A., and Schneider, D. A. (1993). LH* – linear hashing for distributed files. In *Proc. ACM SIGMOD Int. Conf. on Management of Data*, pages 327–336. 618

Liu, B., Zhu, Y., and Rundensteiner, E. (2006). Run-time operator state spilling for memory intensive long running queries. In *Proc. ACM SIGMOD Int. Conf. on Management of Data*, pages 347–358. 740

Liu, L., Pu, C., Barga, R., and Zhou, T. (1996). Differential evaluation of continual queries. In *Proc. IEEE Int. Conf. Dist. Comp. Syst*, pages 458–465. 6

Liu, L., Pu, C., and Tang, W. (1999). Continual queries for internet-scale event-driven information delivery. *IEEE Trans. Knowl. and Data Eng.*, 11(4):610–628. 736

Liu, Z. H., Chandrasekar, S., Baby, T., and Chang, H. J. (2008). Towards a physical XML independent XQuery/sql/xml engine. *Proc. VLDB*, 1(2):1356–1367. 698

Livny, M., Khoshafian, S., and Boral, H. (1987). Multi-disk management. In *Proc. ACM SIGMETRICS Conf. on Measurement and Modeling of Computer Systems*, pages 69–77. 508, 510, 548

Lohman, G. and Mackert, L. F. (1986). R* optimizer validation and performance evaluation for distributed queries. In *Proc. 11th Int. Conf. on Very Large Data Bases*, pages 149–159. 281, 293

Lohman, G., Mohan, C., Haas, L., Daniels, D., Lindsay, B., Selinger, P., and Wilms, P. (1985). Query processing in r*. In Kim et al. [1985], pages 31–47. 250, 277

Longbottom, R. (1980). *Computer System Reliability*. John Wiley & Sons. 410, 455

Lu, H. and Carey, M. J. (1985). Some experimental results on distributed join algorithms in a local network. In *Proc. 10th Int. Conf. on Very Large Data Bases*, pages 292–304. 273

Lu, H., Ooi, B., and Goh, C. (1992). On global multidatabase query optimization. *ACM SIGMOD Rec.*, 21(4):6–11. 307, 331

Lu, H., Ooi, B., and Goh, C. (1993). Multidatabase query optimization: Issues and solutions. In *Proc. 3rd Int. Workshop on Res. Issues in Data Eng*, pages 137–143. 298, 331

Lu, H., Shan, M.-C., and Tan, K.-L. (1991). Optimization of multi-way join queries for parallel execution. In *Proc. 17th Int. Conf. on Very Large Data Bases*, pages 549–560. 530

Lunt, T. F., Denning, D. E., Schell, R. R., Heckman, M., and Shockley, W. R. (1990). The SeaView security model. *IEEE Trans. Softw. Eng.*, 16(6):593–607. 184

Lunt, T. F. and Fernández, E. B. (1990). Database security. *ACM SIGMOD Rec.*, 19(4):90–97. 181, 201, 202

Lv, Q., Cao, P., Cohen, E., Li, K., and Shenker, S. (2002). Search and replication in unstructured peer-to-peer networks. In *Proc. 16th Annual Int. Conf. on Supercmputing*, pages 84–95. 617

Lynch, N. (1983a). Concurrency control for resilient nested transactions. In *Proc. 2nd ACM SIGACT–SIGMOD Symp. on Principles of Database Systems*, pages 166–181. 401

Lynch, N. (1983b). Multilevel atomicity: A new correctness criterion for database concurrency control. *ACM Trans. Database Syst.*, 8(4):484–502. 395, 401

Lynch, N. and Merritt, M. (1986). Introduction to the theory of nested transactions. Technical Report MIT/LCS/TR-367, Massachusetts Institute of Technology, Cambridge, Mass. 401

Lynch, N., Merritt, M., Weihl, W. E., and Fekete, A. (1993). *Atomic Transactions in Concurrent Distributed Systems*. Morgan Kaufmann. 359, 401

Ma, L., Viglas, S., Li, M., and Li, Q. (2005). Stream operators for querying data streams. In *Proc. 6th Int. Conf. on Web-Age Information Management:*, pages 404–415. 727

Mackert, L. F. and Lohman, G. (1986). R* optimizer validation and performance evaluation for local queries. In *Proc. ACM SIGMOD Int. Conf. on Management of Data*, pages 84–95. 264, 281, 291

Madden, S. and Franklin, M. J. (2002). Fjording the stream: An architecture for queries over streaming sensor data. In *Proc. 18th Int. Conf. on Data Engineering*, pages 555–566. 734

Madden, S., Shah, M., Hellerstein, J., and Raman, V. (2002a). Continuously adaptive continuous queries over streams. In *Proc. ACM SIGMOD Int. Conf. on Management of Data*, pages 49–60. 734, 741

Madden, S., Shah, M. A., Hellerstein, J. M., and Raman, V. (2002b). Continuously adaptive continuous queries over streams. In *Proc. ACM SIGMOD Int. Conf. on Management of Data*, pages 49–60. 320

Madhavan, J., Bernstein, P. A., and Rahm, E. (2001). Generic schema matching with cupid. In *Proc. 27th Int. Conf. on Very Large Data Bases*, pages 49–58. 134, 144, 160

Maheshwari, U. and Liskov, B. (1994). Fault-tolerant distributed garbage collection in a client-server object-oriented database. In *Proc. 3rd Int. Conf. on Parallel and Distributed Information Systems*, pages 239–248. 581

Mahmoud, . A. and Riordon, J. S. (1976). Optimal allocation of resources in distributed information networks. *ACM Trans. Database Syst.*, 1(1):66–78. 125

Maier, D. (1986). A logic for objects. Technical Report CS/E-86-012, Oregon Graduate Center. 607

Maier, D. (1989). Why isn't there an object-oriented data model? Technical Report CS/E 89-002, Oregon Graduate Center, Portland, Oregon. 553

Maier, D., Graefe, G., Shapiro, L., Daniels, S., Keller, T., and Vance, B. (1994). Issues in distributed object assembly. In Özsu et al. [1994a], pages 165–181. 592

Maier, D. and Stein, J. (1986). Indexing in an object-oriented dbms. In *Proc. Int. Workshop on Object-Oriented Database Systems*, pages 171–182. 587, 588, 589, 590

Makki, K. and Pissinou, N. (1995). Detection and resolution algorithm for deadlocks in distributed database systems. In *Proc. ACM Int. Conf. on Information and Knowledge Management*, pages 411–416. 401

Malkhi, D., Noar, M., and Ratajczak, D. (2002). Viceroy: A scalable and dynamic emulation of the butterfly. In *Proc. ACM SIGACT-SIGOPS 21st Symp. on the Principles of Distributed Computing*, pages 183–192. 621

Manber, U. and Myers, G. (1990). Suffix arrays: a new method for on-line string searches. In *Proc. 1st Annual ACM-SIAM Symp. on Discrete Algorithms*, pages 319–327. 667

Manolescu, I., Florescu, D., and Kossmann, D. (2001). Answering XML queries on heterogeneous data sources. In *Proc. 27th Int. Conf. on Very Large Data Bases*, pages 241–250. 160

Martin, B. and Pedersen, C. H. (1994). Long-lived concurrent activities. In Özsu et al. [1994a], pages 188–211. 593

Martínez, J. M., editor. MPEG-7 overview (2004). Available from: http://www.chiariglione.org/mpeg/standards/mpeg-7/mpeg-7.htm [Last retrieved: December 2009]. 690

Martins, V., Akbarinia, R., Pacitti, E., and Valduriez, P. (2006a). Reconciliation in the appa p2p system. In *IEEE Int. Conf. on Parallel and Distributed Systems (ICPADS)*, pages 401–410. 651, 654

Martins, V. and Pacitti, E. (2006). Dynamic and distributed reconciliation in p2p-dht networks. In *uropean Conf. on Parallel Computing (Euro-Par)*, pages 337–349. 651, 654

Martins, V., Pacitti, E., Dick, M. E., and Jimenez-Peris, R. (2008). Scalable and topology-aware reconciliation on p2p networks. *Distrib. Parall. Databases*, 24(1–3):1–43. 651

Martins, V., Pacitti, E., and Valduriez, P. (2006b). Survey of data replication in p2p systems. Technical Report 6083, INRIA, Rennes, France. 654

Maymounkov, P. and Mazières, D. (2002). Kademlia: A peer-to-peer information system based on the XOR metric. In *Proc. 1st Int. Workshop Peer-to-Peer Systems*, Lecture Notes in Computer Science 2429, pages 53–65. 621

McBrien, P. and Poulovassilis, A. (2003). Defining peer-to-peer data integration using both as view rules. In *Proc. 1st Int. Workshop on Databases, Information Systems and Peer-to-Peer Computing*, pages 91–107. 627

McCallum, A., Nigam, K., Rennie, J., and Seymore, K. (1999). A machine learning approach to building domain-specific search engines. In *Proc. 16th Int. Joint Conf. on AI*. 666

McCann, R., AlShebli, B., Le, Q., Nguyen, H., Vu, L., and Doan, A. (2005). Mapping maintenance for data integration systems. In *Proc. 31st Int. Conf. on Very Large Data Bases*, pages 1018–1029. 156

McConnel, S. and Siewiorek, D. P. (1982). Evaluation criteria. In Siewiorek and Swarz [1982], pages 201–302. 409

McCormick, W. T., Schweitzer, P. J., and White, T. W. (1972). Problem decomposition and data reorganization by a clustering technique. *Oper. Res.*, 20(5):993–1009. 102

Medina-Mora, R., Wong, H., and Flores, P. (1993). Action workflow as the enterprise integration technology. *Q. Bull. IEEE TC on Data Eng.*, 16(2):49–52. 354

Mehta, M. and DeWitt, D. (1995). Managing intra-operator parallelism in parallel database systems. In *Proc. 21th Int. Conf. on Very Large Data Bases*. 529, 548

Melnik, S., Garcia-Molina, H., and Rahm, E. (2002). Similarity flooding: A versatile graph matching algorithm and its application to schema matching. In *Proc. 18th Int. Conf. on Data Engineering*, pages 117–128. 134, 145, 148, 160

Melnik, S., Raghavan, S., Yang, B., and Garcia-Molina, H. (2001). Building a distributed full-text index for the web. In *Proc. 10th Int. World Wide Web Conf.*, pages 396–406. Available from: citeseer.ist.psu.edu/article/ melnik01building.html. 668

Melton, J. (2002). *Advanced SQL: 1999 - Understanding Object-Relational and Other Advanced Features*. Morgan Kaufmann. 553

Melton, J., Michels, J.-E., Josifovski, V., Kulkarni, K., Schwartz, P., and Zeidenstein, K. (2001). Sql and management of external data. *ACM SIGMOD Rec.*, 30(1):70–77. 314, 328

Menasce, D. A. and Muntz, R. R. (1979). Locking and deadlock detection in distributed databases. *IEEE Trans. Softw. Eng.*, SE-5(3):195–202. 392

Menasce, D. A. and Nakanishi, T. (1982a). Optimistic versus pessimistic concurrency control mechanisms in database management systems. *Inf. Syst.*, 7(1):13–27. 401

Menasce, D. A. and Nakanishi, T. (1982b). Performance evaluation of a two-phase commit based protocol for ddbs. In *Proc. First ACM SIGACT–SIGMOD Symp. on Principles of Database Systems*, pages 247–255. 401

Mendelzon, A. O., Mihaila, G. A., and Milo, T. (1997). Querying the World Wide Web. *Int. J. Digit. Libr.*, 1(1):54–67. 676, 677

Meng, W., Yu, C., Kim, W., Wang, G., Phan, T., and Dao, S. (1993). Construction of relational front-end for object-oriented database systems. In *Proc. 9th Int. Conf. on Data Engineering*, pages 476–483. 331

Merrett, T. H. and Rallis, N. (1985). An analytic evaluation of concurrency control algorithms. In *Proc. CIPS (Canadian Information Processing Society) Congress '85*, pages 435–439. 401

Milán-Franco, J. M., Jiménez-Peris, R., Patiño-Martínez, M., and Kemme, B. (2004). Adaptive middleware for data replication. In *Proc. ACM/IFIP/USENIX Int. Middleware Conf.*, pages 175–194. 542, 548

Miller, G. A. (1995). WordNet: A lexical database for English. *Commun. ACM*, 38(11):39–45. 142

Miller, R. J., Haas, L. M., and Hernández, M. A. (2000). Schema mapping as query discovery. In *Proc. 26th Int. Conf. on Very Large Data Bases*, pages 77–88. 150

Miller, R. J., Hernández, M. A., Haas, L. M., Yan, L., Ho, C. T. H., Fagin, R., and Popa, L. (2001). The Clio project: Managing heterogeneity. *ACM SIGMOD Rec.*, 31(1):78–83. 152

Milo, T. and Suciu, D. (1999). Index structures for path expressions. In *Proc. 7th Int. Conf. on Database Theory*, pages 277–295. 701

Milo, T. and Zohar, S. (1998). Using schema matching to simplify heterogeneous data translation. In *Proc. 24th Int. Conf. on Very Large Data Bases*, pages 122–133. 134, 160

Minoura, T. and Wiederhold, G. (1982). Resilient extended true-copy token scheme for a distributed database system. *IEEE Trans. Softw. Eng.*, SE-8(3):173–189. 456, 493

Mitchell, G., Dayal, U., and Zdonik, S. (1993). Control of an extensible query optimizer: A planning-based approach. In *Proc. 19th Int. Conf. on Very Large Data Bases*, pages 517–528. 584

Mitchell, T. (1997). *Machine Learning*. McGraw-Hill. 666

Mohan, C. (1979). Data base design in the distributed environment. Working Paper WP-7902, Department of Computer Sciences, University of Texas at Austin. 125

Mohan, C. and Lindsay, B. (1983). Efficient commit protocols for the tree of processes model of distributed transactions. In *Proc. ACM SIGACT-SIGOPS 2nd Symp. on the Principles of Distributed Computing*, pages 76–88. 434, 456

Mohan, C., Lindsay, B., and Obermarck, R. (1986). Transaction management in the r* distributed database management system. *ACM Trans. Database Syst.*, 11(4):378–396. 377, 393, 434

Mohan, C. and Yeh, R. T. (1978). *Distributed Data Base Systems: A Framework for Data Base Design. In Distributed Data Bases, Infotech State-of-the-Art Report.* Infotech. 39

Morgan, H. L. and Levin, K. D. (1977). Optimal program and data location in computer networks. *Commun. ACM*, 20(5):315–322. 125

Moss, E. (1985). *Nested Transactions*. M.I.T. Press. 351, 352, 396, 401

Motwani, R., Widom, J., Arasu, A., Babcock, B., Babu, S., Datar, M., Manku, G., Olston, C., Rosenstein, J., and Varma, R. (2003). Query processing, approximation, and resource management in a data stream management system. In *Proc. 1st Biennial Conf. on Innovative Data Systems Research*, pages 245–256. 732

Muro, S., Ibaraki, T., Miyajima, H., and Hasegawa, T. (1983). File redundancy issues in distributed database systems. In *Proc. 9th Int. Conf. on Very Data Bases*, pages 275–277. 124

Muro, S., Ibaraki, T., Miyajima, H., and Hasegawa, T. (1985). Evaluation of file redundancy in distributed database systems. *IEEE Trans. Softw. Eng.*, SE-11(2):199–205. 124

Muth, P., Rakow, T., Weikum, G., Brössler, P., and Hasse, C. (1993). Semantic concurrency control in object-oriented database systems. In *Proc. 9th Int. Conf. on Data Engineering*, pages 233–242. 604, 605

Myers, G. J. (1976). *Software Reliability: Principles and Practices*. John Wiley & Sons. 455

Naacke, H., Tomasic, A., and Valduriez, P. (1999). Validating mediator cost models with DISCO. *Networking and Information Systems Journal*, 2(5):639–663. 307, 310, 331

Najork, M. and Wiener, J. L. (2001). Breadth-first crawling yields high-quality pages. In *Proc. 10th Int. World Wide Web Conf.*, pages 114–118. 665

Naumann, F., Ho, C.-T., Tian, X., Haas, L. M., and Megiddo, N. (2002). Attribute classification using feature analysis. In *Proc. 18th Int. Conf. on Data Engineering*, page 271. 146

Navathe, S. B., Ceri, S., Wiederhold, G., and Dou, J. (1984). Vertical partitioning of algorithms for database design. *ACM Trans. Database Syst.*, 9(4):680–710. 98, 99, 102, 109, 125

NBS (1977). Data encryption standard. Technical Report 46, U. S. Department of Commerce/National Bureau of Standards, Federal Information Processing Standards Publication. 180

Nejdl, W., Siberski, W., and Sintek, M. (2003). Design issues and challenges for rdf- and schema-based peer-to-peer systems. *ACM SIGMOD Rec.*, 32(3):41–46. 624, 628

Nepal, S. and Ramakrishna, M. (1999). Query processing issues in image (multimedia) databases. In *Proc. 15th Int. Conf. on Data Engineering*, pages 22–29. 629, 654

Newton, G. (1979). Deadlock prevention, detection and resolution: An annotated bibliography. *Operating Systems Rev.*, 13(2):33–44. 401

Ng, P. (1988). A commit protocol for checkpointing transactions. In *Proc. 7th. Symp. on Reliable Distributed Systems*, pages 22–31. 456

Niamir, B. (1978). Attribute partitioning in a self–adaptive relational database system. Technical Report 192, Laboratory for Computer Science, Massachusetts Institute of Technology, Cambridge, Mass. 98, 125

Nicola, M. and der Linden, B. V. (2005). Native XML support in db2 universal database. In *Proc. 31st Int. Conf. on Very Large Data Bases*, pages 1164–1174. 699

Nicolas, J. M. (1982). Logic for improving integrity checking in relational data bases. *Acta Informatica*, 18:227–253. 192, 202

Nodine, M. and Zdonik, S. (1990). Cooperative transaction hierarchies: A transaction model to support design applications. In *Proc. 16th Int. Conf. on Very Large Data Bases*, pages 83–94. 354

OASIS UDDI. Universal description discovery & integration (UDDI) (2002). Available from: http://uddi.xml.org/ [Last retrieved: December 2009]. 690

Obermarck, R. (1982). Deadlock detection for all resource classes. *ACM Trans. Database Syst.*, 7(2):187–208. 39, 393, 401

Omiecinski, E. (1991). Performance analysis of a load balancing hash-join algorithm for a shared-memory multiprocessor. In *Proc. 17th Int. Conf. on Very Large Data Bases*, pages 375–385. 528, 548

Ooi, B., Shu, Y., and Tan, K.-L. (2003a). Relational data sharing in peer-based data management systems. *ACM SIGMOD Rec.*, 32(3):59–64. 627

Ooi, B. C., Shu, Y., and Tan, K.-L. (2003b). Db-enabled peers for managing distributed data. In *Proc. 5th Asian-Pacific Web Conference*, pages 10–21. 612

Ordonez, C. (2003). Clustering binary data streams with k-means. In *Proc. ACM SIGMOD Workshop on Research Issues in Data Mining and Knowledge Discovery*. 743

Orenstein, J., Haradvala, S., Margulies, B., and Sakahara, D. (1992). Query processing in the objectstore database system. In *ACM SIGMOD Int. Conf. on Management of Data*, pages 403–412. 586

Orfali, R., Harkey, D., and Edwards, J. (1996). *The Essential Distributed Objects Survival Guide*. John Wiley & Sons. 607

Osborn, S. L. and Heaven, T. E. (1986). The design of a relational database system with abstract data types for domains. *ACM Trans. Database Syst.*, 11(3):357–373. 557

Osterhaug, A. (1989). *Guide to Parallel Programming on Sequent Computer Systems*. Prentice-Hall. 498

O'Toole, J., Nettles, S., and Gifford, D. (1993). Concurrent compacting garbage collection of a persistent heap. In *Proc. 14th ACM Symp. Operating Syst. Principles*, pages 161–174. 581

Ou, Z., Yu, G., Yu, Y., Wu, S., Yang, X., and Deng, Q. (2005). Tick scheduling: A deadline based optimal task scheduling approach for real-time data stream systems. In *Proc. 6th Int. Conf. on Web-Age Information Management:*, pages 725–730. 735

Ouksel, A. M. and Sheth, A. P. (1999). Semantic interoperability in global information systems: A brief introduction to the research area and the special section. *ACM SIGMOD Rec.*, 28(1):5–12. 160

Özsoyoglu, Z. M. and Zhou, N. (1987). Distributed query processing in broadcasting local area networks. In *Proc. 20th Hawaii Int. Conf. on System Sciences*, pages 419–429. 214, 215

Özsu, M. and Barker, K. (1990). Architectural classification and transaction execution models of multidatabase systems. In *Proc. Int. Conf. on Computing and Information*, pages 275–279. 40

Özsu, M., Dayal, U., and Valduriez, P., editors (1994a). *Distributed Object Management*. Morgan Kaufmann, San Mateo, Calif. 607, 784, 785, 787, 789, 793, 800, 801, 807, 809, 814

Özsu, M., Peters, R., Szafron, D., Irani, B., Munoz, A., and Lipka, A. (1995a). Tigukat: A uniform behavioral objectbase management system. *VLDB J.*, 4:445–492. 555, 606

Özsu, M. T. (1985a). Modeling and analysis of distributed concurrency control algorithms using an extended petri net formalism. *IEEE Trans. Softw. Eng.*, SE-11(10):1225–1240. 401

Özsu, M. T. (1985b). Performance comparison of distributed vs centralized locking algorithms in distributed database systems. In *Proc. 5th Int. Conf. on Distributed Computing Systems*, pages 254–261. 401

Özsu, M. T. (1994). Transaction models and transaction management in OODBMSs. In Dogac et al. [1994], pages 275–279. 359, 607

Özsu, M. T. and Blakeley, J. (1994). Query processing in object-oriented database systems. In Kim, W., editor, *Modern Database Management – Object-Oriented and Multidatabase Technologies*, pages 146–174. Addison-Wesley/ACM Press. 582, 607

Özsu, M. T., Dayal, U., and Valduriez, P. (1994b). An introduction to distributed object management. In Özsu et al. [1994a], pages 1–24. 551

Özsu, M. T., Munoz, A., and Szafron, D. (1995b). An extensible query optimizer for an objectbase management system. In *Proc. 4th Int. Conf. on Information and Knowledge Management*, pages 188–196. 584

Özsu, M. T. and Valduriez, P. (1991). Distributed database systems: Where are we now? *Comp.*, 24(8):68–78. 38

Özsu, M. T. and Valduriez, P. (1994). Distributed data management: Unsolved problems and new issues. In Casavant, T. and Singhal, M., editors, *Readings in Distributed Computing Systems*, pages 512–544. IEEE/CS Press. 38

Özsu, M. T. and Valduriez, P. (1997). Distributed and parallel database systems. In Tucker, A., editor, *Handbook of Computer Science and Engineering*, pages 1093–1111. CRC Press. 38

Özsu, M. T., Voruganti, K., and Unrau, R. (1998). An asynchronous avoidance-based cache consistency algorithm for client caching dbmss. In *Proc. 24th Int. Conf. on Very Large Data Bases*, pages 440–451. 573

Pacitti, E., Coulon, C., Valduriez, P., and Özsu, M. T. (2006). Preventive replication in a database cluster. *Distrib. Parall. Databases*, 18(3):223–251. 537, 539, 540, 548

Pacitti, E., Minet, P., and Simon, E. (1999). Fast algorithms for maintaining replica consistency in lazy master replicated databases. In *Proc. 25th Int. Conf. on Very Large Data Bases*, pages 126–137. 463, 482, 484, 537

Pacitti, E., Özsu, M. T., and Coulon, C. (2003). Preventive multi-master replication in a cluster of autonomous databases. In *Proc. 9th Int. Euro-Par Conf.*, pages 318–327. 537, 548

Pacitti, E. and Simon, E. (2000). Update propagation strategies to improve freshness in lazy master replicated databases. *VLDB J.*, 8(3-4):305–318. 462, 493, 537

Pacitti, E., Simon, E., and de Melo, R. (1998). Improving data freshness in lazy master schemes. In *Proc. 18th Int. Conf. on Distributed Computing Systems*, pages 164–171. 463, 493

Pacitti, E., Valduriez, P., and Mattoso, M. (2007a). Grid data management: open problems and new issues. *Journal of Grid Computing*, 5(3):273–281. 654

Pacitti, E., Valduriez, P., and Mattoso, M. (2007b). Grid data management: Open problems and new issues. *J. Grid Comp.*, 5(3):273–281. 750, 763

Page, L., Brin, S., Motwani, R., and Winograd, T. (1998). The pagerank citation ranking: Bringing order to the web. Technical report, Stanford University. 665

Page, T. W. and Popek, G. J. (1985). Distributed data management in local area networks. In *Proc. ACM SIGACT–SIGMOD Symp. on Principles of Database Systems*, pages 135–142. 210, 250

Pal, S., Cseri, I., Seeliger, O., Rys, M., Schaller, G., Yu, W., Tomic, D., Baras, A., Berg, B., Churin, D., and Kogan, E. (2005). Xquery implementation in a relational database system. In *Proc. 31st Int. Conf. on Very Large Data Bases*, pages 1175–1186. 699

Palma, W., Akbarinia, R., Pacitti, E., and Valduriez, P. (2009). Dhtjoin: processing continuous join queries using dht networks. *Distrib. Parall. Databases*, 26(2–3):291–317. 732

Palopoli, L., Saccà, D., Terracina, G., and Ursino, D. (1999). A unified graph-based framework for deriving nominal interscheme properties, type conflicts and object cluster similarities. In *Proc. Int. Conf. on Cooperative Information Systems*, pages 34–45. 134, 142, 160

Palopoli, L., Saccà, D., Terracina, G., and Ursino, D. (2003a). Uniform techniques for deriving similarities of objects and subschemes in heterogeneous databases. *IEEE Trans. Knowl. and Data Eng.*, 15(2):271–294. 145, 160

Palopoli, L., Saccà, D., and Ursino, D. (1998). Semi-automatic semantic discovery of properties from database schemas. In *Proc. Int. Conf. on Database Eng. and Applications*, pages 244–253. 134, 145, 160

Palopoli, L., Terracina, G., and Ursino, D. (2003b). Experiences using DIKE, a system for supporting cooperative information system and data warehouse design. *Inf. Syst.*, 28:835–865. 134, 160

Palpanas, T., Vlachos, M., Keogh, E., Gunopulos, D., and Truppel, W. (2004). Online amnesic approximation of streaming time series. In *Proc. 20th Int. Conf. on Data Engineering*, pages 338–349. 726

Pandey, S., Ramamritham, K., and Chakrabarti, S. (2003). Monitoring the dynamic web to respond to continuous queries. In *Proc. 12th Int. World Wide Web Conf.* 6

Papadimitriou, C. H. (1979). Serializability of concurrent database updates. *J. ACM*, 26(4):631–653. 350

Papadimitriou, C. H. (1986). *The Theory of Concurrency Control*. Computer Science Press. 401

Papakonstantinou, Y., Garcia-Molina, H., and Widom, J. (1995). Object exchange across heterogeneous information sources. In *Proc. 11th Int. Conf. on Data Engineering*, pages 251–260. 671, 673

Pape, C. L., Gançarski, S., and Valduriez, P. (2004). Refresco: Improving query performance through freshness control in a database cluster. In *Proc. Confederated Int. Conf. DOA, CoopIS and ODBASE*, Lecture Notes in Computer Science 3290, pages 174–193. 493, 540, 548

Paris, J. F. (1986). Voting with witnesses: A consistency scheme for replicated files. In *Proc. 6th Int. Conf. on Distributed Computing Systems*, pages 606–612. 493

Park, Y., Scheuermann, P., and Tang, H. (1995). A distributed deadlock detection and resolution algorithm based on a hybrid wait-for graph and probe generation scheme. In *Proc. ACM Int. Conf. Information and Knowledge Management*, pages 378–86. 401

Passerini, A., Frasconi, P., and Soda, G. (2001). Evaluation methods for focused crawling. In *Proc. 7th Congress of the Italian Association for Artificial Intelligence*, pages 33–39. 666

Patiño-Martínez, M., Jiménez-Peris, R., Kemme, B., and Alonso, G. (2005). MIDDLE-R: Consistent database replication at the middleware level. *ACM Trans. Comp. Syst.*, 23(4):375–423. 491

Patiño-Martínez, M., Jiménez-Peris, R., Kemme, B., and Alonso, G. (2000). Scalable replication in database clusters. In *Proc. 14th Int. Symp. on Distributed Computing*, pages 315–329. 482, 489, 548

Pavlo, A., Paulson, E., Rasin, A., Abadi, D. J., DeWitt, D. J., Madden, S., and Stonebraker, M. (2009). A comparison of approaches to large-scale data analysis. In *Proc. ACM SIGMOD Int. Conf. on Management of Data*, pages 165–178. 760

Paxson, V. and Floyd, S. (1995). Wide-area traffic: The failure of poisson modeling. *IEEE/ACM Trans. Networking*, 3(3):226–244. 727

Pease, M., Shostak, R., and Lamport, L. (1980). Reaching agreement in the presence of faults. *J. ACM*, 27(2):228–234. 456

Pedone, F. and Schiper, A. (1998). Optimistic atomic broadcast. In *Proc. 12th Int. Symp. on Distributed Computing*, pages 318–332. 539

Perez-Sorrosal, F., Vuckovic, J., Patiño-Martínez, M., and Jiménez-Peris, R. (2006). Highly available long running transactions and activities for J2EE. In *Proc. 26th Int. Conf. on Distributed Computing Systems*, page 2. 546, 548

Peters, R. J., Lipka, A., Özsu, M. T., and Szafron, D. (1993). An extensible query model and its languages for a uniform behavioral object management system. In *Proc. 2nd International Conference on Information and Knowledge Management*, pages 403–412. 584

Piatetsky-Shapiro, G. and Connell, C. (1984). Accurate estimation of the number of tuples satisfying a condition. In *Proc. ACM SIGMOD Int. Conf. on Management of Data*, pages 256–276. 252

Pinedo, M. (2001). *Scheduling: Theory, Algorithms and Systems*. Integre Technical Publishing, 2 edition. 537

Pirahesh, H., Mohan, C., Cheng, J. M., Liu, T. S., and Selinger, P. G. (1990). Parallelism in rdbms : Architectural issues and design. In *Proc. 2nd Int. Symp. on Databases in Distributed and Parallel Systems*, pages 4–29. 532, 533, 548

Plainfossé, D. and Shapiro, M. (1995). A survey of distributed garbage collection techniques. In *Proc. Int. Workshop on Memory Management*, pages 211–249. 581

Plattner, C. and Alonso, G. (2004). Ganymed: Scalable replication for transactional web applications. In *Proc. ACM/IFIP/USENIX Int. Middleware Conf.*, pages 155–174. 464

Plaxton, C., Rajaraman, R., and Richa, A. (1997). Accessing nearby copies of replicated objects in a distributed environment. In *ACM Symp. on Parallel Algorithms and Architectures (SPAA)*, pages 311–320. 646

Polyzotis, N. and Garofalakis, M. N. (2002). Statistical synopses for graph-structured XML databases. In *Proc. ACM SIGMOD Int. Conf. on Management of Data*, pages 358–369. 701

Polyzotis, N., Garofalakis, M. N., and Ioannidis, Y. E. (2004). Approximate XML query answers. In *Proc. ACM SIGMOD Int. Conf. on Management of Data*, pages 263–274. 701

Polyzotis, N., Skiadopoulos, S., Vassiliadis, P., Simitsis, A., and Frantzell, N.-E. (2008). Meshing streaming updates with persistent data in an active data warehouse. *IEEE Trans. Knowl. and Data Eng.*, 20(7):976–991. 761

Poosala, V., Ioannidis, Y., Haas, P., and Shekita, E. (1996). Improved histograms for selectivity estimation of range predicates. In *Proc. ACM SIGMOD Int. Conf. on Management of Data*, pages 294–305. 256

Popa, L., Velegrakis, Y., Miller, R. J., Hernandez, M. A., and Fagin, R. (2002). Translating web data. In *Proc. 28th Int. Conf. on Very Large Data Bases*. 155

Porto, F., Laber, E. S., and Valduriez, P. (2003). Cherry picking: A semantic query processing strategy for the evaluation of expensive predicates. In *Proc. Brazilian Symposium on Databases*, pages 356–370. 320, 326, 331

Potier, D. and LeBlanc, P. (1980). Analysis of locking policies in database management systems. *Commun. ACM*, 23(10):584–593. 401

Pottinger, R. and Levy, A. Y. (2000). A scalable algorithm for answering queries using views. In *Proc. 26th Int. Conf. on Very Large Data Bases*, pages 484–495. 305, 331

Pradhan, D. K., editor (1986). *Fault-Tolerant Computing: Theory and Techniques*, volume 2. Prentice-Hall. 455

Pu, C. (1988). Superdatabases for composition of heterogeneous databases. In *Proc. 4th Int. Conf. on Data Engineering*, pages 548–555. 147, 352

Pu, C. and Leff, A. (1991). Replica control in distributed systems: An asynchronous approach. In *Proc. ACM SIGMOD Int. Conf. on Management of Data*, pages 377–386. 462

Pugh, W. (1989). Skip lists: A probabilistic alternative to balanced trees. In *Proc. Workshop on Algorithms and Data Structures*, pages 437–449. 622

Qiao, L., Agrawal, D., and Abbadi, A. E. (2003). Supporting sliding window queries for continuous data streams. In *Proc. 15th Int. Conf. on Scientific and Statistical Database Management*, pages 85–94. 737

Raghavan, S. and Garcia-Molina, H. (2001). Crawling the hidden web. In *Proc. 27th Int. Conf. on Very Large Data Bases*, pages 129–138. 657, 686

Raghavan, S. and Garcia-Molina, H. (2003). Representing web graphs. In *Proc. 19th Int. Conf. on Data Engineering*, pages 405–416. 658, 661, 662, 663

Rahal, A., Zhu, Q., and Larson, P.-Å. (2004). Evolutionary techniques for updating query cost models in a dynamic multidatabase environment. *VLDB J.*, 13(2):162–176. 307, 313, 331

Rahimi, S. (1987). Reference architecture for distributed database management systems. In *Proc. 3th Int. Conf. on Data Engineering*. Tutorial Notes. 40

Rahm, E. and Bernstein, P. A. (2001). A survey of approaches to automatic schema matching. *VLDB J.*, 10(4):334–350. 138, 139, 143, 146, 160

Rahm, E. and Do, H. H. (2000). Data cleaning: Problems and current approaches. *Q. Bull. IEEE TC on Data Eng.*, 23(4):3–13. 157

Rahm, E. and Marek, R. (1995). Dynamic multi-resource load balancing in parallel database systems. In *Proc. 21th Int. Conf. on Very Large Data Bases*, pages 395–406. 530, 548

Ramabhadran, S., Ratnasamy, S., Hellerstein, J. M., and Shenker, S. (2004). Brief announcement: prefix hash tree. In *Proc. ACM SIGACT-SIGOPS 23rd Symp. on the Principles of Distributed Computing*, page 368. 622, 643

Ramakrishnan, R. (2009). Data management in the cloud. In *Proc. 25th Int. Conf. on Data Engineering*, page 5. 753, 763

Ramakrishnan, R. and Gehrke, J. (2003). *Database Management Systems*. McGraw-Hill, 3 edition. 70, 189, 201

Ramamoorthy, C. V. and Wah, B. W. (1983). The isomorphism of simple file allocation. *IEEE Trans. Comput.*, C-23(3):221–231. 121

Ramamritham, K. and Pu, C. (1995). A formal characterization of epsilon serializability. *IEEE Trans. Knowl. and Data Eng.*, 7(6):997–1007. 401, 462

Raman, V., Deshpande, A., and Hellerstein, J. M. (2003). Using state modules for adaptive query processing. In *Proc. 19th Int. Conf. on Data Engineering*, pages 353–365. 331

Raman, V. and Hellerstein, J. M. (2001). Potter's wheel: An interactive data cleaning system. In *Proc. 27th Int. Conf. on Very Large Data Bases*, pages 381–390. 158

Ramanathan, P. and Shin, K. G. (1988). Checkpointing and rollback recovery in a distributed system using common time base. In *Proc. 7th Symp. on Reliable Distributed Systems*, pages 13–21. 456

Randell, B., Lee, P. A., and Treleaven, P. C. (1978). Reliability issues in computing system design. *ACM Comput. Surv.*, 10(2):123–165. 406, 455

Rao, P. and Moon, B. (2004). Prix: Indexing and querying XML using prüfer sequences. In *Proc. 20th Int. Conf. on Data Engineering*, pages 288–300. 701

Ratnasamy, S., Francis, P., Handley, M., and Karp, R. (2001a). A scalable content-addressable network. In *Proc. ACM Int. Conf. on Data Communication*, pages 161–172. 620, 646

Ratnasamy, S., Francis, P., Handley, M., Karp, R. M., and Shenker, S. (2001b). A scalable content-addressable network. In *Proc. ACM Int. Conf. on Data Communication*, pages 161–172. 618

Ray, I., Mancini, L. V., Jajodia, S., and Bertino, E. (2000). Asep: A secure and flexible commit protocol for mls distributed database systems. *IEEE Trans. Knowl. and Data Eng.*, 12(6):880–899. 187, 202

Reiss, F. and Hellerstein, J. (2005). Data triage: an adaptive architecture for load shedding in telegraphCQ. In *Proc. 21st Int. Conf. on Data Engineering*, pages 155–156. 740

Ribeiro-Neto, B. A. and Barbosa, R. A. (1998). Query performance for tightly coupled distributed digital libraries. In *Proc. 3rd ACM Int. Conf. on Digital Libraries*, pages 182–190. 668

Ritter, J. Why Gnutella can't scale, no, really (2001). Available from: http://www.darkridge.com/~jpr5/doc/gnutella.html [Last retrieved: December 2009]. 618

Rivera-Vega, P., Varadarajan, R., and Navathe, S. B. (1990). Scheduling data redistribution in distributed databases. In *Proc. Int. Conf. on Data Eng*, pages 166–173. 124

Rivest, R. L., Shamir, A., and Adelman, L. (1978). A method for obtaining digital signatures and public-key cryptosystems. *Commun. ACM*, 21(2):120–126. 180

Rjaibi, W. (2004). An introduction to multilevel secure relational database management systems. In *Proc. Conf. of the IBM Centre for Advanced Studies on Collaborative Research*, pages 232–241. 187, 202

Röhm, U., Böhm, K., and Schek, H.-J. (2000). Olap query routing and physical design in a database cluster. In *Advances in Database Technology, Proc. 7th Int. Conf. on Extending Database Technology*, pages 254–268. 535, 544, 548

Röhm, U., Böhm, K., and Schek, H.-J. (2001). Cache-aware query routing in a cluster of databases. In *Proc. 17th Int. Conf. on Data Engineering*, pages 641–650. 535

Röhm, U., Böhm, K., Schek, H.-J., and Schuldt, H. (2002a). Fas - a freshness-sensitive coordination cocoon for a cluster of olap components. In *Proc. 28th Int. Conf. on Very Large Data Bases*, pages 754–765. 493

Röhm, U., Böhm, K., Schek, H.-J., and Schuldt, H. (2002b). FAS - A freshness-sensitive coordination middleware for a cluster of olap components. In *Proc. 28th Int. Conf. on Very Large Data Bases*, pages 754–765. 462, 541

Roitman, H. and Gal, A. (2006). Ontobuilder: Fully automatic extraction and consolidation of ontologies from web sources using sequence semantics. In *EDBT Workshops*, volume 4254 of *LNCS*, pages 573–576. 152

Rosenkrantz, D. J. and Hunt, H. B. (1980). Processing conjunctive predicates and queries. In *Proc. 6th Int. Conf. on Very Data Bases*, pages 64–72. 224, 241

Rosenkrantz, D. J., Stearns, R. E., and Lewis, P. M. (1978). System level concurrency control for distributed database systems. *ACM Trans. Database Syst.*, 3(2):178–198. 390

Roth, J. P., Bouricius, W. G., Carter, E. C., and Schneider, P. R. (1967). Phase ii of an architectural study for a self-repairing computer. Report SAMSO-TR-67-106, U. S. Air Force Space and Missile Division, El Segundo, Calif. Cited in [Siewiorek and Swarz, 1982]. 410

Roth, M. and Schwartz, P. (1997). Don't scrap it, wrap it! a wrapper architecture for legacy data sources. In *Proc. 23th Int. Conf. on Very Large Data Bases*, pages 266–275. 327

Roth, M. T., Ozcan, F., and Haas, L. M. (1999). Cost models do matter: Providing cost information for diverse data sources in a federated system. In *Proc. 25th Int. Conf. on Very Large Data Bases*, pages 599–610. 307, 310, 331

Rothermel, K. and Mohan, C. (1989). Aries/nt: A recovery method based on write-ahead logging for nested transactions. In *Proc. 15th Int. Conf. on Very Large Data Bases*, pages 337–346. 401

Rothnie, J. B. and Goodman, N. (1977). A survey of research and development in distributed database management. In *Proc. 3rd Int. Conf. on Very Data Bases*, pages 48–62. 116

Rowstron, A. I. T. and Druschel, P. (2001). Pastry: Scalable, decentralized object location, and routing for large-scale peer-to-peer systems. In *Proc. IFIP/ACM Int. Conf. on Distributed Systems Platforms*, pages 329–350. 621

Ryvkina, E., Maskey, A., Adams, I., Sandler, B., Fuchs, C., Cherniack, M., and Zdonik, S. (2006). Revision processing in a stream processing engine: A high-level design. In *Proc. 22nd Int. Conf. on Data Engineering*, page 141. 725

Sacca, D. and Wiederhold, G. (1985). Database partitioning in a cluster of processors. *ACM Trans. Database Syst.*, 10(1):29–56. 99, 115, 125

Sacco, M. S. and Yao, S. B. (1982). Query optimization in distributed data base systems. In Yovits, M., editor, *Advances in Computers*, volume 21, pages 225–273. Academic Press. 39, 209, 211, 220

Saito, Y. and Shapiro, M. (2005). Optimistic replication. *ACM Comput. Surv.*, 37(1):42–81. 462, 466, 493

Salton, G. (1989). *Automatic Text Processing – The Transformation, Analysis, and Retrieval of Information by Computer*. Addison–Wesley. 667

Schlageter, G. and Dadam, P. (1980). Reconstruction of consistent global states in distributed databases. In Delobel, C. and Litwin, W., editors, *Distributed Data Bases*, pages 191–200. North-Holland. 456

Schlichting, R. D. and Schneider, F. B. (1983). Fail–stop processors: An approach to designing fault–tolerant computing systems. *ACM Trans. Comp. Syst.*, 1(3):222–238. 455

Schmidt, C. and Parashar, M. (2004). Enabling flexible queries with guarantees in p2p systems. *IEEE Internet Computing*, 8(3):19–26. 622

Schmidt, S., Berthold, H., and Legler, T. (2004). QStream: Deterministic querying of data streams. In *Proc. 30th Int. Conf. on Very Large Data Bases*, pages 1365–1368. 738

Schmidt, S., Legler, T., Schar, S., and Lehner, W. (2005). Robust real-time query processing with QStream. In *Proc. 31st Int. Conf. on Very Large Data Bases*, pages 1299–1301. 738

Schreiber, F. (1977). A framework for distributed database systems. In *Proc. Int. Computing Symposium*, pages 475–482. 39

Selinger, P. G. and Adiba, M. (1980). Access path selection in distributed data base management systems. In *Proc. First Int. Conf. on Data Bases*, pages 204–215. 250, 254, 277, 292, 293

Selinger, P. G., Astrahan, M. M., Chamberlin, D. D., Lorie, R. A., and Price, T. G. (1979). Access path selection in a relational database management system. In

Proc. ACM SIGMOD Int. Conf. on Management of Data, pages 23–34. 212, 253, 261, 292, 586

Serrano, D., Patiño-Martínez, M., Jiménez-Peris, R., and Kemme, B. (2007). Boosting database replication scalability through partial replication and 1-copy-snapshot-isolation. In *Proc. 13th IEEE Pacific Rim Int. Symp. on Dependable Computing*, pages 290–297. 491

Sevcik, K. C. (1983). Comparison of concurrency control methods using analytic models. In *Information Processing '83*, pages 847–858. 401

Severence, D. G. and Lohman, G. M. (1976). Differential files: Their application to the maintenance of large databases. *ACM Trans. Database Syst.*, 1(3):256–261. 419

Shafer, J. C., Agrawal, R., and Mehta, M. (1996). Sprint: A scalable parallel classifier for data mining. In *Proc. 22th Int. Conf. on Very Large Data Bases*, pages 544–555. 743

Shah, M. A., Hellerstein, J. M., Chandrasekaran, S., and Franklin, M. J. (2003). Flux: An adaptive partitioning operator for continuous query systems. In *Proc. 19th Int. Conf. on Data Engineering*, pages 25–36. 320, 321, 322, 331

Shapiro, L. (1986). oin processing in database systems with large main memories. *ACM Trans. Database Syst.*, 11(3):239–264. 587

Sharaf, M., Labrinidis, A., Chrysanthis, P., and Pruhs, K. (2005). Freshness-aware scheduling of continuous queries in the dynamic web. In *Proc. 8th Int. Workshop on the World Wide Web and Databases*, pages 73–78. 735

Sharp, J. (1987). *An Introduction to Distributed and Parallel Processing*. Blackwell Scientific Publications. 498

Shasha, D. and Wang, T.-L. (1991). Optimizing equijoin queries in distributed databases where relations are hash partitioned. *ACM Trans. Database Syst.*, 16(2):279–308. 292

Shatdal, A. and Naughton, J. F. (1993). Using shared virtual memory for parallel join processing. In *Proc. ACM SIGMOD Int. Conf. on Management of Data*, pages 119–128. 534, 548

Shekita, E. J. and Carey, M. J. (1990). A performance evaluation of pointer-based joins. In *Proc. ACM SIGMOD Int. Conf. on Management of Data*, pages 300–311. 590

Shekita, E. J., Young, H. C., and Tan, K. L. (1993). Multi-join optimization for symmetric multiprocessor. In *Proc. 19th Int. Conf. on Very Large Data Bases*, pages 479–492. 530, 548

Sheth, A. and Larson, J. (1990). Federated databases: Architectures and integration. *ACM Comput. Surv.*, 22(3):183–236. 40, 135, 160, 298

Sheth, A., Larson, J., Cornellio, A., and Navathe, S. B. (1988a). A tool for integrating conceptual schemas and user views. In *Proc. 4th Int. Conf. on Data Engineering*, pages 176–183. 147, 202

Sheth, A., Larson, J., and Watkins, E. (1988b). Tailor, a tool for updating views. In *Advances in Database Technology, Proc. 1st Int. Conf. on Extending Database Technology*, pages 190–213. Springer. 202

Sheth, A. P. and Kashyap, V. (1992). So far (schematically) yet so near (semantically). In *Proc. IFIP WG 2.6 Database Semantics Conf. on Interoperable Database Systems*, pages 283–312. 141

Shivakumar, N. and García-Molina, H. (1997). Wave-indices: indexing evolving databases. In *Proc. ACM SIGMOD Int. Conf. on Management of Data*, pages 381–392. 738

Shrivastava, S. K., editor (1985). *Reliable Computer Systems*. Springer. 455, 768

Sidell, J., Aoki, P. M., Sah, A., Staelin, C., Stonebraker, M., and Yu, A. (1996). Data replication in mariposa. In *Proc. 12th Int. Conf. on Data Eng*, pages 485–494. 456, 493

Siegel, J., editor (1996). *CORBA Fundamentals and Programming*. John Wiley & Sons. 607

Siewiorek, D. P. and Swarz, R. S., editors (1982). *The Theory and Practice of Reliable System Design*. Digital Press. 407, 409, 455, 810

Silberschatz, A., Korth, H., and Sudarshan, S. (2002). *Database System Concepts*. McGraw-Hill, 4 edition. 70

Simon, E. and Valduriez, P. (1984). Design and implementation of an extendible integrity subsystem. In *Proc. ACM SIGMOD Int. Conf. on Management of Data*, pages 9–17. 193, 202

Simon, E. and Valduriez, P. (1986). Integrity control in distributed database systems. In *Proc. 19th Hawaii Int. Conf. on System Sciences*, pages 622–632. 192, 202

Simon, E. and Valduriez, P. (1987). Design and analysis of a relational integrity subsystem. Technical Report DB-015-87, Microelectronics and Computer Corporation, Austin, Tex. 189, 192, 202

Singhal, M. (1989). Deadlock detection in distributed systems. *Comp.*, 22(11):37–48. 401

Sinha, M. K., Nanadikar, P. D., and Mehndiratta, S. L. (1985). Timestamp based certification schemes for transactions in distributed database systems. In *Proc. ACM SIGMOD Int. Conf. on Management of Data*, pages 402–411. 385

Skarra, A. (1989). oncurrency control for cooperating transactions in an object-oriented database. In *Proc. ACM SIGPLAN Workshop on Object-Based Concurrent Programming*, pages 145–147. 401

Skarra, A., Zdonik, S., and Reiss, S. (1986). An object server for an object-oriented database system. In *Proc. of the 1st Int. Workshop on Object-Oriented Database Systems*, pages 196–204. 401

Skeen, D. (1981). Nonblocking commit protocols. In *ACM SIGMOD Int. Conf. on Management of Data*, pages 133–142. 440, 443, 447, 456

Skeen, D. (1982a). *Crash Recovery in a Distributed Database Management System*. Ph.D. thesis, Department of Electrical Engineering and Computer Science, University of California at Berkeley, Berkeley, Calif. 456

Skeen, D. (1982b). A quorum-based commit protocol. In *Proc. 6th Berkeley Workshop on Distributed Data Management and Computer Networks*, pages 69–80. 448, 450

Skeen, D. and Stonebraker, M. (1983). A formal model of crash recovery in a distributed system. *IEEE Trans. Softw. Eng.*, SE-9(3):219–228. 437, 443, 449, 456

Skeen, D. and Wright, D. (1984). Increasing availability in partitioned networks. In *Proc. 3rd ACM SIGACT–SIGMOD Symp. on Principles of Database Systems*, pages 290–299. 456, 493

Smith, J. M. and Chang, P. Y. (1975). Optimizing the performance of a relational algebra database interface. *Commun. ACM*, 18(10):568–579. 228, 241

Somani, A., Choy, D., and Kleewein, J. C. (2002). Bringing together content and data management systems: Challenges and opportunities. *IBM Systems J.*, 41(4):686–696. 159

Sousa, A., Oliveira, R., Moura, F., and Pedone, F. (2001). Partial replication in the database state machine. In *Proc. IEEE Int. Symp. Network Computing and Applications*, pages 298–309. 491, 548

Srivastava, U. and Widom, J. (2004). Memory-limited execution of windowed stream joins. In *Proc. 30th Int. Conf. on Very Large Data Bases*, pages 324–335. 740

Stallings, W. (2011). *Data and Computer Communications*. Prentice-Hall, 9 edition. 70

Stanoi, I., Agrawal, D., and El-Abbadi, A. (1998). Using broadcast primitives in replicated databases. In *Proc. 8th Int. Conf. on Distributed Computing Systems*, pages 148–155. 482

Stearns, R. E., II, P. M. L., and Rosenkrantz, D. J. (1976). Concurrency controls for database systems. In *Proc. 17th Symp. on Foundations of Computer Science*, pages 19–32. 350

Stöhr, T., Märtens, H., and Rahm, E. (2000). Multi-dimensional database allocation for parallel data warehouses. In *Proc. 26th Int. Conf. on Very Large Data Bases*, pages 273–284. 542

Stoica, I., Morris, R., Karger, D. R., Kaashoek, M. F., and Balakrishnan, H. (2001a). Chord: A scalable peer-to-peer lookup service for internet applications. In *Proc. ACM Int. Conf. on Data Communication*, pages 149–160. 618

Stoica, I., Morris, R., Liben-Nowell, D., Karger, D., Kaashoek, M., Dabek, F., and Balakrishnan, H. (2001b). Chord: A scalable peer-to-peer lookup protocol for internet applications. In *Proc. ACM Int. Conf. on Data Communication*, pages 149–160. 621

Stonebraker, M. (1975). Implementation of integrity constraints and views by query modification. In *Proc. ACM SIGMOD Int. Conf. on Management of Data*, pages 65–78. 172, 173, 186, 191, 192, 201, 202

Stonebraker, M. (1981). Operating system support for database management. *Commun. ACM*, 24(7):412–418. 39, 415

Stonebraker, M. (1986). The case for shared nothing. *Q. Bull. IEEE TC on Data Eng.*, 9(1):4–9. 547

Stonebraker, M. (2010). SQL databases v. NoSQL databases. *Commun. ACM*, 53(4):10–11. 753

Stonebraker, M., Abadi, D. J., DeWitt, D. J., Madden, S., Paulson, E., Pavlo, A., and Rasin, A. (2010). MapReduce and parallel DBMSs: friends or foes? *Commun. ACM*, 53(1):64–71. 760, 763

Stonebraker, M. and Brown, P. (1999). *Object-Relational DBMSs*. Morgan Kaufmann, 2nd edition. 552, 607

Stonebraker, M., Kreps, P., Wong, W., and Held, G. (1976). The design and implementation of ingres. *ACM Trans. Database Syst.*, 1(3):198–222. 56, 258

Stonebraker, M. and Neuhold, E. (1977). A distributed database version of ingres. In *Proc. 2nd Berkeley Workshop on Distributed Data Management and Computer Networks*, pages 9–36. 474

Stonebraker, M., Rowe, L., Lindsay, B., Gray, J., Carey, M., Brodie, M., Bernstein, P., and Beech, D. (1990). Third-generation data base system manifesto. *ACM SIGMOD Rec.*, 19(3):31–44. 553

Straube, D. and Özsu, M. T. (1990a). Queries and query processing in object-oriented database systems. *ACM Trans. Information Syst.*, 8(4):387–430. 585

Straube, D. and Özsu, M. T. (1990b). Type consistency of queries in an object-oriented database. In *Proc. Joint ACM OOPSLA/ECOOP '90 Conference on Object-Oriented Programming: Systems, Languages and Applications*, pages 224–233. 585

Straube, D. D. and Özsu, M. T. (1995). Query optimization and execution plan generation in object-oriented database systems. *IEEE Trans. Knowl. and Data Eng.*, 7(2):210–227. 589

Strong, H. R. and Dolev, D. (1983). Byzantine agreement. In *Digest of Papers — COMPCON*, pages 77–81, San Francisco, Calif. 456

Stroustrup, B. (1986). *The C++ Programming Language*. Addison Wesley. 559

Sullivan, M. and Heybey, A. (1998). Tribeca: A system for managing large databases of network traffic. In *Proc. USENIX 1998 Annual Technical Conf.* 726, 730

Swami, A. (1989). Optimization of large join queries: combining heuristics and combinatorial techniques. In *Proc. ACM SIGMOD Int. Conf. on Management of Data*, pages 367–376. 212, 249

Tandem (1987). Nonstop sql – a distributed high-performance, high-availability implementation of sql. In *Proc. Int. Workshop on High Performance Transaction Systems*, pages 60–104. 377, 548

Tandem (1988). A benchmark of nonstop sql on the debit credit transaction. In *Proc. ACM SIGMOD Int. Conf. on Management of Data*, pages 337–341. 377

Tanenbaum, A. (1995). *Distributed Operating Systems*. Prentice-Hall. 180

Tanenbaum, A. S. (2003). *Computer Networks*. Prentice-Hall, 4th edition. 60, 70

Tanenbaum, A. S. and van Renesse, R. (1988). Voting with ghosts. In *Proc. 8th Int. Conf. on Distributed Computing Systems*, pages 456–461. 493

Tanenbaum, A. S. and van Steen, M. (2002). *Distributed Systems: Principles and Paradigms*. Prentice-Hall. 2

Tao, Y. (2010). *Mining Time-Changing Data Streams*. PhD thesis, University of Waterloo. 763

Tao, Y. and Özsu, M. T. (2009). Efficient decision tree construction for mining time-varying data streams. In *Proc. Conf. of the IBM Centre for Advanced Studies on Collaborative Research*. 743

Tao, Y., Yiu, M. L., Papadias, D., Hadjieleftheriou, M., and Mamoulis, N. (2005). RPJ: Producing fast join results on streams through rate-based optimization. In *Proc. ACM SIGMOD Int. Conf. on Management of Data*, pages 371–382. 738

Tatarinov, I., Ives, Z. G., Madhavan, J., Halevy, A. Y., Suciu, D., Dalvi, N. N., Dong, X., Kadiyska, Y., Miklau, G., and Mork, P. (2003). The piazza peer data management project. *ACM SIGMOD Rec.*, 32(3):47–52. 625, 654

Tatbul, N., Cetintemel, U., Zdonik, S., Cherniack, M., and Stonebraker, M. (2003). Load shedding in a data stream manager. In *Proc. 29th Int. Conf. on Very Large Data Bases*, pages 309–320. 739

Terry, D., Goldberg, D., Nichols, D., and Oki, B. (1992). Continuous queries over append-only databases. In *Proc. ACM SIGMOD Int. Conf. on Management of Data*, pages 321–330. 6

Thakkar, S. S. and Sweiger, M. (1990). Performance of an oltp application on symmetry multiprocessor system. In *Proc. 17th Int. Symposium on Computer Architecture*, pages 228–238. 503

Thiran, P., Hainaut, J.-L., Houben, G.-J., and Benslimane, D. (2006). Wrapper-based evolution of legacy information systems. *ACM Trans. Softw. Eng. and Methodology*, 15(4):329–359. 329, 331

Thomas, R. H. (1979). A majority consensus approach to concurrency control for multiple copy databases. *ACM Trans. Database Syst.*, 4(2):180–209. 385, 450, 487

Thomasian, A. (1993). Two-phase locking and its thrashing behavior. *ACM Trans. Database Syst.*, 18(4):579–625. 401

Thomasian, A. (1996). *Database Concurrency Control: Methods, Performance, and Analysis*. Kluwer Academic Publishers. 358, 398, 399, 401

Thomasian, A. (1998). Distributed optimistic concurrency control methods for high performance transaction processing. *IEEE Trans. Knowl. and Data Eng.*, 10(1):173–189. 401

Thuraisingham, B. (2001). Secure distributed database systems. *Information Security Technical Report*, 6(2). 187, 202

Tian, F. and DeWitt, D. (2003a). Tuple routing strategies for distributed Eddies. In *Proc. 29th Int. Conf. on Very Large Data Bases*, pages 333–344. 739

Tian, F. and DeWitt, D. J. (2003b). Tuple routing strategies for distributed eddies. In *Proc. 29th Int. Conf. on Very Large Data Bases*, pages 333–344. 322, 326, 331

Tomasic, A., Amouroux, R., Bonnet, P., Kapitskaia, O., Naacke, H., and Raschid, L. (1997). The distributed information search component (DISCO) and the world-wide web – prototype demonstration. In *Proc. ACM SIGMOD Int. Conf. on Management of Data*, pages 546–548. 319, 329

Tomasic, A., Raschid, L., and Valduriez, P. (1996). Scaling heterogeneous databases and the design of disco. In *Proc. 16th Int. Conf. on Distributed Computing Systems*, pages 449–457. 319, 331

Tomasic, A., Raschid, L., and Valduriez, P. (1998). Scaling access to distributed heterogeneous data sources with Disco. In *IEEE Trans. Knowl. and Data Eng.* in press. 319, 331

Traiger, I. L., Gray, J., Galtieri, C. A., and Lindsay, B. G. (1982). Transactions and recovery in distributed database systems. *ACM Trans. Database Syst.*, 7(3):323–342. 456

Triantafillou, P. and Pitoura, T. (2003). Towards a unifying framework for complex query processing over structured peer-to-peer data networks. In *Int. Workshop on Databases, Information Systems and Peer-to-Peer Computing*, pages 169–183. 641

Triantafillou, P. and Taylor, D. J. (1995). The location-based paradigm for replication: Achieving efficiency and availability in distributed systems. *IEEE Trans. Softw. Eng.*, 21(1):1–18. 493

Tsichritzis, D. and Klug, A. (1978). The ansi/x3/sparc dbms framework report of the study group on database management systems. *Inf. Syst.*, 1:173–191. 22

Tsuchiya, M., Mariani, M. P., and Brom, J. D. (1986). Distributed database management model and validation. *IEEE Trans. Softw. Eng.*, SE-12(4):511–520. 401

Tucker, P., Maier, D., Sheard, T., and Faragas, L. (2003). Exploiting punctuation semantics in continuous data streams. *IEEE Trans. Knowl. and Data Eng.*, 15(3):555–568. 725, 732

Ullman, J. (1997). Information integration using logical views. In *Proc. 6th Int. Conf. on Database Theory*, volume 1186 of *Lecture Notes in Computer Science*, pages 19–40. Springer. 303, 331

Ullman, J. D. (1982). *Principles of Database Systems*. Computer Science Press, 2nd edition. 224, 228, 231, 241, 272

Ullman, J. D. (1988). *Principles of Database and Knowledge Base Systems*, volume 1. Computer Science Press. 300, 301, 337

Ulusoy, Ö. (2007). Research issues in peer-to-peer data management. In *Proc. 22nd Int. Symp. on Computer and Information Science*, pages 1–8. 653

Urhan, T. and Franklin, M. J. (2000). XJoin: A reactively-scheduled pipelined join operator. *Q. Bull. IEEE TC on Data Eng.*, 23(2):27–33. 732

Urhan, T. and Franklin, M. J. (2001). Dynamic pipeline scheduling for improving interactive query performance. In *Proc. 27th Int. Conf. on Very Large Data Bases*, pages 501–510. 738

Urhan, T., Franklin, M. J., and Amsaleg, L. (1998a). Cost based query scrambling for initial delays. In *Proc. ACM SIGMOD Int. Conf. on Management of Data*, pages 130–141. 322, 331

Urhan, T., Franklin, M. J., and Amsaleg, L. (1998b). Cost-based query scrambling for initial delays. In *Proc. ACM SIGMOD Int. Conf. on Management of Data*, pages 130–141. 739

Valduriez, P. (1982). Semi-join algorithms for distributed database machines. In Schneider, J.-J., editor, *Distributed Data Bases*. North-Holland. pages 23–37. 270, 273, 291, 292

Valduriez, P. (1987). Join indices. *ACM Trans. Database Syst.*, 12(2):218–246. 587, 588, 589

Valduriez, P. (1993). Parallel database systems: Open problems and new issues. *Distrib. Parall. Databases*, 1:137–16. 497

Valduriez, P. and Boral, H. (1986). Evaluation of recursive queries using join indices. In *Proc. First Int. Conf. on Expert Database Systems*, pages 197–208. 219

Valduriez, P. and Gardarin, G. (1984). Join and semi-join algorithms for a multi processor database machine. *ACM Trans. Database Syst.*, 9(1):133–161. 291, 292, 513

Valduriez, P., Khoshafian, S., and Copeland, G. (1986). Implementation techniques of complex objects. In *Proc. 11th Int. Conf. on Very Large Data Bases*, pages 101–109. 579

Valduriez, P. and Pacitti, E. (2004). Data management in large-scale p2p systems. In *Proc. 6th Int. Conf. High Performance Comp. for Computational Sci.*, pages 104–118. 612, 653

Varadarajan, R., Rivera-Vega, P., and Navathe, S. B. (1989). Data redistribution scheduling in fully connected networks. In *Proc. 27th Annual Allerton Conf. on Communication, Control, and Computing*. 124

Velegrakis, Y., Miller, R. J., and Popa, L. (2004). Preserving mapping consistency under schema changes. *VLDB J.*, 13(3):274–293. 156, 157

Verhofstadt, J. S. (1978). Recovery techniques for database systems. *ACM Comput. Surv.*, 10(2):168–195. 39, 419, 456

Vermeer, M. (1997). *Semantic Interoperability for Legacy Databases*. Ph.D. thesis, Department of Computer Science, University of Twente, Enschede, Netherlands. 140

Vidal, M.-E., Raschid, L., and Gruser, J.-R. (1998). A meta-wrapper for scaling up to multiple autonomous distributed information sources. In *Proc. Int. Conf. on Cooperative Information Systems*, pages 148–157. 314

Viglas, S. and Naughton, J. (2002). Rate-based query optimization for streaming information sources. In *Proc. ACM SIGMOD Int. Conf. on Management of Data*, pages 37–48. 738, 739

Viglas, S., Naughton, J., and Burger, J. (2003). Maximizing the output rate of multi-join queries over streaming information sources. In *Proc. 29th Int. Conf. on Very Large Data Bases*, pages 285–296. 732, 739

Vossough, E. and Getta, J. R. (2002). Processing of continuous queries over unlimited data streams. In *Proc. 13th Int. Conf. Database and Expert Systems Appl.*, pages 799–809. 733

Voulgaris, S., Jelasity, M., and van Steen, M. (2003). A robust and scalable peer-to-peer gossiping protocol. In *Agents and Peer-to-Peer Computing, Second Int. Workshop, (AP2PC)*, pages 47–58. 618

Vu, Q. H., Lupu, M., and Ooi, B. C. (2009). *Peer-to-Peer Computing: Principles and Applications*. Springer. 653

Wah, B. W. and Lien, Y. N. (1985). Design of distributed databases on local computer systems. *IEEE Trans. Softw. Eng.*, SE-11(7):609–619. 214, 215

Walsh, N., editor. The DocBook schema (2006). Available from: http://www.oasis-open.org/docbook/specs/wd-docbook-docbook-5.0b3.html [Last retrieved: December 2009]. 690

Walton, C., Dale, A., and Jenevin, R. (1991). A taxonomy and performance model of data skew effects in parallel joins. In *Proc. 17th Int. Conf. on Very Large Data Bases*, pages 537–548. 527, 548

Wang, H., Fan, W., Yu, P., and Han, J. (2003a). Mining concept-drifting data streams using ensemble classifiers. In *Proc. 9th ACM SIGKDD Int. Conf. on Knowledge Discovery and Data Mining*, pages 226–235. 743

Wang, H. and Meng, X. (2005). On the sequencing of tree structures for XML indexing. In *Proc. 21st Int. Conf. on Data Engineering*, pages 372–383. 701

Wang, H., Park, S., Fan, W., and Yu, P. S. (2003b). ViST: A dynamic index method for querying XML data by tree structures. In *Proc. ACM SIGMOD Int. Conf. on Management of Data*, pages 110–121. 701

Wang, H., Zaniolo, C., and Luo, R. (2003c). Atlas: A small but complete SQL extension for data mining and data streams. In *Proc. 29th Int. Conf. on Very Large Data Bases*, pages 1113–1116. 732

Wang, S., Rundensteiner, E., Ganguly, S., and Bhatnagar, S. (2006). State-slice: New paradigm of multi-query optimization of window-based stream queries. In *Proc. 32nd Int. Conf. on Very Large Data Bases*. 740

Wang, W., Li, J., Zhang, D., and Guo, L. (2004). Processing sliding window join aggregate in continuous queries over data streams. In *Proc. 8th East European Conf. Advances in Databases and Information Systems*, pages 348–363. 733

Wang, Y. and Rowe, L. (1991). Cache consistency and concurrency control in a client/server dbms architecture. In *Proc. ACM SIGMOD Int. Conf. on Management of Data*, pages 367–376. 573

Weihl, W. (1988). Commutativity-based concurrency control for abstract data types. *IEEE Trans. Comput.*, C-37(12):1488–1505. 594, 595, 604

Weihl, W. (1989). Local atomicity properties: Modular concurrency control for abstract data types. *ACM Trans. Prog. Lang. and Syst.*, 11(2):249–28. 594, 595

Weikum, G. (1986). Pros and cons of operating system transactions for data base systems. In *Proc. AFIPS Fall Joint Computer Conf.*, pages 1219–1225. 397

Weikum, G. (1991). Principles and realization strategies of multilevel transaction management. *ACM Trans. Database Syst.*, 16(1):132–180. 397, 398

Weikum, G. and Hasse, C. (1993). Multi-level transaction management for complex objects: Implementation, performance, parallelism. *VLDB J.*, 2(4):407–454. 397, 604, 605

Weikum, G. and Schek, H. J. (1984). Architectural issues of transaction management in layered systems. In *Proc. 10th Int. Conf. on Very Large Data Bases*, pages 454–465. 397

Weikum, G. and Vossen, G. (2001). *Transactional Information Systems: Theory, Algorithms, and the Practice of Concurrency Control*. Morgan Kaufmann. 358

White, S. and DeWitt, D. (1992). Quickstore: A high performance mapped object store. In *Proc. 18th Int. Conf. on Very Large Data Bases*, pages 419–431. 576

Wiederhold, G. (1982). *Database Design*. McGraw-Hill, 2nd edition. 83

Wiederhold, G. (1992). Mediators in the architecture of future information systems. *Comp.*, 25(3):38–49. 37, 331

Wiesmann, M., Schiper, A., Pedone, F., Kemme, B., and Alonso, G. (2000). Database replication techniques: A three parameter classification. In *Proc. 19th Symp. on Reliable Distributed Systems*, pages 206–215. 493

Wilkinson, K. and Neimat, M. (1990). Maintaining consistency of client-cached data. In *Proc. 16th Int. Conf. on Very Large Data Bases*, pages 122–133. 572

Williams, R., Daniels, D., Haas, L., Lapis, G., Lindsay, B., Ng, P., Obermarck, R., Selinger, P., Walker, A., Wilms, P., and Yost, R. (1982). R*: An overview of the architecture. In *Proc. 2nd Int. Conf. on Databases*, pages 1–28. 175, 214, 215

Wilms, P. F. and Lindsay, B. G. (1981). A database authorization mechanism supporting individual and group authorization. Research Report RJ 3137, IBM Almaden Research Laboratory, San Jose, Calif. 186, 187, 201

Wilschut, A. and Apers, P. (1991). Dataflow query execution in a parallel main-memory environment. In *Proc. 1st Int. Conf. on Parallel and Distributed Information Systems*, pages 68–77. 322, 325, 641, 732

Wilshut, A. N. and Apers, P. (1992). Parallelism in a main-memory system: The performance of prisma/db. In *Proc. 22th Int. Conf. on Very Large Data Bases*, pages 23–27. 526

Wilshut, A. N., Flokstra, J., and Apers, P. (1995). Parallel evaluation of multi-join queries. In *Proc. ACM SIGMOD Int. Conf. on Management of Data*, pages 115–126. 529, 534

Wilson, B. and Navathe, S. B. (1986). An analytical framework for the redesign of distributed databases. In *Proc. 6th Advanced Database Symposium*, pages 77–83. 124

Wolf, J. L., Dias, D., Yu, S., and Turek, J. (1993). Algorithms for parallelizing relational database joins in the presence of data skew. Research Report RC19236 (83710), IBM Watson Research Center, Yorktown Heights, NY. 529, 548

Wolfson, O. (1987). The overhead of locking (and commit) protocols in distributed databases. *ACM Trans. Database Syst.*, 12(3):453–471. 455, 456, 493

Wong, E. (1977). Retrieving dispersed data from sdd-1. In *Proc. 2nd Berkeley Workshop on Distributed Data Management and Computer Networks*, pages 217–235. 281, 293

Wong, E. and Youssefi, K. (1976). Decomposition: A strategy for query processing. *ACM Trans. Database Syst.*, 1(3):223–241. 258, 275, 292

Wright, D. D. (1983). Managing distributed databases in partitioned networks. Technical Report TR83-572, Department of Computer Science, Cornell University, Ithaca, N.Y. 456, 493

Wu, E., Diao, Y., and Rizvi, S. (2006). High-performance complex event processing over streams. In *Proc. ACM SIGMOD Int. Conf. on Management of Data*, pages 407–418. 725

Wu, K.-L., Chen, S.-K., and Yu, P. (2004). Interval query indexing for efficient stream processing. In *Proc. 13th ACM Int. Conf. on Information and Knowledge Management*, pages 88–97. 741

Wu, K.-L., Yu, P. S., and Pu, C. (1997). Divergence control algorithms for epsilon serializability. *IEEE Trans. Knowl. and Data Eng.*, 9(2):262–274. 401, 462

Wu, S., Yu, G., Yu, Y., Ou, Z., Yang, X., and Gu, Y. (2005). A deadline-sensitive approach for real-time processing of sliding windows. In *Proc. 6th Int. Conf. on Web-Age Information Management:*, pages 566–577. 740

Fernández, M., Malhotra, A., Marsh, J., Nagy, M., and Walsh, N., editors. XQuery 1.0 and XPath 2.0 data model (XDM) (2007). Available from: `http://www.w3.org/TR/2007/REC-xpath-datamodel-20070123` [Last retrieved: February 2010]. 712

XHTML. XHTML 1.0 The extensible HyperText markup language (2nd edition) (2002). Available from: `http://www.w3.org/TR/xhtml1/` [Last retrieved: December 2009]. 690

Xie, J., Yang, J., and Chen, Y. (2005). On joining and caching stochastic streams. In *Proc. ACM SIGMOD Int. Conf. on Management of Data*, pages 359–370. 740

Xu, J., Lin, X., and Zhou, X. (2004). Space efficient quantile summary for constrained sliding windows on a data stream. In *Proc. 5th Int. Conf. on Web-Age Information Management:*, pages 34–44. 737

Yan, L. L. (1997). Towards efficient and scalable mediation: The aurora approach. In *Proc. IBM CASCON Conference*, pages 15–29. 134

Yan, L.-L., Miller, R. J., Haas, L. M., and Fagin, R. (2001). Data-driven understanding and refinement of schema mappings. In *Proc. ACM SIGMOD Int. Conf. on Management of Data*, pages 485–496. 152

Yan, L.-L. and Özsu, M. T. (1999). Conflict tolerant queries in aurora. In *Proc. Int. Conf. on Cooperative Information Systems*, pages 279–290. 158

Yan, L. L., Özsu, M. T., and Liu, L. (1997). Accessing heterogeneous data through homogenization and integration mediators. In *Proc. Int. Conf. on Cooperative Information Systems*, pages 130–139. 134

Yang, B. and Garcia-Molina, H. (2002). Improving search in peer-to-peer networks. In *Proc. 22nd Int. Conf. on Distributed Computing Systems*, pages 5–14. 617

Yang, X., Lee, M.-L., and Ling, T. W. (2003). Resolving structural conflicts in the integration of XML schemas: A semantic approach. In *Proc. 22nd Int. Conf. on Conceptual Modeling*, pages 520–533. 134

Yao, S. B., Navathe, S. B., and Weldon, J.-L. (1982a). *An Integrated Approach to Database Design*, pages 1–30. Lecture Notes in Computer Science 132. Springer. 73

Yao, S. B., Waddle, V., and Housel, B. (1982b). View modeling and integration using the functional data model. *IEEE Trans. Softw. Eng.*, SE-8(6):544–554. 149

Yeung, C. and Hung, S. (1995). A new deadlock detection algorithm for distributed real-time database systems. In *Proc. 14th Symp. on Reliable Distributed Systems*, pages 146–153. 401

Yong, V., Naughton, J., and Yu, J. (1994). Storage reclamation and reorganization in client-server persistent object stores. In *Proc. 10th Int. Conf. on Data Engineering*, pages 120–133. 581

Yormark, B. (1977). The ansi/sparc/dbms architecture. In Jardine, D. A., editor, *ANSI/SPARC DBMS Model*, pages 1–21. North-Holland. 22

Yoshida, M., Mizumachi, K., Wakino, A., Oyake, I., and Matsushita, Y. (1985). Time and cost evaluation schemes of multiple copies of data in distributed database systems. *IEEE Trans. Softw. Eng.*, SE-11(9):954–958. 124

Yu, C. and Meng, W. (1998). *Principles of Query Processing for Advanced Database Applictions*. Morgan Kaufmann. 331

Yu, C. T. and Chang, C. C. (1984). Distributed query processing. *ACM Comput. Surv.*, 16(4):399–433. 220

Yu, P. S., Cornell, D., Dias, D. M., and Thomasian, A. (1989). Performance comparison of the io shipping and database call shipping schemes in multi-system partitioned database systems. *Perf. Eval.*, 10:15–33. 401

Zaniolo, C. (1983). The database language gem. In *Proc. ACM SIGMOD Int. Conf. on Management of Data*, pages 207–218. 587

Zdonik, S. and Maier, D., editors (1990). *Readings in Object-Oriented Database Systems*. Morgan Kaufmann. 607

Zezula, P., Amato, G., Debole, F., and Rabitti, F. (2003). Tree signatures for XML querying and navigation. In *Database and XML Technologies, 1st Int. XML Database Symp.*, pages 149–163. 701

Zhang, C., Naughton, J. F., DeWitt, D. J., Luo, Q., and Lohman, G. M. (2001). On supporting containment queries in relational database management systems. In *Proc. ACM SIGMOD Int. Conf. on Management of Data*, pages 425–436. 699, 700

Zhang, J. and Honeyman, P. (2008). A replicated file system for grid computing. *Concurrency and Computation: Practice and Experience*, 20(9):1113–1130. 750

Zhang, N. (2006). *Query Processing and Optimization in Native XML Databases*. PhD thesis, University of Waterloo. 719

Zhang, N., Agarwal, N., Chandrasekar, S., Idicula, S., Medi, V., Petride, S., and Sthanikam, B. (2009a). Binary XML storage and query processing in oracle 11g. *PVLDB*, 2(2):1354–1365. 703

Zhang, N., Kacholia, V., and Özsu, M. T. (2004). A succinct physical storage scheme for efficient evaluation of path queries in XML. In *Proc. 20th Int. Conf. on Data Engineering*, pages 54–65. 699

Zhang, N. and Özsu, M. T. (2010). XML native storage and query processing. In Li, C. and Ling, T.-W., editors, *Advanced Applications and Structures in XML Processing: Label Streams, Semantics Utilization and Data Query Technologies*. IGI Global. 699

Zhang, N., Özsu, M. T., Aboulnaga, A., and Ilyas, I. F. (2006a). XSEED: accurate and fast cardinality estimation for XPath queries. In *Proc. 22nd Int. Conf. on Data Engineering*, page 61. 702

Zhang, N., Özsu, M. T., Ilyas, I. F., and Aboulnaga, A. (2006b). Fix: Feature-based indexing technique for XML documents. In *Proc. 32nd Int. Conf. on Very Large Data Bases*, pages 259–270. 701

Zhang, R., Koudas, N., Ooi, B. C., and Srivastava, D. (2005). Multiple aggregations over data streams. In *Proc. ACM SIGMOD Int. Conf. on Management of Data*, pages 299–310. 740

Zhang, Y. (2010). *XRPC: Efficient Distributed Query Processing on Heterogeneous XQuery Engines*. PhD thesis, Universiteit van Amsterdam. 719

Zhang, Y. and Boncz, P. A. (2007). Xrpc: Interoperable and efficient distributed XQuery. In *Proc. 33rd Int. Conf. on Very Large Data Bases*, pages 99–110. 712

Zhang, Y., Tang, N., and Boncz, P. A. (2009b). Efficient distribution of full-fledged XQuery. In *Proc. 25th Int. Conf. on Data Engineering*, pages 565–576. 710, 712

Zhao, B., Huang, L., Stribling, J., Rhea, S., Joseph, A. D., and Kubiatowicz, J. (2004). Tapestry: A resilient global-scale overlay for service deployment. *IEEE J. Selected Areas in Comm.*, 22(1):41–53. 620, 646

Zhu, Q. (1995). *Estimating Local Cost Parameters for Global Query Optimization in a Multidatabase System*. Ph.D. thesis, Department of Computer Science, University of Waterloo, Waterloo, Canada. 313

Zhu, Q. and Larson, P.-Å. (1994). A query sampling method of estimating local cost parameters in a multidatabase system. In *Proc. 10th Int. Conf. on Data Engineering*, pages 144–153. 307, 308, 331

Zhu, Q. and Larson, P. A. (1996a). Developing regression cost models for multidatabase systems. In *Proc. 4th Int. Conf. on Parallel and Distributed Information Systems*, pages 220–231. 307, 309, 331

Zhu, Q. and Larson, P. A. (1996b). Global query processing and optimization in the cords multidatabase system. In *Proc. Int. Conf. on Parallel and Distributed Computing Systems*, pages 640–647. 308

Zhu, Q. and Larson, P. A. (1998). Solving local cost estimation problem for global query optimization in multidatabase systems. *Distrib. Parall. Databases*, 6(4):373–420. 307, 308, 331

Zhu, Q. and Larson, P.-Å. (2000). Classifying local queries for global query optimization in multidatabase systems. *Int. J. Cooperative Information Syst.*, 9(3):315–355. 309

Zhu, Q., Motheramgari, S., and Sun, Y. (2003). Cost estimation for queries experiencing multiple contention states in dynamic multidatabase environments. *Knowledge and Information Systems*, 5(1):26–49. 307, 314, 331

Zhu, Q., Sun, Y., and Motheramgari, S. (2000). Developing cost models with qualitative variables for dynamic multidatabase environments. In *Proc. 16th Int. Conf. on Data Engineering*, pages 413–424. 307, 313, 331

Zhu, S. and Ravishankar, C. (2004). A scalable approach to approximating aggregate queries over intermittent streams. In *Proc. 16th Int. Conf. on Scientific and Statistical Database Management*, pages 85–94. 727

Zhu, Y., Rundensteiner, E., and Heineman, G. (2004). Dynamic plan migration for continuous queries over data streams. In *Proc. ACM SIGMOD Int. Conf. on Management of Data*, pages 431–442. 739

Zhu, Y. and Shasha, D. (2003). Efficient elastic burst detection in data streams. In *Proc. 9th ACM SIGKDD Int. Conf. on Knowledge Discovery and Data Mining*, pages 336–345. 727

Ziane, M., Zaït, M., and Borla-Salamet, P. (1993). Parallel query processing with zigzag trees. *VLDB J.*, 2(3):277–301. 523, 548

Zloof, M. M. (1977). Query-by-example: A data base language. *IBM Systems J.*, 16(4):324–343. 57

Zobel, D. D. (1983). The deadlock problem: A classifying bibliography. *Operating Systems Rev.*, 17(2):6–15. 401

Index

Printed in the United States
By Bookmasters